GO!

with Microsoft®

Office 2016

Volume 1

**Shelley Gaskin,
Alicia Vargas, Nancy Graviett,
and Debra Geoghan**

PEARSON

Boston   Columbus   Indianapolis   New York   San Francisco
Amsterdam   Cape Town   Dubai   London   Madrid   Milan   Munich   Paris   Montréal   Toronto
Delhi   Mexico City   São Paulo   Sydney   Hong Kong   Seoul   Singapore   Taipei   Tokyo

Vice President, Career Skills: Andrew Gilfillan
Executive Editor: Jenifer Niles
Project Manager: Holly Haydash
Team Lead, Project Management: Laura Burgess
Development Editor: Ginny Munroe
Editorial Assistant: Michael Campbell
Director of Product Marketing: Maggie Waples
Director of Field Marketing: Leigh Ann Sims
Field Marketing Managers: Molly Schmidt and Joanna Conley
Marketing Coordinator: Susan Osterlitz
Operations Specialist: Diane Peirano

Senior Art Director: Diane Ernsberger
Cover Photos: GaudiLab, Rawpixel.com, Pressmaster, Eugenio
    Marongiu, Boggy, Gajus, Rocketclips, Inc
Associate Director of Design: Blair Brown
Director of Media Development: Blaine Christine
Media Project Manager, Production: John Cassar
Full-Service Project Management: Lumina Datamatics, Inc.
Composition: Lumina Datamatics, Inc.
Printer/Binder: LSC Communications/Menasha
Cover Printer: Phoenix Color
Text Font: Times LT Pro

Library of Congress Cataloging-in-Publication Data

Names: Gaskin, Shelley, author.
Title: GO! with Microsoft Office 2016 / Shelley Gaskin, Alicia Vargas,
    Nancy Graviett, and Debra Geoghan.
Description: Boston : Pearson Education, Inc., [2017] | "Volume 1." |
    Includes index.
Identifiers: LCCN 2015040442 | ISBN 9780134320779 (pbk. : volume 1)
Subjects: LCSH: Microsoft Office. | Business—Computer programs.
Classification: LCC HF5548.4.M525 G36733 2017 | DDC 005.5—dc23
LC record available at http://lccn.loc.gov/2015040442

6 18

PEARSON

ISBN 10: 0-13-432077-8
ISBN 13: 978-0-13-432077-9

Brief Contents

MN 12.02 2018 1129

Table of Contents

Introduction to Microsoft Access 2016 **537**

Chapter 1 Getting Started with Microsoft Access 2016 539

About the Authors

Shelley Gaskin, Series Editor, is a professor in the Business and Computer Technology Division at Pasadena City College in Pasadena, California. She holds a bachelor's degree in Business Administration from Robert Morris College (Pennsylvania), a master's degree in Business from Northern Illinois University, and a doctorate in Adult and Community Education from Ball State University (Indiana). Before joining Pasadena City College, she spent 12 years in the computer industry, where she was a systems analyst, sales representative, and director of Customer Education with Unisys Corporation. She also worked for Ernst & Young on the development of large systems applications for their clients. She has written and developed training materials for custom systems applications in both the public and private sector, and has also written and edited numerous computer application textbooks.

This book is dedicated to my students, who inspire me every day.

Alicia Vargas is a faculty member in Business Information Technology at Pasadena City College. She holds a master's and a bachelor's degree in business education from California State University, Los Angeles, and has authored several textbooks and training manuals on Microsoft Word, Microsoft Excel, and Microsoft PowerPoint.

This book is dedicated with all my love to my husband Vic, who makes everything possible; and to my children Victor, Phil, and Emmy, who are an unending source of inspiration and who make everything worthwhile.

Debra Geoghan is a Professor of Computer Science in the STEM department at Bucks County Community College, teaching computer classes ranging from basic computer literacy to cybercrime, computer forensics, and networking. She has certifications from Microsoft, CompTIA, and Apple. Deb has taught at the college level since 1996 and also spent 11 years in the high school classroom. She holds a B.S. in Secondary Science Education from Temple University and an M.A. in Computer Science Education from Arcadia University.

Throughout her teaching career Deb has worked with educators to integrate technology across the curriculum. At BCCC she serves on many technology committees, presents technology workshops for BCCC faculty, and heads the Computer Science Area. Deb is an avid user of technology, which has earned her the nickname "gadget lady."

This book is dedicated to my colleagues and students at Bucks County Community College: for your suggestions and encouragement throughout this process. You inspire me every day. And most importantly—my family. My husband and sons for your patience, help, and love—I couldn't have done this without your love and support.

Nancy Graviett is a professor and department chair in Business Technology at St. Charles Community College in Cottleville, Missouri. She holds a bachelor's degree in marketing and a master's degree in business education from the University of Missouri and has completed a certificate in online education. Nancy has authored textbooks on WordPerfect, Google, Microsoft Outlook and Microsoft Access.

This book is dedicated to my husband, Dave, and my children, Matthew and Andrea. I cannot thank my family enough for the love and support they share everyday.

GO! with Office 2016

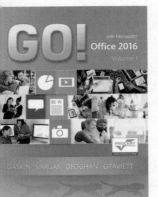

GO! with Office 2016 is the right approach to learning for today's fast-moving, mobile environment. The GO! Series focuses on the job and *success* skills students need to succeed in the workforce. Using job-related projects that put Microsoft Office into context, students learn the *how* and *why* at the moment they need to know, and because the GO! Series uses Microsoft procedural syntax, students never get lost in the instruction. For Office 2016, the hallmark GO! *guided practice-to-skill mastery pathway* is better than ever. Not only do students have multiple opportunities to work live in Microsoft Office to practice and apply the skills they have learned, but also, the *instructional* projects are now Grader projects, so students can work live in Office and receive auto-graded feedback as they learn!

By combining these new instructional Grader projects with the variety of existing Grader projects and the high-fidelity simulations that match the text, students have an effective pathway for learning, practicing, and assessing their abilities. After completing the instructional projects, students are ready to apply the skills with a wide variety of progressively challenging projects that require them to solve problems, think critically, and create projects on their own. The new *GO! with Google* projects also enable students to apply what they have learned in a different environment, and the integrated MOS objectives make this the one resource needed to learn Office, gain critical productivity skills, and prepare to get MOS certified!

What's New

Coverage of new features of Office 2016 ensures that students are learning the skills they need to work in today's job market.

NEW MyITLab 2016 Grader Projects In addition to the homework and assessment Graders already available, the A and B *instructional* projects are now Graders, enabling students to *learn by doing* live in the application *and* receive the instant feedback they need to ensure understanding.

MyITLab HTML 5 Training & Assessment Simulations for Office 2016 These simulations are rewritten by the authors to match the pedagogical approach of the textbook projects and to provide a direct one-to-one learning experience.

NEW Windows 10 Coverage Students practice and learn everything necessary to get up and running with Windows 10, including *GO! Learn How* videos and MyITLab simulation trainings for the Windows 10 skills covered in the textbook.

NEW Google Projects For each A and B instructional project, students construct a parallel project using Google productivity tools. This gives students the opportunity to think critically and apply what they are learning about Microsoft Office to *other* productivity tools, which is an essential job skill.

NEW MOS Preparation MOS objectives are integrated into the text for easy review and reference for students who are preparing for a MOS certification exam. A MOS appendix is also included to provide a comprehensive list of the exam objectives.

NEW Lessons on the GO! How do you teach software that is constantly updated and getting new features all the time? This new project type will cover newer Microsoft apps such as Sway and MIX and things yet to come! These lessons are found in MyITLab and the Instructor Resource Center, and come with instructional content, student data files, solutions files, and rubrics for grading.

GO! To Work Page Here, students can review a summary of the chapter items focused on employability, including a MOS Objective summary, Build Your ePortfolio guidelines, and the GO! For Job Success soft skills videos and discussions.

Application Capstone Projects MyITLab grader Capstone projects for each application provide a variety of opportunities for students to ensure they have reached proficiency.

FOUR Types of Videos Students enjoy video learning, and these videos help students learn and gain skills and insight needed to succeed in the workforce.

- *(NEW) GO! Walk Thru:* Give students a quick 30-second preview of what they will do and create—from beginning to end—by completing each of the A and B Instructional Projects. These videos increase the student's confidence by letting the student see the entire project built quickly.
- *GO! Learn How (formerly Student Training)*: Students learn visually by viewing these instructor-led videos that are broken down by Objective for direct guidance. This is the personal instruction students need—especially outside of the classroom—to answer the *How do I?* questions.
- *GO! to Work*: These videos provide short interviews with real business information workers showing how they use Office in the workplace.
- *GO! for Job Success:* These videos relate to the projects in the chapter and cover important career topics such as *Dressing for Success*, *Time Management*, and *Making Ethical Choices*.

Expanded Project Summary chart This easy-to-use guide outlines all the instructional and end-of-chapter projects by category, including Instruction, Review, Mastery and Transfer of Learning, and Critical Thinking.

In-text boxed content for easy navigation *Another Way*, *Notes*, *More Knowledge*, *Alerts*, and *By Touch* instructions are included in line with the instruction—not in the margins—so students won't miss this important information and will learn it in context with what is on their screen.

MyITLab 2016 for GO!
Let MyITLab do the work by giving students instantaneous feedback and saving hours of grading with GO!'s extensive Grader Project options. And the HTML5 Training and Assessment simulations provide a high-fidelity environment that provide step-by-step summary of student actions and include just-in-time learning aids to assist students: Read, Watch, Practice.

All other end-of-chapter projects, C, D, H, I, J, K, L, M, N, and O, have grading rubrics and solution files for easy hand grading. These are all Content-based, Outcomes-based, Problem-Solving, and Critical Thinking projects that enable you to add a variety of assessments—including authentic assessments—to evaluate a student's proficiency with the application.

IT Innovation Station
Stay current with Office and Windows updates and important Microsoft and office productivity news and trends with help from your Pearson authors! Now that Microsoft Office is in the cloud, automatic updates occur regularly. These can affect how you to teach your course and the resources you are using. To keep you and your students completely up to date on the changes occurring in Office 2016 and Windows 10, we are launching the *IT Innovation Station*. This website will contain monthly updates from our product team and our author-instructors with tips for understanding updates, utilizing new capabilities, implementing new instructional techniques, and optimizing your Office use.

Why the GO! Approach Helps Students Succeed

GO! Provides Personalized Learning

MyITLab from Pearson is an online homework, training, and assessment system that will improve student results by helping students master skills and concepts through immediate feedback and a robust set of tools that allows instructors to easily gauge and address the performance of individuals and classrooms.

MyITLab learning experiences engage students using both realistic, high-fidelity simulations of Microsoft Office as well as auto-graded, live-in-the-application assignments, so they can understand concepts more thoroughly. With the ability to approach projects and problems as they would in real life—coupled with tutorials that adapt based on performance—students quickly complete skills they know and get help when and where they need it.

For educators, MyITLab establishes a reliable learning environment backed by the Pearson Education 24/7, 99.97 percent uptime service level agreement, and that includes the tools educators need to track and support both individual and class-wide student progress.

GO! Engages Students by Combining a Project-Based Approach with the Teachable Moment

GO!'s project-based approach clusters the learning objectives around the projects rather than around the software features. This tested pedagogical approach teaches students to solve real problems as they practice and learn the features.

GO! instruction is organized around student learning outcomes with numbered objectives and two instructional projects per chapter. Students can engage in a wide variety of end-of-chapter projects where they apply what they have learned in outcomes-based, problem-solving, and critical thinking projects— many of which require students to create the project from scratch.

GO! instruction is based on the teachable moment where students learn important concepts at the exact moment they are practicing the skill. The explanations and concepts are woven into the steps— not presented as paragraphs of text at the beginning of the project before students have even seen the software in action.

Each Project Opening Page clearly outlines Project Activities (what the student will do in this project), Project Files (what starting files are needed and how the student will save the files), and Project Results (what the student's finished project will look like). Additionally, to support this page, the GO! Walk Thru video gives students a 30-second overview of how the project will progress and what they will create.

GO! Demonstrates Excellence in Instructional Design

Student Learning Outcomes and Objectives are clearly defined so students understand what they will learn and what they will be able to do when they finish the chapter.

Clear Instruction provided through project steps written following Microsoft® Procedural Syntax to guide students where to go *and then* what to do, so they never get lost!

Teachable moment approach has students learn important concepts when they need to as they work through the instructional projects. No long paragraphs of text.

Clean Design presents textbook pages that are clean and uncluttered, with screenshots that validate the student's actions and that engage visual learners.

Sequential Pagination displays the pages sequentially numbered, like every other textbook a student uses, instead of using letters or abbreviations. Student don't spend time learning a new numbering approach.

Important information is boxed within the text so that students won't miss or skip the Another Way, By Touch, Note, Alert, or More Knowledge details so there are no distracting and "busy-looking" marginal notes.

Color-Coded Steps guide students through the projects with colors coded by project.

End-of-Project Icon helps students know when they have completed the project, which is especially useful in self-paced or online environments. These icons give students a clearly identifiable end point for each project.

GO! Learn How Videos provide step-by-step visual instruction for the A and B instructional projects— delivered by a real instructor! These videos provide the assistance and personal learning students may need when working on their own.

GO! Delivers Easy Course Implementation

Instructor Page

Teach the Course You Want in Less Time

The *GO!* series' one-of-a-kind instructional system provides you with everything you need to prepare for class, teach the material, and assess your students.

Prepare

- **Office 2013 to 2016 Transition Guide** provides an easy-to-use reference for updating your course for Office 2016 using GO!

- **Annotated Instructor Tabs** provide clear guidance on how to implement your course.

- **MyITLab Implementation Guide** is provided for course planning and learning outcome alignment.

- **MyITLab content folders** now organized by *Instruction*, *Practice*, *Review*, and *Assessment*.

- **Syllabus templates** outline various plans for covering the content in an 8-, 12-, or 16-week course.

- **List of Chapter Outcomes and Objectives** is provided for course planning and learning outcome alignment.

- **Student Assignment Tracker** for students to track their own work.

- **Assignment Planning Guide** Description of the *GO!* assignments with recommendations based on class size, delivery method, and student needs.

- **Solution Files** Examples of homework submissions to serve as examples for students.

- **Online Study Guide for Students** Interactive objective-style questions based on chapter content.

Teach

- **The Annotated Instructors Edition** includes the entire student text, spiral-bound and wrapped with teaching notes and suggestions for how to implement your course.

- **Scripted Lectures** present a detailed guide for delivering live in-class demonstrations of the A and B Instructional Projects.

- **PowerPoint Presentations** provide a visual walk-through of the chapter with suggested lecture notes included.

- **Audio PowerPoint Presentations** provide a visual walk-through of the chapter with the lecture notes read out loud.

- **Walk Thru Videos** provide a quick 30-second preview of what the student will do and create—from beginning to end—by completing each of the A and B Instructional projects. These videos increase the student's confidence by letting the student see the entire project built quickly.

Assess

- **A scoring checklist, task-specific rubric, or analytic rubric** accompanies every assignment.

- **Prepared Exams** provide cumulative exams for each project, chapter, and application that are easy to score using the provided scoring checklist and point suggestions for each task.

- **Solution Files** are provided in three formats: native file, PDF, and annotated PDF.

- **Rubrics** provide guidelines for grading open-ended projects.

- **Testbank questions** are available for you to create your own objective-based quizzes for review.

Grader Projects

- **Projects A & B** (Guided Instruction)
- **Project E Homework** (Formative) and Assesment (Summative) (Cover Objectives in Project A)
- **Project F Homework** (Formative) and Assesment (Summative) (Cover Objectives in Project B)
- **Project G Homework** (Formative) and Assesment (Summative) (Cover Objectives in Projects A and B)
- **Application Capstone Homework** (Formative review of core objectives covered in application)
- **Application Capstone Exam** (Summative review of core objectives covered in application—generates badge with 90 percent or higher)

GO! Series Hallmarks

Teach the Course You Want in Less Time

A Microsoft® Office textbook designed for student success!

- **Project-Based** – Students learn by creating projects that they will use in the real world.

- **Microsoft Procedural Syntax** – Steps are written to put students in the right place at the right time.

- **Teachable Moment** – Expository text is woven into the steps—at the moment students need to know it—not chunked together in a block of text that will go unread.

- **Sequential Pagination** – Students have actual page numbers instead of confusing letters and abbreviations.

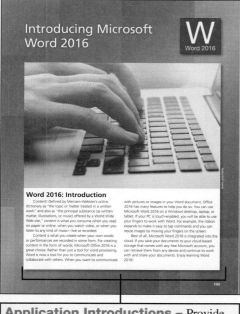

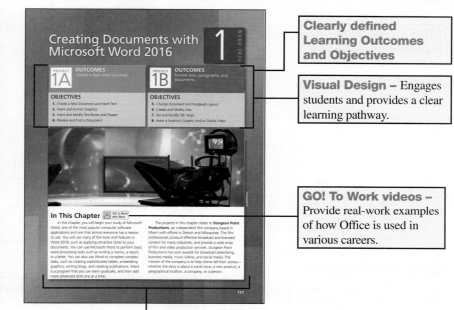

Clearly defined Learning Outcomes and Objectives

Visual Design – Engages students and provides a clear learning pathway.

GO! To Work videos – Provide real-work examples of how Office is used in various careers.

Application Introductions – Provide an overview of the application to prepare students for the upcoming chapters.

Scenario – Each chapter opens with a job-related scenario that sets the stage for the projects the student will create.

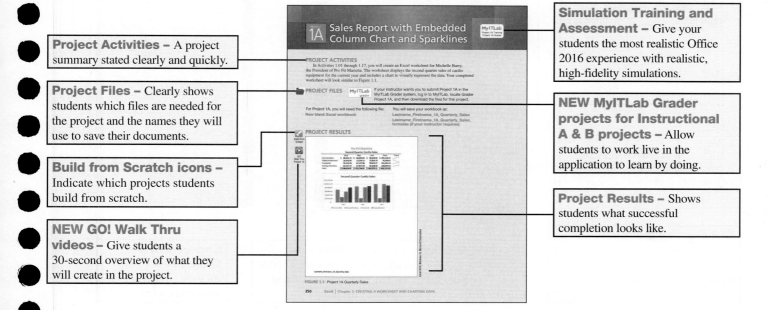

Project Activities – A project summary stated clearly and quickly.

Project Files – Clearly shows students which files are needed for the project and the names they will use to save their documents.

Build from Scratch icons – Indicate which projects students build from scratch.

NEW GO! Walk Thru videos – Give students a 30-second overview of what they will create in the project.

Simulation Training and Assessment – Give your students the most realistic Office 2016 experience with realistic, high-fidelity simulations.

NEW MyITLab Grader projects for Instructional A & B projects – Allow students to work live in the application to learn by doing.

Project Results – Shows students what successful completion looks like.

In-text Features
Another Way, Notes, More Knowledge, Alerts, and By Touch Instructions

Color Coding – Each chapter has two instructional projects, which is less overwhelming for students than one large chapter project. The projects are differentiated by different colored numbering and headings.

MOS Objectives – Are highlighted throughout the text to provide a review and exam prep reference.

Microsoft Procedural Syntax – Steps are written to put the student at the right place at the right time.

Teachable Moment – Expository text is woven into the steps—at the moment students need to know it—not chunked together in a block of text that will go unread.

Intext Callouts – Ensure that students will read this important material—Another Way, Notes, More Knowledge, Alerts, and By Touch instructions.

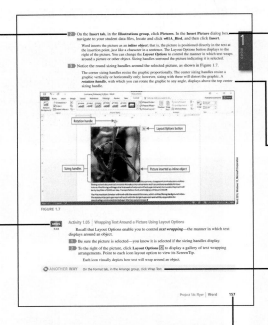

Sequential Pagination – Students are given actual page numbers to navigate through the textbook instead of confusing letters and abbreviations.

End-of-Chapter

MOS Skills Summary – List all the MOS objectives covered in the chapter.

Build Your ePortfolio – Provides guidelines for creating an effective representation of your course work.

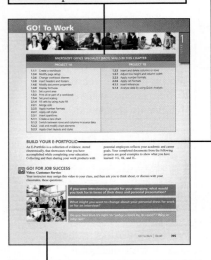

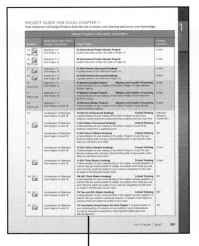

GO! For Job Success – Soft skills, videos, and discussions to prepare students with the soft skills needed for today's work environment.

Review and Assessment Chart – Provides an easy-to-use guide to all the instructional and end-of-chapter projects by category from Mastery and Transfer of Knowledge to Critical Thinking.

End-of-Chapter Glossary – Gives students an easy way to review key terms.

End-of-Chapter

Objective List – Every end-of-chapter project includes a listing of covered Objectives from Projects A and B.

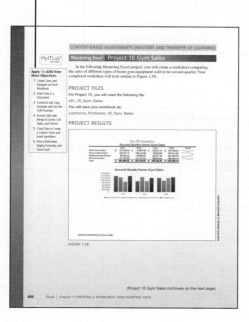

Grader Projects – In addition to the two Grader Projects for the instructional portion of the chapter (Projects A and B), each chapter has six MyITLab Grader projects within the end-of-chapter material—three homework and three assessment—clearly indicated by the MyITLab logo.

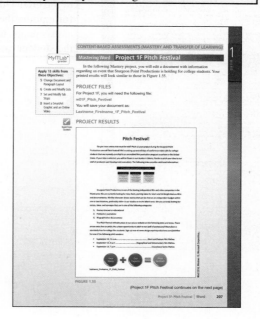

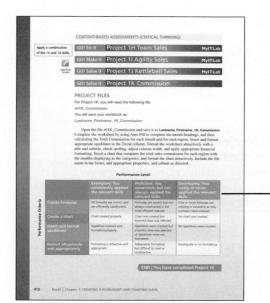

Task-Specific Rubric – A matrix specific to the GO! Solve It projects that states the criteria and standards for grading these defined-solution projects.

End-of-Chapter

Outcomes-Based Assessments – Assessments with open-ended solutions.

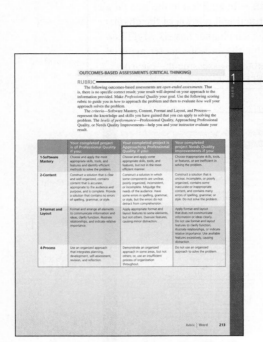

Outcomes-Based Assessments – Assessments with open-ended solutions.

Outcomes Rubric – A standards-based analytic rubric specific to the GO! Think projects that states the criteria and standards for grading these open-ended assessments. For these authentic assessments, an analytic rubric enables the instructor to judge and the student to self assess.

Sample Solution – Outcomes-based assessments include a sample solution so the instructor can compare student work with an example of expert work.

FPCC Career Center

Student and Alumni Workshops

The FPCC Career Center is committed to helping you improve your job potential. We offer a number of workshops that will help you improve your job skills. The following workshops are available to all students and graduates at no fee.

Workshop	Topics Covered
Word, Part 1	Navigating the Word screen Creating and saving documents Creating and modifying lists Using tab stops
Word, Part 2	Creating and formatting tables Editing text Using proofing tools Using templates
Word, Part 3	Creating a report Creating a newsletter Using mail merge
Excel, Part 1	Navigating the Excel screen Creating a worksheet Using formulas Creating charts
Excel, Part 2	Using functions Formatting cells Editing and moving data Performing a what-if analysis
Excel, Part 3	Creating and using tables Using financial functions Formatting worksheets
Business Communication, Part 1	Writing business letters Writing memos
Business Communication, Part 2	Designing visual presentations Delivering effective presentations
Creating a Resume	Creating effective resumes Formatting resumes for different audiences

Lastname_Firstname_2L_Workshops

Google Projects for each A & B instructional project – Provide students the opportunity to think critically and apply what they are learning about Microsoft Office to other productivity tools—an essential job skill.

Student Materials

Student Data Files – All student data files are available in MyITLab for Office 2016 or at www.pearsonhighered.com/go

FOUR Types of Videos help students learn and gain skills and insight needed to succeed in the workforce.

- *(NEW) GO! Walk Thru* is a brief overview of the A & B instructional projects to give students the context of what they will be doing in the projects
- *GO! Learn How (formerly Student Training)* instructor-led videos are broken down by Objective for direct guidance; this personal instruction answers the "how-do-I" questions students ask.
- *GO! to Work* videos provide short interviews with workers showing how they use Office in the workplace.
- *GO! for Job Success* videos relate to the projects in the chapter and cover important career topics such as *Dressing for Success*, *Time Management*, and *Making Ethical Choices*.

Matching and multiple choice questions provide a variety of review options for content in each chapter.

MOS Objective quiz provides a quick assessment of student understanding of the MOS objectives covered in the chapter. Helpful for courses focused on the pathway to MOS certification.

Available in MyITLab for Office 2016.

GO! with MyITLab
Gives you a completely integrated solution

Instruction ▪ Training ▪ Assessment

All of the content in the book and MyITLab is written by the authors, who are instructors, so the instruction works seamlessly with the simulation trainings and grader projects—true 1:1. eText, Training & Assessment Simulations, and Grader Projects.

Instructor Resources

All Instructor Resources found in MyITLab or at pearsonhighered. com/go

Annotated Instructor Edition – This instructor tool includes a full copy of the student textbook and a guide to implementing your course depending on the emphasis you want to place on digital engagement. Also included are teaching tips, discussion topics, and other useful pieces for teaching each chapter.

Assignment Sheets – Lists all the assignments for the chapter. Just add the course information, due dates, and points. Providing these to students ensures they will know what is due and when.

Scripted Lectures – A script to guide your classroom lecture of each instructional project.

Annotated Solution Files – Coupled with the scorecards, these create a grading and scoring system that makes grading easy and efficient.

PowerPoint Lectures – PowerPoint presentations for each chapter.

Audio PowerPoints – Audio versions of the PowerPoint presentations for each chapter.

Scoring Rubrics – Can be used either by students to check their work or by you as a quick check-off for the items that need to be corrected.

Syllabus Templates – For 8-week, 12-week, and 16-week courses.

Test Bank – Includes a variety of test questions for each chapter.

Instruction

Instruction: General

Syllabi templates demonstrate different approaches for covering the content in an 8-, 12-, or 16-week course.

Application Intro Videos provide a quick overview of what the application is and its primary function.

GO! to Work Videos put each chapter into context as related to how people use productivity software in their daily lives and work.

GO! For Success videos and discussions provide real-life scenarios exploring the essential soft skills needed to succeed in the workplace and professional settings.

Instruction: Hands-On *using one or more of the following:*

- **Interactive eText** allows students to read the narrative and instruction and also link directly to the various types of videos included.
- **(NEW) Walk Thru Videos** provide a quick 30-second overview of what students will do in the A & B instructional projects.
- **Scripted Lectures** are a detailed guide through the A & B projects from the book for you to use for in-class demonstration.
- **GO! Learn How** (previously Student Training) videos are instructor-led videos that provide guided instruction through each Objective and the related Activities.
- **PowerPoint Presentations** provide a visual walk-through of the chapter with suggested lecture notes included.
- **Audio PowerPoint Presentations** provide the visual walk-through of chapters with the lecture notes read aloud.
- **(NEW) A & B Instruction Projects** assigned to students. Students can complete the Instructional Projects 1A and 1B and submit for instructor review or manual grading. They can also submit as a MyITLab Grader project, which allows the students to work live in the application starting with files downloaded from MyITLab and then submitted for automatic grading and feedback.
- **(NEW) MOS Objectives** are covered throughout the chapter and are indicated with the **MOS** icon. Instructors use these to point students to content they would encounter on a MOS exam. If a course is focused on MOS preparation, this content would be emphasized in the instruction.

Practice

MyITLab Skill-based Training Simulation provides students with hands-on practice applying the skills they have learned in a simulated environment where they have access to Learning Aids to assist if needed (READ, WATCH, PRACTICE). All of the student's keystrokes are recorded so that instructors can review and provide support to the students. Instructor can set the number of times the students can complete the simulation.

MyITLab Homework Grader Projects (E, F, or G) provide students with live-in-the-application practice with the skills they learned in Projects A and B. These projects provide students with detailed reports showing them where they made errors and also provide "live comments" explaining the details.

Student Assignment Tracker for students to track their work.

Review

GO! Online activities (multiple choice and matching activities) provide objective-based quizzing to allow students to review how they are doing.

Testbank questions are available for instructors to create their own quizzes for review or assessment.

End-of-chapter online projects H–O provide Content-based, Outcome-based, and Critical Thinking projects that you can assign for additional review, practice, or assessments. These are graded manually by the instructor using the provided Solution Files and Grading Scorecards or Rubrics.

MOS Quizzes provide an objective-based quiz to review the MOS objective-related content covered in the chapter. Provides students with review to help if they plan to take a MOS Certification exam.

Assessment

MyITLab Skill-based Exam Simulation provides students with an assessment of their knowledge and ability to apply the skills they have learned. In the Simulated Exams, students do not have access to the Learning Aids. All of the student's keystrokes are recorded so that instructors can review and provide support to the students. Instructors can set the number of times the students can complete the simulation exam.

MyITLab Assessment Grader Projects (E, F, or G) provide students with live-in-the-application practice with the skills they learned in Projects A and B. These projects provide students with detailed reports showing the student where they made errors and also provides "live comments" explaining the details.

Prepared Exams – these are additional projects created specifically for use as exams that the instructor will grade manually. They are available by Project, by Chapter, and by Unit.

Pre-built Chapter quizzes provide objective-based quizzing to allow students to review how they are doing.

Testbank questions are available for instructors to create their own quizzes for review or assessment.

Abul Sheikh	Abraham Baldwin Agricultural College
John Percy	Atlantic Cape Community College
Janette Hicks	Binghamton University
Shannon Ogden	Black River Technical College
Karen May	Blinn College
Susan Fry	Boise State University
Chigurupati Rani	Borough of Manhattan Community College / CUNY
Ellen Glazer	Broward College
Kate LeGrand	Broward College
Mike Puopolo	Bunker Hill Community College
Nicole Lytle-Kosola	California State University, San Bernardino
Nisheeth Agrawal	Calhoun Community College
Pedro Diaz-Gomez	Cameron
Linda Friedel	Central Arizona College
Gregg Smith	Central Community College
Norm Cregger	Central Michigan University
Lisa LaCaria	Central Piedmont Community College
Steve Siedschlag	Chaffey College
Terri Helfand	Chaffey College
Susan Mills	Chambersburg
Mandy Reininger	Chemeketa Community College
Connie Crossley	Cincinnati State Technical and Community College
Marjorie Deutsch	City University of New York - Queensborough Community College
Mary Ann Zlotow	College of Dupage
Christine Bohnsak	College of Lake County
Gertrude Brier	College of Staten Island
Sharon Brown	College of The Albemarle
Terry Rigsby	Columbia College
Vicki Brooks	Columbia College
Donald Hames	Delgado Community College
Kristen King	Eastern Kentucky University
Kathie Richer	Edmonds Community College
Gary Smith	Elmhurst College
Wendi Kappersw	Embry-Riddle Aeronautical University
Nancy Woolridge	Fullerton College
Abigail Miller	Gateway Community & Technical College
Deep Ramanayake	Gateway Community & Technical College
Gwen White	Gateway Community & Technical College
Debbie Glinert	Gloria K School
Dana Smith	Golf Academy of America
Mary Locke	Greenville Technical College
Diane Marie Roselli	Harrisburg Area Community College
Linda Arnold	Harrisburg Area Community College - Lebanon
Daniel Schoedel	Harrisburg Area Community College - York Campus
Ken Mayer	Heald College
Xiaodong Qiao	Heald College
Donna Lamprecht	Hopkinsville Community College
Kristen Lancaster	Hopkinsville Community College
Johnny Hurley	Iowa Lakes Community College
Linda Halverson	Iowa Lakes Community College
Sarah Kilgo	Isothermal Community College
Chris DeGeare	Jefferson College
David McNair	Jefferson College
Diane Santurri	Johnson & Wales
Roland Sparks	Johnson & Wales University
Ram Raghuraman	Joliet Junior College
Eduardo Suniga	Lansing Community College

Kenneth A. Hyatt	Lonestar College - Kingwood
Glenn Gray	Lonestar College North Harris
Gene Carbonaro	Long Beach City College
Betty Pearman	Los Medanos College
Diane Kosharek	Madison College
Peter Meggison	Massasoit Community College
George Gabb	Miami Dade College
Lennie Alice Cooper	Miami Dade College
Richard Mabjish	Miami Dade College
Victor Giol	Miami Dade College
John Meir	Midlands Technical College
Greg Pauley	Moberly Area Community College
Catherine Glod	Mohawk Valley Community College
Robert Huyck	Mohawk Valley Community College
Kevin Engellant	Montana Western
Philip Lee	Nashville State Community College
Ruth Neal	Navarro College
Sharron Jordan	Navarro College
Richard Dale	New Mexico State University
Lori Townsend	Niagara County Community College
Judson Curry	North Park University
Mary Zegarski	Northampton Community College
Neal Stenlund	Northern Virginia Community Colege
Michael Goeken	Northwest Vista College
Mary Beth Tarver	Northwestern State University
Amy Rutledge	Oakland University
Marcia Braddock	Okefenokee Technical College
Richard Stocke	Oklahoma State University - OKC
Jane Stam	Onondaga Community College
Mike Michaelson	Palomar College
Kungwen (Dave) Chu	Purdue University Calumet
Wendy Ford	CUNY - Queensborough CC
Lewis Hall	Riverside City College
Karen Acree	San Juan College
Tim Ellis	Schoolcraft College
Dan Combellick	Scottsdale Community College
Pat Serrano	Scottsdale Community College
Rose Hendrickson	Sheridan College
Kit Carson	South Georgia College
Rebecca Futch	South Georgia State College
Brad Hagy	Southern Illinois University Carbondale
Mimi Spain	Southern Maine Community College
David Parker	Southern Oregon University
Madeline Baugher	Southwestern Oklahoma State University
Brian Holbert	St. Johns River State College
Bunny Howard	St. Johns River State College
Stephanie Cook	State College of Florida
Sharon Wavle	Tompkins Cortland Community College
George Fiori	Tri-County Technical College
Steve St. John	Tulsa Community College
Karen Thessing	University of Central Arkansas
Richard McMahon	University of Houston-Downtown
Shohreh Hashemi	University of Houston-Downtown
Donna Petty	Wallace Community College
Julia Bell	Walters State Community College
Ruby Kowaney	West Los Angeles College
Casey Thompson	Wiregrass Georgia Technical College
DeAnnia Clements	Wiregrass Georgia Technical College

Getting Started with Windows 10

1

PROJECT 1A

OUTCOMES
Sign in and out of Windows 10, identify the features of an operating system, create a folder and save a file, use Windows apps, and customize your Start menu.

OBJECTIVES

1. Explore the Windows 10 Environment
2. Use File Explorer and Desktop Apps to Create a New Folder and Save a File
3. Identify the Functions of the Windows 10 Operating System
4. Discover Windows 10 Features
5. Sign Out of Windows 10, Turn Off Your Computer, and Manage User Accounts
6. Manage Your Windows 10 System

PROJECT 1B

OUTCOMES
Start programs, search for and manage files and folders, copy and move files and folders, and use the Recycle Bin.

OBJECTIVES

7. Download and Extract Files and Folders
8. Use File Explorer to Display Locations, Folders, and Files
9. Start Programs and Open Data Files
10. Create, Rename, and Copy Files and Folders
11. Use OneDrive as Cloud Storage

Eugenio Marongiu/Shutterstock

In This Chapter  GO! to Work with Windows

In this chapter, you will use Microsoft Windows 10, which is software that manages your computer's hardware, software, communications, and data files. You will use the taskbar and Start menu features to get your work done with ease and use Windows apps to get your latest personal information and to find news and entertainment. You will sign in to your computer, explore the features of Windows 10, create folders and save files, use Windows apps, manage multiple windows, sign out of your computer, and examine user accounts.

The projects in this chapter relate to the **Bell Orchid Hotels**, headquartered in Boston, and which own and operate resorts and business-oriented hotels. Resort properties are located in popular destinations, including Honolulu, Orlando, San Diego, and Santa Barbara. The resorts offer deluxe accommodations and a wide array of dining options. Other Bell Orchid hotels are located in major business centers and offer the latest technology in their meeting facilities. Bell Orchid offers extensive educational opportunities for employees. The company plans to open new properties and update existing properties over the next decade.

Getting to Know Windows 10

PROJECT ACTIVITIES

In Activities 1.01 through 1.19, you will participate in training along with Steven Ramos and Barbara Hewitt, both of whom work for the Information Technology Department at the Boston headquarters office of the Bell Orchid Hotels. After completing this part of the training, you will be able to sign in and sign out of your computer, create folders and save files, use Windows apps, and manage your user account. You will capture two screens that will look similar to Figure 1.1.

Please always review the downloaded Grader instructions before beginning.

PROJECT FILES

For Project 1A, you will need the following files:

No Student Data Files are required to begin this project. When prompted to do so, you will create a new Snip file and a new Windows 10 screenshot using features in Windows 10.

You will save your files as:

Lastname_Firstname_1A_Get_Started_Snip
Lastname_Firstname_1A_Graph_Screenshot

PROJECT RESULTS

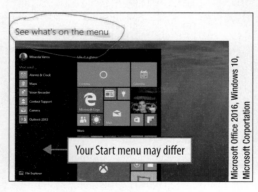

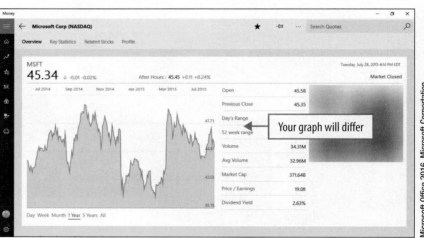

Microsoft Office 2016, Windows 10, Microsoft Corportation

Microsoft Office 2016, Microsoft Corportation

FIGURE 1.1 Project 1A Getting to Know Windows 10

A *program* is a set of instructions that a computer uses to accomplish a task. A computer program that helps you perform a task for a specific purpose is referred to as an *application*. For example, there are applications to create a document using word processing software, to play a game, to view the latest weather report, or to manage information.

An *operating system* is a specific type of computer program that manages the other programs on a computing device such as a desktop computer, a laptop computer, a smartphone, a tablet computer, or a game console. You need an operating system to:

- use application programs
- coordinate the use of your computer hardware such as a keyboard, mouse, touchpad, touchscreen, game controller, or printer
- organize data that you store on your computer and access data that you store on your own computer and in other locations

Windows 10 is an operating system developed by Microsoft Corporation that works with mobile computing devices and also with traditional desktop and laptop PCs.

Activity 1.01 | Identifying Apps and Platforms

The term *desktop app* commonly refers to a computer program that is installed on the hard drive of your personal computer—usually referred to as a PC—and requires a computer operating system like Microsoft Windows or Apple OSX (pronounced O-S-ten) to run. The programs in the full-featured versions of Microsoft Office such as Word and Excel are popular desktop apps. Adobe's Photoshop photo editing software and Adobe's Premiere video editing software are also popular desktop apps. Desktop apps typically have hundreds of features that take time to learn and use efficiently.

The shortened version of the term *application* is *app*, and this is typically a smaller application designed for a single purpose. Apps can run from the device operating system on a PC, a tablet computer, a game console, or a smartphone. You might already be familiar with apps that run on mobile devices like an Apple iPhone, an Apple iPad, an Android phone, an Android tablet, a Windows phone, or a Windows tablet. Examples include games like Monument Valley and Words with Friends; social networking and messaging apps like Instagram, Facebook, and WhatsApp; information apps like The Weather Channel and NFL Mobile; apps provided by your bank to enable you to conduct transactions; and services like Skype or Google Search.

Windows apps are apps that run not only on a Windows phone and a Windows tablet, but also on your Windows desktop PC. Most popular apps have versions for each major *mobile device platform*—the hardware and software environment for smaller-screen devices such as tablets and smartphones. For example, the NFL Mobile app is available for Apple mobile devices, Windows mobile devices, Android devices, and BlackBerry devices.

Increasingly, an operating system environment is referred to simply as a *platform*, which refers to an underlying computer system on which application programs can run. An *application developer*, which is anyone who writes a computer application, must write his or her application for one or more platforms, the most popular of which are the iOS platform, the Android platform, and the Windows platform.

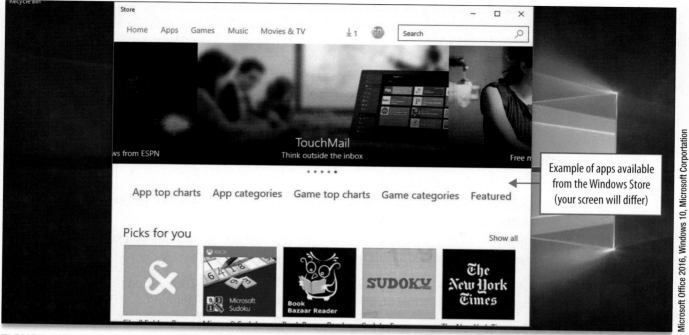

Example of apps available from the Windows Store (your screen will differ)

FIGURE 1.2

Some Windows apps are also referred to as ***universal apps*** because anyone that wants to develop an app for the Windows 10 platform can use a common code base to deliver the app to any Windows device—a desktop or laptop PC, a Windows phone, a Windows tablet, or an Xbox game console.

App developers can also use this code base to develop apps for Microsoft's new ***HoloLens*** see-through holographic computer and for devices on the ***Internet of Things***, which refers to a growing network of physical objects that will have sensors connected to the Internet. Home automation devices like lights and appliances that you can control over the Internet are among the first objects connected to the ***IoT***—the common acronym for the Internet of Things.

FIGURE 1.3

Self-Check | Answer These Questions to Check Your Understanding

1 A set of instructions that a computer uses to accomplish a task is a _____.

2 A specific type of computer program that manages the other programs on a computer is an _____ _____.

3 Computer programs installed on the hard drive of a computer, such as Microsoft Excel and Adobe Photoshop, and that typically have hundreds of features and take time to learn and use efficiently, are referred to as _____ apps.

4 The hardware and software environment for smaller-screen devices such as laptops, tablets, and smartphones is referred to as a mobile device _____.

5 The growing network of physical objects that have sensors connected to the Internet is called the _____ _____ _____.

Activity 1.02 | Recognizing User Accounts in Windows 10

On a single computer, Windows 10 can have multiple user accounts. This is useful because you can share a computer with other people in your family or organization and each person can have his or her own information and settings—none of which others can see. Each user on a single computer is referred to as a *user account*.

ALERT! **Variations in Screen Organization, Colors, and Functionality Are Common in Windows 10**

Individuals and organizations can determine how Windows 10 displays; therefore, the colors and the organization of various elements on the screen can vary. Your college or organization may customize Windows 10 to display a college picture or company logo, or restrict access to certain features. The basic functions and structure of Windows 10 are not changed by such variations. You can be confident that the skills you will practice in this instruction apply to Windows 10 regardless of available functionality or differences between the figures shown and your screen.

NOTE **Comparing Your Screen with the Figures in This Textbook**

Your screen will more closely match the figures shown in this textbook if you set your screen resolution to 1280 × 768. At other resolutions, your screen will closely resemble, but not match, the figures shown. To view your screen's resolution, on the desktop, right-click in a blank area, click *Display settings*, on the right click *Advanced display settings*, click the *Resolution arrow*, and then click the desired setting.

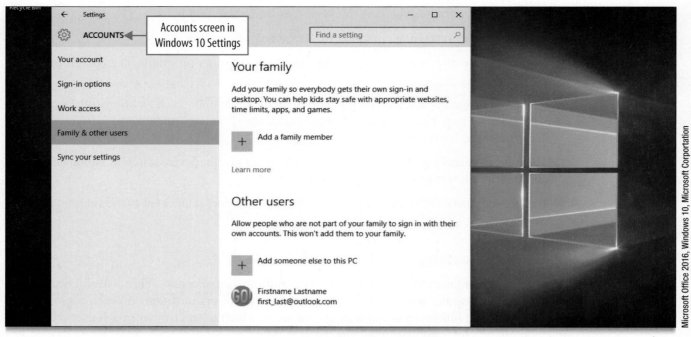

FIGURE 1.4

With Windows 10, you can create a ***Microsoft account***, and then use that account to sign in to *any* Windows 10 computer on which you have, or create, a user account. By signing in with a Microsoft account you can:

- download apps from the Windows Store
- get your online content—email, social network updates, updated news—automatically displayed in an app when you sign in

Optionally, you can create a local account for use only on a specific PC. On your own Windows 10 computer, you must establish and then sign in with either a local account or a Microsoft account. Regardless of which one you select, you must provide an email address to associate with the user account name. If you create and then sign in with a local account, you can still connect to the Internet, but you will not have the advantage of having your personal arrangement of apps displayed on your Start menu every time you sign in to that PC. You can use any email address to create a local account—similar to other online services where an email address is your user ID. You can also use any email address to create a Microsoft account.

To enjoy and get the full benefit from Windows 10, Microsoft Office, Skype, and free unlimited OneDrive cloud storage, if you have not already done so, create a Microsoft account by going to www.microsoft.com/en-us/account and click *Create a free Microsoft account*. Here you can create an account using any email address and, if you want to do so, view a short video to learn about Microsoft accounts.

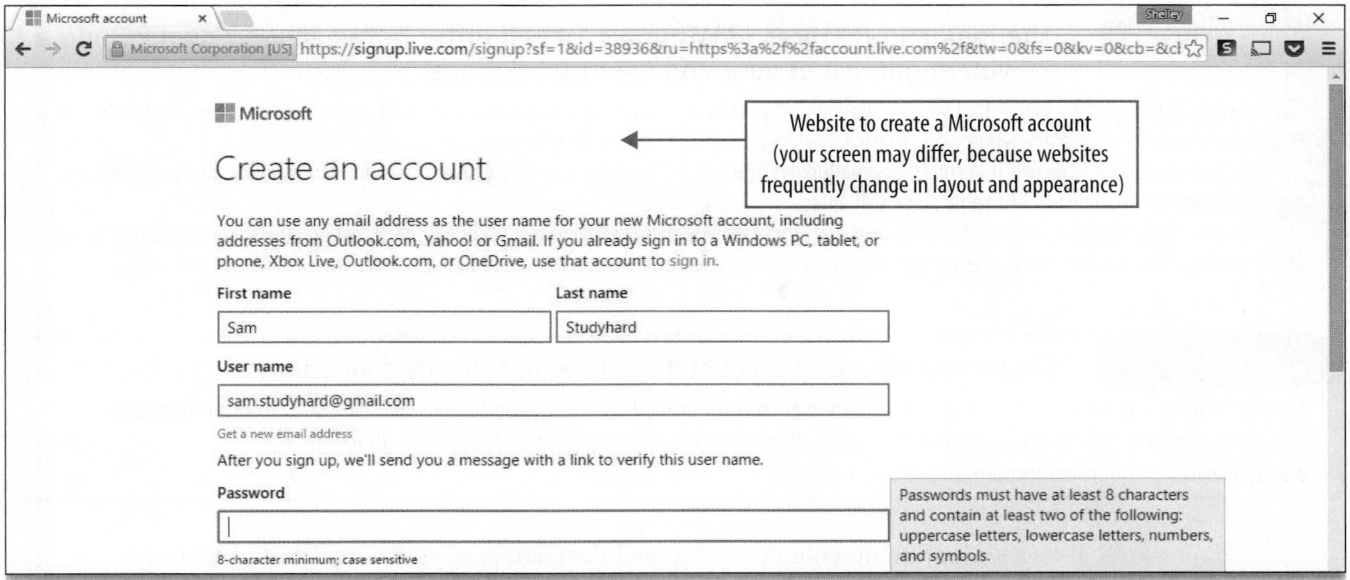

Website to create a Microsoft account (your screen may differ, because websites frequently change in layout and appearance)

FIGURE 1.5

Microsoft Office 2016, Windows 10, Microsoft Corportation

By signing in with a Microsoft account, your computer becomes your connected device where *you*—not your files—are the center of activity. At your college or place of employment, sign-in requirements will vary, because those computers are controlled by the organization's IT (Information Technology) professionals who are responsible for maintaining a secure computing environment for the entire organization.

Self-Check | Answer These Questions to Check Your Understanding

1 On a single Windows 10 computer, multiple people can have a user account with their own information and _____.

2 On your own Windows 10 computer, it is recommended that you create a Microsoft account—if you do not have one—and then use that account to sign in because you will have your personal arrangement of _____ displayed on the Start menu every time you sign in to that PC.

3 To use your own Windows 10 computer, you must establish and then sign in with either a _____ account or a Microsoft account.

4 You can use any _____ address to set up a Microsoft account.

5 Sign-in requirements vary in organizations and colleges, because those computers are _____ by the organization's IT (Information Technology) professionals.

Activity 1.03 | Turning On Your Computer, Signing In, and Exploring the Windows 10 Environment

Before you begin any computer activity, you must, if necessary, turn on your computer. This process is commonly referred to as ***booting the computer***. Because Windows 10 does not require you to completely shut down your computer except to install or repair a hardware device, in most instances moving the mouse or pressing a key will wake your computer in a few seconds. So most of the time you will skip the lengthier boot process.

In this Activity, you will turn on your computer and sign in to Windows 10. Within an organization, the sign-in process may differ from that of your own computer.

The look and features of Windows 10 will differ between your own PC and a PC you might use at your college or workplace.

The Activities in Project 1A assume that you are working on your own PC and signed in with a Microsoft account, or that you are working on a PC at your college or workplace where you are permitted to sign into Windows 10 with your own Microsoft account.

If you do not have a Microsoft account, or are working at a computer where you are unable to sign in with your Microsoft account, you can still complete the Activities but some steps will differ.

On your own computer, you created your user account when you installed Windows 10 or when you set up your new computer that came with Windows 10. In a classroom or lab, check with your instructor to see how you will sign in to Windows 10.

Create your Microsoft account if you have not already done so.

To benefit from this instruction and understand your own computer, be sure that you know your Microsoft account login and password, and use that to set up your user account. If you need to create a Microsoft account, go to www.microsoft.com/en-us/account and click *Create a free Microsoft account*.

1 If necessary, turn on your computer, and then compare your screen with Figure 1.6.

The Windows 10 *lock screen* displays a background—this might be a default picture from Microsoft or a picture that you selected if you have personalized your system already. You can also choose to have a slide show of your own photos display on the lock screen.

Your lock screen displays the time, day, and date. From the Personalization screen of Windows 10 Settings, you can choose *lock screen apps* to display, such as your calendar and mail. A lock screen app runs in the background and shows you quick status and notifications, even when your screen is locked. A lock screen app may also display a *badge*, which is an *icon*—small images that can represent commands, files, applications, or other windows—that shows status information such as your Internet connection or battery time remaining or summary information; for example, how many unread emails are in a mail app or the number of new posts in a social media app.

For example, one lock screen app that you can add is Skype so that you can answer a Skype call without having to sign in.

Your organization might have a custom sign-in screen with a logo or sign-in instructions, which will differ from the one shown. If you are using Windows 10 Pro, in the Accounts section of Settings, there is a feature named *Work access*, from which you may be able to connect to your work or school system based on established policies.

The image shows a Windows 10 lock screen displaying the time "3:20" and "Thursday, September 3" over a photographic background. A callout with an arrow points to the image and reads:

Windows 10 lock screen
(your image will vary)

FIGURE 1.6

2 Determine whether you are working with a mouse and keyboard system or with a touchscreen system. If you are working with a touchscreen, determine whether you will use a stylus pen or the touch of your fingers.

Windows 10 is optimized for touchscreen computers and also works with a mouse and keyboard in the way you are probably most accustomed. If your device has a touchscreen, you can use the following gestures with your fingers in place of mouse and keyboard commands:

NOTE	If You Are Using a Touchscreen
	Tap an item to click it.
	Press and hold for a few seconds to right-click; release when the information or commands display.
	Touch the screen with two or more fingers and then pinch together to zoom in or stretch your fingers apart to zoom out.
	Slide your finger on the screen to scroll—slide left to scroll right and slide right to scroll left.
	Slide to rearrange—similar to dragging with a mouse.
	Swipe to select—slide an item a short distance with a quick movement—to select an item and bring up commands, if any.

3   Press [Enter] to display the Windows 10 sign-in screen.

BY TOUCH   On the lock screen, swipe upward to display the sign-in screen. Tap your user image if necessary to display the Password box.

4   If you are the displayed user, type your password (if you have established one) and press [Enter]. If you are not the displayed user, click your user image if it displays or click the Switch user arrow [→] and then click your user image. Type your password.

BY TOUCH   Tap the Password box to display the onscreen keyboard, type your password using the onscreen keyboard, and then at the right, tap the arrow.

The Windows 10 desktop displays with a default desktop background, a background you have selected, or perhaps a background set by your college or workplace.

5   In the lower left corner of your screen, move the mouse pointer over—***point to***—**Start** ⊞ and then ***click***—press the left button on your mouse pointing device—to display the **Start menu**. Compare your screen with Figure 1.7, and then take a moment to study the table in Figure 1.8.

The ***mouse pointer*** is any symbol that displays on your screen in response to moving your mouse.

The Windows 10 ***Start menu*** displays a list of installed programs on the left and a customizable group of square and rectangular boxes—referred to as ***tiles***—on the right. You can customize the arrangement of tiles from which you can access apps, websites, programs, folders, and tools for using your computer by simply clicking or tapping them.

Think of the right side of the Start menu as your connected ***dashboard***—a one-screen view of links to information and programs that matter to *you*—through which you can connect with the people, activities, places, and apps that you care about.

Some tiles are referred to as ***live tiles***, because they are constantly updated with fresh information relevant to you—the number of new email messages you have, new sports scores that you are interested in, or new updates to social networks such as Facebook or Twitter. Live tiles are at the center of your Windows 10 experience.

As you progress in your study of Windows 10, you will learn to customize the Start menu and add, delete, and organize tiles into meaningful groups. Your Start menu will not look like anyone else's; you will customize it to suit your own information needs.

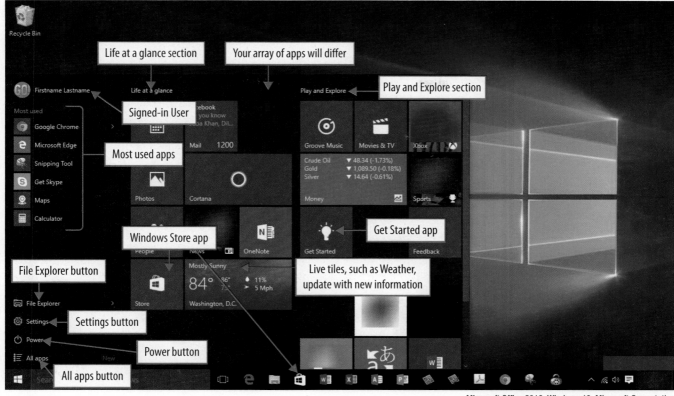

FIGURE 1.7

Microsoft Office 2016, Windows 10, Microsoft Corportation

PARTS OF THE WINDOWS 10 START MENU	
All apps button	Expands the list of apps to show all installed apps in alphabetic sections.
File Explorer button	Opens the File Explorer program.
Get Started app	Displays information to help you learn about Windows 10.
Life at a glance section	Apps pinned to the Start menu that related to your own information; for example, your Mail, your Calendar, and your contacts (People); you can change this heading or delete it.
Most used apps	Displays a list of the apps that you use the most; updates as you use Windows 10.
Play and Explore section	Apps pinned to the Start menu that relate to games or news apps that you have installed; you can change this heading or delete it.
Power button	Enables you to set your computer to Sleep, Shut down, or Restart.
Settings button	Displays the Settings window to change any Windows 10 setting.
Signed-in User	Displays the name of the signed-in user.
Windows Store app	Opens the Windows Store to locate and download more apps.

FIGURE 1.8

Microsoft Office 2016, Windows 10, Microsoft Corportation

6 ▸ Click **Start** ⊞ again to close the Start menu. Compare your screen with Figure 1.9, and then take a moment to study the parts of the Windows desktop as shown in the table in Figure 1.10.

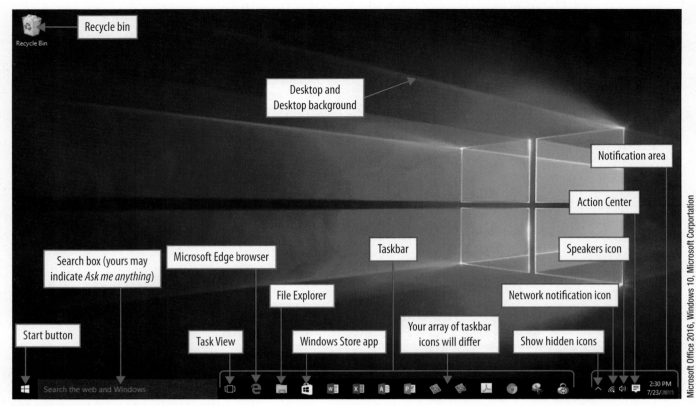

FIGURE 1.9

PARTS OF THE WINDOWS 10 DESKTOP	
Action Center	Displays the Action Center in a vertical pane on the right of your screen where you can see app notifications—such as new mail or new alerts from Microsoft or from social networks like Facebook—at the top and access commonly used settings at the bottom.
Desktop	Serves as a surface for your work, like the top of an actual desk. Here you can arrange icons—small pictures that represent a file, folder, program, or other object.
Desktop background	Displays the colors and graphics of your desktop; you can change the desktop background to look the way you want it, such as using a picture or a solid color. Also referred to as *wallpaper*.
File Explorer	Launches the File Explorer program, which displays the contents of folders and files on your computer and on connected locations, and also enables you to perform tasks related to your files and folders such as copying, moving, and renaming.
Microsoft Edge browser	Launches Microsoft Edge, the web browser program developed by Microsoft that is included with Windows 10.
Network notification icon	Displays the status of your network.
Notification area	Displays notification icons and the system clock and calendar; sometimes referred to as the *system tray*.
Recycle Bin	Contains files and folders that you delete. When you delete a file or folder from a location on your hard disk drive, it is not actually deleted; it stays in the Recycle Bin if you want it back, until you take an action to empty the Recycle Bin.
Search box	Before **Cortana**—Microsoft's intelligent personal assistant—is set up, this will indicate *Search the web and Windows*. After Cortana is set up, this will indicate *Ask me anything*. Regardless, you can type in the box to begin a search of your computer and the web.

FIGURE 1.10 *(continued)*

PARTS OF THE WINDOWS 10 DESKTOP (*continued*)	
Show hidden icons	Displays additional icons related to your notifications.
Speakers icon	Displays the status of your computer's speakers (if any).
Start button	Displays the Start menu.
Task View	Displays your desktop background with a small image of all open programs and apps. Click once to open, click again to close.
Taskbar	Contains buttons to launch programs and buttons for all open programs; by default, it is located at the bottom of the desktop, but you can move it. You can customize the number and arrangement of buttons.
Windows Store	Opens the Windows Store where you can select and download Windows apps.

Microsoft Office 2016, Windows 10, Microsoft Corportation

FIGURE 1.10

> **NOTE** **This Activity Is Optional**
>
> Complete this Activity if you are able to do so. Some college labs may not enable these features. If you cannot practice in your college lab, practice this on another computer if possible.

Activity 1.04 | Changing Your Desktop Background and Lock Screen Image

As a way to personalize your computer, you can change the desktop background to a personal photo. You can also change your lock screen image to a personal photo.

1 Click **Start** 🪟, just above the Start button click **Settings**, click **Personalization**, and then on the left click **Background**.

2 On the right, under **Choose your picture**, click **Browse**, and then select a personal photo from the **Pictures** folder on your PC—or navigate to some other location where you have stored a personal photo.

3 Click the picture, and then at the bottom of the Open dialog box, click **Choose picture**.

4 On the left, click **Lock screen**, on the right, click the **Background arrow**, and then click **Picture**.

5 Click **Browse**, and then select a personal photo from the **Pictures** folder on your PC—or navigate to some other location where you have stored a personal photo.

6 Click the picture, and then at the bottom of the Open dialog box, click **Choose picture**.

7 Close all open windows.

> **NOTE** **This Activity Is Optional**
>
> Complete this Activity if you are able to do so. Some college labs may not enable these features. If you cannot practice in your college lab, practice this on another computer if possible.

Activity 1.05 | Creating a PIN to Use in Place of Passwords

You can create a *PIN*—a personal identification number—to use in place of a password. Having a PIN makes it easier to sign in to Windows, apps, and services because it is short.

1 Click **Start** 🪟, just above the Start button click **Settings**, click **Accounts**, and then on the left click **Sign-in options**.

2 On the right, under **PIN**, click **Add**. If necessary, enter the password for your Microsoft account and click **Sign in**.

3 In the **New PIN** box, type **1234**—or a PIN of your choice so long as you can remember it. In the **Confirm PIN** box, retype your PIN.

4 Click **OK**, and notice that you can use this PIN to sign in to Windows, apps, and services.

5 **Close** ⌧ the **Settings** window.

Objective 2 | Use File Explorer and Desktop Apps to Create a New Folder and Save a File

Activity 1.06 | Pinning a Program and Adding a Toolbar to the Taskbar

Snipping Tool is a program within Windows 10 that captures an image of all or part of your computer's screen. A ***snip***, as the captured image is called, can be annotated, saved, copied, or shared via email.

1 In the lower left corner of your screen, click in the **Search box**.

Recall that your Search box may be set up for Cortana, in which case it will indicate *Ask me anything*; if Cortana is not set up, the Search box will indicate *Search the web and Windows*. If Cortana asks to be set up, you can indicate that you are not interested or go ahead and set it up.

Search relies on ***Bing***, Microsoft's search engine, which enables you to conduct a search on your PC, your apps, and the web.

2 With your insertion point in the search box, type **snipping** Compare your screen with Figure 1.11.

🔄 **BY TOUCH** On a touchscreen, tap in the Search box to display the onscreen keyboard, and then begin to type *snipping*.

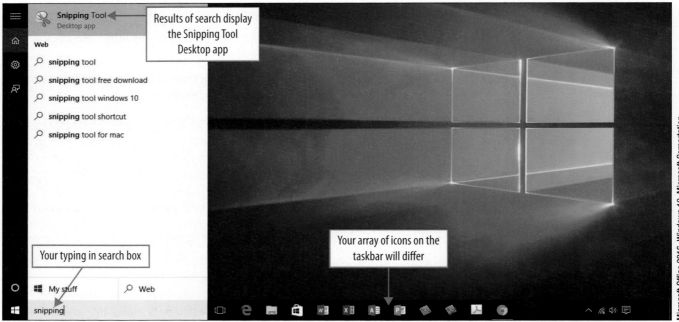

Microsoft Office 2016, Windows 10, Microsoft Corportation

FIGURE 1.11

14 **Windows 10** | Chapter 1: GETTING STARTED WITH WINDOWS 10

3 With **Snipping Tool** shaded and displayed at the top of the search results, press Enter one time.

> The Snipping Tool *dialog box*—a small window that displays options for completing a task—displays on the desktop, and on the taskbar, the Snipping Tool program button displays underlined and framed in a lighter shade to indicate that the program is open.

⟳ BY TOUCH   In the search results, tap the Snipping Tool app.

4 On the taskbar, point to the **Snipping Tool** button 🔍 and then *right-click*—click the right mouse button one time. On the displayed **Jump List**, click **Pin this program to taskbar**.

> A *Jump List* displays destinations and tasks from a program's taskbar icon when you right-click the icon.

⟳ BY TOUCH   On the taskbar, use the *Swipe to select* technique—swipe upward with a short quick movement—to display the Jump List. On the list, tap *Pin this program to taskbar*.

5 Point to the upper right corner of the **Snipping Tool** dialog box, and then click **Close** ☒.

> Because you will use Snipping Tool frequently while completing the projects in this instruction, it is recommended that you leave Snipping Tool pinned to your taskbar.

6 Point to an empty area of the taskbar, and then right-click to display a list that contains *Toolbars*—if your taskbar is crowded, you might have to try several times to find an empty area.

7 Point to **Toolbars**, click **Links**, and then on the taskbar, notice the text *Links*.

8 To the right of the text *Links*, click >> and then notice the links to websites you have visited.

> It is good to know that these taskbar toolbars are available if you want to use them; however, it is now more common to add tiles to the Start menu for frequently used sites. There are some additional toolbars you might want to explore.

9 To remove the taskbar toolbar, right-click again in a blank area of the taskbar, point to **Toolbars**, and then click **Links** again to remove it from the taskbar.

Activity 1.07 | Creating a New Folder to Store a File

A *file* is a collection of information stored on a computer under a single name. Examples of a file include a Word document, an Excel workbook, a picture, a song, or a program. A *folder* is a container in which you can store files. Windows 10 organizes and keeps track of your electronic files by letting you create and label electronic folders into which you can place your files.

In this Activity, you will create a new folder and save it in a location of your choice. You might decide to use a *removable storage device*, such as a USB flash drive, which is commonly used to transfer information from one computer to another. Such devices are also useful when you want to work with your files on different computers. For example, you probably have files that you work with at your college, at home, and possibly at your workplace.

A *drive* is an area of storage that is formatted with a file system compatible with your operating system and is identified by a drive letter. For example, your computer's *hard disk drive*—the primary storage device located inside your computer where some of your files and programs are typically stored—is usually designated as drive *C*. Removable storage devices that you insert into your computer will be designated with a drive letter—the letter designation varies from one computer to another.

As you progress in your study of Windows 10, you will also learn to use *cloud storage*—storage space on an Internet site that can also display as a drive on your computer. When you create a Microsoft account, free cloud storage called *OneDrive* is provided to you. If you are signed in with your Microsoft account, you can access OneDrive from File Explorer.

Increasingly, the use of removable storage devices for file storage is becoming less common, because having your files stored in the cloud where you can retrieve them from any device is more convenient and efficient.

ALERT!

The steps in this Activity use the example of storing on a USB flash drive. If you want to store your file in a different location, such as the Documents folder on your computer's hard drive or a folder on your OneDrive, you can still complete the steps, but your screens will not match exactly those shown.

---

1 Be sure your Windows desktop is still displayed. If you want to do so, insert your USB flash drive. If necessary, close any messages.

> Plugging in a device results in a chime sound—if sound is enabled. You might see a message in the taskbar or on the screen that the device software is being installed.

2 On the taskbar, click **File Explorer** 📁. If necessary, on the ribbon at the top of the window, on the View tab, in the Layout group, click Tiles. (You might have to expand your ribbon, as described in the table in Figure 1.13; also, you might have to scroll within the Layout group to view *Tiles*.) Compare your screen with Figure 1.12, and then take a moment to study the parts of the File Explorer window as shown in the table in Figure 1.13.

NOTE   Does your ribbon show only the tab names?

By default, the ribbon is minimized and appears as a menu bar, displaying only the ribbon tabs. If only the tabs of your ribbon are displayed, click the Expand the Ribbon arrow ⌄ on the right side to display the full ribbon.

The *File Explorer window* displays with the Quick access area selected by default. A File Explorer window displays the contents of the current location, and contains helpful parts so that you can *navigate*—explore within the file organizing structure of Windows. A *location* is any disk drive, folder, network, or cloud storage area in which you can store files and folders.

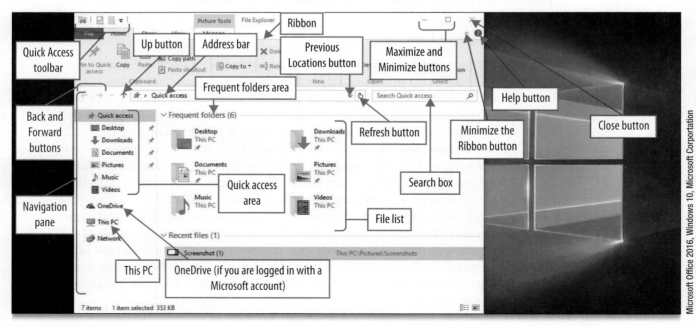

FIGURE 1.12

PARTS OF THE FILE EXPLORER WINDOW	
Address bar	Displays your current location in the folder structure as a series of links separated by arrows.
Back and Forward buttons	Provides the ability to navigate to other folders you have already opened without closing the current folder window. These buttons work with the address bar; that is, after you use the address bar to change folders, you can use the Back button to return to the previous folder.
Close button	Closes the window.
File list	Displays the contents of the current folder or location; if you type text into the Search box, only the folders and files that match your search will display here—including files in subfolders.
Frequent folders area	When Quick access is selected in the navigation pane, displays the folders you use frequently.
Help button	Opens a Bing search for Windows 10 help.
Maximize button	Increases the size of a window to fill the entire screen.
Minimize button	Removes the window from the screen without closing it; minimized windows can be reopened by clicking the associated button in the taskbar.
Minimize the Ribbon button	Collapses the ribbon so that only the tab names display.
Navigation pane	Displays—for the purpose of navigating to locations—the Quick access area, your OneDrive if you have one and are signed in, locations on the PC at which you are working, any connected storage devices, and network locations to which you might be connected.
OneDrive	Provides navigation to your free file storage and file sharing service provided by Microsoft that you get when you sign up for a Microsoft account; this is your personal cloud storage for files.
Previous Locations button	Displays the path to locations you have visited recently so that you can go back to a previously working directory quickly.
Quick access area	Displays commonly accessed locations—such as Documents and Desktop—that you want to access quickly.
Quick Access Toolbar	Displays commonly used commands; you can customize this toolbar by adding and deleting commands and by showing the toolbar below the ribbon instead of above the ribbon.
Refresh button	Refreshes the current path.
Ribbon	Groups common tasks on related tabs at the top of the window; for example, copying and moving, creating new folders, emailing and zipping items, and changing views.
Search box	Locates files stored within the current folder when you type a search term.
This PC	Provides navigation to your internal storage and attached storage devices including optical media such as a DVD drive.
Up button	Opens the location where the folder you are viewing is saved—also referred to as the *parent folder*.

FIGURE 1.13

3 If necessary, in the upper right corner of the **File Explorer** window, click **Expand the Ribbon** ⌄ .

The *ribbon* is a user interface in Windows 10 that groups commands for performing related tasks on tabs across the upper portion of a window. Commands for common tasks include copying and moving, creating new folders, emailing and zipping items, and changing the view.

Use the *navigation pane*—the area on the left side of the File Explorer window—to get to locations—your OneDrive, folders on your PC, devices and drives connected to your PC, and other PCs on your network.

4 In the **navigation pane**, click **This PC**. On the right, under **Devices and drives**, locate **Windows (C:)**—or **OS (C:)**—point to the device name to display the ⌖ pointer, and then right-click to display a shortcut menu. Compare your screen with Figure 1.14.

A *shortcut menu* is a context-sensitive menu that displays commands and options relevant to the active object. The Windows logo on the C: drive indicates this is where the Windows 10 operating system is stored.

↻ BY TOUCH   Press and hold briefly to display a shaded square and then release.

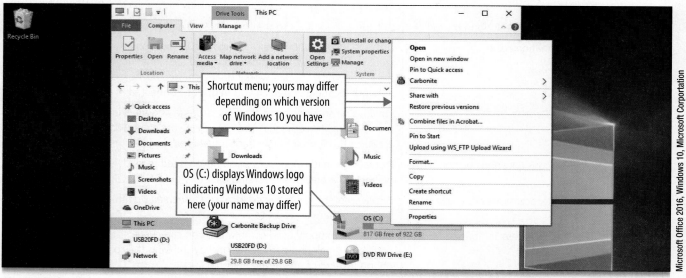

FIGURE 1.14

5 On the shortcut menu, click **Open** to display the *file list* for this drive.

A file list displays the contents of the current location. If you enter a search term in the search box, your results will also display here. Here, in the C: drive, Windows 10 stores various files related to your operating system.

↻ ANOTHER WAY   Point to the device name and double-click to display the file list for the device.

6 On the ribbon, notice that the **Drive Tools tab** displays above the **Manage tab**.

This is a *contextual tab*, which is a tab added to the ribbon automatically when a specific object is selected and that contains commands relevant to the selected object.

7 To the left of the **address bar**, click **Up** ⬆ to move up one level in the drive hierarchy and close the file list.

> The **address bar** displays your current location in the folder structure as a series of links separated by arrows. Use the address bar to enter or select a location. You can tap or click a part of the path to go to that level, or tap or click at the end of the path to select the path for copying.

8 Under **Devices and drives**, click your **USB flash drive** to select it—or click the folder or location where you want to store your files for this Project—and notice that the drive or folder is highlighted in blue, indicating it is selected. At the top of the window, on the ribbon, click the **Computer tab**, and then in the **Location group**, click **Open**. Compare your screen with Figure 1.15.

> The file list for the selected location displays. There may be no files or only a few files in the location you have selected. You can open a location by using the shortcut menu or by using this ribbon command.

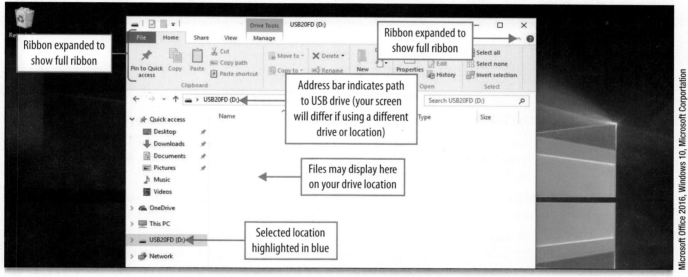

FIGURE 1.15

9 On the ribbon, in the **New group**, click **New folder**.

10 With the text *New folder* highlighted in blue, type **Windows 10 Chapter 1** and press Enter to confirm the folder name and select—highlight in blue—the new folder. With the folder selected, press Enter again to open the File Explorer window for your **Windows 10 Chapter 1** folder. Compare your screen with Figure 1.16.

> A new folder is created in the location you selected. The address bar indicates the *path* from This PC to your folder. A path is a sequence of folders that leads to a specific file or folder.

> To *select* means to specify, by highlighting, a block of data or text on the screen with the intent of performing some action on the selection.

↻ BY TOUCH   You may have to tap the keyboard icon in the lower right corner of the taskbar to display the onscreen keyboard.

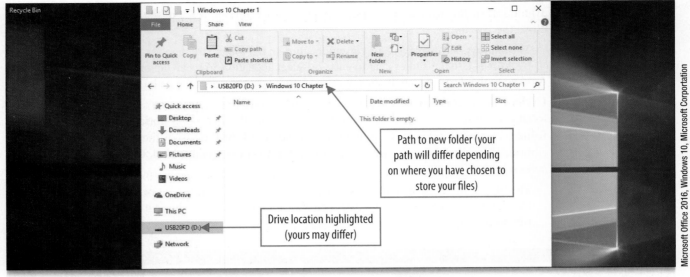

FIGURE 1.16

Activity 1.08 | Creating and Saving a File

1 In the upper right corner of your **Windows 10 Chapter 1** folder window, click **Close** ☒.

2 In the lower left corner, click **Start** ▦, and then at the bottom of the menu, click **All apps**.

The *All apps* command displays the Start menu in an alphabetic arrangement showing every app—both desktop apps and Windows apps—that is installed on your computer. Many apps are installed by default and are part of the Windows 10 operating system.

3 Point to the right edge of the **menu list** to display a **scroll bar**, and then drag the **scroll box** down to view apps listed under **G**. Compare your screen with Figure 1.17.

To *drag* is to move something from one location on the screen to another while holding down the left mouse button; the action of dragging includes releasing the mouse button at the desired time or location.

FIGURE 1.17

More Knowledge — **Jump to a Lettered Section of the All Apps List Quickly**

To move quickly to an alphabetic section of the All apps list, click any alphabetic letter on the list to display an onscreen alphabet, and then click the letter of the alphabet to which you want to jump.

4 Click **Get Started**. If necessary, in the upper right, click **Maximize** ▢ so that the **Get Started** window fills your entire screen. On the list along the left side of the screen, click **Start**, and then click **See what's on the menu**. Then, move your mouse pointer to the right edge of the screen to display the **scroll bar**. Compare your screen with Figure 1.18.

A vertical *scroll bar* displays on the right side of this window. A scroll bar displays when the contents of a window are not completely visible. A scroll bar can be vertical as shown or horizontal and displayed at the bottom of a window.

Within the scroll bar, you can move the *scroll box* to bring the contents of the window into view. The position of the scroll box within the scroll bar indicates your relative position within the window's contents. You can click the *scroll arrow* at either end of the scroll bar to move within the window in small increments.

In any window, the *Maximize* button will maximize the size of the window to fill the entire screen.

It is worth your time to explore this *Get Started* feature in Windows 10 to learn about all the things that Windows 10 can do for you.

FIGURE 1.18

5 On the taskbar, click **Snipping Tool** ✂ to display the small **Snipping Tool** dialog box over the screen.

6 On the **menu bar** of the **Snipping Tool** dialog box, click the **arrow** to the right of *New*— referred to as the **New arrow**—and then compare your screen with Figure 1.19.

An arrow attached to a button will display a menu when clicked. Such a button is referred to as a *split button*—clicking the main part of the button performs a command and clicking the arrow opens a menu with choices. A *menu* is a list of commands within a category, and a group of menus at the top of a program window is referred to as the *menu bar*.

FIGURE 1.19

7 On the menu, notice that there are four types of snips.

A *free-form snip* enables you to draw an irregular line such as a circle around an area of the screen. A *rectangular snip* enables you to draw a precise box by dragging the mouse pointer around an area of the screen to form a rectangle. A *window snip* captures the entire displayed window. A *full-screen snip* captures the entire screen.

8 On the menu, click **Rectangular Snip**, and move your mouse slightly. Notice that the screen dims and your pointer takes the shape of a plus sign ⊞.

9 Move the mouse pointer to the upper left corner of the white portion of the screen, hold down the left mouse button, and then drag down and to the right until you have captured the white portion of the screen with the Start menu picture as shown in Figure 1.20 and then release the mouse button. If you are not satisfied with your result, close the Snipping Tool window and begin again.

Your snip is copied to the Snipping Tool mark-up window. Here you can annotate—mark or make notes on—save, copy, or share the snip.

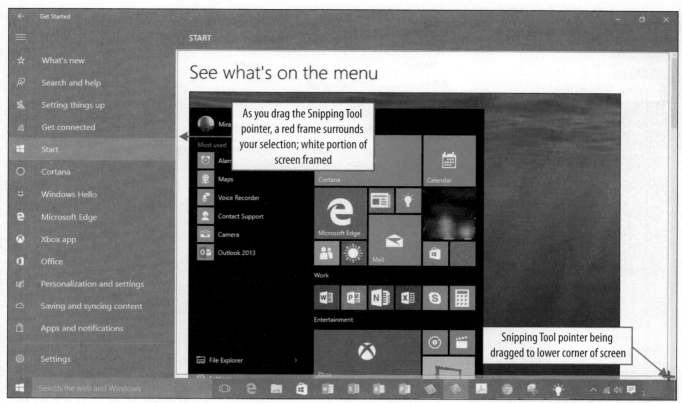

FIGURE 1.20

10 On the toolbar of the displayed **Snipping Tool** mark-up window, click the **Pen button arrow** ✏, and then click **Red Pen**. Notice that your mouse pointer displays as a red dot.

11 At the top of the snip—remember that you are now looking at a picture of the portion of the screen you captured—point to the words *See what's on the menu* and use the red mouse pointer to draw a circle around the text—the circle need not be precise. If you are not satisfied with your circle, on the toolbar, click the Eraser button 🖊, point anywhere on the red circle, click to erase, and then begin again. Compare your screen with Figure 1.21.

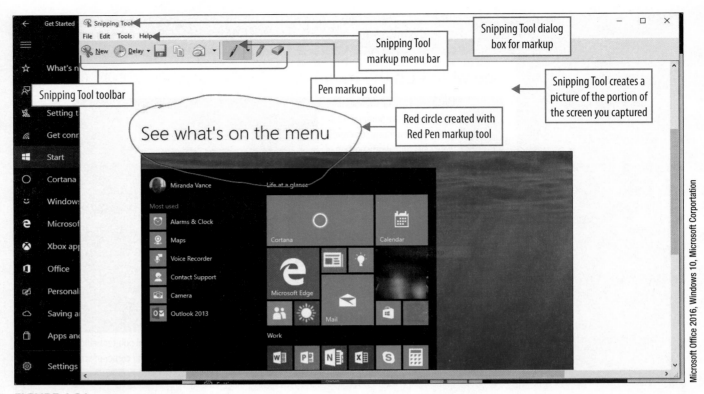

FIGURE 1.21

> **12** On the toolbar of the **Snipping Tool** mark-up window, click **Highlighter** . Notice that your mouse pointer displays as a small yellow rectangle.

> **13** Point to the text *See what's on the menu*, hold down the left mouse button, and then drag over the text to highlight it in yellow. If you are not satisfied with your yellow highlight, on the toolbar, click the Eraser button, point anywhere on the yellow highlight, click to erase, and then begin again. Compare your screen with Figure 1.22.

BY TOUCH   Use your finger to draw the circle and to highlight text.

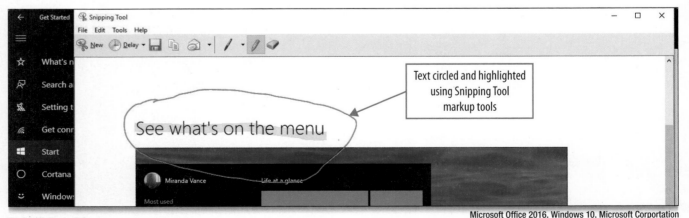

Microsoft Office 2016, Windows 10, Microsoft Corportation

FIGURE 1.22

> **14** On the **Snipping Tool** mark-up window's toolbar, click **Save Snip** to display the **Save As** dialog box.

15 In the **Save As** dialog box, in the **navigation pane**, drag the scroll box down as necessary to find and then click the location where you created your **Windows 10 Chapter 1** folder.

16 In the **file list**, scroll as necessary, locate and *double-click*—press the left mouse button two times in rapid succession while holding the mouse still—your **Windows 10 Chapter 1** folder. Compare your screen with Figure 1.23.

🔄 **ANOTHER WAY**   Right-click the folder name and click Open.

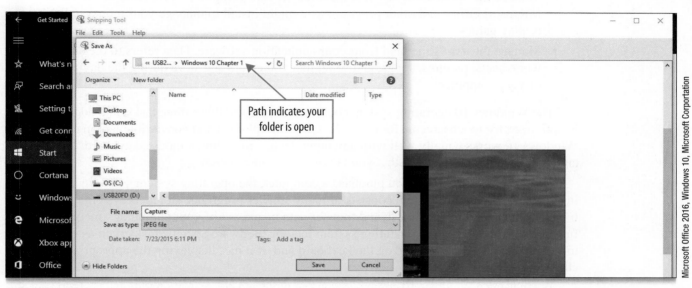

FIGURE 1.23

NOTE   Successful Double-Clicking Requires a Steady Hand

Double-clicking needs a steady hand. The speed of the two clicks is not as important as holding the mouse still between the two clicks. If you are not satisfied with your result, try again.

---

17 At the bottom of the **Save As** dialog box, locate **Save as type**, click anywhere in the box to display a list, and then on the displayed list click **JPEG file**.

JPEG, which is commonly pronounced *JAY-peg* and stands for Joint Photographic Experts Group, is a common file type used by digital cameras and computers to store digital pictures. JPEG is popular because it can store a high-quality picture in a relatively small file.

18 At the bottom of the **Save As** dialog box, click in the **File name** box to select the text *Capture*, and then using your own name, type **Lastname_Firstname_1A_Get_Started_Snip**

Within any Windows-based program, text highlighted in blue—selected—in this manner will be replaced by your typing.

NOTE   File Naming in This Textbook

Windows 10 recognizes file names with spaces. You can use spaces in file names, however, some programs, especially when transferring files over the Internet, may insert the extra characters *%20* in place of a space. In this instruction you will be instructed to save files using an underscore instead of a space. The underscore key is the shift of the ⊡ key—on most keyboards located two keys to the left of Backspace.

---

19 In the lower right corner of the dialog box, click **Save**.

20 **Close** ⊠ the **Snipping Tool** mark-up window, and then **Close** ⊠ the **Get Started** window. Hold this file until you finish Project 1A, and then submit as directed by your instructor.

You have successfully created a folder and saved a file within that folder.

Traditionally, the three major tasks of an operating system are to:

- Manage your computer's hardware—the printers, scanners, disk drives, monitors, and other hardware attached to it.
- Manage the application software installed on your computer—programs like those in Microsoft Office and other programs you might install to manage your money, edit photos, or play games.
- Manage the *data* generated from your application software. Data refers to the documents, worksheets, pictures, songs, and so on that you create and store during the day-to-day use of your computer.

The Windows 10 operating system continues to perform these three tasks, and additionally is optimized for touchscreens; for example, tablets of all sizes and convertible laptop computers. Windows 10 works equally well with any input device, including a mouse, keyboard, touchscreen, and *pen*—a pen-shaped stylus that you tap on a computer screen.

In most instances, when you purchase a computer, the operating system software is already installed. The operating system consists of many smaller programs, stored as system files, which transfer data to and from the disk and transfer data in and out of your computer's memory. Other functions performed by the operating system include hardware-specific tasks such as checking to see if a key has been pressed on the keyboard and, if it has, displaying the appropriate letter or character on the screen.

When using a Windows 10 computer, you can write and create using traditional desktop apps, and you can also read and socialize and communicate by using the Windows Store apps. With Windows 10, as compared to earlier versions of Windows, your PC has some of the characteristics of a smartphone or tablet—it is connected, it is mobile, and it is centered on people and activities. If, as Microsoft predicts, the laptop and tablet will ultimately merge into one device—like the Microsoft Surface—then you will be well prepared by learning to use Windows 10 and the Windows apps.

Activity 1.09 | Identifying Operating System Functions and Windows App Functions

Windows 10, in the same manner as other operating systems and earlier versions of the Windows operating system, has a desktop that uses a *graphical user interface*—abbreviated as *GUI* and pronounced *GOO-ee*. A graphical user interface uses graphics such as an image of a file folder or wastebasket that you click to activate the item represented. A GUI commonly incorporates the following:

- A *pointer*—any symbol that displays on your screen in response to moving your mouse and with which you can select objects and commands.
- A *pointing device*, such as a mouse or touchpad, to control the pointer.
- *Icons*—small images that represent commands, files, applications, or other windows. You can select an object icon and drag it to move it or double-click a program icon to start a program.
- A *desktop*—a simulation of a real desk that represents your work area; here you can arrange icons such as shortcuts to programs, files, folders, and various types of documents in the same manner you would arrange physical objects on top of a desk.

In Windows 10, you also have a Start menu with tiles on the right. The array of tiles serves as a connected dashboard to all of your important programs, sites, and services. On the Start menu, your view is tailored to your information and activities.

The physical parts of your computer such as the central processing unit (CPU), memory, and any attached devices such as a printer, are collectively known as *resources*. The operating system keeps track of the status of each resource and decides when a resource needs attention and for how long.

There will be times when you want and need to interact with the functions of the operating system; for example, when you want to install a new hardware device like a color printer. Windows 10 provides tools with which you can inform the operating system of new hardware that you attach to your computer.

Software application programs are the programs that enable you to do work on, and be entertained by, your computer—programs such as Word and Excel found in the Microsoft Office suite of products, Adobe Photoshop, and computer games. No application program, whether a larger desktop app or smaller Windows app, can run on its own—it must run under the direction of an operating system.

For the everyday use of your computer, the most important and most often used function of the operating system is managing your files and folders—referred to as *data management*. In the same manner that you strive to keep your paper documents and file folders organized so that you can find information when you need it, your goal when organizing your computer files and folders is to group your files so that you can find information easily. Managing your data files so that you can find your information when you need it is one of the most important computing skills you can learn.

FIGURE 1.24

Managing the data on all of your devices is an important computing skill; storing your data in the cloud—for example, on OneDrive—enables you to access your data from any device

Hywards/Shutterstock

To check how well you can identify operating system functions, take a moment to answer the following questions:

Self-Check | Answer These Questions to Check Your Understanding

1 Of the three major functions of the operating system, the first is to manage your computer's _____ such as disk drives, monitors, and printers.

2 The second major function of the operating system is to manage the application _____ such as Microsoft Office, Adobe PhotoShop, and video games.

3 The third major function of the operating system is to manage the _____ generated from your applications—the files such as Word documents, Excel workbooks, pictures, and songs that you create and store during the day-to-day use of your computer.

4 The Start menu's array of tiles is your connected _____ to all of your important programs, sites, and services.

5 One of the most important computing skills you can learn is how to manage your _____ _____ so that you can find your information quickly.

Objective 4 | Discover Windows 10 Features

According to Microsoft, a billion people in the world use Windows and 93 percent of PCs in the world run some version of Windows. Increasingly people want to use Windows in a format that runs easily on mobile computing devices such as laptops, tablets, convertibles, and smartphones; research shows this is where people now spend more time.

With only desktop apps to choose from, Windows is centered around files—typing and creating things—and that will continue to be an important part of what you do on your computer, especially in the workplace.

Additionally, you are doing different kinds of things on your PC, and you probably expect your PC to be more like a smartphone—connected all the time, mobile, to have long battery life if it's a laptop, and be centered on the people and activities that are important to you. It is for those activities that the Windows apps will become important to you.

Think of Windows 10 as a way to do work on your desktop or laptop computer, and then to read and be entertained on your laptop, tablet, or Xbox game console. Windows 10 is both serious for work and fun for entertainment and social networking.

Activity 1.10 | Using Windows Apps

On your own computer, an array of Windows apps displays on the Start menu immediately after you sign in to a Windows 10 computer. Keep in mind that a workplace computer may have a specific, locked-down arrangement of apps, or no apps at all.

On a new computer, the apps might be preselected by your computer manufacturer and by Microsoft. You can use these right away, and later you can add, delete, and rearrange the apps so that your Start menu tiles become your own personal dashboard. Recall that some apps are represented by live tiles that will update with information after you set them to do so. For example, the Mail app will show updates of incoming mail after you connect it to your email account.

Some of the built-in apps that will come with a new installation of Windows 10 on a consumer PC include:

- Mail, from which you can get email from all of your email accounts, all in one place!
- Weather, from which you can get hourly, daily, and 10-day forecasts.

- Sound Recorder, with which you can easily record a sound, and then trim, save, and replay it on your PC.
- Sports, where you can keep up with all the sports and teams you care about with Live Tile updates.
- News, which is a photo-rich app to keep up with what's happening in the world.

1 With your **desktop** displayed, to the right of Start ⊞, click in the Search box to display the insertion point, type **sports** and then compare your screen with Figure 1.25.

> The *insertion point* is a blinking vertical line that indicates where text will be inserted when you type.
>
> At the top of the results, the Windows Store app *Sports* is highlighted.
>
> Windows 10 comes with some Windows apps already built-in—these include Sports, Weather, News, and Money. These are high-quality apps, and you might want to explore them and pin them to your Start menu. There are other apps in the Windows Store for these same categories, but the Microsoft apps are worth investigating.

NOTE	Don't Have the Sports App?

You can use any app available on your system or from the Windows Store to complete this Activity. The Sports app and the Money app are used here as an example.

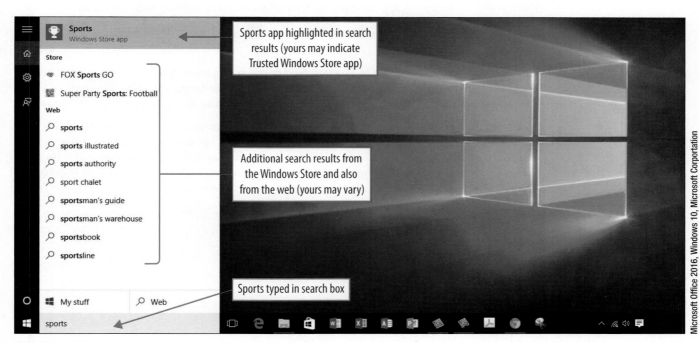

Sports app highlighted in search results (yours may indicate Trusted Windows Store app)

Additional search results from the Windows Store and also from the web (yours may vary)

Sports typed in search box

Microsoft Office 2016, Windows 10, Microsoft Corporation

FIGURE 1.25

2 At the top of the list, point to the text *Sports Trusted Windows Store app*, right-click, and then click **Pin to Start**—or if *Unpin from Start* displays, click anywhere on your desktop to close the search results so that the app remains pinned to your Start menu.

3 Click **Start** ⊞ to display the **Start menu**, and then on the right, locate the **Sports** app, as shown in Figure 1.26.

> Up-to-date information may already begin to display.

Your array of apps will differ

Sports app displaying updated information (yours will differ and may be in a different location)

Microsoft Office 2016, Windows 10, Microsoft Corportation

FIGURE 1.26

4 ▶ Click the **Sports** app tile; if necessary wait a moment if this is the first time you have used this app. In the upper right corner, if necessary, click **Maximize** ▢ to have the app fill the entire window.

> Here you can scroll down and click on many new sports stories. Across the top, you can click on *Scoreboard* to see up-to-date scores of games, or click *Slideshows* or *Videos* to see sports news stories portrayed in images or videos.

> The features in the Sports app are representative of the features in many Windows apps.

5 ▶ In the upper left corner, click the **Hamburger** icon ☰, and then compare your screen with Figure 1.27.

> This icon is commonly referred to as a *hamburger menu* or a *menu icon* or simply a *hamburger*. The name derives from the three lines that bring to mind a hamburger on a bun. This type of button is often used in mobile applications because it is compact to use on smaller screens.

> When you click the hamburger icon, a menu displays that identifies the list of icons on the left so that you can navigate to more specific areas of the Microsoft Sports app. Sometimes this area is referred to as the *app bar*. Regardless of the name, you can see that you can navigate directly to categories such as the NBA (National Basketball Association) or MLB (Major League Baseball). You can also create a list of favorite teams that you want to follow.

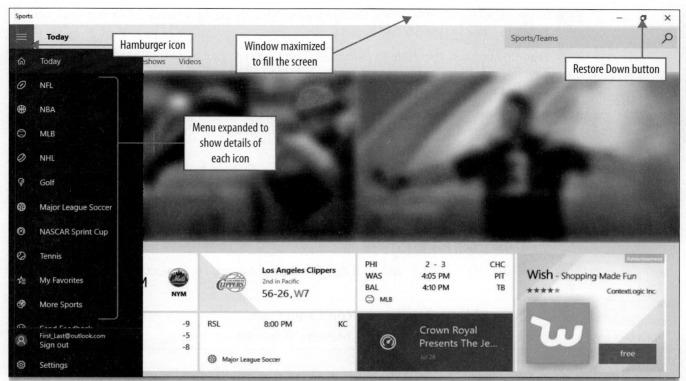

FIGURE 1.27

6 In the upper right corner, click *Restore Down* 🗗 to return the window to its previous size.

Use the Maximize command 🗖 to display a window in a full-screen view; use the *Restore Down command* 🗗 to resize a window to its previous size.

7 **Close** ✕ the Sports app.

8 With your **desktop** displayed, to the right of Start 🔲, click in the Search box to display the insertion point, type **money** and then at the top of the list of results, click the Window Store app **Money**.

9 **Maximize** 🗖 the window, and then on the navigation bar at the top of the window, click **Watchlist**. On the list of stocks, click **MSFT**. If *MSFT* does not display, at the upper right, click +, type MSFT, and then on the list that displays, click MSFT to add it to the list.

Information about Microsoft's stock and a graph displays.

10 Below the graph, click **1 Year** to see a graph representing one year.

11 With your Microsoft graph displayed, press and hold down 🏴 and then press PrintScrn; release the two keys. Notice that your screen dims momentarily; you will view the screenshot at the end of this activity.

Use this technique to create a *screenshot*. The screenshot file is automatically stored in the Pictures folder of your hard drive.

A screenshot captured in this manner from a Windows Store app is saved as a *.png* file, which is commonly pronounced PING, and stands for Portable Network Graphic. This is an image file type that can be transferred over the Internet.

A *keyboard shortcut* is a combination of two or more keyboard keys and is useful to perform a task that would otherwise require a mouse.

12 Point to the right edge of the screen to display a scroll bar, and then scroll down to see news stories about Microsoft.

13 In the upper right corner, click **Restore Down** ⟦⟧ to return the window to its previous size, and then **Close** ⟦×⟧ the Money app.

14 From the taskbar, open **File Explorer** ⟦⟧, and then navigate to **This PC**. In the file list, double-click **Pictures**, and then double-click **Screenshots**. On the ribbon, click the **View tab**, and then in the **Layout group**, if necessary, click **Large icons**.

15 In the **file list**, click one time to select the **Screenshot** file that you captured of the Microsoft graph; if more than one Screenshot file displays, click to select the file that has the highest number.

16 On the ribbon, on the **Home tab**, in the **Organize group**, click **Rename**, and then using your own name, type **Lastname_Firstname_1A_Graph_Screenshot** and then press ⟦Enter⟧.

17 With the renamed screenshot selected, on the **Home tab**, click **Copy**. In the **navigation pane**, navigate to the location of your **Windows 10 Chapter 1 folder**, open the folder, and then on the ribbon, click **Paste**.

18 Close all open windows, and hold this file until you complete Project 1A.

More **Knowledge**	**Where Did the Hamburger Icon Come From?**

For a brief history of the hamburger icon, visit http://blog.placeit.net/history-of-the-hamburger-icon

---

Activity 1.11 │ Using Task View, Snap Assist, and Virtual Desktops

Use the *Task View* button on the taskbar to see and switch between open apps—including desktop apps. Use *Snap Assist* to display a 50/50 split screen view of two apps. Begin by dragging the *title bar*—the bar across the top of the window that displays the program or app name—to the right or left until it snaps into place. Or, hold down ⟦⟧ and press ⟦→⟧ or ⟦←⟧ to snap the window right or left. As soon as you snap the first window, Task View displays all your other open windows, and you need to click only one to have it snap to the other half of the screen. You can also snap four apps by dragging their title bars into the corners of your screen.

1 Be sure all windows are closed, and then on the taskbar, click **File Explorer** ⟦⟧. Navigate to the location for your **Windows 10 Chapter 1** folder, but do not open the folder. With your File Explorer window open, click **Start** ⟦⟧ and then open one of the displayed apps; for example, Weather. From either the taskbar or the Start menu, open the Windows Store.

Three windows are open with the Windows Store app window on top.

2 On the taskbar, click **Task View** ⟦⟧, point to one of the windows, and then compare your screen with Figure 1.28.

Task View displays a *thumbnail*—a reduced image of a graphic—of each open window. This command is convenient when you want to see all of your open windows.

When you point to an open window, a Close button displays in the upper right corner so that you can close the window from Task View.

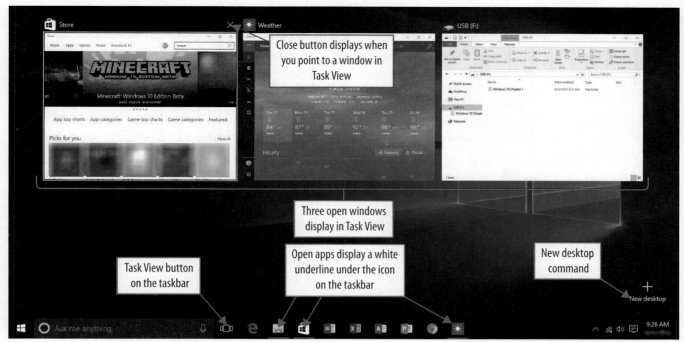

Close button displays when you point to a window in Task View

Three open windows display in Task View

Open apps display a white underline under the icon on the taskbar

New desktop command

Task View button on the taskbar

New desktop

FIGURE 1.28

Microsoft Office 2016, Windows 10, Microsoft Corportation

3 Click the **File Explorer** window, hold down ⊞, and then press →.

The File Explorer window snaps to the right side of the screen, and Snap Assist displays the other two open windows on the left.

4 On the left, click the Weather app, and then compare your screen with Figure 1.29.

The Weather window snaps to the left side of the screen.

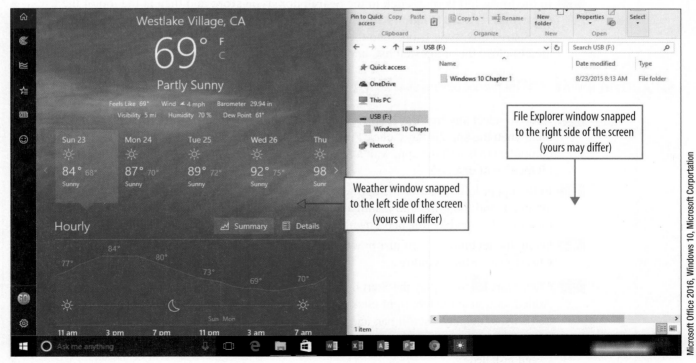

File Explorer window snapped to the right side of the screen (yours may differ)

Weather window snapped to the left side of the screen (yours will differ)

FIGURE 1.29

Microsoft Office 2016, Windows 10, Microsoft Corportation

5 On the taskbar, click **Task View** ⬜ again, in the lower right corner, click **New desktop**, and notice that two thumbnail images display—**Desktop 1** with your two apps snapped and **Desktop 2**.

> If you have a large number of apps open, you can create another *virtual desktop*—an additional desktop to organize and quickly access groups of windows—to work with just the apps you want by clicking + New Desktop in the lower right corner of your screen. This can be a good way to organize and quickly access groups of windows.
>
> For example, you could run your work email and Office apps on your desktop, and then open another virtual desktop for personal work. Then you can use Task View to switch between open desktops.

6 Click **Desktop 1** to bring that desktop back to full screen, and then on the taskbar, click **Task View** ⬜.

7 From your desktop, drag the Windows Store window down to **Desktop 2**.

8 Click **Desktop 2** and maximize ⬜ the window if necessary, and then click **Task View** ⬜. With **Desktop 2** active—its icon is framed above the taskbar—drag the app on the screen back down to **Desktop 1**.

9 Point to **Desktop 2** and click **Close** ✕, and then in the upper right corner of each open window, click **Close** ✕.

> Create virtual desktops when you need to separate a group of windows while working on other things. Then you can close the virtual desktop when you no longer need it.

Activity 1.12 | Organizing Your Start Menu and Getting Apps from the Windows Store

On your own PC, you will want to organize your Start menu to become your personal dashboard. You will probably use your desktop apps like Microsoft Word and Microsoft Excel for work and school, but with the tiles on the Start menu, you can also use your PC like you use your smartphone—centered on the people and notifications that are important to you.

You can pin apps to the Start menu and then group your apps. You can also name your groups.

1 In the lower left corner, click in the **Search** box, type **store** and then at the top of the list, click **Store Trusted Windows Store app**. In the Store app, in the upper right corner, click in the **Search** box, type **travel** and then click the **Search** button 🔍. If necessary, click in a white area to close the suggested list, and then on the right, click **Show all**.

🔄 **ANOTHER WAY**   On the taskbar, click the Store icon 🛒 ; or, on the Start menu, click the Windows Store tile.

2 Click to select any free travel app (good ones include *Fodors*, *TripAdvisor*, and *tripwolf*), and then when the app displays, click **Free** (or click Install if your already own the app on another computer) to install the app; wait a few moments for the download and installation to complete ("Open" will display).

3 In the upper left corner of the app window, click the **Back** button ←. If necessary, click Show all again, and then find and install another travel app of your choice. When "Open" displays, meaning the app has finished downloading, in the upper left corner, click the Back button.

4 Using the techniques you just practiced, install a third travel app of your choice, and then **Close** ✕ the **Store** window.

5 Click **Start** ⊞ to display the Start menu. In the lower left corner, click **All apps**. In the Recently Added section at the top, right-click each travel app and pin it to the Start menu. Point anywhere in the list to display a scroll bar, and then compare your screen with Figure 1.30.

> The *Recently added* section of the Start menu displays apps that you have recently downloaded and installed.
>
> The *All apps* command displays all the apps installed on your computer in alphabetical order. You may see recently added apps display at the top.

FIGURE 1.30

6 ▶ Scroll as necessary to locate one of the first travel apps that you installed, and notice that *New* displays under its name. Right-click the name of the app, and notice that from the All apps list, you can Unpin an app from the Start menu, pin it to the taskbar, or uninstall the app. Compare your screen with Figure 1.31.

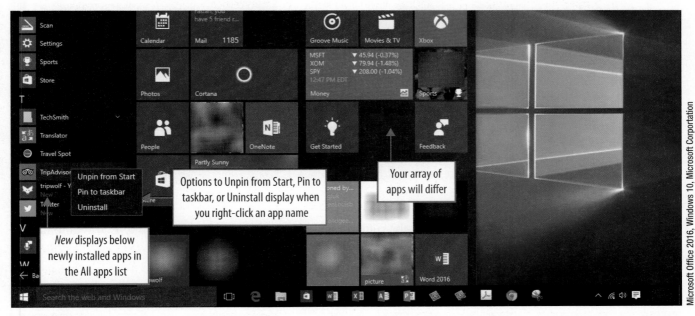

FIGURE 1.31

7 ▶ With your Start menu displayed, use the wheel on your mouse or the scroll bar at the right to scroll and locate one of your travel apps you pinned to the Start menu. Drag the app tile into a blank space, and notice that a shaded bar displays indicating that you can create a new section on your Start menu, as shown in Figure 1.32.

Your array of tiles and amount of space will differ from what is shown, because Windows 10 is *your* personal dashboard!

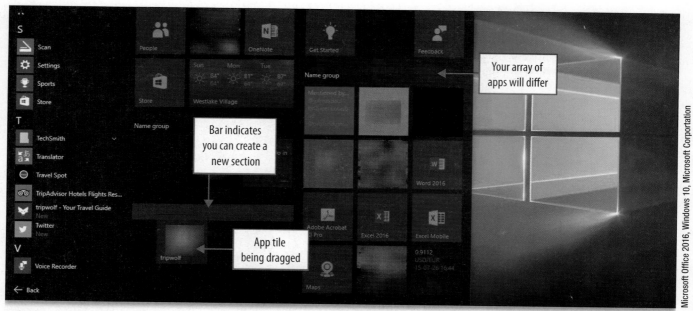

FIGURE 1.32

> 8 ► Drag the two remaining travel apps next to the first one, and then point to the area above the new group to display *Name group*, as shown in Figure 1.33.

FIGURE 1.33

> 9 ► Click the double lines at the right or click the text *New group*, and then type **Travel** to name the group. Press ⊞Enter, and then compare your screen with Figure 1.34.
>
> You can use the techniques you just learned with the Windows Store, the All apps menu, and the tiles on the Start menu to customize Windows 10 to be your personal dashboard.

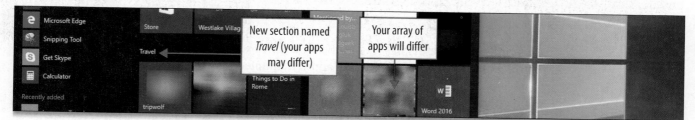

FIGURE 1.34

Microsoft Office 2016, Windows 10, Microsoft Corportation

10 Point to one of the Travel app tiles, right-click, point to **Resize**, and then click **Small**. Point to another of the Travel app tiles, right-click, point to **Resize**, and then click **Wide**.

> You might want to resize tiles on your Start menu to make them more or less visible—this is another way to personalize Windows 10 to make it work for you.

Activity 1.13 | Using the Windows 10 Action Center

You probably want your PC to give you notifications—just like your smartphone does—and the Windows 10 Action Center does that. The **Action Center** is a vertical panel that displays on the right side of your screen when you click the icon in the notifications area of the taskbar. The upper portion displays notifications from apps you have installed and from which you have elected to receive notifications. The bottom portion displays Quick Actions—buttons that take you to frequently used system commands.

Both areas of the Action Center are customizable to suit your needs. When you have a new notification, the icon on the taskbar will light up white. There is even a Quiet Hours setting to turn off notifications when you don't want them.

1 At the right edge of your taskbar, to the left of the date and time, click **Action Center** 🗨 to display the **Action Center** pane on the right side of your screen. Compare your screen with Figure 1.35.

> Although your arrangement and list will differ from what is shown in the Figure, you can see that this is a convenient way to check mail and messages without leaving whatever you are working on.

> You can add sites like Facebook and Twitter to your Action Center.

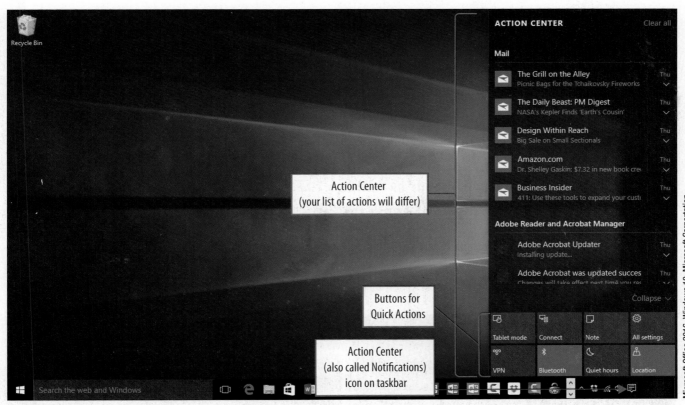

FIGURE 1.35

2 At the bottom of the **Action Center**, click **All settings**, and then in the **Settings** window, click **System**. On the left, click **Notifications & actions**, scroll down toward the bottom of the list on the right, and then compare your screen with Figure 1.36.

> Here you can make decisions about what apps can send you notifications in the Action Center.

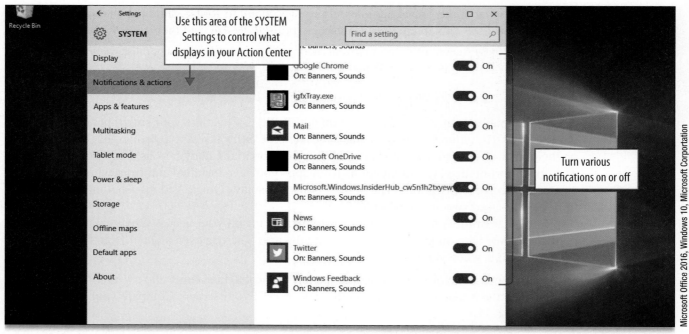

FIGURE 1.36

3 ▶ **Close** ⊠ the **Settings** window.

Activity 1.14 │ Using Cortana and Searching for Help

Cortana, the name for the intelligent female character in the *Halo* video game series, is also the name for the personal digital assistant in Windows 10. With use, Cortana becomes more useful to you, and you can add features—such as reminders—that Cortana delivers to you.

On your own PC, when you first use Windows 10 on a new installation or on a new system, Cortana might not be activated. You will benefit from activating and using this powerful feature that can search the web, find things on your PC, and keep track of your calendar.

ALERT!   **Is Cortana Already Installed on Your System?**

If Cortana is already active on your system—*Ask me anything* displays to the right of the Start button—skip to Step 5 of this Activity.

---

1 ▶ In the lower left corner of your desktop, determine whether Cortana is active, as shown in Figure 1.37.

If this area indicates *Search the web and Windows*, then Cortana is not yet active on your system.

FIGURE 1.37

2 ▶ If Cortana is not active, click **Start** ⊞, click **All apps**, scroll down to apps that begin with the letter **C**, and then point to **Cortana** as shown in Figure 1.38.

Cortana on the All apps list

Cortana might also display as a tile

FIGURE 1.38

3 Click **Cortana**, and then in the upper left corner, click the **menu** icon ≡ to display the menu commands. At the bottom of the menu, click **Try Cortana**.

4 As necessary, (note that the following sequence of steps may vary, but in general this is what you can expect) click **Next**, click **I agree**, and then type your first name or nickname. Click **Next**, as necessary click **Got it**. Notice that your Search box now indicates *Ask me anything*, as shown in Figure 1.39.

> Usually you will also see a microphone icon so that you can speak your requests to Cortana instead of typing them.

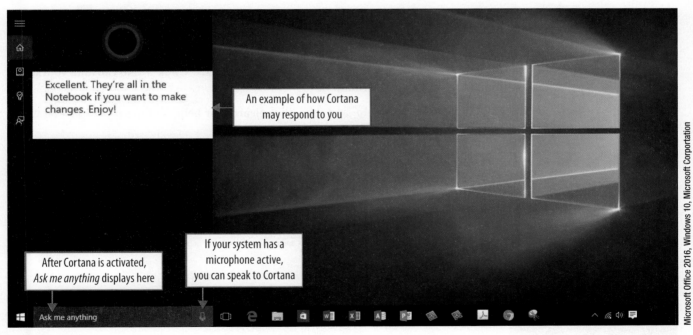

Excellent. They're all in the Notebook if you want to make changes. Enjoy!

An example of how Cortana may respond to you

After Cortana is activated, *Ask me anything* displays here

If your system has a microphone active, you can speak to Cortana

Ask me anything

FIGURE 1.39

5 Click in the **Ask me anything** box, and then type **who is Cortana?** Then press Enter. If necessary, click *See more results on Bing.com*.

> Your *web browser*—software with which you display webpages and navigate the Internet—displays a Bing search with web links to information about Cortana.

6 **Close** ✕ the browser window.

7 Click again in the **Ask me anything** box, and then in the upper left corner, click the **menu** icon ≡. Compare your screen with Figure 1.40.

> On this menu, you can add Reminders to Cortana or add information to Cortana's notebook.

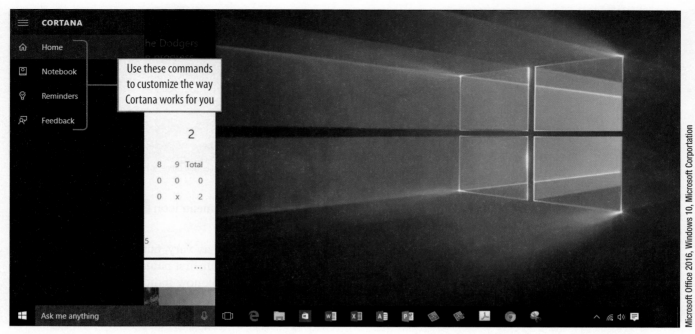

FIGURE 1.40

8 ▸ Click in an empty area of the desktop to dismiss Cortana, and then click **Start** ⊞. Locate and click the tile **Get Started**. If you do not see this tile, ask Cortana to find it for you by typing *Get Started*.

9 ▸ **Maximize** ☐ the window, and then on the left, click **Cortana**. Click **Make Cortana yours**, and take a moment to read this information.

10 ▸ On the left, click **Search and help**, and then click **Search for help**. Compare your screen with Figure 1.41.

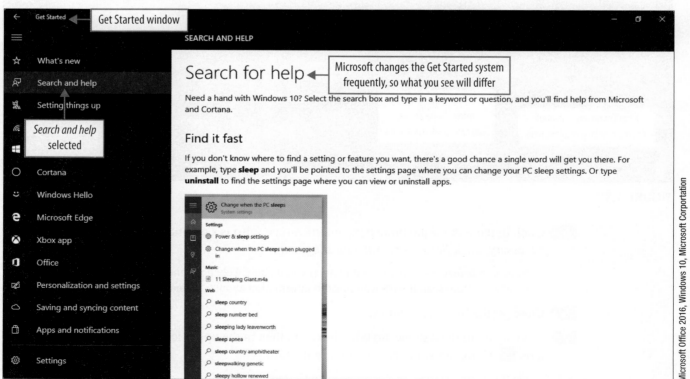

FIGURE 1.41

11 Scroll down and take a moment to read all of the important information.

Because Windows 10 will continue to grow and change and add new security features, rely on Cortana and the web information listed on this page to get help using Windows 10. You will always get the most current information.

12 **Close** ☒ the **Get Started** window and any other open windows.

Activity 1.15 | Using the Microsoft Edge Browser

Microsoft Edge is the web browser program that comes with Windows 10. Among its many features are the ability to:

- Enter a search directly into the address bar
- Save sites and favorites and reading lists in the *Hub* feature
- Take notes and highlight directly on a webpage and then share that page with someone
- Pin a website to your Start menu

1 On the taskbar, click **Microsoft Edge** ⬛. If the icon is not on your taskbar, search for the app in the search box. **Maximize** ☐ the window.

2 In the **Search or enter web address** box, or in the address bar, type the name of your college and then press [Enter].

It is not necessary to type a web address; Edge will search for you and present the results.

3 In the search results, locate and click the link for your college's official website. On your college website, search for or navigate to information about the college library.

4 With the webpage for your college library displayed, in the upper right corner, click **Make a Web Note** ✎, and then compare your screen with Figure 1.42.

The Web Note toolbar displays tools for marking a webpage. Tools include a Pen, a Highlighter, an Eraser, a Note maker, and a Clip for cutting out a portion of a webpage as a file. On the right of the toolbar, there are tools for saving and sharing a webpage on which you have made markups or notes.

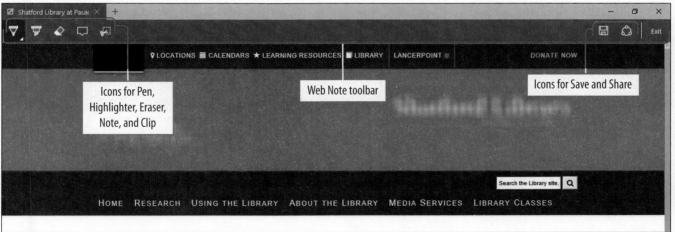

FIGURE 1.42

5 On the toolbar, point to the **Pen** ▽, click the **small white triangle** in the lower right corner, and then on the displayed gallery, click the **yellow square**. Click the **white triangle** again, and then click the largest size.

6 With your mouse pointer, circle the name of—or some other information about—your college library. Compare your screen with Figure 1.43.

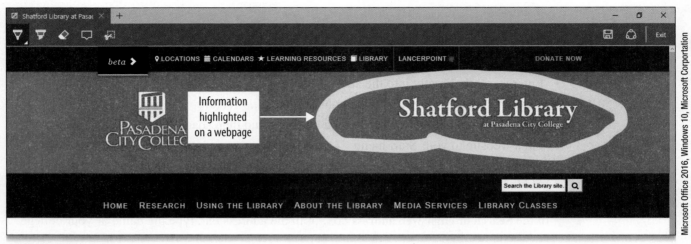

FIGURE 1.43

7 On the toolbar, click **Share** 🌀 to display the **Share** pane on the right, and notice the various ways you can share this marked-up webpage with others.

8 Click in a blank area of the webpage to close the Share pane. On the toolbar, click **Exit**.

9 In the upper right corner, click **More actions** ⋯ and then on the list, click **Pin to Start**. **Close** ✕ the browser window.

10 Click **Start** ⊞, and then scroll as necessary to locate the pinned website on your Start menu. Compare your screen with Figure 1.44.

Use this technique to pin websites that you visit often to your Start menu.

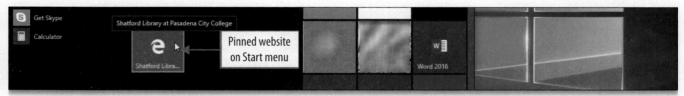

FIGURE 1.44

On your own computer, when you are done working, sign out from Windows 10, and then set your computer properly so that your data is saved, you save energy, and your computer remains secure.

When you turn off your computer by using the *Sleep* command, Windows 10 automatically saves your work, the screen goes dark, the computer's fan stops, and your computer goes to sleep. You need not close your programs or files because your work is saved. When you wake your computer by pressing a key, moving the mouse, or using whatever method is appropriate for your device, you need only to dismiss the lock screen and then enter your password; your screen will display exactly like it did when you initiated the Sleep command.

When you *shut down* your computer, all open programs and files close, network connections close, and the hard disk stops. No power is used. According to Microsoft, about half of all Windows users like to shut down so that they get a "fresh start" each time they turn on the computer. The other half use sleep.

Activity 1.16 | Locking, Signing Out of, and Shutting Down Your Computer

In an organization, there might be a specific process for signing out from Windows 10 and turning off the computer. The following steps will work on your own PC.

1 Click **Start** ⊞, and then in the upper left corner, click your user name. Compare your screen with Figure 1.45.

> Here you can sign out of or lock your computer, in addition to changing your account settings. If you click Sign out, the lock screen will display, and then on the lock screen, if you press Enter, all the user accounts on the computer will display and you are able to sign in.
>
> If you click Lock, the lock screen will display.

FIGURE 1.45

Microsoft Office 2016, Windows 10, Microsoft Corportation

2 Click **Lock**, and then with the lock screen displayed, press Enter. Sign in to your computer again if necessary.

3 If you want to shut down your computer, click **Start** ⊞, click Power, and then click Shut down.

Activity 1.17 | Customizing and Managing User Accounts

Windows 10 supports multiple local account users on a single computer, and at least one user is the administrator—the initial administrator that was established when the system was purchased or when Windows 10 was installed.

As the administrator of your own computer, you can restrict access to your computer so that only people you authorize can use your computer or view its files. This access is managed through a local *user account*, which is a collection of information that tells Windows 10 what files and folders the account holder can access, what changes the account holder can make to the computer system, and what the account holder's personal preferences are.

Each person accesses his or her user account with a user name and password, and each user has his or her own desktop, files, and folders. Users with a local account should also establish a Microsoft account so that their Start menu arrangement—personal dashboard of tiles—displays when they sign in.

An *administrator account* allows complete access to the computer. Administrators can make changes that affect other users, change security settings, install software and hardware, access all files on the computer, and make changes to other user accounts.

1 Click **Start** ▦. Above the Start button, click **Settings**, and then click **Accounts**. Compare your screen with Figure 1.46.

Here you can manage your Microsoft account, set various sign-in options, and change your account picture.

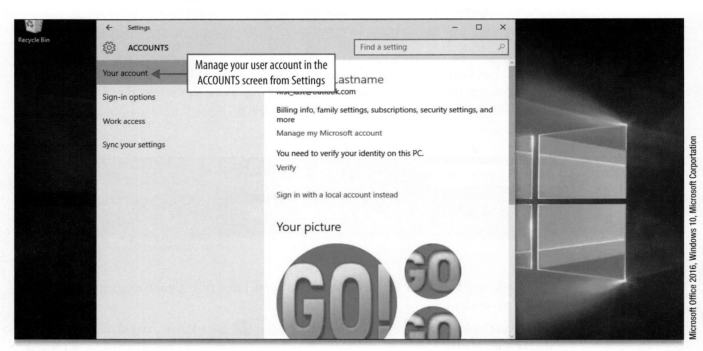

FIGURE 1.46

2 **Close** ☒ the **Settings** window.

3 As directed by your instructor, submit the two files you created in this project: **Lastname_Firstname_1A_Get_Started_Snip** and **Lastname_Firstname_1A_Graph_Screenshot**.

On your own computer, you can change the default settings of some basic functions that will help you manage your Windows 10 system.

Activity 1.18 │ Managing Windows Updates, Notifications, and Backup

Windows 10 is a modern operating system, and just like the operating system on your smartphone or tablet, Windows 10 will receive regular updates. These updates will include improvements, new features, and new security updates to address new security issues that emerge. Apps in the Windows Store will also be continuously updated.

Because updates will be automatically installed, you will not have to be concerned about keeping your Windows 10 system up to date; however, you can still view updates and see when they will be installed.

In Windows 10, notifications keep you informed about your apps and messages. You can manage what notifications you get and see in the notifications area of the taskbar from the Settings window.

The backup and recovery tools available in Windows 10 include: *File History*, which can automatically back up your most important files to a separate location; *PC Reset*, which lets you return your PC to the condition it was in the day you bought it; and *system image backup*, which creates a full system image backup from which you can restore your entire PC.

1 On the taskbar, click **Action Center** 🗩, and then at the bottom, in the **Quick Actions** area, click **All settings**. In the **Settings** window, *point to* **System**, and then notice that in this group of settings you can manage your display, your notifications, your apps, and the computer's power. Compare your screen with Figure 1.47.

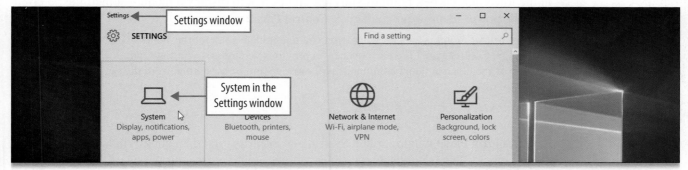

FIGURE 1.47

Microsoft Office 2016, Windows 10, Microsoft Corportation

2 Click **System**, and then on the left, click **Notifications & actions**. On the right, click **Select which icons appear on the taskbar**.

Here you can select the On and Off buttons to determine which icons display on your taskbar.

3 Without making any changes, click **Back** ← as many times as necessary to redisplay the **Settings** window. Click **Update & security**, and then on the left, click **Backup**. On the right, click **Add a drive**. (This may vary depending on what drives are attached to your system.)

> A list of drives connected to your computer displays, and you can select a drive onto which you could make a backup.

4 **Close** × the **Settings** window without making a backup.

More Knowledge	**Consider a Commercial Backup Service Instead**

The backup system in Windows 10 is useful, but you might find it easier to use a commercial backup system like Carbonite or Mozy. For a small annual fee, these systems back up your files automatically on their servers—in the cloud—and if your computer suffers a misfortune, you can get your files back easily by simply downloading them to your new or repaired system.

N O T E	**This Activity Is Optional**

Complete this Activity if you are able to do so. Some college labs may not enable these features. If you cannot practice in your college lab, practice this on another computer if possible.

Activity 1.19 | Managing Windows Defender and Windows Firewall

Windows Defender is protection built into Windows 10 that helps prevent viruses, spyware, and malicious or unwanted software from being installed on your PC without your knowledge. You can rely on Windows Defender without assistance from other software products that might come preinstalled on a PC you purchase; you can confidently uninstall and not pay for these products.

Windows Firewall is protection built into Windows 10 that can prevent hackers or malicious software from gaining access to your computer through a network or the Internet.

1 In the lower left corner of your screen, click in the search box, type **windows defender** and then press Enter to display the **Windows Defender** dialog box.

> Here you can change settings related to real-time and cloud-based protection.

2 **Close** × the **Windows Defender** window.

3 In the lower left corner, point to **Start** ▦, right-click to display a menu—sometimes referred to as the power menu—and then click **Control Panel**.

> The *Control Panel* is an area where you can manipulate some of the Windows 10 basic system settings. Control Panel is a carryover from previous versions of Windows, and over time, more and more of the Control Panel commands will move to and be accessible from the Settings window.

⟳ ANOTHER WAY   Type *control panel* in the search box.

---

4 In the **Control Panel** window, click **System and Security**, and then click **Windows Firewall**. On the left, click **Change notification settings**—if necessary, enter your password; or, if you are unable to enter a password, just read the remaining steps in this activity.

5 In the **Customize Settings** window, notice that you can receive notifications when Windows Firewall blocks a new app.

6 **Close** × the window.

7 If you have not already done so, as directed by your instructor, submit the two files you created in this project: **Lastname_Firstname_1A_Get_Started_Snip** and **Lastname_Firstname_1A_Graph_Screenshot**.

> **END | You have completed Project 1A**

Managing Files and Folders

In Activities 1.20 through 1.32, you will assist Barbara Hewitt and Steven Ramos, who work for the Information Technology Department at the Boston headquarters office of the Bell Orchid Hotels. Barbara and Steven have been asked to organize some of the files and folders that comprise the corporation's computer data. You will capture screens that will look similar to Figure 1.48.

PROJECT FILES

For Project 1B, you will need the following student data files:

Student Data Files may be provided by your instructor, or you can download them from www.pearsonhighered.com/go which you will learn to do in the next Activity. If you already have the Student Data Files stored in a location that you can access, then begin with Activity 1.21.

win10_01_Student_Data_Files

You will save your files as:

Lastname_Firstname_1B_WordPad_Snip

Lastname_Firstname_1B_Europe_ Folders_Snip

Lastname_Firstname_1B_HR_Snip

Lastname_Firstname_1B_OneDrive_Snip (Optional)

Please always review the downloaded Grader instructions before beginning.

PROJECT RESULTS

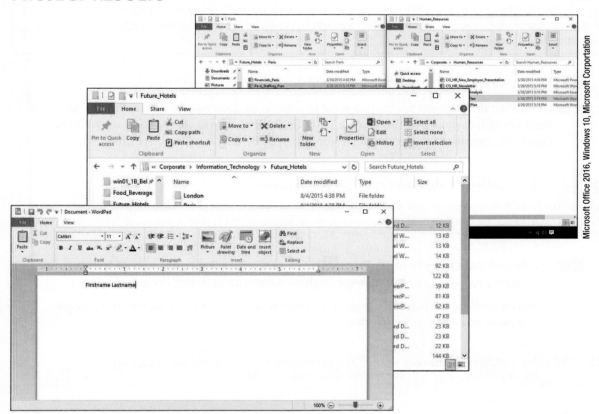

FIGURE 1.48 Project 1B Managing Files and Folders

Objective 7 | Download and Extract Files and Folders

Download refers to the action of transferring or copying a file from another location—such as a cloud storage location or from an Internet site—to your computer. Files that you download are frequently *compressed files*, which are files that have been reduced in size, take up less storage space, and can be transferred to other computers faster than uncompressed files.

A compressed folder might contain a group of files that were combined into one compressed folder, which makes it easier to share a group of files. To *extract* means to decompress, or pull out, files from a compressed form. The terms *zip* and *unzip* refer to the process of compressing (zipping) and extracting (unzipping). File Explorer includes *Compressed Folder Tools*, available on the ribbon, to assist you in extracting compressed files.

ALERT!   **Already Have the Student Data Files?**

If your instructor has already provided you with the Student Data Files that accompany this chapter and you have stored them in a location that you can access, then skip to Activity 1.21. However, you can refer to these instructions when downloading files from other sites.

Activity 1.20 | Downloading Files from a Website

To complete this Project and the Projects at the end of this chapter, you will need the Student Data Files that accompany this chapter. Follow the steps in this Activity to download the Student Data Files from the publisher's website; or, your instructor might provide the Student Data Files to you, for example, in your learning management system.

NOTE   **Using a Touchscreen**

If you are using a touchscreen device to complete this Project, continue to use the tap and swipe gestures presented in Project 1A. The remainder of this instruction will assume that you are using a mouse and keyboard setup, but all the Projects can be completed using a touchscreen without a mouse or keyboard.

---

1 If necessary, sign in to your computer and display the Windows 10 desktop.

2 Determine the location where you want to store your downloaded Student Data Files; this example will assume you are using a USB flash drive. If you are working on your own computer, consider the Documents folder on This PC or your OneDrive cloud storage.

ALERT!   **In a College Lab, Use Your USB Flash Drive**

If you are completing these Activities in a college lab, store your Student Data Files on a USB flash drive and use it to complete the steps, because in a college lab, any work you store on the computer at which you are working will likely be deleted as soon as you sign off the lab computer.

---

3 On the taskbar, click **Microsoft Edge** , click in the **Search or enter web address** box or in the address bar—type **www.pearsonhighered.com/go** and then press Enter.

Microsoft Edge is Microsoft's Windows 10 *web browser*—software with which you display webpages and navigate the Internet.

ANOTHER WAY   You can use other browsers, such as Chrome or Firefox, to go to this website. Use the download techniques associated with that browser to download the files.

---

4 At the Pearson site, on the right, locate and then click the cover image for the book you are using. In the window that opens, under **Student Resources**, click **Organized by chapter**.

5 ▶ Click the link for **win10_01_Student_Data_Files**. At the bottom of the screen, when the file has finished downloading, click **Open** to display the **File Explorer** window for the downloaded files, and then notice the path in the address bar.

> Typically, files that you download from an Internet site are stored in the ***Downloads folder*** on your PC.

6 ▶ In the **file list**, click the **win10_01_Student_Data_Files** folder one time to select it, and then on the right edge of the ribbon, with the **Compressed Folder Tools** active, click **Extract all**. In the displayed dialog box, click **Browse**.

7 ▶ In the **Select a destination** window, in the **navigation pane**, if necessary expand **This PC**, and then click your **USB flash drive** one time to select it—or click your desired storage location. In the lower right corner, click **Select Folder**. In the lower right corner of the displayed window, click **Extract**.

> After a few moments, the folder is extracted and placed in the location you selected.

8 ▶ **Close** ☒ all open windows to redisplay your desktop.

Objective 8 | Use File Explorer to Display Locations, Folders, and Files

A file is the fundamental unit of storage that enables Windows 10 to distinguish one set of information from another. A folder is the basic organizing tool for files. In a folder, you can store files that are related to one another. You can also place a folder inside another folder, which is then referred to as a ***subfolder***.

Windows 10 arranges folders in a structure that resembles a ***hierarchy***—an arrangement where items are ranked and where each level is lower in rank than the item above it. The hierarchy of folders is referred to as the ***folder structure***. A sequence of folders in the folder structure that leads to a specific file or folder is a ***path***.

Activity 1.21 | Navigating with File Explorer

Recall that File Explorer is the program that displays the contents of locations, folders, and files on your computer and also in your OneDrive and other cloud storage locations. File Explorer also enables you to perform tasks related to your files and folders such as copying, moving, and renaming. When you open a folder or location, a window displays to show its contents. The design of the window helps you navigate—explore within the file structure for the purpose of finding files and folders—so that you can save and find your files and folders efficiently.

In this Activity, you will open a folder and examine the parts of its window.

1 ▶ Close any open windows. With your desktop displayed, on the taskbar, *point to* but do not click **File Explorer** 📁, and notice the ScreenTip *File Explorer*.

> A ***ScreenTip*** displays useful information when you perform various mouse actions, such as pointing to screen elements.

2 ▶ Click **File Explorer** 📁 to display the **File Explorer** window.

> File Explorer is at work anytime you are viewing the contents of a location or the contents of a folder stored in a specific location. By default, the File Explorer button on the taskbar opens with the ***Quick access*** location—a list of files you have been working on and folders you use often— selected in the navigation pane and in the address bar.

> The default list will likely display the Desktop, Downloads, Documents, Pictures, Music, Videos, and OneDrive folders, and then folders you worked on recently or work on frequently will be added automatically, although you can change this behavior.

The benefit of the Quick access list is that you can customize a list of folders that you go to often. To add a folder to the list quickly, you can right-click a folder in the file list and click Pin to Quick Access.

For example, if you are working on a project, you can pin it—or simply drag it—to the Quick access list. When you are done with the project and not using the folder so often, you can remove it from the list. Removing it from the list does not delete the folder, it simply removes it from the Quick access list.

<table>
<tr><td>**NOTE**</td><td>**You Can Change the Behavior of the Quick Access List in File Explorer**</td></tr>
</table>

If you prefer to have File Explorer default to the This PC view—which was the default in Windows 8—on the View tab, click Options to display the Folder Options dialog box. On the General tab, click the Open File Explorer to arrow, and then click This PC. If you want to prevent recently and frequently used items from displaying on the Quick access list, on the same tab, at the bottom under Privacy, clear the check boxes and then clear the File Explorer history.

3 On the left, in the **navigation pane**, scroll down if necessary, and then click **This PC** to display folders, devices, and drives in the **file list** on the right. Compare your screen with Figure 1.49.

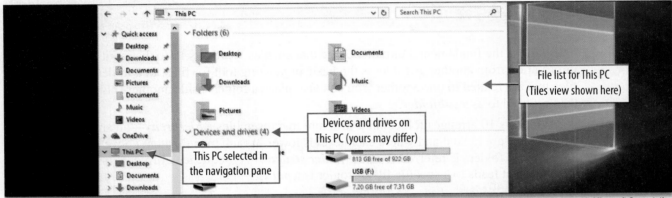

Microsoft Office 2016, Windows 10, Microsoft Corportation

FIGURE 1.49

4 If necessary, in the upper right corner, click Expand the Ribbon ⌄. In the **File List,** under **Folders,** click **Documents** one time to select it, and then on the ribbon, on the **Computer tab,** in the **Location group,** click **Open.** On the ribbon, click the **View tab,** and then in the **Layout group,** if necessary, click **Details.**

The window for the Documents folder displays. You may or may not have files and folders already stored here.

ANOTHER WAY   Point to Documents, right-click to display a shortcut menu, and then click Open; or, point to Documents and double-click.

5 Compare your screen with Figure 1.50, and then take a moment to study the parts of the window as described in the table in Figure 1.51.

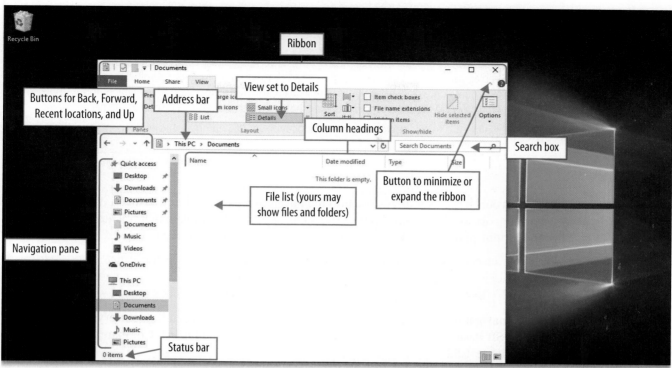

FIGURE 1.50

Microsoft Office 2016, Windows 10, Microsoft Corportation

PARTS OF THE FILE EXPLORER WINDOW	
WINDOW PART	**FUNCTION**
Address bar	Displays your current location in the file structure as a series of links separated by arrows. Tap or click a part of the path to go to that level or tap or click at the end to select the path for copying.
Back, Forward, Recent locations, and Up buttons	Enable you to navigate to other folders you have already opened without closing the current window. These buttons work with the address bar; that is, after you use the address bar to change folders, you can use the Back button to return to the previous folder. Use the Up button to open the location where the folder you are viewing is saved—also referred to as the ***parent folder***.
Column headings	Identify the columns in Details view. By clicking the column heading name, you can change how the files in the file list are organized; by clicking the arrow on the right, you can select various sort arrangements in the file list. By right-clicking a column heading, you can select other columns to add to the file list.
File list	Displays the contents of the current folder or location. If you type text into the Search box, a search is conducted on the folder or location only, and only the folders and files that match your search will display here—including files in subfolders.
Minimize the Ribbon or Expand the Ribbon button	Changes the display of the ribbon. When minimized, the ribbon shows only the tab names and not the full ribbon.
Navigation pane	Displays locations to which you can navigate; for example, your OneDrive, folders on This PC, devices and drives connected to your PC, folders listed under Quick access, and possibly other PCs on your network. Use Quick access to open your most commonly used folders and searches. If you have a folder that you use frequently, you can drag it to the Quick access area so that it is always available.
Ribbon	Groups common tasks such as copying and moving, creating new folders, emailing and zipping items, and changing views of the items in the file list.

FIGURE 1.51 *(continued)*

PARTS OF THE FILE EXPLORER WINDOW (*continued*)	
WINDOW PART	**FUNCTION**
Search box	Enables you to type a word or phrase and then searches for a file or subfolder stored in the current folder that contains matching text. The search begins as soon as you begin typing; for example, if you type *G*, all the file and folder names that start with the letter *G* display in the file list.
Status bar	Displays the total number of items in a location, or the number of selected items and their total size.

Microsoft Office 2016, Windows 10, Microsoft Corportation

FIGURE 1.51

6 ▶ Move your ⬉ pointer anywhere into the **navigation pane**, and notice that a downward pointing arrow ✓ displays to the left of *Quick access* to indicate that this item is expanded, and a right-pointing arrow ❯ displays to the left of items that are collapsed.

You can click these arrows to collapse and expand areas in the navigation pane.

Activity 1.22 | Using File Explorer to Display Locations, Folders, and Files

1 ▶ In the **navigation pane**, if necessary expand **This PC**, scroll down if necessary, and then click your **USB flash drive** one time to display its contents in the **file list**. Compare your screen with Figure 1.52.

In the navigation pane, *This PC* displays all of the drive letter locations attached to your computer, including the internal hard drives, CD or DVD drives, and any connected devices such as a USB flash drive.

Your extracted student data files display if this is your storage location.

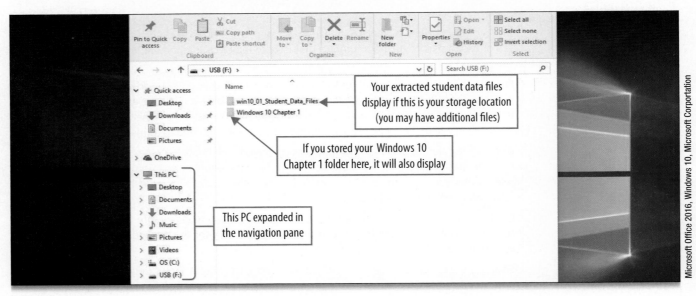

Microsoft Office 2016, Windows 10, Microsoft Corporation

FIGURE 1.52

2 In the **file list**, double-click the uncompressed **win10_01_Student_Data_Files** folder to display the subfolders and files. Then double-click the folder for this Project—**win01_1B_Bell_Orchid**.

Recall that the corporate office of the Bell Orchid Hotels is in Boston. The corporate office maintains subfolders labeled for each of its large hotels in Honolulu, Orlando, San Diego, and Santa Barbara.

🔁 **ANOTHER WAY**   Right-click the folder, and then click Open; or, select the folder and then on the ribbon, on the Home tab, in the Open group, click Open.

3 In the **file list**, double-click **Orlando** to display the subfolders, and then look at the **address bar** to view the path. Compare your screen with Figure 1.53.

Within each city's subfolder, there is a structure of subfolders for the Accounting, Engineering, Food and Beverage, Human Resources, Operations, and Sales and Marketing departments.

Because folders can be placed inside other folders, such an arrangement is common when organizing files on a computer.

In the address bar, the path from the flash drive to the win01_1B_Bell_Orchid folder to the Orlando folder displays as a series of links.

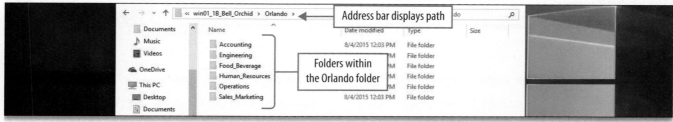

FIGURE 1.53

Microsoft Office 2016, Windows 10, Microsoft Corportation

4 In the **address bar**, to the right of **win01_1B_Bell_Orchid**, click the ▶ arrow to display a list of the subfolders in the **win01_1B_Bell_Orchid** folder. On the list that displays, notice that **Orlando** displays in bold, indicating it is open in the file list. Then, on the list, click **Honolulu**.

The subfolders within the Honolulu folder display.

5 In the **address bar**, to the right of **win01_1B_Bell_Orchid**, click the ▶ arrow again to display the subfolders in that folder. Then, on the **address bar**—not on the list—point to **Honolulu** and notice that the list of subfolders in the **Honolulu** folder displays.

After you display one set of subfolders in the address bar, all of the links are active and you need only point to them to display the list of subfolders.

Clicking an arrow to the right of a folder name in the address bar displays a list of the subfolders in that folder. You can click a subfolder name to display its contents. In this manner, the address bar is not only a path, but it is also an active control with which you can step from the current folder directly to any other folder above it in the folder structure just by clicking a folder name.

6 On the list of subfolders for **Honolulu**, click **Sales_Marketing** to display its contents in the **file list**. On the **View tab**, in the **Layout group**, if necessary, click **Details**. Compare your screen with Figure 1.54.

ANOTHER WAY   In the file list, double-click the Sales_Marketing folder.

The files in the Sales_Marketing folder for Honolulu display in the Details layout. To the left of each file name, an icon indicates the program that created each file. Here, there is one PowerPoint file, one Excel file, one Word file, and four JPEG images.

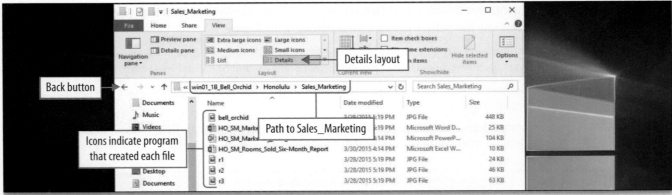

Microsoft Office 2016, Windows 10, Microsoft Corportation

FIGURE 1.54

7 In the upper left portion of the window, click **Back** ← one time.

The Back button retraces each of your clicks in the same manner as clicking the Back button when you are browsing the Internet.

8 In the **file list**, point to the **Human_Resources** folder, and then double-click to open the folder.

9 In the **file list**, click one time to select the PowerPoint file **HO_HR_New_Employee_Presentation**, and then on the ribbon, click the **View tab**. In the **Panes group**, click **Details pane**, and then compare your screen with Figure 1.55.

The *Details pane* displays the most common *file properties* associated with the selected file. File properties refer to information about a file, such as the author, the date the file was last changed, and any descriptive *tags*—properties that you create to help you find and organize your files.

Additionally, a thumbnail image of the first slide in the presentation displays, and the status bar displays the number of items in the folder.

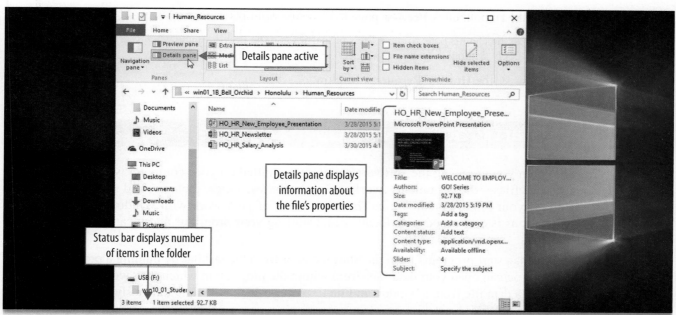

FIGURE 1.55

10 On the right, in the **Details pane**, click **Add a tag**, type **New Employee meeting** and then at the bottom of the pane click **Save**.

You can add tags to files to make them easier to find, because you can search for tags.

⟳ ANOTHER WAY   With the file selected, on the Home tab, in the Open group, click Properties to display the Properties dialog box for the file.

11 On the ribbon, on the **View tab**, in the **Panes group**, click **Preview pane** to replace the **Details pane** with the **Preview pane**. Compare your screen with Figure 1.56.

In the Preview pane that displays on the right, you can use the scroll bar to scroll through the slides in the presentation; or, you can click the up or down scroll arrow to view the slides as a miniature presentation.

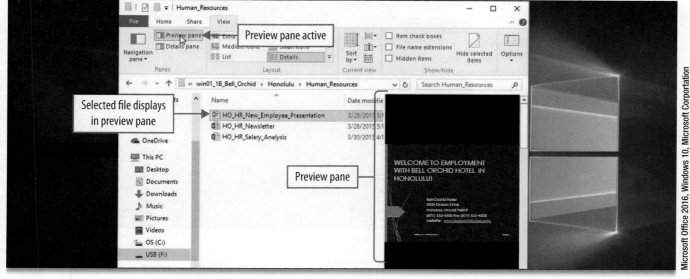

FIGURE 1.56

12 On the ribbon, click **Preview pane** to close the right pane.

Use the Details pane to see a file's properties and the Preview pane when you want to look at a file quickly without actually opening it.

13 **Close** ⌧ the **Human_Resources** window.

Objective 9 | Start Programs and Open Data Files

When you are using the software programs installed on your computer, you create and save data files—the documents, workbooks, databases, songs, pictures, and so on that you need for your job or personal use. Therefore, most of your work with Windows 10 desktop applications is concerned with locating and starting your programs and locating and opening your files.

You can start programs from the Start menu or from the taskbar by pinning a program to the taskbar. You can open your data files from within the program in which they were created, or you can open a data file from a window in File Explorer, which will simultaneously start the program and open your file.

Activity 1.23 | Starting Programs

1 Close any open windows. Click **Start** ⊞ to place the insertion point in the search box, and then type **paint** Compare your screen with Figure 1.57.

The Windows 10 search feature will immediately begin searching your PC and the web when you type in the search box. Here, Windows 10 searches your computer for applications and Documents containing the term *paint*, and searches Windows Store apps and the Web for the word *paint*.

Paint is a Windows desktop application that comes with Windows 10 with which you can create and edit drawings and display and edit stored photos.

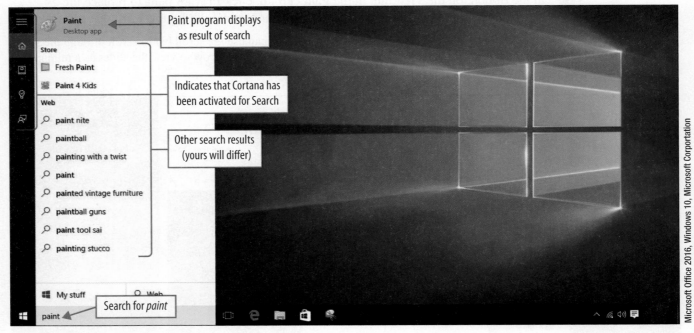

FIGURE 1.57

2 With the **Paint Desktop app** selected—also referred to as *in focus*—as the result of your search, press [Enter] to open this Windows desktop application.

3 On the ribbon of the Paint program, with the **Home tab** active, in the **Tools group**, click the **Pencil** icon. Move your mouse pointer into the white drawing area, hold down the left mouse button, and then with your mouse, try drawing the letters of your first name in the white area of the window.

↻ BY TOUCH   Use your finger to draw on the screen.

4 In the upper left corner, to the left of the **Home tab**, click the **File tab** to display a menu of commands for things you can do with your picture.

5 At the bottom of the menu, click **Exit**. In the displayed message, click **Don't Save**.

Messages like this display in most programs to prevent you from forgetting to save your work. A file saved in the Paint program creates a graphic file in the JPEG format.

6 Click **Start** ⊞ to place the insertion point in the search box, type **wordpad** and then open the **WordPad Desktop app**. Notice that this program window has characteristics similar to the Paint program window; for example, it has a ribbon of commands.

7 With the insertion point blinking in the document window, type your first and last name.

8 From the taskbar, start **Snipping Tool**, and then create a **Window Snip**. Click anywhere in the WordPad window to display the **Snipping Tool** mark-up window. **Save** the snip as a **JPEG** in your **Windows 10 Chapter 1** folder as **Lastname_Firstname_1B_WordPad_Snip** Hold this file until you finish this project, and then submit this file as directed by your instructor.

9 **Close** ☒ the **Snipping Tool** window. **Close** ☒ **WordPad**, and then click **Don't Save**.

10 Search for the **windows journal** desktop app and open it—click **Cancel** if asked to install print information. Search for the **alarms & clock** Windows Store app and open it. Search for the **calculator** Windows Store app and open it. Search for **network and sharing center** and open it. Compare your screen with Figure 1.58.

Windows Journal is a desktop app that comes with Windows 10 with which you can type or handwrite—on a touch screen—notes and then store them or email them. The *Network and Sharing Center* is a Windows 10 feature in the Control Panel where you can view your basic network information.

You can open multiple programs and apps, and each one displays in its own window. Each open program displays an icon on the taskbar.

You can see that for both desktop apps that come with Windows 10 and Windows Store apps, the easiest way to find a program is to simply search for it, and then open it from the list of results.

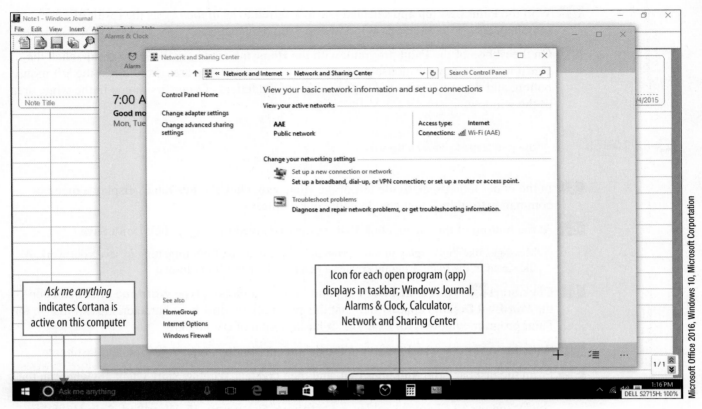

FIGURE 1.58

11 Click **Start** ▪, and then directly above the Start button, click **All apps**. Click the letter **A** to display an onscreen alphabet, and then click **W** to quickly jump to the W section of the list. Click **Windows Accessories**. Compare your screen with Figure 1.59.

These are programs that come with Windows 10. You can open them from this list or search for them as you just practiced. Additionally, use the technique you just practiced to quickly jump to a section of the All apps list without scrolling.

FIGURE 1.59

Microsoft Office 2016, Windows 10, Microsoft Corportation

12 On the taskbar, click the **Windows Journal** icon, and then on the taskbar, click the **Alarms & Clocks** icon.

Use the taskbar to quickly move among open apps.

13 **Close** ☒ all open windows and redisplay the desktop.

Activity 1.24 | Opening Data Files

NOTE	You Need Microsoft Word 2016 or Word 2013
For this Project you need Microsoft Word 2016 or Word 2013 on your computer; you can use a trial version if necessary.

1 Click **Start**, type **word 2016** (or type *word 2013* if that is the version of Word on your computer) and then open the **Word** desktop app. Maximize the window if necessary. Compare your screen with Figure 1.60.

The Word program window has features that are common to other programs you have opened; for example, commands are arranged on tabs. When you create and save data in Word, you create a Word document file.

FIGURE 1.60

Microsoft Office 2016, Windows 10, Microsoft Corportation

2 On the left, click **Open Other Documents**. Notice the list of places from which you can open a document, including your OneDrive if you are logged in. Click **Browse** to display the **Open** dialog box. Compare your screen with Figure 1.61, and then take a moment to study the table in Figure 1.62.

Recall that a dialog box is a window containing options for completing a task; its layout is similar to that of a File Explorer window. When you are working in a desktop application, use the Open dialog box to locate and open existing files that were created in the desktop application.

When you click Browse, typically the Documents folder on This PC displays. You can use the skills you have practiced to navigate to other locations on your computer, such as your removable USB flash drive.

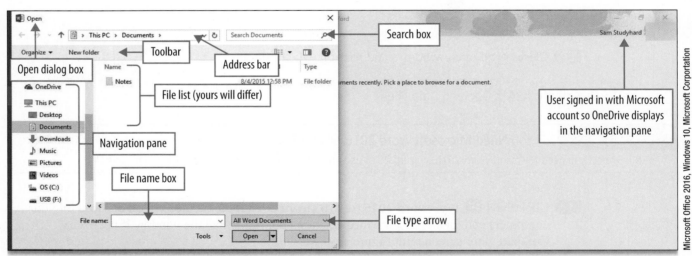

FIGURE 1.61

Microsoft Office 2016, Windows 10, Microsoft Corporation

DIALOG BOX ELEMENT	FUNCTION
Address bar	Displays the path in the folder structure.
File list	Displays the list of files and folders that are available in the folder indicated in the address bar.
File name box	Enables you to type the name of a specific file to locate it—if you know it.
File type arrow	Enables you to restrict the type of files displayed in the file list; for example, the default *All Word Documents* restricts (filters) the type of files displayed to only Word documents. You can click the arrow and adjust the restrictions (filters) to a narrower or wider group of files.
Navigation pane	Navigate to files and folders and get access to Quick access, OneDrive, and This PC.
Search box	Search for files in the current folder. Filters the file list based on text that you type; the search is based on text in the file name (and for files on the hard drive or OneDrive, in the file itself), and on other properties that you can specify. The search takes place in the current folder, as displayed in the address bar, and in any subfolders within that folder.
Toolbar	Displays relevant tasks; for example, creating a new folder.

FIGURE 1.62

3 In the **navigation pane**, scroll down as necessary, and then under **This PC**, click your **USB flash drive**. In the **file list**, double-click your **win10_01_Student_Data_Files** folder to open it and display its contents. Then double-click the **win01_1B_Bell_Orchid** folder to open it and display its contents.

4 In the upper right portion of the **Open** dialog box, click the **More options arrow** ▾, and then set the view to **Large icons**. Compare your screen with Figure 1.63.

The Live Preview feature indicates that each folder contains additional subfolders.

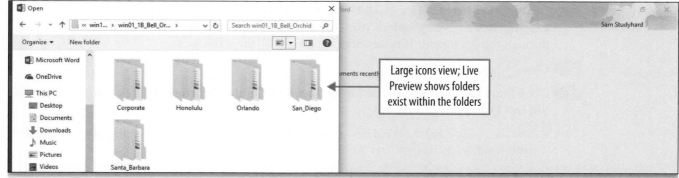

FIGURE 1.63

5 In the **file list**, double-click the **Corporate** folder, and then double-click the **Accounting** folder.

The view returns to the Details view.

6 In the **file list**, notice that only one document—a Word document—displays. In the lower right corner, locate the **File type** button, and notice that *All Word Documents* displays as the file type. Click the **File type arrow**, and then on the displayed list, click **All Files**. Compare your screen with Figure 1.64.

> When you change the file type to *All Files*, you can see that the Word file is not the only file in this folder. By default, the Open dialog box displays only the files created in the *active program*; however, you can display variations of file types in this manner.
>
> Microsoft Office file types are identified by small icons, which is a convenient way to differentiate one type of file from another. Although you can view all the files in the folder, you can open only the files that were created in the active program, which in this instance is Microsoft Word.

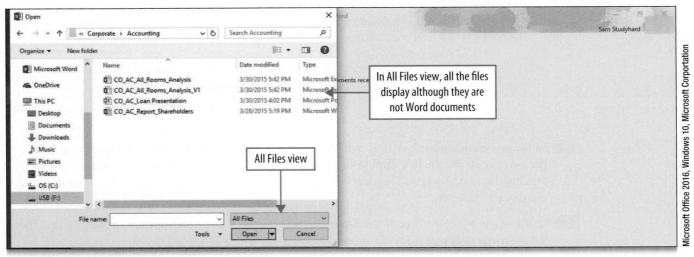

FIGURE 1.64

7 Change the file type back to **All Word Documents**. Then in the **file list**, double-click the **CO_AC_Report_Shareholders** Word file to open the document. Take a moment to scroll through the document. If necessary, Maximize ☐ the window.

8 Close ☒ the Word window.

9 Click **Start** ⊞, and then search for **.txt** Open one of the **Structure.txt** files, which are in your Student Data Files several times.

> The file opens using the Windows 10 *Notepad* desktop app—a basic text-editing program included with Windows 10 that you can use to create simple documents.
>
> In the search box, you can search for files on your computer, and you can search for a file by its *file name extension*—a set of characters at the end of a file name that helps Windows understand what kind of information is in a file and what program should open it. A *.txt file* is a simple file consisting of lines of text with no formatting and that almost any computer can open and display.

10 Close ☒ all open windows.

Storing Files and Creating Desktop Shortcuts for a Program on Your Desktop

On your desktop, you can add or remove *desktop shortcuts*, which are desktop icons that can link to items accessible on your computer such as a program, file, folder, disk drive, printer, or another computer. In previous versions of Windows, many computer users commonly did this.

Now the Start menu is your personal dashboard for all your programs and online activities, and increasingly you will access programs and your own files in the cloud. So do not clutter your desktop with shortcuts—doing so is more confusing than useful. Placing desktop shortcuts for frequently used programs or folders directly on your desktop may seem convenient, but as you add more icons, your desktop becomes cluttered and the shortcuts are not easy to find. A better organizing method is to use the taskbar for shortcuts to programs. For folders and files, the best organizing structure is to create a logical structure of folders within your Documents folder.

You can also drag frequently-used folders to the Quick access area in the navigation pane so that they are available any time you open File Explorer. As you progress in your use of Windows 10, you will discover techniques for using the taskbar and the Quick access area of the navigation pane to streamline your work, instead of cluttering your desktop.

Activity 1.25 | Searching, Pinning, Sorting, and Filtering in File Explorer

1 Click **File Explorer**. On the right, at the bottom, notice that under **Recent files**, you can see files that you have recently opened.

2 In the **navigation pane**, click your **USB flash drive**—or click the location where you have stored your student data files for this Project. In the upper right, click in the **Search** box, and then type **pool** Compare your screen with Figure 1.65.

Files that contain the word *pool* in the title display. If you are searching a folder on your hard drive or OneDrive, files that contain the word *pool* within the document will also display. Additionally, Search Tools display on the ribbon.

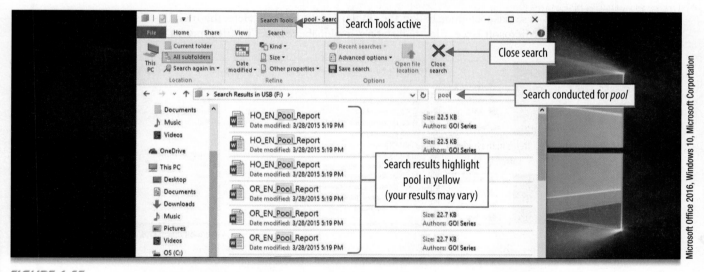

FIGURE 1.65

3 In the search box, clear the search by clicking ☒, and then in the search box type **dogs.jpg** Notice that you can also search by using a file extension as part of the search term.

4 **Clear** ☒ the search. In the **file list**, double-click your **win10_01_Student_Data_Files** folder to open it in the file list, and then click one time on your **win01_1B_Bell_Orchid** folder to select it.

5 On the **Home tab**, in the **Clipboard group**, click **Pin to Quick access**. Compare your screen with Figure 1.66.

> You can pin frequently used folders to the Quick access area, and then unpin them when you no longer need frequent access. Folders that you access frequently will also display in the Quick access area without the pin image. Delete them by right-clicking the name and clicking Unpin from Quick access.

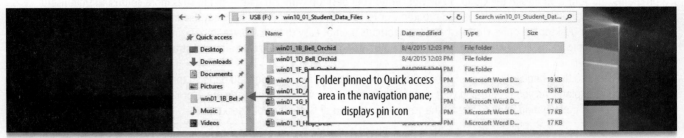

FIGURE 1.66

🔄 **ANOTHER WAY**   In the file list, right-click a folder name, and then click Pin to Quick access; or, drag the folder to the Quick access area in the navigation pain and release the mouse button when the ScreenTip displays Pin to Quick access.

---

6 In the **file list**—or from the Quick access area—double-click your **win01_1B_Bell_Orchid** folder to display its contents in the file list. Double-click the **Corporate** folder and then double-click the **Engineering** folder.

7 Point to an empty area of the **file list**, right-click, point to **Sort by**, and then click **Type**. Compare your screen with Figure 1.67.

> Use this technique to sort files in the file list by type. Here, the JPG files display first, and then the Microsoft Excel files, and so on—in alphabetic order by file type.

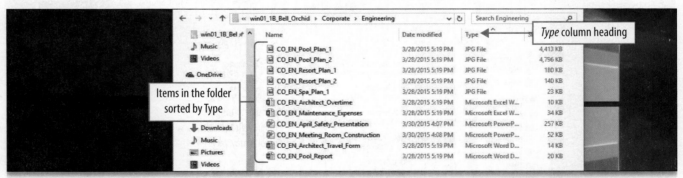

FIGURE 1.67

8 Point to the column heading **Type**, and then click ∧.

9 Point to the column heading **Type** again, and on the right, click ▾. On the displayed list, click **Microsoft PowerPoint Presentation**, and notice that the file list is filtered to show only PowerPoint files.

> A **filtered list** is a display of files that is limited based on specified criteria.

10 Click the check box to clear the Microsoft PowerPoint filter and redisplay all of the files.

11 **Close** ✕ all open windows.

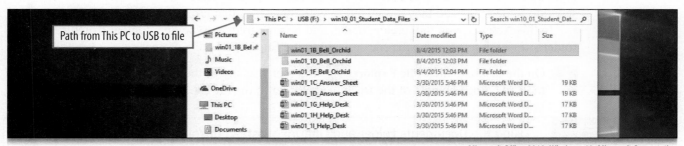

> **A L E R T !** **Allow Time to Complete the Remainder of This Project in One Session**
>
> If you are working on a computer that is not your own, for example, in a college lab, plan your time to complete the remainder of this Project in one working session. Allow 45 to 60 minutes.
>
>   Because you will need to store and then delete files on the hard disk drive of the computer at which you are working, it is recommended that you complete this project in one working session—*unless you are working on your own computer or you know that the files will be retained.* In your college lab, files you store on the computer's hard drive will not be retained after you sign off.

Objective 10 Create, Rename, and Copy Files and Folders

File management includes organizing, copying, naming, renaming, moving, and deleting the files and folders you have stored in various locations—both locally and in the cloud.

Activity 1.26 | **Copying Files from a Removable Storage Device to the Documents Folder on the Hard Disk Drive**

Barbara and Steven have the assignment to transfer and then organize some of the corporation's files to a computer that will be connected to the corporate network. Data on such a computer can be accessed by employees at any of the hotel locations through the use of sharing technologies. For example, *SharePoint* is a Microsoft technology that enables employees in an organization to access information across organizational and geographic boundaries.

1 Close any open windows. If necessary, insert the USB flash drive that contains the Student Data Files that accompany this chapter that you downloaded from the Pearson website or obtained from your instructor.

2 Open **File Explorer** . In the **navigation pane**, if necessary expand **This PC**, and then click your USB flash drive to display its contents in the file list.

   Recall that in the navigation pane, under This PC, you have access to all the storage areas inside your computer, such as your hard disk drives, and to any devices with removable storage, such as CDs, DVDs, or USB flash drives.

3 In the **file list**, double-click **win10_01_Student_Data_Files** (not the zipped folder if you still have it) to open it, and then click one time on the **win01_1B_Bell_Orchid** to select the folder. Compare your screen with Figure 1.68.

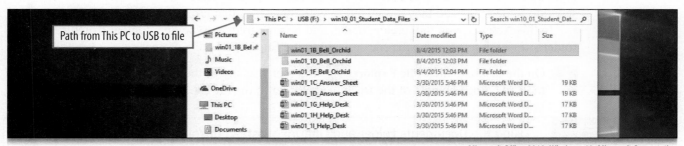

FIGURE 1.68

Microsoft Office 2016, Windows 10, Microsoft Corportation

4 With the **win01_1B_Bell_Orchid** folder on your USB drive selected, on the ribbon, on the **Home tab**, in the **Clipboard group**, click **Copy**.

The Copy command places a copy of your selected file or folder on the *Clipboard* where it will be stored until you use the Paste command to insert the copy somewhere else. The Clipboard is a temporary storage area for information that you have copied or moved from one place and plan to use somewhere else.

In Windows 10, the Clipboard can hold only one piece of information at a time. Whenever something is copied to the Clipboard, it replaces whatever was there before. In Windows 10, you cannot view the contents of the Clipboard nor place multiple items there in the manner that you can in Microsoft Word.

ANOTHER WAY   With the item selected in the file list, press [Ctrl] + [C] to copy the item to the clipboard.

5 To the left of the address bar, click **Up** [↑] two times. In the **file list**, double-click your **Documents** folder to open it, and then on the **Home tab**, in the **Clipboard group**, click **Paste**.

A *progress bar* displays in a dialog box, and also displays on the File Explorer taskbar button with green shading. A progress bar indicates visually the progress of a task such as a copy process, a download, or a file transfer.

The Documents folder is one of several folders within your *personal folder* stored on the hard disk drive. For each user account—even if there is only one user on the computer—Windows 10 creates a personal folder labeled with the account holder's name.

ANOTHER WAY   With the destination location selected, press [Ctrl] + [V] to paste the item from the clipboard to the selected location. Or, on the Home tab, in the Organize group, click Copy to, find and then click the location to which you want to copy. If the desired location is not on the list, use the Choose location command at the bottom.

6 Close [×] the **Documents** window.

Activity 1.27 | Creating Folders, Renaming Folders, and Renaming Files

Barbara and Steven can see that various managers have been placing files related to the new European hotels in the *Future_Hotels* folder. They can also see that the files have not been organized into a logical structure. For example, files that are related to each other are not in separate folders; instead they are mixed in with other files that are not related to the topic.

In this Activity, you will create, name, and rename folders to begin a logical structure of folders in which to organize the files related to the European hotels project.

1 On the taskbar, click **File Explorer** 📁, and then use any of the techniques you have practiced to display the contents of the **Documents** folder in the **file list**.

NOTE   Using the Documents Folder and OneDrive Instead of Your USB Drive

In this modern computing era, you should limit your use of USB drives to those times when you want to quickly take some files to another computer without going online. Instead of using a USB drive, use your computer's hard drive, or better yet, your free OneDrive cloud storage that comes with your Microsoft account.

There are two good reasons to stop using USB flash drives. First, searching is limited on a USB drive—search does not look at the content inside a file. When you search files on your hard drive or OneDrive, the search extends to words and phrases actually *inside* the files. Second, if you delete a file or folder from a USB drive, it is gone and cannot be retrieved. Files you delete from your hard drive or OneDrive go to the Recycle Bin where you can retrieve them later.

---

2 In the **file list**, double-click the **win01_1B_Bell_Orchid** folder, double-click the **Corporate** folder, double-click the **Information_Technology** folder, and then double-click the **Future_Hotels** folder to display its contents in the file list; sometimes this navigation is written as *Documents > win01_1B_Bell_Orchid > Corporate > Information_Technology > Future_Hotels*.

Some computer users prefer to navigate a folder structure by double-clicking in this manner. Others prefer using the address bar as described in the following Another Way box. Use whatever method you prefer—double-clicking in the file list, clicking in the address bar, or expanding files in the navigation pane.

ANOTHER WAY In the navigation pane, click Documents, and expand each folder in the navigation pane. Or, In the address bar, to the right of Documents, click >, and then on the list, click win01_1B_Bell_Orchid. To the right of win01_1B_Bell_Orchid, click > and then click Corporate. To the right of Corporate, click > and then click Information_Technology. To the right of Information_Technology, click >, and then click Future_Hotels.

3 In the **file list**, be sure the items are in alphabetical order by **Name**. If the items are not in alphabetical order, recall that by clicking the small arrow in the column heading name, you can change how the files in the file list are ordered.

4 On the ribbon, click the **View tab**, and then in the **Layout group**, be sure **Details** is selected.

The ***Details view*** displays a list of files or folders and their most common properties.

ANOTHER WAY Right-click in a blank area of the file list, point to View, and then click Details.

5 On the ribbon, click the **Home tab**, and then in the **New group**, click **New folder**. With the text *New folder* selected, type **Paris** and press [Enter]. Click **New folder** again, and then type **Venice** and press [Enter]. Create a third **New folder** named **London**

In a Windows 10 file list, folders are listed first, in alphabetic order, followed by individual files in alphabetic order.

6 Click the **Venice** folder one time to select it, and then on the ribbon, in the **Organize group**, click **Rename**. Notice that the text *Venice* is selected. Type **Rome** and press [Enter].

ANOTHER WAY Point to a folder or file name, right-click, and then on the shortcut menu, click Rename.

7 In the **file list**, click one time to select the Word file **Architects**. With the file name selected, click the file name again to select all the text. Click the file name again to place the insertion point within the file name, edit the file name to **Architects_Local** and press [Enter]. Compare your screen with Figure 1.69.

You can use any of the techniques you just practiced to change the name of a file or folder.

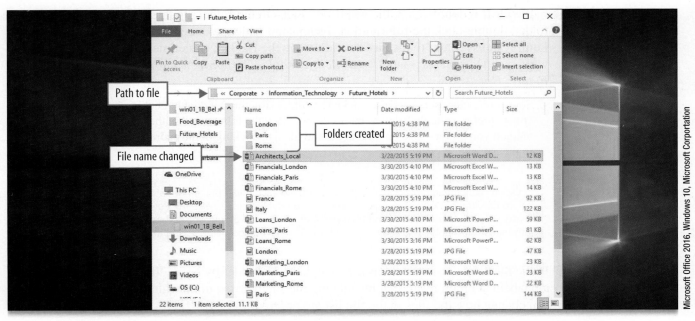

FIGURE 1.69

---

8 From the taskbar, start **Snipping Tool**; if necessary drag the *title bar*—the bar across the top of a window that displays the program name—of Snipping Tool into a blank area of the desktop. Click the **New arrow**, and then click **Window Snip**. Point anywhere in the **Future_Hotels** window and click one time. In the **Snipping Tool** mark-up window, click **Save Snip** 🖫.

9 In the **Save As** dialog box, in the **navigation pane**, scroll down as necessary, and then click your USB flash drive so that it displays in the **address bar**.

10 In the **file list**, double-click your **Windows 10 Chapter 1** folder to open it. Click in the **File name** box, and then replace the selected text by typing **Lastname_Firstname_1B_Europe_Folders_Snip**

11 Be sure the file type is **JPEG**. Click **Save** or press Enter. **Close** × the **Snipping Tool** window. Hold this file until you finish this Project.

12 **Close** × all open windows.

Activity 1.28 | Copying Files

Copying, moving, renaming, and deleting files and folders comprise the most heavily used features within File Explorer. Probably half or more of the steps you complete in File Explorer relate to these tasks, so mastering these techniques will increase your efficiency.

When you *copy* a file or a folder, you make a duplicate of the original item and then store the duplicate in another location. In this Activity, you will assist Barbara and Steven in making copies of the Staffing_Plan file and then placing the copies in each of the three folders you created—London, Paris, and Rome.

1 From the taskbar, open **File Explorer** 📁, and then by double-clicking in the file list or following the links in the address bar, navigate to **This PC > Documents > win01_1B_Bell_Orchid > Corporate > Information_Technology > Future_Hotels**.

2 **Maximize** ☐ the window. On the **View tab**, if necessary set the **Layout** to **Details**, and then in the **Current view group**, click **Size all columns to fit** 🖽.

3 In the **file list**, click the file **Staffing_Plan** one time to select it, and then on the **Home tab**, in the **Clipboard group**, click **Copy**.

> **4** At the top of the **file list**, double-click the **London folder** to open it, and then in the **Clipboard group**, click **Paste**. Notice that the copy of the **Staffing_Plan** file displays. Compare your screen with Figure 1.70.

FIGURE 1.70

Microsoft Office 2016, Windows 10, Microsoft Corportation

🔄 ANOTHER WAY   Right-click the file you want to copy, and on the menu click Copy. Then right-click the folder into which you want to place the copy, and on the menu click Paste. Or, select the file you want to copy, press Ctrl + C to activate the Copy command, open the folder into which you want to paste the file, and then press Ctrl + V to activate the Paste command.

> **5** With the **London** window open, by using any of the techniques you have practiced, rename this copy of the **Staffing_Plan** file to **London_Staffing_Plan**

> **6** To the left of the **address bar**, click **Up** ⬆ to move up one level in the folder structure and redisplay the file list for the **Future_Hotels** folder.

🔄 ANOTHER WAY   In the address bar, click Future_Hotels to redisplay this window and move up one level in the folder structure.

> **7** Click the **Staffing_Plan** file one time to select it, hold down Ctrl, and then drag the file upward over the **Paris** folder until the ScreenTip + *Copy to Paris* displays, and then release the mouse button and release Ctrl.

When dragging a file into a folder, holding down Ctrl engages the Copy command and places a *copy* of the file at the location where you release the mouse button. This is another way to copy a file or copy a folder.

> **8** Open the **Paris** folder, and then rename the **Staffing_Plan** file **Paris_Staffing_Plan** Then, move up one level in the folder structure to display the **Future_Hotels** window.

> **9** Double-click the **Rome** folder to open it. With your mouse pointer anywhere in the **file list**, right-click, and then from the shortcut menu click **Paste**.

A copy of the Staffing_Plan file is copied to the folder. Because a copy of the Staffing_Plan file is still on the Clipboard, you can continue to paste the item until you copy another item on the Clipboard to replace it.

> **10** Rename the file **Rome_Staffing_Plan**

> **11** On the **address bar**, click **Future_Hotels** to move up one level and open the **Future_Hotels** window—or click Up ⬆ to move up one level. Leave this folder open for the next activity.

Activity 1.29 | Moving Files

When you move a file or folder, you remove it from the original location and store it in a new location. In this Activity, you will move items from the Future_Hotels folder into their appropriate folders.

1 With the **Future_Hotels** folder open, in the **file list**, click the Excel file **Financials_London** one time to select it. On the **Home tab**, in the **Clipboard group**, click **Cut**.

The file's Excel icon dims. This action places the item on the Clipboard.

ANOTHER WAY   Right-click the file or folder, and on the shortcut menu, click Cut; or, select the file or folder, and then press Ctrl + X.

2 Double-click the **London** folder to open it, and then on the **Home tab**, in the **Clipboard group**, click **Paste**.

ANOTHER WAY   Right-click the folder, and on the shortcut menu, click Paste; or, select the folder, and then press Ctrl + V.

3 Click **Up** ↑ to move up one level and redisplay the **Future_Hotels** folder window. In the **file list**, point to **Financials_Paris**, hold down the left mouse button, and then drag the file upward over the **Paris** folder until the ScreenTip →*Move to Paris* displays, and then release the mouse button.

4 Open the **Paris** folder, and notice that the file was moved to this folder. Click **Up** ↑—or on the address bar, click Future_Hotels to return to that folder.

5 In the **file list**, click **Loans_London**, hold down Ctrl, and then click **London** and **Marketing_London** to select the three files. Release the Ctrl key. Compare your screen with Figure 1.71.

Use this technique to select a group of noncontiguous items in a list.

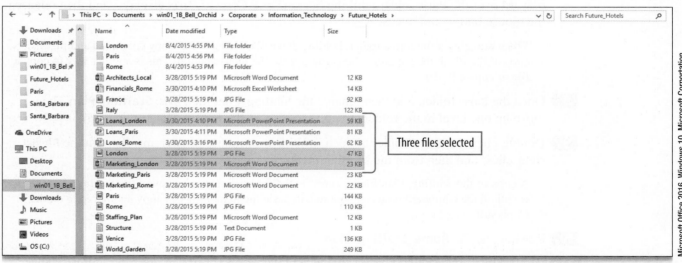

FIGURE 1.71

6 Point to any of the selected files, hold down the left mouse button, and then drag upward over the **London** folder until the ScreenTip ➔*Move to London* displays and *3* displays over the files being moved, and then release the mouse button.

You can see that by keeping related files together—for example, all the files that relate to the London hotel—in folders that have an appropriately descriptive name, it will be easier to locate information later.

7 By dragging, move the **Architects_Local** file into the **London** folder.

8 In an empty area of the file list, right-click, and then click **Undo Move**. Leave the **Future_Hotels** window open for the next activity.

Any action that you make in a file list can be undone in this manner.

🔄 ANOTHER WAY   Press Ctrl + Z to undo an action in the file list.

More Knowledge	**Using Shift + Click to Select Files**

If files to be selected are contiguous (next to each other in the file list), click the first file to be selected and then press Shift and click the left mouse button on the last file to select all of the files between the top and bottom file selections.

Activity 1.30 | **Copying and Moving Files by Snapping Two Windows**

Sometimes you will want to open, in a second window, another instance of a program that you are using; that is, two copies of the program will be running simultaneously. This capability is especially useful in the File Explorer program, because you are frequently moving or copying files from one location to another.

In this Activity, you will open two instances of File Explorer, and then use the *Snap* feature to display both instances on your screen.

To copy or move files or folders into a different level of a folder structure, or to a different drive location, the most efficient method is to display two windows side by side and then use drag and drop or copy (or cut) and paste commands.

In this Activity, you will assist Barbara and Steven in making copies of the Staffing_Plan files for the corporate office.

1 In the upper right corner, click **Restore Down** ⬜ to restore the **Future_Hotels** window to its previous size and not maximized on the screen.

2 Hold down ⊞ and press ← to snap the window so that it occupies the left half of the screen.

3 On the taskbar, right-click **File Explorer** ▭, and then on the list, click **File Explorer** to open another instance of the program. With the new window active, hold down ⊞ and press → to snap the window so that it occupies the right half of the screen.

🔄 ANOTHER WAY   Drag the title bar of a window to the left or right side of the screen and when your mouse pointer reaches the edge, it will snap it into place.

4 In the window on the right, click in a blank area to make the window active. Then navigate to **Documents > win01_1B_Bell_Orchid > Corporate > Human_Resources**. Compare your screen with Figure 1.72.

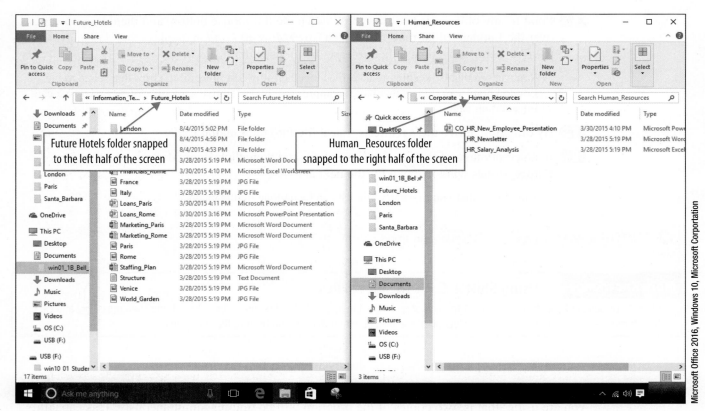

FIGURE 1.72

5 In the left window, double-click to open the **Rome** folder, and then click one time to select the file **Rome_Staffing_Plan**.

6 Hold down Ctrl, and then drag the file into the right window, into an empty area of the **Human_Resources file list**, until the ScreenTip + *Copy to Human_Resources* displays and then release the mouse button and Ctrl.

7 In the left window, on the **address bar**, click **Future_Hotels** to redisplay that folder. Open the **Paris** folder, point to **Paris_Staffing_Plan** and right-click, and then click **Copy**.

> You can access the Copy command in various ways; for example, from the shortcut menu, on the ribbon, or by using the keyboard shortcut Ctrl + C.

8 In the right window, point anywhere in the **file list**, right-click, and then click **Paste**.

9 Start the **Snipping Tool** program, click the **New arrow**, and then click **Full-screen Snip**. In the **Snipping Tool** mark-up window, click **Save Snip** 💾.

10 In the displayed **Save As** dialog box, notice the path in the **address bar**. If necessary, in the navigation pane, under **This PC**, click your USB flash drive, and then display the window for your **Windows 10 Chapter 1** folder.

11 Be sure the file type is **JPEG**. Using your own name, as the file name type **Lastname_Firstname_1B_HR_Snip** and press Enter. Hold this file until you have completed this Project.

12 **Close** ⊠ all open windows.

Activity 1.31 | Deleting Files and Using the Recycle Bin

It is good practice to delete files and folders that you no longer need from your hard disk drive and removable storage devices. Doing so makes it easier to keep your data organized and also frees up storage space.

When you delete a file or folder from any area of your computer's hard disk drive or from OneDrive, the file or folder is not immediately deleted. Instead, the deleted item is stored in the *Recycle Bin* and remains there until the Recycle Bin is emptied. Thus, you can recover an item deleted from your computer's hard disk drive or OneDrive so long as the Recycle Bin has not been emptied. Items deleted from removable storage devices like a USB flash drive and from some network drives are immediately deleted and cannot be recovered from the Recycle Bin.

To permanently delete a file without first moving it to the Recycle Bin, click the item, hold down [Shift], and then press [Del]. A message will display indicating *Are you sure you want to permanently delete this file?* Use caution when using [Shift] + [Del] to permanently delete a file because this action is not reversible.

You can restore items by dragging them from the file list of the Recycle Bin window to the file list of the folder window in which you want to restore them. Or, you can restore them to the location from which they were deleted by right-clicking the items in the file list of the Recycle Bin window and selecting Restore.

Self-Check | Answer These Questions to Check Your Understanding

1 When you delete a file or folder from any area of your computer's hard disk drive or from OneDrive, the file or folder is not deleted; it is automatically stored in the _____ _____.

2 Files deleted from the computer's hard drive or OneDrive can be recovered from the Recycle Bin until the Recycle Bin is _____.

3 Items deleted from removable storage devices such as a USB flash drive are immediately deleted and cannot be _____ from the Recycle Bin.

4 You can permanently delete a file from the hard drive or OneDrive without first moving it to the Recycle Bin, but a warning message will indicate *Are you sure you want to _____ delete this file?*

5 To restore items from the Recycle Bin to the location from which they were deleted, right-click the items and then click _____.

Objective 11 Use OneDrive as Cloud Storage

OneDrive is Microsoft's *cloud storage* product. Cloud storage means that your data is stored on a remote server that is maintained by a company so that you can access your files from anywhere and from any device. The idea of having all of your data on a single device—your desktop or laptop PC—has become old fashioned. Because cloud storage from large companies like Microsoft is secure, many computer users now store their information on cloud services like OneDrive. Anyone with a Microsoft account has a large amount of free storage on OneDrive, and if you have an Office 365 account—free to many college students if your college offers such a program—you have 1 terabyte or more of OneDrive storage that you can use across all Microsoft products. That amount of storage is probably all you will ever need—even if you store lots of photos on your OneDrive.

OneDrive is no longer just an app, as it was in Windows 8. Rather, OneDrive is integrated into the Windows 10 operating system. Similarly, Google's cloud storage called *Google Drive* is integrated into its Chrome operating system, and Apple's cloud storage called *iCloud* is integrated into both the Mac and iOS operating systems.

Activity 1.32 | Using OneDrive as Cloud Storage

When you install Windows 10 or use it for the first time, you will be prompted to set up your OneDrive. The setup process involves determining which folders—if not all—that you want to *sync* to OneDrive. Syncing—also called synchronizing—is the process of updating OneDrive data to match any updates you make on your device, and vice versa. This setup is optional, and you can always come back to it later. Your OneDrive storage, however, will be available from the navigation pane in File Explorer. Additionally, you will always have instant access to your OneDrive from any web browser.

1 **Close** ⊠ any open windows. From the taskbar, start **File Explorer** 🗔 and then navigate to **Documents > win01_1B_Bell_Orchid > Santa_Barbara > Sales_Marketing > Media**.

2 Hold down Ctrl, click **Scenic1** and **Scenic2**, and then release Ctrl. With the two files selected, press Ctrl + C, which is the keyboard shortcut for the Copy command.

Although you see no screen action, the two files are copied to the Clipboard.

3 In the **navigation pane**, click **OneDrive**. If a dialog box regarding Customizing your OneDrive settings displays, in the lower right corner, click Cancel.

If you have decided on syncing options, you can do so in this dialog box; or, postpone these decisions by clicking Cancel.

Your OneDrive folders display in the file list.

4 On the ribbon, on the **Home tab**, in the **New group**, click **New folder**. Name the new folder **Marketing Photos** and then press Enter. Double-click the new folder to open it.

5 Press Ctrl + V, which is the keyboard shortcut for the Paste command, to paste the two photos into the folder. On the **View tab**, set the **Layout** to **Details**. Compare your screen with Figure 1.73.

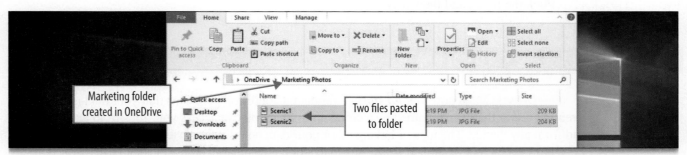

FIGURE 1.73

Microsoft Office 2016, Windows 10, Microsoft Corportation

6 Using the techniques you have practiced, create a window snip and save the snip in your chapter folder. Be sure the file type is **JPEG**. Using your own name, as the file name type **Lastname_Firstname_1B_OneDrive_Snip** and press Enter.

7 **Close** ⊠ all open windows.

END | You have completed Project 1B

END OF CHAPTER

SUMMARY

Windows 10 is optimized for touchscreens and also works with a mouse and keyboard. You will probably use touch when you are reading or communicating on the web and a keyboard when creating files.

The Windows 10 Start menu is your connected dashboard—this is your one-screen view of information that updates continuously with new information and personal communications that are important to you.

The Windows Store apps you use from the Start menu display in separate Windows, similar to your other files, so you can move them on the desktop or display them side by side. These apps typically have a single purpose.

File Explorer is at work anytime you are viewing the contents of a location, a folder, or a file. Use File Explorer to navigate your Windows 10 structure that stores and organizes the files you create.

GO! LEARN IT ONLINE

Review the concepts and key terms in this chapter by completing these online challenges, which you can find in **MyITLab**.

Matching and Multiple Choice: Answer matching and multiple choice questions to test what you learned in this chapter.

Lessons on the GO!: Learn how to use all the new apps and features as they are introduced by Microsoft.

GO! FOR JOB SUCCESS

Video: Email Etiquette

Your instructor may assign this video to your class, and then ask you to think about, or discuss with your classmates, these questions:

FotolEdhar/Fotolia

Why do you think it is important to follow specific etiquette when composing email?

Why is it important to include a greeting and sign every email you send?

What are the differences between sending a business email and a personal email, and what are three specific things you should never do in a business email?

Review and Assessment Guide for Windows 10 Chapter 1			
Project	**Apply Skills from These Chapter Objectives**	**Project Type**	**Project Location**
1C	Objectives 1-6 from Project 1A	**1C Chapter Review** A guided review of the skills from Project 1A.	On the following pages
1D	Objectives 7-11 from Project 1B	**1D Chapter Review** A guided review of the skills from Project 1B.	On the following pages
1E	Objectives 1-6 from Project 1A	**1E Mastery** **Mastery and Transfer of Learning** A demonstration of your mastery of the skills in Project 1A with decision-making.	On the following pages
1F	Objectives 7-11 from Project 1B	**1F Mastery** **Mastery and Transfer of Learning** A demonstration of your mastery of the skills in Project 1B with decision-making.	On the following pages
1G	Combination of Objectives from Projects 1A and 1B	**1G GO! Think** **Critical Thinking** A demonstration of your understanding of the chapter concepts applied in a manner that you would outside of college. An analytic rubric helps you and your instructor grade the quality of your work by comparing it to the work an expert in the discipline would create.	On the following pages
1H	Combination of Objectives from Projects 1A and 1B	**1H GO! Think** **Critical Thinking** A demonstration of your understanding of the chapter concepts applied in a manner that you would outside of college. An analytic rubric helps you and your instructor grade the quality of your work by comparing it to the work an expert in the discipline would create.	On the following pages
1I	Combination of Objectives from Projects 1A and 1B	**1I GO! Think** **Critical Thinking** A demonstration of your understanding of the chapter concepts applied in a manner that you would outside of college. An analytic rubric helps you and your instructor grade the quality of your work by comparing it to the work an expert in the discipline would create.	On the following pages

GLOSSARY

GLOSSARY OF CHAPTER KEY TERMS

.png An image file format, commonly pronounced *PING*, that stands for Portable Network Graphic; this is an image file type that can be transferred over the Internet.

.txt file A simple file consisting of lines of text with no formatting that almost any computer can open and display.

Action Center A vertical panel that displays on the right side of your screen when you click the icon in the notifications area of the taskbar; the upper portion displays notifications you have elected to receive such as mail and social network updates and the lower portion displays buttons for frequently used system commands.

Address bar (File Explorer) The area at the top of a File Explorer window that displays your current location in the folder structure as a series of links separated by arrows.

Administrator account A user account that lets you make changes that will affect other users of the computer; the most powerful of the three types of accounts, because it permits the most control over the computer.

All apps A command that displays all the apps installed on your computer in alphabetical order on the Start menu.

App The shortened version of the term *application*, and which typically refers to a smaller application designed for a single purpose.

App bar A term used to describe a horizontal or vertical array of command icons in a Windows app.

Application A set of instructions that a computer uses to accomplish a task; also called a program.

Application developer An individual who writes computer applications.

Badge An icon that displays on the Lock screen for lock screen apps that you have selected.

Bing Microsoft's search engine, which powers Cortana.

Booting the computer The process of turning on a computer when the computer has been completely shut down and during which the BIOS program will run.

Click The action of pressing the left mouse button.

Clipboard A temporary storage area for information that you have copied or moved from one place and plan to use somewhere else.

Cloud storage Storage space on an Internet site that may also display as a drive on your computer.

Compressed file A file that has been reduced in size and that takes up less storage space and can be transferred to other computers faster than uncompressed files.

Compressed Folder Tools File Explorer tools, available on the ribbon, to assist you in extracting compressed files.

Contextual tab A tab added to the ribbon in Windows Explorer that contains context-sensitive commands and options that are relevant to the active object.

Control Panel An area of Windows 10 where you can manipulate some of the Windows 10 basic system settings—a carryover from previous versions of Windows.

Cortana Microsoft's intelligent personal assistant that is part of the Windows 10 operating system.

Dashboard A descriptive term for the Windows 10 Start menu because it provides a one-screen view of links to information and programs that matter most to the signed-in user.

Data All the files—documents, spreadsheets, pictures, songs, and so on—that you create and store during the day-to-day use of your computer.

Data management The process of managing your files and folders in an organized manner so that you can find information when you need it.

Desktop The main Windows 10 screen that serves as a starting point and surface for your work, like the top of an actual desk.

Desktop app A computer program that is installed on the hard drive of a personal computer and that requires a computer operating system like Microsoft Windows or Apple OSX to run.

Desktop background Displays the colors and graphics of your desktop; you can change the desktop background to look the way you want.

Desktop shortcuts Desktop icons that link to any item accessible on your computer or on a network, such as a program, file, folder, disk drive, printer, or another computer.

Details pane Displays the most common properties associated with the selected file.

Details view A view in File Explorer that displays a list of files or folders and their most common properties.

Dialog box A small window that displays options for completing a task.

Double-click The action of pressing the left mouse button twice in rapid succession while holding the mouse still.

Download The action of transferring or copying a file from another location—such as a cloud storage location or from an Internet site—to your computer.

Downloads folder A folder that holds items that you have downloaded from the Internet.

Drag The action of moving something from one location on the screen to another while holding down the left mouse button; the action of dragging includes releasing the mouse button at the desired time or location.

Drive An area of storage that is formatted with a file system compatible with your operating system and is identified by a drive letter.

Extract The action of decompressing—pulling out—files from a compressed form.

File A collection of information that is stored on a computer under a single name, for example, a text document, a picture, or a program.

File Explorer window A window that displays the contents of the current location and contains helpful parts so that you can navigate within the file organizing structure of Windows.

File History A backup and recovery tool that automatically backs up your files to a separate location.

File list Displays the contents of the current folder or location; if you type text into the Search box, only the folders and files that match your search will display here—including files in subfolders.

File name extension A set of characters at the end of a file name that helps Windows 10 understand what kind of information is in a file and what program should open it.

File properties Information about a file such as its author, the date the file was last changed, and any descriptive tags.

Filtered list A display of files that is limited based on specified criteria.

Folder A container in which you store files.

Folder structure The hierarchy of folders in Windows 10.

Free-form snip When using Snipping Tool, the type of snip that lets you draw an irregular line, such as a circle, around an area of the screen.

Full-screen snip When using Snipping Tool, the type of snip that captures the entire screen.

Get Started A feature in Windows 10 to learn about all the things that Windows 10 can do for you.

Google Drive Google's cloud storage.

Graphical user interface The system by which you interact with your computer and which uses graphics such as an image of a file folder or wastebasket that you click to activate the item represented.

GUI The acronym for a graphical user interface, pronounced *GOO-ee*.

Hamburger Another name for the hamburger menu.

Hamburger menu An icon made up of three lines that evoke a hamburger on a bun.

Hard disk drive The primary storage device located inside your computer and where most of your files and programs are typically stored; usually labeled as drive C.

Hierarchy An arrangement where items are ranked and where each level is lower in rank than the item above it.

HoloLens A see-through holographic computer developed by Microsoft.

Hub A feature in Microsoft Edge where you can save favorite websites and create reading lists.

iCloud Apple's cloud storage that is integrated into its Mac and iOS operating systems.

Icons Small images that represent commands, files, or other windows.

Insertion point A blinking vertical line that indicates where text or graphics will be inserted.

Internet of Things A growing network of physical objects that will have sensors connected to the Internet.

IoT The common acronym for the Internet of Things.

JPEG An acronym for Joint Photographic Experts Group, and which is a common file type used by digital cameras and computers to store digital pictures; JPEG is popular because it can store a high-quality picture in a relatively small file.

Jump list A list that displays when you right-click a button on the taskbar, and which displays locations (in the upper portion) and tasks (in the lower portion) from a program's taskbar button.

Keyboard shortcut A combination of two or more keyboard keys, used to perform a task that would otherwise require a mouse.

Live tiles Tiles on the Windows 10 Start menu that are constantly updated with fresh information relevant to the signed-in user; for example, the number of new email messages, new sports scores of interest, or new updates to social networks such as Facebook or Twitter.

Location Any disk drive, folder, or other place in which you can store files and folders.

Lock screen The first screen that displays after turning on a Windows 10 device and that displays the time, day, and date, and one or more icons representing the status of the device's Internet connection, battery status on a tablet or laptop, and any lock screen apps that are installed such as email notifications.

Lock screen apps Apps that display on a Windows 10 lock screen and that show quick status and notifications, even if the screen is locked.

Maximize The command to display a window in full-screen view.

Menu A list of commands within a category.

Menu bar A group of menus.

Menu icon Another name for the hamburger menu.

Microsoft account A single login account for Microsoft systems and services.

Microsoft Edge The web browser program included with Windows 10.

Mobile device platform The hardware and software environment for smaller-screen devices such as tablets and smartphones.

Mouse pointer Any symbol that displays on your screen in response to moving your mouse.

Navigate Explore within the file organizing structure of Windows 10.

Navigation pane The area on the left side of a folder window in File Explorer that displays the Quick Access area and an expandable list of drives and folders.

Network and Sharing Center A Windows 10 feature in the Control Panel where you can view your basic network information.

Notepad A basic text-editing program included with Windows 10 that you can use to create simple documents.

OneDrive A free file storage and file sharing service provided by Microsoft when you sign up for a free Microsoft account.

Operating system A specific type of computer program that manages the other programs on a computer—including computer devices such as desktop computers, laptop computers, smartphones, tablet computers, and game consoles.

Parent folder In the file organizing structure of File Explorer, the location where the folder you are viewing is saved—one level up in the hierarchy.

Path A sequence of folders (directories) that leads to a specific file or folder.

PC Reset A backup and recovery tool that returns your PC to the condition it was in the day you purchased it.

Pen A pen-shaped stylus that you tap on a computer screen.

Personal folder A folder created for each user account on a Windows 10 computer, labeled with the account holder's name, and which contains the subfolders *Documents, Pictures, Music*.

PIN Acronym for personal identification number; in Windows 10 Settings, you can create a PIN to use in place of a password.

Platform An underlying computer system on which application programs can run.

Point to The action of moving the mouse pointer over a specific area.

Pointer Any symbol that displays on your screen in response to moving your mouse and with which you can select objects and commands.

Pointing device A mouse, touchpad, or other device that controls the pointer position on the screen.

Program A set of instructions that a computer uses to accomplish a task; also called an application.

Progress bar In a dialog box or taskbar button, a bar that indicates visually the progress of a task such as a download or file transfer.

Quick access The navigation pane area in File Explorer where you can pin folders you use frequently and that also adds folders you are accessing frequently.

Quick Access Toolbar (File Explorer) The small row of buttons in the upper left corner of a File Explorer window from which you can perform frequently used commands.

Recently added On the Start menu, a section that displays apps that you have recently downloaded and installed.

Rectangular snip When using Snipping Tool, the type of snip that lets you draw a precise box by dragging the mouse pointer around an area of the screen to form a rectangle.

Recycle Bin A folder that stores anything that you delete from your computer, and from which anything stored there can be retrieved until the contents are permanently deleted by activating the Empty Recycle Bin command.

Removable storage device A portable device on which you can store files, such as a USB flash drive, a flash memory card, or an external hard drive, commonly used to transfer information from one computer to another.

Resources A term used to refer collectively to the parts of your computer such as the central processing unit (CPU), memory, and any attached devices such as a printer.

Restore Down A command to restore a window to its previous size before it was maximized.

Ribbon The area at the top of a folder window in File Explorer that groups common tasks such as copying and moving, creating new folders, emailing and zipping items, and changing views on related tabs.

Right-click The action of clicking the right mouse button.

Screenshot Another name for a screen capture.

ScreenTip Useful information that displays in a small box on the screen when you perform various mouse actions, such as pointing to screen elements.

Scroll arrow An arrow at the top, bottom, left, or right, of a scroll bar that when clicked, moves the window in small increments.

Scroll bar A bar that displays on the bottom or right side of a window when the contents of a window are not completely visible; used to move the window up, down, left, or right to bring the contents into view.

Scroll box The box in a vertical or horizontal scroll bar that you drag to reposition the document on the screen.

Select To specify, by highlighting, a block of data or text on the screen with the intent of performing some action on the selection.

SharePoint A Microsoft technology that enables employees in an organization to access information across organizational and geographic boundaries.

Shortcut menu A context-sensitive menu that displays commands and options relevant to the active object.

Shut down Turning off your computer in a manner that closes all open programs and files, closes your network connections, stops the hard disk, and discontinues the use of electrical power.

Sleep Turning off your computer in a manner that automatically saves your work, stops the fan, and uses a small amount of electrical power to maintain your work in memory.

Snap Assist The ability to drag windows to the edges or corners of your screen, and then having Task View display thumbnails of other open windows so that you can select what other windows you want to snap into place.

Snip The image captured using Snipping Tool.

Snipping Tool A program included with Windows 10 with which you can capture an image of all or part of a computer screen, and then annotate, save, copy, or share the image via email.

Split button A button that has two parts—a button and an arrow; clicking the main part of the button performs a command and clicking the arrow opens a menu with choices.

Start menu The menu that displays when you click the Start button, which consists of a list of installed programs on the left and a customizable group of app tiles on the right.

Subfolder A folder within another folder.

System image backup A backup and recovery tool that creates a full system image backup from which you can restore your entire PC.

System tray Another name for the notification area on the taskbar.

Tags A property that you create and add to a file to help you find and organize your files.

Taskbar The area of the desktop that contains program buttons, and buttons for all open programs; by default, it is located at the bottom of the desktop, but you can move it.

This PC An area on the navigation pane that provides navigation to your internal storage and attached storage devices including optical media such as a DVD drive.

Thumbnail A reduced image of a graphic.

Tiles Square and rectangular boxes on the Windows 10 Start menu from which you can access apps, websites, programs, and tools for using the computer by simply clicking or tapping them.

Title bar The bar across the top of the window that displays the program name.

Universal apps Windows apps that use a common code base to deliver the app to any Windows device.

Unzip Extracting files.

User account A collection of information that tells Windows 10 what files and folders the account holder can access, what changes the account holder can make to the computer system, and what the account holder's personal preferences are.

Virtual desktop An additional desktop display to organize and quickly access groups of windows.

Wallpaper Another term for the desktop background.

Web browser Software with which you display webpages and navigate the Internet.

Window snip When using Snipping Tool, the type of snip that captures the entire displayed window.

Windows 10 An operating system developed by Microsoft Corporation designed to work with mobile computing devices of all types and also with traditional PCs.

Windows apps Apps that run not only on a Windows phone and a Windows tablet, but also on your Windows desktop PC.

Windows Defender Protection built into Windows 10 that helps prevent viruses, spyware, and malicious or unwanted software from being installed on your PC without your knowledge.

Windows Firewall Protection built into Windows 10 that can prevent hackers or malicious software from gaining access to your computer through a network or the Internet.

Windows Journal A desktop app that comes with Windows 10 with which you can type or handwrite—on a touchscreen—notes and then store them or email them.

Windows Store The program where you can find and download Windows apps.

Work access A Windows 10 feature with which you can connect to your work or school system based on established policies.

Zip Compressing files.

Apply 1A skills from these Objectives:

1 Explore the Windows 10 Environment

2 Use File Explorer and Desktop Apps to Create a New Folder and Save a File

3 Identify the Functions of the Windows 10 Operating System

4 Discover Windows 10 Features

5 Sign Out of Windows 10, Turn Off Your Computer, and Manage User Accounts

6 Manage Your Windows 10 System

PROJECT FILES

For Project 1C, you will need the following files:

Your USB flash drive—or other location—containing the student data files
win01_1C_Answer_Sheet (Word document)

You will save your file as:

Lastname_Firstname_1C_Answer_Sheet

1 Close all open windows. On the taskbar, click **File Explorer**, navigate to the location where you are storing your student data files for this chapter, and then open the file **win01_1C_Answer_Sheet**. If necessary, at the top click Enable editing; be sure the window is maximized.

In the upper left corner, click **File**, click **Save As**, click **Browse**, and then navigate to your **Windows 10 Chapter 1** folder. Using your own name, save the document as **Lastname_Firstname_1C_Answer_Sheet**

With the Word document displayed, on the taskbar, click the **Word** button to minimize the window and leave your Word document accessible from the taskbar. **Close** the **File Explorer** window. As you complete each step in this project, write the letter of your answer on a piece of paper; you will fill in your Answer Sheet after you complete all the steps in this project.

Click **Start**, and then with the insertion point blinking in the search box, type **lock screen** Which of the following is true?

A. Search terms that include the text *lock screen* display in the search results.

B. The System settings dialog opens on the desktop.

C. From this screen, you can remove or change your lock screen picture from your computer.

2 At the top of the search results, click **Lock screen settings**. What is your result?

A. Your lock screen picture fills the screen.

B. The PERSONALIZATION window displays with Background selected on the left.

C. The PERSONALIZATION window displays with Lock screen selected on the left.

3 **Close** the **Settings** window. Click **Start**, click **All apps**, scroll to the **G** section, click **Get Started**, and then on the left, click **Windows Hello**. According to this information, which of the following is true?

A. You cannot activate Windows Hello by using a fingerprint.

B. Windows Hello enables you to sign in to your computer without typing a password.

C. To set up Windows Hello, you must open a Windows Store app.

4 **Close** the **Get Started** window. On the taskbar, click **File Explorer**. What is your result?

A. The window for your USB flash drive displays.

B. The File Explorer window displays.

C. The Documents window displays.

(Project 1C Exploring Windows 10 continues on the next page)

5 On **This PC**, locate and open **Documents**. What is your result?

A. The first document in the folder opens in its application.

B. The contents of the Documents folder display in the file list.

C. The contents of the Documents folder display in the address bar.

6 In the **navigation pane**, click **This PC**. What is your result?

A. The storage devices attached to your computer display in the file list.

B. All of the files on the hard drive display in the file list.

C. Your computer restarts.

7 **Close** the **This PC** window. Click **Start**, and then in the search box, type **paint** Open the **Paint desktop app**, and then pin the program to the taskbar. **Close** the **Paint** window. Which of the following is true?

A. On the taskbar, the Paint program icon on the taskbar displays with shading and a white line under it.

B. The Paint program tile displays on the right side of the Start menu.

C. The Paint program icon displays on the taskbar with no shading.

8 On the taskbar, point to the **Paint** button, right-click, and then click **Unpin this program from taskbar**. Click **Start**, type **store** and then with the **Store app** at the top of the search results, press Enter. What is your result?

A. All the storage devices attached to your computer display on the Start menu.

B. The Store app displays.

C. A list of games that you can download displays.

9 **Close** the **Store** app. Click **Start**, type **maps** and press Enter; if necessary, enable your current location. Click **Start**, type **weather** and then press Enter. On the taskbar, click **Task View**. What is your result?

A. The Start menu displays.

B. The Weather app opens and fills the screen.

C. All the open apps display as smaller images.

10 Point to the **Weather** app, and then click its **Close** button. In the same manner, close the **Maps** app. What is your result?

A. Your Word document displays as a small image on the desktop.

B. The search results for *Weather* redisplay.

C. The Start menu displays.

To complete this project: On the taskbar, click the Word icon to redisplay your Word document. Type your answers into the correct boxes. Save and close your Word document, and submit as directed by your instructor. **Close** all open windows.

END | You have completed Project 1C

| Apply **1B** skills from these Objectives: | **Skills Review** | **Project 1D Working with Windows, Programs, and Files** |

Apply 1B skills from these Objectives:

7 Download and Extract Files and Folders

8 Use File Explorer to Display Locations, Folders, and Files

9 Start Programs and Open Data Files

10 Create, Rename, and Copy Files and Folders

11 Use OneDrive as Cloud Storage

Skills Review   Project 1D Working with Windows, Programs, and Files

PROJECT FILES

For Project 1D, you will need the following files:

Your USB flash drive—or other location—containing the student data files
win01_1D_Answer_Sheet (Word document)

You will save your file as:

Lastname_Firstname_1D_Answer_Sheet

1 Close all open windows. On the taskbar, click **File Explorer**, navigate to the location where you are storing your student data files for this chapter, and then open the file **win01_1D_Answer_Sheet**. If necessary, at the top click Enable Editing; be sure the window is maximized.

In the upper left corner, click **File**, click **Save As**, click **Browse**, and then navigate to your **Windows 10 Chapter 1** folder. Using your own name, save the document as **Lastname_Firstname_1D_Answer_Sheet**

With the Word document displayed, on the taskbar, click the **Word** button to minimize the window and leave your Word document accessible from the taskbar. **Close** the **File Explorer** window. As you complete each step in this project, write the letter of your answer on a piece of paper; you will fill in your Answer Sheet after you complete all the steps in this project.

Open **File Explorer**, navigate to your student data files, and then open your **win01_1D_Bell_Orchid** folder. If necessary, on the **View tab**, set the **Layout** to **Details**.

In the **file list**, how many *folders* display?

A. Four

B. Five

C. Six

2 Navigate to **Corporate ▸ Food_Beverage**. If necessary, change the view to **Details**. How many *folders* are in the **Food_Beverage** folder?

A. Three

B. Two

C. One

3 Open the **Restaurants** folder, and then click one time to select the file **Breakfast_Continental**. On the ribbon, click the **Home tab**. In which group of commands can you change the name of this file?

A. New

B. Select

C. Organize

(Project 1D Working with Windows, Programs, and Files continues on the next page)

Skills Review | **Project 1D Working with Windows, Programs, and Files** (continued)

4 ▶ With the **Breakfast_Continental** file still selected, point to the file name and right-click. Which of the following is *not* true?

A. From this menu, you can rename the file.

B. From this menu, you can print the file.

C. From this menu, you can move the folder to another folder within Corporate.

5 ▶ Click on the desktop to close the shortcut menu, and then click the **Up** button to move up one level in the hierarchy and display the file list for the **Food_Beverage** folder. On the ribbon, click the **View tab**. In the **Layout group**, click **Large icons**. What is your result?

A. The window fills the entire screen.

B. Files that are pictures are visible as pictures.

C. Only picture files display in the file list.

6 ▶ On the **View tab**, return the **Layout** to **Details**. In the **file list**, click one time to select the file **CO_FB_Menu_Presentation**. In the **Panes group**, click the **Details pane** button. (*Hint*: You can point to a button to see its ScreenTip). By looking at the displayed details about this file on the right, which of the following is an information item you can determine about this file?

A. The number of words on each slide

B. The number of slides in the presentation

C. The slide layout used in the title slide

7 ▶ In the **Panes group**, click **Preview pane**. In the **Preview pane**, *slowly* drag the scroll box to the bottom of the scroll bar. Which of the following is *not* true?

A. The slide title displays as you drag the scroll box.

B. The PowerPoint program opens as you drag the scroll box.

C. The slide number displays as you drag the scroll box.

8 ▶ On the ribbon, click **Preview pane** to turn off the display of the pane. Point to an empty area of the **file list**, right-click, point to **Sort by**, and then click **Type**. In the Type column, if necessary, click the arrow so that the column is sorted in ascending order. Which of the following is true?

A. The Restaurants folder displays at the bottom of the list.

B. The files are in alphabetic order by name.

C. The files are in alphabetic order by Type.

9 ▶ In the **Corporate ▶ Food_Beverage** folder, create a new folder named **Dining_Rooms** Select the three JPG files, and then move them into the new folder. Which of the following is true?

A. The status bar indicates that there are five items in the current folder.

B. The three JPG files display in the file list for Food_Beverage.

C. The Dining_Rooms folder is selected.

(Project 1D Working with Windows, Programs, and Files continues on the next page)

Skills Review | ## Project 1D Working with Windows, Programs, and Files (continued)

10 Open the **Restaurants** folder, and then in the upper right portion of the window, in the **search** box, type **sales** and press Enter. How many files display with the word *Sales* in the document name?

A. Three

B. Four

C. Five

To complete this project: Close all open windows. On the taskbar, click the Word icon to redisplay your Word document. Type your answers into the correct boxes. Save and close your Word document, and submit as directed by your instructor. **Close** any open windows.

> **END | You have completed Project 1D**

Mastering Windows 10 | **Project 1E Create a File and Use Windows Apps**

PROJECT ACTIVITIES

In the following Mastering Windows 10 project, you will capture and save a snip that will look similar to Figure 1.74.

PROJECT FILES

For Project 1E, you will need the following files:

Two new Snip files that you will create during the project

You will save your files as:

Lastname_Firstname_1E_Cortana_Snip

Lastname_Firstname_1E_Snap_Snip

PROJECT RESULTS

Microsoft Office 2016, Windows 10, Microsoft Corportation

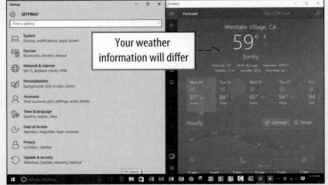

Microsoft Office 2016, Windows 10, Microsoft Corportation

FIGURE 1.74

(Project 1E Create a File and Use Windows Apps continues on the next page)

Mastering Windows 10 | **Project 1E Create a File and Use Windows Apps** (continued)

1 Click **Start**, click **All apps**, click any letter to display an onscreen alphabet, click **G** to jump to the G section, and then click **Get Started**.

2 On the left, click **Cortana**, and then click **What is Cortana?** Scroll down to view the information about setting a reminder.

3 On the taskbar, click **Snipping Tool**, click the **New button arrow**, and then click **Window Snip**. Click anywhere in the window to capture the snip.

4 On the toolbar of the **Snipping Tool** mark-up window, click the **Highlighter**, and then highlight the text *Set a reminder*. Use the red **Pen** to circle the **hamburger menu** icon in the upper left corner. Click the **Save Snip** button.

5 In the displayed **Save As** dialog box, navigate to your **Windows 10 Chapter 1** folder. Using the jpeg file type and your own name, save the snip as **Lastname_Firstname_1E_Cortana_Snip**

6 **Close** the **Snipping Tool** window, and then **Close** the **Get Started** window.

7 Click **Start**, click **All apps**, click any letter to display an onscreen alphabet, click **S** to jump to the S section, and then click **Settings**. Display the **All apps** list again, jump to the W section, and then click **Weather**.

8 Press ⊞ + → to snap the Weather app to the right side of the screen. Click the **Settings** window to snap it to the left side of the screen.

9 On the taskbar, click **Snipping Tool**, click the **New button arrow**, and then click **Full-screen Snip**.

10 Click the **Save Snip** button. In the displayed **Save As** dialog box, navigate to your **Windows 10 Chapter 1** folder. Using the jpeg file type and your own name, save the snip as **Lastname_Firstname_1E_Snap_Assist_Snip**

11 Close all open windows, and then submit your two snip files to your instructor as directed.

END | You have completed Project 1E

Mastering Windows 10 | **Project 1F Working with Windows, Programs, and Files**

Apply 1B skills from these Objectives:

7 Download and Extract Files and Folders

8 Use File Explorer to Display Locations, Folders, and Files

9 Start Programs and Open Data Files

10 Create, Rename, and Copy Files and Folders

11 Use OneDrive as Cloud Storage

PROJECT ACTIVITIES

In the following Mastering Windows 10 project, you will capture and save a snip that will look similar to Figure 1.75.

PROJECT FILES

For Project 1F, you will need the following files:

Two new Snip files that you will create during the project

You will save your files as:

Lastname_Firstname_1F_San_Diego_Snip
Lastname_Firstname_1F_Filter_Snip

PROJECT RESULTS

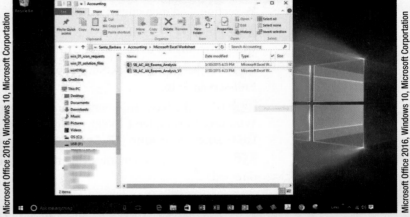

FIGURE 1.75

(Project 1F Working with Windows, Programs, and Files continues on the next page)

Project 1F Working with Windows, Programs, and Files (continued)

1 Close all open windows, and then on the taskbar, click **File Explorer**. Display the window for your **USB flash drive**—or the location of your student data files—and then navigate to **win01_1F_Bell_Orchid** ▸ **San_Diego** ▸ **Sales_Marketing** ▸ **Media**.

2 From the **View tab**, change the **Layout** to **Large icons**, and then in the **file list**, click one time to select the file **SanDiego1**.

3 Display the **Preview pane** for this file.

4 Start **Snipping Tool**, create a **Window Snip**, click anywhere in the **Media** window to capture it, and then click the **Save Snip** button.

5 In the displayed **Save As** dialog box, navigate to and open your **Windows 10 Chapter 1** folder so that its name displays in the **address bar**. Using the jpeg file type and your own name, save the snip as **Lastname_Firstname_1F_San_Diego_Snip**

6 **Close** the **Snipping Tool** window. Turn off the display of the **Preview pane**. **Close** the window.

7 Open **File Explorer**, and then from your student data files, navigate to **win01_1F_Bell_Orchid** ▸ **Santa_Barbara** ▸ **Accounting**.

8 From the **Type** column heading, filter the list to display only **Microsoft Excel Worksheet** files.

9 Create a **Full-screen snip**. Using the **jpeg** file type and your own name, save the snip as **Lastname_Firstname_1F_Filter_Snip**

10 **Close** the **Snipping Tool** window. **Close** the **File Explorer** window. Submit your two snip files as directed by your instructor.

END | You have completed Project 1F

RUBRIC

The following outcomes-based assessments are *open-ended assessments*. That is, there is no specific correct result; your result will depend on your approach to the information provided. Make *Professional Quality* your goal. Use the following scoring rubric to guide you in *how* to approach the problem, and then to evaluate *how well* your approach solves the problem.

The *criteria*—Software Mastery, Content, Format and Layout, and Process—represent the knowledge and skills you have gained that you can apply to solving the problem. The *levels of performance*—Professional Quality, Approaching Professional Quality, or Needs Quality Improvements—help you and your instructor evaluate your result.

	Your completed project is of Professional Quality if you:	Your completed project is Approaching Professional Quality if you:	Your completed project Needs Quality Improvements if you:
1-Software Mastery	Choose and apply the most appropriate skills, tools, and features and identify efficient methods to solve the problem.	Choose and apply some appropriate skills, tools, and features, but not in the most efficient manner.	Choose inappropriate skills, tools, or features, or are inefficient in solving the problem.
2-Content	Construct a solution that is clear and well organized, contains content that is accurate, appropriate to the audience and purpose, and is complete. Provide a solution that contains no errors of spelling, grammar, or style.	Construct a solution in which some components are unclear, poorly organized, inconsistent, or incomplete. Misjudge the needs of the audience. Have some errors in spelling, grammar, or style, but the errors do not detract from comprehension.	Construct a solution that is unclear, incomplete, or poorly organized, contains some inaccurate or inappropriate content, and contains many errors of spelling, grammar, or style. Do not solve the problem.
3-Format and Layout	Format and arrange all elements to communicate information and ideas, clarify function, illustrate relationships, and indicate relative importance.	Apply appropriate format and layout features to some elements, but not others. Overuse features, causing minor distraction.	Apply format and layout that does not communicate information or ideas clearly. Do not use format and layout features to clarify function, illustrate relationships, or indicate relative importance. Use available features excessively, causing distraction.
4-Process	Use an organized approach that integrates planning, development, self-assessment, revision, and reflection.	Demonstrate an organized approach in some areas, but not others; or, use an insufficient process of organization throughout.	Do not use an organized approach to solve the problem.

GO! Think   Project 1G Help Desk

In this project, you will construct a solution by applying any combination of the skills you practiced from the Objectives in Projects 1A and 1B.

PROJECT FILES

For Project 1G, you will need the following file:

win01_1G_Help_Desk (Word file)

You will save your document as:

Lastname_Firstname_1G_Help_Desk

From the student files that accompany this chapter, open the Word document **win01_1G_Help_Desk**. Save the document in your chapter folder as **Lastname_Firstname_1G_Help_Desk**

The following email question arrived at the Help Desk from an employee at the Bell Orchid Hotel's corporate office. In the Word document, construct a response based on your knowledge of Windows 10. Although an email response is not as formal as a letter, you should still use good grammar, good sentence structure, professional language, and a polite tone. Save your document and submit the response as directed by your instructor.

To: Help Desk

We have a new employee in our department, and as her user picture, she wants to use a picture of her dog. I know that Corporate Policy says it is OK to use an acceptable personal picture on a user account. Can she change the picture herself within her standard user account, or does she need an administrator account to do that?

END | You have completed Project 1G

GO! Think | Project 1H Help Desk

In this project, you will construct a solution by applying any combination of the skills you practiced from the Objectives in Projects 1A and 1B.

PROJECT FILES

For Project 1H, you will need the following file:

win01_1H_Help_Desk (Word file)

You will save your document as:

Lastname_Firstname_1H_Help_Desk

From the student files that accompany this chapter, open the Word document **win01_1H_Help_Desk**. Save the document in your chapter folder as **Lastname_Firstname_1H_Help_Desk**

The following email question arrived at the Help Desk from an employee at the Bell Orchid Hotel's corporate office. In the Word document, construct a response based on your knowledge of Windows 10. Although an email response is not as formal as a letter, you should still use good grammar, good sentence structure, professional language, and a polite tone. Save your document and submit the response as directed by your instructor.

To: Help Desk

When I'm done using my computer at the end of the day, should I use the Sleep option or the Shut down option, and what's the difference between the two?

END | You have completed Project 1H

GO Think! Project 1I Help Desk

In this project, you will construct a solution by applying any combination of the skills you practiced from the Objectives in Projects 1A and 1B.

PROJECT FILES

For Project 1I, you will need the following file:

win01_1I_Help_Desk (Word file)

You will save your document as:

Lastname_Firstname_1I_Help_Desk

From the student files that accompany this chapter, open the Word document **win01_1I_Help_Desk**. Save the document in your chapter folder as **Lastname_Firstname_1I_Help_Desk**

The following email question has arrived at the Help Desk from an employee at the Bell Orchid Hotel's corporate office. In the Word document, construct a response based on your knowledge of Windows 10. Although an email response is not as formal as a letter, you should still use good grammar, good sentence structure, professional language, and a polite tone. Save your document and submit the response as directed by your instructor.

To: Help Desk

I am not sure about the differences between copying and moving files and folders. When is it best to copy a file or a folder and when is it best to move a file or folder? Can you also describe some techniques that I can use for copying or moving files and folders? Which do you think is the easiest way to copy or move files and folders?

> **END | You have completed Project 1I**

Introduction to Microsoft Office 2016 Features

OFFICE 2016 · **1**

PROJECT 1A

OUTCOMES
Create, save, and print a Microsoft Office 2016 document.

OBJECTIVES

1. Explore Microsoft Office 2016
2. Enter, Edit, and Check the Spelling of Text in an Office 2016 Program
3. Perform Commands from a Dialog Box
4. Create a Folder and Name and Save a File
5. Insert a Footer, Add Document Properties, Print a File, and Close a Desktop App

---

PROJECT 1B

OUTCOMES
Perform commands, apply formatting, and install apps for Office in Microsoft Office 2016

OBJECTIVES

6. Open an Existing File and Save it with a New Name
7. Sign in to Office and Explore Options for a Microsoft Office Desktop App
8. Perform Commands from the Ribbon and Quick Access Toolbar
9. Apply Formatting in Office Programs and Inspect Documents
10. Compress Files and Get Help with Office
11. Install Apps for Office and Create a Microsoft Account

Imagewell10/Fotolia

In This Chapter

In this chapter, you will practice using features in Microsoft Office 2016 that work similarly across Word, Excel, Access, and PowerPoint. These features include managing files, performing commands, adding document properties, signing in to Office, applying formatting to text, and searching for Office commands quickly. You will also practice installing apps from the Office Store and setting up a free Microsoft account so that you can use OneDrive.

The projects in this chapter relate to **Skyline Metro Grill**, which is a chain of 25 casual, full-service restaurants based in Boston. The Skyline Metro Grill owners are planning an aggressive expansion program. To expand by 15 additional restaurants in Chicago, San Francisco, and Los Angeles by 2020, the company must attract new investors, develop new menus, develop new marketing strategies, and recruit new employees, all while adhering to the company's quality guidelines and maintaining its reputation for excellent service. To succeed, the company plans to build on its past success and maintain its quality elements.

PROJECT 1A Note Form

PROJECT ACTIVITIES

In Activities 1.01 through 1.08, you will create a note form using Microsoft Word 2016, save it in a folder that you create by using File Explorer, and then print the note form or submit it electronically as directed by your instructor. Your completed note form will look similar to Figure 1.1.

PROJECT FILES

 If your instructor wants you to submit Project 1A in the MyITLab Grader system, log in to MyITLab, locate Grader Project1A, and then download the files for this project.

For Project 1A, you will need the following file:
New blank Word document

You will save your file as:
Lastname_Firstname_1A_Note_Form

Please always review the downloaded Grader instructions before beginning.

PROJECT RESULTS

Build From Scratch

GO! Walk Thru Project 1A

Skyline Metro Grill, Chef's Notes
Executive Chef, Sarah Jackson

Lastname_Firstname_1A_Note_Form

Word 2016, Windows 10, Microsoft Corporation

FIGURE 1.1 Project 1A Note Form

Objective 1 Explore Microsoft Office 2016

GO! Learn How
Video OF1.1

The term *desktop application* or *desktop app* refers to a computer program that is installed on your PC and that requires a computer operating system such as Microsoft Windows. The programs in Microsoft Office 2016 are considered to be desktop apps. A desktop app typically has hundreds of features and takes time to learn.

An *app* refers to a self-contained program usually designed for a single purpose and that runs on smartphones and other mobile devices—for example, looking at sports scores or booking a flight on a particular airline. Microsoft's Windows 10 operating system supports both desktop apps that run only on PCs and *Windows apps* that run on all Windows device families—including PCs, Windows phones, Windows tablets, and the Xbox gaming system.

ALERT!	**To submit as an autograded project, log into MyITLab, download the files for this project, and then begin with those files instead of a new blank document.**

1 On the computer you are using, start Microsoft Word 2016, and then compare your screen with Figure 1.2.

Depending on which operating system you are using and how your computer is set up, you might start Word from the taskbar in Windows 7, Windows 8, or Windows 10, or from the Start screen in Windows 8, or from the Start menu in Windows 10. On an Apple Mac computer, the program will display in the dock.

Documents that you have recently opened, if any, display on the left. On the right, you can select either a blank document or a *template*—a preformatted document that you can use as a starting point and then change to suit your needs.

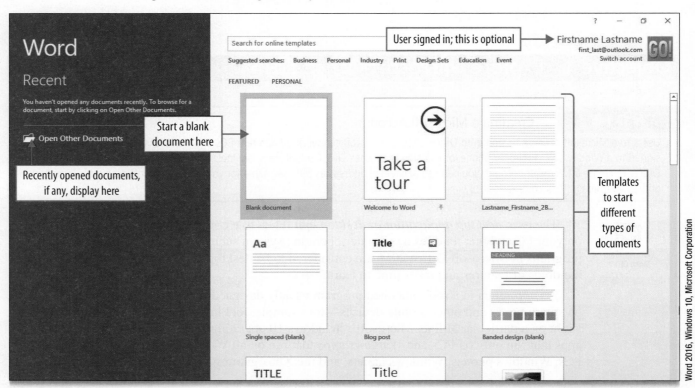

FIGURE 1.2

2 Click **Blank document**. Compare your screen with Figure 1.3, and then take a moment to study the description of these screen elements in the table in Figure 1.4.

NOTE	Displaying the Full Ribbon

If your full ribbon does not display, click any tab, and then at the right end of the ribbon, click 📌 to pin the ribbon to keep it open while you work.

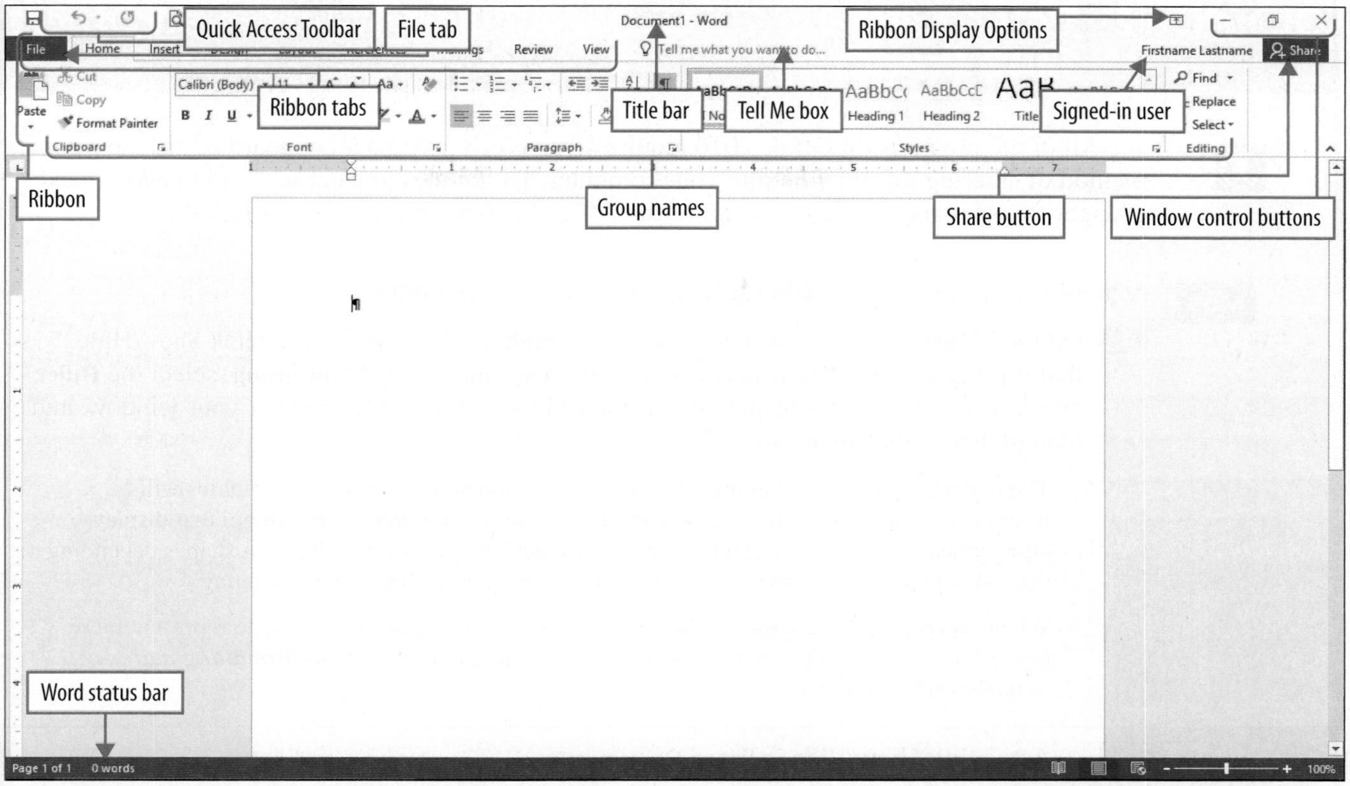

FIGURE 1.3

Word 2016, Windows 10, Microsoft Corporation

SCREEN ELEMENT	DESCRIPTION
File tab	Displays Microsoft Office Backstage view, which is a centralized space for all of your file management tasks such as opening, saving, printing, publishing, or sharing a file—all the things you can do *with* a file.
Group names	Indicate the name of the groups of related commands on the displayed tab.
Quick Access Toolbar	Displays buttons to perform frequently used commands and resources with a single click. The default commands include Save, Undo, and Redo. You can add and delete buttons to customize the Quick Access Toolbar for your convenience.
Ribbon	Displays a group of task-oriented tabs that contain the commands, styles, and resources you need to work in an Office 2016 desktop app. The look of your ribbon depends on your screen resolution. A high resolution will display more individual items and button names on the ribbon.
Ribbon Display Options	Displays three ways you can display the ribbon: Auto-hide Ribbon, Show Tabs, or Show Tabs and Commands.
Ribbon tabs	Display the names of the task-oriented tabs relevant to the open program.
Share button	Opens the Share pane from which you can save your file to the cloud—your OneDrive—and then share it with others so you can collaborate.
Signed-in user	Identifies the signed-in user.
Status bar	Displays file information on the left; on the right displays buttons for Read Mode, Print Layout, and Web Layout views; on the far right displays Zoom controls.
Tell Me box	Provides a search feature for Microsoft Office commands that you activate by typing what you are looking for in the Tell Me box; as you type, every keystroke refines the results so that you can click the command as soon as it displays.
Title bar	Displays the name of the file and the name of the program; the window control buttons are grouped on the right side of the title bar.
Window control buttons	Displays buttons for commands to change the Ribbon Display Options, Minimize, Restore Down, or Close the window.

FIGURE 1.4

Word 2016, Windows 10, Microsoft Corporation

GO! Learn How
Video OF1.2

All of the programs in Office 2016 require some typed text. Your keyboard is still the primary method of entering information into your computer. Techniques to enter text and to *edit*—make changes to—text are similar across all of the Office 2016 programs.

1.4.6

Activity 1.02 | Entering and Editing Text in an Office 2016 Program

1 On the ribbon, on the **Home tab**, in the **Paragraph group**, if necessary, click **Show/Hide** ¶ so that it is active—shaded. If necessary, on the **View tab**, in the **Show group**, select the **Ruler** check box so that rulers display below the ribbon and on the left side of your window, and then redisplay the **Home tab**.

The *insertion point*—a blinking vertical line that indicates where text or graphics will be inserted—displays. In Office 2016 programs, the mouse *pointer*—any symbol that displays on your screen in response to moving your mouse device—displays in different shapes depending on the task you are performing and the area of the screen to which you are pointing.

When you press Enter, Spacebar, or Tab on your keyboard, characters display to represent these keystrokes. These screen characters do not print, and are referred to as *formatting marks* or *nonprinting characters*.

> **NOTE** Activating Show/Hide in Word Documents
>
> When Show/Hide is active—the button is shaded—formatting marks display. Because formatting marks guide your eye in a document—like a map and road signs guide you along a highway—these marks will display throughout this instruction. Many expert Word users keep these marks displayed while creating documents.

2 Type **Skyline Grille Info** and notice how the insertion point moves to the right as you type. Point slightly to the right of the letter *e* in *Grille* and click one time to place the insertion point there. Compare your screen with Figure 1.5.

A *paragraph symbol* (¶) indicates the end of a paragraph and displays each time you press Enter. This is a type of formatting mark and does not print.

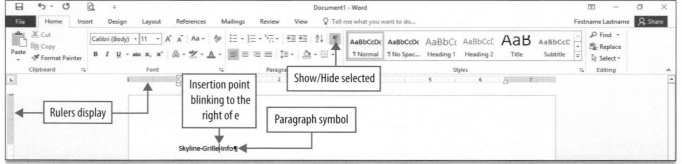

Word 2016, Windows 10, Microsoft Corporation

FIGURE 1.5

3 On your keyboard, locate and then press the Backspace key to delete the letter *e*.

Pressing Backspace removes a character to the left of the insertion point.

4 Press → one time to place the insertion point to the left of the *I* in *Info*. Type **Chef's** and then press Spacebar one time.

By *default*, when you type text in an Office program, existing text moves to the right to make space for new typing. Default refers to the current selection or setting that is automatically used by a program unless you specify otherwise.

5 Press ⌈Del⌉ four times to delete *Info* and then type **Notes**

Pressing ⌈Del⌉ removes a character to the right of the insertion point.

6 With your insertion point blinking after the word *Notes*, on your keyboard, hold down the ⌈Ctrl⌉ key. While holding down ⌈Ctrl⌉, press ⌈←⌉ three times to move the insertion point to the beginning of the word *Grill*. Release ⌈Ctrl⌉.

This is a ***keyboard shortcut***—a key or combination of keys that performs a task that would otherwise require a mouse. This keyboard shortcut moves the insertion point to the beginning of the previous word.

A keyboard shortcut is indicated as ⌈Ctrl⌉ + ⌈←⌉ (or some other combination of keys) to indicate that you hold down the first key while pressing the second key. A keyboard shortcut can also include three keys, in which case you hold down the first two and then press the third. For example, ⌈Ctrl⌉ + ⌈Shift⌉ + ⌈←⌉ selects one word to the left.

7 With the insertion point blinking at the beginning of the word *Grill*, type **Metro** and press ⌈Spacebar⌉.

8 Press ⌈Ctrl⌉ + ⌈End⌉ to place the insertion point after the letter *s* in *Notes*, and then press ⌈Enter⌉ one time. With the insertion point blinking, type the following and include the spelling error: **Exective Chef, Madison Dunham**

9 With your mouse, point slightly to the left of the *M* in *Madison*, hold down the left mouse button, and then ***drag***—hold down the left mouse button while moving your mouse—to the right to select the text *Madison Dunham* but not the paragraph mark following it, and then release the mouse button. Compare your screen with Figure 1.6.

The ***mini toolbar*** displays commands that are commonly used with the selected object, which places common commands close to your pointer. When you move the pointer away from the mini toolbar, it fades from view.

Selecting refers to highlighting—by dragging or clicking with your mouse—areas of text or data or graphics so that the selection can be edited, formatted, copied, or moved. The action of dragging includes releasing the left mouse button at the end of the area you want to select.

The Office programs recognize a selected area as one unit to which you can make changes. Selecting text may require some practice. If you are not satisfied with your result, click anywhere outside of the selection, and then begin again.

⟳ BY TOUCH   Double-tap on *Madison* to display the gripper—a small circle that acts as a handle—directly below the word. This establishes the start gripper. If necessary, with your finger, drag the gripper to the beginning of the word. Then drag the gripper to the end of *Dunham* to select the text and display the end gripper.

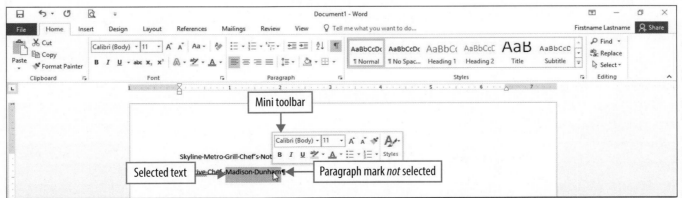

FIGURE 1.6

10 With the text *Madison Dunham* selected, type **Sarah Jackson**

In any Windows-based program, such as the Microsoft Office 2016 programs, selected text is deleted and then replaced when you begin to type new text. You will save time by developing good techniques for selecting and then editing or replacing selected text, which is easier than pressing the [Del] key numerous times to delete text.

Activity 1.03 | Checking Spelling

Office 2016 has a dictionary of words against which all entered text is checked. In Word and PowerPoint, words that are not in the dictionary display a wavy red line, indicating a possible misspelled word, a proper name, or an unusual word—none of which are in the Office 2016 dictionary.

In Excel and Access, you can initiate a check of the spelling, but red underlines do not display.

1 Notice that the misspelled word *Exective* displays with a wavy red underline.

2 Point to *Exective* and then *right-click*—click your right mouse button one time.

A *shortcut menu* displays, which displays commands and options relevant to the selected text or object. These are *context-sensitive commands* because they relate to the item you right-clicked. These shortcut menus are also referred to as *context menus*. Here, the shortcut menu displays commands related to the misspelled word.

BY TOUCH   Tap and hold a moment—when a square displays around the misspelled word, release your finger to display the shortcut menu.

3 Press [Esc] to cancel the shortcut menu, and then in the lower left corner of your screen, on the status bar, click the *Proofing* icon ▯, which displays an *X* because some errors are detected. Compare your screen with Figure 1.7.

The Spelling pane displays on the right. Here you have many more options for checking spelling than you have on the shortcut menu. The suggested correct word, *Executive*, is highlighted.

You can click the speaker icon to hear the pronunciation of the selected word. If you have not already installed a dictionary, you can click *Get a Dictionary*—if you are signed in to Office with a Microsoft account—to find and install one from the online Office store; or if you have a dictionary app installed, it will display here and you can search it for more information.

In the Spelling pane, you can ignore the word one time or in all occurrences, change the word to the suggested word, select a different suggestion, or add a word to the dictionary against which Word checks.

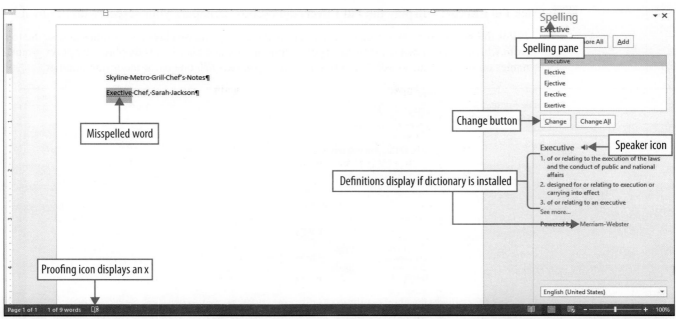

FIGURE 1.7

Word 2016, Windows 10, Microsoft Corporation

ANOTHER WAY Press F7 to display the Spelling pane; or, on the Review tab, in the Proofing group, click Spelling & Grammar.

4 In the *Spelling* pane, click **Change** to change the spelling to *Executive*. In the message box that displays, click **OK**.

Objective 3 Perform Commands from a Dialog Box

GO! Learn How
Video OF1.3

In a dialog box, you make decisions about an individual object or topic. In some dialog boxes, you can make multiple decisions in one place.

Activity 1.04 | Performing Commands from a Dialog Box

1.3.6

1 On the ribbon, click the **Design tab**, and then in the **Page Background group**, click **Page Color**.

2 At the bottom of the menu, notice the command *Fill Effects* followed by an **ellipsis** (...). Compare your screen with Figure 1.8.

An *ellipsis* is a set of three dots indicating incompleteness. An ellipsis following a command name indicates that a dialog box will display when you click the command.

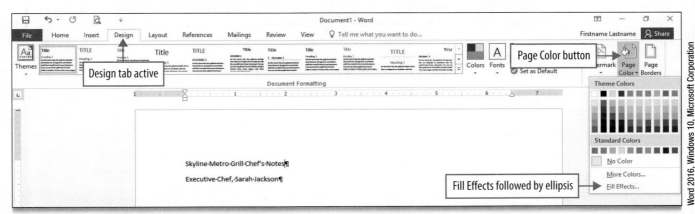

FIGURE 1.08

Word 2016, Windows 10, Microsoft Corporation

Project 1A: Note Form | **Office**   **103**

3 Click **Fill Effects** to display the **Fill Effects** dialog box. Compare your screen with Figure 1.9.

Fill is the inside color of a page or object. Here, the dialog box displays a set of tabs across the top from which you can display different sets of options. Some dialog boxes display the option group names on the left. The Gradient tab is active. In a *gradient fill*, one color fades into another.

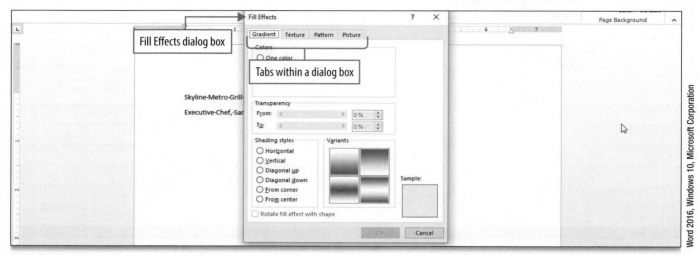

FIGURE 1.9

4 Under **Colors**, click the **One color** option button.

The dialog box displays settings related to the One color option. An *option button* is a round button that enables you to make one choice among two or more options.

5 Click the **Color 5 arrow**—the arrow under the text *Color 5*—and then in the third column, point to the second color to display the ScreenTip *Light Gray-25%, Background 2, Darker 10%*.

When you click an arrow in a dialog box, additional options display. A *ScreenTip* displays useful information about mouse actions, such as pointing to screen elements or dragging.

6 Click **Gray-25%, Background 2, Darker 10%**, and then notice that the fill color displays in the **Color 1** box. In the **Dark Light** bar, click the **Light arrow** as many times as necessary until the scroll box is all the way to the right. Under **Shading styles**, click the **Diagonal down** option button. Under **Variants**, click the **upper right variant**. Compare your screen with Figure 1.10.

This dialog box is a good example of the many different elements you may encounter in a dialog box. Here you have option buttons, an arrow that displays a menu, a slider bar, and graphic options that you can select.

BY TOUCH

In a dialog box, you can tap option buttons and other commands just as you would click them with a mouse. When you tap an arrow to display a color palette, a larger palette displays than if you used your mouse. This makes it easier to select colors in a dialog box.

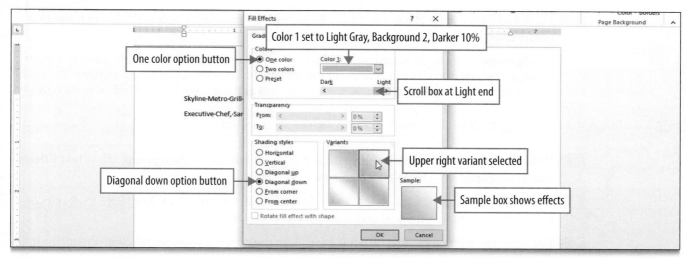

FIGURE 1.10

7 At the bottom of the dialog box, click **OK**, and notice the subtle page color.

In Word, the gray shading page color will not print—even on a color printer—unless you set specific options to do so. However, a subtle background page color is effective if people will be reading the document on a screen. Microsoft's research indicates that two-thirds of people who open Word documents on a screen never print them; they only read them.

MOS
2.2.6

Activity 1.05 | **Using Undo and Applying a Built-In Style to Text**

1 Point to the *S* in *Skyline*, and then drag down and to the right to select both paragraphs of text and include the paragraph marks. On the mini toolbar, click **Styles**, and then *point to* but do not click **Title**. Compare your screen with Figure 1.11.

A **style** is a group of **formatting** commands, such as font, font size, font color, paragraph alignment, and line spacing that can be applied to a paragraph with one command. Formatting is the process of establishing the overall appearance of text, graphics, and pages in an Office file— for example, in a Word document.

Live Preview is a technology that shows the result of applying an editing or formatting change as you point to possible results—before you actually apply it.

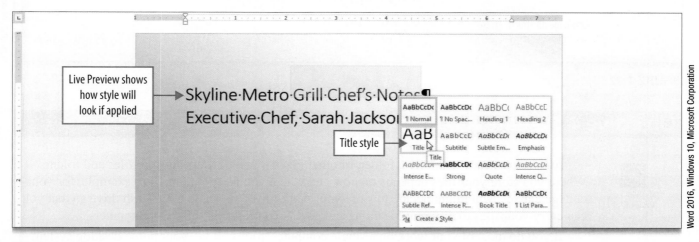

FIGURE 1.11

2 In the **Styles** gallery, click **Title**.

A **gallery** is an Office feature that displays a list of potential results.

3 ▶ On the ribbon, on the **Home tab**, in the **Paragraph group**, click **Center** 🔲 to center the two paragraphs.

> *Alignment* refers to the placement of paragraph text relative to the left and right margins. *Center alignment* refers to text that is centered horizontally between the left and right margins. You can also align text at the left margin, which is the default alignment for text in Word, or at the right.

🔄 ANOTHER WAY   Press Ctrl + E as the keyboard shortcut for the Center command.

4 ▶ With the two paragraphs still selected, on the **Home tab**, in the **Font group**, click **Text Effects and Typography** 🅰 to display a gallery.

5 ▶ In the second row, click the first effect—**Gradient Fill – Gray**. Click anywhere to *deselect*— cancel the selection—the text and notice the text effect.

6 ▶ Because this effect might be difficult to read, in the upper left corner of your screen, on the *Quick Access Toolbar*, click **Undo** ↩.

> The *Undo* command reverses your last action.

🔄 ANOTHER WAY   Press Ctrl + Z as the keyboard shortcut for the Undo command.

7 ▶ With all of the text still selected, display the **Text Effects and Typography** 🅰 gallery again, and then in the second row, click the second effect—**Gradient Fill – Blue, Accent 1, Reflection**. Click anywhere to deselect the text and notice the text effect. Compare your screen with Figure 1.12.

> As you progress in your study of Microsoft Office, you will practice using many dialog boxes and commands to apply interesting effects such as this to your Word documents, Excel worksheets, Access database objects, and PowerPoint slides.

FIGURE 1.12

Objective 4   Create a Folder and Name and Save a File

GO! Learn How
Video OF1.4

A *location* is any disk drive, folder, or other place in which you can store files and folders. Where you store your files depends on how and where you use your data. For example, for your college classes, you might decide to store your work on a removable USB flash drive so that you can carry your files to different locations and access your files on different computers.

If you do most of your work on a single computer, for example, your home desktop system or your laptop computer that you take with you to school or work, then you can store your files in one of the folders—Documents, Music, Pictures, or Videos—on your hard drive provided by your Windows operating system.

The best place to store files if you want them to be available anytime, anywhere, from almost any device is on your *OneDrive*, which is Microsoft's free *cloud storage* for anyone with a free Microsoft account. Cloud storage refers to online storage of data so that you can access your data from different places and devices. *Cloud computing* refers to applications and services that are accessed over the Internet, rather than accessing applications installed on your local computer.

If you have an *Office 365* account—one of the versions of Microsoft Office to which you subscribe for an annual fee—your storage capacity on OneDrive is a terabyte or more, which is more than most individuals would ever require.

Because many people now have multiple computing devices—desktop, laptop, tablet, smartphone—it is common to store data *in the cloud* so that it is always available. *Synchronization*, also called *syncing*—pronounced SINK-ing—is the process of updating computer files that are in two or more locations according to specific rules. So if you create and save a Word document on your OneDrive using your laptop, you can open and edit that document on your tablet in OneDrive. When you close the document again, the file is properly updated to reflect your changes. Your OneDrive account will guide you in setting options for syncing files to your specifications.

You need not be connected to the Internet to access documents stored on OneDrive because an up-to-date version of your content is synched to your local system and available on OneDrive. You must, however, be connected to the Internet for the syncing to occur. Saving to OneDrive will keep the local copy on your computer and the copy in the cloud synchronized for as long as you need it. You can open and edit Office files by using Office apps available on a variety of device platforms, including iOS, Android, and Windows.

The Windows operating system helps you to create and maintain a logical folder structure, so always take the time to name your files and folders consistently.

Activity 1.06 | Creating a Folder and Naming and Saving a File

A Word document is an example of a file. In this Activity, you will create a folder in the storage location you have chosen to use for your files and then save your file. This example will use the Documents folder on the PC at which you are working. If you prefer to store on your OneDrive or on a USB flash drive, you can use similar steps.

1 Decide where you are going to store your files for this Project.

> As the first step in saving a file, determine where you want to save the file, and if necessary, insert a storage device.

2 At the top of your screen, in the title bar, notice that *Document1 – Word* displays.

> The Blank option on the opening screen of an Office 2016 program displays a new unsaved file with a default name— *Document1, Presentation1*, and so on. As you create your file, your work is temporarily stored in the computer's memory until you initiate a Save command, at which time you must choose a file name and a location in which to save your file.

3 In the upper left corner of your screen, click the **File tab** to display **Backstage** view. Compare your screen with Figure 1.13.

> *Backstage view* is a centralized space that groups commands related to *file* management; that is why the tab is labeled *File*. File management commands include opening, saving, printing, publishing, or sharing a file. The *Backstage tabs*—*Info, New, Open, Save, Save As, Print, Share, Export*, and *Close*—display along the left side. The tabs group file-related tasks together.
>
> Here, the *Info tab* displays information—*info*—about the current file, and file management commands display under Info. For example, if you click the Protect Document button, a list of options that you can set for this file that relate to who can open or edit the document displays.
>
> On the right, you can also examine the *document properties*. Document properties, also known as *metadata*, are details about a file that describe or identify it, such as the title, author name, subject, and keywords that identify the document's topic or contents. To close Backstage view and return to the document, you can click ◄ in the upper left corner or press [Esc].

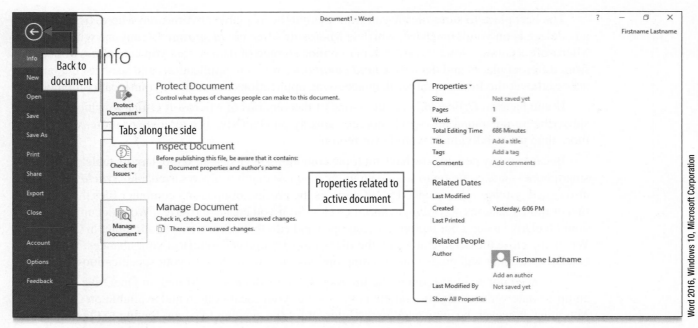

FIGURE 1.13

> **4** On the left, click **Save As**, and notice that the default location for storing Office files is your **OneDrive**—if you are signed in. Compare your screen with Figure 1.14.
>
> > When you are saving something for the first time, for example, a new Word document, the Save and Save As commands are identical. That is, the Save As commands will display if you click Save or if you click Save As.

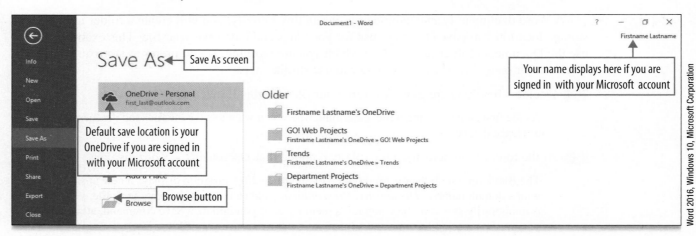

FIGURE 1.14

NOTE Saving After Your File Is Named

After you name and save a file, the Save command on the Quick Access Toolbar saves any changes you make to the file without displaying Backstage view. The Save As command enables you to name and save a *new* file based on the current one—in a location that you choose. After you name and save the new document, the original document closes, and the new document—based on the original one—displays.

---

5 To store your Word file in the **Documents** folder on your PC, click **Browse** to display the **Save As** dialog box. On the left, in the **navigation pane**, scroll down; if necessary click > to expand This PC, and then click **Documents**, or navigate to your USB flash drive or other location. In a college lab, your work may be lost if you store in the Documents folder. Compare your screen with Figure 1.15.

In the Save As dialog box, you must indicate the name you want for the file and the location where you want to save the file. When working with your own data, it is good practice to pause at this point and determine the logical name and location for your file.

In the Save As dialog box, a *toolbar* displays, which is a row, column, or block of buttons or icons, that displays across the top of a window and that contains commands for tasks you perform with a single click.

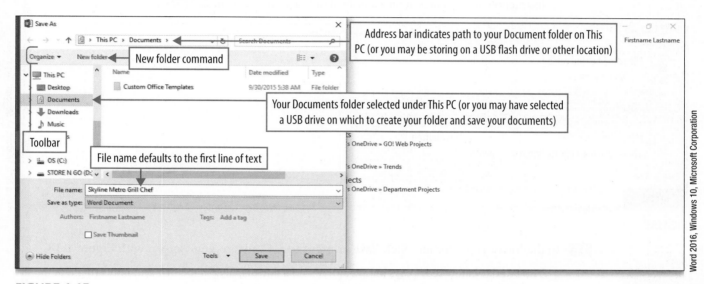

FIGURE 1.15

6 On the toolbar, click **New folder**.

In the file list, Windows creates a new folder, and the text *New folder* is selected.

7 Type **Office Features Chapter 1** and press Enter. Compare your screen with Figure 1.16.

In Windows-based programs, the Enter key confirms an action.

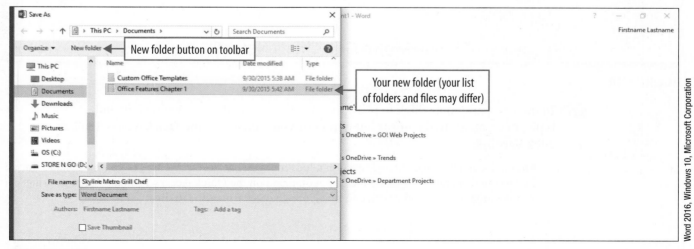

FIGURE 1.16

8 In the **file list**, double-click the name of your new folder to open it and display its name in the **address bar**.

9 In the lower portion of the dialog box, click in the **File name** box to select the existing text. Notice that as the suggested file name, Office inserts the text at the beginning of the document.

10 On your keyboard, locate the ⬚ key, to the right of zero on the number row. Notice that the Shift of this key produces the underscore character. With the text still selected and using your own name, type **Lastname_Firstname_1A_Note_Form** Compare your screen with Figure 1.17.

> You can use spaces in file names, however, some people prefer not to use spaces. Some programs, especially when transferring files over the Internet, may insert the extra characters *%20* in place of a space. In general, however, unless you encounter a problem, it is OK to use spaces. In this instruction, underscores are used instead of spaces in file names.

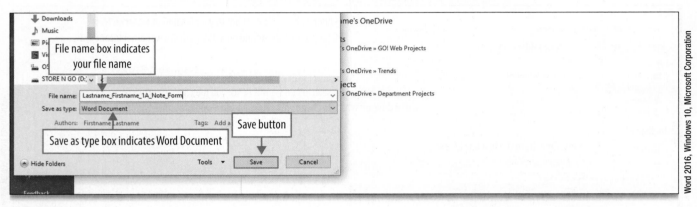

FIGURE 1.17

11 In the lower right corner, click **Save** or press Enter. Compare your screen with Figure 1.18.

> The Word window redisplays and your new file name displays in the title bar, indicating that the file has been saved to the location that you have specified.

FIGURE 1.18

12 In the first paragraph, click to place the insertion point after the word *Grill* and type **,** (a comma). In the upper left corner of your screen, on the **Quick Access Toolbar**, click **Save** 🖫.

> After a document is named and saved in a location, you can save any changes you have made since the last Save operation by using the Save command on the Quick Access Toolbar. When working on a document, it is good practice to save your changes from time to time.

GO! Learn How
Video OF1.5

MOS
1.3.4, 1.4.5

For most of your files, especially in a workplace setting, it is useful to add identifying information to help in finding files later. You might also want to print your file on paper or create an electronic printout. The process of printing a file is similar in all of the Office applications.

Activity 1.07 | Inserting a Footer, Inserting Document Info, and Adding Document Properties

> **NOTE** | What Does Your Instructor Require for Submission? A Paper Printout, an Image That Looks Like a Printed Document, or Your Word File?
>
> In this Activity, you can produce a paper printout or an electronic image of your document that looks like a printed document. Or, your instructor may want only your completed Word file.

1 On the ribbon, click the **Insert tab**, and then in the **Header & Footer group**, click **Footer**.

2 At the bottom of the list, click **Edit Footer**. On the ribbon, notice that the **Header & Footer Tools** display.

The *Header & Footer Tools Design* tab displays on the ribbon. The ribbon adapts to your work and will display additional tabs like this one—referred to as ***contextual tabs***—when you need them.

A *footer* is a reserved area for text or graphics that displays at the bottom of each page in a document. Likewise, a *header* is a reserved area for text or graphics that displays at the top of each page in a document. When the footer (or header) area is active, the document area is dimmed, indicating it is unavailable.

3 On the ribbon, under **Header & Footer Tools**, on the **Design tab**, in the **Insert group**, click **Document Info**, and then click **File Name** to insert the name of your file in the footer, which is a common business practice. Compare your screen with Figure 1.19.

Ribbon commands that display ⯆ will, when clicked, display a list of options for the command.

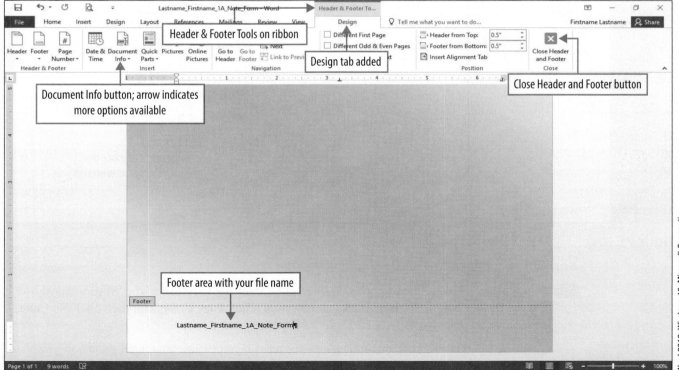

FIGURE 1.19

Word 2016, Windows 10, Microsoft Corporation

4 At the right end of the ribbon, click **Close Header and Footer**.

🔄 **ANOTHER WAY** Double-click anywhere in the dimmed document to close the footer.

5 Click the **File tab** to display **Backstage** view. On the right, at the bottom of the **Properties** list, click **Show All Properties**.

🔄 **ANOTHER WAY** Click the arrow to the right of Properties, and then click Advanced Properties to show and edit properties at the top of your document window.

6 On the list of **Properties**, click to the right of *Tags* to display an empty box, and then type **chef, notes, form**

> *Tags*, also referred to as *keywords*, are custom file properties in the form of words that you associate with a document to give an indication of the document's content. Adding tags to your documents makes it easier to search for and locate files in File Explorer, on your OneDrive, and in systems such as Microsoft *SharePoint* document libraries. SharePoint is collaboration software with which people in an organization can set up team sites to share information, manage documents, and publish reports for others to see.

🔄 **BY TOUCH** Tap to the right of Tags to display the Tags box and the onscreen keyboard.

7 Click to the right of *Subject* to display an empty box, and then type your course name and section #; for example, *CIS 10, #5543.*

8 Under **Related People**, be sure that your name displays as the author. If necessary, right-click the author name, click Edit Property, type your name, click outside of the Edit person dialog box, and then click OK. Compare your screen with Figure 1.20.

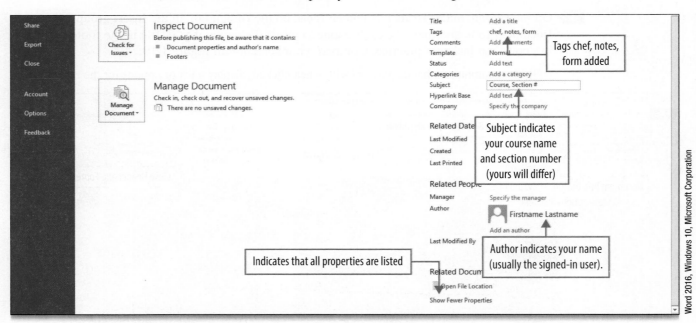

FIGURE 1.20

Activity 1.08 | Printing a File and Closing a Desktop App

1 In **Backstage** view, in the upper left corner, click **Back** 🔙 to return to the Word window. On the **Design tab**, in the **Page Background group**, click **Page Color**, and then click **No Color** to remove the fill effects.

> It's easy to remove formatting from your documents if you change your mind about how you want your document to look.

2 ▶ Click the **File tab** to return to **Backstage** view, on the left click **Print**, and then compare your screen with Figure 1.21.

> Here you can select any printer connected to your system and adjust the settings related to how you want to print. On the right, the **Print Preview** displays, which is a view of a document as it will appear on paper when you print it.
>
> At the bottom of the Print Preview area, in the center, the number of pages and page navigation arrows with which you can move among the pages in Print Preview display. On the right, the Zoom slider enables you to shrink or enlarge the Print Preview. **Zoom** is the action of increasing or decreasing the viewing area of the screen.

🔄 **ANOTHER WAY**   From the document screen, press Ctrl + P or Ctrl + F2 to display Print in Backstage view.

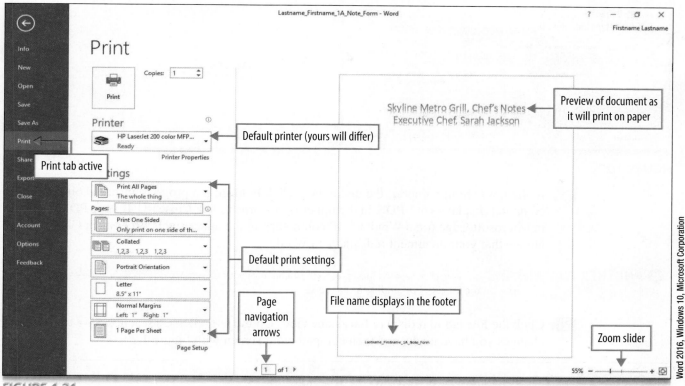

FIGURE 1.21

3 ▶ To create an electronic image of your document that looks like a printed document, skip this step and continue to Step 4. To print your document on paper using the default printer on your system, in the upper left portion of the screen, click **Print**.

> The document will print on your default printer; if you do not have a color printer, the blue text will print in shades of gray. Backstage view closes and your file redisplays in the Word window.

4 ▶ To create an electronic image of your document that looks like a printed document, in **Backstage** view, on the left click **Export**. On the right, click the **Create PDF/XPS** button to display the **Publish as PDF or XPS** dialog box.

> **PDF** stands for **Portable Document Format**, which is a technology that creates an image that preserves the look of your file. This is a popular format for sending documents electronically, because the document will display on most computers.
>
> **XPS** stands for **XML Paper Specification**—a Microsoft file format that also creates an image of your document and that opens in the XPS viewer.

5 On the left in the **navigation pane**, if necessary expand > This PC, and then navigate to your **Office Features Chapter 1** folder in your **Documents** folder—or in whatever location you have created your Office Features Chapter 1 folder. Compare your screen with Figure 1.22.

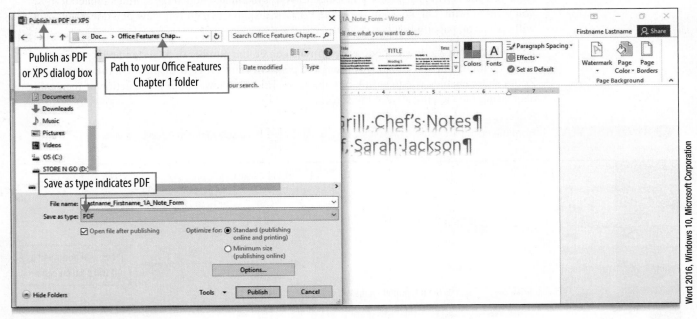

FIGURE 1.22

6 In the lower right corner of the dialog box, click **Publish**; if a program installed on your computer displays your PDF, in the upper right corner, click Close ☒. If your PDF displays in Microsoft Edge (on a Windows 10 computer), in the upper right corner click Close ☒. Notice that your document redisplays in Word.

🔄 **ANOTHER WAY**   In Backstage view, click Save As, navigate to the location of your Chapter folder, click the Save as type arrow, on the list click PDF, and then click Save.

7 Click the **File tab** to redisplay **Backstage** view. On the left, click **Close**, click **Save** to save the changes you have made, and then compare your screen with Figure 1.23.

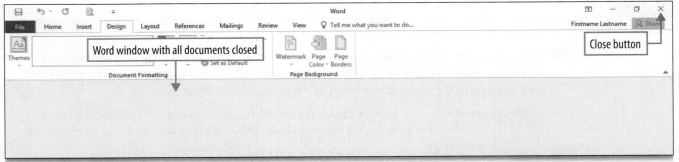

FIGURE 1.23

Word 2016, Windows 10, Microsoft Corporation

8 In the upper right corner of the Word window, click **Close** ☒. If directed by your instructor to do so, submit your paper printout, your electronic image of your document that looks like a printed document, or your original Word file.

> **END | You have completed Project 1A**

PROJECT

1B Memo

MyITLab
Project 1B Grader

PROJECT ACTIVITIES

In Activities 1.09 through 1.24, you will open, edit, and then compress a Word file. You will also use the Tell Me help feature and install an app for Office. Your completed document will look similar to Figure 1.24.

PROJECT FILES

MyITLab grader

If your instructor wants you to submit Project 1B in the MyITLab Grader system, log in to MyITLab, locate Grader Project1B, and then download the files for this project.

For Project 1B, you will need the following file:
of01B_Rehearsal_Dinner

You will save your file as:
Lastname_Firstname_1B_Rehearsal_Dinner

Please always review the downloaded Grader instructions before beginning.

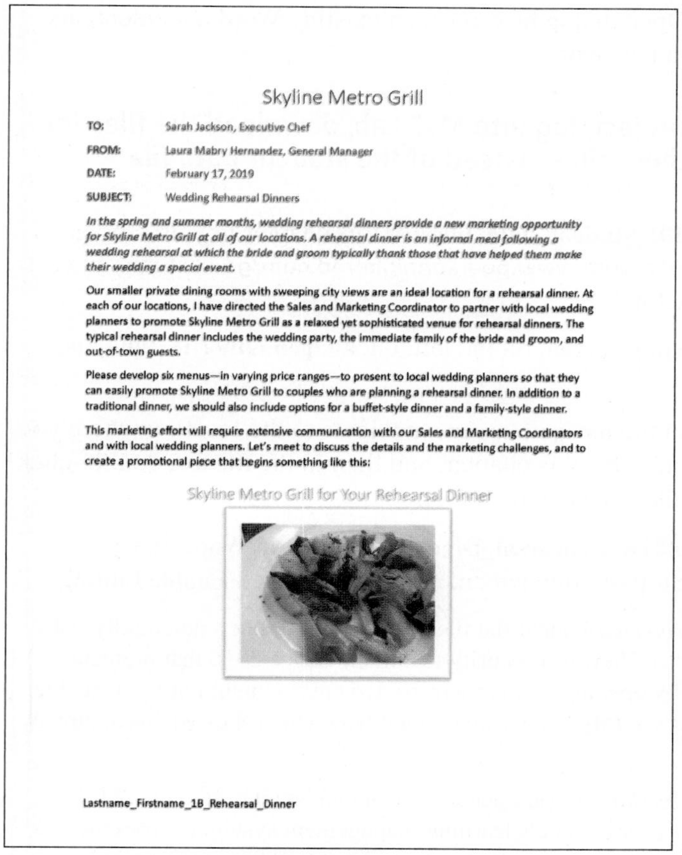

PROJECT RESULTS

GO! Walk Thru Project 1B

Skyline Metro Grill

TO: Sarah Jackson, Executive Chef

FROM: Laura Mabry Hernandez, General Manager

DATE: February 17, 2019

SUBJECT: Wedding Rehearsal Dinners

In the spring and summer months, wedding rehearsal dinners provide a new marketing opportunity for Skyline Metro Grill at all of our locations. A rehearsal dinner is an informal meal following a wedding rehearsal at which the bride and groom typically thank those that have helped them make their wedding a special event.

Our smaller private dining rooms with sweeping city views are an ideal location for a rehearsal dinner. At each of our locations, I have directed the Sales and Marketing Coordinator to partner with local wedding planners to promote Skyline Metro Grill as a relaxed yet sophisticated venue for rehearsal dinners. The typical rehearsal dinner includes the wedding party, the immediate family of the bride and groom, and out-of-town guests.

Please develop six menus—in varying price ranges—to present to local wedding planners so that they can easily promote Skyline Metro Grill to couples who are planning a rehearsal dinner. In addition to a traditional dinner, we should also include options for a buffet-style dinner and a family-style dinner.

This marketing effort will require extensive communication with our Sales and Marketing Coordinators and with local wedding planners. Let's meet to discuss the details and the marketing challenges, and to create a promotional piece that begins something like this:

Skyline Metro Grill for Your Rehearsal Dinner

Lastname_Firstname_1B_Rehearsal_Dinner

Word 2016, Windows 10, Microsoft Corporation

FIGURE 1.24 Project 1B Memo

Objective 6 | Open an Existing File and Save It with a New Name

GO! Learn How
Video OF1.6

In any Office program, you can display the **Open dialog box**, from which you can navigate to and then open an existing file that was created in that same program.

The Open dialog box, along with the Save and Save As dialog boxes, is a common dialog box. These dialog boxes, which are provided by the Windows programming interface, display in all Office programs in the same manner. So the Open, Save, and Save As dialog boxes will all look and perform the same regardless of the Office program in which you are working.

> **ALERT!** **To Complete This Project, You Will Need the Student Data Files That Accompany This Chapter**
>
> To complete this project, you will need the Student Data Files that accompany this chapter. Possibly your instructor has provided these to you already; for example, in the learning management system used by your college. Alternatively, to download the files, go to **www.pearsonhighered.com/go** On the left, narrow your choice by selecting the appropriate topic, and then on the right, locate and click the image of this book. In the window that displays, click Download Data Files, and then click the chapter name. Using the commands for your browser, store the zipped file in your storage location, and then use the Extract tools in File Explorer to extract the zipped folder. Instructions for extracting can be found in the Getting Started with Windows 10 chapter.

Activity 1.09 | Opening an Existing File and Saving It with a New Name

In this Activity, you will display the Open dialog box, open an existing Word document, and then save it in your storage location with a new name.

> **ALERT!** **To submit as an autograded project, log into MyITLab, download the files for this project, and begin with those files instead of the student data file.**

1 Be sure you have saved the folder **of01_student_data_files** for this chapter in your storage location; you can download this folder from **www.pearsonhighered.com/go** or it may have been provided to you by your instructor.

2 Start Word, and then on Word's opening screen, on the left, click **Open Other Documents**. Under **Open**, click **Browse**.

3 In the **Open** dialog box, on the left in the **navigation pane**, navigate to the location where you stored the **of01_student_data_files** folder for this chapter, and then in the **file list**, double-click the folder name **of01_student_data_files** to open the folder.

4 In the **file list**, double-click the file **of01B_Rehearsal_Dinner** to open it in Word. If **PROTECTED VIEW** displays at the top of your screen, in the center click **Enable Editing**.

In Office 2016, a file will open in **Protected View** if the file appears to be from a potentially risky location, such as the Internet. Protected View is a security feature in Office 2016 that protects your computer from malicious files by opening them in a restricted environment until you enable them. **Trusted Documents** is another security feature that remembers which files you have already enabled.

You might encounter these security features if you open a file from an email or download files from the Internet; for example, from your college's learning management system or from the Pearson website. So long as you trust the source of the file, click Enable Editing or Enable Content—depending on the type of file you receive—and then go ahead and work with the file.

5 With the document displayed in the Word window, be sure that **Show/Hide** is active; if necessary, on the Home tab, in the Paragraph group, click Show/Hide to activate it; on the View tab, be sure that Rulers are active. Compare your screen with Figure 1.25.

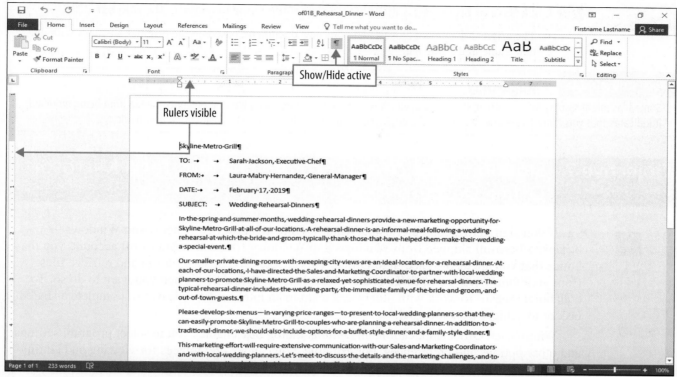

FIGURE 1.25

6 ▶ Click the **File tab** to display **Backstage** view, and then on the left, click **Save As**. Under **Save As**, click **Browse**.

7 ▶ In the **Save As** dialog box, use the **navigation pane** to navigate to and open the **Office Features Chapter 1** folder that you created to store your work from this chapter.

In Backstage view, on the right, you might also see your Office Features Chapter 1 folder listed, and if so, you can open it directly from there. The common dialog boxes Open, Save, and Save As remember your recently used locations and display them in Backstage view.

↻ ANOTHER WAY From the Word window, press [F12] to display the Save As dialog box.

8 ▶ Click in the **File name** box to select the existing text, and then, using your own name, type **Lastname_Firstname_1B_Rehearsal_Dinner** Compare your screen with Figure 1.26.

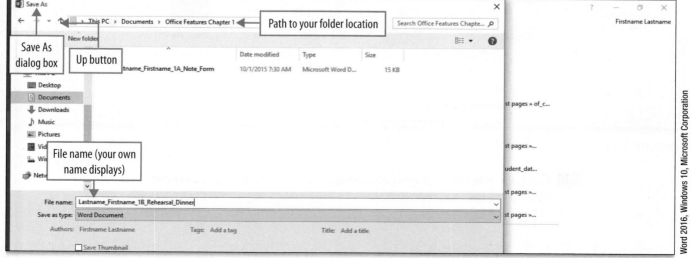

FIGURE 1.26

9 ▶ Click **Save** or press Enter; notice that your new file name displays in the title bar.

The original document closes, and your new document, based on the original, displays with the new name in the title bar.

Objective 7 | Sign In to Office and Explore Options for a Microsoft Office Desktop App

GO! Learn How
Video OF1.7

If you sign in to a computer using Windows 8 or Windows 10—there is no Windows 9, because Microsoft skipped from Windows 8 to Windows 10—with a Microsoft account, you may notice that you are also signed in to Office. This enables you to save files to and retrieve files from your OneDrive and to ***collaborate*** with others on Office files when you want to do so. To collaborate means to work with others as a team in an intellectual endeavor to complete a shared task or to achieve a shared goal.

Within each Office application, an ***Options dialog box*** enables you to select program settings and other options and preferences. For example, you can set preferences for viewing and editing files.

Activity 1.10 | Signing In to Office and Viewing Application Options

1 ▶ In the upper right corner of your screen, if you are signed in with a Microsoft account, click your name, and then compare your screen with Figure 1.27.

Here you can change your photo, go to About me to edit your profile, examine your Account settings, or switch accounts to sign in with a different Microsoft account.

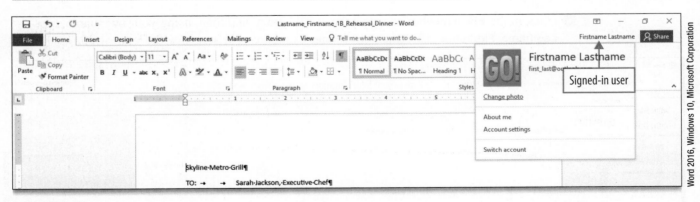

FIGURE 1.27

2 ▶ Click the **File tab** to display **Backstage** view. On the left, click **Options**.

3 In the **Word Options** dialog box, on the left, click **Display**, and then on the right, locate the information under **Always show these formatting marks on the screen**.

The Word Options dialog box—or the similar Options dialog box in any of the Office applications—controls nearly every aspect of the application. Next to many of the items, you will see small *i* icons, which when you point to them display a ScreenTip.

If you click each of the categories on the left side of the dialog box, you will see that the scope of each application is quite large and that you have a great deal of control over how the application behaves. For example, you can customize the tab names and group names in the ribbon.

If you are not sure what a setting or option does, in the upper right corner of the title bar, click the Help button—the question mark icon.

4 Under **Always show these formatting marks on the screen**, be sure the last check box, **Show all formatting marks**, is selected—select it if necessary. Compare your screen with Figure 1.28.

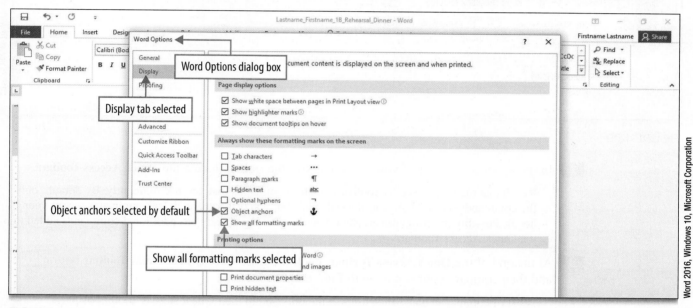

FIGURE 1.28

5 In the lower right corner of the dialog box, click **OK**.

Objective 8 Perform Commands from the Ribbon and Quick Access Toolbar

GO! Learn How
Video OF1.8

The ribbon that displays across the top of the program window groups commands in the way that you would most logically use them. The ribbon in each Office program is slightly different, but all contain the same three elements: *tabs*, *groups*, and *commands*.

Tabs display across the top of the ribbon, and each tab relates to a type of activity; for example, laying out a page. Groups are sets of related commands for specific tasks. Commands—instructions to computer programs—are arranged in groups and might display as a button, a menu, or a box in which you type information.

You can also minimize the ribbon so only the tab names display, which is useful when working on a smaller screen such as a tablet computer where you want to maximize your screen viewing area.

Activity 1.11 | Performing Commands from and Customizing the Quick Access Toolbar

1.4.3

1 ▸ Take a moment to examine the document on your screen. If necessary, on the ribbon, click the View tab, and then in the Show group, click to place a check mark in the Ruler check box. Compare your screen with Figure 1.29.

> This document is a memo from the General Manager to the Executive Chef regarding a new restaurant promotion for wedding rehearsal dinners.

> When working in Word, display the rulers so that you can see how margin settings affect your document and how text and objects align. Additionally, if you set a tab stop or an indent, its location is visible on the ruler.

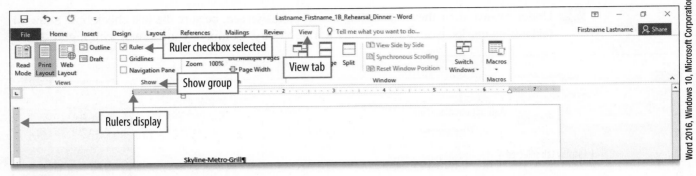

FIGURE 1.29

2 ▸ In the upper left corner of your screen, above the ribbon, locate the **Quick Access Toolbar**.

> Recall that the Quick Access Toolbar contains commands that you use frequently. By default, only the commands Save, Undo, and Redo display, but you can add and delete commands to suit your needs. Possibly the computer at which you are working already has additional commands added to the Quick Access Toolbar.

3 ▸ At the end of the **Quick Access Toolbar**, click the **Customize Quick Access Toolbar** button , and then compare your screen with Figure 1.30.

> A list of commands that Office users commonly add to their Quick Access Toolbar displays, including New, Open, Email, Quick Print, and Print Preview and Print. Commands already on the Quick Access Toolbar display a check mark. Commands that you add to the Quick Access Toolbar are always just one click away.

> Here you can also display the More Commands dialog box, from which you can select any command from any tab to add to the Quick Access Toolbar.

 **BY TOUCH**   Tap once on Quick Access Toolbar commands.

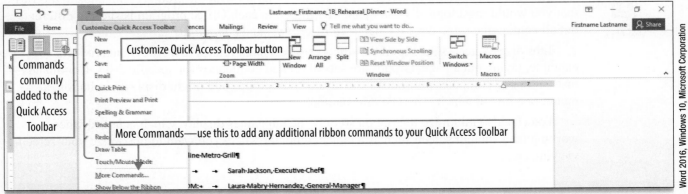

FIGURE 1.30

4 On the list, click **Print Preview and Print**, and then notice that the icon is added to the **Quick Access Toolbar**. Compare your screen with Figure 1.31.

The icon that represents the Print Preview command displays on the Quick Access Toolbar. Because this is a command that you will use frequently while building Office documents, you might decide to have this command remain on your Quick Access Toolbar.

↻ **ANOTHER WAY**   Right-click any command on the ribbon, and then on the shortcut menu, click Add to Quick Access Toolbar.

FIGURE 1.31   Word 2016, Windows 10, Microsoft Corporation

MOS
5.2.5

Activity 1.12 | Performing Commands from the Ribbon

1 In the first line of the document, if necessary, click to the left of the *S* in *Skyline* to position the insertion point there, and then press Enter one time to insert a blank paragraph. Press ↑ one time to position the insertion point in the new blank paragraph. Compare your screen with Figure 1.32.

FIGURE 1.32   Word 2016, Windows 10, Microsoft Corporation

2 On the ribbon, click the **Insert tab**. In the **Illustrations group**, *point* to **Online Pictures** to display its ScreenTip.

Many buttons on the ribbon have this type of *enhanced ScreenTip*, which displays useful descriptive information about the command.

3 Click **Online Pictures**, and then compare your screen with Figure 1.33.

In the Insert Pictures dialog box, you can search for online pictures using Bing Image Search, and, if you are signed in with your Microsoft account, you can also find images on your OneDrive by clicking Browse. At the bottom, you can click a logo to download pictures from your Facebook and other types of accounts if you have them.

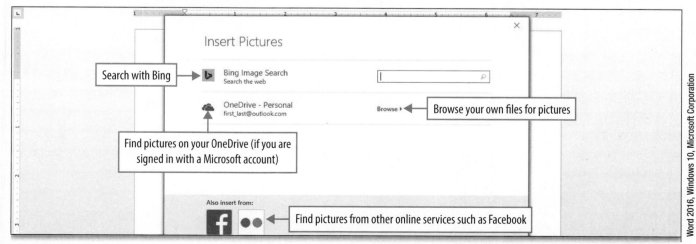

FIGURE 1.33

4 With the insertion point positioned in the **Bing Image Search** box, type **salad** and press Enter. Point to any of the results, and notice that keywords display. Compare your screen with Figure 1.34.

> You can use various keywords to find images that are appropriate for your documents. The results shown indicate the images are licensed under **Creative Commons**, which, according to **www.creativecommons.org** is "a nonprofit organization that enables the sharing and use of creativity and knowledge through free legal tools."

> Creative Commons helps people share and use their photographs, but does not allow companies to sell them. For your college assignments, you can use these images so long as you are not profiting by selling the photographs.

> To find out more about Creative Commons, go to **https://creativecommons.org/about** and watch the video.

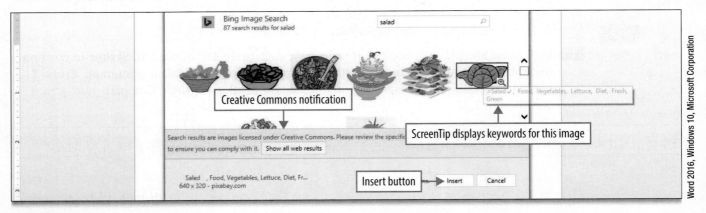

FIGURE 1.34

5 Locate an attractive picture of a salad on a plate or in a bowl that has a horizontal orientation—the picture is wider than it is tall—and then click that picture to select it. In the lower right corner, click **Insert**. In the upper right corner of the picture, point to the **Layout Options** button to display its ScreenTip, and then compare your screen with Figure 1.35.

> **Layout Options** enable you to choose how the **object**—in this instance an inserted picture—interacts with the surrounding text. An object is a picture or other graphic such as a chart or table that you can select and then move and resize.

> When a picture is selected, the Picture Tools become available on the ribbon. Additionally, **sizing handles**—small circles or squares that indicate an object is selected—surround the selected picture.

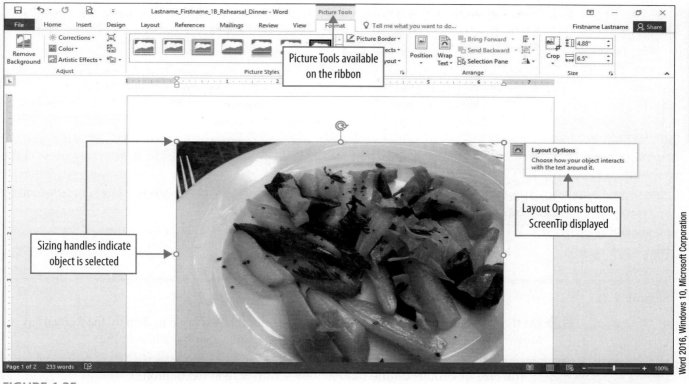

FIGURE 1.35

6 With the image selected, click **Layout Options** 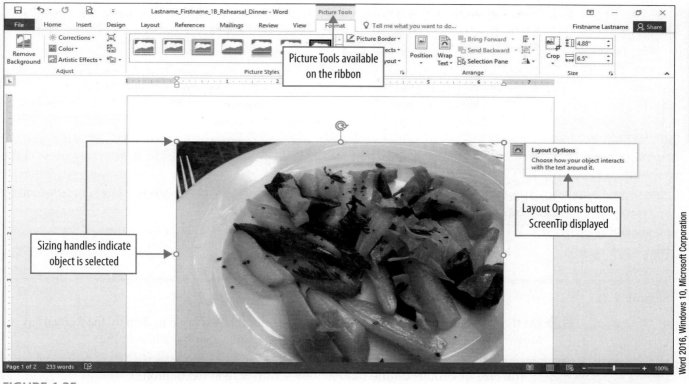, and then under **With Text Wrapping**, in the second row, click the first layout—**Top and Bottom**.

7 On the ribbon, with the **Picture Tools Format tab** active, at the right, in the **Size group**, click in the **Shape Height** box to select the existing text. Type **2** and press Enter.

8 Point to the image to display the pointer, hold down the left mouse button to display a green line at the left margin, and then drag the image to the right and slightly upward until a green line displays in the center of the image and at the top of the image, as shown in Figure 1.36, and then release the left mouse button. If you are not satisfied with your result, on the Quick Access Toolbar, click Undo and begin again.

Alignment guides are green lines that display to help you align objects with margins or at the center of a page.

Inserted pictures anchor—attach to—the paragraph at the insertion point location—as indicated by an anchor symbol.

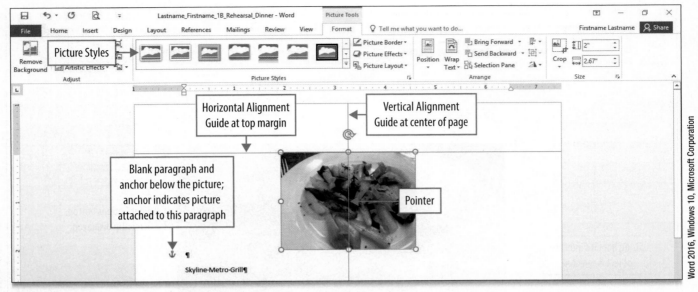

FIGURE 1.36

9 On the ribbon, in the **Picture Styles group**, point to the first style to display the ScreenTip *Simple Frame, White*, and notice that the image displays with a white frame.

> **NOTE**   The Size of Groups on the Ribbon Varies with Screen Resolution
>
> Your monitor's screen resolution might be set higher than the resolution used to capture the figures shown here. At a higher resolution, the ribbon expands some groups to show more commands than are available with a single click, such as those in the Picture Styles group. Or, the group expands to add descriptive text to some buttons, such as those in the Arrange group. Regardless of your screen resolution, all Office commands are available to you. In higher resolutions, you will have a more robust view of the ribbon commands.

10 Watch the image as you point to the second picture style, and then to the third, and then to the fourth.

Recall that Live Preview shows the result of applying an editing or formatting change as you point to possible results—*before* you actually apply it.

11 In the **Picture Styles group**, click the second style—**Beveled Matte, White**—and then click anywhere outside of the image to deselect it. Notice that the Picture Tools no longer display on the ribbon. Compare your screen with Figure 1.37.

Contextual tabs on the ribbon display only when you need them.

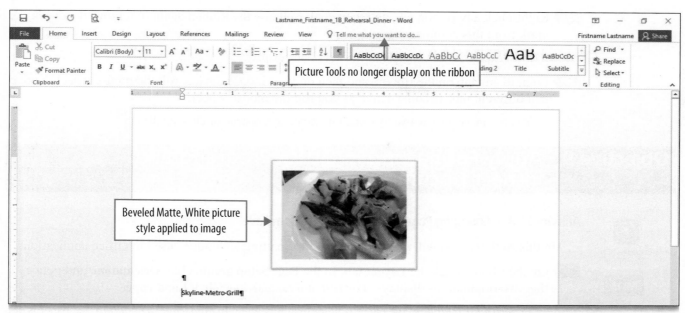

Beveled Matte, White picture style applied to image

Picture Tools no longer display on the ribbon

Skyline-Metro-Grill¶

FIGURE 1.37

Word 2016, Windows 10, Microsoft Corporation

12 On the **Quick Access Toolbar**, click **Save** 🖫 to save the changes you have made.

Activity 1.13 | Minimizing the Ribbon and Using the Keyboard to Control the Ribbon

Instead of a mouse, some individuals prefer to navigate the ribbon by using keys on the keyboard.

1 On your keyboard, press [Alt], and then on the ribbon, notice that small labels display on the tabs. Press [N] to activate the commands on the **Insert tab**, and then compare your screen with Figure 1.38.

Each label represents a *KeyTip*—an indication of the key that you can press to activate the command. For example, on the Insert tab, you can press [F] to open the Online Pictures dialog box.

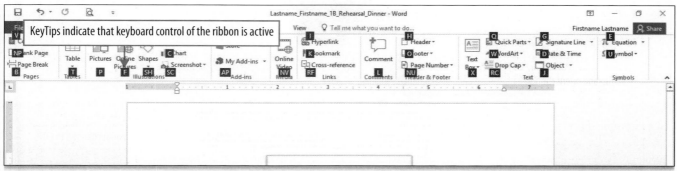

KeyTips indicate that keyboard control of the ribbon is active

FIGURE 1.38

Word 2016, Windows 10, Microsoft Corporation

2 Press [Esc] to redisplay the KeyTips for the tabs. Then, press [Alt] or [Esc] again to turn off keyboard control of the ribbon.

3 Point to any tab on the ribbon and right-click to display a shortcut menu.

Here you can choose to display the Quick Access Toolbar below the ribbon or collapse the ribbon to maximize screen space. You can also customize the ribbon by adding, removing, renaming, or reordering tabs, groups, and commands, although this is not recommended until you become an expert Word user.

4 Click **Collapse the Ribbon**. Notice that only the ribbon tabs display. Click the **Home tab** to display the commands. Click anywhere in the document, and notice that the ribbon goes back to the collapsed display.

5 Right-click any ribbon tab, and then click **Collapse the Ribbon** again to remove the check mark from this command.

Most expert Office users prefer the full ribbon display.

6 Point to any tab on the ribbon, and then on your mouse device, roll the mouse wheel. Notice that different tabs become active as you roll the mouse wheel.

You can make a tab active by using this technique, instead of clicking the tab.

Objective 9 Apply Formatting in Office Programs and Inspect Documents

GO! Learn How
Video OF1.9

MOS
1.4.2

Activity 1.14 | Changing Page Orientation and Zoom Level

In this Activity, you will practice common formatting techniques used in Office applications.

1 On the ribbon, click the **Layout tab**. In the **Page Setup group**, click **Orientation**, and notice that two orientations display—*Portrait* and *Landscape*. Click **Landscape**.

In ***portrait orientation***, the paper is taller than it is wide. In ***landscape orientation***, the paper is wider than it is tall.

2 In the lower right corner of the screen, locate the **Zoom slider**.

Recall that to zoom means to increase or decrease the viewing area. You can zoom in to look closely at a section of a document, and then zoom out to see an entire page on the screen. You can also zoom to view multiple pages on the screen.

3 Drag the **Zoom slider** to the left until you have zoomed to approximately *60%*. Compare your screen with Figure 1.39.

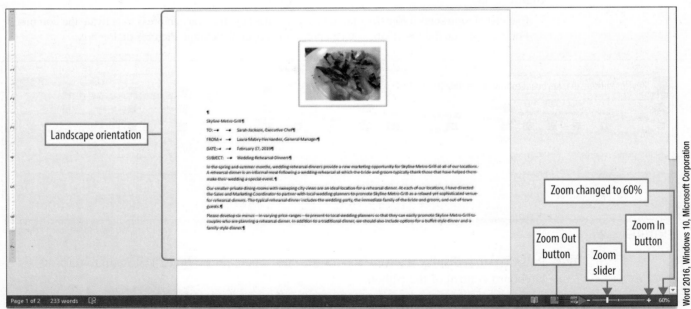

Landscape orientation

Zoom changed to 60%

Zoom Out button

Zoom slider

Zoom In button

FIGURE 1.39

🔄 **BY TOUCH**   Drag the Zoom slider with your finger.

Word 2016, Windows 10, Microsoft Corporation

4 Use the technique you just practiced to change the **Orientation** back to **Portrait**.

The default orientation in Word is Portrait, which is commonly used for business documents such as letters and memos.

5 In the lower right corner, click the **Zoom In** button ➕ as many times as necessary to return to the **100%** zoom setting.

Use the zoom feature to adjust the view of your document for editing and for your viewing comfort.

🔄 **ANOTHER WAY** You can also control Zoom from the ribbon. On the View tab, in the Zoom group, you can control the Zoom level and also zoom to view multiple pages.

6 On the **Quick Access Toolbar**, click **Save** 🖫.

More Knowledge   **Zooming to Page Width**

Some Office users prefer *Page Width*, which zooms the document so that the width of the page matches the width of the window. Find this command on the View tab, in the Zoom group.

Activity 1.15 | Formatting Text by Using Fonts, Alignment, Font Colors, and Font Styles

1 If necessary, on the right edge of your screen, drag the vertical scroll box to the top of the scroll bar. To the left of *Skyline Metro Grill*, point in the margin area to display the ⬚ pointer and click one time to select the entire paragraph. Compare your screen with Figure 1.40.

Use this technique to select complete paragraphs from the margin area—drag downward to select multiple-line paragraphs—which is faster and more efficient than dragging through text.

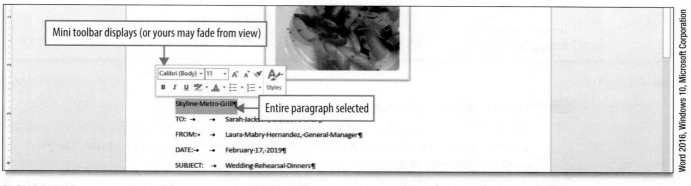

Mini toolbar displays (or yours may fade from view)

Entire paragraph selected

Word 2016, Windows 10, Microsoft Corporation

FIGURE 1.40

2 On the ribbon, click the **Home tab**, and then in the **Paragraph group**, click **Center** ☰ to center the paragraph.

3 On the **Home tab**, in the **Font group**, click the **Font button arrow** `Calibri (Body) ▾`. On the alphabetical list of font names, scroll down and then locate and *point to* **Cambria**.

A *font* is a set of characters with the same design and shape. The default font in a Word document is Calibri, which is a *sans serif font*—a font design with no lines or extensions on the ends of characters.

The Cambria font is a *serif font*—a font design that includes small line extensions on the ends of the letters to guide the eye in reading from left to right.

The list of fonts displays as a gallery showing potential results. For example, in the Font gallery, you can point to see the actual design and format of each font as it would look if applied to text.

4 Point to several other fonts and observe the effect on the selected text. Then, scroll back to the top of the **Font** gallery. Under **Theme Fonts**, click **Calibri Light**.

A ***theme*** is a predesigned combination of colors, fonts, line, and fill effects that look good together and is applied to an entire document by a single selection. A theme combines two sets of fonts— one for text and one for headings. In the default Office theme, Calibri Light is the suggested font for headings.

5 With the paragraph *Skyline Metro Grill* still selected, on the **Home tab**, in the **Font group**, click the **Font Size button arrow** 11 ▼, point to **36**, and then notice how Live Preview displays the text in the font size to which you are pointing. Compare your screen with Figure 1.41.

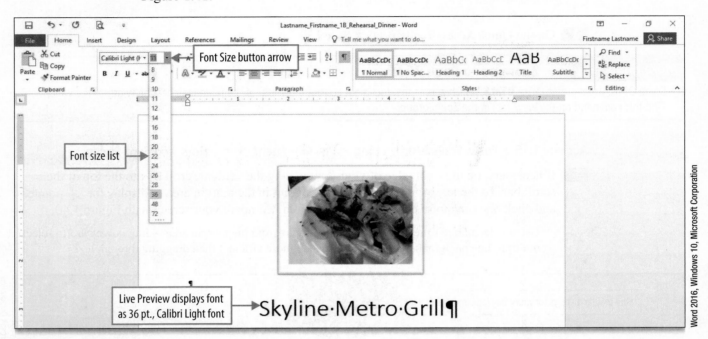

FIGURE 1.41

6 On the list of font sizes, click **20**.

Fonts are measured in ***points***, with one point equal to 1/72 of an inch. A higher point size indicates a larger font size. Headings and titles are often formatted by using a larger font size. The word *point* is abbreviated as ***pt***.

7 With *Skyline Metro Grill* still selected, on the **Home tab**, in the **Font group**, click the **Font Color button arrow** A̲ ▼. Under **Theme Colors**, in the last column, click the last color— **Green, Accent 6, Darker 50%**. Click anywhere to deselect the text.

8 To the left of *TO:*, point in the left margin area to display the ⤢ pointer, hold down the left mouse button, drag down to select the four memo headings, and then release your mouse button. Compare your screen with Figure 1.42.

Use this technique to select complete paragraphs from the margin area—drag downward to select multiple paragraphs—which is faster and more efficient than dragging through text.

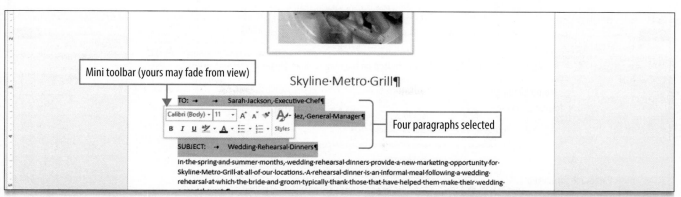

FIGURE 1.42

9 With the four paragraphs selected, on the mini toolbar, click the **Font Color** button ▲ ▾, and notice that the text color of the four paragraphs changes.

> The font color button retains its most recently used color—Green, Accent 6, Darker 50%. As you progress in your study of Microsoft Office, you will use other commands that behave in this manner; that is, they retain their most recently used format. This is commonly referred to as *MRU*—most recently used.

> Recall that the mini toolbar places commands that are commonly used for the selected text or object close by so that you reduce the distance that you must move your mouse to access a command. If you are using a touch screen device, most commands that you need are close and easy to touch.

10 On the right edge of your screen, if necessary drag the vertical scroll box down slightly to position more of the text on the screen. Click anywhere in the paragraph that begins *In the spring*, and then *triple-click*—click the left mouse button three times—to select the entire paragraph. If the entire paragraph is not selected, click in the paragraph and begin again.

11 With the entire paragraph selected, on the mini toolbar, locate and then click the **Font Color button arrow** ▲ ▾, and then under **Theme Colors**, in the sixth column, click the last color—**Orange, Accent 2, Darker 50%**.

12 In the memo headings, select the guide word **TO:** and then on the mini toolbar, click **Bold** B and **Italic** I .

> *Font styles* include bold, italic, and underline. Font styles emphasize text and are a visual cue to draw the reader's eye to important text.

13 On the mini toolbar, click **Italic** I again to turn off the Italic formatting.

> A *toggle button* is a button that can be turned on by clicking it once, and then turned off by clicking it again.

MOS
2.2.2

Activity 1.16 | Using Format Painter

Use the Format Painter to copy the formatting of specific text or of a paragraph and then apply it in other locations in your document.

1 With TO: still selected, on the mini toolbar, click **Format Painter** ✷ . Then, move your mouse under the word *Sarah*, and notice the ▲I mouse pointer. Compare your screen with Figure 1.43.

> The pointer takes the shape of a paintbrush, and contains the formatting information from the paragraph where the insertion point is positioned. Information about the Format Painter and how to turn it off displays in the status bar.

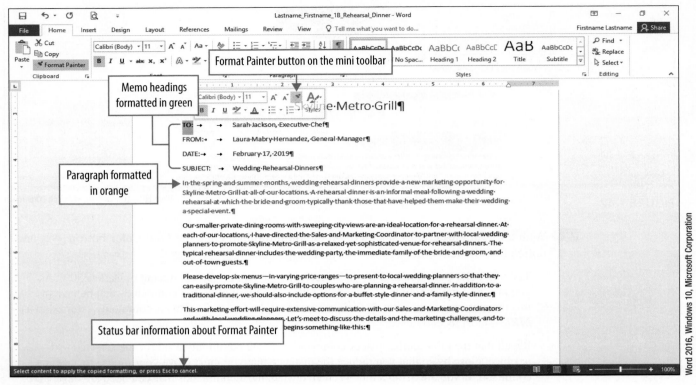

FIGURE 1.43

2 ▸ With the ‸I pointer, drag to select the guide word **FROM:** and notice that Bold formatting is applied. Then, point to the selected text *FROM:* and on the mini toolbar, *double-click* **Format Painter** ☞.

3 ▸ Select the guide word **DATE:** to copy the Bold formatting, and notice that the pointer retains the ‸I shape.

> When you *double-click* the Format Painter button, the Format Painter feature remains active until you either click the Format Painter button again, or press (Esc) to cancel it—as indicated on the status bar.

4 ▸ With **Format Painter** still active, select the guide word **SUBJECT:**, and then on the ribbon, on the **Home tab**, in the **Clipboard group**, notice that **Format Painter** ☞ is selected, indicating that it is active. Compare your screen with Figure 1.44.

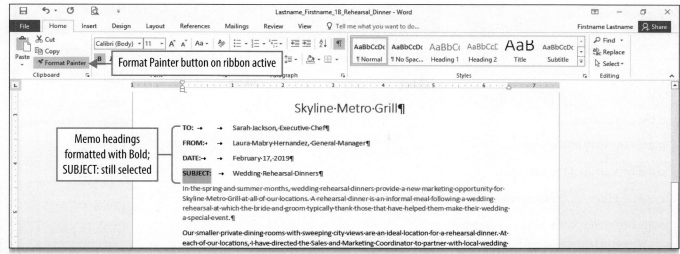

FIGURE 1.44

5 On the ribbon, click **Format Painter** to turn the command off.

ANOTHER WAY Press Esc to turn off Format Painter.

6 In the paragraph that begins *In the spring*, triple-click again to select the entire paragraph. On the mini toolbar, click **Bold** B and **Italic** I. Click anywhere to deselect.

7 On the **Quick Access Toolbar**, click **Save** to save the changes you have made to your document.

MOS
2.1.2

Activity 1.17 | Using Keyboard Shortcuts and Using the Clipboard to Copy, Cut, and Paste

The **Clipboard** is a temporary storage area that holds text or graphics that you select and then cut or copy. When you **copy** text or graphics, a copy is placed on the Clipboard and the original text or graphic remains in place. When you **cut** text or graphics, a copy is placed on the Clipboard, and the original text or graphic is removed—cut—from the document.

After copying or cutting, the contents of the Clipboard are available for you to **paste**—insert—in a new location in the current document, or into another Office file.

1 On your keyboard, hold down Ctrl and press Home to move to the beginning of your document, and then take a moment to study the table in Figure 1.45, which describes similar keyboard shortcuts with which you can navigate quickly in a document.

TO MOVE	PRESS
To the beginning of a document	Ctrl + Home
To the end of a document	Ctrl + End
To the beginning of a line	Home
To the end of a line	End
To the beginning of the previous word	Ctrl + ←
To the beginning of the next word	Ctrl + →
To the beginning of the current word (if insertion point is in the middle of a word)	Ctrl + ←
To the beginning of the previous paragraph	Ctrl + ↑
To the beginning of the next paragraph	Ctrl + ↓
To the beginning of the current paragraph (if insertion point is in the middle of a paragraph)	Ctrl + ↑
Up one screen	PgUp
Down one screen	PgDn

Word 2016, Windows 10, Microsoft Corporation

FIGURE 1.45

2 To the left of *Skyline Metro Grill*, point in the left margin area to display the 🔏 pointer, and then click one time to select the entire paragraph. On the **Home tab**, in the **Clipboard group**, click **Copy** 📋.

Because anything that you select and then copy—or cut—is placed on the Clipboard, the Copy command and the Cut command display in the Clipboard group of commands on the ribbon. There is no visible indication that your copied selection has been placed on the Clipboard.

ANOTHER WAY Right-click the selection, and then click Copy on the shortcut menu; or, use the keyboard shortcut Ctrl + C.

3 On the **Home tab**, in the **Clipboard group**, to the right of the group name *Clipboard*, click the **Dialog Box Launcher** button 🔲, and then compare your screen with Figure 1.46.

The Clipboard pane displays with your copied text. In any ribbon group, the *Dialog Box Launcher* displays either a dialog box or a pane related to the group of commands. It is not necessary to display the Clipboard in this manner, although sometimes it is useful to do so.

Word 2016, Windows 10, Microsoft Corporation

FIGURE 1.46

4 In the upper right corner of the **Clipboard** pane, click **Close** ⊠.

5 Press Ctrl + End to move to the end of your document. Press Enter one time to create a new blank paragraph. On the **Home tab**, in the **Clipboard group**, point to **Paste**, and then click the *upper* portion of this split button.

> The Paste command pastes the most recently copied item on the Clipboard at the insertion point location. If you click the lower portion of the Paste button, a gallery of Paste Options displays. A ***split button*** is divided into two parts; clicking the main part of the button performs a command, and clicking the arrow displays a list or gallery with choices.

🔄 ANOTHER WAY | Right-click, on the shortcut menu under Paste Options, click the desired option button; or, press Ctrl + V.

6 Below the pasted text, click **Paste Options** 📋 as shown in Figure 1.47.

> Here you can view and apply various formatting options for pasting your copied or cut text. Typically you will click Paste on the ribbon and paste the item in its original format. If you want some other format for the pasted item, you can choose another format from the ***Paste Options gallery***.

> The Paste Options gallery provides a Live Preview of the various options for changing the format of the pasted item with a single click. The Paste Options gallery is available in three places: on the ribbon by clicking the lower portion of the Paste button—the Paste button arrow; from the Paste Options button that displays below the pasted item following the paste operation; or on the shortcut menu if you right-click the pasted item.

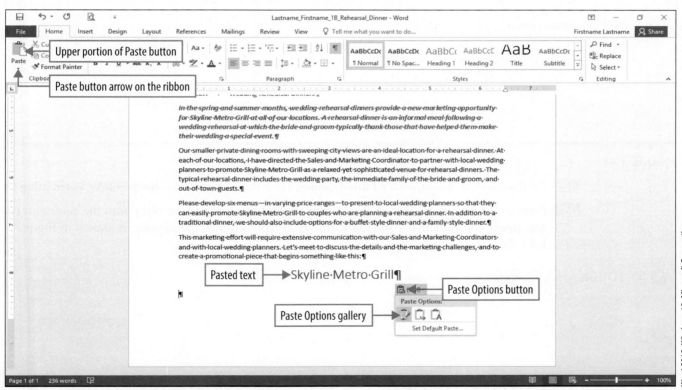

FIGURE 1.47

7 In the **Paste Options** gallery, *point* to each option to see the Live Preview of the format that would be applied if you clicked the button.

> The contents of the Paste Options gallery are contextual; that is, they change based on what you copied and where you are pasting.

8 ▶ Press Esc to close the gallery; the button will remain displayed until you take some other screen action.

9 ▶ On your keyboard, press Ctrl + Home to move to the top of the document, and then click the **salad image** one time to select it. While pointing to the selected image, right-click, and then on the shortcut menu, click **Cut**.

Recall that the Cut command cuts—removes—the selection from the document and places it on the Clipboard.

↻ **ANOTHER WAY**   On the Home tab, in the Clipboard group, click the Cut button; or use the keyboard shortcut Ctrl + X.

10 ▶ Press Del one time to remove the blank paragraph from the top of the document, and then press Ctrl + End to move to the end of the document.

11 ▶ With the insertion point blinking in the blank paragraph at the end of the document, right-click, and notice that the **Paste Options** gallery displays on the shortcut menu. Compare your screen with Figure 1.48.

FIGURE 1.48

12 ▶ On the shortcut menu, under **Paste Options**, click the first button—**Keep Source Formatting**.

13 ▶ Point to the picture to display the pointer, and then drag to the right until the center green **Alignment Guide** displays and the blank paragraph is above the picture, as shown in Figure 1.49. Release the left mouse button.

↻ **BY TOUCH**   Drag the picture with your finger to display the Alignment Guide.

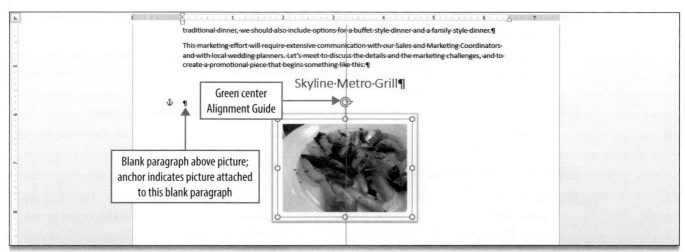

MOS

2.2.7, 5.2.8

Activity 1.18 | Changing Text to WordArt and Adding Alternative Text for Accessibility

1 Above the picture, click to position the insertion point at the end of the word *Grill*, press Spacebar one time, and then type **for Your Rehearsal Dinner**

2 Select the text *Skyline Metro Grill for Your Rehearsal Dinner*, and then on the **Insert tab**, in the **Text group**, click **Insert WordArt** *4 -*.

> ***WordArt*** is an Office feature available in Word, Excel, and PowerPoint that enables you to change normal text into decorative stylized text.

3 In the displayed gallery, use the ScreenTips to locate and then click **Fill - Gold, Accent 4, Soft Bevel**.

4 With the WordArt surrounded with a solid line, on the **Home tab**, in the **Font group**, change the font size to **16**.

5 Point to the solid line surrounding the WordArt to display the pointer, and then drag the WordArt slightly to the right until the green center alignment guides display, as shown in Figure 1.50, and then release the mouse button to center the WordArt above your picture. Click outside of the WordArt to deselect.

6 Point to the picture of the salad and right-click. On the shortcut menu, click **Format Picture**.

7 In the **Format Picture** pane that displays on the right, under **Format Picture**, click **Layout & Properties** 🖼, and then click **Alt Text**.

Alternative text helps people using a *screen reader*, which is software that enables visually impaired users to read text on a computer screen to understand the content of pictures. *Alt text* is the term commonly used for this feature.

8 As the Title, type **Salad** and as the Description, type **Picture of salad on a plate**

Anyone viewing the document with a screen reader will see the alternative text displayed instead of the picture.

9 **Close** ✕ the **Format Picture** pane.

10 On the **Insert tab**, in the **Header & Footer group**, click **Footer**. At the bottom of the list, click **Edit Footer**, and then with the **Header & Footer Tools Design tab** active, in the **Insert group**, click **Document Info**. Click **File Name** to add the file name to the footer.

11 On the right end of the ribbon, click **Close Header and Footer**.

12 On the **Quick Access Toolbar**, point to the **Print Preview and Print icon** 🔍 you placed there, right-click, and then click **Remove from Quick Access Toolbar**.

If you are working on your own computer and you want to do so, you can leave the icon on the toolbar; in a college lab, you should return the software to its original settings.

13 Click **Save** 💾 and then click the **File tab** to display **Backstage** view. With the **Info tab** active, in the lower right corner, click **Show All Properties**. As **Tags**, type **weddings, rehearsal dinners, marketing**

14 As the **Subject**, type your course name and number—for example, *CIS 10, #5543*. Under **Related People**, be sure your name displays as the author (edit it if necessary), and then on the left, click **Print** to display the Print Preview. Compare your screen with Figure 1.51.

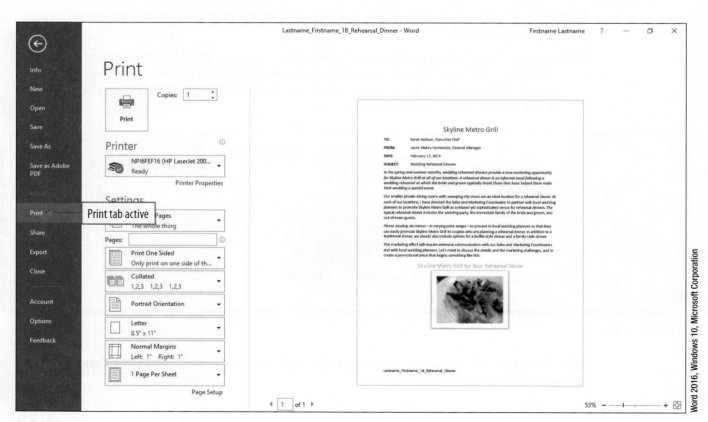

FIGURE 1.51

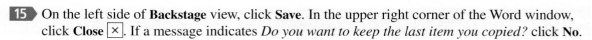

15 On the left side of **Backstage** view, click **Save**. In the upper right corner of the Word window, click **Close** ⊠. If a message indicates *Do you want to keep the last item you copied?* click **No**.

> This message displays if you have copied some type of image to the Clipboard. If you click Yes, the items on the Clipboard will remain for you to use in another program or document.

16 As directed by your instructor, create and submit a paper printout or an electronic image of your document that looks like a printed document; or, submit your completed Word file. If necessary, refer to Activity 1.08 in Project 1A.

1.5.4, 1.5.5, 1.5.6

Activity 1.19 | Inspecting a Document

Word, Excel, and PowerPoint all have the same commands to inspect a file before sharing it.

1 If necessary, open your **Lastname_Firstname_1B_Rehearsal_Dinner** document.

2 Click the **File tab**, on the left, if necessary, click **Info**, and then on the right, click **Check for Issues**.

3 On the list, click **Inspect Document**.

> The *Inspect Document* command searches your document for hidden data or personal information that you might not want to share publicly. This information could reveal company details that should not be shared.

4 In the lower right corner of the **Document Inspector** dialog box, click **Inspect**.

> The Document Inspector runs and lists information that was found and that you could choose to remove.

5 Click **Close**, click **Check for Issues** again, and then click **Check Accessibility**.

> The *Check Accessibility* command checks the document for content that people with disabilities might find difficult to read. The Accessibility Checker pane displays on the right and lists two objects that might require attention: a text box (your WordArt) and your picture.

6 **Close** ⊠ the **Accessibility Checker** pane, and then click the **File tab**.

7 Click **Check for Issues**, and then click **Check Compatibility**.

> The *Check Compatibility* command checks for features in your document that may not be supported by earlier versions of the Office program. This is only a concern if you are sharing documents with individuals with older software.

8 Click **OK**. Leave your Word document displayed for the next Activity.

1.2.3

Activity 1.20 | Inserting a Bookmark

A *bookmark* identifies a word, section, or place in your document so that you can find it quickly without scrolling. This is especially useful in a long document.

1 In the paragraph that begins *Please develop*, select the text *six menus*.

2 On the **Insert tab**, in the **Links group**, click **Bookmark**.

3 In the Bookmark name box, type **menus** and then click **Add**.

4 Press [Ctrl] + [Home] to move to the top of your document.

5 Press [Ctrl] + [G], which is the keyboard shortcut for the Go To command.

6 Under **Go to what**, click **Bookmark**, and then with menus selected, click **Go To**. **Close** the **Find and Replace** dialog box, and notice that your bookmarked text is selected for you.

7 **Close** ⊠ Word, and then click **Save**. Close any open windows.

GO! Learn How
Video OF1.10

A ***compressed file*** is a file that has been reduced in size. Compressed files take up less storage space and can be transferred to other computers faster than uncompressed files. You can also combine a group of files into one compressed folder, which makes it easier to share a group of files.

Within each Office program, you will see the ***Tell Me*** feature at the right end of the ribbon tabs, which is a search feature for Microsoft Office commands that you activate by typing what you are looking for in the Tell Me box.

Another method to get help with an Office command is to point to the command on the ribbon, and then at the bottom of the displayed ScreenTip, click Tell me more, which will display step-by-step assistance.

Activity 1.21 | Compressing Files

In this Activity, you will combine the two files you created in this chapter into one compressed file.

1 On the Windows taskbar, click **File Explorer** ▣. On the left, in the **navigation pane**, navigate to your storage location, and then open your **Office Features Chapter 1** folder. If you have been using this folder, in might appear under Quick access. Compare your screen with Figure 1.52.

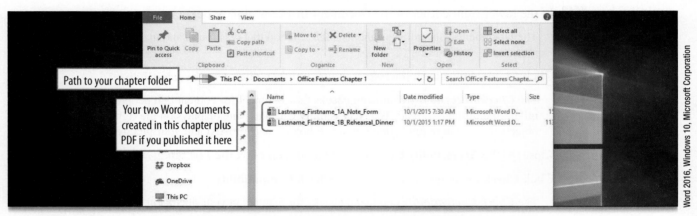

FIGURE 1.52

2 In the **file list,** click your **Lastname_Firstname_1A_Note_Form** Word file one time to select it. Then, hold down Ctrl, and click your **Lastname_Firstname_1B_Rehearsal_Dinner** file to select both files in the list.

In any Windows-based program, holding down Ctrl while selecting enables you to select multiple items.

3 On the **File Explorer** ribbon, click **Share,** and then in the **Send group,** click **Zip.** Compare your screen with Figure 1.53.

Windows creates a compressed folder containing a *copy* of each of the selected files. The folder name is selected—highlighted in blue—so that you can rename it. The default folder name is usually the name of the first file in the group that you select.

↻ BY TOUCH Tap the ribbon commands.

FIGURE 1.53

Word 2016, Windows 10, Microsoft Corporation

> **↺ ANOTHER WAY** Point to the selected files in the File List, right-click, point to Send to, and then click Compressed (zipped) folder.

4 With the folder name selected—highlighted in blue—using your own name, type **Lastname_Firstname_Office_Features_Chapter_1** and press Enter.

The compressed folder is ready to attach to an email or share in some other format.

5 In the upper right corner of the folder window, click **Close** ×.

Activity 1.22 | Using Microsoft Office Tell Me and Tell Me More to Get Help

In this Activity, you will use Tell Me to find information about formatting currency in Excel.

1 Start Excel and open a **Blank workbook**. With cell **A1** active, type **456789** and press Enter. Click cell **A1** again to make it the active cell.

2 At the top of the screen, click in the **Tell me what you want to do** box, and then type **format as currency** In the displayed list, point to **Accounting Number Formats**, and then click **$ English (United States)**.

As you type, every keystroke refines the results so that you can click the command as soon as it displays. This feature helps you apply the command immediately; it does not explain how to locate the command.

3 On the **Home tab**, in the **Alignment group**, *point to* **Merge & Center**, and then at the bottom of the displayed ScreenTip, click **Tell me more**. At the right edge of the displayed **Excel 2016 Help** window, use the scroll bar to scroll about halfway down the window, and then compare your screen with Figure 1.54.

The ***Tell me more*** feature opens the Office online Help system with explanations about how to perform the task.

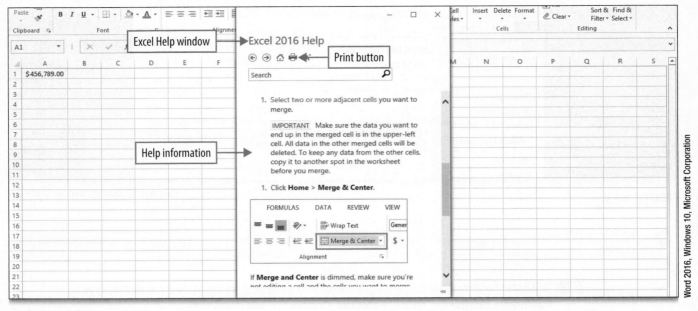

FIGURE 1.54

4 If you want to do so, at the top of the **Excel Help** window, click Print 🖶 to print a copy of this information for your reference.

5 In the upper right corner of the Help window, click **Close** ☒.

6 Leave Excel open for the next Activity.

Objective 11 | Install Apps for Office and Create a Microsoft Account

GO! Learn How
Video OF1.11

Apps for Office are a collection of downloadable apps that enable you to create and view information within your familiar Office programs. Apps for Office combine cloud services and web technologies within the user interface of Office. Some of these apps are developed by Microsoft, but many more are developed by specialists in different fields. As new apps are developed, they will be available from the online *Office Store*—a public marketplace that Microsoft hosts and regulates on Office.com.

A *task pane app* works side-by-side with an Office document by displaying a separate pane on the right side of the window. For example, a task pane app can look up and retrieve product information from a web service based on the product name or part number selected in the document.

A *content app* integrates web-based features as content within the body of a document. For example, in Excel, you can use an app to look up and gather search results for a new apartment by placing the information in an Excel worksheet, and then use maps to determine the distance of each apartment to work and to family members. *Mail apps* display next to an Outlook item. For example, a mail app could detect a purchase order number in an email message and then display information about the order or the customer.

Activity 1.23 | Installing Apps for Office

1 With cell **A1** active, on your keyboard, press Delete to clear the cell. On the Excel ribbon, click the **Insert tab**. In the **Add-ins group**, click **Store**.

2 In the **Office Add-ins** dialog box, in the upper right, click in the **Search the Office Store** box, type **bing maps** and then press Enter.

3 Click the **Bing logo**, and then in the lower right corner, click **Trust It**.

4 If necessary, click Update. On the Welcome message, click **Insert Sample Data**.

> Here, the Bing map displays information related to the sample data—this is a *content app*. Each city in the sample data displays a small pie chart that represents the two sets of data—revenue and expenses. Compare your screen with Figure 1.55.

> This is just one example of many apps downloadable from the Office Store.

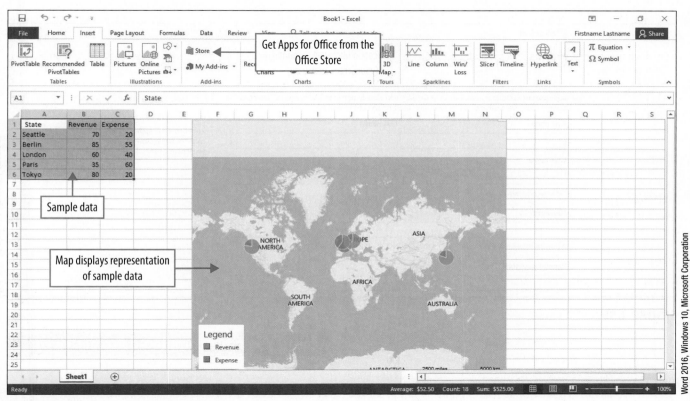

FIGURE 1.55

5 In the upper right corner of your screen, **Close** ⊠ Excel without saving.

Activity 1.24 | Creating a Microsoft Account

> **ALERT!**   **This is an optional activity.**
>
> You will find both Windows and Office to be much more useful if you sign in with a Microsoft account. If you already have an email account from **msn.com**, **hotmail.com**, **live.com**, or **outlook.com**, then you already have a Microsoft account. If you do not, you can create a free Microsoft account by following the steps in this activity.

In Windows 8 and Windows 10, you can use a Microsoft account to sign in to *any* Windows PC. Signing in with a Microsoft account is recommended because you can:

- Download Windows apps from the Windows Store.
- Get your online content—email, social network updates, updated news—automatically displayed in an app when you sign in.
- Synch settings online to make every Windows computer you use look and feel the same.
- Sign in to Office so that you can store documents on your OneDrive.

1 Use an Internet search engine to search for **create a microsoft account** or go to **signup.live.com** and at the bottom click **Sign up now**. You will see a screen similar to Figure 1.56. Complete the form to create your account.

You can use any email address that you currently have for your Microsoft account. Or, on this screen, you can create a new outlook.com account.

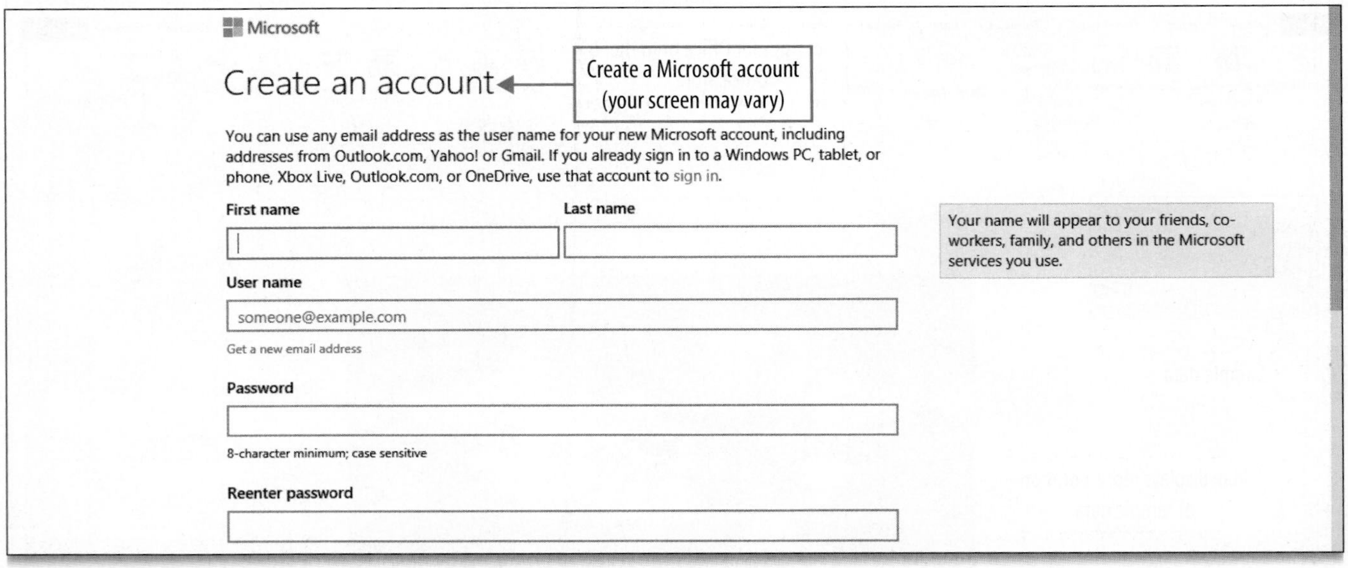

Microsoft

Create an account ◄ Create a Microsoft account (your screen may vary)

You can use any email address as the user name for your new Microsoft account, including addresses from Outlook.com, Yahoo! or Gmail. If you already sign in to a Windows PC, tablet, or phone, Xbox Live, Outlook.com, or OneDrive, use that account to sign in.

First name

Last name

Your name will appear to your friends, co-workers, family, and others in the Microsoft services you use.

User name

someone@example.com

Get a new email address

Password

8-character minimum; case sensitive

Reenter password

Word 2016, Windows 10, Microsoft Corporation

FIGURE 1.56

END | You have completed Project 1B

GO! To Work

MICROSOFT OFFICE SPECIALIST (MOS) SKILLS IN THIS CHAPTER

PROJECT 1A

1.1.1 Create a blank document
1.3.4 Insert headers and footers
1.3.6 Format page background elements
1.4.5 Add document properties
1.4.6 Show or hide formatting symbols
2.2.6 Apply built-in styles to text

PROJECT 1B

1.2.3 Create bookmarks
1.4.2 Customize views by using zoom settings
1.4.3 Customize the Quick Access toolbar
1.5.4 Inspect a document for hidden properties or personal information
1.5.5 Inspect a document for accessibility issues
1.5.6 Inspect a document for compatibility issues
2.1.2 Cut, copy, and paste text
2.2.2 Apply formatting by using Format Painter
2.2.7 Change text to WordArt
5.2.5 Apply a picture style
5.2.8 Add alternative text to objects for accessibility

BUILD YOUR E-PORTFOLIO

An E-Portfolio is a collection of evidence, stored electronically, that showcases what you have accomplished while completing your education. Collecting and then sharing your work products with potential employers reflects your academic and career goals. Your completed documents from the following projects are good examples to show what you have learned: 1A and 1B.

END OF CHAPTER

SUMMARY

Many Office features and commands, such as accessing the Open and Save As dialog boxes, performing commands from the ribbon and from dialog boxes, and using the Clipboard are the same in all Office desktop apps.

A desktop app is installed on your computer and requires a computer operating system such as Microsoft Windows or Apple's Mac OS-X to run. The programs in Microsoft Office 2016 are considered to be desktop apps.

An app refers to a self-contained program usually designed for a single purpose and that runs on smartphones and other mobile devices—for example, looking at sports scores or booking a flight on a particular airline.

Within an Office app, you can add Apps for Office from the Office Store, which combine cloud services and web technologies within the Office user interface. Apps can be task pane apps, content apps, or mail apps.

GO! LEARN IT ONLINE

Review the concepts, key terms, and MOS skills in this chapter by completing these online challenges, which you can find at **MyITLab**.

Matching and Multiple Choice: Answer matching and multiple-choice questions to test what you learned in this chapter.

Lessons on the GO!: Learn how to use all the new apps and features as they are introduced by Microsoft.

MOS Prep Quiz: Answer questions to review the MOS skills that you practiced in this chapter.

GLOSSARY

GLOSSARY OF CHAPTER KEY TERMS

Alignment The placement of text or objects relative to the left and right margins.

Alignment guides Green lines that display when you move an object to assist in alignment.

Alt text Another name for alternative text.

Alternative text Text added to a picture or object that helps people using a screen reader understand what the object is.

App A self-contained program usually designed for a single purpose and that runs on smartphones and other mobile devices.

Apps for Office A collection of downloadable apps that enable you to create and view information within Office programs, and that combine cloud services and web technologies within the user interface of Office.

Backstage tabs The area along the left side of Backstage view with tabs to display screens with related groups of commands.

Backstage view A centralized space for file management tasks; for example, opening, saving, printing, publishing, or sharing a file. A navigation pane displays along the left side with tabs that group file-related tasks together.

Bookmark A command that identifies a word, section, or place in a document so that you can find it quickly without scrolling.

Center alignment The alignment of text or objects that is centered horizontally between the left and right margin.

Clipboard A temporary storage area that holds text or graphics that you select and then cut or copy.

Check Accessibility A command that checks the document for content that people with disabilities might find difficult to read.

Check Compatibility A command that searches your document for features that may not be supported by older versions of Office.

Cloud computing Applications and services that are accessed over the Internet, rather than accessing applications that are installed on your local computer.

Cloud storage Online storage of data so that you can access your data from different places and devices.

Collaborate To work with others as a team in an intellectual endeavor to complete a shared task or to achieve a shared goal.

Commands Instructions to a computer program that cause an action to be carried out.

Compressed file A file that has been reduced in size and thus takes up less storage space and can be transferred to other computers quickly.

Content app An app for Office that integrates web-based features as content within the body of a document.

Context menus Menus that display commands and options relevant to the selected text or object; also called *shortcut menus*.

Context-sensitive commands Commands that display on a shortcut menu that relate to the object or text that you right-clicked.

Contextual tabs Tabs that are added to the ribbon automatically when a specific object, such as a picture, is selected, and that contain commands relevant to the selected object.

Copy A command that duplicates a selection and places it on the Clipboard.

Creative Commons A nonprofit organization that enables sharing and use of images and knowledge through free legal tools.

Cut A command that removes a selection and places it on the Clipboard.

Default The term that refers to the current selection or setting that is automatically used by a computer program unless you specify otherwise.

Deselect The action of canceling the selection of an object or block of text by clicking outside of the selection.

Desktop app A computer program that is installed on your PC and requires a computer operating system such as Microsoft Windows; also known as a *desktop application*.

Desktop application A computer program that is installed on your PC and requires a computer operating system such as Microsoft Windows; also known as a *desktop app*.

Dialog Box Launcher A small icon that displays to the right of some group names on the ribbon and that opens a related dialog box or pane providing additional options and commands related to that group.

Document properties Details about a file that describe or identify it, including the title, author name, subject, and keywords that identify the document's topic or contents; also known as *metadata*.

Drag The action of holding down the left mouse button while moving your mouse.

Edit The process of making changes to text or graphics in an Office file.

Ellipsis A set of three dots indicating incompleteness; an ellipsis following a command name indicates that a dialog box will display if you click the command.

Enhanced ScreenTip A ScreenTip that displays more descriptive text than a normal ScreenTip.

Fill The inside color of an object.

Font A set of characters with the same design and shape.

Font styles Formatting emphasis such as bold, italic, and underline.

Footer A reserved area for text or graphics that displays at the bottom of each page in a document.

Formatting The process of establishing the overall appearance of text, graphics, and pages in an Office file—for example, in a Word document.

Formatting marks Characters that display on the screen, but do not print, indicating where the Enter key, the Spacebar, and the Tab key were pressed; also called *nonprinting characters*.

Gallery An Office feature that displays a list of potential results instead of just the command name.

Gradient fill A fill effect in which one color fades into another.

Groups On the Office ribbon, the sets of related commands that you might need for a specific type of task.

Header A reserved area for text or graphics that displays at the top of each page in a document.

Info tab The tab in Backstage view that displays information about the current file.

Inspect Document A command that searches your document for hidden data or personal information that you might not want to share publicly.

Insertion point A blinking vertical line that indicates where text or graphics will be inserted.

Keyboard shortcut A combination of two or more keyboard keys, used to perform a task that would otherwise require a mouse.

KeyTip The letter that displays on a command in the ribbon and that indicates the key you can press to activate the command when keyboard control of the Ribbon is activated.

Keywords Custom file properties in the form of words that you associate with a document to give an indication of the document's content; used to help find and organize files. Also called *tags*.

Landscape orientation A page orientation in which the paper is wider than it is tall.

Layout Options A button that displays when an object is selected and that has commands to choose how the object interacts with surrounding text.

Live Preview A technology that shows the result of applying an editing or formatting change as you point to possible results—*before* you actually apply it.

Location Any disk drive, folder, or other place in which you can store files and folders.

Mail app An app for Office that displays next to an Outlook item.

Metadata Details about a file that describe or identify it, including the title, author name, subject, and keywords that identify the document's topic or contents; also known as *document properties*.

Mini toolbar A small toolbar containing frequently used formatting commands that displays as a result of selecting text or objects.

MRU Acronym for *most recently used*, which refers to the state of some commands that retain the characteristic most recently applied; for example, the Font Color button retains the most recently used color until a new color is chosen.

Nonprinting characters Characters that display on the screen, but do not

print, indicating where the Enter key, the Spacebar, and the Tab key were pressed; also called *formatting marks*.

Object A text box, picture, table, or shape that you can select and then move and resize.

Office 365 A version of Microsoft Office to which you subscribe for an annual fee.

Office Store A public marketplace that Microsoft hosts and regulates on Office.com.

OneDrive Microsoft's free cloud storage for anyone with a free Microsoft account.

Open dialog box A dialog box from which you can navigate to, and then open on your screen, an existing file that was created in that same program.

Option button In a dialog box, a round button that enables you to make one choice among two or more options.

Options dialog box A dialog box within each Office application where you can select program settings and other options and preferences.

Page Width A view that zooms the document so that the width of the page matches the width of the window. Find this command on the View tab, in the Zoom group.

Paragraph symbol The symbol ¶ that represents the end of a paragraph.

Paste The action of placing text or objects that have been copied or cut from one location to another location.

Paste Options gallery A gallery of buttons that provides a Live Preview of all the Paste options available in the current context.

PDF The acronym for *Portable Document Format*, which is a file format that creates an image that preserves the look of your file, but that cannot be easily changed; a popular format for sending documents electronically, because the document will display on most computers.

Pointer Any symbol that displays on your screen in response to moving your mouse.

Points A measurement of the size of a font; there are 72 points in an inch.

Portable Document Format A file format that creates an image that preserves the look of your file, but that cannot be easily changed; a popular format for sending documents electronically, because the document

will display on most computers; also called a *PDF*.

Portrait orientation A page orientation in which the paper is taller than it is wide.

Print Preview A view of a document as it will appear when you print it.

Protected View A security feature in Office 2016 that protects your computer from malicious files by opening them in a restricted environment until you enable them; you might encounter this feature if you open a file from an e-mail or download files from the Internet.

pt The abbreviation for *point*; for example, when referring to a font size.

Quick Access Toolbar In an Office program window, the small row of buttons in the upper left corner of the screen from which you can perform frequently used commands.

Read-only A property assigned to a file that prevents the file from being modified or deleted; it indicates that you cannot save any changes to the displayed document unless you first save it with a new name.

Right-click The action of clicking the right mouse button one time.

Sans serif font A font design with no lines or extensions on the ends of characters.

Screen reader Software that enables visually impaired users to read text on a computer screen to understand the content of pictures.

ScreenTip A small box that that displays useful information when you perform various mouse actions such as pointing to screen elements or dragging.

Selecting Highlighting, by dragging with your mouse, areas of text or data or graphics, so that the selection can be edited, formatted, copied, or moved.

Serif font A font design that includes small line extensions on the ends of the letters to guide the eye in reading from left to right.

Share button Opens the Share pane from which you can save your file to the cloud—your OneDrive—and then share it with others so you can collaborate.

SharePoint Collaboration software with which people in an organization can set up team sites to share information, manage documents, and publish reports for others to see.

Shortcut menu A menu that displays commands and options relevant to the selected text or object; also called a *context menu*.

Sizing handles Small squares or circles that indicate a picture or object is selected.

Split button A button divided into two parts and in which clicking the main part of the button performs a command and clicking the arrow opens a menu with choices.

Status bar The area along the lower edge of an Office program window that displays file information on the left and buttons to control how the window looks on the right.

Style A group of formatting commands, such as font, font size, font color, paragraph alignment, and line spacing that can be applied to a paragraph with one command.

Synchronization The process of updating computer files that are in two or more locations according to specific rules—also called *syncing*.

Syncing The process of updating computer files that are in two or more locations according to specific rules—also called *synchronization*.

Tabs (ribbon) On the Office ribbon, the name of each task-oriented activity area.

Tags Custom file properties in the form of words that you associate with a document to give an indication of the document's content; used to help find and organize files. Also called *keywords*.

Task pane app An app for Office that works side-by-side with an Office document by displaying a separate pane on the right side of the window.

Tell Me A search feature for Microsoft Office commands that you activate by typing what you are looking for in the Tell Me box.

Tell me more A prompt within a ScreenTip that opens the Office online Help system with explanations about how to perform the command referenced in the ScreenTip.

Template A preformatted document that you can use as a starting point and then change to suit your needs.

Theme A predesigned combination of colors, fonts, and effects that looks good together and is applied to an entire document by a single selection.

Title bar The bar at the top edge of the program window that indicates the name of the current file and the program name.

Toggle button A button that can be turned on by clicking it once, and then turned off by clicking it again.

Toolbar In a folder window, a row of buttons with which you can perform common tasks, such as changing the view of your files and folders.

Triple-click The action of clicking the left mouse button three times in rapid succession.

Trusted Documents A security feature in Office that remembers which files you have already enabled; you might encounter this feature if you open a file from an e-mail or download files from the Internet.

Windows apps An app that runs on all Windows device families—including PCs, Windows phones, Windows tablets, and the Xbox gaming system.

WordArt An Office feature in Word, Excel, and PowerPoint that enables you to change normal text into decorative stylized text.

XML Paper Specification A Microsoft file format that creates an image of your document and that opens in the XPS viewer.

XPS The acronym for XML Paper Specification—a Microsoft file format that creates an image of your document and that opens in the XPS viewer.

Zoom The action of increasing or decreasing the size of the viewing area on the screen.

Introducing Microsoft Word 2016

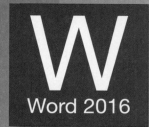

W Word 2016

devrim_pinar/fotolia

Word 2016: Introduction

Content! Defined by Merriam-Webster's online dictionary as "the topic or matter treated in a written work" and also as "the principal substance (as written matter, illustrations, or music) offered by a World Wide Web site," content is what you consume when you read on paper or online, when you watch video, or when you listen to any kind of music—live or recorded.

Content is what you *create* when your own words or performances are recorded in some form. For creating content in the form of words, Microsoft Office 2016 is a great choice. Rather than just a tool for word processing, Word is now a tool for you to communicate and collaborate with others. When you want to communicate with pictures or images in your Word document, Office 2016 has many features to help you do so. You can use Microsoft Word 2016 on a Windows desktop, laptop, or tablet. If your PC is touch-enabled, you will be able to use your fingers to work with Word. For example, the ribbon expands to make it easy to tap commands and you can resize images by moving your fingers on the screen.

Best of all, Microsoft Word 2016 is integrated into the cloud. If you save your documents to your cloud-based storage that comes with any free Microsoft account, you can retrieve them from any device and continue to work with and share your documents. Enjoy learning Word 2016!

Creating Documents with Microsoft Word 2016

PROJECT 1A

OUTCOMES
Create a flyer with a picture.

PROJECT 1B

OUTCOMES
Format text, paragraphs, and documents.

OBJECTIVES

1. Create a New Document and Insert Text
2. Insert and Format Graphics
3. Insert and Modify Text Boxes and Shapes
4. Preview and Print a Document

OBJECTIVES

5. Change Document and Paragraph Layout
6. Create and Modify Lists
7. Set and Modify Tab Stops
8. Insert a SmartArt Graphic and an Online Video

IvicaNS/Fotolia

In This Chapter

GO! to Work with Word

In this chapter, you will begin your study of Microsoft Word, one of the most popular computer software applications and one that almost everyone has a reason to use. You will use many of the tools and features in Word 2016, such as applying attractive styles to your documents. You can use Microsoft Word to perform basic word processing tasks such as writing a memo, a report, or a letter. You can also use Word to complete complex tasks, such as creating sophisticated tables, embedding graphics, writing blogs, and creating publications. Word is a program that you can learn gradually, and then add more advanced skills one at a time.

The projects in this chapter relate to **Sturgeon Point Productions**, an independent film company based in Miami with offices in Detroit and Milwaukee. The film professionals produce effective broadcast and branded content for many industries, and provide a wide array of film and video production services. Sturgeon Point Productions has won awards for broadcast advertising, business media, music videos, and social media. The mission of the company is to help clients tell their stories—whether the story is about a social issue, a new product, a geographical location, a company, or a person.

PROJECT ACTIVITIES

In Activities 1.01 through 1.16, you will create a flyer announcing two internships for a short documentary by Sturgeon Point Productions. Your completed document will look similar to Figure 1.1.

PROJECT FILES

 If your instructor wants you to submit Project 1A in the **MyITLab** grader MyITLab Grader system, log in to MyITLab, locate Grader Project 1A, and then download the files for this project.

For Project 1A, you will need the following files:

New blank Word document
w01A_Text
w01A_Bird

You will save your document as:

Lastname_Firstname_1A_Flyer

Please always review the downloaded Grader instructions before beginning.

PROJECT RESULTS

Build From
Scratch

GO!
Walk Thru
Project 1A

Internships Available

Interviews will be held:

Friday and Saturday, January 14 and 15

In the Career Services Conference Room

This summer, Sturgeon Point Productions will be filming a short documentary in Costa Rica about its native birds and has positions available for two interns. The filming will begin the first week of July and will last approximately two weeks. Payment will be by Day Rate of $100 per day. Transportation, food, and lodging will be provided.

The First Assistant Director will work with the second film crew, which will be filming background video. The Assistant Script Supervisor will work with the Script Supervisor and will be responsible for coordinating communication between the two camera crews.

You must have a valid U. S. passport; no inoculations are necessary. Details are available on the company website.

To set up an interview, apply online at:

www.SturgeonPointProductions.com

Lastname_Firstname_1A_Flyer

Word 2016, Windows 10, Microsoft Corporation

FIGURE 1.1 Project 1A Internship Flyer

NOTE If You Are Using a Touchscreen

	Tap an item to click it.
	Press and hold for a few seconds to right-click; release when the information or commands displays.
	Touch the screen with two or more fingers and then pinch together to zoom out or stretch your fingers apart to zoom in.
	Slide your finger on the screen to scroll—slide left to scroll right and slide right to scroll left.
	Slide to rearrange—similar to dragging with a mouse.
	Swipe to select—slide an item a short distance with a quick movement—to select an item and bring up commands, if any.

Objective 1 Create a New Document and Insert Text

GO! Learn How
Video W1-1

When you start Word, documents you have recently opened, if any, display on the left. On the right, you can select a *template*—a preformatted document that you can use as a starting point and then change to suit your needs. If you want to start a new, blank document, you can select the blank document template. When you create a new document, you can type all of the text, or you can type some of the text and then insert additional text from another source.

1.1.1, 1.4.6

Activity 1.01 │ Starting a New Word Document

> **ALERT!** To submit as an autograded project, log into MyITLab and download the files for this project, and begin with those files instead of a new blank document.

1 Start Word and then click **Blank document**. On the **Home tab**, in the **Paragraph group**, if necessary click **Show/Hide** ¶ so that it is active and the formatting marks display. If the rulers do not display, click the View tab, and then in the Show group, select the Ruler check box.

2 Type **Internships Available** and then press Enter two times. Then type the following text: **This summer, Sturgeon Point Productions will be filming a short documentary in Costa Rica about its native birds and has positions available for two interns.**

As you type, the insertion point moves to the right, and when it approaches the right margin, Word determines whether the next word in the line will fit within the established right margin. If the word does not fit, Word moves the entire word down to the next line. This is *wordwrap* and means that you press Enter *only* when you reach the end of a paragraph—it is not necessary to press Enter at the end of each line of text.

NOTE Spacing Between Sentences

Although you might have learned to add two spaces following end-of-sentence punctuation, the common practice now is to space only one time at the end of a sentence. Be sure to press Spacebar only one time following end-of-sentence punctuation.

3 Press Spacebar and then take a moment to study the table in Figure 1.2 to become familiar with the default document settings in Microsoft Word. Compare your screen with Figure 1.3.

When you press Enter, Spacebar, or Tab on your keyboard, characters display in your document to represent these keystrokes. These characters do not print and are referred to as *formatting marks* or *nonprinting characters*. These marks will display throughout this instruction.

DEFAULT DOCUMENT SETTINGS IN A NEW WORD DOCUMENT	
SETTING	**DEFAULT FORMAT**
Font and font size	The default font is Calibri, and the default font size is 11 points.
Margins	The default left, right, top, and bottom page margins are 1 inch.
Line spacing	The default line spacing is 1.08, which provides slightly more space between lines than single spacing does.
Paragraph spacing	The default spacing after a paragraph is 8 points, which is slightly less than the height of one blank line of text.
View	The default view is Print Layout view, which displays the page borders and displays the document as it will appear when printed.

FIGURE 1.2

FIGURE 1.3

More **Knowledge**   **Word's Default Settings Are Easier to Read Online**

Until just a few years ago, word processing programs used single spacing, an extra blank paragraph to separate paragraphs, and 12 pt Times New Roman as the default formats. Now, studies show that individuals find the Word default formats described in Figure 1.2 to be easier to read online, where many documents are now viewed and read.

1.1.4

Activity 1.02 | **Inserting Text from Another Document**

1 ▶ On the ribbon, click the **Insert tab**. In the **Text group**, click the **Object button arrow**, and then click **Text from File**.

ALERT!   **Does the Object dialog box display?**

If the Object dialog box displays, you probably clicked the Object *button* instead of the Object *button arrow*. Close the Object dialog box, and then in the Text group, click the Object button arrow, as shown in Figure 1.4. Click *Text from File*, and then continue with Step 2.

2 ▶ In the **Insert File** dialog box, navigate to the student files that accompany this textbook, locate and select **w01A_Text**, and then click **Insert**. Compare your screen with Figure 1.4.

A *copy* of the text from the w01A_Text file displays at the insertion point location; the text is not removed from the original file.

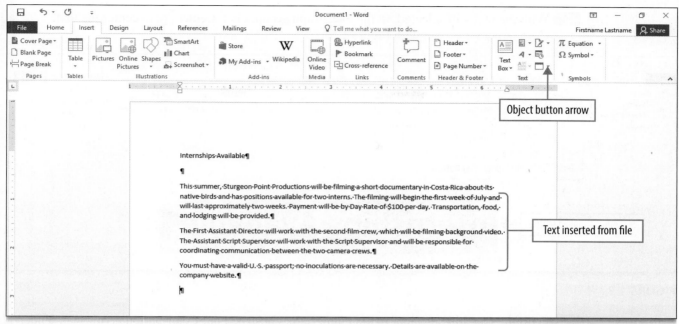

Object button arrow

Text inserted from file

FIGURE 1.4

Word 2016, Windows 10, Microsoft Corporation

ANOTHER WAY   Open the file, copy the required text, close the file, and then paste the text into the current document.

3 On the **Quick Access Toolbar**, click **Save** 🔲, and then under **Save As**, click **Browse**. Navigate to the location where you are saving your files for this chapter, and then create and open a new folder named **Word Chapter 1** In the **File name** box, using your own name, replace the existing text with **Lastname_Firstname_1A_Flyer** and then click **Save**.

Objective 2   Insert and Format Graphics

GO! Learn How
Video W1-2

To add visual interest to a document, insert *graphics*. Graphics include pictures, online pictures, charts, and *drawing objects*—shapes, diagrams, lines, and so on. For additional visual interest, you can apply an attractive graphic format to text; add, resize, move, and format pictures; and add a page border.

2.2.6 and 2.2.10

Activity 1.03 | Formatting Text by Using Text Effects

Text effects are decorative formats, such as shadowed or mirrored text, text glow, 3-D effects, and colors that make text stand out.

1 Including the paragraph mark, select the first paragraph of text—*Internships Available*. On the **Home tab**, in the **Font group**, click **Text Effects and Typography** Ⓐ ·.

2 In the **Text Effects and Typography** gallery, in the third row, point to the first effect to display the ScreenTip *Fill – Black, Text 1, Outline – Background 1, Hard Shadow – Background 1*, and then click this effect.

3 With the text still selected, in the **Font group**, click in the **Font Size** box 11 · to select the existing font size. Type **52** and then press Enter.

When you want to change the font size of selected text to a size that does not display in the Font Size list, type the number in the Font Size box and press Enter to confirm the new font size.

4 With the text still selected, in the **Paragraph group**, click **Center** ▤ to center the text. Compare your screen with Figure 1.5.

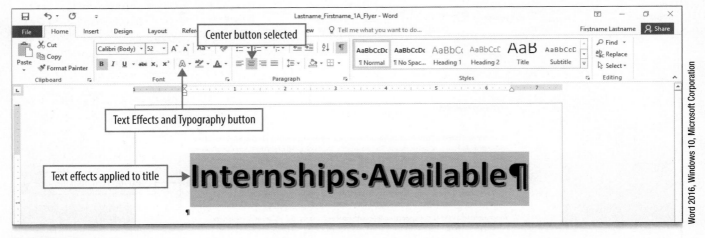

FIGURE 1.5

5 With the text still selected, in the **Font group**, click the **Font Color button arrow** ⏷. Under **Theme Colors**, in the sixth column, click the first color—**Orange, Accent 2**.

6 With the text still selected, in the **Font group**, click **Text Effects and Typography** ⏷. Point to **Shadow**, and then under **Outer**, in the second row, click the third style—**Offset Left**.

7 Click anywhere in the document to deselect the text, click **Save** 🖫, and then compare your screen with Figure 1.6.

FIGURE 1.6

More Knowledge **Clear Existing Formatting**

If you do not like your text effect, you can remove all formatting from any selected text. To do so, on the Home tab, in the Font group, click Clear All Formatting 📎.

MOS
5.1.2

Activity 1.04 | **Inserting Pictures**

1 In the paragraph that begins *This summer*, click to position the insertion point at the beginning of the paragraph.

2 On the **Insert tab**, in the **Illustrations group**, click **Pictures**. In the **Insert Picture** dialog box, navigate to your student data files, locate and click **w01A_Bird**, and then click **Insert**.

> Word inserts the picture as an *inline object*; that is, the picture is positioned directly in the text at the insertion point, just like a character in a sentence. The Layout Options button displays to the right of the picture. You can change the *Layout Options* to control the manner in which text wraps around a picture or other object. Sizing handles surround the picture indicating it is selected.

3 Notice the round sizing handles around the selected picture, as shown in Figure 1.7.

> The corner sizing handles resize the graphic proportionally. The center sizing handles resize a graphic vertically or horizontally only; however, sizing with these will distort the graphic. A *rotation handle*, with which you can rotate the graphic to any angle, displays above the top center sizing handle.

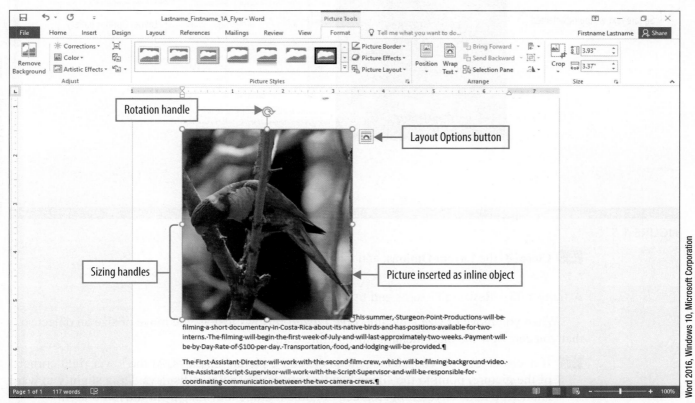

FIGURE 1.7

MOS
5.2.6

Activity 1.05 | Wrapping Text Around a Picture Using Layout Options

Recall that Layout Options enable you to control *text wrapping*—the manner in which text displays around an object.

1 Be sure the picture is selected—you know it is selected if the sizing handles display.

2 To the right of the picture, click **Layout Options** 🖼 to display a gallery of text wrapping arrangements. Point to each icon layout option to view its ScreenTip.

> Each icon visually depicts how text will wrap around an object.

⟳ ANOTHER WAY   On the Format tab, in the Arrange group, click Wrap Text.

3 From the gallery, under **With Text Wrapping**, click the first layout—**Square**. Compare your screen with Figure 1.8.

Select Square text wrapping when you want to wrap the text to the left or right of an image. To the left of the picture, an *object anchor* displays, indicating that the selected object is anchored to the text at this location in the document.

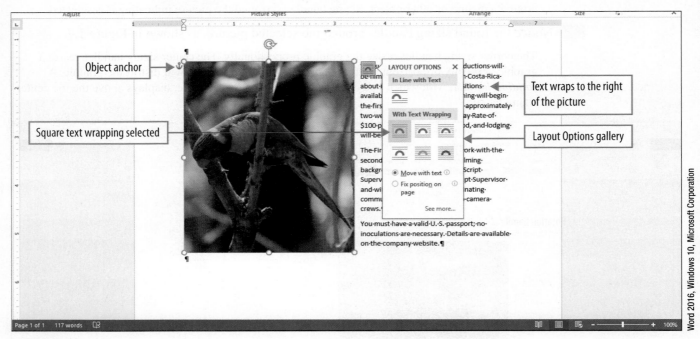

Object anchor

Square text wrapping selected

Text wraps to the right of the picture

Layout Options gallery

LAYOUT OPTIONS

In Line with Text

With Text Wrapping

Move with text
Fix position on page

See more...

Word 2016, Windows 10, Microsoft Corporation

FIGURE 1.8

4 **Close** ☒ the **Layout Options**, and then **Save** 🔲 your document.

Activity 1.06 | **Resizing Pictures and Using Live Layout**

When you move or size a picture, ***Live Layout*** reflows text as you move or size an object so that you can view the placement of surrounding text.

1 If necessary, scroll your document so the entire picture displays. At the lower right corner of the picture, point to the sizing handle until the 🔓 pointer displays. Drag slightly upward and to the left. As you drag, a green alignment guide may display at the left margin. Compare your screen with Figure 1.9.

Alignment guides may display when you are moving or sizing a picture to help you with object placement, and Live Layout shows you how the document text will flow and display on the page.

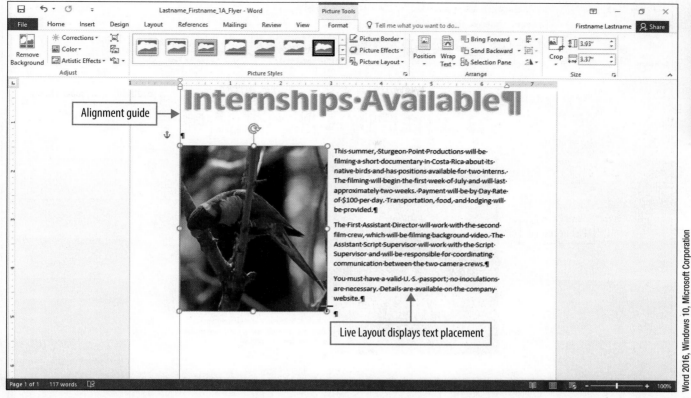

FIGURE 1.9

2 Continue to drag up and to the left until the bottom of the graphic is aligned at approximately **4 inches on the vertical ruler**. Notice that the graphic is proportionally resized.

3 On the **Quick Access Toolbar**, click **Undo** to restore the picture to its original size.

ANOTHER WAY   On the Format tab, in the Adjust group, click Reset Picture.

4 On the ribbon, under **Picture Tools**, on the **Format tab**, in the **Size group**, click in the **Shape Height** box. Type **3.8** and then press Enter. If necessary, scroll down to view the entire picture on your screen, and then compare your screen with Figure 1.10.

When you use the Shape Height and Shape Width boxes to change the size of a graphic, the graphic will always resize proportionally; that is, the width adjusts as you change the height and vice versa.

ANOTHER WAY   A *spin box* is a small box with an upward- and downward-pointing arrow that lets you move rapidly through a set of values by clicking. You can change the height or width of a picture object by clicking the Shape Height or Shape width spin box arrows.

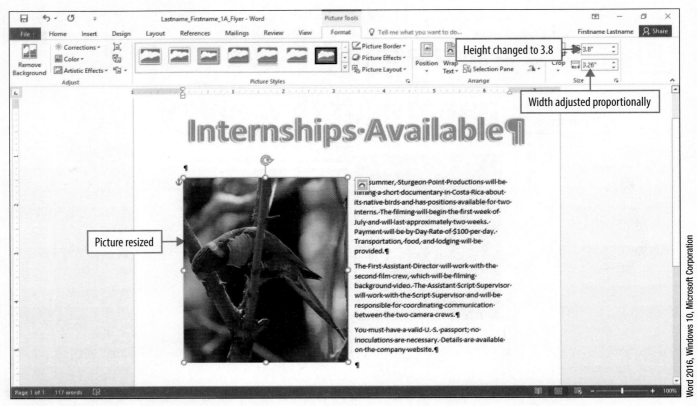

FIGURE 1.10

5 **Save** your document.

Word 2016, Windows 10, Microsoft Corporation

MOS
5.2.7

Activity 1.07 | Positioning a Picture

There are two ways to move a picture in a document. You can point to the picture and then drag it to a new position. You can also change the picture settings in a dialog box, which gives you more precise control over the picture location.

1 Be sure the picture is selected. On the ribbon, click the **Format tab**. In the **Arrange group**, click **Position**, and then click **More Layout Options**.

2 In the **Layout** dialog box, be sure the **Position tab** is selected. Under **Horizontal**, click the **Alignment** option button. To the right of **Alignment**, click the **arrow**, and then click **Right**. To the right of **relative to**, click the **arrow**, and then click **Margin**.

3 Under **Vertical**, click the **Alignment** option button. Change the **Alignment** options to **Top relative to Line**. Compare your screen with Figure 1.11.

With these alignment settings, the picture will move to the right margin of the page and the top edge will align with the top of the first line of the paragraph to which it is anchored.

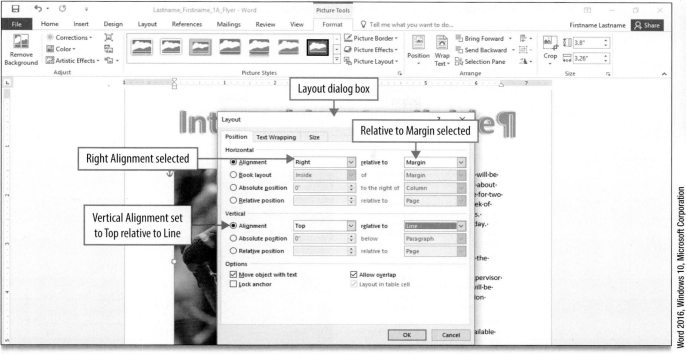

FIGURE 1.11

4 ▶ At the bottom of the **Layout** dialog box, click **OK**, and then on the **Quick Access Toolbar**, click **Save** 🖫. Notice that the picture moves to the right margin, and the text wraps on the left side of the picture. Compare your screen with Figure 1.12.

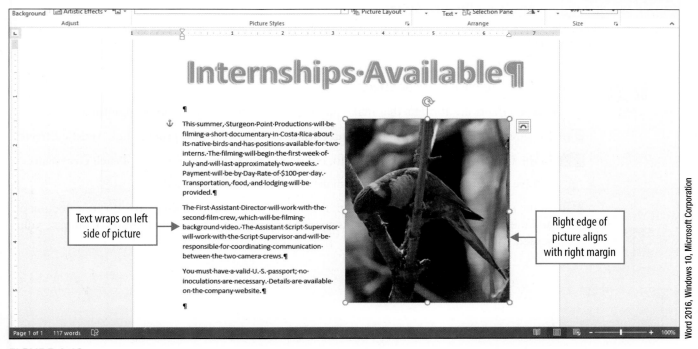

FIGURE 1.12

MOS
5.2.2

Activity 1.08 │ Applying Picture Effects

Picture styles include shapes, shadows, frames, borders, and other special effects with which you can stylize an image. ***Picture Effects*** enhance a picture with effects such as a shadow, glow, reflection, or 3-D rotation.

1 Be sure the picture is selected. On the **Format tab**, in the **Picture Styles group**, click **Picture Effects**.

2 Point to **Soft Edges**, and then click **5 Point**.

The Soft Edges feature fades the edges of the picture. The number of points you choose determines how far the fade goes inward from the edges of the picture.

3 Compare your screen with Figure 1.13, and then **Save** 🖫 your document.

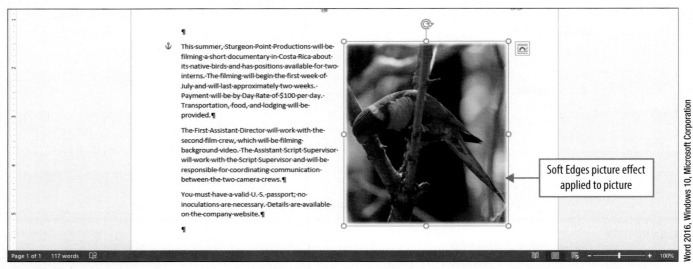

FIGURE 1.13

More Knowledge | **Applying Picture Styles**

To apply a picture style, select the picture. On the Picture Tools Format tab, in the Picture Styles group, click More, and then click the Picture Style that you want to apply.

MOS
5.2.1

Activity 1.09 │ Applying Artistic Effects

Artistic effects are formats that make pictures look more like sketches or paintings.

1 Be sure the picture is selected. On the **Format tab**, in the **Adjust group**, click **Artistic Effects**.

2 In the first row of the gallery, point to, but do not click, the third effect—**Pencil Grayscale**.

Live Preview displays the picture with the *Pencil Grayscale* effect added.

3 In the second row of the gallery, click the third effect—**Paint Brush**. **Save** 🖫 your document, and then notice that the picture looks more like a painting than a photograph. Compare your screen with Figure 1.14.

FIGURE 1.14

Activity 1.10 | Adding a Page Border

Page borders frame a page and help to focus the information on the page.

1 Click anywhere outside the picture to deselect it. On the **Design tab**, in the **Page Background group**, click **Page Borders**.

2 In the **Borders and Shading** dialog box, on the **Page Border tab**, under **Setting**, click **Box**. Under **Style**, scroll the list and click the seventh style—double lines.

3 Click the **Color arrow**, and then in the sixth column, click the first color—**Orange, Accent 2**.

4 Under **Apply to**, be sure *Whole document* is selected, and then compare your screen with Figure 1.15.

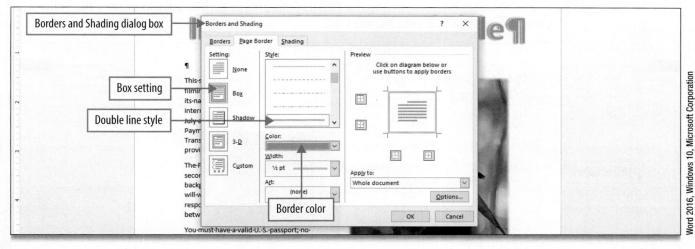

FIGURE 1.15

5 At the bottom of the **Borders and Shading** dialog box, click **OK**.

6 Press Ctrl + Home to move to the top of the document, click **Save** , and then compare your screen with Figure 1.16.

FIGURE 1.16

GO! Learn How
Video W1-3

Word has predefined **shapes** and **text boxes** that you can add to your documents. A shape is an object such as a line, arrow, box, callout, or banner. A text box is a movable, resizable container for text or graphics. Use these objects to add visual interest to your document.

5.1.1, 5.2.7

Activity 1.11 │ **Inserting, Sizing, and Positioning a Shape**

> **1** Press ↓ one time to move to the blank paragraph below the title. Press Enter four times to create additional space for a text box, and notice that the picture anchored to the paragraph moves with the text.

> **2** Press Ctrl + End to move to the bottom of the document, and notice that your insertion point is positioned in the empty paragraph at the end of the document. Press Delete to remove the blank paragraph.

> **3** Click the **Insert tab**, and then in the **Illustrations group**, click **Shapes** to display the gallery. Compare your screen with Figure 1.17.

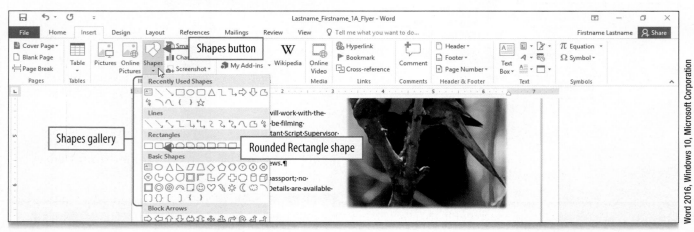

FIGURE 1.17

> **4** Under **Rectangles**, click the second shape—**Rounded Rectangle**, and then move your pointer. Notice that the ⊞ pointer displays.

> **5** Position the ⊞ pointer near the left margin at approximately **8 inches on the vertical ruler**. Click one time to insert a 1-inch by 1-inch rounded rectangle. The exact location is not important.

A blue rectangle with rounded edges displays.

6 To the right of the rectangle object, click **Layout Options** 🔳, and then at the bottom of the gallery, click **See more** to display the Layout dialog box.

♻ ANOTHER WAY   On the Format tab, in the Arrange group, click Position, and then click More Layout Options.

7 In the **Layout** dialog box, under **Horizontal**, click **Alignment**. To the right of **Alignment**, click the **arrow**, and then click **Centered**. To the right of **relative to**, click the **arrow**, and then click **Page**. Under **Vertical**, select the existing number in the **Absolute position** box, and then type **1** To the right of **below**, be sure that **Paragraph** displays. Click **OK**.

This action centers the rectangle on the page and positions the rectangle one inch below the last paragraph.

8 On the **Format tab**, click in the **Shape Height box** ↕ 0.29" ⬍ to select the existing text. Type **1.5** and then click in the **Shape Width box** ⬌ 1.07" ⬍. Type **4.5** and then press Enter.

9 Compare your screen with Figure 1.18, and then **Save** 🖫 your document.

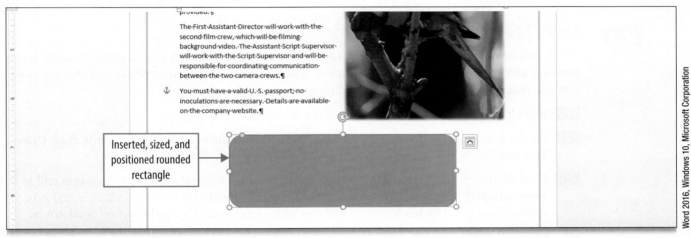

provided. ¶

The·First·Assistant·Director·will·work·with·the·
second·film·crew,·which·will·be·filming·
background·video.·The·Assistant·Script·Supervisor·
will·work·with·the·Script·Supervisor·and·will·be·
responsible·for·coordinating·communication·
between·the·two·camera·crews.¶

⚓ You·must·have·a·valid·U.·S.·passport;·no·
inoculations·are·necessary.·Details·are·available·
on·the·company·website.¶

Inserted, sized, and positioned rounded rectangle →

Word 2016, Windows 10, Microsoft Corporation

FIGURE 1.18

MOS
5.2.4

Activity 1.12 │ **Typing Text in a Shape and Formatting a Shape**

1 If necessary, select the rectangle shape. Type **To set up an interview, apply online at:** and then press Enter. Type **www.SturgeonPointProductions.com**

2 Press Ctrl + A to select the text you just typed. Right-click over the selected text to display the mini toolbar, and then click **Bold** B. With the text still selected, click **Increase Font Size** A˄ three times to increase the font size to **16 pt**.

Use the keyboard shortcut Ctrl + A to select all of the text in a text box.

3 With the text still selected, on the mini toolbar, click the **Font Color button arrow**. Under **Theme Colors**, click **Black, Text 1**.

4 Click outside the shape to deselect the text. Click the border of the shape to select the shape but not the text. On the **Format tab**, in the **Shape Styles group**, click **Shape Fill**. In the sixth column, click the fourth color—**Orange, Accent 2, Lighter 40%**.

5 With the shape still selected, in the **Shape Styles group**, click **Shape Outline**. In the sixth column, click the first color—**Orange, Accent 2**. Compare your screen with Figure 1.19, and then **Save** 🖫 your document.

Text typed and formatted, shape fill and outline applied →

To·set·up·an·interview,·apply·online·at:¶

www.SturgeonPointProductions.com¶

Word 2016, Windows 10, Microsoft Corporation

FIGURE 1.19

5.1.4

Activity 1.13 | **Inserting a Text Box**

A text box is useful to differentiate portions of text from other text on the page. Because it is a *floating object*—a graphic that can be moved independently of the surrounding text characters—you can place a text box anywhere on the page.

1 ⟩ Press Ctrl + Home to move to the top of the document.

2 ⟩ On the **Insert tab**, in the **Text group**, click **Text Box**. At the bottom of the gallery, click **Draw Text Box**.

3 ⟩ Position the ⊞ pointer over the first blank paragraph—aligned with the left margin and at approximately 1 inch on the vertical ruler. Drag down and to the right to create a text box approximately **1.5 inches** high and **4 inches** wide—the exact size and location need not be precise.

4 ⟩ With the insertion point blinking in the text box, type the following, pressing Enter after each of the first *two* lines to create a new paragraph:

Interviews will be held:
Friday and Saturday, January 14 and 15
In the Career Services Conference Room

5 ⟩ Compare your screen with Figure 1.20, and then **Save** 🖫 your document.

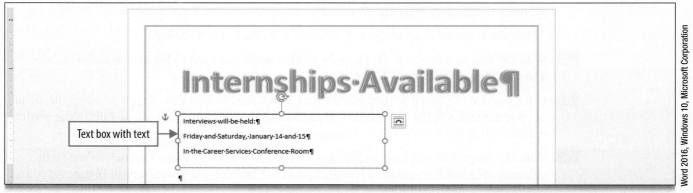

Internships·Available¶

Text box with text →

Interviews·will·be·held:¶

Friday·and·Saturday,·January·14·and·15¶

In·the·Career·Services·Conference·Room¶

¶

Word 2016, Windows 10, Microsoft Corporation

FIGURE 1.20

MOS

5.2.4

Activity 1.14 | Sizing and Positioning a Text Box and Formatting a Text Box Using Shape Styles

1 ▶ Point to the text box border to display the 🔁 pointer. In the space below the *Internships Available* title, by dragging, move the text box until a horizontal green alignment guide displays above the first blank paragraph mark and a vertical green alignment guide displays in the center of the page, as shown in Figure 1.21. If the alignment guides do not display, drag the text box to position it approximately as shown in the Figure.

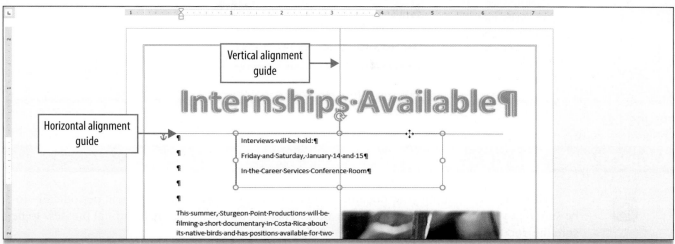

Word 2016, Windows 10, Microsoft Corporation

FIGURE 1.21

2 ▶ To place the text box precisely, on the **Format tab**, in the **Arrange group**, click **Position**, and then click **More Layout Options**.

3 ▶ In the **Layout** dialog box, under **Horizontal**, click **Alignment**. To the right of **Alignment**, click the **arrow**, and then click **Centered**. To the right of **relative to**, click the **arrow**, and then click **Page**.

4 ▶ Under **Vertical**, click in the **Absolute position** box, select the existing number, and then type **1.25** To the right of **below**, click the **arrow**, and then click **Margin**.

5 ▶ In the **Layout** dialog box, click the **Size tab**. Under **Height**, select the number in the **Absolute** box. Type **1.25** and then under **Width**, select the number in the **Absolute** box. Type **4** and then click **OK**.

> The text box is sized correctly, centered horizontally, and the top edge is positioned 1.25 inches below the top margin of the document.

6 ▶ On the ribbon, under **Drawing Tools**, click the **Format tab**. In the **Shape Styles group**, click **More** ⏷, and then in the first row, click the third style—**Colored Outline – Orange, Accent 2**.

7 ▶ On the **Format tab**, in the **Shape Styles group**, click **Shape Effects**. Point to **Shadow**, and then under **Outer**, in the first row, click the first effect—**Offset Diagonal Bottom Right**.

8 ▶ Click in the text box, and then press Ctrl + A to select all of the text. Right-click over the selected text to display the mini toolbar, change the **Font Size** to **16** and apply **Bold** B . Press Ctrl + E to center the text.

> Ctrl + E is the keyboard shortcut to center text in a document or object.

9 ▶ Click anywhere in the document to deselect the text box. Compare your screen with Figure 1.22, and then **Save** 💾 your document.

Text formatted and centered, text box sized and positioned, Shape Style and Shadow effect applied

Interviews·will·be·held:¶

Friday·and·Saturday,·January·14·and·15¶

In·the·Career·Services·Conference·Room¶

This·summer,·Sturgeon·Point·Productions·will·be·

FIGURE 1.22

Objective 4 | Preview and Print a Document

GO! Learn How
Video W1-4

While you are creating your document, it is useful to preview your document periodically to be sure that you are getting the result you want. Then, before printing, make a final preview to be sure the document layout is what you intended.

1.3.4

Activity 1.15 | Adding a File Name to the Footer by Inserting a Field

Information in headers and footers helps to identify a document when it is printed or displayed electronically. Recall that a header is information that prints at the top of every page; a footer is information that prints at the bottom of every page. In this textbook, you will insert the file name in the footer of every Word document.

1 Click the **Insert tab**, and then in the **Header & Footer group**, click **Footer**.

2 At the bottom of the gallery, click **Edit Footer**.

The footer area displays with the insertion point blinking at the left edge, and on the ribbon, the Header & Footer Tools display.

ANOTHER WAY At the bottom edge of the page, right-click; from the shortcut menu, click Edit Footer.

3 On the ribbon, under the **Header & Footer Tools**, on the **Design tab**, in the **Insert group**, click **Document Info**, and then click **File Name**. Compare your screen with Figure 1.23.

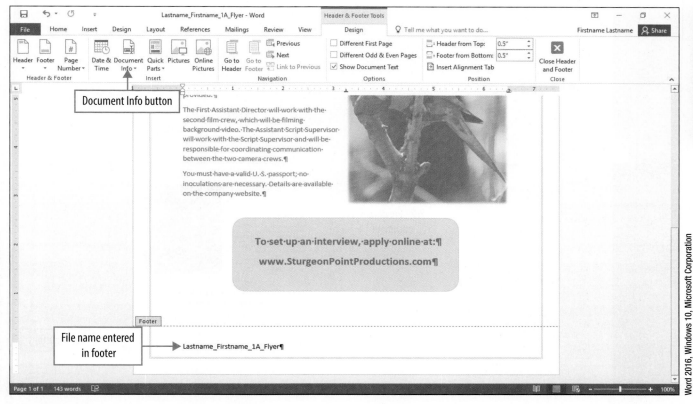

FIGURE 1.23

4 On the **Design tab**, click **Close Header and Footer**, and then **Save** 🖫 your document.

When the body of the document is active, the footer text is dimmed—it displays in gray. Conversely, when the footer area is active, the footer text is not dimmed; instead, the document text is dimmed.

🔄 **ANOTHER WAY**   Double-click in the document outside of the footer area to close the footer and return to the document.

MOS
1.4.5, 1.5.3

Activity 1.16 | Adding Document Properties and Previewing and Printing a Document

1 Press Ctrl + Home to move the insertion point to the top of the document. In the upper left corner of your screen, click the **File tab** to display **Backstage** view. On the right, at the bottom of the **Properties** list, click **Show All Properties**.

2 On the list of **Properties**, click to the right of **Tags** to display an empty box, and then type **internship, documentary**

3 Click to the right of **Subject** to display an empty box, and then type your course name and section number. Under **Related People**, be sure that your name displays as the author. If necessary, right-click the author name, click Edit Property, type your name, and click OK.

4 On the left, click **Print** to display the **Print Preview**. Compare your screen with Figure 1.24.

Here you can select any printer connected to your system and adjust the settings related to how you want to print. On the right, Print Preview displays your document exactly as it will print; the formatting marks do not display. At the bottom of the Print Preview area, in the center, the number of pages and arrows with which you can move among the pages in Print Preview displays. On the right, Zoom settings enable you to shrink or enlarge the Print Preview.

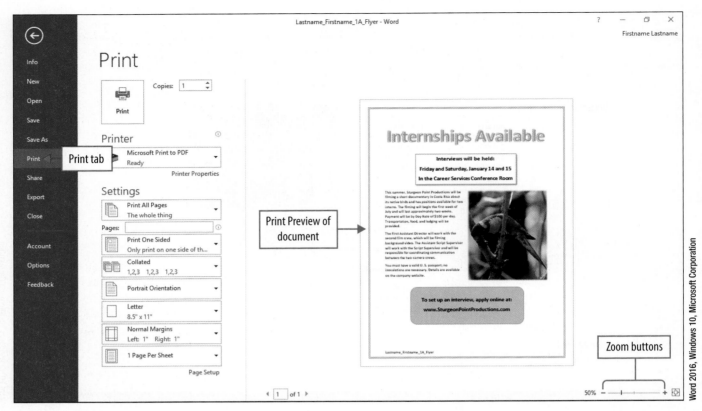

FIGURE 1.24

5 In the lower right corner of the window, click **Zoom In** several times to view the document at a larger size, and notice that a larger preview is easier to read. Click **Zoom to Page** 🖽 to view the entire page.

6 If you want to print your document on paper using the default printer on your system, in the upper left portion of the screen, click **Print**.

   The document will print on your default printer; if you do not have a color printer, colors will print in shades of gray. Backstage view closes and your file redisplays in the Word window.

7 **Save** 🖫 your document. In the upper right corner of the Word window, click **Close** ⊠. If directed by your instructor to do so, submit your paper printout, your electronic image of your document that looks like a printed document, or your completed Word file.

> **END | You have completed Project 1A**

GO! With Google

Objective | Create a Flyer Using Google Docs

A L E R T ! | **Working with Web-Based Applications and Services**

Computer programs and services on the web receive continuous updates and improvements, so the steps to complete this web-based activity may differ from the ones shown. You can often look at the screens and the information presented to determine how to complete the activity.

If you do not already have a Google account, you will need to create one before you begin this activity. Go to http://google.com and, in the upper right corner, click Sign In. On the Sign In screen, click Create Account. On the Create your Google Account page, complete the form, read and agree to the Terms of Service and Privacy Policy, and then click Next step. On the Welcome screen, click Get Started.

Build from Scratch

Activity | Creating a Flyer

In this Activity, you will use Google Docs to create a flyer.

1 From the desktop, open your browser, navigate to http://google.com, and then sign in to your Google account. In the upper right corner of your screen, click **Google Apps** and then click **Drive**.

2 To create a folder in which to store your web projects, click **NEW**, and then click **Folder**. In the **New folder** box, type **GO! Web Projects** and then click **Create** to create a folder on your Google drive. Double-click your **GO! Web Projects** folder to open it.

3 In the left pane, click **NEW**, and then click **Google Docs** to open a new tab in your browser and to start an Untitled document. At the top of the window, click **Untitled document** and then, using your own name as the file name, type **Lastname_Firstname_1A_Google_Doc** and then press Enter to change the file name.

4 To the right of the file name, point to the small file folder to display the ScreenTip **Move to folder**. Click the file folder and notice that your file is saved in the GO! Web Projects folder. Compare your screen with Figure A.

5 Click in your document to close the Move to folder dialog box and to position the insertion point at the top of the document. Type **Internships Available** and then press Enter two times. Type **Interviews will be held Friday and Saturday, January 14 and 15 in the Career Services Conference Room.**

6 Press Ctrl + A to select all of the text. Click the **Font size arrow**, and then click **24**. With the text still selected, click **Center**.

7 Press Ctrl + End to move to the end of the document, and then press Enter. Click **Insert**, and then click **Image**. With **Upload** selected, click **Choose an image to upload**. Navigate to your student data files, click **w01A_Bird**, and then click **Open** to insert the picture.

8 Click the picture to select it, and then point to the square sizing handle at the upper left corner of the picture. Drag down and to the right until the sizing handle aligns with approximately **3 inches on the ruler**.

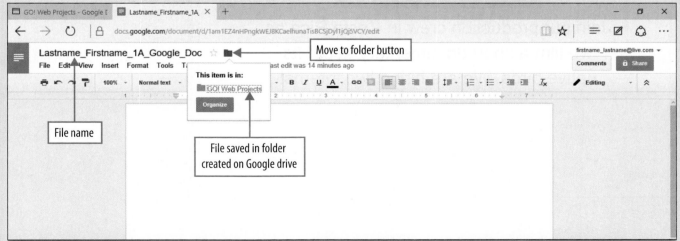

FIGURE A

(GO! With Google continues on the next page)

9 Click to the right of the picture and then press Enter twice. Type **Join our production crew in Costa Rica as we film a short documentary about its native birds. We are hiring two interns!**

10 Select the title **Internships Available** and then click **Text color** 🔲. In the third column, click the sixth color—**dark orange 1**, and then apply **Bold** 🔲. Your document will look similar to Figure B.

11 Your document will be saved automatically. Sign out of your Google account. Submit as instructed by your instructor.

Internships Available

Interviews will be held Friday and Saturday, January 14 and 15 in the Career Services Conference Room.

Join our production crew in Costa Rica as we film a short documentary about its native birds. We are hiring two interns!

FIGURE B

Information Handout

PROJECT ACTIVITIES

In Activities 1.17 through 1.29, you will format an information handout from Sturgeon Point Productions that describes internships available to students. Your completed document will look similar to Figure 1.25.

PROJECT FILES

MyITLab grader

If your instructor wants you to submit Project 1B in the MyITLab Grader system, log in to MyITLab, locate Grader Project 1B, and then download the files for this project.

For Project 1B, you will need the following file:
w01B_Programs

You will save your document as:
Lastname_Firstname_1B_Programs

Please always review the downloaded Grader instructions before beginning.

PROJECT RESULTS

GO!
Walk Thru
Project 1B

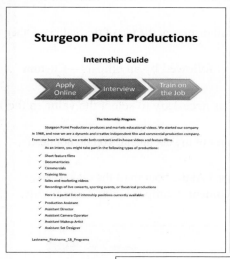

Word 2016, Windows 10, Microsoft Corporation

FIGURE 1.25 Project 1B Information Handout

Objective 5 | Change Document and Paragraph Layout

GO! Learn How
Video W1-5

Document layout includes *margins*—the space between the text and the top, bottom, left, and right edges of the paper. Paragraph layout includes line spacing, indents, and tabs. In Word, the information about paragraph formats is stored in the paragraph mark at the end of a paragraph. When you press Enter, the new paragraph mark contains the formatting of the previous paragraph, unless you take steps to change it.

1.3.1

Activity 1.17 | Setting Margins

> **ALERT!** **To submit as an autograded project, log into MyITLab and download the files for this project, and begin with those files instead of w01B_Programs.**

1 Start Word, and then click **Open Other Documents**. Navigate to the student files that accompany this textbook, and then open the document **w01B_Programs**. On the **Home tab**, in the **Paragraph group**, be sure **Show/Hide** ¶ is active so that you can view the formatting marks.

2 Click the **File tab**, and then click **Save As**. Navigate to your **Word Chapter 1** folder, and then using your own name, **Save** the document as **Lastname_Firstname_1B_Programs**

3 Click the **Layout tab**. In the **Page Setup group**, click **Margins**, and then take a moment to study the settings in the Margins gallery.

> If you have recently used custom margins settings, they will display at the top of this gallery. Other commonly used settings also display.

4 At the bottom of the **Margins** gallery, click the command followed by an ellipsis—**Custom Margins** to display the **Page Setup** dialog box.

5 In the **Page Setup** dialog box, under **Margins**, press Tab as necessary to select the value in the **Left** box, and then, with *1.25"* selected, type **1**

> This action will change the left margin to 1 inch on all pages of the document. You do not need to type the inch (") mark.

6 Press Tab to select the margin in the **Right** box, and then type **1** At the bottom of the dialog box, notice that the new margins will apply to the **Whole document**. Compare your screen with Figure 1.26.

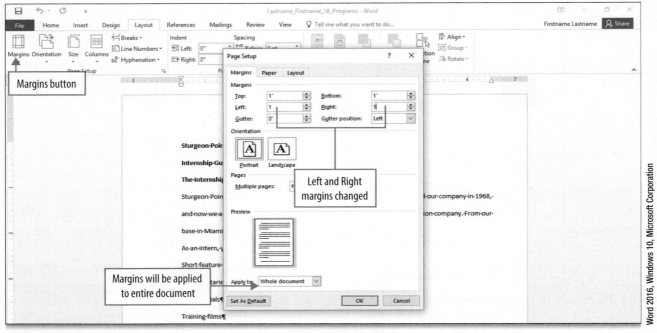

FIGURE 1.26

Word 2016, Windows 10, Microsoft Corporation

7 Click **OK** to apply the new margins and close the dialog box. If the ruler below the ribbon is not displayed, on the View tab, in the Show group, select the Ruler check box.

8 Scroll to position the bottom of **Page 1** and the top of **Page 2** on your screen. Notice that the page edges display, and the page number and total number of pages display on the left side of the status bar.

9 Near the bottom edge of **Page 1**, point anywhere in the bottom margin area, right-click, and then click **Edit Footer** to display the footer area.

10 On the ribbon, under the **Header & Footer Tools**, on the **Design tab**, in the **Insert group**, click **Document Info**, and then click **File Name**.

11 Double-click anywhere in the document to close the footer area, and then **Save** 🖫 your document.

Activity 1.18 | Aligning Paragraphs

Alignment refers to the placement of paragraph text relative to the left and right margins. Most paragraph text uses *left alignment*—aligned at the left margin, leaving the right margin uneven. Three other types of paragraph alignment are: *center alignment*—centered between the left and right margins; *right alignment*—aligned at the right margin with an uneven left margin; and *justified alignment*—text aligned evenly at both the left and right margins. The table in Figure 1.27 shows examples of these alignment types.

TYPES OF PARAGRAPH ALIGNMENT		
ALIGNMENT	**BUTTON**	**DESCRIPTION AND EXAMPLE**
Align Left	☰	Align Left is the default paragraph alignment in Word. Text in the paragraph aligns at the left margin, and the right margin is uneven.
Center	☰	Center alignment aligns text in the paragraph so that it is centered between the left and right margins.
Align Right	☰	Align Right aligns text at the right margin. Using Align Right, the left margin, which is normally even, is uneven.
Justify	☰	The Justify alignment option adds additional space between words so that both the left and right margins are even. Justify is often used when formatting newspaper-style columns.

Word 2016, Windows 10, Microsoft Corporation

FIGURE 1.27

1 Scroll to position the middle of **Page 2** on your screen, look at the left and right margins, and notice that the text is justified—both the right and left margins of multiple-line paragraphs are aligned evenly at the margins. On the **Home tab**, in the **Paragraph group**, notice that **Justify** ☰ is active.

> To achieve a justified right margin, Word adjusts the size of spaces between words, which can result in unattractive spacing in a document that spans the width of a page. Many individuals find such spacing difficult to read.

2 Press Ctrl + A to select all of the text in the document, and then on the **Home tab**, in the **Paragraph group**, click **Align Left** ☰.

🔄 **ANOTHER WAY**   On the Home tab, in the Editing group, click Select, and then click Select All.

3 Press Ctrl + Home to move to the beginning of the document. In the left margin area, point to the left of the first paragraph—*Sturgeon Point Productions*—until the 🔾 pointer displays, and then click one time to select the paragraph.

> Use this technique to select entire lines of text.

4 On the mini toolbar, in the **Font Size** box, select the existing number, type **40** and then press Enter.

Use this technique to change the font size to a size that is not available on the Font Size list.

5 Select the second paragraph—*Internship Guide*—and then on the mini toolbar, change the **Font Size** to **26 pt**. Point to the left of the first paragraph—*Sturgeon Point Productions*—to display the pointer again, and then drag down to select the first two paragraphs, which form the title and subtitle of the document.

6 On the **Home tab**, in the **Paragraph group**, click **Center** to center the title and subtitle between the left and right margins, and then compare your screen with Figure 1.28.

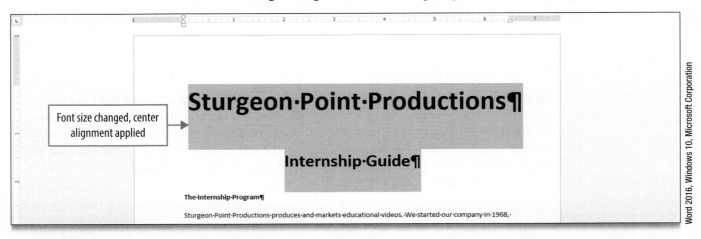

Font size changed, center alignment applied

Sturgeon·Point·Productions¶

Internship·Guide¶

The·Internship·Program¶

Sturgeon·Point·Productions·produces·and·markets·educational·videos.·We·started·our·company·in·1968,·

FIGURE 1.28

7 Near the top of **Page 1**, locate the first bold subheading—*The Internship Program*. Point to the left of the paragraph to display the pointer, and then click one time to select the text.

8 With *The Internship Program* selected, use your mouse wheel or the vertical scroll bar to bring the bottom portion of **Page 1** into view. Locate the subheading *Requirements*. Move the pointer to the left of the paragraph to display the pointer, hold down Ctrl, and then click one time. Release Ctrl, and then scroll to the middle of **Page 2**. Use the same technique to select the third subheading—*Introduction to Upcoming Internships*.

Three subheadings are selected; in Windows-based programs, you can hold down Ctrl to select multiple items.

9 Click **Center** to center all three subheadings, and then click **Save**.

2.2.3

Activity 1.19 | Setting Line Spacing

Line spacing is the distance between lines of text in a paragraph. Three of the most commonly used line spacing options are shown in the table in Figure 1.29.

LINE SPACING OPTIONS	
ALIGNMENT	**DESCRIPTION, EXAMPLE, AND INFORMATION**
Single spacing	**This text in this example uses single spacing**. Single spacing was once the most commonly used spacing in business documents. Now, because so many documents are read on a computer screen rather than on paper, single spacing is becoming less popular.
Multiple 1.08 spacing	**This text in this example uses multiple 1.08 spacing**. The default line spacing in Microsoft Word 2016 is 1.08, which is slightly more than single spacing to make the text easier to read on a computer screen. Many individuals now prefer this spacing, even on paper, because the lines of text appear less crowded.
Double spacing	**This text in this example uses double spacing**. College research papers and draft documents that need space for notes are commonly double-spaced; there is space for a full line of text between each document line.

FIGURE 1.29

1 Press Ctrl + Home to move to the beginning of the document. Press Ctrl + A to select all of the text in the document.

2 With all of the text in the document selected, on the **Home tab**, in the **Paragraph group**, click **Line and Paragraph Spacing** , and notice that the text in the document is double-spaced—**2.0** is checked. Compare your screen with Figure 1.30.

BY TOUCH   Tap the ribbon commands.

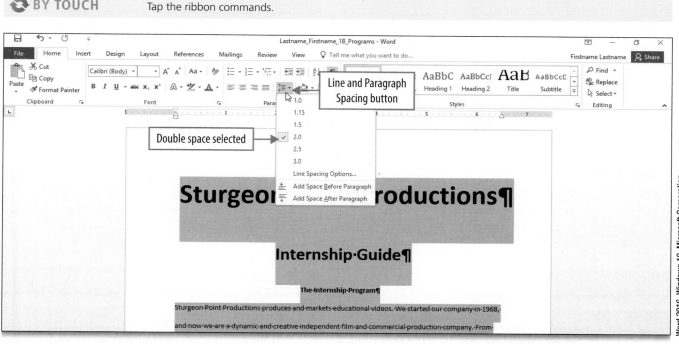

FIGURE 1.30

3 On the **Line Spacing** menu, click the *third* setting—**1.5**—and then click anywhere in the document to deselect the text. Compare your screen with Figure 1.31, and then **Save** your document.

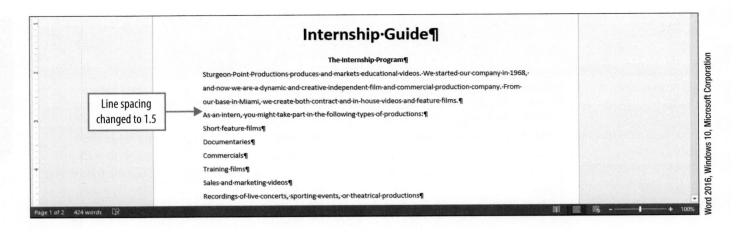

FIGURE 1.31

 MOS
2.2.3

Activity 1.20 | Indenting Text

Indenting the first line of each paragraph is a common technique to distinguish paragraphs.

1 Below the title and subtitle of the document, click anywhere in the paragraph that begins *Sturgeon Point Productions produces*.

2 On the **Home tab**, in the **Paragraph group**, click the **Dialog Box Launcher** ▣.

3 In the **Paragraph** dialog box, on the **Indents and Spacing tab**, under **Indentation**, click the **Special arrow**, and then click **First line** to indent the first line by 0.5", which is the default indent setting. Compare your screen with Figure 1.32.

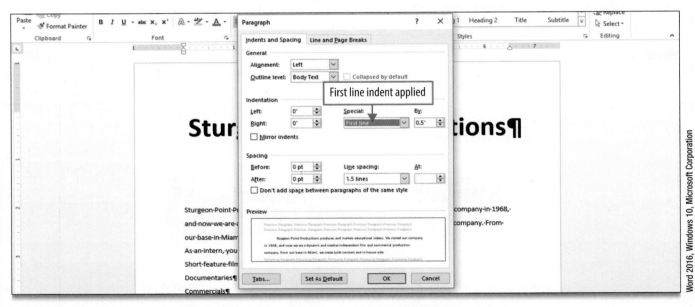

FIGURE 1.32

4 Click **OK**, and then click anywhere in the next paragraph, which begins *As an intern*. On the ruler under the ribbon, drag the **First Line Indent** marker ▽ to **0.5 inches on the horizontal ruler**, and then compare your screen with Figure 1.33.

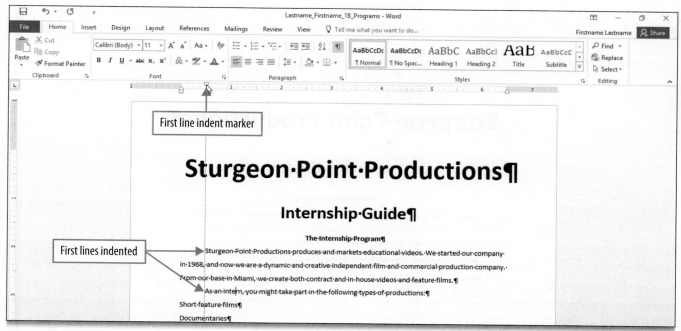

FIGURE 1.33

Word 2016, Windows 10, Microsoft Corporation

5 By using either of the techniques you just practiced, or by using the Format Painter, apply a first line indent of **0.5"** to the paragraph that begins *Here is a partial* to match the indent of the remaining paragraphs in the document.

6 **Save** 🖫 your document.

MOS
1.2.3

Activity 1.21 | Setting Space Before and After Paragraphs

Adding space after each paragraph is another technique to differentiate paragraphs.

1 Press Ctrl + A to select all of the text in the document. Click the **Layout tab**, and then in the **Paragraph group**, under **Spacing**, click the **After spin box up arrow** one time to change the value to **6 pt**.

> To change the value in the box, you can also select the existing number, type a new number, and then press Enter. This document will use 6 pt spacing after paragraphs to add space.

🔄 **ANOTHER WAY**   On either the Home tab or the Layout tab, display the Paragraph dialog box from the Paragraph group, and then under Spacing, click the spin box arrows as necessary.

2 Press Ctrl + Home, and then compare your screen with Figure 1.34.

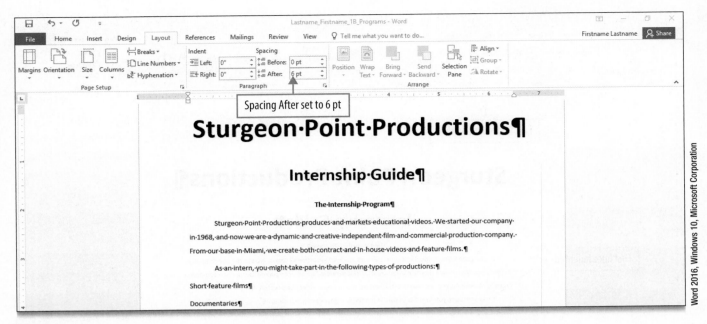

FIGURE 1.34

3 Near the top of **Page 1**, select the subheading **The Internship Program**, including the paragraph mark following it. Scroll down using the vertical scroll bar, hold down Ctrl, and then select the **Requirements** and **Introduction to Upcoming Internships** subheadings.

> **ALERT!** **Did your screen zoom when you were selecting?**
>
> Holding down Ctrl and using the mouse wheel at the same time will zoom your screen.

4 With all three subheadings selected, in the **Paragraph group**, under **Spacing**, click the **Before up spin box arrow** two times to set the **Spacing Before** to **12 pt**. Compare your screen with Figure 1.35, and then **Save** 🖫 your document.

This action increases the amount of space above each of the subheadings, which will make them easy to distinguish in the document. The formatting is applied only to the selected paragraphs.

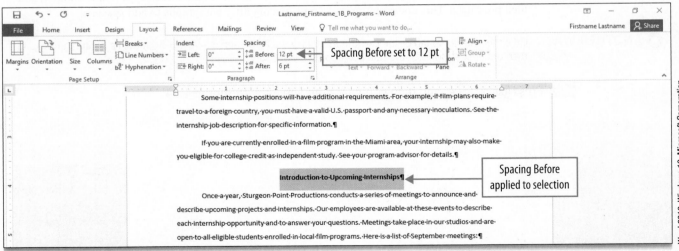

FIGURE 1.35

GO! Learn How
Video W1-6

To display a list of information, you can choose a **bulleted list**, which uses **bullets**—text symbols such as small circles or check marks—to introduce each item in a list. You can also choose a **numbered list**, which uses consecutive numbers or letters to introduce each item in a list.

Use a bulleted list if the items in the list can be introduced in any order; use a numbered list for items that have definite steps, a sequence of actions, or are in chronological order.

3.3.1

Activity 1.22 | Creating a Bulleted List

1 In the upper portion of **Page 1**, locate the paragraph *Short feature films*, and then point to this paragraph from the left margin area to display the pointer. Drag down to select this paragraph and the next five paragraphs—ending with the paragraph *Recordings of live concerts*.

2 On the **Home tab**, in the **Paragraph group**, click **Bullets** to change the selected text to a bulleted list.

> The 6 pt spacing between each of the bulleted points is removed and each bulleted item is automatically indented.

3 On the ruler, point to **First Line Indent** and read the ScreenTip, and then point to **Hanging Indent**. Compare your screen with Figure 1.36.

> By default, Word formats bulleted items with a first line indent of 0.25" and adds a Hanging Indent at 0.5". The hanging indent maintains the alignment of text when a bulleted item is more than one line.

> You can modify the list indentation by using Decrease Indent or Increase Indent. Decrease Indent moves your paragraph closer to the margin. Increase Indent moves your paragraph farther away from the margin.

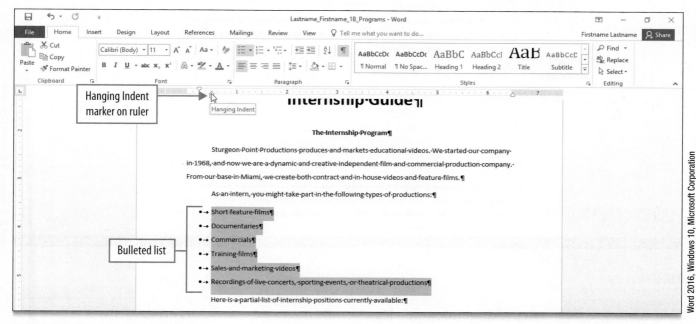

FIGURE 1.36

4 Scroll down slightly, and then by using the pointer from the left margin area, select the five internship positions, beginning with *Production Assistant* and ending with *Assistant Set Designer*. In the **Paragraph group**, click **Bullets** .

5 Scroll down to view **Page 2**. Apply bullets to all of the paragraphs that indicate the September meetings and meeting dates, beginning with *Technical* and ending with *Music*.

6 **Save** 🖫 your document.

MOS

3.3.1

Activity 1.23 | Creating a Numbered List

1 Under the subheading *Requirements*, in the paragraph that begins *The exact requirements*, click to position the insertion point at the *end* of the paragraph, following the colon. Press Enter to create a blank paragraph. Notice that the paragraph is indented because the First Line Indent from the previous paragraph carried over to the new paragraph.

2 To change the indent formatting for this paragraph, on the ruler, drag the **First Line Indent** marker ▽ to the left so that it is positioned directly above the lower button.

3 Being sure to include the period, type **1.** and press Spacebar. Compare your screen with Figure 1.37.

Word determines that this paragraph is the first item in a numbered list and formats the new paragraph accordingly, indenting the list in the same manner as the bulleted list. The space after the number changes to a tab, and the AutoCorrect Options button displays to the left of the list item. The tab is indicated by a right arrow formatting mark.

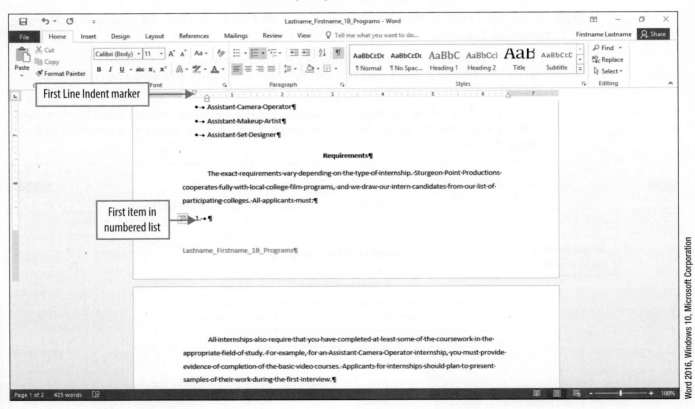

FIGURE 1.37

ALERT!	**Activating Automatic Numbered Lists**

If a numbered list does not begin automatically, click the File tab, and then click the Options tab. On the left side of the Word Options dialog box, click Proofing. Under AutoCorrect options, click the AutoCorrect Options button. In the AutoCorrect dialog box, click the AutoFormat As You Type tab. Under *Apply as you type*, select the *Automatic numbered lists* check box, and then click OK two times to close both dialog boxes.

4 Click **AutoCorrect Options** ⚡, and then compare your screen with Figure 1.38.

From the displayed list, you can remove the automatic formatting here, or stop using the automatic numbered lists option in this document. You also have the option to open the AutoCorrect dialog box to *Control AutoFormat Options*.

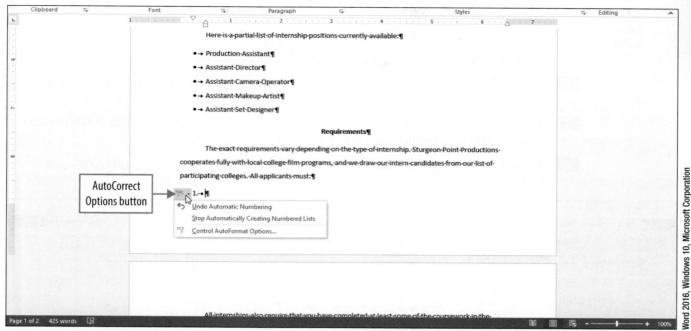

FIGURE 1.38

5 Click **AutoCorrect Options** ⚡ again to close the menu without selecting any of the commands. Type **Be enrolled in an accredited film program** and press Enter. Notice that the second number and a tab are added to the next line.

6 Type **Be available during the entire production schedule** and press Enter. Type **Submit two faculty recommendation letters** and then compare your screen with Figure 1.39. **Save** 💾 your document.

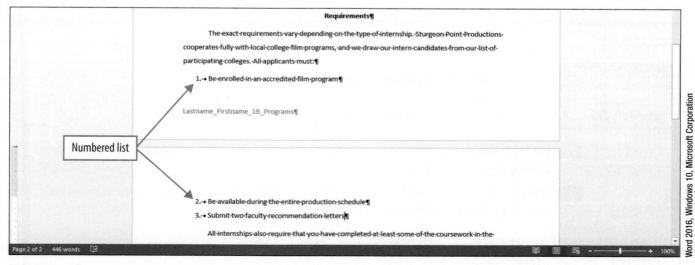

FIGURE 1.39

Activity 1.24 | Customizing Bullets

3.3.2

You can use any symbol from any font for your bullet characters.

1 Press Ctrl + End to move to the end of the document, and then scroll up as necessary to display the bulleted list containing the list of meetings.

2 Point to the left of the first list item to display the ↗ pointer, and then drag down to select all six meetings in the list—the bullet symbols are not selected.

3 On the mini toolbar, click the **Bullets button arrow** ≡▾ to display the Bullet Library, and then compare your screen with Figure 1.40.

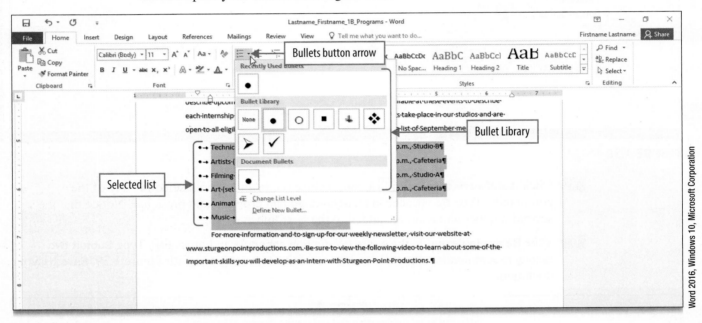

FIGURE 1.40

4 Under **Bullet Library**, click the **check mark** symbol. If the check mark is not available, choose another bullet symbol.

5 With the bulleted list still selected, right-click over the list, and then on the mini toolbar, double-click **Format Painter** ▾ to activate it for multiple use.

ANOTHER WAY   On the Home tab, in the Clipboard group, double-click Format Painter.

6 ▸ Use the vertical scroll bar or your mouse wheel to scroll to view **Page 1**. Move the pointer to the left of the first item in the first bulleted list to display the ⬜ pointer, and then drag down to select all six items in the list and to apply the format of the third bulleted list—the check mark bullets—to this list. Repeat this procedure to change the bullets in the second list to check marks. Press Esc to turn off **Format Painter**, and then **Save** ⬜ your document. Compare your screen with Figure 1.41.

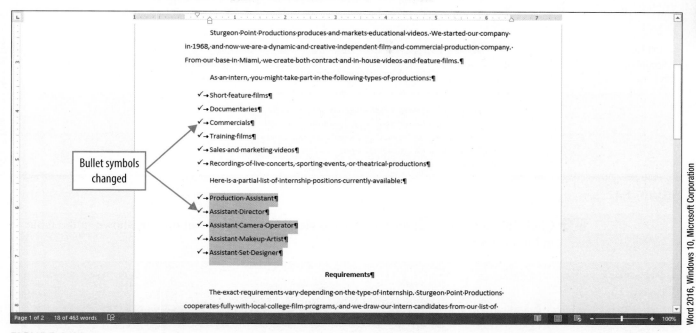

Word 2016, Windows 10, Microsoft Corporation

FIGURE 1.41

Objective 7 | Set and Modify Tab Stops

GO! Learn How
Video W1-7

Tab stops mark specific locations on a line of text. Use tab stops to indent and align text, and use the Tab key to move to tab stops.

Activity 1.25 | Setting Tab Stops

1 ▸ Scroll to view the lower portion of **Page 2**, and then by using the ⬜ pointer at the left of the first item, select all of the items in the bulleted list. Notice that there is a tab mark between the name of the meeting and the date.

The arrow that indicates a tab is a nonprinting formatting mark.

2 ▸ To the left of the horizontal ruler, point to **Tab Alignment** ⬜ to display the *Left Tab* ScreenTip, and then compare your screen with Figure 1.42.

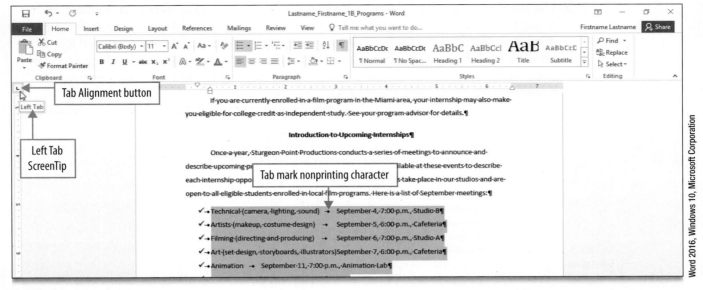

FIGURE 1.42

> **3** Click **Tab Alignment** [⌐] several times to view the tab alignment options shown in the table in Figure 1.43.

TAB ALIGNMENT OPTIONS

TYPE	TAB ALIGNMENT BUTTON DISPLAYS THIS MARKER	DESCRIPTION
Left	[⌐]	Text is left aligned at the tab stop and extends to the right.
Center	[⊥]	Text is centered around the tab stop.
Right	[⌐]	Text is right aligned at the tab stop and extends to the left.
Decimal	[⊥]	The decimal point aligns at the tab stop.
Bar	[⌐]	A vertical bar displays at the tab stop.
First Line Indent	[▽]	Text in the first line of a paragraph indents.
Hanging Indent	[⌂]	Text in all lines except the first line in the paragraph indents.

FIGURE 1.43

> **4** Display **Left Tab** [⌐]. Along the lower edge of the horizontal ruler, point to and then click at **3.5 inches on the horizontal ruler**. Notice that all of the dates left align at the new tab stop location, and the right edge of the column is uneven.

> **5** Compare your screen with Figure 1.44, and then **Save** [💾] your document.

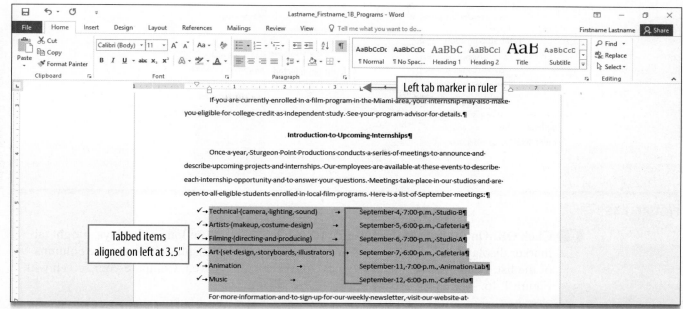

FIGURE 1.44

Activity 1.26 | Modifying Tab Stops

Tab stops are a form of paragraph formatting. Therefore, the information about tab stops is stored in the paragraph mark in the paragraphs to which they were applied.

1 With the bulleted list still selected, on the ruler, point to the new tab marker at *3.5 inches on the horizontal ruler*, and then when the *Left Tab* ScreenTip displays, drag the tab marker to **4 inches on the horizontal ruler**.

In all of the selected lines, the text at the tab stop left aligns at 4 inches.

2 On the ruler, point to the tab marker that you moved to display the *Left Tab* ScreenTip, and then double-click to display the **Tabs** dialog box.

ANOTHER WAY On the Home tab, in the Paragraph group, click the Dialog Box Launcher. At the bottom of the Paragraph dialog box, click the Tabs button.

3 In the **Tabs** dialog box, under **Tab stop position**, if necessary select *4"* and then type **6**

4 Under **Alignment**, click the **Right** option button. Under **Leader**, click the **2** option button. Near the bottom of the **Tabs** dialog box, click **Set**.

Because the Right tab will be used to align the items in the list, the tab stop at 4" is no longer necessary.

5 In the **Tabs** dialog box, in the **Tab stop position** box, click **4"** to select this tab stop, and then in the lower portion of the **Tabs** dialog box, click the **Clear** button to delete this tab stop, which is no longer necessary. Compare your screen with Figure 1.45.

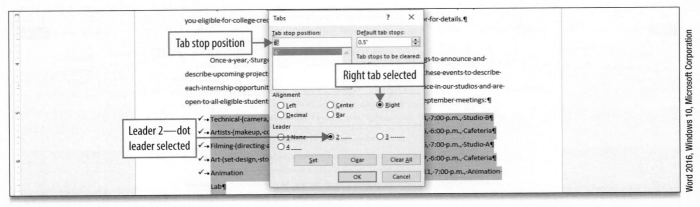

FIGURE 1.45

> **6** Click **OK**. On the ruler, notice that the left tab marker at *4"* no longer displays, a right tab marker displays at *6"*, and a series of dots—a ***dot leader***—displays between the columns of the list. Notice also that the right edge of the column is even. Compare your screen with Figure 1.46.

> A ***leader character*** creates a solid, dotted, or dashed line that fills the space to the left of a tab character and draws the reader's eyes across the page from one item to the next. When the character used for the leader is a dot, it is commonly referred to as a dot leader.

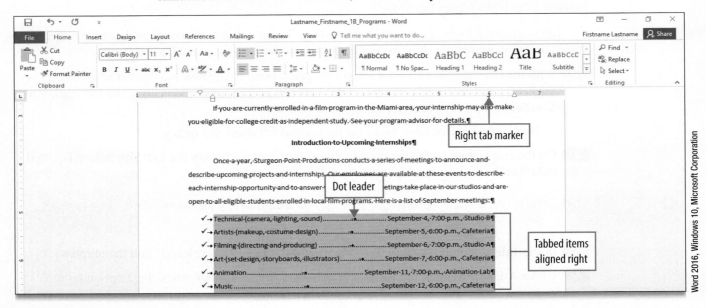

FIGURE 1.46

> **7** In the bulleted list that uses dot leaders, locate the *Art* meeting, and then click to position the insertion point at the end of that line, after the word *Cafeteria*. Press Enter to create a new blank bullet item.

> **8** Type **Video Editing** and press Tab. Notice that a dot leader fills the space to the tab marker location.

> **9** Type **September 10, 7:00 p.m., Cafeteria** and notice that the text moves to the left to maintain the right alignment of the tab stop.

> **10** **Save** 🖫 your document.

GO! Learn How
Video W1-8

SmartArt graphics are designer-quality visual representations of information, and Word provides many different layouts from which you can choose. You can also insert a link to an online video from a variety of online sources, thus enabling the reader to view the video when connected to the Internet. SmartArt graphics and videos can communicate your messages or ideas more effectively than plain text, and these objects add visual interest to a document or web page.

MOS

5.3.1

Activity 1.27 | Inserting a SmartArt Graphic

1 Press Ctrl + Home to move to the top of the document, and then click to the right of the subtitle *Internship Guide*.

2 Click the **Insert tab**, and then in the **Illustrations group**, point to **SmartArt** to display its ScreenTip. Read the ScreenTip, and then click **SmartArt**.

3 In the center portion of the **Choose a SmartArt Graphic** dialog box, scroll down and examine the numerous types of SmartArt graphics available.

4 On the left, click **Process**, and then by using the ScreenTips, locate and click **Basic Chevron Process**. Compare your screen with Figure 1.47.

At the right of the dialog box, a preview and description of the SmartArt displays.

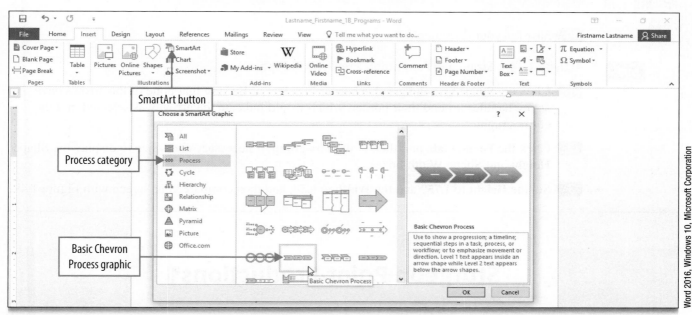

FIGURE 1.47

Word 2016, Windows 10, Microsoft Corporation

5 Click **OK** to insert the SmartArt graphic.

To the left of the inserted SmartArt graphic, the text pane may display. The text pane provides one method for entering text into your SmartArt graphic. If you choose not to use the text pane to enter text, you can close it.

6 On the ribbon, under **SmartArt Tools**, on the **Design tab**, in the **Create Graphic group**, notice the **Text Pane** button. If the text pane button is selected, click Text Pane to close the pane.

7 In the SmartArt graphic, in the first blue arrow, click **[Text]**, and notice that *[Text]* is replaced by a blinking insertion point.

The word *[Text]* is called *placeholder text*, which is nonprinting text that indicates where you can type.

8 ▸ Type **Apply Online**

9 ▸ Click the placeholder text in the middle arrow. Type **Interview** and then click the placeholder text in the third arrow. Type **Train on the Job** and then compare your screen with Figure 1.48.

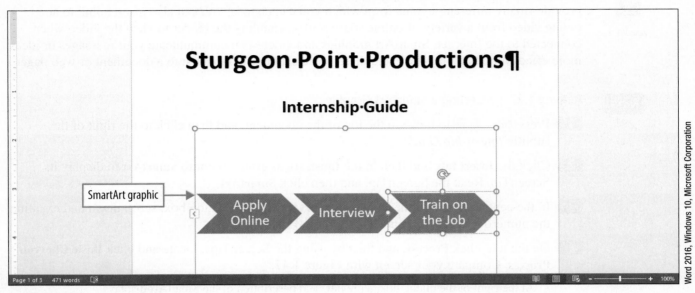

FIGURE 1.48

10 ▸ **Save** 🖫 your document.

MOS
5.3.2

Activity 1.28 | Sizing and Formatting a SmartArt Graphic

1 ▸ Click the **SmartArt solid graphic border** to select it. Be sure that none of the arrows have sizing handles around their border, which would indicate the arrow was selected, not the entire graphic.

2 ▸ Click the **Format tab**, and then in the **Size group**, if necessary click Size to display the Shape Height and Shape Width boxes.

3 ▸ Set the **Height** to **1.75"** and the **Width** to **6.5"**, and then compare your screen with Figure 1.49.

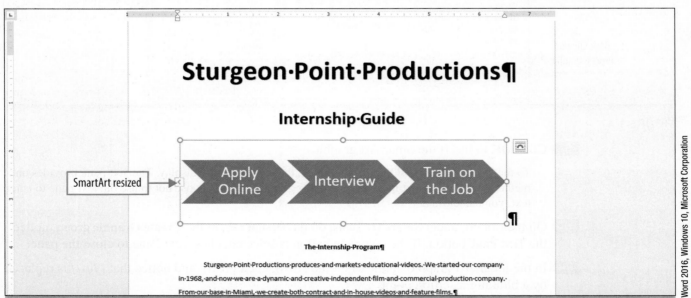

FIGURE 1.49

4 With the SmartArt graphic still selected, click the **SmartArt Tools Design tab**, and then in the **SmartArt Styles group**, click **Change Colors**. Under **Colorful**, click the fourth style—**Colorful Range - Accent Colors 4 to 5**.

5 On the **SmartArt Tools Design tab**, in the **SmartArt Styles group**, click **More** ⊽. Under **3-D**, click the second style—**Inset**. Click **Save** 🖫, and then compare your screen with Figure 1.50.

FIGURE 1.50

Activity 1.29 | Inserting an Online Video

Microsoft's research indicates that two-thirds of people who open Word documents never edit them; they only read them. So with more and more documents being read online—and not on paper—it makes sense that you may want to include videos in your Word documents.

1 Press Ctrl + End to move to the end of the document.

2 On the **Insert tab**, in the **Media group**, click **Online Video**.

Here you can search the web for an online video, search YouTube, or enter an *embed code* to insert a link to a video from a website. An embed code is a code that creates a link to a video, picture, or other type of *rich media* content. Rich media, also called *interactive media*, refers to computer interaction that responds to your actions; for example, by presenting text, graphics, animation, video, audio, or games.

3 In the **Bing Video Search** box, type **Go 1B Video** and then press Enter.

Several videos display based on the search term that you typed.

4 Point to several of the videos and notice that a ScreenTip displays a description of the video. Click one of the videos that includes the words *Go 1B Video* in the ScreenTip, and then click **Insert**. Compare your screen with Figure 1.51.

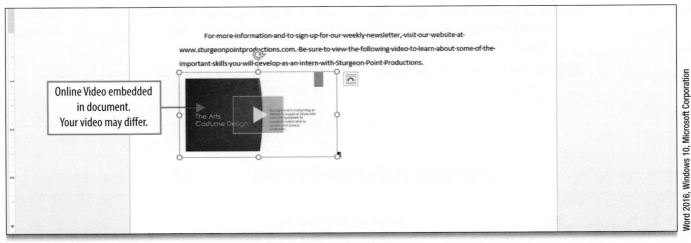

For·more·information·and·to·sign·up·for·our·weekly·newsletter,·visit·our·website·at·
www.sturgeonpointproductions.com.·Be·sure·to·view·the·following·video·to·learn·about·some·of·the·
important·skills·you·will·develop·as·an·intern·with·Sturgeon·Point·Productions.

Online Video embedded
in document.
Your video may differ.

The·Arts·
Costume·Design

Word 2016, Windows 10, Microsoft Corporation

FIGURE 1.51

ALERT! **Are you unable to locate or play the video?**

If you are unable to locate a video using the search words that you entered in Step 3, in the Bing Video Search box, type MyITLab and then insert the first video that displays. Depending upon your computer configuration, the video may not play.

---

5 On the **Picture Tools Format** tab, in the **Size** group, click in the **Height** box to select the value. Type **1.5** and then press Enter to change the size of the video.

6 Click **Save** 💾, and then press Ctrl + Home to move to the top of your document.

7 Click the **File tab**, and then in the lower right portion of the screen, click **Show All Properties**. In the **Tags** box, type **internship** and in the **Subject** box, type your course name and section number. In the **Author** box, replace the existing text with your first and last name.

8 On the left, click **Print** to display **Print Preview**. At the bottom of the preview, click the **Next Page** ▶ and **Previous Page** ◀ buttons to move between pages. If necessary, return to the document and make any necessary changes.

9 Save 💾 your document. In the upper right corner of the Word window, click **Close** ✕. If directed by your instructor to do so, submit your paper printout, your electronic image of your document that looks like a printed document, or your completed Word file.

END | You have completed Project 1B

GO! With Google

Objective | Create an Information Handout

ALERT! **Working with Web-Based Applications and Services**

Computer programs and services on the web receive continuous updates and improvements, so the steps to complete this web-based activity may differ from the ones shown. You can often look at the screens and the information presented to determine how to complete the activity.

If you do not already have a Google account, you will need to create one before you begin this activity. Go to http://google.com and, in the upper right corner, click Sign In. On the Sign In screen, click Create Account. On the Create your Google Account page, complete the form, read and agree to the Terms of Service and Privacy Policy, and then click Next step. On the Welcome screen, click Get Started.

Activity | Creating a Handout with Bulleted and Numbered Lists

In this Activity, you will use Google Docs to create an information handout.

1 From the desktop, open your browser, navigate to **http://google.com**, and then sign in to your Google account. In the upper right corner of your screen, click **Google Apps** ▦, and then click **Drive** △. Double-click your **GO! Web Projects** folder to open it. If you have not created this folder, refer to the instructions in the first Google Docs project in this chapter.

2 In the left pane, click **NEW**, and then click **Google Docs**. Click **File**, and then click **Open**. Click **Upload**, and then click **Select a file from your computer**. From your student data files, click **w01_1B_Web** and then click **Open** to open the file and upload it to your GO! Web Projects folder.

3 In the upper left corner of the Google Docs window, select **w01_1B_Web** and then type **Lastname_Firstname_1B_Google_Doc** and then press Enter to rename the file.

4 Press Ctrl + A to select all of the text. Click **Line spacing** ⬚▾, and then click **1.5**. Click **Left align** ▤.

5 Select the six lines of text beginning with *Short feature films* and ending with *Recording of live concerts*, and then click **Bulleted list** ⬚ to apply bullets to the selected text. Select the list of internship positions beginning with *Production Assistant* and ending with *Assistant Set Designer*, and then click **Bulleted list** ⬚. Compare your screen with Figure A.

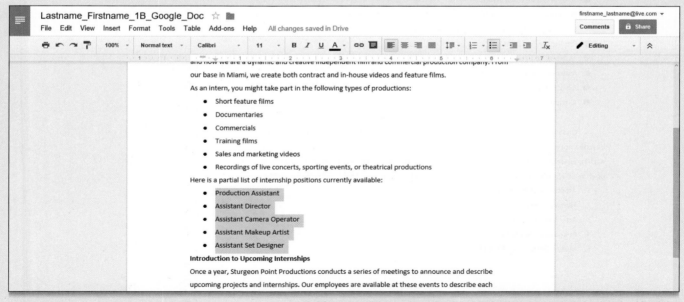

FIGURE A

(GO! With Google continues on the next page)

6 Select the last five lines of the document beginning with *Artists* and ending with *Music*. To create a numbered list from the selection, click **Numbered list** 📄.

7 Select the first three lines of text in the document, and then click **Center** ▤. Click in the *Introduction to Upcoming Internships* heading, and then click **Center** ▤.

8 Click at the beginning of the paragraph that begins *Sturgeon Point Production produces and markets*, and then press Tab. Look at the ruler and notice that the first line indent is applied.

9 With the insertion point in the same paragraph, double-click **Paint format** 🖌. Then, click in the paragraphs that begin *As an intern*, *Here is a partial list*, and *Once a year* to apply the first line indent to each of the paragraphs. Click **Paint format** 🖌 to turn it off. Compare your screen with Figure B.

10 Your document will be saved automatically. Sign out of your Google account, and then submit as instructed by your instructor.

Sturgeon Point Productions

Internship Guide

The Internship Program

Sturgeon Point Productions produces and markets educational videos. We started our company in 1968, and now we are a dynamic and creative independent film and commercial production company. From our base in Miami, we create both contract and in-house videos and feature films.

As an intern, you might take part in the following types of productions:

- Short feature films
- Documentaries
- Commercials
- Training films
- Sales and marketing videos
- Recordings of live concerts, sporting events, or theatrical productions

Here is a partial list of internship positions currently available:

- Production Assistant
- Assistant Director
- Assistant Camera Operator
- Assistant Makeup Artist
- Assistant Set Designer

Introduction to Upcoming Internships

Once a year, Sturgeon Point Productions conducts a series of meetings to announce and describe upcoming projects and internships. Our employees are available at these events to describe each internship opportunity and to answer your questions. Meetings take place in our studios and are open to all eligible students enrolled in local film programs. Here is a list of September meetings:

1. Artists—September 5, 6:00 p.m.
2. Filming—September 6, 7:00 p.m.
3. Art—September 7, 6:00 p.m.
4. Animation—September 11, 7:00 p.m.
5. Music—September 12, 6:00 p.m.

FIGURE B

GO! To Work

MICROSOFT OFFICE SPECIALIST (MOS) SKILLS IN THIS CHAPTER

PROJECT 1A	PROJECT 1B
1.1.1 Create a blank document	**1.3.1** Modify page setup
1.1.4 Insert text from a file or external source	**2.2.3** Set line and paragraph spacing and indentation
1.3.4 Insert headers and footers	**3.3.1** Create a numbered or bulleted list
1.4.5 Add document properties	**3.3.2** Change bullet characters or number formats for a list level
1.4.6 Show or hide formatting symbols	
1.5.3 Print all or part of a document	**5.3.1** Create a SmartArt graphic
5.1.1 Insert shapes	**5.3.2** Format a SmartArt graphic
5.1.2 Insert pictures	**5.3.3** Modify SmartArt graphic content
5.1.4 Insert text boxes	
5.2.1 Apply artistic effects	
5.2.2 Apply picture effects	
5.2.4 Format objects	
5.2.6 Wrap text around objects	
5.2.7 Position objects	

BUILD YOUR E-PORTFOLIO

An E-Portfolio is a collection of evidence, stored electronically, that showcases what you have accomplished while completing your education. Collecting and then sharing your work products with potential employers reflects your academic and career goals. Your completed documents from the following projects are good examples to show what you have learned: 1G, 1K, and 1L.

GO! FOR JOB SUCCESS

Video: Personal Branding

Your instructor may assign this video to your class, and then ask you to think about, or discuss with your classmates, these questions:

FotolEdhar / Fotolia

> How do you suggest job seekers communicate their unique value—their personal brand—to potential employers online?

> What are the best ways to network online and offline?

> What are some of the biggest pitfalls in using social media to communicate a personal brand?

END OF CHAPTER

SUMMARY

In this chapter, you started Word and practiced navigating the Word window, and you entered, edited, and formatted text. You also inserted text from another Word file.

Graphics include pictures, shapes, and text boxes. In this chapter, you formatted objects by applying styles, effects, and text-wrapping options, and you sized and positioned objects on the page.

SmartArt graphics visually represent your ideas, and there are many SmartArt graphics from which to choose. You can also use online videos in your documents to provide visual information to the reader.

Word documents can be formatted to display your information attractively. You can add a page border, add bulleted and numbered lists, change margins and tabs, and modify paragraph and line spacing.

GO! LEARN IT ONLINE

Review the concepts, key terms, and MOS skills in this chapter by completing these online challenges, which you can find at **MyITLab**.

Matching and Multiple Choice: Answer matching and multiple choice questions to test what you learned in this chapter.

Lessons on the GO!: Learn how to use all the new apps and features as they are introduced by Microsoft.

MOS Prep Quiz: Answer questions to review the MOS skills that you practiced in this chapter.

GO! COLLABORATIVE TEAM PROJECT (Available in **MyITLab** and Instructor Resource Center)

If your instructor assigns this project to your class, you can expect to work with one or more of your classmates—either in person or by using Internet tools—to create work products similar to those that you created in this chapter. A team is a group of workers who work together to solve a problem, make a decision, or create a work product. Collaboration is when you work together with others as a team in an intellectual endeavor to complete a shared task or achieve a shared goal.

Your instructor will assign Projects from this list to ensure your learning and assess your knowledge.

		Project Guide for Word Chapter 1	
Project	**Apply Skills from These Chapter Objectives**	**Project Type**	**Project Location**
1A **MyITLab**	Objectives 1-4 from Project 1A	**1A Instructional Project (Grader Project)** A guided review of the skills from Project.	In MyITLab and in text
1B **MyITLab**	Objectives 5-8 from Project 1B	**1B Instructional Project (Grader Project)** A guided review of the skills from Project.	In MyITLab and in text
1C	Objectives 1-4 from Project 1A	**1C Skills Review (Scorecard Grading)** A guided review of the skills from Project 2A.	In text
1D	Objectives 5-8 from Project 1B	**1D Skills Review (Scorecard Grading)** A guided review of the skills from Project 2B.	In text
1E **MyITLab**	Objectives 1-4 from Project 1A	**1E Mastery (Grader Project)** **Mastery and Transfer of Learning** A demonstration of your mastery of the skills in Project 2A with extensive decision making.	In MyITLab and in text
1F **MyITLab**	Objectives 5-8 from Project 1B	**1F Mastery (Grader Project)** **Mastery and Transfer of Learning** A demonstration of your mastery of the skills in Project 2B with extensive decision making.	In MyITLab and in text
1G **MyITLab**	Objectives 1-8 from Project 1A and 1B	**1G Mastery (Grader Project)** **Mastery and Transfer of Learning** A demonstration of your mastery of the skills in Projects 2A and 2B with extensive decision making.	In MyITLab and in text
1H	Combination of Objectives from Projects 1A and 1B	**1H GO! Fix It (Scorecard Grading)** **Critical Thinking** A demonstration of your mastery of the skills in Projects 1A and 1B by creating a correct result from a document that contains errors you must find.	Instructor Resource Center (IRC) and MyITLab
1I	Combination of Objectives from Projects 1A and 1B	**1I GO! Make It (Scorecard Grading)** **Critical Thinking** A demonstration of your mastery of the skills in Projects 1A and 1B by creating a result from a supplied picture.	IRC and MyITLab
1J	Combination of Objectives from Projects 1A and 1B	**1J GO! Solve It (Rubric Grading)** **Critical Thinking** A demonstration of your mastery of the skills in Projects 1A and 1B, your decision-making skills, and your critical thinking skills. A task-specific rubric helps you self-assess your result.	IRC and MyITLab
1K	Combination of Objectives from Projects 1A and 1B	**1K GO! Solve It (Rubric Grading)** **Critical Thinking** A demonstration of your mastery of the skills in Projects 1A and 1B, your decision-making skills, and your critical thinking skills. A task-specific rubric helps you self-assess your result.	In text
1L	Combination of Objectives from Projects 1A and 1B	**1L GO! Think (Rubric Grading)** **Critical Thinking** A demonstration of your understanding of the chapter concepts applied in a manner that you would outside of college. An analytic rubric helps you and your instructor grade the quality of your work by comparing it to the work an expert in the discipline would create.	In text
1M	Combination of Objectives from Projects 1A and 1B	**1M GO! Think (Rubric Grading)** **Critical Thinking** A demonstration of your understanding of the chapter concepts applied in a manner that you would outside of college. An analytic rubric helps you and your instructor grade the quality of your work by comparing it to the work an expert in the discipline would create.	IRC and MyITLab
1N	Combination of Objectives from Projects 1A and 1B	**1N You and GO! (Rubric Grading)** **Critical Thinking** A demonstration of your understanding of the chapter concepts applied in a manner that you would in a personal situation. An analytic rubric helps you and your instructor grade the quality of your work.	IRC and MyITLab
1O	Combination of Objectives from Projects 1A and 1B	**1O Collaborative Team Project for WORD Chapter 1** **Critical Thinking** A demonstration of your understanding of concepts and your ability to work collaboratively in a group role-playing assessment, requiring both collaboration and self-management.	IRC and MyITLab

GLOSSARY

GLOSSARY OF CHAPTER KEY TERMS

Alignment The placement of paragraph text relative to the left and right margins.

Alignment guide A green vertical or horizontal line that displays when you are moving or sizing an object to assist you with object placement.

Artistic effects Formats applied to images that make pictures resemble sketches or paintings.

Bulleted list A list of items with each item introduced by a symbol such as a small circle or check mark, and which is useful when the items in the list can be displayed in any order.

Bullets Text symbols such as small circles or check marks that precede each item in a bulleted list.

Center alignment The alignment of text or objects that is centered horizontally between the left and right margin.

Dot leader A series of dots preceding a tab that guides the eye across the line.

Drawing objects Graphic objects, such as shapes, diagrams, lines, or circles.

Embed code A code that creates a link to a video, picture, or other type of rich media content.

Floating object A graphic that can be moved independently of the surrounding text characters.

Formatting marks Characters that display on the screen, but do not print, indicating where the Enter key, the Spacebar, and the Tab key were pressed; also called nonprinting characters.

Graphics Pictures, charts, or drawing objects.

Inline object An object or graphic inserted in a document that acts like a character in a sentence.

Interactive media Computer interaction that responds to your actions; for example, by presenting text, graphics, animation, video, audio, or games. Also referred to as rich media.

Justified alignment An arrangement of text in which the text aligns evenly on both the left and right margins.

Layout Options Picture formatting options that control the manner in which text wraps around a picture or other object.

Leader character Characters that form a solid, dotted, or dashed line that fills the space preceding a tab stop.

Left alignment An arrangement of text in which the text aligns at the left margin, leaving the right margin uneven.

Line spacing The distance between lines of text in a paragraph.

Live Layout A feature that reflows text as you move or size an object so that you can view the placement of surrounding text.

Margins The space between the text and the top, bottom, left, and right edges of the paper.

Nonprinting characters Characters that display on the screen, but do not print; also called formatting marks.

Numbered list A list that uses consecutive numbers or letters to introduce each item in a list.

Object anchor The symbol that indicates to which paragraph an object is attached.

Picture effects Effects that enhance a picture, such as a shadow, glow, reflection, or 3-D rotation.

Picture styles Frames, shapes, shadows, borders, and other special effects that can be added to an image to create an overall visual style for the image.

Placeholder text Nonprinting text that holds a place in a document where you can type.

Rich media Computer interaction that responds to your actions; for example, by presenting text, graphics, animation, video, audio, or games. Also referred to as interactive media.

Right alignment An arrangement of text in which the text aligns at the right margin, leaving the left margin uneven.

Rotation handle A symbol with which you can rotate a graphic to any angle; displays above the top center sizing handle.

Shapes Lines, arrows, stars, banners, ovals, rectangles, and other basic shapes with which you can illustrate an idea, a process, or a workflow.

SmartArt A designer-quality visual representation of your information that you can create by choosing from among many different layouts to effectively communicate your message or ideas.

Spin box A small box with an upward- and downward-pointing arrow that lets you move rapidly through a set of values by clicking.

Tab stop A specific location on a line of text, marked on the Word ruler, to which you can move the insertion point by pressing the Tab key, and which is used to align and indent text.

Template A preformatted document that you can use as a starting point and then change to suit your needs.

Text box A movable resizable container for text or graphics.

Text effects Decorative formats, such as shadowed or mirrored text, text glow, 3-D effects, and colors that make text stand out.

Text wrapping The manner in which text displays around an object.

Toggle button A button that can be turned on by clicking it once, and then turned off by clicking it again.

Wordwrap The feature that moves text from the right edge of a paragraph to the beginning of the next line as necessary to fit within the margins.

Apply **1A skills** from these Objectives:

1 Create a New Document and Insert Text
2 Insert and Format Graphics
3 Insert and Modify Text Boxes and Shapes
4 Preview and Print a Document

Skills Review　Project 1C Photography

In the following Skills Review, you will create a flyer advertising a photography internship with Sturgeon Point Productions. Your completed document will look similar to Figure 1.52.

PROJECT FILES

For Project 1C, you will need the following files:

New blank Word document
w01C_Building
w01C_Photographer

You will save your document as:

Lastname_Firstname_1C_Photography

Build from Scratch

PROJECT RESULTS

Internship Available for Still Photographer

This position requires skill in the use of:

Professional full-frame DSLR cameras

Tilt-shift lenses for tall buildings

This fall, Sturgeon Point Productions will film a documentary on the historic architecture in and around Milwaukee, Wisconsin.

The filming will take place during the last two weeks of September. If the weather is not conducive to outdoor shooting, it is possible that filming will continue into the first week of October.

The still photographer will accompany the director during the first two weeks of September to scout locations and take photographs for the purpose of planning the filming schedule. The photographer will also accompany the film crew throughout filming.

Photographs taken during pre-production and filming will be used for advertising and marketing and published in an upcoming book on the history of the city of Milwaukee.

Submit Your Application by June 30!

Lastname_Firstname_1C_Photography

Word 2016, Windows 10, Microsoft Corporation

FIGURE 1.52

(Project 1C Photography continues on the next page)

1 Start Word and then click **Blank document**. On the **Home tab**, in the **Paragraph group**, if necessary, click Show/Hide to display the formatting marks. If the rulers do not display, click the View tab, and then in the Show group, select the Ruler check box.

a. Type **Internship Available for Still Photographer** and then press Enter two times. Type the following text: **This fall, Sturgeon Point Productions will film a documentary on the historic architecture in and around Milwaukee, Wisconsin.** Press Enter.

b. On the ribbon, click the **Insert tab**. In the **Text group**, click the **Object button arrow**, and then click **Text from File**. In the **Insert File** dialog box, navigate to the student files that accompany this chapter, locate and select **w01C_Photographer**, and then click **Insert**. Delete the blank paragraph at the end of the document.

c. Including the paragraph mark, select the first paragraph of text—*Internship Available for Still Photographer*. On the **Home tab**, in the **Font group**, click **Text Effects and Typography**. In the **Text Effects and Typography** gallery, in the first row, click the fourth effect—**Fill – White, Outline – Accent 5, Shadow**.

d. With the text still selected, in the **Font group**, click in the **Font Size** box to select the existing font size. Type **44** and then press Enter. In the **Font group**, click the **Font Color button arrow**. Under **Theme Colors**, in the fourth column, click the first color—**Blue-Gray, Text 2**.

e. With the text still selected, in the **Font group**, click **Text Effects and Typography**. Point to **Shadow**, and then under **Outer**, in the second row, click the third style—**Offset Left**. In the **Paragraph group**, click **Center**.

f. On the **Quick Access Toolbar**, click **Save**. Under **Save As**, click **Browse**. Navigate to your **Word Chapter 1** folder. In the **File name** box, replace the existing text with **Lastname_Firstname_1C_Photography** and then click **Save**.

2 In the paragraph that begins *The filming*, click to position the insertion point at the beginning of the paragraph. On the **Insert tab**, in the **Illustrations group**, click **Pictures**. In the **Insert Picture** dialog box, navigate to your student data files, locate and click **w01C_Building**, and then click **Insert**.

a. To the right of the selected picture, click the **Layout Options** button, and then under **With Text Wrapping**, click the first option—**Square**. **Close** the Layout Options.

b. On the **Format tab**, in the **Size group**, click in the **Shape Height** box to select the value, type **2.7** and then press Enter.

c. With the picture selected, on the **Format tab**, in the **Arrange group**, click **Position**, and then click **More Layout Options**. In the **Layout** dialog box, on the **Position tab**, in the middle of the dialog box under **Vertical**, click the **Alignment** option button. To the right of **Alignment**, click the arrow, and then click **Top**. To the right of **relative to**, click the arrow, and then click **Line**. Click **OK**.

d. On the **Format tab**, in the **Picture Styles group**, click **Picture Effects**. Point to **Soft Edges**, and then click **5 Point**. On the **Format tab**, in the **Adjust group**, click **Artistic Effects**. In the fourth row, click the third effect—**Crisscross Etching**.

e. Click anywhere outside the picture to deselect it. On the **Design tab**, in the **Page Background group**, click **Page Borders**. In the **Borders and Shading** dialog box, on the **Page Border tab**, under **Setting**, click **Box**. Under **Style**, scroll the list and then click the third style from the bottom—a black line that fades to gray.

f. Click the **Color arrow**, and then in the next to last column, click the first color—**Blue, Accent 5**. Under **Apply to**, be sure **Whole document** is selected, and then click **OK**. Click **Save**.

3 Click the **Insert tab**, and then in the **Illustrations group**, click **Shapes** to display the gallery. Under **Basic Shapes**, in the second row, click the fifth shape—**Frame**.

a. Position the ⊞ pointer anywhere in the blank area at the bottom of the document. Click one time to insert a 1" by 1" frame. The exact location need not be precise. To the right of the shape, click the **Layout Options** button, and at the bottom click **See more**.

b. In the **Layout** dialog box, under **Horizontal**, click the **Alignment** option button. To the right of **Alignment**, click the arrow, and then click **Centered**. To the right of **relative to**, click the arrow, and then click **Page**. Under **Vertical**, click the **Absolute**

(Project 1C Photography continues on the next page)

position option button. In the **Absolute position** box, select the existing number, and then type **1** To the right of **below**, click the arrow, and then click **Paragraph**. Click **OK**.

c. On the **Format tab**, click in the **Shape Height** box. Type **1.5** and then click in the **Shape Width** box. Type **5.5** and then press Enter.

d. If necessary, select the frame shape. On the **Format tab**, in the **Shape Styles group**, click **More** ⬇. In the **Shape Styles** gallery, in the first row, click the sixth style—**Colored Outline - Blue, Accent 5**. Type **Submit Your Application by June 30!** Select the text you just typed, and then on the mini toolbar, change the **Font Size** to **22**.

4 Click outside of the frame to deselect it, and then press Ctrl + Home to move to the top of the document. Press ↓ two times to move to the blank paragraph below the title. Press Enter four times to make space for a text box.

a. On the **Insert tab**, in the **Text group**, click **Text Box**. At the bottom of the gallery, click **Draw Text Box**. Position the ➕ pointer over the first blank paragraph at the left margin. Drag down and to the right to create a text box approximately 1.5 inches high and 4 inches wide—the exact size and location need not be precise.

b. With the insertion point blinking in the text box, type the following, pressing Enter after the first two lines to create a new paragraph:

This position requires skill in the use of:
Professional full-frame DSLR cameras
Tilt-shift lenses for tall buildings

c. To precisely place the text box, on the **Format tab**, in the **Arrange group**, click **Position**, and then click **More Layout Options**. In the **Layout** dialog box, under **Horizontal**, click the **Alignment** button. To the right of **Alignment**, click the arrow, and then click **Centered**. To the right of **relative to**, click the arrow, and then click **Page**.

d. Under **Vertical**, click the **Absolute position** button. In the **Absolute position** box, select the existing number. Type **2** To the right of **below**, click the arrow, and then click **Margin**.

e. In the **Layout** dialog box, click the **Size tab**. Under **Height**, select the number in the **Absolute** box. Type **1** and then under **Width**, select the number in the **Absolute** box. Type **3.75** and then click **OK**.

f. In the text box, select all of the text. If necessary, right-click over the selected text to display the mini toolbar. Change the **Font Size** to **12**, apply **Bold**, and then press Ctrl + E to **Center** the text.

g. On the **Format tab**, in the **Shape Styles group**, click **Shape Effects**. Point to **Shadow**, and then under **Outer**, in the first row, click the first style—**Offset Diagonal Bottom Right**.

h. In the **Shape Styles group**, click **Shape Outline**. In the fifth column, click the first color—**Blue, Accent 1** to change the color of the text box border. Click **Shape Fill**, and then in the fifth column, click the second color—**Blue, Accent 1, Lighter 80%**. Click **Save**.

5 Click the **Insert tab**, and then in the **Header & Footer group**, click **Footer**. At the bottom of the menu, click **Edit Footer**. On the **Header & Footer Tools Design tab**, in the **Insert group**, click **Document Info**, and then click **File Name**. Double-click in the document outside of the footer area to close the footer and return to the document.

a. Press Ctrl + Home to move the insertion point to the top of the document. In the upper left corner of your screen, click the **File tab** to display **Backstage** view. On the right, at the bottom of the **Properties list**, click **Show All Properties**.

b. On the list of Properties, click to the right of **Tags** to display an empty box, and then type **internship, documentary** Click to the right of **Subject** to display an empty box, and then type your course name and section #. Under **Related People**, be sure that your name displays as the author. If necessary, right-click the author name, click Edit Property, type your name, and click OK.

c. **Save** your document. In the upper right corner of the Word window, click **Close**. If directed by your instructor to do so, submit your paper printout, your electronic image of your document that looks like a printed document, or your completed Word file.

END | You have completed Project 1C

Skills Review   Project 1D Internship

In the following Skills Review, you will edit an information handout regarding production and development internships with Sturgeon Point Productions. Your completed document will look similar to Figure 1.53.

PROJECT FILES

For Project 1D, you will need the following file:

w01D_Internship

You will save your document as:

Lastname_Firstname_1D_Internship

PROJECT RESULTS

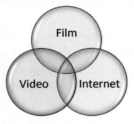

STURGEON POINT PRODUCTIONS

Sturgeon Point Productions is a full service film and video production facility located in Miami, Florida. Celebrating over 45 years of producing top quality commercial and independent film, our projects range from award winning documentaries and live action short features, to live concert and sporting events, to popular educational and training series of videos for schools, businesses, trade shows and multi-media presentations. We currently offer internships to film students in participating local colleges and universities, in both our development and production departments.

In-House Office Internships

Sturgeon Point Productions is looking for story analysts, research, post production and production assistants to work in our offices. We offer college credit as independent study at participating schools for one semester, which can be repeated for up to one year from the start date of the internship. To receive credit, interns must:

1. Be enrolled as a film major at a participating local college or university
2. Maintain a 3.0 GPA
3. Receive satisfactory monthly progress reports from their direct supervisor

Lastname_Firstname_1D_Internship

Following is a list of departments in our Miami office, currently seeking development and production interns:

✓ Development Department.. Researcher
✓ Development Department..................................Asst. to Producer
✓ Development Department..............................Writer's Assistant
✓ Post Production...Asst. Editor
✓ Post Production..Asst. Sound Editor
✓ Production...Asst. Office Manager

Additional Information

For more information and to sign up for our weekly newsletter, visit our website at www.sturgeonpointproductions.com. Be sure to view the following video to learn about some of the important skills you will develop as an intern with Sturgeon Point Productions.

Lastname_Firstname_1D_Internship

FIGURE 1.53

(Project 1D Internship continues on the next page)

1 Start Word, click **Open Other Documents**, and then click **Browse**. Navigate to your student files, and then open **w01D_Internship**. On the **Home tab**, in the **Paragraph group**, be sure **Show/Hide** is active. Click the **File tab**, and then click **Save As**. Navigate to your **Word Chapter 1** folder, and then **Save** the document as **Lastname_Firstname_1D_Internship**

a. Click the **Layout tab**. In the **Page Setup group**, click **Margins**, and then click **Custom Margins**. In the **Page Setup** dialog box, press Tab as necessary to select the value in the **Left** box. Type **1** and then press Tab to select the value in the **Right** box. Type **1** and then click **OK**.

b. Scroll down to view the bottom of **Page 1**, point anywhere in the bottom margin area, right-click, and then click **Edit Footer** to display the footer area. On the **Header & Footer Tools Design tab**, in the **Insert group**, click **Document Info**, and then click **File Name**. Double-click anywhere in the document to close the footer area.

c. Press Ctrl + A to select all of the text in the document, and then on the **Home tab**, in the **Paragraph group**, click **Align Left**.

d. Press Ctrl + Home. Select the document title, and then on the **Home tab**, in the **Paragraph group**, click **Center**.

e. Locate the first bold subheading—*In-House Office Internships*. Point to the left of the paragraph to display the 🔏 pointer, and then click one time to select the text. With *In-House Office Internships* selected, locate the subheading *Additional Information*. Move the pointer to the left of the paragraph to display the 🔏 pointer, hold down Ctrl, and then click one time to select both paragraphs. In the **Paragraph group**, click **Center**.

f. Press Ctrl + A to select all of the text in the document. On the **Home tab**, in the **Paragraph group**, click **Line and Paragraph Spacing**, and then click **1.5**.

2 Below the title of the document, click anywhere in the paragraph that begins *Sturgeon Point Productions is a full service*. On the **Home tab**, in the **Paragraph group**, click the **Dialog Box Launcher**.

a. In the **Paragraph** dialog box, on the **Indents and Spacing tab**, under **Indentation**, click the **Special**

arrow, and then click **First line** to indent the first line by 0.5". Click **OK**, and then click anywhere in the paragraph that begins *Sturgeon Point Productions is looking for*. On the ruler under the ribbon, drag the **First Line Indent** marker to **0.5 inches on the horizontal ruler**.

b. Press Ctrl + A to select all of the text in the document. Click the **Layout tab**, and then in the **Paragraph group**, under **Spacing**, click the **After spin box up arrow** one time to change the value to **6 pt**.

c. Select the subheading **In-House Office Internships**, including the paragraph mark following it. Scroll down, hold down Ctrl, and then select the subheading **Additional Information**. With both subheadings selected, in the **Paragraph group**, under **Spacing**, click the **Before up spin box arrow** two times to set the **Spacing Before** to **12 pt**. **Save** your document.

3 Locate the first paragraph that begins *Development Department*, and then point to this paragraph from the left margin area to display the 🔏 pointer. Drag down to select this paragraph and the next five paragraphs so that six paragraphs are selected. On the **Home tab**, in the **Paragraph group**, click **Bullets** to change the selected text to a bulleted list.

a. Under the subheading *In-House Office Internships*, in the paragraph that begins *Sturgeon Point Productions is looking*, click to position the insertion point at the *end* of the paragraph, following the colon. Press Enter to create a blank paragraph. On the ruler, drag the **First Line Indent** marker to the left so that it is positioned directly above the lower button. Being sure to include the period, type **1.** and then press Spacebar to create the first item in a numbered list.

b. Type **Be enrolled as a film major at a participating local college or university** and then press Enter. Type **Maintain a 3.0 GPA** and then press Enter. Type **Receive satisfactory monthly progress reports from their direct supervisor**

c. Scroll down to view the bulleted list of departments, and then select all six bulleted items in the list. On the mini toolbar, click the **Bullets button arrow**, and then under **Bullet Library**, click the **check mark** symbol. If the check mark is not available, choose another bullet symbol.

(Project 1D Internship continues on the next page)

4 ▶ With the list selected, move the pointer to the horizontal ruler, and then point to and click at **3.5 inches on the horizontal ruler** to align the job titles at the tab mark.

a. With the bulleted list still selected, on the ruler, point to the new tab marker at **3.5 inches on the horizontal ruler**, and then when the *Left Tab* ScreenTip displays, drag the tab marker to **4 inches on the horizontal ruler**.

b. On the ruler, point to the tab marker that you moved to display the *Left Tab* ScreenTip, and then double-click to display the **Tabs** dialog box.

c. In the **Tabs** dialog box, under **Tab stop position**, if necessary select *4″*, and then type **6** Under **Alignment**, click the **Right** option button. Under **Leader**, click the **2** option button. Near the bottom of the **Tabs** dialog box, click **Set**.

d. Under **Tab stop position**, select **4″**, and then click **Clear** to delete the tab stop. Click **OK**. **Save** your document.

5 ▶ Press Ctrl + Home to move to the top of the document, and then in the title, click to the right of the *S* in *PRODUCTIONS*.

a. Click the **Insert tab**, and then in the **Illustrations group**, click **SmartArt**. On the left, click **Relationship**, and then scroll the list to the bottom. Locate and then click **Basic Venn**. Click **OK** to insert the SmartArt graphic. If necessary, close the Text Pane.

b. In the SmartArt graphic, click **[Text]** in the top circle shape. Type **Film** and then in the lower left shape, click the placeholder **[Text]**. Type **Video** and then in the third circle, type **Internet**

c. Click the SmartArt graphic border to select it. Click the **Format tab**, and then in the **Size group**, if

necessary click **Size** to display the **Shape Height** and **Shape Width** boxes. Set the **Height** to **3″** and the **Width** to **6.5″**.

d. With the SmartArt graphic still selected, on the ribbon, under **SmartArt Tools**, click the **Design tab**, and then in the **SmartArt Styles group**, click **Change Colors**. Under **Colorful**, click the third style—**Colorful Range - Accent Colors 3 to 4**. On the **Design tab**, in the **SmartArt Styles group**, click **More** ⤓. Under **3-D**, in the first row, click the third style—**Cartoon**.

6 ▶ Hold down Ctrl and then press End to move to the end of the document. On the **Insert tab**, in the **Media group**, click **Online Video**. Click in the **Bing Video Search** box. Including the quotation marks, type **"Go 2013 1B video"** and then press Enter. In the first row, click the first video, and then click **Insert**.

a. On the **Format tab**, in the **Size group**, change the **Height** to **2.0**

b. Click the **File tab**, and then on the right, click **Show All Properties**. In the **Tags** box, type **internship** and in the **Subject** box type your course name and section number. If necessary, in the **Author** box, replace the existing text with your first and last name. Click **Save**.

c. Click the **File tab**, and then click **Print** to display **Print Preview**. At the bottom of the preview, click the **Next Page** and **Previous Page** buttons to move between pages. If necessary, return to the document and make any necessary changes.

d. **Save** your document. In the upper right corner of the Word window, click **Close**. If directed by your instructor to do so, submit your paper printout, your electronic image of your document that looks like a printed document, or your completed Word file.

END | You have completed Project 1D

Mastering Word **Project 1E Documentary**

In the following Mastery project, you will create a flyer announcing a special event being hosted by Sturgeon Point Productions. Your printed results will look similar to Figure 1.54.

PROJECT FILES

For Project 1E, you will need the following files:

New blank Word document

w01E_Antarctica

w01E_Filmmaker

You will save your document as:

Lastname_Firstname_1E_Documentary

Build from Scratch

PROJECT RESULTS

FIGURE 1.54

(Project 1E Documentary continues on the next page)

Mastering Word   Project 1E Documentary (continued)

1 Start Word and display a **Blank document** with the ruler and formatting marks displayed.

2 Type **Sturgeon Point Productions Presents Aria Pacheco** and then press Enter. From your student data files, insert the text file **w01E_Filmmaker**. Using your own name, **Save** the document in your **Word Chapter 1** folder as **Lastname_Firstname_1E_Documentary**

3 To the document title, apply the **Fill – White, Outline – Accent 1, Glow – Accent 1** text effect, and then change the **Font Size** to **36**.

4 Change the title **Font Color** to **Blue-Gray, Text 2**—in the fourth column, the first color. Apply an **Outer Shadow** using **Offset Left**—in the second row, the third style. **Center** the title.

5 Position the insertion point at the beginning of the paragraph that begins with *This year*, and then from your student data files, insert the picture **w01E_Antarctica**.

6 Change the **Layout Options** to **Square** and then change the **Height** of the picture to **2.25** Using the **Position** command, display the **Layout** dialog box, and then change the **Horizontal Alignment** to **Right relative to** the **Margin**.

7 Apply a **10 Point Soft Edges** picture effect to the image, and then display the **Artistic Effects** gallery. In the third row, apply the fourth effect—**Mosaic Bubbles**.

8 Deselect the picture. Apply a **Page Border** to the document using the **Shadow** setting. Select the first style,

and change the **Color** to **Blue-Gray, Text 2**. Change the **Width** to **3 pt**.

9 Below the last paragraph, draw a **Text Box** and then change the **Height** to **1.5** and the **Width** to **4.5**

10 To precisely place the text box, display the **Layout** dialog box. Change the **Horizontal Alignment** to **Centered**, **relative to** the **Page**, and then change the **Vertical Absolute position** to **0.5** below the **Paragraph**.

11 In the text box, type the following text:

> **Date: April 5**
>
> **Time: 8 p.m.**
>
> **Place: Studio G Screening Room**

12 In the text box, change the font size of all the text to **18**. Apply **Bold** and **Center**. Apply a **Shape Style** to the text box—under **Theme Styles**, in the last row, select the second style—**Intense Effect – Blue, Accent 1**. Change the **Shape Outline** to **Black, Text 1**.

13 Insert the **File Name** in the footer, and then display the document properties. As the **Tags** type **documentary, interview** and as the **Subject** type your course and section number. Be sure your name is indicated as the **Author**. **Save** your file.

14 Display the **Print Preview** and, if necessary, return to the document and make any necessary changes. **Save** your document and **Close** Word. If directed by your instructor to do so, submit your paper printout, your electronic image of your document that looks like a printed document, or your completed Word file.

> **END | You have completed Project 1E**

MyITLab® grader

Mastering Word Project 1F Pitch Festival

In the following Mastery project, you will edit a document with information regarding an event that Sturgeon Point Productions is holding for college students. Your printed results will look similar to Figure 1.55.

Apply 1B skills from these Objectives:

5 Change Document and Paragraph Layout

6 Create and Modify Lists

7 Set and Modify Tab Stops

8 Insert a SmartArt Graphic and an Online Video

PROJECT FILES

For Project 1F, you will need the following file:

w01F_Pitch_Festival

You will save your document as:

Lastname_Firstname_1F_Pitch_Festival

PROJECT RESULTS

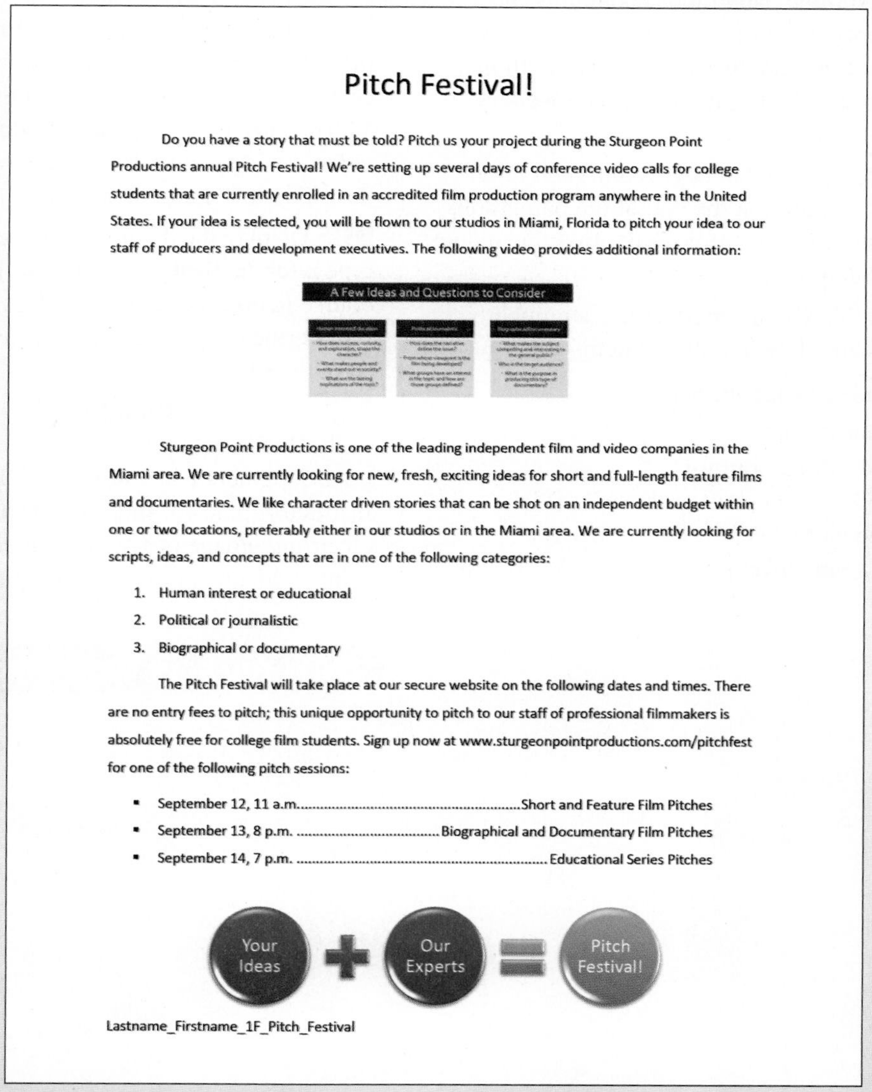

Pitch Festival!

Do you have a story that must be told? Pitch us your project during the Sturgeon Point Productions annual Pitch Festival! We're setting up several days of conference video calls for college students that are currently enrolled in an accredited film production program anywhere in the United States. If your idea is selected, you will be flown to our studios in Miami, Florida to pitch your idea to our staff of producers and development executives. The following video provides additional information:

A Few Ideas and Questions to Consider

Sturgeon Point Productions is one of the leading independent film and video companies in the Miami area. We are currently looking for new, fresh, exciting ideas for short and full-length feature films and documentaries. We like character driven stories that can be shot on an independent budget within one or two locations, preferably either in our studios or in the Miami area. We are currently looking for scripts, ideas, and concepts that are in one of the following categories:

1. Human interest or educational
2. Political or journalistic
3. Biographical or documentary

The Pitch Festival will take place at our secure website on the following dates and times. There are no entry fees to pitch; this unique opportunity to pitch to our staff of professional filmmakers is absolutely free for college film students. Sign up now at www.sturgeonpointproductions.com/pitchfest for one of the following pitch sessions:

- September 12, 11 a.m...Short and Feature Film Pitches
- September 13, 8 p.m. ....Biographical and Documentary Film Pitches
- September 14, 7 p.m. ....Educational Series Pitches

Lastname_Firstname_1F_Pitch_Festival

Word 2016, Windows 10, Microsoft Corporation

FIGURE 1.55

(Project 1F Pitch Festival continues on the next page)

Mastering Word   Project 1F Pitch Festival (continued)

1 Start Word, and then from your student files, open **w01F_Pitch_Festival**. Display formatting marks, and then **Save** the file in your **Word Chapter 1** folder as **Lastname_Firstname_1F_Pitch_Festival**

2 Insert the **File Name** in the footer, and then change the **Line Spacing** for the entire document to **1.5**. **Center** the document title, and then change the title font size to **24**. Change the **Top** and **Bottom** margins to **0.5**

3 Select the three paragraphs below the title, and then apply a **First line** indent of **0.5"**.

4 Select the entire document, and then change the **Spacing Before** to **6 pt** and the **Spacing After** to **6 pt**.

5 Select the last three paragraphs containing the dates, and then apply filled square bullets. If the bullets are not available, choose another bullet style. With the bulleted list selected, set a **Right** tab with **dot leaders** at **6"**.

6 Locate the paragraph that begins *Sturgeon Point Productions*, and then click at the end of the paragraph, after the colon. Press Enter and remove the first line indent from the new paragraph.

7 In the blank line you inserted, create a numbered list with the following three numbered items:

Human interest or educational

Political or journalistic

Biographical or documentary

8 Position the insertion point at the end of the document after the word *Pitches*. Do *not* insert a blank line. Insert a **SmartArt** graphic from the **Process**

category. Toward the bottom of the gallery, select and insert the **Equation** SmartArt. Select the outside border of the SmartArt, and then change the **Height** of the SmartArt to **1** and the **Width** to **6.5**

9 With the SmartArt selected, change the layout to **Square**, and change the **Horizontal Alignment** to **Centered relative to** the **Page**. Change the **Vertical Alignment** to **Bottom relative to** the **Margin**.

10 In the first circle type **Your Ideas** and in the second circle type **Our Experts** In the third circle type **Pitch Festival!**

11 Change the SmartArt color to **Colorful Range – Accent Colors 4 to 5**. Apply the **3-D Polished** style.

12 Click at the end of the first paragraph below the title. Press Enter, remove the first line indent, and then center the blank line. Insert an **Online Video**. In the **Bing Video Search** box, type **Go 1F Video** and then insert the video that displays a blue SmartArt. Change the height of the video to **1.5** and then **Save**.

13 Display the document properties. In the **Tags** box, type **pitch festival** and in the **Subject** box, type your course name and section number. In the **Author** box, replace the existing text with your first and last name. **Save** the file.

14 Display the **Print Preview** and if necessary, return to the document and make any necessary changes. **Save** your document and **Close** Word. If directed by your instructor to do so, submit your paper printout, your electronic image of your document that looks like a printed document, or your completed Word file.

> **END | You have completed Project 1F**

Mastering Word   Project 1G Educational Website

In the following Mastery project, you will create a flyer that details a new educational website that Sturgeon Point Productions has developed for instructors. Your printed results will look similar to those in Figure 1.56.

Apply 1A and 1B skills from these Objectives:

1 Create a New Document and Insert Text
2 Insert and Format Graphics
3 Insert and Modify Text Boxes and Shapes
4 Preview and Print a Document
5 Change Document and Paragraph Layout
6 Create and Modify Lists
7 Set and Modify Tab Stops
8 Insert a SmartArt Graphic and an Online Video

Build from Scratch

PROJECT FILES

For Project 1G, you will need the following files:

New blank Word document
w01G_Education
w01G_Media

You will save your document as:

Lastname_Firstname_1G_Educational_Website

PROJECT RESULTS

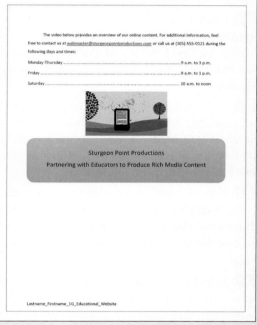

Word 2016, Windows 10, Microsoft Corporation

FIGURE 1.56

(Project 1G Educational Website continues on the next page)

1 Start Word and display a blank document. Display formatting marks and the ruler. **Save** the document in your **Word Chapter 1** folder as **Lastname_Firstname_1G_Educational_Website**

2 Type **Educational Websites** and then press Enter. Type **Sturgeon Point Productions is offering website tie-ins with every educational video title in our catalog, at no additional cost.** Press Spacebar, and then with the insertion point positioned at the end of the sentence that you typed, insert the text from your student data file **w01G_Education**.

3 Change the **Line Spacing** for the entire document to **1.5** and the spacing **After** to **6 pt**. To each of the four paragraphs that begin *Sturgeon Point Productions*, *As educators*, *When submitting*, and *The video*, apply a **First Line** indent of **0.5"**.

4 Change the **font size** of the title to **50** and the **Line Spacing** to **1.0**. **Center** the title. With the title selected, display the **Text Effects and Typography** gallery. In the first row, apply the second effect—**Fill – Blue, Accent 1, Shadow**.

5 Click at the beginning of the paragraph below the title, and then from your student data files, insert the picture **w01G_Media**. Change the picture **Height** to **2** and the **Layout Options** to **Square**. Format the picture with **Soft Edges** in **10 Point**.

6 Use the **Position** command to display the **Layout** dialog box. Change the picture position so that the **Horizontal Alignment** is **Right relative to** the **Margin**. Change the **Vertical Alignment** to **Top relative to** the **Line**.

7 Select the five paragraphs beginning with *Historic interactive timelines* and ending with *Quizzes and essay exams*, and then apply check mark bullets.

8 In the paragraph below the bulleted list, click after the colon. Press Enter and remove the first line indent. Type a numbered list with the following three numbered items:

    The title in which you are interested
    The name of the class and subject
    Online tools you would like to see created

9 With the insertion point located at the end of the numbered list, insert a **SmartArt** graphic. In the **Process** category, locate and select the **Basic Chevron Process**. In the first shape type **View** In the second shape type **Interact** and in the third shape type **Assess**

10 Change the SmartArt color to **Colorful Range – Accent Colors 4 to 5**, and then apply the **3-D Flat Scene** style. Change the **Height** of the SmartArt to **1** and the **Width** to **6.5** Change the **Layout Options** to **Square**, the **Horizontal Alignment** to **Centered relative to** the **Page**, and the **Vertical Alignment** to **Bottom relative to** the **Margin**.

11 Select the days and times at the end of the document, and then set a **Right** tab with **dot leaders** at **6"**.

12 Click in the blank line below the tabbed list, and **Center** the line. Insert an **Online Video**. In the **Bing Video Search** box, type **Pearson Higher Education Learning** and then insert the first video that displays. Change the video **Height** to **1.5**

13 Below the video, insert a **Rounded Rectangle** shape. The exact location need not be precise. Change the **Shape Height** to **1.5** and the **Shape Width** to **6.5** Display the **Shape Styles** gallery, and then in the fourth row, apply the second style—**Subtle Effect - Blue, Accent 1**.

14 Use the **Position** command to display the **Layout** dialog box, and then change the position so that both the **Horizontal** and **Vertical Alignment** are **Centered relative to** the **Margin**. In the rectangle, type **Sturgeon Point Productions** and then press Enter. Type **Partnering with Educators to Produce Rich Media Content** and then change the font size of all of the text in the text box to **16**.

15 Move to the top of the document and insert a **Text Box** above the title. The exact location need not be precise. Change the **Height** of the text box to **0.5** and the width to **3.7** Type **Sturgeon Point Productions** and then change the font size to **22 Center** the text.

16 Use the **Position** command to display the **Layout** dialog box, and then position the text box so that the **Horizontal Alignment** is **Centered relative to** the **Page** and the **Vertical Absolute position** is **0.5 below** the **Page**.

17 With the text box selected, display the **Shape Fill** gallery, and then in the next to last column, select the second color—**Blue, Accent 5, Lighter 80%**. Change

(Project 1G Educational Website continues on the next page)

Mastering Word   Project 1G Educational Website (continued)

the **Shape Outline** to the same color—**Blue, Accent 5, Lighter 80%**.

18 Deselect the text box. Apply a **Page Border** to the document. Use the **Box** setting, and choose the first style. Change the **Color** to **Blue, Accent 5**.

19 Change the **Top** margin to **1.25** and insert the **File Name** in the footer.

20 Display the document properties. As the **Tags** type **website** and as the **Subject** type your course and section number. Be sure your name displays in the **Author** box. **Save** your document and **Close** Word. If directed by your instructor to do so, submit your paper printout, your electronic image of your document that looks like a printed document, or your completed Word file.

END | You have completed Project 1G

Apply a combination of the 1A and 1B skills.

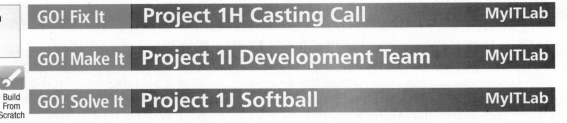

Build From Scratch

| GO! Fix It | **Project 1H Casting Call** | MyITLab |

| GO! Make It | **Project 1I Development Team** | MyITLab |

| GO! Solve It | **Project 1J Softball** | MyITLab |

| GO! Solve It | **Project 1K Production** | |

PROJECT FILES

For Project 1K, you will need the following files:

w01K_Production
w01K_Studio

You will save your document as:

Lastname_Firstname_1K_Production

From the student files that accompany this textbook, locate and open the file w01K_Production. Format the document using techniques you learned in this chapter to create an appropriate flyer aimed at filmmakers. From your student data files, insert the picture w01K_Studio, and then format the picture with an artistic effect. Insert a SmartArt graphic that illustrates two or three important points about the company. Use text effects and text wrapping so that the flyer is easy to read and understand and has an attractive design. Save the file in your Word Chapter 1 folder as **Lastname_Firstname_1K_Production** and submit it as directed.

Performance Level

Performance Criteria		Exemplary: You consistently applied the relevant skills	Proficient: You sometimes, but not always, applied the relevant skills	Developing: You rarely or never applied the relevant skills
	Use text effects	Text effects applied to text in an attractive and appropriate manner.	Text effects are applied but do not appropriately display text.	Text effects not used.
	Insert and format a picture	The picture is inserted and text wrapping and an artistic effect are applied.	The picture is inserted but not formatted properly.	No picture is inserted in the document.
	Insert and format SmartArt	The SmartArt is inserted and appropriately formatted.	The SmartArt is inserted but no formatting is applied.	No SmartArt is inserted in the document.

END | You have completed Project 1K

RUBRIC

The following outcomes-based assessments are *open-ended assessments*. That is, there is no specific correct result; your result will depend on your approach to the information provided. Make *Professional Quality* your goal. Use the following scoring rubric to guide you in *how* to approach the problem and then to evaluate *how well* your approach solves the problem.

The *criteria*—Software Mastery, Content, Format and Layout, and Process— represent the knowledge and skills you have gained that you can apply to solving the problem. The *levels of performance*—Professional Quality, Approaching Professional Quality, or Needs Quality Improvements—help you and your instructor evaluate your result.

	Your completed project is of Professional Quality if you:	Your completed project is Approaching Professional Quality if you:	Your completed project Needs Quality Improvements if you:
1-Software Mastery	Choose and apply the most appropriate skills, tools, and features and identify efficient methods to solve the problem.	Choose and apply some appropriate skills, tools, and features, but not in the most efficient manner.	Choose inappropriate skills, tools, or features, or are inefficient in solving the problem.
2-Content	Construct a solution that is clear and well organized, contains content that is accurate, appropriate to the audience and purpose, and is complete. Provide a solution that contains no errors of spelling, grammar, or style.	Construct a solution in which some components are unclear, poorly organized, inconsistent, or incomplete. Misjudge the needs of the audience. Have some errors in spelling, grammar, or style, but the errors do not detract from comprehension.	Construct a solution that is unclear, incomplete, or poorly organized, contains some inaccurate or inappropriate content, and contains many errors of spelling, grammar, or style. Do not solve the problem.
3-Format and Layout	Format and arrange all elements to communicate information and ideas, clarify function, illustrate relationships, and indicate relative importance.	Apply appropriate format and layout features to some elements, but not others. Overuse features, causing minor distraction.	Apply format and layout that does not communicate information or ideas clearly. Do not use format and layout features to clarify function, illustrate relationships, or indicate relative importance. Use available features excessively, causing distraction.
4-Process	Use an organized approach that integrates planning, development, self-assessment, revision, and reflection.	Demonstrate an organized approach in some areas, but not others; or, use an insufficient process of organization throughout.	Do not use an organized approach to solve the problem.

Apply a combination of the 1A and 1B skills.

Build from Scratch

GO! Think Project 1L Classes

PROJECT FILES

For Project 1L, you will need the following file:

New blank Word document

You will save your document as:

Lastname_Firstname_1L_Classes

The Human Resources director at Sturgeon Point Productions needs to create a flyer to inform full-time employees of educational opportunities beginning in September. The courses are taught each year by industry professionals and are designed to improve skills in motion picture and television development and production. Employees who have been with Sturgeon Point Productions for at least two years are eligible to take the courses free of cost. The classes provide employees with opportunities to advance their careers, gain valuable skills, and achieve technical certification. All courses take place in Studio G. Interested employees should contact Elana Springs in Human Resources to sign up. Information meetings are being held at 5:30 according to the following schedule: television development on June 15; motion picture production on June 17; and recording services on June 21.

Create a flyer with basic information about the courses and information meetings. Be sure the flyer is easy to read and understand and has an attractive design. Save the document as **Lastname_Firstname_1L_Classes** and submit it as directed.

> END | You have completed Project 1L

Build from Scratch

GO! Think Project 1M Store   MyITLab

Build from Scratch

You and GO! Project 1N Family Flyer   MyITLab

Build from Scratch

GO! Collaborative Team Project Project 1O Bell Orchid Hotels   MyITLab

Creating Cover Letters and Using Tables to Create Resumes

2

PROJECT 2A

OUTCOMES
Write a resume by using a Word table.

OBJECTIVES
1. Create a Table
2. Format a Table
3. Present a Word Document Online

PROJECT 2B

OUTCOMES
Write a cover letter and print an envelope.

OBJECTIVES
4. Create a Custom Word Template
5. Correct and Reorganize Text
6. Use the Proofing Options and Print an Envelope

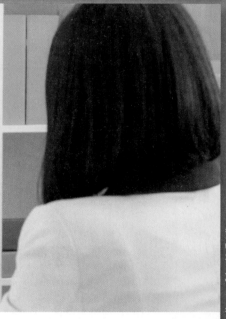

Kaspars Grinvalds/Fotolia

In This Chapter
GO! to Work with Word

Tables are useful for organizing and presenting data. Because a table is so easy to use, many individuals prefer to arrange tabular information in a Word table rather than setting a series of tabs. For example, you can use a table when you want to present rows and columns of information or to create a format for a document such as a resume.

When using Word to write business or personal letters, use a commonly approved letter format, and always use a clear writing style. You will make a good impression on prospective employers if you use a standard business letter style when you are writing a cover letter for a resume.

The projects in this chapter relate to the **College Career Center at Florida Port Community College** in St. Petersburg, Florida, a coastal port city near the Florida High Tech Corridor. With 60 percent of Florida's high tech companies and a third of the state's manufacturing companies located in the St. Petersburg and Tampa Bay areas, the college partners with businesses to play a vital role in providing a skilled workforce. The College Career Center assists students in exploring careers, finding internships, and applying for jobs. The Center offers workshops for resume and cover letter writing and for practice interviews.

Resume

PROJECT
2A

MyITLab
Project 2A Training
Project 2A Grader

PROJECT ACTIVITIES

In Activities 2.01 through 2.11, you will create a table to use as the format for a resume. The director of the Career Center, Mary Walker-Huelsman, will use this model when assisting students with building their resumes. Your completed document will look similar to Figure 2.1.

PROJECT FILES

MyITLab
grader

If your instructor wants you to submit Project 2A in the MyITLab Grader system, log in to MyITLab, locate Grader Project 2A, and then download the files for this project.

For Project 2A, you will need the following file:

New blank Word document
w02A_Experience

You will save your document as:

Lastname_Firstname_2A_Resume

Please always review the downloaded Grader instructions before beginning.

PROJECT RESULTS

Build From
Scratch

GO!
Walk Thru
Project 2A

Josh Hayes
1541 Dearborn Lane, St. Petersburg, FL 33713

(727) 555-0313
jhayes@alcona.net

OBJECTIVE — Technology writing and editing position in the robotics industry, using research and advanced editing skills to communicate with customers.

SUMMARY OF QUALIFICATIONS
- Two years' experience in robotics lab for Aerospace Instruction Team
- Excellent interpersonal and communication skills
- Proficiency using Microsoft Word
- Proficiency using page layout and design software
- Fluency in spoken and written Spanish

EXPERIENCE — **Instructional Lab Assistant**, Florida Port Community College, St. Petersburg, FL July 2013 to June 2015
- Assist robotics professors with sophisticated experiments
- Set up robotics practice sessions for Aerospace Instruction Team

Assistant Executive Editor, Tech Today Newsletter, St. Petersburg, FL September 2012 to June 2013
- Wrote and edited articles for popular college technology newsletter
- Responsible for photo editing, cropping, and resizing photos for newsletter
- Received Top College Technology Publication Award

Teacher's Assistant, Florida Port Community College, Aerospace Department, St. Petersburg, FL July 2013 to June 2015
- Helped students with homework, explained assignments, organized materials for professor
- Set up robotics lab assignments for students

EDUCATION — **University of South Florida, Tampa, FL**
Bachelor of Science, Mechanical Engineering, June 2015

Florida Port Community College, St. Petersburg, FL
Associate of Arts, Journalism, June 2013

HONORS AND ACTIVITIES
- Elected to Pi Tau Sigma, honor society for mechanical engineers
- Qualified for Dean's List, six semesters
- Student Mentor, help other students in engineering programs

Lastname_Firstname_2A_Resume

Word 2016, Windows 10, Microsoft Corporation

FIGURE 2.1 Project 2A Resume

GO! Learn How
Video W2-1

MOS
3.1.3

A ***table*** is an arrangement of information organized into rows and columns. The intersection of a row and a column in a table creates a box called a ***cell*** into which you can type. Tables are useful to present information in a logical and orderly format.

Activity 2.01 | Creating a Table by Specifying Rows and Columns

> **ALERT!**
>
> **To submit as an autograded project, log into MyITLab, download the files for this project, and begin with those files instead of a new blank document.**

1 Start Word and then click **Blank document**. On the **Home tab**, in the **Paragraph group**, if necessary click Show/Hide to display the formatting marks. If the rulers do not display, click the View tab, and then in the Show group, select the Ruler check box.

2 Click the **File tab** to display **Backstage** view, click **Save As**, and then click **Browse**. In the **Save As** dialog box, navigate to the location where you are storing your projects for this chapter. Create a new folder named **Word Chapter 2**

3 **Save** the file in the **Word Chapter 2** folder as **Lastname_Firstname_2A_Resume**

4 On the **Insert tab**, in the **Header & Footer group**, click **Footer**, and then at the bottom of the list, click **Edit Footer**. On the ribbon, in the **Insert group**, click **Document Info**, click **File Name**, and then at the right end of the ribbon, click **Close Header and Footer**.

5 On the **Insert tab**, in the **Tables group**, click **Table**. In the **Insert Table** grid, in the fourth row, point to the second square, and notice that the cells are bordered in orange and *2x4 Table* displays at the top of the grid. Compare your screen with Figure 2.2.

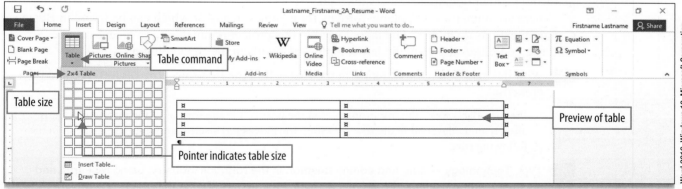

FIGURE 2.2

6 Click one time to create the table. Notice that formatting marks in each cell indicate the end of the contents of each cell; the mark to the right of each *row* indicates the row end. **Save** 🖫 your document, and then compare your screen with Figure 2.3.

A table with four rows and two columns displays at the insertion point location, and the insertion point displays in the upper left cell. The table fills the width of the page, from the left margin to the right margin. On the ribbon, Table Tools and two additional tabs—*Design* and *Layout*— display. Borders display around each cell in the table.

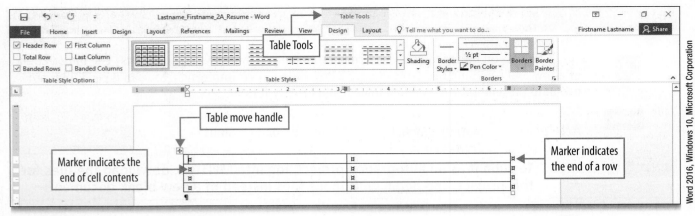

FIGURE 2.3

More Knowledge | **Converting Text to a Table and Converting a Table to Text**

You can convert text you have already typed to a table. To do so, if necessary, first use commas or tabs within paragraphs to signal Word to create a column. Then, on the Insert tab, click Table, and click Convert Text to Table. In the Convert Text to Table dialog box, confirm the number of columns you want, indicate the delimiter character you used (e.g. Tab or Paragraph mark), and then click OK. You can convert a table to regular text and choose which text character to use to separate the columns. To do so, on the Table Tools Layout tab, in the Data group, click Convert to Text.

Activity 2.02 | Typing Text in a Table

In a Word table, each cell behaves similarly to a document. For example, as you type in a cell, when you reach the right border of the cell, wordwrap moves the text to the next line. When you press Enter, the insertion point moves down to a new paragraph in the same cell. You can also insert text from another document into a table cell.

There are numerous acceptable formats for resumes, many of which can be found in Business Communications textbooks. The layout used in this project is suitable for a recent college graduate and places topics in the left column and details in the right column.

1 With the insertion point blinking in the first cell in the first row, type **OBJECTIVE** and then press Tab.

Pressing Tab moves the insertion point to the next cell in the row, or, if the insertion point is already in the last cell in the row, pressing Tab moves the insertion point to the first cell in the following row.

2 Type **Technology writing and editing position in the robotics industry, using research and advanced editing skills to communicate with customers.** Notice that the text wraps in the cell and the height of the row adjusts to fit the text.

3 Press Tab to move to the first cell in the second row. Type **SUMMARY OF QUALIFICATIONS** and then press Tab. Type the following, pressing Enter at the end of each line *except* the last line:

Two years' experience in robotics lab for Aerospace Instruction Team
Excellent interpersonal and communication skills
Proficiency using Microsoft Word
Proficiency using page layout and design software
Fluency in spoken and written Spanish

The default font and font size in a table are the same as for a document—Calibri 11 pt. The default line spacing in a table is single spacing with no space before or after paragraphs, which differs from the defaults for a document.

4 **Save** 🖫 your document, and then compare your screen with Figure 2.4.

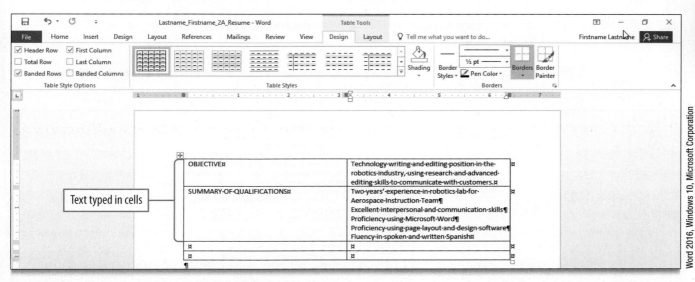

FIGURE 2.4

Activity 2.03 | Inserting Text from a File and Removing Blank Paragraphs

MOS
1.1.4

1 Press Tab to move to the first cell in the third row. Type **EXPERIENCE** and then press Tab.

2 Type the following, pressing Enter after each item, including the last item:

Instructional Lab Assistant, Florida Port Community College, St. Petersburg, FL July 2013 to June 2015
Assist robotics professors with sophisticated experiments
Set up robotics practice sessions for Aerospace Instruction Team

3 Be sure your insertion point is positioned in the second column to the left of the cell marker below *Instruction Team*. Compare your screen with Figure 2.5.

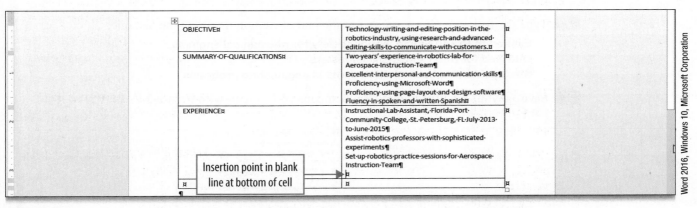

FIGURE 2.5

4 On the **Insert tab**, in the **Text group**, click the **Object button arrow**, and then click **Text from File**. Navigate to your student data files, select **w02A_Experience**, and then click **Insert**.

All of the text from the w02A_Experience document is added to the document at the insertion point.

🔄 **ANOTHER WAY**   Open the second document and select the text you want. Copy the text, and then paste at the desired location.

5 Press Backspace one time to remove the blank line at the end of the inserted text, and then compare your screen with Figure 2.6.

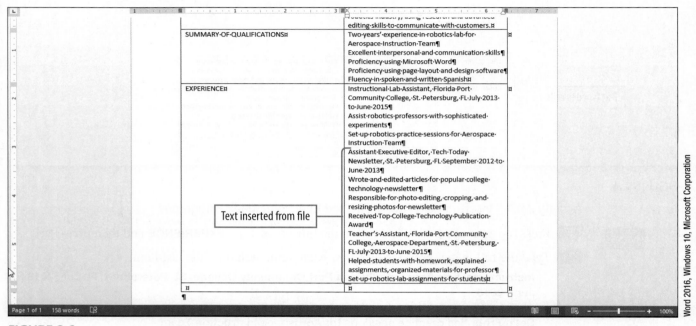

FIGURE 2.6

6 Press Tab to move to the first cell in the fourth row. Type **HONORS AND ACTIVITIES** and then press Tab.

7 Type the following, pressing Enter at the end of each item *except* the last one:

Elected to Pi Tau Sigma, honor society for mechanical engineers
Qualified for Dean's List, six semesters
Student Mentor, help other students in engineering programs

8 **Save** 🖫 your document, and then compare your screen with Figure 2.7.

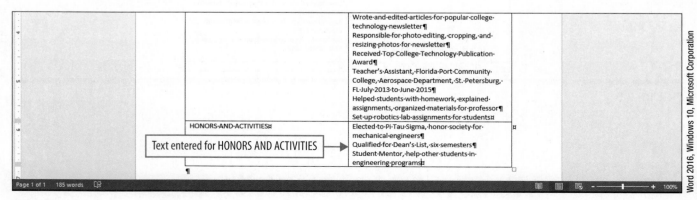

FIGURE 2.7

Activity 2.04 | Creating Bulleted Lists in a Table

1 Press Ctrl + Home to move to the top of your document, and then in the cell to the right of *SUMMARY OF QUALIFICATIONS*, select all of the text.

2 On the **Home tab**, in the **Paragraph group**, click **Bullets** :≡ ⌄.

The selected text displays as a bulleted list to make each qualification more distinctive.

3 Click anywhere in the cell to deselect the bulleted text, and then drag to select all of the bulleted text again. In the **Paragraph group**, click **Decrease Indent** ⌷ one time to align the bullets at the left edge of the cell.

4 Scroll as necessary so that you can view the entire *EXPERIENCE* and *HONORS AND ACTIVITIES* sections on your screen. With the bulleted text still selected, in the **Clipboard group**, double-click **Format Painter**.

5 In the cell to the right of *EXPERIENCE*, select the second and third paragraphs—beginning with *Assist* and *Set up*—to create the same style of bulleted list as you did in the previous step.

6 In the same cell, under *Assistant Executive Editor*, select the three paragraphs that begin *Wrote* and *Responsible* and *Received* to create another bulleted list aligned at the left edge of the cell.

7 In the same cell, select the paragraphs that begin *Helped* and *Set up* to create the same type of bulleted list.

8 In the cell below, select the paragraphs that begin *Elected*, *Qualified*, and *Student* to create a bulleted list.

9 Press Esc to turn off the **Format Painter**. Click anywhere in the table to deselect the text, **Save** 🖫 your document, and then compare your screen with Figure 2.8.

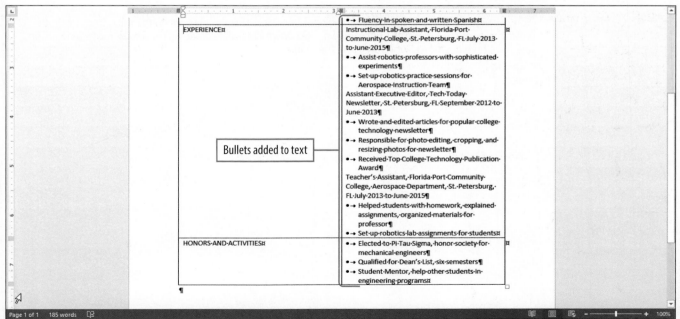

FIGURE 2.8

Objective 2 Format a Table

GO! Learn How
Video W2-2

Use Word's formatting tools to make your tables attractive and easy to read. Types of formatting you can add to a table include changing the row height and the column width, removing or adding borders, increasing or decreasing the paragraph or line spacing, and enhancing the text.

MOS
3.2.4

Activity 2.05 │ Changing the Width of Table Columns and Using AutoFit

When you create a table, all of the columns are of equal width. In this Activity, you will change the width of the columns.

1 ▶ Press Ctrl + Home. Click anywhere in the first column, and then on the ribbon, under **Table Tools**, click the **Layout tab**. In the **Cell Size group**, notice the **Width** box, which displays the width of the active column.

2 ▶ Look at the horizontal ruler and locate the **1.5-inch mark**. Then, in the table, in any row, point to the vertical border between the two columns to display the ⊞ pointer.

3 ▶ Hold down the left mouse button and drag the column border to the left until the white arrow on the ruler is at approximately **1.5 inches on the horizontal ruler** and then release the left mouse button.

4 ▶ In the **Cell Size group**, click the **Width box down spin arrow** as necessary to set the column width to **1.4"** and notice that the right border of the table moves to the right.

Adjusting column width by dragging a column border adjusts only the width of the column; adjusting column width with the Width box simultaneously adjusts the right border of the table.

5 ▶ In the **Cell Size group**, click **AutoFit**, and then click **AutoFit Window** to stretch the table across the page within the margins so that the right border of the table is at the right margin. **Save** 🖫 and then compare your screen with Figure 2.9.

ANOTHER WAY   You can adjust column widths by dragging the Move Table Column markers on the ruler. To maintain the right border of the table at the right margin, hold down Shift while dragging. To display measurements on the ruler, hold down Alt while dragging the marker.

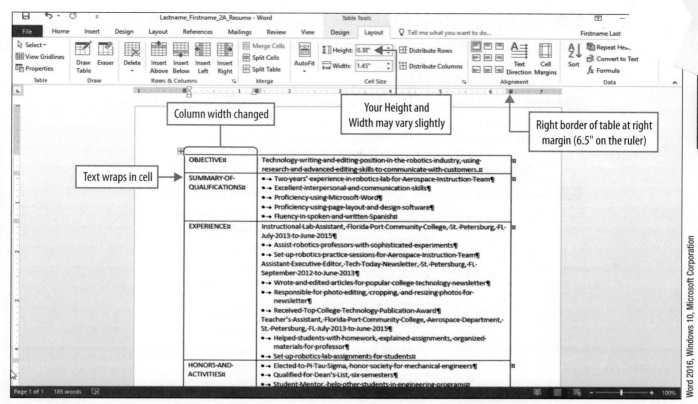

FIGURE 2.9

More Knowledge | **Changing Column Widths**

You will typically get the best results if you change the column widths starting at the left side of the table, especially in tables with three or more columns. Word can also calculate the best column widths for you. To do this, select the table. Then, on the Layout tab, in the Cell Size group, click the AutoFit button and click AutoFit Contents.

Activity 2.06 | **Using One-Click Row/Column Insertion to Modify Table Dimensions**

One of the most common actions you will take in a table is adding another row or another column. By using **One-click Row/Column Insertion** you can do so in context by pointing to the left or top edge where you want the row or column to appear and then clicking the ⊕ button to add it.

1 Scroll to view the lower portion of the table. On the left border of the table, *point* to the upper left corner of the cell containing the text *HONORS AND ACTIVITIES* to display the **One-click Row/Column Insertion** button. Compare your screen with Figure 2.10.

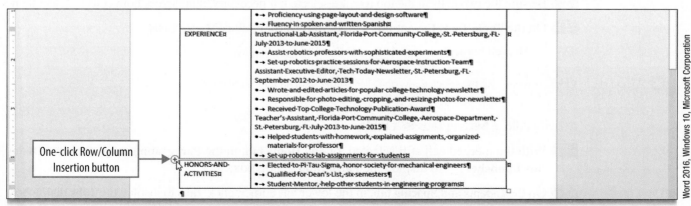

FIGURE 2.10

2 Click ⊕ one time to insert a new row above the *HONORS AND ACTIVITIES* row.

3 Click in the left cell of the new row, type **EDUCATION** and then press Tab. If a bullet character displays in the table cell, on the ribbon, on the **Home tab**, in the **Paragraph group**, click **Bullets** to turn off Bullets.

4 Type the following, pressing Enter at the end of each item *except* the last one:

> **University of South Florida, Tampa, FL**
> **Bachelor of Science, Mechanical Engineering, June 2015**
> **Florida Port Community College, St. Petersburg, FL**
> **Associate of Arts, Journalism, June 2013**

5 **Save** 🖫 your document, and then compare your screen with Figure 2.11.

Word 2016, Windows 10, Microsoft Corporation

FIGURE 2.11

ANOTHER WAY   When the insertion point is in the last cell in the bottom row of a table, you can add a row by pressing the Tab key; the insertion point will display in the first cell of the new row.

3.2.3

Activity 2.07 | Merging Table Cells

The title of a table typically spans all of the columns. In this Activity, you will merge cells so that you can position the personal information across both columns.

1 Press Ctrl + Home to move to the top of your document, and then click anywhere in the top row of the table.

2 On the **Table Tools Layout tab**, in the **Rows & Columns group**, click **Insert Above**.

A new row displays above the row that contained the insertion point, and the new row is selected. This is another method to insert rows and columns in a table; use this method to insert a new row at the top of a table.

ANOTHER WAY   Right-click in the top row, point to Insert, and then click Insert Rows Above.

3 Be sure the two cells in the top row are selected; if necessary, drag across both cells to select them.

4 On the **Table Tools Layout tab**, in the **Merge group**, click **Merge Cells**.

The cell border between the two cells no longer displays.

ANOTHER WAY   Right-click the selected row and click Merge Cells on the shortcut menu.

Activity 2.08 | Setting Tabs in a Table

1 With the merged cell still selected, on the **Home tab**, in the **Paragraph group**, click the **Dialog Box Launcher** 🗔 to display the **Paragraph** dialog box.

2 On the **Indents and Spacing tab**, in the lower left corner, click **Tabs** to display the **Tabs** dialog box.

3 Under **Tab stop position**, type **6.5** and then under **Alignment**, click the **Right** option button. Click **Set**, and then click **OK** to close the dialog box.

4 Type **Josh Hayes** Hold down Ctrl and then press Tab. Notice that the insertion point moves to the right-aligned tab stop at 6.5".

> In a Word table, you must use Ctrl + Tab to move to a tab stop, because pressing Tab is reserved for moving the insertion point from cell to cell.

5 Type **(727) 555-0313** and then press Enter.

6 Type **1541 Dearborn Lane, St. Petersburg, FL 33713** Hold down Ctrl and then press Tab.

7 Type **jhayes@alcona.net Save** 🖫 your document, and then compare your screen with Figure 2.12.

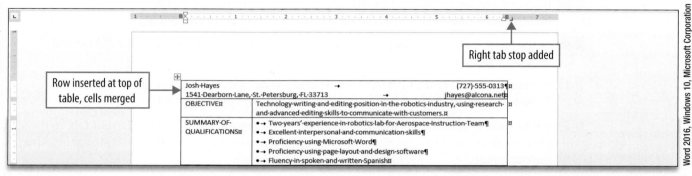

FIGURE 2.12

Activity 2.09 | Using Spacing After in a Table

1 In the first row of the table, select the name *Josh Hayes*, and then on the mini toolbar, apply **Bold** B and change the **Font Size** to **16**.

2 Under *Josh Hayes*, click anywhere in the second line of text, which contains the address and email address.

3 On the **Layout tab**, in the **Paragraph group**, click the **Spacing After up spin arrow** three times to add **18 pt** spacing between the first row of the table and the second row. Compare your screen with Figure 2.13.

> This action separates the personal information from the body of the resume and adds focus to the name.

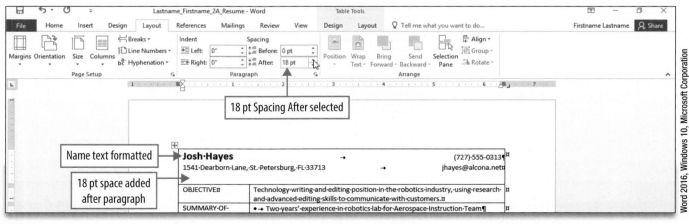

FIGURE 2.13

4 Using the technique you just practiced, in the second column, click in the last paragraph of *every cell* and add **18 pt Spacing After** including the last row; a border will be added to the bottom of the table, and spacing will be needed between the last row and the border.

5 In the second row, point to the word *OBJECTIVE*, hold down the left mouse button, and then drag downward in the first column only to select all the headings in uppercase letters. On the mini toolbar, click **Bold** B.

NOTE   Selecting Only One Column

When you drag downward to select the first column, a fast mouse might also begin to select the second column when you reach the bottom. If this happens, drag upward slightly to deselect the second column and select only the first column.

---

6 In the cell to the right of *EXPERIENCE*, without selecting the following comma, select *Instructional Lab Assistant* and then on the mini toolbar, click **Bold** B.

7 In the same cell, apply **Bold** B to the other job titles—*Assistant Executive Editor* and *Teacher's Assistant*.

8 In the cell to the right of *EDUCATION*, apply **Bold** B to *University of South Florida, Tampa, FL* and *Florida Port Community College, St. Petersburg, FL*.

9 In the same cell, click anywhere in the line beginning *Bachelor*. On the **Layout tab**, in the **Paragraph group**, click the **Spacing After up spin arrow** two times to add **12 pt** spacing after the paragraph.

10 In the cell to the right of *EXPERIENCE*, under *Instructional Lab Assistant*, click anywhere in the second bulleted item, and then add **12 pt Spacing After** the item.

11 In the same cell, repeat this process for the last bulleted item under *Assistant Executive Editor*.

12 Scroll to view the top of your document, **Save** 🖫 your document, and then compare your screen with Figure 2.14.

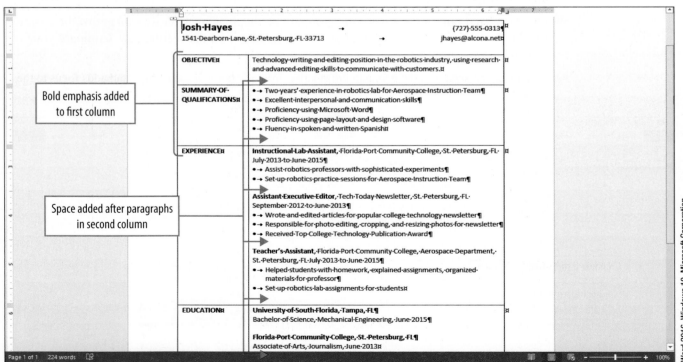

FIGURE 2.14

Activity 2.10 | Modifying Table Borders and Using Spacing Before

When you create a table, all of the cells have black 1/2-point, single-line, solid line borders that print unless you remove them. Most resumes do not display any cell borders. A border at the top and bottom of the resume, however, is attractive and adds a professional look to the document.

1 Scroll as necessary to view the top margin area above the table, and then point slightly outside of the upper left corner of the table to display the **table move handle** ⊞.

2 Click the ⊠ pointer one time to select the entire table, and notice that the row markers at the end of each row are also selected.

> Shaded row markers indicate that the entire row is selected. Use this technique to select the entire table.

3 On the ribbon, under **Table Tools**, click the **Design tab**. In the **Borders group**, click the **Borders button arrow**, and then click **No Border**.

> The black borders no longer display.

4 Press Ctrl + P, which is the keyboard shortcut to view the Print Preview, and notice that no borders display in the preview. Then, press **Back** ⊖ to return to your document.

5 With the table still selected, on the **Design tab**, in the **Borders group**, click the **Borders button arrow**, and then at the bottom of the **Borders** gallery, click **Borders and Shading**.

6 In the **Borders and Shading** dialog box, on the **Borders tab**, under **Setting**, click **Custom**. Under **Style**, scroll down about one-third of the way, and then click the style with a **thick upper line and a thin lower line**.

7 In the **Preview** box at the right, point to the *top* border of the small preview and click one time.

🔄 **ANOTHER WAY**   Click the top border button, which is one of the buttons that surround the Preview.

8 Under **Style**, scroll down if necessary, click the opposite style—with the **thin upper line and the thick lower line**, and then in the **Preview** box, click the *bottom* border of the preview. Compare your screen with Figure 2.15.

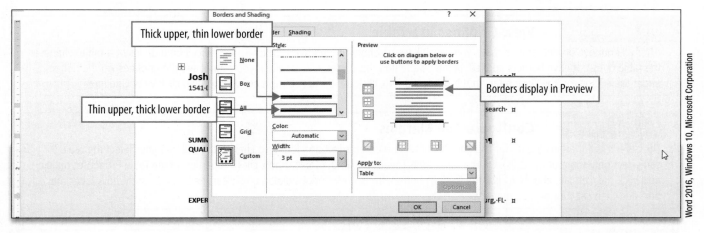

FIGURE 2.15

9 Click **OK**, click anywhere to cancel the selection, and then notice that there is only a small amount of space between the upper border and the first line of text.

10 ▶ Click anywhere in the text *Josh Hayes*, and then on the **Layout tab**, in the **Paragraph group**, click the **Spacing Before up spin arrow** as necessary to add **18 pt** spacing before the first paragraph.

11 ▶ Press Ctrl + P to display **Print Preview**. Compare your screen with Figure 2.16.

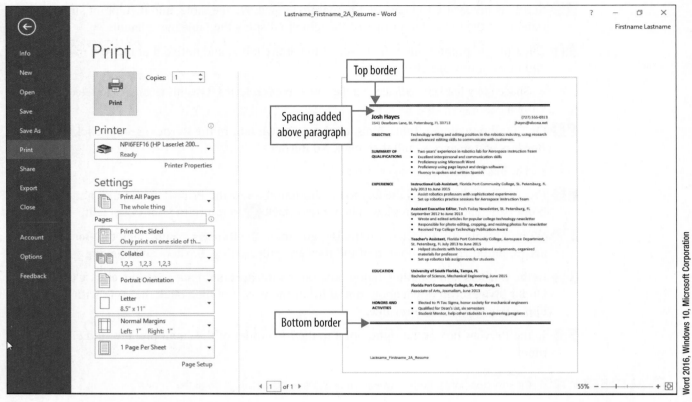

FIGURE 2.16

12 ▶ Press **Back** ⊙ to return to your document, and then on the Quick Access Toolbar, click **Save** 💾.

More Knowledge   **View Gridlines in a Table**

After you remove borders from a table, you can still view nonprinting gridlines, which show the cell boundaries of a table whenever the table does not have borders applied. Some people find this a useful visual aid. If you cannot see the gridlines, on the ribbon, under Table Tools, on the Design tab, in the Borders group, click the Borders button arrow, and then click View Gridlines.

More Knowledge   **Configure Cell Margins**

The default cell margins are 0" for Top and Bottom and 0.08" for Left and Right. To change the cell margins: Select the table (or you can select only some of the cells). On the Table Tools Layout tab, in the Table group, click Properties. In the Table Properties dialog box, click the Cell tab, and then click the Options button. In the Cell Options dialog box, clear the Same as the Whole Table check box, and then set your desired margins.

More Knowledge   **Sorting Data in a Table**

You can sort information in a table. To do so, click anywhere in the table, and then on the Table Tools Layout tab, click Sort. In the Sort dialog box, if the first row contains header information, select the Header Row option button in the lower left corner of the dialog box. In the Sort By list, select the column on which you want to sort, select the Type if necessary, select Ascending or Descending, and then click OK.

GO! Learn How
Video W2-3

Office Presentation Service enables you to present your Word document to others who can watch in a web browser. No preliminary setup is necessary; Word creates a link to your document that you can share with others via email or instant message. Anyone to whom you send the link can see your document while you are presenting online.

Individuals watching your presentation can navigate within the document independently of you or others in the presentation, so they can use a mouse, keyboard, or touch input to move around in the document while you are presenting it. If an individual is viewing a different portion of the document than the presenter, an alert displays on his or her screen. To return to the portion of the document that the presenter is showing, a Follow Presenter button displays.

While you are presenting, you can make minor edits to the document. If you want to share a copy of the document to the presentation attendees, you can select *Enable remote viewers to download the document* when you start the presentation. You can also share any meeting notes that you or others created in OneNote.

Activity 2.11 | Presenting a Word Document Online

If you are creating your own resume, it will be valuable to get feedback from your friends, instructors, or Career Center advisors before you submit your resume for a job application. In this Activity, you will present the resume document online for others to look at.

> **NOTE**   **You may be asked to sign in with your Microsoft account.**
>
> You may be asked to sign in with your Microsoft account, even if you are already signed in, to present your document online.

1 With your resume document displayed, click **Save** 🖫.

2 Click the **File tab**, on the left click **Share**, and then under **Share**, click **Present Online**.

3 On the right, click **Present Online**. Wait a moment for the service to connect, and then compare your screen with Figure 2.17.

There are several methods to send your meeting invitation to others. You can click Copy Link to copy and paste the hyperlink; for example, you could copy the link into a ***Skype*** window. Skype is a Microsoft product with which you can make voice calls, make video calls, transfer files, or send messages—including instant messages and text messages—over the Internet.

You can also select Send in Email, which will open your Outlook email window if you use Outlook as your mail client.

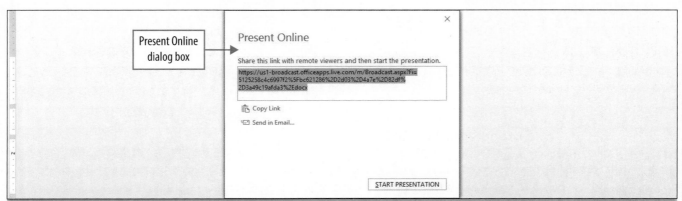

FIGURE 2.17

4 If you want to do so, identify a classmate or friend who is at a computer and available to view your presentation, select one of the methods to share, click **START PRESENTATION**, and when you are finished, on the ribbon, click **End Online Presentation**. If you are not ready to share your document right now, **Close** ☒ the **Present Online** dialog box.

> If you present online, you will need to initiate voice communication using Skype or by simply phoning the other person.

5 Be sure you have closed the Present Online dialog box. On the ribbon, on the **Present Online tab**, click **End Online Presentation**, and then in the message, click **End Online Presentation**.

6 Press Ctrl + Home to move to the top of your document. In the lower right corner, click **Zoom In** ➕ as necessary to set the Zoom level to **100%**. If necessary, on the **Home tab**, redisplay the formatting marks by clicking **Show/Hide**.

7 Click the **File tab**, and then in the lower right portion of the screen, click **Show All Properties**. In the **Tags** box, type **resume, Word table** and in the **Subject** box, type your course name and section number. In the **Author** box, be sure your name is indicated and edit if necessary.

8 On the left, click **Print** to display **Print Preview**. If necessary, return to the document and make any necessary changes.

9 **Save** your document. In the upper right corner of the Word window, click **Close** ☒. If directed by your instructor to do so, submit your paper printout, your electronic image of your document that looks like a printed document, or your original Word file.

END | You have completed Project 2A

GO! With Google

Objective | Edit a Resume in Google Docs

ALERT! **Working with Web-Based Applications and Services**

Computer programs and services on the web receive continuous updates and improvements, so the steps to complete this web-based activity may differ from the ones shown. You can often look at the screens and the information presented to determine how to complete the activity.

If you do not already have a Google account, you will need to create one before you begin this activity. Go to http://google.com and, in the upper right corner, click Sign In. On the Sign In screen, click Create Account. On the Create your Google Account page, complete the form, read and agree to the Terms of Service and Privacy Policy, and then click Next step. On the Welcome screen, click Get Started.

Activity | Editing a Resume in Google Docs

In this Activity, you will use Google Docs to open and edit a Word table containing a resume similar to the resume you created in Project 2A.

1 From the desktop, open your browser, navigate to **http://google.com**, and then click the **Google Apps** menu ⊞. Click **Drive**, and then if necessary, sign in to your Google account.

2 Open your **GO! Web Projects** folder—or click New to create and then open this folder if necessary.

3 In the left pane, click **NEW**, and then click **File upload**. In the **Open** dialog box, navigate to your Student Data Files for this chapter, and then in the **File List**, double-click to open **w02_2A_Web**.

4 When the upload is complete, in the **Google Drive file list**, point to the file name, right-click, point to **Open with**, and then click **Google Docs** to open it in Google Docs.

5 Click anywhere in the word *OBJECTIVE*, right-click, and then click **Table properties**.

Under **Table border**, click the **Table border width arrow**, and then click **0.5 pt**. Click **OK** to display the table and cell borders in the default black color.

6 On the menu bar, click **Table**, and then click **Insert row above**. In the first cell of the new row, type **Daniela Frank** Select the text you just typed, and then on the toolbar, click the **Font size arrow**, and then click **18**.

7 Press Tab to move to the second cell of the new row, and then type **1343 Siena Lane, Deerfield, WI 53531** Hold down Shift and press Enter. Type **(608) 555-0588** Hold down Shift and press Enter. Type **dfrank@alcona.net** Select all the text in the second cell that you just typed, and then on the toolbar, click **Right align**. In Google Docs, the phone number and possibly the email address may remain as hyperlinks. Compare your screen with Figure A.

(GO! With Google continues on the next page)

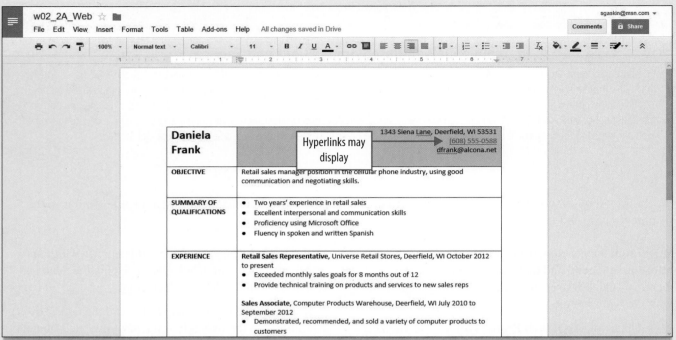

FIGURE A

8 Drag to select the two cells in the top row, right-click over the selection, and then click **Table properties**. Under **Cell background color**, click the arrow, and then in the top row, click the seventh color—**light gray 1**. Click **OK**.

9 Scroll down and click anywhere in the *EXPERIENCE* cell. Right-click, and then click **Insert row below**. In the first cell of the new row, type **EDUCATION**

10 Press `Tab` to move to the second cell in the new row, and then type **Madison Area Technical College, Madison, WI** Hold down `Shift` and press `Enter`.

11 On the toolbar, click **Bold** to turn off bold formatting, and then type **Associate of Arts in Information Systems, June 2014** and press `Enter`.

12 Right-click, click **Table properties**, and then change the **Table border width** to **0 pt** to remove the borders. Click **OK**.

13 Scroll as necessary to view the top of your document, and then compare your screen with Figure B.

(GO! With Google continues on the next page)

GO! With Google

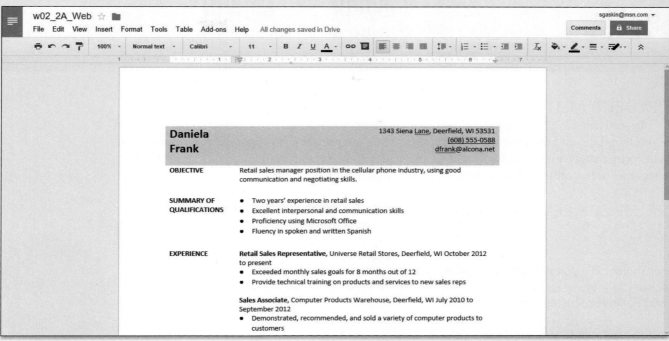

FIGURE B

14 Submit the file as directed by your instructor. In the upper right, click your user name, and then click

Sign out. **Close** your browser window. Your file is automatically saved in your Google Drive.

Cover Letter and Envelope

PROJECT ACTIVITIES

In Activities 2.12 through 2.22, you will create a letterhead, save the letterhead as a custom Word template, and then use the letterhead to create a cover letter to accompany a resume. You will format an envelope, and if you have an envelope and printer available, you can print an envelope. Your completed document will look similar to Figure 2.18.

 ## PROJECT FILES

 If your instructor wants you to submit Project 2B in the MyITLab Grader system, log in to MyITLab, locate Grader Project 2B, and then download the files for this project.

For Project 2B, you will need the following files:

New blank Word document
w02B_Cover_Letter_Text

You will save your document as:

Lastname_Firstname_2B_Cover_Letter

Please always review the downloaded Grader instructions before beginning.

PROJECT RESULTS

Build
From
Scratch

GO!
Walk Thru
Project 2B

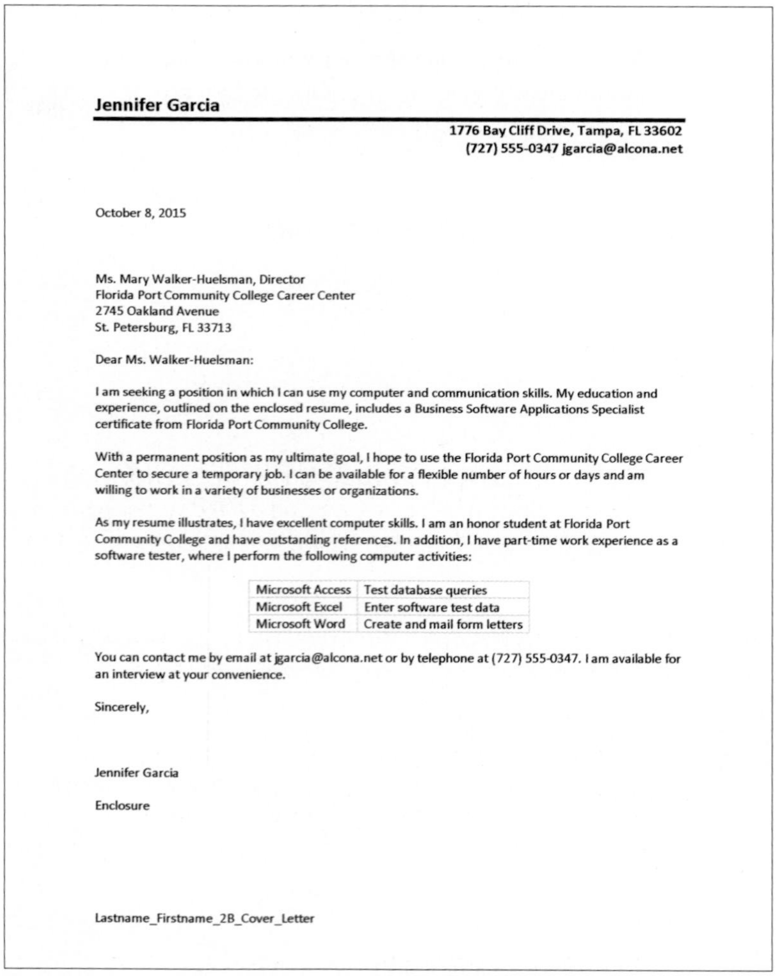

Jennifer Garcia

1776 Bay Cliff Drive, Tampa, FL 33602
(727) 555-0347 jgarcia@alcona.net

October 8, 2015

Ms. Mary Walker-Huelsman, Director
Florida Port Community College Career Center
2745 Oakland Avenue
St. Petersburg, FL 33713

Dear Ms. Walker-Huelsman:

I am seeking a position in which I can use my computer and communication skills. My education and experience, outlined on the enclosed resume, includes a Business Software Applications Specialist certificate from Florida Port Community College.

With a permanent position as my ultimate goal, I hope to use the Florida Port Community College Career Center to secure a temporary job. I can be available for a flexible number of hours or days and am willing to work in a variety of businesses or organizations.

As my resume illustrates, I have excellent computer skills. I am an honor student at Florida Port Community College and have outstanding references. In addition, I have part-time work experience as a software tester, where I perform the following computer activities:

Microsoft Access	Test database queries
Microsoft Excel	Enter software test data
Microsoft Word	Create and mail form letters

You can contact me by email at jgarcia@alcona.net or by telephone at (727) 555-0347. I am available for an interview at your convenience.

Sincerely,

Jennifer Garcia

Enclosure

Lastname_Firstname_2B_Cover_Letter

Word 2016, Windows 10, Microsoft Corporation

FIGURE 2.18 Project 2B—Cover Letter and Envelope

Objective 4 | Create a Custom Word Template

GO! Learn How
Video W2-4

A *template* is a file you use as a starting point for a *new* document. A template has a predefined document structure and defined settings, such as font, margins, and available styles. On Word's opening screen, you can select from among many different templates—or you can create your own custom template.

When you open a template as the starting point for a new document, the template file opens a copy of itself, unnamed, and then you use the structure—and possibly some content, such as headings—as the starting point for a new document.

All documents are based on a template. When you create a new blank document, it is based on Word's *Normal template*, which serves as the starting point for all blank Word documents.

1.3.3

Activity 2.12 | Changing the Document Style Set for Paragraph Spacing and Applying a Bottom Border to a Paragraph

> **ALERT!**   **To submit as an autograded project, log into MyITLab, download the files for this project and then begin with those files instead of a new blank document.**

A *letterhead* is the personal or company information that displays at the top of a letter, and which commonly includes a name, address, and contact information. The term also refers to a piece of paper imprinted with such information at the top. In this Activity, you will create a custom template for a personal letterhead.

1 Start Word and display a blank document; be sure that formatting marks and rulers display.

2 On the **Design tab**, in the **Document Formatting group**, click **Paragraph Spacing**.

The Paragraph Spacing command offers various options for setting the line and paragraph spacing of your entire document. A gallery of predefined values displays; or you can create your own custom paragraph spacing.

3 On the list *point* to **Default** and notice the settings in the ScreenTip.

Recall that the default spacing for a new Word document is 0 points of blank space before a paragraph, 8 points of blank space following a paragraph, and line spacing of 1.08.

4 Point to **No Paragraph Space** and notice the settings in the ScreenTip.

The *No Paragraph Space* style inserts *no* extra space before or after a paragraph and uses line spacing of 1. This is the same format used for the line spacing commonly referred to as *single spacing*. A *style set* is a collection of character and paragraph formatting that is stored and named.

5 Click **No Paragraph Space**.

By using the No Paragraph Space style, you will be able to follow the prescribed format of a letter, which Business Communications texts commonly describe in terms of single spacing.

ANOTHER WAY   On Word's opening screen, select the Single-spaced (blank) document; or, in a blank document, select the entire document, and then on the Home tab, in the Styles group, click No Spacing. Also, so long as you leave an appropriate amount of space between the elements of the letter, you can use Word's default spacing. Finally, you could use one of Word's predesigned templates for a cover letter and observe all spacing requirements for a letter.

6 Type **Jennifer Garcia** and then press Enter.

7 Type **1776 Bay Cliff Drive, Tampa, FL 33602** and then press Enter.

8 Type **(727) 555-0347 jgarcia@alcona.net** and then press ⏎. If the web address changes to blue text, right-click the web address, and then click **Remove Hyperlink**.

9 Select the first paragraph—*Jennifer Garcia*—and then on the mini toolbar, apply **Bold** ⓑ and change the **Font Size** to **16**.

10 Select the second and third paragraphs. On the mini toolbar, apply **Bold** ⓑ and change the **Font Size** to **12**.

11 With the two paragraphs still selected, on the **Home tab**, in the **Paragraph group**, click **Align Right** ▤.

🔁 **ANOTHER WAY**   Press Ctrl + R to align text to the right.

12 Click anywhere in the first paragraph—*Jennifer Garcia*. In the **Paragraph group**, click the **Borders button arrow** ▦ ▾, and then at the bottom, click **Borders and Shading**.

13 In the **Borders and Shading** dialog box, on the **Borders tab**, under **Style**, be sure the first style—a single solid line—is selected.

14 Click the **Width arrow**, and then click **3 pt**. To the right, under **Preview**, click the bottom border of the diagram. Under **Apply to**, be sure *Paragraph* displays. Compare your screen with Figure 2.19.

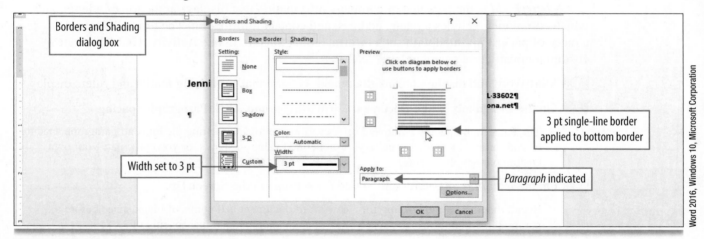

FIGURE 2.19

🔁 **ANOTHER WAY**   Alternatively, under Preview, click the bottom border button ▦.

15 Click **OK** to display a 3 pt line below *Jennifer Garcia*, which extends from the left margin to the right margin.

The border is a paragraph command and uses the same margins of the paragraph to which it is applied.

MOS
1.1.2

Activity 2.13 | Saving a Document as a Custom Word Template

After you create a document format that you like and will use again, for example, a letterhead for personal letters during a job search, you can save it as a template and then use it as the starting point for any letter.

1 Display the **Save As** dialog box. In the lower portion of the dialog box, in the **Save as type** box, at the right edge, click the **arrow**, and then click **Word Template**.

2 At the top of the **Save As** dialog box, notice the path, and then compare your screen with Figure 2.20.

By default, Word stores template files on your hard drive in your user folder, in a folder named Custom Office Templates. By doing so, the template is available to you from the Word opening screen.

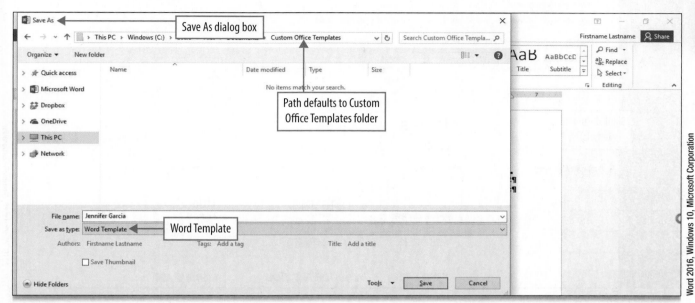

FIGURE 2.20

Word 2016, Windows 10, Microsoft Corporation

3 Click in the **File name** box, using your own name, type **Lastname_Firstname_2B_Letterhead_Template** and then click **Save**.

ALERT! **Are you unable to save in the Custom Word Templates folder?**

Some college computer labs block you from saving on the hard drive. If you are unable to save your template in the Custom Word Templates folder, navigate to your Word Chapter 2 folder in your storage location and save there. If you want to open a template that you stored in a location other than Word's default path, you must open the template directly from File Explorer—not from within Word—for it to open a new unnamed document based on the template.

---

4 Click the **File tab** to display **Backstage** view, and then click **Close** to close the file but leave Word open.

Activity 2.14 | Creating a Cover Letter from a Custom Word Template

A *cover letter* is a document that you send with your resume to provide additional information about your skills and experience. An effective cover letter includes specific information about why you are qualified for the job for which you are applying. Use the cover letter to explain your interest in the position and the organization.

ALERT! **Were you unable to save in the Custom Word Templates folder?**

If you saved your template file at your storage location because you were blocked from saving in the default folder on the hard drive, open your saved document, press [F12] to display the Save As dialog box, and then in your storage location, save the document—using your own name—as Lastname_Firstname_2B_Cover_Letter. Then move to Activity 2.15.

---

1 With Word open but no documents displayed, click the **File tab** to display **Backstage** view, and then click **New** to display the new document options. Compare your screen with Figure 2.21.

Here you can create a new document from a blank document or from one of Word's many built-in or online templates.

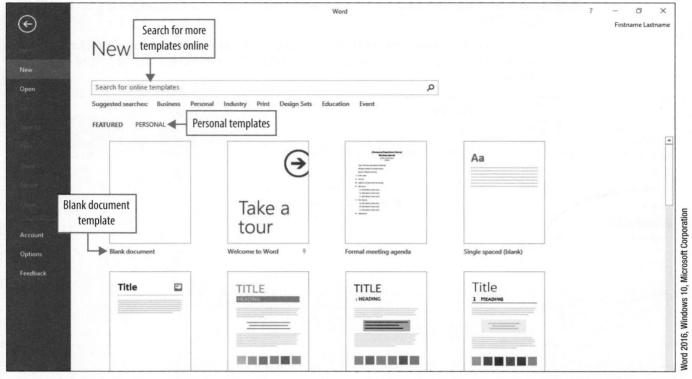

FIGURE 2.21

2 Under **Suggested searches**, click **Personal**, *point* to the name of your letterhead template, and then compare your screen with Figure 2.22.

Custom templates that you create and that are stored in the Custom Word Templates folder on your hard drive are accessible to you here whenever you want to create a new document from your stored template.

FIGURE 2.22

3 Click your letterhead template (or retrieve it from your storage location if you stored it elsewhere).

Word opens a copy of your 2B_Letterhead_Template in the form of a new Word document—the title bar indicates *Document* followed by a number. You are not opening the original template file, and changes that you make to this new document will not affect the contents of your stored 2B_Letterhead_Template file.

4 ▸ Display the **Save As** dialog box, and then navigate to your **Word Chapter 2** folder. Using your own first and last name, **Save** the file as **Lastname_Firstname_2B_Cover_Letter**

5 ▸ On the **Insert tab**, in the **Header & Footer** group, click **Footer**, at the bottom click **Edit Footer**, and then in the **Insert group**, click **Document Info**. Click **File Name**, and then click **Close Header and Footer**.

6 ▸ **Save** 🖫 your document.

Objective 5 | Correct and Reorganize Text

GO! Learn How
Video W2-5

Business letters follow a standard format and contain the following parts: the current date, referred to as the ***dateline***; the name and address of the person receiving the letter, referred to as the ***inside address***; a greeting, referred to as the ***salutation***; the text of the letter, usually referred to as the ***body*** of the letter; a closing line, referred to as the ***complimentary closing***; and the ***writer's identification***, which includes the name or job title (or both) of the writer and which is also referred to as the ***writer's signature block***.

Some letters also include the initials of the person who prepared the letter, an optional ***subject line*** that describes the purpose of the letter, or a list of ***enclosures***—documents included with the letter.

2.1.3

Activity 2.15 | Adding AutoCorrect Entries

Word's ***AutoCorrect*** feature corrects commonly misspelled words automatically; for example, *teh* instead of *the*. If you have words that you frequently misspell, you can add them to the list for automatic correction.

1 ▸ Click the **File tab** to display **Backstage** view. On the left, click **Options** to display the **Word Options** dialog box.

2 ▸ On the left side of the **Word Options** dialog box, click **Proofing**, and then under **AutoCorrect options**, click the **AutoCorrect Options** button.

3 ▸ In the **AutoCorrect** dialog box, click the **AutoCorrect tab**. Under **Replace**, type **resumee** and under **With**, type **resume**

> If another student has already added this AutoCorrect entry, a Replace button will display.

4 ▸ Click **Add**. If the entry already exists, click Replace instead, and then click Yes.

5 ▸ In the **AutoCorrect** dialog box, under **Replace**, type **computr** and under **With**, type **computer** Compare your screen with Figure 2.23.

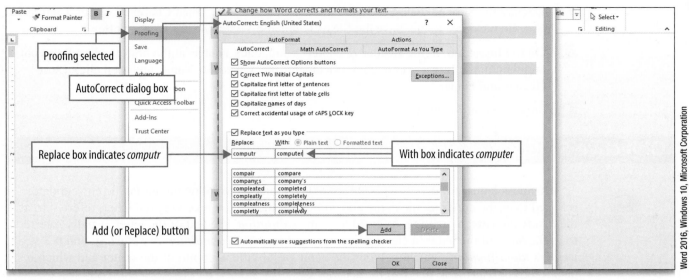

FIGURE 2.23

6 Click **Add** (or Replace) and then click **OK** two times to close the dialog boxes.

Activity 2.16 | Inserting the Current Date and Creating a Cover Letter

By using the ***Date & Time*** command, you can select from a variety of formats to insert the current date and time in a document.

For cover letters, there are a variety of accepted letter formats that you will see in reference manuals and Business Communications texts. The one used in this chapter is a block style cover letter following the style in Courtland Bovee and John Thill, *Business Communication Today*, Twelfth Edition, Pearson, 2014, p. 570.

1 Press Ctrl + End to move the insertion point to the blank line below the letterhead, and then press Enter three times.

2 On the **Insert tab**, in the **Text group**, click **Insert Date & Time** , and then click the third date format. Click **OK** to create the dateline.

> Most Business Communication texts recommend that the dateline be positioned at least 0.5 inch (3 blank lines) below the letterhead; or, position the dateline approximately 2 inches from the top edge of the paper.

3 Press Enter four times, which leaves three blank lines. Type the following inside address on four lines, but do *not* press Enter following the last line:

Ms. Mary Walker-Huelsman, Director

Florida Port Community College Career Center

2745 Oakland Avenue

St. Petersburg, FL 33713

> The recommended space between the dateline and inside address varies slightly among experts in Business Communication texts and office reference manuals. However, all indicate that the space can be from one to 10 blank lines depending on the length of your letter.

4 Press Enter two times to leave one blank line, and then compare your screen with Figure 2.24.

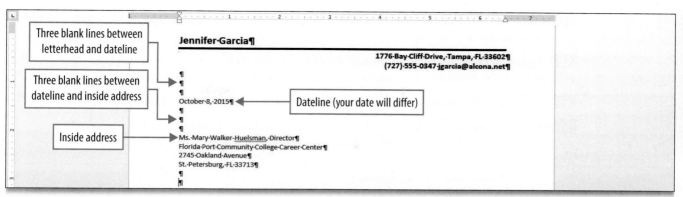

FIGURE 2.24

5 Type the salutation **Dear Ms. Walker-Huelsman:** and then press Enter two times.

Always leave one blank line above and below the salutation.

6 Type, exactly as shown, the following opening paragraph that includes an intentional word usage error: **I am seeking a position in witch I can use my** and press Spacebar. Type, exactly as shown, **computr** and then watch *computr* as you press Spacebar.

The AutoCorrect feature recognizes the misspelled word, and then changes *computr* to *computer* when you press Spacebar, Enter, or a punctuation mark.

7 Type the following, including the misspelled last word: **and communication skills. My education and experience, outlined on the enclosed resumee** and then type **,** (a comma). Notice that when you type the comma, AutoCorrect replaces *resumee* with *resume*.

8 Press Spacebar, and then complete the paragraph by typing **includes a Business Software Applications Specialist certificate from FPCC.** Compare your screen with Figure 2.25.

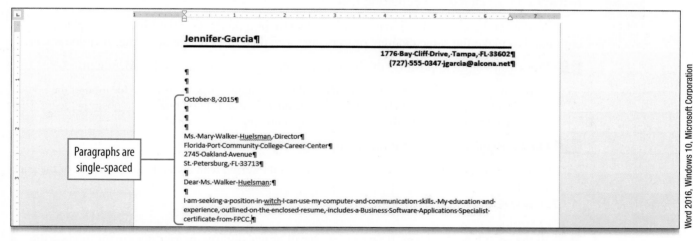

FIGURE 2.25

9 Press Enter two times. On the **Insert tab**, in the **Text group**, click the **Object button arrow**, and then click **Text from File**. From your student data files, locate and **Insert** the file **w02B_Cover_Letter_Text**.

Some of the words in the cover letter text display red or blue wavy underlines. These indicate potential spelling, grammar, or word usage errors, and will be addressed before the end of this project.

10 Scroll as necessary to display the lower half of the letter on your screen, and be sure your insertion point is positioned in the blank paragraph at the end of the document.

11 Press [Enter] one time to leave one blank line between the last paragraph of the letter and the complimentary closing.

12 Type **Sincerely,** as the complimentary closing, and then press [Enter] four times to leave three blank lines between the complimentary closing and the writer's identification.

13 Type **Jennifer Garcia** as the writer's identification, and then press [Enter] two times.

14 Type **Enclosure** to indicate that a document is included with the letter. **Save** 🖫 your document, and then compare your screen with Figure 2.26.

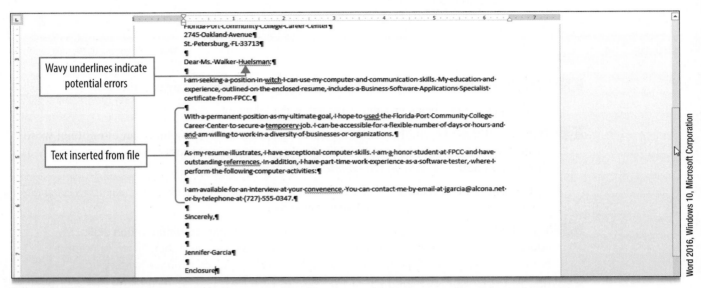

FIGURE 2.26

1.2.1, 2.1.1

Activity 2.17 | Finding and Replacing Text

Use the Find command to locate text in a document quickly. Use the Find and Replace command to make the same change, or to make more than one change at a time, in a document.

1 Press [Ctrl] + [Home] to position the insertion point at the beginning of the document.

Because a find operation—or a find and replace operation—begins from the location of the insertion point and proceeds to the end of the document, it is good practice to position the insertion point at the beginning of the document before initiating the command.

2 On the **Home tab**, in the **Editing group**, click **Find**.

The Navigation pane displays on the left side of the screen with a search box at the top of the pane.

↻ **ANOTHER WAY**   Hold down [Ctrl] and press [F].

---

3 In the search box, type **ac** If necessary, scroll down slightly in your document to view the entire body text of the letter, and then compare your screen with Figure 2.27.

In the document, the search letters *ac* are selected and highlighted in yellow for both words that begin with the letters *ac* and also for the word *contact*, which contains this letter combination. In the Navigation pane, the three instances are shown in context—*ac* displays in bold.

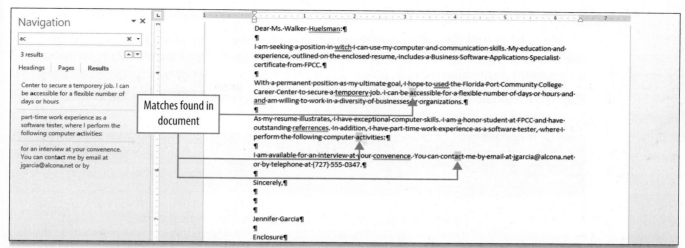

FIGURE 2.27

Word 2016, Windows 10, Microsoft Corporation

4 Click in the search box again, and type as necessary to display the word *accessible* in the search box.

> One match for the search term displays in context in the Navigation pane and is highlighted in the document.

5 In the document, double-click the yellow highlighted word *accessible*, and then type **available** to replace the word.

6 Close ✕ the **Navigation** pane, and then on the **Home tab**, in the **Editing group**, click **Replace**.

7 In the **Find and Replace** dialog box, in the **Find what** box, replace the existing text by typing **FPCC** In the **Replace with** box, type **Florida Port Community College** and then compare your screen with Figure 2.28.

FIGURE 2.28

Word 2016, Windows 10, Microsoft Corporation

8 In the lower left corner of the dialog box, click **More** to expand the dialog box, and then under **Search Options**, select the **Match case** check box.

> The acronym *FPCC* appears in the document two times. In a formal letter, the reader may not know what the acronym means, so you should include the full text instead of an acronym. In this instance, you must select the *Match case* check box so that the replaced text will match the case you typed in the Replace with box, and *not* display in all uppercase letters in the manner of *FPCC*.

9 In the **Find and Replace** dialog box, click **Replace All** to replace both instances of *FPCC*. Click **OK** to close the message box.

10 In the **Find and Replace** dialog box, clear the **Match case** check box, click **Less**, and then **Close** the dialog box.

> The Find and Replace dialog box opens with the settings used the last time it was open. Therefore, it is good practice to reset this dialog box to its default settings each time you use it.

11 Save 🖫 your document.

Activity 2.18 | Selecting Text and Moving Text by Using Drag and Drop

By using Word's **drag-and-drop** feature, you can use the mouse to drag selected text from one location to another. This method is most useful when the text you are moving is on the same screen as the destination location.

1 Take a moment to study the table in Figure 2.29 to become familiar with the techniques you can use to select text in a document quickly.

SELECTING TEXT IN A DOCUMENT	
TO SELECT THIS:	**DO THIS:**
A portion of text	Click to position the insertion point at the beginning of the text you want to select, hold down Shift, and then click at the end of the text you want to select. Alternatively, hold down the left mouse button and drag from the beginning to the end of the text you want to select.
A word	Double-click the word.
A sentence	Hold down Ctrl and click anywhere in the sentence.
A paragraph	Triple-click anywhere in the paragraph; or, move the pointer to the left of the paragraph, into the margin area. When the ⟰ pointer displays, double-click.
A line	Move the pointer to the left of the line. When the ⟰ pointer displays, click one time.
One character at a time	Position the insertion point to the left of the first character, hold down Shift, and press ← or → as many times as desired.
A string of words	Position the insertion point to the left of the first word, hold down Shift and Ctrl, and then press ← or → as many times as desired.
Consecutive lines	Position the insertion point to the left of the first word, hold down Shift and press ↑ or ↓.
Consecutive paragraphs	Position the insertion point to the left of the first word, hold down Shift and Ctrl and press ↑ or ↓.
The entire document	Hold down Ctrl and press A. Alternatively, move the pointer to the left of any line in the document. When the ⟰ pointer displays, triple-click.

FIGURE 2.29

2 Be sure you can view the entire body of the letter on your screen. In the paragraph that begins *With a permanent position*, in the second line, locate and double-click *days*.

3 Point to the selected word to display the ⬚ pointer.

4 Drag to the right until the dotted vertical line that floats next to the pointer is positioned to the right of the word *hours* in the same line, as shown in Figure 2.30.

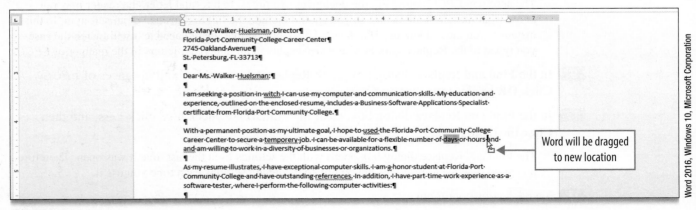

FIGURE 2.30

5 Release the mouse button to move the text. Select the word *hours* and drag it to the left of the word *or*—the previous location of the word *days*. Click anywhere in the document to deselect the text.

6 Examine the text that you moved, and add or remove spaces as necessary.

7 Hold down Ctrl, and then in the paragraph that begins *I am available*, click anywhere in the first sentence to select the entire sentence.

8 Release Ctrl. Drag the selected sentence to the end of the paragraph by positioning the small vertical line that floats with the pointer to the left of the paragraph mark. **Save** 🖫 your document, and then compare your screen with Figure 2.31.

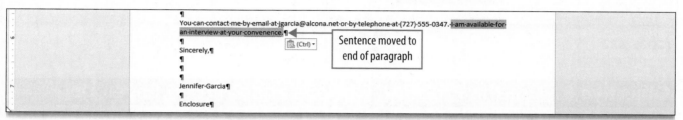

FIGURE 2.31

MOS
3.1.4

Activity 2.19 | Inserting a Table into a Document and Applying a Table Style

1 Locate the paragraph that begins *You can contact me*, and then click to position the insertion point in the blank paragraph above that paragraph. Press Enter one time.

2 On the **Insert tab**, in the **Tables group**, click **Table**. In the **Table** grid, in the third row, click the second square to insert a 2x3 table.

3 In the first cell of the table, type **Microsoft Access** and then press Tab. Type **Test database queries** and then press Tab. Complete the table using the following information:

Microsoft Excel	Enter software test data
Microsoft Word	Create and mail form letters

4 Point slightly outside of the upper left corner of the table to display the **table move handle** button ⊞. With the 🔩 pointer, click one time to select the entire table.

5 On the ribbon, under **Table Tools**, click the **Layout tab**. In the **Cell Size group**, click **AutoFit**, and then click **AutoFit Contents** to have Word choose the best column widths for the two columns based on the text you entered.

6 With the table still selected, under **Table Tools**, click the **Design tab**. In the **Table Styles group**, click **More** ⊽. Under **Plain Tables**, click the second style—**Table Grid Light**.

Use Table Styles to change the visual style of a table.

7 With the table still selected, on the **Home tab**, in the **Paragraph group**, click **Center** ≣ to center the table between the left and right margins. Click anywhere to deselect the table.

8 Save 🖫 and then compare your screen with Figure 2.32.

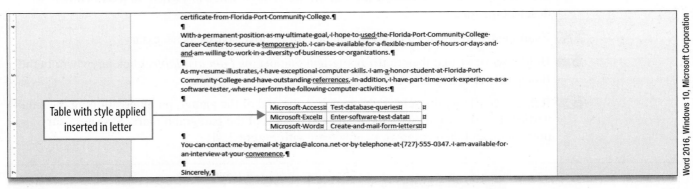

FIGURE 2.32

Objective 6 | Use the Proofing Options and Print an Envelope

GO! Learn How
Video W2-6

Word compares the words you type to words in the Office dictionary and also compares the phrases and punctuation that you type to a list of grammar rules. This automatic proofing is set by default. Words that are not in the dictionary and words, phrases, and punctuation that differ from the grammar rules are marked with wavy underlines; for example, the misuse of *their*, *there*, and *they're*.

Word will not flag the word *sign* as misspelled even though you intended to type *sing a song* rather than *sign a song*, because both are words contained within Word's dictionary. Your own knowledge and proofreading skills are still required, even when using a sophisticated word processing program like Word.

Activity 2.20 | Checking for Spelling and Grammar Errors

There are two ways to respond to spelling and grammar errors flagged by Word. You can right-click a flagged word or phrase, and then from the shortcut menu choose a correction or action. Or, you can initiate the Spelling & Grammar command to display the Spelling and Grammar pane, which provides more options than the shortcut menus.

> **ALERT!** **Activating Spelling and Grammar Checking**
>
> If you do not see any wavy red or blue lines under words, the automatic spelling and/or grammar checking has been turned off on your system. To activate the spelling and grammar checking, display Backstage view, click Options, click Proofing, and then under *When correcting spelling in Microsoft Office programs*, select the first four check boxes. Under *When correcting spelling and grammar in Word*, select the first four check boxes, and then click the Writing Style arrow and click Grammar. Under *Exceptions for*, clear both check boxes. To display the flagged spelling and grammar errors, click the Recheck Document button, and then close the dialog box.

1 Position the body of the letter on your screen, and then examine the text to locate wavy underlines.

A list of grammar rules applied by a computer program like Word can never be exact, and a computer dictionary cannot contain all known words and proper names. Therefore, you will need to check any words flagged by Word with wavy underlines, and you will also need to proofread for content errors.

2 In the lower left corner of your screen, in the status bar, locate and point to but do not click the 🔲 icon to display the ScreenTip *Word found proofing errors. Click or tap to correct them.* Compare your screen with Figure 2.33.

If this button displays, you know there are potential errors identified in the document.

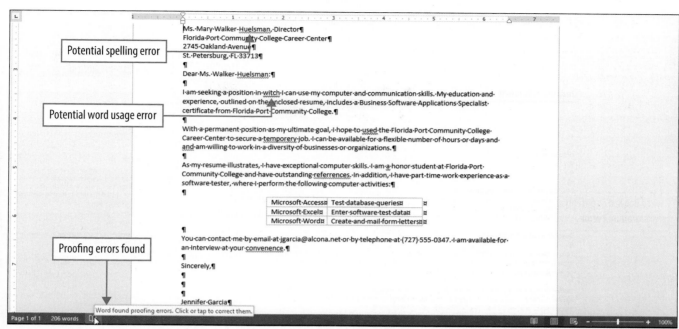

Potential spelling error

Potential word usage error

Proofing errors found

FIGURE 2.33

3 In the paragraph that begins *With a permanent*, in the second line, locate the word *temporery* with the wavy red underline. Point to the word and right-click, and then click **temporary** to correct the spelling error.

4 In the next line, locate the word *and* that displays with a wavy red underline, point to the word and right-click, and then on the shortcut menu, click **Delete Repeated Word** to delete the duplicate word.

5 Press [Ctrl] + [Home] to move the insertion point to the beginning of the document. Click the **Review tab**, and then in the **Proofing group**, click **Spelling & Grammar** to check the spelling and grammar of the text in the document.

The Spelling pane displays on the right, and the proper name *Huelsman* is flagged. Word's dictionary contains only very common proper names—unusual names like this one will typically be flagged as a potential spelling error. If this is a name that you frequently type, consider adding it to the dictionary.

⟳ ANOTHER WAY Press [F7] to start the Spelling & Grammar command.

6 In the **Spelling** pane, click **Ignore All**. Compare your screen with Figure 2.34.

The word *witch* is highlighted as a grammar error, and in the Grammar pane, *which* is suggested.

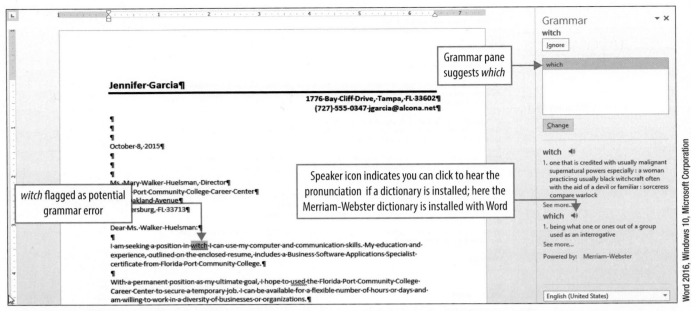

FIGURE 2.34

Grammar
witch
Ignore
which

Change

witch 🔊
1. one that is credited with usually malignant supernatural powers especially : a woman practicing usually black witchcraft often with the aid of a devil or familiar : sorceress compare warlock
See more...
which 🔊
1. being what one or ones out of a group used as an interrogative
See more...
Powered by: Merriam-Webster

English (United States)

Grammar pane suggests which

Speaker icon indicates you can click to hear the pronunciation if a dictionary is installed; here the Merriam-Webster dictionary is installed with Word

witch flagged as potential grammar error

Jennifer·Garcia¶

1776·Bay·Cliff·Drive,·Tampa,·FL·33602¶
(727)·555-0347·jgarcia@alcona.net¶

October·8,·2015¶

Ms.·Mary·Walker-Huelsman,·Director¶
·Port·Community·College·Career·Center¶
·akland·Avenue¶
·ersburg,·FL·33713¶

Dear·Ms.·Walker-Huelsman:¶

I·am·seeking·a·position·in·witch·I·can·use·my·computer·and·communication·skills.·My·education·and·experience,·outlined·on·the·enclosed·resume,·includes·a·Business·Software·Applications·Specialist·certificate·from·Florida·Port·Community·College.¶

With·a·permanent·position·as·my·ultimate·goal,·I·hope·to·used·the·Florida·Port·Community·College·Career·Center·to·secure·a·temporary·job.·I·can·be·available·for·a·flexible·number·of·hours·or·days·and·am·willing·to·work·in·a·diversity·of·businesses·or·organizations.¶

Word 2016, Windows 10, Microsoft Corporation

---

7 In the **Grammar** pane, click **Change** to change to the correct usage *which*.

The next marked word—a possible grammar error—displays.

8 Click **Change** to change *used* to *use*. Notice that the next error is a potential Spelling error. In the **Spelling** pane, change *referrences* to the suggestion *references*. Notice that the next error is a possible grammar error.

9 Click **Change** to change *a* to *an*. Continue the spelling and grammar check and correct the spelling of *convenence*.

10 When Word displays the message *Spelling and grammar check is complete*, click **OK**.

11 Save 🖫 your document.

Activity 2.21 | Using the Thesaurus

A *thesaurus* is a research tool that lists *synonyms*—words that have the same or similar meaning to the word you selected.

1 Scroll so that you can view the body of the letter. In the paragraph that begins *With a permanent*, double-click to select the word *diversity*, and then in the **Proofing** group, click **Thesaurus**.

The Thesaurus pane displays on the right with a list of synonyms; the list will vary in length depending on the selected word.

🔄 **ANOTHER WAY**   Right-click the word, on the shortcut menu, point to Synonyms, and then click Thesaurus.

2 In the **Thesaurus** pane, under **variety (n.)**, point to the word *variety*, and then click the arrow that displays. Click **Insert** to change *diversity* to *variety*.

3 In the paragraph that begins *As my resume*, double-click the word *exceptional*, and then on the ribbon, click **Thesaurus** again.

4 In the **Thesaurus** pane, under **excellent (adj.)**, point to *excellent*, click the **arrow**, and then click **Insert**. Compare your screen with Figure 2.35.

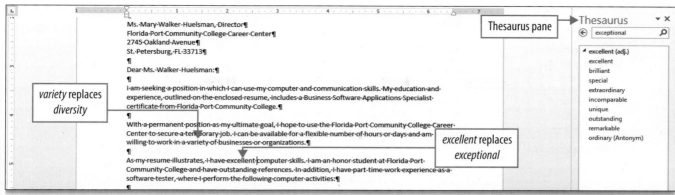

FIGURE 2.35

Word 2016, Windows 10, Microsoft Corporation

5 ▸ **Close** ☒ the **Thesaurus** pane.

6 ▸ Click the **File tab** to display **Backstage** view, and then on the **Info tab**, in the lower right portion of the screen, click **Show All Properties**. If you used your template, notice that it is indicated to the right of *Template*.

7 ▸ In the **Tags** box, type **cover letter** and in the **Subject** box, type your course name and section number. In the **Author** box, be sure your name is indicated and edit if necessary.

8 ▸ On the left, click **Print** to display **Print Preview**. If necessary, return to the document and make any necessary changes.

9 ▸ **Save** your document. If directed by your instructor to do so, submit your paper printout, your electronic image of your document that looks like a printed document, or your original Word file. In the upper right corner of the Word window, click **Close** ☒.

ALERT! **Because the next Activity is optional, if you are submitting your work in MyITLab, this is the file you will upload.**

Activity 2.22 | Addressing and Printing an Envelope

Use Word's Envelopes command on the Mailings label to format and print an envelope.

NOTE **This Is an Optional Activity**

This activity is optional. If you do not have an envelope and printer, or do not want to complete the activity at this time, then this project is complete.

1 ▸ Display your **2B_Cover_Letter**, and then select the four lines that comprise the inside address.

2 ▸ On the **Mailings tab**, in the **Create group**, click **Envelopes**. Notice that the **Delivery address** contains the selected inside address.

3 ▸ Click in the **Return address** box, and then type **Jennifer Garcia** and press Enter. Type **1776 Bay Cliff Drive** and then press Enter. Type **Tampa, FL 33602**

4 ▸ In the lower portion of the **Envelopes and Labels** dialog box, click **Options**, and then compare your screen with Figure 2.36.

The default envelope size is a standard business envelope referred to as a Size 10.

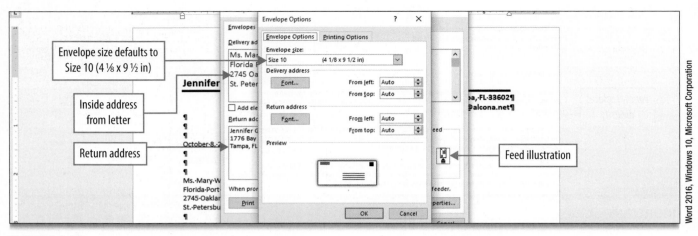

FIGURE 2.36

> **5** Click **OK** to close the **Envelope Options** dialog box. As shown under **Feed**, insert an envelope in your printer and then click **Print**.

> Depending on the type and brand of printer you are using, your feed area may vary.

> **6** Close your **2B_Cover_Letter**, and then close Word.

END | You have completed Project 2B

GO! With Google

Objective | Create a Table in Google Docs

ALERT! **Working with Web-Based Applications and Services**

Computer programs and services on the web receive continuous updates and improvements, so the steps to complete this web-based activity may differ from the ones shown. You can often look at the screens and the information presented to determine how to complete the activity.

If you do not already have a Google account, you will need to create one before you begin this activity. Go to http://google.com and, in the upper right corner, click Sign In. On the Sign In screen, click Create Account. On the Create your Google Account page, complete the form, read and agree to the Terms of Service and Privacy Policy, and then click Next step. On the Welcome screen, click Get Started.

Activity | Creating a Table in Google Docs

In this Activity, you will use Google Docs to create a table within a document similar to Project 2B.

1 From the desktop, open your browser, navigate to **http://google.com**, and then click the **Google Apps** menu ⊞. Click **Drive**, and then if necessary, sign in to your Google account.

2 Open your **GO! Web Projects** folder—or click New to create and then open this folder if necessary.

3 In the left pane, click **NEW**, and then click **File upload**. In the **Open** dialog box, navigate to your Student Data Files for this chapter, and then in the **File List**, double-click to open **w02_2B_Web**.

4 When the upload is complete, in the **Google Drive file list**, point to the document name, right-click, point

to **Open with**, and then click **Google Docs** to open it in Google Docs.

5 Click in the document and then press Ctrl + End to move to the end of the document, and then press Enter.

6 On the menu bar, click **Table**, point to **Insert table**, and then insert a **3x4 Table**.

7 Type **Position** and press Tab. Type **Type** and press Tab. Type **Location** and press Tab.

8 In the second row type **Paralegal** and press Tab. Type **Part-time** and press Tab. Type **Tampa** and press Tab. Compare your screen with Figure A.

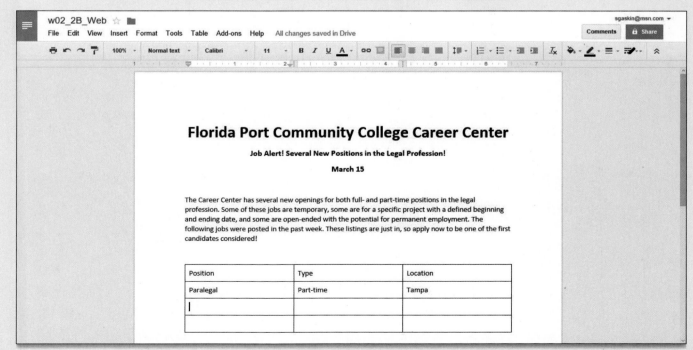

FIGURE A

(GO! With Google continues on the next page)

9 Type **Legal Records Clerk** and press `Tab`. Type **Full-time, 2 months** and press `Tab`. Type **North Tampa** and press `Tab`.

11 Right-click in the last row of the table, and then click **Delete row**.

12 Drag to select all the cells in the first row, and then on the toolbar, click the **Normal text button arrow**, and then click **Heading 2**. With the three column titles still selected, on the toolbar, click **Center**.

13 Press `Ctrl` + `Home` to move to the top of the document, and then compare your screen with Figure B.

14 Submit the file as directed by your instructor. In the upper right, click your user name, and then click **Sign out**. **Close** your browser window. Your file is automatically saved in your Google Drive.

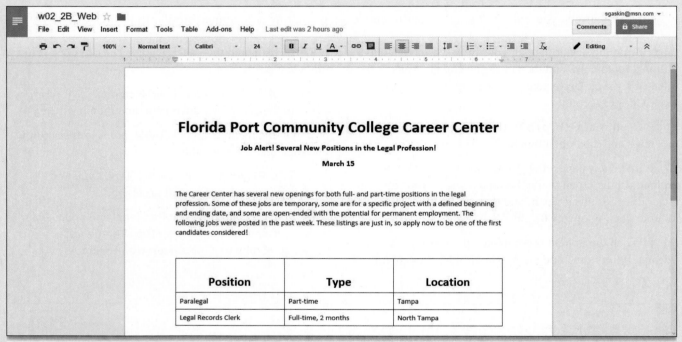

FIGURE B

GO! To Work

MICROSOFT OFFICE SPECIALIST (MOS) SKILLS IN THIS CHAPTER

PROJECT 2A	PROJECT 2B
1.1.4 Insert text from a file or external source	**1.2.1** Search for text
3.1.3 Create a table by specifying rows and columns	**1.3.3** Apply document style sets
3.2.3 Merge and split cells	**2.1.1** Find and replace text
3.2.4 Resize tables, rows, and columns	**2.1.3** Replace text by using AutoCorrect
	3.1.4 Apply table styles

BUILD YOUR E-PORTFOLIO

An E-Portfolio is a collection of evidence, stored electronically, that showcases what you have accomplished while completing your education. Collecting and then sharing your work products with potential employers reflects your academic and career goals. Your completed documents from the following projects are good examples to show what you have learned: 2G, 2K, and 2L.

GO! FOR JOB SUCCESS

Video: Cover Letter and Resume Tips

Your instructor may assign this video to your class, and then ask you to think about, or discuss with your classmates, these questions:

FotolEdhar / Fotolia

A cover letter should contain information that is different from but complementary to the information and facts on your resume and be tailored to the specific job you are applying for. Name two different things that you could mention in a cover letter.

What type of information belongs in the Career Objective portion of your resume?

When is it best to use a chronological resume layout, and when is it appropriate to use a functional resume layout?

END OF CHAPTER

SUMMARY

Word tables enable you to present information in a logical and orderly format. Each cell in a Word table behaves like a document; as you type in a cell, wordwrap moves text to the next line.

A good source of information for resume formats is a business communications textbook. A simple two-column table created in Word is suitable to create an appropriate resume for a recent college graduate.

Use Word's Office Presentation Service to present a Word document to others who can watch in a web browser. Word automatically creates a link to your document that you can share with others via email.

A template is useful because it has a predefined document structure and defined settings such as font and margins. Create your own custom template or, from Word's opening screen, select from thousands of templates.

GO! LEARN IT ONLINE

Review the concepts, key terms, and MOS skills in this chapter by completing these online challenges, which you can find at **MyITLab**.

Matching and Multiple Choice: Answer matching and multiple-choice questions to test what you learned in this chapter.

Lessons on the GO: Learn how to use all the new apps and features as they are introduced by Microsoft.

MOS Prep Quiz: Answer questions to review the MOS skills that you practiced in this chapter.

GO! COLLABORATIVE TEAM PROJECT (Available in **MyITLab** and Instructor Resource Center)

If your instructor assigns this project to your class, you can expect to work with one or more of your classmates—either in person or by using Internet tools—to create work products similar to those that you created in this chapter. A team is a group of workers who work together to solve a problem, make a decision, or create a work product. Collaboration is when you work together with others as a team in an intellectual endeavor to complete a shared task or achieve a shared goal.

PROJECT GUIDE FOR WORD CHAPTER 2

Your instructor will assign Projects from this list to ensure your learning and assess your knowledge.

REVIEW AND ASSESSMENTS GUIDE FOR WORD CHAPTER 2

Project	Apply Skills from These Chapter Objectives	Project Type	Project Location
2A **MyITLab**	Objectives 1–3 from Project 2A	**2A Instructional Project (Grader Project)** Guided instruction to learn the skills in Project 2A.	In MyITLab and in text
2B **MyITLab**	Objectives 4–6 from Project 2B	**2B Instructional Project (Grader Project)** Guided instruction to learn the skills in Project 2B.	In MyITLab and in text
2C	Objectives 1–3 from Project 2A	**2C Skills Review (Scorecard Grading)** A guided review of the skills from Project 2A.	In text
2D	Objectives 4–6 from Project 2B	**2D Skills Review (Scorecard Grading)** A guided review of the skills from Project 2B.	In text
2E **MyITLab**	Objectives 1–3 from Project 2A	**2E Mastery (Grader Project)** **Mastery and Transfer of Learning** A demonstration of your mastery of the skills in Project 2A with extensive decision making.	In MyITLab and in text
2F **MyITLab**	Objectives 4–6 from Project 2B	**2F Mastery (Grader Project)** **Mastery and Transfer of Learning** A demonstration of your mastery of the skills in Project 2B with extensive decision making.	In MyITLab and in text
2G **MyITLab**	Objectives 1–6 from Projects 2A and 2B	**2G Mastery (Grader Project)** **Mastery and Transfer of Learning** A demonstration of your mastery of the skills in Projects 2A and 2B with extensive decision making.	In MyITLab and in text
2H	Combination of Objectives from Projects 2A and 2B	**2H GO! Fix It (Scorecard Grading)** **Critical Thinking** A demonstration of your mastery of the skills in Projects 2A and 2B by creating a correct result from a document that contains errors you must find.	Instructor Resource Center (IRC and MyITLab)
2I	Combination of Objectives from Projects 2A and 2B	**2I GO! Make It (Scorecard Grading)** **Critical Thinking** A demonstration of your mastery of the skills in Projects 2A and 2B by creating a result from a supplied picture.	IRC and MyITLab
2J	Combination of Objectives from Projects 2A and 2B	**2J GO! Solve It (Rubric Grading)** **Critical Thinking** A demonstration of your mastery of the skills in Projects 2A and 2B, your decision-making skills, and your critical-thinking skills. A task-specific rubric helps you self-assess your result.	IRC and MyITLab
2K	Combination of Objectives from Projects 2A and 2B	**2K GO! Solve It (Rubric Grading)** **Critical Thinking** A demonstration of your mastery of the skills in Projects 2A and 2B, your decision-making skills, and your critical-thinking skills. A task-specific rubric helps you self-assess your result.	In text
2L	Combination of Objectives from Projects 2A and 2B	**2L GO! Think (Rubric Grading)** **Critical Thinking** A demonstration of your understanding of the chapter concepts applied in a manner that you would outside of college. An analytic rubric helps you and your instructor grade the quality of your work by comparing it to the work an expert in the discipline would create.	In text
2M	Combination of Objectives from Projects 2A and 2B	**2M GO! Think (Rubric Grading)** **Critical Thinking** A demonstration of your understanding of the chapter concepts applied in a manner that you would outside of college. An analytic rubric helps you and your instructor grade the quality of your work by comparing it to the work an expert in the discipline would create.	IRC and MyITLab
2N	Combination of Objectives from Projects 2A and 2B	**2N You and GO! (Rubric Grading)** **Critical Thinking** A demonstration of your understanding of the chapter concepts applied in a manner that you would in a personal situation. An analytic rubric helps you and your instructor grade the quality of your work.	IRC and MyITLab
2O	Combination of Objectives from Projects 2A and 2B	**2O Collaborative Team Project for Word Chapter 2 Critical Thinking** A demonstration of your understanding of concepts and your ability to work collaboratively in a group role-playing assessment, requiring both collaboration and self-management.	IRC and MyITLab

GLOSSARY

GLOSSARY OF CHAPTER KEY TERMS

AutoCorrect A feature that corrects common typing and spelling errors as you type, for example, changing *teh* to *the*.

Body The text of a letter.

Cell The box at the intersection of a row and column in a Word table.

Complimentary closing A parting farewell in a business letter.

Cover letter A document that you send with your resume to provide additional information about your skills and experience.

Date & Time A command with which you can automatically insert the current date and time into a document in a variety of formats.

Dateline The first line in a business letter that contains the current date and which is positioned just below the letterhead if a letterhead is used.

Drag-and-drop A technique by which you can move, by dragging, selected text from one location in a document to another.

Enclosures Additional documents included with a business letter.

Inside address The name and address of the person receiving the letter and positioned below the date line.

Letterhead The personal or company information that displays at the top of a letter.

No Paragraph Space Style The built-in paragraph style—available from the Paragraph Spacing command—that inserts *no* extra space before or after a paragraph and uses line spacing of 1.

Normal template The template that serves as a basis for all Word documents.

Office Presentation Service A Word feature to present your Word document to others who can watch in a web browser.

One-click Row/Column Insertion A Word table feature with which you can insert a new row or column by pointing to the desired location and then clicking.

Salutation The greeting line of a business letter.

Single spacing The common name for line spacing in which there is *no* extra space before or after a paragraph and uses line spacing of 1.

Skype A Microsoft product with which you can make voice calls, make video calls, transfer files, or send messages—including instant messages and text messages—over the Internet.

Style set A collection of character and paragraph formatting that is stored and named.

Subject line The optional line following the inside address in a business letter that states the purpose of the letter.

Synonyms Words with the same or similar meaning.

Table An arrangement of information organized into rows and columns.

Template An existing document that you use as a starting point for a new document; it opens a copy of itself, unnamed, and then you use the structure—and possibly some content, such as headings—as the starting point for new a document.

Thesaurus A research tool that provides a list of synonyms.

Writer's identification The name and title of the author of a letter, placed near the bottom of the letter under the complimentary closing—also referred to as the *writer's signature block*.

Writer's signature block The name and title of the author of a letter, placed near the bottom of the letter, under the complimentary closing—also referred to as the *writer's identification*.

Skills Review   Project 2C Student Resume

Apply 2A skills from these Objectives:

1 Create a Table
2 Format a Table
3 Present a Word Document Online

In the following Skills Review, you will use a table to create a resume for Ashley Kent. Your completed resume will look similar to the one shown in Figure 2.37.

PROJECT FILES

For Project 2C, you will need the following files:

New blank Word document
w02C_Skills
w02C_Experience

You will save your document as:

Lastname_Firstname_2C_Student_Resume

PROJECT RESULTS

Build From Scratch

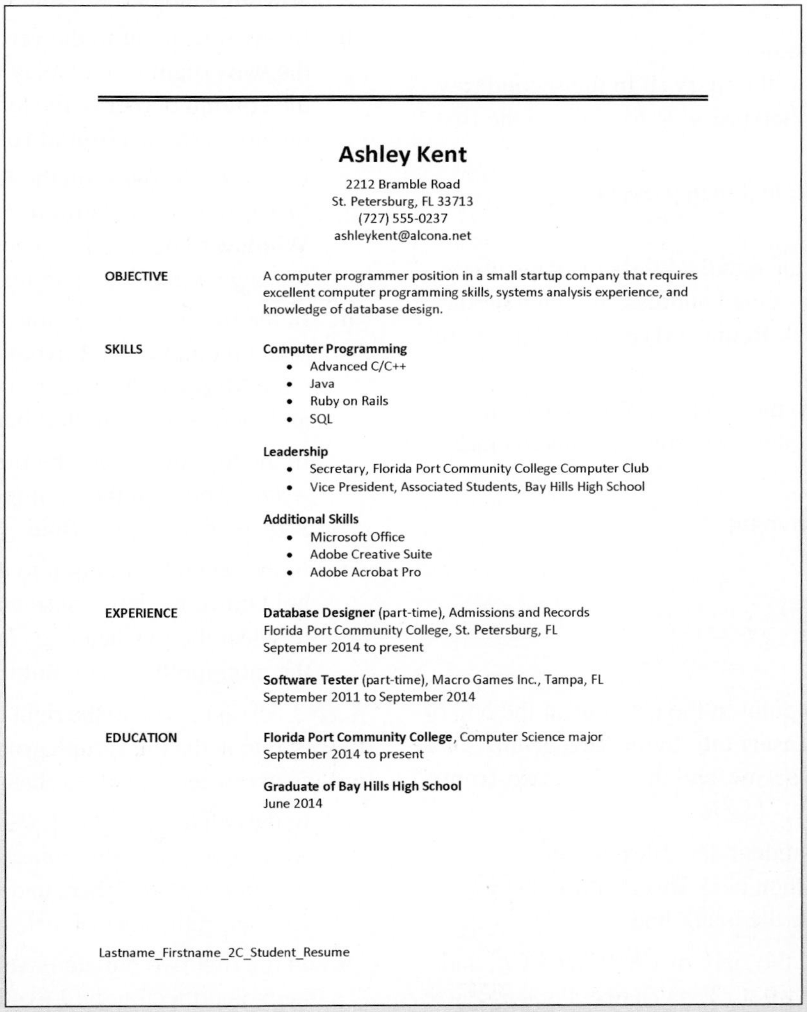

Ashley Kent

2212 Bramble Road
St. Petersburg, FL 33713
(727) 555-0237
ashleykent@alcona.net

OBJECTIVE A computer programmer position in a small startup company that requires excellent computer programming skills, systems analysis experience, and knowledge of database design.

SKILLS **Computer Programming**
- Advanced C/C++
- Java
- Ruby on Rails
- SQL

Leadership
- Secretary, Florida Port Community College Computer Club
- Vice President, Associated Students, Bay Hills High School

Additional Skills
- Microsoft Office
- Adobe Creative Suite
- Adobe Acrobat Pro

EXPERIENCE **Database Designer** (part-time), Admissions and Records
Florida Port Community College, St. Petersburg, FL
September 2014 to present

Software Tester (part-time), Macro Games Inc., Tampa, FL
September 2011 to September 2014

EDUCATION **Florida Port Community College**, Computer Science major
September 2014 to present

Graduate of Bay Hills High School
June 2014

Lastname_Firstname_2C_Student_Resume

Word 2016, Windows 10, Microsoft Corporation

FIGURE 2.37

(Project 2C Student Resume continues on the next page)

1 Start Word and display a blank document. Be sure that formatting marks and rulers display. **Save** the document in your **Word Chapter 2** folder as **Lastname_Firstname_2C_Student_Resume**

a. Add the file name to the footer, and then close the footer area. Click the **Insert tab**, and then in the **Tables group**, click **Table**. In the **Table** grid, in the fourth row, click the second square to insert a **2x4** table.

b. In the first cell of the table, type **Ashley Kent** and then press Enter. Type the following text, pressing Enter after each line *except* the last line:

   2212 Bramble Road

   St. Petersburg, FL 33713

   (727) 555-0237

   ashleykent@alcona.net

c. Press ↓ to move to the first cell in the second row. Type **SKILLS** and then press ↓ to move to the first cell in the third row.

d. Type **EXPERIENCE** and then press ↓. Type **EDUCATION**

e. In the first cell, if the email address displays in blue, right-click the email address, and then on the shortcut menu, click **Remove Hyperlink**. **Save** your document.

2 Click in the cell to the right of *SKILLS*, and then type the following, pressing Enter after each line *including* the last line:

   Computer Programming

   Advanced C/C++

   Java

   Ruby on Rails

   SQL

a. With the insertion point in the new line at the end of the cell, click the **Insert tab**. In the **Text group**, click the **Object button arrow**, and then click **Text from File**.

b. Navigate to your student data files, select **w02C_Skills**, and then click **Insert**. Press Backspace one time to remove the blank line.

c. Click in the cell to the right of *EXPERIENCE*, and then insert the file **w02C_Experience**. Press Backspace one time to remove the blank line.

d. Click in the cell to the right of *EDUCATION*, and then type the following, pressing Enter after all lines *except* the last line:

   Florida Port Community College, Computer Science major

   September 2014 to present

   Graduate of Bay Hills High School

   June 2014

3 Point to the upper left corner of the *SKILLS* cell, and then click the **Row Insertion** button. In the first cell of the new row, type **OBJECTIVE** and then press Tab.

a. Type **A computer programmer position in a small startup company that requires excellent computer programming skills, systems analysis experience, and knowledge of database design.**

b. In any row, point to the vertical border between the two columns to display the ⊹ pointer. Drag the column border to the left to approximately **1.5 inches on the horizontal ruler**.

c. Under **Table Tools**, on the **Layout tab**, in the **Cell Size group**, click **AutoFit**, and then click **AutoFit Window** to be sure that your table stretches across the page within the margins.

d. In the first row of the table, drag across both cells to select them. On the **Layout tab**, in the **Merge group**, click **Merge Cells**. Right-click over the selected cell, and then on the mini toolbar, click **Center**.

e. In the top row, select the first paragraph of text— *Ashley Kent*. On the mini toolbar, increase the **Font Size** to **20** and apply **Bold**.

f. In the second row, point to the word *OBJECTIVE*, hold down the left mouse button, and then drag down to select the row headings in uppercase letters. On the mini toolbar, click **Bold**. **Save** your document.

4 Click in the cell to the right of *OBJECTIVE*. On the **Layout tab**, in the **Paragraph group**, click the **Spacing After up spin arrow** three times to change the spacing to **18 pt**.

a. In the cell to the right of *SKILLS*, apply **Bold** to the words *Computer Programming*, *Leadership*, and *Additional Skills*. Then, under each bold heading in the cell, select the lines of text, and create a bulleted list.

b. In the first two bulleted lists, click in the last bullet item, and then on the **Layout tab**, in the **Paragraph group**, set the **Spacing After** to **12 pt**.

(Project 2C Student Resume continues on the next page)

c. In the last bulleted list, click in the last bullet item, and then set the **Spacing After** to **18 pt**.

d. In the cell to the right of *EXPERIENCE*, apply **Bold** to *Database Designer* and *Software Tester*. Click in the line *September 2014 to present* and apply **Spacing After** of **12 pt**. Click in the line *September 2011 to September 2014* and apply **Spacing After** of **18 pt**.

e. In the cell to the right of *EDUCATION*, apply **Bold** to *Florida Port Community College* and *Graduate of Bay Hills High School*.

f. In the same cell, click in the line *September 2014 to present* and apply **Spacing After** of **12 pt**.

g. In the first row, click in the last line—*ashleykent@ alcona.net*—and then change the **Spacing After** to **18 pt**. Click in the first line—*Ashley Kent*—and set the **Spacing Before** to **30 pt** and the **Spacing After** to **6 pt**.

5 Point to the upper left corner of the table, and then click the **table move handle** ⊞ to select the entire table. Under **Table Tools**, on the **Design tab**, in the **Borders group**, click the **Borders button arrow**, and then click **No Border**.

a. In the **Borders group**, click the **Borders button arrow** again, and then at the bottom of the gallery, click **Borders and Shading**. In the **Borders and Shading** dialog box, under **Setting**, click **Custom**. Under **Style**, scroll down slightly, and then click the style with two equal lines.

b. Click the **Width arrow**, and then click **1 1/2 pt**. Under **Preview**, click the top border of the preview box, and then click **OK**.

c. Click the **File tab** to display **Backstage** view, and then in the lower right portion of the screen, click **Show All Properties**. In the **Tags** box, type **resume, table** and in the **Subject** box, type your course name and section number. In the **Author** box, be sure your name is indicated and edit if necessary.

d. On the left, click **Print** to display **Print Preview**. If necessary, return to the document and make any necessary changes.

e. **Save** 🖫 your document, and then if you want to do so, present your document online to a fellow classmate. If directed by your instructor to do so, submit your paper printout, your electronic image of your document that looks like a printed document, or your original Word file. Close Word.

END | You have completed Project 2C

Apply **2B** skills from these Objectives:

4 Create a Custom Word Template

5 Correct and Reorganize Text

6 Use the Proofing Options and Print an Envelope

Skills Review   Project 2D Cover Letter

In the following Skills Review, you will create a letterhead, save the letterhead as a custom Word template, and then use the letterhead to create a cover letter to accompany a resume. If you have an envelope and printer available, you will format and print an envelope. Your completed document will look similar to Figure 2.38.

PROJECT FILES

For Project 2D, you will need the following files:

New blank Word document
w02D_Cover_Letter_Text

You will save your documents as:

Lastname_Firstname_2D_Cover_Letter

Build From Scratch

PROJECT RESULTS

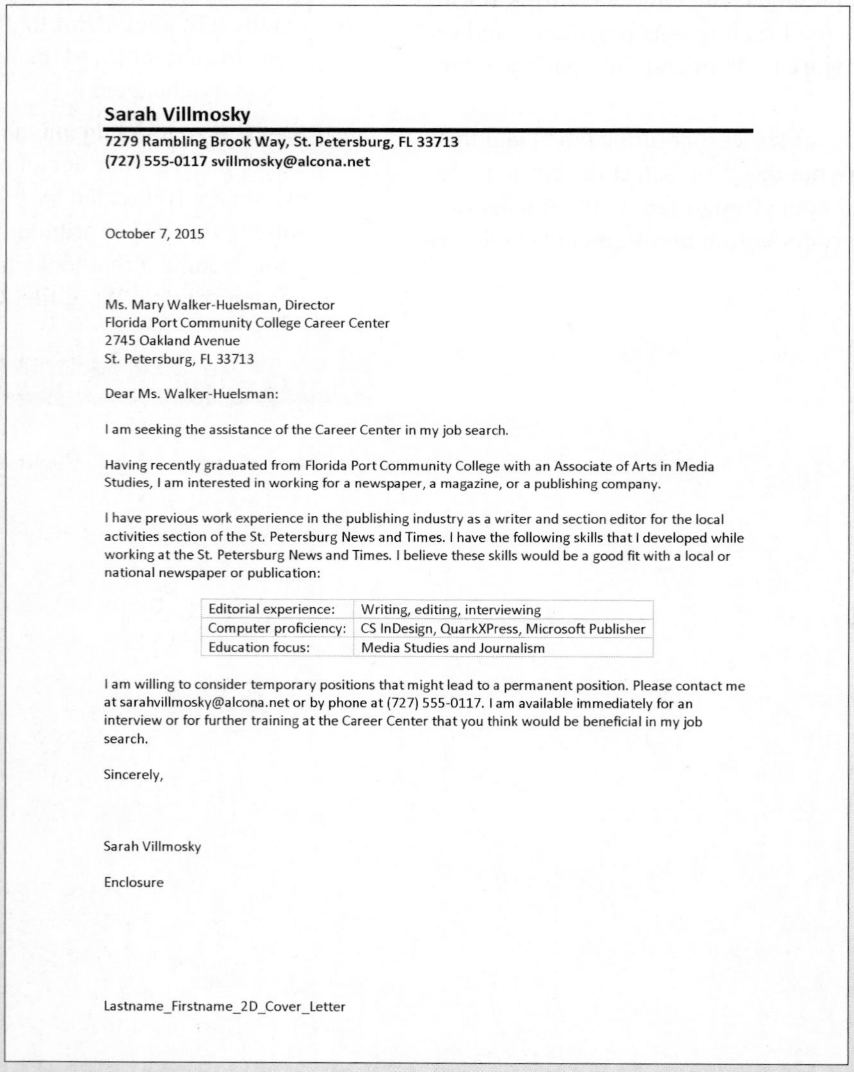

Sarah Villmosky
7279 Rambling Brook Way, St. Petersburg, FL 33713
(727) 555-0117 svillmosky@alcona.net

October 7, 2015

Ms. Mary Walker-Huelsman, Director
Florida Port Community College Career Center
2745 Oakland Avenue
St. Petersburg, FL 33713

Dear Ms. Walker-Huelsman:

I am seeking the assistance of the Career Center in my job search.

Having recently graduated from Florida Port Community College with an Associate of Arts in Media Studies, I am interested in working for a newspaper, a magazine, or a publishing company.

I have previous work experience in the publishing industry as a writer and section editor for the local activities section of the St. Petersburg News and Times. I have the following skills that I developed while working at the St. Petersburg News and Times. I believe these skills would be a good fit with a local or national newspaper or publication:

Editorial experience:	Writing, editing, interviewing
Computer proficiency:	CS InDesign, QuarkXPress, Microsoft Publisher
Education focus:	Media Studies and Journalism

I am willing to consider temporary positions that might lead to a permanent position. Please contact me at sarahvillmosky@alcona.net or by phone at (727) 555-0117. I am available immediately for an interview or for further training at the Career Center that you think would be beneficial in my job search.

Sincerely,

Sarah Villmosky

Enclosure

Lastname_Firstname_2D_Cover_Letter

Word 2016, Windows 10, Microsoft Corporation

FIGURE 2.38   (Project 2D Cover Letter continues on the next page)

Skills Review   Project 2D Cover Letter (continued)

1 Start Word and display a blank document; be sure that formatting marks and rulers display. On the **Design tab**, in the **Document Formatting group**, click **Paragraph Spacing**, and then click **No Paragraph Space**.

a. Type **Sarah Villmosky** and then press Enter. Type **7279 Rambling Brook Way, St. Petersburg, FL 33713** and then press Enter.

b. Type **(727) 555-0117 svillmosky@alcona.net** and then press Enter. If the web address changes to blue text, right-click the web address, and then click **Remove Hyperlink**.

c. Select the first paragraph—*Sarah Villmosky*—and then on the mini toolbar, apply **Bold**, and change the **Font Size** to **16**.

d. Select the second and third paragraphs, and then on the mini toolbar, apply **Bold**, and change the **Font Size** to **12**.

e. Click anywhere in the first paragraph—*Sarah Villmosky*. On the **Home tab**, in the **Paragraph group**, click the **Borders button arrow**, and then click **Borders and Shading**. Under **Style**, click the first style—a single solid line. Click the **Width arrow**, and then click **3 pt**. In the **Preview** area, click the bottom border, and then click **OK**.

f. Click the **File tab**, click **Save As**, and then click **Browse** to display the **Save As** dialog box. In the lower portion of the dialog box, in the **Save as type** box, click the arrow, and then click **Word Template**. In the **File name** box, using your own name, type **Lastname_Firstname_2D_Letterhead_Template** and then click **Save** to save the custom Word template in the default path, which is the Templates folder on the hard drive of your computer.

g. Click the **File tab** to display **Backstage** view, and then click **Close** to close the file but leave Word open.

h. With Word open but no documents displayed, click the **File tab**, and then click **New**. Under **Suggested searches**, click **PERSONAL**, and then locate and click the letterhead template that you just created.

i. Click the **File tab**, click **Save As**, click **Browse** to display the **Save As** dialog box, navigate to your **Word Chapter 2** folder, and then using your own name **Save** the file as **Lastname_Firstname_2D_Cover_Letter**

j. On the **Insert tab**, in the **Header & Footer group**, click **Footer**, click **Edit Footer**, and then in the

Insert group, click **Document Info**. Click **File Name**, and then click **Close Header and Footer**. Click **Save**.

2 Click the **File tab**. On the left, click **Options**. On the left side of the **Word Options** dialog box, click **Proofing**, and then under **AutoCorrect options**, click the **AutoCorrect Options** button.

a. In the **AutoCorrect** dialog box, click the **AutoCorrect tab**. Under **Replace**, type the misspelled word **assistence** and under **With**, type **assistance** Click **Add**. If the entry already exists, click Replace instead, and then click Yes. Click **OK** two times to close the dialog boxes.

b. Press Ctrl + End, and then press Enter three times. On the **Insert tab**, in the **Text group**, click **Date & Time**, and then click the third date format. Click **OK**.

c. Press Enter four times. Type the following inside address using four lines, but do *not* press Enter after the last line:

Ms. Mary Walker-Huelsman, Director
Florida Port Community College Career Center
2745 Oakland Avenue
St. Petersburg, FL 33713

d. Press Enter two times, type **Dear Ms. Walker-Huelsman:** and then press Enter two times. Type, exactly as shown with the intentional misspelling, and then watch *assistence* as you press Spacebar after typing it: **I am seeking the assistence**

e. Type **of the Career Center in my job search.** Press Enter two times.

f. On the **Insert tab**, in the **Text Group**, click the **Object button arrow**, and then click **Text from File**. From your student data files, locate and insert the file **w02D_Cover_Letter_Text**.

g. Scroll to view the lower portion of the page, and be sure your insertion point is in the empty paragraph mark at the end. Press Enter, type **Sincerely,** and then press Enter four times. Type **Sarah Villmosky** and press Enter two times. Type **Enclosure** and then **Save** your document.

h. Press Ctrl + Home. On the **Home tab**, in the **Editing group**, click **Find**. In the **Navigation** pane that opens on the left, click in the search box, and then type **journalism** In the letter, double-click the yellow highlighted word *Journalism* and type **Media Studies**

(Project 2D Cover Letter continues on the next page)

i. **Close** the **Navigation** pane, and then on the **Home tab**, in the **Editing group**, click **Replace**. In the **Find and Replace** dialog box, in the **Find what** box, replace the existing text by typing **SPNT** In the **Replace with** box, type **St. Petersburg News and Times** Click **More** to expand the dialog box, select the **Match case** check box, click **Replace All**, and then click **OK**. Two replacements are made. **Close** the **Find and Replace** dialog box.

j. In the paragraph that begins *I am available*, hold down Ctrl, and then click anywhere in the first sentence. Drag the selected sentence to the end of the paragraph by positioning the small vertical line that floats with the point to the left of the paragraph mark.

3 Below the paragraph that begins *I have previous*, click to position the insertion point in the blank paragraph, and then press Enter one time. On the **Insert tab**, in the **Tables group**, click **Table**. In the **Table grid**, in the third row, click the second square to insert a **2×3** table. Type the following information in the table:

Editorial experience:	Writing, editing, interviewing
Computer proficiency:	CS InDesign, QuarkXPress, Microsoft Publisher
Education focus:	Media Studies and Journalism

a. Point outside of the upper left corner of the table and click the **table move handle** button to select the entire table. On the **Layout tab**, in the **Cell Size group**, click **AutoFit**, and then click **AutoFit Contents**.

b. With the table selected, on the **Table Tools Design tab**, in the **Table Styles group**, click **More** ⬇. Under **Plain Tables**, click the second style—**Table Grid Light**.

c. With the table still selected, on the **Home tab**, in the **Paragraphs group**, click **Center**. **Save** your document.

4 Press Ctrl + Home. On the **Review tab**, in the **Proofing group**, click **Spelling & Grammar**. For the spelling of *Villmosky*, in the **Spelling** pane, click **Ignore All**. For the spelling of *Huelsman*, click **Ignore All**.

a. For the grammar error *a*, click **Change**. Click **Change** to correct the misspelling of *intrested*. Click **Delete** to delete the duplicated word *for*. Change *activitys* to *activities*. Change *benificial* to *beneficial*. Click **OK** when the Spelling & Grammar check is complete.

b. In the paragraph that begins *I am willing*, in the third line, double-click the word *preparation*. In the **Proofing group**, click **Thesaurus**.

c. In the **Thesaurus** pane, point to *training*, click the arrow, and then click **Insert**. **Close** the **Thesaurus** pane.

d. Click **File tab**, and then in the lower right portion of the screen, click **Show All Properties**. In the **Tags** box, type **cover letter** and in the **Subject** box, type your course name and section number.

e. In the **Author** box, be sure your name is indicated and edit if necessary. On the left, click **Print**. If necessary, return to the document and make any necessary changes. Save your document. If directed by your instructor to do so, submit your paper printout, your electronic image of your document that looks like a printed document, or your original Word file. **Close** Word.

END | You have completed Project 2D

MyITLab grader

Apply 2A skills from these Objectives:

1 Create a Table
2 Format a Table
3 Present a Word Document Online

In the following Mastering Word project, you will create an announcement for new job postings at the Career Center. Your completed document will look similar to Figure 2.39.

PROJECT FILES

For Project 2E, you will need the following files:

New blank Word document
w02E_New_Jobs

You will save your document as:

Lastname_Firstname_2E_Job_Listings

PROJECT RESULTS

Build From Scratch

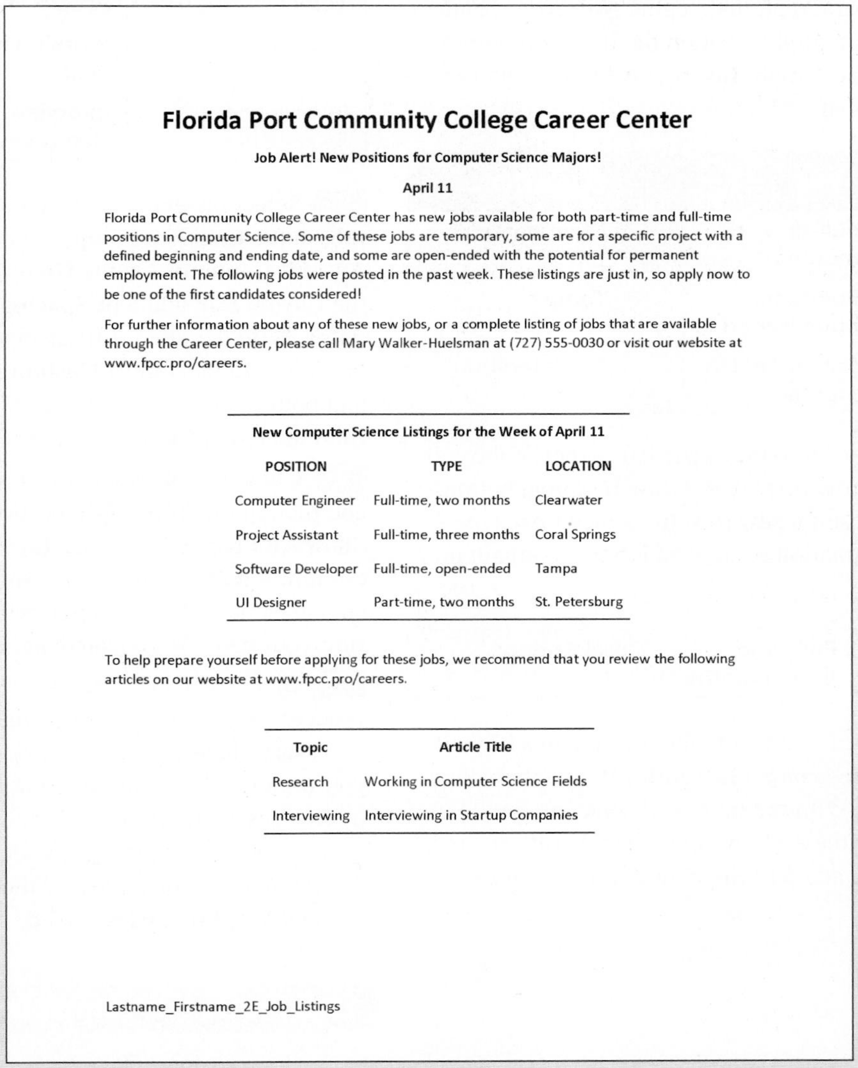

Florida Port Community College Career Center

Job Alert! New Positions for Computer Science Majors!

April 11

Florida Port Community College Career Center has new jobs available for both part-time and full-time positions in Computer Science. Some of these jobs are temporary, some are for a specific project with a defined beginning and ending date, and some are open-ended with the potential for permanent employment. The following jobs were posted in the past week. These listings are just in, so apply now to be one of the first candidates considered!

For further information about any of these new jobs, or a complete listing of jobs that are available through the Career Center, please call Mary Walker-Huelsman at (727) 555-0030 or visit our website at www.fpcc.pro/careers.

New Computer Science Listings for the Week of April 11		
POSITION	TYPE	LOCATION
Computer Engineer	Full-time, two months	Clearwater
Project Assistant	Full-time, three months	Coral Springs
Software Developer	Full-time, open-ended	Tampa
UI Designer	Part-time, two months	St. Petersburg

To help prepare yourself before applying for these jobs, we recommend that you review the following articles on our website at www.fpcc.pro/careers.

Topic	Article Title
Research	Working in Computer Science Fields
Interviewing	Interviewing in Startup Companies

Lastname_Firstname_2E_Job_Listings

Word 2016, Windows 10, Microsoft Corporation

FIGURE 2.39

(Project 2E Table of Job Listings continues on the next page)

Mastering Word | **Project 2E Table of Job Listings** (continued)

1 Start Word and display a blank document; display formatting marks and rulers. **Save** the document in your **Word Chapter 2** folder as **Lastname_Firstname_2E_Job_Listings** and then add the file name to the footer.

2 Type **Florida Port Community College Career Center** and press Enter. Type **Job Alert! New Positions for Computer Science Majors!** and press Enter. Type **April 11** and press Enter. **Insert** the file **w02E_New_Jobs**.

3 At the top of the document, select and **Center** the three title lines. Select the title *Florida Port Community College Career Center*, change the **Font Size** to **20 pt** and apply **Bold**. Apply **Bold** to the second and third title lines. Locate the paragraph that begins *For further*, and then below that paragraph, position the insertion point in the second blank paragraph. **Insert** a **3x4** table. Enter the following in the table:

POSITION	TYPE	LOCATION
Computer Engineer	Full-time, two months	Clearwater
Software Developer	Full-time, open-ended	Tampa
UI Designer	Part-time, two months	St. Petersburg

4 In the table, point to the upper left corner of the cell *Software Developer* to display the **Row Insertion** button, and then click to insert a new row. In the new row, type the following information so that the job titles remain in alphabetic order:

Project Assistant	Full-time, three months	Coral Springs

5 Select the entire table. On the **Table Tools Layout tab**, in the **Cell Size group**, click **AutoFit**, and then click **AutoFit Contents**. With the table still selected, on the **Home tab**, **Center** the table. With the table still selected, on the **Layout tab**, add **6 pt Spacing Before** and **6 pt Spacing After**.

6 With the table still selected, remove all table borders, and then add a **Custom 1 pt** solid line top border and bottom border. Select all three cells in the first row, apply **Bold**, and then **Center** the text. Click anywhere in the first row, and then on the **Table Tools Layout tab**, in the **Rows & Columns group**, insert a row above. Merge the three cells in the new top row, and then type **New Computer Science Listings for the Week of April 11** Notice that the new row keeps the formatting of the row from which it was created.

7 In the last blank paragraph at the bottom of the document, **Insert** a **2×3** table. Enter the following:

Topic	Article Title
Research	Working in Computer Science Fields
Interviewing	Interviewing in Startup Companies

8 Select the entire table. On the **Table Tools Layout tab**, in the **Cell Size group**, use the **AutoFit** button to **AutoFit Contents**. On the **Home tab**, **Center** the table. On the **Layout tab**, add **6 pt Spacing Before** and **6 pt Spacing After**. With the table still selected, remove all table borders, and then add a **Custom 1 pt** solid line top border and bottom border. Select the cells in the first row, apply **Bold**, and then **Center** the text.

9 Click the **File tab** to display **Backstage** view, and then in the lower right portion of the screen, click **Show All Properties**. In the **Tags** box type **new listings, computer science** and in the **Subject** box type your course name and section number. In the **Author** box, be sure your name is indicated and edit if necessary.

10 On the left, click **Print** to display **Print Preview**. If necessary, return to the document and make any necessary changes. **Save** your document, and then if you want to do so, present your document online to a fellow classmate. If directed by your instructor to do so, submit your paper printout, your electronic image of your document that looks like a printed document, or your original Word file. **Close** Word.

END | You have completed Project 2E

MyITLab grader

Apply 2B skills from these Objectives:

4 Create a Custom Word Template

5 Correct and Reorganize Text

6 Use the Proofing Options and Print an Envelope

In the following Mastering Word project, you will create a memo that includes job tips for students and graduates using the services of the Florida Port Community College Career Center. Your completed document will look similar to Figure 2.40.

PROJECT FILES

For Project 2F, you will need the following files:

w02F_Memo_Template
w02F_Memo_Text

You will save your documents as:

Lastname_Firstname_2F_Career_Tips

PROJECT RESULTS

Florida Port Community College Career Center

Memo

DATE:	January 12, 2019
TO:	Florida Port Community College Students and Graduates
FROM:	Mary Walker-Huelsman, Director
SUBJECT:	Using the Career Center

Tips for Students and Recent Graduates of Florida Port Community College

It is no surprise that after you leave college, you will be entering one of the most competitive job markets on record. That doesn't mean it's impossible to get your dream job. It does, however, mean that it's critical that you know how to put your best self forward to job interviewers and that you highlight all of your academic, personal, and professional achievements in a way that will help you stand out from the crowd. An Associate degree from Florida Port Community College is just the first step on your journey to getting the professional career that you want.

Give 100 Percent to Every Job

Treat every job as a career. Be willing to go beyond your assignment and complete tasks not delegated to you. Take the initiative to see ways to contribute to the company. Be willing to stay if there is unfinished work. You never know who you will meet on any job. Making a positive impression every time will give you a network of people who may help you down the road. Networking is an established means professionals use to further their careers. You can always benefit from networking. You will distinguish yourself from potential competitors if you truly give 100 percent to each job. Always remember these job basics:

Job Item	Tip for Success
Time Management	Show up on time and don't hurry to leave
Attire	Dress appropriately for the job
Work Area	Keep your work area neat and organized

Use the Career Center

Here at the Career Center and on our website, we offer tips on how to write a stellar resume and a cover letter that puts your hard work up front and center. Have you volunteered somewhere? Have you participated at a club at school? Were you a TA or a tutor? Did you make the Dean's list or graduate with honors? These are the kinds of achievements interviewers want to see. Meet with your career guidance counselor and together, come up with a plan to find the jobs that you want and get the important interview.

Lastname_Firstname_2F_Career_Tips

Word 2016, Windows 10, Microsoft Corporation

FIGURE 2.40

(Project 2F Career Tips Memo continues on the next page)

Mastering Word | **Project 2F Career Tips Memo** (continued)

1 Start Word. From your student data files, open the file **02F_Memo_Template**.

2 Display the **Save As** dialog box. Navigate to your **Word Chapter 2** folder, and then in the **File name** box, using your own name, type **Lastname_Firstname_2F_Career_Tips**

3 Add the file name to the footer. At the top of your document, in the *DATE* paragraph, click to the right of the tab formatting mark, and then type **January 12, 2019** Use a similar technique to add the following information:

TO:	Florida Port Community College Students and Graduates
FROM:	Mary Walker-Huelsman, Director
SUBJECT:	Using the CC

4 Position the insertion point in the blank paragraph below the memo heading. **Insert** the file **w02F_Memo_Text**, and then press Backspace one time to remove the blank line at the end of the inserted text.

5 Press Ctrl + Home to move to the top of the document. By using either the **Spelling & Grammar** command on the Review tab or by right-clicking words that display blue or red wavy underlines, correct or ignore words flagged as spelling, grammar, or word usage errors. *Note*: If you are checking an entire document, it is usually preferable to move to the top of the document, and then use the Spelling & Grammar command so that you do not overlook any flagged words.

6 In the paragraph that begins *Treat every job*, in the second line of the paragraph, locate and double-click **donate**. On the **Review tab**, in the **Proofing group**, click **Thesaurus**, and then from the **Thesaurus** pane, change

the word to *contribute*. In the last line of the same paragraph, point to **fundamentals**, right-click, point to **Synonyms**, and then click **basics**.

7 In the paragraph that begins *An Associate degree*, move the first sentence to the end of the paragraph.

8 At the end of the paragraph that begins *Treat every job*, click in the blank paragraph, and then **Insert** a **2x4** table. Type the following information in the table:

Job Item	Tip for Success
Time Management	Show up on time and don't hurry to leave
Attire	Dress appropriately for the job
Work Area	Keep your work area neat and organized

9 Select the entire table. **AutoFit Contents**, and then apply the **Grid Table 1 Light – Accent 1** table style—under **Grid Tables**, in the first row, the second style. **Center** the table.

10 Press Ctrl + Home to move to the top of your document. Using Match Case, replace all instances of *CC* with *Career Center*.

11 Click the **File tab**, and then click **Show All Properties**. As the **Tags**, type **memo, job tips** As the **Subject**, type your course name and section number. Be sure your name is indicated as the **Author**, and edit if necessary. View the Print Preview, and make any necessary changes. Save your document. If directed by your instructor to do so, submit your paper printout, your electronic image of your document that looks like a printed document, or your original Word file. **Close** Word.

END | You have completed Project 2F

Mastering Word **Project 2G Application Letter and Resume**

In the following Mastering Word project, you will create a letter and resume. Your completed document will look similar to Figure 2.41.

Apply 2A and 2B skills from these Objectives:

1 Create a Table
2 Format a Table
3 Present a Word Document Online
4 Create a Custom Word Template
5 Correct and Reorganize Text
6 Use the Proofing Options and Print an Envelope

PROJECT FILES

For Project 2G, you will need the following files:

w02G_Letter_and_Resume
w02G_Letter_Text

You will save your documents as:

You will save your document as
Lastname_Firstname_2G_Letter_and_Resume

PROJECT RESULTS

FIGURE 2.41

Word 2016, Windows 10, Microsoft Corporation

(Project 2G Application Letter and Resume continues on the next page)

Mastering Word | Project 2G Application Letter and Resume (continued)

1 Start Word. From your student data files, open the file **w02G_Letter_and_Resume**.

2 Display the **Save As** dialog box. Navigate to your **Word Chapter 2** folder, and then in the **File name** box, using your own name, type **Lastname_Firstname_2G_Letter_and_Resume**

3 Add the file name to the footer. Be sure that rulers and formatting marks display. On **Page 1**, click in the blank paragraph below the letterhead, and then press Enter three times. Use the **Date & Time** command to insert the current date using the third format, and then press Enter four times. Type the following:

> **Ms. Mary Walker-Huelsman, Director**
>
> **Florida Port Community College Career Center**
>
> **2745 Oakland Avenue**
>
> **St. Petersburg, FL 33713**

4 Press Enter two times, type **Dear Ms. Walker-Huelsman:** and press Enter two times. **Insert** the text from the file **w02G_Letter_Text** and press Backspace one time to remove the blank line at the bottom of the selected text.

5 Press Ctrl + Home to move to the top of the document. By using either the **Spelling & Grammar** command on the **Review tab** or by right-clicking words that display blue or red wavy underlines, correct or ignore words flagged as spelling, grammar, or word usage errors. *Hint*: If you are checking an entire document, it is usually preferable to move to the top of the document, and then use the Spelling & Grammar command so that you do not overlook any flagged words.

6 Press Ctrl + Home to move to the top of the document again, and then replace all instances of **posting** with **listing**

7 In the paragraph that begins *The job description*, use the Thesaurus pane or the Synonyms command on the shortcut menu to change *specific* to *explicit* and *credentials* to *qualifications*.

8 In the paragraph that begins *I currently live in Tampa*, select the first sentence of the paragraph and drag it to the end of the same paragraph.

9 Click to position your insertion point in the *second* blank line below the paragraph that begins *The job description*. **Insert** a **2x3** table, and then type the text shown in Table 1.

TABLE 1

Education	Bachelor of Science, Business Management
Experience	Two years Computer Support experience at a major university
Required Certifications	MCITP, MCDST

10 Select the entire table. **AutoFit Contents**, and then apply the **Table Grid Light** table style—under **Plain Tables**, in the first row, the first style. **Center** the table.

11 In the resume on **Page 2**, insert a new second row in the table. In the first cell of the new row, type **OBJECTIVE** and then apply **Bold** to the text you just typed. Press Tab. Type **To obtain a Business Programmer Analyst position that will use my technical and communications skills and computer support experience.** In the same cell, add **12 pt Spacing After**.

12 Select the entire table. On the **Layout tab**, **AutoFit Contents**. Remove the table borders, and then display the **Borders and Shading** dialog box. With the table selected, create a **Custom** single solid line **1 1/2 pt** top border.

13 In the first row of the resume table, select both cells and then **Merge Cells**. **Center** the five lines and apply **Bold**. In the first row, select **William Franklin** and change the **Font Size** to **20 pt** and add **24 pt Spacing Before**. In the email address at the bottom of the first row, add **24 pt Spacing After**.

14 In the cell to the right of *RELEVANT EXPERIENCE*, below the line that begins *January 2014*, apply bullets to the six lines that comprise the job duties. Create a similar bulleted list for the duties as a Computer Technician. In the cell to the right of *CERTIFICATIONS*, select all four lines and create a bulleted list.

15 Click the **File tab**, and then click **Show All Properties**. As the **Tags**, type **cover letter, resume** As the **Subject**, type your course name and section number. Be sure your name is indicated as the **Author**, and edit if necessary. View the Print Preview, and make any necessary changes. If directed by your instructor to do so, submit your paper printout, your electronic image of your document that looks like a printed document, or your original Word file. **Close** Word.

> **END | You have completed Project 2G**

Apply a combination of the **2A** and **2B** skills.	**GO! Fix It** Project 2H New Jobs **MyITLab**
	GO! Make It Project 2I Training **MyITLab**
	GO! Solve It Project 2J Job Postings **MyITLab**
	GO! Solve It Project 2K Agenda

Build From Scratch

PROJECT FILES

For Project 2K, you will need the following file:

Agenda template from Word's Online templates

You will save your document as:

Lastname_Firstname_2K_Agenda

On Word's opening screen, search for an online template using the search term **formal meeting agenda** Create the agenda and then save it in your Word Chapter 2 folder as **Lastname_Firstname_2K_Agenda** Use the following information to prepare an agenda for an FPCC Career Center meeting.

The meeting will be chaired by Mary Walker-Huelsman. It will be the monthly meeting of the Career Center's staff—Kevin Rau, Marilyn Kelly, André Randolph, Susan Nguyen, and Charles James. The meeting will be held on March 15, 2016, at 3:00 p.m. The old business agenda items (open issues) include 1) seeking more job listings related to the printing and food service industries; 2) expanding the alumni website, and 3) the addition of a part-time trainer. The new business agenda items will include 1) writing a grant so the center can serve more students and alumni; 2) expanding the training area with 20 additional workstations; 3) purchase of new computers for the training room; and 4) renewal of printing service contract.

Add the file name to the footer, add your name, your course name, the section number, and then add the keywords **agenda, monthly staff meeting** to the Properties area. Submit as directed.

Performance Level

Performance Criteria		Exemplary: You consistently applied the relevant skills.	Proficient: You sometimes, but not always, applied the relevant skills.	Developing: You rarely or never applied the relevant skills.
	Select an agenda template	Agenda template is appropriate for the information provided for the meeting.	Agenda template is used, but does not fit the information provided.	No template is used for the agenda.
	Add appropriate information to the template	All information is inserted in the appropriate places.	All information is included, but not in the appropriate places.	Information is missing.
	Format template information	All text in the template is properly aligned and formatted.	All text is included, but alignment or formatting is inconsistent.	No additional formatting has been added.

END | You have completed Project 2K

RUBRIC

The following outcomes-based assessments are *open-ended assessments*. That is, there is no specific correct result; your result will depend on your approach to the information provided. Make *Professional Quality* your goal. Use the following scoring rubric to guide you in *how* to approach the problem and then to evaluate *how well* your approach solves the problem.

The *criteria*—Software Mastery, Content, Format and Layout, and Process—represent the knowledge and skills you have gained that you can apply to solving the problem. The *levels of performance*—Professional Quality, Approaching Professional Quality, or Needs Quality Improvements—help you and your instructor evaluate your result.

	Your completed project is of Professional Quality if you:	Your completed project is Approaching Professional Quality if you:	Your completed project Needs Quality Improvements if you:
1-Software Mastery	Choose and apply the most appropriate skills, tools, and features and identify efficient methods to solve the problem.	Choose and apply some appropriate skills, tools, and features, but not in the most efficient manner.	Choose inappropriate skills, tools, or features, or are inefficient in solving the problem.
2-Content	Construct a solution that is clear and well organized, contains content that is accurate, appropriate to the audience and purpose, and is complete. Provide a solution that contains no errors of spelling, grammar, or style.	Construct a solution in which some components are unclear, poorly organized, inconsistent, or incomplete. Misjudge the needs of the audience. Have some errors in spelling, grammar, or style, but the errors do not detract from comprehension.	Construct a solution that is unclear, incomplete, or poorly organized, contains some inaccurate or inappropriate content, and contains many errors of spelling, grammar, or style. Do not solve the problem.
3-Format and Layout	Format and arrange all elements to communicate information and ideas, clarify function, illustrate relationships, and indicate relative importance.	Apply appropriate format and layout features to some elements, but not others. Overuse features, causing minor distraction.	Apply format and layout that does not communicate information or ideas clearly. Do not use format and layout features to clarify function, illustrate relationships, or indicate relative importance. Use available features excessively, causing distraction.
4-Process	Use an organized approach that integrates planning, development, self-assessment, revision, and reflection.	Demonstrate an organized approach in some areas, but not others; or, use an insufficient process of organization throughout.	Do not use an organized approach to solve the problem.

Apply a combination of the 2A and 2B skills.

Build
From
Scratch

GO! Think | Project 2L Workshops

PROJECT FILES

For Project 2L, you will need the following files:

New blank Word document
w02L_Workshop_Information

You will save your document as:

Lastname_Firstname_2L_Workshops

The Florida Port Community College Career Center offers a series of workshops for both students and alumni. Any eligible student or graduate can attend the workshops, and there is no fee. Currently, the Career Center offers a three-session workshop covering Excel and Word, a two-session workshop covering Business Communication, and a one-session workshop covering Creating a Resume.

Print the w02L_Workshop_Information file and use the information to complete this project. Create an announcement with a title, an introductory paragraph, and a table listing the workshops and the topics covered in each workshop. Use the file w02L_Workshop_Information for help with the topics covered in each workshop. Format the table cells appropriately. Add an appropriate footer and document properties. Save the document as **Lastname_Firstname_2L_Workshops** and submit it as directed.

> **END | You have completed Project 2L**

Build from
Scratch

GO! Think! | Project 2M Schedule   MyITLab

Build from
Scratch

You and GO! | Project 2N Personal Resume   MyITLab

Build from
Scratch

GO! Collaborative Team Project | Project 2O Bell Orchid Hotels   MyITLab

Creating Research Papers, Newsletters, and Merged Mailing Labels

PROJECT 3A

OUTCOMES
Create a research paper that includes citations and a bibliography.

PROJECT 3B

OUTCOMES
Create a multiple-column newsletter and merged mailing labels.

OBJECTIVES

1. Create a Research Paper
2. Insert Footnotes in a Research Paper
3. Create Citations and a Bibliography in a Research Paper
4. Use Read Mode and PDF Reflow

OBJECTIVES

5. Format a Multiple-Column Newsletter
6. Use Special Character and Paragraph Formatting
7. Create Mailing Labels Using Mail Merge

Guschenkova/Fotolia

In This Chapter

Microsoft Word provides many tools for creating complex documents. For example, Word has tools that enable you to create a research paper that includes citations, footnotes, and a bibliography. You can also create multiple-column newsletters, format the nameplate at the top of the newsletter, use special character formatting to create distinctive title text, and add borders and shading to paragraphs to highlight important information.

In this chapter, you will edit and format a research paper, create a two-column newsletter, and optionally create a set of mailing labels to mail the newsletter to multiple recipients.

The projects in this chapter relate to **University Medical Center**, which is a patient-care and research institution serving the metropolitan area of Memphis, Tennessee. Because of its outstanding reputation in the medical community and around the world, University Medical Center is able to attract top physicians, scientists, and researchers in all fields of medicine and achieve a level of funding that allows it to build and operate state-of-the-art facilities. A program in biomedical research was recently added. Individuals throughout the eastern United States travel to University Medical Center for diagnosis and care.

Research Paper

PROJECT
3A

MyITLab
Project 3A Training
Project 3A Grader

PROJECT ACTIVITIES

In Activities 3.01 through 3.13, you will edit and format a research paper that contains an overview of a new area of study. This paper was created by Gerard Foster, a medical intern at University Medical Center, for distribution to his classmates studying various physiologic monitoring devices. Your completed document will look similar to Figure 3.1.

Please always review the downloaded Grader instructions before beginning.

PROJECT FILES

MyITLab grader

If your instructor wants you to submit Project 3A in the MyITLab Grader system, log in to MyITLab, locate Grader Project 3A, and then download the files for this project.

For Project 3A, you will need the following file:

w03A_Quantitative_Technology

You will save your document as:

Lastname_Firstname_3A_Quantitative_Technology

PROJECT RESULTS

GO!
Walk Thru
Project 3A

Word 2016, Windows 10, Microsoft Corporation

FIGURE 3.1 Project 3A Quantitative Technology

GO! Learn How
Video W3-1

When you write a research paper or a report for college or business, follow a format prescribed by one of the standard *style guides*—a manual that contains standards for the design and writing of documents. The two most commonly used styles for research papers are those created by the ***Modern Language Association (MLA)*** and the ***American Psychological Association (APA)***; there are several others.

Activity 3.01 | Formatting the Spacing and First-Page Information for a Research Paper

> **ALERT!** To submit as an autograded project, log into MyITLab, download the files for this project, and then use those files instead of w03A_Quantitative_Technology.

When formatting the text for your research paper, refer to the standards for the style guide that you have chosen. In this Activity, you will create a research paper using the MLA style. The MLA style uses 1-inch margins, a 0.5" first line indent, and double spacing throughout the body of the document with no extra space above or below paragraphs.

1 Start Word. On the left, click **Open Other Documents**, click **Browse**, and then navigate to the student data files that accompany this chapter. Locate and open the document **w03A_Quantitative_Technology**. If necessary, display the formatting marks and rulers. In the location where you are storing your projects for this chapter, create a new folder named **Word Chapter 3** and then **Save** the file in the folder as **Lastname_Firstname_3A_Quantitative_Technology**

2 Press [Ctrl] + [A] to select the entire document. On the **Home tab**, in the **Paragraph group**, click **Line and Paragraph Spacing** [icon], and then change the line spacing to **2.0**. On the **Layout tab**, in the **Paragraph group**, change the **Spacing After** to **0 pt**.

3 Press [Ctrl] + [Home] to deselect and move to the top of the document. Press [Enter] one time to create a blank paragraph at the top of the document, and then click to position the insertion point in the blank paragraph. Type **Gerard Foster** and press [Enter].

4 Type **Dr. Hillary Kim** and press [Enter]. Type **Biomedical Research 617** and press [Enter]. Type **February 15, 2016** and press [Enter].

5 Type **Quantified Self Movement Gains Momentum** and then press [Ctrl] + [E], which is the keyboard shortcut to center a paragraph of text. Click **Save** [icon], and then compare your screen with Figure 3.2.

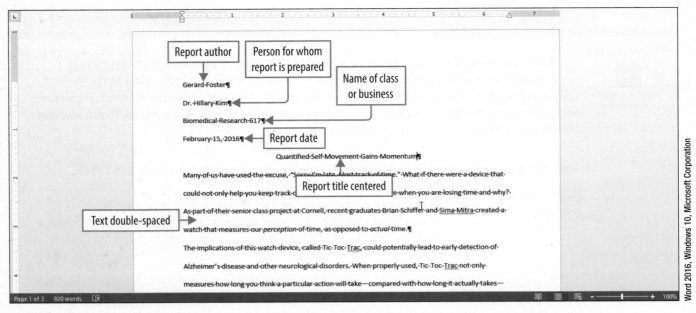

FIGURE 3.2

Word 2016, Windows 10, Microsoft Corporation

More Knowledge | **Creating a Document Heading for a Research Paper**

On the first page of an MLA-style research paper, on the first line, type the report author. On the second line, type the person for whom the report is prepared—for example, your professor or supervisor. On the third line, type the name of the class or business. On the fourth line, type the date. On the fifth line, type the report title and center it.

Activity 3.02 | Formatting the Page Numbering and Paragraph Indents for a Research Paper

MOS
1.3.5, 2.2.3

1 On the **Insert tab**, in the **Header & Footer group**, click **Header**, and then at the bottom of the list, click **Edit Header**.

2 Type **Foster** and then press Spacebar.

Recall that the text you insert into a header or footer displays on every page of a document. Within a header or footer, you can insert many different types of information; for example, automatic page numbers, the date, the time, the file name, or pictures.

3 Under **Header and Footer Tools**, on the **Design tab**, in the **Header & Footer group**, click **Page Number**, and then point to **Current Position**. In the gallery, under **Simple**, click **Plain Number**. Compare your screen with Figure 3.3.

Word will automatically number the pages using this number format.

Word 2016, Windows 10, Microsoft Corporation

FIGURE 3.3

4 On the **Home tab**, in the **Paragraph group**, click **Align Right** 📄. Double-click anywhere in the document to close the Header area.

5 Near the top of **Page 1**, locate the paragraph beginning *Many of us*, and then click to position the insertion point at the beginning of the paragraph. By moving the vertical scroll bar, scroll to view the end of the document, hold down Shift, and then click to the right of the last paragraph mark to select all of the text from the insertion point to the end of the document. Release Shift.

6 With the text selected, in the **Paragraph group**, click the **Dialog Box Launcher** button 📄 to display the **Paragraph** dialog box.

7 On the **Indents and Spacing tab**, under **Indentation**, click the **Special arrow**, and then click **First line**. In the **By** box, be sure **0.5"** displays. Click **OK**. Compare your screen with Figure 3.4.

The MLA style uses 0.5-inch indents at the beginning of the first line of every paragraph. *Indenting*—moving the beginning of the first line of a paragraph to the right or left of the rest of the paragraph—provides visual cues to the reader to help divide the document text and make it easier to read.

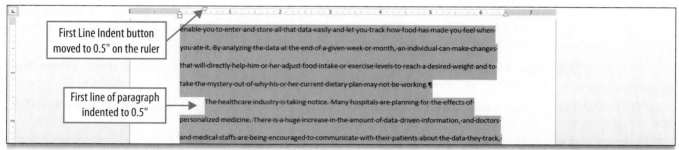

FIGURE 3.4

Word 2016, Windows 10, Microsoft Corporation

🔄 **ANOTHER WAY**   On the ruler, point to the First Line Indent button 📄, and then drag the button to 0.5" on the horizontal ruler.

8 Press Ctrl + Home to deselect and move to the top of the document. On the **Insert tab**, in the **Header & Footer group**, click **Footer**, and then at the bottom of the list click **Edit Footer**.

9 In the **Insert group**, click **Document Info**, and then click **File Name**. On the ribbon, click **Close Header and Footer**.

The file name in the footer is *not* part of the research report format, but it is included in projects in this chapter so that you and your instructor can identify your work.

10 **Save** 💾 your document.

More **Knowledge**   **Suppressing the Page Number on the First Page of a Document**

Some style guidelines require that the page number and other header and footer information on the first page be hidden from view—*suppressed*. To hide the information contained in the header and footer areas on Page 1 of a document, double-click in the header or footer area. Then, under Header and Footer Tools, on the Design tab, in the Options group, select the Different First Page check box.

GO! Learn How
Video W3-2

Within report text, numbers mark the location of **notes**—information that expands on the topic being discussed but that does not fit well in the document text. The numbers refer to **footnotes**—notes placed at the bottom of the page containing the note, or to **endnotes**—notes placed at the end of a document or chapter.

Activity 3.03 │ Inserting Footnotes

MOS
4.1.1

You can add footnotes as you type your document or after your document is complete. Word renumbers the footnotes automatically, so footnotes do not need to be entered in order, and if one footnote is removed, the remaining footnotes automatically renumber.

1 Scroll to view the upper portion of **Page 2**, and then locate the paragraph that begins *Accurate records*. In the third line of the paragraph, click to position the insertion point to the right of the period after *infancy*.

2 On the **References tab**, in the **Footnotes group**, click **Insert Footnote**.

Word creates space for a footnote in the footnote area at the bottom of the page and adds a footnote number to the text at the insertion point location. Footnote *1* displays in the footnote area, and the insertion point moves to the right of the number. A short black line is added just above the footnote area. You do not need to type the footnote number.

3 Type **The Department of Health & Human Services indicates that the use of Health Information Technology will improve the quality of health care.**

This is an explanatory footnote; the footnote provides additional information that does not fit well in the body of the report.

4 Click the **Home tab**, and then in the **Font group** and **Paragraph group**, examine the font size and line spacing settings. Notice that the new footnote displays in 10 pt font size and is single-spaced, even though the font size of the document text is 11 pt and the text is double-spaced, as shown in Figure 3.5.

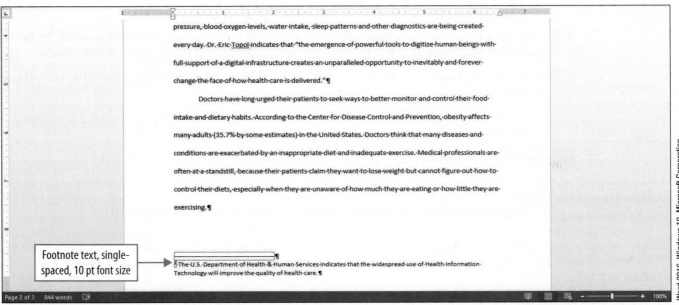

Footnote text, single-spaced, 10 pt font size

Word 2016, Windows 10, Microsoft Corporation

FIGURE 3.5

5 Scroll to view the top of **Page 1**, and then locate the paragraph that begins *Many of us*. At the end of the paragraph, click to position the insertion point to the right of the period following *time*.

6 On the **References tab**, in the **Footnotes group**, click **Insert Footnote**. Type **Organizations such as airlines and the military could benefit because many employees are involved in time-sensitive operations.** Notice that the footnote you just added becomes the new footnote *1*. Click **Save** 🖫, and then compare your screen with Figure 3.6.

The first footnote that you typed, which is on Page 2 and begins *The Department of Health*, is renumbered as footnote *2*.

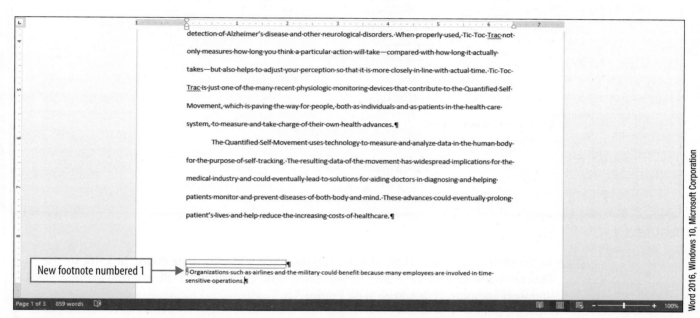

detection of Alzheimer's disease and other neurological disorders. When properly used, Tic-Toc-Trac not only measures how long you think a particular action will take—compared with how long it actually takes—but also helps to adjust your perception so that it is more closely in line with actual time. Tic-Toc-Trac is just one of the many recent physiologic monitoring devices that contribute to the Quantified Self Movement, which is paving the way for people, both as individuals and as patients in the health care system, to measure and take charge of their own health advances. ¶

The Quantified Self Movement uses technology to measure and analyze data in the human body for the purpose of self-tracking. The resulting data of the movement has widespread implications for the medical industry and could eventually lead to solutions for aiding doctors in diagnosing and helping patients monitor and prevent diseases of both body and mind. These advances could eventually prolong patient's lives and help reduce the increasing costs of healthcare. ¶

New footnote numbered 1 → ¹ Organizations such as airlines and the military could benefit because many employees are involved in time-sensitive operations. ¶

FIGURE 3.6

More Knowledge | **Using Symbols Rather Than Numbers for Notes**

Instead of using numbers to designate footnotes, you can use standard footnote symbols. The seven traditional symbols, available from the Footnote and Endnote dialog box, in order, are * (asterisk), † (dagger), ‡ (double dagger), § (section mark), || (parallels), ¶ (paragraph mark), and # (number or pound sign). This sequence can be continuous (this is the default setting), or it can begin anew with each page.

Activity 3.04 | Modifying a Footnote Style

4.1.2

Microsoft Word contains built-in paragraph formats called *styles*—groups of formatting commands, such as font, font size, font color, paragraph alignment, and line spacing—that can be applied to a paragraph with one command.

The default style for footnote text is a single-spaced paragraph that uses a 10-point Calibri font and no paragraph indents. MLA style specifies double-spaced text in all areas of a research paper—including footnotes. According to the MLA style, first lines of footnotes must also be indented 0.5 inch and use the same font size as the report text.

1 At the bottom of **Page 1**, point anywhere in the footnote text you just typed, right-click, and then on the shortcut menu, click **Style**. Compare your screen with Figure 3.7.

The Style dialog box displays, listing the styles currently in use in the document, in addition to some of the word processing elements that come with special built-in styles. Because you right-clicked in the footnote text, the selected style is the Footnote Text style.

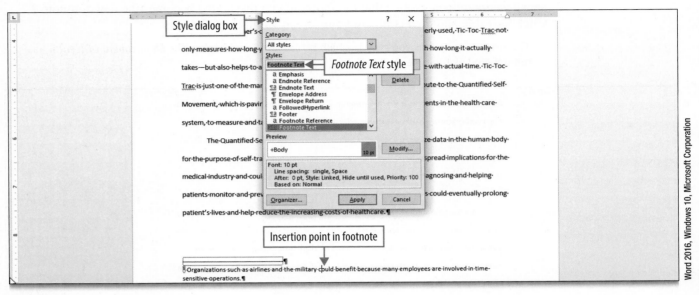

FIGURE 3.7

2 In the **Style** dialog box, click **Modify**, and then in the **Modify Style** dialog box, locate the **Formatting** toolbar in the center of the dialog box. Click the **Font Size button arrow**, click **11**, and then compare your screen with Figure 3.8.

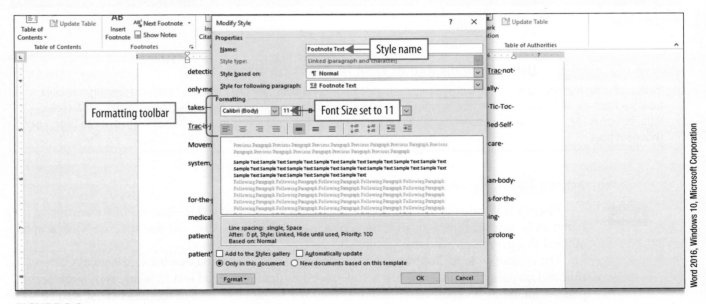

FIGURE 3.8

3 In the lower left corner of the dialog box, click **Format**, and then click **Paragraph**. In the **Paragraph** dialog box, on the **Indents and Spacing tab**, under **Indentation**, click the **Special arrow**, and then click **First line**.

4 Under **Spacing**, click the **Line spacing arrow**, and then click **Double**. Compare your dialog box with Figure 3.9.

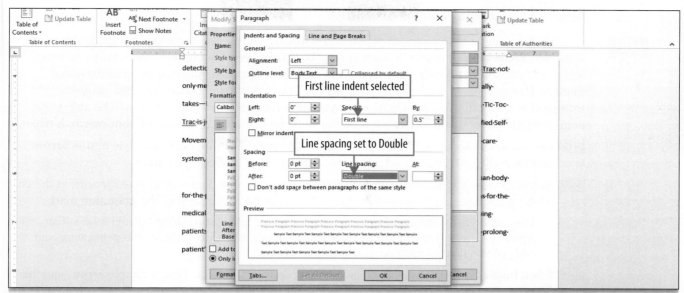

FIGURE 3.9

5 ⟩ Click **OK** to close the **Paragraph** dialog box, click **OK** to close the **Modify Style** dialog box, and then click **Apply** to apply the new style and close the dialog box. Compare your screen with Figure 3.10.

Your inserted footnotes are formatted with the modified Footnote Text paragraph style; any new footnotes that you insert will also use this format.

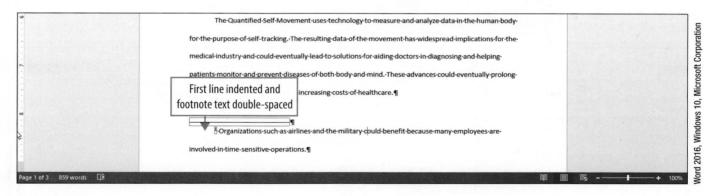

FIGURE 3.10

6 ⟩ Scroll to view the bottom of **Page 2** to confirm that the new format was also applied to the second footnote, and then **Save** 💾 your document.

Objective 3   Create Citations and a Bibliography in a Research Paper

GO! Learn How
Video W3-3

Reports and research papers typically include information that you find in other sources, and these sources of information must be credited. When you use quotations from or detailed summaries of other people's work, you must specify the source of the information. A *citation* is a note inserted into the text of a report or research paper that refers the reader to a source in the bibliography. Create a *bibliography* at the end of a research paper to list the sources you have referenced. Such a list is typically titled *Works Cited* (in MLA style), *Bibliography*, *Sources*, or *References*.

Activity 3.05 | Adding Citations for a Book

When writing a long research paper, you will likely reference numerous books, articles, and websites. Some of your research sources may be referenced many times, others only one time. References to sources within the text of your research paper are indicated in an *abbreviated* manner. However, as you enter a citation for the first time, you can also enter the *complete* information about the source. Then, when you have finished your paper, you will be able to automatically generate the list of sources that must be included at the end of your research paper.

1 On the **References tab**, in the **Citations & Bibliography group**, click the **Style button arrow**, and then click **MLA** to insert a reference using MLA bibliography style.

2 Scroll to view the middle of **Page 2**. In the paragraph that begins *Accurate records*, at the end of the paragraph, click to position the insertion point to the right of the quotation mark.

> The citation in the document points to the full source information in the bibliography, which typically includes the name of the author, the full title of the work, the year of publication, and other publication information.

3 Click **Insert Citation**, and then click **Add New Source**. Click the **Type of Source arrow**, and then if necessary, click **Book**. Add the following information, and then compare your screen with Figure 3.11:

Author	Sopol, Eric J.
Title	The Creative Destruction of Medicine
Year	2012
City	New York
Publisher	Basic Books
Medium	Print

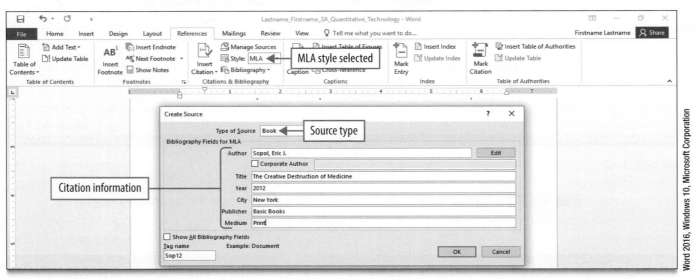

FIGURE 3.11

4 Click **OK** to insert the citation. Point to *(Sopol)* and click one time to select the citation.

> In the MLA style, citations that refer to items on the *Works Cited* page are placed in parentheses and are referred to as ***parenthetical references***—references that include the last name of the author or authors and the page number in the referenced source, which you add to the reference. No year is indicated, and there is no comma between the name and the page number.

> Both MLA and APA styles use parenthetical references for source citations rather than using footnotes.

5 **Save** the document.

If the author of a document is only identified as the name of an organization, select the Corporate Author check box and type the name of the organization in the Corporate Author box.

In the 7th edition of the *MLA Handbook for Writers of Research Papers*, the category Medium was added and must be included for any item on the Works Cited page. Entries for this category can include Print, Web, Performance, and Photograph, among many others.

Activity 3.06 | Editing Citations

1 In the lower right corner of the box that surrounds the selected reference, point to the small arrow to display the ScreenTip *Citation Options*. Click the **Citation Options arrow**, and then on the list of options, click **Edit Citation**.

2 In the **Edit Citation** dialog box, under **Add**, in the **Pages** box, type **5** to indicate that you are citing from page 5 of this source. Compare your screen with Figure 3.12.

FIGURE 3.12

Word 2016, Windows 10, Microsoft Corporation

3 Click **OK** to display the page number of the citation. Click outside of the citation box to deselect it.

4 Type a period to the right of the citation, and delete the period to the left of the quotation mark.

> In the MLA style, if the reference occurs at the end of a sentence, the parenthetical reference always displays to the left of the punctuation mark that ends the sentence.

5 Press [Ctrl] + [End] to move to the end of the document, and then click to position the insertion point after the letter *e* in *disease* and to the left of the period.

6 In the **Citations & Bibliography group**, click **Insert Citation**, and then click **Add New Source**. Click the **Type of Source arrow**, if necessary scroll to the top of the list, click **Book**, and then add the following information:

Author	**Glaser, John P., and Claudia Salzberg**
Title	**The Strategic Application of Information Technology in Health Care Organizations**
Year	**2011**
City	**San Francisco**
Publisher	**Jossey-Bass**
Medium	**Print**

In the Create Source dialog box, if you prefer, you can enter each author name separately by using the Edit command to the right of the Author box. Initiate the command for each author of the work, and then Word will automatically format all the names properly and in the correct order in the Works Cited list.

> ### N O T E MLA Style for Two or More Authors
> According to MLA Style, to cite a book by two or more authors, reverse only the name of the first author, add a comma, and give the other name or names in normal form. Place a period after the last name.

7 ▸ Click **OK**. Click the inserted citation to select it, click the **Citation Options arrow**, and then click **Edit Citation**.

8 ▸ In the **Edit Citation** dialog box, under **Add**, in the **Pages** box, type **28** to indicate that you are citing from page 28 of this source. Click **OK**.

9 ▸ On the **References tab**, in the **Citations & Bibliography group**, click **Manage Sources**, and then compare your screen with Figure 3.13.

> The Source Manager dialog box displays. Other citations on your computer display in the Master List box. The citations for the current document display in the Current List box. Word maintains the Master List so that if you use the same sources regularly, you can copy sources from your Master List to the current document. A preview of the bibliography entry also displays at the bottom of the dialog box.

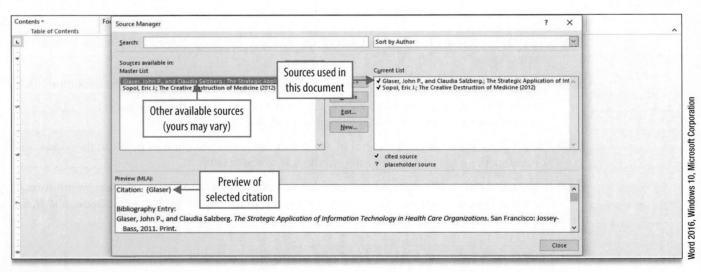

FIGURE 3.13

10 ▸ At the bottom of the **Source Manager** dialog box, click **Close**. Click anywhere in the document to deselect the parenthetical reference, and then **Save** 🔲 your document.

Activity 3.07 │ Adding Citations for a Website

MOS
4.1.3

1 ▸ In the lower portion of **Page 2**, in the paragraph that begins *Doctors have long urged*, in the third line, click to position the insertion point after the s in *States* and to the left of the period.

2 In the **Citations & Bibliography group**, click **Insert Citation**, and then click **Add New Source**. Click the **Type of Source arrow**, scroll down as necessary, and then click **Web site**. Type the following information:

Author	**Ogden, C. L.**
Name of Web Page	**NCHS Data Brief Number 82**
Year	**2012**
Month	**January**
Day	**01**
Year Accessed	**2016**
Month Accessed	**January**
Day Accessed	**17**
Medium	**Web**

3 Click **OK**. **Save** 🖫, and then compare your screen with Figure 3.14.

> A parenthetical reference is added. Because the cited Web page has no page numbers, only the author name is used in the parenthetical reference.

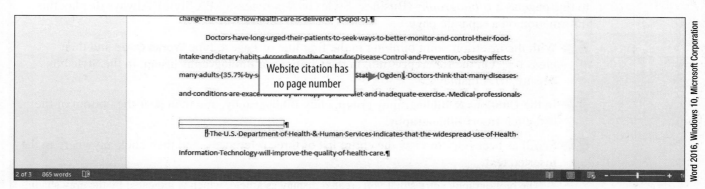

FIGURE 3.14

Word 2016, Windows 10, Microsoft Corporation

More Knowledge **Including URLs of Web Sources**

With the 7th edition of the *MLA Handbook for Writers of Research Papers*, including the URL of Web sources is recommended only when the reader would have difficulty finding the source without it or if your instructor requires it. Otherwise, readers will likely find the resource by using search tools. If you include the URL, enclose it in angle brackets and end with a period.

Activity 3.08 | Inserting Page Breaks

Your bibliography must begin on a new page, so at the bottom of the last page of your report, you must insert a manual page break.

1 Press Ctrl + End to move the insertion point to the end of the document.

> If there is a footnote on the last page, the insertion point will display at the end of the final paragraph, but above the footnote—a footnote is always associated with the page that contains the footnote information.

2 Press `Ctrl` + `Enter` to insert a manual page break.

A ***manual page break*** forces a page to end at the insertion point location, and then places any subsequent text at the top of the next page. Recall that the new paragraph retains the formatting of the previous paragraph, so in this instance the first line is indented.

A ***page break indicator***, which shows where a manual page break was inserted, displays at the bottom of Page 3.

3 On the **Home tab**, in the **Paragraph group**, click the **Dialog Box Launcher** button ⌐ to display the **Paragraph** dialog box.

4 On the **Indents and Spacing tab**, under **Indentation**, click the **Special arrow**, and then click **(none)**. Click **OK**, and then **Save** 🖫 your document.

↻ ANOTHER WAY On the ruler, point to the First Line Indent button ▽ , and then drag the button to 0" on the horizontal ruler.

Activity 3.09 | Creating a Reference Page

At the end of a report or research paper, include a list of each source referenced. *Works Cited* is the reference page heading used in the MLA style guidelines. Other styles may refer to this page as a *Bibliography* (Business Style) or *References* (APA Style). Always display this information on a separate page.

1 With the insertion point blinking in the first line of **Page 4**, type **Works Cited** and then press `Enter`. On the **References tab**, in the **Citations & Bibliography group**, in the **Style** box, be sure *MLA* displays.

2 In the **Citations & Bibliography group**, click **Bibliography**, and then near the bottom of the list, click **Insert Bibliography**.

3 Scroll as necessary to view the entire list of three references, and then click anywhere in the inserted text.

The bibliography entries that you created display as a field, which is indicated by the gray shading. This field links to the Source Manager for the citations. The references display alphabetically by the author's last name.

4 In the bibliography, point to the left of the first entry—beginning *Glaser, John P.*—to display the ⮥ pointer. Drag down to select all three references in the field but not the blank paragraph.

5 On the **Home tab**, in the **Paragraph group**, change the **Line spacing** to **2.0**, and then on the **Layout tab**, in the **Paragraph group**, change the **Spacing After** to **0 pt**.

The entries display according to MLA guidelines; the text is double-spaced, the extra space between paragraphs is removed, and each entry uses a ***hanging indent***—the first line of each entry extends 0.5 inch to the left of the remaining lines of the entry.

↻ ANOTHER WAY Display the Paragraph dialog box. Under Spacing, click the Line spacing arrow, and then click Double. Under Spacing, in the After box, type 0.

---

6 At the top of **Page 4**, click anywhere in the title text *Works Cited*, and then press `Ctrl` + `E` to center the title. Compare your screen with Figure 3.15, and then **Save** 🖫 your document.

In MLA style, the *Works Cited* title is centered.

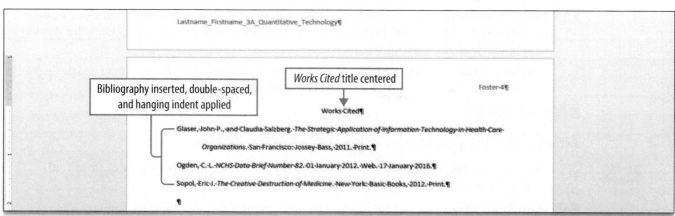

FIGURE 3.15

Word 2016, Windows 10, Microsoft Corporation

Activity 3.10 | Managing and Modifying Sources for a Document

Use the Source Manager to organize the sources cited in your document. For example, in the Source Manager dialog box, you can copy sources from the master list to the current list, delete a source, edit a source, or search for a source. You can also display a preview of how your citations will appear in your document.

1 On the **References tab**, in the **Citations & Bibliography group**, click **Manage Sources**.

2 On the left, in the **Master List**, click the entry for *Sopol, Eric J.* and then between the **Master List** and the **Current List**, click **Edit**.

The name of this source should be *Topol* instead of *Sopol*.

3 In the **Edit Source** dialog box, in the **Author** box, delete *S* and type **T**

4 Click **OK**. When the message box indicates *This source exists in your master list and current document. Do you want to update both lists with these changes?* click **Yes**. Compare your screen with Figure 3.16.

In the lower portion of the Source Manager dialog box, a preview of the corrected entry displays.

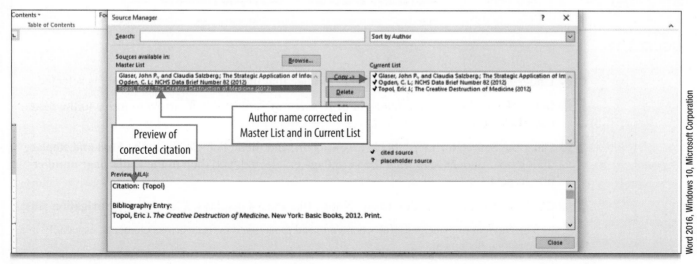

FIGURE 3.16

5 In the lower right corner, click **Close**. On your **Works Cited page**, notice that the author name is *not* corrected. Scroll to view the lower portion of **Page 2**, and notice that the author name *is* corrected and the citation is selected.

6 On the selected citation *(Topol 5)*, click the **Citation Options arrow**, and then click **Update Citations and Bibliography**. Press Ctrl + End, and notice that this action updates the Works Cited page with the corrected name.

> Editing a source in Source Manager updates only the sources in the document; to update the Works Cited page, use the Update Citations and Bibliography command on the citation.

7 Click **Save** 🖫.

Activity 3.11 | Using the Navigation Pane to Go to a Specific Page

In a multipage document, use the Navigation pane to move to a specific page or to find specific objects in the document.

1 Press Ctrl + Home to move to the top of the document. Click the **View tab**, and then in the **Show group**, select the **Navigation Pane** check box.

2 In the **Navigation** pane, on the right end of the **Search document** box, click the **Search for more things arrow**, and then compare your screen with Figure 3.17.

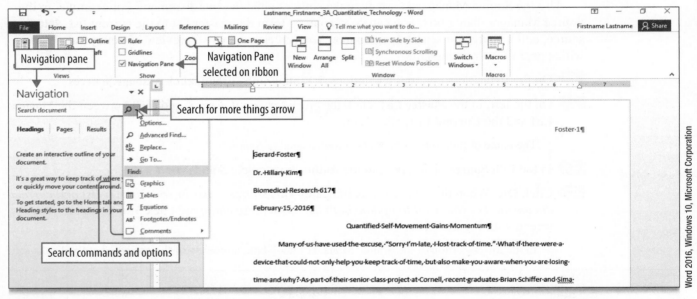

FIGURE 3.17

3 Under **Find**, click **Footnotes/Endnotes**. Notice that the first numbered footnote is selected.

4 In the **Navigation** pane, to the right of *Result 1 of 2*, click the ▼ arrow to move to the next numbered footnote.

5 Click the **Search for more things arrow** again, and then click **Go To**. In the **Find and Replace** dialog box, under **Go to what**, be sure **Page** is selected, and then in the **Enter page number** box, type **4**

6 Click **Go To**, and then click **Close**. Notice that **Page 4** displays. **Close** ☒ the **Navigation** pane.

> The Navigation pane is useful when you need to navigate to find various elements, especially in a very long document.

⟳ ANOTHER WAY   You can also initiate the Go To command from the ribbon or by using a keyboard shortcut. To do so, on the Home tab, in the Editing group, click the Find arrow, and then click Go To; or, hold down Ctrl and press G to display the Go To tab of the Find and Replace dialog box.

Activity 3.12 | Managing Document Properties

MOS
3.1.2

For a research paper, you may want to add additional document properties.

1 Press **Ctrl** + **Home** to return to the top of your document. Click the **File tab** to display **Backstage** view, and then in the lower right corner of the screen, click **Show All Properties**.

2 As the document **Title**, type **Quantified Self Movement Gains Momentum** and then as the **Tags**, type **quantified self, research paper**

3 Click in the **Comments** box and type **draft copy of report for class** and then in the **Categories** box, type **biomedical research**

4 In the **Subject** box, type your course name and section number. In the **Company** box, select and delete any existing text, and then type **University Medical Center**

5 Click in the **Manager** box and type **Dr. Hillary Kim** Be sure your name displays as the **Author** and edit if necessary.

6 At the top of the **Properties** list, click the text *Properties*, and then click **Advanced Properties**. In the dialog box, if necessary click the **Summary tab**, and then compare your screen with Figure 3.18.

In the Advanced Properties dialog box, you can view and modify additional document properties.

FIGURE 3.18

7 Click the **Statistics tab**.

The document statistics show the number of revisions made to the document, the last time the document was edited, and the number of paragraphs, lines, words, and characters in the document. Additional information categories are available by clicking the Custom tab.

8 **Close** ⊠ the dialog box, and then on the left, click **Save** to save and return to your document.

***More* Knowledge** **Inserting a Watermark**

A **watermark** is a text or graphic element that displays behind document text. Until you know your research paper is final—for example, you have others reviewing it—you might want to display the word DRAFT on each page. To do so, on the Design tab, in the Page Background group, click Watermark, and then at the bottom, click Custom Watermark. In the Printed Watermark dialog box, click the Text watermark option button, click the Text arrow, and then click DRAFT. Click OK. To remove the watermark—after you are sure your research paper is final—click the Watermark command again, and then click Remove Watermark.

Objective 4 Use Read Mode and PDF Reflow

GO! Learn How
Video W3-4

Read Mode optimizes the view of the Word screen for the times when you are *reading* Word documents on the screen and not creating or editing them. Microsoft's research indicates that two-thirds of user sessions in Word contain no editing—meaning that people are simply reading the Word document on the screen. The Column Layout feature of Read Mode reflows the document to fit the size of the device you are reading so that the text is as easy to read on a tablet device as on a 24-inch screen. The Object Zoom feature of Read Mode resizes graphics to fit the screen you are using, but you can click or tap to zoom in on the graphic.

PDF Reflow provides the ability to import PDF files into Word so that you can transform a PDF back into a fully editable Word document. This is useful if you have lost the original Word file or if someone sends you a PDF that you would like to modify. PDF Reflow is not intended to act as a viewer for PDF files—for that you will still want to use a PDF reader such as Adobe Reader. In Windows 10, the Microsoft Edge browser also serves as a PDF reader.

1.4.1

Activity 3.13 │ Using Read Mode

1 ▶ If necessary, press ⎡Ctrl⎤ + ⎡Home⎤ to move to the top of your document. On the **View tab**, in the **Views group**, click **Read Mode**, and notice that Read Mode keeps footnotes displayed on the page associated with the footnote.

⟲ ANOTHER WAY On the right side of the status bar, click the Read Mode button 📖.

2 ▶ In the upper left corner, click **Tools**.

You can use these tools to find something within the document or use Bing to conduct an Internet search.

3 ▶ Click **Find**, and then in the **Search** box, type **Topol** Notice that Word displays the first page where the search term displays and highlights the term in yellow. Compare your screen with Figure 3.19.

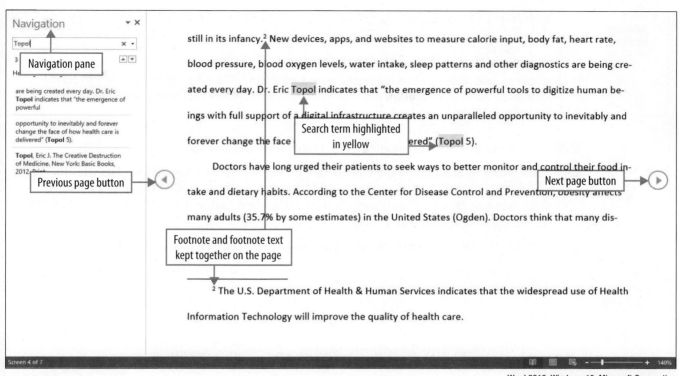

FIGURE 3.19

Word 2016, Windows 10, Microsoft Corporation

4 In the upper left corner, click **View**, and then take a moment to study the table in Figure 3.20.

VIEW COMMANDS IN READ MODE	
VIEW COMMAND	**ACTION**
Edit Document	Return to Print Layout view to continue editing the document.
Navigation Pane	Search for specific text or click a heading or page to move to that location.
Show Comments	See comments, if any, within the document.
Column Width	Change the display of the document to fit more or less text on each line.
Page Color	Change the colors used to show the document to make it easier to read. Some readers prefer a sepia (brownish-gray) shading as the background or a black background with white text.
Layout	Read in different layouts. Select Column Layout, which is the default, or Paper Layout, which mimics the 8.5 x 11 format but without the ribbon.

FIGURE 3.20

5 On the **View** menu, click **Edit Document** to return to **Print Layout** view. **Close** ☒ the **Navigation** pane.

6 In the upper right corner of the Word window, click **Close** ☒. If directed by your instructor to do so, submit your paper printout, your electronic image of your document that looks like a printed document, or your original Word file. If you are submitting this Project as a MyITLab grader, submit this file.

More **Knowledge**   **Highlighting Text in a Word Document**

You can highlight text in a Word document. Select the text you want to highlight, and then on the Home tab, in the Font group, click the Text Highlight Color arrow ✎ ▾ . Click the color you want to use for your highlight to apply it to the selected text. Or, click the Text Highlight Color button arrow ✎ ▾ , click a color, and then use the ✎ pointer to select text that you want to highlight.

ACTIVITY 3.14 | Using PDF Reflow

1.1.3, 1.5.2

1 Start Word, and then on the left, click **Open Other Documents**.

2 Click **Browse**, and then in the **Open** dialog box, navigate to your student data files for this chapter. Click **w03A_PDF_optional**. In the lower right corner, click **Open**. If a message indicates that *Word will now convert the PDF to an editable Word document …*, click OK. Compare your screen with Figure 3.21.

With the PDF displayed in Word, you can make edits, and then re-save as a PDF.

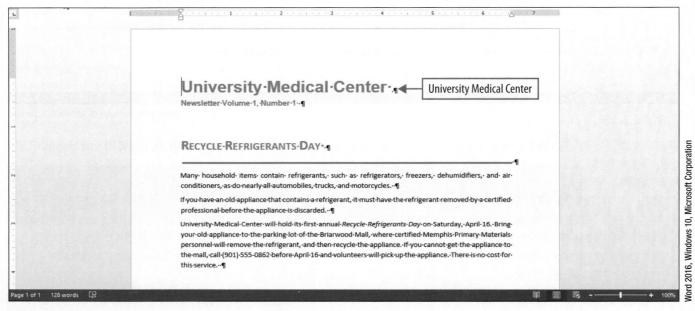

FIGURE 3.21

3 **Close** ☒ Word.

More Knowledge   **Saving Documents in Alternative File Formats**

You can save a Word document in a variety of other document formats, including a PDF. To do so, with your Word document open, display the Save As dialog box. Click the Save as type arrow, and then click the desired file type. Commonly used file types are PDF and Rich Text Format.

END | You have completed Project 3A

GO! With Google

Objective | Use the Research Bar in Google Docs

> **ALERT!** | **Working with Web-Based Applications and Services**
>
> Computer programs and services on the web receive continuous updates and improvements, so the steps to complete this web-based Activity may differ from the ones shown. You can often look at the screens and the information presented to determine how to complete the Activity.
>
> If you do not already have a Google account, you will need to create one before you begin this Activity. Go to http://google.com and, in the upper right corner, click Sign In. On the Sign In screen, click Create Account. On the Create your Google Account page, complete the form, read and agree to the Terms of Service and Privacy Policy, and then click Next step. On the Welcome screen, click Get Started.

Activity | Using the Research Bar in Google Docs

Google Docs provides a research tool that you can use to find studies and academic papers on many topics. You can narrow your search results by selecting "Scholar" from the menu in the search bar. After you find the study, you can insert it as a citation or a footnote. You can also choose to use the MLA, APA, or Chicago citation formatting.

1 From the desktop, open your browser, navigate to **http://google.com**, and then click the **Google Apps** menu ⊞. Click **Drive**, and then if necessary, sign in to your Google account.

2 Open your **GO! Web Projects** folder—or click NEW to create and then open this folder if necessary.

3 In the left pane, click **NEW**, and then click **File upload**. In the **Open** dialog box, navigate to your student data files for this chapter, and then in the **File List**, double-click to open **w03_3A_Web**.

4 Point to the uploaded file **w03_3A_Web**, and then right-click. On the shortcut menu, scroll as necessary, and then click **Rename**. Using your own last name and first name, type **Lastname_Firstname_WD_3A_Web** and use the default .docx extension. Click **OK** to rename the file.

5 Point to the file you just renamed, right-click, point to **Open with**, and then click **Google Docs**.

6 Press [Ctrl] + [End] to move to the end of the document, and then press [Enter] one time. Type **There are many studies related to the quantified self movement conducted by Melanie Swan, who is interested in crowdsourced health research.**

7 On the menu bar, click **Tools**, and then click **Research** to open the **Research pane** on the right. At the top of the **Research pane**, click the arrow to the right of *G*, click the arrow a second time to filter the results, and then on the list click **Scholar**.

8 In the search box at the top, delete any existing text, type **Melanie Swan** and then press [Enter]. *Point* to the first item in the list, and then compare your screen with Figure A.

(GO! With Google continues on the next page)

GO! With Google

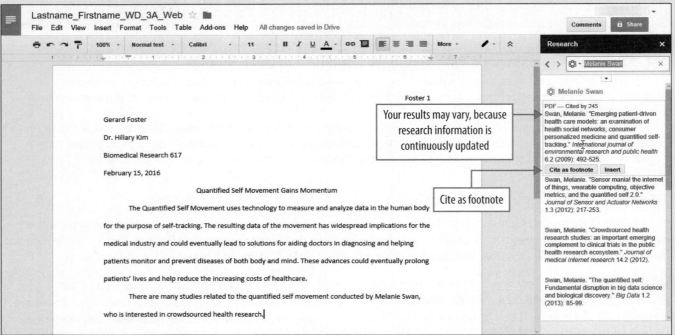

FIGURE A

9 Click **Cite as footnote**. Notice that a footnote number is inserted at the end of the sentence. Scroll down to view the bottom of the page, and then compare your screen with Figure B.

10 Submit the file as directed by your instructor. In the upper right, click your user name, and then click **Sign out**. **Close** your browser window. Your file is automatically saved in your Google Drive.

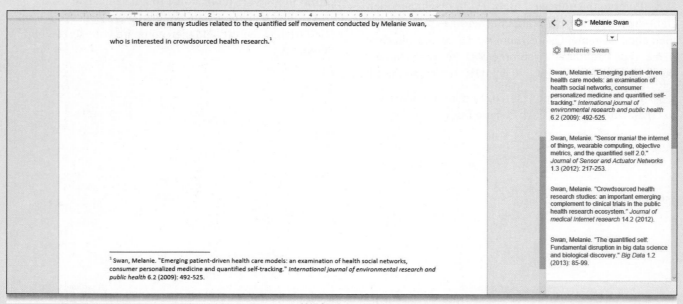

FIGURE B

Newsletter with Optional Mailing Labels

MyITLab
Project 3B Training
Project 3B Grader

PROJECT ACTIVITIES

In Activities 3.15 through 3.29, you will edit a newsletter that University Medical Center is sending to the board of directors; optionally, you can create the necessary mailing labels. Your completed documents will look similar to Figure 3.22.

Please always review the downloaded Grader instructions before beginning.

PROJECT FILES

MyITLab grader If your instructor wants you to submit Project 3B in the MyITLab Grader system, log in to MyITLab, locate Grader Project 3B, and then download the files for this project.

For Project 3B, you will need the following files:
w03B_Environment_Newsletter
w03B_Addresses (Optional if assigned)

You will save your documents as:
Lastname_Firstname_3B_Environment_Newsletter
Lastname_Firstname_3B_Mailing_Labels (Optional if assigned)

GO! Walk Thru Project 3B

PROJECT RESULTS

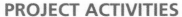

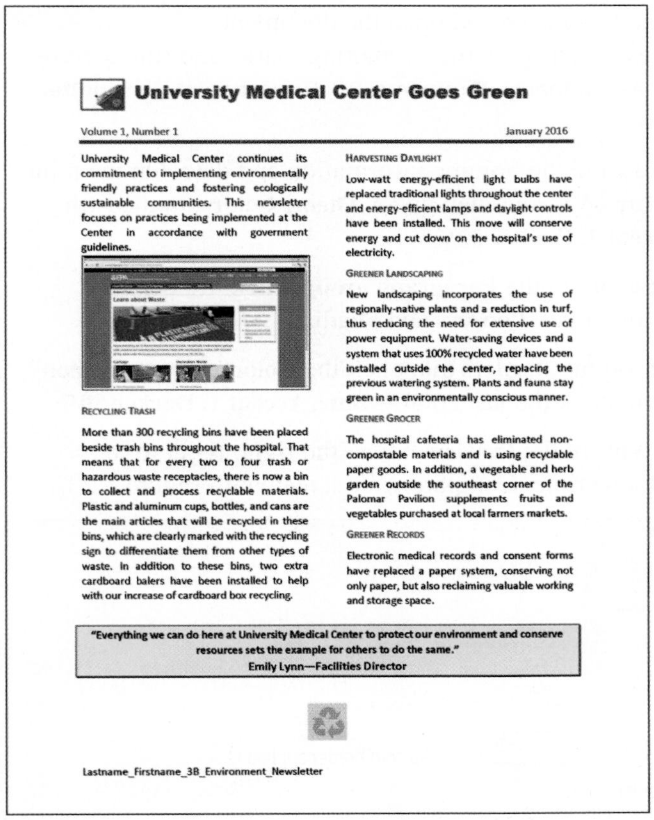

University Medical Center Goes Green

Volume 1, Number 1 January 2016

University Medical Center continues its commitment to implementing environmentally friendly practices and fostering ecologically sustainable communities. This newsletter focuses on practices being implemented at the Center in accordance with government guidelines.

RECYCLING TRASH

More than 300 recycling bins have been placed beside trash bins throughout the hospital. That means that for every two to four trash or hazardous waste receptacles, there is now a bin to collect and process recyclable materials. Plastic and aluminum cups, bottles, and cans are the main articles that will be recycled in these bins, which are clearly marked with the recycling sign to differentiate them from other types of waste. In addition to these bins, two extra cardboard balers have been installed to help with our increase of cardboard box recycling.

HARVESTING DAYLIGHT

Low-watt energy-efficient light bulbs have replaced traditional lights throughout the center and energy-efficient lamps and daylight controls have been installed. This move will conserve energy and cut down on the hospital's use of electricity.

GREENER LANDSCAPING

New landscaping incorporates the use of regionally-native plants and a reduction in turf, thus reducing the need for extensive use of power equipment. Water-saving devices and a system that uses 100% recycled water have been installed outside the center, replacing the previous watering system. Plants and fauna stay green in an environmentally conscious manner.

GREENER GROCER

The hospital cafeteria has eliminated non-compostable materials and is using recyclable paper goods. In addition, a vegetable and herb garden outside the southeast corner of the Palomar Pavilion supplements fruits and vegetables purchased at local farmers markets.

GREENER RECORDS

Electronic medical records and consent forms have replaced a paper system, conserving not only paper, but also reclaiming valuable working and storage space.

"Everything we can do here at University Medical Center to protect our environment and conserve resources sets the example for others to do the same."
Emily Lynn—Facilities Director

Lastname_Firstname_3B_Environment_Newsletter

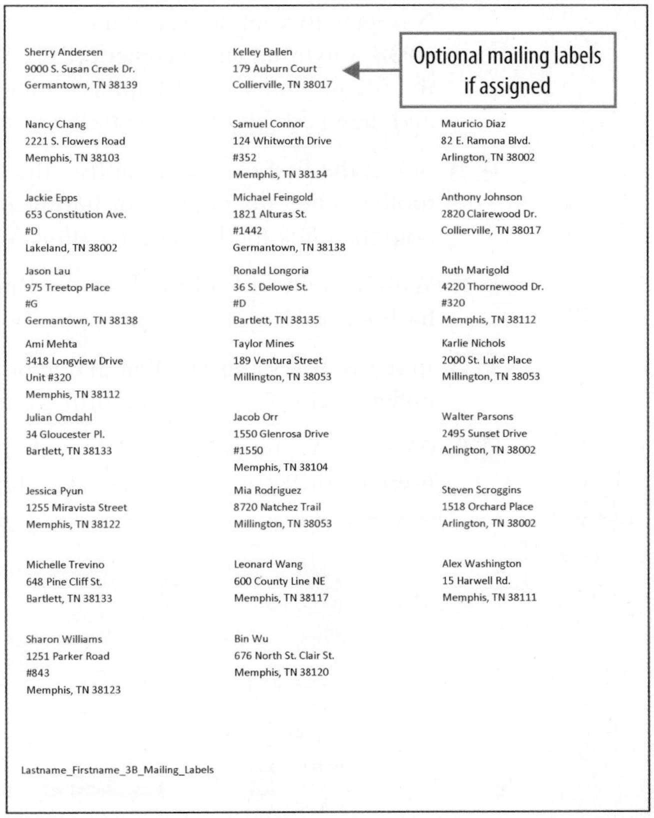

Optional mailing labels if assigned

Sherry Andersen 9000 S. Susan Creek Dr. Germantown, TN 38139	Kelley Ballen 179 Auburn Court Collierville, TN 38017	
Nancy Chang 2221 S. Flowers Road Memphis, TN 38103	Samuel Connor 124 Whitworth Drive #352 Memphis, TN 38134	Mauricio Diaz 82 E. Ramona Blvd. Arlington, TN 38002
Jackie Epps 653 Constitution Ave. #D Lakeland, TN 38002	Michael Feingold 1821 Alturas St. #1442 Germantown, TN 38138	Anthony Johnson 2820 Clairewood Dr. Collierville, TN 38017
Jason Lau 975 Treetop Place #G Germantown, TN 38138	Ronald Longoria 36 S. Delowe St. #D Bartlett, TN 38135	Ruth Marigold 4220 Thornewood Dr. #320 Memphis, TN 38112
Ami Mehta 3418 Longview Drive Unit #320 Memphis, TN 38112	Taylor Mines 189 Ventura Street Millington, TN 38053	Karlie Nichols 2000 St. Luke Place Millington, TN 38053
Julian Omdahl 34 Gloucester Pl. Bartlett, TN 38133	Jacob Orr 1550 Glenrosa Drive #1550 Memphis, TN 38104	Walter Parsons 2495 Sunset Drive Arlington, TN 38002
Jessica Pyun 1255 Miravista Street Memphis, TN 38122	Mia Rodriguez 8720 Natchez Trail Millington, TN 38053	Steven Scroggins 1518 Orchard Place Arlington, TN 38002
Michelle Trevino 648 Pine Cliff St. Bartlett, TN 38133	Leonard Wang 600 County Line NE Memphis, TN 38117	Alex Washington 15 Harwell Rd. Memphis, TN 38111
Sharon Williams 1251 Parker Road #843 Memphis, TN 38123	Bin Wu 676 North St. Clair St. Memphis, TN 38120	

Lastname_Firstname_3B_Mailing_Labels

FIGURE 3.22 Project 3B Environment Newsletter

GO! Learn How
Video W3-5

A *newsletter* is a periodical that communicates news and information to a specific group. Newsletters, as well as all newspapers and most magazines, use multiple columns for articles because text in narrower columns is easier to read than text that stretches across a page.

You can create a newsletter in Word by changing a single column of text into two or more columns. If a column does not end where you want it to, you can end the column at a location of your choice by inserting a *manual column break*—an artificial end to a column to balance columns or to provide space for the insertion of other objects.

Activity 3.15 | Changing One Column of Text to Two Columns

> **ALERT!** To submit as an autograded project, log into MyITLab, download the files for this project, and then begin with those files instead of with w03B_Environment_Newsletter.

MOS
2.3.1

Newsletters are usually two or three columns wide. When using 8.5 × 11-inch paper in portrait orientation, avoid creating four or more columns because they are so narrow that word spacing looks awkward, often resulting in one long word on a line by itself.

1 Start Word. On Word's opening screen, in the lower left, click **Open Other Documents**. Navigate to your student data files, and then locate and open the document **w03B_Environment_Newsletter**. If necessary, display the formatting marks and rulers. **Save** the file in your **Word Chapter 3** folder as **Lastname_Firstname_3B_Environment_Newsletter** and then add the file name to the footer.

2 Select the first two paragraphs—the title and the Volume information and date. On the mini toolbar, click the **Font Color button arrow** ⬛, and then under **Theme Colors**, in the fifth column, click the last color—**Blue, Accent 1, Darker 50%**.

3 With the text still selected, on the **Home tab**, in the **Paragraph group**, click the **Borders button arrow** ⬛, and then at the bottom, click **Borders and Shading**.

4 In the **Borders and Shading** dialog box, on the **Borders tab**, click the **Color arrow**, and then under **Theme Colors**, in the fifth column, click the last color—**Blue, Accent 1, Darker 50%**.

5 Click the **Width arrow**, and then click **3 pt**. In the **Preview** box at the right, point to the *bottom* border of the preview and click one time. Compare your screen with Figure 3.23.

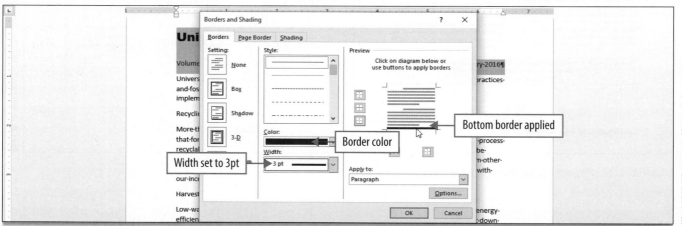

FIGURE 3.23

Word 2016, Windows 10, Microsoft Corporation

6 In the **Borders and Shading** dialog box, click **OK**.

The line visually defines the newsletter's ***nameplate***—the banner on the front page of a newsletter that identifies the publication.

7 Below the Volume information, click at the beginning of the paragraph that begins *University Medical Center continues*. By using the vertical scroll box, scroll to view the lower portion of the document, hold down ⌷Shift⌷, and then click after the paragraph mark at the end of the paragraph that begins *Electronic medical records* to select all of the text between the insertion point and the sentence ending with the word *space*. Be sure that the paragraph mark is included in the selection. Compare your screen with Figure 3.24.

Use ⌷Shift⌷ to define a selection that may be difficult to select by dragging.

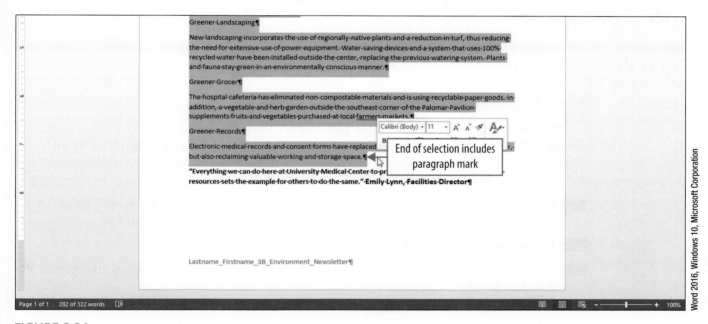

Greener·Landscaping¶

New·landscaping·incorporates·the·use·of·regionally-native·plants·and·a·reduction·in·turf,·thus·reducing·the·need·for·extensive·use·of·power·equipment.·Water-saving·devices·and·a·system·that·uses·100%·recycled·water·have·been·installed·outside·the·center,·replacing·the·previous·watering·system.·Plants·and·fauna·stay·green·in·an·environmentally-conscious·manner.¶

Greener·Grocer¶

The·hospital·cafeteria·has·eliminated·non-compostable·materials·and·is·using·recyclable·paper·goods.·In·addition,·a·vegetable·and·herb·garden·outside·the·southeast·corner·of·the·Palomar·Pavilion·supplements·fruits·and·vegetables·purchased·at·local·farmers·markets.¶

Greener·Records¶

Electronic·medical·records·and·consent·forms·have·replaced
but·also·reclaiming·valuable·working·and·storage·space.¶

End of selection includes paragraph mark

"Everything·we·can·do·here·at·University·Medical·Center·to·pr
resources·sets·the·example·for·others·to·do·the·same."·Emily·Lynn,·Facilities·Director¶

Lastname_Firstname_3B_Environment_Newsletter¶

Page 1 of 1   282 of 322 words

FIGURE 3.24

8 On the **Layout tab**, in the **Page Setup group**, click **Columns**, and then click **Two**. Compare your screen with Figure 3.25, and then **Save** 🖫 your newsletter.

Word divides the selected text into two columns and inserts a ***section break*** at the end of the selection, dividing the one-column section of the document from the two-column section of the document. A ***section*** is a portion of a document that can be formatted differently from the rest of the document. A section break marks the end of one section and the beginning of another section.

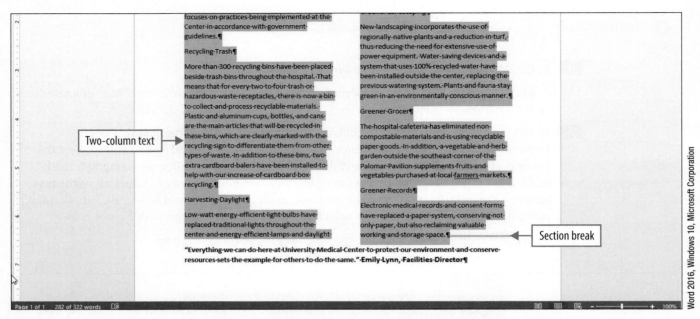

FIGURE 3.25

Activity 3.16 | Formatting Multiple Columns

The uneven right margin of a single page-width column is easy to read. When you create narrow columns, justified text is sometimes preferable. Depending on the design and layout of your newsletter, you might decide to reduce extra space between paragraphs and between columns to improve the readability of the document.

1 With the two columns of text still selected, on the **Layout tab**, in the **Paragraph group**, click the **Spacing After down spin arrow** one time to change the spacing after to **6 pt**.

2 On the **Home tab**, in the **Paragraph group**, click **Justify** ▤.

3 Click anywhere in the document to deselect the text, compare your screen with Figure 3.26, and then **Save** 🖫.

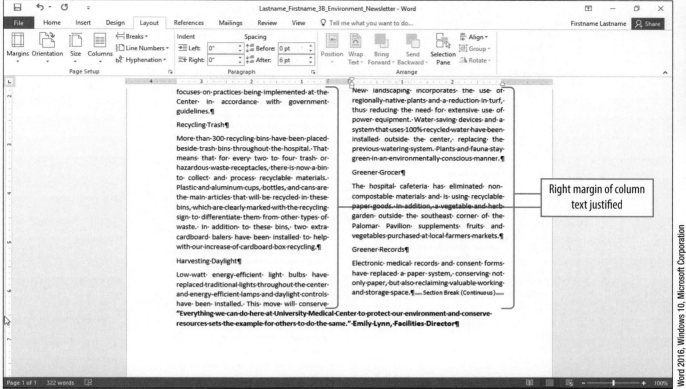

Right margin of column text justified

FIGURE 3.26

More Knowledge   **Justifying Column Text**

Although many magazines and newspapers still justify text in columns, there are a variety of opinions about whether to justify the columns, or to use left alignment and leave the right edge uneven. Justified text tends to look more formal and cleaner, but in a word processing document, it also results in uneven spacing between words. It is the opinion of some authorities that justified text is more difficult to read, especially in a page-width document. Let the overall look and feel of your newsletter be your guide.

2.3.2

Activity 3.17 | Inserting a Column Break

1 ▶ Near the bottom of the first column, click to position the insertion point at the beginning of the line *Harvesting Daylight*.

2 ▶ On the **Layout tab**, in the **Page Setup group**, click **Breaks**. Under **Page Breaks**, click **Column**, and then if necessary, scroll to view the bottom of the first column.

A column break displays at the bottom of the first column; text to the right of the column break moves to the top of the next column.

3 ▶ Compare your screen with Figure 3.27, and then **Save** 🖫.

A *column break indicator*—a dotted line containing the words *Column Break*—displays at the bottom of the column.

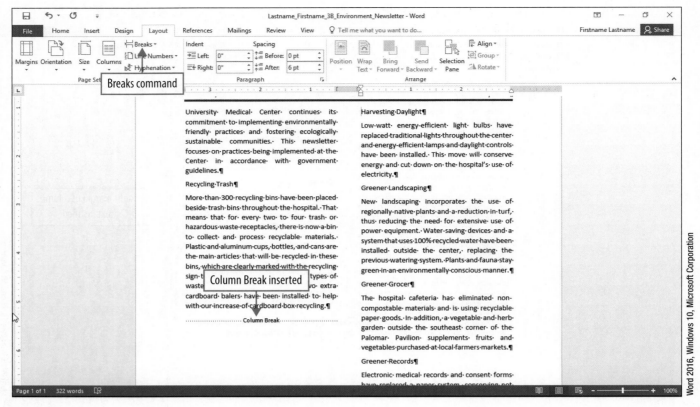

FIGURE 3.27

Activity 3.18 | Inserting an Online Picture

MOS
5.2.6, 5.2.7

You can search for and insert online pictures in your document without saving the images to your computer. Pictures can make your document visually appealing and more interesting.

1 Press Ctrl + End to move to the end of the document. Compare your screen with Figure 3.28.

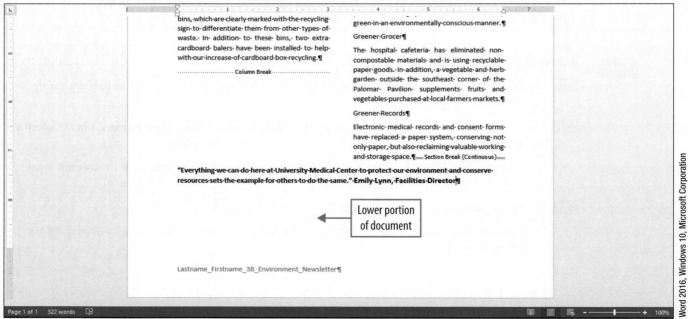

FIGURE 3.28

2 On the **Insert tab**, in the **Illustrations group**, click **Online Pictures**. With your insertion point blinking in the **Bing Image Search** box, type **green recycling symbol** and then press Enter. Compare your screen with Figure 3.29.

You can use various keywords to find images that are appropriate for your documents. The results shown indicate the images are licensed under *Creative Commons*, which, according to **www.creativecommons.org** is "a nonprofit organization that enables the sharing and use of creativity and knowledge through free legal tools."

Creative Commons helps people share and use their photographs, but does not allow users to sell them. For your college assignments, you can use these images so long as you are not profiting by selling the images.

To find out more about Creative Commons, go to **https://creativecommons.org/about** and watch their video.

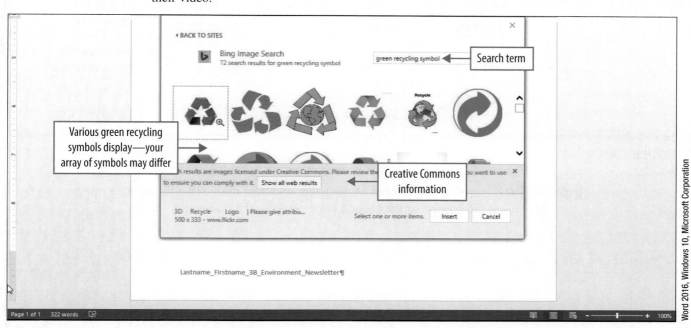

FIGURE 3.29

▶ **3** Click one of the green recycling symbols in the first row, and then in the lower right corner click **Insert**; your picture may display in a large size and create a new page.

▶ **4** With the picture selected, on the **Picture Tools Format tab**, in the **Size group**, click in the **Height** box. Type **0.5** and then press Enter. To the right of the picture, click **Layout Options** 🔳, and then click **Square** 🔳, which is the first button under **With Text Wrapping**. At the bottom of the **Layout Options gallery**, click **See more** to display the **Layout** dialog box. Compare your screen with Figure 3.30.

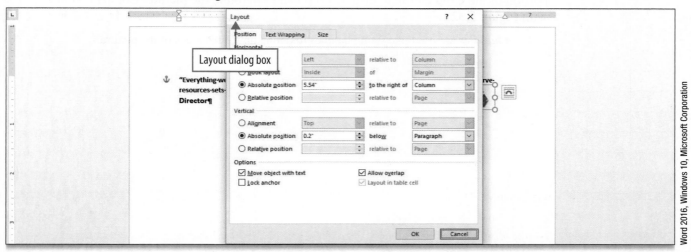

FIGURE 3.30

5 In the **Layout** dialog box, on the **Position tab**, under **Horizontal**, click the **Alignment** option button. Click the **Alignment arrow**, and then click **Centered**. Click the **relative to arrow** and then click **Page**. Under **Vertical**, click the **Alignment** option button. Click the **Alignment arrow**, and then click **Bottom**. Click the **relative to arrow**, and then click **Margin**. Compare your screen with Figure 3.31.

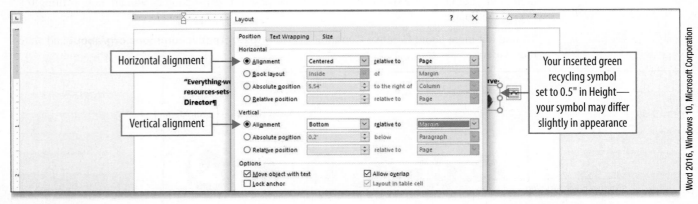

FIGURE 3.31

6 Click **OK**, scroll to the bottom of the page, and then notice that the recycle image displays at the bottom of the second page. **Save** 🖫 the document.

↻ ANOTHER WAY   Drag the image to visually position the image.

Activity 3.19 | Cropping a Picture and Resizing a Picture by Scaling

In this Activity, you will insert a picture and edit the picture by cropping and scaling. When you *crop* a picture, you remove unwanted or unnecessary areas of the picture. When you *scale* a picture, you resize it to a percentage of its size.

1 Press Ctrl + Home to move to the top of the document. On the **Insert tab**, in the **Illustrations group**, click **Pictures**. In the **Insert Picture** dialog box, navigate to the location of your student data files, and then double-click **w03B_Recycling** to insert it.

2 With the picture selected, on the **Picture Tools Format tab**, in the **Size group**, click the upper portion of the **Crop** button to display crop handles around the picture. Compare your screen with Figure 3.32.

Crop handles are used like sizing handles to define unwanted areas of the picture.

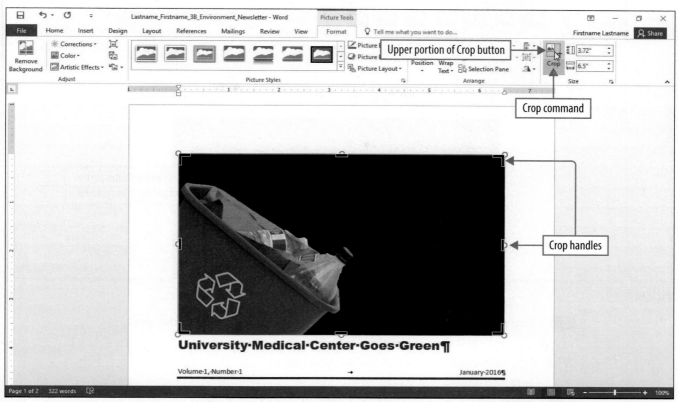

FIGURE 3.32

Word 2016, Windows 10, Microsoft Corporation

3 ▶ Point to the center right crop handle to display the ⊢ pointer. Compare your screen with Figure 3.33.

Use the *crop pointer* to crop areas of a picture.

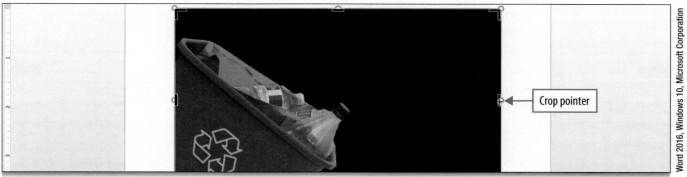

FIGURE 3.33

Word 2016, Windows 10, Microsoft Corporation

4 ▶ With the crop pointer displayed, hold down the left mouse button and drag to the left to approximately **5 inches on the horizontal ruler**, and then release the mouse button. Compare your screen with Figure 3.34.

The portion of the image to be removed displays in gray.

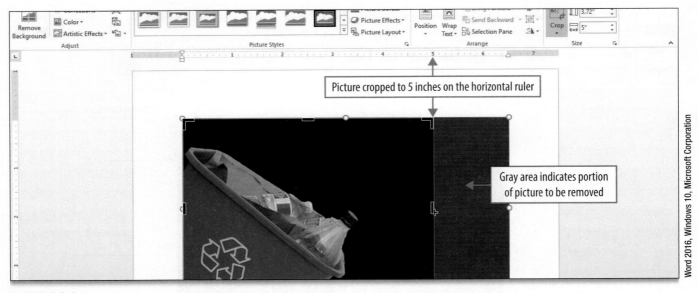

FIGURE 3.34

5 Click anywhere in the document outside of the image to apply the crop.

ANOTHER WAY   Click the upper portion of the Crop button to apply the crop.

6 Click to select the picture again. On the **Picture Tools Format tab**, in the **Size group**, click the **Dialog Box Launcher** button ⌐.

7 In the **Layout** dialog box, on the **Size tab**, under **Scale**, be sure that the **Lock aspect ratio** and **Relative to original picture size** check boxes are selected. Under **Scale**, select the percentage in the **Height box**, type **10** and then press Tab. Compare your screen with Figure 3.35.

When *Lock aspect ratio* is selected, the height and width of the picture are sized proportionately and only one scale value is necessary. The second value—in this instance Width—adjusts proportionately. When *Relative to original picture size* is selected, the scale is applied as a percentage of the original picture size.

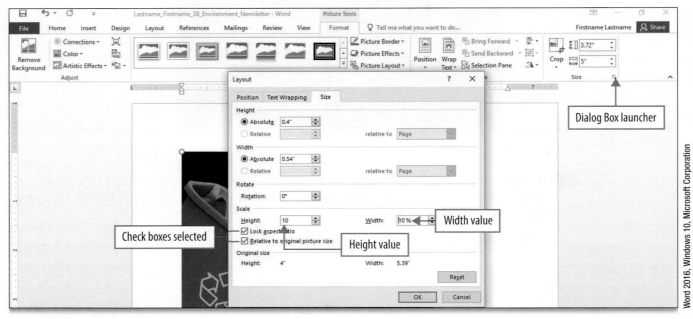

FIGURE 3.35

8 In the **Layout** dialog box, click the **Text Wrapping tab**. Under **Wrapping style**, click **Square**.

9 Click the **Position tab**, and then under **Horizontal**, click the **Alignment** option button. Be sure that the **Alignment** indicates **Left** and **relative to Column**. Under **Vertical**, click the **Alignment** option button, and then change the alignment to **Top relative to Margin**. Click **OK**, and then compare your screen with Figure 3.36.

Picture cropped, scaled, and positioned →

...iversity·Medical·Center·Goes·Green¶

FIGURE 3.36

Word 2016, Windows 10, Microsoft Corporation

Activity 3.20 | Setting Transparent Color and Recoloring a Picture

1.4.2, 5.2.3

You can make one color in a picture transparent using the Set Transparent Color command. When you *recolor* a picture, you change all the colors in the picture to shades of a single color.

1 On the **View tab**, in the **Zoom group**, click **Zoom**, and then click **200%**. Click **OK**. Drag the scroll bars as necessary so that you can view the recycle bin picture at the top of the document.

2 If necessary, select the recycle bin picture. Click the **Picture Tools Format tab**. In the **Adjust group**, click **Color**, and then below the gallery, click **Set Transparent Color**. Move the pointer into the document to display the ☑ pointer.

3 Point anywhere in the black background of the recycle bin picture, and then click to apply the transparent color to the background. Compare your screen with Figure 3.37.

Transparent color applied to black background →

University·Medical·Center·Goes·G

Volume·1,·Number·1

Word 2016, Windows 10, Microsoft Corporation

FIGURE 3.37

4 Press [Ctrl] + [End] to move to the end of your document, and then select the picture of the recycle symbol. On the **Format tab**, in the **Adjust group**, click **Color** to display a gallery of recoloring options. Under **Recolor**, in the last row, click the fourth option—**Olive Green, Accent color 3 Light**. Compare your screen with Figure 3.38, and then **Save** 🖫 the document.

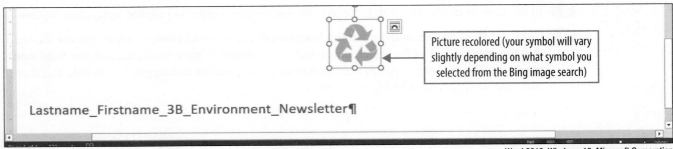

FIGURE 3.38

Activity 3.21 | Adjusting the Brightness and Contrast of a Picture

Brightness is the relative lightness of a picture. *Contrast* is the difference between the darkest and lightest area of a picture.

1 If necessary, select the recycle symbol. On the **Format tab**, in the **Adjust group**, click **Corrections**. Under **Brightness/Contrast**, point to several of the options to view the effect that the settings have on the picture.

2 Under **Brightness/Contrast**, in the last row, click the first setting—**Brightness: –40% Contrast: +40%**. Compare your screen with Figure 3.39.

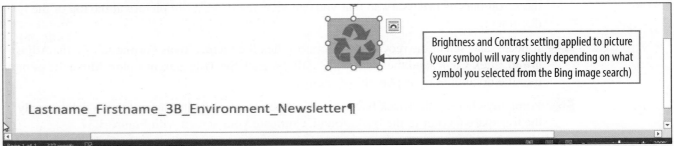

FIGURE 3.39

3 On the **View tab**, in the **Zoom group**, click **100%**, if necessary click **OK**, and then **Save** the document.

Activity 3.22 | Applying a Border to a Picture and Flipping a Picture

The *flip* commands create a reverse image of a picture or object.

1 Press Ctrl + Home to move to the top of the document, and then select the picture of the recycle bin. On the **Format tab**, in the **Picture Styles group**, click **Picture Border**. Under **Theme Colors**, in the fourth column, click the first color—**Dark Blue, Text 2**.

2 Click **Picture Border** again, and then point to **Weight**. Click **1 ½ pt** to change the thickness of the border.

3 On the **Format tab**, in the **Arrange group**, click **Rotate Objects**, and then click **Flip Horizontal**. Click anywhere in the document to deselect the picture. **Save**, and then compare your screen with Figure 3.40.

FIGURE 3.40

3.2.3, 1.2.2, 5.1.3

Activity 3.23 | Inserting and Formatting a Screenshot

A *screenshot* is an image of an active window on your computer that you can paste into a document. Screenshots are especially useful when you want to insert an image of a website into your Word document. You can insert a screenshot of any open window on your computer.

1 In the paragraph that begins *University Medical Center continues*, click after the period at the end of the paragraph. Start your web browser, and then navigate to **www.epa.gov** and press Enter.

2 From the taskbar, redisplay your **3B_Environment_Newsletter** document.

3 With the insertion point positioned at the end of the paragraph, on the **Insert tab**, in the **Illustrations group**, click **Screenshot**.

All of your open windows display in the Available Windows gallery and are available to paste into the document.

ALERT! **If No Windows Display**

If no windows display when you click the Screenshot command, possibly your browser does not support this feature. Instead, on the menu that displays, click Screen Clipping, position the + pointer in the upper right corner of the web window, and then drag down to the lower right corner. Release the mouse button to insert the screenshot.

---

4 In the **Screenshot** gallery, click the browser window that contains the EPA site to insert the screenshot at the insertion point. If a message box displays asking if you want to hyperlink the screenshot, click No, and then notice that the image is inserted and is sized to fit between the margins of the first column. Compare your screen with Figure 3.41.

By selecting No in the message box, you are inserting a screenshot without links to the actual website. Choose Yes if you want to link the image to the website.

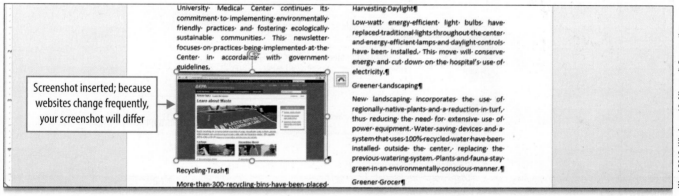

FIGURE 3.41

5 With the inserted screenshot selected, on the **Format tab**, in the **Picture Styles group**, click **Picture Border**, and then under **Theme Colors**, in the second column, click the first color—**Black, Text 1**.

6 **Save** the document.

More Knowledge **Inserting a Hyperlink in a Document**

You can create a link in your document for quick access to webpages and files. To insert a link in a document, first position the insertion point where you want the link to appear. On the Insert tab, in the Links group, click Hyperlink. In the Insert Hyperlink dialog box, in the Text to display box, type the text that will display in the document as a blue hyperlink. At the bottom, in the Address box, type the URL and then click OK.

GO! Learn How
Video W3-6

By using special text and paragraph formatting, you can emphasize text and make your newsletter look more professional. For example, you can place a border around one or more paragraphs or add shading to a paragraph. When adding shading, use light colors; dark shading can make the text difficult to read.

Activity 3.24 | Applying the Small Caps Font Effect

For headlines and titles, *small caps* is an attractive font effect. The effect changes lowercase letters to uppercase letters, but with the height of lowercase letters.

1 Under the screenshot, select the paragraph *Recycling Trash* including the paragraph mark.

2 Right-click the selected text, and then on the shortcut menu, click **Font** to display the **Font** dialog box. Click the **Font color arrow**, and then change the color to **Blue, Accent 1, Darker 50%**—in the fifth column, the last color.

3 Under **Font style**, click **Bold**. Under **Effects**, select the **Small caps** check box. Compare your screen with Figure 3.42.

> The Font dialog box provides more options than are available on the ribbon and enables you to make several changes at the same time. In the Preview box, the text displays with the selected formatting options applied.

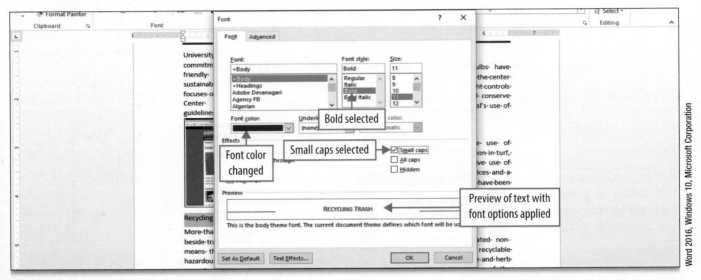

FIGURE 3.42

4 Click **OK**. With the text still selected, right-click, and then on the mini toolbar, double-click **Format Painter** so that you can apply the format multiple times. Then, in the second column, with the pointer, select each of the heading paragraphs—*Harvesting Daylight*, *Greener Landscaping*, *Greener Grocer*, and *Greener Records*—to apply the same formats. Press [Esc] to turn off Format Painter.

5 In the first column, below the screenshot, notice that the space between the *Recycling Trash* subheading and the screenshot is fairly small. Click anywhere in the *Recycling Trash* subheading, and then on the **Layout tab**, in the **Paragraph group**, click the **Before up spin arrow** two times to set the spacing to **12 pt**.

6 Compare your screen with Figure 3.43, and then **Save** your document.

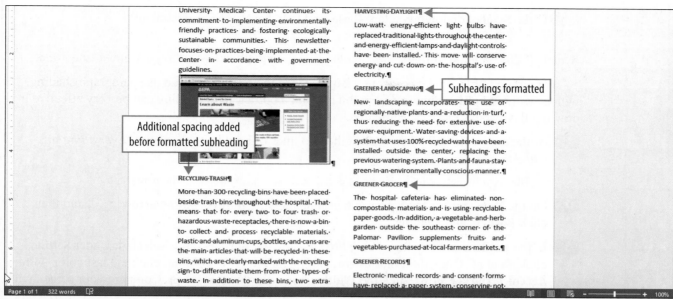

University Medical Center continues its commitment to implementing environmentally-friendly practices and fostering ecologically sustainable communities. This newsletter focuses on practices being implemented at the Center in accordance with government guidelines.

Additional spacing added before formatted subheading

RECYCLING·TRASH¶

More·than·300·recycling·bins·have·been·placed· beside·trash·bins·throughout·the·hospital.··That· means· that· for· every· two· to· four· trash· or· hazardous-waste-receptacles,·there·is·now·a·bin· to· collect· and· process· recyclable· materials.· Plastic·and·aluminum·cups,·bottles,·and·cans·are· the·main·articles·that·will·be·recycled·in·these· bins,·which·are·clearly·marked·with·the·recycling· sign· to· differentiate· them· from· other· types· of· waste.· In· addition· to· these· bins,· two· extra·

HARVESTING·DAYLIGHT¶

Low-watt· energy-efficient· light· bulbs· have· replaced·traditional·lights·throughout·the·center· and·energy-efficient·lamps·and·daylight·controls· have· been· installed.·· This· move· will· conserve· energy· and· cut· down· on· the· hospital's· use· of· electricity.¶

Subheadings formatted

GREENER·LANDSCAPING¶

New· landscaping· incorporates· the· use· of· regionally-native·plants·and·a·reduction·in·turf,· thus· reducing· the· need· for· extensive· use· of· power· equipment.· Water-saving· devices· and· a· system·that·uses·100%·recycled·water·have·been· installed· outside· the· center,· replacing· the· previous·watering·system.·Plants·and·fauna·stay· green·in·an·environmentally-conscious·manner.¶

GREENER·GROCER¶

The· hospital· cafeteria· has· eliminated· non-compostable· materials· and· is· using· recyclable· paper·goods.·In·addition,·a·vegetable·and·herb· garden· outside· the· southeast· corner· of· the· Palomar· Pavilion· supplements· fruits· and· vegetables·purchased·at·local·farmers·markets.¶

GREENER·RECORDS¶

Electronic· medical· records· and· consent· forms· have· replaced· a· paper· system,· conserving· not·

Page 1 of 1   322 words

FIGURE 3.43

Activity 3.25 | Inserting Symbols and Special Characters

MOS
3.2.5

You can insert symbols and special characters in a Word document, including copyright symbols, trademark symbols, and em dashes. An ***em dash*** is a punctuation symbol used to indicate an explanation or emphasis.

1 Press Ctrl + End to move to the end of the document, and then after the name *Emily Lynn* delete the comma and the space that separates her name from her job title—*Facilities Director*.

2 With the insertion point positioned before the *F* in *Facilities*, on the **Insert tab**, in the **Symbols group**, click **Symbol**. Below the gallery, click **More Symbols** to display the **Symbol** dialog box.

Here you can choose the symbol that you want to insert in your document.

3 In the **Symbol** dialog box, click the **Special Characters tab**. Scroll the list to view the types of special characters that you can insert; notice that some of the characters can be inserted using a Shortcut key.

4 Click **Em Dash**, and then in the lower right portion of the dialog box, click **Insert**. If necessary, drag the title bar of the Symbol window up or to the side, and then compare your screen with Figure 3.44.

An em dash displays between the name *Lynn* and the word *Facilities*.

FIGURE 3.44

5 In the **Symbol** dialog box, click **Close**, and then **Save** 🔲 your document.

Activity 3.26 | Adding Borders and Shading to a Paragraph and Inserting a Manual Line Break

Paragraph borders provide strong visual cues to the reader. You can use paragraph shading with or without borders; however, combined with a border, light shading can be very effective in drawing the reader's eye to specific text.

1 At the end of the document, select the two lines of bold text that begin *"Everything we can do.*

> The recycle picture may also be selected because it is anchored to the paragraph.

2 On the **Home tab**, in the **Paragraph group**, click the **Borders button arrow** ⊞ ▾, and then click **Borders and Shading**.

3 In the **Borders and Shading** dialog box, be sure the **Borders tab** is selected. Under **Setting**, click **Shadow**. Click the **Color arrow**, and then in the fifth column, click the last color—**Blue, Accent 1, Darker 50%**. Click the **Width arrow**, and then click **1 pt**. Compare your screen with Figure 3.45.

> In the lower right portion of the Borders and Shading dialog box, the *Apply to* box indicates *Paragraph*. The *Apply to* box directs where the border will be applied—in this instance, the border will be applied only to the selected paragraph.

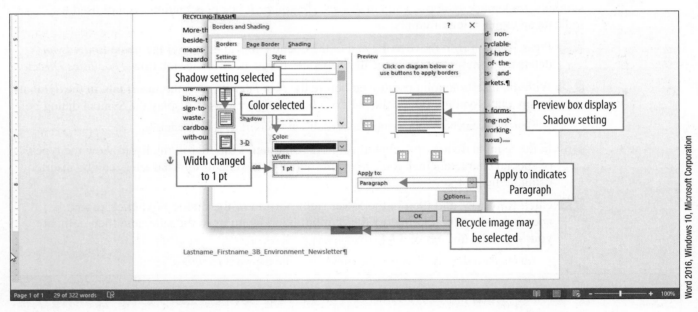

FIGURE 3.45

N O T E   Adding Simple Borders to Text

You can add simple borders from the Borders button gallery, located in the Paragraph group. This button offers less control over the border appearance, however, because the line thickness and color applied will match the most recently used on the computer at which you are working. The Borders and Shading dialog box enables you to make your own custom selections.

---

4 At the top of the **Borders and Shading** dialog box, click the **Shading tab**.

5 Click the **Fill arrow**, and then in the fifth column, click the second color—**Blue, Accent 1, Lighter 80%**. Notice that the shading change is reflected in the Preview area on the right side of the dialog box.

6 Click **OK**. On the **Home tab**, in the **Paragraph group**, click **Center** ▤.

7 Click anywhere in the document to deselect, and then compare your screen with Figure 3.46.

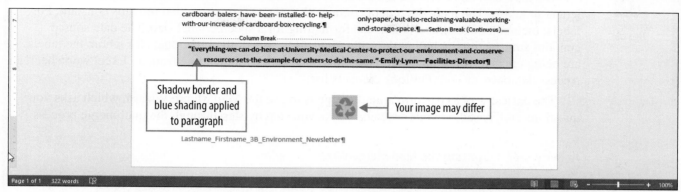

FIGURE 3.46

Word 2016, Windows 10, Microsoft Corporation

8 In the shaded paragraph, in the second line, click in front of the *E* in the name *Emily*. Hold down [Shift] and then press [Enter].

> Holding down [Shift] while pressing [Enter] inserts a ***manual line break***, which moves the text to the right of the insertion point to a new line while keeping the text in the same paragraph. A ***line break indicator***, in the shape of a bent arrow, indicates a manual line break.

9 Press [Ctrl] + [Home] to move the insertion point to the top of the document. Click the **File tab** to display **Backstage** view. On the right, at the bottom of the **Properties** list, click **Show All Properties**.

10 On the list of **Properties**, click to the right of **Tags**, and then type **newsletter, January**

11 Click to the right of **Subject**, and then type your course name and section number. Under **Related People**, be sure that your name displays as the author. If necessary, right-click the author name, click Edit Property, type your name, and click OK.

12 On the left, click **Print** to display the **Print Preview**, and then on the left click Save to save your document and return to the document window. In the upper right corner of the Word window, click **Close** ☒. If directed by your instructor to do so, submit your paper printout, your electronic image of your document that looks like a printed document, or your completed Word file. If you are submitting this Project as a MyITLab grader, submit this file.

ALERT!   **The Remaining Activities in This Chapter Are Optional**

Activities 3.27, 3.28, and 3.29, in which you create a set of mailing labels for the newsletter, are optional. Check with your instructor to see if you should complete these three Activities. These Activities *are* included in the MyITLab Grader system as a separate Grader exercise.

Objective 7 Create Mailing Labels Using Mail Merge

GO! Learn How
Video W3-7

Word's *mail merge* feature joins a *main document* and a *data source* to create customized letters or labels. The main document contains the text or formatting that remains constant. For labels, the main document contains the formatting for a specific label size. The data source contains information including the names and addresses of the individuals for whom the labels are being created. Names and addresses in a data source might come from an Excel worksheet, an Access database, or your Outlook contacts list.

The easiest way to perform a mail merge is to use the Mail Merge Wizard, which asks you questions and, based on your answers, walks you step by step through the mail merge process.

Activity 3.27 | Starting the Mail Merge Wizard Template

In this Activity, you will open the data source for the mail merge, which is an Excel worksheet containing names and addresses.

1 Start Word and display a new blank document. Display formatting marks and rulers. **Save** the document in your **Word Chapter 3** folder as **Lastname_Firstname_3B_Mailing_Labels**

2 With your new document open on the screen, from the taskbar, open **File Explorer** . Navigate to the student data files that accompany this chapter, and then double-click the Word file **w03B_Addresses** to open it in Excel. Compare your screen with Figure 3.47.

This Excel worksheet contains the addresses. Each row of information that contains data for one person is referred to as a *record*. The column headings, for example *First Name* and *Last Name*, are referred to as *fields*.

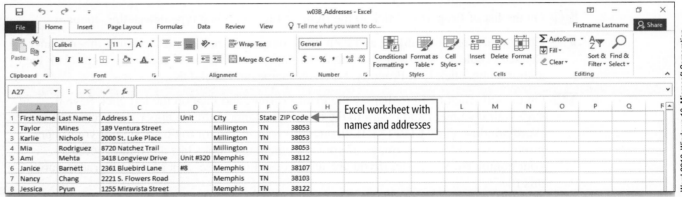

FIGURE 3.47

3 **Close** Excel and if necessary, close the File Explorer window. Be sure that your blank **Lastname_Firstname_3B_Mailing_Labels** document displays.

4 Click the **Mailings tab**. In the **Start Mail Merge group**, click **Start Mail Merge**, and then click **Step-by-Step Mail Merge Wizard** to display the **Mail Merge** pane on the right.

5 In the **Mail Merge** pane, under **Select document type**, click **Labels**. At the bottom of the **Mail Merge** pane, click **Next: Starting document** to display Step 2 of 6.

6 Under **Select starting document**, be sure **Change document layout** is selected, and then under **Change document layout**, click **Label options**.

7 ▶ In the **Label Options** dialog box, under **Printer information**, click the **Tray arrow**, and then if necessary, click **Default tray (Automatically Select)**—the exact wording may vary depending on your printer, but select the *Default* or *Automatic* option so that you can print the labels on regular paper rather than manually inserting labels in the printer.

8 ▶ Under **Label information**, click the **Label vendors arrow**, and then click **Avery US Letter**. Under **Product number**, scroll about halfway down the list, and then click **5160 Easy Peel Address Labels**. Compare your screen with Figure 3.48.

The Avery 5160 address label is a commonly used label. The precut sheets contain three columns of 10 labels each—for a total of 30 labels per sheet.

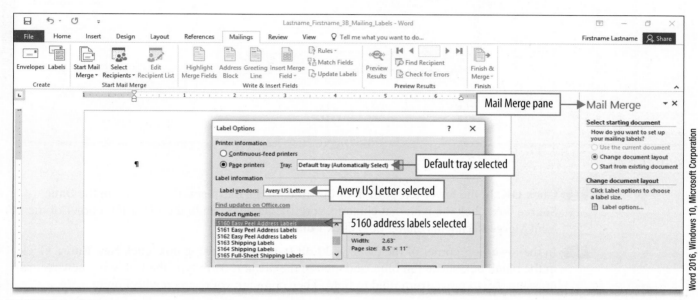

FIGURE 3.48

9 ▶ At the bottom of the **Label Options** dialog box, click **OK**. If a message box displays, click OK to set up the labels. If the gridlines do not display, on the Table Tools Layout tab, in the Table group, click View Gridlines. At the bottom of the **Mail Merge** pane, click **Next: Select recipients**.

The label page is set up with three columns and ten rows. Here, in Step 3 of the Mail Merge Wizard, you must identify the recipients—the data source. For your recipient data source, you can choose to use an existing list—for example, a list of names and addresses that you have in an Access database, an Excel worksheet, or your Outlook contacts list. If you do not have an existing data source, you can type a new list at this point in the wizard.

10 ▶ In the **Mail Merge** pane, under **Select recipients**, be sure the **Use an existing list** option button is selected. Under **Use an existing list**, click **Browse**.

11 ▶ In the **Select Data Source** dialog box, navigate to the student data files that accompany this chapter, click the Excel file **w03B_Addresses** one time to select it, and then click **Open** to display the **Select Table** dialog box. Compare your screen with Figure 3.49.

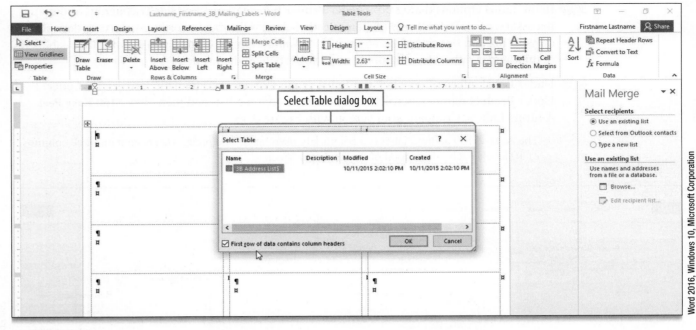

FIGURE 3.49

> **12** Click **OK**. In the lower left portion of the **Mail Merge Recipients** dialog box, in the **Data Source** box, click the path that contains your file name. Then in the lower left corner of the **Mail Merge Recipients** dialog box, click **Edit**.

> **13** In the lower left corner of the displayed **Edit Data Source** dialog box, click **New Entry**. Click in the blank box shaded in blue, and then in the blank record, type the following new record, pressing [Tab] to move from field to field. Then compare your screen with Figure 3.50.

FIRST_NAME	LAST_NAME	ADDRESS_1	UNIT	CITY	STATE	ZIP CODE
Sharon	Williams	1251 Parker Road	#843	Memphis	TN	38123

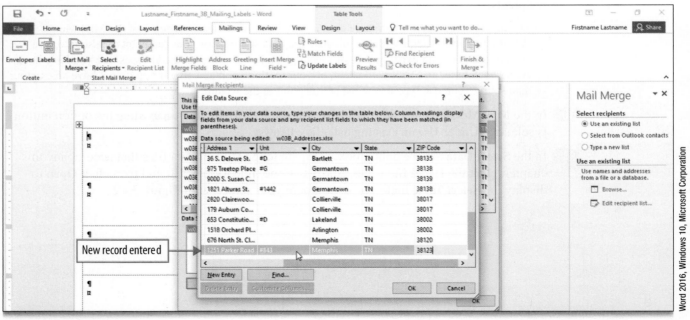

FIGURE 3.50

14 In the lower right corner of the **Edit Data Source** dialog box, click **OK**, and then in the displayed message, click **Yes**. Scroll to the end of the recipient list to confirm that the record for *Sharon Williams* that you just added is in the list. At the bottom of the **Mail Merge Recipients** dialog box, click **OK**.

Activity 3.28 | Completing the Mail Merge

Not only can you add and edit names and addresses while completing the Mail Merge, but you can also match your column names with preset names used in Mail Merge.

1 At the bottom of the **Mail Merge** pane, click **Next: Arrange your labels**.

2 Under **Arrange your labels**, click **Address block**. In the **Insert Address Block** dialog box, under **Specify address elements**, examine the various formats for names. If necessary, under *Insert recipient's name in this format*, select the *Joshua Randall Jr.* format. Compare your dialog box with Figure 3.51.

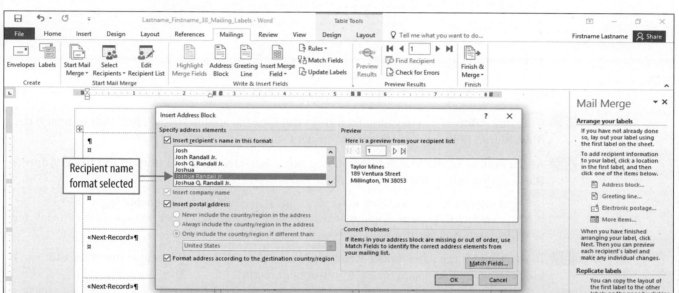

FIGURE 3.51

3 In the lower right corner of the **Insert Address Block** dialog box, click **Match Fields**, and then compare your screen with Figure 3.52.

If your field names are descriptive, the Mail Merge program will identify them correctly, as is the case with most of the information in the *Required for Address Block* section. However, the Address 2 field is unmatched—in the source file, this column is named *Unit*.

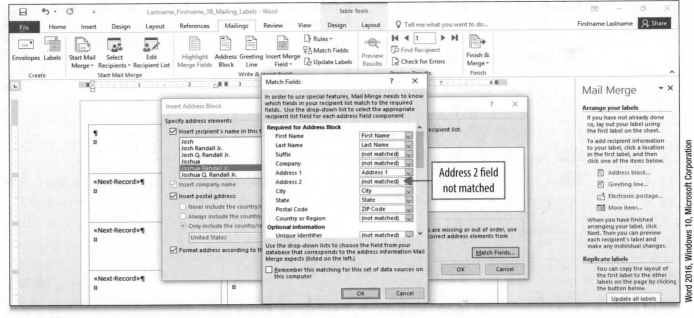

FIGURE 3.52

4 ▶ Click the **Address 2 arrow**, and then from the list of available fields, click **Unit** to match the Mail Merge field with the field in your data source.

5 ▶ At the bottom of the **Match Fields** dialog box, click **OK**. At the bottom of the **Insert Address Block** dialog box, click **OK**.

Word inserts the Address block in the first label space surrounded by double angle brackets. The *AddressBlock* field name displays, which represents the address block you saw in the Preview area of the Insert Address Block dialog box.

6 ▶ In the **Mail Merge** pane, under **Replicate labels**, click **Update all labels** to insert an address block in each label space for each subsequent record.

7 ▶ At the bottom of the **Mail Merge** pane, click **Next: Preview your labels**. Notice that for addresses with four lines, the last line of the address is cut off.

8 ▶ Press Ctrl + A to select all of the label text, click the **Layout tab**, and then in the **Paragraph group**, click in the **Spacing Before** box. Type **3** and press Enter.

9 ▶ Click in any label to deselect, and notice that 4-line addresses are no longer cut off. Compare your screen with Figure 3.53.

FIGURE 3.53

10 At the bottom of the **Mail Merge** pane, click **Next: Complete the merge**.

Step 6 of the Mail Merge displays. At this point you can print or edit your labels, although this is done more easily in the document window.

11 **Save** 🖫 your labels, and then on the right, **Close** ⊠ the **Mail Merge** pane.

Activity 3.29 | Previewing and Printing Mail Merge Results

If you discover that you need to make further changes to your labels, you can still make them even though the Mail Merge task pane is closed.

1 Add the file name to the footer, close the footer area, and then move to the top of **Page 2**. Click anywhere in the empty table row, and then click the **Table Tools Layout tab**. In the **Rows & Columns group**, click **Delete**, and then click **Delete Rows**.

Adding footer text to a label sheet replaces the last row of labels on a page with the footer text, and moves the last row of labels to the top of the next page. In this instance, a blank second page is created, which you can delete by deleting the blank row.

2 Notice that the labels do not display in alphabetical order. Click the **Mailings tab**, and then in the **Start Mail Merge group**, click **Edit Recipient List** to display the list of names and addresses.

3 In the **Mail Merge Recipients** dialog box, click the **Last Name** field heading, and notice that the names are sorted alphabetically by the recipient's last name.

Mailing labels are often sorted by either last name or by ZIP Code.

4 Click the **Last Name** field heading again, and notice that the last names are sorted in descending order. Click the **Last Name** field one more time to return to ascending order, and then click **OK**. Press Ctrl + Home, and then compare your screen with Figure 3.54.

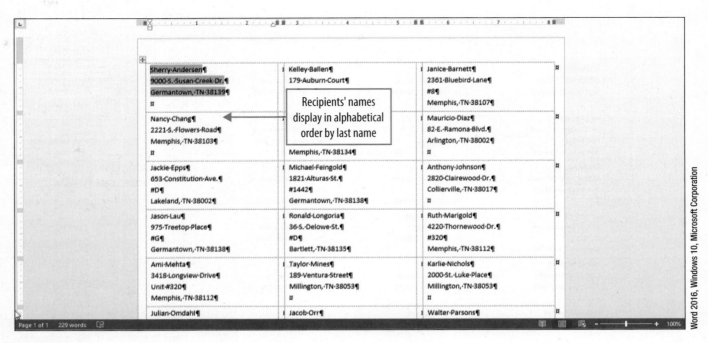

FIGURE 3.54

Word 2016, Windows 10, Microsoft Corporation

5 ▶ Click the **File tab**. On the right, at the bottom of the **Properties** list, click **Show All Properties**. On the list of **Properties**, click to the right of **Tags**, and then type **labels**

6 ▶ Click to the right of **Subject**, and then type your course name and section number. Be sure that your name displays as the author. If necessary, right-click the author name, click Edit Property, type your name, and click OK.

7 ▶ On the left, click **Save**. In the upper right corner of the Word window, click **Close** ☒. If directed by your instructor to do so, submit your Lastname_Firstname_3B_Mailing_Labels file as a paper printout, an electronic image of your document that looks like a printed document, or your completed Word file.

   If you print, the labels will print on whatever paper is in the printer; unless you have preformatted labels available, the labels will print on a sheet of paper. Printing the labels on plain paper enables you to proofread the labels before you print them on more expensive label sheets.

END | You have completed Project 3B

GO! With Google

Objective Format a Single-Column Newsletter in Google Docs

ALERT! **Working with Web-Based Applications and Services**

Computer programs and services on the web receive continuous updates and improvements, so the steps to complete this web-based activity may differ from the ones shown. You can often look at the screens and the information presented to determine how to complete the activity.

If you do not already have a Google account, you will need to create one before you begin this activity. Go to http://google.com and, in the upper right corner, click Sign In. On the Sign In screen, click Create Account. On the Create your Google Account page, complete the form, read and agree to the Terms of Service and Privacy Policy, and then click Next step. On the Welcome screen, click Get Started.

Activity | Formatting a Single-Column Newsletter in Google Docs

In this Activity, you will use Google Docs to edit a single-column newsletter similar to the one you edited in Project 3B. You can create columns in a Google Doc by inserting a table with two columns, and then typing in the two columns.

1 From the desktop, open your browser, navigate to **http://google.com**, and then click the **Google Apps** menu ▦. Click **Drive**, and then if necessary, sign in to your Google account.

2 Open your **GO! Web Projects** folder—or click New to create and then open this folder if necessary.

3 In the left pane, click **NEW**, and then click **File upload**. In the **Open** dialog box, navigate to your student data files for this chapter, and then in the **File List**, double-click to open **w03_3B_Web**.

4 Point to the uploaded file **w03_3B_Web**, and then right-click. On the shortcut menu, scroll as necessary, and then click **Rename**. Using your own last name and first name, type **Lastname_Firstname_WD_3B_Web** (leave the file extension .docx) and then click **OK** to rename the file.

5 Right-click the file you just renamed, point to **Open with**, and then click **Google Docs.**

6 Drag to select the newsletter title—*University Medical Center Goes Green*. On the toolbar, click the **Font size arrow**, and then click **18**. With the newsletter title still selected, on the toolbar, click the **Text color arrow**, and then in the second row, click the third from last color—**blue**.

7 Apply the same **Font Color** to the five subheadings—*Recycling Trash*, *Harvesting Daylight*, *Greener Landscaping*, *Greener Grocer*, and *Greener Records*. Compare your screen with Figure A.

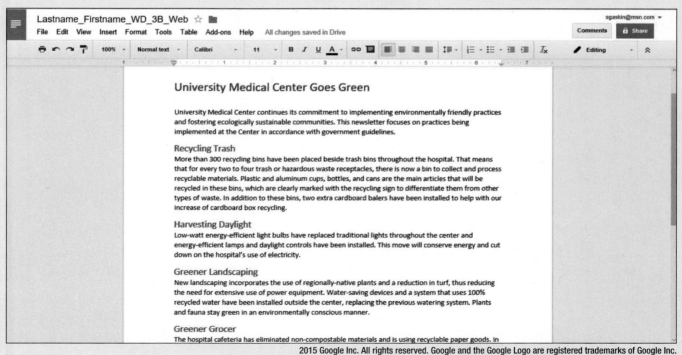

FIGURE A

(GO! With Google continues on the next page)

GO! With Google

8 Press Ctrl + End to move to the end of the document, and then press Enter. On the menu bar, click **Insert**, and then click **Image**. In the **Insert image** dialog box, in the upper right, click **Search**, and then click in the Google search box. Type **green recycle symbol** and then press Enter.

9 Click an image of a green recycle symbol similar to the one you used in Project 3B, and then at the bottom click **Select**.

10 Click the inserted image to select it, point to a corner of the image to display the sizing arrow, and then drag to resize the image until it displays at the bottom of the first page. On the toolbar, click the **Center** icon to center the image. Click anywhere in the text to deselect the image.

11 Submit the file as directed by your instructor. In the upper right, click your user name, and then click **Sign out**. **Close** your browser window. Your file is automatically saved in your Google Drive.

GO! To Work

Andrew Rodriguez / Fotolia; FotolEdhar/ Fotolia; apops/ Fotolia; Yuri Arcurs/ Fotolia

MICROSOFT OFFICE SPECIALIST (MOS) SKILLS IN THIS CHAPTER

PROJECT 3A	PROJECT 3B
1.2.4 Move to a specific location in a document	**1.1.3** Open a PDF in Word for editing
1.3.5 Insert page numbers	**1.2.2** Insert hyperlinks
1.4.1 Change document views	**1.4.2** Customize views by using zoom settings
1.4.5 Add document properties	**1.5.2** Save documents in alternative file formats
2.2.3 Set line and paragraph spacing and indentation	**2.1.4** Insert special characters
4.1.1 Insert footnotes and endnotes	**2.2.1** Apply font formatting
4.1.2 Modify footnote and endnote properties	**2.3.1** Format text in multiple columns
4.1.3 Create bibliography citation sources	**2.3.2** Insert page, section, or column breaks
4.1.4 Modify bibliography citation sources	**5.1.3** Insert a screen shot or screen clipping
4.1.5 Insert citations for bibliographies	**5.2.3** Remove picture backgrounds
	5.2.4 Format objects
	5.2.6 Wrap text around objects
	5.2.7 Position objects

BUILD YOUR E-PORTFOLIO

An E-Portfolio is a collection of evidence, stored electronically, that showcases what you have accomplished while completing your education. Collecting and then sharing your work products with potential employers reflects your academic and career goals. Your completed documents from the following projects are good examples to show what you have learned: 3G, 3K, 3L.

GO! FOR JOB SUCCESS

Video: Email Etiquette

Your instructor may assign this video to your class, and then ask you to think about, or discuss with your classmates, these questions:

FotolEdhar / Fotolia

Why do you think it is important to follow specific etiquette when composing email?

Why is it important to include a greeting and sign every email that you send?

What are the differences between sending a business email and a personal email, and what are three specific things you should never do in a business email?

GO! COLLABORATIVE TEAM PROJECT

If your instructor assigns this project to your class, you can expect to work with one or more of your classmates—either in person or by using Internet tools—to create work products similar to those that you created in this chapter. A team is a group of workers who work together to solve a problem, make a decision, or create a work product. Collaboration is when you work together with others as a team in an intellectual endeavor to complete a shared task or achieve a shared goal.

END OF CHAPTER

SUMMARY

Word assists you in formatting a research paper for college or business by providing built-in styles and formats for the most commonly used footnote and citation styles for research papers—MLA and APA.

Word helps you create the bibliography for your research paper by recording all of your citations in the Source Manager, and then generating the bibliography—in MLA, called Works Cited—for you.

Newsletters are often used by organizations to communicate information to a specific group. A newsletter can be formatted in two columns with a nameplate at the top that identifies the publication.

The Mail Merge Wizard enables you to easily merge a main document and a data source to create customized letters or labels. The data source can be an Excel spreadsheet, an Access database, or Outlook contacts.

GO! LEARN IT ONLINE

Review the concepts, key terms, and MOS skills in this chapter by completing these online challenges, which you can in **MyITLab**.

Matching and Multiple Choice: Answer matching and multiple-choice questions to test what you learned in this chapter.

Lessons on the GO!: Learn how to use all the new apps and features as they are introduced by Microsoft.

MOS Prep Quiz: Answer questions to review the MOS skills that you practiced in this chapter

PROJECT GUIDE FOR WORD CHAPTER 3

Your instructor will assign Projects from this list to ensure your learning and assess your knowledge.

	REVIEW AND ASSESSMENTS GUIDE FOR WORD CHAPTER 3		
Project	**Apply Skills from These Chapter Objectives**	**Project Type**	**Project Location**
3A **MyITLab**	Objectives 1–4 from Project 3A	**3A Instructional Project (Grader Project)** Guided instruction to learn the skills in Project 3A	In MyITLab and in text
3B **MyITLab**	Objectives 5–7 from Project 3B	**3B Instructional Project (Grader Project)** Guided instruction to learn the skills in Project 3B	In MyITLab and in text
3C	Objectives 1–4 from Project 3A	**3C Skills Review** A guided review of the skills from Project 3A.	In text
3D	Objectives 5–7 from Project 3B	**3D Skills Review** A guided review of the skills from Project 3B.	In text
3E **MyITLab**	Objectives 1–4 from Project 3A	**3E Mastery (Grader Project)** **Mastery and Transfer of Learning** A demonstration of your mastery of the skills in Project 3A with extensive decision making.	In MyITLab and in text
3F **MyITLab**	Objectives 5–7 from Project 3B	**3F Mastery (Grader Project)** **Mastery and Transfer of Learning** A demonstration of your mastery of the skills in Project 3B with extensive decision making.	In MyITLab and in text
3G **MyITLab**	Objectives 1–7 from Projects 3A and 3B	**3G Mastery (Grader Project)** **Mastery and Transfer of Learning** A demonstration of your mastery of the skills in Projects 3A and 3B with extensive decision making.	In MyITLab and in text
3H	Combination of Objectives from Projects 3A and 3B	**3H GO! Fix It** **Critical Thinking** A demonstration of your mastery of the skills in Projects 3A and 3B by creating a correct result from a document that contains errors you must find.	Instructor Resource Center (IRC) and MyITLab
3I	Combination of Objectives from Projects 3A and 3B	**3I GO! Make It** **Critical Thinking** A demonstration of your mastery of the skills in Projects 3A and 3B by creating a result from a supplied picture.	IRC and MyITLab
3J	Combination of Objectives from Projects 3A and 3B	**3J GO! Solve It** **Critical Thinking** A demonstration of your mastery of the skills in Projects 3A and 3B, your decision-making skills, and your critical-thinking skills. A task-specific rubric helps you self-assess your result.	IRC and MyITLab
3K	Combination of Objectives from Projects 3A and 3B	**3K GO! Solve It** **Critical Thinking** A demonstration of your mastery of the skills in Projects 3A and 3B, your decision-making skills, and your critical-thinking skills. A task-specific rubric helps you self-assess your result.	In text
3L	Combination of Objectives from Projects 3A and 3B	**3L GO! Think** **Critical Thinking** A demonstration of your understanding of the chapter concepts applied in a manner that you would outside of college. An analytic rubric helps you and your instructor grade the quality of your work by comparing it to the work an expert in the discipline would create.	In text
3M	Combination of Objectives from Projects 3A and 3B	**3M GO! Think** **Critical Thinking** A demonstration of your understanding of the chapter concepts applied in a manner that you would outside of college. An analytic rubric helps you and your instructor grade the quality of your work by comparing it to the work an expert in the discipline would create.	IRC and MyITLab
3N	Combination of Objectives from Projects 3A and 3B	**3N You and GO!** **Critical Thinking** A demonstration of your understanding of the chapter concepts applied in a manner that you would in a personal situation. An analytic rubric helps you and your instructor grade the quality of your work.	IRC and MyITLab
3O	Combination of Objectives from Projects 3A and 3B	**3O Cumulative Team Project for Word Chapter 3** **Critical Thinking** A demonstration of your understanding of concepts and your ability to work collaboratively in a group role-playing assessment, requiring both collaboration and self-management.	IRC and MyITLab
Capstone Project for Word Chapters 1–3	Combination of Objectives from Projects 1A, 1B, 2A, 2B, 3A, and 3B	A demonstration of your mastery of the skills in Chapters 1–3 with extensive decision making. **(Grader Project)**	IRC and MyITLab

GLOSSARY

GLOSSARY OF CHAPTER KEY TERMS

American Psychological Association (APA) One of two commonly used style guides for formatting research papers.

Bibliography A list of cited works in a report or research paper; also referred to as Works Cited, Sources, or References, depending upon the report style.

Brightness The relative lightness of a picture.

Citation A note inserted into the text of a research paper that refers the reader to a source in the bibliography.

Column break indicator A dotted line containing the words *Column Break* that displays at the bottom of the column.

Contrast The difference between the darkest and lightest area of a picture.

Crop A command that removes unwanted or unnecessary areas of a picture.

Crop handles Handles used to define unwanted areas of a picture.

Crop pointer The pointer used to crop areas of a picture.

Data source A document that contains a list of variable information, such as names and addresses, that is merged with a main document to create customized form letters or labels.

Em dash A punctuation symbol used to indicate an explanation or emphasis.

Endnote In a research paper, a note placed at the end of a document or chapter.

Fields In a mail merge, the column headings in the data source.

Flip A command that creates a reverse image of a picture or object.

Footnote In a research paper, a note placed at the bottom of the page.

Hanging indent An indent style in which the first line of a paragraph extends to the left of the remaining lines and that is commonly used for bibliographic entries.

Line break indicator A nonprinting character in the shape of a bent arrow that indicates a manual line break.

Mail merge A feature that joins a main document and a data source to create customized letters or labels.

Main document In a mail merge, the document that contains the text or formatting that remains constant.

Manual column break An artificial end to a column to balance columns or to provide space for the insertion of other objects.

Manual line break A break that moves text to the right of the insertion point to a new line while keeping the text in the same paragraph.

Manual page break The action of forcing a page to end and placing subsequent text at the top of the next page.

Modern Language Association (MLA) One of two commonly used style guides for formatting research papers.

Nameplate The banner on the front page of a newsletter that identifies the publication.

Newsletter A periodical that communicates news and information to a specific group.

Note In a research paper, information that expands on the topic, but that does not fit well in the document text.

Page break indicator A dotted line with the text *Page Break* that indicates where a manual page break was inserted.

Parenthetical references References that include the last name of the author or authors, and the page number in the referenced source.

PDF Reflow The ability to import PDF files into Word so that you can transform a PDF back into a fully editable Word document.

Read Mode A view in Word that optimizes the Word screen for the times when you are reading Word documents on the screen and not creating or editing them.

Recolor A feature that enables you to change all colors in the picture to shades of a single color.

Record Each row of information that contains data for one person.

Scale A command that resizes a picture to a percentage of its size.

Screenshot An image of an active window on your computer that you can paste into a document.

Section A portion of a document that can be formatted differently from the rest of the document.

Section break A double dotted line that indicates the end of one section and the beginning of another section.

Small caps A font effect that changes lowercase letters to uppercase letters, but with the height of lowercase letters.

Style A group of formatting commands, such as font, font size, font color, paragraph alignment, and line spacing, that can be applied to a paragraph with one command.

Style guide A manual that contains standards for the design and writing of documents.

Suppress A Word feature that hides header and footer information, including the page number, on the first page of a document.

Watermark A text or graphic element that displays behind document text.

Works Cited In the MLA style, a list of cited works placed at the end of a research paper or report.

Apply 3A skills from these Objectives:

1 Create a Research Paper
2 Insert Footnotes in a Research Paper
3 Create Citations and a Bibliography in a Research Paper
4 Use Read Mode and PDF Reflow

Skills Review   Project 3C Diet and Exercise Report

In the following Skills Review, you will edit and format a research paper that contains information about the effects of diet and exercise. This paper was created by Rachel Holder, a medical intern at University Medical Center, for distribution to her classmates studying physiology. Your completed document will look similar to the one shown in Figure 3.55.

PROJECT FILES

For Project 3C, you will need the following file:

w03C_Diet_Exercise

You will save your document as:

Lastname_Firstname_3C_Diet_Exercise

PROJECT RESULTS

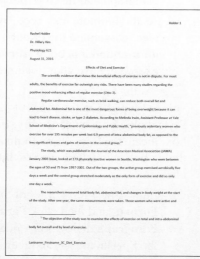

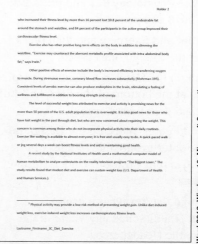

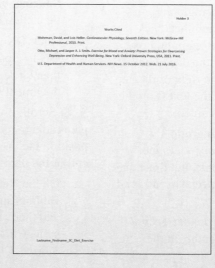

Word 2016, Windows 10, Microsoft Corporation

FIGURE 3.55

(Project 3C Diet and Exercise Report continues on the next page)

Skills Review | Project 3C Diet and Exercise Report (continued)

1 Start Word. On Word's opening screen, in the lower left, click **Open Other Documents**. Navigate to your student data files, and then locate and open the document **w03C_Diet_Exercise**. Display the formatting marks and rulers. Save the file in your **Word Chapter 3** folder as **Lastname_Firstname_3C_Diet_Exercise**

a. Press Ctrl + A to select all the text. On the **Home tab**, in the **Paragraph group**, click **Line and Paragraph Spacing**, and then change the line spacing to **2.0**. On the **Layout tab**, in the **Paragraph group**, change the **Spacing After** to **0 pt**.

b. Press Ctrl + Home, press Enter to create a blank line at the top of the document, and then click to position the insertion point in the new blank line. Type **Rachel Holder** and press Enter. Type **Dr. Hillary Kim** and press Enter. Type **Physiology 621** and press Enter. Type **August 31, 2016** and press Enter.

c. Type **Effects of Diet and Exercise** and then press Ctrl + E to center the title you just typed.

2 On the **Insert tab**, in the **Header & Footer group**, click **Header**, and then at the bottom of the list, click **Edit Header**. Type **Holder** and then press Spacebar.

a. Under **Header and Footer Tools**, on the **Design tab**, in the **Header & Footer group**, click **Page Number**, and then point to **Current Position**. Under **Simple**, click **Plain Number**.

b. On the **Home tab**, in the **Paragraph group**, click **Align Right**. Double-click anywhere in the document to close the Header area.

c. Near the top of **Page 1**, locate the paragraph beginning *The scientific evidence*, and then click to position the insertion point at the beginning of that paragraph. Scroll to the end of the document, hold down Shift, and then click to the right of the last paragraph mark to select all of the text from the insertion point to the end of the document.

d. On the **Home tab**, in the **Paragraph group**, click the **Dialog Box Launcher** button. In the **Paragraph** dialog box, on the **Indents and Spacing tab**, under **Indentation**, click the **Special arrow**, and then click **First line**. Click **OK**.

e. On the **Insert tab**, in the **Header & Footer group**, click **Footer**, and then click **Edit Footer**. In the **Insert group**, click **Document Info**, and then click **File Name**. Click **Close Header and Footer**.

3 Scroll to view the top of **Page 2**, locate the paragraph that begins *Exercise also has*, and then at the end of that paragraph, click to position the insertion point to the right of the period following *Irwin*. On the **References tab**, in the **Footnotes group**, click **Insert Footnote**.

a. As the footnote text, type **Physical activity may provide a low-risk method of preventing weight gain. Unlike diet-induced weight loss, exercise-induced weight loss increases cardiorespiratory fitness levels.**

b. In the upper portion of **Page 1**, locate the paragraph that begins *Regular cardiovascular exercise*. Click to position the insertion point at the end of the paragraph and insert a footnote.

c. As the footnote text, type **The objective of the study was to examine the effects of exercise on total and intra-abdominal body fat overall and by level of exercise. Save** your document.

4 At the bottom of **Page 1**, right-click in the footnote you just typed. On the shortcut menu, click **Style**. In the **Style** dialog box, click **Modify**. In the **Modify Style** dialog box, locate the Formatting toolbar in the center of the dialog box, click the **Font Size button arrow**, and then click **11**.

a. In the lower left corner of the dialog box, click **Format**, and then click **Paragraph**. In the **Paragraph** dialog box, under **Indentation**, click the **Special arrow**, and then click **First line**. Under **Spacing**, click the **Line spacing button arrow**, and then click **Double**.

b. Click **OK** to close the **Paragraph** dialog box, click **OK** to close the **Modify Style** dialog box, and then click **Apply** to apply the new style. **Save** your document.

5 Scroll to view the top of **Page 1**, and then in the paragraph that begins *The scientific evidence*, click to position the insertion point to the left of the period at the end of the paragraph.

a. On the **References tab**, in the **Citations & Bibliography group**, click the **Style button arrow**, and then click **MLA** to insert a reference using MLA style. Click **Insert Citation**, and then click **Add New Source**. Click the **Type of Source arrow**, scroll as

(Project 3C Diet and Exercise Report continues on the next page)

necessary to locate and click **Book**, and then add the following information:

Author	Otto, Michael, and Jasper A. J. Smits
Title	Exercise for Mood and Anxiety: Proven Strategies for Overcoming Depression and Enhancing Well-Being
Year	2011
City	New York
Publisher	Oxford University Press, USA
Medium	Print

b. Click **OK** to insert the citation. In the paragraph, click to select the citation, click the **Citation Options arrow**, and then click **Edit Citation**. In the **Edit Citation** dialog box, under **Add**, in the **Pages** box, type **3** and then click **OK**.

c. On the upper portion of **Page 2**, in the paragraph that begins *Other positive effects*, in the second line, click to position the insertion point to the left of the period following *substantially*. In the **Citations & Bibliography group**, click **Insert Citation**, and then click **Add New Source**. Click the **Type of Source arrow**, click **Book**, and then add the following information:

Author	Lohrman, David, and Lois Heller
Title	Cardiovascular Physiology, Seventh Edition
Year	2010
City	New York
Publisher	McGraw-Hill Professional
Medium	Print

d. Click **OK**. Click to select the citation in the paragraph, click the **Citation Options arrow**, and then click **Edit Citation**. In the **Edit Citation** dialog box, under **Add**, in the **Pages** box, type **195** and then click **OK**.

6 Press Ctrl + End to move to the end of the last paragraph in the document. Click to the left of the period following *loss*. In the **Citations & Bibliography group**, click **Insert Citation**, and then click **Add New Source**. Click the **Type of Source arrow**,

click **Web site**, and then select the **Corporate Author** check box. Add the following information:

Corporate Author	U.S. Department of Health and Human Services
Name of Web Page	NIH News
Year	2012
Month	October
Day	15
Year Accessed	2016
Month Accessed	July
Day Accessed	21
Medium	Web

a. Click **OK**. Press Ctrl + End to move the insertion point to the end of the document. Press Ctrl + Enter to insert a manual page break. On the **Home tab**, in the **Paragraph group**, click the **Dialog Box Launcher** button. In the **Paragraph** dialog box, on the **Indents and Spacing tab**, under **Indentation**, click the **Special arrow**, and then click **(none)**. Click **OK**.

b. Type **Works Cited** and then press Enter. On the **References tab**, in the **Citations & Bibliography group**, be sure **MLA** displays in the **Style** box. In the **Citations & Bibliography group**, click **Bibliography**, and then at the bottom, click **Insert Bibliography**.

c. In the bibliography, move the pointer to the left of the first entry—beginning *Lohrman*—to display the pointer. Drag down to select all three references in the field. On the **Home tab**, in the **Paragraph group**, set the **Line spacing** to **2.0**. On the **Layout tab**, set the **Spacing After** to **0 pt**.

d. Click anywhere in the *Works Cited* title, and then press Ctrl + E to center the title. **Save** your document.

7 On the **References tab**, in the **Citations & Bibliography group**, click **Manage Sources**. On the left, on the **Master List**, click the entry for *Lohrman, David*, and then click **Edit**. In the **Edit Source** dialog box, in the **Author** box, change the *L* in *Lohrman* to **M** Click **OK**, click **Yes**, and then click **Close**.

a. On **Page 2**, in the paragraph that begins *Other positive effects*, in the second line, on the selected citation, click the **Citation Options arrow**, and then click **Update Citations and Bibliography**.

(Project 3C Diet and Exercise Report continues on the next page)

b. Click the **File tab**, and then in the lower right corner, click **Show All Properties**. Add the following information:

Title	Diet and Exercise
Tags	weight loss, exercise, diet
Comments	Draft copy of report for class
Categories	biomedical research
Company	University Medical Center
Manager	Dr. Hillary Kim

c. In the **Subject** box, type your course name and section number. Be sure that your name displays as the Author and edit if necessary. On the left, click **Save** to redisplay your document. On the **View tab**, in the **Views group**, click **Read Mode**. In the upper left, click **Tools**, click **Find**, and then in the search box, type **Yale** and notice that the text you searched for is highlighted in the document.

d. In the upper left, click **View**, and then click **Edit Document** to return to Print Layout view. **Close** the **Navigation** pane. **Save** your document, and view the Print Preview. If directed by your instructor to do so, submit your paper printout, your electronic image of your document that looks like a printed document, or your original Word file. **Close** Word.

END | You have completed Project 3C

Apply **3B** skills from these Objectives:

5 Format a Multiple-Column Newsletter

6 Use Special Character and Paragraph Formatting

7 Create Mailing Labels Using Mail Merge

Skills Review   Project 3D Career Newsletter

In the following Skills Review, you will format a newsletter regarding professional development opportunities offered by University Medical Center, and you will create mailing labels for staff interested in these opportunities. Your completed document will look similar to Figure 3.56.

PROJECT FILES

For Project 3D, you will need the following files:

w03D_Career_Newsletter

w03D_Career_Sign (optional)

w03D_Medical_Symbol

w03D_Addresses (Optional: Use only if you are completing the Mailing Labels portion of this project)

You will save your documents as:

Lastname_Firstname_3D_Career_Newsletter

Lastname_Firstname_3D_Mailing_Labels (Optional: Create only if you are completing the Mailing Labels portion of this project)

PROJECT RESULTS

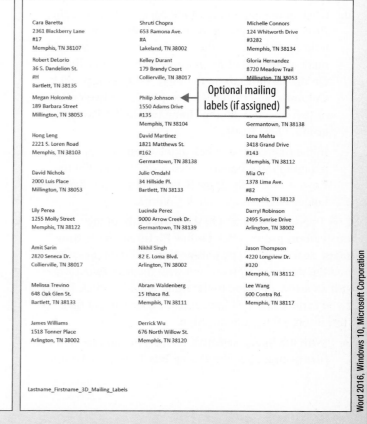

Lastname_Firstname_3D_Career_Newsletter

Lastname_Firstname_3D_Mailing_Labels

FIGURE 3.56

Word 2016, Windows 10, Microsoft Corporation

(Project 3D Career Newsletter continues on the next page)

1 ▶ Start Word. On Word's opening screen, in the lower left, click **Open Other Documents**. Navigate to your student files, and then locate and open **w03D_Career_Newsletter**. Save the file in your **Word Chapter 3** folder as **Lastname_Firstname_3D_Career_Newsletter** and then add the file name to the footer.

a. Select the first two lines of the document. On the mini toolbar, change the **Font** to **Arial Black** and the **Font Size** to **18**. Select the first three lines of the document. Click the **Font Color button arrow**, and then under **Theme Colors**, in the fifth column, click the last color—**Blue, Accent 1, Darker 50%**.

b. With the text still selected, on the **Home tab**, in the **Paragraph group**, click the **Borders button arrow**, and then at the bottom, click **Borders and Shading**. In the **Borders and Shading** dialog box, on the **Borders tab**, click the **Color arrow**, and then under **Theme Colors**, in the fifth column, click the last color—**Blue, Accent 1, Darker 50%**.

c. Click the **Width arrow**, and then click **3 pt**. In the **Preview** box, click the bottom border. Click **OK**.

d. Click at the beginning of the paragraph that begins *Professional Development*. Scroll the document, hold down Shift, and then click after the paragraph mark at the end of the *Internship Essentials* line. On the **Layout tab**, in the **Page Setup group**, click **Columns**, and then click **Two**. With the two columns of text selected, on the **Home tab**, in the **Paragraph group**, click **Justify**.

e. In the first column, click at the beginning of the paragraph that begins *Courses are taught*. On the **Layout tab**, in the **Page Setup group**, click **Breaks**. Under **Page Breaks**, click **Column**.

2 ▶ Press Ctrl + Home. On the **Insert tab**, in the **Illustrations group**, click **Online Pictures**. In the **Bing Image Search** box, type **career sign** and then press Enter. Find the image of a green sign with the text *Your Career* with an arrow pointing to the right, and then click **Insert**. If you cannot find this image, from your student data files, insert w03D_Career_Sign.

a. With the image selected, on the **Format tab**, in the **Size group**, click the **Dialog Box Launcher** button.

In the **Layout** dialog box, on the **Size tab**, under **Scale**, be sure the **Lock aspect ratio** and **Relative to original picture size** check boxes are selected. Under **Scale**, select the percentage in the **Height box**, type **90** and then press Tab.

b. In the **Layout** dialog box, click the **Text Wrapping tab**. Under **Wrapping style**, click **Square**.

c. Click the **Position tab**, and then under **Horizontal**, click the **Alignment** option button. Be sure that the **Alignment** indicates **Left** and **relative to Column**. Under **Vertical**, click the **Alignment** option button, and then change the alignment to **Top relative to Margin**. Click **OK**. Compare the picture size and placement with Figure 3.56 and adjust the size of the image if necessary. **Save** your newsletter.

3 ▶ Press Ctrl + End to move to the end of the document. On the **Insert tab**, in the **Illustrations group**, click **Pictures**, and then from your student data files, insert the picture **w03D_Medical_Symbol**.

a. With the image still selected, on the **Format tab**, in the **Adjust group**, click **Color**, and then under **Recolor**, in the last row, click **Blue, Accent color 1 Light**.

b. With the picture selected, on the **Format tab**, in the **Size group**, click in the **Height** box. Type **1** and then press Enter. To the right of the picture, click **Layout Options**, and then click **Square**. At the bottom of the **Layout Options** gallery, click **See more** to display the **Layout** dialog box.

c. On the **Position tab**, under **Horizontal**, click the **Alignment** option button, and then change the **Alignment** to **Centered relative to Page**. Under **Vertical**, click the **Alignment** option button, and then change **Alignment** to **Bottom relative to Margin**. Click **OK**.

d. On the **Format tab**, in the **Picture Styles group**, click **Picture Border**. Under **Theme Colors**, in the fifth column, click the second color—**Blue Accent 1, Lighter 80%**. Click **Picture Border** again, and then point to **Weight**. Click **1 pt**.

(Project 3D Career Newsletter continues on the next page)

4 In the paragraph that begins *University Medical Center is a dynamic*, click after the period at the end of the paragraph, and then press [Enter] one time. With the insertion point in the new blank paragraph, open your web browser, and then navigate to **www.ahrq.gov/clinic/**

a. From the taskbar, redisplay your **3D_Career_Newsletter** document. With the insertion point positioned at the end of the first paragraph in the body of the newsletter, on the **Insert tab**, in the **Illustrations group**, click **Screenshot**. In the **Screenshot** gallery, click the browser window that contains the website you just opened.

b. Select the subheading **Professional Development at UMC** including the paragraph mark. Right-click the selected text, and then on the shortcut menu, click **Font**. In the **Font** dialog box, click the **Font color arrow**, and then in the fifth column, click the last color—**Blue, Accent 1, Darker 50%**. Under **Font style**, click **Bold**, and then under **Effects**, select **Small caps**. Click **OK**.

c. With the text still selected, right-click, and then on the mini toolbar, double-click **Format Painter**. In the second column, with the [🔎I] pointer, select each of the subheadings—**What to Expect from Coursework at UMC** and **Examples of Courses at UMC**. Press [Esc] to turn off Format Painter.

5 Press [Ctrl] + [End] to move to the end of the document, and then select the two lines of bold text—the graphic will also be selected. On the **Home tab**, in the **Paragraph group**, click the **Borders button arrow**, and then click **Borders and Shading**.

a. In the **Borders and Shading** dialog box, on the **Borders tab**, under **Setting**, click **Shadow**. Click the **Color arrow**, and then in the fifth column, click the last color—**Blue, Accent 1, Darker 50%**. Click the **Width arrow**, and then click **1 pt**.

b. In the **Borders and Shading** dialog box, click the **Shading tab**. Click the **Fill arrow**, and then in the fifth column, click the second color—**Blue, Accent 1, Lighter 80%**. Click **OK**. On the **Home tab**, in the **Paragraph group**, click **Center**. In the shaded paragraph, click in front of the *D* in the word *Director*. Hold down [Shift] and then press [Enter].

c. Press [Ctrl] + [Home], and then click the **File tab**. At the bottom of the **Properties** list, click **Show All Properties**. Click to the right of **Tags**, and then type **newsletter, careers** Click to the right of **Subject**, and then type your course name and section number. Under **Related People**, if necessary, type your name in the Author box. Display the **Print Preview** and make any necessary corrections. **Save** the document; close Word and close your browser window.

6 (NOTE: The remainder of this project, which is the creation of mailing labels, is optional. Complete if assigned by your instructor.) Start Word and display a new blank document. **Save** the document in your **Word Chapter 3** folder as **Lastname_Firstname_3D_Mailing_Labels**.

a. Click the **Mailings tab**. In the **Start Mail Merge group**, click **Start Mail Merge**, and then click **Step-by-Step Mail Merge Wizard**. In the **Mail Merge** pane, under **Select document type**, click **Labels**. At the bottom of the **Mail Merge** pane, click **Next: Starting document**.

b. Under **Select starting document**, under **Change document layout**, click **Label options**. In the **Label Options** dialog box, under **Printer information**, be sure that the **Default tray** is selected.

c. Under **Label information**, click the **Label vendors arrow**, and then click **Avery US Letter**. Under **Product number**, scroll about halfway down the list, and then click **5160 Easy Peel Address Labels**. At the bottom of the **Label Options** dialog box, click **OK**. At the bottom of the **Mail Merge** pane, click **Next: Select recipients**.

d. In the **Mail Merge** pane, under **Select recipients**, under **Use an existing list**, click **Browse**. In the **Select Data Source** dialog box, navigate to the student data files that accompany this chapter, click the Excel file **w03D_Addresses** one time to select it, and then click **Open** to display the **Select Table** dialog box. Click **OK**.

7 In the lower left portion of the **Mail Merge Recipients** dialog box, in the **Data Source** box, click the path that contains your file name. Then, at the bottom of the **Mail Merge Recipients** dialog box, click **Edit**. In the lower left corner of the displayed **Edit Data Source** dialog box, click **New Entry**. In the blank record, which

(Project 3D Career Newsletter continues on the next page)

is shaded, type the following, pressing Tab to move from field to field:

First Name	Mia
Last Name	Orr
Address 1	1378 Lima Ave.
Unit	#82
City	Memphis
State	TN
ZIP Code	38123

a. In the lower right corner of the **Edit Data Source** dialog box, click **OK**, and then in the displayed message, click **Yes**. At the bottom of the **Mail Merge Recipients** dialog box, click **OK**.

b. At the bottom of the **Mail Merge** pane, click **Next: Arrange your labels**. Under **Arrange your labels**, click **Address block**. In the lower right corner of the **Insert Address Block** dialog box, click **Match Fields**.

c. Click the **Address 2 arrow**, and then from the list of available fields, click **Unit**. Click **OK** two times.

d. In the **Mail Merge** pane, under **Replicate labels**, click **Update all labels**. At the bottom of the **Mail**

Merge pane, click **Next: Preview your labels**. Press Ctrl + A to select all of the label text, click the **Layout tab**, and then in the **Paragraph group**, click in the **Spacing Before** box. Type **3** and press Enter. At the bottom of the **Mail Merge** pane, click **Next: Complete the merge**.

e. Click the **Mailings tab**, and then in the **Start Mail Merge group**, click **Edit Recipient List** to display the list of names and addresses. In the **Mail Merge Recipients** dialog box, click the **Last Name** field heading to sort the names. Click **OK**. **Close** the **Mail Merge** pane.

f. Scroll the document and then click anywhere in the empty table row at the bottom. Click the **Table Tools Layout tab**. In the **Rows & Columns group**, click **Delete**, and then click **Delete Rows**. Add the file name to the footer, close the footer area, and then click the **File tab**. Click **Show All Properties**. As the **Tags**, type **labels** and as the **Subject**, type your course name and section number. Be sure your name displays as the **Author**, and then **Save** your file.

g. If directed by your instructor to do so, submit your paper printout, your electronic image of your document, or your original Word file. **Close** Word.

END | You have completed Project 3D

Mastering Word | Project 3E Skin Protection Report

In the following Mastering Word project, you will edit and format a research paper that contains information about skin protection and the use of sunblocks and sunscreens. This paper was created by Rachel Holder, a medical intern at University Medical Center, for distribution to her classmates studying dermatology. Your completed document will look similar to the one shown in Figure 3.57.

Apply 3A skills from these Objectives:

1. Create a Research Paper
2. Insert Footnotes in a Research Paper
3. Create Citations and a Bibliography in a Research Paper
4. Use Read Mode and PDF Reflow

PROJECT FILES

For Project 3E, you will need the following file:

w03E_Skin_Protection

You will save your document as:

Lastname_Firstname_3E_Skin_Protection

PROJECT RESULTS

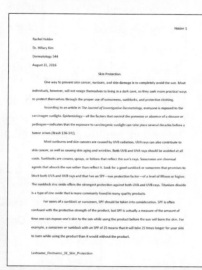
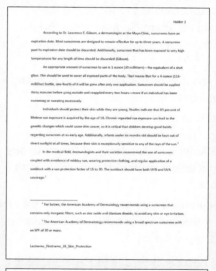

Word 2016, Windows 10, Microsoft Corporation

FIGURE 3.57

(Project 3E Skin Protection Report continues on the next page)

Mastering Word Project 3E Skin Protection Report (continued)

1 Start Word, and on the left click **Open Other Documents**. From your student data files, locate and open the document **w03E_Skin_Protection**. Display formatting marks and rulers. Save the file in your **Word Chapter 3** folder as **Lastname_Firstname_3E_Skin_Protection**

2 Select all the text, change the **Line Spacing** to **2.0**, and then change the **Spacing After** to **0 pt**.

3 At the top of the document, insert a new blank paragraph, and then in the new paragraph, type **Rachel Holder** Press Enter. Type **Dr. Hillary Kim** and press Enter. Type **Dermatology 544** and press Enter. Type **August 31, 2016** and press Enter. Type **Skin Protection** and then press Ctrl + E to center the title you just typed.

4 Insert a header, type **Holder** and then press Spacebar. Display the **Page Number gallery**, and then in the **Current Position**, add the **Plain Number** style. Apply **Align Right** formatting to the header. Insert a footer with the file name.

5 To the paragraph that begins *One way to prevent*, apply a **First line** indent of **0.5"**.

6 On **Page 2**, at the end of the paragraph that begins *In the medical field*, insert a footnote with the following text: **The American Academy of Dermatology recommends using a broad spectrum sunscreen with an SPF of 30 or more.**

7 Modify the **Footnote Text** style so that the **Font Size** is **11**, there is a **First line indent** of **0.5"**, and the spacing is **Double**, and then apply the style.

8 On **Page 1**, at the end of the paragraph that begins *According to an article*, click to the left of the period, and then using **MLA** format, insert a citation for a **Journal Article** with the following information:

Author	Brash, D. E.
Title	Sunlight and Sunburn in Human Skin Cancer
Journal Name	The Journal of Investigative Dermatology
Year	1996
Pages	136-142
Medium	Print

9 In the report, select the citation you just created, display the **Citation Options**, and then edit the citation to include **Pages 136-142**

10 At the top of **Page 2**, at the end of the paragraph that begins *According to Dr.*, click to the left of the period, and then insert a citation for a **Web site** with the following information:

Author	Gibson, Lawrence E.
Name of Web Page	Does Sunscreen Expire?
Year	2011
Month	April
Day	01
Year Accessed	2016
Month Accessed	June
Day Accessed	30
Medium	Web

11 On **Page 3**, at the end of the last paragraph of the report that begins *Because the effect*, click to the left of the period, and then insert a citation for a **Book** with the following information:

Author	Leffell, David.
Title	Total Skin: The Definitive Guide to Whole Skin Care for Life
Year	2000
City	New York
Publisher	Hyperion
Medium	Print

12 In the report, select the citation you just created, display the **Citation Options**, and then edit the citation to include **Page 96**

13 Move to the end of the document, and then insert a manual page break to create a new page. Display the **Paragraph** dialog box, and then change the **Indentation** under **Special** to **(none)**. Add a **Works Cited** title, press Enter, and then **Insert Bibliography**. Select the references, apply **Double** line spacing, and then set the **Spacing After** paragraphs to **0 pt. Center** the *Works Cited* title.

(Project 3E Skin Protection Report continues on the next page)

Mastering Word | Project 3E Skin Protection Report (continued)

14 Update the **Document Properties** with the following information:

Title	Skin Protection
Tags	sunscreen, sun exposure
Comments	Draft copy of report for class
Categories	Dermatology
Company	University Medical Center
Manager	Dr. Hillary Kim

15 In the **Subject** box, type your course name and section number. Be sure that your name displays as the **Author** and edit if necessary. On the left, click **Print** to view the **Print Preview**. Click **Save** to redisplay your document. If directed by your instructor to do so, submit your paper printout, your electronic image of your document that looks like a printed document, or your original Word file. **Close** Word.

END | You have completed Project 3E

Mastering Word | **Project 3F Dogs Newsletter and Mailing Labels**

Apply 3B skills from these Objectives:

5 Format a Multiple-Column Newsletter

6 Use Special Character and Paragraph Formatting

7 Create Mailing Labels Using Mail Merge

In the following Mastering Word project, you will format a newsletter with information about the therapy dogs handled by volunteers at the University Medical Center. Optionally, you will create mailing labels so that the newsletter can be sent to the volunteer staff. Your completed documents will look similar to Figure 3.58.

PROJECT FILES

For Project 3F, you will need the following files:

w03F_Dogs_Newsletter

w03F_Dog

w03F_Addresses (Optional: Use only if you are completing the Mailing Labels portion of this project)

You will save your documents as:

Lastname_Firstname_3F_Dogs_Newsletter

Lastname_Firstname_3F_Mailing_Labels (Optional: Create only if you are completing the Mailing Labels portion of this project)

PROJECT RESULTS

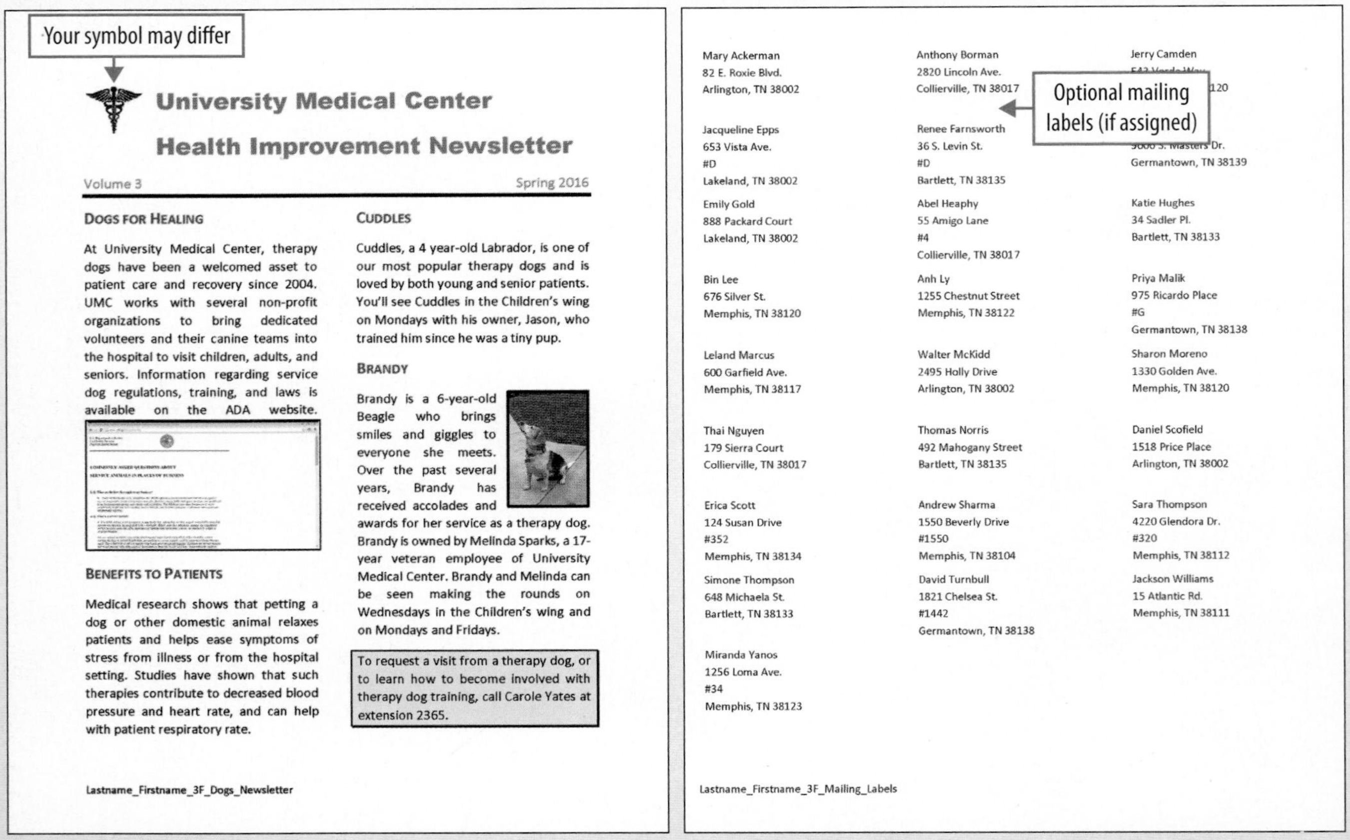

Your symbol may differ

University Medical Center
Health Improvement Newsletter

Volume 3   Spring 2016

DOGS FOR HEALING

At University Medical Center, therapy dogs have been a welcomed asset to patient care and recovery since 2004. UMC works with several non-profit organizations to bring dedicated volunteers and their canine teams into the hospital to visit children, adults, and seniors. Information regarding service dog regulations, training, and laws is available on the ADA website.

BENEFITS TO PATIENTS

Medical research shows that petting a dog or other domestic animal relaxes patients and helps ease symptoms of stress from illness or from the hospital setting. Studies have shown that such therapies contribute to decreased blood pressure and heart rate, and can help with patient respiratory rate.

CUDDLES

Cuddles, a 4 year-old Labrador, is one of our most popular therapy dogs and is loved by both young and senior patients. You'll see Cuddles in the Children's wing on Mondays with his owner, Jason, who trained him since he was a tiny pup.

BRANDY

Brandy is a 6-year-old Beagle who brings smiles and giggles to everyone she meets. Over the past several years, Brandy has received accolades and awards for her service as a therapy dog. Brandy is owned by Melinda Sparks, a 17-year veteran employee of University Medical Center. Brandy and Melinda can be seen making the rounds on Wednesdays in the Children's wing and on Mondays and Fridays.

To request a visit from a therapy dog, or to learn how to become involved with therapy dog training, call Carole Yates at extension 2365.

Lastname_Firstname_3F_Dogs_Newsletter

Mary Ackerman
82 E. Roxie Blvd.
Arlington, TN 38002

Jacqueline Epps
653 Vista Ave.
#D
Lakeland, TN 38002

Emily Gold
888 Packard Court
Lakeland, TN 38002

Bin Lee
676 Silver St.
Memphis, TN 38120

Leland Marcus
600 Garfield Ave.
Memphis, TN 38117

Thai Nguyen
179 Sierra Court
Collierville, TN 38017

Erica Scott
124 Susan Drive
#352
Memphis, TN 38134

Simone Thompson
648 Michaela St.
Bartlett, TN 38133

Miranda Yanos
1256 Loma Ave.
#34
Memphis, TN 38123

Anthony Borman
2820 Lincoln Ave.
Collierville, TN 38017

Renee Farnsworth
36 S. Levin St.
#D
Bartlett, TN 38135

Abel Heaphy
55 Amigo Lane
#4
Collierville, TN 38017

Anh Ly
1255 Chestnut Street
Memphis, TN 38122

Walter McKidd
2495 Holly Drive
Arlington, TN 38002

Thomas Norris
492 Mahogany Street
Bartlett, TN 38135

Andrew Sharma
1550 Beverly Drive
#1550
Memphis, TN 38104

David Turnbull
1821 Chelsea St.
#1442
Germantown, TN 38138

Jerry Camden
543 Vanda Way
120

Optional mailing labels (if assigned)

5000 S. Masters Dr.
Germantown, TN 38139

Katie Hughes
34 Sadler Pl.
Bartlett, TN 38133

Priya Malik
975 Ricardo Place
#G
Germantown, TN 38138

Sharon Moreno
1330 Golden Ave.
Memphis, TN 38120

Daniel Scofield
1518 Price Place
Arlington, TN 38002

Sara Thompson
4220 Glendora Dr.
#320
Memphis, TN 38112

Jackson Williams
15 Atlantic Rd.
Memphis, TN 38111

Lastname_Firstname_3F_Mailing_Labels

Word 2016, Windows 10, Microsoft Corporation

FIGURE 3.58

(Project 3F Dogs Newsletter and Mailing Labels continues on the next page)

Mastering Word | Project 3F Dogs Newsletter and Mailing Labels (continued)

1 Start Word. From your student files, open **w03F_Dogs_Newsletter**. **Save** the file in your **Word Chapter 3** folder as **Lastname_Firstname_3F_Dogs_Newsletter** and then add the file name to the footer. Select the first three lines of the document, and then change the **Font Color** to **Olive Green, Accent 3, Darker 25%**—in the seventh column, the fifth color. With the text selected, display the **Borders and Shading** dialog box. Apply a **3 pt** bottom border using the color **Black, Text 1**.

2 Click at the beginning of the newsletter title *University Medical Center*. Insert an online picture from **Bing Image Search** by searching for **physician symbol** and then insert one of the symbols that is not bordered or framed.

3 Set the image **Height** to **1"**. Change the **Brightness/Contrast** to **Brightness: 0% (Normal) Contrast: +40%**.

4 Change the **Text Wrapping** to **Square**. Change the **Horizontal Alignment** to **Left relative** to **Margin** and the **Vertical Alignment** to **Top relative** to **Margin**. If necessary, drag a corner of the inserted physician symbol to decrease its size so that the newsletter title displays on two lines.

5 Starting with the paragraph that begins *Dogs for Healing*, select all of the text from that point to the end of the document. Change the **Spacing After** to **10 pt**, format the text in two columns, and apply **Justify** alignment. Insert a **Column** break before the subheading *Cuddles*.

6 Click at the beginning of the sentence that begins with *Brandy is a 6-year-old Beagle*. From your student data files, insert the picture **w03F_Dog**. Rotate the picture using **Flip Horizontal**.

7 Change the picture **Width** to **1** and then apply the **Square** layout option. Change the **Horizontal Alignment** to **Right relative** to **Margin** and the **Vertical Alignment** to **Top relative** to **Line**. Apply a **Black, Text 1 Picture Border** and change the **Weight** to **2 ¼ pt**.

8 Start your web browser and if necessary, maximize the window. Navigate to **www.ada.gov/qasrvc.htm** From the taskbar, redisplay your **Lastname_Firstname_3F_Dogs_Newsletter** file, click at the end of the paragraph below the *Dogs for Healing* subheading. Insert a **Screenshot** of the website. Apply a **Black, Text 1 Picture Border** and change the **Weight** to **1 pt**.

9 Select the subheading **Dogs for Healing** including the paragraph mark. By using the **Font** dialog box, change the **Size** to **16**, apply **Bold**, apply the **Small caps** effect, and change the **Font color** to **Olive Green, Accent 3, Darker 50%**—in the seventh column, the last color. Apply the same formatting to the subheadings **Benefits to Patients**, **Cuddles**, and **Brandy**.

10 Select the last paragraph in the newsletter including the paragraph mark, and then apply a **1 pt Shadow** border, in **Black, Text 1**. Shade the paragraph with a **Fill** color of **Olive Green, Accent 3, Lighter 80%**—in the seventh column, the second color.

11 Click the **File tab**, and then click **Show All Properties**. As the **Tags**, type **dogs, newsletter** As the **Subject**, type your course name and section number. Under **Related People**, if necessary, type your name in the Author box. **Print Preview** the document and make any necessary corrections.

12 On the left, click **Print** to view the **Print Preview**. Click **Save** to redisplay your document. If directed by your instructor to do so, submit your paper printout, your electronic image of your document that looks like a printed document, or your original Word file. **Close** Word.

> **END | You have completed Project 3F**

ALERT!   **Optional Project to Produce Mailing Labels**

Your instructor may ask you to complete the optional project on the following page to produce mailing labels. Check with your instructor to see if you should complete the mailing labels. This project is not included in the MyITLab Grader system.

1 Start Word and display a new blank document. **Save** the document in your **Word Chapter 3** folder as **Lastname_Firstname_3F_Mailing_Labels** From your student files, **Open** the file **w03F_Addresses**. **Save** the address file in your **Word Chapter 3** folder as **Lastname_Firstname_3F_Addresses**.

2 Start the **Step-by-Step Mail Merge Wizard** to create **Labels**. Display the **Label Options** dialog box, and be sure that the **Default tray** is selected and that the label vendor is **Avery US Letter**. The **Product number** is **5160 Easy Peel Address Labels**. Select the **Use an existing list** option, click **Browse**, and then in the **Select Data Source** dialog box, navigate to your student data files and open **w03F_Addresses**. In the **Select Table** dialog box, click **OK**. Add the following record to your file:

First Name	Miranda
Last Name	Yanos
Address 1	1256 Loma Ave.
Unit	#34
City	Memphis
State	TN
ZIP Code	38123

3 Insert an **Address block** and match the fields. Match the **Address 2** field to the **Unit** field, and then update the labels. Preview the labels, and then select the entire document. Change the **Spacing Before** to **3** and then **Complete the merge**. Delete the last row from the bottom of the table, and then add the file name to the footer.

4 Display the document properties. As the **Tags** type **labels** and as the **Subject** type your course name and section number. Be sure your name displays in the **Author box**, and then **Save** your file. As directed by your instructor, print or submit electronically. **Close** Word and close your browser window.

END | You have completed the optional portion of this project

MyITLab grader

Mastering Word Project 3G Research Paper, Newsletter, and Mailing Labels

Apply 3A and 3B skills from these Objectives:

1 Create a Research Paper
2 Insert Footnotes in a Research Paper
3 Create Citations and a Bibliography in a Research Paper
4 Use Read Mode and PDF Reflow
5 Format a Multiple-Column Newsletter
6 Use Special Character and Paragraph Formatting
7 Create Mailing Labels Using Mail Merge

In the following Mastering Word project, you will edit and format a research paper and a newsletter. Optionally, you will create mailing labels. Your completed documents will look similar to Figure 3.59.

PROJECT FILES

For Project 3G, you will need the following files:

w03G_Newsletter_and_Research_Paper

w03G_Addresses (Optional: For use if you are completing the Mailing Labels portion of this project)

You will save your documents as:

Lastname_Firstname_3G_Research_Paper_and_Newsletter

Lastname_Firstname_3G_Mailing_Labels (Optional: Create only if you are completing the Mailing Labels portion of this project)

PROJECT RESULTS

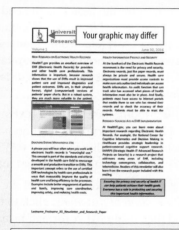

FIGURE 3.59

Word 2016, Windows 10, Microsoft Corporation

(Project 3G Research Paper, Newsletter, and Mailing Labels continues on the next page)

Mastering Word **Project 3G Research Paper, Newsletter, and Mailing Labels** (continued)

1 From your student files, open **w03G_Newsletter_and_Research_Paper**. **Save** the file in your **Word Chapter 3** folder as **Lastname_Firstname_3G_Newsletter_and_Research_Paper** and then add the file name to the footer. Click anywhere on Page 2, and because this is a separate section, add the File Name to the footer again so that it appears in both sections of the document. Redisplay **Page 1**, select the first three lines of the newsletter heading, and then apply a **3 pt** bottom border in **Black, Text 1**.

2 Click at the beginning of the newsletter title *University Medical Center*. Insert an online picture from **Bing Image Search** by searching for **microscope** and then insert an image of a black—or a black and white—microscope. Set the **Height** of the image to **.7"** and then **Recolor** the picture by applying **Blue, Accent color 1 Light**. Apply a **Black, Text 1 Picture Border** and change the **Weight** to **2 ¼ pt**.

3 Change the **Text Wrapping** of the inserted image to **Square**. Change the **Horizontal Alignment** to **Left** relative to **Margin** and the **Vertical Alignment** to **Top** relative to **Margin**.

4 Starting with the subheading paragraph *New Research on Electronic Health Records*, select all of the text from that point to the end of the page—include the paragraph mark but do not include the Section Break in your selection. Format the text in two columns, and apply **Justify** alignment. Insert a **Column** break before the subheading *Health Information Privacy and Security*.

5 Start your web browser, and then navigate to **www.healthit.gov** If necessary, close the message about subscribing. Redisplay your document, click at the end of the paragraph below the *New Research on Electronic Health Records* subheading. Insert a **Screenshot** of the website. Apply a **Black, Text 1 Picture Border** and change the **Weight** to **1 pt**.

6 Select the subheading *New Research on Electronic Health Records* including the paragraph mark. From the **Font** dialog box, apply **Bold** and **Small Caps** and change the **Font color** to **Dark Blue, Text 2**—in the fourth column, the first color. Apply the same formatting to the subheadings *Doctors Define Meaningful Use*, *Health Information and Privacy and Security* and *Research*

Sources Aid in EHR Implementation. Select the *Doctors Define Meaningful Use* subheading and then change the **Spacing Before** to **18 pt**.

7 Select the last paragraph in the newsletter—the text in bold italic that begins *Ensuring the privacy* including the paragraph mark but not the Section Break lines—and then apply a **1 pt Shadow** border using **Black, Text 1**. Shade the paragraph with the **Fill** color **Dark Blue, Text 2, Lighter 80%**—in the fourth column, the second color. **Center** the text. **Save** your document.

8 On **Page 2**, beginning with **Janet Eisler**, select all of the text on the page. With the text on Page 2 selected, change the **Line Spacing** to **2.0**, and then change the **Spacing After** to **0 pt**. To the paragraph that begins *There is often a discrepancy*, apply a **First line** indent of **0.5"** inches.

9 At the bottom of **Page 2**, in the next to last line of text, after the period at the end of the sentence that ends *if they had it*, insert a footnote with the following text: **The EMR (electronic medical record) is the patient record created in hospitals and ambulatory environments; it serves as a data source for other systems.**

10 Modify the **Footnote Text** style to set the **Font Size** to **11** and the format of the Footnote Text paragraph to include a **First line** indent of **0.5"** and **Double** spacing. Apply the new style to the footnote text.

11 On **Page 2**, at the end of the paragraph that begins *Those clinical practices*, click to the left of the period, and then using **MLA** format, insert a citation for a **Web site** with the following information:

Author	**Gabriel, Barbara A.**
Name of Web Page	**Do EMRS Make You a Better Doctor?**
Year	**2008**
Month	**July**
Day	**15**
Year Accessed	**2016**
Month Accessed	**June**
Day Accessed	**30**
Medium	**Web**

(Project 3G Research Paper, Newsletter, and Mailing Labels continues on the next page)

12 On **Page 3**, at the end of the paragraph that begins *Further research*, click to the left of the period, and then using **MLA** format, insert a citation for a **Book** with the following information:

Author	DeVore, Amy.
Title	The Electronic Health Record for the Physician's Office, 1e
Year	2010
City	Maryland Heights
Publisher	Saunders
Medium	Print

13 In the report, select the citation you just created, display the **Citation Options**, and then edit the citation to include **Pages 253**

14 On **Page 4**, click in the blank paragraph. On the **References tab**, click **Bibliography**, and then click **Insert Bibliography**.

15 Update the **Document Properties** with the following information:

Title	Electronic Health Records
Tags	EMR, health records
Subject	(insert your course name and section number)
Company	University Medical Center
Manager	Dr. Hillary Kim

16 On the left, click **Print** to display the **Print Preview**, and then click **Save** to redisplay your document. If directed by your instructor to do so, submit your paper printout, your electronic image of your document that looks like a printed document, or your original Word file. **Close** Word.

END | You have completed Project 3G

ALERT! | **Optional Project to Produce Mailing Labels**

Your instructor may ask you to complete the optional project on the next page to produce mailing labels. Check with your instructor to see if you should complete the mailing labels. This project is not included in the MyITLab Grader system.

1 Start Word and display a new blank document. **Save** the document in your **Word Chapter 3** folder as **Lastname_Firstname_3G_Mailing_Labels**

2 Start the **Step-by-Step Mail Merge Wizard** to create **Labels**. Display the **Label Options** dialog box, and be sure that the **Default tray** is selected and that the label vendor is **Avery US Letter**. The **Product number** is **5160 Easy Peel Address Labels**. Select the **Use an existing list option**, click **Browse**, and then in the **Select Data Source** dialog box, navigate to your student data files and open **w03G_Addresses**. In the **Select Table** dialog box, click **OK**. Add the following record to your file:

First Name	Mason
Last Name	Zepeda
Address 1	134 Atlantic Ave.
Unit	#21
City	Memphis
State	TN
ZIP Code	38123

3 Insert an **Address block** and match the fields. Match the **Address 2** field to the **Unit** field, and then update the labels. Preview the labels, and then select the entire document. Change the **Spacing Before** to **3** and then **Complete the merge**. Delete the last row from the bottom of the table, and then add the file name to the footer.

4 Display the document properties. As the **Tags** type **labels** and as the **Subject** type your course name and section number. Be sure your name displays in the **Author box**, and then **Save** your file. As directed by your instructor, print or submit your work electronically. Close all open windows.

> **END | You have completed the optional portion of this project**

CONTENT-BASED ASSESSMENTS (CRITICAL THINKING)

GO! Fix It	Project 3H Hospital Materials	MyITLab
GO! Make It	Project 3I Health Newsletter	MyITLab
GO! Solve It	Project 3J Colds and Flu	MyITLab
GO! Solve It	Project 3K Cycling Newsletter	

PROJECT FILES

For Project 3K, you will need the following file:

w03K_Cycling_Newsletter

You will save your document as:

Lastname_Firstname_3K_Cycling_Newsletter

The University Medical Center Emergency Department publishes a monthly newsletter focusing on safety and injury prevention. The topic for the current newsletter is bicycle safety. From your student data files, open **w03K_Cycling_Newsletter**, add the file name to the footer, and then save the file in your **Word Chapter 3** folder as **Lastname_Firstname_3K_Cycling_Newsletter**

Using the techniques that you practiced in this chapter, format the document in two-column newsletter format. Format the nameplate so that it is clearly separate from the body of the newsletter and is easily identified as the nameplate. Insert column breaks as necessary and apply appropriate formatting to subheadings. Insert and format at least one online picture that is appropriate to the topic, and insert a screenshot of a relevant website. Apply a border and shading to the last paragraph so that it is formatted attractively.

Add your name, your course name and section number, and the keywords **agenda, monthly staff meeting** to the Properties area. Submit as directed.

(Project 3K Cycling Newsletter continues on the next page)

GO! Solve It | Project 3K Cycling Newsletter (continued)

Performance Level

	Exemplary: You consistently applied the relevant skills	Proficient: You sometimes, but not always, applied the relevant skills	Developing: You rarely or never applied the relevant skills
Format nameplate	The nameplate is formatted attractively and in a manner that clearly indicates that it is the nameplate.	The nameplate includes some formatting but is not clearly separated from the body of the newsletter.	The newsletter does not include a nameplate.
Insert and format at least one online picture	An appropriate online picture image is included. The image is sized and positioned appropriately.	A clip art image is inserted but is either inappropriate, or is formatted or positioned poorly.	No clip art image is included.
Border and shading added to a paragraph	The last paragraph displays an attractive border with shading that enables the reader to read the text.	A border or shading is displayed but not both; or the shading is too dark to enable the reader to easily read the text.	No border or shading is added to a paragraph.
Insert a screenshot	A screenshot is inserted in one of the columns; the screenshot is related to the content of the article.	A screenshot is inserted in the document but does not relate to the content of the article.	No screenshot is inserted.

Performance Criteria

END | You have completed Project 3K

RUBRIC

The following outcomes-based assessments are *open-ended assessments*. That is, there is no specific correct result; your result will depend on your approach to the information provided. Make *Professional Quality* your goal. Use the following scoring rubric to guide you in *how* to approach the problem and then to evaluate *how well* your approach solves the problem.

The *criteria*—Software Mastery, Content, Format and Layout, and Process— represent the knowledge and skills you have gained that you can apply to solving the problem. The *levels of performance*—Professional Quality, Approaching Professional Quality, or Needs Quality Improvements—help you and your instructor evaluate your result.

	Your completed project is of Professional Quality if you:	Your completed project is Approaching Professional Quality if you:	Your completed project Needs Quality Improvements if you:
1-Software Mastery	Choose and apply the most appropriate skills, tools, and features and identify efficient methods to solve the problem.	Choose and apply some appropriate skills, tools, and features, but not in the most efficient manner.	Choose inappropriate skills, tools, or features, or are inefficient in solving the problem.
2-Content	Construct a solution that is clear and well organized, contains content that is accurate, appropriate to the audience and purpose, and is complete. Provide a solution that contains no errors in spelling, grammar, or style.	Construct a solution in which some components are unclear, poorly organized, inconsistent, or incomplete. Misjudge the needs of the audience. Have some errors in spelling, grammar, or style, but the errors do not detract from comprehension.	Construct a solution that is unclear, incomplete, or poorly organized; contains some inaccurate or inappropriate content; and contains many errors in spelling, grammar, or style. Do not solve the problem.
3-Format & Layout	Format and arrange all elements to communicate information and ideas, clarify function, illustrate relationships, and indicate relative importance.	Apply appropriate format and layout features to some elements, but not others. Overuse features, causing minor distraction.	Apply format and layout that does not communicate information or ideas clearly. Do not use format and layout features to clarify function, illustrate relationships, or indicate relative importance. Use available features excessively, causing distraction.
4-Process	Use an organized approach that integrates planning, development, self-assessment, revision, and reflection.	Demonstrate an organized approach in some areas, but not others; or, use an insufficient process of organization throughout.	Do not use an organized approach to solve the problem.

| Apply a combination of the **3A** and **3B** skills. | **GO! Think**   Project 3L Influenza Report |

PROJECT FILES

Build from Scratch

For Project 3L, you will need the following file:

New blank Word document

You will save your document as:

Lastname_Firstname_3L_Influenza

As part of the ongoing research conducted by University Medical Center in the area of community health and contagious diseases, Dr. Hillary Kim has asked Sarah Stanger to create a report on influenza—how it spreads, and how it can be prevented in the community.

Create a new Word document and save it as **Lastname_Firstname_3L_Influenza** Conduct your research and then create the report in MLA format. The report should include at least two footnotes, at least two citations, and should include a *Works Cited* page.

The report should contain an introduction, and then information about what influenza is, how it spreads, and how it can be prevented. A good place to start is at **http://health.nih.gov/topic/influenza**.

Add the file name to the footer. Add appropriate information to the Document Properties and submit as directed.

END | You have completed Project 3L

Build From Scratch

| **GO! Think!**   Project 3M Volunteer Newsletter | **MyITLab** |

Build from Scratch

| **You and GO!**   Project 3N College Newsletter | **MyITLab** |

| **GO! Collaborative Team Project** | Project 3O Bell Orchid Hotels   **MyITLab** |

Introducing Microsoft Excel 2016

E
Excel 2016

Georgejmclittle/Fotolia

Excel 2016: Introduction

Quantitative information! Defined as a type of information that can be counted or that communicates the quantity of something, quantitative information can be either easy or hard to understand—depending on how it is presented. According to Stephen Few, in his book *Show Me the Numbers*: "Quantitative information forms the core of what businesses must know to operate effectively."

Excel 2016 is a tool to communicate quantitative business information effectively. Sometimes you need to communicate quantitative relationships. For example, the number of units sold per geographic region shows a relationship of sales to geography. Sometimes you need

to summarize numbers. A list of every student enrolled at your college with his or her major indicated is not as informative as a summary of the total number of students in each major. In business, the most common quantitative information is some measure of money—costs, sales, payroll, expenses—and so on.

Rather than just a tool for making calculations, Excel is now a tool for you to communicate and collaborate with others. When you want to communicate visually with tables and graphs, Excel 2016 has many features to help you do so. If you engage in Business Intelligence activities, you will find rich tools for forecasting and analysis. Excel is the world's most widely used and familiar data analysis tool.

Creating a Worksheet and Charting Data

1

PROJECT 1A

OUTCOMES
Create a sales report with an embedded column chart and sparklines.

OBJECTIVES

1. Create, Save, and Navigate an Excel Workbook
2. Enter Data in a Worksheet
3. Construct and Copy Formulas and Use the SUM Function
4. Format Cells with Merge & Center, Cell Styles, and Themes
5. Chart Data to Create a Column Chart and Insert Sparklines
6. Print a Worksheet, Display Formulas, and Close Excel

PROJECT 1B

OUTCOMES
Calculate the value of an inventory.

OBJECTIVES

7. Check Spelling in a Worksheet
8. Enter Data by Range
9. Construct Formulas for Mathematical Operations
10. Edit Values in a Worksheet
11. Format a Worksheet

Lee Torrens/Shutterstock

In This Chapter GO! to Work with Excel

In this chapter, you will use Microsoft Excel 2016 to create and analyze data organized into columns and rows. After entering data in a worksheet, you can perform complex calculations, analyze the data to make logical decisions, and create attractive charts that help readers visualize your data in a way they can understand and that is meaningful. In this chapter, you will create and modify Excel workbooks. You will practice the basics of worksheet design, create a footer, enter and edit data in a worksheet, and chart data. You will save, preview, and print workbooks, and you will construct formulas for mathematical operations.

The projects in this chapter relate to **Pro Fit Marietta**, a distributor of fitness equipment and apparel to private gyms, personal trainers, health clubs, corporate wellness centers, hotels, college athletic facilities, physical therapy practices, and multi-unit residential properties. The company's mission is to find, test, and distribute the highest-quality fitness products in the world to its customers for the benefit of consumers. Their popular blog provides useful tips on how to use the latest workout and fitness equipment. The company is located in Marietta, Georgia, which is metropolitan Atlanta's largest suburb.

PROJECT

Sales Report with Embedded Column Chart and Sparklines

PROJECT ACTIVITIES

In Activities 1.01 through 1.17, you will create an Excel worksheet for Michelle Barry, the President of Pro Fit Marietta. The worksheet displays the second quarter sales of cardio equipment for the current year and includes a chart to visually represent the data. Your completed worksheet will look similar to Figure 1.1.

PROJECT FILES

If your instructor wants you to submit Project 1A in the MyITLab Grader system, log in to MyITLab, locate Grader Project 1A, and then download the files for this project.

For Project 1A, you will need the following file:
New blank Excel workbook

You will save your workbook as:
Lastname_Firstname_1A_Quarterly_Sales
Lastname_Firstname_1A_Quarterly_Sales_formulas (if your instructor requires)

Please always review the downloaded Grader instructions before beginning.

PROJECT RESULTS

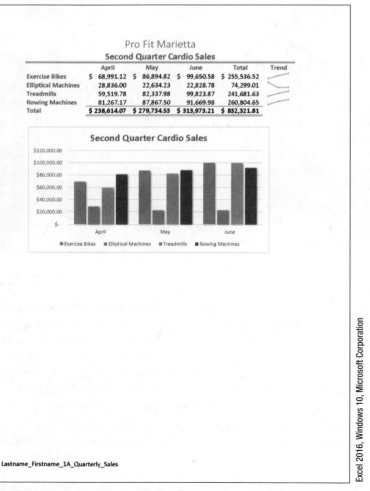

Excel 2016, Windows 10, Microsoft Corporation

FIGURE 1.1 Project 1A Quarterly Sales

NOTE	If You Are Using a Touchscreen
	Tap an item to click it.
	Press and hold for a few seconds to right-click; release when the information or commands display.
	Touch the screen with two or more fingers and then pinch together to zoom out or stretch your fingers apart to zoom in.
	Slide your finger on the screen to scroll—slide left to scroll right and slide right to scroll left.
	Slide to rearrange—similar to dragging with a mouse.
	Swipe to select—slide an item a short distance with a quick movement—to select an item and bring up commands, if any.

Objective 1 | Create, Save, and Navigate an Excel Workbook

GO! Learn How
Video E1-1

On startup, Excel displays a new blank *workbook*—the Excel document that stores your data—which contains one or more pages called a *worksheet*. A worksheet—or *spreadsheet*—is stored in a workbook, and is formatted as a pattern of uniformly spaced horizontal rows and vertical columns. The intersection of a column and a row forms a box referred to as a *cell*.

1.1.1

Activity 1.01 | Starting Excel, Navigating Excel, and Naming and Saving a Workbook

> **ALERT!** To submit as an autograded project, log into MyITLab, download the files for this project, and begin with those files instead of a new blank workbook.

1 Start Excel, and on the opening screen, click **Blank workbook**. In the lower right corner of the window, on the status bar, if necessary, click the Normal button ⊞, and then to the right, locate the zoom—magnification—level.

> Your zoom level should be 100%, although some figures in this textbook may be shown at a higher zoom level. The *Normal view* maximizes the number of cells visible on your screen and keeps the column letters and row numbers closer to the cells.

🔄 **BY TOUCH** On Excel's opening screen, tap Blank workbook.

2 On the ribbon, click the **File tab**, on the left click **Save As**, under **Save As**, click **Browse** to display the **Save As** dialog box, and then navigate to the location where you will store your workbooks for this chapter.

3 In your storage location, create a new folder named **Excel Chapter 1** and then open the new folder to display its folder window. In the **File name** box, notice that *Book1* displays as the default file name.

4 In the **File name** box, click **Book1** to select it, and then using your own name, type **Lastname_Firstname_1A_Quarterly_Sales** being sure to include the underscore (_) instead of spaces between words.

5 Click **Save**. Compare your screen with Figure 1.2, and then take a moment to study the parts of the Excel window described in the table in Figure 1.3.

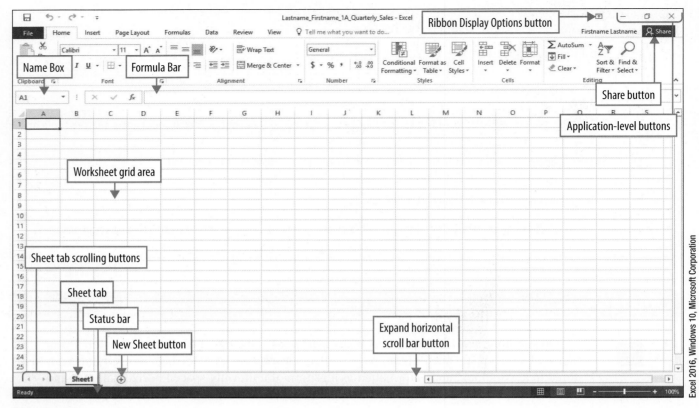

FIGURE 1.2

PARTS OF THE EXCEL WINDOW	
SCREEN PART	**DESCRIPTION**
Horizontal scroll bar button	Increases or decreases the width of the horizontal scroll bar by sliding left or right.
Formula Bar	Displays the value or formula contained in the active cell; also permits entry or editing.
Sheet tab	Identifies the worksheet in the workbook.
New sheet button	Inserts an additional worksheet.
Name Box	Displays the name of the selected cell, table, chart, or object.
Share button	Opens the Share pane from which you can save your file to the cloud—your OneDrive—and then share it with others so you can collaborate.
Sheet tab scrolling buttons	Display sheet tabs that are not in view when there are numerous sheet tabs.
Status bar	Displays the current cell mode, page number, worksheet information, view and zoom buttons, and for numerical data, common calculations such as Sum and Average.
Application-level buttons	Minimize, close, or restore the previous size of the displayed workbook window.
Ribbon Display Options button	Displays various ways you can display the ribbon—the default is Show Tabs and Commands.
Worksheet grid area	Displays the columns and rows that intersect to form the worksheet's cells.

FIGURE 1.3

6 ▸ Take a moment to study Figure 1.4 and the table in Figure 1.5 to become familiar with the Excel worksheet window.

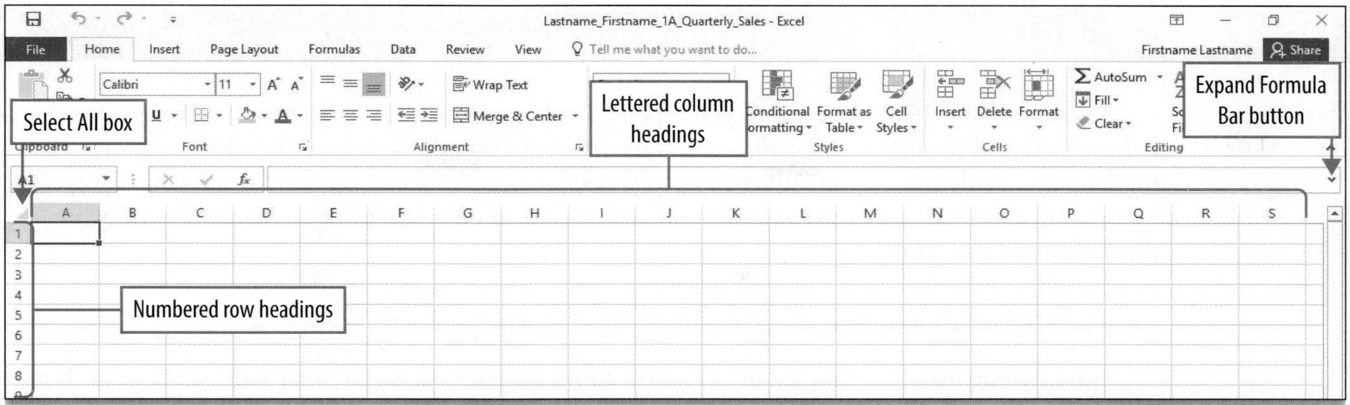

FIGURE 1.4

Excel 2016, Windows 10, Microsoft Corporation

PARTS OF THE EXCEL WORKSHEET WINDOW	
WORKBOOK WINDOW ELEMENT	**DESCRIPTION**
Excel pointer	Displays the location of the pointer.
Expand Formula Bar button	Increases the height of the Formula Bar to display lengthy cell content.
Lettered column headings	Indicate the column letter.
Numbered row headings	Indicate the row number.
Select All box	Selects all the cells in a worksheet.

FIGURE 1.5

7 In the lower right corner of the screen, in the horizontal scroll bar, click the **right scroll arrow** one time to shift **column A** out of view.

A *column* is a vertical group of cells in a worksheet. Beginning with the first letter of the alphabet, *A*, a unique letter identifies each column—this is called the *column heading*. Clicking one of the horizontal scroll bar arrows shifts the window either left or right one column at a time.

8 Point to the **right scroll arrow**, and then hold down the left mouse button until the columns begin to scroll rapidly to the right; release the mouse button when you begin to see pairs of letters as the column headings.

BY TOUCH   Anywhere on the worksheet, slide your finger to the left to view columns to the right.

9 Slowly drag the horizontal scroll box to the left, and notice that just above the scroll box, ScreenTips with the column letters display as you drag. Drag the horizontal scroll box left or right—or click the left or right scroll arrow—as necessary to position **column Z** near the center of your screen.

Column headings after column Z use two letters starting with AA, AB, and so on through ZZ. After that, columns begin with three letters beginning with AAA. This pattern provides 16,384 columns. The last column is XFD.

10 In the vertical scroll bar, click the **down scroll arrow** one time to move **Row 1** out of view.

A *row* is a horizontal group of cells. Beginning with number 1, a unique number identifies each row—this is the *row heading*, located at the left side of the worksheet. A single worksheet can have 1,048,576 rows of data.

11 Use the skills you just practiced to scroll horizontally to display **column A**, and if necessary, **row 1**.

12 Click **Save** 🖫.

Objective 2 | Enter Data in a Worksheet

GO! Learn How
Video E1-2

Cell content, which is anything you type in a cell, can be one of two things: either a *constant value*—referred to simply as a *value*—or a *formula*. A formula is an equation that performs mathematical calculations on values in your worksheet. The most commonly used values are *text values* and *number values*, but a value can also include a date or a time of day. A text value is also referred to as a *label*.

Activity 1.02 | Entering Text, Using AutoComplete, and Using the Name Box to Select a Cell

A text value usually provides information about number values in other worksheet cells. For example, a title such as Second Quarter Cardio Sales gives the reader an indication that the data in the worksheet relates to information about sales of cardio equipment during the three-month period April through June.

1 Point to and then click the cell at the intersection of **column A** and **row 1** to make it the *active cell*—the cell is outlined and ready to accept data.

The intersecting column letter and row number form the *cell reference*—also called the *cell address*. When a cell is active, its column letter and row number are highlighted. The cell reference of the selected cell, *A1*, displays in the Name Box.

2 With cell **A1** as the active cell, type the worksheet title **Pro Fit Marietta** and then press Enter. Compare your screen with Figure 1.6.

Text or numbers in a cell are referred to as *data*. You must confirm the data you type in a cell by pressing Enter or by some other keyboard movement, such as pressing Tab or an arrow key. Pressing Enter moves the active cell to the cell below.

Excel 2016, Windows 10, Microsoft Corporation

FIGURE 1.6

3 In cell **A1**, notice that the text does not fit; the text extends into cell **B1** to the right.

If text is too long for a cell and cells to the right are empty, the text will display. If the cells to the right contain other data, only the text that will fit in the cell displays.

4 In cell **A2**, type the worksheet subtitle **Second Quarter Cardio Sales** and then press Enter. Compare your screen with Figure 1.7.

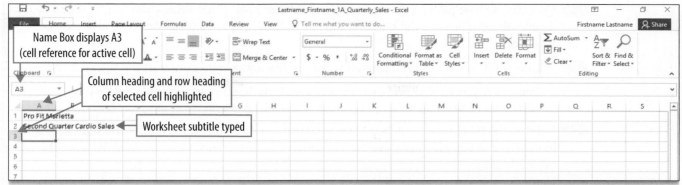

FIGURE 1.7

5 Above **column A**, click in the **Name Box** to select the cell reference *A3*. Type **a4** and then press Enter to make cell **A4** the active cell. In cell **A4**, type **Exercise Bikes** to form the first row title, and then press Enter.

> The text characters that you typed align at the left edge of the cell—referred to as ***left alignment***—and cell A5 becomes the active cell. Left alignment is the default for text values. You can type a cell address in the Name Box and press Enter to move to a specific cell quickly.

6 In cell **A5**, type **E** and notice the text from the previous cell displays.

> If the first characters you type in a cell match an existing entry in the column, Excel fills in the remaining characters for you. This feature, called ***AutoComplete***, assists only with alphabetic values.

7 Continue typing the remainder of the row title **lliptical Machines** and press Enter.

> The AutoComplete suggestion is removed when the entry you are typing differs from the previous value.

8 In cell **A6**, type **Treadmills** and press Enter. In cell **A7**, type **Rowing Machines** and press Enter. In cell **A8**, type **Total** and press Enter. On the Quick Access Toolbar, click **Save** 💾.

ANOTHER WAY Use the keyboard shortcut Ctrl + S to save changes to your workbook.

Activity 1.03 | Using Auto Fill and Keyboard Shortcuts

MOS
2.1.4

1 Click cell **B3**. Type **A** and notice that when you begin to type in a cell, on the **Formula Bar**, the **Cancel** and **Enter** buttons become active, as shown in Figure 1.8.

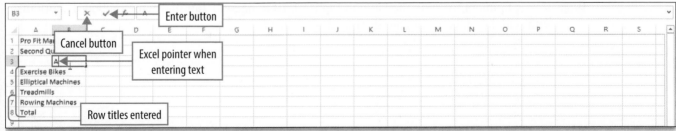

FIGURE 1.8

2 Continue to type **pril** and then on the **Formula Bar**, notice that values you type in a cell also display there. Then, on the **Formula Bar**, click **Enter** ✓ to confirm the entry and keep cell **B3** active.

3 With cell **B3** active, locate the small square in the lower right corner of the selected cell.

You can drag this *fill handle*—the small square in the lower right corner of a selected cell—to adjacent cells to fill the cells with values based on the first cell.

4 Point to the **fill handle** until the ⊞ pointer displays, hold down the left mouse button, drag to the right to cell **D3**, and as you drag, notice the ScreenTips *May* and *June*. Release the mouse button.

5 Under the text that you just filled, click the **Auto Fill Options** button ⊞ that displays, and then compare your screen with Figure 1.9.

Auto Fill generates and extends a *series* of values into adjacent cells based on the value of other cells. A series is a group of things that come one after another in succession; for example, *April*, *May*, *June*.

The Auto Fill Options button displays options to fill the data; options vary depending on the content and program from which you are filling, and the format of the data you are filling.

Fill Series is selected, indicating the action that was taken. Because the options are related to the current task, the button is referred to as being *context sensitive*.

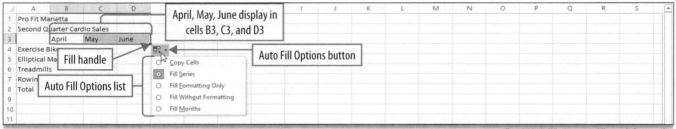

FIGURE 1.9

Excel 2016, Windows 10, Microsoft Corporation

6 Click in any cell to cancel the display of the list.

The list no longer displays; the button will display until you perform some other screen action.

7 Press Ctrl + Home, which is the keyboard shortcut to make cell **A1** active.

8 On the Quick Access Toolbar, click **Save** 🖫 to save the changes you have made to your workbook.

9 Take a moment to study the table in Figure 1.10 to become familiar with keyboard shortcuts with which you can navigate the Excel worksheet.

KEYBOARD SHORTCUTS TO NAVIGATE THE EXCEL WORKSHEET	
TO MOVE THE LOCATION OF THE ACTIVE CELL:	**PRESS:**
Up, down, right, or left one cell	↑, ↓, →, ←
Down one cell	Enter
Up one cell	Shift + Enter
Up one full screen	PageUp
Down one full screen	PageDown
To column A of the current row	Home
To the last cell in the last column of the active area (the rectangle formed by all the rows and columns in a worksheet that contain entries)	Ctrl + End
To cell A1	Ctrl + Home
Right one cell	Tab
Left one cell	Shift + Tab
To the cell one worksheet window to the right	Alt + PageDown
To the cell one worksheet window to the left	Alt + PageUp
To the cell containing specific content that you enter in the Find and Replace dialog box	Shift + F5
To the cell that corresponds with the cell reference you enter in the Go To dialog box	F5

FIGURE 1.10

Excel 2016, Windows 10, Microsoft Corporation

Activity 1.04 | Aligning Text and Adjusting the Size of Columns

MOS
5.1.4

> 1 ▶ In the **column heading area**, point to the vertical line between **column A** and **column B** to display the ⊹ pointer, press and hold down the left mouse button, and then compare your screen with Figure 1.11.

> A ScreenTip displays information about the width of the column. The default width of a column is 64 *pixels*. A pixel, short for *picture element*, is a point of light measured in dots per square inch. Sixty-four pixels equal 8.43 characters, which is the average number of characters that will fit in a cell using the default font. The default font in Excel is Calibri and the default font size is 11.

FIGURE 1.11

Excel 2016, Windows 10, Microsoft Corporation

> 2 ▶ Drag to the right, and when the number of pixels indicated in the ScreenTip reaches **120 pixels**, release the mouse button. If you are not satisfied with your result, click Undo ⟲ on the Quick Access Toolbar and begin again.

> This width accommodates the longest row title in cells A4 through A8—*Elliptical Machines*. The worksheet subtitle in cell A2 spans more than one column and still does not fit in column A.

3 Point to cell **B3** and then drag across to select cells **B3**, **C3**, and **D3**. Compare your screen with Figure 1.12; if you are not satisfied with your result, click anywhere and begin again.

The three cells, B3 through D3, are selected and form a *range*—two or more cells on a worksheet that are adjacent (next to each other) or nonadjacent (not next to each other). This range of cells is referred to as *B3:D3*. When you see a colon (:) between two cell references, the range includes all the cells between the two cell references.

A range of cells you select this way is indicated by a dark border, and Excel treats the range as a single unit so you can make the same changes to more than one cell at a time. The selected cells in the range are highlighted except for the first cell in the range, which displays in the Name Box.

When you select a range of data, the ***Quick Analysis tool*** displays in the lower right corner of the selected range, with which you can analyze your data by using Excel tools such as charts, color-coding, and formulas.

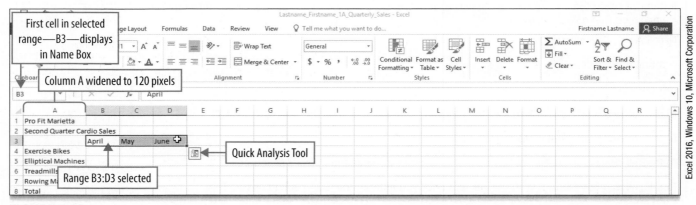

FIGURE 1.12

BY TOUCH To select a range, tap a cell to display a circular gripper in the upper left and lower right corners of the cell, and then drag one of the grippers as necessary to select the desired range.

4 With the range **B3:D3** selected, point anywhere over the selected range, right-click, and then on the mini toolbar, click **Center** ☰. On the Quick Access Toolbar, click **Save** 🖫.

The column titles *April*, *May*, *June* align in the center of each cell.

Activity 1.05 | Entering Numbers

To type number values, use either the number keys across the top of your keyboard or the numeric keypad if you have one—laptop computers might not have a numeric keypad.

1 Under *April*, click cell **B4**, type **68991.12** and then on the **Formula Bar**, click **Enter** ✓ to maintain cell **B4** as the active cell. Compare your screen with Figure 1.13.

By default, *number* values align at the right edge of the cell. The default ***number format***—a specific way in which Excel displays numbers—is the ***general format***. In the default general format, whatever you type in the cell will display, with the exception of trailing zeros to the right of a decimal point. For example, in the number 237.50 the *0* following the *5* is a trailing zero and would not display.

Data that displays in a cell is the ***displayed value***. Data that displays in the Formula Bar is the ***underlying value***. The number of digits or characters that display in a cell—the displayed value—depends on the width of the column. Calculations on numbers will always be based on the underlying value, not the displayed value.

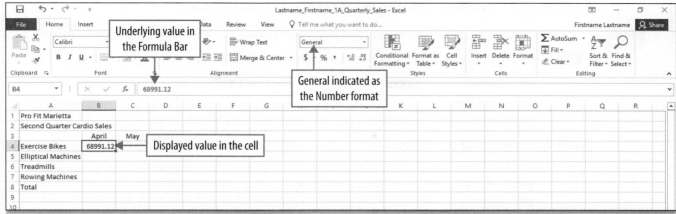

FIGURE 1.13

Excel 2016, Windows 10, Microsoft Corporation

2 Press Tab to make cell **C4** active. Type **86894.82** and then press Tab to move to cell **D4**. Type **99650.58** and then press Enter to move to cell **B5** in the next row. Then, by using the same technique, enter the remaining sales numbers as shown:

	APRIL	MAY	JUNE
Elliptical Machines	28836	22634.23	22828.78
Treadmills	59519.78	82337.98	99823.87
Rowing Machines	81267.17	87867.50	91669.98

3 Compare the numbers you entered with Figure 1.14, and then **Save** 💾 your workbook.

In the default General format, trailing zeros to the right of a decimal point will not display. For example, when you type *87867.50*, the cell displays 87867.5 instead.

FIGURE 1.14

Excel 2016, Windows 10, Microsoft Corporation

Objective 3 Construct and Copy Formulas and Use the SUM Function

GO! Learn How
Video E1-3

A cell contains either a constant value (text or numbers) or a formula. A formula is an equation that performs mathematical calculations on values in other cells, and then places the result in the cell containing the formula. You can create formulas or use a *function*—a prewritten formula that looks at one or more values, performs an operation, and then returns a value.

Activity 1.06 | **Constructing a Formula and Using the SUM Function**

In this Activity, you will practice three different ways to sum a group of numbers in Excel.

1 Click cell **B8** to make it the active cell and type **=**

The equal sign (=) displays in the cell with the insertion point blinking, ready to accept more data.

All formulas begin with the = sign, which signals Excel to begin a calculation. The Formula Bar displays the = sign, and the Formula Bar Cancel and Enter buttons display.

2 At the insertion point, type **b4** and then compare your screen with Figure 1.15.

A list of Excel functions that begin with the letter *B* may briefly display—as you progress in your study of Excel, you will use functions of this type. A blue border with small corner boxes surrounds cell B4, which indicates that the cell is part of an active formula. The color used in the box matches the color of the cell reference in the formula.

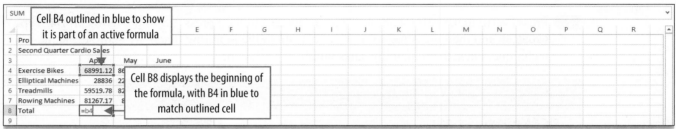

FIGURE 1.15

Excel 2016, Windows 10, Microsoft Corporation

3 At the insertion point, type **+** and then type **b5**

A border of another color surrounds cell B5, and the color matches the color of the cell reference in the active formula. When typing cell references, it is not necessary to use uppercase letters.

4 At the insertion point, type **+b6+b7** and then press Enter.

The result of the formula calculation—*238614.1*—displays in the cell. Recall that in the default General format, trailing zeros do not display.

5 Click cell **B8** again, look at the **Formula Bar**, and then compare your screen with Figure 1.16.

The formula adds the values in cells B4 through B7, and the result displays in cell B8. In this manner, you can construct a formula by typing. Although cell B8 displays the *result* of the formula, the formula itself displays in the Formula Bar. This is referred to as the ***underlying formula***.

Always view the Formula Bar to be sure of the exact content of a cell—*a displayed number may actually be a formula.*

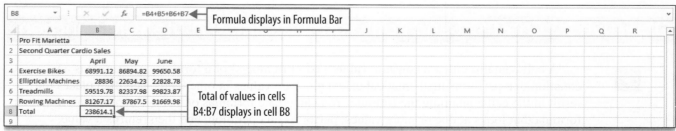

FIGURE 1.16

Excel 2016, Windows 10, Microsoft Corporation

6 Click cell **C8** and type **=** to signal the beginning of a formula. Then, point to cell **C4** and click one time.

> The reference to the cell C4 is added to the active formula. A moving border surrounds the referenced cell, and the border color and the color of the cell reference in the formula are color coded to match.

7 At the insertion point, type **+** and then click cell **C5**. Repeat this process to complete the formula to add cells **C6** and **C7**, and then press Enter.

> The result of the formula calculation—*279734.5*—displays in the cell. This method of constructing a formula is the ***point and click method***.

8 Click cell **D8**. On the **Home tab**, in the **Editing group**, click **AutoSum**, and then compare your screen with Figure 1.17.

> SUM is an Excel function—a prewritten formula. A moving border surrounds the range D4:D7 and *=SUM(D4:D7)* displays in cell D8.

> The = sign signals the beginning of a formula, *SUM* indicates the type of calculation that will take place (addition), and *(D4:D7)* indicates the range of cells on which the sum calculation will be performed. A ScreenTip provides additional information about the action.

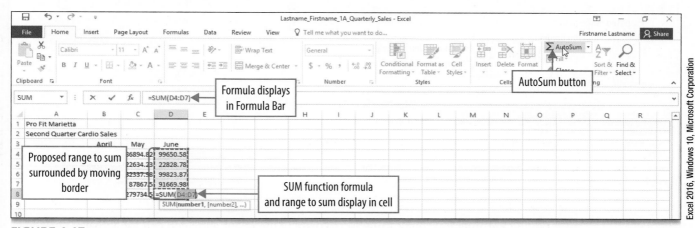

FIGURE 1.17

ANOTHER WAY Use the keyboard shortcut Alt + = ; or, on the Formulas tab, in the Function Library group, click the AutoSum button.

---

9 Look at the **Formula Bar**, and notice that the formula also displays there. Then, look again at the cells surrounded by the moving border.

> When you activate the ***Sum function***, Excel first looks *above* the active cell for a range of cells to sum. If no range is above the active cell, Excel will look to the *left* for a range of cells to sum. If the proposed range is not what you want to calculate, you can select a different group of cells.

10 Press Enter to construct a formula by using the prewritten SUM function.

> Your total is *313973.2*. Because the Sum function is frequently used, it has its own button in the Editing group on the Home tab of the ribbon. A larger version of the button also displays on the Formulas tab in the Function Library group. This button is also referred to as ***AutoSum***.

11 Notice that the totals in the range **B8:D8** display only one decimal place. Click **Save** 🔲.

> Number values that are too long to fit in the cell do *not* spill over into the unoccupied cell to the right in the same manner as text values. Rather, Excel rounds the number to fit the space.

> ***Rounding*** is a procedure that determines which digit at the right of the number will be the last digit displayed and then increases it by one if the next digit to its right is 5, 6, 7, 8, or 9.

Activity 1.07 | Copying a Formula by Using the Fill Handle

You have practiced three ways to create a formula—by typing, by using the point-and-click technique, and by using a Function button from the ribbon. You can also copy formulas. When you copy a formula from one cell to another, Excel adjusts the cell references to fit the new location of the formula.

1 ▶ Click cell **E3**, type **Total** and then press Enter.

The text in cell E3 is centered because the centered format continues from the adjacent cell.

2 ▶ With cell **E4** as the active cell, hold down Alt, and then press =. Compare your screen with Figure 1.18.

Alt + = is the keyboard shortcut for the SUM function. Recall that Excel first looks above the selected cell for a proposed range of cells to sum, and if no data is detected, Excel looks to the left and proposes a range of cells to sum.

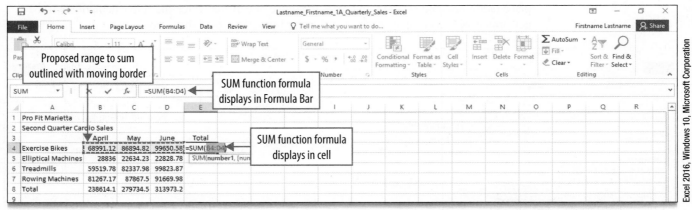

FIGURE 1.18

3 ▶ On the **Formula Bar**, click **Enter** ✓ to display the result and keep cell **E4** active.

The total dollar amount of *Exercise Bikes* sold in the quarter is *255536.5*. In cells E5:E8, you can see that you need a formula similar to the one in E4, but formulas that refer to the cells in row 5, row 6, and so on.

4 ▶ With cell **E4** active, point to the fill handle in the lower right corner of the cell until the ➕ pointer displays. Then, drag down through cell **E8**; if you are not satisfied with your result, on the Quick Access Toolbar, click Undo ↺ and begin again. Compare your screen with Figure 1.19.

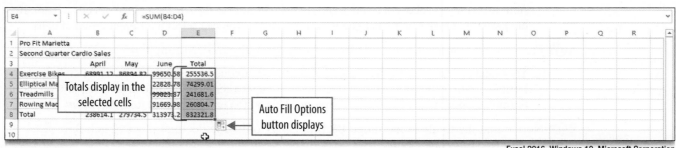

FIGURE 1.19

5 ▶ Click cell **E5**, look at the **Formula Bar**, and notice the formula *=SUM(B5:D5)*. Click cell **E6**, look at the **Formula Bar**, and then notice the formula *=SUM(B6:D6)*.

In each row, Excel copied the formula but adjusted the cell references *relative to* the row number. This is called a ***relative cell reference***—a cell reference based on the relative position of the cell that contains the formula and the cells referred to in the formula.

The calculation is the same, but it is performed on the cells in that particular row. Use this method to insert numerous formulas into spreadsheets quickly.

6 ▶ Click cell **F3**, type **Trend** and then press Enter. **Save** 🖫 your workbook.

Objective 4 | Format Cells with Merge & Center, Cell Styles, and Themes

GO! Learn How
Video E1-4

Format—change the appearance of—cells to make your worksheet attractive and easy to read.

Activity 1.08 | Using Merge & Center and Applying Cell Styles

MOS
2.2.1, 2.2.7

1 ▶ Select the range **A1:F1**, and then in the **Alignment group**, click **Merge & Center**. Then, select the range **A2:F2** and click **Merge & Center**.

The ***Merge & Center*** command joins selected cells into one larger cell and centers the contents in the merged cell; individual cells in the range B1:F1 and B2:F2 can no longer be selected—they are merged into cell A1 and A2, respectively.

🔄 **ANOTHER WAY** Select the range, right-click over the selection, and then on the mini toolbar, click the Merge & Center command.

2 ▶ Click cell **A1**. In the **Styles group**, click **Cell Styles**, and then compare your screen with Figure 1.20.

A ***cell style*** is a defined set of formatting characteristics, such as font, font size, font color, cell borders, and cell shading.

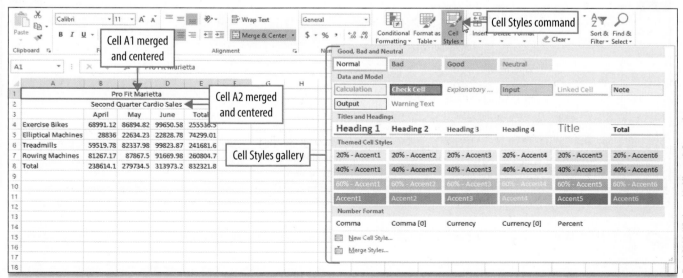

FIGURE 1.20

3 In the displayed gallery, under **Titles and Headings**, click **Title** and notice that the row height adjusts to accommodate the larger font size.

4 Click cell **A2**, display the **Cell Styles** gallery, and then under **Titles and Headings**, click **Heading 1**.

Use cell styles to maintain a consistent look in a worksheet and across worksheets in a workbook.

5 Select the horizontal range **B3:F3**, hold down Ctrl, and then select the vertical range **A4:A8** to select the column titles and the row titles. Release Ctrl.

Use this technique to select two or more ranges that are nonadjacent—not next to each other.

6 With the two ranges selected, display the **Cell Styles** gallery, click **Heading 4** to apply this cell style to the column titles and row titles, and then **Save** 🖫 your workbook.

Activity 1.09 | Formatting Financial Numbers

1 Select the range **B4:E4**, hold down Ctrl, and then select the range **B8:E8**. Release Ctrl.

This range is referred to as *b4:e4,b8:e8* with a comma separating the references to the two nonadjacent ranges.

ANOTHER WAY   In the Name Box type b4:e4,b8:e8 and then press Enter.

2 With the two ranges selected, on the **Home tab**, in the **Number group**, click **Accounting Number Format** 🖸. Compare your screen with Figure 1.21.

The *Accounting Number Format* applies a thousand comma separator where appropriate, inserts a fixed U.S. dollar sign aligned at the left edge of the cell, applies two decimal places, and leaves a small amount of space at the right edge of the cell to accommodate a parenthesis when negative numbers are present. Excel widens the columns to accommodate the formatted numbers.

At the bottom of your screen, in the status bar, Excel displays the results for some common calculations that might be made on the range; for example, the Average of the numbers selected and the Count—the number of items selected.

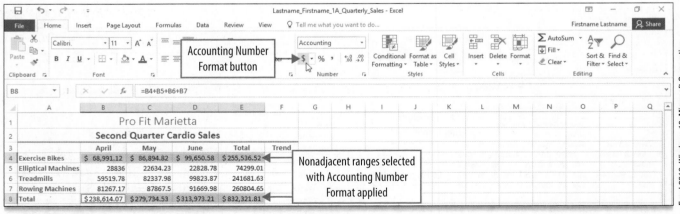

FIGURE 1.21

ANOTHER WAY   Display the Cell Styles gallery, and under Number Format, click Currency.

3 > Select the range **B5:E7**, and then in the **Number group**, click **Comma Style** .

The ***Comma Style*** inserts a thousand comma separator where appropriate and applies two decimal places. Comma Style also leaves space at the right to accommodate a parenthesis when negative numbers are present.

When preparing worksheets with financial information, the first row of dollar amounts and the total row of dollar amounts are formatted in the ***Accounting Number Format***; that is, with thousand comma separators, dollar signs, two decimal places, and space at the right to accommodate a parenthesis for negative numbers, if any. Rows that are *not* the first row or the total row should be formatted with the Comma Style.

4 > Select the range **B8:E8**. In the **Styles group**, display the **Cell Styles** gallery, and then under **Titles and Headings**, click **Total**. Click any blank cell to cancel the selection, and then compare your screen with Figure 1.22.

This is a common way to apply borders to financial information. The single border indicates that calculations were performed on the numbers above, and the double border indicates that the information is complete. Sometimes financial documents do not display values with cents; rather, the values are rounded up. You can do this by selecting the cells, and then clicking the Decrease Decimal button two times.

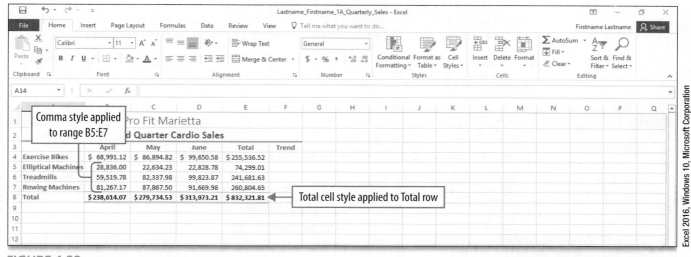

FIGURE 1.22

Activity 1.10 | Changing the Workbook Theme

1.3.6

A ***theme*** is a predefined set of colors, fonts, lines, and fill effects that coordinate for an attractive look.

1 > Click the **Page Layout tab**, and then in the **Themes group**, click **Themes**.

2 > Click the **Retrospect** theme, and notice that the cell styles change to match the new theme. Click **Save** .

More **Knowledge**   **Formatting a Cell's Font, Style, Size, or Color with Individual Commands**

Instead of using Cell Styles, you could use a combination of individual commands to format a cell. For example, on the Home tab, in the Font group, you can change a cell's font by clicking the Font arrow and selecting a different font. You can change the font size by clicking the Font Size arrow and selecting a size. From the same group, you can apply various styles to the cell—such as Bold or Italic or Underline. To change a cell's font color, in the Font Group, click the Font Color arrow and select a different color.

GO! Learn How
Video E1-5

MOS
5.1.1, 5.1.3

A **chart** is a graphic representation of data in a worksheet. Data in a chart is easier to understand than a table of numbers. **Sparklines** are tiny charts embedded in a cell that give a visual trend summary alongside your data. A sparkline makes a pattern more obvious to the eye.

Activity 1.11 | Charting Data and Using Recommended Charts to Select and Insert a Column Chart

Recommended Charts is an Excel feature that displays a customized set of charts that, according to Excel's calculations, will best fit your data based on the range of data that you select. In this Activity, you will create a **column chart** showing the monthly sales of cardio equipment by category during the second quarter. A column chart is useful for illustrating comparisons among related numbers. The chart will enable the company president, Michelle Barry, to see a pattern of overall monthly sales.

1 Select the range **A3:D7**.

When charting data, typically you should *not* include totals—include only the data you want to compare.

2 With the data that you want to compare selected, click the **Insert tab**, and then in the **Charts group**, click **Recommended Charts**. Compare your screen with Figure 1.23.

The Insert Chart dialog box displays a list of recommended charts on the left and a preview of the first chart, which is selected, on the right. The second tab of the Insert Chart dialog box includes all chart types—even those that are not recommended by Excel for this type of data.

By using different **chart types**, you can display data in a way that is meaningful to the reader—common examples are column charts, pie charts, and line charts.

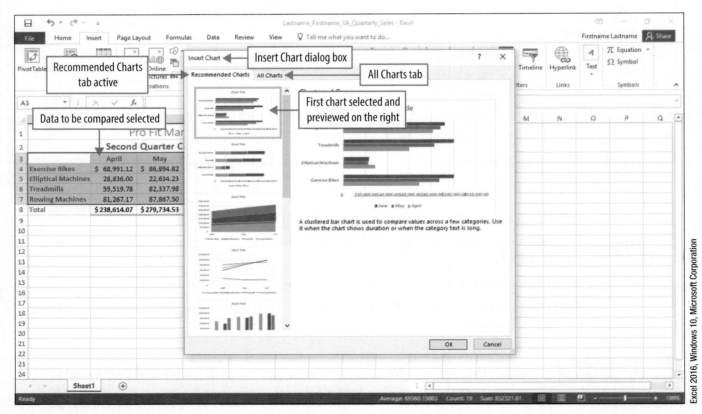

FIGURE 1.23

3 In the **Insert Chart** dialog box, use the scroll bar to scroll down about one-third of the way, and then click the second Clustered Column chart. Compare your screen with Figure 1.24.

Here, *each type of cardio equipment* displays its *sales for each month*. A clustered column chart is useful to compare values across a few categories, especially if the order of categories is not important.

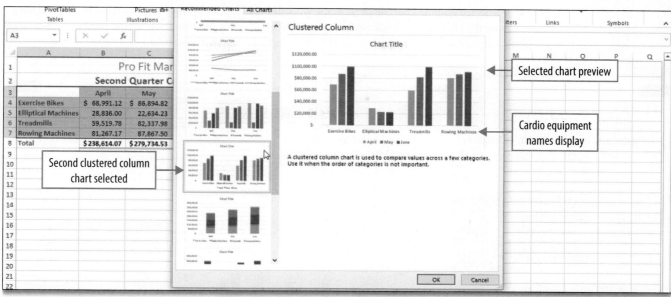

FIGURE 1.24

Excel 2016, Windows 10, Microsoft Corporation

4 In the **Insert Chart** dialog box, click the chart directly above the selected chart—the first clustered column chart. Compare your screen with Figure 1.25.

In this clustered column chart, *each month* displays its *sales for each type of cardio equipment*. When constructing a chart, you can switch the row and column data in this manner to display the data in a way that is most useful to the reader. Here, the president of Pro Fit Marietta wants to compare sales of each type of equipment by month to detect patterns.

The comparison of data—either by month or by type of equipment—depends on the type of analysis you want to perform. You can select either chart, or, after your chart is complete, you can use the *Switch/Row Column* command on the ribbon to swap the data over the axis; that is, data being charted on the vertical axis will move to the horizontal axis and vice versa.

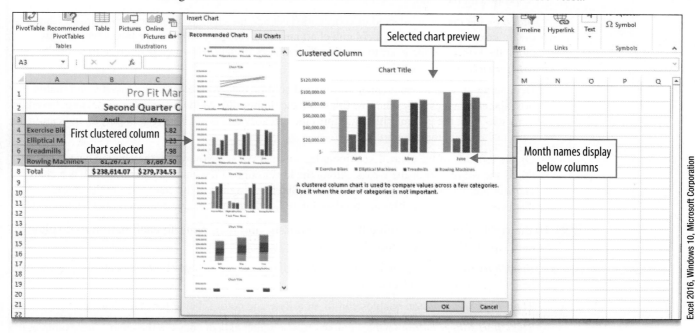

FIGURE 1.25

Excel 2016, Windows 10, Microsoft Corporation

5 In the lower right corner of the **Insert Chart** dialog box, click **OK** to insert the selected chart into the worksheet. Compare your screen with Figure 1.26.

Your selected column chart displays in the worksheet, and the charted data is bordered by colored lines. Because the chart object is selected—surrounded by a border and displaying sizing handles—contextual tools named *Chart Tools* display and add contextual tabs next to the standard tabs on the ribbon.

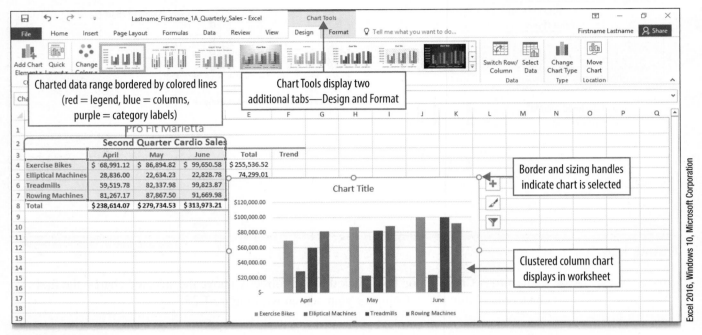

FIGURE 1.26

Activity 1.12 | Using the Chart Tools to Apply Chart Styles

1 On the ribbon, locate the contextual tabs under **Chart Tools—Design** and **Format**.

When a chart is selected, Chart Tools become available and these two tabs provide commands for working with the chart.

Based on the data you selected in your worksheet and the chart you selected in the Insert Chart dialog box, Excel constructs a column chart and adds *category labels*—the labels that display along the bottom of the chart to identify the category of data. This area is referred to as the *category axis* or the *x-axis*.

Depending on which arrangement of row and column data you select in the Insert Chart dialog box, Excel arranges either the row titles or the column titles as the category names. Here, based on your selection, the column titles that form the category labels are bordered in purple, indicating the cells that contain the category names.

On the left side of the chart, Excel includes a numerical scale on which the charted data is based; this is the *value axis* or the *y-axis*. Along the lower edge of the chart, a *legend*, which is a chart element that identifies the patterns or colors that are assigned to the categories in the chart, displays. Here, the row titles are bordered in red, indicating the cells containing the legend text.

2 To the right of the chart, notice the three buttons, and then point to each button to display its ScreenTip, as shown in Figure 1.27.

The *Chart Elements button* enables you to add, remove, or change chart elements such as the title, legend, gridlines, and data labels.

The *Chart Styles button* enables you to set a style and color scheme for your chart.

The *Chart Filters button* enables you to change which data displays in the chart—for example, to see only the data for *May* and *June* or only the data for *Treadmills* and *Rowing Machines*.

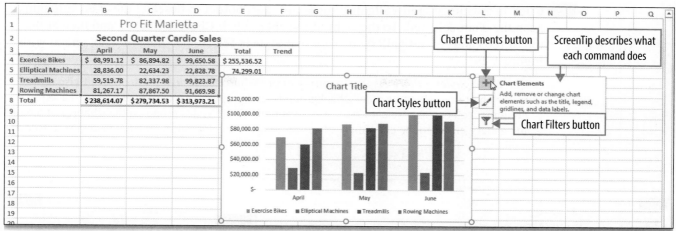

FIGURE 1.27

3 In the worksheet data, locate the group of cells bordered in blue.

> Each of the twelve cells bordered in blue is referred to as a *data point*—a value that originates in a worksheet cell. Each data point is represented in the chart by a *data marker*—a column, bar, area, dot, pie slice, or other symbol in a chart that represents a single data point.

> Related data points form a *data series*; for example, there is a data series for *April*, for *May*, and for *June*. Each data series has a unique color or pattern represented in the chart legend.

4 On the **Design tab**, in the **Chart Layouts group**, click **Quick Layout**, and then compare your screen with Figure 1.28.

> In the Quick Layout gallery, you can change the overall layout of the chart by selecting a predesigned *chart layout*—a combination of chart elements, which can include a title, legend, labels for the columns, and the table of charted cells.

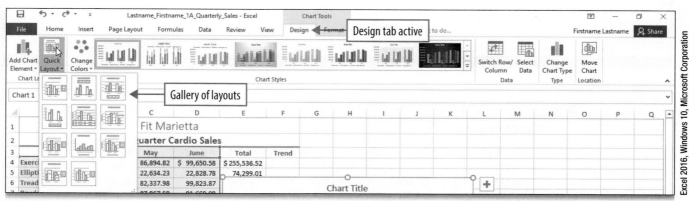

FIGURE 1.28

5 *Point* to several different layouts to see how Live Preview displays the effect on your chart, and then click the **Quick Layout** button again without changing the layout.

6 In the chart, click anywhere in the text *Chart Title* to select the title box, watch the **Formula Bar** as you begin to type **Second** and notice that AutoComplete fills in the subtitle for you. Press Enter at any point to insert the worksheet subtitle as the chart title.

7 Click in a white area just slightly *inside* the chart border to deselect the chart title but keep the chart selected. To the right of the chart, click **Chart Styles** 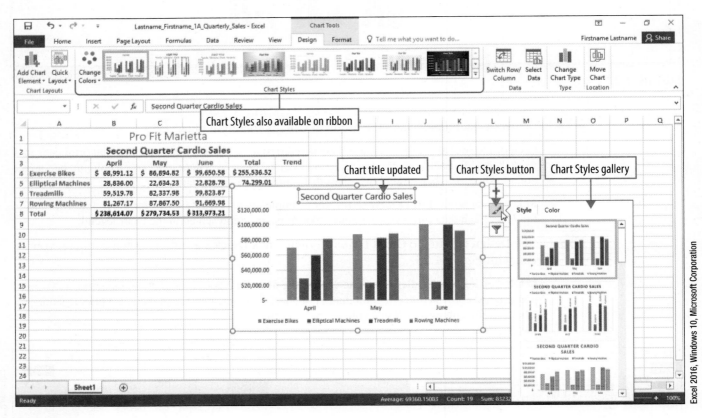, and then at the top of the **Chart Styles** gallery, be sure that **Style** is selected. Compare your screen with Figure 1.29.

> The ***Chart Styles gallery*** displays an array of predefined ***chart styles***—the overall visual look of the chart in terms of its colors, backgrounds, and graphic effects such as flat or shaded columns. You can also select Chart Styles from the Chart Styles group on the ribbon, but having the gallery closer to the chart makes it easier to use a touch gesture on a touch device to format a chart.

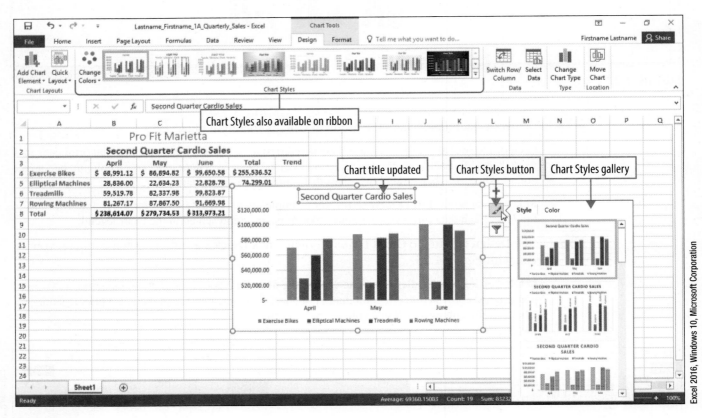

FIGURE 1.29

8 On the right side of the **Style** gallery, scroll down about halfway, and then by using the ScreenTips as your guide, locate and click **Style 6**.

> This style uses a white background, formats the columns with theme colors, and applies a slight shadowed effect to the columns. With this clear visual representation of the data, the president can see the sales of all product categories in each month, and can see that the sale of exercise bikes and treadmills has risen markedly during the quarter.

9 At the top of the gallery, click **Color**. Under **Colorful**, point to the third row of colors to display the ScreenTip *Color 3*, and then click to apply the **Color 3** variation of the theme colors.

10 Point to the top border of the chart to display the 🔾 pointer, and then drag the upper left corner of the chart just inside the upper left corner of cell **A10**, approximately as shown in Figure 1.30.

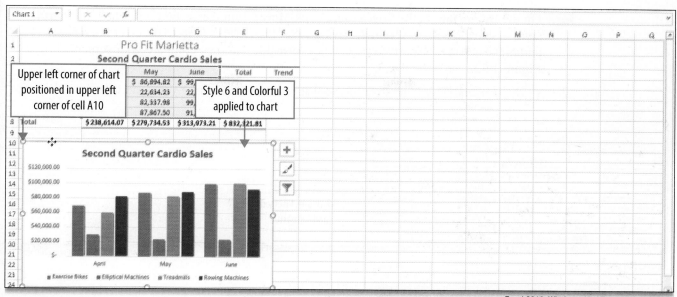

FIGURE 1.30

11 Click any cell to deselect the chart, and notice that the chart buttons no longer display to the right of the chart and the Chart Tools no longer display on the ribbon. Click **Save** 🖫.

Contextual tabs display when an object is selected and then are removed from view when the object is deselected.

Activity 1.13 | Creating and Formatting Sparklines

By creating sparklines, you provide a context for your numbers. Your readers will be able to see the relationship between a sparkline and its underlying data quickly.

1 Select the range **B4:D7**, which represents the monthly sales figures for each product and for each month. Click the **Insert tab**, and then in the **Sparklines group**, click **Line**. In the displayed **Create Sparklines** dialog box, notice that the selected range *B4:D7* displays.

2 With the insertion point blinking in the **Location Range** box, type **f4:f7** which is the range of cells where you want the sparklines to display. Compare your screen with Figure 1.31.

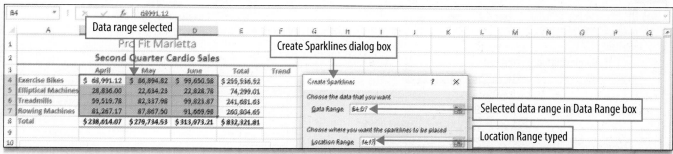

FIGURE 1.31

🔄 **ANOTHER WAY**   In the worksheet, select the range F4:F7 to insert it into the Location Range box.

3 Click **OK** to insert the sparklines in the range **F4:F7**, and then on the **Design tab**, in the **Show group**, click the **Markers** check box to select it.

Alongside each row of data, the sparkline provides a quick visual trend summary for sales of each cardio item over the three-month period. For example, you can see instantly that of the four items, only Elliptical Machines had declining sales for the period.

4 On the **Design tab**, in the **Style group**, click **More** ▾. In the second row, click the fourth style—**Sparkline Style Accent 4, Darker 25%**. Press Ctrl + Home to deselect the range and make cell **A1** the active range. Click **Save** 🖫, and then compare your screen with Figure 1.32.

Use markers, colors, and styles in this manner to further enhance your sparklines.

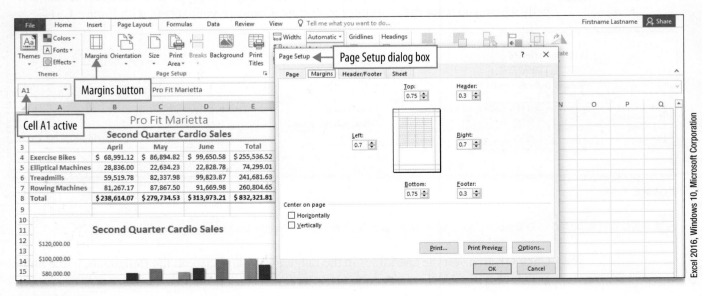

FIGURE 1.32

Excel 2016, Windows 10, Microsoft Corporation

Objective 6 Print a Worksheet, Display Formulas, and Close Excel

GO! Learn How
Video E1-6

Use the ***Show Formulas*** command to display the formula in each cell instead of the resulting value. Use the commands on the Page Layout tab to prepare for printing.

Activity 1.14 | Creating a Footer and Centering a Worksheet

1.3.8, 1.3.4

For each Excel project in this textbook, you will create a footer containing the file name, which includes your name and the project name. You will also center the data horizontally on the page to create an attractive result if your worksheet is printed.

1 If necessary, click cell **A1** to deselect the chart. Click the **Page Layout tab**, and then in the **Page Setup group**, click **Margins**. At the bottom of the **Margins** gallery, click **Custom Margins**, to display the **Page Setup** dialog box. Compare your screen with Figure 1.33.

FIGURE 1.33

2 On the **Margins tab**, under **Center on page**, select the **Horizontally** check box.

This action will center the data and chart horizontally on the page, as shown in the Preview area.

3 In the **Page Setup** dialog box, click the **Header/Footer tab**, and then in the center of the dialog box, click **Custom Footer**. In the **Footer** dialog box, with your insertion point blinking in the **Left section**, on the row of buttons, click **Insert File Name** 📄. Compare your screen with Figure 1.34.

&[File] displays in the Left section. Here you can type or insert information from the row of buttons into the left, middle, or right section of the footer. The Custom Header button displays a similar screen to enter information in the header of the worksheet.

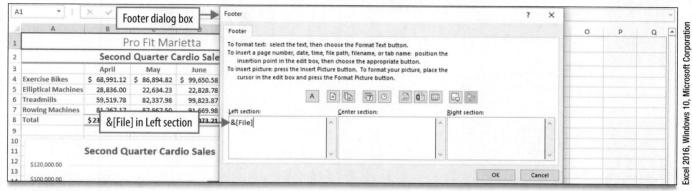

FIGURE 1.34

4 Click **OK** two times.

The vertical dotted line between columns indicates that as currently arranged, only the columns to the left of the dotted line will print on the first page. The exact position of the vertical line may depend on your default printer setting.

🔄 **ANOTHER WAY** — Deselect the chart. On the Insert tab, in the Text group, click Header & Footer to display Page Layout view. Click in the left section of the displayed footer, and then in the Header & Footer Elements group, click File Name. Click any cell in the workbook to deselect the footer area, and then on the status bar, click the Normal button to return to Normal view.

Activity 1.15 | **Adding Document Properties and Printing a Workbook**

1.4.6, 1.5.3

1 In the upper left corner of your screen, click the **File tab** to display **Backstage** view. In the lower right corner, click **Show All Properties**.

2 As the **Tags**, type **cardio sales** In the **Subject** box, type your course name and section number. Be sure your name displays in the **Author** box and edit if necessary.

3 On the left, click **Print** to view the **Print Preview**. Compare your screen with Figure 1.35.

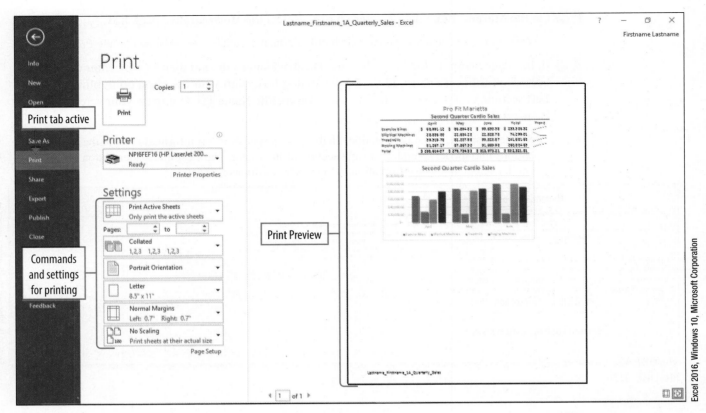

FIGURE 1.35

4 ▸ Note any adjustments that need to be made, and then on the left, click **Save** to save and return to the workbook.

> **NOTE** **What Does Your Instructor Require for Submission? A Paper Printout, an Image That Looks Like a Printed Document, or Your Excel File?**
>
> You can produce a paper printout of your worksheet or an electronic image of your worksheet that looks like a printed document. Or, your instructor may want only your completed Excel file.

5 ▸ If you are directed to print on paper, be sure that a printer is available to your system. Press Ctrl + F2, which is the keyboard shortcut to display the **Print Preview**, and then under **Print**, click the **Print** button.

6 ▸ If you are directed to create an electronic image of your worksheet that looks like a printed document, click the **File tab**, on the left click **Export**, and then on the right, click **Create PDF/XPS**. In the **Publish as PDF or XPS** dialog box, navigate to your storage location, in the **Save as type** box, be sure **PDF** is indicated, and then click **Publish** to create the PDF file.

Activity 1.16 | Printing a Section of the Worksheet

From Backstage view, you can print only the portion of the worksheet that you select, and there are times you might want to do this.

1 ▸ Select the range **A2:F5** to select only the subtitle and the data for *Exercise Bikes* and *Elliptical Machines* and the column titles

2 Press Ctrl + F2, which is the keyboard shortcut to display **Print Preview**, and then under **Settings**, click the first arrow, which currently displays *Print Active Sheets*. On the list that displays, click **Print Selection**, and then compare your screen with Figure 1.36.

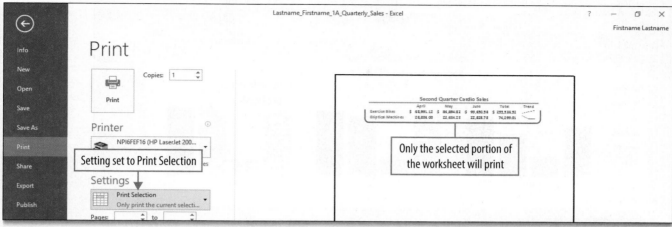

FIGURE 1.36

Excel 2016, Windows 10, Microsoft Corporation

3 If directed by your instructor, print the selection on paper; otherwise, in the upper left corner, click **Back** ← to return to your workbook.

4 Press Ctrl + Home, and then click **Save** 🖫.

Activity 1.17 | Changing Page Orientation and Displaying, Printing, and Hiding Formulas

1.4.8, 1.5.4

When you type a formula in a cell, the cell displays the *results* of the formula calculation. Recall that this value is called the displayed value. You can view and print the underlying formulas in the cells. When you do so, a formula often takes more horizontal space to display than the result of the calculation.

1 If necessary, redisplay your worksheet. Because you will make some temporary changes to your workbook, on the Quick Access Toolbar, click **Save** 🖫 to be sure your work is saved up to this point.

2 On the **Formulas tab**, in the **Formula Auditing group**, click **Show Formulas**.

🔄 **ANOTHER WAY** Hold down Ctrl, and then press ~ (usually located below Esc).

3 In the **column heading area**, point to the **column A** heading to display the ↓ pointer, hold down the left mouse button, and then drag to the right to select columns **A:F**. Compare your screen with Figure 1.37.

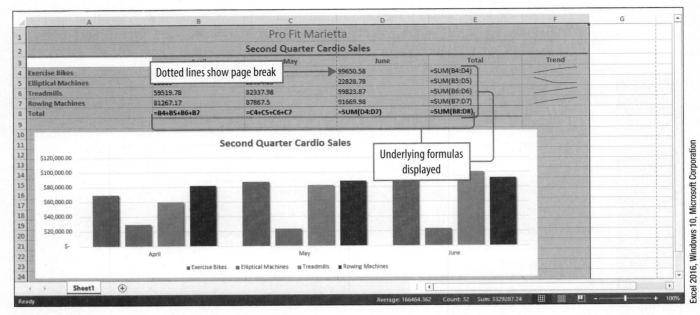

FIGURE 1.37

> **NOTE** | **Turning the Display of Formulas On and Off**
>
> The Show Formulas button is a toggle button. Clicking it once turns the display of formulas on—the button will be shaded. Clicking the button again turns the display of formulas off.

---

4 ▶ Point to the column heading boundary between any two of the selected columns to display the ⊞ pointer, and then double-click to AutoFit the selected columns.

   AutoFit adjusts the width of a column to fit the cell content of the *widest* cell in the column.

🔁 **ANOTHER WAY** | With the columns selected, on the Home tab, in the Cells group, click Format, and then click AutoFit Column Width.

---

5 ▶ On the **Page Layout tab**, in the **Page Setup group**, click **Orientation**, and then click **Landscape**. In the **Scale to Fit** group, click the **Width arrow**, and then click **1 page** to scale the data to fit onto one page.

   Scaling shrinks the width or height of the printed worksheet to fit a maximum number of pages and is convenient for printing formulas. Although it is not always the case, formulas frequently take up more space than the actual data.

🔁 **ANOTHER WAY** | In the Scale to Fit group, click the Dialog Box Launcher button to display the Page tab of the Page Setup dialog box. Then, under Scaling, click the Fit to option button.

---

6 ▶ In the **Page Setup group**, click **Margins**, click **Custom Margins**, and then on the **Margins tab**, under **Center on page**, be sure the **Horizontally** check box is selected—select it if necessary.

7 ▶ Click **OK** to close the dialog box. Check to be sure your chart is centered below the data and the left and right edges are slightly inside column A and column F—use the 🔧 pointer to drag a chart edge and then deselect the chart if necessary.

8 ▶ Click any cell so that the chart is not selected, and then press ⌘Ctrl + F2 to display the **Print Preview**. Under **Settings**, if necessary switch back to the option to **Print Active Sheets**. If directed to do so by your instructor, print on paper; or, to save the workbook in this format, click Save As and name the worksheet **Lastname_Firstname_1A_Quarterly_Sales_formulas**

> If you save the workbook with this new name, your original workbook is automatically saved and closed.

9 ▶ If you did not save your formulas worksheet, on the left, click **Close**, and when prompted, click **Don't Save** so that you do *not* save the changes you made—displaying formulas, changing column widths and orientation, and scaling—to print your formulas.

10 ▶ In the upper right corner of your screen, click **Close** ⌧ to close Excel.

END | You have completed Project 1A

GO! With Google

Objective   Create a Sales Report with an Embedded Column Chart Using Google Sheets

> **ALERT!**   **Working with Web-Based Applications and Services**
>
> Computer programs and services on the web receive continuous updates and improvements, so the steps to complete this web-based Activity may differ from the ones shown. You can often look at the screens and the information presented to determine how to complete the Activity.
>
> If you do not already have a Google account, you will need to create one before you begin this activity. Go to http://google.com and in the upper right corner, click Sign In. On the Sign In screen, click Create Account. On the Create your Google Account page, complete the form, read and agree to the Terms of Service and Privacy Policy, and then click Next step. On the Welcome screen, click Get Started.

Activity │ Creating a Sales Report with an Embedded Column Chart Using Google Sheets

In this Activity, you will use Google Sheets to create a sales report and chart similar to the one you created in Project 1A.

1 From the desktop, open your browser, (use a browser other than Edge), navigate to **http://google.com** and then click the **Google Apps** menu ⊞. Click **Drive**, and then if necessary, sign in to your Google account.

2 Open your **GO! Web Projects** folder—or click NEW to create and then open this folder if necessary.

3 In the left pane, click **NEW**, and then click **Google Sheets**. From your Windows taskbar, open **File Explorer**, navigate to your Student Data Files for this chapter, and then in the **File List**, double-click to open **e01A_Web**.

4 In the displayed Excel worksheet, select the range **A1:E8**, right-click over the selection, click **Copy**, and then **Close** Excel. **Close** the **File Explorer** window.

5 In your blank Google Sheet, with cell **A1** active, point to cell **A1**, right-click, and then click **Paste**; by copying and pasting the data, you can create this project more quickly without having to do extra typing. In the column heading area, point to the border between **column A** and **column B** to display the ↔ pointer, and then widen **column A** slightly so that all of the data in rows 4–8 displays.

6 Select the range **A1:E1**. On the toolbar, click **Merge cells** ⊞. On the toolbar, click the **Align arrow** ▼, and then click **Center** ≣. Repeat for the range **A2:E2**, and then apply **Bold** **B** to cells **A1** and **A2**.

7 Select the range with the month names, center them, and apply **Bold** **B**. Apply **Bold** **B** to the totals in the range **B8:E8**.

8 Select the range **A3:D7** (the data without the totals and without the titles). On the menu bar, click **Insert**, and

then click **Chart**. In the **Chart Editor** dialog box, notice the three tabs.

9 In the **Chart Editor** window, with the first chart type selected, click the **Chart types tab**, and then select the **Switch rows/columns** check box.

10 Click the **Customization tab**. In the **Title** box, replace the existing text with **Second Quarter Cardio Sales**

11 Click the **Legend arrow**, and then click **None**. Click the **Background arrow**, and then in the fourth column, click the third color—**light yellow 3**.

12 In the lower left corner, click **Insert**. Point anywhere inside the selected chart, hold down the left mouse button to display the 🖐 pointer, and then drag the chart slightly below the data. Then using the corner sizing handles resize and reposition the chart attractively below the data.

13 At the top of the worksheet, click the text *Untitled spreadsheet*, and then using your own name, type **Lastname_Firstname_EX_1A_Web** and press ENTER.

14 If you are instructed to submit your file to your instructor, you can either share the file through Google Drive, or create a PDF or Excel file. Click the File menu, point to Download as, and click the format you want. The file will download to your default download folder as determined by your browser settings. Ask your instructor in what format he or she would like to receive your file.

15 **Close** the browser tab—a new Google Sheet always opens in a new window in your browser; your work is automatically saved. Notice that your new Google Sheet displays in the file list on your Google Drive. Sign out of your Google account.

PROJECT 1B Inventory Valuation

MyITLab
Project 1B Training
Project 1B Grader

PROJECT ACTIVITIES

In Activities 1.18 through 1.27 you will create a workbook for Josh Feingold, Operations Manager, which calculates the retail value of an inventory of plyometric training products. Your completed worksheet will look similar to Figure 1.38.

PROJECT FILES

MyITLab grader

If your instructor wants you to submit Project 1B in the MyITLab Grader system, log in to MyITLab, locate Grader Project 1B, and then download the files for this project.

Please always review the downloaded Grader instructions before beginning.

For Project 1B, you will need the following file:
New blank Excel workbook

You will save your workbook as:
Lastname_Firstname_1B_Plyo_Products

PROJECT RESULTS

Build From Scratch

GO! Walk Thru Project 1B

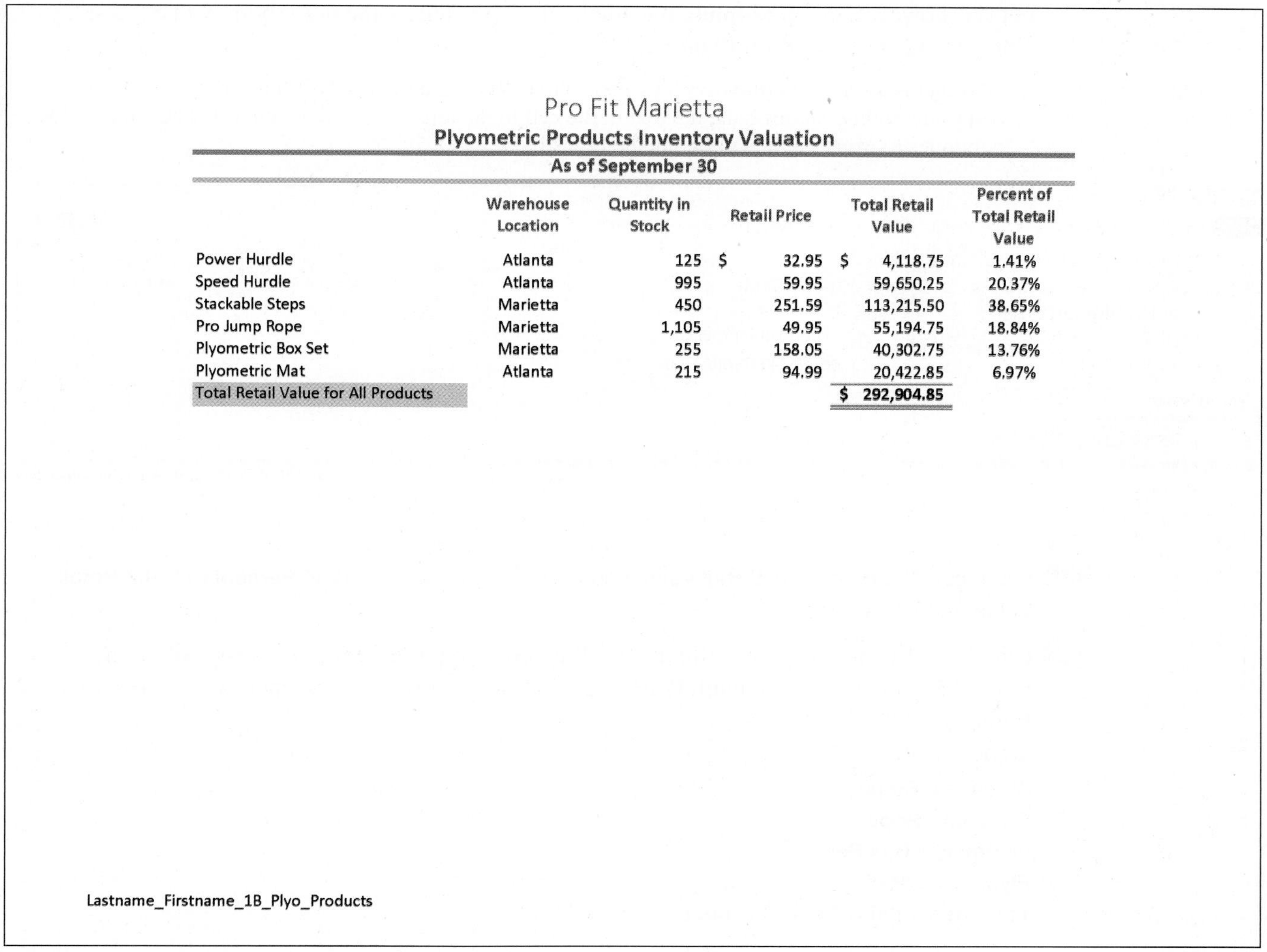

Pro Fit Marietta
Plyometric Products Inventory Valuation
As of September 30

	Warehouse Location	Quantity in Stock	Retail Price	Total Retail Value	Percent of Total Retail Value
Power Hurdle	Atlanta	125	$ 32.95	$ 4,118.75	1.41%
Speed Hurdle	Atlanta	995	59.95	59,650.25	20.37%
Stackable Steps	Marietta	450	251.59	113,215.50	38.65%
Pro Jump Rope	Marietta	1,105	49.95	55,194.75	18.84%
Plyometric Box Set	Marietta	255	158.05	40,302.75	13.76%
Plyometric Mat	Atlanta	215	94.99	20,422.85	6.97%
Total Retail Value for All Products				$ 292,904.85	

Lastname_Firstname_1B_Plyo_Products

Excel 2016, Windows 10, Microsoft Corporation

FIGURE 1.38 Project 1B Plyo Products

GO! Learn How
Video E1-7

In Excel, the spelling checker performs similarly to the other Microsoft Office programs.

Activity 1.18 | Checking Spelling in a Worksheet

> **ALERT!** To submit as an autograded project, log into MyITLab, download the files for this project, and begin with those files instead of a new blank workbook.

1 Start Excel and display a new blank workbook. In cell **A1**, type **Pro Fit Marietta** and press Enter. In cell **A2**, type **Plyometric Products Inventory** and press Enter.

2 Click the **File tab**, on the left click **Save As**, under **Save As**, click **Browse** to display the **Save As** dialog box, and then navigate to your **Excel Chapter 1** folder. As the **File name**, using your own name, type **Lastname_Firstname_1B_Plyo_Products** and then click **Save**.

3 Press Tab to move to cell **B3**, type **Quantity** and press Tab. In cell **C3**, type **Average Cost** and press Tab. In cell **D3**, type **Retail Price** and press Tab.

4 Click cell **C3**, and then look at the **Formula Bar**. Notice that in the cell, the displayed value is cut off; however, in the **Formula Bar**, the entire text value—the underlying value—displays. Compare your screen with Figure 1.39.

> Text that is too long to fit in a cell extends into cells on the right only if they are empty. If the cell to the right contains data, the text in the cell to the left is truncated—cut off. The entire value continues to exist, but it is not completely visible.

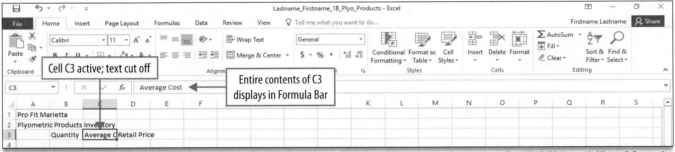

Excel 2016, Windows 10, Microsoft Corporation

FIGURE 1.39

5 Click cell **E3**, type **Total Retail Value** and press Tab. In cell **F3**, type **Percent of Total Retail Value** and press Enter.

6 Click cell **A4**. *Without* correcting the spelling error, type **Powr Hurdle** Press Enter. In the range **A5:A10**, type the remaining row titles shown below. Then compare your screen with Figure 1.40.

Speed Hurdle
Stackable Steps
Pro Jump Rope
Plyometric Box Set
Plyometric Mat
Total Retail Value for All Products

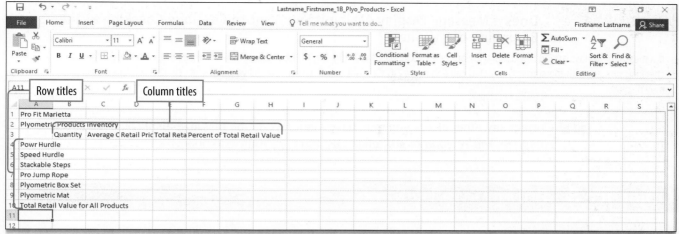

FIGURE 1.40

Excel 2016, Windows 10, Microsoft Corporation

7 In the **column heading area**, point to the right boundary of **column A** to display the 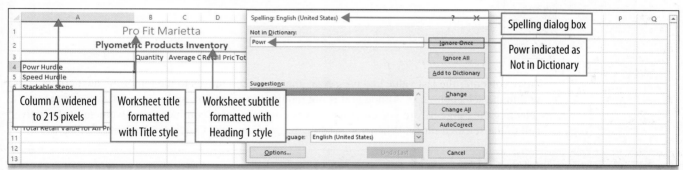 pointer, and then drag to the right to widen **column A** to **215** pixels.

8 Select the range **A1:F1**, **Merge & Center** the text, and then from the **Cell Styles** gallery, apply the **Title** style.

9 Select the range **A2:F2**, **Merge & Center** the text, and then from the **Cell Styles** gallery, apply the **Heading 1** style. Press Ctrl + Home to move to the top of your worksheet.

10 With cell **A1** as the active cell, click the **Review tab**, and then in the **Proofing group**, click **Spelling**. Compare your screen with Figure 1.41.

FIGURE 1.41

Excel 2016, Windows 10, Microsoft Corporation

ANOTHER WAY Press F7, which is the keyboard shortcut for the Spelling command.

11 In the **Spelling** dialog box, under **Not in Dictionary**, notice the word *Powr*.

The spelling tool does not have this word in its dictionary. Under *Suggestions*, Excel provides a list of suggested spellings.

12 Under **Suggestions**, click **Power**, and then click **Change**.

Powr, a typing error, is changed to *Power*. A message box displays *The spelling check is complete for the entire sheet*—unless you have additional unrecognized words. Because the spelling check begins its checking process starting with the currently selected cell, it is good practice to return to cell A1 before starting the Spelling command.

13 ▸ Correct any other errors you may have made. When the message displays, *Spell check complete. You're good to go!*, click **OK**. **Save** 🖫 your workbook.

Objective 8 Enter Data by Range

GO! Learn How
Video E1-8

You can enter data by first selecting a range of cells. This is a time-saving technique, especially if you use the numeric keypad to enter the numbers.

Activity 1.19 | Entering Data by Range

1 ▸ Select the range **B4:D9**, type **125** and then press Enter.

The value displays in cell B4, and cell B5 becomes the active cell.

2 ▸ With cell **B5** active in the range, and pressing Enter after each entry, type the following, and then compare your screen with Figure 1.42:

1125
450
1105
255
215

After you enter the last value and press Enter, the active cell moves to the top of the next column within the selected range. Although it is not required to enter data in this manner, you can see that selecting the range before you enter data saves time because it confines the movement of the active cell to the selected range. When you select a range of data, the Quick Analysis button displays.

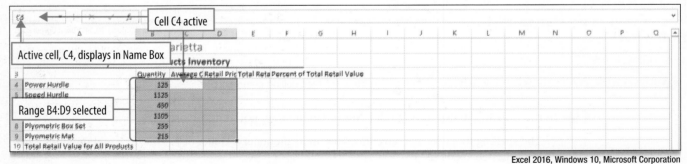

FIGURE 1.42

Excel 2016, Windows 10, Microsoft Corporation

3 ▸ With the selected range still active, from the following table, beginning in cell **C4** and pressing Enter after each entry, enter the data for the **Average Cost** column and then the **Retail Price** column. If you prefer, deselect the range to enter the values—typing in a selected range is optional.

AVERAGE COST	RETAIL PRICE
15.50	32.95
29.55	59.95
125.95	251.59
18.75	49.95
85.25	159.05
49.95	94.99

Recall that the default number format for cells is the *General* number format, in which numbers display exactly as you type them and trailing zeros do not display, even if you type them.

4 Click any blank cell, and then compare your screen with Figure 1.43. Correct any errors you may have made while entering data, and then click **Save** 🖫.

	A	B	C	D	E	F	G	H	I	J	K	L	M	N	O	P	Q
1	Pro Fit Marietta																
2	Plyometric Products Inventory																
3		Quantity	Average C	Retail Pric	Total Reta	Percent of Total Retail Value											
4	Power Hurdle	125	15.5	32.95													
5	Speed Hurdle	1125	29.55	59.95													
6	Stackable Steps	450	125.95	251.59													
7	Pro Jump Rope	1105	18.75	49.95													
8	Plyometric Box Set	255	85.25	159.05													
9	Plyometric Mat	215	49.95	94.99													
10	Total Retail Value for All Products																
11																	

Data entered

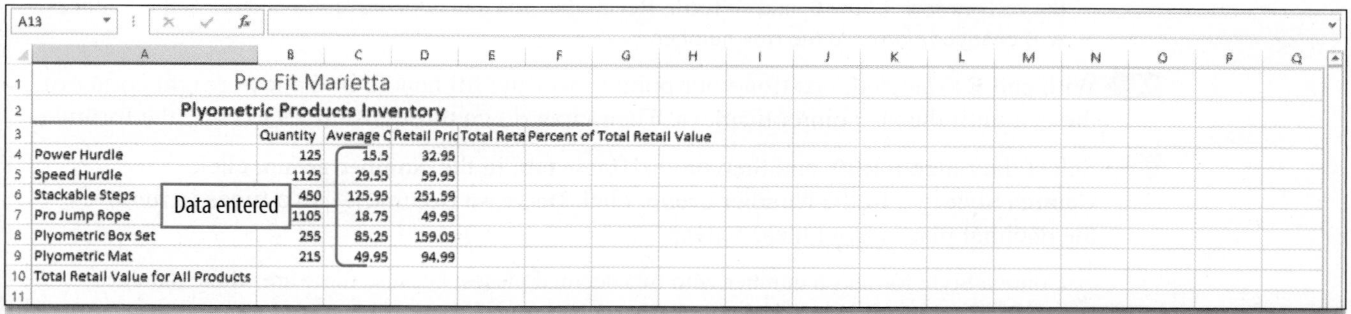

Excel 2016, Windows 10, Microsoft Corporation

FIGURE 1.43

Objective 9 Construct Formulas for Mathematical Operations

GO! Learn How
Video E1-9

Operators are symbols with which you can specify the type of calculation you want to perform in a formula.

Activity 1.20 | Using Arithmetic Operators

1 Click cell **E4**, type **=b4*d4** and notice that the two cells are outlined as part of an active formula. Then press Enter.

The *Total Retail Value* of all *Power Hurdle* items in inventory—*4118.75*—equals the *Quantity* (125) times the *Retail Price* (selling price) of 32.95. In Excel, the asterisk (*) indicates multiplication.

2 Take a moment to study the symbols you will use to perform basic mathematical operations in Excel as shown in the table in Figure 1.44, which are referred to as *arithmetic operators*.

SYMBOLS USED IN EXCEL FOR ARITHMETIC OPERATORS	
OPERATOR SYMBOL	**OPERATION**
+	Addition
−	Subtraction (also negation)
*	Multiplication
/	Division
%	Percent
^	Exponentiation

Excel 2016, Windows 10, Microsoft Corporation

FIGURE 1.44

3 Click cell **E4**.

> You can see that in cells E5:E9 you need a formula similar to the one in E4, but one that refers to the cells in row 5, row 6, and so forth. Recall that you can copy formulas and the cell references will change *relative to* the row number.

4 With cell **E4** selected, position your pointer over the fill handle in the lower right corner of the cell until the ⊞ pointer displays. Then, drag down through cell **E9** to copy the formula.

5 Select the range **B4:B9**, and then on the **Home tab**, in the **Number group**, click **Comma Style** ⟨,⟩. In the **Number group**, click **Decrease Decimal** ⟨.00→.0⟩ two times to remove the decimal places from these values.

> Comma Style formats a number with two decimal places; because these are whole numbers referring to quantities, no decimal places are necessary.

⟳ ANOTHER WAY   Select the range, display the Cell Styles gallery, and then under Number Format, click Comma [0].

6 Select the range **E4:E9**, and then at the bottom of your screen, in the status bar, notice the displayed values for **Average**, **Count**, and **Sum**—*50158.89167, 6* and *300953.35*.

> When you select a range of numerical data, Excel's ***AutoCalculate*** feature displays three calculations in the status bar by default—Average, Count, and Sum. Here, Excel indicates that if you averaged the selected values, the result would be *50158.89167*, there are *6* cells in the selection that contain values, and that if you added the values the result would be *300953.35*.

> You can display three additional calculations to this area by right-clicking the status bar and selecting them—Numerical Count, Minimum, and Maximum.

Activity 1.21 │ Using the Quick Analysis Tool

5.1.4

Recall that the Quick Analysis button displays when you select a range of data. Quick Analysis is convenient because it keeps common commands close to your mouse pointer and also displays commands in a format that is easy to touch with your finger if you are using a touchscreen device.

1 Be sure the range **E4:E9** is still selected. In the lower right corner of the selected range, click **Quick Analysis** 📧, and then in the displayed gallery, click **Totals**. *Point to*, but do not click, the first **Sum** button, which shows blue cells at the bottom. Compare your screen with Figure 1.45.

> Here, the shaded cells on the button indicate what will be summed and where the result will display, and a preview of the result displays in the cell bordered with a gray shadow.

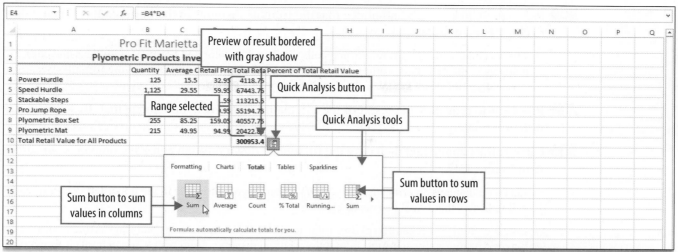

FIGURE 1.45

2 ▸ Click the first **Sum** button to display the column total *300953.4* formatted in Bold.

Sums calculated using the Quick Analysis tool are formatted in Bold.

3 ▸ Select the range **C5:E9** and apply the **Comma Style** ⟦,⟧; notice that Excel widens the columns to accommodate the data.

4 ▸ Select the range **C4:E4**, hold down Ctrl, and then click cell **E10**. Release Ctrl, and then apply the **Accounting Number Format** ⟦$ ▾⟧. Notice that Excel widens the columns as necessary.

5 ▸ Click cell **E10**, and then from the **Cell Styles** gallery, apply the **Total** style. Click any blank cell, **Save** ⟦💾⟧ your workbook, and then compare your screen with Figure 1.46.

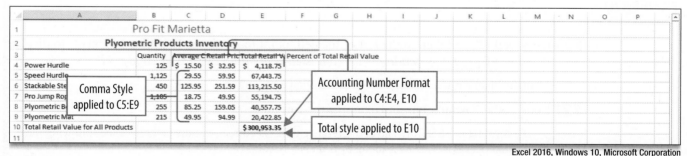

FIGURE 1.46

Activity 1.22 | Copying Formulas Containing Absolute Cell References

4.1.1

In a formula, a relative cell reference refers to a cell by its position *relative to* the cell that contains the formula. An **absolute cell reference**, on the other hand, refers to a cell by its *fixed* position in the worksheet, for example, the total in cell E10.

A relative cell reference automatically adjusts when a formula is copied. In some calculations, you do *not* want the cell reference to adjust; rather, you want the cell reference to remain the same when the formula is copied.

1 ▸ Click cell **F4**, type **=** and then click cell **E4**. Type **/** and then click cell **E10**.

The formula *=E4/E10* indicates that the value in cell E4 will be *divided* by the value in cell E10. Why? Because Mr. Feingold wants to know the percentage by which each product's Total Retail Value makes up the Total Retail Value for All Products.

Arithmetically, the percentage is computed by dividing the *Total Retail Value* for each product by the *Total Retail Value for All Products*. The result will be a percentage expressed as a decimal.

2 Press [Enter]. Click cell **F4** and notice that the formula displays in the **Formula Bar**. Then, point to cell **F4** and double-click.

The formula, with the two referenced cells displayed in color and bordered with the same color, displays in the cell. This feature, called the **range finder**, is useful for verifying formulas because it visually indicates which workbook cells are included in a formula calculation.

3 Press [Enter] to redisplay the result of the calculation in the cell, and notice that .013686, which is approximately 1% of the total retail value of the inventory, is made up of Power Hurdles.

4 Click cell **F4** again, and then drag the fill handle down through cell **F9**. Compare your screen with Figure 1.47.

Each cell displays an error message—*#DIV/0!* and a green triangle in the upper left corner of each cell indicates that Excel detects an error.

Like a grammar checker, Excel uses rules to check for formula errors and flags errors in this manner. Additionally, the Auto Fill Options button displays, from which you can select formatting options for the copied cells.

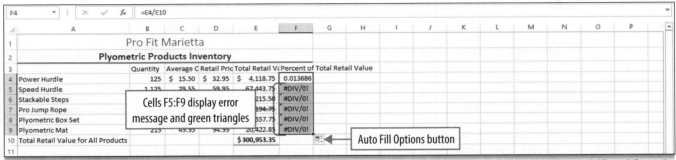

FIGURE 1.47

5 Click cell **F5**, and then to the left of the cell, point to the **Error Checking** button ⚠ to display its ScreenTip—*The formula or function used is dividing by zero or empty cells.*

In this manner, Excel suggests the cause of an error.

6 Look at the **Formula Bar** and examine the formula.

The formula is =E5/E11. The cell reference to E5 is correct, but the cell reference following the division operator (/) is *E11*, and E11 is an *empty* cell.

7 Click cell **F6**, point to the **Error Checking** button ⚠, and in the **Formula Bar** examine the formula.

Because the cell references are relative, Excel builds the formulas by increasing the row number for each equation. But in this calculation, the divisor must always be the value in cell E10—the *Total Retail Value for All Products*.

8 Point to cell **F4**, and then double-click to place the insertion point within the cell.

9 Within the cell, use the arrow keys as necessary to position the insertion point to the left of *E10*, and then press [F4]. Compare your screen with Figure 1.48.

Dollar signs ($) display, which changes the reference to cell E10 to an absolute cell reference. The use of the dollar sign to denote an absolute reference is not related in any way to whether or not the values you are working with are currency values. It is simply the symbol that Excel uses to denote an absolute cell reference.

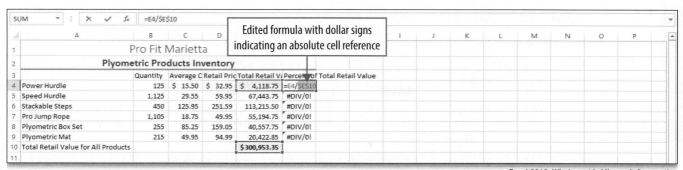

FIGURE 1.48

⟳ ANOTHER WAY   Edit the formula so that it indicates *=E4/$E$10*.

10 On the **Formula Bar**, click **Enter** ✓ so that **F4** remains the active cell. Then, drag the fill handle to copy the new formula down through cell **F9**. Compare your screen with Figure 1.49.

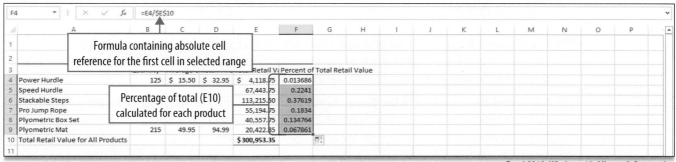

FIGURE 1.49

11 Click cell **F5**, examine the formula in the **Formula Bar**, and then examine the formulas for cells **F6**, **F7**, **F8**, and **F9**.

> For each formula, the cell reference for the *Total Retail Value* of each product changed relative to its row; however, the value used as the divisor—*Total Retail Value for All Products* in cell E10—remained absolute. You can see that by using either relative or absolute cell references, it is easy to duplicate formulas without typing them.

12 Save 🖫 your workbook.

More Knowledge   **Calculate a Percentage if You Know the Total and the Amount**

Using the equation *amount/total = percentage*, you can calculate the percentage by which a part makes up a total—with the percentage formatted as a decimal. For example, if on a test you score 42 points correctly out of 50, your percentage of correct answers is 42/50 = 0.84 or 84%.

Objective 10   Edit Values in a Worksheet

GO! Learn How
Video E1-10

Excel performs calculations on numbers; that is why you use Excel. If you make changes to the numbers, Excel automatically *re*-calculates the results. This is one of the most powerful and valuable features of Excel.

Activity 1.23 | Editing Values in a Worksheet

You can edit text and number values directly within a cell or in the Formula Bar.

1 In cell **E10**, notice the column total *$300,953.35*. Click cell **B5**. To change its value, type **995** and watch cell E5 as you press Enter.

Excel formulas *recalculate* if you change the value in a cell that is referenced in a formula. It is not necessary to delete the old value in a cell; selecting the cell and typing a new value replaces the old value with your new typing.

The *Total Retail Value* of all *Speed Hurdle* items recalculates to *59,650.25* and the total in cell E10 recalculates to *$293,159.85*. Additionally, all of the percentages in column F recalculate.

2 Point to cell **D8**, and then double-click to place the insertion point within the cell. Use the arrow keys to move the insertion point to the left or right of *9*, and use either Del or Backspace to delete *9* and then type **8** so that the new Retail Price is *158.05*.

3 Watch cell **E8** and **E10** as you press Enter, and then notice the recalculation of the formulas in those two cells.

Excel recalculates the value in cell E8 to *40,302.75* and the value in cell E10 to *$292,904.85*. Additionally, all of the percentages in column F recalculate because the *Total Retail Value for All Products* recalculated.

4 Point to cell **A2** so that the ⊕ pointer is positioned slightly to the right of the word *Inventory*, and then double-click to place the insertion point in the cell. Edit the text to add the word **Valuation** pressing Spacebar as necessary, and then press Enter.

5 Click cell **B3**, and then in the **Formula Bar**, click to place the insertion point after the letter *y*. Press Spacebar one time, type **in Stock** and then on the **Formula Bar**, click **Enter** ✓. Click **Save** 🖫, and then compare your screen with Figure 1.50.

Recall that if text is too long to fit in the cell and the cell to the right contains data, the text is truncated—cut off—but the entire value still exists as the underlying value.

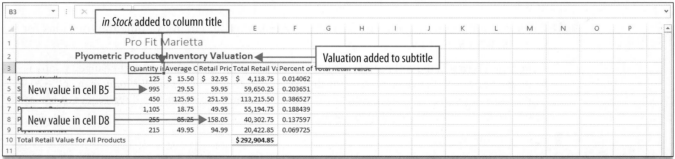

Excel 2016, Windows 10, Microsoft Corporation

FIGURE 1.50

Activity 1.24 | Formatting Cells with the Percent Style

MOS
2.2.5

A percentage is part of a whole expressed in hundredths. For example, 75 cents is the same as 75 percent of one dollar. The Percent Style button formats the selected cell as a percentage rounded to the nearest hundredth.

1 Click cell **F4**, and then in the **Number group**, click **Percent Style** %.

Your result is 1%, which is *0.014062* rounded to the nearest hundredth and expressed as a percentage. Percent Style displays the value of a cell as a percentage.

2 Select the range **F4:F9**, right-click over the selection, and then on the mini toolbar, click **Percent Style** %, click **Increase Decimal** .00 two times, and then click **Center** ≡.

Percent Style may not offer a percentage precise enough to analyze important financial information—adding additional decimal places to a percentage makes data more precise.

3 Click any cell to cancel the selection, **Save** your workbook, and then compare your screen with Figure 1.51.

	A	B	C	D	E	F	G
1	Pro Fit Marietta						
2	Plyometric Products Inventory Valuation						
3		Quantity ir	Average C	Retail Pric	Total Retail Vá	Percent of Total Retail Value	
4	Power Hurdle	125	$ 15.50	$ 32.95	$ 4,118.75	1.41%	
5	Speed Hurdle	995	29.55	59.95	59,650.25	20.37%	
6	Stackable Steps	450	*Percentages formatted*		5.50	38.65%	
7	Pro Jump Rope	1,105			.75	18.84%	
8	Plyometric Box Set	255	85.25	158.05	40,302.75	13.76%	
9	Plyometric Mat	215	49.95	94.99	20,422.85	6.97%	
10	Total Retail Value for All Products				$ 292,904.85		
11							

FIGURE 1.51

Excel 2016, Windows 10, Microsoft Corporation

Objective 11 | Format a Worksheet

Formatting refers to the process of specifying the appearance of cells and the overall layout of your worksheet. Formatting is accomplished through various commands on the ribbon, for example, applying Cell Styles, and also from commands on shortcut menus, using keyboard shortcuts, and in the Format Cells dialog box.

Activity 1.25 | Inserting and Deleting Rows and Columns

MOS
1.3.5

1 In the **row heading area** on the left side of your screen, point to the row heading for **row 3** to display the → pointer, and then right-click to simultaneously select the row and display a shortcut menu.

2 On the shortcut menu, click **Insert** to insert a new **row 3** above the selected row.

The rows below the new row 3 move down one row, and the Insert Options button displays. By default, the new row uses the formatting of the row *above*.

ANOTHER WAY   Select the row, on the Home tab, in the Cells group, click the Insert button arrow, and then click Insert Sheet Rows. Or, select the row and click the Insert button—the default setting of the button inserts a new sheet row above the selected row.

3 Click cell **E11**. On the **Formula Bar**, notice that the range changed to sum the new range **E5:E10**. Compare your screen with Figure 1.52.

If you move formulas by inserting additional rows or columns in your worksheet, Excel automatically adjusts the formulas. Excel adjusted all of the formulas in the worksheet that were affected by inserting this new row.

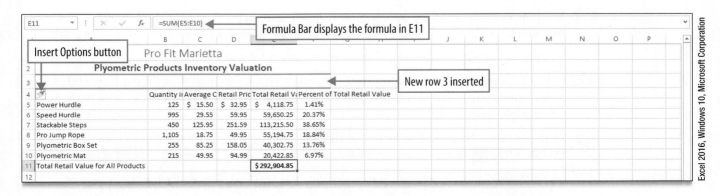

FIGURE 1.52

4 Click cell **A3**, type **As of September 30** and then on the **Formula Bar**, click **Enter** ☑ to maintain **A3** as the active cell. **Merge & Center** the text across the range **A3:F3**, and then apply the **Heading 2** cell style.

5 In the **column heading area**, point to **column B** to display the ⬇ pointer, right-click, and then click **Insert**.

> A column is inserted to the left of column B. By default, the new column uses the formatting of the column to the *left*.

🔄 **ANOTHER WAY**   Select the column, on the Home tab, in the Cells group, click the Insert button arrow, and then click Insert Sheet Columns. Or, select the column and click the Insert button—the default setting of the button inserts a new sheet column to the right of the selected column.

6 Click cell **B4**, type **Warehouse Location** and then press Enter.

7 In cell **B5**, type **Atlanta** and then type **Atlanta** again in cells **B6** and **B10**. Use AutoComplete to speed your typing by pressing Enter as soon as the AutoComplete suggestion displays. In cells **B7**, **B8**, and **B9**, type **Marietta**

8 In the **column heading area**, point to **column D**, right-click, and then click **Delete**.

> The remaining columns shift to the left, and Excel adjusts all the formulas in the worksheet accordingly. You can use a similar technique to delete a row in a worksheet.

9 Compare your screen with Figure 1.53, and then **Save** 💾 your workbook.

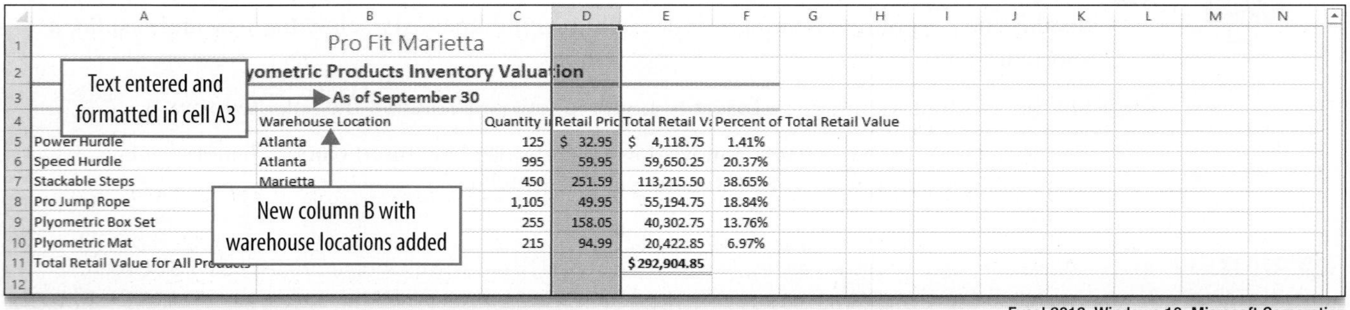

	A	B	C	D	E	F	G	H	I	J	K	L	M	N
1			Pro Fit Marietta											
2	Text entered and	...yometric Products Inventory Valua...ion												
3	formatted in cell A3	➤ As of September 30												
4		Warehouse Location	Quantity i...	Retail Pric...	Total Retail V...	Percent of Total Retail Value								
5	Power Hurdle	Atlanta	125	$ 32.95	$ 4,118.75	1.41%								
6	Speed Hurdle	Atlanta	995	59.95	59,650.25	20.37%								
7	Stackable Steps	Marietta	450	251.59	113,215.50	38.65%								
8	Pro Jump Rope		1,105	49.95	55,194.75	18.84%								
9	Plyometric Box Set	New column B with	255	158.05	40,302.75	13.76%								
10	Plyometric Mat	warehouse locations added	215	94.99	20,422.85	6.97%								
11	Total Retail Value for All Pr...				$ 292,904.85									
12														

Excel 2016, Windows 10, Microsoft Corporation

FIGURE 1.53

Activity 1.26 | Adjusting Column Widths and Wrapping Text

MOS
1.3.7, 2.2.4

Use the Wrap Text command to display the contents of a cell on multiple lines.

1 In the **column heading area**, point to the **column B** heading to display the ⬇ pointer, and then drag to the right to select **columns B:F**.

2 With the columns selected, in the **column heading area**, point to the right boundary of any of the selected columns to display the ✛ pointer, and then drag to set the width to **95 pixels**.

> Use this technique to format multiple columns or rows simultaneously.

3 Select the range **B4:F4** that comprises the column headings, and then on the **Home tab**, in the **Alignment group**, click **Wrap Text** 📄. Notice that the row height adjusts to display the titles on multiple lines.

4 With the range **B4:F4** still selected, in the **Alignment group**, click **Center** ☰ and **Middle Align** 📶. With the range **B4:F4** still selected, apply the **Heading 4** cell style.

> The Middle Align command aligns text so that it is centered between the top and bottom of the cell.

5 Select the range **B5:B10**, right-click, and then on the mini toolbar, click **Center** ▤. Click cell **A11**, and then from the **Cell Styles** gallery, under **Themed Cell Styles**, click **40% - Accent1**. **Save** 🖫 your workbook.

Activity 1.27 | Changing Theme Colors

You can change only the theme *colors* of a workbook—without changing the theme fonts or effects.

1 On the **Page Layout tab**, in the **Themes group**, click **Colors**, and then click **Green** to change the Theme Color. Click any blank cell, and then compare your screen with Figure 1.54.

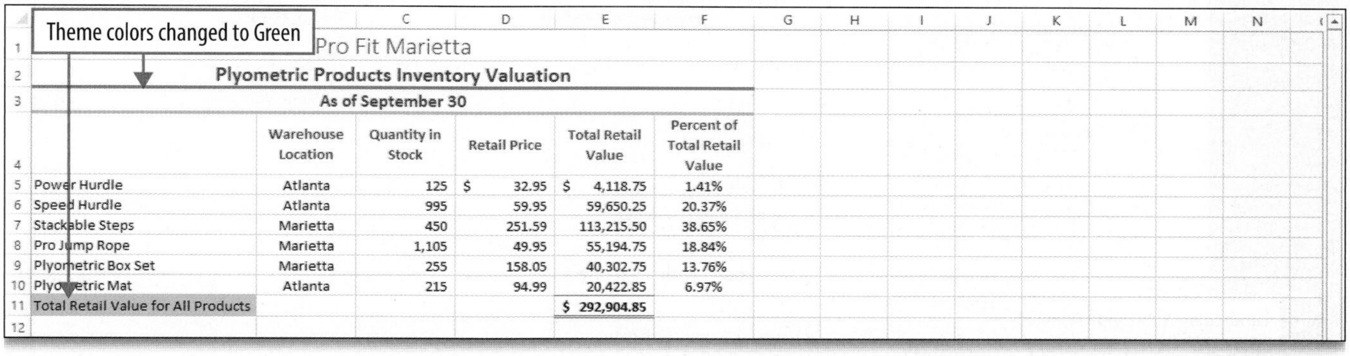

Theme colors changed to Green

	Pro Fit Marietta					
	Plyometric Products Inventory Valuation					
	As of September 30					
		Warehouse Location	Quantity in Stock	Retail Price	Total Retail Value	Percent of Total Retail Value
Power Hurdle		Atlanta	125	$ 32.95	$ 4,118.75	1.41%
Speed Hurdle		Atlanta	995	59.95	59,650.25	20.37%
Stackable Steps		Marietta	450	251.59	113,215.50	38.65%
Pro Jump Rope		Marietta	1,105	49.95	55,194.75	18.84%
Plyometric Box Set		Marietta	255	158.05	40,302.75	13.76%
Plyometric Mat		Atlanta	215	94.99	20,422.85	6.97%
Total Retail Value for All Products					$ 292,904.85	

Excel 2016, Windows 10, Microsoft Corporation

FIGURE 1.54

2 On the **Page Layout tab**, in the **Page Setup group**, click **Margins**, and then click **Custom Margins**.

3 In the **Page Setup** dialog box, on the **Margins tab**, under **Center on page**, select the **Horizontally** check box.

This action will center the data horizontally on the page, as shown in the Preview area.

4 Click the **Header/Footer tab**, and then in the center of the dialog box, click **Custom Footer**. In the **Footer** dialog box, with your insertion point blinking in the **Left section**, on the row of buttons, click **Insert File Name** 🗐.

&[File] displays in the Left section. Here you can type or insert information from the row of buttons into the left, middle, or right section of the footer. The Custom Header button displays a similar screen to enter information in the header of the worksheet.

5 Click **OK** two times.

6 Click the **File tab** to display Backstage view, and then in the lower right corner, click **Show All Properties**.

7 As the **Tags**, type **plyo products, inventory** and as the **Subject**, type your course name and section number. Be sure your name displays in the **Author** box, or edit it if necessary.

8 On the left, click **Print** to view the **Print Preview**. At the bottom of the **Print Preview**, click **Next Page** ▶, and notice that as currently formatted, the worksheet occupies two pages.

9 Under **Settings**, click **Portrait Orientation**, and then click **Landscape Orientation**. Compare your screen with Figure 1.55.

You can change the orientation on the Page Layout tab, or here, in Print Preview. Because it is in the Print Preview that you will often see adjustments that need to be made, commonly used settings display on the Print tab in Backstage view.

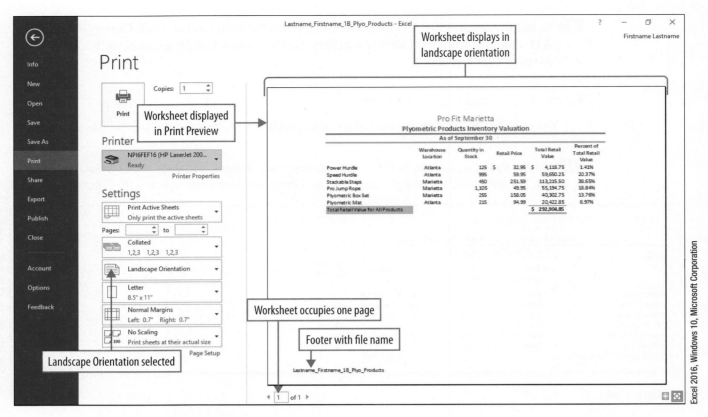

FIGURE 1.55

10 ▸ On the left, click **Save**. By using the techniques you practiced in Project 1A and as directed by your instructor, print, create a PDF image that looks like a printed document, or submit your completed Excel file. If required by your instructor, print or create an electronic version of your worksheet with formulas displayed.

11 ▸ In **Backstage** view, click **Close** to close your workbook, and then **Close** ⓧ Excel.

END | You have completed Project 1B

GO! With Google

Objective | Creating an Inventory Valuation Report

> **ALERT!** **Working with Web-Based Applications and Services**
>
> Computer programs and services on the web receive continuous updates and improvements, so the steps to complete this web-based Activity may differ from the ones shown. You can often look at the screens and the information presented to determine how to complete the Activity.
>
> If you do not already have a Google account, you will need to create one before you begin this activity. Go to http://google.com and in the upper right corner, click Sign In. On the Sign In screen, click Create Account. On the Create your Google Account page, complete the form, read and agree to the Terms of Service and Privacy Policy, and then click Next step. On the Welcome screen, click Get Started.

Activity | Creating an Inventory Valuation Report Using Google Sheets

In this Activity, you will use Google Sheets to create an inventory valuation report similar to the one you created in Project 1B.

1 From the desktop, open your browser (a browser other than Edge), navigate to **http://google.com** and then click the **Google Apps** menu. Click **Drive**, and then if necessary, sign in to your Google account.

2 Open your **GO! Web Projects** folder—or click New to create and then open this folder if necessary.

3 In the left pane, click **NEW**, and then click **Google Sheets**. From your Windows taskbar, open **File Explorer**, navigate to your Student Data Files for this chapter, and then in the **File List**, double-click the Word document **e01B_Web**; to complete this project quickly and eliminate extra typing, you will copy the data from a Word document.

4 In the displayed Word document, click anywhere in the text, and then in the upper left corner, click to select the **Table Select** to select the entire Word table. Right-click anywhere over the selection, and then click **Copy**. **Close** Word. **Close** the **File Explorer** window.

5 In your blank Google Sheet, with cell **A1** active, point to cell **A1**, right-click, and then click **Paste**. In the column heading area, point to the border between **column A** and **column B** to display the pointer, and then widen **column A** slightly so that all of the data in rows 4–10 displays.

6 Select the range **A1:E1**. On the toolbar, click **Merge cells**. On the toolbar, click the **Align arrow**, and then click **Center**. Repeat for the range **A2:E2**, and then apply **Bold** to cells **A1** and **A2**.

7 Select the range **B3:E3**, on the menu bar click **Format**, point to **Text wrapping**, and then click **Wrap**. **Center** these column titles and apply **Bold**.

8 Select the range **C4:C9**, on the menu bar click **Format**, point to **Number**, on the fly-out menu click **Number**, and then if necessary, on the toolbar, click **Decrease decimal places** two times.

9 Click cell **E4**, type **=** and then click cell **C4**. Type ***** and then click cell **D4**. Press Enter. Click cell **E4**, point to the fill handle in the lower right corner of the cell, and then drag down to cell **E9**.

10 Select the range **E4:E9**. On the toolbar, click **Functions**, click **SUM**, and then press Enter.

11 Select the range **D4:E4**, hold down Ctrl, and then select cell **E10**. On the menu bar, click **Format**, point to **Number**, and then in the fly-out menu click **Currency**.

12 Select cell **A10**, hold down Ctrl, and then click cell **E10**. Apply **Bold**.

13 Click cell **A1**, hold down Ctrl, and then click cell **A2**, cell **A10**, and cell **E10**. With the four cells selected, on the toolbar, click **Fill color**, and then in the fourth column, click the third color—**light yellow 3**.

14 At the top of the worksheet, click the text *Untitled spreadsheet*, and then using your own name, type **Lastname_Firstname_EX_1B_Web** and press ENTER.

(GO! With Google continues on the next page)

GO! With Google

15 If you are instructed to submit your file to your instructor, you can either share the file through Google Drive, or create a PDF or Excel file as described in the Note box below. Ask your instructor in what format he or she would like to receive your file.

16 **Close** the browser tab—a new Google Sheet always opens in a new window in your browser; your work is automatically saved. Notice that your new Google Sheet displays in the file list on your Google Drive. Sign out of your Google account.

N O T E Downloading Google Files

You can download your file in several formats, including PDF or PowerPoint. Click the File menu, point to Download as, and click the format directed by your instructor. The file will download to your default download folder as determined by your browser settings.

Lastname_Firstname_EX_1B_Web

File   Edit   View   Insert   Format   Data   Tools   Add-ons   Help

	A	B	C	D	E
1			Pro Fit Marietta		
2			Plyometric Products Inventory Valuation		
3		Warehouse Location	Quantity In Stock	Retail Price	Total Retail Value
4	Power Hurdle	Atlanta	125	$32.95	$4,118.75
5	Speed Hurdle	Atlanta	995	59.95	59650.25
6	Stackable Steps	Marietta	450	251.59	113215.5
7	Pro Jump Rope	Marietta	1,105	49.95	55194.75
8	Plyometric Box Set	Marietta	255	158.05	40302.75
9	Plyometric Mat	Atlanta	215	94.99	20422.85
10	Total Retail Value for All Products				$292,904.85
11					

FIGURE A

GO! To Work

MICROSOFT OFFICE SPECIALIST (MOS) SKILLS IN THIS CHAPTER	
PROJECT 1A	**PROJECT 1B**
1.1.1 Create a workbook	**1.3.5** Insert and delete columns or rows
1.3.4 Modify page setup	**1.3.7** Adjust row height and column width
1.3.6 Change workbook themes	**2.2.5** Apply number formats
1.3.8 Insert headers and footers	**2.2.6** Apply cell formats
1.4.6 Modify document properties	**4.1.1** Insert references
1.4.8 Display formulas	**5.1.4** Analyze data by using Quick Analysis
1.5.1 Set a print area	
1.5.3 Print all or part of a workbook	
1.5.4 Set print scaling	
2.1.4 Fill cells by using Auto Fill	
2.2.1 Merge cells	
2.2.5 Apply number formats	
2.2.7 Apply cell styles	
2.3.1 Insert sparklines	
5.1.1 Create a new chart	
5.1.3 Switch between rows and columns in source data	
5.2.2 Add and modify chart elements	
5.2.3 Apply chart layouts and styles	

BUILD YOUR E-PORTFOLIO

An E-Portfolio is a collection of evidence, stored electronically, that showcases what you have accomplished while completing your education. Collecting and then sharing your work products with potential employers reflects your academic and career goals. Your completed documents from the following projects are good examples to show what you have learned: 1G, 1K, and 1L.

GO! FOR JOB SUCCESS

Video: Interview Success

Your instructor may assign this video to your class, and then ask you to think about, or discuss with your classmates, these questions:

FotolEdhar / Fotolia

If you were interviewing people for your company, what would you look for in terms of their dress and personal presentation?

What might you want to change about your personal dress for work or for an interview?

Do you feel that it's right to "judge a book by its cover"? Why or why not?

END OF CHAPTER

SUMMARY

In Excel, you work with worksheets that are contained in a workbook. A worksheet is formatted as a pattern of uniformly spaced horizontal rows and vertical columns, the intersection of which forms a cell.

A cell can contain a constant value—referred to as a value—or a formula, which is an equation that performs mathematical calculations on the values in your worksheet. Common values are text and numbers.

You can insert sparklines in an Excel worksheet, which are tiny charts embedded in a cell that give a visual trend summary alongside your data. A sparkline makes a pattern more obvious to the eye.

Charts provide a graphic representation of data in a worksheet. Use the Recommended Charts feature to display customized charts that, according to Excel's calculations, will best represent your data.

GO! LEARN IT ONLINE

Review the concepts, key terms, and MOS skills in this chapter by completing these online challenges, which you can find at **MyITLab**.

Matching and Multiple Choice: Answer matching and multiple choice questions to test what you learned in this chapter.

Lessons on the GO!: Learn how to use all the new apps and features as they are introduced by Microsoft.

MOS Prep Quiz: Answer questions to review the MOS skills that you practiced in this chapter.

GO! COLLABORATIVE TEAM PROJECT (Available in **MyITLab** and Instructor Resource Center)

If your instructor assigns this project to your class, you can expect to work with one or more of your classmates—either in person or by using Internet tools—to create work products similar to those that you created in this chapter. A team is a group of workers who work together to solve a problem, make a decision, or create a work product. Collaboration is when you work together with others as a team in an intellectual endeavor to complete a shared task or achieve a shared goal.

PROJECT GUIDE FOR EXCEL CHAPTER 1

Your instructor will assign Projects from this list to ensure your learning and assess your knowledge.

	PROJECT GUIDE FOR EXCEL CHAPTER 1		
Project	**Apply Skills from These Chapter Objectives**	**Project Type**	**Project Location**
1A MyITLab	Objectives 1–6 from Project 1A	**1A Instructional Project (Grader Project)** Guided instruction to learn the skills in Project 1A.	In text
1B MyITLab	Objectives 7–11 from Project 1B	**1B Instructional Project (Grader Project)** Guided instruction to learn the skills in Project 1B.	In text
1C	Objectives 1–6 from Project 1A	**1C Skills Review (Scorecard Grading)** A guided review of the skills from Project 1A.	In text
1D	Objectives 7–11 from Project 1B	**1D Skills Review (Scorecard Grading)** A guided review of the skills from Project 1B.	In text
1E MyITLab	Objectives 1–6 from Project 1A	**1E Mastery (Grader Project)** **Mastery and Transfer of Learning** A demonstration of your mastery of the skills in Project 1A with extensive decision making.	In text
1F MyITLab	Objectives 7–11 from Project 1B	**1F Mastery (Grader Project)** **Mastery and Transfer of Learning** A demonstration of your mastery of the skills in Project 1B with extensive decision making.	In text
1G MyITLab	Objectives 1–11 from Projects 1A and 1B	**1G Mastery (Grader Project)** **Mastery and Transfer of Learning** A demonstration of your mastery of the skills in Projects 1A and 1B with extensive decision making.	In text
1H	Combination of Objectives from Projects 1A and 1B	**1H GO! Fix It (Scorecard Grading)** **Critical Thinking** A demonstration of your mastery of the skills in Projects 1A and 1B by creating a correct result from a document that contains errors you must find.	Instructor Resource Center (IRC)
1I	Combination of Objectives from Projects 1A and 1B	**1I GO! Make It (Scorecard Grading)** **Critical Thinking** A demonstration of your mastery of the skills in Projects 1A and 1B by creating a result from a supplied picture.	IRC and MyITLab
1J	Combination of Objectives from Projects 1A and 1B	**1J GO! Solve It (Rubric Grading)** **Critical Thinking** A demonstration of your mastery of the skills in Projects 1A and 1B, your decision-making skills, and your critical-thinking skills. A task-specific rubric helps you self-assess your result.	IRC and MyITLab
1K	Combination of Objectives from Projects 1A and 1B	**1K GO! Solve It (Rubric Grading)** **Critical Thinking** A demonstration of your mastery of the skills in Projects 1A and 1B, your decision-making skills, and your critical-thinking skills. A task-specific rubric helps you self-assess your result.	In text
1L	Combination of Objectives from Projects 1A and 1B	**1L GO! Think (Rubric Grading)** **Critical Thinking** A demonstration of your understanding of the chapter concepts applied in a manner that you would outside of college. An analytic rubric helps you and your instructor grade the quality of your work by comparing it to the work an expert in the discipline would create.	In text
1M	Combination of Objectives from Projects 1A and 1B	**1M GO! Think (Rubric Grading)** **Critical Thinking** A demonstration of your understanding of the chapter concepts applied in a manner that you would outside of college. An analytic rubric helps you and your instructor grade the quality of your work by comparing it to the work an expert in the discipline would create.	IRC and MyITLab
1N	Combination of Objectives from Projects 1A and 1B	**1N You and GO! (Rubric Grading)** **Critical Thinking** A demonstration of your understanding of the chapter concepts applied in a manner that you would in a personal situation. An analytic rubric helps you and your instructor grade the quality of your work.	IRC and MyITLab
1O	Combination of Objectives from Projects 1A and 1B	**1O Cumulative Group Project for Excel Chapter 1** A demonstration of your understanding of concepts and your ability to work collaboratively in a group role-playing assessment, requiring both collaboration and self-management.	IRC and MyITLab

GLOSSARY

GLOSSARY OF CHAPTER KEY TERMS

Absolute cell reference A cell reference that refers to cells by their fixed position in a worksheet; an absolute cell reference remains the same when the formula is copied.

Accounting Number Format The Excel number format that applies a thousand comma separator where appropriate, inserts a fixed U.S. dollar sign aligned at the left edge of the cell, applies two decimal places, and leaves a small amount of space at the right edge of the cell to accommodate a parenthesis for negative numbers.

Active cell The cell, surrounded by a border, ready to receive data or be affected by the next Excel command.

Arithmetic operators The symbols +, −, *, /, %, and ^ used to denote addition, subtraction (or negation), multiplication, division, percentage, and exponentiation in an Excel formula.

Auto Fill An Excel feature that generates and extends values into adjacent cells based on the values of selected cells.

AutoCalculate A feature that displays three calculations in the status bar by default—Average, Count, and Sum—when you select a range of numerical data.

AutoComplete A feature that speeds your typing and lessens the likelihood of errors; if the first few characters you type in a cell match an existing entry in the column, Excel fills in the remaining characters for you.

AutoFit An Excel feature that adjusts the width of a column to fit the cell content of the widest cell in the column.

AutoSum A button that provides quick access to the SUM function.

Category axis The area along the bottom of a chart that identifies the categories of data; also referred to as the x-axis.

Category labels The labels that display along the bottom of a chart to identify the categories of data; Excel uses the row titles as the category names.

Cell The intersection of a column and a row.

Cell address Another name for a cell reference.

Cell content Anything typed into a cell.

Cell reference The identification of a specific cell by its intersecting column letter and row number.

Cell style A defined set of formatting characteristics, such as font, font size, font color, cell borders, and cell shading.

Chart The graphic representation of data in a worksheet; data presented as a chart is usually easier to understand than a table of numbers.

Chart Elements button A button that enables you to add, remove, or change chart elements such as the title, legend, gridlines, and data labels.

Chart Filters button A button that enables you to change which data displays in the chart.

Chart layout The combination of chart elements that can be displayed in a chart such as a title, legend, labels for the columns, and the table of charted cells.

Chart style The overall visual look of a chart in terms of its graphic effects, colors, and backgrounds; for example, you can have flat or beveled columns, colors that are solid or transparent, and backgrounds that are dark or light.

Chart Styles button A button that enables you to set a style and color scheme for your chart.

Chart Styles gallery A group of predesigned chart styles that you can apply to an Excel chart.

Chart types Various chart formats used in a way that is meaningful to the reader; common examples are column charts, pie charts, and line charts.

Column A vertical group of cells in a worksheet.

Column chart A chart in which the data is arranged in columns and that is useful for showing data changes over a period of time or for illustrating comparisons among items.

Column heading The letter that displays at the top of a vertical group of cells in a worksheet; beginning with the first letter of the alphabet, a unique letter or combination of letters identifies each column.

Comma Style The Excel number format that inserts thousand comma separators where appropriate and applies two decimal places; Comma Style also leaves space at the right to accommodate a parenthesis when negative numbers are present.

Constant value Numbers, text, dates, or times of day that you type into a cell.

Context sensitive A command associated with the currently selected or active object; often activated by right-clicking a screen item.

Data Text or numbers in a cell.

Data marker A column, bar, area, dot, pie slice, or other symbol in a chart that represents a single data point; related data points form a data series.

Data point A value that originates in a worksheet cell and that is represented in a chart by a data marker.

Data series Related data points represented by data markers; each data series has a unique color or pattern represented in the chart legend.

Displayed value The data that displays in a cell.

Excel pointer An Excel window element with which you can display the location of the pointer.

Expand Formula Bar button An Excel window element with which you can increase the height of the Formula Bar to display lengthy cell content.

Expand horizontal scroll bar button An Excel window element with which you can increase the width of the horizontal scroll bar.

Fill handle The small square in the lower right corner of a selected cell.

Format Changing the appearance of cells and worksheet elements to make a worksheet attractive and easy to read.

Formula An equation that performs mathematical calculations on values in a worksheet.

Formula Bar An element in the Excel window that displays the value or formula contained in the active cell; here you can also enter or edit values or formulas.

Function A predefined formula—a formula that Excel has already built for you—that performs calculations by using specific values in a particular order.

General format The default format that Excel applies to numbers; this format has no specific characteristics—whatever you type in the cell will display, with the exception that trailing zeros to the right of a decimal point will not display.

Label Another name for a text value, and which usually provides information about number values.

Left alignment The cell format in which characters align at the left edge of the cell; this is the default for text entries and is an example of formatting information stored in a cell.

Legend A chart element that identifies the patterns or colors that are assigned to the categories in the chart.

Lettered column headings The area along the top edge of a worksheet that identifies each column with a unique letter or combination of letters.

Merge & Center A command that joins selected cells in an Excel worksheet into one larger cell and centers the contents in the merged cell.

Name Box An element of the Excel window that displays the name of the selected cell, table, chart, or object.

Normal view A screen view that maximizes the number of cells visible on your screen and keeps the column letters and row numbers close to the columns and rows.

Number format A specific way in which Excel displays numbers in a cell.

Number values Constant values consisting of only numbers.

Numbered row headings The area along the left edge of a worksheet that identifies each row with a unique number.

Operators The symbols with which you can specify the type of calculation you want to perform in an Excel formula.

Picture element A point of light measured in dots per square inch on a screen; 64 pixels equals 8.43 characters, which is the average number of characters that will fit in a cell in an Excel worksheet using the default font.

Pixel The abbreviated name for a picture element.

Point and click method The technique of constructing a formula by pointing to and then clicking cells; this method

is convenient when the referenced cells are not adjacent to one another.

Quick Analysis Tool A tool that displays in the lower right corner of a selected range, with which you can analyze your data by using Excel tools such as charts, color-coding, and formulas.

Range Two or more selected cells on a worksheet that are adjacent or nonadjacent; because the range is treated as a single unit, you can make the same changes or combination of changes to more than one cell at a time.

Range finder An Excel feature that outlines cells in color to indicate which cells are used in a formula; useful for verifying which cells are referenced in a formula.

Recommended Charts An Excel feature that displays a customized set of charts that, according to Excel's calculations, will best fit your data based on the range of data that you select.

Relative cell reference In a formula, the address of a cell based on the relative positions of the cell that contains the formula and the cell referred to in the formula.

Rounding A procedure in which you determine which digit at the right of the number will be the last digit displayed and then increase it by one if the next digit to its right is 5, 6, 7, 8, or 9.

Row A horizontal group of cells in a worksheet.

Row heading The numbers along the left side of an Excel worksheet that designate the row numbers.

Scaling The process of shrinking the width and/or height of printed output to fit a maximum number of pages.

Select All box A box in the upper left corner of the worksheet grid that, when clicked, selects all the cells in a worksheet.

Series A group of things that come one after another in succession; for example, January, February, March, and so on.

Sheet tab scrolling buttons Buttons to the left of the sheet tabs used to display Excel sheet tabs that are not in view; used when there are more sheet tabs than will display in the space provided.

Sheet tabs The labels along the lower border of the Excel window that identify each worksheet.

Show Formulas A command that displays the formula in each cell instead of the resulting value.

Sparkline A tiny chart in the background of a cell that gives a visual trend summary alongside your data; makes a pattern more obvious.

Spreadsheet Another name for a worksheet.

Status bar The area along the lower edge of the Excel window that displays, on the left side, the current cell mode, page number, and worksheet information; on the right side, when numerical data is selected, common calculations such as Sum and Average display.

SUM function A predefined formula that adds all the numbers in a selected range of cells.

Switch Row/Column A charting command to swap the data over the axis—data being charted on the vertical axis will move to the horizontal axis and vice versa.

Text values Constant values consisting of only text, and which usually provide information about number values; also referred to as labels.

Theme A predefined set of colors, fonts, lines, and fill effects that coordinate with each other.

Underlying formula The formula entered in a cell and visible only on the Formula Bar.

Underlying value The data that displays in the Formula Bar.

Value Another name for a constant value.

Value axis A numerical scale on the left side of a chart that shows the range of numbers for the data points; also referred to as the Y-axis.

Workbook An Excel file that contains one or more worksheets.

Worksheet The primary document that you use in Excel to work with and store data, and which is formatted as a pattern of uniformly spaced horizontal and vertical lines.

Worksheet grid area A part of the Excel window that displays the columns and rows that intersect to form the worksheet's cells.

X-axis Another name for the horizontal (category) axis.

Y-axis Another name for the vertical (value) axis.

Skills Review | Project 1C Step Sales

In the following Skills Review, you will create a new Excel worksheet with a chart that summarizes the first quarter sales of fitness equipment for step training. Your completed worksheet will look similar to Figure 1.56.

PROJECT FILES

For Project 1C, you will need the following file:

New blank Excel workbook

You will save your workbook as:

Lastname_Firstname_1C_Step_Sales

PROJECT RESULTS

Build From Scratch

Lastname_Firstname_1C_Step_Sales

Excel 2016, Windows 10, Microsoft Corporation

FIGURE 1.56

(Project 1C Step Sales continues on the next page)

1 Start Excel and open a new blank workbook. Click the **File tab** to display **Backstage** view, click **Save As**, and then navigate to your **Excel Chapter 1** folder. In the **File name** box, using your own name, type **Lastname_Firstname_1C_Step_Sales** and then press Enter.

a. With cell **A1** as the active cell, type the worksheet title **Pro Fit Marietta** and then press Enter. In cell **A2**, type the worksheet subtitle **First Quarter Step Sales** and then press Enter.

b. Click in cell **A4**, type **Basic Step Box** and then press Enter. In cell **A5**, type **Step Storage Box** and then press Enter. In cell **A6**, type **Stackable Steps** and then press Enter. In cell **A7**, type **Step Mats** and then press Enter. In cell **A8**, type **Total** and then press Enter.

c. Click cell **B3**. Type **January** and then in the **Formula Bar**, click **Enter** to keep cell **B3** the active cell. With **B3** as the active cell, point to the fill handle in the lower right corner of the selected cell, drag to the right to cell **D3**, and then release the mouse button to enter the text *February* and *March*.

d. Press Ctrl + Home to make cell **A1** the active cell. In the **column heading area**, point to the vertical line between **column A** and **column B** to display the ✛ pointer, hold down the left mouse button, and drag to the right to increase the column width to **130 pixels**.

e. Point to cell **B3**, and then drag across to select cells **B3** and **C3** and **D3**. With the range **B3:D3** selected, point anywhere over the selected range, right-click, and then on the mini toolbar, click **Center**.

f. Click cell **B4**, type **75826.99** and press Tab to make cell **C4** active. Enter the remaining values, as shown in **Table 1**, pressing Tab to move across the rows and Enter to move down the columns.

2 Click cell **B8** to make it the active cell and type =

a. At the insertion point, type **b4** and then type + Type **b5** and then type **+b6+b7** Press Enter. Your result is *293079.6*.

b. Click in cell **C8**. Type = and then click cell **C4**. Type + and then click cell **C5**. Repeat this process to complete the formula to add cells **C6** and **C7** to the formula, and then press Enter. Your result is *305016.4*.

c. Click cell **D8**. On the **Home tab**, in the **Editing group**, click **AutoSum**, and then press Enter to construct a formula by using the SUM function. Your result is *307715.3*.

d. In cell **E3** type **Total** and press Enter. With cell **E4** as the active cell, hold down Alt, and then press =. On the **Formula Bar**, click **Enter** to display the result and keep cell **E4** active.

e. With cell **E4** active, point to the fill handle in the lower right corner of the cell. Drag down through cell **E8**, and then release the mouse button to copy the formula with relative cell references down to sum each row.

3 Click cell **F3**. Type **Trend** and then press Enter.

a. Select the range **A1:F1**, and then on the **Home tab**, in the **Alignment group**, click **Merge & Center**. Select the range **A2:F2** and **Merge & Center** the selection.

b. Click cell **A1**. In the **Styles group**, click **Cell Styles**. Under **Titles and Headings**, click **Title**. Click cell **A2**, display the **Cell Styles** gallery, and then click **Heading 1**.

c. Select the range **B3:F3**, hold down Ctrl, and then select the range **A4:A8**. From the **Cell Styles** gallery, click **Heading 4** to apply this cell style to the column and row titles.

d. Select the range **B4:E4**, hold down Ctrl, and then select the range **B8:E8**. On the **Home tab**, in the **Number group**, click **Accounting Number Format**. Select the range **B5:E7**, and then in the **Number group**, click **Comma Style**. Select the range **B8:E8**. From the **Styles group**, display the **Cell Styles** gallery, and then under **Titles and Headings**, click **Total**.

e. On the ribbon, click the **Page Layout tab**, and then in the **Themes group**, click **Themes** to display the **Themes** gallery. Click the **Basis** theme. (This theme widens the columns slightly). On the Quick Access Toolbar, click **Save**.

TABLE 1

	January	February	March
Basic Step Box	75826.99	81657.32	72431.22
Step Storage Box	85245.90	92618.95	88337.68
Stackable Steps	68751.64	71997.48	78951.23
Step Mats	63255.10	58742.67	67995.20

(Project 1C Step Sales continues on the next page)

4 Select the range **A3:D7**, which includes the row titles, the column titles, and the data without the totals. Click the **Insert tab**, and then in the **Charts group**, click **Recommended Charts**. In the **Insert Chart** dialog box, scroll down and click the fifth recommended chart—a **Clustered Column** chart in which *each month* displays its *sales for each type of step training equipment*. Click **OK**.

a. In the chart, click anywhere in the text *Chart Title* to select the text box. Watch the **Formula Bar** as you type **First** and then let AutoComplete complete the title by pressing Enter.

b. Click in a white area just slightly *inside* the chart border to deselect the chart title but keep the chart selected. To the right of the chart, click the second button—the **Chart Styles** button 🖌.

Be sure the **Style** tab is selected. Use the scroll bar to scroll down, and then by using the ScreenTips, locate and click **Style 6**.

c. At the top of the gallery, click **COLOR**. Under **Colorful**, point to the fourth row of colors to display the ScreenTip *Color 4*, and then click to apply the **Color 4** variation of the theme colors.

d. Point to the top border of the chart to display the ⭢ pointer, and then drag the upper left corner of the chart just to the center of cell **A10** to visually center it below the data.

5 Select the range **B4:D7**. Click the **Insert tab**, and then in the **Sparklines group**, click **Line**. In the **Create Sparklines** dialog box, in the **Location Range** box, type **f4:f7** and then click **OK** to insert the sparklines.

a. On the **Design tab**, in the **Show group**, select the **Markers** check box to display markers in the sparklines.

b. On the **Design tab**, in the **Style group**, click **More** ▾ and then in the second row, click the fourth style—**Sparkline Style Accent 4, Darker 25%**.

6 Click cell **A1** to deselect the chart. Click the **Page Layout tab**, and then in the **Page Setup group**, click **Margins**. Click **Custom Margins**. In the **Page Setup** dialog box, on the **Margins tab**, under **Center on page**, select the **Horizontally** check box.

a. Click the **Header/Footer tab**, and then click **Custom Footer**. With your insertion point in the **Left section**, click **Insert File Name**. Click **OK** two times.

b. Click the **File tab** to display **Backstage** view. In the lower right corner, click **Show All Properties**. As the **Tags**, type **step sales, 1st quarter** In the **Subject** box, type your course name and section number. Be sure your name displays as the author—edit if necessary.

c. On the left, click **Save**.

d. By using the techniques you practiced in Project 1A and as directed by your instructor, print, create a PDF image that looks like a printed document, or submit your completed Excel file. If required by your instructor, print or create an electronic version of your worksheet with formulas displayed. In the upper right corner of your Excel window, click Close.

END | You have completed Project 1C

Apply **1B** skills from these Objectives:

7 Check Spelling in a Worksheet

8 Enter Data by Range

9 Construct Formulas for Mathematical Operations

10 Edit Values in a Worksheet

11 Format a Worksheet

Skills Review   Project 1D Band and Tubing Inventory

In the following Skills Review, you will create a worksheet that summarizes the inventory of band and tubing exercise equipment. Your completed worksheet will look similar to Figure 1.57.

PROJECT FILES

For Project 1D, you will need the following file:

New blank Excel workbook

You will save your workbook as:

Lastname_Firstname_1D_Band_Inventory

Build From
Scratch

PROJECT RESULTS

Pro Fit Marietta
Band and Tubing Inventory

As of June 30

	Material	Quantity in Stock	Retail Price	Total Retail Value	Percent of Total Retail Value
Super Strength Bands	Latex	225	$ 48.98	$ 11,020.50	25.16%
Medium Tubing	Rubber	198	27.95	5,534.10	12.64%
Resistance Band, Average	Latex	165	42.95	7,086.75	16.18%
Mini Bands, Medium	Latex	245	25.95	6,357.75	14.52%
Mini Bands, Heavy	Rubber	175	32.95	5,766.25	13.17%
Heavy Tubing	Latex	187	42.95	8,031.65	18.34%
Total Retail Value for All Products				$ 43,797.00	

Lastname_Firstname_1D_Band_Inventory

Excel 2016, Windows 10, Microsoft Corporation

FIGURE 1.57

(Project 1D Band and Tubing Inventory continues on the next page)

1 Start Excel and display a new blank workbook. **Save** the workbook in your **Excel Chapter 1** folder as **Lastname_Firstname_1D_Band_Inventory** In cell **A1** type **Pro Fit Marietta** and in cell **A2** type **Band and Tubing Inventory**

a. Click cell **B3**, type **Quantity in Stock** and press **Tab**. In cell **C3** type **Average Cost** and press **Tab**. In cell **D3**, type **Retail Price** and press **Tab**. In cell **E3**, type **Total Retail Value** and press **Tab**. In cell **F3** type **Percent of Total Retail Value** and press **Enter**.

b. Click cell **A4**, type **Super Strength Bands** and press **Enter**. In the range **A5:A10**, type the remaining row titles as shown below, including any misspelled words.

   Medium Tubing

   Resistnce Band, Average

   Mini Bands, Medium

   Mini Bands, Heavy

   Heavy Tubing

   Total Retail Value for All Products

c. Press **Ctrl** + **Home** to move to the top of your worksheet. On the **Review tab**, in the **Proofing group**, click **Spelling**. Correct *Resistnce* to **Resistance** and any other spelling errors you may have made, and then when the message displays, *Spell check complete. You're good to go!* click **OK**.

d. In the **column heading area**, point to the right boundary of **column A** to display the ➕ pointer, and then drag to the right to widen **column A** to **225** pixels.

e. In the **column heading area**, point to the **column B** heading to display the ⬇ pointer, and then drag to the right to select **columns B:F**. With the columns selected, in the **column heading area**, point to the right boundary of any of the selected columns, and then drag to the right to set the width to **100 pixels**.

f. Select the range **A1:F1**. On the **Home tab**, in the **Alignment group**, click **Merge & Center**, and then in the **Cell Styles** gallery, apply the **Title** style. Select the range **A2:F2**. **Merge & Center** the text across the selection, and then in the **Cell Styles** gallery, apply the **Heading 1** style.

2 On the **Page Layout tab**, in the **Themes group**, change the **Colors** to **Blue Green**. Select the empty range

B4:D9. With cell **B4** active in the range, type **225** and then press **Enter**.

a. With cell **B5** active in the range, and pressing **Enter** after each entry, type the following data in the *Quantity in Stock* column:

   198
   265
   245
   175
   187

b. With the selected range still active, from the following table, beginning in cell **C4** and pressing **Enter** after each entry, enter the following data for the **Average Cost** column and then the **Retail Price** column. If you prefer, type without selecting the range first; recall that this is optional.

Average Cost	Retail Price
22.75	48.98
15.95	27.95
26.90	42.95
12.95	25.95
18.75	32.95
26.90	42.95

3 In cell **E4**, type **=b4*d4** and then press **Enter** to construct a formula that calculates the *Total Retail Value* of the *Super Strength Bands* (Quantity in Stock X Retail Price).

a. Click cell **E4**, position your pointer over the fill handle, and then drag down through cell **E9** to copy the formula with relative cell references.

b. Select the range **B4:B9**, and then on the **Home tab**, in the **Number group**, click **Comma Style**. Then, in the **Number group**, click **Decrease Decimal** two times to remove the decimal places from these non-currency values.

c. To calculate the *Total Retail Value for All Products*, select the range **E4:E9**, and then in the lower right corner of the selected range, click the **Quick Analysis** button 📧.

(Project 1D Band and Tubing Inventory continues on the next page)

d. In the gallery, click **Totals**, and then click the *first* **Sum** button, which visually indicates that the column will be summed with a result at the bottom of the column.

e. Select the range **C5:E9** and apply the **Comma Style**. Select the range **C4:E4**, hold down Ctrl, and then click cell **E10**. With the nonadjacent cells selected, apply the **Accounting Number Format**. Click cell **E10**, and then from the **Cell Styles** gallery, apply the **Total** style.

f. Click cell **F4**, type **=** and then click cell **E4**. Type **/** and then click cell **E10**. Press F4 to make the reference to cell *E10* absolute, and then on the **Formula Bar**, click **Enter** so that cell **F4** remains the active cell. Drag the fill handle to copy the formula down through cell **F9**.

g. Point to cell **B6**, and then double-click to place the insertion point within the cell. Use the arrow keys to move the insertion point to the left or right of *2*, and use either Delete or Backspace to delete *2*, and then type **1** and press Enter so that the new *Quantity in Stock* is *165*. Notice the recalculations in the worksheet.

4 Select the range **F4:F9**, right-click over the selection, and then on the mini toolbar, click **Percent Style**. Click **Increase Decimal** two times, and then **Center** the selection.

a. In the **row heading area** on the left side of your screen, point to **row 3** to display the → pointer, and then right-click to simultaneously select the row and display a shortcut menu. On the shortcut menu, click **Insert** to insert a new **row 3**.

b. Click cell **A3**, type **As of June 30** and then on the **Formula Bar**, click **Enter** to keep cell **A3** as the active cell. **Merge & Center** the text across the range **A3:F3**, and then apply the **Heading 2** cell style.

5 In the **column heading area**, point to **column B**. When the ↓ pointer displays, right-click, and then click **Insert** to insert a new column.

a. Click cell **B4**, type **Material** and then press Enter. In cell **B5**, type **Latex** and then press Enter. In cell **B6,** type **Rubber** and then press Enter.

b. Using AutoComplete to speed your typing by pressing Enter as soon as the AutoComplete suggestion displays, in cells **B7**, **B8**, and **B10** type **Latex** and in cell **B9** type **Rubber**

c. In the **column heading area**, point to the right boundary of **column B**, and then drag to the left and set the width to **90 pixels**. In the **column heading area**, point to **column D**, right-click, and then click **Delete**.

d. Select the column titles in the range **B4:F4**, and then on the **Home tab**, in the **Alignment group**, click **Wrap Text**, **Center**, and **Middle Align**. With the range still selected, apply the **Heading 4** cell style.

e. Click cell **A11**, and then in the **Cell Styles** gallery, under **Themed Cell Styles**, click **40% - Accent1**.

6 Click the **Page Layout tab**, and then in the **Page Setup group**, click **Margins**. Click **Custom Margins**. In the **Page Setup** dialog box, on the **Margins tab**, under **Center on page**, select the **Horizontally** check box.

a. Click the **Header/Footer tab**, and then click **Custom Footer**. With your insertion point in the **Left section**, click **Insert File Name**. Click **OK** two times.

b. In the **Page Setup group**, click **Orientation**, and then click **Landscape**.

c. Click the **File tab** to display **Backstage** view. In the lower right corner, click **Show All Properties**. As the **Tags**, type **bands, tubing, inventory** In the **Subject** box, type your course name and section number. Be sure your name displays as the author—edit if necessary.

d. On the left, click **Save**.

e. By using the techniques you practiced in Project 1A and as directed by your instructor, print, create a PDF image that looks like a printed document, or submit your completed Excel file. If required by your instructor, print or create an electronic version of your worksheet with formulas displayed. In the upper right corner of your Excel window, click Close.

End | You have completed Project 1D

Mastering Excel Project 1E Gym Sales

In the following Mastering Excel project, you will create a worksheet comparing the sales of different types of home gym equipment sold in the second quarter. Your completed worksheet will look similar to Figure 1.58.

Apply 1A skills from these Objectives:

1 Create, Save, and Navigate an Excel Workbook

2 Enter Data in a Worksheet

3 Construct and Copy Formulas and Use the SUM Function

4 Format Cells with Merge & Center, Cell Styles, and Themes

5 Chart Data to Create a Column Chart and Insert Sparklines

6 Print a Worksheet, Display Formulas, and Close Excel

PROJECT FILES

For Project 1E, you will need the following file:

e01E_Gym_Sales

You will save your workbook as:

Lastname_Firstname_1E_Gym_Sales

PROJECT RESULTS

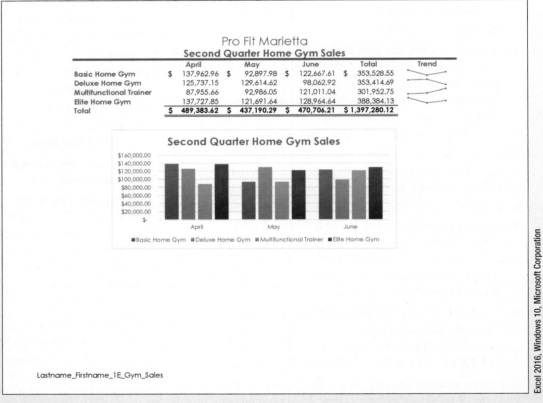

FIGURE 1.58

Excel 2016, Windows 10, Microsoft Corporation

(Project 1E Gym Sales continues on the next page)

Mastering Excel Project 1E Gym Sales (continued)

1 Start Excel, and then on the opening screen, in the lower left, click **Open Other Workbooks**. Click **Browse**, and then navigate to your student data files for this chapter. Open the file **e01_1E_Gym_Sales**. Click the **File tab**, on the left click **Save As**, and then click **Browse**. In the **Save As** dialog box, navigate to your **Excel Chapter 1** folder, and then using your own name, save the file as **Lastname_Firstname_1E_Gym_Sales**

2 Change the theme to **Wisp**.

3 In cell **B3**, use the fill handle to fill the months *May* and *June* in the range **C3:D3**.

4 **Merge & Center** the title across the range **A1:F1**, and then apply the **Title** cell style. **Merge & Center** the subtitle across the range **A2:F2**, and then apply the **Heading 1** cell style. **Center** the column titles in the range **B3:F3**.

5 Widen **column A** to **180 pixels**, and then widen columns **B:F** to **115 pixels**. In the range **B7:D7**, enter the monthly sales figures for the Elite Home Gym as shown in the table below:

	April	May	June
Elite Home Gym	137727.85	121691.64	128964.64

6 In cell **B8**, on the **Home tab**, use the **AutoSum** command to sum the April sales. Copy the resulting formula across to cells **C8:D8** to sum the May monthly sales and the June monthly sales. In cell **E4**, use the **AutoSum** button to sum the *Basic Home Gym* sales. Copy the formula down to cells **E4:E8**.

7 Apply the **Heading 4** cell style to the row titles and the column titles. Apply the **Total** cell style to the totals in the range **B8:E8**.

8 Apply the **Accounting Number Format** to the first row of sales figures and to the total row. Apply the **Comma Style** to the remaining sales figures.

9 To compare the monthly sales of each product visually, select the range that represents the sales figures for the three months, including the month names and the product names—do not include any totals in the range. With this data selected, use the **Recommended Charts** command to insert a **Clustered Column** chart with the month names displayed on the category axis and the product names displayed in the legend.

10 Move the chart so that its upper left corner is positioned in the center of cell **A10**. Then drag the center right sizing handle to the right until the right edge of the chart aligns with the right edge of **column E**; this will display the legend on one row and, after you add the sparklines, center the chart below the data.

11 Apply **Chart Style 6** and **Color 2** under **Colorful**. Change the **Chart Title** to **Second Quarter Home Gym Sales**

12 In the range **F4:F7**, insert **Line** sparklines that compare the monthly data. Do not include the totals. Show the sparkline **Markers** and apply **Sparkline Style Accent 2, Darker 50%** in the first row, the second style.

13 Center the worksheet **Horizontally** on the page, and then insert a **Footer** with the **File Name** in the **left section**.

14 Change the **Orientation** to **Landscape**. Display the document properties, and then as the **Tags** type **home gym, sales** As the **Subject**, type your course name and section number. Be sure your name displays as the **Author**. Check your worksheet by previewing it in **Print Preview**, and then make any necessary corrections.

15 **Save** your workbook. By using the techniques you practiced in Project 1A and as directed by your instructor, print, create a PDF image that looks like a printed document, or submit your completed Excel file. If required by your instructor, print or create an electronic version of your worksheet with formulas displayed. In the upper right corner of your Excel window, click **Close**.

END | You have completed Project 1E

CONTENT-BASED ASSESSMENTS (MASTERY AND TRANSFER OF LEARNING)

MyITLab® grader

Mastering Excel | Project 1F Balance Sales

Apply 1B skills from these Objectives:

- **7** Check Spelling in a Worksheet
- **8** Enter Data by Range
- **9** Construct Formulas for Mathematical Operations
- **10** Edit Values in a Worksheet
- **11** Format a Worksheet

In the following Mastering Excel project, you will create a worksheet that summarizes the sales of balance and stabilization equipment that Pro Fit Marietta is marketing. Your completed worksheet will look similar to Figure 1.59.

PROJECT FILES

For Project 1F, you will need the following file:

e01F_Balance_Sales

You will save your workbook as:

Lastname_Firstname_1F_Balance_Sales

PROJECT RESULTS

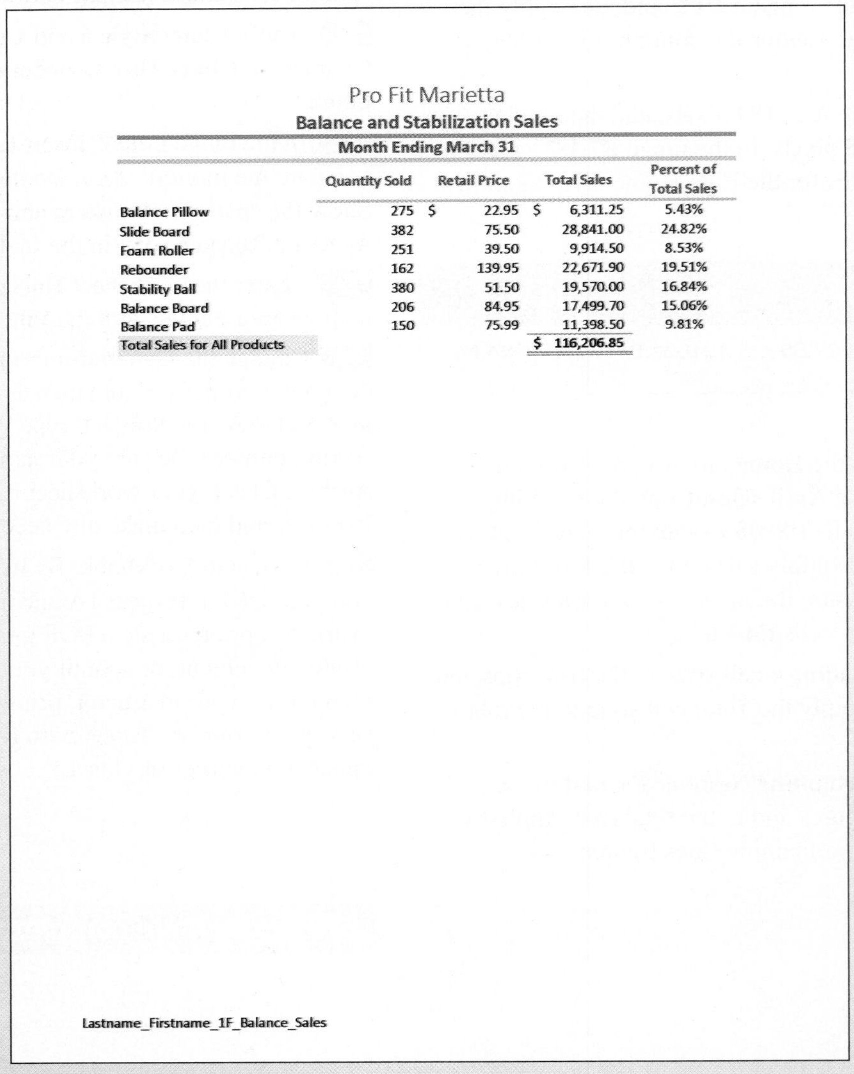

Pro Fit Marietta

Balance and Stabilization Sales

Month Ending March 31

	Quantity Sold	Retail Price	Total Sales	Percent of Total Sales
Balance Pillow	275	$ 22.95	$ 6,311.25	5.43%
Slide Board	382	75.50	28,841.00	24.82%
Foam Roller	251	39.50	9,914.50	8.53%
Rebounder	162	139.95	22,671.90	19.51%
Stability Ball	380	51.50	19,570.00	16.84%
Balance Board	206	84.95	17,499.70	15.06%
Balance Pad	150	75.99	11,398.50	9.81%
Total Sales for All Products			$ 116,206.85	

Lastname_Firstname_1F_Balance_Sales

Excel 2016, Windows 10, Microsoft Corporation

FIGURE 1.59

(Project 1F Balance Sales continues on the next page)

Mastering Excel Project 1F Balance Sales (continued)

1 Start Excel, and then on the opening screen, in the lower left, click **Open Other Workbooks**. Click **Browse**, and then navigate to your student data files for this chapter. Open the file **e01_1F_Balance_Sales**. Click the **File tab**, on the left click **Save A**s, and then click **Browse**. In the **Save As** dialog box, navigate to your **Excel Chapter 1** folder, and then using your own name, save the file as **Lastname_Firstname_1F_Balance_Sales**

2 **Merge & Center** the title and the subtitle across **columns A:F**. Apply the **Title** and **Heading 1** cell styles respectively.

3 Make cell **A1** the active cell, and then check spelling in your worksheet. Correct *Silde* to **Slide**. Widen **column A** to **180 pixels** and **columns B:F** to **95 pixels**.

4 In cell **E4**, construct a formula to calculate the *Total Sales* of the *Balance Pillow* by multiplying the *Quantity Sold* times the *Retail Price*. Copy the formula down for the remaining products.

5 Select the range **E4:E10**, and then use the **Quick Analysis** tool to **Sum** the *Total Sales for All Products*, which will be formatted in Bold. To the total in cell **E11**, apply the **Total** cell style.

6 Using absolute cell references as necessary so that you can copy the formula, in cell **F4**, construct a formula to calculate the *Percent of Total Sales* for the first product. Copy the formula down for the remaining products.

7 To the computed percentages, apply **Percent Style** with two decimal places, and then **Center** the percentages.

8 Apply the **Comma Style** with no decimal places to the *Quantity Sold* figures. To cells **D4**, **E4**, and **E11** apply the **Accounting Number Format**.

9 To the range **D5:E10**, apply the **Comma Style**.

10 Change the *Retail Price* of the *Slide Board* to **75.50** and the *Quantity Sold* of the *Balance Pad* to **150**

11 Delete **column B**.

12 Insert a new **row 3**. In cell **A3**, type **Month Ending March 31** and then **Merge & Center** the text across the range **A3:E3**. Apply the **Heading 2** cell style.

13 To cell **A12**, apply the **20%-Accent1** cell style.

14 Select the four column titles, apply **Wrap Text**, **Middle Align**, and **Center** formatting, and then apply the **Heading 3** cell style.

15 Center the worksheet **Horizontally** on the page, and then insert a **Footer** with the **File Name** in the **left section**.

16 Display the document properties, and then as the **Tags**, type **balance, stability, sales** In the **Subject** box, add your course name and section number. Be sure your name displays as the Author.

17 **Save** your workbook. By using the techniques you practiced in Project 1A and as directed by your instructor, print, create a PDF image that looks like a printed document, or submit your completed Excel file. If required by your instructor, print or create an electronic version of your worksheet with formulas displayed. In the upper right corner of your Excel Window, click **Close**.

> **END | You have completed Project 1F**

Mastering Excel Project 1G Regional Sales

In the following Mastering Excel project, you will create a new worksheet that compares annual sales by region. Your completed worksheet will look similar to Figure 1.60.

Apply a combination of 1A and 1B skills:

1 Create, Save, and Navigate an Excel Workbook

2 Enter Data in a Worksheet

3 Construct and Copy Formulas and Use the SUM Function

4 Format Cells with Merge & Center, Cell Styles, and Themes

5 Chart Data to Create a Column Chart and Insert Sparklines

6 Print a Worksheet, Display Formulas, and Close Excel

7 Check Spelling in a Worksheet

8 Enter Data by Range

9 Construct Formulas for Mathematical Operations

10 Edit Values in a Worksheet

11 Format a Worksheet

PROJECT FILES

For Project 1G, you will need the following file:

e01G_Regional_Sales

You will save your workbook as

Lastname_Firstname_1G_Regional_Sales

PROJECT RESULTS

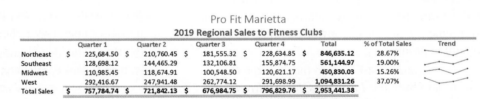

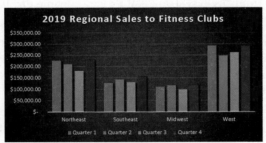

Lastname_Firstname_1G_Regional_Sales

FIGURE 1.60

(Project 1G Regional Sales continues on the next page)

Mastering Excel | Project 1G Regional Sales Project 1G (continued)

1 Start Excel, and then on the opening screen, in the lower left, click **Open Other Workbooks**. Click **Browse**, and then navigate to your student data files for this chapter. Open the file **e01_1G_Regional_Sales**. Click the **File tab**, on the left click **Save As**, and then click **Browse**. In the **Save As** dialog box, navigate to your **Excel Chapter 1** folder, and then using your own name, save the file as **Lastname_Firstname_1G_Regional_Sales**

2 Change the **Theme** to **Retrospect**. Set the width of **column A** to **80 pixels** and the width of columns **B:H** to **110 pixels**.

3 **Merge & Center** the title across the range **A1:H1**, and then apply the **Title** cell style. **Merge & Center** the subtitle across the range **A2:H2**, and then apply the **Heading 1** cell style.

4 Select the seven column titles, apply **Center** formatting, and then apply the **Heading 4** cell style.

5 By using the **Quick Analysis** tool, **Sum** the *Quarter 1* sales, and then copy the formula across for the remaining Quarters; the Quick Analysis tool formats totals in Bold.

6 Select the *Northeast* sales for the four quarters, and then display the **Quick Analysis** gallery for **Totals**. Click the second **Sum** option—the sixth item in the gallery—which displays the column selection in yellow. Copy the formula down through cell **F7**; recall that the Quick Analysis tool formats sums in Bold.

7 Apply the **Accounting Number Format** to the first row of sales figures and to the total row. Apply the **Comma Style** to the remaining sales figures. Format the totals in **row 7** with the **Total** cell style.

8 **Insert** a new **row 6** with the row title **Midwest** and the following sales figures for each quarter: **110985.45** and **118674.91** and **100548.50** and **120621.17** Copy the formula in cell **F5** down to cell **F6** to sum the new row.

9 Using absolute cell references as necessary so that you can copy the formula, in cell **G4** construct a formula to calculate the *Percent of Total Sales* for the first region. Copy the formula down for the remaining regions.

10 To the computed percentages, apply **Percent Style** with two decimal places, and then **Center** the percentages.

11 Insert **Line** sparklines in the range **H4:H7** that compare the quarterly data. Do not include the totals. Show the sparkline **Markers** and apply the second style in the second row—**Sparkline Style Accent 2, Darker 25%**.

12 **Save** your workbook. To compare the quarterly sales of each region visually, select the range that represents the sales figures for the four quarters, including the quarter names and each region—do not include any totals in the range. With this data selected, by using the **Recommended Charts** command, insert a **Clustered Column** with the regions as the category axis and the Quarters as the legend.

13 Apply **Chart Style 8** and **Color 3** under **Colorful**. Position the chart so that its upper right corner aligns with the upper right corner of cell **F10**.

14 Change the **Chart Title** to **2019 Regional Sales to Fitness Clubs**

15 Deselect the chart. Change the page **Orientation** to **Landscape**, center the worksheet **Horizontally** on the page, and then insert a footer with the file name in the left section.

16 Show the document properties. As the **Tags**, type **fitness clubs, sales** In the **Subject** box, type your course name and section number. Be sure your name displays as the Author.

17 **Save** your workbook. By using the techniques you practiced in Project 1A and as directed by your instructor, print, create a PDF image that looks like a printed document, or submit your completed Excel file. If required by your instructor, print or create an electronic version of your worksheet with formulas displayed. In the upper right corner of your Excel Window, click **Close**.

> **END | You have completed Project 1G**

GO! Fix It	Project 1H Team Sales	MyITLab
GO! Make It	Project 1I Agility Sales	MyITLab
GO! Solve It	Project 1J Kettlebell Sales	MyITLab
GO! Solve It	Project 1K Commission	

PROJECT FILES

For Project 1K, you will need the following file:

e01K_Commission

You will save your workbook as:

Lastname_Firstname_1K_Commission

Open the file e01K_Commission and save it as **Lastname_Firstname_1K_Commission** Complete the worksheet by using Auto Fill to complete the month headings, and then calculating the Total Commission for each month and for each region. Insert and format appropriate sparklines in the Trend column. Format the worksheet attractively with a title and subtitle, check spelling, adjust column width, and apply appropriate financial formatting. Insert a chart that compares the total sales commission for each region with the months displaying as the categories, and format the chart attractively. Include the file name in the footer, add appropriate properties, and submit as directed.

Performance Level

Performance Criteria		Exemplary: You consistently applied the relevant skills	Proficient: You sometimes, but not always, applied the relevant skills	Developing: You rarely or never applied the relevant skills
	Create formulas	All formulas are correct and are efficiently constructed.	Formulas are correct but not always constructed in the most efficient manner.	One or more formulas are missing or incorrect; or only numbers were entered.
	Create a chart	Chart created properly.	Chart was created but incorrect data was selected.	No chart was created.
	Insert and format sparklines	Sparklines inserted and formatted properly.	Sparklines were inserted but incorrect data was selected or sparklines were not formatted.	No sparklines were inserted.
	Format attractively and appropriately	Formatting is attractive and appropriate.	Adequately formatted but difficult to read or unattractive.	Inadequate or no formatting.

END | You have completed Project 1K

RUBRIC

The following outcomes-based assessments are *open-ended assessments*. That is, there is no specific correct result; your result will depend on your approach to the information provided. Make *Professional Quality* your goal. Use the following scoring rubric to guide you in *how* to approach the problem and then to evaluate *how well* your approach solves the problem.

The *criteria*—Software Mastery, Content, Format and Layout, and Process—represent the knowledge and skills you have gained that you can apply to solving the problem. The *levels of performance*—Professional Quality, Approaching Professional Quality, or Needs Quality Improvements—help you and your instructor evaluate your result.

	Your completed project is of Professional Quality if you:	Your completed project is Approaching Professional Quality if you:	Your completed project Needs Quality Improvements if you:
1-Software Mastery	Choose and apply the most appropriate skills, tools, and features and identify efficient methods to solve the problem.	Choose and apply some appropriate skills, tools, and features, but not in the most efficient manner.	Choose inappropriate skills, tools, or features, or are inefficient in solving the problem.
2-Content	Construct a solution that is clear and well organized, contains content that is accurate, appropriate to the audience and purpose, and is complete. Provide a solution that contains no errors of spelling, grammar, or style.	Construct a solution in which some components are unclear, poorly organized, inconsistent, or incomplete. Misjudge the needs of the audience. Have some errors in spelling, grammar, or style, but the errors do not detract from comprehension.	Construct a solution that is unclear, incomplete, or poorly organized, contains some inaccurate or inappropriate content, and contains many errors of spelling, grammar, or style. Do not solve the problem.
3-Format and Layout	Format and arrange all elements to communicate information and ideas, clarify function, illustrate relationships, and indicate relative importance.	Apply appropriate format and layout features to some elements, but not others. Overuse features, causing minor distraction.	Apply format and layout that does not communicate information or ideas clearly. Do not use format and layout features to clarify function, illustrate relationships, or indicate relative importance. Use available features excessively, causing distraction.
4-Process	Use an organized approach that integrates planning, development, self-assessment, revision, and reflection.	Demonstrate an organized approach in some areas, but not others; or, use an insufficient process of organization throughout.	Do not use an organized approach to solve the problem.

| Apply a combination of the **1A** and **1B** skills. | **GO! Think**   Project 1L Video Sales |

PROJECT FILES

Build From Scratch

For Project 1L, you will need the following file:

New blank Excel workbook

You will save your workbook as:

Lastname_Firstname_1L_Video_Sales

Michelle Barry, President of Pro Fit Marietta, needs a worksheet that summarizes the following data regarding the first quarter sales of training videos. Michelle would like the worksheet to include a calculation of the total sales for each type of video and a total of the sales of all of the videos. She would also like to know each type of video's percentage of total sales.

	Number Sold	Price
Pilates	156	29.99
Step	392	14.99
Weight Training	147	54.99
Kickboxing	282	29.99
Yoga	165	34.99

Create a worksheet that provides Michelle with the information needed. Include appropriate worksheet, column, and row titles. Using the formatting skills that you practiced in this chapter, format the worksheet in a manner that is professional and easy to read and understand. Insert a footer with the file name and add appropriate document properties. Save the file as **Lastname_Firstname_1L_Video_Sales** and print or submit as directed by your instructor.

END | You have completed Project 1L

Build From Scratch

| **GO! Think**   Project 1M Expenses | **MyITLab** |

Build From Scratch

| **You and GO!**   Project 1N Personal Expenses | **MyITLab** |

Build From Scratch

| **GO! Collaborative Team Project** | **Project 1O Bell Orchid Hotels**   **MyITLab** |

Using Functions, Creating Tables, and Managing Large Workbooks

2

PROJECT 2A

OUTCOMES
Analyze inventory by applying statistical and logical calculations to data and by sorting and filtering data.

OBJECTIVES

1. Use Flash Fill and the SUM, AVERAGE, MEDIAN, MIN, and MAX Functions
2. Move Data, Resolve Error Messages, and Rotate Text
3. Use COUNTIF and IF Functions and Apply Conditional Formatting
4. Use Date & Time Functions and Freeze Panes
5. Create, Sort, and Filter an Excel Table
6. View, Format, and Print a Large Worksheet

PROJECT 2B

OUTCOMES
Summarize the data on multiple worksheets.

OBJECTIVES

7. Navigate a Workbook and Rename Worksheets
8. Enter Dates, Clear Contents, and Clear Formats
9. Copy and Paste by Using the Paste Options Gallery
10. Edit and Format Multiple Worksheets at the Same Time
11. Create a Summary Sheet with Column Sparklines
12. Format and Print Multiple Worksheets in a Workbook

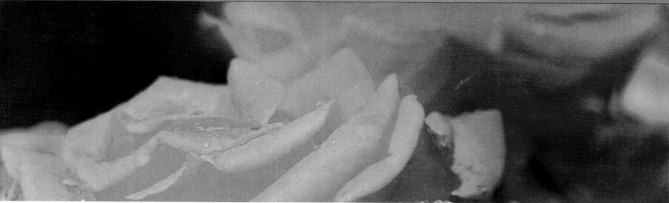

Jbd30/Shutterstock

In This Chapter GO! to Work with Excel

In this chapter, you will use the Statistical functions to calculate the average of a group of numbers and perform other summary calculations. You will also use Logical and Date & Time functions. Excel's statistical functions are useful for common calculations that you probably encounter frequently. You will also use Excel's Flash Fill feature to automatically fill in values, use the counting functions, and apply different types of conditional formatting to make data easy to visualize. You will create a table to organize related information and analyze the table's information by sorting and filtering. You will summarize a workbook that contains multiple worksheets.

The projects in this chapter relate to **Rosedale Landscape and Garden**, which grows and sells trees and plants suitable for all areas of North America. Throughout its 75-year history, the company has introduced many new plants for the enjoyment of home gardeners. The company has nurseries and stores in the major metropolitan areas in the United States and Canada. In addition to high-quality plants and trees, Rosedale sells garden tools and outdoor furniture. Rosedale also offers professional landscape design and installation for both commercial and residential clients. The company headquarters is in Pasadena, California.

PROJECT
2A

Inventory Status Report

MyITLab
Project 2A Training
Project 2A Grader

PROJECT ACTIVITIES

In Activities 2.01 through 2.20, you will edit a worksheet for Holman Hill, President of Rosedale Landscape and Garden, detailing the current inventory of trees at the Pasadena nursery. Your completed worksheet will look similar to Figure 2.1.

PROJECT FILES

MyITLab
grader

If your instructor wants you to submit Project 2A in the MyITLab Grader system, log in to MyITLab, locate Grader Project 2A, and then download the files for this project.

For Project 2A, you will need the following file:

e02A_Tree_Inventory

You will save your workbook as:

Lastname_Firstname_2A_Tree_Inventory

Please always review the downloaded Grader instructions before beginning.

PROJECT RESULTS

GO!
Walk Thru
Project 2A

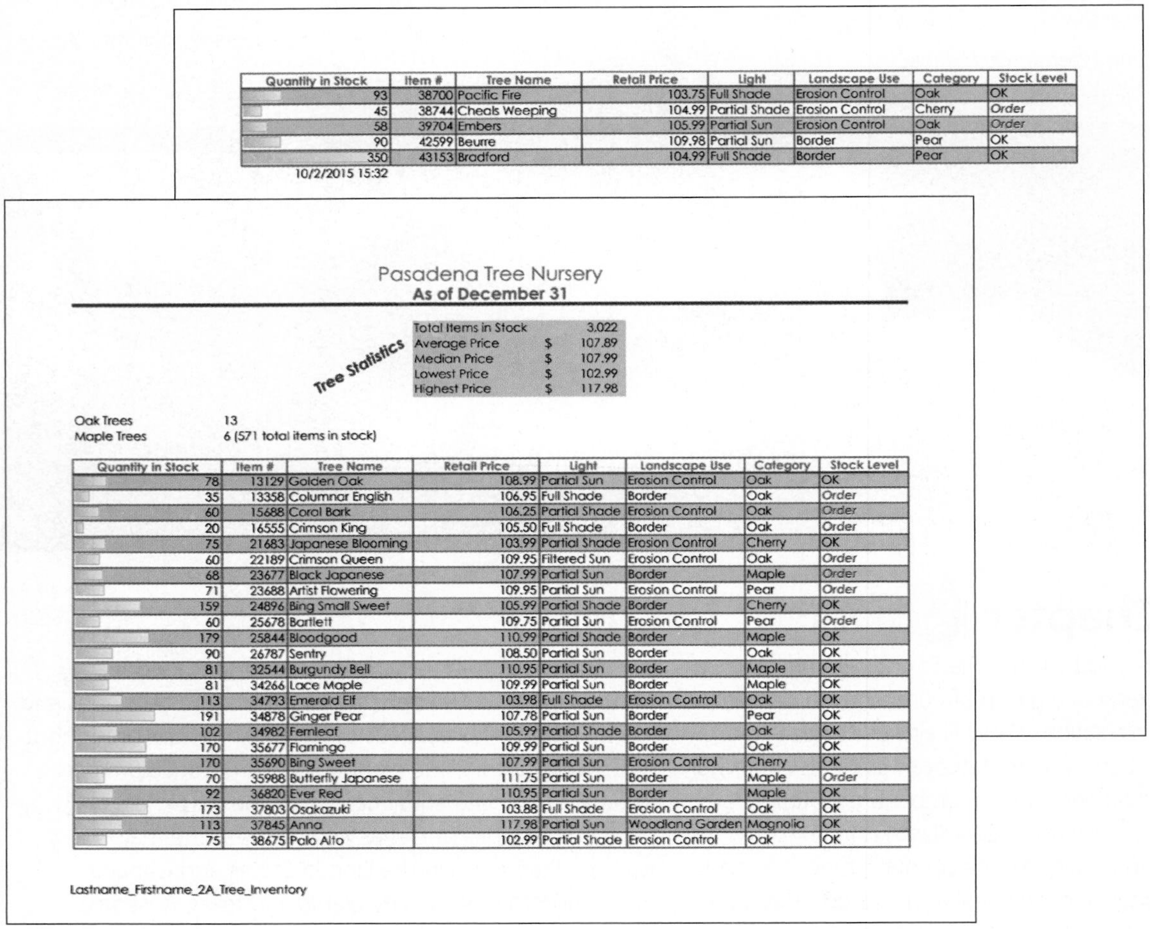

Quantity in Stock	Item #	Tree Name	Retail Price	Light	Landscape Use	Category	Stock Level
93	38700	Pacific Fire	103.75	Full Shade	Erosion Control	Oak	OK
45	38744	Cheals Weeping	104.99	Partial Shade	Erosion Control	Cherry	Order
58	39704	Embers	105.99	Partial Sun	Erosion Control	Oak	Order
90	42599	Beurre	109.98	Partial Sun	Border	Pear	OK
350	43153	Bradford	104.99	Full Shade	Border	Pear	OK

10/2/2015 15:32

Pasadena Tree Nursery
As of December 31

Tree Statistics

Total Items in Stock	3,022
Average Price	$ 107.89
Median Price	$ 107.99
Lowest Price	$ 102.99
Highest Price	$ 117.98

Oak Trees 13
Maple Trees 6 (571 total items in stock)

Quantity in Stock	Item #	Tree Name	Retail Price	Light	Landscape Use	Category	Stock Level
78	13129	Golden Oak	108.99	Partial Sun	Erosion Control	Oak	OK
35	13358	Columnar English	106.95	Full Shade	Border	Oak	Order
60	15688	Coral Bark	106.25	Partial Shade	Erosion Control	Oak	Order
20	16555	Crimson King	105.50	Full Shade	Border	Oak	Order
75	21683	Japanese Blooming	103.99	Partial Shade	Erosion Control	Cherry	OK
60	22189	Crimson Queen	109.95	Filtered Sun	Erosion Control	Oak	Order
68	23677	Black Japanese	107.99	Partial Sun	Border	Maple	Order
71	23688	Artist Flowering	109.95	Partial Sun	Erosion Control	Pear	Order
159	24896	Bing Small Sweet	105.99	Partial Shade	Border	Cherry	OK
60	25678	Bartlett	109.75	Partial Sun	Erosion Control	Pear	Order
179	25844	Bloodgood	110.99	Partial Shade	Border	Maple	OK
90	26787	Sentry	108.50	Partial Sun	Border	Oak	OK
81	32544	Burgundy Bell	110.95	Partial Sun	Border	Maple	OK
81	34266	Lace Maple	109.99	Partial Sun	Border	Maple	OK
113	34793	Emerald Elf	103.98	Full Shade	Erosion Control	Oak	OK
191	34878	Ginger Pear	107.78	Partial Sun	Border	Pear	OK
102	34982	Fernleaf	105.99	Partial Shade	Border	Oak	OK
170	35677	Flamingo	109.99	Partial Sun	Border	Oak	OK
170	35690	Bing Sweet	107.99	Partial Sun	Erosion Control	Cherry	OK
70	35988	Butterfly Japanese	111.75	Partial Sun	Border	Maple	Order
92	36820	Ever Red	110.95	Partial Sun	Border	Maple	OK
173	37803	Osakazuki	103.88	Full Shade	Erosion Control	Oak	OK
113	37845	Anna	117.98	Partial Sun	Woodland Garden	Magnolia	OK
75	38675	Palo Alto	102.99	Partial Shade	Erosion Control	Oak	OK

Lastname_Firstname_2A_Tree_Inventory

Excel 2016, Windows 10, Microsoft Corporation

FIGURE 2.1

GO! Learn How
Video E2-1

Flash Fill recognizes a pattern in your data, and then automatically fills in values when you enter examples of the output that you want. Use Flash Fill to split data into two or more cells or to combine data from two cells.

A *function* is the name given to a predefined formula—a formula that Excel has already built for you—that performs calculations by using specific values that you insert in a particular order or structure. *Statistical functions*, which include the AVERAGE, MEDIAN, MIN, and MAX functions, are useful to analyze a group of measurements.

Activity 2.01 | Using Flash Fill

ALERT!   **To submit as an autograded project, log into MyITLab and download the files for this project, and begin with those files instead of e02A_Tree_Inventory.**

1 Start Excel, and then in the lower left corner of Excel's opening screen, click **Open Other Workbooks**.

2 Click **Browse**. Navigate to the student files that accompany this chapter, and then locate and open **e02A_Tree_Inventory**. Press F12 to display the **Save As** dialog box, and then navigate to the location where you are storing your projects for this chapter.

3 Create a new folder named **Excel Chapter 2** and then open the new folder. In the **File name** box, type **Lastname_Firstname_2A_Tree_Inventory** and then click **Save** or press Enter.

4 Scroll down. Notice that the worksheet contains data related to types of trees in inventory, including information about the *Quantity in Stock*, *Item #/Category*, *Tree Name*, *Retail Price*, *Light*, and *Landscape Use*.

5 In the **column heading area**, point to **column C** to display the ↓ pointer, and then drag to the right to select **columns C:D**. On the **Home tab**, in the **Cells group**, click the **Insert button arrow**, and then click **Insert Sheet Columns**.

New columns for C and D display and the remaining columns move to the right.

↻ ANOTHER WAY   Select the columns, right-click anywhere over the selected columns, and then on the shortcut menu, click Insert.

6 Click cell **C11**, type **13129** and then on the **Formula Bar**, click **Enter** ✓ to confirm the entry and keep **C11** as the active cell.

7 On the **Home tab**, in the **Editing group**, click **Fill**, and then click **Flash Fill**. Compare your screen with Figure 2.2.

Use this technique to split a column of data based on what you type. Flash Fill looks to the left and sees the pattern you have established, and then fills the remaining cells in the column with only the Item #. The Flash Fill Options button displays.

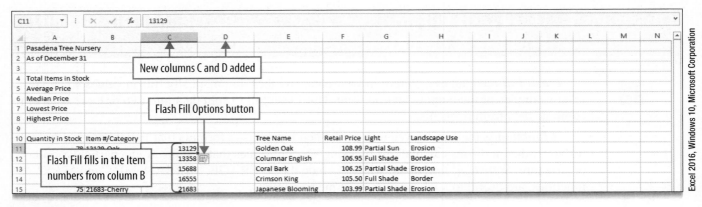

FIGURE 2.2

8 Near the lower right corner of cell **C11**, click the **Flash Fill Options** button, and notice that here you can *Undo Flash Fill*, *Accept suggestions*, or *Select all 28 changed cells*, for example, to apply specific formatting. Click the button again to close it.

> If Excel is not sure what pattern to use, it suggests a pattern by filling with pale gray characters, and then you can use the Accept suggestions command to accept or start again.

9 Click cell **D11**, type **Oak** and then on the **Formula Bar**, click ✓ to confirm the entry and keep **D11** as the active cell. Press Ctrl + E, which is the keyboard shortcut for Flash Fill.

> Flash Fill extracts the text from the *Item#/Category* column and also inserts *Category* as the column name. Now that *Item #* and *Category* are in two separate columns, the data can be sorted and filtered by both Item # and Category.

10 Select **column B**, and then in the **Cells group**, click the **Delete button arrow**. Click **Delete Sheet Columns**. On the Quick Access Toolbar, click **Save** 🖫.

🔁 ANOTHER WAY   Select the column, right-click anywhere over the selected column, and then on the shortcut menu, click Delete.

Activity 2.02 | Moving a Column

1 In cell **B10**, type **Item #** and then press Enter. Select **column C**, and then on the **Home tab**, in the **Clipboard group**, click **Cut** ✂. Click cell **H1**, and then in the **Clipboard group**, click the upper portion of the **Paste** button.

🔁 ANOTHER WAY   Press Ctrl + X to cut and Ctrl + V to paste.

2 Select and then delete **column C**. Select **columns A:G**. In the **Cells group**, click **Format**, and then click **AutoFit Column Width**.

🔁 ANOTHER WAY   Select the columns, in the column heading area point to any of the selected column borders to display the ✛ pointer, and then double-click to AutoFit the columns.

3 **Merge & Center** cell **A1** across the range **A1:H1**, and then apply the **Title** cell style. **Merge & Center** cell **A2** across the range **A2:H2**, and then apply the **Heading 1** cell style. Compare your screen with Figure 2.3. **Save** 🖫 your workbook.

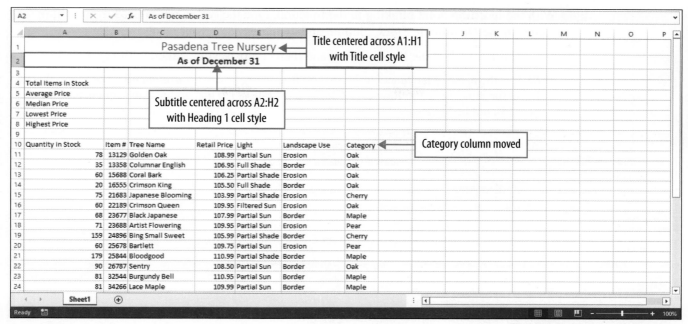

FIGURE 2.3

Excel 2016, Windows 10, Microsoft Corporation

Activity 2.03 | Using the SUM and AVERAGE Functions

In this Activity, you will use the SUM and AVERAGE functions to gather information about the product inventory.

MOS
4.1.2, 4.1.5

1 Click cell **B4**. Click the **Formulas tab**, and then in the **Function Library group**, click the upper portion of the **AutoSum** button. Compare your screen with Figure 2.4.

The **SUM function** is a predefined formula that adds all the numbers in a selected range of cells. Because it is frequently used, there are several ways to insert the function. For example, you can insert the function from the Home tab's Editing group, or by using the keyboard shortcut [Alt] + [=], or from the Function Library group on the Formulas tab, or from the Math & Trig button in that group.

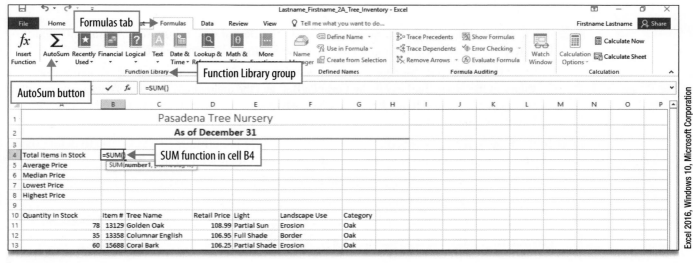

FIGURE 2.4

2 With the insertion point blinking in the function, type the cell range **a11:a39** to sum all the values in the *Quantity in Stock* column, and then press Enter; your result is *3022*.

3 Click cell **B4**, look at the **Formula Bar**, and then compare your screen with Figure 2.5.

> *SUM* is the name of the function. The values in parentheses are the ***arguments***—the values that an Excel function uses to perform calculations or operations. In this instance, the argument consists of the values in the range A11:A39.

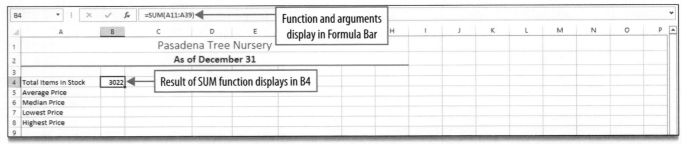

FIGURE 2.5

4 Click cell **B5**. In the **Function Library group**, click **More Functions**, point to **Statistical**, point to **AVERAGE**, and notice the ScreenTip. Compare your screen with Figure 2.6.

> The ScreenTip describes how the AVERAGE function will compute the calculation.

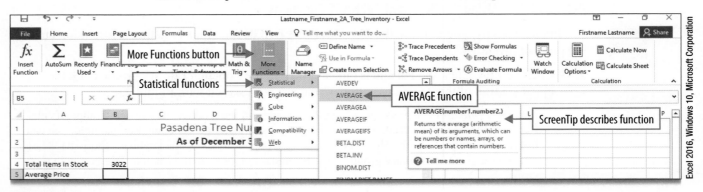

FIGURE 2.6

5 Click **AVERAGE**, and then if necessary, drag the title bar of the Function Arguments dialog box down and to the right so you can view the Formula Bar and cell B5.

> The ***AVERAGE function*** adds a group of values, and then divides the result by the number of values in the group. In the cell, the Formula Bar, and the dialog box, Excel proposes to average the value in cell B4. Recall that Excel functions will propose a range if there is data above or to the left of a selected cell.

6 In the **Function Arguments** dialog box, notice that *B4* is highlighted. Press Del to delete the existing text, type **d11:d39** and then compare your screen with Figure 2.7.

> Because you want to average the Retail Price values in the range D11:D39—and not cell B4—you must edit the proposed range.

Excel 2016, Windows 10, Microsoft Corporation

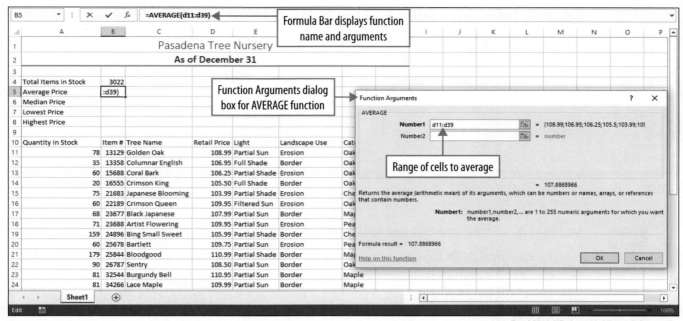

FIGURE 2.7

7 In the **Function Arguments** dialog box, click **OK**, and then click **Save**.

The result indicates that the average Retail Price of all products is *107.89*.

Activity 2.04 | Using the MEDIAN Function

The ***MEDIAN function*** is a statistical function that describes a group of data—it is commonly used to describe the price of houses in a particular geographical area. The MEDIAN function finds the middle value that has as many values above it in the group as are below it. It differs from AVERAGE in that the result is not affected as much by a single value that is greatly different from the others.

1 Click cell **B6**. In the **Function Library group**, click **More Functions**, display the list of **Statistical** functions, scroll down as necessary, and then click **MEDIAN**.

2 Press Del to delete the text in the **Number1** box. Type **d11:d39** and then compare your screen with Figure 2.8.

When indicating which cells you want to use in the function's calculation—known as *defining the arguments*—you can either select the values with your mouse or type the range of values, whichever you prefer.

Excel 2016, Windows 10, Microsoft Corporation

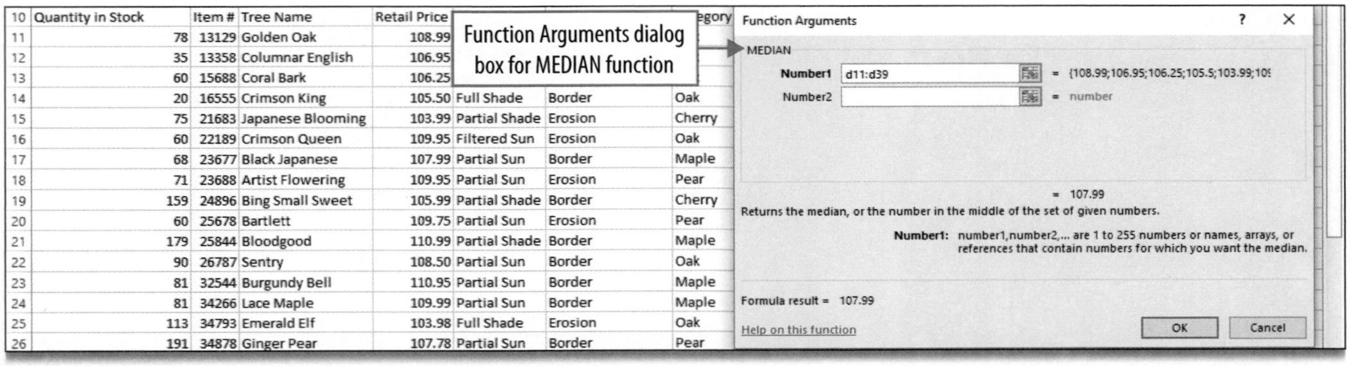

FIGURE 2.8

3 Click **OK** to display *107.99* in cell **B6**. Click **Save** 🖫 and compare your screen with Figure 2.9.

In the range of prices, 107.99 is the middle value. Half of all trees in inventory are priced *above* 107.99 and half are priced *below* 107.99.

	A	B	C	D	E	F	G	H	I	J	K	L	M	N	O	P
4	Total Items in Stock	3022														
5	Average Price	107.89														
6	Median Price	107.99	Median Price													
7	Lowest Price															
8	Highest Price															
9																

B6 ▾ : × ✓ fx =MEDIAN(D11:D39)

FIGURE 2.9

MOS
4.1.3

Activity 2.05 | Using the MIN and MAX Functions

The statistical ***MIN function*** determines the smallest value in a selected range of values. The statistical ***MAX function*** determines the largest value in a selected range of values.

1 Click cell **B7**. On the **Formulas tab**, in the **Function Library group**, click **More Functions**, display the list of **Statistical** functions, scroll as necessary, and then click **MIN**.

2 Press ⌈Del⌉, and then in the **Number1** box, type **d11:d39** Click **OK**.

The lowest Retail Price is *102.99*.

3 Click cell **B8**, and then by using a similar technique, insert the **MAX** function to determine the highest **Retail Price**, and then check to see that your result is *117.98*.

4 Press ⌈Ctrl⌉ + ⌈Home⌉. Point to cell **B4**, right-click, and then on the mini toolbar, click **Comma Style** ⌈ ʼ ⌉ one time and **Decrease Decimal** ⌈.00→.0⌉ two times.

5 Select the range **B5:B8**, apply the **Accounting Number Format** ⌈$ ▾⌉, click **Save** 🖫, and then compare your screen with Figure 2.10.

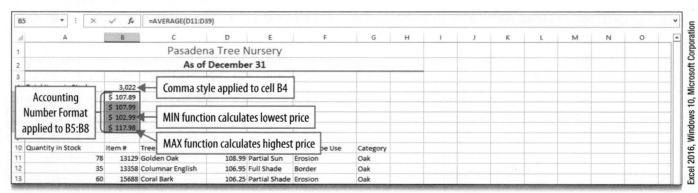

B5 ▾ : × ✓ fx =AVERAGE(D11:D39)

	A	B	C	D	E	F	G	H	I	J	K	L	M	N	O
1			Pasadena Tree Nursery												
2			As of December 31												
3															
	Total Items in Stock	3,022	Comma style applied to cell B4												
5	Average Price	$ 107.89													
6	Median Price	$ 107.99													
7	Lowest Price	$ 102.99	MIN function calculates lowest price												
8	Highest Price	$ 117.98													
			MAX function calculates highest price				Use	Category							
10	Quantity in Stock	Item #	Tree												
11	78	13129	Golden Oak	108.99	Partial Sun	Erosion	Oak								
12	35	13358	Columnar English	106.95	Full Shade	Border	Oak								
13	60	15688	Coral Bark	106.25	Partial Shade	Erosion	Oak								

Accounting Number Format applied to B5:B8

FIGURE 2.10

GO! Learn How
Video E2-2

When you move a formula, the cell references within the formula do not change, no matter what type of cell reference you use.

If you move cells into a column that is not wide enough to display number values, Excel will display a message so that you can adjust as necessary.

You can reposition data within a cell at an angle by rotating the text.

Activity 2.06 | Moving Data and Resolving a # # # # # Error Message

1 Select **column E** and set the width to **50 pixels**. Select the range **A4:B8**. Point to the right edge of the selected range to display the pointer, and then compare your screen with Figure 2.11.

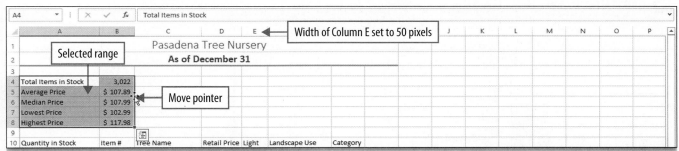

Excel 2016, Windows 10, Microsoft Corporation

FIGURE 2.11

2 Drag the selected range to the right until the ScreenTip displays *D4:E8*, release the mouse button, and then notice that a series of # symbols displays in **column E**. Point to any of the cells that display # symbols, and then compare your screen with Figure 2.12.

Using this technique, cell contents can be moved from one location to another; this is referred to as *drag and drop*.

If a cell width is too narrow to display the entire number, Excel displays the ##### message, because displaying only a portion of a number would be misleading. The underlying values remain unchanged and are displayed in the Formula Bar for the selected cell. An underlying value also displays in the ScreenTip if you point to a cell containing # symbols.

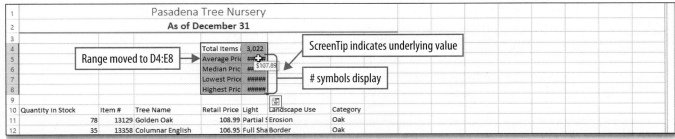

Excel 2016, Windows 10, Microsoft Corporation

FIGURE 2.12

3 Select **columns D:E**, and then in the **column heading area**, point to the right boundary of **column E** to display the pointer. Double-click to AutoFit the column to accommodate the widest entry.

4 Select the range **D4:E8**. On the **Home tab**, in the **Styles group**, display the **Cell Styles** gallery. Under **Themed Cell Styles**, click **20%-Accent1**. Click **Save**.

Activity 2.07 | Rotating Text

1 In cell **C6**, type **Tree Statistics** and then press Enter.

2 Select cell **C6**. On the **Home tab**, in the **Font group**, change the **Font Size** `11 ▾` to **14**, and then apply **Bold** `B` and **Italic** `I`. Click the **Font Color arrow** `A ▾`, and then in the fifth column, click the first color—**Blue, Accent 1**.

3 In the **Alignment group**, apply **Align Right** `≡`.

4 Select the range **C4:C8**, right-click over the selection, and then on the shortcut menu, click **Format Cells**. In the **Format Cells** dialog box, click the **Alignment tab**. Under **Text control**, select the **Merge cells** check box.

5 Under **Orientation**, click in the **Degrees** box to select the value, type **30** and then compare your screen with Figure 2.13.

⟳ **ANOTHER WAY**   In the upper right portion of the dialog box, under Orientation, point to the red diamond, and then drag the diamond upward until the Degrees box indicates 30.

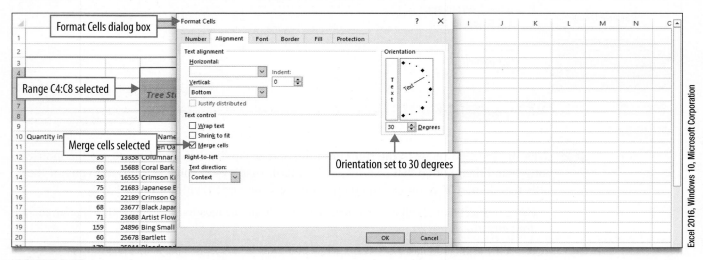

FIGURE 2.13

6 In the lower right corner of the **Format Cells** dialog box, click **OK**. Press Ctrl + Home, **Save** `💾` your workbook, and then compare your screen with Figure 2.14.

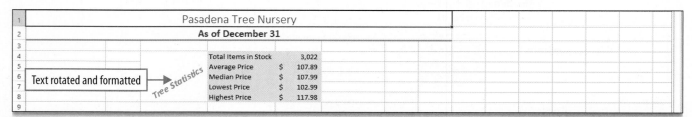

FIGURE 2.14

Excel 2016, Windows 10, Microsoft Corporation

7 In the **row heading area**, point to **row 9** and right-click to select the row and display the shortcut menu. Click **Insert**, and then press F4 two times to repeat the last action and insert two additional blank rows.

> F4 is useful to repeat commands in Microsoft Office programs. Most commands can be repeated in this manner.

8 ▸ From the **row heading area**, select **rows 9:11**. On the **Home tab**, in the **Editing group**, click **Clear** and then click **Clear Formats** to remove the blue accent color in columns D and E from the new rows. Click **Save** 🔲.

> When you insert rows or columns, formatting from adjacent rows or columns repeats in the new cells.

9 ▸ Click cell **E4**, look at the **Formula Bar**, and then notice that the arguments of the **SUM** function adjusted and refer to the appropriate cells in rows 14:42.

> The referenced range updates to *A14:A42* after you insert the three new rows. In this manner, Excel adjusts the cell references in a formula relative to their new locations.

Objective 3 | Use COUNTIF and IF Functions and Apply Conditional Formatting

GO! Learn How
Video E2-3

Recall that statistical functions analyze a group of measurements. Another group of Excel functions, referred to as *logical functions*, test for specific conditions. Logical functions typically use conditional tests to determine whether specified conditions—called *criteria*—are true or false.

Activity 2.08 | Using the COUNTIF Function

MOS
4.1.4, 4.2.4

The *COUNT function* counts the number of cells in a range that contain numbers. The *COUNTIF function* is a statistical function that counts the number of cells within a range that meet the given condition—the criteria that you provide. The COUNTIF function has two arguments—the range of cells to check and the criteria.

The trees of Rosedale Landscape and Garden will be featured on an upcoming segment of a TV gardening show. In this Activity, you will use the COUNTIF function to determine the number of *Oak* trees currently available in inventory that can be featured in the TV show.

1 ▸ In cell **A10**, type **Oak Trees** and then press Tab.

2 ▸ With cell **B10** as the active cell, on the **Formulas tab**, in the **Function Library group**, click **More Functions**, and then display the list of **Statistical** functions. Click **COUNTIF**.

> Recall that the COUNTIF function counts the number of cells within a range that meet the given condition.

3 ▸ In the **Range** box, type **g14:g42** Click in the **Criteria** box, type **Oak** and then compare your screen with Figure 2.15.

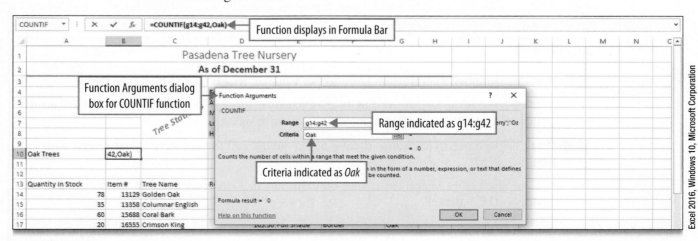

FIGURE 2.15

4 In the lower right corner of the **Function Arguments** dialog box, click **OK**.

There are *13* different *Oak* trees available to feature on the TV show.

5 On the **Home tab**, in the **Alignment group**, click **Align Left** ☰ to place the result closer to the row title. **Save** 🖫 your workbook.

Activity 2.09 | Using the IF Function

A *logical test* is any value or expression that you can evaluate as being true or false. The *IF function* uses a logical test to check whether a condition is met, and then returns one value if true, and another value if false.

For example, *C14=228* is an expression that can be evaluated as true or false. If the value in cell C14 is equal to 228, the expression is true. If the value in cell C14 is not 228, the expression is false.

In this Activity, you will use the IF function to evaluate the inventory levels and determine if more products should be ordered.

1 Click cell **H13**, type **Stock Level** and then press [Enter].

2 In cell **H14**, on the **Formulas tab**, in the **Function Library group**, click **Logical**, and then in the list, click **IF**. Drag the title bar of the **Function Arguments** dialog box up or down to view **row 14** on your screen.

3 With the insertion point in the **Logical_test** box, type **a14<75**

This logical test will look at the value in cell A14, which is *78*, and then determine if the number is less than 75. The expression *<75* includes the *comparison operator*, which means *less than*. Comparison operators compare values.

4 Examine the table in Figure 2.16 for a list of comparison operator symbols and their definitions.

COMPARISON OPERATORS	
COMPARISON OPERATORS	**SYMBOL DEFINITION**
=	Equal to
>	Greater than
<	Less than
>=	Greater than or equal to
<=	Less than or equal to
<>	Not equal to

FIGURE 2.16

5 Press [Tab] to move the insertion point to the **Value_if_true** box, and then type **Order**

If the result of the logical test is true—the Quantity in Stock is less than 75—cell H14 will display the text *Order* indicating that additional trees must be ordered.

6 Press [Tab] to move to the **Value_if_false** box, type **OK** and then compare your screen with Figure 2.17.

If the result of the logical test is false—the Quantity in Stock is *not* less than 75—then Excel will display *OK* in the cell.

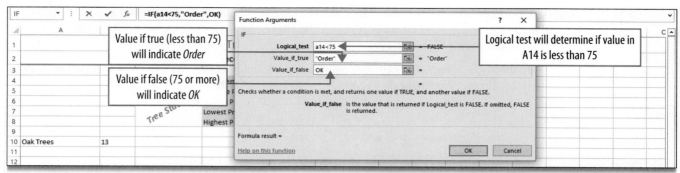

FIGURE 2.17

7 Click **OK** to display the result *OK* in cell **H14**.

8 Using the fill handle, copy the function in cell **H14** down through cell **H42**. Then scroll as necessary to view cell **A18**, which contains the value *75*. Look at cell **H18** and notice that the **Stock Level** is indicated as *OK*. **Save** 🖫 your workbook. Compare your screen with Figure 2.18.

The comparison operator indicated <75 (less than 75) and therefore a value of *exactly* 75 is indicated as OK.

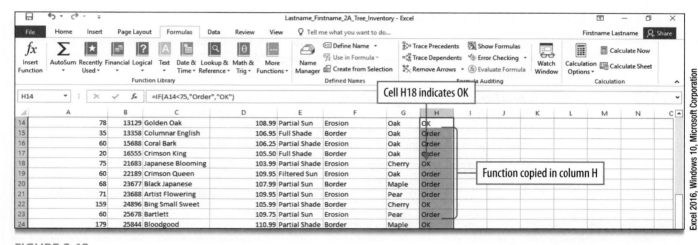

FIGURE 2.18

Activity 2.10 | Applying Conditional Formatting by Using Highlight Cells Rules and Data Bars

2.3.4

A *conditional format* changes the appearance of a cell based on a condition—a criteria. If the condition is true, the cell is formatted based on that condition; if the condition is false, the cell is *not* formatted. In this Activity, you will use conditional formatting as another way to draw attention to the Stock Level of trees.

1 Be sure the range **H14:H42** is selected. On the **Home tab**, in the **Styles group**, click **Conditional Formatting**. In the list, point to **Highlight Cells Rules**, and then click **Text That Contains**.

2 In the **Text That Contains** dialog box, with the insertion point blinking in the first box, type **Order** and notice that in the selected range, the text *Order* displays with the default format— Light Red Fill with Dark Red Text.

3 In the second box, click the **arrow**, and then in the list, click **Custom Format**.

Here, in the Format Cells dialog box, you can select any combination of formats to apply to the cell if the condition is true. The custom format you specify will be applied to any cell in the selected range if it contains the text *Order*.

4 On the **Font tab**, under **Font style**, click **Bold Italic**. Click the **Color arrow**, and then under **Theme Colors**, in the last column, click the first color—**Green, Accent 6**. Click **OK**. Compare your screen with Figure 2.19.

> In the range, if the cell meets the condition of containing *Order*, the font color will change to Bold Italic, Green, Accent 6.

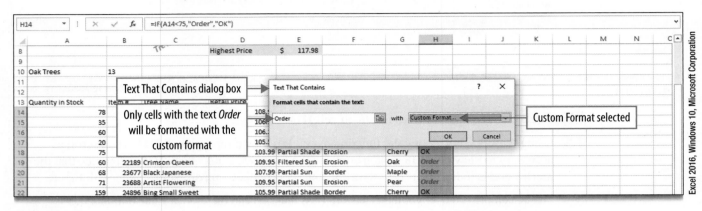

FIGURE 2.19

5 In the **Text That Contains** dialog box, click **OK**.

6 Select the range **A14:A42**. In the **Styles group**, click **Conditional Formatting**. Point to **Data Bars**, and then under **Gradient Fill**, click **Orange Data Bar**. Click anywhere to cancel the selection, click **Save** 🔲, and then compare your screen with Figure 2.20.

> A *data bar* provides a visual cue to the reader about the value of a cell relative to other cells. The length of the data bar represents the value in the cell. A longer bar represents a higher value and a shorter bar represents a lower value. Data bars are useful for identifying higher and lower numbers quickly within a large group of data, such as very high or very low levels of inventory.

FIGURE 2.20

Excel 2016, Windows 10, Microsoft Corporation

1.2.1 and 2.1.1

Activity 2.11 | Using Find and Replace

The **Find and Replace** feature searches the cells in a worksheet—or in a selected range—for matches, and then replaces each match with a replacement value of your choice.

Comments from customers on the company's blog indicate that using the term *Erosion Control* would be clearer than *Erosion* when describing the best landscape use for specific trees. Therefore, all products of this type will be relabeled accordingly. In this Activity, you will replace all occurrences of *Erosion* with *Erosion Control*.

1 Select the range **F14:F42**. On the **Home tab**, in the **Editing group**, click **Find & Select**, and then click **Replace**.

> Restrict the find and replace operation to a specific range in this manner, especially if there is a possibility that the name occurs elsewhere.

2 Type **Erosion** to fill in the **Find what** box. In the **Replace with** box, type **Erosion Control** and then compare your screen with Figure 2.21.

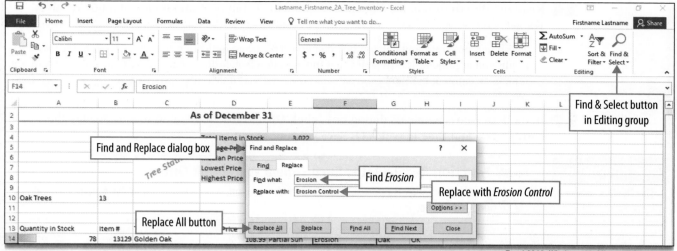

FIGURE 2.21

Excel 2016, Windows 10, Microsoft Corporation

3 Click **Replace All**. In the message box, notice that 13 replacements were made, and then click **OK**. In the lower right corner of the **Find and Replace** dialog box, click **Close**. Click **Save** 🖫.

Objective 4 Use Date & Time Functions and Freeze Panes

GO! Learn How
Video E2-4

Excel can obtain the date and time from your computer's calendar and clock and display this information on your worksheet.

By freezing or splitting panes, you can view two areas of a worksheet and lock rows and columns in one area. When you freeze panes, you select the specific rows or columns that you want to remain visible when scrolling in your worksheet.

Activity 2.12 | Using the NOW Function to Display a System Date

The ***NOW function*** retrieves the date and time from your computer's calendar and clock and inserts the information into the selected cell. The result is formatted as a date and time.

1 To the left of the **Formula Bar**, click in the **Name Box**, type **a44** and then press Enter. Notice that cell A44 is the active cell.

2 With cell **A44** as the active cell, on the **Formulas tab**, in the **Function Library group**, click **Date & Time**. In the list of functions, click **NOW**. Compare your screen with Figure 2.22.

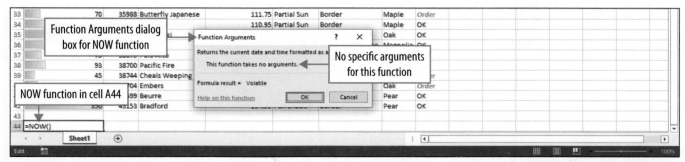

FIGURE 2.22

Excel 2016, Windows 10, Microsoft Corporation

> **3** Read the description in the **Function Arguments** dialog box, and notice that this result is *Volatile*.

> The Function Arguments dialog box displays a message indicating that this function does not require an argument. It also states that this function is ***volatile***, meaning the date and time will not remain as entered, but rather the date and time will automatically update each time you open this workbook.

> **4** In the **Function Arguments** dialog box, click **OK** to close the dialog box to display the current date and time in cell **A44**. **Save** 🖫 your workbook.

More **Knowledge**	**NOW Function Recalculates Each Time a Workbook Opens**

The NOW function updates each time the workbook is opened. With the workbook open, you can force the NOW function to update by pressing F9, for example, to update the time.

1.4.5

Activity 2.13 │ Freezing and Unfreezing Panes

In a large worksheet, if you scroll down more than 25 rows or scroll beyond column O (the exact row number and column letter varies, depending on your screen size and screen resolution), you will no longer see the top rows or first column of your worksheet where identifying information about the data is usually placed. You will find it easier to work with your data if you can always view the identifying row or column titles.

The *Freeze Panes* command enables you to select one or more rows or columns and then freeze (lock) them into place. The locked rows and columns become separate panes. A *pane* is a portion of a worksheet window bounded by and separated from other portions by vertical or horizontal bars.

> **1** Press Ctrl + Home to make cell **A1** the active cell. Scroll down until **row 21** displays at the top of your Excel window, and notice that all of the identifying information in the column titles is out of view.

> **2** Press Ctrl + Home again, and then from the **row heading area**, select **row 14**. Click the **View tab**, and then in the **Window group**, click **Freeze Panes**. In the list, click **Freeze Panes**. Click any cell to deselect the row, and then notice that a line displays along the upper border of **row 14**.

> By selecting row 14, the rows above—rows 1–13—are frozen in place and will not move as you scroll down.

> **3** Watch the row numbers below **row 13**, and then begin to scroll down to bring **row 21** into view again. Notice that rows 1:13 are frozen in place. Compare your screen with Figure 2.23.

> The remaining rows of data continue to scroll. Use this feature when you have long or wide worksheets.

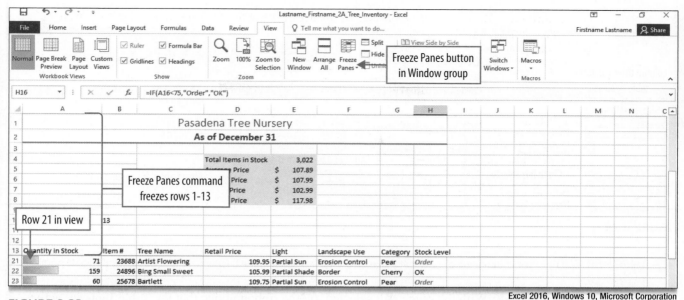

Excel 2016, Windows 10, Microsoft Corporation

FIGURE 2.23

> **4** In the **Window group**, click **Freeze Panes**, and then click **Unfreeze Panes** to unlock all rows and columns. **Save** 🖫 your workbook.

More Knowledge **Freeze Columns or Freeze Both Rows and Columns**

You can freeze columns that you want to remain in view on the left. Select the column to the right of the column(s) that you want to remain in view while scrolling to the right, and then click the Freeze Panes command. You can also use the command to freeze both rows and columns; click a *cell* to freeze the rows *above* the cell and the columns to the *left* of the cell.

Objective 5 | Create, Sort, and Filter an Excel Table

GO! Learn How
Video E2-5

To analyze a group of related data, you can convert a range of cells to an *Excel table*. An Excel table is a series of rows and columns that contains related data that is managed independently from the data in other rows and columns in the worksheet.

3.1.1, 3.2.1

Activity 2.14 | Creating an Excel Table and Applying a Table Style

> **1** Be sure that you have applied the Unfreeze Panes command—no rows on your worksheet are locked. Click any cell in the data below row 13. Click the **Insert tab**. In the **Tables group**, click **Table**. In the **Create Table** dialog box, if necessary, click to select the My table has headers check box, and then compare your screen with Figure 2.24.
>
> The column titles in row 13 will form the table headers. By clicking in a range of contiguous data, Excel will suggest the range as the data for the table. You can adjust the range if necessary.

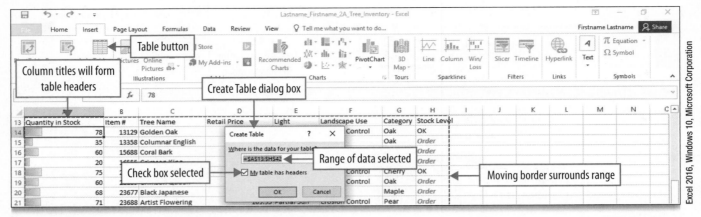

FIGURE 2.24

🔄 **ANOTHER WAY**   Select the range of cells that make up the table, including the header row, and then click the Table button.

▸ 2 ▸ Click **OK**. With the range still selected, on the ribbon notice that the **Table Tools** are active.

▸ 3 ▸ On the **Design tab**, in the **Table Styles group**, click **More** 🔽, and then under **Light**, locate and click **Table Style Light 16**.

▸ 4 ▸ Press Ctrl + Home. Click **Save** 💾, and then compare your screen with Figure 2.25.

Sorting and filtering arrows display in the table's header row.

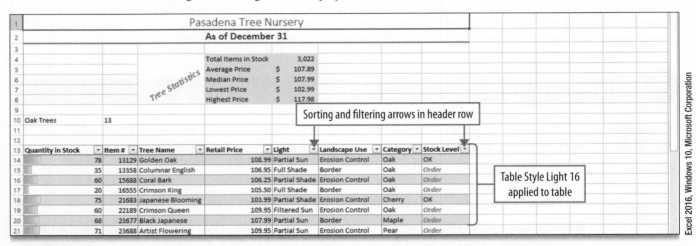

FIGURE 2.25

3.3.2, 3.3.3

Activity 2.15 │ Sorting an Excel Table

You can **sort** tables—arrange all the data in a specific order—in ascending or descending order.

▸ 1 ▸ In the header row of the table, click the **Retail Price arrow**, and then on the menu, click **Sort Smallest to Largest**. Next to the arrow, notice the small **up arrow** indicating an ascending (smallest to largest) sort.

This action sorts the rows in the table from the lowest retail price to highest retail price.

▸ 2 ▸ In the table's header row, click the **Category arrow**, and then click **Sort Z to A**.

This action sorts the rows in the table in reverse alphabetic order by Category name, and the small arrow points downward, indicating a descending (Z to A) sort. The Retail Price continues to be sorted from smallest to largest within each category.

3 Click the **Category arrow**, and then sort from **A to Z**. Next to the arrow, notice the small **up arrow** indicating an ascending (A to Z) sort.

This action sorts the rows in the table alphabetically by Category, and within a Category sorts the rows from smallest to largest by Retail Price.

4 In the table header row, click the **Item # arrow**, and then click **Sort Smallest to Largest**, which will apply an ascending sort to the data using the *Item #* column.

Activity 2.16 | Filtering an Excel Table and Displaying a Total Row

3.2.3, 3.3.1

You can *filter* tables—display only a portion of the data based on matching a specific value—to show only the data that meets the criteria that you specify.

1 Click the **Category arrow**. On the menu, click the **(Select All)** check box to clear all the check boxes. Click to select only the **Maple** check box, and then click **OK**. Compare your screen with Figure 2.26.

Only the rows containing *Maple* in the Category column display—the remaining rows are hidden from view. A small funnel—the filter icon—indicates that a filter is applied to the data in the table. Additionally, the row numbers display in blue to indicate that some rows are hidden from view. A filter hides entire rows in the worksheet.

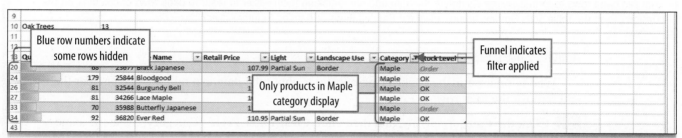

FIGURE 2.26

Excel 2016, Windows 10, Microsoft Corporation

2 Point to the right of *Category*, and notice that *Equals "Maple"* displays to indicate the filter criteria.

3 Click any cell in the table so that the table is selected. Click the **Design tab**, and then in the **Table Style Options group**, select the **Total Row** check box.

Total displays in cell A43. In cell H43, the number *6* indicates that six rows currently display.

4 Click cell **A43**, click the **arrow** that displays to the right of cell **A43**, and then in the list, click **Sum**.

Excel sums only the visible rows in Column A, and indicates that 571 products in the Maple category are in stock. In this manner, you can use an Excel table to quickly find information about a group of data.

5 Click cell **A11**, type **Maple Trees** and press Tab. In cell **B11**, type **6 (571 total items in stock)** and then press Enter.

6 In the table header row, click the **Category arrow**, and then on the menu, click **Clear Filter From "Category"**.

All the rows in the table redisplay.

7 Click the **Landscape Use arrow**, click the **(Select All)** check box to clear all the check boxes, and then click to select the **Erosion Control** check box. Click **OK**.

8 ▶ Click the **Category arrow**, click the **(Select All)** check box to clear all the check boxes, and then click the **Oak** check box. Click **OK**, **Save** 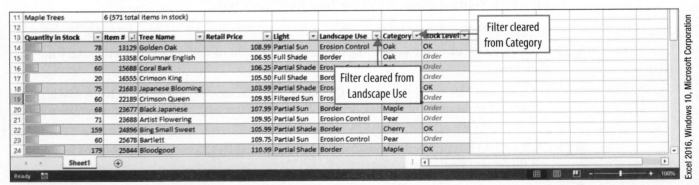 your workbook, and then compare your screen with Figure 2.27.

By applying multiple filters, you can determine quickly that eight tree names identified with a *Landscape Use* of *Erosion Control* are in the *Oak* tree category with a total of 710 such trees in stock.

11	Maple Trees	6 (571 total items in stock)						
12								
13	Quantity in Stock ▾	Item # ▾	Tree Name ▾	Retail Price ▾	Light ▾	Landscape Use ▾	Category ▾	Stock Level ▾
14	78	13129	Golden Oak	108.99	Partial Sun	Erosion Control	Oak	OK
16	60	15688	Coral Bark	106.25	Partial Shade	Erosion Control	Oak	Order
19	60	22189	Crimson Queen	109.95	Filtered Sun	Erosion Control	Oak	Order
28	113	34793	Emerald Elf	103.98	Full Shade	Erosion Control	Oak	OK
35	173	37803	Osakazuki	103.88	Full Shade	Erosion Control	Oak	OK
37	75	38675	Palo Alto	102.99	Partial Shade	Erosion Control	Oak	OK
38	93	38700	Pacific Fire	103.75	Full Shade	Erosion Control	Oak	OK
40	58	39704	Embers	105.99	Partial Sun	Erosion Control	Oak	Order
43	710							8
44	10/1/2015 15:38							

8 tree types in Oak category can be used for Erosion Control

FIGURE 2.27

More **Knowledge** **Band Rows and Columns in a Table**

You can band rows to format even rows differently from odd rows, making them easier to read. To band rows or columns, on the Design tab, in the Table Style Options group, select the Banded Rows or Banded Columns check box.

Activity 2.17 | Clearing Filters

When you are finished answering questions about the data in a table, you can clear the filters and remove the total row.

1 ▶ Click the **Category arrow**, and then click **Clear Filter From "Category"**. Use the same technique to remove the filter from the **Landscape Use** column.

2 ▶ Click anywhere in the table to activate the table and display the **Table Tools** on the ribbon. Click the **Design tab**, and then in the **Table Style Options group**, click the **Total Row** check box to clear the check mark and remove the Total row from the table.

3 ▶ Click **Save** 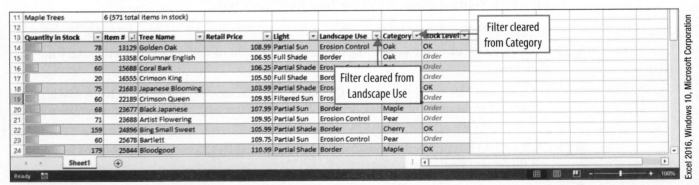, and then compare your screen with Figure 2.28.

11	Maple Trees	6 (571 total items in stock)						
12								
13	Quantity in Stock ▾	Item # ▾	Tree Name ▾	Retail Price ▾	Light ▾	Landscape Use ▾	Category ▾	Stock Level ▾
14	78	13129	Golden Oak	108.99	Partial Sun	Erosion Control	Oak	OK
15	35	13358	Columnar English	106.95	Full Shade	Border	Oak	Order
16	60	15688	Coral Bark	106.25	Partial Shade	Eros		Order
17	20	16555	Crimson King	105.50	Full Shade	Bord		Order
18	75	21683	Japanese Blooming	103.99	Partial Shade	Eros		OK
19	60	22189	Crimson Queen	109.95	Filtered Sun	Eros		Order
20	68	23677	Black Japanese	107.99	Partial Sun	Border	Maple	Order
21	71	23688	Artist Flowering	109.95	Partial Sun	Erosion Control	Pear	Order
22	159	24896	Bing Small Sweet	105.99	Partial Shade	Border	Cherry	OK
23	60	25678	Bartlett	109.75	Partial Sun	Erosion Control	Pear	Order
24	179	25844	Bloodgood	110.99	Partial Shade	Border	Maple	OK

Filter cleared from Category

Filter cleared from Landscape Use

FIGURE 2.28

More **Knowledge** **Converting a Table to a Range**

When you are finished answering questions about the data in a table by sorting, filtering, and totalling, you can convert the table into a normal range. Doing so is useful if you want to use the Table feature only to apply an attractive Table Style to a range of cells. For example, you can insert a table, apply a Table Style, and then convert the table to a normal range of data but keep the formatting. To convert a table to a range, on the Design tab, in the Tools group, click Convert to Range. In the message box, click Yes. Or, with any table cell selected, right-click, point to Table, and then click Convert to Range.

Objective 6 | View, Format, and Print a Large Worksheet

GO! Learn How
Video E2-6

You can magnify or shrink the view of a worksheet on your screen to either zoom in to view specific data or zoom out to see the entire worksheet. You can also split a worksheet window into panes to view different parts of a worksheet at the same time.

A worksheet might be too wide, too long—or both—to print on a single page. Use Excel's *Print Titles* and *Scale to Fit* commands to create pages that are attractive and easy to read.

The Print Titles command enables you to specify rows and columns to repeat on each printed page. Scale to Fit commands enable you to stretch or shrink the width, height, or both, of printed output to fit a maximum number of pages.

1.4.7

Activity 2.18 | Modifying and Shrinking the Worksheet View

1 Press [Ctrl] + [Home] to display the top of your worksheet. On the **View tab**, in the **Zoom group**, click **Zoom**.

2 In the **Zoom** dialog box, click the **75%** option button, and then click **OK.** Notice that by zooming out in this manner, you can see additional rows of your worksheet on the screen.

3 In the lower right corner of your worksheet, in the status bar, click **Zoom In** ➕ until the worksheet redisplays at 100%.

Activity 2.19 | Splitting a Worksheet Window into Panes

1.4.5

The *Split* command splits the window into multiple resizable panes that contain views of your worksheet. This is useful to view multiple distant parts of your worksheet at one time.

1 Click cell **F9**. On the **View tab**, in the **Window group**, click **Split**.

Horizontal and vertical split bars display. You can drag the split bars to view any four portions of the worksheet. On the right, separate vertical scroll bars display for the upper and lower panes and at the bottom, separate horizontal scroll bars display for the left and right panes.

2 Drag the lower vertical scroll box down to the bottom of the scroll bar to view **row 43**. Compare your screen with Figure 2.29.

Here it could be useful to isolate the Tree Statistics at the top and then scroll to the bottom to browse the inventory items.

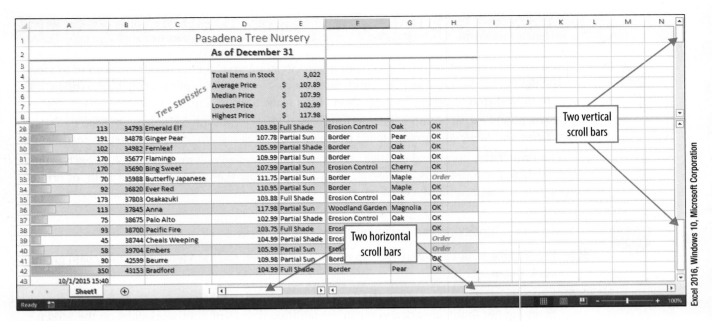

FIGURE 2.29

3 Click **Split** again to remove the split bars.

4 Press Ctrl + Home to display the top of your worksheet. On the **Page Layout tab**, in the **Themes group**, click **Themes**, and then click **Slice**.

5 Select the range **A13:H13**. On the **Home tab**, from the **Styles group**, apply the **Heading 4** cell style, and then apply **Center** ≡. Click cell **A1**.

Activity 2.20 | Printing Titles and Scaling to Fit

1 Click the **Page Layout tab**, and then in the **Page Setup group**, click **Margins**. At the bottom of the gallery, click **Custom Margins** to display the **Page Setup** dialog box. Under **Center on page**, select the **Horizontally** check box.

2 Click the **Header/Footer tab**, and then in the center of the dialog box, click **Custom Footer**. In the **Footer** dialog box, with your insertion point blinking in the **Left section**, on the row of buttons, click **Insert File Name** 🗋. Click **OK** two times.

3 In the **Page Setup group**, click **Orientation**, and then click **Landscape**.

The dotted line indicates that as currently formatted, column H will not fit on the page.

4 Press Ctrl + F2 to display the **Print Preview**. At the bottom of the **Print Preview**, click **Next Page** ▶.

As currently formatted, the worksheet will print on four pages, and the columns will span multiple pages. Additionally, after Page 1, no column titles are visible to identify the data in the columns.

5 Click **Next Page** ▶ two times to display **Page 4**, and notice that one column moves to an additional page.

6 In the upper left corner of **Backstage** view, click **Back** ⊙ to return to the worksheet. In the **Page Setup group**, click **Print Titles**. Under **Print titles**, click in the **Rows to repeat at top** box, and then at the right, click **Collapse Dialog** 🖾.

7 From the **row heading area**, select **row 13**, and then in the **Page Setup – rows to repeat at top:** dialog box, click **Expand Dialog**. Click **OK** to print the column titles in row 13 at the top of every page.

You can collapse and then expand dialog boxes on your screen to enable a better view of your data.

8 Press Ctrl + F2 to display the **Print Preview** again. At the bottom of the **Settings group**, click the **No Scaling arrow**, and then on the displayed list, point to **Fit All Columns on One Page**. Compare your screen with Figure 2.30.

This action will shrink the width of the printed output to fit all the columns on one page. You can make adjustments like this on the Page Layout tab, or here, in the Print Preview.

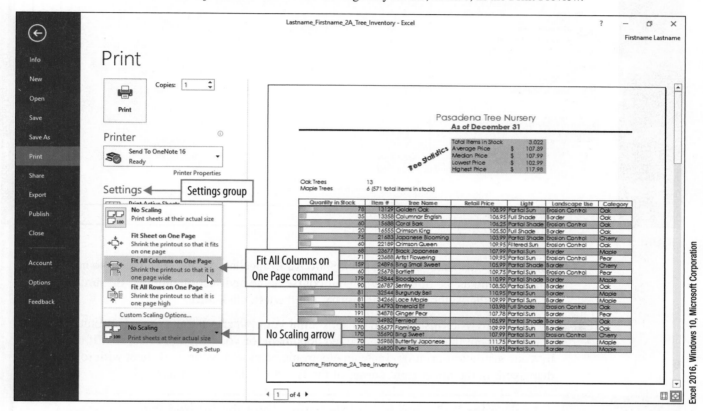

FIGURE 2.30

9 Click **Fit All Columns on One Page**. Notice in the **Print Preview** that all the columns display on one page.

ANOTHER WAY With the worksheet displayed, on the Page Layout tab, in the Scale to Fit group, click the Width button arrow, and then click 1 page.

10 At the bottom of the **Print Preview**, click **Next Page** one time. Notice that the output will now print on two pages and that the column titles display at the top of **Page 2**. Compare your screen with Figure 2.31.

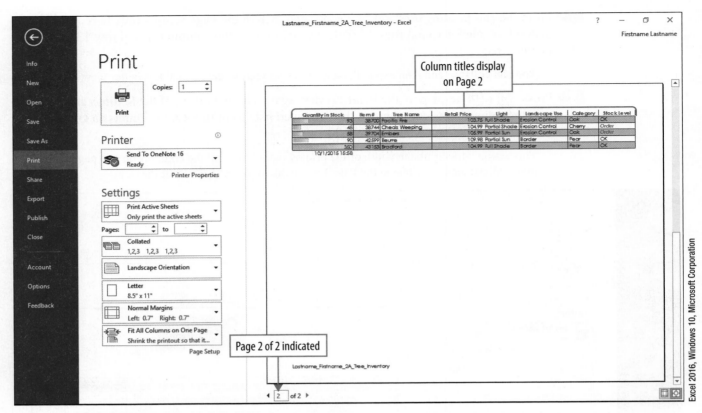

FIGURE 2.31

11 ▸ On the left, click **Info**, and then click **Show All Properties**. As the **Tags**, type **tree inventory, Pasadena** and as the **Subject**, type your course name and section number. Be sure your name displays as the Author; edit if necessary. On the left, click **Save**.

12 ▸ If directed by your instructor to do so, submit your paper printout, your electronic image of your document that looks like a printed document, or your original Excel file. If required by your instructor, print or create an electronic version of your worksheet with formulas displayed. In the upper right corner of the Excel window, click **Close** ⊠.

More Knowledge   **Scaling for Data That Is Slightly Larger Than the Printed Page**

If your data is just a little too large to fit on a printed page, you can scale the worksheet to make it fit. Scaling reduces both the width and height of the printed data to a percentage of its original size or by the number of pages that you specify. On the Page Layout tab, in the Scale to Fit group, click the Scale arrows to select a percentage.

END | You have completed Project 2A

GO! With Google

Objective | Summarize an Inventory List

> **ALERT!** **Working with Web-Based Applications and Services**
>
> Computer programs and services on the web receive continuous updates and improvements, so the steps to complete this web-based activity may differ from the ones shown. You can often look at the screens and the information presented to determine how to complete the activity.
>
> If you do not already have a Google account, you will need to create one before you begin this activity. Go to http://google.com and, in the upper right corner, click Sign In. On the Sign In screen, click Create Account. On the Create your Google Account page, complete the form, read and agree to the Terms of Service and Privacy Policy, and then click Next step. On the Welcome screen, click Get Started.

Activity | Create SUM, AVERAGE, COUNTIF, and IF functions

1 From the desktop, open your browser, navigate to **http://google.com**, and then click the **Google Apps** menu ▦. Click **Drive** △, and then if necessary, sign in to your Google account.

2 Open your **GO! Web Projects** folder—or click New to create and then open this folder if necessary. In the left pane, click **NEW**, and then click **File upload**. Navigate to your student data files, click **e02_2A_Web**, and then click **Open**.

3 Right-click the file you uploaded, point to **Open with**, and then click **Google Sheets**.

4 Select the range **A1:H1**. Click **Merge cells** ⊞. Click **Format**, point to **Align**, and then click **Center**. With **A1** selected, click **Paint format** ⊤, and then click cell **A2**.

5 Select **A1:A2**, and then click the **Font size arrow** ▾. Click **18**.

6 Click cell **B4**. On the ribbon, click **Functions** Σ ▾, and then click **SUM**. Within the formula's parentheses, type **a11:a33** and press Enter for a result of *2311*. Click **B4**, and then on the ribbon, click **More formats** 123 ▾. Click **Number**, and then click **Decrease decimal places** ⊶ two times.

7 Click cell **B5**, click **Functions** Σ ▾, and then click **AVERAGE**. Within the parentheses, type **d11:d33** and press Enter. Click **B5**, and then on the ribbon, click **Format as currency** ⑂.

8 Click cell **B7**. Type **=countif(g11:g33,"Oak")** and then press Enter to create a function that counts the number of Oak trees in the category column.

9 Click cell **H11**. Type **=if(a11<75,"Order","OK")** and then press Enter. Click cell **H11**, and then drag the fill handle down through cell **H33**.

10 With the range **H11:H33** selected, click **Format**, and then click **Conditional formatting**. On the right side of the window, in the **Apply to range** box, make sure that **H11:H33** displays. Under **Format cells if…**, click the displayed box, and then click **Text contains**. Click in the **Value or formula** box, and then type **Order** Under **Formatting style,** click **Bold**. Click **Done** to apply the default green background conditional format and bold to all cells containing the word *Order*. Click cell **A1** and compare your screen with Figure A.

11 Submit your file as directed by your instructor. Sign out of your Google account and close your browser.

1			Austin Tree Nursery				
2			As of March 30				
3							
4	Total Items in Stock	2,311					
5	Average Price	$108.52					
6							
7	Oak Trees:	10					
8							
9							
10	Quantity in Stock	Item #	Tree Name	Retail Price	Light	Landscape Use	Category	Stock Level
11	78	13129	Golden Oak	108.99	Partial Sun	Erosion	Oak	OK
12	35	13358	Columnar English	106.95	Full Shade	Border	Oak	Order
13	60	15688	Coral Bark	106.25	Partial Shade	Erosion	Oak	Order
14	20	16555	Crimson King	105.5	Full Shade	Border	Oak	Order
15	75	21683	Japanese Blooming	103.99	Partial Shade	Erosion	Cherry	OK
16	60	22189	Crimson Queen	109.95	Filtered Sun	Erosion	Oak	Order

FIGURE A

PROJECT 2B

Weekly Sales Summary

MyITLab
Project 2B Training
Project 2B Grader

PROJECT ACTIVITIES

In Activities 2.21 through 2.35, you will edit an existing workbook for the Sales Director, Mariam Daly. The workbook summarizes the online and in-store sales of products during a one-week period in April. The worksheets of your completed workbook will look similar to Figure 2.32.

PROJECT FILES

MyITLab grader

If your instructor wants you to submit Project 2B in the MyITLab Grader system, log in to MyITLab, locate Grader Project 2B, and then download the files for this project.

Please always review the downloaded Grader instructions before beginning.

For Project 2B, you will need the following file:
e02B_Weekly_Sales

You will save your workbook as:
Lastname_Firstname_2B_Weekly_Sales

PROJECT RESULTS

GO! Walk Thru Project 2B

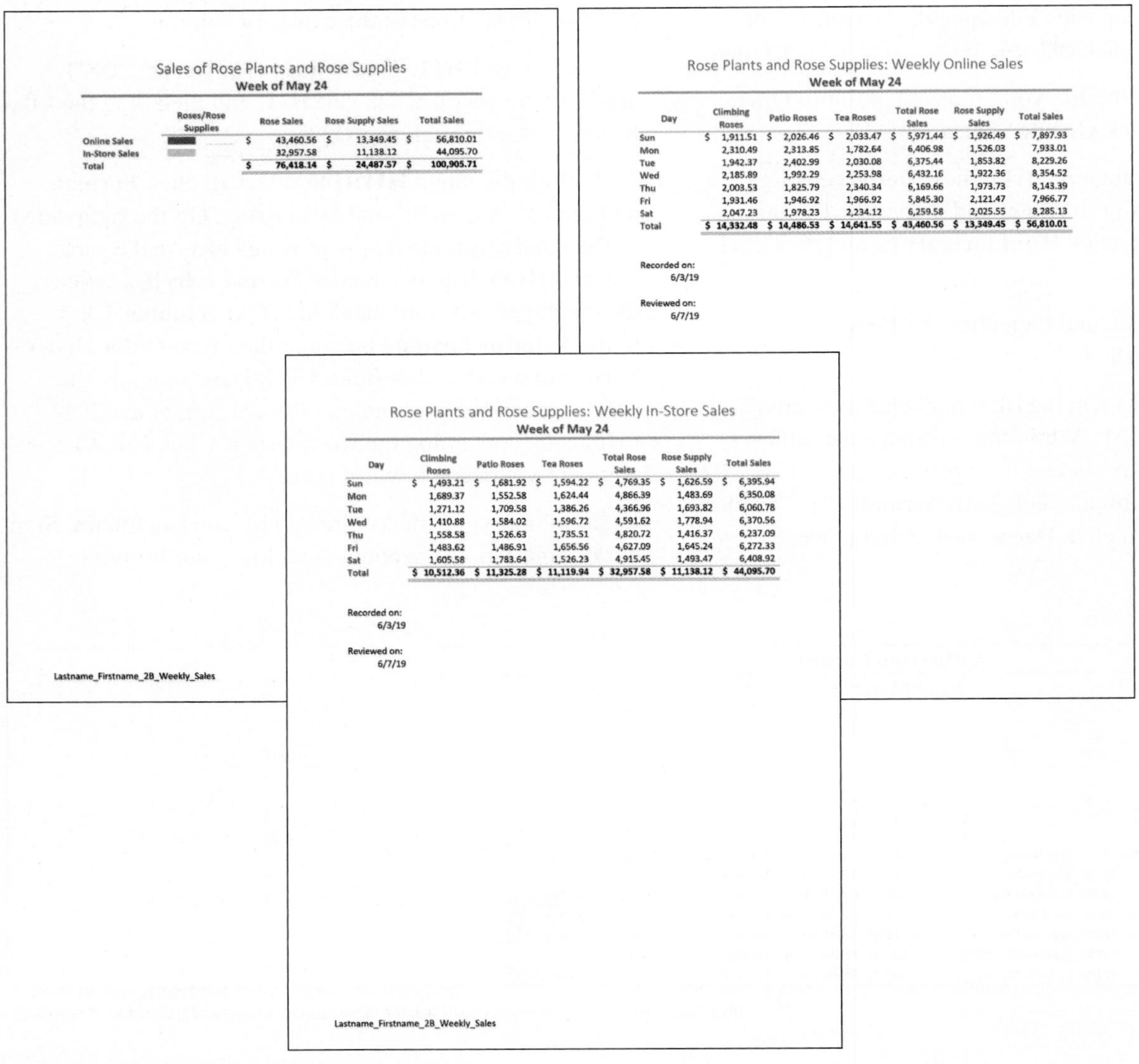

Sales of Rose Plants and Rose Supplies
Week of May 24

	Roses/Rose Supplies	Rose Sales	Rose Supply Sales	Total Sales
Online Sales		$ 43,460.56	$ 13,349.45	$ 56,810.01
In-Store Sales		32,957.58	11,138.12	44,095.70
Total		$ 76,418.14	$ 24,487.57	$ 100,905.71

Lastname_Firstname_2B_Weekly_Sales

Rose Plants and Rose Supplies: Weekly Online Sales
Week of May 24

Day	Climbing Roses	Patio Roses	Tea Roses	Total Rose Sales	Rose Supply Sales	Total Sales
Sun	$ 1,911.51	$ 2,026.46	$ 2,033.47	$ 5,971.44	$ 1,926.49	$ 7,897.93
Mon	2,310.49	2,313.85	1,782.64	6,406.98	1,526.03	7,933.01
Tue	1,942.37	2,402.99	2,030.08	6,375.44	1,853.82	8,229.26
Wed	2,185.89	1,992.29	2,253.98	6,432.16	1,922.36	8,354.52
Thu	2,003.53	1,825.79	2,340.34	6,169.66	1,973.73	8,143.39
Fri	1,931.46	1,946.92	1,966.92	5,845.30	2,121.47	7,966.77
Sat	2,047.23	1,978.23	2,234.12	6,259.58	2,025.55	8,285.13
Total	$ 14,332.48	$ 14,486.53	$ 14,641.55	$ 43,460.56	$ 13,349.45	$ 56,810.01

Recorded on:
6/3/19

Reviewed on:
6/7/19

Rose Plants and Rose Supplies: Weekly In-Store Sales
Week of May 24

Day	Climbing Roses	Patio Roses	Tea Roses	Total Rose Sales	Rose Supply Sales	Total Sales
Sun	$ 1,493.21	$ 1,681.92	$ 1,594.22	$ 4,769.35	$ 1,626.59	$ 6,395.94
Mon	1,689.37	1,552.58	1,624.44	4,866.39	1,483.69	6,350.08
Tue	1,271.12	1,709.58	1,386.26	4,366.96	1,693.82	6,060.78
Wed	1,410.88	1,584.02	1,596.72	4,591.62	1,778.94	6,370.56
Thu	1,558.58	1,526.63	1,735.51	4,820.72	1,416.37	6,237.09
Fri	1,483.62	1,486.91	1,656.56	4,627.09	1,645.24	6,272.33
Sat	1,605.58	1,783.64	1,526.23	4,915.45	1,493.47	6,408.92
Total	$ 10,512.36	$ 11,325.28	$ 11,119.94	$ 32,957.58	$ 11,138.12	$ 44,095.70

Recorded on:
6/3/19

Reviewed on:
6/7/19

Lastname_Firstname_2B_Weekly_Sales

Excel 2016, Windows 10, Microsoft Corporation

FIGURE 2.32 Project 2B Weekly Sales

GO! Learn How
Video E2-7

Use multiple worksheets in a workbook to organize data in a logical arrangement. When you have more than one worksheet in a workbook, you can *navigate* (move) among worksheets by clicking the *sheet tabs*. Sheet tabs identify each worksheet in a workbook and display along the lower left edge of the workbook window. When you have more worksheets in the workbook than can display in the sheet tab area, use the sheet tab scrolling buttons to move sheet tabs into and out of view.

Activity 2.21 | Navigating Among Worksheets, Renaming Worksheets, and Changing the Tab Color of Worksheets

ALERT! To submit as an autograded project, log into MyITLab and download the files for this project, and begin with those files instead of e02B_Weekly_Sales.

MOS
1.3.1, 1.3.2

Excel names the first worksheet in a workbook *Sheet1* and each additional worksheet that you add in order—*Sheet2*, *Sheet3*, and so on. Most Excel users rename their worksheets with meaningful names. In this Activity, you will navigate among worksheets, rename worksheets, and change the tab color of sheet tabs.

1 Start Excel. In the lower left corner of Excel's opening screen, click **Open Other Workbooks**, and then click **Browse**.

ANOTHER WAY Press Ctrl + F12 to display the Open dialog box.

2 Navigate to the student files that accompany this chapter, and then open **e02B_Weekly_Sales**. Press F12 to display the **Save As** dialog box, and then navigate to your **Excel Chapter 2** folder. In the **File name** box, using your own name, type **Lastname_Firstname_2B_Weekly_Sales** and then click **Save** or press Enter.

In this workbook, two worksheets display, into which some data has already been entered. For example, on the first worksheet, the days of the week and sales data for the one-week period display.

3 Along the bottom of the Excel window, point to and then click the **Sheet2 tab**.

The second worksheet in the workbook displays and becomes the active worksheet. *Sheet2* displays in bold.

4 In cell **A1**, notice the text *In-Store*—this worksheet will contain data for in-store sales.

5 Click the **Sheet1 tab**. Then, point to the **Sheet1 tab**, and double-click to select the sheet tab name. Type **Online Sales** and press Enter.

The first worksheet becomes the active worksheet, and the sheet tab displays *Online Sales*.

6 Point to the **Online Sales sheet tab** and right-click. Point to **Tab Color**, and then in the next to last column, point to the first color—**Blue, Accent 5**. Compare your screen with Figure 2.33.

ANOTHER WAY On the Home tab, in the Cells group, click the Format button, and then on the displayed list, point to Tab Color.

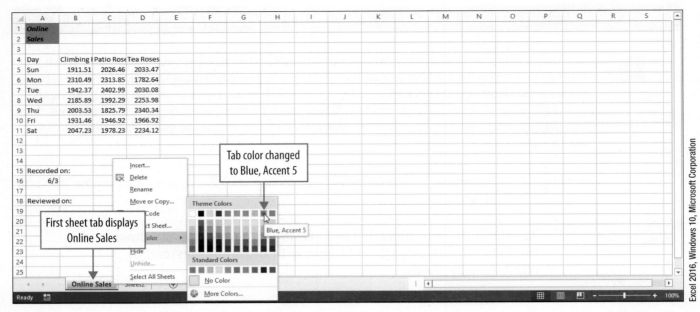

FIGURE 2.33

> **7** ▶ Click **Blue, Accent 5** to change the tab color.

> **8** ▶ Point to the **Sheet2 tab**, right-click, and then from the shortcut menu, click **Rename**. Type **In-Store Sales** and press Enter.

> You can either double-click the sheet name or use the shortcut menu to rename a sheet tab.

> **9** ▶ Point to the **In-Store Sales sheet tab** and right-click. Point to **Tab Color**, and then in the last column, click the first color—**Green, Accent 6**. **Save** 🖫 your workbook.

More Knowledge | **Copying a Worksheet**

To copy a worksheet to the same workbook, right-click the sheet tab, on the shortcut menu click Move or Copy, click the sheet before which you want to insert the copied sheet, select the Create a copy check box, and then click OK. To copy to a different, opened workbook, in the Move or Copy dialog box, click the To book arrow, and then select the workbook into which you want to insert the copy.

Objective 8 | Enter Dates, Clear Contents, and Clear Formats

GO! Learn How
Video E2-8

Dates represent a type of value that you can enter in a cell. When you enter a date, Excel assigns a serial value—a number—to the date. This makes it possible to treat dates like other numbers. For example, if two cells contain dates, you can find the number of days between the two dates by subtracting the older date from the more recent date.

Activity 2.22 | Entering and Formatting Dates

In this Activity, you will examine the various ways that Excel can format dates in a cell. Date values entered in any of the following formats will be recognized by Excel as a date:

VALUE TYPED	EXAMPLE
m/d/yy	7/4/2016
d-mmm	4-Jul
d-mmm-yy	4-Jul-16
mmm-yy	Jul-16

On your keyboard, ⊡ (the hyphen key) and ⊡ (the forward slash key) function identically in any of these formats and can be used interchangeably. You can abbreviate the month name to three characters or spell it out. You can enter the year as two digits, four digits, or even leave it off. When left off, the current year is assumed but does not display in the cell.

A two-digit year value of 30 through 99 is interpreted by the Windows operating system as the four-digit years of 1930 through 1999. All other two-digit year values are assumed to be in the 21st century. If you always type year values as four digits, even though only two digits may display in the cell, you can be sure that Excel interprets the year value as you intended. Examples are shown in Figure 2.34.

HOW EXCEL INTERPRETS DATES	
DATE TYPED AS:	**COMPLETED BY EXCEL AS:**
7/4/15	7/4/2015
7/4/98	7/4/1998
7/4	4-Jul (current year assumed)
7-4	4-Jul (current year assumed)
July 4	4-Jul (current year assumed)
Jul 4	4-Jul (current year assumed)
Jul/4	4-Jul (current year assumed)
Jul-4	4-Jul (current year assumed)
July 4, 1998	4-Jul-98
July 2012	Jul-12 (first day of month assumed)
July 1998	Jul-98 (first day of month assumed)

Excel 2016, Windows 10, Microsoft Corporation

FIGURE 2.34

1 Click the **Online Sales sheet tab** to make it active. Click cell **A16** and notice that the cell displays *6/3*. In the **Formula Bar**, notice that the full date of June 3, 2016, displays in the format *6/3/2016*.

2 With cell **A16** selected, on the **Home tab**, in the **Number group**, click the **Number Format arrow**. At the bottom, click **More Number Formats** to display the **Number tab** of the **Format Cells** dialog box.

Under Category, *Date* is selected, and under Type, *3/14* is selected. Cell A16 uses this format type; that is, only the month and day display in the cell.

3 In the displayed dialog box, under **Type**, click several other date types and watch the **Sample** area to see how applying the selected date format will format your cell. When you are finished, click the **3/14/12** type, and then compare your screen with Figure 2.35.

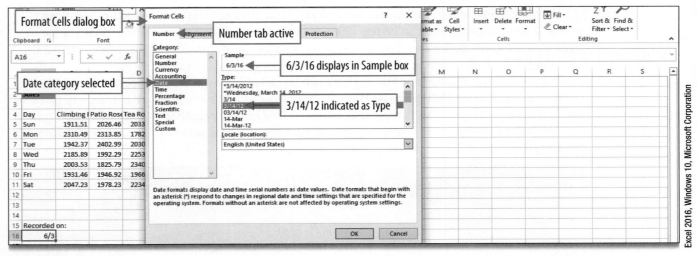

FIGURE 2.35

4 At the bottom of the dialog box, click **OK**. Click cell **A19**, type **6-7-16** and then press Enter.

Cell A19 has no special date formatting applied, and displays in the default date format *6/7/2016*.

ALERT! **The Date Does Not Display as 6/7/2016?**

Settings in your Windows operating system determine the default format for dates. If your result is different, it is likely that the formatting of the default date was adjusted on the computer at which you are working.

---

5 Click cell **A19** again. Hold down Ctrl and press ; (semicolon). Press Enter to confirm the entry.

Excel enters the current date, obtained from your computer's internal calendar, in the selected cell using the default date format. Ctrl + ; is a quick method to enter the current date.

6 Click cell **A19** again, type **6/7/16** and then press Enter.

Because the year *16* is less than 30, Excel assumes a 21st century date and changes *16* to *2016* to complete the four-digit year. Typing *98* would result in *1998*. For two-digit years that you type that are between 30 and 99, Excel assumes a 20th century date.

7 Click cell **A16**, and then on the **Home tab**, in the **Clipboard group**, click **Format Painter** 🖌. Click cell **A19**, and notice that the date format from cell **A16** is copied to cell **A19**. **Save** 🖫 your workbook.

Activity 2.23 | Clearing Cell Contents and Formats

A cell has *contents*—a value or a formula—and a cell may also have one or more *formats* applied, for example, bold and italic font styles, fill color, font color, and so on. You can choose to clear—delete—the *contents* of a cell, the *formatting* of a cell, or both.

Clearing the contents of a cell deletes the value or formula typed there, but it does *not* clear formatting applied to a cell. In this Activity, you will clear the contents of a cell and then clear the formatting of a cell that contains a date to see its underlying content.

1 In the **Online Sales** worksheet, click cell **A1**. In the **Editing group**, click **Clear** 🧹, and then click **Clear Contents**. Notice that the text is cleared, but the green formatting remains.

2 Click cell **A2**, and then press Delete.

You can use either of these two methods to delete the *contents* of a cell. Deleting the contents does not, however, delete the formatting of the cell; you can see that the green fill color format applied to the two cells still displays.

3 In cell **A1**, type **Online Sales** and then on the **Formula Bar**, click **Enter** ✓ so that cell **A1** remains the active cell.

In addition to the green fill color, the bold italic text formatting remains with the cell.

4 In the **Editing group**, click **Clear** ✒, and then click **Clear Formats**.

Clearing the formats deletes formatting from the cell—the green fill color and the bold and italic font styles—but does not delete the cell's contents.

5 Use the same technique to clear the green fill color from cell **A2**. Click cell **A16**, click **Clear** ✒, and then click **Clear Formats**. In the **Number group**, notice that *General* displays as the number format of the cell.

The box in the Number group indicates the current Number format of the selected cell. Clearing the date formatting from the cell displays the date's serial number. The date, June 3, 2016, is stored as a serial number that indicates the number of days since January 1, 1900. This date is the 42,524th day since the reference date of January 1, 1900.

6 On the Quick Access Toolbar, click **Undo** ↶ to restore the date format. **Save** 🖫 your workbook, and then compare your screen with Figure 2.36.

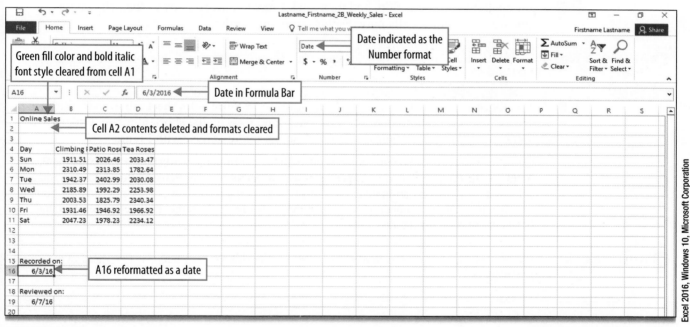

FIGURE 2.36

Excel 2016, Windows 10, Microsoft Corporation

More Knowledge   **Clearing an Entire Worksheet**

To clear an entire worksheet, in the upper left corner of the worksheet, click the Select All button, and then on the Home tab, in the Editing group, click Clear, and then click Clear All.

GO! Learn How
Video E2-9

Data in cells can be copied to other cells in the same worksheet, to other sheets in the same workbook, or to sheets in another workbook. The action of placing cell contents that have been copied or moved to the Clipboard into another location is called **paste**.

Activity 2.24 | Copying and Pasting by Using the Paste Options Gallery

2.1.2, 2.1.3

Recall that the Clipboard is a temporary storage area maintained by your Windows operating system. When you select one or more cells, and then perform the Copy command or the Cut command, the selected data is placed on the Clipboard. From the Clipboard storage area, the data is available for pasting into other cells, other worksheets, other workbooks, and even into other Office programs. When you paste, the **Paste Options gallery** displays, which includes Live Preview to preview the Paste formatting that you want.

1 With the **Online Sales** worksheet active, select the range **A4:A19**.

> A range of cells identical to this one is required for the *In-Store Sales* worksheet.

2 Right-click over the selection, and then click **Copy** to place a copy of the cells on the Clipboard. The copied cells may display a moving border.

ANOTHER WAY Use the keyboard shortcut for Copy, which is Ctrl + C; or click the Copy button in the Clipboard group on the Home tab.

3 At the bottom of the workbook window, click the **In-Store Sales sheet tab** to make it the active worksheet. Point to cell **A4**, right-click, and then on the shortcut menu, under **Paste Options**, *point* to the first button—**Paste**. Compare your screen with Figure 2.37.

> Live Preview displays how the copied cells will be placed in the worksheet if you click the Paste button. In this manner, you can experiment with different paste options, and then be sure you are selecting the paste operation that you want. When pasting a range of cells, you need only point to or select the cell in the upper left corner of the **paste area**—the target destination for data that has been cut or copied using the Clipboard.

ANOTHER WAY Use the keyboard shortcut for Paste, which is Ctrl + V; or click the Paste button in the Clipboard group on the Home tab.

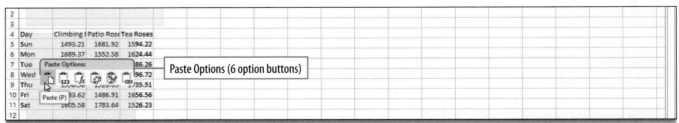

FIGURE 2.37

Excel 2016, Windows 10, Microsoft Corporation

4 Click the first button, **Paste**. In the status bar, notice the message that displays, indicating that your selected range remains available on the Office Clipboard.

5 Display the **Online Sales** worksheet. Press Esc to cancel the moving border. **Save** 🖫 your workbook.

> The status bar no longer displays the message.

Objective 10 Edit and Format Multiple Worksheets at the Same Time

GO! Learn How
Video E2-10

You can enter or edit data on several worksheets at the same time by selecting and grouping multiple worksheets. Data that you enter or edit on the active sheet is reflected in all selected sheets. If the sheet tab displays with a solid background color, you know the sheet is not selected.

Activity 2.25 | Grouping Worksheets for Editing

In this Activity, you will group the two worksheets, and then format both worksheets at the same time.

1 With the **Online Sales** sheet active, press Ctrl + Home to make cell **A1** the active cell. Point to the **Online Sales sheet tab**, right-click, and then click **Select All Sheets**.

2 At the top of your screen, notice that *[Group]* displays in the title bar. Compare your screen with Figure 2.38.

> Both worksheets are selected, as indicated by *[Group]* in the title bar and the sheet tab names underlined. Data that you enter or edit on the active sheet will also be entered or edited in the same manner on all the selected sheets in the same cells.

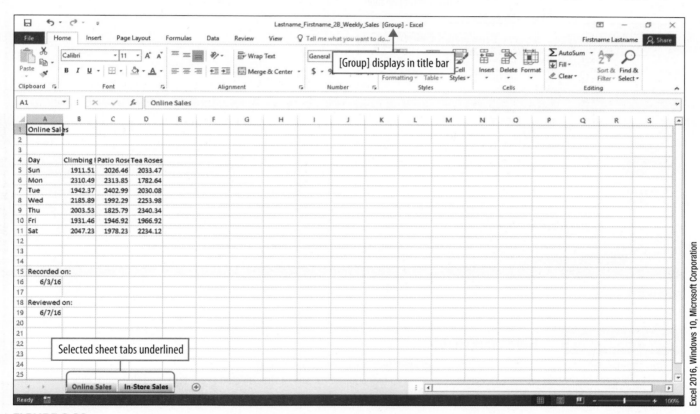

FIGURE 2.38

3 Select **columns A:G**, and then set their width to **85 pixels**.

4 Click cell **A2**, type **Week of May 24** and then on the **Formula Bar**, click **Enter** ✓ to keep cell **A2** as the active cell. **Merge & Center** the text across the range **A2:G2**, and then apply the **Heading 1** cell style.

5 Click cell **E4**, type **Total Rose Sales** and then press Tab. In cell **F4**, type **Rose Supply Sales** and then press Tab. In cell **G4**, type **Total Sales** and then press Enter.

6 Select the range **A4:G4**, and then apply the **Heading 3** cell style. In the **Alignment group**, click **Center** ☰, **Middle Align** ☰, and **Wrap Text**. **Save** 🖫 your workbook.

7 Display the **In-Store Sales** worksheet to cancel the grouping, and then compare your screen with Figure 2.39.

> As soon as you select a single sheet, the grouping of the sheets is cancelled and *[Group]* no longer displays in the title bar. Because the sheets were grouped, the same new text and formatting were applied to both sheets. In this manner, you can make the same changes to all the sheets in a workbook at one time.

🗘 ANOTHER WAY   Right-click any sheet tab, and then click Ungroup Sheets.

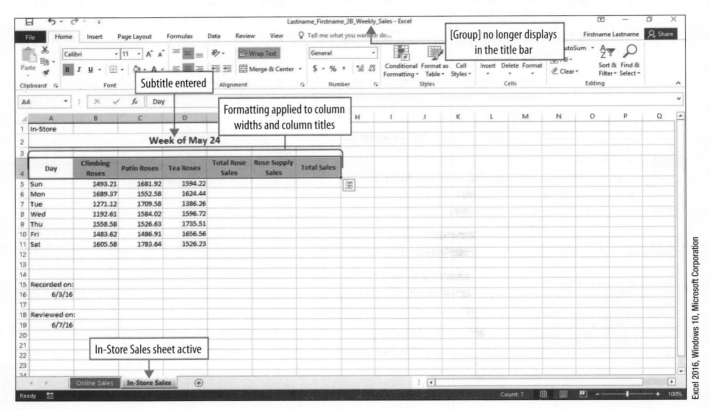

FIGURE 2.39

More **Knowledge**	**Hide Worksheets**

You can hide any worksheet in a workbook to remove it from view using this technique:
Select the sheet tabs of the worksheets you want to hide, right-click any of the selected sheet tabs, and then click Hide.

Activity 2.26 | Formatting and Constructing Formulas on Grouped Worksheets

Recall that formulas are equations that perform calculations on values in your worksheet and that a formula starts with an equal sign (=). Operators are the symbols with which you specify the type of calculation that you want to perform on the elements of a formula. In this Activity, you will enter sales figures for Rose Supply items from both Online and In-Store sales, and then calculate the total sales.

1 Display the **Online Sales** worksheet. Verify that the sheets are not grouped—*[Group]* does *not* display in the title bar.

2 Click cell **A1**, replace *Online Sales* by typing **Rose Plants and Rose Supplies: Weekly Online Sales** and then on the **Formula Bar**, click **Enter** ✓ to keep cell **A1** as the active cell. **Merge & Center** the text across the range **A1:G1**, and then apply the **Title** cell style.

3 In the column titled *Rose Supply Sales*, click cell **F5**. In the range **F5:F11**, type the following data for Rose Supply Sales, and then compare your screen with Figure 2.40.

	ROSE SUPPLY SALES
Sun	1926.49
Mon	1526.03
Tue	1853.82
Wed	1922.36
Thu	1973.73
Fri	2121.47
Sat	2025.55

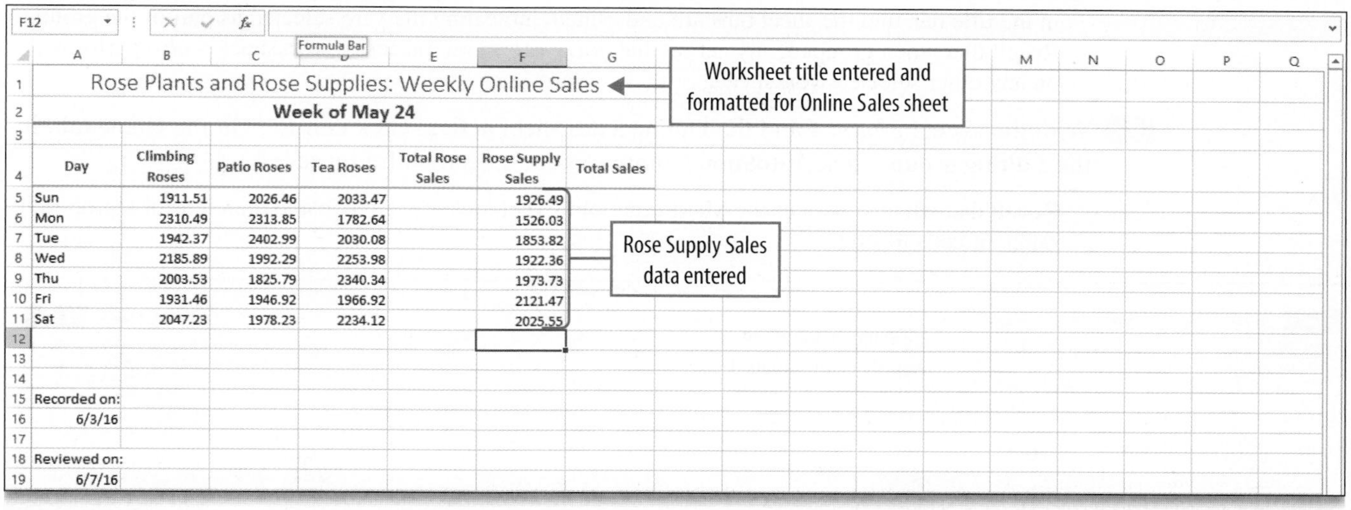

	A	B	C	D	E	F	G
1	Rose Plants and Rose Supplies: Weekly Online Sales						
2	Week of May 24						
3							
4	Day	Climbing Roses	Patio Roses	Tea Roses	Total Rose Sales	Rose Supply Sales	Total Sales
5	Sun	1911.51	2026.46	2033.47		1926.49	
6	Mon	2310.49	2313.85	1782.64		1526.03	
7	Tue	1942.37	2402.99	2030.08		1853.82	
8	Wed	2185.89	1992.29	2253.98		1922.36	
9	Thu	2003.53	1825.79	2340.34		1973.73	
10	Fri	1931.46	1946.92	1966.92		2121.47	
11	Sat	2047.23	1978.23	2234.12		2025.55	
12							
13							
14							
15	Recorded on:						
16	6/3/16						
17							
18	Reviewed on:						
19	6/7/16						

FIGURE 2.40

4 Display the **In-Store Sales** sheet. In cell **A1**, replace *In-Store* by typing **Rose Plants and Rose Supplies: Weekly In-Store Sales** and then on the **Formula Bar**, click **Enter** ✓ to keep cell **A1** as the active cell. **Merge & Center** the text across the range **A1:G1**, and then apply the **Title** cell style.

5 In the column titled *Rose Supply Sales*, click cell **F5**. In the range **F5:F11**, type the following data for Rose Supply Sales, and then compare your screen with Figure 2.41.

	ROSE SUPPLY SALES
Sun	1626.59
Mon	1483.69
Tue	1693.82
Wed	1778.94
Thu	1416.37
Fri	1645.24
Sat	1493.47

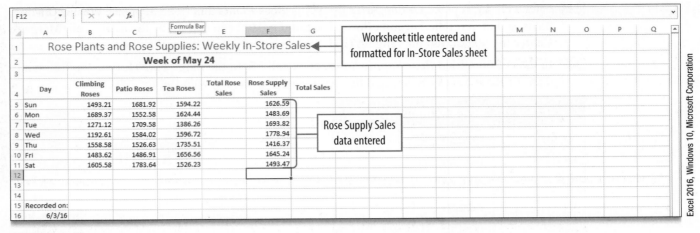

FIGURE 2.41

6 ▸ **Save** 🖫 your workbook. Right-click the **Online Sales sheet tab**, and then click **Select All Sheets**.

The first worksheet becomes the active sheet, and the worksheets are grouped. *[Group]* displays in the title bar, and the sheet tabs are underlined, indicating they are selected as part of the group. Recall that when grouped, any action that you perform on the active worksheet is *also* performed on any other selected worksheets.

7 ▸ With the sheets *grouped* and the **Online Sales** sheet active, click cell **E5**. On the **Home tab**, in the **Editing group**, click **AutoSum**. Compare your screen with Figure 2.42.

Recall that when you enter the SUM function, Excel looks first above and then left for a proposed range of cells to sum.

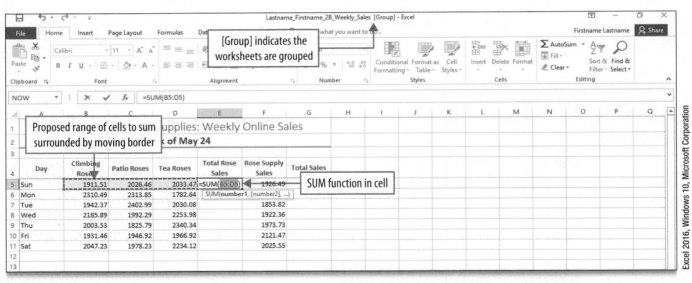

FIGURE 2.42

8 ▸ Press Enter to display Total Rose Sales for Sunday, which is *5971.44*.

9 ▸ Click cell **E5**, and then drag the fill handle down to copy the formula through cell **E11**.

10 ▸ Click cell **G5**, type = click cell **E5**, type + click cell **F5**, and then compare your screen with Figure 2.43.

Using the point-and-click technique to construct this formula is only one of several techniques you can use. Alternatively, you could use any other method to enter the SUM function to add the values in these two cells.

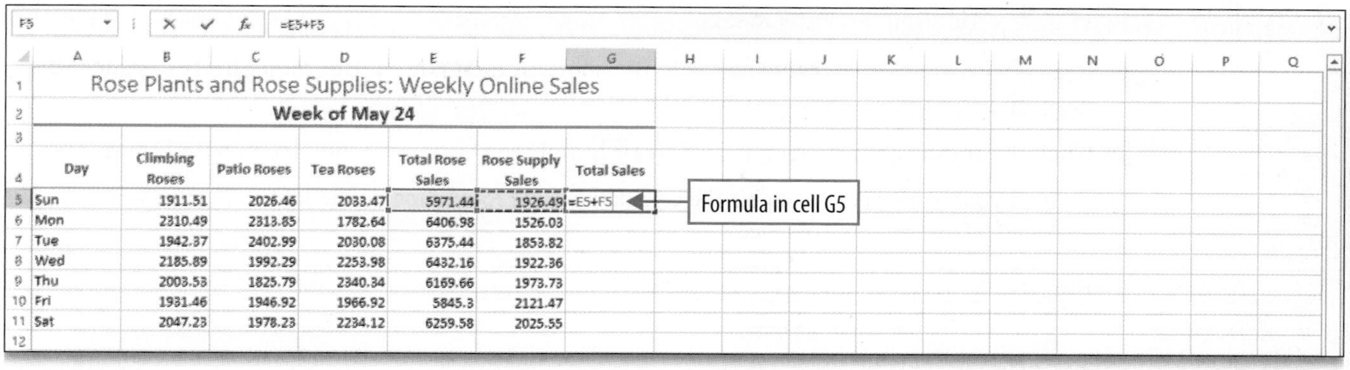

	A	B	C	D	E	F	G	H	I	J	K	L	M	N	O	P	Q
	F5	▾ : × ✓ fx	=E5+F5														
1		Rose Plants and Rose Supplies: Weekly Online Sales															
2		Week of May 24															
3																	
4	Day	Climbing Roses	Patio Roses	Tea Roses	Total Rose Sales	Rose Supply Sales	Total Sales										
5	Sun	1911.51	2026.46	2033.47	5971.44	1926.49	=E5+F5										
6	Mon	2310.49	2313.85	1782.64	6406.98	1526.03											
7	Tue	1942.37	2402.99	2030.08	6375.44	1853.82											
8	Wed	2185.89	1992.29	2253.98	6432.16	1922.36											
9	Thu	2003.53	1825.79	2340.34	6169.66	1973.73											
10	Fri	1931.46	1946.92	1966.92	5845.3	2121.47											
11	Sat	2047.23	1978.23	2234.12	6259.58	2025.55											
12																	

Formula in cell G5

FIGURE 2.43

11 Press Enter to display the result *7897.93,* and then copy the formula down through cell **G11**. **Save** 💾 your workbook.

Activity 2.27 | Determining Multiple Totals at the Same Time

You can select a contiguous range of cells adjacent to rows or columns of numbers and then click the AutoSum button—or use [Alt] + [=]—to enter the SUM function for each row or column.

1 With the two worksheets still grouped, in cell **A12**, type **Total** and then select the range **B5:G12**, which is all of the sales data and the empty cells at the bottom of each column of sales data.

2 With the range **B5:G12** selected, hold down [Alt] and press [=] to enter the **SUM** function in each empty cell. Click **Save** 💾.

Selecting a range in this manner and then clicking the AutoSum button, or entering the SUM function with the keyboard shortcut [Alt] + [=], places the SUM function in the empty cells at the bottom of each column.

Activity 2.28 | Formatting Grouped Worksheets

1 With the two worksheets still grouped, select the range **A5:A12**, and then apply the **Heading 4** cell style.

2 To apply financial formatting to the worksheets, select the range **B5:G5**, hold down [Ctrl], and then select the range **B12:G12**. With the nonadjacent ranges selected, apply the **Accounting Number Format** [$ ▾].

3 Select the range **B6:G11** and apply **Comma Style** [,]. Select the range **B12:G12** and apply the **Total** cell style. Press [Ctrl] + [Home] to move to the top of the worksheet; compare your screen with Figure 2.44.

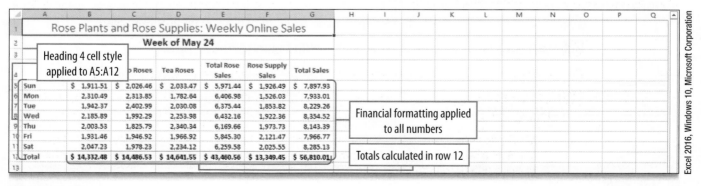

FIGURE 2.44

Activity 2.29 | Ungrouping Worksheets

1 Right-click the **Online Sales sheet**. On the shortcut menu, click **Ungroup Sheets** to cancel the grouping.

2 Click the **In-Store Sales sheet**. Click **Save** 🖫, and then compare your screen with Figure 2.45.

With your worksheets grouped, the calculations and formatting on the first worksheet were also added on the second worksheet.

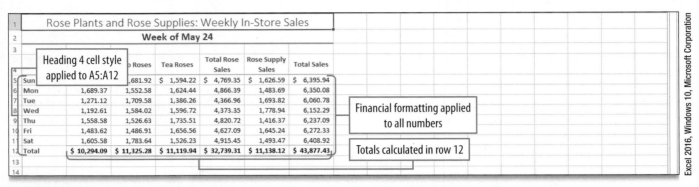

FIGURE 2.45

Objective 11 Create a Summary Sheet with Column Sparklines

GO! Learn How
Video E2-11

A ***summary sheet*** is a worksheet where totals from other worksheets are displayed and summarized. Recall that sparklines are tiny charts within a single cell that show a data trend.

Activity 2.30 | Inserting a Worksheet

1.1.3

1 To the right of the **In-Store Sales** sheet tab, click **New sheet** ⊕.

2 Rename the new worksheet tab **Summary** and change its **Tab Color** to **Gold, Accent 4**—in the eighth column, the first color.

3 Widen **columns A:E** to **110** pixels. In cell **A1**, type **Sales of Rose Plants and Rose Supplies** and then **Merge & Center** the title across the range **A1:E1**. Apply the **Title** cell style.

4 In cell **A2**, type **Week of May 24** and then **Merge & Center** across **A2:E2**; apply the **Heading 1** cell style.

5 Leave **row 3** blank. To form column titles, in cell **B4**, type **Roses/Rose Supplies** and press Tab. In cell **C4**, type **Rose Sales** and press Tab. In cell **D4**, type **Rose Supply Sales** and press Tab. In cell **E4**, type **Total Sales** and press Enter.

6 Select the range **B4:E4**. Apply the **Heading 3** cell style. In the **Alignment group**, click **Center** ≡, **Middle Align** ≡, and **Wrap Text**.

7 To form row titles, in cell **A5**, type **Online Sales** In cell **A6**, type **In-Store Sales**

8 **Save** 🖫, and then compare your screen with Figure 2.46.

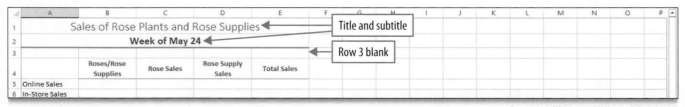

FIGURE 2.46

Excel 2016, Windows 10, Microsoft Corporation

4.1.1

Activity 2.31 | Constructing Formulas that Refer to Cells in Another Worksheet

In this Activity, you will construct formulas in the Summary worksheet to display the total sales for both online sales and in-store sales that will update the Summary worksheet whenever changes are made to the other worksheet totals.

1 Click cell **C5**. Type = and then click the **Online Sales sheet tab**. On the **Online Sales** worksheet, click cell **E12**, and then press Enter to redisplay the **Summary** worksheet and insert the total **Rose Sales** amount of *$43,460.56*.

2 Click cell **C5** to select it again. Look at the **Formula Bar**, and notice that instead of a value, the cell contains a formula that is equal to the value in another cell in another worksheet. Compare your screen with Figure 2.47.

> The value in this cell is equal to the value in cell E12 of the *Online Sales* worksheet. The Accounting Number Format applied to the referenced cell is carried over. By using a formula of this type, changes in cell E12 on the *Online Sales* worksheet will be automatically updated in this *Summary* worksheet.

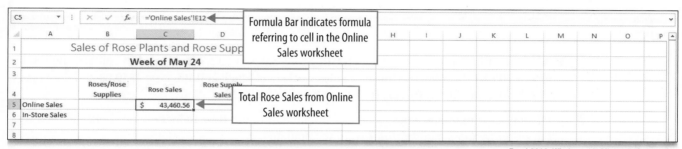

FIGURE 2.47

Excel 2016, Windows 10, Microsoft Corporation

3 Click cell **D5**. Type = and then click the **Online Sales sheet tab**. Click cell **F12**, and then press Enter to redisplay the **Summary** worksheet and insert the total **Rose Supply Sales** amount of *$13,349.45*.

4 By using the techniques you just practiced, in cells **C6** and **D6** insert the total **Rose Sales** and **Rose Supply Sales** data from the **In-Store Sales** worksheet. Click **Save**, and then compare your screen with Figure 2.48.

FIGURE 2.48

Excel 2016, Windows 10, Microsoft Corporation

Activity 2.32 | Changing Values in a Detail Worksheet to Update a Summary Worksheet

The formulas in cells C5:D6 display the totals from the other two worksheets. Changes made to any of the other two worksheets—sometimes referred to as *detail sheets* because the details of the information are contained there—that affect their totals will display on this Summary worksheet. In this manner, the Summary worksheet accurately displays the current totals from the other worksheets.

1 In cell **A7**, type **Total** Select the range **C5:E6**, and then on the **Home tab**, in the **Editing group**, click **AutoSum** to total the two rows.

This technique is similar to selecting the empty cells at the bottom of columns and then inserting the SUM function for each column. Alternatively, you could use any other method to sum the rows. Recall that cell formatting carries over to adjacent cells unless two cells are left blank.

2 Select the range **C5:E7**, and then click **AutoSum** to total the three columns. Compare your screen with Figure 2.49.

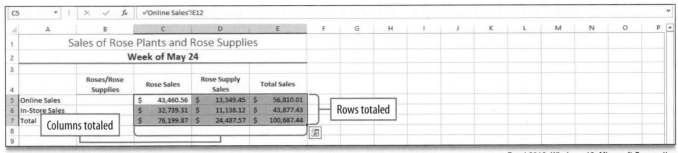

FIGURE 2.49

Excel 2016, Windows 10, Microsoft Corporation

3 Notice that in cell C6, Rose Sales for In-Store Sales is $32,739.31, and in cell C7, the total is $76,199.87. Display the **In-Store Sales** worksheet, click cell **B8**, type **1410.88** and then press Enter. Notice that the formulas in the worksheet recalculate.

4 Display the **Summary** worksheet, and notice that in the **Rose Sales** column, both the total for the *In-Store Sales* and the *Total* were recalculated.

In this manner, a Summary sheet recalculates any changes made in the other worksheets.

5 On the **Summary** worksheet, select the range **C6:E6** and change the format to **Comma Style**. Select the range **C7:E7**, and then apply the **Total** cell style. Select the range **A5:A7** and apply the **Heading 4** cell style. **Save** 🖫 your workbook. Click cell **A1**, and then compare your screen with Figure 2.50.

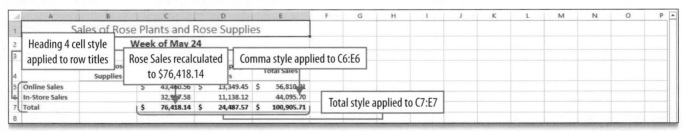

FIGURE 2.50

Excel 2016, Windows 10, Microsoft Corporation

MOS

2.3.1

Activity 2.33 | Inserting Column Sparklines

In this Activity, you will insert column sparklines to visualize the ratio of Rose sales to Rose Supply sales for both Online and In-Store.

1 On the **Summary** worksheet, click cell **B5**. On the **Insert tab**, in the **Sparklines group**, click **Column**. In the **Create Sparklines** dialog box, with the insertion point blinking in the **Data Range** box, type **c5:d5** and then compare your screen with Figure 2.51.

FIGURE 2.51

2 Click **OK**. Click cell **B6**, and then **Insert** a **Column Sparkline** for the range **c6:d6**

3 With cell **B6** selected, on the **Design tab**, in the **Style group**, click **More** ⊡, and then click **Sparkline Style Accent 4, (no dark or light)**—in the third row, the fourth style. Press Ctrl + Home, click **Save** 🖫, and then compare your screen with Figure 2.52.

> You can see, at a glance, that for both Online and In-Store sales, Rose sales are greater than Rose Supply sales.

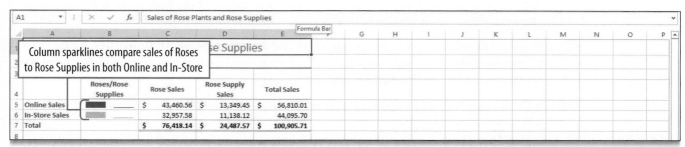

FIGURE 2.52

Objective 12 | Format and Print Multiple Worksheets in a Workbook

GO! Learn How
Video E2-12

Each worksheet within a workbook can have different formatting, for example, different headers or footers. If all the worksheets in the workbook will have the same header or footer, you can select all the worksheets and apply formatting common to all of the worksheets; for example, you can set the same footer in all of the worksheets.

1.1.4, 1.3.3

Activity 2.34 | Moving a Worksheet, Repeating Footers, and Formatting Multiple Worksheets in a Workbook

In this Activity, you will move the Summary sheet to become the first worksheet in the workbook. Then you will format and prepare your workbook for printing. The three worksheets containing data can be formatted simultaneously.

1 Point to the **Summary sheet tab**, hold down the left mouse button to display a small black triangle—a caret—and then notice that a small paper icon attaches to the mouse pointer.

2 Drag to the left until the caret and mouse pointer are to the left of the **Online Sales sheet tab**, as shown in Figure 2.53, and then release the left mouse button.

> Use this technique to rearrange the order of worksheets within a workbook.

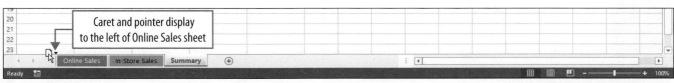

FIGURE 2.53

3 Be sure the **Summary** worksheet is the active sheet, point to its sheet tab, right-click, and then click **Select All Sheets** to display *[Group]* in the title bar.

4 Click the **Page Layout tab**. In the **Page Setup group**, click **Margins**, and then at the bottom of the gallery, click **Custom Margins** to display the **Page Setup** dialog box.

5 In the **Page Setup** dialog box, on the **Margins tab**, under **Center on page**, select the **Horizontally** check box.

6 Click the **Header/Footer tab**, and then in the center of the dialog box, click **Custom Footer**. In the **Footer** dialog box, with your insertion point blinking in the **Left section**, on the row of buttons, click **Insert File Name** ▣.

7 Click **OK** two times.

The dotted line indicates the page break as currently formatted.

8 Press Ctrl + Home; verify that *[Group]* still displays in the title bar.

By selecting all sheets, you can apply the same formatting to all the worksheets at the same time, for example, to repeat headers or footers.

9 Click the **File tab** to display **Backstage** view, and then click **Show All Properties**. As the **Tags**, type **weekly sales** and in the **Subject** box, type your course name and section number. Be sure your name displays as the **Author**; edit if necessary.

10 On the left, click **Print** to display the **Print Preview**, and then compare your screen with Figure 2.54.

By grouping, you can view all sheets in Print Preview. If you do not see *1 of 3* at the bottom of the Preview, redisplay the workbook, select all the sheets again, and then redisplay Print Preview.

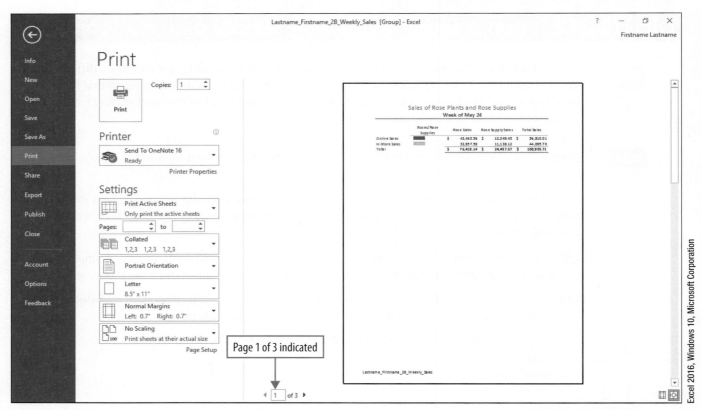

FIGURE 2.54

11 At the bottom of the **Print Preview**, click **Next Page** ▶ as necessary and take a moment to view each page of your workbook.

1.5.3

Activity 2.35 | Printing All or Individual Worksheets in a Workbook

1 In **Backstage** view, click **Save** to save your workbook before printing. In the displayed workbook, right-click the **Summary sheet tab**, and then click **Ungroup Sheets**.

2 Press Ctrl + F2 to display **Print Preview**, and then at the bottom of the window, notice that *1 of 1* is indicated.

> Because the worksheets are no longer grouped, only the active sheet is available for printing.

3 On the left, under **Settings**, click **Print Active Sheets**, and then click **Print Entire Workbook**.

> At the bottom of the window, *1 of 3* is indicated. You can use this command to print an entire workbook.

4 If directed by your instructor to do so, submit your paper printout, your electronic image of your document that looks like a printed document, or your original Excel file. If required by your instructor, print or create an electronic version of your worksheet with formulas displayed. In the upper right corner of the Excel window, click **Close** ☒.

END | You have completed Project 2B

GO! With Google

A L E R T !	**Working with Web-Based Applications and Services**

Computer programs and services on the web receive continuous updates and improvements, so the steps to complete this web-based activity may differ from the ones shown. You can often look at the screens and the information presented to determine how to complete the activity.

If you do not already have a Google account, you will need to create one before you begin this activity. Go to http://google.com and, in the upper right corner, click Sign In. On the Sign In screen, click Create Account. On the Create your Google Account page, complete the form, read and agree to the Terms of Service and Privacy Policy, and then click Next step. On the Welcome screen, click Get Started.

Activity | Calculating Weekly Sales with Google Sheets

1 From the desktop, open your browser, navigate to **http://google.com**, and then click the **Google Apps** menu ⊞. Click **Drive**, and then if necessary, sign in to your Google account.

2 Open your **GO! Web Projects** folder—or click New to create and then open this folder if necessary. In the left pane, click **NEW**, and then click **File upload**. Navigate to your student data files, click **e02_2B_Web**, and then click **Open**.

3 Right-click the file you uploaded, point to **Open with**, and then click **Google Sheets**.

4 Click cell **E5**. On the ribbon, click **Functions** Σ ⌄, and then click **SUM**. Select **B5:D5** and then press Enter to total the rose sales for Sunday. Click cell **E5**, and then drag the fill handle down through cell **E11**. Select **E6:E11**, and then on the ribbon, click **More Formats** 123 ⌄. Click **Number**.

5 Click cell **G5** and then enter a formula to add cells **E5** and **F5**. Fill the formula down through cell **G11**, and then format the range **G6:G11** with **Number** format.

6 Select the range **B5:B11**. Click **Functions** Σ ⌄, click **SUM**, and then press Enter to sum the selected range and place the result in cell **B12**. With **B12** selected, fill the formula across to cell **G12**.

7 Click cell **H5**. To calculate the percent that the Sunday sales are of the total sales, type **=g5/g12** and then press F4 to make the cell reference to G12 absolute. Press Enter and then fill the formula down through cell **H11**. With the range **H5:H11** selected, click **Format as percent** % .

8 Click cell **A1** and then compare your screen with Figure A.

9 Submit your file as directed by your instructor. Sign out of your Google account and close your browser.

	A	B	C	D	E	F	G	H	I	J	K	L	M	N	O	P	Q
1		**Rose Plants and Rose Supplies: Austin Sales**															
2				**Week of May 24**													
3																	
4	Day	Climbing Roses	Patio Roses	Tea Roses	Total Rose Sales	Rose Supply Sales	Total Sales	Percent of Sales									
5	Sun	$911.51	$26.46	$33.47	$971.44	$1,926.49	$2,897.93	12.17%									
6	Mon	310.49	313.85	782.64	1,406.98	1,526.03	2,933.01	12.32%									
7	Tue	942.37	402.99	30.08	1,375.44	1,853.82	3,229.26	13.56%									
8	Wed	185.89	992.29	253.98	1,432.16	1,922.36	3,354.52	14.09%									
9	Thu	3.53	825.79	340.34	1,169.66	1,973.73	3,143.39	13.20%									
10	Fri	931.46	946.92	966.92	2,845.30	2,121.47	4,966.77	20.86%									
11	Sat	47.23	978.23	234.12	1,259.58	2,025.55	3,285.13	13.80%									
12	Total Sales	$3,332.48	$4,486.53	$2,641.55	$10,460.56	$13,349.45	$23,810.01										
13																	
14																	
15																	

FIGURE A

GO! To Work

MICROSOFT OFFICE SPECIALIST (MOS) SKILLS IN THIS CHAPTER

PROJECT 2A

1.2.1 Search for data within a workbook
1.4.5 Change window views
1.4.7 Change magnification by using zoom tools
1.5.4 Set print scaling
1.5.5 Display repeating row and column titles on multipage worksheets
2.1.1 Replace data
2.3.4 Apply conditional formatting
3.1.1 Create an Excel table from a cell range
3.2.1 Apply styles to tables
3.2.3 Insert total rows
3.3.1 Filter records
3.3.2 Sort data by multiple columns
3.3.3 Change sort order
4.1.2 Perform calculations by using the SUM function
4.1.3 Perform calculations by using MIN and MAX functions
4.1.5 Perform calculations by using the AVERAGE function
4.2.1 Perform logical operations by using the IF function
4.2.4 Perform statistical operations by using the COUNTIF function

PROJECT 2B

1.1.3 Add a worksheet to an existing workbook
1.1.4 Copy and move a worksheet
1.3.1 Change worksheet tab color
1.3.2 Rename a worksheet
1.3.3 Change worksheet order
1.5.3 Print all or part of a workbook
2.1.2 Cut, copy, or paste data
2.1.3 Paste data by using special paste options
2.3.1 Insert sparklines
4.1.1 Insert references

BUILD YOUR E-PORTFOLIO

An E-Portfolio is a collection of evidence, stored electronically, that showcases what you have accomplished while completing your education. Collecting and then sharing your work products with potential employers reflects your academic and career goals. Your completed documents from the following projects are good examples to show what you have learned: 2G, 2K, and 2L.

GO! FOR JOB SUCCESS

Video: Customer Service

Your instructor may assign this video to your class, and then ask you to think about, or discuss with your classmates, these questions:

FotolEdhar / Fotolia

How could Lee have been more helpful to the customer?

What did the supervisor, Christine, do to calm the customer?

What might SunTel do on a company-wide basis to create a better customer service experience?

END OF CHAPTER

SUMMARY

Use Flash Fill to recognize a pattern in data and automatically fill in values when you enter examples of desired output. Flash Fill can split data from two or more cells or combine data from two cells.

Functions are formulas that Excel provides and that perform calculations by using specific values in a particular order or structure. Statistical functions are useful to analyze a group of measurements.

You can navigate among worksheets in a workbook by clicking the sheet tabs, which identify each worksheet in a workbook. Use multiple worksheets in a workbook to organize data in a logical arrangement.

Dates are a value you can enter in a cell to which Excel assigns a serial value—a number—so that you can treat dates like other numbers. For example, you can find the number of days between two dates.

GO! LEARN IT ONLINE

Review the concepts, key terms, and MOS skills in this chapter by completing these online challenges, which you can find at **MyITLab**.

Matching and Multiple Choice: Answer matching and multiple choice questions to test what you learned in this chapter.

Lessons on the GO!: Learn how to use all the new apps and features as they are introduced by Microsoft.

MOS Prep Quiz: Answer questions to review the MOS skills that you practiced in this chapter.

GO! COLLABORATIVE TEAM PROJECT (Available in **MyITLab** and Instructor Resource Center)

If your instructor assigns this project to your class, you can expect to work with one or more of your classmates—either in person or by using Internet tools—to create work products similar to those that you created in this chapter. A team is a group of workers who work together to solve a problem, make a decision, or create a work product. Collaboration is when you work together with others as a team in an intellectual endeavor to complete a shared task or achieve a shared goal.

Your instructor will assign Projects from this list to ensure your learning and assess your knowledge.

Project	Apply Skills from These Chapter Objectives	Project Type	Project Location
2A **MyITLab**	Objectives 1–6 from Project 2A	**2A Instructional Project (Grader Project)** Guided instruction to learn the skills in Project 2A.	In MyITLab and in text
2B **MyITLab**	Objectives 7–12 from Project 2B	**2B Instructional Project (Grader Project)** Guided instruction to learn the skills in Project 2B.	In MyITLab and in text
2C	Objectives 1–6 from Project 2A	**2C Skills Review (Scorecard Grading)** A guided review of the skills from Project 2A.	In text
2D	Objectives 7–12 from Project 2B	**2D Skills Review (Scorecard Grading)** A guided review of the skills from Project 2B.	In text
2E **MyITLab**	Objectives 1–6 from Project 2A	**2E Mastery (Grader Project)** **Mastery and Transfer of Learning** A demonstration of your mastery of the skills in Project 2A with extensive decision making.	In MyITLab and in text
2F **MyITLab**	Objectives 7–12 from Project 2B	**2F Mastery (Grader Project)** **Mastery and Transfer of Learning** A demonstration of your mastery of the skills in Project 2B with extensive decision making.	In MyITLab and in text
2G **MyITLab**	Objectives 1–12 from Projects 2A and 2B	**2G Mastery (Grader Project)** **Mastery and Transfer of Learning** A demonstration of your mastery of the skills in Projects 2A and 2B with extensive decision making.	In MyITLab and in text
2H	Combination of Objectives from Projects 2A and 2B	**2H GO! Fix It (Scorecard Grading)** **Critical Thinking** A demonstration of your mastery of the skills in Projects 2A and 2B by creating a correct result from a document that contains errors you must find.	Instructor Resource Center (IRC) and MyITLab
2I	Combination of Objectives from Projects 2A and 2B	**2I GO! Make It (Scorecard Grading)** **Critical Thinking** A demonstration of your mastery of the skills in Projects 2A and 2B by creating a result from a supplied picture.	IRC and MyITLab
2J	Combination of Objectives from Projects 2A and 2B	**2J GO! Solve It (Rubric Grading)** **Critical Thinking** A demonstration of your mastery of the skills in Projects 2A and 2B, your decision-making skills, and your critical-thinking skills. A task-specific rubric helps you self-assess your result.	IRC and MyITLab
2K	Combination of Objectives from Projects 2A and 2B	**2K GO! Solve It (Rubric Grading)** **Critical Thinking** A demonstration of your mastery of the skills in Projects 2A and 2B, your decision-making skills, and your critical-thinking skills. A task-specific rubric helps you self-assess your result.	In text
2L	Combination of Objectives from Projects 2A and 2B	**2L GO! Think (Rubric Grading)** **Critical Thinking** A demonstration of your understanding of the chapter concepts applied in a manner that you would outside of college. An analytic rubric helps you and your instructor grade the quality of your work by comparing it to the work an expert in the discipline would create.	In text
2M	Combination of Objectives from Projects 2A and 2B	**2M GO! Think (Rubric Grading)** **Critical Thinking** A demonstration of your understanding of the chapter concepts applied in a manner that you would outside of college. An analytic rubric helps you and your instructor grade the quality of your work by comparing it to the work an expert in the discipline would create.	IRC and MyITLab
2N	Combination of Objectives from Projects 2A and 2B	**2N You and GO! (Rubric Grading)** **Critical Thinking** A demonstration of your understanding of the chapter concepts applied in a manner that you would in a personal situation. An analytic rubric helps you and your instructor grade the quality of your work.	IRC and MyITLab
2O	Combination of Objectives from Projects 2A and 2B	**2O Collaborative Team Project for EXCEL Chapter 2** **Critical Thinking** A demonstration of your understanding of concepts and your ability to work collaboratively in a group role-playing assessment, requiring both collaboration and self-management.	IRC and MyITLab

GLOSSARY

GLOSSARY OF CHAPTER KEY TERMS

Arguments The values that an Excel function uses to perform calculations or operations.

AVERAGE function An Excel function that adds a group of values, and then divides the result by the number of values in the group.

Comparison operators Symbols that evaluate each value to determine if it is the same (=), greater than (>), less than (<), or in between a range of values as specified by the criteria.

Conditional format A format that changes the appearance of a cell—for example, by adding cell shading or font color—based on a condition; if the condition is true, the cell is formatted based on that condition, and if the condition is false, the cell is *not* formatted.

COUNT function A statistical function that counts the number of cells in a range that contains numbers.

COUNTIF function A statistical function that counts the number of cells within a range that meet the given condition and that has two arguments—the range of cells to check and the criteria.

Criteria Conditions that you specify in a logical function.

Data bar A cell format consisting of a shaded bar that provides a visual cue to the reader about the value of a cell relative to other cells; the length of the bar represents the value in the cell—a longer bar represents a higher value and a shorter bar represents a lower value.

Detail sheet The worksheets that contain the details of the information summarized on a summary sheet.

Drag and drop The action of moving a selection by dragging it to a new location.

Excel table A series of rows and columns that contains related data that is managed independently from the data in other rows and columns in the worksheet.

Filter The process of displaying only a portion of the data based on matching a specific value to show only the data that meets the criteria that you specify.

Find and Replace A command that searches the cells in a worksheet—or in a selected range—for matches and then replaces each match with a replacement value of your choice.

Flash Fill Recognizes a pattern in your data, and then automatically fills in values when you enter examples of the output that you want. Use it to split data from two or more cells or to combine data from two cells.

Freeze Panes A command that enables you to select one or more rows or columns and freeze (lock) them into place; the locked rows and columns become separate panes.

Function A predefined formula—a formula that Excel has already built for you—that performs calculations by using specific values in a particular order or structure.

IF function A function that uses a logical test to check whether a condition is met, and then returns one value if true, and another value if false.

Logical functions A group of functions that test for specific conditions and that typically use conditional tests to determine whether specified conditions are true or false.

Logical test Any value or expression that can be evaluated as being true or false.

MAX function An Excel function that determines the largest value in a selected range of values.

MEDIAN function An Excel function that finds the middle value that has as many values above it in the group as are below it; it differs from AVERAGE in that the result is not affected as much by a single value that is greatly different from the others.

MIN function An Excel function that determines the smallest value in a selected range of values.

Navigate The process of moving within a worksheet or workbook.

NOW function An Excel function that retrieves the date and time from your computer's calendar and clock and inserts the information into the selected cell.

Pane A portion of a worksheet window bounded by and separated from other portions by vertical and horizontal bars.

Paste The action of placing cell contents that have been copied or moved to the Clipboard into another location.

Paste area The target destination for data that has been cut or copied using the Office Clipboard.

Paste Options gallery A gallery of buttons that provides a Live Preview of all the Paste options available in the current context.

Print Titles An Excel command that enables you to specify rows and columns to repeat on each printed page.

Scale to Fit Excel commands that enable you to stretch or shrink the width, height, or both, of printed output to fit a maximum number of pages.

Sheet tabs The labels along the lower border of the workbook window that identify each worksheet.

Sort The process of arranging data in a specific order based on the value in each field.

Split Splits the window into multiple resizable panes that contain views of your worksheet. This is useful to view multiple distant parts of your worksheet at one time.

Statistical functions Excel functions, including the AVERAGE, MEDIAN, MIN, and MAX functions, which are useful to analyze a group of measurements.

SUM function A predefined formula that adds all the numbers in a selected range of cells.

Summary sheet A worksheet where totals from other worksheets are displayed and summarized.

Volatile A term used to describe an Excel function that is subject to change each time the workbook is reopened; for example, the NOW function updates itself to the current date and time each time the workbook is opened.

Apply 2A skills from these Objectives:

1 Use Flash Fill and the SUM, AVERAGE, MEDIAN, MIN, and MAX Functions

2 Move Data, Resolve Error Messages, and Rotate Text

3 Use COUNTIF and IF Functions and Apply Conditional Formatting

4 Use Date & Time Functions and Freeze Panes

5 Create, Sort, and Filter an Excel Table

6 View, Format, and Print a Large Worksheet

Skills Review Project 2C Roses

In the following Skills Review, you will edit a worksheet detailing the current inventory of roses at the Pasadena nursery. Your completed workbook will look similar to Figure 2.55.

PROJECT FILES

For Project 2C, you will need the following file:

e02C_Roses

You will save your workbook as:

Lastname_Firstname_2C_Roses

PROJECT RESULTS

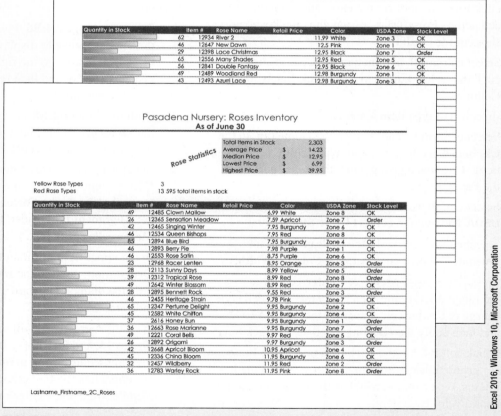

FIGURE 2.55

Excel 2016, Windows 10, Microsoft Corporation

(Project 2C Roses continues on the next page)

1 Start Excel. From your student files, locate and open **e02C_Roses**. **Save** the file in your **Excel Chapter 2** folder as **Lastname_Firstname_2C_Roses**

a. In the **column heading area**, point to **column C** to display the ⬇ pointer, and then drag to the right to select **columns C:D**. On the **Home tab**, in the **Cells group**, click the **Insert button arrow**, and then click **Insert Sheet Columns**.

b. Click cell **C14**, type **12113** and then on the **Formula Bar**, click **Enter** to confirm the entry and keep cell **C14** as the active cell. On the **Home tab**, in the **Editing group**, click **Fill**, and then click **Flash Fill**.

c. Click cell **D14**, type **Zone 5** On the **Formula Bar**, click **Enter** to confirm the entry and keep the cell active. Press Ctrl + E, which is the keyboard shortcut for Flash Fill.

d. Select **column B**, and then in the **Cells group**, click the **Delete button arrow**. Click **Delete Sheet Columns**.

2 In cell **B13** type **Item #** and press Enter.

a. Select **column C**, and then on the **Home tab**, in the **Clipboard group**, click **Cut**. Click cell **G1**, and then in the **Clipboard group**, click the upper portion of the **Paste** button.

b. Select and then delete **column C**. In cell **F13** type **USDA Zone** and in cell **G13** type **Stock Level**

c. Select columns **A:G**. In the **Cells group**, click **Format**, and then click **AutoFit Column Width**.

d. Press Ctrl + Home. **Merge & Center** cell **A1** across the range **A1:G1**, and then apply the **Title** cell style. **Merge & Center** cell **A2** across the range **A2:G2**, and then apply the **Heading 1** cell style. Click **Save**.

3 Click cell **B4**. On the **Formulas tab**, in the **Function Library group**, click **AutoSum**, and then within the parentheses, type **a14:a68** which is the range containing the quantities for each item.

a. Click cell **B5**. On the **Formulas tab**, in the **Function Library group**, click **More Functions**. Point to **Statistical**, click **AVERAGE**, and then in the **Number1** box, type **d14:d68** which is the range containing the *Retail Price* for each item. Click **OK**.

b. Click cell **B6**. In the **Function Library group**, click **More Functions**, point to **Statistical**, and then click **MEDIAN**. In the **Function Arguments** dialog box,

to the right of the **Number1** box, click **Collapse Dialog**, and then select the range **D14:D68**. Click **Expand Dialog**, and then click **OK**. Recall that you can select or type a range and that you can collapse the dialog box to make it easier to view your selection.

c. Click cell **B7**, and then by typing or selecting, insert the **MIN** function to determine the lowest **Retail Price**. Click cell **B8**, and then insert the **MAX** function to determine the highest **Retail Price**.

4 Select cell **B4**. On the **Home tab**, apply **Comma Style**, and then click **Decrease Decimal** two times. Select the range **B5:B8**, and then apply the **Accounting Number Format**.

a. Select the range **A4:B8**. Point to the right edge of the selected range to display the 🔭 pointer. Drag the selected range to the right until the ScreenTip displays *D4:E8*, and then release the mouse button. AutoFit **column D**.

b. With the range **D4:E8** selected, on the **Home tab**, in the **Styles group**, display the **Cell Styles** gallery, and then apply **20% - Accent1**.

c. In cell **C6**, type **Rose Statistics** Select the range **C4:C8**, right-click over the selection, and then click **Format Cells**. In the **Format Cells** dialog box, click the **Alignment tab**. Under **Text control**, select the **Merge cells** check box.

d. In the upper right portion of the dialog box, under **Orientation**, point to the **red diamond**, and then drag the diamond upward until the **Degrees** box indicates *20*. Click **OK**.

e. With the merged cell still selected, change the **Font Size** to **14**, and then apply **Bold** and **Italic**. Click the **Font Color button arrow**, and then in the fifth column, click the first color—**Blue, Accent 1**. Apply **Middle Align** and **Center** to the cell.

5 Click cell **B10**. On the **Formulas tab**, in the **Function Library group**, click **More Functions**, and then display the list of **Statistical** functions. Click **COUNTIF**.

a. As the range, type **e14:e68** which is the range with the color of each item. Click in the **Criteria** box, type **Yellow** and then click **OK** to calculate the number of yellow rose types.

(Project 2C Roses continues on the next page)

b. Click cell **G14**. On the **Formulas tab**, in the **Function Library group**, click **Logical**, and then on the list, click **IF**. If necessary, drag the title bar of the **Function Arguments** dialog box up or down so that you can view **row 14** on your screen.

c. With the insertion point in the **Logical_test** box, click cell **A14**, and then type **<40** Press ⟨Tab⟩ to move the insertion point to the **Value_if_true** box, and then type **Order** Press ⟨Tab⟩ to move the insertion point to the **Value_if_false** box, type **OK** and then click **OK**. Using the fill handle, copy the function in cell **G14** down through cell **G68**.

6 With the range **G14:G68** selected, on the **Home tab**, in the **Styles group**, click **Conditional Formatting**. In the list, point to **Highlight Cells Rules**, and then click **Text that Contains**.

a. In the **Text That Contains** dialog box, with the insertion point blinking in the first box, type **Order** and then in the second box, click the **arrow**. On the list, click **Custom Format**.

b. In the **Format Cells** dialog box, on the **Font tab**, under **Font style**, click **Bold Italic**. Click the **Color arrow**, and then under **Theme Colors**, in the fourth column, click the first color—**Blue-Gray, Text 2**. Click **OK** two times to apply the font color, bold, and italic to the cells that contain the word *Order*.

c. Select the range **A14:A68**. In the **Styles group**, click **Conditional Formatting**. In the list, point to **Data Bars**, and then under **Gradient Fill**, click **Red Data Bar**. Click anywhere to cancel the selection.

d. Select the range **E14:E68**. On the **Home tab**, in the **Editing group**, click **Find & Select**, and then click **Replace**. In the **Find and Replace** dialog box, in the **Find what** box, type **Deep Burgundy** and then in the **Replace with** box type **Burgundy** Click **Replace All** and then click **OK**. In the lower right corner of the **Find and Replace** dialog box, click **Close**.

e. Scroll down as necessary, and then click cell **A70**. Type **Edited by Maria Rios** and then press ⟨Enter⟩. With cell **A71** as the active cell, on the **Formulas tab**, in the **Function Library group**, click **Date & Time**. In the list of functions, click **NOW**, and then click **OK** to enter the current date and time. **Save** your workbook.

7 Click any cell in the data below row 13. Click the **Insert tab**, and then in the **Tables group**, click **Table**. In the **Create Table** dialog box, be sure the **My table has headers** check box is selected, and then click **OK**. On the **Design tab**, in the **Table Styles group**, click **More** ⟨▾⟩ and then under **Light**, locate and click **Table Style Light 9**.

a. In the header row of the table, click the **Retail Price arrow**, and then from the menu, click **Sort Smallest to Largest**. Click the **Color arrow**. On the menu, click the **(Select All)** check box to clear all the check boxes. Scroll as necessary and then select only the **Red** check box. Click **OK**.

b. Click anywhere in the table. On the **Design tab**, in the **Table Style Options group**, select the **Total Row** check box. Click cell **A69**, click the arrow that displays to the right of cell **A69**, and then click **Sum**. In cell **B11**, type the result **13** and then press ⟨Tab⟩. In cell **C11**, type **595 total items in stock** and then press ⟨Enter⟩.

c. In the header row of the table, click the **Color arrow** and then click **Clear Filter From "Color"** to redisplay all of the data. Click anywhere in the table. Click the **Design tab**, in the **Table Style Options group**, clear the **Total Row** check box.

8 On the **Page Layout tab**, in the **Themes group**, click **Themes** and then click the **Ion** theme. Change the **Orientation** to **Landscape**.

a. In the **Page Setup group**, click **Margins**, and then click **Custom Margins** to display the **Page Setup** dialog box.

b. On the **Margins tab**, under **Center on page**, select the **Horizontally** check box. On the **Header/Footer tab**, display the **Custom Footer**, and then in the **Left section**, insert the file name. Click **OK** two times.

c. In the **Page Setup** group, click **Print Titles** to redisplay the **Page Setup** dialog box. Under **Print titles**, click in the **Rows to repeat at top** box, and then at the right, click **Collapse Dialog**. From the **row heading area**, select **row 13**, and then click **Expand Dialog**. Click **OK** to print the column titles in row 13 at the top of every page.

d. Press ⟨Ctrl⟩ + ⟨F2⟩ to display the **Print Preview**. At the bottom of the **Settings group**, click **No Scaling**, and then on the displayed list, click **Fit All Columns on One Page**.

(Project 2C Roses continues on the next page)

e. On the left, click **Info**, and then in the lower right corner, click **Show All Properties**. As the **Tags**, type **inventory, Pasadena, roses** In the **Subject** box, type your course name and section number. Be sure your name displays as the author.

9 ▸ **Save** your workbook. If directed by your instructor to do so, submit your paper printout, your electronic image of your document that looks like a printed document, or your original Excel file. If required by your instructor, print or create an electronic version of your worksheet with formulas displayed. In the upper right corner of the Excel window, click **Close**.

END | You have completed Project 2C

Skills Review   Project 2D Canada

In the following Skills Review, you will edit a workbook that summarizes sales in the Eastern and Western region of Canada. Your completed workbook will look similar to Figure 2.56.

PROJECT FILES

For Project 2D, you will need the following file:

e02D_Canada

You will save your workbook as:

Lastname_Firstname_2D_Canada

PROJECT RESULTS

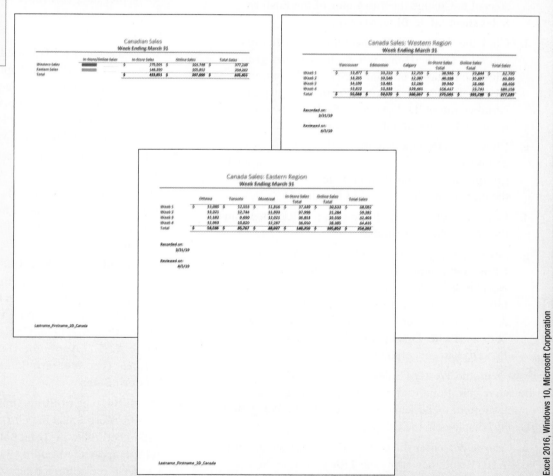

FIGURE 2.56

(Project 2D Canada continues on the next page)

1 Start Excel. From your student files, open **e02D_Canada**. **Save** the file in your **Excel Chapter 2** folder as **Lastname_Firstname_2D_Canada**

a. Point to the **Sheet1 tab**, and then double-click to select the sheet tab name. Type **Western Sales** and then press Enter.

b. Point to the **Sheet2 tab**, right-click, and then from the shortcut menu, click **Rename**. Type **Eastern Sales** and press Enter.

c. Point to the **Western Sales sheet tab** and right-click. On the shortcut menu, point to **Tab Color**, and then in the last column, click the first color—**Green, Accent 6**. Change the **Tab Color** of the **Eastern Sales sheet tab** to **Blue, Accent 5**.

d. Click the **Western Sales sheet tab**, and then click cell **A13**. On the **Home tab**, in the **Number group**, click the **Number Format arrow**. At the bottom of the list, click **More Number Formats** to display the **Number tab** of the **Format Cells** dialog box. Click the **3/14/12** type, and then click **OK**.

e. Click cell **A16**, type **4/5/19** and then press Enter. Click cell **A13**, and then on the **Home tab**, in the **Clipboard group**, click **Format Painter**. Click cell **A16** to copy the date format from cell **A13** to cell **A16**.

f. Click cell **A1**. In the **Editing group**, click **Clear**, and then click **Clear Formats**.

g. Select the range **A5:A16**. On the **Home tab**, in the **Clipboard group**, click **Copy**. At the bottom of the workbook window, click the **Eastern Sales sheet tab** to make it the active worksheet. Right-click cell **A5**, and then under **Paste Options**, click the first button—**Paste**. Display the **Western Sales** sheet. Press Esc to cancel the moving border.

2 With the **Western Sales** sheet active, make cell **A1** the active cell. Point to the sheet tab, right-click, and then on the shortcut menu, click **Select All Sheets**. Verify that *[Group]* displays in the title bar.

a. **Merge & Center** the text in cell **A1** across the range **A1:G1**, and then apply the **Title** cell style. Select **columns A:G**, and then set their widths to **100 pixels**.

b. Click cell **A2**, type **Week Ending March 31** and then on the **Formula Bar**, click the **Enter** button to keep cell **A2** as the active cell. **Merge & Center** the text across the range **A2:G2**, and then apply the **Heading 1** cell style.

c. Select the range **B4:G4**, and then apply the **Heading 3** cell style. In the **Alignment group**, click **Center**, **Middle Align**, and **Wrap Text**.

d. With the sheets still grouped and the **Western Sales** sheet active, click cell **E5**. On the **Home tab**, in the **Editing group**, click the **AutoSum** button, and then press Enter. Click cell **E5**, and then drag the fill handle down to copy the formula through cell **E8**.

e. Click cell **G5**, type = click cell **E5**, type + click cell **F5**, and then press Enter. Copy the formula down through cell **G8**. In cell **A9**, type **Total** Select the range **B5:G9**, and then hold down Alt and press = to enter the SUM function for all the columns. Select the range **A5:A9**, and then apply the **Heading 4** cell style.

f. Select the range **B5:G5**, hold down Ctrl, and then select the range **B9:G9**. Apply the **Accounting Number Format** and decrease the decimal places to zero. Select the range **B6:G8**, and then apply **Comma Style** with zero decimal places. Select the range **B9:G9**, and then apply the **Total** cell style.

3 Click the **Eastern Sales sheet tab** to cancel the grouping and display the second worksheet.

a. To the right of the **Eastern Sales sheet tab**, click the **New sheet** button. **Rename** the new worksheet tab **Summary** and then change the **Tab Color** to **Gold, Accent 4**.

b. Widen **columns A:E** to **150** pixels. In cell **A1**, type **Canadian Sales** and then **Merge & Center** the title across the range **A1:E1**. Apply the **Title** cell style. In cell **A2**, type **Week Ending March 31** and then **Merge & Center** the text across the range **A2:E2**. Apply the **Heading 1** cell style. In cell **A5**, type **Western Sales** and in cell **A6**, type **Eastern Sales**

c. In cell **B4**, type **In-Store/Online Sales** and in cell **C4**, type **In-Store Sales** In cell **D4**, type **Online Sales** and in cell **E4**, type **Total Sales** Select the range **B4:E4**, apply the **Heading 3** cell style, and then **Center** these column titles.

d. Click cell **C5**. Type = and then click the **Western Sales sheet tab**. In the **Western Sales** worksheet, click cell **E9**, and then press Enter. Click cell **D5**. Type = and then click the **Western Sales sheet tab**. Click cell **F9**, and then press Enter.

(Project 2D Canada continues on the next page)

e. By using the same technique, in cells **C6** and **D6**, insert the total **In-Store Sales** and **Online Sales** data from the **Eastern Sales** worksheet.

f. Select the range **C5:E6**, and then click **AutoSum** to total the two rows. In cell **A7**, type **Total** and then in **C7** sum the range **C5:C6**. Fill the formula across to **D7:E7**.

g. Select the nonadjacent ranges **C5:E5** and **C7:E7**, and then apply **Accounting Number Format** with zero decimal places. Select the range **C6:E6**, and then apply **Comma Style** with zero decimal places. Select the range **C7:E7**, and then apply the **Total** cell style. Select the range **A5:A7** and apply the **Heading 4** cell style.

h. Click cell **B5**. On the **Insert tab**, in the **Sparklines group**, click **Column**. In the **Create Sparklines** dialog box, with the insertion point blinking in the **Data Range** box, select the range **C5:D5** and then click **OK**.

i. Click cell **B6**, and then insert a **Column Sparkline** for the range **C6:D6**. With the **Eastern Sales** sparkline selected, in the **Style group**, apply the second style in the third row—**Sparkline Style Accent 2, (no dark or light)**.

4 Point to the **Summary sheet tab**, hold down the left mouse button to display a small black triangle, drag to the left until the triangle and mouse pointer are to the left of the **Western Sales sheet tab**, and then release the left

mouse button to move the sheet to the first position in the workbook.

a. Be sure the **Summary** worksheet is the active sheet. Point to the **Summary sheet tab**, right-click, and then click **Select All Sheets** to display [*Group*] in the title bar. Press Ctrl + Home to move to cell A1. On the **Page Layout tab**, in the **Page Setup group**, click **Margins**, and then click **Custom Margins** to display the **Page Setup** dialog box. On the **Margins tab**, center the worksheets **Horizontally**. On the **Header/Footer tab**, insert the file name in the **left section** of the footer.

b. Display the **Print Preview** of the worksheets. Under **Settings**, click **No Scaling**, and then click **Fit All Columns on One Page**. Use the **Next** button to view all three worksheets.

c. On the left, click **Info**, and then in the lower right corner of the screen, click **Show All Properties**. As the **Tags**, type **Canada, sales** In the **Subject** box, type your course name and section number. Be sure your name displays as the author.

d. **Save** your workbook. If directed by your instructor to do so, submit your paper printout, your electronic image of your document that looks like a printed document, or your original Excel file. If required by your instructor, print or create an electronic version of your worksheet with formulas displayed. In the upper right corner of the Excel window, click **Close**.

END | You have completed Project 2D

Mastering Excel Project 2E Plants

In the following project, you will edit a worksheet detailing the current inventory of plants at the Pasadena facility. Your completed worksheet will look similar to Figure 2.57.

Apply 2A skills from these Objectives:

1 Use Flash Fill and the SUM, AVERAGE, MEDIAN, MIN, and MAX Functions

2 Move Data, Resolve Error Messages, and Rotate Text

3 Use COUNTIF and IF Functions and Apply Conditional Formatting

4 Use Date & Time Functions and Freeze Panes

5 Create, Sort, and Filter an Excel Table

6 View, Format, and Print a Large Worksheet

PROJECT FILES

For Project 2E, you will need the following file:

e02E_Plants

You will save your workbook as:

Lastname_Firstname_2E_Plants

PROJECT RESULTS

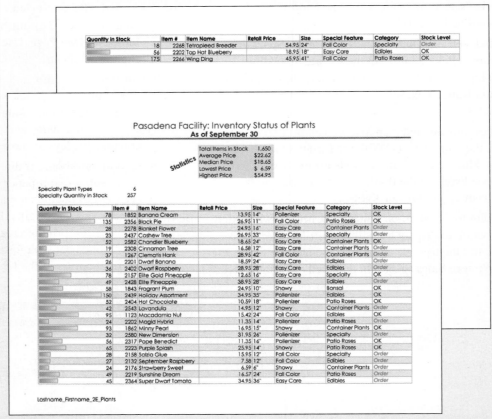

FIGURE 2.57

Excel 2016, Windows 10, Microsoft Corporation

(Project 2E Plants continues on the next page)

Mastering Excel Project 2E Plants (continued)

1 Start Excel. From your student files, locate and open **e02E_Plants**, and then **Save** the file in your **Excel Chapter 2** folder as **Lastname_Firstname_2E_Plants**

2 To the right of **column B**, insert two new columns to create **new blank columns C and D**. By using **Flash Fill** in the two new columns, split the data in **column B** into a column for *Item #* in **column C** and *Category* in **column D**. As necessary, type **Item #** as the column title in **column C** and **Category** as the column title in **column D**. Delete **column B**.

3 By using the **Cut** and **Paste** commands, cut **column C**—*Category*—and paste it to **column H**, and then delete the empty **column C**. Apply **AutoFit** to **columns A:G**.

4 In cell **B4**, insert a function to calculate the **Total Items in Stock** by summing the **Quantity in Stock** data, and then apply **Comma Style** with zero decimal places to the result.

5 In each cell in the range **B5:B8**, insert functions to calculate the Average, Median, Lowest, and Highest retail prices, and then apply the **Accounting Number Format** to each result.

6 Move the range **A4:B8** to the range **D4:E8**, apply the **40% - Accent4** cell style to the range, and then select **columns D:E** and **AutoFit**.

7 In cell **C6**, type **Statistics** and then select the range **C4:C8**. In the **Format Cells** dialog box, merge the selected cells, and change the text **Orientation to 25 Degrees**. Format the cell with **Bold**, a **Font Size of 14 pt**, and then change the **Font Color** to **Blue-Gray, Text 2**. Apply **Middle Align** and **Align Right**.

8 In the **Category** column, **Replace All** occurrences of **Vine Roses** with **Patio Roses**

9 In cell **B10**, use the **COUNTIF** function to count the number of **Specialty** plant types in the **Category** column.

10 In cell **H13**, type **Stock Level** In cell **H14**, enter an **IF** function to determine the items that must be ordered.

If the **Quantity in Stock** is less than **50** the **Value_if_true** is **Order** Otherwise the **Value_if_false** is **OK** Fill the formula down through cell **H42**.

11 Apply **Conditional Formatting** to the **Stock Level** column so that cells that contain the text *Order* are formatted with **Bold Italic** and with a **Color** of **Green, Accent 6**. Apply conditional formatting to the **Quantity in Stock** column by applying a **Gradient Fill Green Data Bar**.

12 Format the range **A13:H42** as a **Table** with headers, and apply the style **Table Style Light 20**. Sort the table from **A to Z** by **Item Name**, and then filter on the **Category** column to display the **Specialty** types.

13 Display a **Total Row** in the table, and then in cell **A43**, **Sum** the **Quantity in Stock** for the **Specialty** items. Type the result in cell **B11**. Click in the table, and then on the **Design tab**, remove the total row from the table. Clear the **Category** filter.

14 **Merge & Center** the title and subtitle across **columns A:H**, and apply **Title** and **Heading 1** styles, respectively. Change the theme to **Mesh**, and then select and **AutoFit** all the columns.

15 Set the orientation to **Landscape**. In the **Page Setup** dialog box, center the worksheet **Horizontally**, insert a custom footer in the **left section** with the file name, and set **row 13** to repeat at the top of each page. Display the **Print Preview**. Apply the **Fit All Columns on One Page** setting.

16 As the **Tags**, type **plants inventory, Pasadena** As the **Subject**, type your course name and section number. Be sure your name displays as the **Author**.

17 **Save** your workbook. If directed by your instructor to do so, submit your paper printout, your electronic image of your document that looks like a printed document, or your original Excel file. If required by your instructor, print or create an electronic version of your worksheet with formulas displayed. In the upper right corner of the Excel window, click **Close**.

> **END | You have completed Project 2E**

Mastering Excel   Project 2F Bonus

In the following project, you will edit a workbook that summarizes the compensation for the commercial salespersons who qualified for bonuses in the Western and Eastern Canadian regions. Your completed worksheets will look similar to Figure 2.58.

Apply 2B skills from these Objectives:

7 Navigate a Workbook and Rename Worksheets

8 Enter Dates, Clear Contents, and Clear Formats

9 Copy and Paste by Using the Paste Options Gallery

10 Edit and Format Multiple Worksheets at the Same Time

11 Create a Summary Sheet with Column Sparklines

12 Format and Print Multiple Worksheets in a Workbook

PROJECT FILES

For Project 2F, you will need the following file:

e02F_Bonus

You will save your workbook as:

Lastname_Firstname_2F_Bonus

PROJECT RESULTS

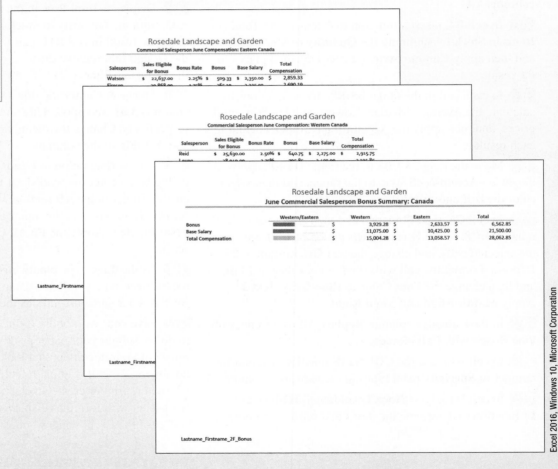

FIGURE 2.58

(Project 2F Bonus continues on the next page)

1 Start Excel. From your student files, open **e02F_Bonus**, and then save the file in your **Excel Chapter 2** folder as **Lastname_Firstname_2F_Bonus**

2 Rename **Sheet1** as **Western** and change the **Tab Color** to **Brown, Accent 2**. Rename **Sheet2** as **Eastern** and change the **Tab Color** to **Orange, Accent 1**.

3 Click the **Western sheet tab** to make it the active sheet, and then group the worksheets. In cell **A1**, type **Rosedale Landscape and Garden** and then **Merge & Center** the text across the range **A1:F1**. Apply the **Title** cell style. **Merge & Center** the text in cell **A2** across the range **A2:F2**, and then apply the **Heading 3** cell style.

4 With the sheets still grouped, in cell **D5** calculate the **Bonus** for *Reid* by multiplying the **Sales Eligible for Bonus** by the **Bonus Rate**. **Copy** the formula down through cell **D8**.

5 In cell **F5**, calculate **Total Compensation** by summing the **Bonus** and **Base Salary** for *Reid*. Copy the formula down through the cell **F8**.

6 In **row 9**, sum the columns for **Sales Eligible for Bonus**, **Bonus**, **Base Salary**, and **Total Compensation**. Apply the **Accounting Number Format** with two decimal places to the appropriate cells in **row 5** and **row 9** (do not include the percentages).

7 Apply the **Comma Style** with two decimal places to the appropriate cells in **rows 6:8** (do not include the percentages). Apply the **Total** cell style to the appropriate cells in the Total row.

8 Click the Eastern sheet tab to ungroup the sheets, and then insert a new worksheet. Change the sheet name to **Summary** and then change the **Tab Color** to **Brown, Text 2**. Widen **column A** to **210** pixels, widen **columns B:E** to **155** pixels.

9 Move the **Summary** sheet so that it is the first sheet in the workbook. In cell **A1** of the **Summary** sheet, type **Rosedale Landscape and Garden** and then **Merge & Center** the title across the range **A1:E1**. Apply the **Title** cell style. In cell **A2**, type **June Commercial Salesperson Bonus Summary: Canada** and then **Merge & Center** the text across the range **A2:E2**. Apply the **Heading 1** cell style.

10 In the range **A5:A7**, type the following row titles and then apply the **Heading 4** cell style:

Bonus

Base Salary

Total Compensation

11 In the range **B4:E4**, type the following column titles, and then **Center** and apply the **Heading 3** cell style.

Western/Eastern

Western

Eastern

Total

12 In cell **C5**, enter a formula that references cell **D9** in the **Western** worksheet so that the total bonus amount for the Western region displays in cell **C5**. Create similar formulas to enter the total **Base Salary** for the Western region in cell **C6**. Using the same technique, enter formulas in the range **D5:D6** so that the **Eastern** totals display.

13 Sum the **Bonus** and **Base Salary** rows, and then calculate **Total Compensation** for the **Western**, **Eastern**, and **Total** columns.

14 In cell **B5**, insert a **Column Sparkline** for the range **C5:D5**. In cells **B6** and **B7**, insert **Column** sparklines for the appropriate ranges to compare Western totals with Eastern totals.

15 To the sparkline in cell **B5**, apply the second style in the third row—**Sparkline Style Accent 2, (no dark or light)**. To the sparkline in cell **B6**, apply the first style in the fifth row—**Sparkline Style Dark #1**. To the sparkline in cell **B7**, apply the first style in the fourth row—**Sparkline Style Accent 1, Lighter 40%**.

16 **Group** the three worksheets, and then center the worksheets **Horizontally** on the page, and insert a **Custom Footer** in the **left section** with the file name. Change the **Orientation** to **Landscape**.

17 As the **Tags**, type **June, bonus, compensation** As the **Subject**, type your course name and section number. Be sure your name displays as the **Author** and then **Save**. If directed by your instructor to do so, submit your paper printout, your electronic image of your document that looks like a printed document, or your original Excel file. If required by your instructor, print or create an electronic version of your worksheet with formulas displayed. In the upper right corner of the Excel window, click **Close**.

END | You have completed Project 2F

MyITLab® grader

Mastering Excel | Project 2G Inventory

In the following project, you will edit a worksheet that summarizes the inventory of bulbs and trees at the Pasadena facility. Your completed workbook will look similar to Figure 2.59.

Apply a combination of 2A and 2B skills:

1 Use Flash Fill and the SUM, AVERAGE, MEDIAN, MIN, and MAX Functions

2 Move Data, Resolve Error Messages, and Rotate Text

3 Use COUNTIF and IF Functions and Apply Conditional Formatting

4 Use Date & Time Functions and Freeze Panes

5 Create, Sort, and Filter an Excel Table

6 View, Format and Print a Large Worksheet

7 Navigate a Workbook and Rename Worksheets

8 Enter Dates, Clear Contents, and Clear Formats

9 Copy and Paste by Using the Paste Options Gallery

10 Edit and Format Multiple Worksheets at the Same Time

11 Create a Summary Sheet with Column Sparklines

12 Format and Print Multiple Worksheets in a Workbook

PROJECT FILES

For Project 2G, you will need the following file:

e02G_Inventory

You will save your workbook as:

Lastname_Firstname_2G_Inventory

PROJECT RESULTS

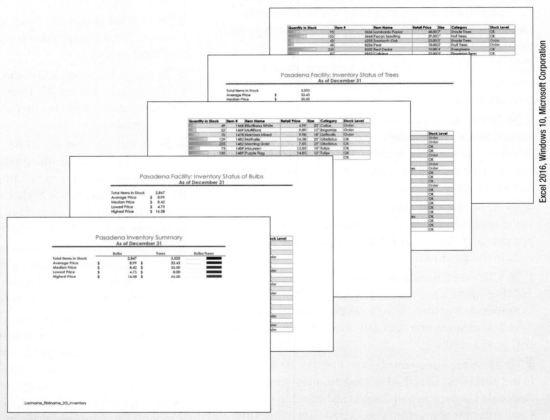

Excel 2016, Windows 10, Microsoft Corporation

FIGURE 2.59

(Project 2G Inventory continues on the next page)

1 Start Excel. From your student files, open **e02G_Inventory**. Save the file in your **Excel Chapter 2** folder as **Lastname_Firstname_2G_Inventory**

2 Change the **Theme** to **Slice**. Rename **Sheet1** as **Bulbs** and **Sheet2** as **Trees** and then make the **Bulbs sheet** the active sheet.

3 To the right of **column B**, insert two new columns to create **new blank columns C and D**. By using **Flash Fill** in the two new columns, split the data in **column B** into a column for *Item #* in **column C** and *Category* in **column D**. Type **Item #** as the column title in **column C** and **Category** as the column title in **column D**.

4 Delete **column B**. By using the **Cut** and **Paste** commands, cut **column C**—*Category*—and paste it to **column G**, and then delete the empty **column C**. Apply **AutoFit** to **columns A:F**.

5 Display the **Trees** worksheet, and then repeat Steps 3 and 4 on this worksheet.

6 Group the worksheets and then make the following calculations:

- In cell **B4**, enter a function to sum the **Quantity in Stock** data, and then apply **Comma Style** with zero decimal places to the result.
- In cells **B5:B8**, enter formulas to calculate the Average, Median, Lowest, and Highest retail prices, and then apply the **Accounting Number Format**.

7 Ungroup the worksheets. In each of the two worksheets, make the following calculations *without* grouping the sheets:

- In cell **B10**, enter a COUNTIF function to determine how many different types of **Tulips** are in stock on the **Bulbs** sheet and how many different types of **Evergreens** are in stock on the **Trees** worksheet.
- In cell **G14**, type **Stock Level** In cell **G15**, enter an **IF** function to determine the items that must be ordered. If the **Quantity in Stock** is less than **75** the **Value_if_true** is **Order** Otherwise the **Value_if_false** is **OK** Fill the formula down through all the rows.
- Apply **Conditional Formatting** to the **Stock Level** column so that cells that contain the text *Order* are formatted with **Bold Italic** with a **Font Color** of **Dark Blue, Text 2**. Apply **Gradient Fill Blue Data Bars** to the **Quantity in Stock** column.

8 In the **Bulbs** sheet, format the range **A14:G42** as a table with headers and apply **Table Style Light 20**. Insert a **Total Row**, filter by **Category** for **Tulips**, and then **Sum** the **Quantity in Stock** column. Record the result in cell **B11**.

9 Select the table, clear the filter, **Sort** the table on the **Item #** column from **Smallest to Largest**, and then remove the **Total Row**. On the **Page Layout tab**, set **Print Titles** so that **row 14** repeats at the top of each page.

10 In the **Trees** sheet, format the range **A14:G42** as a table with headers and apply **Table Style Light 19**. Insert a **Total Row**, filter by **Category** for **Evergreens**, and then **Sum** the **Quantity in Stock** column. Record the result in cell **B11**.

11 Select the table, clear the filter, **Sort** the table on the **Item #** column from **Smallest to Largest**, and then remove the **Total Row**. On the **Page Layout tab**, set **Print Titles** so that **row 14** repeats at the top of each page, and then **Save** your workbook.

12 Group the two worksheets. **Merge & Center** the title in cell **A1** across the range **A1:G1** and apply the **Title** cell style. **Merge & Center** the subtitle in cell **A2** across the range **A2:G2** and apply the **Heading 1** cell style. **AutoFit** Column A. **Center** the worksheets **Horizontally**, change the **Orientation** to **Landscape**, display the **Print Preview**, and then change the **Settings** to **Fit All Columns on One Page**.

13 In **Backstage** view, on the left click **Save**, and then ungroup the sheets. Make the **Trees** sheet the active sheet, and then insert a new worksheet. Change the sheet name to **Summary** and then widen **columns A:D** to **170** pixels. Move the **Summary** sheet so that it is the first sheet in the workbook.

14 In cell **A1**, type **Pasadena Inventory Summary** and then **Merge & Center** the title across the range **A1:D1**. Apply the **Title** cell style. In cell **A2**, type **As of December 31** and then **Merge & Center** the text across the range **A2:D2**. Apply the **Heading 1** cell style.

15 On the **Bulbs sheet**, **Copy** the range **A4:A8**. Display the **Summary sheet** and **Paste** the selection to cell **A5**. Apply the **Heading 4** cell style to the selection.

16 In the **Summary sheet**, in cell **B4**, type **Bulbs** In cell **C4** type **Trees** In cell **D4** type **Bulbs/Trees** and then **Center** the column titles. Apply the **Heading 3** cell style.

(Project 2G Inventory continues on the next page)

17 In cell **B5**, enter a formula that references cell **B4** in the **Bulbs sheet** so that the **Bulbs Total Items in Stock** displays in **B5**. Create similar formulas to enter the **Average Price**, **Median Price**, **Lowest Price**, and **Highest Price** from the **Bulbs sheet** into the **Summary** sheet in the range **B6:B9**.

18 Enter formulas in the range **C5:C9** that reference the appropriate cells in the **Trees** worksheet.

19 In cells **D5**, **D6**, **D7**, **D8**, and **D9**, insert **Column** sparklines using the values in the *Bulbs* and *Trees* columns. Format each sparkline using the first five Sparkline styles in the first row.

20 To the range **B5:C5**, apply **Comma Style** with zero decimal places, and to the range **B6:C9**, apply

Accounting Number Format. Center the **Summary** worksheet **Horizontally** and change the **Orientation** to **Landscape**. **Group** the worksheets and insert a footer in the left section with the **File Name**.

21 As the **Tags**, type **Pasadena inventory** As the **Subject**, type your course name and section number. Be sure your name displays as the **Author**.

22 In **Backstage** view, on the left click **Save**. If directed by your instructor to do so, submit your paper printout, your electronic image of your document that looks like a printed document, or your original Excel file. If required by your instructor, print or create an electronic version of your worksheet with formulas displayed. In the upper right corner of the Excel window, click **Close**.

END | You have completed Project 2G

Apply a combination of the 2A and 2B skills.

| GO! Fix It | Project 2H Planters | MyITLab |

| GO! Make It | Project 2I Salary | MyITLab |

| GO! Solve It | Project 2J Sod | MyITLab |

| GO! Solve It | Project 2K Products | MyITLab |

PROJECT FILES

For Project 2K, you will need the following file:

e02K_Products

You will save your workbook as:

Lastname_Firstname_2K_Products

From your student data files, open the file e02K_Products and save it as **Lastname_Firstname_2K_Products** This workbook contains two worksheets: one for U.S. sales data by product and one for Canadian sales data by product. Complete the two worksheets by calculating totals by product and by month. Then calculate the Percent of Total for each product, using absolute cell references as necessary. Format the worksheet, percentages, and values appropriately. Insert a new worksheet that summarizes the monthly totals for the United States and Canada. Enter the months as the column titles and the countries as the row titles. Include a Product Total column and a column for sparklines comparing the months. Format the Summary worksheet appropriately, including a title and subtitle. Include the file name in the footer, add appropriate document properties, and submit as directed.

Performance Level

Performance Criteria		Exemplary: You consistently applied the relevant skills.	Proficient: You sometimes, but not always, applied the relevant skills.	Developing: You rarely or never applied the relevant skills.
	Create formulas	All formulas are correct and are efficiently constructed.	Formulas are correct but not always constructed in the most efficient manner.	One or more formulas are missing or incorrect; or only numbers were entered.
	Create Summary worksheet	Summary worksheet created properly.	Summary worksheet was created but some elements were incorrect.	No Summary worksheet was created.
	Format appropriately	Formatting is appropriate.	Not all worksheets were appropriately formatted.	No formatting was applied.

END | You have completed Project 2K

OUTCOMES-BASED ASSESSMENTS

RUBRIC

The following outcomes-based assessments are open-ended assessments. That is, there is no specific correct result; your result will depend on your approach to the information provided. Make Professional Quality your goal. Use the following scoring rubric to guide you in how to approach the problem and then to evaluate how well your approach solves the problem.

The *criteria*—Software Mastery, Content, Format and Layout, and Process—represent the knowledge and skills you have gained that you can apply to solving the problem. The *levels of performance*—Professional Quality, Approaching Professional Quality, or Needs Quality Improvements—help you and your instructor evaluate your result.

	Your completed project is of Professional Quality if you:	Your completed project is Approaching Professional Quality if you:	Your completed project Needs Quality Improvements if you:
1-Software Mastery	Choose and apply the most appropriate skills, tools, and features and identify efficient methods to solve the problem.	Choose and apply some appropriate skills, tools, and features, but not in the most efficient manner.	Choose inappropriate skills, tools, or features, or are inefficient in solving the problem.
2-Content	Construct a solution that is clear and well organized, contains content that is accurate, appropriate to the audience and purpose, and is complete. Provide a solution that contains no errors in spelling, grammar, or style.	Construct a solution in which some components are unclear, poorly organized, inconsistent, or incomplete. Misjudge the needs of the audience. Have some errors in spelling, grammar, or style, but the errors do not detract from comprehension.	Construct a solution that is unclear, incomplete, or poorly organized; contains some inaccurate or inappropriate content; and contains many errors in spelling, grammar, or style. Do not solve the problem.
3-Format & Layout	Format and arrange all elements to communicate information and ideas, clarify function, illustrate relationships, and indicate relative importance.	Apply appropriate format and layout features to some elements, but not others. Overuse features, causing minor distraction.	Apply format and layout that does not communicate information or ideas clearly. Do not use format and layout features to clarify function, illustrate relationships, or indicate relative importance. Use available features excessively, causing distraction.
4-Process	Use an organized approach that integrates planning, development, self-assessment, revision, and reflection.	Demonstrate an organized approach in some areas, but not others; or, use an insufficient process of organization throughout.	Do not use an organized approach to solve the problem.

Apply a combination of the 2A and 2B skills.

GO! Think   Project 2L Palms

PROJECT FILES

For Project 2L, you will need the following file:

e02L_Palms

You will save your workbook as:

Lastname_Firstname_2L_Palms

Melanie Castillo, Product Manager for Rosedale Landscape and Garden, has requested a worksheet that summarizes the current palm tree inventory data. Melanie would like the worksheet to include the total Quantity in Stock and Number of Items for each of the four categories of palm trees, and she would like the items to be sorted from lowest to highest retail price. She would also like a separate column for Item # and for Category.

Edit the file e02L_Palms to provide Melanie with the information requested, and use the Table feature to find the data requested. Format the worksheet titles and data and include an appropriately formatted table so that the worksheet is professional and easy to read and understand. Insert a footer with the file name and add appropriate document properties. Save the file as **Lastname_Firstname_2L_Palms** and print or submit as directed by your instructor.

END | You have completed Project 2L

GO! Think   Project 2M Contracts   **MyITLab**

Build from Scratch

You and GO!   Project 2N Annual Expenses   **MyITLab**

Build from Scratch

GO! Collaborative Team Project   Project 2O Bell Orchid Hotels   **MyITLab**

Analyzing Data with Pie Charts, Line Charts, and What-If Analysis Tools

PROJECT **3A**

OUTCOMES
Present fund data in a pie chart.

PROJECT **3B**

OUTCOMES
Make projections using what-if analysis and present projections in a line chart.

OBJECTIVES

1. Chart Data with a Pie Chart
2. Format a Pie Chart
3. Edit a Workbook and Update a Chart
4. Use Goal Seek to Perform What-If Analysis

OBJECTIVES

5. Design a Worksheet for What-If Analysis
6. Answer What-If Questions by Changing Values in a Worksheet
7. Chart Data with a Line Chart

EuToch/Fotolia

In This Chapter GO! to Work with Excel

In this chapter, you will work with two different types of commonly used charts that make it easy to visualize data. You will create a pie chart in a separate chart sheet to show how the parts of a fund contribute to a total fund. Pie charts are one type of chart you can use to show part-to-whole relationships. You will also practice using parentheses in a formula, calculate the percentage rate of an increase, answer what-if questions, and then chart data in a line chart to show the flow of data over time. In this chapter, you will also practice formatting the axes in a line chart.

The projects in this chapter relate to the city of **Pacifica Bay**, a coastal city south of San Francisco. The city's access to major transportation provides both residents and businesses an opportunity to compete in the global marketplace. The city's mission is to create a more beautiful and more economically viable community for its residents. Each year the city welcomes a large number of tourists who enjoy exploring the rocky coastline and seeing the famous landmarks in San Francisco. The city encourages best environmental practices and partners with cities in other countries to promote sound government at the local level.

PROJECT ACTIVITIES

In Activities 3.01 through 3.12, you will edit a worksheet for Michael Larsen, City Manager, that reports the adjusted figures for Enterprise Fund Expenditures for the next fiscal year, and then present the data in a pie chart. Your completed worksheets will look similar to Figure 3.1.

PROJECT FILES

MyITLab
grader

If your instructor wants you to submit Project 3A in the MyITLab Grader system, log in to MyITLab, locate Grader Project 3A, and then download the files for this project.

For Project 3A, you will need the following file:
e03A_Enterprise_Fund

You will save your workbook as:
Lastname_Firstname_3A_Enterprise_Fund

Please always review the downloaded Grader instructions before beginning.

PROJECT RESULTS

GO!
Walk Thru
Project 3A

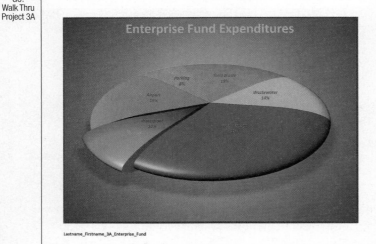

Enterprise Fund Expenditures

Lastname_Firstname_3A_Enterprise_Fund

Pacifica Bay
Enterprise Fund Expenditures

| | Recommended Adjustments | | |
	Originally Proposed	Adjusted	% of Total Fund Expenditures
Airport	$ 17,610,810	$ 18,121,067	18.12%
Parking	6,824,865	7,897,526	7.90%
Solid Waste	18,695,222	17,845,287	17.85%
Wastewater	12,657,765	13,985,695	13.99%
Water Usage	30,457,903	32,356,236	32.36%
Waterfront	10,976,843	9,794,189	9.79%
Total	$ 97,223,408	$ 100,000,000	

Lastname_Firstname_3A_Enterprise_Fund

FIGURE 3.1 Project 3A Enterprise Fund Pie Chart

Objective 1 Chart Data with a Pie Chart

GO! Learn How
Video E3-1

A *pie chart* shows the relationship of each part to a whole. The size of each pie slice is equal to its value compared to the total value of all the slices. A pie chart displays data that is arranged in a single column or single row, and shows the size of items in a single data series proportional to the sum of the items. Whereas a column or bar chart can have two or more data series in the chart, a pie chart can have only one data series.

Consider using a pie chart when you have only one data series to plot, you do not have more than seven categories, and the categories represent parts of a total value.

Activity 3.01 | Calculating Values for a Pie Chart

ALERT!   **To submit as an autograded project, log into MyITLab and download the files for this project, and begin with those files instead of e03A_Enterprise_Fund.**

A *fund* is a sum of money set aside for a specific purpose. In a municipal government like the city of Pacifica Bay, the *general fund* is money set aside for the normal operating activities of the city, such as police, fire, and administering the everyday functions of the city.

Municipal governments also commonly establish an *enterprise fund* to report income and expenditures related to municipal services for which a fee is charged in exchange for goods or services. For example, Pacifica Bay receives income from airport landing fees, parking fees, water usage fees, and rental fees along public beaches, but there are costs—expenditures—related to building and maintaining these facilities and services from which income is received.

1 Start Excel. From the student files that accompany this chapter, open **e03A_Enterprise_Fund**. Display the **Save As** dialog box, and then navigate to the location where you are storing projects for this chapter. Create and open a new folder named **Excel Chapter 3**. In the **File name** box, type **Lastname_Firstname_3A_Enterprise_Fund** and then click **Save** or press Enter.

The worksheet indicates the originally proposed and adjusted expenditures from the Enterprise Fund for the next fiscal year.

2 Click cell **D5**, and then type **=** to begin a formula.

3 Click cell **C5**, which is the first value that is part of the total adjusted Fund Expenditures, to insert it into the formula. Type **/** to indicate division, and then click cell **C11**, which is the total adjusted expenditures.

Recall that to determine the percentage by which a value makes up a total, you must divide the value by the total. The result will be a percentage expressed as a decimal.

4 Press F4 to make the reference to the value in cell **C11** absolute, which will enable you to copy the formula. Compare your screen with Figure 3.2.

Recall that an *absolute cell reference* refers to a cell by its fixed position in the worksheet—the cell reference will not change when you copy the formula. The reference to cell C5 is a *relative cell reference*, because when you copy the formula, you want the reference to change *relative* to its row. In the formula, the dollar signs display to indicate that a cell reference is absolute.

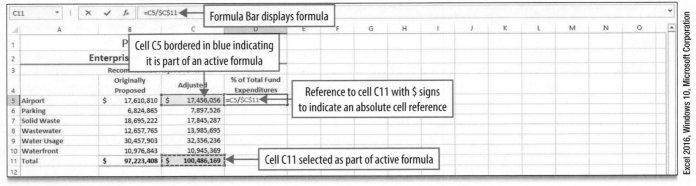

FIGURE 3.2

> **5** On the **Formula Bar**, click **Enter** ✓ to confirm the entry and to keep cell **D5** the active cell.

> **6** Copy the formula down through cell **D10**, and then compare your screen with Figure 3.3.

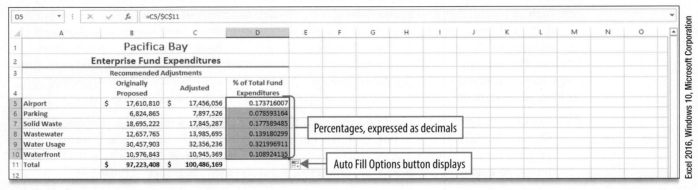

FIGURE 3.3

> **7** With the range **D5:D10** still selected, right-click over the selection, and then on the mini toolbar, click **Percent Style** % and **Center** ≡. Click cell **A1** to cancel the selection, and then **Save** 🖫 your workbook. Compare your screen with Figure 3.4.

Pacifica Bay
Enterprise Fund Expenditures
Recommended Adjustments

A	Originally Proposed	Adjusted	% of Total Fund Expenditures
5 Airport	$ 17,610,810	$ 17,456,056	17%
6 Parking	6,824,865	7,897,526	8%
7 Solid Waste	18,695,222	17,845,287	18%
8 Wastewater	12,657,765	13,985,695	14%
9 Water Usage	30,457,903	32,356,236	32%
10 Waterfront	10,976,843	10,945,369	11%
11 Total	$ 97,223,408	$ 100,486,169	

Percent of Total for each item calculated, expressed as percentages

Excel 2016, Windows 10, Microsoft Corporation

FIGURE 3.4

Activity 3.02 | Creating a Pie Chart and Moving a Chart to a Chart Sheet

5.1.1, 5.2.4

1 Select the range **A5:A10**, hold down Ctrl, and then select the range **C5:C10** to select the nonadjacent ranges with the item names and the adjusted expenditure for each item.

To create a pie chart, you must select two ranges. One range contains the labels for each slice of the pie chart, and the other range contains the values that add up to a total. The two ranges must have the same number of cells and the range with the values should *not* include the cell with the total.

The item names (Airport, Parking, and so on) are the category names and will identify the slices of the pie chart. Each adjusted expenditure is a *data point*—a value that originates in a worksheet cell and that is represented in a chart by a *data marker*. In a pie chart, each pie slice is a data marker. Together, the data points form the *data series*—related data points represented by data markers—and determine the size of each pie slice.

2 With the nonadjacent ranges selected, click the **Insert tab**, and then in the **Charts group**, click **Insert Pie or Doughnut Chart** . Under **3-D Pie**, click the chart **3-D Pie** to create the chart on your worksheet and to display the Chart Tools contextual tabs on the ribbon.

3 On the **Design tab**, at the right end of the ribbon in the **Location group**, click **Move Chart**. In the **Move Chart** dialog box, click the **New sheet** option button.

4 In the **New sheet** box, replace the highlighted text *Chart1* by typing **Expenditures Chart** and then click **OK** to display the chart on a separate worksheet in your workbook. Compare your screen with Figure 3.5.

The pie chart displays on a separate new sheet in your workbook, and a *legend* identifies the pie slices. Recall that a legend is a chart element that identifies the patterns or colors assigned to the categories in the chart.

A *chart sheet* is a workbook sheet that contains only a chart; it is useful when you want to view a chart separately from the worksheet data. The sheet tab indicates *Expenditures Chart*.

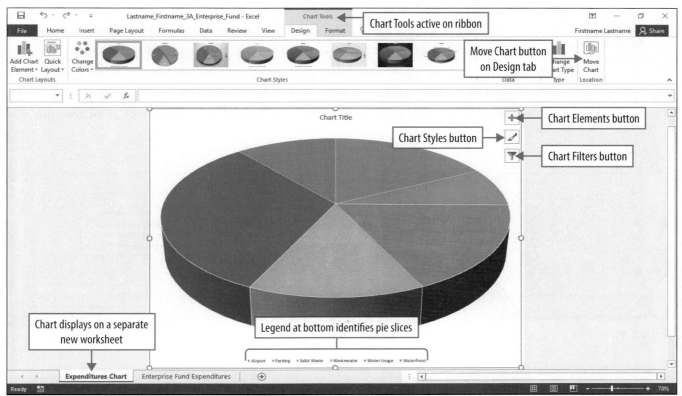

FIGURE 3.5

GO! Learn How
Video E3-2

Activity 3.03 | Formatting a Chart Title by Applying a WordArt Style and Changing Font Size

1 Click the text **Chart Title** to surround it with selection handles, and then watch the **Formula Bar** as you type **Enterprise Fund Expenditures** Press Enter to create the new chart title in the box.

2 Click the **Format tab**, and then in the **WordArt Styles group**, click **More** ⏷. In the first row, click the last style—**Fill – Gold, Accent 4, Soft Bevel**.

3 With the ⌶ pointer, drag to select the chart title text, and then on the mini toolbar, change the **Font Size** to **32**. Click the edge of the chart to deselect the title, and then compare your screen with Figure 3.6.

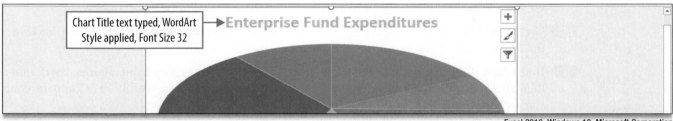

Chart Title text typed, WordArt Style applied, Font Size 32 → **Enterprise Fund Expenditures**

Excel 2016, Windows 10, Microsoft Corporation

FIGURE 3.6

4 **Save** 🖫 your workbook.

Activity 3.04 | Formatting Chart Elements by Removing a Legend and Adding and Formatting Data Labels

MOS
5.2.2

In your worksheet, for each budget item, you calculated the percent of the total in column D. These percentages can also be calculated by the Chart feature and added to the pie slices as labels.

1 If necessary, click the edge of the chart to display the three chart buttons on the right, and then click **Chart Elements** ⊞. Compare your screen with Figure 3.7.

Use the Chart Elements button to add, remove, or change chart elements such as the chart title, the legend, and the data labels.

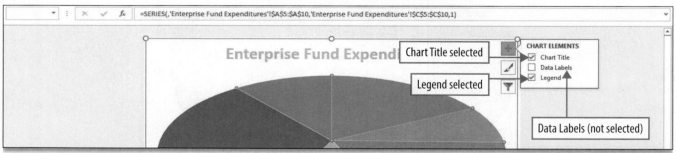

=SERIES(,'Enterprise Fund Expenditures'!$A$5:$A$10,'Enterprise Fund Expenditures'!$C$5:$C$10,1)

Enterprise Fund Expend | Chart Title selected

Legend selected

CHART ELEMENTS
- ☑ Chart Title
- ☐ Data Labels
- ☑ Legend

Data Labels (not selected)

Excel 2016, Windows 10, Microsoft Corporation

FIGURE 3.7

2 Click the **Legend** check box to deselect it and remove the legend from the bottom of the chart.

3 *Point* to **Data Labels**, and then click the ▶ **arrow** to display a menu. At the bottom of the menu, click **More Options** to display the **Format Data Labels** pane on the right.

The Format Data Labels pane displays and data labels representing the values display on each pie slice.

4 In the **Format Data Labels** pane, under **Label Options**, click as necessary to select the **Category Name** and **Percentage** check boxes. Click to *clear* any other check boxes in this group. Under **Label Position**, click the **Center** option button. Compare your screen with Figure 3.8.

All of the data labels are selected and display both the category name and the percentage. In the worksheet, you calculated the percent of the total in column D. Here, the percentage will be calculated by the Chart feature and added to the chart as a label.

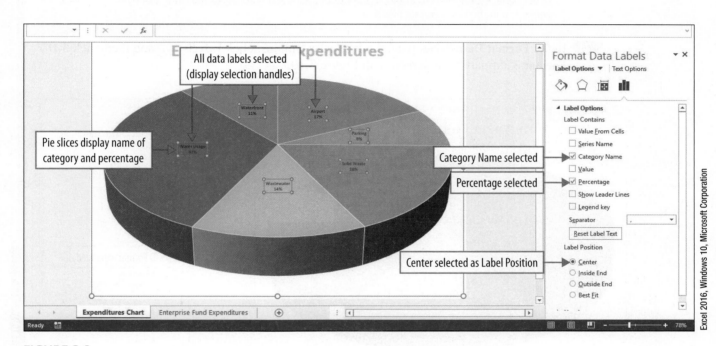

FIGURE 3.8

5 Point to any of the selected data labels, right-click to display a shortcut menu, and then click **Font** to display the **Font** dialog box.

6 On the **Font tab**, click the **Font style arrow**, and then click **Bold Italic**. In the **Size** box, drag to select **9** and type **11** Compare your screen with Figure 3.9.

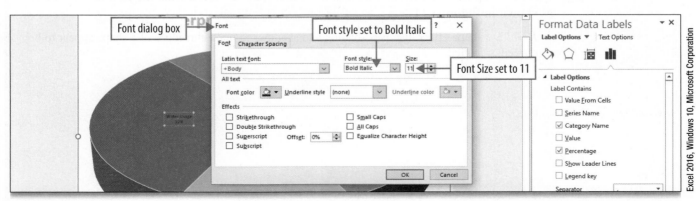

FIGURE 3.9

7 Click **OK** to close the dialog box and apply the formatting to the data labels. In the upper right corner of the **Format Data Labels** pane, click **Close** ☒. **Save** 🖫 your workbook.

Activity 3.05 | Formatting a Data Series with 3-D Effects

3-D, which is short for *three-dimensional*, refers to an image that appears to have all three spatial dimensions—length, width, and depth.

1 In any pie slice, point anywhere outside of the selected label, and then double-click to display the **Format Data Series** pane on the right.

> **ANOTHER WAY**   Right-click outside the label of any pie slice, and then click Format Data Series to display the Format Data Series pane. Or, on the Format tab, in the Current Selection group, click the Chart Elements arrow, click Series 1, and then click Format Selection.

2 In the **Format Data Series** pane, under **Series Options**, click **Effects** ◌, and then click **3-D Format**. Compare your screen with Figure 3.10.

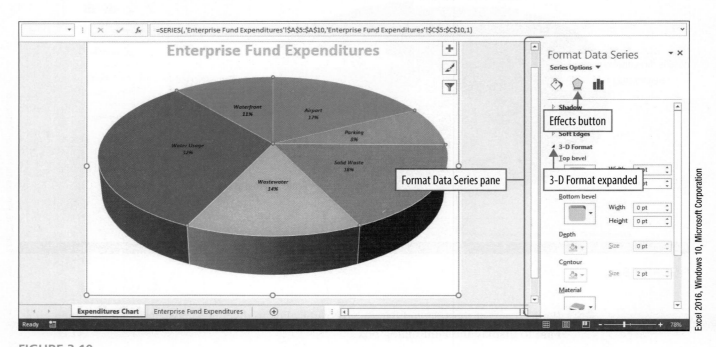

FIGURE 3.10

3 Click the **Top bevel arrow**, and then in the gallery, under **Bevel**, click the first bevel—**Circle**—as shown in Figure 3.11.

> *Bevel* is a shape effect that uses shading and shadows to make the edges of a shape appear to be curved or angled.

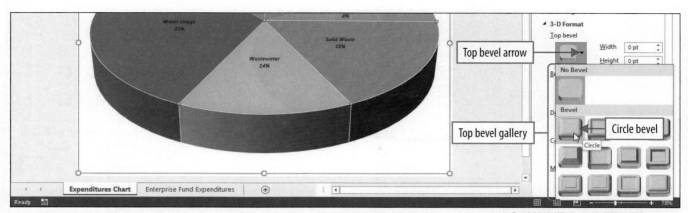

FIGURE 3.11

4 ▶ Under **Top bevel**, in the **Width** box, select the existing text and type **512** Change the **Height** to **512** and then press Enter.

5 ▶ Under **Bottom bevel**, use the technique you just practiced to apply a **Circle** bevel with **Width** of **512** and **Height** of **512** Compare your screen with Figure 3.12.

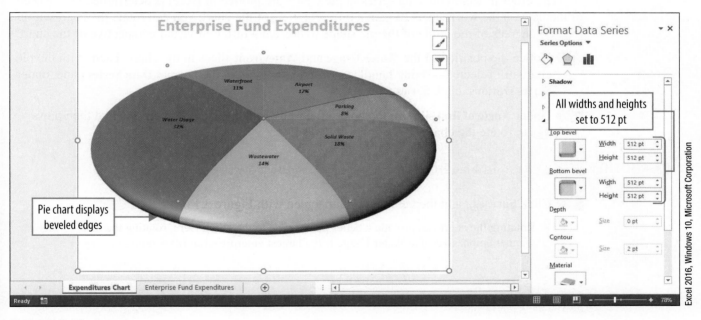

FIGURE 3.12

6 ▶ In the **Format Data Series** pane, scroll down as necessary, and then click the **Material arrow**. Under **Standard**, click the third material—**Plastic**.

7 ▶ **Save** 🖫 your workbook.

Activity 3.06 | Formatting a Data Series with a Shadow Effect

1 ▶ In the **Format Data Series** pane, scroll back to the top of the pane, and then click **Shadow** to expand the options for this effect.

2 ▶ Under **Shadow**, click the **Presets arrow**, use the scroll bar to move to the bottom of the gallery, and then under **Perspective**, in the first row, point to the third effect to display the ScreenTip *Below*. Compare your screen with Figure 3.13.

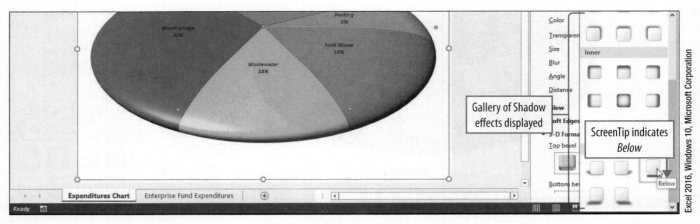

FIGURE 3.13

Excel 2016, Windows 10, Microsoft Corporation

3 ▶ Click **Below** to apply the shadow to the chart. **Save** 🔲 your workbook.

Activity 3.07 │ Rotating a Pie Chart by Changing the Angle of the First Slice

The order in which the data series in pie charts are plotted in Excel is determined by the order of the data on the worksheet. To gain a different view of the chart, you can rotate the chart within the 360 degrees of the circle of the pie shape to present a different visual perspective of the chart.

1 ▶ Notice the position of the **Water Usage** and **Waterfront** slices in the chart. Then, with the pie chart still selected—sizing handles surround the pie—in the **Format Data Series** pane, under **Series Options**, click **Series Options** 📊.

2 ▶ Under **Angle of first slice**, in the box to the right, drag to select **0°**, type **250** and then press Enter to rotate the chart 250 degrees to the right.

🔄 **ANOTHER WAY**   Drag the slider to 250°, or click the spin box up arrow as many times as necessary.

3 ▶ Click **Save** 🔲, and then compare your screen with Figure 3.14.

Rotating the chart can provide a better perspective to the chart. Here, rotating the chart in this manner emphasizes that Water Usage is the largest enterprise fund expenditure.

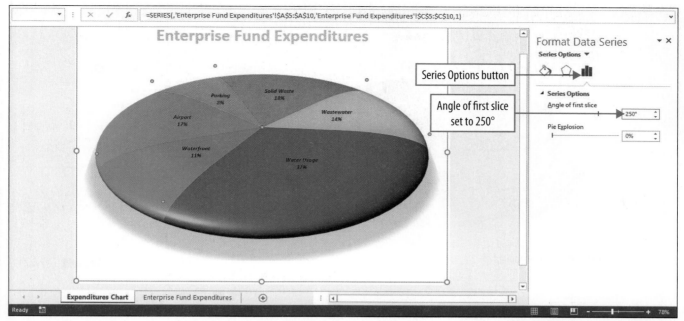

FIGURE 3.14

Activity 3.08 | Exploding and Coloring a Pie Slice

You can pull out—*explode*—one or more slices of a pie chart to emphasize a specific slice or slices.

1 In the **Format Data Series** pane, under **Series Options**, notice the slider and box for *Pie Explosion*.

When all the pie slices are selected, as they currently are, you can use this command to explode *all* of the pie pieces away from the center by varying degrees to emphasize all the individual slices of the pie chart. An exploded pie chart visualizes the contribution of each value to the total, while at the same time emphasizing individual values.

2 On the pie chart, click the **Waterfront** slice to select only that slice, and then on the right, notice that the **Format Data Point** pane displays.

Excel adjusts the pane, depending on what you have selected, so that the commands you need are available.

3 In the **Format Data Point** pane, in the **Point Explosion** box, select the existing text, type **10%** and then press Enter.

4 With the **Waterfront** slice still selected, in the **Format Data Point** pane, under **Series Options**, click **Fill & Line** ⬙, and then click **Fill** to expand its options.

5 Click the **Gradient fill** option button, click the **Preset gradients arrow**, and then in the fourth row, click the last gradient—**Bottom Spotlight – Accent 6**. Click **Save** 🖫, and then compare your screen with Figure 3.15.

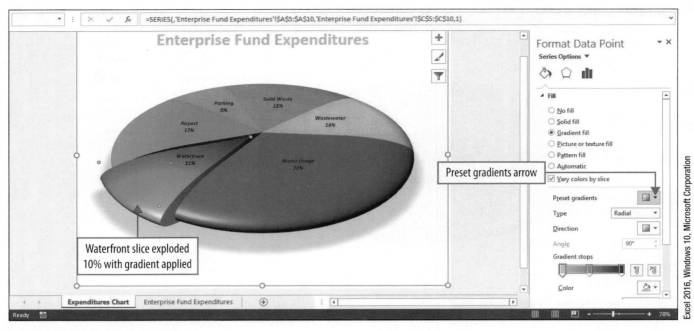

FIGURE 3.15

Activity 3.09 | Formatting the Chart Area

The entire chart and all of its elements comprise the ***chart area***.

1 Point to the white area just inside the border of the chart to display the ScreenTip *Chart Area*. Click one time, and notice that on the right, the **Format Chart Area** pane displays.

2 Under **Chart Options**, click **Fill & Line** 🖾, and be sure the **Fill** options are still displayed.

3 Click the **Gradient fill** option button, click the **Preset gradients arrow**, and then in the fourth row, click the first gradient—**Bottom Spotlight – Accent 1**.

4 In the **Format Chart Area** pane, click **Fill** to collapse the options, and then click **Border** to expand its options.

5 Under **Border**, click **Solid line**, click the **Color arrow** to display the Outline colors, and then in the fourth column, click the first color—**Blue – Gray, Text 2**. In the **Width** box, drag to select the existing width, and then type **5**

6 **Close** ⊠ the **Format Chart Area** pane, and then click outside of the Chart Area to deselect the chart. Click **Save** 🖫, and then compare your screen with Figure 3.16.

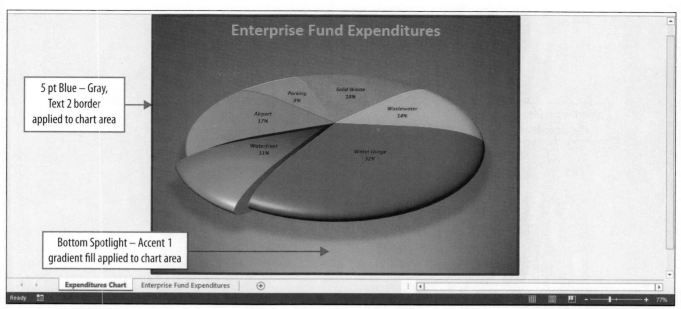

5 pt Blue – Gray, Text 2 border applied to chart area

Bottom Spotlight – Accent 1 gradient fill applied to chart area

FIGURE 3.16

Excel 2016, Windows 10, Microsoft Corporation

Objective 3 Edit a Workbook and Update a Chart

GO! Learn How
Video E3-3

Activity 3.10 | Editing a Workbook and Updating a Chart

If you edit the data in your worksheet, the chart data markers—in this instance, the pie slices—will adjust automatically to accurately represent the new values.

1 On the pie chart, notice that *Airport* represents 17% of the total projected expenses.

2 In the sheet tab area at the bottom of the workbook, click the **Enterprise Fund Expenditures tab** to redisplay the worksheet.

3 Click cell **C5**, type **18,121,067** and then press Enter. Notice that the Accounting Number Format is retained in the cell.

🔄 **ANOTHER WAY**   Double-click the cell to position the insertion point in the cell and edit.

4 Notice that the total in cell **C11** recalculated to *$101,151,180* and the percentages in **column D** also recalculated.

5 Display the **Expenditures Chart** sheet. Notice that the pie slices adjust to show the recalculation—*Airport* is now *18%* of the adjusted expenditures. Click **Save** 🖫, and then compare your screen with Figure 3.17.

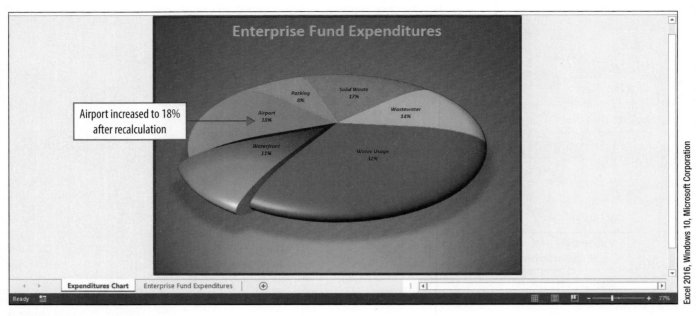

FIGURE 3.17

Activity 3.11 | Using Goal Seek to Perform What-If Analysis

GO! Learn How
Video E3-4

MOS
Expert 3.4.2

The process of changing the values in cells to see how those changes affect the outcome of formulas in your worksheet is referred to as **what-if analysis**. One what-if analysis tool in Excel is **Goal Seek**, which finds the input needed in one cell to arrive at the desired result in another cell.

1 Click the **Enterprise Fund Expenditures sheet tab** to redisplay the worksheet.

2 Select the range **D5:D10**, and then increase the number of decimal places to two. Compare your screen with Figure 3.18.

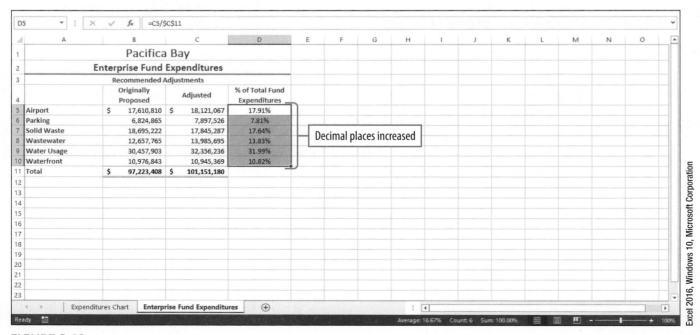

FIGURE 3.18

3 Click cell **C11**. On the **Data tab**, in the **Forecast group**, click **What-If Analysis**, and then click **Goal Seek**.

4 In the **Goal Seek** dialog box, notice that the active cell, **C11**, is indicated in the **Set cell** box. Press `Tab` to move to the **To value** box, and then type **100,000,000**

> C11 is the cell in which you want to set a specific value; $100,000,000 is the total expenditures budgeted for the Enterprise Fund. The Set cell box contains the formula that calculates the information you seek.

5 Press `Tab` to move the insertion point to the **By changing cell** box, and then click cell **C10**. Compare your screen with Figure 3.19.

> Cell C10 contains the value that Excel changes to reach the goal. In the Goal Seek dialog box, Excel formats this cell as an absolute cell reference.

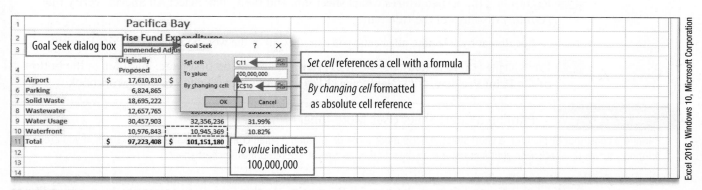

FIGURE 3.19

6 Click **OK**. In the displayed **Goal Seek Status** dialog box, click **OK**.

7 Press `Ctrl` + `Home`, click **Save** 🖫, and then compare your screen with Figure 3.20.

> Excel calculates that the city must budget for *$9,794,189* in Waterfront expenditures in order to maintain a total Enterprise Fund Expenditure budget of $100,000,000.

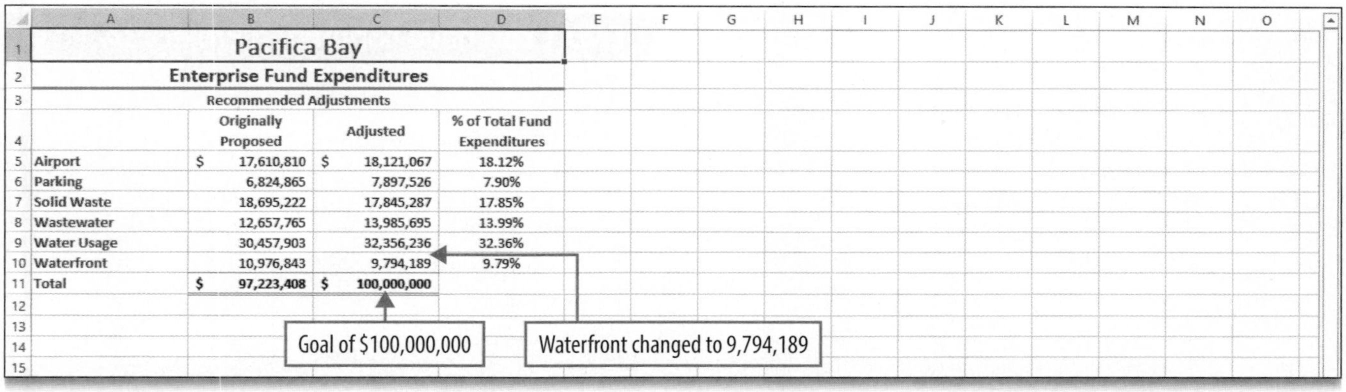

	A	B	C	D
1		Pacifica Bay		
2		Enterprise Fund Expenditures		
3		Recommended Adjustments		
4		Originally Proposed	Adjusted	% of Total Fund Expenditures
5	Airport	$ 17,610,810	$ 18,121,067	18.12%
6	Parking	6,824,865	7,897,526	7.90%
7	Solid Waste	18,695,222	17,845,287	17.85%
8	Wastewater	12,657,765	13,985,695	13.99%
9	Water Usage	30,457,903	32,356,236	32.36%
10	Waterfront	10,976,843	9,794,189	9.79%
11	Total	$ 97,223,408	$ 100,000,000	

Goal of $100,000,000 — Waterfront changed to 9,794,189

FIGURE 3.20

Activity 3.12 | Preparing and Printing a Workbook with a Chart Sheet

1 Click the **Page Layout tab**. In the **Page Setup group**, click the Dialog Box Launcher ⌸.

2 In the **Page Setup** dialog box, on the **Margins tab**, under **Center on page**, select the **Horizontally** check box.

3 Click the **Header/Footer tab**, and then in the center of the dialog box, click **Custom Footer**. In the **Footer** dialog box, with the insertion point blinking in the **Left section**, on the row of buttons, click **Insert File Name** 🗐. Click **OK** two times.

> The dotted line indicates the page break as currently formatted.

4 Display the **Expenditures Chart**, which must have its footer formatted separately. In the **Page Setup group**, click the **Dialog Box Launcher** 🖼.

> Chart sheets are automatically centered on the page.

5 Click the **Header/Footer tab**, and then in the center of the dialog box, click **Custom Footer**. In the **Footer** dialog box, with the insertion point blinking in the **Left section**, on the row of buttons, click **Insert File Name** 🗐. Click **OK** two times.

6 Right-click the **Expenditures Chart sheet tab**, and then click **Select All Sheets**. Verify that *[Group]* displays in the title bar.

> Recall that by selecting all sheets, you can view all of the workbook pages in Print Preview.

7 Press [Ctrl] + [F2] to display the **Print Preview**. Examine the first page, and then at the bottom of the **Print Preview**, click **Next Page** ▶ to view the second page of your workbook.

NOTE | Printing a Chart Sheet Uses More Toner

Printing a chart that displays on a chart sheet will use more toner or ink than a small chart that is part of a worksheet. If you are printing your work, check with your instructor to verify whether or not you should print the chart sheet.

---

8 Click **Info**, and then click **Show All Properties**. As the **Tags**, type **enterprise fund, expenditures** As the **Subject**, type your course name and section number. Be sure your name displays as the **Author. Save** 🖫 the workbook.

9 If directed by your instructor to do so, submit your paper printout, your electronic image of your document that looks like a printed document, or your original Excel file. If required by your instructor, print or create an electronic version of your worksheet with formulas displayed. In the upper right corner of the Excel window, click **Close** ⊠.

END | You have completed Project 3A

Go! With Google

Objective | Analyze Expenditures with a Pie Chart

> **ALERT!** | **Working with Web-Based Applications and Services**
>
> Computer programs and services on the web receive continuous updates and improvements, so the steps to complete this web-based activity may differ from the ones shown. You can often look at the screens and the information presented to determine how to complete the activity.
>
> If you do not already have a Google account, you will need to create one before you begin this Activity. Go to http://google.com and, in the upper right corner, click Sign In. On the Sign In screen, click Create Account. On the Create your Google Account page, complete the form, read and agree to the Terms of Service and Privacy Policy, and then click Next step. On the Welcome screen, click Get Started.

Activity | Create a Pie Chart

1 From the desktop, open your browser, navigate to **http://google.com**, and then click the **Google Apps** menu . Click **Drive**, and then if necessary, sign in to your Google account.

2 Open your **GO! Web Projects** folder—or click New to create and then open this folder if necessary. In the left pane, click **NEW**, and then click **File upload**. Navigate to your student data files, click **e03_3A_Web**, and then click **Open**.

3 Right-click the file you uploaded, point to **Open with**, and then click **Google Sheets**.

4 Click cell **D5**. Type = and then click cell **C5**. Type / and then click **C11** and press F4 to make the cell reference absolute. Press Enter to create a formula to calculate % of Total Fund Expenditures.

5 Click cell **D5**, and then apply percent formatting. Fill the formula down through cell **D10**. Click **Format**, point to **Align**, and then click **Center**.

6 Select the range **A5:A10**, hold down Ctrl, and then select **C5:C10**. Click **Insert**, and then click **Chart**. To the right of the chart gallery, point to the vertical scroll bar

and drag down to display the Pie charts. Click the third chart—**3D pie chart**, and then click **Insert**.

7 Point to the chart and then drag down and to the left to position the pie chart under the worksheet data so that its left edge aligns with the left edge of cell **A13**. Click the **Chart title** to display a box in which you can type the chart title. Type **Enterprise Fund Expenditures** and then press Enter. In the chart title ribbon, click the **Font Size arrow**, and then click **20**. Click anywhere in the chart outside of the title so that the title is not selected.

8 In the upper right corner of the chart area, click the **down-pointing triangle**, and then click **Advanced edit**. Under **Legend**, click **Right**, and then in the list, click **Labeled**. To the right of **Background**, click the **Background color arrow**, and then in the seventh column, click the third color—**light cornflower blue 3**. Click **Update** to apply the formatting changes and close the **Chart Editor**.

9 Click cell **A1** and then scroll down to view the entire chart. Compare your screen with Figure A.

10 Submit your file as directed by your instructor. Sign out of your Google account and close your browser.

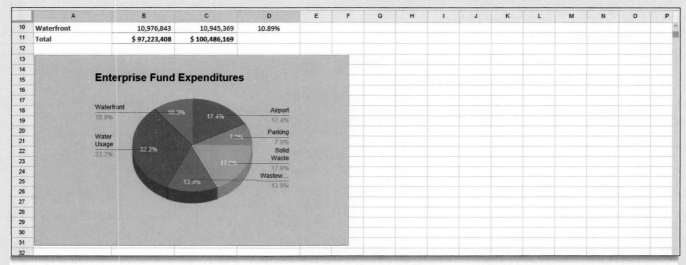

FIGURE A

Tourism Spending Projection with Line Chart

PROJECT ACTIVITIES

In Activities 3.13 through 3.20, you will assist Michael Larsen, City Manager, in creating a worksheet to estimate future tourism spending based on two possible growth rates. You will also create a line chart to display past visitor spending. Your resulting worksheet and chart will look similar to Figure 3.21.

PROJECT FILES

If your instructor wants you to submit Project 3B in the MyITLab Grader system, log in to MyITLab, locate Grader Project 3B, and then download the files for this project.

For Project 3B, you will need the following files:
e03B_Tourism
e03B_Surfers

You will save your workbook as:
Lastname_Firstname_3B_Tourism

Please always review the downloaded Grader instructions before beginning.

PROJECT RESULTS

GO!
Walk Thru
Project 3B

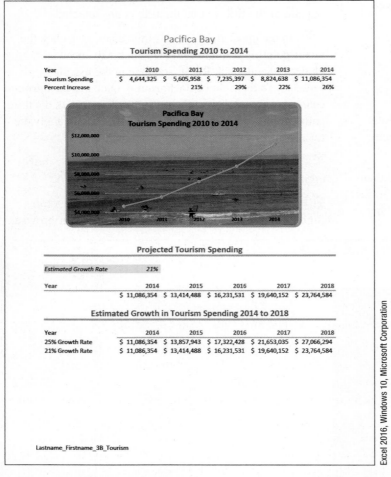

FIGURE 3.21 Project 3B Tourism Spending Projection with Line Chart

GO! Learn How
Video E3-5

If you change the value in a cell referenced in a formula, Excel automatically recalculates the result of the formula. This means that you can change cell values to see what would happen if you tried different values. Recall that this process of changing the values in cells to see how those changes affect the outcome of formulas in your worksheet is referred to as *what-if analysis*.

Activity 3.13 | Using Parentheses in a Formula to Calculate a Percentage Rate of Increase

ALERT!   **To submit as an autograded project, log into MyITLab and download the files for this project, and begin with those files instead of e03B_Tourism.**

Mr. Larsen has the city's tourism spending figures for the recent 5-year period. In each year, tourism spending has increased. In this Activity, you will construct a formula to calculate the ***percentage rate of increase***—the percent by which one number increases over another number—for each year since 2010. From this information, future tourism spending growth can be estimated.

Excel follows a set of mathematical rules called the ***order of operations***, which has four basic parts:

- Expressions within parentheses are processed first.
- Exponentiation, if present, is performed before multiplication and division.
- Multiplication and division are performed before addition and subtraction.
- Consecutive operators with the same level of precedence are calculated from left to right.

1 Start Excel. From your student data files, open **e03B_Tourism**. **Save** the file in your **Excel Chapter 3** folder as **Lastname_Firstname_3B_Tourism**

2 In cell **B4**, type **2010** and then press `Tab`. In cell **C4**, type **2011** and then press `Tab`. Select the range **B4:C4**, and then drag the fill handle to the right through cell **F4** to extend the series to *2014*. Compare your screen with Figure 3.22.

By establishing a pattern of 1-year intervals with the first two cells, you can use the fill handle to continue the series. The AutoFill feature will do this for any pattern that you establish with two or more cells.

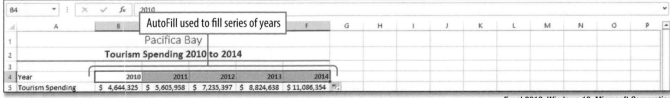

Excel 2016, Windows 10, Microsoft Corporation

FIGURE 3.22

3 Click cell **C6**. Being sure to include the parentheses, type **=(c5-b5)/b5** and then on the **Formula Bar**, click **Enter** ✓ to keep cell **C6** active. Notice that your result displays as *$0.21* because Excel retains the Accounting Number Format of the cells referenced in the formula.

As you type, a list of Excel functions that begin with the letters *C* and *B* may briefly display. This is ***Formula AutoComplete***, an Excel feature which, after typing an = (equal sign) and the beginning letter or letters of a function name, displays a list of function names that match the typed letter(s). In this instance, the letters represent cell references, *not* the beginning of a function name.

4 With cell **C6** selected, apply **Percent Style** %, and then compare your screen with Figure 3.23.

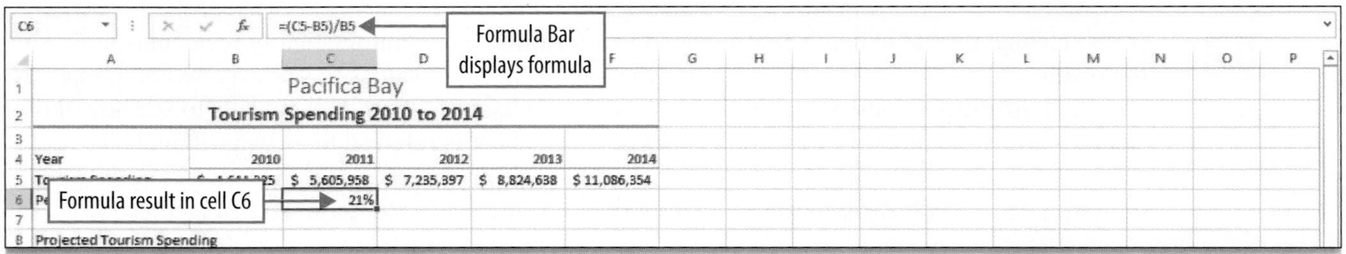

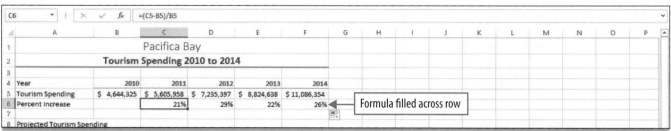

FIGURE 3.23

5 With cell **C6** selected, drag the fill handle to the right to copy the formula through cell **F6**.

Because this formula uses relative cell references—that is, for each year, the formula is the same but the values used are relative to the formula's location—you can copy the formula in this manner. For example, the result for 2012 uses the 2011 value as the base, the result for 2013 uses the 2012 value as the base, and the result for 2014 uses the 2013 value as the base.

6 Click cell **C6** and look at the **Formula Bar**.

The mathematical formula *rate = amount of increase/base* is used to calculate the percentage rate of tourism spending increase from 2010 to 2011. The formula is applied as follows:

First, determine the *amount of increase* by subtracting the *base*—the starting point represented by the 2010 tourism spending—from the 2011 tourism spending. Therefore, the *amount of increase* = $5,605,958 – $4,644,325 or $961,633. Between 2010 and 2011, tourism spending increased by $961,633. In the formula, this calculation is represented by *C5-B5*.

Second, calculate the *rate*—what the amount of increase ($961,633) represents as a percentage of the base (2010's tourism spending of $4,644,325). Determine this by dividing the amount of increase ($961,633) by the base ($4,644,325). Therefore, $961,633 divided by $4,644,325 is equal to *0.207055492* or, when formatted as a percent and rounded up, 21%.

7 In the **Formula Bar**, locate the parentheses enclosing *C5-B5*.

Recall that Excel follows a set of mathematical rules called the order of operations, in which expressions within parentheses are processed first, multiplication and division are performed before addition and subtraction, and consecutive operators with the same level of precedence are calculated from left to right.

8 **Save** 🖫 your workbook, and then compare your screen with Figure 3.24.

FIGURE 3.24

Activity 3.14 | Using Format Painter

2.2.3

In this Activity, you will use Format Painter to copy formatting.

1 Point to cell **A2**, right-click, on the mini toolbar, click **Format Painter** , and then click cell **A8** to copy the format.

> The format of cell A2 is *painted*—applied to—cell A8, including the merging and centering of the text across the range A8:F8.

ANOTHER WAY On the Home tab, in the Clipboard group, click the Format Painter button.

2 Point to cell **F5**, right-click, and then click **Copy**. Point to cell **B13**, right-click, and then on the shortcut menu, under **Paste Options**, click **Paste** . Compare your screen with Figure 3.25, and then **Save** your workbook.

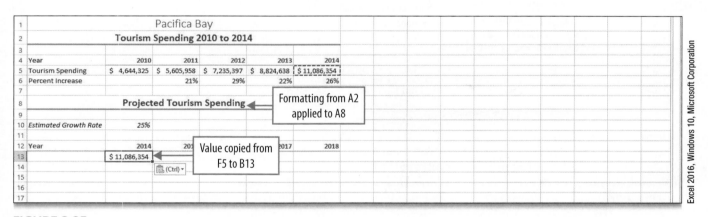

FIGURE 3.25

Activity 3.15 | Calculating a Value After an Increase

A growth in tourism spending means that the city can plan for additional revenues and also plan more hotel and conference space to accommodate the increasing number of visitors. Therefore, city planners in Pacifica Bay want to estimate how much tourism spending will increase in the future. The calculations you made in the previous Activity show that tourism spending has increased at varying rates during each year from 2010 to 2014, ranging from a low of 21% to a high of 29% per year.

Economic data suggests that future growth will trend close to that of the recent past. To plan for the future, Mr. Larsen wants to prepare a forecast of tourism spending based on the percentage increase halfway between the high of 29% and the low of 21%; that is, for 25%. In this Activity, you will calculate the tourism spending that would result from a 25% increase.

1 Click cell **C13**. Type **=b13*(100%+b10)** and then on the **Formula Bar**, click **Enter** ✓ to display a result of *13857942.5*.

2 Point to cell **B13**, right-click, click **Format Painter** ⟨⟩, and then click cell **C13** to copy the format. Compare your screen with Figure 3.26.

This formula calculates what tourism spending will be in the year 2015 assuming an increase of 25% over 2014's tourism spending. Use the mathematical formula *value after increase = base × percent for new value* to calculate a value after an increase as follows:

First, establish the *percent for new value*. The **percent for new value = base percent + percent of increase**. The *base percent* of 100% represents the base tourism spending and the *percent of increase*—in this instance, 25%. Therefore, the tourism spending will equal 100% of the base year plus 25% of the base year. This can be expressed as 125% or 1.25. In this formula, you will use 100% + the rate in cell B10, which is 25%, to equal 125%.

Second, enter a reference to the cell that contains the *base*—the tourism spending in 2014. The base value resides in cell B13—*$11,086,354*.

Third, calculate the *value after increase*. Because in each future year the increase will be based on 25%—an absolute value located in cell B10—this cell reference can be formatted as absolute by typing dollar signs.

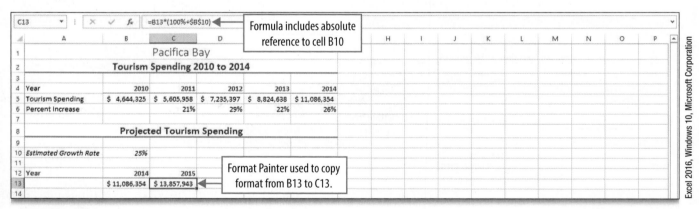

FIGURE 3.26

3 With cell **C13** as the active cell, drag the fill handle to copy the formula to the range **D13:F13**. Click an empty cell to cancel the selection, click **Save** 🖫 and then compare your screen with Figure 3.27.

The formula in cell C13 uses a relative cell address—B13—for the *base*; the tourism spending in the previous year is used in each of the formulas in cells D13:F13 as the *base* value. Because the reference to the *percent of increase* in cell B10 is an absolute reference, each *value after increase* is calculated with the value from cell B10.

The tourism spending projected for 2015—*$13,857,943*—is an increase of 25% over the spending in 2014. The projected spending in 2016—*$17,322,428*—is an increase of 25% over the spending in 2015, and so on.

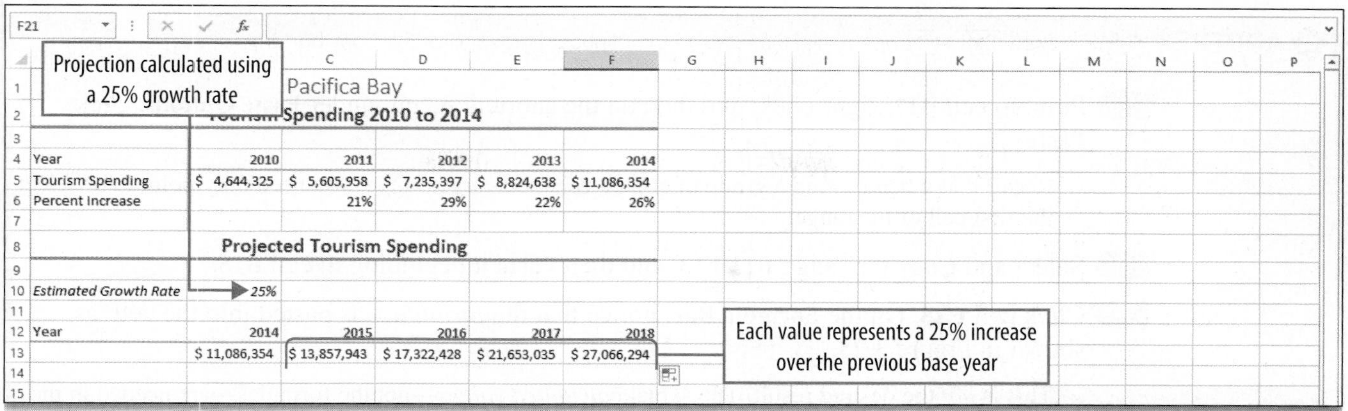

F21	:	×	✓	fx															
⊿			C	D	E	F	G	H	I	J	K	L	M	N	O	P			

Projection calculated using a 25% growth rate

1		Pacifica Bay
2		Tourism Spending 2010 to 2014
3		
4	Year	2010	2011	2012	2013	2014
5	Tourism Spending	$ 4,644,325	$ 5,605,958	$ 7,235,397	$ 8,824,638	$ 11,086,354
6	Percent Increase		21%	29%	22%	26%
7		
8		Projected Tourism Spending
9		
10	Estimated Growth Rate	→25%
11		
12	Year	2014	2015	2016	2017	2018
13		$ 11,086,354	$ 13,857,943	$ 17,322,428	$ 21,653,035	$ 27,066,294
14		
15		

Each value represents a 25% increase over the previous base year

Excel 2016, Windows 10, Microsoft Corporation

FIGURE 3.27

More Knowledge | **Percent Increase or Decrease**

The basic formula for calculating an increase or decrease can be done in two parts. First determine the percent by which the base value will be increased or decreased, and then add or subtract the results to the base. The formula can be simplified by using (1+amount of increase) or (1−amount of decrease), where 1, rather than 100%, represents the whole. Therefore, the formula used in Step 1 of Activity 3.15 could also be written =b13*(1+b10), or =(b13*b10)+b13.

Objective 6 | Answer What-If Questions by Changing Values in a Worksheet

GO! Learn How
Video E3-6

If a formula depends on the value in a cell, you can see what effect it will have if you change the value in that cell. Then, you can copy the value computed by the formula and paste it into another part of the worksheet where you can compare it to other values.

Activity 3.16 | Answering What-If Questions and Using Paste Special

2.1.3

A growth rate of 25% in tourism spending in each year will result in tourism spending of approximately $27 million by 2018. The city planners will likely ask: *What if* tourism spending grows at the lowest rate of 21%?

Because the formulas are constructed to use the growth rate displayed in cell B10, Mr. Larsen can answer that question quickly by entering a different percentage into that cell. To keep the results of the new calculation so it can be compared, you will paste the results of the what-if question into another area of the worksheet.

1 Leave **row 14** blank, and then click cell **A15**. Type **Estimated Growth in Tourism Spending 2014 to 2018** and then press Enter. Use **Format Painter** ⚡ to copy the format from cell **A8** to cell **A15**.

2 Select the range **A10:B10**, right-click to display the mini toolbar, click the **Fill Color button arrow** ◌ ▾, and then under **Theme Colors**, in the first column, click the third color—**White, Background 1, Darker 15%**.

3 Leave **row 16** blank, and then in the range **A17:A19**, type the following row titles:
Year
25% Growth Rate
21% Growth Rate

4 Select the range **B12:F12**, right-click over the selection, and then on the shortcut menu, click **Copy**.

5 Point to cell **B17**, right-click, and then on the shortcut menu, under **Paste Options**, click **Paste**.

> Recall that when pasting a group of copied cells to a target range, you need only point to or select the first cell of the range.

6 Select and **Copy** the range **B13:F13**, and then **Paste** it beginning in cell **B18**.

7 Click cell **C18**. On the **Formula Bar**, notice that the *formula* was pasted into the cell, as shown in Figure 3.28.

> This is *not* the desired result. The actual *calculated values*—not the formulas—are needed in the range.

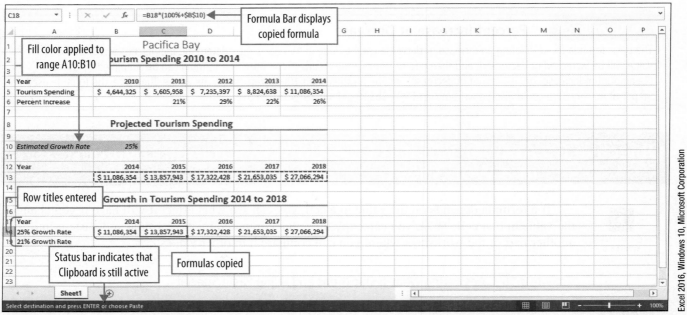

FIGURE 3.28

8 On the Quick Access Toolbar, click **Undo**. With the range **B13:F13** still copied to the Clipboard—as indicated by the message in the status bar and the moving border—point to cell **B18**, and then right-click to display the shortcut menu.

9 Under **Paste Options**, point to **Paste Special** to display another gallery, and then under **Paste Values**, point to **Values & Number Formatting** to display the ScreenTip as shown in Figure 3.29.

> The ScreenTip *Values & Number Formatting (A)* indicates that you can paste the calculated values that result from the calculation of formulas along with the formatting applied to the copied cells. *(A)* is the keyboard shortcut for this command.

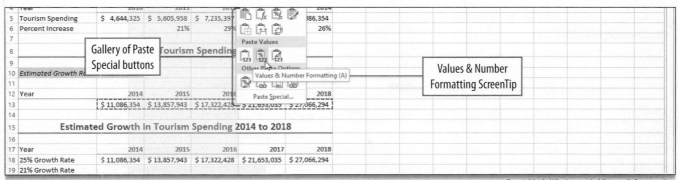

FIGURE 3.29

10 ▶ Click **Values & Number Formatting** 🖼️, click cell **C18** and notice on the **Formula Bar** that the cell contains a *value*, not a formula. Press [Esc] to cancel the moving border. Compare your screen with Figure 3.30.

The calculated estimates based on a 25% growth rate are pasted along with their formatting.

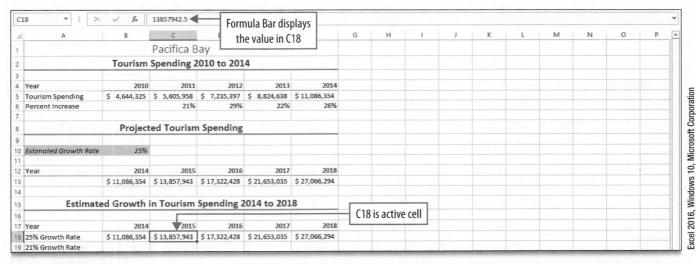

FIGURE 3.30

11 ▶ Click cell **B10**. Type **21** and then watch the values in **C13:F13** *recalculate* as, on the **Formula Bar**, you click **Enter** ✓.

The value *21%* is the lowest percent increase for the past 5-year period.

12 ▶ Select and **Copy** the new values in the range **B13:F13**. Point to cell **B19**, right-click, and then on the shortcut menu, point to **Paste Special**. Under **Paste Values**, click **Values & Number Formatting** 🖼️.

13 ▶ Press [Esc] to cancel the moving border, click cell **A1**, click **Save** 💾, and then compare your screen with Figure 3.31.

With this information, Mr. Larsen can answer what-if questions about the projected increase in tourism spending based on the rates of increase over the past five years.

8	Projected Tourism Spending					
9						
10	*Estimated Growth Rate*	21%				
11						
12	Year	2014	2015	2016	2017	2018
13		$ 11,086,354	$ 13,414,488	$ 16,231,531	$ 19,640,152	$ 23,764,584
14						
15	Estimated Growth in Tourism Spending 2014 to 2018					
16						
17	Year	2014	2015	2016	2017	2018
18	25% Growth Rate	$ 11,086,354	$ 13,857,943	$ 17,322,428	$ 21,653,035	$ 27,066,294
19	21% Growth Rate	$ 11,086,354	$ 13,414,488	$ 16,231,531	$ 19,640,152	$ 23,764,584
20						

Values copied for each what-if question

FIGURE 3.31

Objective 7 | Chart Data with a Line Chart

GO! Learn How
Video E3-7

A *line chart* displays trends over time. Time is displayed along the bottom axis and the data point values connect with a line. The curve and direction of the line make trends obvious to the reader.

The columns in a column chart and the pie slices in a pie chart emphasize the distinct values of each data point. A line chart, on the other hand, emphasizes the flow from one data point value to the next.

Activity 3.17 | Inserting Multiple Rows and Creating a Line Chart

1.3.5, 5.1.1

So that City Council members can see how tourism spending has increased over a 5-year period, in this Activity, you will chart the actual tourism spending from 2010 to 2014 in a line chart.

1 Click the **Page Layout tab**. In the **Themes group**, click **Colors**, and then change the **Theme Colors** to **Orange**.

2 In the **row header area**, point to **row 8** to display the ➡ pointer, and then drag down to select **rows 8:24**. Right-click over the selection, and then click **Insert** to insert the same number of blank rows as you selected. Compare your screen with Figure 3.32.

Use this technique to insert multiple rows quickly.

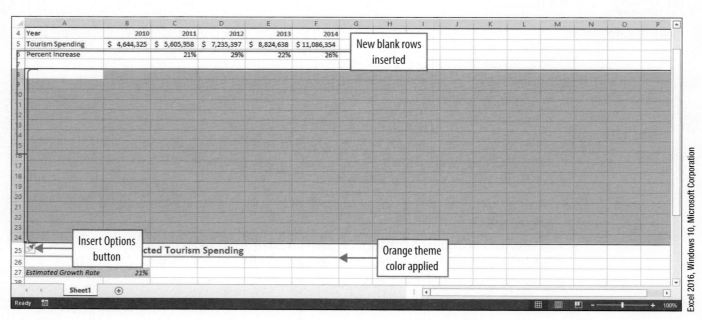

FIGURE 3.32

3 Near **row 25**, click **Insert Options** 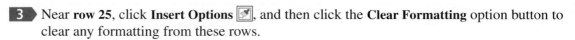, and then click the **Clear Formatting** option button to clear any formatting from these rows.

> You will use this blank area to position your line chart.

4 Press `Ctrl` + `Home` to deselect the rows and move to the top of your worksheet. Select the range **A5:F5**. On the **Insert tab**, in the **Charts group**, click **Insert Line or Area Chart**.

5 In the gallery of line charts, under **2-D Line**, point to the fourth chart type to display the ScreenTip *Line with Markers*. Compare your screen with Figure 3.33.

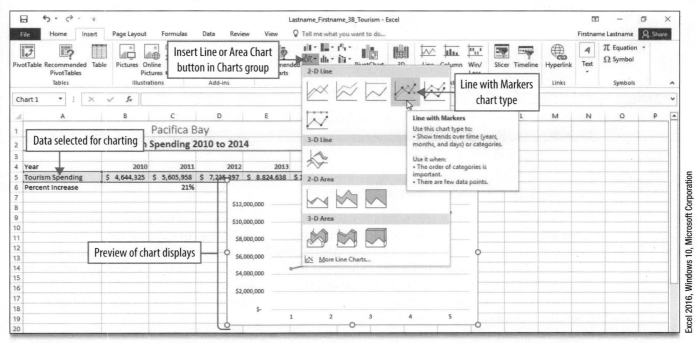

FIGURE 3.33

6 Click the **Line with Markers** chart type to create the chart in the worksheet.

7 Point to the border of the chart to display the pointer, and then drag the chart so that its upper left corner is positioned in cell **A8**, aligned approximately under the *t* in the word *Percent* above.

> Excel uses the label in cell A5—*Tourism Spending*—as the suggested chart title.

8 Point to the **Chart Title** *Tourism Spending* and right-click. On the shortcut menu, click **Edit Text** to place the insertion point at the beginning of the title. Type **Pacifica Bay** and press `Enter`. Press `End` to move to the end of *Spending*, press `Spacebar`, and then type **2010 to 2014**

9 Click the dashed border surrounding the **Chart Title** so that it is a solid line, indicating the entire title is selected. Right-click over the title, and then click **Font**. In the **Font** dialog box, click the **Font style arrow**, and then click **Bold**. Click the **Font color arrow**, and then in the second column, click the first color—**Black, Text 1**. Click **OK**.

10 On the right side of the chart, click **Chart Elements**, and then compare your screen with Figure 3.34.

> Three of the available chart elements are included for this chart by default—the axes, the chart title, and the gridlines.

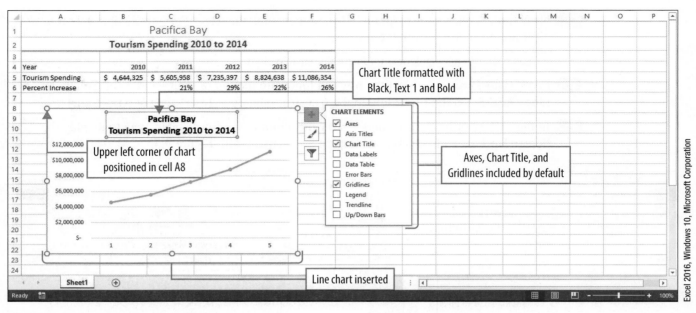

FIGURE 3.34

Activity 3.18 | Formatting Axes in a Line Chart

An *axis* is a line that serves as a frame of reference for measurement; it borders the chart *plot area*. The plot area is the area bounded by the axes, including all the data series. In a line chart, the area along the bottom of a chart that identifies the categories of data is referred to as the *category axis* or the *x-axis*. The area along the left side of a chart that shows the range of numbers for the data points is referred to as the *value axis* or the *y-axis*.

In this Activity, you will change the category axis to include the years 2010 to 2014 and adjust the numeric scale of the value axis.

1 Be sure the chart is still selected. At the bottom of the chart, point to any of the numbers *1* through *5* to display the ScreenTip *Horizontal (Category) Axis*, and then right-click. On the shortcut menu, click **Select Data**.

ANOTHER WAY   Click the Design tab, and then in the Data group, click Select Data.

2 On the right side of the **Select Data Source** dialog box, under **Horizontal (Category) Axis Labels**, locate **Edit**, as shown in Figure 3.35.

Here you can change the labels on the category axis to the years that are represented in the chart.

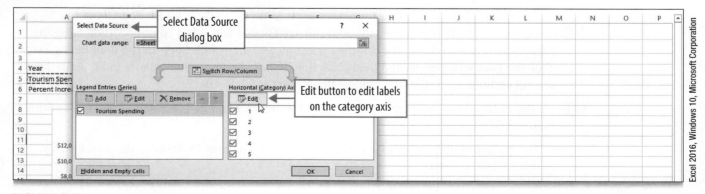

FIGURE 3.35

3 In the right column, click **Edit**. If necessary, drag the title bar of the Axis Labels dialog box to the right of the chart so that it is not blocking your view of the data. Select the years in the range **B4:F4**. Compare your screen with Figure 3.36.

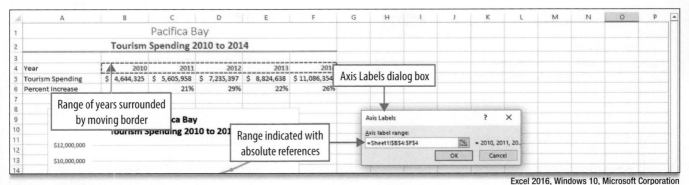

FIGURE 3.36

4 In the **Axis Labels** dialog box, click **OK**, and notice that in the right column of the **Select Data Source** dialog box, the years display as the category labels. Click **OK** to close the **Select Data Source** dialog box. Compare your screen with Figure 3.37.

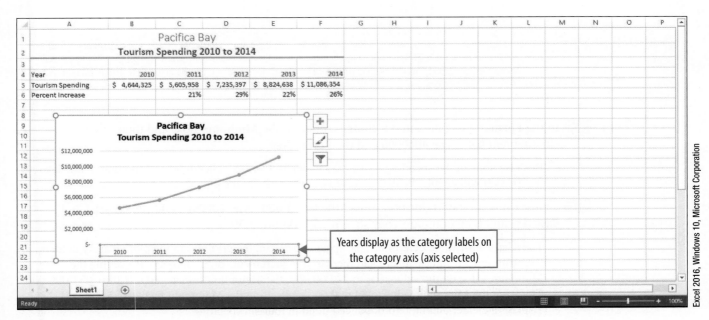

FIGURE 3.37

5 With the **Horizontal (Category) Axis** still selected, click the **Chart Elements** button ⊞, point to **Axes**, click the ▶ arrow, and then click **More Options** to display the **Format Axis** pane.

6 Under **Axis Options**, click **Fill & Line** ◇, if necessary click Line to expand the options. Click the **No line** option button and then **Close** ☒ the **Format Axis** pane.

7 On the chart, notice that the orange line—the data series—does not display in the lower portion of the chart. On the left side of the chart, point to any of the dollar values to display the ScreenTip *Vertical (Value) Axis*, and then right-click. On the shortcut menu, click **Format Axis** to display the **Format Axis** pane on the right. Compare your screen with Figure 3.38.

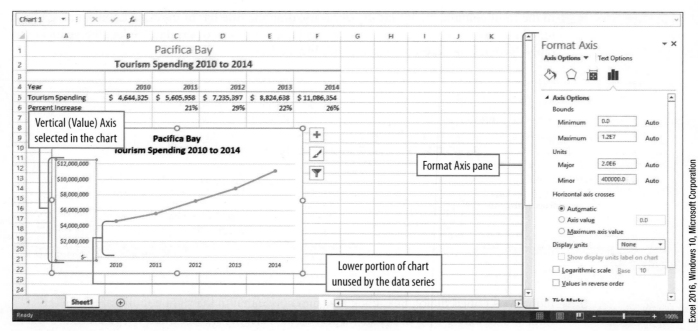

FIGURE 3.38

Excel 2016, Windows 10, Microsoft Corporation

ANOTHER WAY   On the Format tab, in the Current Selection group, click the Chart Elements arrow, click Vertical (Value) Axis, and then click Format Selection. Or, click the Chart Elements button, point to Axes, click the arrow, click More Options, and then in the Format Axis pane, click the Axis Options arrow. On the displayed list, click Vertical (Value) Axis.

8 ▶ In the **Format Axis** pane, under **Bounds**, click in the **Minimum** box, and then select the existing text **0.0**. Type **4000000** and then press Enter.

Because none of the spending figures are under $4,000,000, changing the Minimum number to $4,000,000 will enable the data series to occupy more of the plot area.

9 ▶ Under **Units**, in the **Major** box, select the text **1.0E6**, type **2000000** and press Enter. Click **Save** 🖫, and then compare your screen with Figure 3.39.

The *Major unit* value determines the spacing between the gridlines in the plot area. By default, Excel started the values at zero and increased in increments of $2,000,000. By setting the Minimum value on the value axis to $4,000,000, the Major unit is changed to 1.0E6—$1,000,000. Changing the Minimum value to $4,000,000 and setting the Major unit back to $2,000,000 displays a clearer and more pronounced trend in tourism spending.

Numbers that display E + a number are expressed by Excel in the Scientific format, which displays a number in exponential notation.

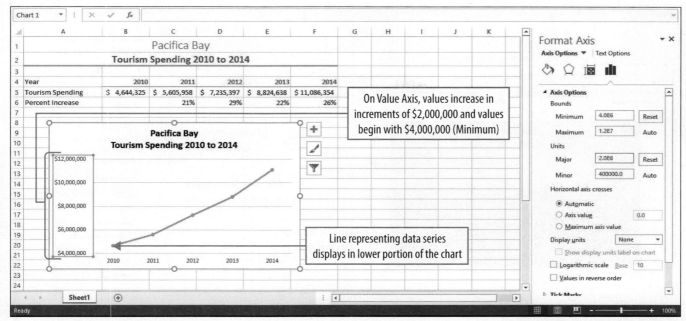

Excel 2016, Windows 10, Microsoft Corporation

FIGURE 3.39

Activity 3.19 | Formatting the Chart Area in a Line Chart

An Excel chart has two background elements—the plot area and the chart area—which by default display a single fill color. To add visual appeal to a chart, you can insert a graphic image as the background.

1 Near the top of the **Format Axis** pane, click the **Axis Options arrow**, and then click **Chart Area** to display the **Format Chart Area** pane. Click **Fill & Line** 🖍️.

When formatting chart elements, Excel provides multiple ways to display the panes that you need. You can right-click the area you want to format and choose a command on the shortcut menu. You can use an existing pane to move to a different pane. And you can use the Format tab on the ribbon to navigate among various chart elements in the Current Selection group. Use whatever method is easiest for you.

🔄 **ANOTHER WAY**   On the Format tab, in the Current Selection group, click the Chart Elements arrow, click Chart Area, and then click Format Selection. Or, right-click slightly inside the chart to display the shortcut menu, and then click Format Chart Area.

2 In the **Format Chart Area** pane, click **Fill** to expand the options, and then click the **Picture or texture fill** option button.

A default texture displays in the chart area.

3 In the **Format Chart Area** pane, under **Insert picture from**, click **File**. In the **Insert Picture** dialog box, navigate to the student data files that accompany this textbook, and then click **e03B_Surfers**. Click **Insert**. Compare your screen with Figure 3.40.

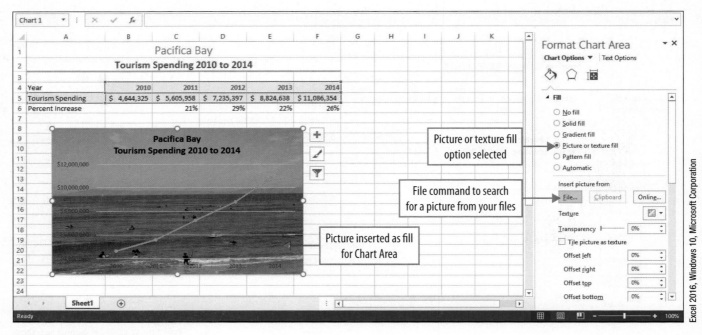

FIGURE 3.40

4 In the **Format Chart Area** pane, click **Fill** to collapse the options, and then if necessary, click Border to expand the options. Click the **Solid line** option button, click the **Color arrow**, and then under **Theme Colors**, in the fifth column, notice that the first color—**Orange, Accent 1**—is already selected by default.

5 Click the **Color arrow** again to accept the default color and close the color palette.

6 Set the **Width** to **4 pt** either by selecting the existing text in the Width box and typing or by clicking the up spin box arrow as necessary.

7 Use the scroll bar on the right side of the Format Chart Area pane if necessary to scroll to the bottom of the pane, and then select the **Rounded corners** check box. On the Quick Access Toolbar, click **Save** 🖫, and then compare your screen with Figure 3.41.

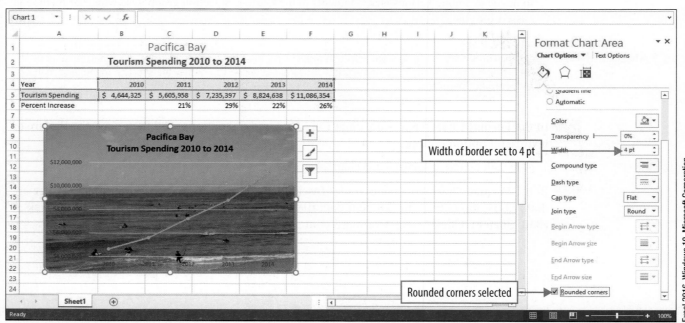

FIGURE 3.41

Activity 3.20 | Formatting the Plot Area Gridlines and Axis Fonts in a Line Chart

1 To the right of the chart, if necessary click Chart Elements ➕ to display the list of elements. Point to **Gridlines**, click the **arrow**, and then click **More Options** to display the **Format Major Gridlines** pane. Compare your screen with Figure 3.42.

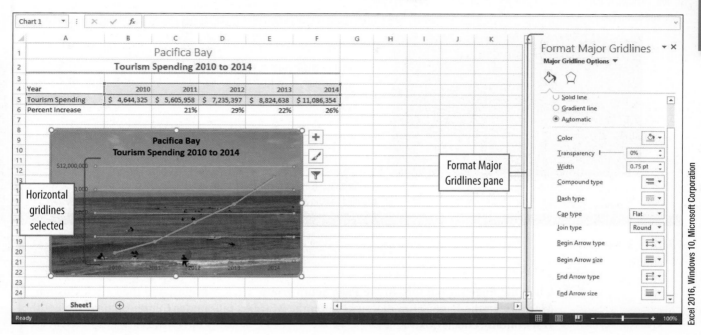

FIGURE 3.42

2 Click the **Solid line** option button. Click the **Color arrow**, and be sure that **Orange, Accent 1**—in the fifth column, the first color—is selected.

3 Set the **Width** to **1 pt**.

4 In the chart, point to any of the dollar values on the **Vertical (Value) Axis**, right-click, and then click **Font**.

5 In the **Font** dialog box, change the **Font style** to **Bold**, and then change the **Font color** to **Black, Text 1**—in the second column, the first color. Click **OK**.

6 Use the same technique to format the font of the **Horizontal (Category) Axis** to **Bold** with **Black, Text 1**.

7 **Close** ✕ the **Format Axis** pane. Click cell **A1** to deselect the chart. Click **Save** 💾, and then compare your screen with Figure 3.43.

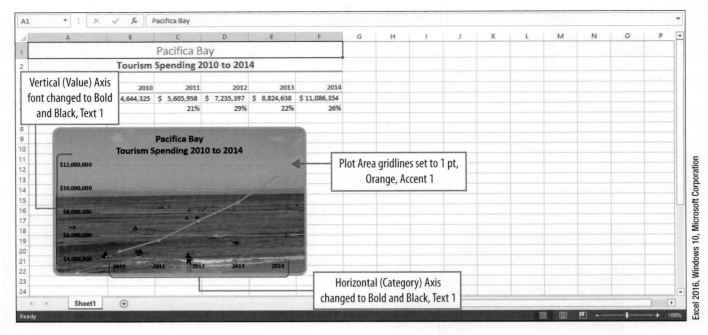

FIGURE 3.43

8 Click the **Page Layout tab**. In the **Page Setup group**, click **Margins**, and then click **Custom Margins**. In the **Page Setup** dialog box, on the **Margins tab**, under **Center on page**, select the **Horizontally** check box.

9 Click the **Header/Footer tab**, and then in the center of the dialog box, click **Custom Footer**. In the **Footer** dialog box, with your insertion point blinking in the **Left section**, on the row of buttons, click **Insert File Name** ⬚.

10 Click **OK** two times. Click the **File tab**, and then click **Show All Properties**. As the **Tags**, type **tourism spending** and as the **Subject**, type your course name and section number. Be sure your name displays as the **Author**.

11 On the left, click **Print** to display the **Print Preview**, and then compare your screen with Figure 3.44. If necessary, return to the worksheet and make any corrections.

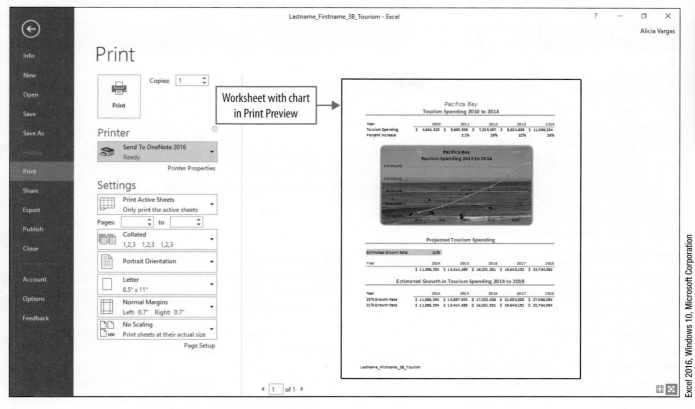

Excel 2016, Windows 10, Microsoft Corporation

FIGURE 3.44

12 On the left, click **Save** to redisplay the workbook.

13 If directed by your instructor to do so, submit your paper printout, your electronic image of your document that looks like a printed document, or your original Excel file. If required by your instructor, print or create an electronic version of your worksheet with formulas displayed. In the upper right corner of the Excel window, click **Close** ☒.

More Knowledge | **Resizing a Chart**

To resize a chart, on the Chart Tools Format tab, in the Size group, type the dimensions in the Shape Height or Shape Width box. Or:

- To change the width of a chart, drag a left or right sizing handle.
- To change the height of a chart, drag a top or bottom sizing handle.
- To size a chart proportionately, hold down Shift and drag a corner sizing handle.

END | You have completed Project 3B

GO! With Google

> **ALERT!** **Working with Web-Based Applications and Services**
>
> Computer programs and services on the web receive continuous updates and improvements, so the steps to complete this web-based activity may differ from the ones shown. You can often look at the screens and the information presented to determine how to complete the activity.
>
> If you do not already have a Google account, you will need to create one before you begin this Activity. Go to http://google.com and, in the upper right corner, click Sign In. On the Sign In screen, click Create Account. On the Create your Google Account page, complete the form, read and agree to the Terms of Service and Privacy Policy, and then click Next step. On the Welcome screen, click Get Started.

Activity | Create a Line Chart

1 From the desktop, open your browser, navigate to **http://google.com**, and then click the **Google Apps** menu ⏶. Click **Drive** △, and then if necessary, sign in to your Google account.

2 Open your **GO! Web Projects** folder—or click New to create and then open this folder if necessary. In the left pane, click **NEW**, and then click **File upload**. Navigate to your student data files, click **e03_3B_Web**, and then click **Open**.

3 Right-click the file you uploaded, point to **Open with**, and then click **Google Sheets**.

4 Drag to select the years and values in the range **A4:F5**, and then on the menu bar, click **Insert**. On the menu, click **Chart**. With the **Recommendations** tab selected, click the **Line chart**, and then click **Insert**.

5 Point to the chart, and then drag down and to the left to position the chart so that its upper left corner is aligned with the upper left corner of cell **A21**.

6 In the upper right corner of the chart area, click the **down-pointing triangle**, and then click **Advanced edit**. Under **Title**, select the existing text. Type **Tourism Spending 2010 to 2014** and then press Enter.

7 Under **Legend**, click **Right**, and then click **None**. In the **Chart Editor**, to the right of the chart options, drag the vertical scroll bar down to display the **Axis** options. To the right of **Axis**, click **Horizontal**, and then click **Left vertical**. Click in the **Min** box, type **3000000** and then press Enter.

8 In the **Chart Editor**, scroll down to display all of the **Series** options. Click the **Point size arrow**, and then click **7px**. In the **Chart Editor**, click **Update**, and then compare your screen with Figure A.

9 Submit your file as directed by your instructor. Sign out of your Google account and close your browser.

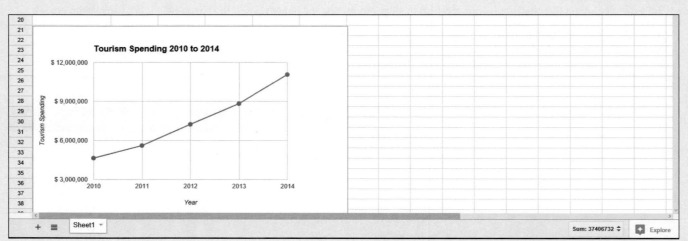

FIGURE A

MICROSOFT OFFICE SPECIALIST (MOS) SKILLS IN THIS CHAPTER	
PROJECT 3A	**PROJECT 3B**
5.1.1 Create a new chart	**1.3.5** Insert or delete columns or rows
5.2.2 Add and modify chart elements	**2.1.3** Paste data by using special paste options
5.2.4 Move charts to a chart sheet	**2.2.3** Format cells by using Format Painter

BUILD YOUR E-PORTFOLIO

An E-Portfolio is a collection of evidence, stored electronically, that showcases what you have accomplished while completing your education. Collecting and then sharing your work products with potential employers reflects your academic and career goals. Your completed documents from the following projects are good examples to show what you have learned: 3G, 3K, and 3L.

GO! FOR JOB SUCCESS

Video: Planning and Managing Your Career

Your instructor may assign this video to your class, and then ask you to think about, or discuss with your classmates, these questions:

FotolEdhar / Fotolia

When did you start career planning and what were the main steps you took to plan your career?

What have been your best sources for networking?

What advice would you give to others about how to stay employable throughout your career?

END OF CHAPTER

SUMMARY

Use pie charts when you want to show the relationship of each part to a whole. Consider using a pie chart when you have only one data series to plot and you do not have more than seven categories.	To create a pie chart, you must select two ranges. One range contains the labels for each pie slice; the other contains the values that add up to a total. Both ranges must have the same number of cells.	In formulas, Excel follows rules called the order of operations; expressions within parentheses are processed first, and multiplication and division are performed before addition and subtraction.	Use a line chart when you want to show trends over time. Time displays along the bottom axis and the data point values connect with a line. The curve and direction of the line make trends obvious.

GO! LEARN IT ONLINE

Review the concepts, key terms, and MOS skills in this chapter by completing these online challenges, which you can find at **MyITLab**.

Matching and Multiple Choice: Answer matching and multiple-choice questions to test what you learned in this chapter.	**Lesson on the GO!** Learn how to use all the new apps and features as they are introduced by Microsoft.	**MOS Prep Quiz:** Answer questions to review the MOS skills that you practiced in this chapter.

GO! COLLABORATIVE TEAM PROJECT (Available in **MyITLab** and Instructor Resource Center)

If your instructor assigns this project to your class, you can expect to work with one or more of your classmates—either in person or by using Internet tools—to create work products similar to those that you created in this chapter. A team is a group of workers who work together to solve a problem, make a decision, or create a work product. Collaboration is when you work together with others as a team in an intellectual endeavor to complete a shared task or achieve a shared goal.

Your instructor will assign Projects from this list to ensure your learning and assess your knowledge.

PROJECT GUIDE FOR EXCEL CHAPTER 3

Project	Apply Skills from These Chapter Objectives	Project Type	Project Location
3A **MyITLab**	Objectives 1–4 from Project 3A	**3A Instructional Project (Grader Project)** Guided instruction to learn the skills in Project 3A.	In MyITLab and in text
3B **MyITLab**	Objectives 5–7 from Project 3B	**3B Instructional Project (Grader Project)** Guided instruction to learn the skills in Project 3B.	In MyITLab and in text
3C	Objectives 1–4 from Project 3A	**3C Skills Review (Scorecard Grading)** A guided review of the skills from Project 3A.	In text
3D	Objectives 5–7 from Project 3B	**3D Skills Review (Scorecard Grading)** A guided review of the skills from Project 3B.	In text
3E **MyITLab**	Objectives 1–4 from Project 3A	**3E Mastery (Grader Project)** **Mastery and Transfer of Learning** A demonstration of your mastery of the skills in Project 3A with extensive decision making.	In MyITLab and in text
3F **MyITLab**	Objectives 5–7 from Project 3B	**3F Mastery (Grader Project)** **Mastery and Transfer of Learning** A demonstration of your mastery of the skills in Project 3B with extensive decision making.	In MyITLab and in text
3G **MyITLab**	Objectives 1–7 from Projects 3A and 3B	**3G Mastery (Grader Project)** **Mastery and Transfer of Learning** A demonstration of your mastery of the skills in Projects 3A and 3B with extensive decision making.	In MyITLab and in text
3H	Combination of Objectives from Projects 3A and 3B	**3H GO! Fix It (Scorecard Grading)** **Critical Thinking** A demonstration of your mastery of the skills in Projects 3A and 3B by creating a correct result from a document that contains errors you must find.	Instructor Resource Center (IRC) and MyITLab
3I	Combination of Objectives from Projects 3A and 3B	**3I GO! Make It (Scorecard Grading)** **Critical Thinking** A demonstration of your mastery of the skills in Projects 3A and 3B by creating a result from a supplied picture.	IRC and MyITLab
3J	Combination of Objectives from Projects 3A and 3B	**3J GO! Solve It (Rubric Grading)** **Critical Thinking** A demonstration of your mastery of the skills in Projects 3A and 3B, your decision-making skills, and your critical-thinking skills. A task-specific rubric helps you self-assess your result.	IRC and MyITLab
3K	Combination of Objectives from Projects 3A and 3B	**3K GO! Solve It (Rubric Grading)** **Critical Thinking** A demonstration of your mastery of the skills in Projects 3A and 3B, your decision-making skills, and your critical-thinking skills. A task-specific rubric helps you self-assess your result.	In text
3L	Combination of Objectives from Projects 3A and 3B	**3L GO! Think (Rubric Grading)** **Critical Thinking** A demonstration of your understanding of the chapter concepts applied in a manner that you would outside of college. An analytic rubric helps you and your instructor grade the quality of your work by comparing it to the work an expert in the discipline would create.	In text
3M	Combination of Objectives from Projects 3A and 3B	**3M GO! Think (Rubric Grading)** **Critical Thinking** A demonstration of your understanding of the chapter concepts applied in a manner that you would outside of college. An analytic rubric helps you and your instructor grade the quality of your work by comparing it to the work an expert in the discipline would create.	IRC and MyITLab
3N	Combination of Objectives from Projects 3A and 3B	**3N You and GO! (Rubric Grading)** **Critical Thinking** A demonstration of your understanding of the chapter concepts applied in a manner that you would in a personal situation. An analytic rubric helps you and your instructor grade the quality of your work.	IRC and MyITLab
3O	Combination of Objectives from Projects 3A and 3B	**3O Collaborative Team Project for Excel Chapter 3** **Critical Thinking** A demonstration of your understanding of concepts and your ability to work collaboratively in a group role-playing assessment, requiring both collaboration and self-management.	IRC and MyITLab
Capstone Project for EXCEL Chapters 1–3	Combination of Objectives from Chapters 1–3	A demonstration of your mastery of the skills in Chapters 1–3 with extensive decision making. **(Grader Project)**	IRC and MyITLab

GLOSSARY

GLOSSARY OF CHAPTER KEY TERMS

3-D The shortened term for *three-dimensional*, which refers to an image that appears to have all three spatial dimensions—length, width, and depth.

Absolute cell reference A cell reference that refers to cells by their fixed position in a worksheet; an absolute cell reference remains the same when the formula is copied.

Axis A line that serves as a frame of reference for measurement and which borders the chart plot area.

Base The starting point when you divide the amount of increase by it to calculate the rate of increase.

Bevel A shape effect that uses shading and shadows to make the edges of a shape appear to be curved or angled.

Category axis The area along the bottom of a chart that identifies the categories of data; also referred to as the x-axis.

Chart area The entire chart and all of its elements.

Chart sheet A workbook sheet that contains only a chart.

Data marker A column, bar, area, dot, pie slice, or other symbol in a chart that represents a single data point; related data points form a data series.

Data point A value that originates in a worksheet cell and that is represented in a chart by a data marker.

Data series Related data points represented by data markers; each data series has a unique color or pattern represented in the chart legend.

Enterprise fund A municipal government fund that reports income and expenditures related to municipal services for which a fee is charged in exchange for goods or services.

Explode The action of pulling out one or more pie slices from a pie chart for emphasis.

Formula AutoComplete An Excel feature which, after typing an = (equal sign) and the beginning letter or letters of a function name, displays a list of function names that match the typed letter(s).

Fund A sum of money set aside for a specific purpose.

General fund The term used to describe money set aside for the normal operating activities of a government entity such as a city.

Goal Seek A what-if analysis tool that finds the input needed in one cell to arrive at the desired result in another cell.

Legend A chart element that identifies the patterns or colors that are assigned to the categories in the chart.

Line chart A chart type that displays trends over time; time displays along the bottom axis and the data point values are connected with a line.

Major unit The value in a chart's value axis that determines the spacing between tick marks and between the gridlines in the plot area.

Order of operations The mathematical rules for performing multiple calculations within a formula.

Percent for new value = base percent + percent of increase The formula for calculating a percentage by which a value increases by adding the base percentage—usually 100%—to the percent increase.

Percentage rate of increase The percent by which one number increases over another number.

Pie chart A chart that shows the relationship of each part to a whole.

Plot area The area bounded by the axes of a chart, including all the data series.

Rate = amount of increase/base The mathematical formula to calculate a rate of increase.

Relative cell reference In a formula, the address of a cell based on the relative positions of the cell that contains the formula and the cell referred to in the formula.

Value after increase = base x percent for new value The formula for calculating the value after an increase by multiplying the original value—the base—by the percent for new value (see the *Percent for new value* formula).

Value axis A numerical scale on the left side of a chart that shows the range of numbers for the data points; also referred to as the y-axis.

What-if analysis The process of changing the values in cells to see how those changes affect the outcome of formulas in a worksheet.

x-axis Another name for the category axis.

y-axis Another name for the value axis.

<table>
<tr><td>

Apply 3A skills from these Objectives:

1 Chart Data with a Pie Chart

2 Format a Pie Chart

3 Edit a Workbook and Update a Chart

4 Use Goal Seek to Perform What-If Analysis

</td><td>

Skills Review | Project 3C Parks

In the following Skills Review, you will edit a worksheet for Jerry Silva, City Parks Manager, which details the revenue generated from city parks and structures. Your completed worksheets will look similar to Figure 3.45.

</td></tr>
</table>

PROJECT FILES

For Project 3C, you will need the following file:

e03C_Parks

You will save your workbook as:

Lastname_Firstname_3C_Parks

PROJECT RESULTS

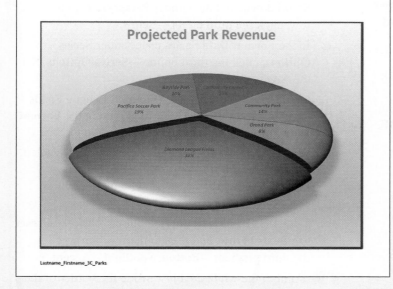

FIGURE 3.45

(Project 3C Parks continues on the next page)

1 Start Excel. From your student data files, open the file **e03C_Parks**. Save the file in your **Excel Chapter 3** folder as **Lastname_Firstname_3C_Parks**

a. Click cell **D5**, and then type = to begin a formula. Click cell **C5**, type **/** and then click cell **C11**. Press F4 to make the reference to the value in cell **C11** absolute. On the **Formula Bar**, click **Enter**, and then fill the formula down through cell **D10**.

b. With the range **D5:D10** selected, right-click over the selection, and then on the mini toolbar, click **Percent Style** and **Center**.

2 Select the nonadjacent ranges **A5:A10** and **C5:C10** to select the park names and the projected revenue. Click the **Insert tab**, and then in the **Charts group**, click **Insert Pie or Doughnut Chart**. Under **3-D Pie**, click the chart type **3-D Pie**.

a. On the **Design tab**, in the **Location group**, click **Move Chart**. In the **Move Chart** dialog box, click the **New sheet** option button. In the **New sheet** box, replace the highlighted text *Chart1* by typing **Projected Park Revenue Chart** and then click **OK**.

b. Click the text *Chart Title*. Type **Projected Park Revenue** and then press Enter to create the new chart title.

c. With the title selected, on the **Format tab**, in the **WordArt Styles group**, click **More** to display the gallery. In the second row, select the fifth style—**Fill – Olive Green, Accent 3, Sharp Bevel**. Drag to select the chart title text, and then on the mini toolbar, change the **Font Size** to **32**.

d. Click in a white area of the chart to deselect the chart title. Click **Chart Elements**, and then click the **Legend** check box to remove the legend.

e. In the list of **Chart Elements**, point to **Data Labels**, click the **arrow** that displays, and then click **More Options**. In the **Format Data Labels** pane on the right, under **Label Options**, select the **Category Name** and **Percentage** check boxes, and *clear* all other check boxes. Under **Label Position**, click **Center**.

f. Point to any of the selected labels, right-click to display a shortcut menu, and then click **Font**. In the **Font** dialog box, on the **Font tab**, change the **Font style** to **Bold Italic** and change the **Size** to **11** Click **OK**.

3 In any pie slice, point anywhere outside the selected label, and then double-click to display the **Format Data Series** pane. Under **Series Options**, click **Effects**, and then click **3-D Format**.

a. Click the **Top bevel arrow**, and then under **Bevel**, click the first button—**Circle**. Apply the **Circle** bevel to the **Bottom bevel**.

b. Set the **Width** and **Height** of both the **Top bevel** and the **Bottom bevel** to **512 pt**

c. Scroll down, click the **Material arrow**, and then under **Standard**, click the third material—**Plastic**.

d. Scroll to the top of the **Format Data Series** pane, click **Shadow**, and then click the **Presets arrow**. Scroll down, and then under **Perspective**, in the first row, click the third effect—**Below**.

e. In the **Format Data Series** pane, under **Series Options**, click the third button—**Series Options**. Set the **Angle of first slice** to **50**

f. On the pie chart, click the **Diamond League Fields** slice to select only that slice, and then in the **Format Data Point** pane, set the **Point Explosion** to **10%**

g. With the **Diamond League Fields** slice still selected, in the **Format Data Point** pane, under **Series Options**, click **Fill & Line**, and then click **Fill** to expand the options.

h. Click the **Gradient fill** option button, click the **Preset gradients arrow**, and then in the fourth row, click the third gradient—**Bottom Spotlight – Accent 3**.

4 Point to the white area just inside the border of the chart to display the ScreenTip *Chart Area*, and then click one time to display the **Format Chart Area** pane.

a. Under **Chart Options**, click **Fill & Line**, and be sure the **Fill** options are still displayed.

b. Click the **Gradient fill** option button, click the **Preset gradients arrow**, and then in the first row, click the fifth gradient—**Light Gradient – Accent 5**.

c. In the **Format Chart Area** pane, click **Fill** to collapse the options, and then click **Border** to expand the options.

d. Click the **Solid line** option button, click the **Color arrow**, and then in the fifth column, click the last color—**Ice Blue, Accent 1, Darker 50%**. Set the **Width** of the border to **5 pt** Close the pane, and then **Save** your workbook.

(Project 3C Parks continues on the next page)

5 In the sheet tab area at the bottom of the workbook, click the **Sheet1 tab**.

a. Click cell **C11**. On the **Data tab**, in the **Forecast group**, click **What-If Analysis**, and then click **Goal Seek**. In the **Goal Seek** dialog box, press Tab to move to the **To value** box, and then type **17,800,000**

b. Press Tab to move the insertion point to the **By changing cell** box, and then click cell **C10**. Click **OK**. In the displayed **Goal Seek Status** dialog box, click **OK** to set the total projected revenue to $17,800,000 by changing the projected revenue for the Community Center.

6 With your worksheet displayed, in the sheet tab area, double-click *Sheet1* to select the text, and then type **Projected Park Revenue Data** and press Enter.

a. Click the **Page Layout tab**. In the **Page Setup Group**, click **Margins**, click **Custom Margins**, and then in the **Page Setup** dialog box, on the **Margins tab**, under **Center on page**, select the **Horizontally** check box.

b. Click the **Header/Footer tab**, click **Custom Footer**, and then with your insertion point in the **Left**

section, on the row of buttons, click **Insert File Name**. Click **OK** two times.

c. Display the **Projected Park Revenue Chart**, and then display the **Page Setup** dialog box.

d. Click the **Header/Footer tab**, click **Custom Footer**, and then in the **Left section**, click the **Insert File Name** button. Click **OK** two times.

e. Click the **File tab**, and then click **Show All Properties**. As the **Tags**, type **park revenue** As the **Subject**, type your course name and section number. Be sure your name displays as the **Author**.

f. **Save** your workbook. If directed by your instructor to do so, submit your paper printout, your electronic image of your document that looks like a printed document, or your original Excel file. If required by your instructor, print or create an electronic version of your worksheet with formulas displayed. In the upper right corner of the Excel window, click **Close**.

END | You have completed Project 3C

Skills Review   Project 3D Housing Permits

In the following Skills Review, you will edit a worksheet that forecasts the revenue from new housing permits that the City of Pacifica Bay expects to collect in the five-year period 2014–2018. Your completed worksheet will look similar to Figure 3.46.

PROJECT FILES

For Project 3D, you will need the following files:

e03D_Housing_Permits

e03D_Housing

You will save your workbook as:

Lastname_Firstname_3D_Housing_Permits

PROJECT RESULTS

Pacifica Bay
Housing Permit Revenue Forecast

	2010	2011	2012	2013	2014
Permit Revenue	$ 1,945,923	$ 2,025,684	$ 2,115,783	$ 2,234,897	$ 2,397,445
Projected Increase		4%	4%	6%	7%

Projected Future Housing Permit Revenue

Forecasted Increase 8%

Year	2014	2015	2016	2017	2018
Projected Permit Revenue	$ 2,397,445	$ 2,589,241	$ 2,796,380	$ 3,020,090	$ 3,261,697

Forecasted Revenue Estimates 2014 to 2018

Year	2014	2015	2016	2017	2018
7% Increase	$ 2,397,445	$ 2,565,266	$ 2,744,835	$ 2,936,973	$ 3,142,561
8% Increase	$ 2,397,445	$ 2,589,241	$ 2,796,380	$ 3,020,090	$ 3,261,697

Lastname_Firstname_3D_Housing_Permits

Excel 2016, Windows 10, Microsoft Corporation

FIGURE 3.46

(Project 3D Housing Permits continues on the next page)

1 Start Excel. From your student data files, open **e03D_Housing_Permits**. Using your own name, save the file in your **Excel Chapter 3** folder as **Lastname_Firstname_3D_Housing_Permits**

a. In cell **B4**, type **2010** and then press Tab. In cell **C4**, type **2011** and then press Enter.

b. Use the fill handle to fill the remaining years through **column F** so that the last year that displays is 2014.

2 Click cell **C6**. Being sure to include the parentheses, type **=(c5-b5)/b5** and then press Enter. Select cell **C6**, and then apply **Percent Style**.

a. With cell **C6** selected, drag the fill handle to the right through cell **F6**.

b. In cell **A8**, type **Projected Future Housing Permit Revenue** and then press Enter. Point to cell **A2**, right-click, on the mini toolbar, click **Format Painter**, and then click cell **A8**. In cell **A10**, type **Forecasted Increase** and then click cell **A12**. Type **Year**

c. In cell **A13**, type **Projected Permit Revenue** and then in cell **B12**, type **2014** and press Tab. In cell **C12**, type **2015** and then press Tab. Select the range **B12:C12**, and then drag the fill handle through cell **F12** to extend the pattern of years to *2018*. Apply **Bold** to the selection.

d. Right-click cell **F5**, and then click **Copy**. Right-click over cell **B13**, and then click **Paste**.

e. In cell **B10**, type **7%** which is the percent of increase from 2013 to 2014. Select the range **A10:B10**, and then from the mini toolbar, apply **Bold** and **Italic**.

3 Click cell **C13**. Type **=b13*(100%+b10)** and then on the **Formula Bar**, click **Enter** to keep the cell active. With cell **C13** as the active cell, drag the fill handle to copy the formula to the range **D13:F13**.

a. Point to cell **B13**, right-click, click **Format Painter**, and then select the range **C13:F13**.

b. Click cell **A15**. Type **Forecasted Revenue Estimates 2014 to 2018** and then press Enter. Use **Format Painter** to copy the format from cell **A8** to cell **A15**.

c. In the range **A17:A19**, type the following row titles:

Year

7% Increase

8% Increase

4 Select the range **B12:F12**, right-click over the selection, and then on the shortcut menu, click **Copy**. **Paste** the selection to the range **B17:F17**.

a. Select the range **B13:F13**, right-click over the selection, and then on the shortcut menu, click **Copy**. Point to cell **B18**, right-click, and then from the shortcut menu, point to **Paste Special**. Under **Paste Values**, click the second button—**Values & Number Formatting**. Press Esc to cancel the moving border.

b. Click cell **B10**. Type **8** and then press Enter. Copy the new values in the range **B13:F13**. Point to cell **B19**, right-click, and then point to **Paste Special**. Under **Paste Values**, click **Values & Number Formatting**. **Save** your workbook.

5 In the **row header area**, point to **row 8** to display the pointer, and then drag down to select **rows 8:24**. Right-click over the selection, and then click **Insert** to insert the same number of blank rows as you selected. Under the selection area near cell **A25**, click **Insert Options**, and then click the **Clear Formatting** option button to clear any formatting from these rows.

a. On the **Page Layout tab**, in the **Themes group**, click the **Colors arrow**, and then click **Yellow**. Select the range **A5:F5**. On the **Insert tab**, in the **Charts group**, click **Insert Line or Area Chart**. In the displayed gallery of line charts, click the **Line with Markers** chart type to create the chart.

b. Point to the border of the chart to display the ⟦⟧ pointer, and then drag the chart so that its upper left corner is positioned in cell **A9**, aligned approximately under the *c* in the word *Projected* above.

c. Point to the Chart Title *Permit Revenue* and right-click. On the shortcut menu, click **Edit Text**. Type **Pacifica Bay Housing** and then press Spacebar. Press End and then press Enter to create a second line. Type **2010 to 2014**

d. Click the dashed border around the chart title to change it to a solid border, right-click over the title, and then on the shortcut menu, click **Font**. In the **Font** dialog box, change the **Font style** to **Bold**, change the **Size** to **16**, and change the **Font color** to **White, Background 1, Darker 5%**—in the first column, the second color. Click **OK**.

(Project 3D Housing Permits continues on the next page)

Skills Review Project 3D Housing Permits (continued)

6 At the bottom of the chart, point to any of the numbers *1* through *5*, and then right-click. On the shortcut menu, click **Select Data**. On the right side of the **Select Data Source** dialog box, click **Edit**. In the worksheet, select the years in the range **B4:F4**, and then click **OK** two times to enter the years as the category labels.

a. With the **Horizontal (Category) Axis** still selected, click **Chart Elements**, point to **Axes**, click the **arrow**, and then click **More Options**. In the **Format Axis** pane, under **Axis Options**, click **Fill & Line**. If necessary, click Line to expand the options. Click the **No line** option button, and then **close** the **Format Axis** pane.

b. On the left side of the chart, point to any of the dollar values, right-click, and then click **Format Axis**. In the **Format Axis** pane, under **Bounds**, select the text in the **Minimum** box, and then type **1900000**

c. Under **Units**, in the **Major** box, select the existing text, and then type **50000**

d. Near the top of the **Format Axis** pane, click the **Axis Options arrow**, and then click **Chart Area** to display the **Format Chart Area** pane. Click **Fill & Line**.

e. In the **Format Chart Area** pane, click **Fill** to expand the options, and then click the **Picture or texture fill** option button. Under **Insert picture from**, click **File**. In the **Insert Picture** dialog box, navigate to the student data files, and then click **e03D_Housing**. Click **Insert**.

f. In the **Format Chart Area** pane, click **Fill** to collapse the options, and then if necessary click Border to expand the Border section. Click the **Solid line** option button, click the **Color arrow**, and then under **Theme Colors**, in the fifth column, click the first color—**Gold, Accent 1**. Set the **Width** to **4 pt** Scroll to the bottom of the pane, and then select the **Rounded corners** check box.

7 To the right of the chart, click **Chart Elements**, point to **Gridlines**, click the **arrow**, and then click **More Options** to display the **Format Major Gridlines** pane.

a. Under **Line**, click the **Solid line** option button. Click the **Color arrow**, and be sure that **Gold, Accent 1** is the selected color. Set the **Width** to **1 pt**

b. In the chart, point to any of the dollar values on the **Vertical (Value) Axis**, right-click, and then click **Font**. In the **Font** dialog box, change the **Font style** to **Bold**, and then change the **Font color** to **White, Background 1**—in the first column, the first color. Click **OK**.

c. By using the same technique, format the **Font** of the **Horizontal (Category) Axis** to **Bold** with **White, Background 1** as the font color.

d. **Close** the **Format Axis** pane, and then click cell **A1** to deselect the chart. Click the **Page Layout tab**. In the **Page Setup group**, click **Margins**, and then click **Custom Margins**. On the **Margins tab**, select the **Horizontally** check box. Click the **Header/Footer tab**, click **Custom Footer**, and then in the **Left section**, insert the file name. Click **OK** two times.

e. Click the **File tab**, and then click **Show All Properties**. As the **Tags**, type **housing permit revenue** In the **Subject** box, type your course name and section number. Be sure your name displays as the **Author**.

f. **Save** your workbook. If directed by your instructor to do so, submit your paper printout, your electronic image of your document that looks like a printed document, or your original Excel file. If required by your instructor, print or create an electronic version of your worksheet with formulas displayed. In the upper right corner of the Excel window, click **Close**.

END | You have completed Project 3D

Mastering Excel | **Project 3E Revenue**

Apply 3A skills from these Objectives:

1 Chart Data with a Pie Chart

2 Format a Pie Chart

3 Edit a Workbook and Update a Chart

4 Use Goal Seek to Perform What-If Analysis

In the following project, you will edit a worksheet that summarizes the revenue budget for the City of Pacifica Bay. Your completed worksheets will look similar to Figure 3.47.

PROJECT FILES

For Project 3E, you will need the following file:

e03E_Revenue

You will save your workbook as:

Lastname_Firstname_3E_Revenue

PROJECT RESULTS

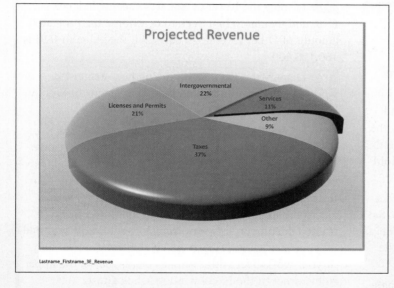

FIGURE 3.47

Excel 2016, Windows 10, Microsoft Corporation

(Project 3E Revenue continues on the next page)

Mastering Excel   Project 3E Revenue (continued)

1 Start Excel. From your student data files, locate and open **e03E_Revenue**. **Save** the file in your **Excel Chapter 3** folder as **Lastname_Firstname_3E_Revenue**

2 In cell **D5**, construct a formula to calculate the **% of Total Projected Revenue** from **Taxes** by dividing the **Projected Revenue for Next Fiscal Year** for **Taxes** by the **Total Projected Revenue for Next Fiscal Year**. Use absolute cell references as necessary, format the result in **Percent Style**, and **Center** the percentage. Fill the formula down through cell **D9**.

3 Select the nonadjacent ranges **A5:A9** and **C5:C9** as the data for a pie chart, and then insert a **3-D Pie** chart. Move the chart to a **New sheet** named **Projected Revenue Chart**

4 As the text for the **Chart Title** element, type **Projected Revenue** Format the **Chart Title** using the **WordArt Style Fill – Aqua, Accent 1, Shadow**—in the first row, the second style and a **Font Size** of **32**.

5 Remove the **Legend** chart element, and then add the **Data Labels** chart element formatted so that only the **Category Name** and **Percentage** display positioned in the **Center**. Format the data labels with a **Font style** of **Bold** and a **Font Size** of **14**.

6 Format the **Data Series** using a **3-D Format** effect. Change the **Top bevel** and **Bottom bevel** to **Art Deco**. Set the **Top bevel Width** and **Height** to **350 pt** and then set the **Bottom bevel Width** and **Height** to **0 pt** Change the **Material** to the second **Special Effect—Soft Edge**.

7 Display the **Series Options**, and then set the **Angle of first slice** to **115** so that the **Taxes** slice is in the front of the pie.

8 Select the **Services** slice, and then explode the slice **10%**. Change the **Fill Color** of the **Services** slice to a **Solid fill** using **Gray-50%, Accent 4**—in the eighth column, the first color.

9 Format the **Chart Area** by applying a **Gradient fill** using the **Preset gradients Light Gradient – Accent 4**. Format the **Border** of the **Chart Area** by applying a **Solid line** border using **Gray-50%, Accent 4** and a **5 pt Width**. Close any panes that are open on the right.

10 Display the **Page Setup** dialog box, and then for this chart sheet, insert a **Custom Footer** in the **left section** with the file name.

11 Display the **Revenue Sources sheet**. Click cell **C10**, and then use **Goal Seek** to determine the projected amount of Other revenue in cell **C9** if the value in **C10** is **150,125,000**

12 Display the **Page Setup** dialog box, center the worksheet **Horizontally**, and then insert a custom footer in the **left section** with the file name.

13 Show all the properties, and then as the **Tags**, type **revenue sources** As the **Subject**, type your course name and section number. Be sure your name displays as the **Author**. **Save** your workbook. If directed by your instructor to do so, submit your paper printout, your electronic image of your document that looks like a printed document, or your original Excel file. If required by your instructor, print or create an electronic version of your worksheet with formulas displayed. In the upper right corner of the Excel window, click **Close**.

END | You have completed Project 3E

Mastering Excel   Project 3F Streets

Apply 3B skills from these Objectives:

5 Design a Worksheet for What-If Analysis

6 Answer What-If Questions by Changing Values in a Worksheet

7 Chart Data with a Line Chart

In the following project, you will edit a worksheet that the City of Pacifica Bay Facilities Director will use to prepare a five-year forecast of the costs associated with street maintenance. Your completed worksheet will look similar to Figure 3.48.

PROJECT FILES

For Project 3F, you will need the following file:

New blank Excel workbook

You will save your workbook as:

Lastname_Firstname_3F_Streets

PROJECT RESULTS

Build from
Scratch

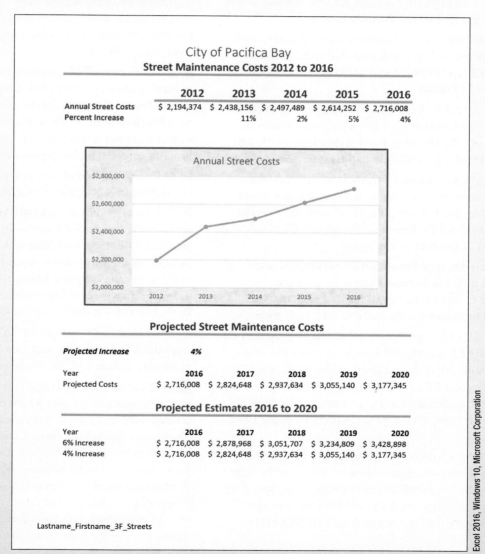

City of Pacifica Bay
Street Maintenance Costs 2012 to 2016

	2012	2013	2014	2015	2016
Annual Street Costs	$ 2,194,374	$ 2,438,156	$ 2,497,489	$ 2,614,252	$ 2,716,008
Percent Increase		11%	2%	5%	4%

Projected Street Maintenance Costs

Projected Increase	4%

Year	2016	2017	2018	2019	2020
Projected Costs	$ 2,716,008	$ 2,824,648	$ 2,937,634	$ 3,055,140	$ 3,177,345

Projected Estimates 2016 to 2020

Year	2016	2017	2018	2019	2020
6% Increase	$ 2,716,008	$ 2,878,968	$ 3,051,707	$ 3,234,809	$ 3,428,898
4% Increase	$ 2,716,008	$ 2,824,648	$ 2,937,634	$ 3,055,140	$ 3,177,345

Lastname_Firstname_3F_Streets

Excel 2016, Windows 10, Microsoft Corporation

FIGURE 3.48

(Project 3F Streets continues on the next page)

Mastering Excel   Project 3F Streets (continued)

1 Start Excel and display a new **Blank workbook**. **Save** the file in your **Excel Chapter 3** folder as **Lastname_Firstname_3F_Streets**

2 Change the **Theme Colors** to **Paper**. In cell **A1**, type the title **City of Pacifica Bay** and then **Merge & Center** the title across **columns A:F**. Apply the **Title** cell style.

3 In cell **A2** type the subtitle **Street Maintenance Costs 2012 to 2016** and then **Merge & Center** the subtitle across **columns A:F**. Apply the **Heading 1** cell style.

4 In the range **B4:F4**, fill the year range with the values 2012 through 2016. In cell **A5** type **Annual Street Costs** and in cell **A6** type **Percent Increase**

5 Change the width of **column A** to **145 pixels**, and then change the width of **columns B:F** to **82 pixels**. In the range **B5:F5** type **2194374** and **2438156** and **2497489** and **2614252** and **2716008**

6 Select **B5:F5**, display the **Cell Styles** gallery, and then apply the **Currency [0]** cell style to the values in **B5:F5**. Apply the **Heading 1** cell style to the years, and apply the **Heading 4** cell style to the range **A5:A6**.

7 In cell **C6**, construct a formula to calculate the percent of increase in annual street maintenance costs from 2012 to 2013. Format the result with the **Percent Style** and then fill the formula through cell **F6** to calculate the percent of increase in each year.

8 In cell **A8**, type **Projected Street Maintenance Costs** and then use **Format Painter** to copy the formatting from cell **A2** to cell **A8**. In cell **A10**, type **Projected Increase** and then in cell **A12**, type **Year**

9 In cell **A13**, type **Projected Costs** and then in the range **B12:F12**, use the fill handle to enter the years 2016 through 2020. Apply **Bold** to the years. **Copy** the value in cell **F5** to cell **B13**. In cell **B10**, type **6%** which is the projected increase estimated by the City financial analysts. To the range **A10:B10**, apply **Bold** and **Italic**.

10 In cell **C13**, construct a formula to calculate the annual projected street maintenance costs for the year 2017 after the projected increase of 6% is applied. Fill the formula through cell **F13**, and then use **Format Painter** to copy the formatting from cell **B13** to the range **C13:F13**.

11 In cell **A15**, type **Projected Estimates 2016 to 2020** and then use **Format Painter** to copy the format from cell **A8** to cell **A15**. In cells **A17:A19**, type the following row titles:

> **Year**
>
> **6% Increase**
>
> **4% Increase**

12 **Copy** the range **B12:F12**, and then **Paste** the selection to **B17:F17**. Copy the range **B13:F13** and then paste the **Values & Number Formatting** to the range **B18:F18**. Complete the Projected Estimates section of the worksheet by changing the *Projected Increase* in **B10** to **4%** and then copying and pasting the **Values & Number Formatting** to the appropriate range in the worksheet. **Save** your workbook.

13 Select **rows 8:24**, and then **Insert** the same number of blank rows as you selected. **Clear Formatting** from the inserted rows. By using the data in **A4:F5**, insert a **Line with Markers** chart in the worksheet. Move the chart so that its upper left corner is positioned in cell **A9** and visually centered under the data above.

14 Format the **Bounds** of the **Vertical (Value) Axis** so that the **Minimum** is **2000000** and the **Major unit** is **200000**

15 Format the **Fill** of the **Chart Area** with a **Texture fill** by applying the **Parchment** texture—in the third row, the fifth texture. Format the **Chart Area** with a **Border** by applying a **Solid line** using **Olive Green, Accent 1, Darker 50%**—in the fifth column, the last color. Change the **Width** of the border to **2 pt**. Format the **Plot Area** with a **Solid fill** using **White, Background 1**—in the first column, the first color.

16 Click cell **A1** to deselect the chart. Center the worksheet **Horizontally**, and then insert a **Custom Footer** in the **left section** with the file name.

17 Show all the properties, and then as the **Tags**, type **street maintenance costs** As the **Subject**, type your course name and section number. Be sure your name displays as the **Author**. **Save** your workbook. If directed by your instructor to do so, submit your paper printout, your electronic image of your document that looks like a printed document, or your original Excel file. If required by your instructor, print or create an electronic version of your worksheet with formulas displayed. In the upper right corner of the Excel window, click **Close**.

END | You have completed Project 3F

Mastering Excel   Project 3G Expenses

In the following project, you will edit a workbook for Jennifer Carson, City Finance Manager. Your completed worksheets will look similar to Figure 3.49.

PROJECT FILES

For Project 3G, you will need the following file:

e03G_Expenses

You will save your workbook as

Lastname_Firstname_3G_Expenses

PROJECT RESULTS

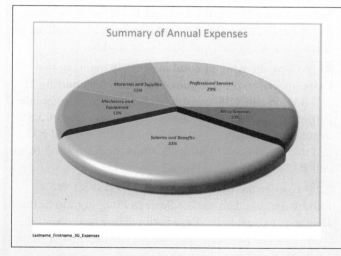

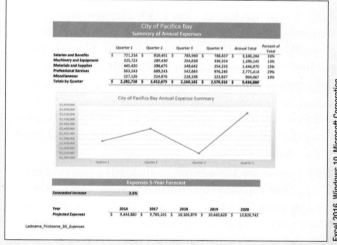

FIGURE 3.49

Excel 2016, Windows 10, Microsoft Corporation

(Project 3G Expenses continues on the next page)

Mastering Excel | **Project 3G Operations** (continued)

1 Start Excel. From your student data files, open **e03G_Expenses**. **Save** the file in your **Excel Chapter 3** folder as **Lastname_Firstname_3G_Expenses**

2 In the **Expenses** worksheet, calculate row totals for each Expense item in the range **F5:F9**. Calculate column totals for each quarter and for the Annual Total in the range **B10:F10**. Be sure that **F6:F9** are formatted with **Comma Style** and zero decimal places.

3 In cell **G5**, construct a formula to calculate the **Percent of Total** by dividing the **Annual Total** for **Salaries and Benefits** by the **Annual Total** for all quarters. Use absolute cell references as necessary, format the result in **Percent Style**, and then **Center**. Fill the formula down through cell **G9**.

4 Use a **3-D Pie** chart to chart the **Annual Total** for each item. Move the chart to a **New sheet**; name the sheet **Annual Expenses Chart**

5 As the text for the **Chart Title** element, type **Summary of Annual Expenses** Format the **Chart Title** using **WordArt Style Fill - Blue, Accent 1, Shadow**—in the first row, the second style and a **Font Size** of **28**.

6 Remove the **Legend** from the chart, and then add **Data Labels** formatted so that only the **Category Name** and **Percentage** display positioned in the **Center**. Format the data labels by applying a **Font style** of **Bold** and **Italic** and a **Font Size** of **12**.

7 Format the **Data Series** using a **3-D Format** effect. Change the **Top bevel** and **Bottom bevel** to **Circle**. Set the **Top bevel Width** and **Height** to **50 pt** and then set the **Bottom bevel Width** and **Height** to **256 pt** Change the **Material** to the fourth **Standard Effect**—**Metal**.

8 Display the **Series Options**, and then set the **Angle of first slice** to **125** so that the **Salaries and Benefits** slice is in the front of the pie. Select the **Salaries and Benefits** slice, and then explode the slice **10%**. Change the **Fill Color** of the **Salaries and Benefits** slice to a **Solid fill** using **Green, Accent 6, Lighter 40%**—in the last column, the fourth color.

9 Format the **Chart Area** by applying a **Gradient fill** using the **Preset gradients Light Gradient – Accent 4**. Format the **Border** of the **Chart Area** by adding a **Solid line** border using **Gold, Accent 4** and a **5 pt Width**.

10 Display the **Page Setup** dialog box, and then for this chart sheet, insert a **Custom Footer** in the **left section** with the file name. **Save** your workbook.

11 Display the **Expenses** worksheet, and then by using the Quarter names and the Totals by Quarter, insert a **Line with Markers** chart in the worksheet. Do *not* include the Annual Total. Move the chart so that its upper left corner is positioned slightly inside the upper left corner of cell **A12**, and then drag the center-right sizing handle so that the chart extends to slightly inside the right border of **column G**. As the **Chart Title**, type **City of Pacifica Bay Annual Expense Summary**

12 Format the **Bounds** of the **Vertical (Value) Axis** so that the **Minimum** is **2100000** and the **Major unit** is **50000** Format the **Fill** of the **Chart Area** with a **Gradient fill** by applying the **Preset gradient Light Gradient - Accent 3**—in the first row, the third gradient. Format the **Plot Area** with a **Solid fill** using **White, Background 1**—in the first column, the first color. Close any panes on the right, click cell **A1** to deselect the chart, and then **Save** your workbook.

13 Copy the **Annual Total** in cell **F10** and then use **Paste Special** to paste **Values & Number Formatting** in cell **B35**. In cell **C35**, construct a formula to calculate the **Projected Expenses** after the forecasted increase of **3.5%** in cell **B31** is applied. Fill the formula through cell **F35**, and then use **Format Painter** to copy the formatting from cell **B35** to the range **C35:F35**.

14 Change the **Orientation** of this worksheet to **Landscape**, and then use the **Scale to Fit** options to fit the **Height** to **1 page**. In the **Page Setup** dialog box, center this worksheet **Horizontally**, and insert a **Custom Footer** in the **left section** with the file name. **Save** your workbook.

15 Show all the properties, and then as the **Tags**, type **annual expense summary** As the **Subject**, type your course name and section number. Be sure your name displays as the **Author**. **Save** your workbook. If directed by your instructor to do so, submit your paper printout, your electronic image of your document that looks like a printed document, or your original Excel file. If required by your instructor, print or create an electronic version of your worksheet with formulas displayed. In the upper right corner of the Excel window, click **Close**.

END | You have completed Project 3G

| GO! Fix It | Project 3H Schools | MyITLab |

| GO! Make It | Project 3I Tax | MyITLab |

| GO! Solve It | Project 3J Staffing | MyITLab |

| GO! Solve It | Project 3K Water Usage |

Build from
Scratch

PROJECT FILES

For Project 3K, you will need the following file:

New blank Excel workbook

You will save your workbook as:

Lastname_Firstname_3K_Water_Usage

Pacifica Bay is a growing community and the City Council has requested an analysis of future resource needs. In this project, you will create a worksheet for the Department of Water and Power that illustrates residential water usage over a five-year period. Create a worksheet with the following data:

	2014	2015	2016	2017	2018
Water Use in Acre Feet	62518	65922	71864	76055	82542

Calculate the percent increase for the years 2015 to 2018. Below the Percent Increase, insert a line chart that illustrates the city's water usage from 2014 to 2018. Format the chart and worksheet attractively with a title and subtitle, and apply appropriate formatting. Include the file name in the footer and enter appropriate document properties. Save the workbook as **Lastname_Firstname_3K_Water_Usage** and submit as directed.

Performance Level

Performance Criteria	Exemplary: You consistently applied the relevant skills	Proficient: You sometimes, but not always, applied the relevant skills	Developing: You rarely or never applied the relevant skills
Create formulas	All formulas are correct and are efficiently constructed.	Formulas are correct but not always constructed in the most efficient manner.	One or more formulas are missing or incorrect or only numbers were entered.
Insert and format line chart	Line chart created correctly and is attractively formatted.	Line chart was created but the data was incorrect or the chart was not appropriately formatted.	No line chart was created.
Format attractively and appropriately	Formatting is attractive and appropriate.	Adequately formatted but difficult to read or unattractive.	Inadequate or no formatting.

END | You have completed Project 3K

RUBRIC

The following outcomes-based assessments are open-ended assessments. That is, there is no specific correct result; your result will depend on your approach to the information provided. Make Professional Quality your goal. Use the following scoring rubric to guide you in how to approach the problem and then to evaluate how well your approach solves the problem.

The *criteria*—Software Mastery, Content, Format and Layout, and Process—represent the knowledge and skills you have gained that you can apply to solving the problem. The *levels of performance*—Professional Quality, Approaching Professional Quality, or Needs Quality Improvements—help you and your instructor evaluate your result.

	Your completed project is of Professional Quality if you:	Your completed project is Approaching Professional Quality if you:	Your completed project Needs Quality Improvements if you:
1-Software Mastery	Choose and apply the most appropriate skills, tools, and features and identify efficient methods to solve the problem.	Choose and apply some appropriate skills, tools, and features, but not in the most efficient manner.	Choose inappropriate skills, tools, or features, or are inefficient in solving the problem.
2-Content	Construct a solution that is clear and well organized, contains content that is accurate, appropriate to the audience and purpose, and is complete. Provide a solution that contains no errors in spelling, grammar, or style.	Construct a solution in which some components are unclear, poorly organized, inconsistent, or incomplete. Misjudge the needs of the audience. Have some errors in spelling, grammar, or style, but the errors do not detract from comprehension.	Construct a solution that is unclear, incomplete, or poorly organized; contains some inaccurate or inappropriate content; and contains many errors in spelling, grammar, or style. Do not solve the problem.
3-Format & Layout	Format and arrange all elements to communicate information and ideas, clarify function, illustrate relationships, and indicate relative importance.	Apply appropriate format and layout features to some elements, but not others. Overuse features, causing minor distraction.	Apply format and layout that does not communicate information or ideas clearly. Do not use format and layout features to clarify function, illustrate relationships, or indicate relative importance. Use available features excessively, causing distraction.
4-Process	Use an organized approach that integrates planning, development, self-assessment, revision, and reflection.	Demonstrate an organized approach in some areas, but not others; or, use an insufficient process of organization throughout.	Do not use an organized approach to solve the problem.

Apply a combination of the 3A and 3B skills.

GO! Think   Project 3L Employment

PROJECT FILES

For Project 3L, you will need the following file:

New blank Excel workbook

You will save your workbook as:

Lastname_Firstname_3L_Employment

Sandy Ingram, the Director of the Employment Development Department for the city of Pacifica Bay, has requested an analysis of employment sectors in the city. Employment data for the previous two years is listed below:

Job Sector	2015 Employment	2016 Employment
Government	1,795	1,524
Healthcare	2,832	2,952
Retail	2,524	2,480
Food Service	3,961	3,753
Industrial	1,477	1,595
Professional	2,515	2,802

Create a workbook to provide Sandy with the employment information for each sector and the total employment for each year. Insert a column to calculate the percent change from 2015 to 2016. Note that some of the results will be negative numbers. Format the percentages with two decimal places. Insert a pie chart in its own sheet that illustrates the 2016 employment figures, and format the chart attractively. Format the worksheet so that it is professional and easy to read and understand. Insert a footer with the file name and add appropriate document properties. Save the file as **Lastname_Firstname_3L_Employment** and print or submit as directed by your instructor.

> END | You have completed Project 3L

GO! Think   Project 3M Population   **MyITLab**

You and GO!   Project 3N Expense Analysis   **MyITLab**

GO! Collaborative Team Project   Project 3O Bell Orchid Hotels   **MyITLab**

Introduction to Microsoft Access 2016

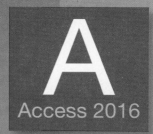

A

Access 2016

Bigpa/Fotolia

Introduction to Access 2016

Microsoft Access 2016 provides a convenient way to organize data that makes it easy for you to utilize and present information. Access uses tables to store the data; like Excel spreadsheets, data is stored in rows and columns in a table. So why use a database rather than an Excel spreadsheet? By using a database, you can manipulate and work with data in a more robust manner. For example, if you have thousands of records about patients in a hospital, you can easily find all of the records that pertain to the patients who received a specific type of medicine on a particular day. Information from one table can be used to retrieve information from another table. For example, by knowing a patient's ID number, you can

view immunization records or view insurance information or view hospitalization records. Having information stored in an Access database enables you to make bulk changes to data at one time even when it is stored in different tables.

It's easy to get started with Access by using one of the many prebuilt database templates. For example, a nonprofit organization can track events, donors, members, and donations for a nonprofit organization. A small business can use a prebuilt database to track inventory, create invoices, monitor projects, manage pricing, track competitors, and manage quotes.

Getting Started with Microsoft Access 2016

1

ACCESS 2016

PROJECT 1A

OUTCOMES
Create a new database.

OBJECTIVES

1. Identify Good Database Design
2. Create a Table and Define Fields in a Blank Desktop Database
3. Change the Structure of Tables and Add a Second Table
4. Create a Query, Form, and Report
5. Close a Database and Close Access

PROJECT 1B

OUTCOMES
Create a database from a template.

OBJECTIVES

6. Use a Template to Create a Database
7. Organize Objects in the Navigation Pane
8. Create a New Table in a Database Created with a Template
9. Print a Report and a Table

Tyler Olson/Fotolia

In This Chapter

GO! to Work with Access

In this chapter, you will use Microsoft Access 2016 to organize a collection of related information. You will create new databases, create tables, and enter data into the tables. You will create a query, a form, and a report—all of which are Access objects that make a database useful for locating and analyzing information. You will also create a complete database from a template that you can use as provided, or that you can modify to meet your needs. In this chapter, you will also learn how to apply good database design principles to your Access database and to define the structure of a database.

The projects in this chapter relate to **Texas Lakes Community College**, which is located in the Austin, Texas, area. Its four campuses serve over 30,000 students and offer more than 140 certificate programs and degrees. The college has a highly acclaimed Distance Education program and an extensive Workforce Development program. The college makes positive contributions to the community through cultural and athletic programs and has significant partnerships with businesses and nonprofit organizations. Popular fields of study include nursing and health care, solar technology, computer technology, and graphic design.

Student Advising Database with Two Tables

MyITLab
Project 1A Training
Project 1A Grader

PROJECT ACTIVITIES

In Activities 1.01 through 1.17, you will assist Dr. Daniel Martinez, Vice President of Student Services at Texas Lakes Community College, in creating a new database for tracking students and their faculty advisors. Your completed database objects will look similar to Figure 1.1.

PROJECT FILES

 If your instructor wants you to submit Project 1A in the MyITLab grader system, log in to MyITLab, locate grader Project1A, and then download the files for this project.

For Project 1A, you will need the following files:

Blank desktop database
a01A_Students (Excel workbook)
a01A_Faculty_Advisors (Excel workbook)

You will save your database as:

Lastname_Firstname_1A_Advising

Please always review the downloaded Grader instructions before beginning.

PROJECT RESULTS

Build From
Scratch

GO!
Walk Thru
Project 1A

Access 2016, Windows 10, Microsoft Corporation

FIGURE 1.1 Project 1A Advising

NOTE	If You Are Using a Touchscreen
	Tap an item to click it.
	Press and hold for a few seconds to right-click; release when the information or command displays.
	Touch the screen with two or more fingers and then pinch together to zoom out or stretch your fingers apart to zoom in.
	Slide your finger on the screen to scroll—slide left to scroll right and slide right to scroll left.
	Slide to rearrange—similar to dragging with a mouse.
	Swipe to select—slide an item a short distance with a quick movement—to select an item and bring up commands, if any.

PROJECT RESULTS

In this project, using your own name, you will create the following database and objects. Your instructor may ask for printouts or PDF electronic images:

Lastname_Firstname_1A_Advising	Database file
Lastname Firstname 1A Students	Table
Lastname Firstname 1A Faculty Advisors	Table
Lastname Firstname 1A All Students Query	Query
Lastname Firstname 1A Student Form	Form
Lastname Firstname 1A Faculty Advisors Report	Report

Objective 1   Identify Good Database Design

GO! Learn How
Video A1-1

A *database* is an organized collection of *data*—facts about people, events, things, or ideas—related to a specific topic or purpose. *Information* is data that is accurate, timely, and organized in a useful manner. Your contact list is a type of database, because it is a collection of data about one topic—the people with whom you communicate. A simple database of this type is called a *flat database* because it is not related or linked to any other collection of data. Another example of a simple database is your music collection. You do not keep information about your music collection in your contact list because the data is not related to the people in your contact list.

A more sophisticated type of database is a *relational database*, because multiple collections of data in the database are related to one another—for example, data about the students, the courses, and the faculty members at a college. Microsoft Access 2016 is a relational *database management system*—also referred to as a *DBMS*—which is software that controls how related collections of data are stored, organized, retrieved, and secured.

Activity 1.01   Using Good Design Techniques to Plan a Database

ALERT!	To submit as an autograded project, log into MyITLab and download the files for this project, and begin with those files instead of a new, blank database. For Project 1A using Grader, read Activity 1.01 carefully, and refer to the Grader instructions for Activity 1.02. Begin working with the database in Activity 1.03. For Grader to award points accurately, when saving an object, do not include your Lastname Firstname at the beginning of the object name.

Before creating a new database, the first step is to determine the information you want to keep track of by asking yourself, *What questions should this database be able to answer?* The purpose of a database is to store the data in a manner that makes it easy to find the information you need by asking questions. For example, in a student database for Texas Lakes Community College, the questions to be answered might include:

- How many students are enrolled at the college?
- How many students have not yet been assigned a faculty advisor?
- Which students live in Austin, Texas?
- Which students owe money for tuition?
- Which students are majoring in Information Systems Technology?

Tables are the foundation of an Access database because all of the data is stored in one or more tables. A table is similar in structure to an Excel worksheet because data is organized into rows and columns. Each table row is a *record*—all of the categories of data pertaining to one person, place, event, thing, or idea. Each table column is a *field*—a single piece of information for every record. For example, in a table storing student contact information, each row forms a record for only one student. Each column forms a field for every record—for example, the student ID number or the student last name.

When organizing the fields of information in your table, break each piece of information into its smallest, most useful part. For example, create three fields for the name of a student—one field for the last name, one field for the first name, and one field for the middle name or initial.

The *first principle of good database design* is to organize data in the tables so that *redundant*—duplicate—data does not occur. For example, record the student contact information in only *one* table, so that if a student's address changes, you can change the information in just one place. This conserves space, reduces the likelihood of errors when inputting new data, and does not require remembering all of the places where a student's address is stored.

The *second principle of good database design* is to use techniques that ensure the accuracy and consistency of data as it is entered into the table. Proofreading data is critical to maintaining accuracy in a database. Typically, many different people enter data into a database—think of all the people who enter data about students at your college. When entering a state in a student contacts table, one person might enter the state as *Texas*, while another might enter the state as *TX*. Use design techniques to help those who enter data into a database to enter the data more accurately and consistently.

Normalization is the process of applying design rules and principles to ensure that your database performs as expected. Taking the time to plan and create a database that is well designed will ensure that you can retrieve meaningful information from the database.

The tables of information in a relational database are linked or joined to one another by a *common field*—a field in two or more tables that stores the same data. For example, a Students table includes the Student ID, name, and full address of every student. The Student Activities table includes the club name and the Student ID of members, but not the name or address, of each student in the club. Because the two tables share a common field—Student ID—you can use the data together to create a list of names and addresses of all of the students in a particular club. The names and addresses are stored in the Students table, and the Student IDs of the club members are stored in the Student Activities table.

GO! Learn How
Video A1-2

Three methods are used to create a new Access database. One method is to create a new database using a ***database template***—a preformatted database designed for a specific purpose. A second method is to create a new database from a ***blank desktop database***. A blank desktop database is stored on your computer or other storage device. Initially, it has no data and has no database tools; you create the data and the tools as you need them. A third method is to create a ***custom web app*** database from scratch or by using a template that you can publish and share with others over the Internet.

Regardless of the method you use, you must name and save the database before you can create any ***objects*** in it. Objects are the basic parts of a database; you create objects to store your data, to work with your data, and to display your data. The most common database objects are tables, queries, forms, and reports. Think of an Access database as a container for the objects that you create.

1.1.1

Activity 1.02 | Starting with a Blank Desktop Database

1 Start Microsoft Access 2016. Take a moment to compare your screen with Figure 1.2 and study the parts of the Microsoft Access opening screen described in the table in Figure 1.3.

From this Access opening screen, you can open an existing database, create a custom web app, create a blank desktop database, or create a new database from a template.

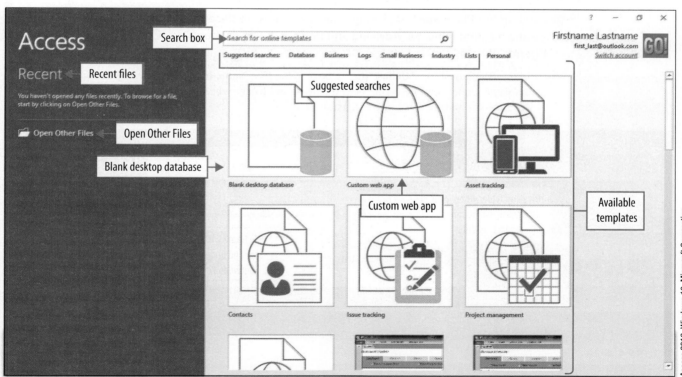

FIGURE 1.2

MICROSOFT ACCESS OPENING SCREEN ELEMENTS	
SCREEN ELEMENT	**DESCRIPTION**
Available templates	Starts a database for a specific purpose that includes built-in objects and tools ready for use.
Blank desktop database	Starts a blank database that is stored on your computer or on a portable storage device.
Custom web app	Starts a web app database that can be published and shared on the Internet.
Open Other Files	Enables you to open a database file from your computer, a shared location, or other location that you have designated.
Recent files	Displays a list of database files that have been recently opened.
Search box	Enables you to search the Microsoft Office website for templates.
Suggested searches	Enables you to click a category to start an online search for a template.

Access 2016, Windows 10, Microsoft Corporation

FIGURE 1.3

2 In the Access opening screen, click **Blank desktop database**. In the **Blank desktop database** dialog box, to the right of the **File Name** box, click **Browse** 🔲. In the **File New Database** dialog box, navigate to the location where you are saving your databases for this chapter, create a **New folder** named **Access Chapter 1** and then press Enter.

3 In the **File name** box, notice that *Database1* displays as the default file name—the number at the end of your file name might differ if you have saved a database previously with the default name. In the **Save as type** box, notice that the default database type is *Microsoft Access 2007 – 2016 Databases*, which means that you can open a database created in Access 2016 by using Access 2007, Access 2010, or Access 2013.

4 Click in the **File name** box. Using your own name, replace the existing text with **Lastname_Firstname_1A_Advising** and then click **OK** or press Enter. Compare your screen with Figure 1.4.

> In the Blank desktop database dialog box, in the File Name box, the name of your database displays. Under the File Name box, the drive and folder where the database will be stored displays. An Access database has a file extension of *.accdb*.

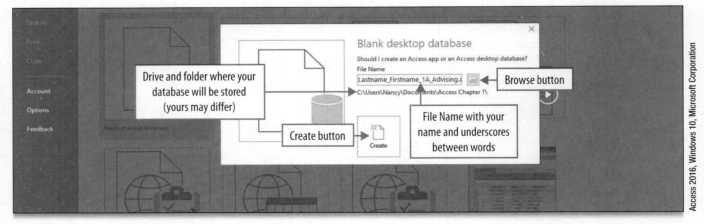

Access 2016, Windows 10, Microsoft Corporation

FIGURE 1.4

5 In the **Blank desktop database** dialog box, click **Create**. Compare your screen with Figure 1.5, and then take a moment to study the screen elements described in the table in Figure 1.6.

> Access creates the new database and opens *Table1*. Recall that a table is an Access object that stores data in columns and rows, similar to the format of an Excel worksheet. Table objects are the foundation of a database because tables store data that is used by other database objects.

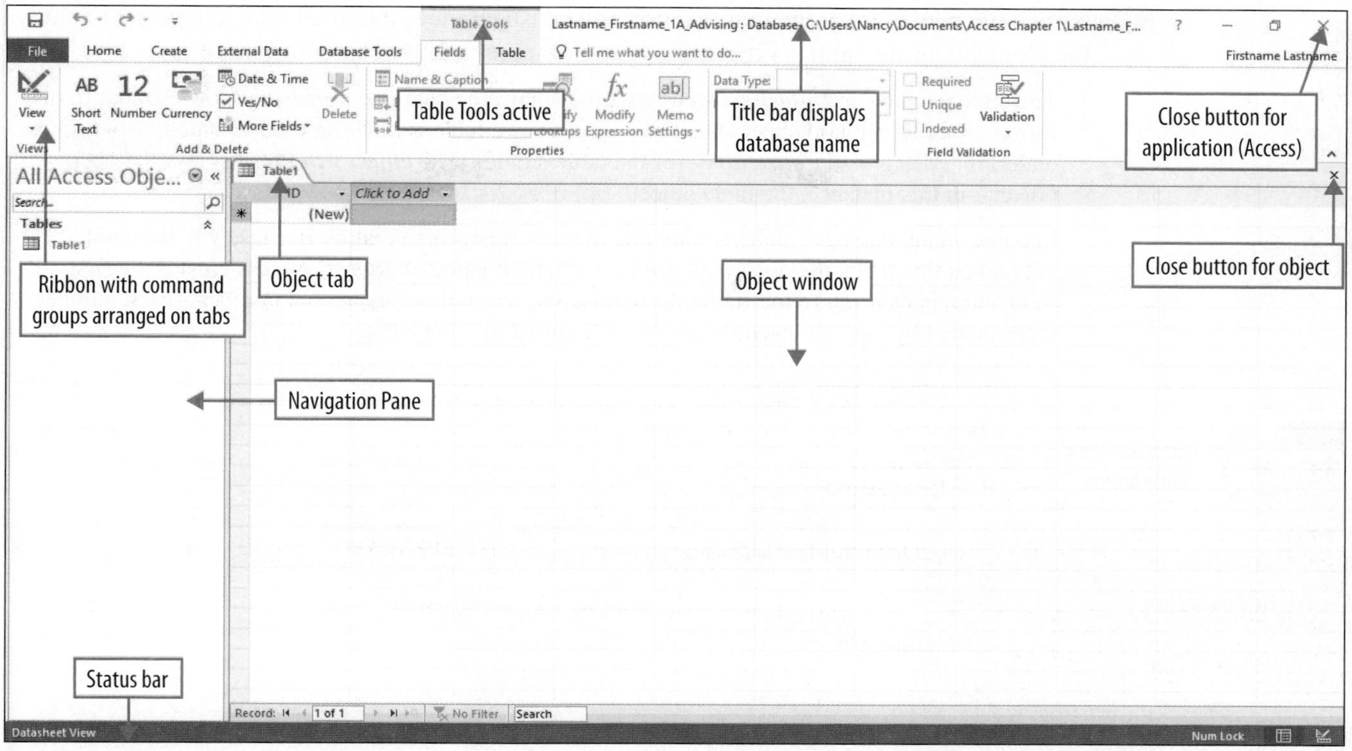

![Access window diagram with labels: Table Tools active, Title bar displays database name, Close button for application (Access), Ribbon with command groups arranged on tabs, Object tab, Object window, Close button for object, Navigation Pane, Status bar]

FIGURE 1.5

Access 2016, Windows 10, Microsoft Corporation

MICROSOFT ACCESS DATABASE WINDOW ELEMENTS	
ACCESS WINDOW ELEMENT	**DESCRIPTION**
Navigation Pane	Displays the database objects that can be opened in the object window.
Object tab	Identifies the open object.
Object window	Displays the active or open object(s), including tables, queries, or other objects.
Close button for object	Closes the active object.
Ribbon	Displays commands grouped by related tasks and stored on different tabs.
Status bar	Indicates the active view and the status of action occurring within the database on the left; provides buttons on the right to switch between Datasheet view and Design view.
Table Tools	Provides tools on two tabs for working with the active table object, these are contextual tabs—only available when a table object is active.
Close button for application (Access)	Closes the active database and Access.

FIGURE 1.6

Access 2016, Windows 10, Microsoft Corporation

2.1.1, 2.4.1

Activity 1.03 | Assigning the Data Type and Name to Fields

After you have named and saved your database, the next step is to consult your database design plan and then create the tables for your data. Limit the data in each table to *one* subject. For example, in this project, your database will have two tables—one for student information and one for faculty advisor information.

Recall that each column in a table is a field; field names display at the top of each column of the table. Recall also that each row in a table is a record—all of the data pertaining to one person, place, thing, event, or idea. Each record is broken up into its smallest usable parts—the fields. Use meaningful names for fields; for example, *Last Name*.

1 Notice the new blank table that displays in Datasheet view, and then take a moment to study the elements of the table's object window. Compare your screen with Figure 1.7.

The table displays in *Datasheet view*, which displays the data in columns and rows similar to the format of an Excel worksheet. Another way to view a table is in *Design view*, which displays the underlying design—the *structure*—of the table's fields. The *object window* displays the open object—in this instance, the table object.

In a new blank database, there is only one object—a new blank table. Because you have not yet named this table, the object tab displays a default name of *Table1*. Access creates the first field and names it *ID*. In the ID field, Access assigns a unique sequential number—each number incremented by one—to each record as it is entered into the table.

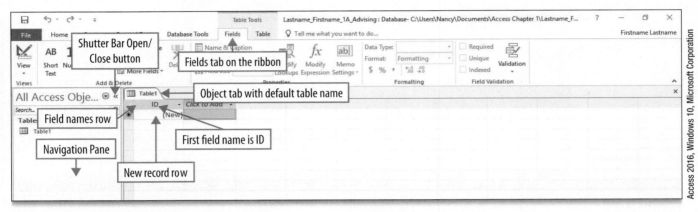

FIGURE 1.7

2 In the **Navigation Pane**, click **Shutter Bar Open/Close** ⟨«⟩ to collapse the **Navigation Pane** to a narrow bar on the left.

The *Navigation Pane* displays and organizes the names of the objects in a database. From the Navigation Pane, you can open objects. Collapse or close the Navigation Pane to display more of the object—in this case, the table.

ANOTHER WAY   Press **F11** to close or open the Navigation Pane.

3 In the field names row, click anywhere in the text *Click to Add* to display a list of data types. Compare your screen with Figure 1.8.

A *data type* classifies the kind of data that you can store in a field, such as numbers, text, or dates. A field in a table can have only one data type. The data type of each field should be included in your database design. After selecting the data type, you can name the field.

ANOTHER WAY   To the right of *Click to Add*, click the arrow.

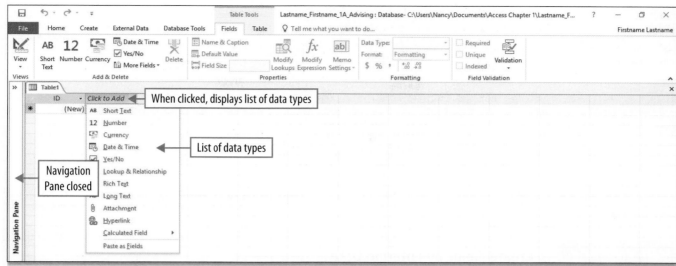

FIGURE 1.8

Access 2016, Windows 10, Microsoft Corporation

4 ▸ In the list of data types, click **Short Text**, and notice that in the second column, *Click to Add* changes to *Field1*, which is selected. Type **Last Name** and then press Enter.

The second column displays *Last Name* as the field name, and, in the third column, the data types list displays. The **Short Text data type** describes text, a combination of text and numbers, or numbers that do not represent a quantity or are not used in calculations, such as the Postal Code. This data type enables you to enter up to 255 characters in the field.

↻ ANOTHER WAY   With the list of data types displayed, type the character that is underscored to select the data type. For example, type *t* to select Short Text or type *u* to select Currency.

5 ▸ In the third field name box, type **t** to select *Short Text*, type **First Name** and then press Enter.

6 ▸ In the fourth field name box, click **Short Text**, type **Middle Initial** and then press Enter.

7 ▸ Create the remaining fields from the table below by first selecting the data type, typing the field name, and then pressing Enter. The field names in the table will display on one line—do not be concerned if the field names do not completely display in the column; you will adjust the column widths later.

Data Type		Short Text	Short Text	Short Text	Short Text	Short Text	Short Text	Short Text	Short Text	Short Text	Short Text	Currency
Field Name	ID	Last Name	First Name	Middle Initial	Address	City	State	Postal Code	Phone	Email	Faculty Advisor ID	Amount Owed

The Postal Code and Phone fields are assigned a data type of Short Text because the numbers are never used in calculations. The Amount Owed field is assigned the **Currency data type**, which describes monetary values and numeric data that can be used in calculations and that have one to four decimal places. A U.S. dollar sign ($) and two decimal places are automatically included for all of the numbers in a field with the Currency data type.

8 ▸ If necessary, scroll to bring the first column—ID—into view, and then compare your screen with Figure 1.9.

Access automatically created the ID field, and you created 11 additional fields in the table.

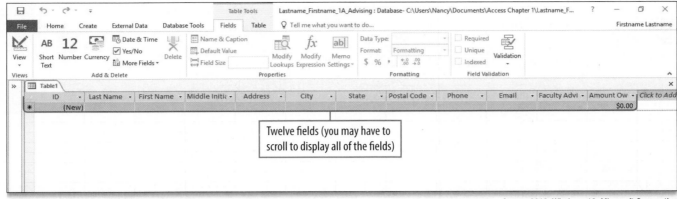

FIGURE 1.9

Access 2016, Windows 10, Microsoft Corporation

More Knowledge **Create Fields by Entering Data**

You can create a new field in Datasheet view by typing the data in a new column. Access automatically assigns a data type based on the data you enter. For example, if you enter a date, Access assigns the Date & Time data type. If you enter a monetary amount, Access assigns the Currency data type. If Access cannot determine the data type based on the data entered, the Short Text data type is assigned. You can always change the data type if an incorrect data type is assigned. If you use this method to create fields, you must check the assigned data types to be sure they are correct. You must also rename the fields because Access assigns the names as *Field1*, *Field2*, and so on.

2.4.3, 2.4.6

Activity 1.04 | Renaming Fields and Changing Data Types in a Table

1 ▶ In the first column, click anywhere in the text *ID*. On the ribbon, under **Table Tools**, on the **Fields tab**, in the **Properties group**, click **Name & Caption**. In the **Enter Field Properties** dialog box, in the **Name** box, change *ID* to **Student ID**

The field name *Student ID* is a more precise description of the data contained in this field. In the Enter Field Properties dialog box, you have the option to use the ***Caption*** property to display a name for a field different from the one that displays in the Name box. Many database designers do not use spaces in field names; instead, they might name a field *LastName* or *LName* and then create a caption for the field so it displays as *Last Name* in tables, forms, or reports. In the Enter Field Properties dialog box, you can also provide a description for the field.

⟳ ANOTHER WAY   Right-click the field name to display the shortcut menu, and then click Rename Field; or, double-click the field name to select the existing text, and then type the new field name.

2 ▶ Click **OK** to close the **Enter Field Properties** dialog box. On the ribbon, in the **Formatting group**, notice that the **Data Type** for the **Student ID** field is *AutoNumber*. Click the **Data Type arrow**, click **Short Text**, and then compare your screen with Figure 1.10.

In the new record row, the Student ID field is selected. By default, Access creates an ID field for all new tables and sets the data type for the field to AutoNumber. The ***AutoNumber data type*** describes a unique sequential or random number assigned by Access as each record is entered. Changing the data type of this field to Short Text enables you to enter a custom student ID number.

When records in a database have *no* unique value, such as a book ISBN or a license plate number, the AutoNumber data type is a useful way to automatically create a unique number. In this manner, you are sure that every record is different from the others.

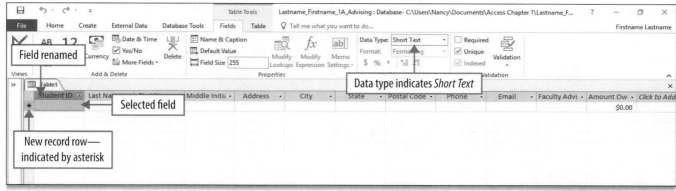

FIGURE 1.10

Access 2016, Windows 10, Microsoft Corporation

Activity 1.05 | Adding a Record to a Table

A new contact list is not useful until you fill it with names and phone numbers. Likewise, a new database is not useful until you **populate** it by filling one or more tables with data. You can populate a table with records by typing data directly into the table.

1 In the new record row, click in the **Student ID** field to display the insertion point, type **1023045** and then press Enter. Compare your screen with Figure 1.11.

The pencil icon in the **record selector box** indicates that a record is being entered or edited. The record selector box is the small box at the left of a record in Datasheet view. When clicked, the entire record is selected.

ANOTHER WAY Press Tab to move the insertion point to the next field.

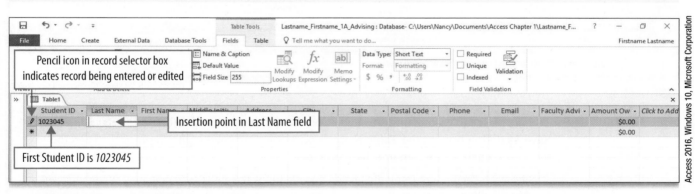

Access 2016, Windows 10, Microsoft Corporation

FIGURE 1.11

2 With the insertion point positioned in the **Last Name** field, type **Fresch** and then press Enter.

NOTE | **Correcting Typing Errors**

Correct any typing errors you make by using the techniques you have practiced in other Office applications. For example, use Backspace to remove characters to the left of the insertion point. Use Del to remove characters to the right of the insertion point. Or select the text you want to replace and type the correct information. Press Esc to exit out of a record that has not been completely entered.

---

3 In the **First Name** field, type **Jenna** and then press Enter.

4 In the **Middle Initial** field, type **A** and then press Enter.

5 In the **Address** field, type **7550 Douglas Ln** and then press Enter.

> Do not be concerned if the data does not completely display in the column. As you progress in your study of Access, you will adjust column widths so that you can view all of the data.

6 Continue entering data in the fields as indicated in the table below, pressing Enter to move to the next field.

City	State	Postal Code	Phone	Email	Faculty Advisor ID
Austin	**TX**	**78749**	**(512) 555-7550**	**jfresch@tlcc.edu**	**FAC-2289**

NOTE | Format for Typing Telephone Numbers in Access

Access does not require a specific format for typing telephone numbers in a record. The examples in this textbook use the format of Microsoft Outlook. Using such a format facilitates easy transfer of Outlook information to and from Access.

---

7 In the **Amount Owed** field, type **250** and then press Enter. Compare your screen with Figure 1.12.

> Pressing Enter or Tab in the last field moves the insertion point to the next row to begin a new record. Access automatically saves the record as soon as you move to the next row; you do not have to take any specific action to save a record.

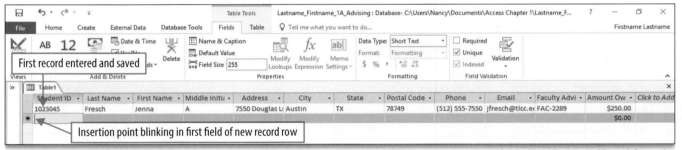

FIGURE 1.12

Access 2016, Windows 10, Microsoft Corporation

8 To give your table a meaningful name, on the Quick Access Toolbar, click **Save** 🖫. In the **Save As** dialog box, in the **Table Name** box, using your own name, replace the selected text by typing **Lastname Firstname 1A Students**

> Save each database object with a name that identifies the data that it contains. When you save objects within a database, it is not necessary to use underscores in place of the spaces between words. Your name is included as part of the object name so that you and your instructor can identify your printouts or electronic files easily.

9 In the **Save As** dialog box, click **OK**. Notice that the object tab—located directly above the *Student ID* field name—displays the new table name that you just entered.

More Knowledge | **Renaming or Deleting a Table**

To change the name of a table, close the table, display the Navigation Pane, right-click the table name, and then click Rename. Type the new name or edit as you would any selected text. To delete a table, close the table, display the Navigation Pane, right-click the table name, and then click Delete.

2.3.2

Activity 1.06 | Adding Additional Records to a Table

1 In the new record row, click in the **Student ID** field, and then enter the data for two additional students as shown in the table below. Press Enter or Tab to move from field to field. The data in each field will display on one line in the table.

Student ID	Last Name	First Name	Middle Initial	Address	City	State	Postal Code	Phone	Email	Faculty Advisor ID	Amount Owed
2345677	Ingram	Joseph	S	621 Hilltop Dr	Leander	TX	78646	(512) 555-0717	jingram@tlcc.edu	FAC-2377	378.5
3456689	Snyder	Amanda	J	4786 Bluff St	Buda	TX	78610	(512) 555-9120	asnyder@tlcc.edu	FAC-9005	0

 2 Press [Enter], and compare your screen with Figure 1.13

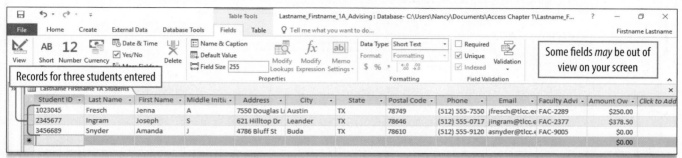

FIGURE 1.13

Access 2016, Windows 10, Microsoft Corporation

 **Activity 1.07** | Importing Data from an Excel Workbook into an Existing Access Table

2.3.4

You can type records directly into a table. You can also ***import*** data from a variety of sources. Importing is the process of copying data from one source or application to another application. For example, you can import data from a Word table or an Excel spreadsheet into an Access database because the data is arranged in columns and rows, similar to a table in Datasheet view.

In this Activity, you will ***append***—add on—data from an Excel spreadsheet to your *1A Students* table. To append data, the table must already be created, and it must be closed.

1 In the upper right corner of the table, below the ribbon, click **Object Close** ☒ to close your **1A Students** table. Notice that no objects are open.

2 On the ribbon, click the **External Data tab**. In the **Import & Link group**, click **Excel**. In the **Get External Data – Excel Spreadsheet** dialog box, click **Browse**.

3 In the **File Open** dialog box, navigate to the student data files that accompany this chapter, double-click the Excel file **a01A_Students**, and then compare your screen with Figure 1.14.

The path to the ***source file***—the file being imported—displays in the File name box. There are three options for importing data from an Excel spreadsheet: import the data into a *new* table in the current database, append a copy of the records to an existing table, or link the data from the spreadsheet to a linked table in the database. A ***link*** is a connection to data in another file. When linking, Access creates a table that maintains a link to the source data, so that changes to the data in one file are automatically made in the other—linked—file.

ANOTHER WAY Click the file name, and then in the File Open dialog box, click Open.

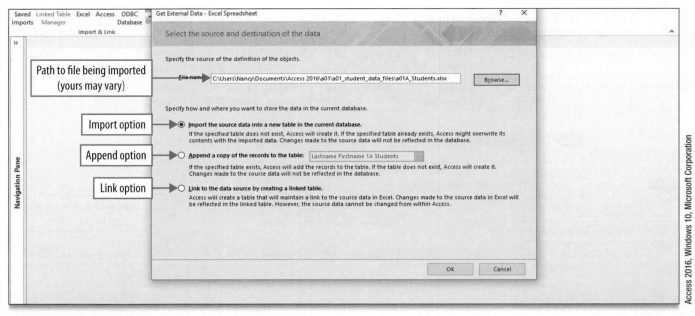

Path to file being imported
(yours may vary)

Import option

Append option

Link option

FIGURE 1.14

4 Click the **Append a copy of the records to the table** option button, and then, in the box to the right, click the **arrow**.

Currently, your database has only one table, so no other tables display on the list. However, when a database has multiple tables, click the arrow to select the table to which you want to append records. The table into which you import or append data is referred to as the *destination table*.

5 Press Esc to cancel the list, and in the dialog box, click **OK**. If a security message displays, click Open. Compare your screen with Figure 1.15.

The first screen of the Import Spreadsheet Wizard displays. A *wizard* is a feature in a Microsoft Office program that walks you step by step through a process. The presence of scroll bars in the window indicates that records and fields are out of view. To append records from an Excel workbook to an existing database table, the column headings in the Excel worksheet or spreadsheet must be identical to the field names in the table. The wizard identified the first row of the spreadsheet as column headings, which are equivalent to field names.

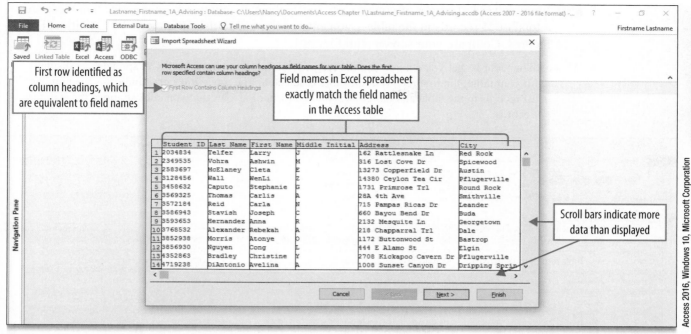

First row identified as column headings, which are equivalent to field names

Field names in Excel spreadsheet exactly match the field names in the Access table

Scroll bars indicate more data than displayed

Access 2016, Windows 10, Microsoft Corporation

FIGURE 1.15

6 In the lower right corner of the wizard, click **Next**. Notice that the name of your table displays under **Import to Table**. In the lower right corner of the wizard, click **Finish**.

7 In the **Get External Data – Excel Spreadsheet** dialog box, click **Close**. Open ⟩⟩ the **Navigation Pane**.

8 Point to the right edge of the **Navigation Pane** to display the ⟷ pointer. Drag to the right to increase the width of the **Navigation Pane** so that the entire table name displays, and then compare your screen with Figure 1.16.

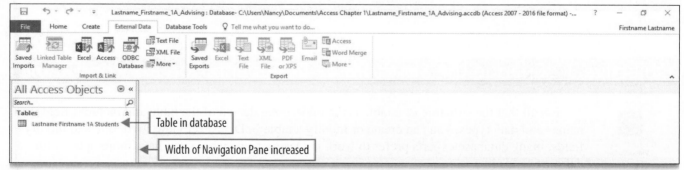

Table in database

Width of Navigation Pane increased

FIGURE 1.16

Access 2016, Windows 10, Microsoft Corporation

9 In the **Navigation Pane**, double-click your **1A Students** table to open the table in Datasheet view, and then **Close** ⟨⟨ the **Navigation Pane**.

ANOTHER WAY To open an object from the Navigation Pane, right-click the object name, and then click Open.

10 In the lower left corner of your screen, locate the navigation area, and notice that there are a total of **25** records in the table—you entered three records and imported 22 additional records. Compare your screen with Figure 1.17.

The records that you entered and the records you imported from the Excel spreadsheet display in your table; the first record in the table is selected. The ***navigation area*** indicates the number of records in the table and has controls in the form of arrows that you click to move through the records.

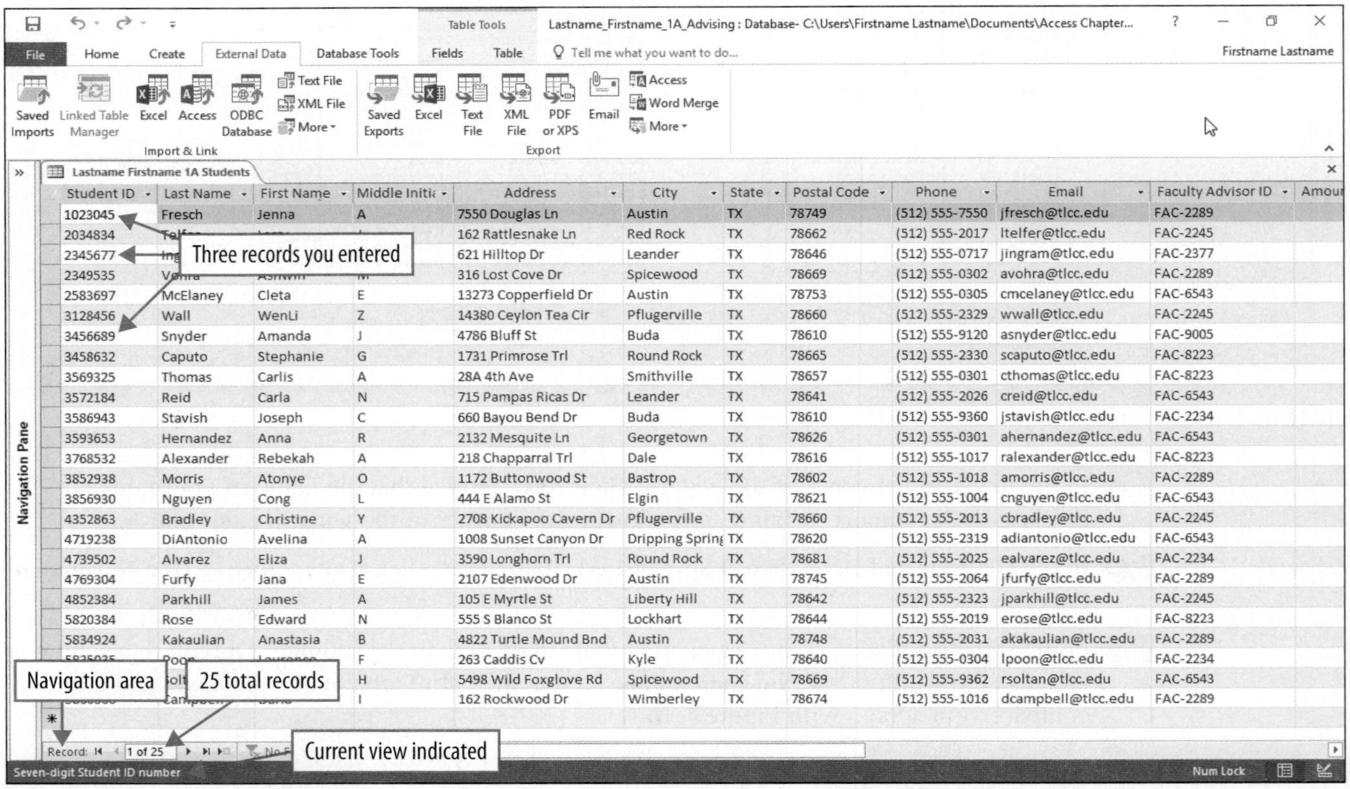

Student ID	Last Name	First Name	Middle Initial	Address	City	State	Postal Code	Phone	Email	Faculty Advisor ID	Amount
1023045	Fresch	Jenna	A	7550 Douglas Ln	Austin	TX	78749	(512) 555-7550	jfresch@tlcc.edu	FAC-2289	
2034834	Telfer			162 Rattlesnake Ln	Red Rock	TX	78662	(512) 555-2017	ltelfer@tlcc.edu	FAC-2245	
2345677	Ingram			621 Hilltop Dr	Leander	TX	78646	(512) 555-0717	jingram@tlcc.edu	FAC-2377	
2349535	Vohra	Ashwin	M	316 Lost Cove Dr	Spicewood	TX	78669	(512) 555-0302	avohra@tlcc.edu	FAC-2289	
2583697	McElaney	Cleta	E	13273 Copperfield Dr	Austin	TX	78753	(512) 555-0305	cmcelaney@tlcc.edu	FAC-6543	
3128456	Wall	WenLi	Z	14380 Ceylon Tea Cir	Pflugerville	TX	78660	(512) 555-2329	wwall@tlcc.edu	FAC-2245	
3456689	Snyder	Amanda	J	4786 Bluff St	Buda	TX	78610	(512) 555-9120	asnyder@tlcc.edu	FAC-9005	
3458632	Caputo	Stephanie	G	1731 Primrose Trl	Round Rock	TX	78665	(512) 555-2330	scaputo@tlcc.edu	FAC-8223	
3569325	Thomas	Carlis	A	28A 4th Ave	Smithville	TX	78657	(512) 555-0301	cthomas@tlcc.edu	FAC-8223	
3572184	Reid	Carla	N	715 Pampas Ricas Dr	Leander	TX	78641	(512) 555-2026	creid@tlcc.edu	FAC-6543	
3586943	Stavish	Joseph	C	660 Bayou Bend Dr	Buda	TX	78610	(512) 555-9360	jstavish@tlcc.edu	FAC-2234	
3593653	Hernandez	Anna	R	2132 Mesquite Ln	Georgetown	TX	78626	(512) 555-0301	ahernandez@tlcc.edu	FAC-6543	
3768532	Alexander	Rebekah	A	218 Chapparral Trl	Dale	TX	78616	(512) 555-1017	ralexander@tlcc.edu	FAC-8223	
3852938	Morris	Atonye	O	1172 Buttonwood St	Bastrop	TX	78602	(512) 555-1018	amorris@tlcc.edu	FAC-2289	
3856930	Nguyen	Cong	L	444 E Alamo St	Elgin	TX	78621	(512) 555-1004	cnguyen@tlcc.edu	FAC-6543	
4352863	Bradley	Christine	Y	2708 Kickapoo Cavern Dr	Pflugerville	TX	78660	(512) 555-2013	cbradley@tlcc.edu	FAC-2245	
4719238	DiAntonio	Avelina	A	1008 Sunset Canyon Dr	Dripping Spring	TX	78620	(512) 555-2319	adiantonio@tlcc.edu	FAC-6543	
4739502	Alvarez	Eliza	J	3590 Longhorn Trl	Round Rock	TX	78681	(512) 555-2025	ealvarez@tlcc.edu	FAC-2234	
4769304	Furfy	Jana	E	2107 Edenwood Dr	Austin	TX	78745	(512) 555-2064	jfurfy@tlcc.edu	FAC-2289	
4852384	Parkhill	James	A	105 E Myrtle St	Liberty Hill	TX	78642	(512) 555-2323	jparkhill@tlcc.edu	FAC-2245	
5820384	Rose	Edward	N	555 S Blanco St	Lockhart	TX	78644	(512) 555-2019	erose@tlcc.edu	FAC-8223	
5834924	Kakaulian	Anastasia	B	4822 Turtle Mound Bnd	Austin	TX	78748	(512) 555-2031	akakaulian@tlcc.edu	FAC-2289	
5825025	Poon	Lawrence	F	263 Caddis Cv	Kyle	TX	78640	(512) 555-0304	lpoon@tlcc.edu	FAC-2234	
	Soltan		H	5498 Wild Foxglove Rd	Spicewood	TX	78669	(512) 555-9362	rsoltan@tlcc.edu	FAC-6543	
	Campbell	Dana	I	162 Rockwood Dr	Wimberley	TX	78674	(512) 555-1016	dcampbell@tlcc.edu	FAC-2289	

Record: 1 of 25 — Current view indicated

Navigation area — 25 total records

Three records you entered

Seven-digit Student ID number

Access 2016, Windows 10, Microsoft Corporation

FIGURE 1.17

Objective 3 Change the Structure of Tables and Add a Second Table

GO! Learn How
Video A1-3

Recall that the structure of a table is the underlying design of the table and includes field names and data types. You can create or modify a table in Datasheet view. To define and modify fields, many database experts prefer to work in Design view, where you have more options for defining fields in a table.

MOS
2.4.9, 1.3.5

Activity 1.08 | Deleting a Table Field in Design View

In this Activity, you will delete the *Middle Initial* field from the table.

1 Click the **Home tab**, and then in the **Views group**, click the **View arrow** to display a list of views.

There are two views for tables: Datasheet view and Design view. Other objects have different views. On the list, Design view is represented by a picture of a pencil, a ruler, and an angle. Datasheet view is represented by a picture of a table arranged in columns and rows. In the Views group, if the top of the View button displays the pencil, ruler, and angle, clicking View will switch your view to Design view. Likewise, clicking the top of the View button that displays as a datasheet will switch your view to Datasheet view.

2 On the list, click **Design View**, and then compare your screen with Figure 1.18.

Design view displays the underlying design—the structure—of the table and its fields. In Design view, the records in the table do not display. You can only view the information about each field's attributes. Each field name is listed, along with its data type. You can add explanatory information about a field in the Description column, but it is not required.

You can decide how each field should look and behave in the Field Properties area. For example, you can set a specific field size in the Field Properties area. In the lower right corner, information displays about the active selection—in this case, the Field Name.

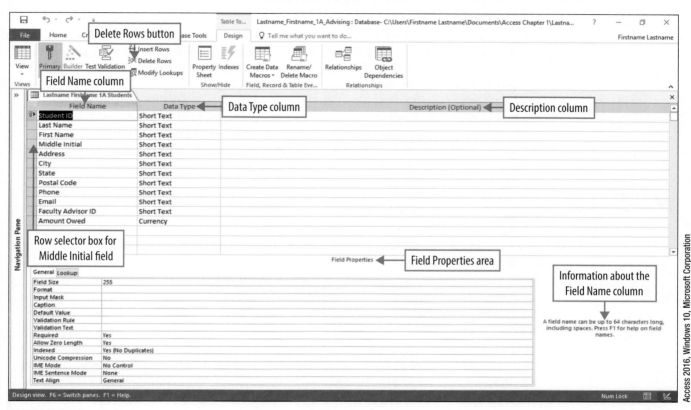

FIGURE 1.18

3 In the **Field Name** column, to the left of **Middle Initial**, point to the row selector box to display the ➡ pointer, and then click one time to select the entire row.

4 On the **Design tab**, in the **Tools group**, click **Delete Rows**. Read the warning in the message box, and then click **Yes**.

Deleting a field deletes both the field and its data. After you save the changes, you cannot undo this action, so Access prompts you to be sure you want to proceed. If you change your mind after deleting a field and saving the changes, you must add the field back into the table and then reenter the data for that field for every record.

🔄 **ANOTHER WAY**   In Design view, right-click the selected row, and then click Delete Rows; or, in Datasheet view, select the field—column—and on the Home tab, in the Records group, click Delete.

Activity 1.09 | Changing a Field Size and Adding a Description

2.4.4, 2.2.3

Typically, many different individuals have the ability to enter data into a table. For example, at your college, many Registration Assistants enter and modify student and course information daily. Two ways to help reduce errors are to restrict what can be typed in a field and to add descriptive information to help the individuals when entering the data.

1 With your table still displayed in **Design** view, in the **Field Name** column, click anywhere in the **Student ID** field name.

2 In the lower area of the screen, under **Field Properties**, click **Field Size** to select the text **255**, and then type **7**

> This action limits the size of the Student ID field to no more than seven characters. *Field properties* control how the field displays and how data can be entered into the field. You can define properties for each field in the Field Properties area by first clicking the field name to display the properties for that specific data type.

> The default field size for a Short Text field is 255. Limiting the Field Size property to seven ensures that no more than 7 characters can be entered for each Student ID. However, this does not prevent someone from entering seven characters that are incorrect or entering fewer than seven characters. Setting the proper data type for the field and limiting the field size are two ways to help reduce errors during data entry.

↻ ANOTHER WAY   In Datasheet view, click in the field. Under Table Tools, on the Fields tab, in the Properties group, click in the Field Size box, and then type the number that represents the maximum number of characters for that field.

3 In the **Student ID** row, click in the **Description** box, type **Seven-digit Student ID number** and then press Enter. Compare your screen with Figure 1.19.

> Descriptions for fields in a table are optional. Include a description if the field name does not provide an obvious explanation of the type of data to be entered. If a description is provided for a field, when data is being entered in that field in Datasheet view, the text in the Description displays on the left side of the status bar to provide additional information for the individuals who are entering the data.

> When you enter a description for a field, a Property Update Options button displays below the text you typed, which enables you to copy the description for the field to all other database objects that use this table as an underlying source.

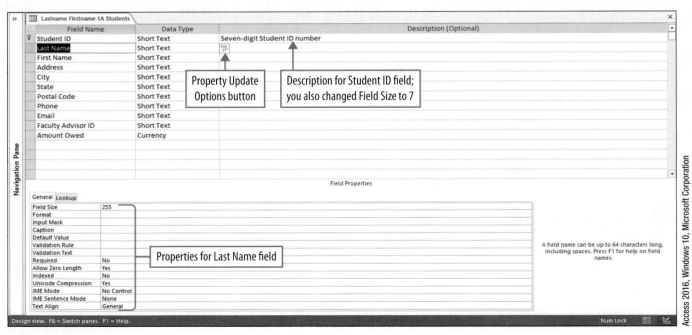

FIGURE 1.19

4 Click in the **State** field name box. In the **Field Properties** area, change the **Field Size** to **2** and in the **Description** box for this field, type **Two-character state abbreviation** and then press Enter.

5 Click in the **Faculty Advisor ID** field name box. In the **Field Properties** area, change the **Field Size** to **8** and in the **Description** box for this field, type **Eight-character ID of the instructor assigned as advisor** and then press Enter.

6 On the Quick Access Toolbar, click **Save** 🖫 to save the design changes to your table, and then notice the message.

> The message indicates that the field size property of one or more fields has changed to a shorter size. If more characters are currently present in the Student ID, State, or Faculty Advisor ID fields than you have allowed, the data will be *truncated*—cut off or shortened—because the fields were not previously restricted to these specific number of characters.

7 In the message box, click **Yes**.

More Knowledge | **Add a Table Description**

You can create a description to provide more information to users regarding the entire table. With the table displayed in Design view, click the Design tab. In the Show/Hide group, click Property Sheet. Click in the Description box, type the table description, and then press Enter. Close the Property Sheet.

Activity 1.10 | Viewing the Primary Key in Design View

Primary key refers to the required field in the table that uniquely identifies a record. For example, in a college registration database, your Student ID number identifies you as a unique individual—every student has a student number and no other student at the college has your exact student number. In the 1A Students table, the Student ID uniquely identifies each student.

When you create a table using the blank desktop database template, Access designates the first field as the primary key field and names the field ID. It is good database design practice to establish a primary key for every table, because doing so ensures that you do not enter the same record more than once. You can imagine the confusion if another student at your college had the same Student ID number as you do.

1 With your table still displayed in **Design** view, in the **Field Name** column, click in the **Student ID** box. To the left of the box, notice the small icon of a key, as shown in Figure 1.20.

> Access automatically designates the first field as the primary key field, but you can set any field as the primary key by clicking the field name, and then in the Tools group, clicking Primary Key.

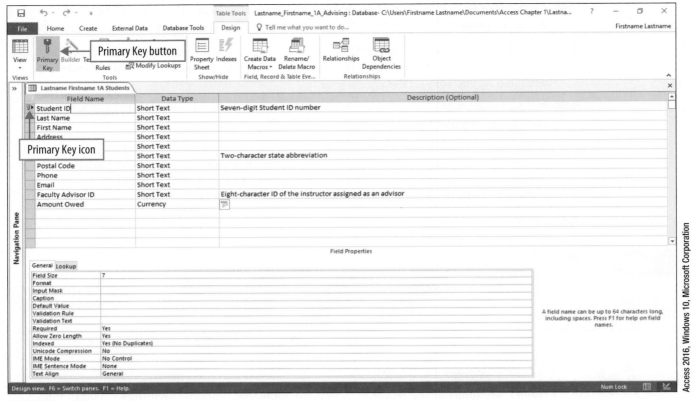

FIGURE 1.20

> **2** On the **Design tab**, in the **Views group**, notice that the View button displays a picture of a datasheet, indicating that clicking View will switch the view to Datasheet view. Click the top of the **View** button.

> If you make design changes to a table and switch views without first saving the table, Access will prompt you to save the table before changing views.

MOS
2.1.2

Activity 1.11 | Adding a Second Table to a Database by Importing an Excel Spreadsheet

Many Microsoft Office users track data in an Excel spreadsheet. The sorting and filtering capabilities of Excel are useful for a simple database where all of the information resides in one large Excel spreadsheet. However, Excel is limited as a database management tool because it cannot *relate* the information in multiple spreadsheets in a way that you can ask a question and get a meaningful result. Because data in an Excel spreadsheet is arranged in columns and rows, the spreadsheet can easily convert to an Access table by importing the spreadsheet.

> **1** On the ribbon, click the **External Data tab**, and then in the **Import & Link group**, click **Excel**. In the **Get External Data – Excel Spreadsheet** dialog box, to the right of the **File name** box, click **Browse**.

> **2** In the **File Open** dialog box, navigate to the location where your student data files are stored, and then double-click **a01A_Faculty_Advisors**. Compare your screen with Figure 1.21.

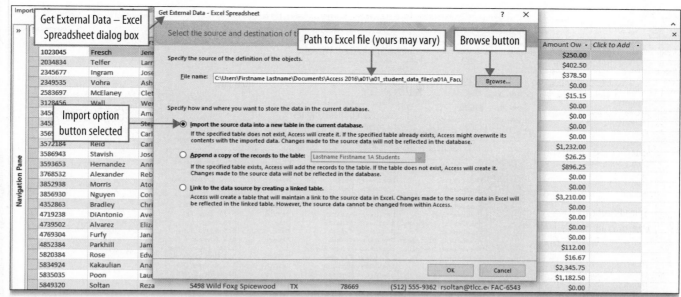

Access 2016, Windows 10, Microsoft Corporation

FIGURE 1.21

3 Be sure that the **Import the source data into a new table in the current database** option button is selected, click **OK**. If a security message displays, click Open.

The Import Spreadsheet Wizard displays the spreadsheet data.

4 In the upper left corner of the wizard, select the **First Row Contains Column Headings** check box.

The Excel data is framed, indicating that the first row of Excel column titles will become the Access table field names, and the remaining rows will become the individual records in the new Access table.

5 Click **Next**. Notice that the first column—*Faculty ID*—is selected, and in the upper area of the wizard, the **Field Name** and the **Data Type** display. Compare your screen with Figure 1.22.

In this step, under Field Options, you can review and change the name or the data type of each selected field. You can also identify fields in the spreadsheet that you do not want to import into the Access table by selecting the Do not import field (Skip) check box.

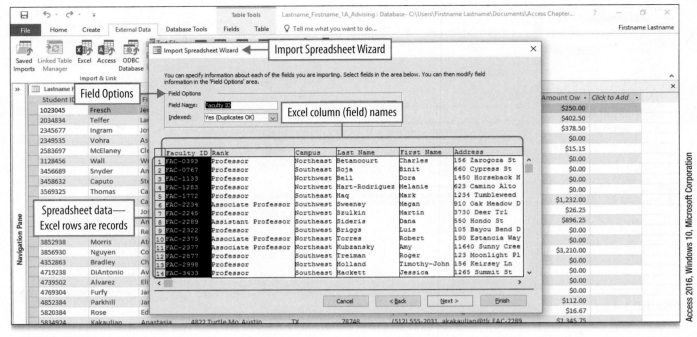

FIGURE 1.22

6 ▶ Click **Next**. In the upper area of the wizard, click the **Choose my own primary key** option button, and then be sure that **Faculty ID** displays.

In the new table, Faculty ID will be the primary key. Every faculty member has a Faculty ID and no two faculty members have the same Faculty ID. By default, Access selects the first field as the primary key, but you can click the arrow and select a different field.

7 ▶ Click **Next**. In the **Import to Table** box, using your own name, type **Lastname Firstname 1A Faculty Advisors** and then click **Finish**.

8 ▶ In the **Get External Data – Excel Spreadsheet** dialog box, click **Close**. Open ⏵ the **Navigation Pane**.

9 ▶ In the **Navigation Pane**, double-click your **1A Faculty Advisors** table to open it in Datasheet view, and then **Close** ⏴ the **Navigation Pane**.

Two tables that are identified by their object tabs are open in the object window. Your 1A Faculty Advisors table is the active table and displays the 29 records that you imported from the Excel spreadsheet.

10 ▶ In your **1A Faculty Advisors** table, click in the **Postal Code** field in the first record. On the ribbon, under **Table Tools**, click the **Fields tab**. In the **Formatting group**, click the **Data Type arrow**, and then click **Short Text**. Compare your screen with Figure 1.23.

When you import data from an Excel spreadsheet, check the data types of all fields to ensure they are correct. Recall that if a field, such as the Postal Code, contains numbers that do not represent a quantity or are not used in calculations, the data type should be set to Short Text. To change the data type of a field, click in the field in any record.

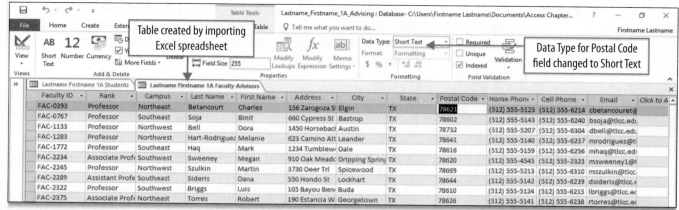

FIGURE 1.23

Activity 1.12 | Adjusting Column Widths

You can adjust the column widths in a table displayed in Datasheet view by using techniques similar to those you use for Excel spreadsheets.

1 In the object window, click the **object tab** for your **1A Students** table to make it the active object and to display it in the object window.

Clicking an object tab along the top of the object window enables you to display the open object and make it active so that you can work with it. All of the columns in the datasheet are the same width, regardless of the length of the data in the field, the length of the field name, or the field size that was set. If you print the table as currently displayed, some of the data or field names will not print completely, so you will want to adjust the column widths.

2 In the column headings row, point to the right edge of the **Address** field to display the ✛ pointer, and then compare your screen with Figure 1.24.

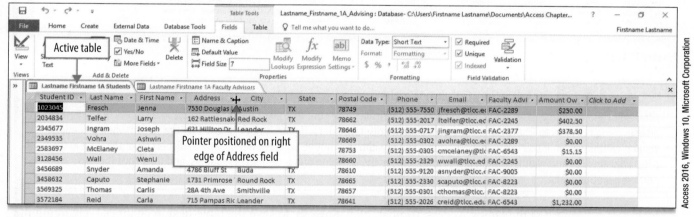

FIGURE 1.24

3 With the ✛ pointer positioned as shown in Figure 1.24, double-click the right edge of the **Address** field.

The column width of the Address field widens to display the longest entry in the field fully. In this manner, the width of a column can be increased or decreased to fit its contents in the same manner as a column in an Excel spreadsheet. In Access, adjusting the column width to fit the contents is referred to as *Best Fit*.

4 Point to the **City** field name to display the ⬇ pointer, right-click to select the entire column and display the shortcut menu. Click **Field Width**, and then in the **Column Width** dialog box, click **Best Fit**.

This is a second way to adjust column widths.

5 If necessary, scroll to the right to view the last three fields. Point to the **Email** field name to display the ⬇ pointer, hold down the left mouse button, and then drag to the right to select this column, the **Faculty Advisor ID** column, and the **Amount Owed** column. Point to the right edge of any of the selected columns to display the ➕ pointer, and then double-click to apply **Best Fit** to all three columns.

You can select multiple columns and adjust the widths of all of them at one time by using this technique or by right-clicking any of the selected columns, clicking Field Width, and clicking Best Fit in the Column Width dialog box.

6 If necessary, scroll to the left to view the **Student ID** field. To the left of the **Student ID** field name, click **Select All** ⬜. Notice that all of the fields are selected.

7 On the ribbon, click the **Home tab**. In the **Records group**, click **More**, and then click **Field Width**. In the **Column Width** dialog box, click **Best Fit**. Click anywhere in the **Student ID** field, and then compare your screen with Figure 1.25.

Using the More command is a third way to adjust column widths. By using Select All, you can adjust the widths of all of the columns at one time. Adjusting the width of columns does not change the data in the table's records; it only changes the *display* of the data.

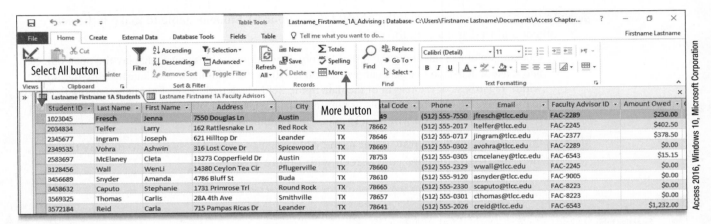

FIGURE 1.25

NOTE   Adjusting Column Widths

After adjusting column widths, scroll horizontally and vertically to be sure that all of the data displays in all of the fields. Access adjusts column widths to fit the screen size based on the displayed data. If data is not displayed on the screen when you adjust column widths—even if you use Select All—the column width may not be adjusted adequately to display all of the data in the field. After adjusting column widths, click in any field to remove the selection of the column or columns, and then save the table before performing other tasks.

---

8 On the Quick Access Toolbar, click **Save** 🖫 to save the table design changes—changing the column widths.

If you do not save the table after making design changes, Access prompts you to save it when you close the table.

MOS
1.5.2

Activity 1.13 | Printing a Table

There are times when you will want to print a table, even though a report may look more professional. For example, you may need a quick reference, or you may want to proofread the data that has been entered.

1 On the ribbon, click the **File tab**, click **Print**, and then click **Print Preview**. Compare your screen with Figure 1.26.

The table displays in Print Preview with the default zoom setting of One Page, a view that enables you to see how your table will print on the page. It is a good idea to view any object in Print Preview before printing so that you can make changes to the object if needed before actually printing it. In the navigation area, the Next Page button is darker (available), an indication that more than one page will print.

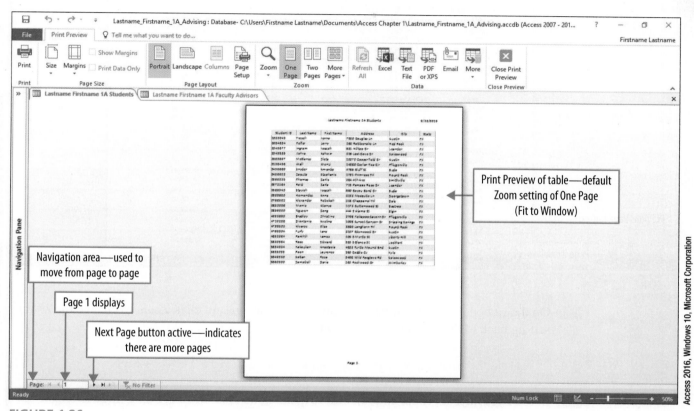

FIGURE 1.26

2 In the navigation area, click **Next Page** ▶ to display Page 2. Point to the top of the page to display the 🔍 pointer, click one time to zoom in, and then compare your screen with Figure 1.27.

The Print Preview display enlarges, and the Zoom Out pointer displays. The second page of the table displays the last five fields. The Next Page button is dimmed, indicating that the button is unavailable because there are no more pages after Page 2. The Previous Page button is available, indicating that a page exists before this page.

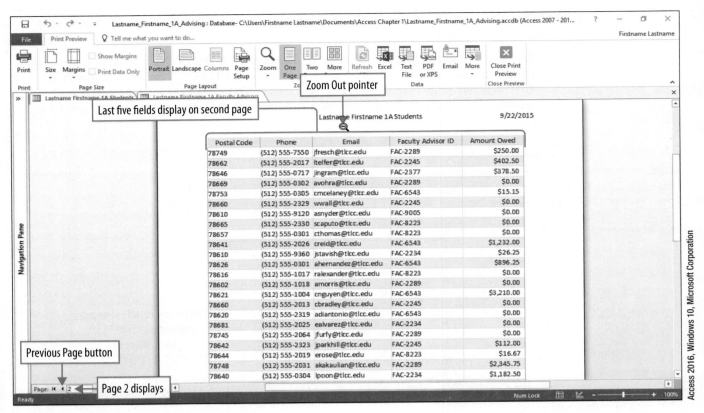

FIGURE 1.27

3 ▸ On the ribbon, on the **Print Preview tab**, in the **Zoom group**, click **Zoom** to change the zoom setting back to the default setting of One Page.

🔁 ANOTHER WAY   With the 🔍 pointer displayed on the page, click to zoom back to the One Page setting.

4 ▸ In the **Page Layout group**, click **Landscape**, and notice that there are only three fields on Page 2. In the navigation area, click **Previous Page** ◄ to display Page 1, and then compare your screen with Figure 1.28.

The orientation of the page to be printed changes. The header on the page includes the table name and current date, and the footer displays the page number. The change in orientation from portrait to landscape is not saved with the table. Each time you print, you must check the page orientation, the margins, and any other print parameters so that the object prints as you intend.

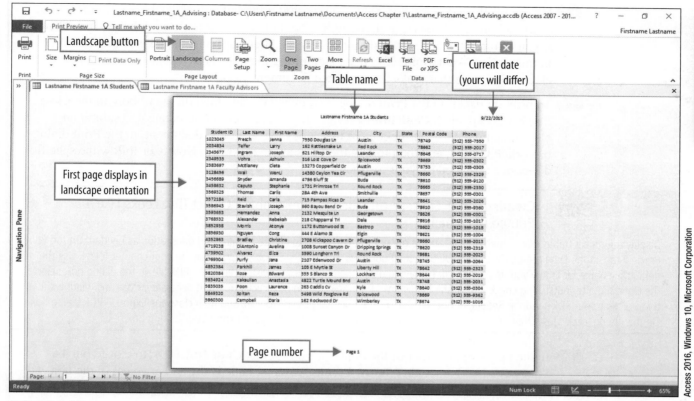

FIGURE 1.28

Access 2016, Windows 10, Microsoft Corporation

> **NOTE**   Headers and Footers in Access Objects
>
> The headers and footers in Access tables and queries are controlled by default settings; you cannot enter additional information or edit the information. The object name displays in the center of the header area, and the current date displays on the right. Adding your name to the object name is helpful in identifying your paper printouts or electronic results. The page number displays in the center of the footer area. The headers and footers in Access forms and reports are more flexible; you can add to and edit the information.

5 On the **Print Preview tab**, in the **Print group**, click **Print**. In the **Print** dialog box, under **Print Range**, verify that **All** is selected. Under **Copies**, verify that the **Number of Copies** is **1**. Compare your screen with Figure 1.29.

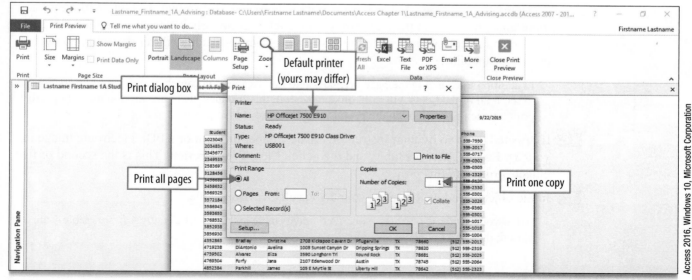

FIGURE 1.29

Access 2016, Windows 10, Microsoft Corporation

6 Determine if your instructor wants you to submit the individual database objects that you create within this Project, or if you will submit only your completed database file. Then, if you are creating and submitting the individual database objects—this is the first of five in this Project—determine if you are submitting the objects as a paper printout or as an electronic image that looks like a printed document.

7 To print on paper, in the **Print** dialog box, click **OK**, and then on the ribbon, in the **Close Preview group**, click **Close Print Preview**. If you are required to create and submit an electronic image of your document that looks like a printed document, in the Print dialog box, click Cancel, and then follow the steps in the following Note—or follow the specific directions provided by your instructor.

> **NOTE** Creating a PDF Electronic Image of Your Database Object That Looks Like a Printed Document
>
> Display the object (table, query, form, report, and so on) in Print Preview and adjust margins and orientation as needed. On the Print Preview tab, in the Data group, click PDF or XPS. In the Publish as PDF or XPS dialog box, navigate to your chapter folder. Use the default file name, or follow your instructor's directions to name the object. If you wish to view the PDF file, in the dialog box, select the Open file after publishing check box. In the Publish as PDF or XPS dialog box, click Publish. If necessary, close any windows that try to display your PDF—Adobe Reader, Adobe Acrobat, or the Microsoft Edge browser, and then close the Export – PDF dialog box. On the ribbon, click Close Print Preview; your electronic image is saved. Close the Save Export Steps dialog box.

8 In the upper right corner of the object window, click **Close Object** ☒ to close your **1A Students** table. Notice that the **1A Faculty Advisors** table is the active object in the object window.

> ⟳ **ANOTHER WAY**   In the object window, right-click the 1A Students object tab, and then click Close.

9 In your **1A Faculty Advisors** table, to the left of the **Faculty ID** field name, click **Select All** ☐ to select all of the columns. On the **Home tab**, in the **Records group**, click **More**, and then click **Field Width**. In the **Column Width** dialog box, click **Best Fit** to adjust the widths of all of the columns so that all of the data displays. Click in any field in the table to cancel the selection. Scroll horizontally and vertically to be sure that all of the data displays in each field; if necessary, use the techniques you practiced to apply Best Fit to individual columns. **Save** 🖫 the changes you made to the table's column widths, and then click in any record to cancel the selection, if necessary

10 On the ribbon, click the **File tab**, click **Print**, and then click **Print Preview**. On the **Print Preview tab**, in the **Page Layout group**, click **Landscape**. Notice that the table will print on more than one page. In the **Page Size group**, click **Margins**, click **Normal**, and then notice that one more column moved to the first page—your results may differ depending on your printer's capabilities.

> In addition to changing the page orientation to Landscape, you can change the margins to Normal to see if all of the fields will print on one page. In this instance, there are still too many fields to print on one page, although the Postal Code field moved from Page 2 to Page 1.

11 If directed to do so by your instructor, create a paper printout or a PDF electronic image of your **1A Faculty Advisors** table, and then click **Close Print Preview**. This is the second of five objects printed in this project.

12 In the object window, **Close** ☒ your **1A Faculty Advisors** table.

> All of your database objects—your *1A Students* table and your *1A Faculty Advisors* table—are closed; the object window is empty.

GO! Learn How
Video A1-4

Recall that tables are the foundation of an Access database because all of the data is stored in one or more tables. You can use the data stored in tables in other database objects such as queries, forms, and reports.

3.1.1

Activity 1.14 | Creating a Query by Using the Simple Query Wizard

A **query** is a database object that retrieves specific data from one or more database objects—either tables or other queries—and then, in a single datasheet, displays only the data that you specify when you design the query. Because the word *query* means *to ask a question*, think of a query as a question formed in a manner that Access can answer.

A **select query** is one type of Access query. A select query, also called a **simple select query**, retrieves (selects) data from one or more tables or queries and then displays the selected data in a datasheet. A select query creates a subset of the data to answer specific questions; for example, *Which students live in Austin, TX?*

The objects from which a query selects the data are referred to as the query's **data source**. In this Activity, you will create a simple query using a wizard that walks you step by step through the process. The process involves selecting the data source and indicating the fields that you want to include in the query results. The query—the question you want to ask—is *What is the name, email address, phone number, and Student ID of every student?*

> **1** On the ribbon, click the **Create tab**, and then in the **Queries group**, click **Query Wizard**. In the **New Query** dialog box, be sure **Simple Query Wizard** is selected, and then click **OK**. If a security message displays, click Open. Compare your screen with Figure 1.30.

In the wizard, the displayed table or query name is the object that was last selected on the Navigation Pane. The last object you worked with was your 1A Faculty Advisors table, so that object name displayed in the wizard.

FIGURE 1.30

> **2** In the wizard, click the **Tables/Queries arrow**, and then click your **Table: Lastname Firstname 1A Students**.

To create a query, first select the data source—the object from which the query is to select the data. The information you need to answer the question is stored in your 1A Students table, so this table is your data source.

3 Under **Available Fields**, click **Last Name**, and then click **Add Field** > to move the field to the **Selected Fields** list on the right. Double-click the **First Name** field to add the field to the **Selected Fields** list.

Use either method to add fields to the Selected Fields list—you can add fields in any order.

4 By using **Add Field** > or by double-clicking the field name, add the following fields to the **Selected Fields** list in the order specified: **Email**, **Phone**, and **Student ID**. Compare your screen with Figure 1.31.

Selecting these five fields will answer the question, *What is the name, email address, phone number, and Student ID of every student?*

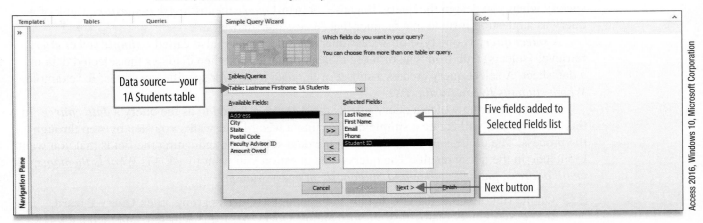

FIGURE 1.31

5 In the wizard, click **Next**. Click in the **What title do you want for your query?** box. Using your own name, edit as necessary so that the query name is **Lastname Firstname 1A All Students Query** and then compare your screen with Figure 1.32.

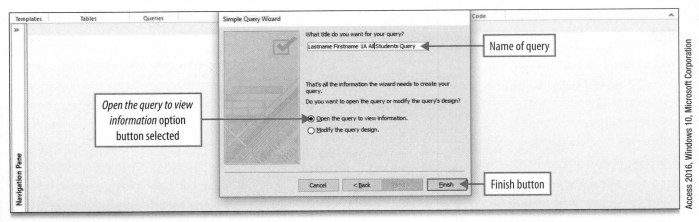

FIGURE 1.32

6 In the wizard, click **Finish**. Select all of the columns, apply **Best Fit**, and then **Save** 🖫 the query. In the first record, click in the **Last Name** field to cancel the selection. Compare your screen with Figure 1.33.

Access *runs* the query—performs the actions indicated in your query design—by searching the records in the specified data source, and then finds the records that match specified criteria. The records that match the criteria display in a datasheet. A select query *selects*—pulls out and displays—*only* the information from the data source that you request, including the specified fields.

In the object window, Access displays every student from your 1A Students table—the data source—but displays *only* the five fields that you moved to the Selected Fields list in the Simple Query Wizard.

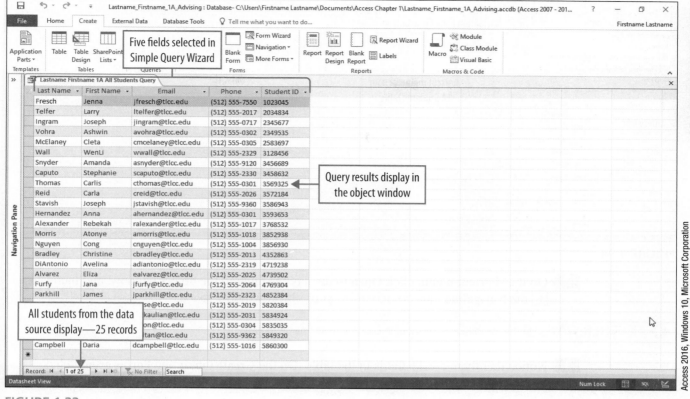

FIGURE 1.33

7 On the ribbon, click the **File tab**, click **Print**, and then click **Print Preview**. Notice that the query results will print on one page. As directed by your instructor, create a paper printout or PDF electronic image. Click **Close Print Preview**. This is the third of five objects printed in this project.

8 In the object window, **Close** ☒ the query.

4.1.1, 4.1.3

Activity 1.15 | **Creating and Printing a Form**

A *form* is an Access object with which you can enter data, edit data, or display data from a table or query. In a form, the fields are laid out in an attractive format on the screen, which makes working with the database easier for those who must enter and look up data.

One type of form displays only one record at a time. Such a form is useful not only to the individual who performs the data entry—typing in the records—but also to anyone who has the job of viewing information in the database. For example, when you visit the Records office at your college to obtain a transcript, someone displays your record on the screen. For the viewer, it is much easier to look at one record at a time using a form than to look at all of the student records in the database table.

1 **Open** ⯈ the **Navigation Pane**. Drag the right edge of the **Navigation Pane** to the right to increase the width of the pane so that all object names display fully. Notice that a table name displays with a datasheet icon, and a query name displays an icon of two overlapping datasheets. Right-click your **1A Students** table, and then compare your screen with Figure 1.34.

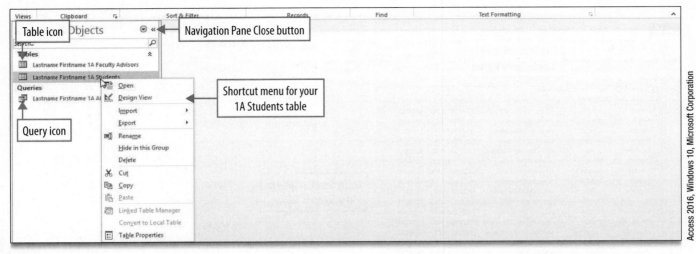

FIGURE 1.34

> **2** On the shortcut menu, click **Open** to display the table in the object window, and then **Close** [«] the **Navigation Pane** to maximize your object window space.

ANOTHER WAY   In the Navigation Pane, double-click the object name to open it.

> **3** Notice that there are 11 fields in the table. On the **Create tab**, in the **Forms group**, click **Form**. Compare your screen with Figure 1.35.

The Form tool creates a form based on the currently selected object—your 1A Students table. The form displays all of the fields from the underlying data source—one record at a time—in a simple top-to-bottom format with all 11 fields in a single column. You can use this form as it displays, or you can modify it. Records that you create or edit in a form are automatically added to or updated in the underlying table or data source.

The new form displays in *Layout view*—the Access view in which you can make changes to elements of an object while it is open and displaying the data from the data source. Each field in the form displayed in Figure 1.35 displays the data for the first student record—*Jenna Fresch*—in your 1A Students table.

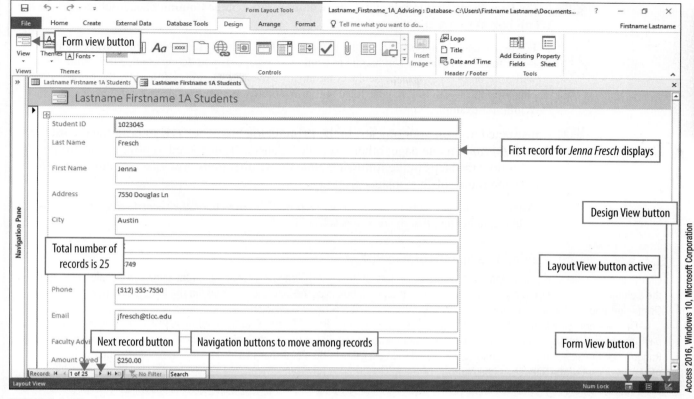

FIGURE 1.35

4 ▶ At the right side of the status bar, notice the three buttons. Point to each button to display its ScreenTip, and notice that **Layout View** ▣ is active, indicating that the form is displayed in Layout view.

5 ▶ In the status bar, click **Form View** ▣.

In *Form view*, you can view the records, create a new record, edit a record, and delete a record. You cannot change the layout or design of the form. Form view is useful for individuals who *access records* in your database. Layout view is useful for individuals who *design* the form.

🔄 **ANOTHER WAY** On the Design tab, or on the Home tab, in the Views group, click View when the button displays an icon of a form.

6 ▶ In the navigation area, click **Next record** ▶ two times to display the third record—the record for *Joseph Ingram*.

Use the navigation buttons to scroll among the records and to display any single record.

7 ▶ Using your own name, **Save** ▣ the form as **Lastname Firstname 1A Student Form**

8 ▶ On the ribbon, click the **File tab**, click **Print**, and then on the right, click **Print**—do *not* click Print Preview because you are going to print a *single* record—not all of the records.

9 ▶ In the **Print** dialog box, under **Print Range**, click the **Selected Record(s)** option button, and then click **Setup**.

10 In the **Page Setup** dialog box, click the **Columns tab**. Under **Column Size**, double-click in the **Width** box, type **7.5** and then click **OK**.

> Forms are usually not printed, so the default width for a form created with the Form command is larger than most printers can handle to print on one page. If you do not change the width, the form will print on two pages because the column flows over the margins allowed by the printer. If, after changing the Width to 7.5, your form still prints on two pages, try entering a different value for Width; for example, 7 or 6.5.

11 If instructed to print your objects, in the **Print** dialog box, click **OK** to print the record for *Joseph Ingram* on one page; otherwise, click Cancel. If instructed to print an electronic copy, follow the steps in the following Note or the directions provided by your instructor. This is the fourth of five objects printed in this project.

> After printing, along the left edge of the record, the narrow bar—the *record selector bar*—displays in black, indicating that the record is selected.

NOTE | **Printing a Single Form in PDF**

On the File tab, click Print, and then on the right, click Print. In the Print dialog box, click Setup. In the Page Setup dialog box, click the Columns tab. Under Column Size, double-click in the Width box, type **7.5** and then click OK. In the Print dialog box, click Cancel. On the left edge of the form, click the record selector bar so that it is black—selected.

On the ribbon, click the External Data tab. In the Export group, click PDF or XPS. In the Publish as PDF or XPS dialog box, navigate to your chapter folder, and at the lower right corner of the dialog box, click Options. In the Options dialog box, under Range, click the Selected records option button, and then click OK. In the Publish as PDF or XPS dialog box, click Publish. If necessary, close Adobe Reader, Adobe Acrobat, or the Microsoft Edge browser.

---

12 **Close** ☒ the form object; leave your **1A Students** table open.

Activity 1.16 | **Creating, Modifying, and Printing a Report**

5.1.1, 1.5.1

A *report* is a database object that displays the fields and records from a table or query in an easy-to-read format suitable for printing. Create professional-looking reports to summarize database information.

1 **Open** ☒ the **Navigation Pane**, and then open your **1A Faculty Advisors** table by double-clicking the table name or by right-clicking the table name and clicking Open. **Close** ☒ the **Navigation Pane**.

2 On the **Create tab**, in the **Reports group**, click **Report**.

> The Report tool creates a report in Layout view and includes all of the fields and all of the records in the data source—your 1A Faculty Advisors table. Dotted lines indicate how the report would break across pages if you print it now. In Layout view, you can make quick changes to the report layout while viewing the data from the table.

3 Click the **Faculty ID** field name, and then on the ribbon, under **Report Layout Tools**, click the **Arrange tab**. In the **Rows & Columns group**, click **Select Column**, and then press ⌷Del⌷. Using the same technique, delete the **Rank** field.

> The Faculty ID and Rank fields, along with the data, are deleted from the report. The fields readjust by moving to the left. Deleting the fields from the report does *not* delete the fields and data from the data source—your 1A Faculty Advisors table.

↻ **ANOTHER WAY** | Right-click the field name, click Select Entire Column, and then press ⌷Del⌷.

---

4 Click the **Address** field name, and then by using the scroll bar at the bottom of the screen, scroll to the right to display the **Cell Phone** field; be careful not to click in the report.

5 Hold down `Shift`, and then click the **Cell Phone** field name to select all of the fields from *Address* through *Cell Phone*. With the field names selected—surrounded by a colored border—in the **Rows & Columns group**, click **Select Column**, and then press `Del`.

Use this method to select and delete multiple columns in Layout view.

6 Scroll to the left, and notice that the four remaining fields display within the dotted lines— they are within the margins of the report. Click the **Campus** field name. Hold down `Shift`, and then click the **First Name** field name to select the first three fields. In the **Rows & Columns group**, click **Select Column** to select all three fields.

7 On the ribbon, click the **Design tab**, and then in the **Tools group**, click **Property Sheet**.

The *Property Sheet* for the selected columns displays on the right side of the screen. Every object and every item in an object has an associated Property Sheet where you can make precise changes to the properties—characteristics—of selected items.

8 In the **Property Sheet**, if necessary, click the **Format tab**. Click **Width**, type **1.5** and then press `Enter`. Compare your screen with Figure 1.36.

The width of the three selected fields changes to 1.5", and the fields readjust by moving to the left. You can change the Width property if you need to move columns within the margins of a report. In this report, the fields already displayed within the margins, but some reports may need this minor adjustment to print on one page.

🔄 **ANOTHER WAY**   Select the column, and then drag the right edge of the column to the left to decrease the width of the field, or drag to the right to increase the width of the field.

FIGURE 1.36

9 Close ☒ the **Property Sheet**. Click the **Last Name** field name. On the ribbon, click the **Home tab**, and then in the **Sort & Filter group**, click **Ascending**.

Access sorts the report in ascending alphabetical order by the Last Name field. By default, tables are sorted in ascending order by the primary key field—in this instance, the Faculty ID field. Changing the sort order in the report does *not* change the sort order in the underlying table.

10 At the top of the report, to the right of the green report icon, click anywhere in the title of the report to select the title placeholder. On the **Home tab**, in the **Text Formatting group**, click the **Font Size arrow**, and then click **14**. **Save** 🖫 the report. In the **Save As** dialog box, in the **Report Name** box, add **Report** to the end of *Lastname Firstname 1A Faculty Advisors*, and then click **OK**.

11 On the **File tab**, click **Print**, and then click **Print Preview**. On the **Print Preview tab**, in the **Zoom group**, click **Two Pages**, and then compare your screen with Figure 1.37.

As currently formatted, the report will print on two pages, because the page number at the bottom of the report is positioned beyond the right margin of the report.

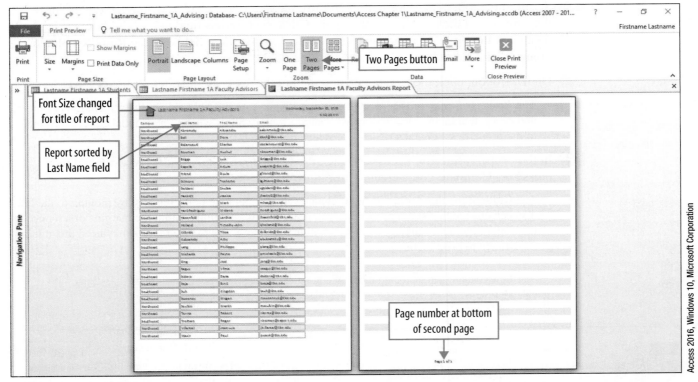

FIGURE 1.37

12 In the **Close Preview group**, click **Close Print Preview**. Scroll down to display the bottom of the report, and then, if necessary, scroll right to display the page number. Click the page number—**Page 1 of 1**—and then press Del.

Because all of the data will print on one page, the page number is not necessary for this report. If you want the page number to display, you can drag it within the margins of the report.

13 Display the report in **Print Preview**, and notice that the report will now print on one page. In the **Zoom group**, click **One Page**. Click **Save** to save the changes to the design of the report, and then create a paper printout or PDF electronic image as directed. Click **Close Print Preview**. This is the fifth or last object printed in this project.

When you create a report by using the Report tool, the default margins are 0.25 inch. Some printers require a greater margin, so your printed report may result in two pages. As you progress in your study of Access, you will practice making these adjustments. Also, if a printer is not installed on your system, the electronic PDF printout might result in a two-page report.

14 In the object window, right-click any **object tab**, and then click **Close All** to close all of the open objects. Notice that the object window is empty.

GO! Learn How
Video A1-5

When you close a table, any changes made to the records are saved automatically. If you made changes to the structure or adjusted column widths, you will be prompted to save the table when you close the table or when you switch views. Likewise, you will be prompted to save queries, forms, and reports if you make changes to the layout or design. If the Navigation Pane is open when you close Access, it will display when you reopen the database. When you are finished using your database, close the database, and then close Access.

Activity 1.17 │ Closing a Database and Closing Access

1 **Open** [»] the **Navigation Pane**. If necessary, increase the width of the Navigation Pane so that all object names display fully. Notice that your report object displays with a green report icon. Compare your screen with Figure 1.38.

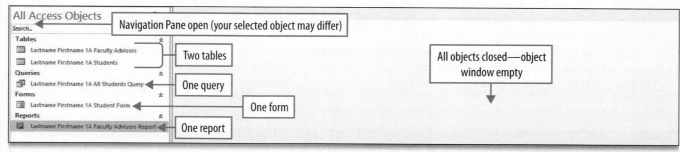

FIGURE 1.38

Access 2016, Windows 10, Microsoft Corporation

2 On the **File tab**, click **Close** to close the database but leave Access open. This action enables you to continue working in Access with another database if you want to do so. In the Access application window, in the upper right corner, click **Close** [X] to close Access. As directed by your instructor, submit your database and the paper printouts or PDF electronic images of the five objects—two tables, one query, one form, and one report—that are the results of this project.

> **END | You have completed Project 1A**

GO! With Google

Objective	Export an Access Table to an Excel Spreadsheet, Open as a Google Sheet, Edit a Record, and Save to Your Computer

Access web apps are designed to work with Microsoft's **SharePoint**, a service for setting up websites to share and manage documents. Your college may not have SharePoint installed, so you will use other tools to share objects from your database so that you can work collaboratively with others. Recall that Google Drive is Google's free, web-based word processor, spreadsheet, slide show, form, and data storage and sharing service. For Access, you can **export** a database object to an Excel worksheet, a PDF file, or a text file, and then save the file to Google Drive.

> **ALERT!** **Working with Web-Based Applications and Services**
>
> Computer programs and services on the web receive continuous updates and improvements. Therefore, the steps to complete this web-based Activity may differ from the ones shown. You can often look at the screens and the information presented to determine how to complete the activity.
>
> If you do not already have a Google account, you will need to create one before you begin this activity. Go to http://google.com and, in the upper right corner, click Sign In. On the Sign In screen, click Create Account. On the Create your Google Account page, complete the form, read and agree to the Terms of Service and Privacy Policy, and then click Next step. On the Welcome screen, click Get Started.

Activity | Exporting an Access Table to an Excel Spreadsheet, Saving the Spreadsheet to Google Drive, Editing a Record in Google Drive, and Saving to Your Computer

In this Activity, you will export your 1A Faculty Advisors table to an Excel spreadsheet, upload your Excel file to Google Drive as a Google Sheet, edit a record in the Google Sheet, and then download a copy of the edited spreadsheet to your computer.

1 Start Access, navigate to your **Access Chapter 1** folder, and then **Open** your **1A_Advising** database file. If necessary, on the Message Bar, click **Enable Content**. In the **Navigation Pane**, click your **1A Faculty Advisors** table to select it—do not open it.

2 On the ribbon, click the **External Data tab**, and then in the **Export group**, click **Excel**. In the **Export – Excel Spreadsheet** dialog box, click **Browse**, and then navigate to your **Access Chapter 1** folder. In the **File Save** dialog box, click in the **File name** box, type **Lastname_Firstname_a1A_Web** and then click **Save**.

3 In the **Export – Excel Spreadsheet** dialog box, under **Specify export options**, select the first two check boxes—**Export data with formatting and layout** and **Open the destination file after the export operation is complete**—and then click **OK**. Take a moment to examine the data in the file, and then **Close** Excel. In the **Export – Excel Spreadsheet** dialog box, click **Close**, and then **Close** Access. **Close** Excel.

4 Open your browser software, navigate to **http://drive.google.com**, and sign in to your Google account.

On the right side of the screen, click **Settings** [⚙], and then click **Settings**. In the **Settings** dialog box, to the right of *Convert uploads*, if necessary, select the **Convert uploaded files to Google Docs editor format** check box. In the upper right, click **Done**.

It is necessary to select this setting; otherwise, your document will upload as a pdf file and cannot be edited without further action.

5 Open your **GO! Web Projects** folder—or create and then open this folder by clicking **NEW** and then **Folder**. On the left, click **NEW**, and then click **File upload**. In the **Open** dialog box, navigate to your **Access Chapter 1** folder, and then double-click your **a1A_Web** Excel file to upload it to Google Drive. When the message *Uploads completed* displays, **Close** the message box.

6 Double-click your **Lastname_Firstname_a1A_Web** file to display the file, and then compare your screen with Figure A.

The worksheet displays column letters, row numbers, and data.

(GO! With Google continues on the next page)

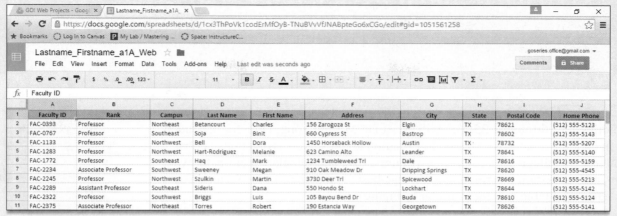

FIGURE A

7 Click in cell **C2**, and replace the current Campus with **Southwest** Click in cell **D2** and replace Betancourt with your last name. Press Tab and then replace Charles with your first name.

8 Above row **1** and to the left of column **A**, click **Select All** [ ]. On the menu bar, click **Format**, and then click **Clear formatting** so that the font is the same for all data; the cell borders are removed, and the formatting of the field names is removed.

9 In the column headings row, click **I** to select the entire column. On the menu bar, click **Format**, point to **Number**, and then click **Plain text** to format every number in the columns as text. Click in cell **A1** to deselect the column.

Recall that in Access, numbers that are not used in calculations should be formatted as Short Text. Because the formatting is cleared, you can enter new records into the spreadsheet in the same format as the existing records.

10 Click **File** to display the menu, point to **Download as**, and then click **Microsoft Excel (.xlsx)**. In the message box—usually displayed at the bottom of your screen—click the **Save arrow**, and then click **Save as**. In the **Save As** dialog box, navigate to your **Access Chapter 1** folder, click in the **File name** box, and type **Lastname_Firstname_a1A_Web_Download** and then click **Save**. **Close** the message box.

> **NOTE** **Saving the Downloaded File to the Access Chapter 1 Folder**
>
> Depending on the browser you are using, you may need to open the file in Excel and then save the a1A_Web_Download worksheet to your Access Chapter 1 folder.

11 In Google Drive, at the upper right corner of your screen, click your user name, and then click **Sign out**. **Close** your browser window.

12 Start Excel. In the Excel opening screen, click **Open Other Workbooks**, and then click **Browse**. Navigate to your **Access Chapter 1** folder, and then double-click your **a1A_Web** Excel file. Notice that this file is the original file—the new record is not entered. If

you are required to print your documents, use one of the methods in the following Note. **Close** your Excel file; and, if prompted, save the changes to your worksheet. Then **Open** and print your a **1A_Web_Download** Excel file using one of the methods in the following Note. **Close** Excel; and, if prompted, save the changes to your worksheet. As directed by your instructor, submit your two workbooks and the two paper printouts or PDF electronic images that are the results of this project.

> **NOTE** **Adding the File Name to the Footer and Printing or Creating a PDF Electronic Image of an Excel Spreadsheet on One Page**
>
> Click the File tab, click Print, and then click Page Setup. In the Page Setup dialog box, on the Page tab, under Orientation, click Landscape. Under Scaling, click the Fit to option button. In the Page Setup dialog box, click the Header/Footer tab, and then click Custom Footer. With the insertion point blinking in the Left section box, click the Insert File Name button, and then click OK. In the Page Setup dialog box, click OK.
>
> To print on paper, click Print. To create a PDF electronic image, on the left side of your screen, click Export. Under Export, be sure Create PDF/XPS Document is selected, and then click Create PDF/XPS. Navigate to your Access Chapter 1 folder, and then click Publish to save the file with the default name and an extension of pdf.

Student Workshops Database

PROJECT
1B

MyITLab
Project 1B Training
Project 1B Grader

PROJECT ACTIVITIES

In Activities 1.18 through 1.25, you will assist Dr. Miriam Yong, Director of Student Activities, in creating a database to store information about student workshops held at Texas Lakes Community College campuses. You will use a database template that tracks event information, add workshop information to the database, and then print the results. Your completed report and table will look similar to Figure 1.39.

Please always review the downloaded Grader instructions before beginning.

PROJECT FILES

MyITLab grader

If your instructor wants you to submit Project 1B in the MyITLab Grader system, log in to MyITLab, locate Grader Project1B, and then download the files for this project.

For Project 1B, you will need the following files:
Desktop event management template
a01B_Workshops (Excel workbook)

You will save your database as:
Lastname_Firstname_1B_Student_Workshops

PROJECT RESULTS

Build From Scratch

GO!
Walk Thru
Project 1B

Lastname Firstname 1B All Events   Tuesday, July 28, 2015   11:41:10 AM

Title	Start Time	End Time	Location
Your Online Reputation	3/9/2021 7:00:00 PM	3/9/2021 9:00:00 PM	Northeast Campus
Internet Safety			
Writing a Research Paper	3/10/2021 4:00:00 PM	3/10/2021 6:00:00 PM	Southwest Campus
Computer Skills			
Resume Writing	3/18/2021 2:00:00 PM	3/18/2021 4:00:00 PM	Northwest Campus
Job Skills			
Careers in the Legal Profession	3/19/2021 2:00:00 PM	3/19/2021 4:00:00 PM	Southeast Campus
Careers			
Transferring to a 4-Year University	4/8/2021 11:00:00 AM	4/8/2021 12:30:00 PM	Northeast Campus
Transfer			
Financial Aid	4/14/2021 7:00:00 PM	4/14/2021 8:30:00 PM	Southeast Campus
CC Info			
Sensitivity Training	4/15/2021 8:00:00 AM	4/15/2021 9:00:00 AM	Northwest Campus
Human Behavior			
Preparing for the Job Interview	4/15/2021 12:30:00 PM	4/15/2021 2:00:00 PM	Northwest Campus
Job Skills			
Class Note Taking	4/18/2021 12:30:00 PM	4/18/2021 1:30:00 PM	Southeast Campus
Study Skills			
Managing Time and Stress	4/18/2021 6:00:00 PM	4/18/2021 7:30:00 PM	Southwest Campus
Study Skills			
Work Smart at Your Computer	4/20/2021 10:00:00 AM	4/20/2021 11:00:00 AM	Northeast Campus
Computer Skills			
Preparing for Tests	4/20/2021 4:00:00 PM	4/20/2021 5:00:00 PM	Southeast Campus
Study Skills			

Page 1 of 1

Lastname Firstname 1B Workshop Locations   5/30/2015

Room ID	Campus/Location	Room	Seats	Room Arrangement	Equipment
NE-01	Northeast Campus	H265	150	Theater	Computer Projector, Surround Sound, Microphone
NE-02	Northeast Campus	B105	25	U-shaped	25 Computers, Projector
NW-01	Northwest Campus	C202	50	Lecture Classroom	Smart Board
SE-01	Southeast Campus	D148	20	U-shaped	White Board
SW-01	Southwest Campus	A15	35	Lecture Classroom	Computer Projector

Page 1

Access 2016, Windows 10, Microsoft Corporation

FIGURE 1.39 Project 1B Student Workshops

PROJECT RESULTS

In this project, using your own name, you will create the following database and objects. Your instructor may ask for printouts or PDF electronic images:

Lastname_Firstname_1B_Student Workshops	Database file
Lastname Firstname 1B All Events	Report
Lastname Firstname 1B Workshop Locations	Table

Objective 6 | Use a Template to Create a Database

GO! Learn How
Video A1-6

A *database template* contains prebuilt tables, queries, forms, and reports that perform a specific task, such as tracking events. For example, your college may hold events such as athletic contests, plays, lectures, concerts, and club meetings. Using a predefined template, your college's Activities Director can quickly create a database to manage these events. The advantage of using a template to start a new database is that you do not have to create the objects—all you need to do is enter the data and modify the prebuilt objects to suit your needs.

The purpose of the database in this project is to track the student workshops that are held by Texas Lakes Community College. The questions to be answered might include:

- What workshops will be offered, and when will they be offered?
- In what rooms and on what campuses will the workshops be held?
- Which workshop locations have a computer projector for PowerPoint presentations?

MOS
1.1.2

Activity 1.18 | Using a Template to Create a Database

ALERT!	**To submit as an autograded project, log into MyITLab and download the files for this project, and begin with those files instead of the Desktop event managment template database. For Project 1B using Grader, read Activity 1.18 carefully. Begin working with the database in Activity 1.19. For Grader to award points accurately, when saving an object, do not include your Lastname Firstname at the beginning of the object name.**

There are two types of database templates—those that will be stored on your desktop and those that are designed to share with others over the Internet. In this Activity, you will use a desktop template to create your database.

1 Start Access. In the Access opening screen, scroll down to display a **Desktop vehicle maintenance** template and an **Asset tracking** template. Compare your screen with Figure 1.40.

These templates are included with the Access program. To store a database to manage vehicle maintenance on your desktop, select the *Desktop Vehicle maintenance* template. To publish a database to track assets and share it with others, select the *Asset tracking* template—the one that displays a globe image. The names of templates designed to create databases stored on your computer start with the word *Desktop*.

You can search the Microsoft Office website for more templates. You can also click a category under the search box, where templates will be suggested.

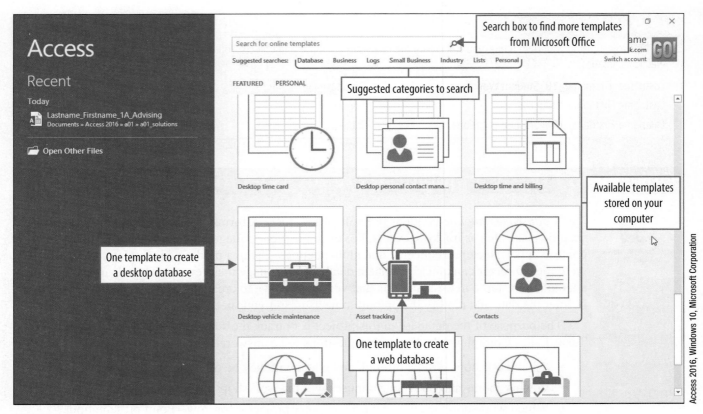

FIGURE 1.40

> Access 2016, Windows 10, Microsoft Corporation

2 At the top of the window, click in the **Search for online templates** box, type **event** and then press Enter. Compare your screen with Figure 1.41.

> You must have an Internet connection to search for online templates. Access displays several templates, including the event management template.

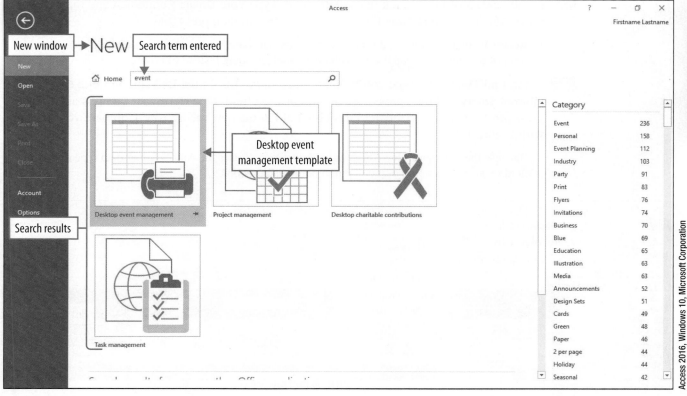

FIGURE 1.41

Access 2016, Windows 10, Microsoft Corporation

3 Click the **Desktop event management** template, and notice the description of the template. In the dialog box, to the right of the **File Name** box, click **Browse** , and then navigate to your **Access Chapter 1** folder.

4 In the **File New Database** dialog box, click in the **File name** box to select the existing text. Using your own name, type **Lastname_Firstname_1B_Student_Workshops** and then press Enter.

5 In the **Desktop event management** dialog box, click **Create** to download the template and to save the database. If a welcome message box displays, click Get Started.

Access creates the *1B_Student_Workshops* database, and the database name displays in the title bar. A predesigned *form*—Event List—displays in the object window. Although you can enter events for any date, when you open the database in the future, the Event List form will display only those events for the current date and future dates.

6 Under the ribbon, on the **Message Bar**, a *SECURITY WARNING* may display. If it is, on the **Message Bar**, click **Enable Content**.

Databases provided by Microsoft are safe to use on your computer.

MOS
2.3.1

Activity 1.19 | Building a Table by Entering Records in a Multiple-Items Form and a Single-Record Form

One purpose of a form is to simplify the entry of data into a table—either for you or for others who enter data. In Project 1A, you created a simple form that enabled you to display or enter records in a table one record at a time. The Desktop Event management template creates a *multiple-items form* that enables you to display or enter *multiple* records in a table, but with an easier and simplified layout rather than typing directly into the table itself.

1 In the new record row, click in the **Title** field. Type **Your Online Reputation** and then press Tab. In the **Start Time** field, type **3/9/21 7p** and then press Tab.

> Access formats the date and time. As you enter dates and times, a small calendar displays to the right of the field. You can use the calendar to select a date instead of typing it.

2 In the **End Time** field, type **3/9/21 9p** and then press Tab. In the **Description** field, type **Internet Safety** and then press Tab. In the **Location** field, type **Northeast Campus** and then press Tab three times to move to the **Title** field in the new record row. Compare your screen with Figure 1.42.

> Because the workshops have no unique value, Access uses the AutoNumber data type in the ID field to assign a unique, sequential number to each record.

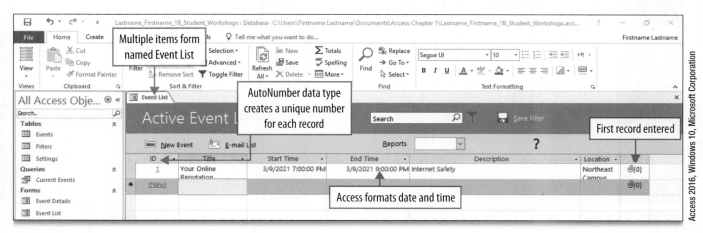

FIGURE 1.42

3 In the form, directly above the field names row, click **New Event**.

> A *single-record form* with the name *Event Details* displays, similar to the simple form you created in Project 1A. A single-record form enables you to display or enter one record at a time into a table.

4 Using Tab to move from field to field, enter the following record in the **Event Details** form—after entering the **End Time**, click in the **Description** field. Then compare your screen with Figure 1.43.

Title	Location	Start Time	End Time	Description
Writing a Research Paper	**Southwest Campus**	**3/10/21 4p**	**3/10/21 6p**	**Computer Skills**

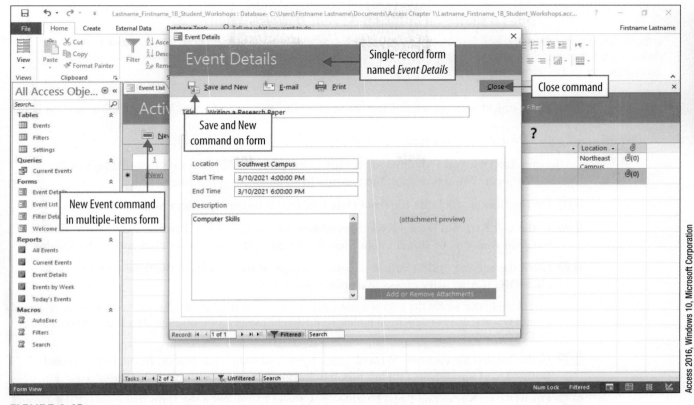

FIGURE 1.43

5 In the **Event Details** single-record form, in the upper right corner, click **Close**, and notice that the new record displays in the multiple-items form—*Event List*.

6 Enter the following records by using either the **Event List** form—the multiple-items form— or the **Event Details** form—the single-record form that is accessed by clicking the *New Event* command on the Event List form. Be sure the multiple-items form displays, and then compare your screen with Figure 1.44.

ID	Title	Start Time	End Time	Description	Location
3	**Resume Writing**	**3/18/21 2p**	**3/18/21 4p**	**Job Skills**	**Northwest Campus**
4	**Careers in the Legal Profession**	**3/19/21 2p**	**3/19/21 4p**	**Careers**	**Southeast Campus**

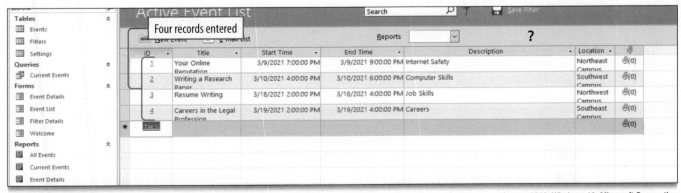

FIGURE 1.44

Access 2016, Windows 10, Microsoft Corporation

<table>
<tr><td>**ALERT!**</td><td>**Does a single-record form—*Event Details*—open?**</td></tr>
</table>

In the multiple-items form, pressing Enter three times at the end of the row to begin a new record will display the single-record form—*Event Details*. If you prefer to use the multiple-items form—Event List—close the single-record form and continue entering records, using the Tab key to move from field to field.

7 In the object window, click **Close** ☒ to close the **Event List** form. Close ☒ the Navigation Pane.

2.3.4

Activity 1.20 | Appending Records by Importing from an Excel Spreadsheet

In this Activity, you will append records to the table storing the data that displays in the Events List form. You will import the records from an Excel spreadsheet.

1 On the ribbon, click the **External Data tab**. In the **Import & Link group**, click **Excel**.

2 In the **Get External Data – Excel Spreadsheet** dialog box, click **Browse**. Navigate to the location where your student data files are stored, and then double-click **a01B_Workshops**.

3 Click the second option button—**Append a copy of the records to the table**—and then click **OK**. If a security message displays, click Open.

> The table that stores the data is named *Events*. Recall that other objects, such as forms, queries, and reports, display data from tables; so the Event Details form displays data that is stored in the Events table.

4 In the **Import Spreadsheet Wizard**, click **Next**, and then click **Finish**. In the **Get External Data – Excel Spreadsheet** dialog box, click **Close**.

5 **Open** ☒ the **Navigation Pane**. Double-click **Event List** to open the form that displays data from the Events table, and then **Close** ☒ the **Navigation Pane**. Compare your screen with Figure 1.45.

> A total of 12 records display; you entered four records, and you appended eight records from the a01B_Workshops Excel workbook. The data displays truncated in several fields because the columns are not wide enough to display all of the data.

ID	Title	Start Time	End Time	Description	Location	
1	Your Online Reputation	3/9/2021 7:00:00 PM	3/9/2021 9:00:00 PM	Internet Safety	Northeast Campus	ⓤ(0)
2	Writing a Research Paper	3/10/2021 4:00:00 PM	3/10/2021 6:00:00 PM	Computer Skills	Southwest Campus	ⓤ(0)
3	Resume Writing	3/18/2021 2:00:00 PM	3/18/2021 4:00:00 PM	Job Skills	Northwest Campus	ⓤ(0)
4	Careers in the Legal Profession	3/19/2021 2:00:00 PM	3/19/2021 4:00:00 PM	Careers	Southeast Campus	ⓤ(0)
5	Transferring to a 4-Year University	4/8/2021 11:00:00 AM	4/8/2021 12:30:00 PM	Transfer	Northeast Campus	ⓤ(0)
6	Financial Aid	4/14/2021 7:00:00 PM	4/14/2021 8:30:00 PM	CC Info	Southeast Campus	ⓤ(0)
7	Sensitivity Training	4/15/2021 8:00:00 AM	4/15/2021 9:00:00 AM	Human Behavior	Northwest Campus	ⓤ(0)
8	Preparing for the Job Interview	4/15/2021 12:30:00 PM	4/15/2021 2:00:00 PM	Job Skills	Northwest Campus	ⓤ(0)
9	Class Note Taking	4/18/2021 12:30:00 PM	4/18/2021 1:30:00 PM	Study Skills	Southeast Campus	ⓤ(0)
10	Managing Time and Stress	4/18/2021 6:00:00 PM	4/18/2021 7:30:00 PM	Study Skills	Southwest Campus	ⓤ(0)
11	Work Smart at Your Computer	4/20/2021 10:00:00 AM	4/20/2021 11:00:00 AM	Computer Skills	Northeast Campus	ⓤ(0)
12	Preparing for Tests	4/20/2021 4:00:00 PM	4/20/2021 5:00:00 PM	Study Skills	Southeast Campus	ⓤ(0)
* (New)						ⓤ(0)

Eight records appended from Excel spreadsheet

Columns not wide enough to display all of the data

FIGURE 1.45

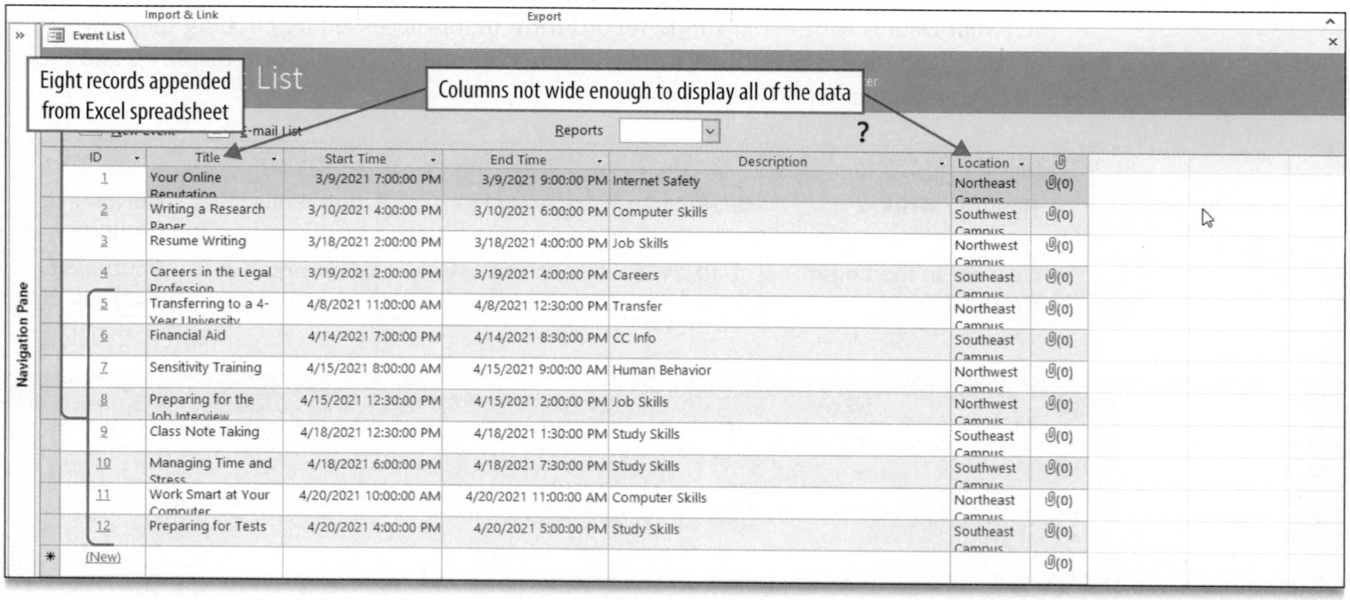

Access 2016, Windows 10, Microsoft Corporation

6 To the left of the **ID** field name, click **Select All** ☐ to select all of the columns and rows.

7 In the field names row, point to the right edge of any of the selected columns to display the ✛ pointer, and then double-click to apply Best Fit to all of the columns. Click in any field to cancel the selection, and then **Save** ☐ the form.

GO! Learn How
Video A1-7

1.3.4

Use the Navigation Pane to open objects, organize database objects, and perform common tasks, such as renaming an object or deleting an object.

Activity 1.21 | Grouping Database Objects in the Navigation Pane

The Navigation Pane groups and displays your database objects and can do so in predefined arrangements. In this Activity, you will group your database objects using the *Tables and Related Views* category, which groups objects by the table to which the objects are related. This grouping is useful because you can determine easily the table that is the data source of queries, forms, and reports.

1 Open » the **Navigation Pane**. At the top of the **Navigation Pane**, click **All Access Objects** arrow . On the list, under **Navigate To Category**, click **Tables and Related Views**. Compare your screen with Figure 1.46.

In the Navigation Pane, you can see the number of objects that are included in the Desktop Events Management template, including the table named *Events*. Other objects in the database that display data from the Events table include one query, two forms, and five reports. In the Navigation Pane, the Event List form is selected because it is open in the object window and is the active object.

Other objects might display on the Navigation Pane; for example, Filters and Unrelated Objects. These filters are objects created for use by the Desktop Event management template.

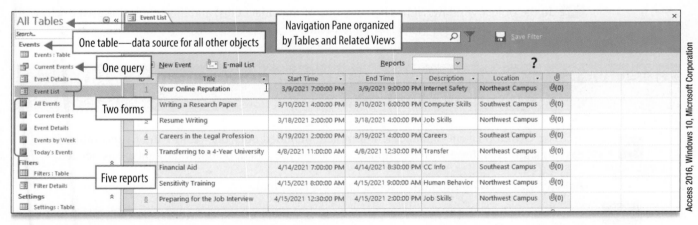

FIGURE 1.46

2 In the **Navigation Pane**, point to **Events: Table**, right-click, and then click **Open** to display the records in the underlying table.

The Events table is the active object in the object window. Use the Navigation Pane to open objects for use. The 12 records that display in the Event List multiple-items form are stored in this table. Recall that tables are the foundation of your database because your data must be stored in a table. You can enter records directly into a table or you can use a form to enter records.

ANOTHER WAY   Double-click the table name to open it in the object window.

3 In the object window, click the **Event List tab** to display the form as the active object in the object window.

Recall that a form presents a more user-friendly screen for entering records into a table.

4 In the **Navigation Pane**, double-click the **Current Events** *report* (green icon) to open the report. Compare your screen with Figure 1.47.

> An advantage of using a template to create a database is that many objects, such as reports, are already designed for you.

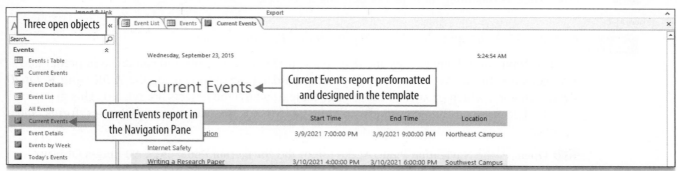

FIGURE 1.47

5 In the object window, **Close** ☒ the **Current Events** report.

6 By double-clicking or right-clicking, from the **Navigation Pane**, open the **Events by Week** report.

> In this predesigned report, the events are displayed by week. After entering records in the form or table, the preformatted reports are updated with the records from the table.

7 In the object window, right-click any one of the **object tabs**, and then click **Close All** to close all of the objects. **Close** ☒ the **Navigation Pane**.

Objective 8 Create a New Table in a Database Created with a Template

GO! Learn How
Video A1-8

The Desktop Event management template included only one table—the *Events* table. It is easy to start a database with a template, and then you can add additional objects as needed.

Activity 1.22 | Using the Table Tool to Create a New Table

2.1.1, 2.1.5

Dr. Yong has information about the various locations where workshops are held. For example, on the Northeast Campus, she has information about the room, seating arrangements, number of seats, and multimedia equipment. In the Events table, workshops are scheduled in rooms at each of the four campuses. It would not make sense to store information about the campus rooms multiple times in the same table. It is *not* considered good database design to have duplicate information in a table.

When data becomes redundant, it is usually an indication that you need a new table to contain that information. In this Activity, you will create a table to track the workshop locations, the equipment, and the seating arrangements in each location.

1 On the ribbon, click the **Create tab**, and then in the **Tables group**, click **Table**.

2 In the field names row, click **Click to Add**, click **Short Text**, type **Campus/Location** and then press [Enter].

3 In the third column, click **Short Text**, type **Room** and then press [Enter]. In the fourth column, click **Number**, type **Seats** and then press [Enter].

> The *Number data type* describes numbers that represent a quantity and may be used in calculations. For the Seats field, you may need to determine how many seats remain after reservations are booked for a room. In the new record row, a *0* displays in the field.

4 In the fifth column, type **t** to select *Short Text*, type **Room Arrangement** and then press Enter. In the sixth column, type **t** and then type **Equipment** On your keyboard, press ↓.

> With the data type list displayed, you can select the data type by either clicking it or typing the letter that is underscored for the data type.
>
> This table has six fields. Access automatically creates the first field in the table—the ID field—to ensure that every record has a unique value. Before naming each field, you must define the data type for the field.

5 Right-click the **ID** field name, and then click **Rename Field**. Type **Room ID** and then press Enter. On the **Fields tab**, in the **Formatting group**, click the **Data Type arrow**, and then click **Short Text**. On the ribbon, in the **Field Validation group**, notice that **Unique** is selected.

> Recall that, by default, Access creates the ID field with the AutoNumber data type so that the field can be used as the primary key. Here, this field will store a unique room ID that is a combination of letters, symbols, and numbers; therefore, it is appropriate to change the data type to Short Text. In Datasheet view, the primary key field is identified by the selection of the Unique check box.

More **Knowledge** | **Create a Table from a Template with Application Parts**

To create a table using the Application Parts gallery, click the Create tab, and in the Templates group click Application Parts. Under Quick Start, click Comments. In the Create Relationship dialog box, specify a relationship between the Comments table and an associated table, and click Next to choose the lookup column, and then click Create to create the table. If you choose No relationship, click Create to create the table. The Comments table displays in the Navigation Pane.

2.3.2

Activity 1.23 | Entering Records Into a New Table

1 In the new record row, click in the **Room ID** field. Enter the following record, pressing Enter or Tab to move from one field to the next. Do not be concerned that all of your text does not display; you will adjust the column widths later. After entering the record, compare your screen with Figure 1.48.

> Recall that Access saves a record when you move to another row within the table. You can press either Enter or Tab to move between fields in a table.

Room ID	Campus/Location	Room	Seats	Room Arrangement	Equipment
NE-01	**Northeast Campus**	**H265**	**150**	**Theater**	**Computer Projector, Surround Sound, Microphone**

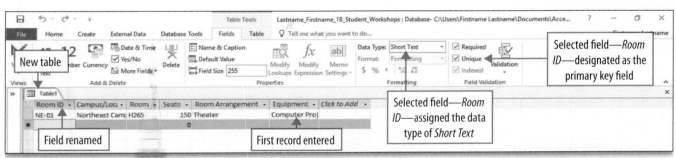

FIGURE 1.48

Access 2016, Windows 10, Microsoft Corporation

2 In the **Views group**, click the top of the **View** button to switch to **Design** view. In the **Save As** dialog box, in the **Table Name** box, using your own name, type **Lastname Firstname 1B Workshop Locations** and then click **OK**.

> Recall that when you switch views or when you close a table, Access prompts you to save the table if you have not previously saved it.

ANOTHER WAY   On the right side of the status bar, click Design View ⬛ to switch to Design view.

3 ▶ In the **Field Name** column, to the left of **Room ID**, notice the key icon.

In Design view, the key icon indicates that the field—Room ID—is the primary key field.

4 ▶ In the **Views group**, click the top of the **View** button to switch back to **Datasheet** view.

ANOTHER WAY   On the right side of the status bar, click Datasheet View ⬛ to switch to Datasheet view.

5 ▶ In the new record row, click in the **Room ID** field. Enter the following records, pressing Enter or Tab to move from one field to the next.

Room ID	Campus/Location	Room	Seats	Room Arrangement	Equipment
SW-01	Southwest Campus	A15	35	Lecture Classroom	Computer Projector
NW-01	Northwest Campus	C202	50	Lecture Classroom	Smart Board
SE-01	Southeast Campus	D148	20	U-shaped	White Board
NE-02	Northeast Campus	B105	25	U-shaped	25 Computers, Projector

6 ▶ To the left of the **Room ID** field name, click **Select All** ⬜ to select all of the columns and rows in the table. On the **Home tab**, in the **Records group,** click **More,** and then click **Field Width.** In the **Column Width** dialog box, click **Best Fit** to display all of the data in each column. Click in any field to cancel the selection, and then **Save** 🖫 the changes to the table. In the object window, **Close** ✕ your **1B Workshop Locations** table.

7 ▶ **Open** 》 the **Navigation Pane**, and notice that your new table displays in its own group. Point to the right edge of the **Navigation Pane** to display the ↔ pointer. Drag to the right to increase the width of the **Navigation Pane** so that your entire table name displays. Compare your screen with Figure 1.49.

Recall that organizing the Navigation Pane by Tables and Related Views groups the objects by each table and displays the related objects under each table name.

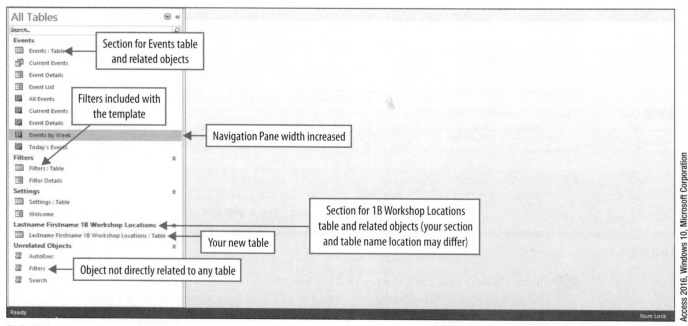

FIGURE 1.49

GO! Learn How
Video A1-9

1.5.1

Recall that one advantage to starting a new database with a template, instead of from a blank database, is that many report objects are already created for you.

Activity 1.24 | Viewing Reports and Printing a Report

1 In the **Navigation Pane**, double-click the report (not the form) name **Event Details** to open it in the object window.

This prebuilt Event Details report displays in an attractively arranged format.

2 **Close** ☒ the **Event Details** report. Open the **All Events** report, and then **Close** ☒ the **Navigation Pane**. On the **Home** tab, in the **Views group**, click the top of the **View** button to switch to **Layout** view.

Recall that Layout view enables you to make changes to an object while viewing the data in the fields. Each prebuilt report displays the records in the table in different useful formats.

⟳ ANOTHER WAY On the right side of the status bar, click Layout View ▤ to switch to Layout view.

3 At the top of the report, click the title—*All Events*—to display a colored border around the title. Click to the left of the letter *A* to place the insertion point there. Using your own name, type **Lastname Firstname 1B** and then press ⌴Spacebar⌴. Press ⌴Enter⌴, and then **Save** ⊟ the report.

Including your name in the title will help you and your instructor identify any submitted work.

4 On right side of the status bar, click **Print Preview** ⌕. In the navigation area, notice that the navigation arrows are unavailable, an indication that this report will print on one page.

⟳ ANOTHER WAY On the Home tab, in the Views group, click the View arrow, and then click Print Preview. Or, on the File tab, click Print, and then click Print Preview. Or, right-click the object tab, and then click Print Preview.

5 Create a paper printout or PDF electronic image as instructed. Click **Close Print Preview**, and then **Close** ☒ the report, saving any changes. This is the first of two objects printed in this project.

1.5.2

Activity 1.25 | Printing a Table

When printing a table, use the Print Preview command to determine if the table will print on one page or if you need to adjust column widths, margins, or page orientation. Recall that there will be occasions when you print a table for a quick reference or for proofreading. For a more professional-looking format, create and print a report.

1 **Open** ☒ the **Navigation Pane**, double-click your **1B Workshop Locations** table to open it in the object window, and then **Close** ☒ the **Navigation Pane**.

2 On the ribbon, click the **File tab**, click **Print**, and then click **Print Preview**.

The table displays how it will look when printed. Generally, tables are not printed, so there is no Print Preview option on the View button or on the status bar.

The navigation area displays *1* in the Pages box, and the navigation arrows to the right of the box are active, an indication that the table will print on more than one page.

3 In the navigation area, click **Next Page** ▸.

The second page of the table displays the last field. Whenever possible, try to print all of the fields horizontally on one page. Of course, if there are many records, more than one page may be needed to print all of the records and all of the fields.

4 On the **Print Preview tab**, in the **Page Layout group**, click **Landscape**, and then compare your screen with Figure 1.50. In landscape orientation, notice that the entire table will print on one page—all of the navigation buttons are unavailable.

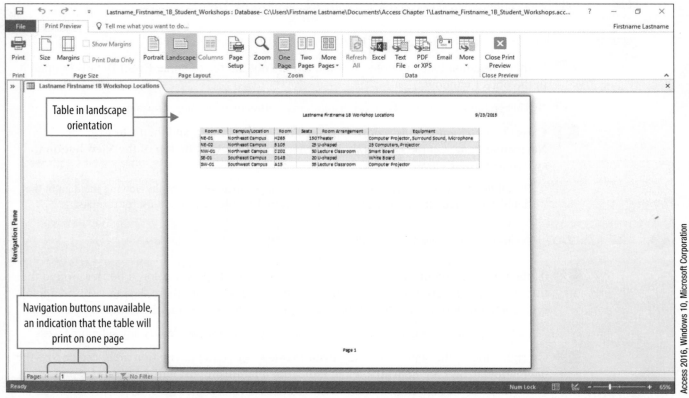

FIGURE 1.50

5 Create a paper printout or PDF electronic image as instructed, and then click **Close Print Preview**. This is the second or last object printed in this project.

6 **Close** ⊠ your **1B Workshop Locations** table. For the convenience of the next individual opening the database, **Open** » the **Navigation Pane**.

7 On the right side of the title bar, click **Close** ⊠ to close the database and to close Access. As directed by your instructor, submit your database and the paper printout or PDF electronic images of the two objects—one report and one table—that are the results of this project.

END | You have completed Project 1B

GO! With Google

Objective | Export an Access Table to a Word Document, Save to Google Drive, Add a Record, and Save to Your Computer

Access web apps are designed to work with Microsoft's SharePoint, a service for setting up websites to share and manage documents. Your college may not have SharePoint installed, so you will use other tools to share objects from your database so that you can work collaboratively with others. Recall that Google Drive is Google's free, web-based word processor, spreadsheet, slide show, form, and data storage and sharing service. For Access, you can export a database object to an Excel worksheet, a PDF file, or a text file, and then save the file to Google Drive.

> **ALERT!** **Working with Web-Based Applications and Services**
>
> Computer programs and services on the web receive continuous updates and improvements. Therefore, the steps to complete this web-based activity may differ from the ones shown. You can often look at the screens and the information presented to determine how to complete the activity.
>
> If you do not already have a Google account, you will need to create one before you begin this activity. Go to http://google.com and, in the upper right corner, click Sign In. On the Sign In screen, click Create Account. On the Create your Google Account page, complete the form, read and agree to the Terms of Service and Privacy Policy, and then click Next step. On the Welcome screen, click Get Started.

Activity | Exporting an Access Table to a Word Document, Saving the Document to Google Drive, Adding a Record in Google Drive, and Saving to Your Computer

In this Activity, you will export your 1B Workshop Locations table to a Word document, upload your Word file to Google Drive as a Google Doc, add a record in Google Drive, and then download a copy of the edited document to your computer.

1 Start Access, navigate to your **Access Chapter 1** folder, and then **Open** your **1B_Student_Workshops** database file. If necessary, on the Message Bar, click **Enable Content**, and then **Close** the **Event List** form. In the **Navigation Pane**, click your **1B Workshop Locations** table to select it—do not open it.

2 On the ribbon, click the **External Data tab**. In the **Export group**, click **More**, and then click **Word**. In the **Export – RTF File** dialog box, click **Browse**, and then navigate to your **Access Chapter 1** folder. In the **File Save** dialog box, click in the **File name** box, using your own name, type **Lastname_Firstname_a1B_Web** and then click **Save**.

3 In the **Export – RTF File** dialog box, under **Specify export options**, select the second check box—**Open the destination file after the export operation is complete**—and then click **OK**. Take a moment to examine the data in the file, and then **Close** Word. In the **Export – RTF File** dialog box, click **Close**, and then **Close** Access.

Notice that the table is too wide to display fully with Portrait orientation

4 Open your browser software, navigate to **http://drive.google.com**, and sign in to your Google account. On the right side of the screen, click **Settings** ⚙, and then click **Settings**. In the **Settings** dialog box, to the right of *Convert uploads*, if necessary, select the **Convert uploaded files to Google Docs editor format** check box. In the upper right, click **Done**.

It is necessary to select this setting; otherwise, your document will upload as a pdf file and cannot be edited without further action.

5 Open your **GO! Web Projects** folder—or create and then open this folder by clicking **NEW** and then clicking **New folder**. On the left, click **NEW**, and then click **File upload**. In the **Choose File to Upload** dialog box, navigate to your **Access Chapter 1** folder, and then double-click your **a1B_Web** Word file to upload it to Google Drive. When the title bar of the message box indicates *Upload complete*, **Close** the message box.

6 Double-click your **a1B_Web** file to open the file in Google Docs. Notice that the table is not fully displayed on the page.

(GO! With Google continues on the next page)

GO! With Google

7 Click **File** to display a menu, and then click **Page setup**. In the **Page setup** dialog box, under **Orientation**, click **Landscape**. Click **OK**.

The table displays fully with Landscape orientation.

8 Click in the last cell in the table, and press Tab. Add the following record, and compare with Figure A

Field	Room ID	Campus/Location	Room	Seats	Room Arrangement	Equipment
	SE-02	**Southeast Campus**	**D120**	**20**	**Testing Lab**	**20 Computers**

Room ID	Campus/Location	Room	Seats	Room Arrangement	Equipment
NE-01	Northeast Campus	H265	150	Theater	Computer Projector, Surround Sound, Microphone
NE-02	Northeast Campus	B105	25	U-shaped	25 Computers, Projector
NW-01	Northwest Campus	C202	50	Lecture Classroom	Smart Board
SE-01	Southeast Campus	D148	20	U-shaped	White Board
SW-01	Southwest Campus	A15	35	Lecture Classroom	Computer Projector
SE-02	Southeast Campus	D120	20	Testing Lab	20 Computers

FIGURE A

9 On the menu, click **File**, point to **Download as**, and then click **Microsoft Word (.docx)**. In the message box—usually displays at the bottom of your screen—click the **Save arrow**, and then click **Save as**. In the **Save As** dialog box, navigate to your **Access Chapter 1** folder, click in the **File name** box, and type **Lastname_Firstname_a1B_Web_Download** and then click **Save**. **Close** the message box.

10 In Google Drive, at the upper right corner of your screen, click your user name, and then click **Sign out**. **Close** your browser window.

11 Start Word. In the Word opening screen, click **Open**. Under **Open**, click **Browse**. Navigate to your **Access Chapter 1** folder, and then double-click your **a1B_Web** Word file. Notice that this file is the original

file—the new record is not entered. If you are required to print your documents, use one of the methods in the following Note. **Close** your Word file; and, if prompted, save the changes to your document. Then **Open** and print your **a1B_Web_Download** Word file using one of the methods in the following Note. **Close** Word; and, if prompted, save the changes to your document. As directed by your instructor, submit your two documents and the two paper printouts or PDF electronic images that are the results of this project.

NOTE — Adding the File Name to the Footer and Printing or Creating a PDF Electronic Image

Click the Insert tab. In the Header & Footer group, click Footer, and then click Blank. With Type here selected, in the Insert group, click Document Info, and then click File Name. Close the Footer window. Click the Layout tab. In the Page Setup group, click Orientation, and then click Landscape.

To print on paper, click File, and then click Print. To create a pdf electronic image of your printout, click File, and then click Export. Under Export, be sure Create PDF/XPS Document is selected, and then click Create PDF/XPS. Navigate to your Access Chapter 1 folder, and then click Publish to save the file with the default name and an extension of pdf.

GO! To Work

MICROSOFT OFFICE SPECIALIST (MOS) SKILLS IN THIS CHAPTER

PROJECT 1A

1.1.1 Create a blank desktop database
1.3.5 Change views of objects
1.5.1 Print reports
1.5.2 Print records
2.1.1 Create a table
2.1.2 Import data into tables
2.2.3 Add table descriptions
2.3.2 Add records
2.3.4 Append records from external data
2.4.1 Add fields to tables
2.4.3 Change field captions
2.4.4 Change field sizes
2.4.5 Change field data types
2.4.6 Configure fields to auto-increment
2.4.9 Delete fields
3.1.1 Run a query
4.1.1 Create a form
4.1.3 Save a form
5.1.1 Create a report based on a query or table

PROJECT 1B

1.1.2 Create a database from a template
1.3.4 Display objects in the Navigation Pane
1.5.1 Print reports
1.5.2 Print records
2.1.1 Create a table
2.1.5 Create a table from a template with application parts
2.3.1 Update records
2.3.4 Append records from external data

BUILD YOUR E-PORTFOLIO

An E-Portfolio is a collection of evidence, stored electronically, that showcases what you have accomplished while completing your education. Collecting and then sharing your work products with potential employers reflects your academic and career goals. Your completed documents from the following projects are good examples to show what you have learned: 1G, 1K, and 1L.

GO! FOR JOB SUCCESS

Video: Goal Setting

Your instructor may assign this video to your class, and then ask you to think about, or discuss with your classmates, these questions:

FotolEdhar / Fotolia

Is there anything you would change about Theo's behavior at his performance evaluation? Why or why not?

SMART goals are goals that are specific, measurable, achievable, realistic, and time-frame specific. Is Theo's first goal of beating his sales numbers by 10 percent next year a SMART goal?

How important do you think it is to set career development goals for yourself? Why?

END OF CHAPTER

SUMMARY

Principles of good database design, also known as normalization, help ensure that the data in your database is accurate and organized in a way that you can retrieve information that is useful.

You can create a database from scratch by using the blank desktop database template or a custom web app or by using a template that contains prebuilt tables, queries, forms, reports, and other objects.

Tables are the foundation of a database, but before entering records in a table, you must define the data type and name the field. Common data types are Short Text, Number, Currency, and Date/Time.

Use forms to enter data into a table or view the data in a table. Use queries to retrieve information from tables. Reports display information from tables in a professional-looking format.

GO! LEARN IT ONLINE

Review the concepts and key terms in this chapter by completing these online challenges, which you can find at **MyITLab**.

Matching and Multiple Choice: Answer matching and multiple-choice questions to test what you learned in this chapter.

Lessons on the GO!: Learn how to use all the new apps and features as they are introduced by Microsoft.

MOS Prep Quiz: Answer questions to review the MOS skills that you have practiced in this chapter.

GO! COLLABORATIVE TEAM PROJECT (Available in **MyITLab** and Instructor Resource Center)

If your instructor assigns this project to your class, you can expect to work with one or more of your classmates—either in person or by using Internet tools—to create work products similar to those that you created in this chapter. A team is a group of workers who work together to solve a problem, make a decision, or create a work product. Collaboration is when you work together with others as a team in an intellectual endeavor to complete a shared task or achieve a shared goal.

Your instructor will assign Projects from this list to ensure your learning and assess your knowledge.

REVIEW AND ASSESSMENT GUIDE FOR ACCESS CHAPTER 1

Project	Apply Skills from These Chapter Objectives	Project Type	Project Location
1A **MyITLab**	Objectives 1–5 from Project 1A	**1A Instructional Project (Grader Project)** Guided instruction to learn the skills in Project 1A.	In MyITLab and in text
1B **MyITLab**	Objectives 6–9 from Project 1B	**1B Instructional Project (Grader Project)** Guided instruction to learn the skills in Project 1B.	In MyITLab and in text
1C	Objectives 1–5 from Project 1A	**1C Skills Review (Scorecard Grading)** A guided review of the skills from Project 1A.	In text
1D	Objectives 6–9 from Project 1B	**1D Skills Review (Scorecard Grading** A guided review of the skills from Project 1B.	In text
1E **MyITLab**	Objectives 1–5 from Project 1A	**1E Mastery (Grader Project)** **Mastery and Transfer of Learning** A demonstration of your mastery of the skills in Project 1A with extensive decision making.	In MyITLab and in text
1F **MyITLab**	Objectives 6–9 from Project 1B	**1F Mastery (Grader Project)** **Mastery and Transfer of Learning** A demonstration of your mastery of the skills in Project 1B with extensive decision making.	In MyITLab and in text
1G **MyITLab**	Combination of Objectives from Projects 1A and 1B	**1G Mastery (Grader Project)** **Mastery and Transfer of Learning** A demonstration of your mastery of the skills in Projects 1A and 1B with extensive decision making.	In MyITLab and in text
1H	Combination of Objectives from Projects 1A and 1B	**1H GO! Fix It (Scorecard Grading)** **Critical Thinking** A demonstration of your mastery of the skills in Projects 1A and 1B by creating a correct result from a document that contains errors you must find.	Instructor Resource Center (IRC) and MyITLab
1I	Combination of Objectives from Projects 1A and 1B	**1I GO! Make It (Scorecard Grading)** **Critical Thinking** A demonstration of your mastery of the skills in Projects 1A and 1B by creating a result from a supplied picture.	IRC and MyITLab
1J	Combination of Objectives from Projects 1A and 1B	**1J GO! Solve It (Rubric Grading)** **Critical Thinking** A demonstration of your mastery of the skills in Projects 1A and 1B, your decision-making skills, and your critical-thinking skills. A task-specific rubric helps you self-assess your result.	IRC and MyITLab
1K	Combination of Objectives from Projects 1A and 1B	**1K GO! Solve It (Rubric Grading)** **Critical Thinking** A demonstration of your mastery of the skills in Projects 1A and 1B, your decision-making skills, and your critical thinking skills. A task-specific rubric helps you self-assess your result.	In text
1L	Combination of Objectives from Projects 1A and 1B	**1L GO! Think (Rubric Grading)** **Critical Thinking** A demonstration of your understanding of the Chapter concepts applied in a manner that you would outside of college. An analytic rubric helps you and your instructor grade the quality of your work by comparing it to the work an expert in the discipline would create.	In text
1M	Combination of Objectives from Projects 1A and 1B	**1M GO! Think (Rubric Grading)** **Critical Thinking** A demonstration of your understanding of the Chapter concepts applied in a manner that you would outside of college. An analytic rubric helps you and your instructor grade the quality of your work by comparing it to the work an expert in the discipline would create.	IRC and MyITLab
1N	Combination of Objectives from Projects 1A and 1B	**1N You and GO! (Rubric Grading)** **Critical Thinking** A demonstration of your understanding of the Chapter concepts applied in a manner that you would in a personal situation. An analytic rubric helps you and your instructor grade the quality of your work.	IRC and MyITLab
1O	Combination of Objectives from Project 1A and 1B	**1O Collaborative Team Project for ACCESS Chapter 1 Critical Thinking** A demonstration of your understanding of concepts and your ability to work collaboratively in a group role-playing assessment, requiring both collaboration and self-management.	IRC and MyITLab

GLOSSARY

GLOSSARY OF CHAPTER KEY TERMS

Append To add on to the end of an object; for example, to add records to the end of an existing table.

AutoNumber data type A data type that describes a unique sequential or random number assigned by Access as each record is entered and that is useful for data that has no distinct field that can be considered unique.

Best Fit An Access command that adjusts the width of a column to accommodate the column's longest entry.

Blank desktop database A database that has no data and has no database tools—you must create the data and tools as you need them; the database is stored on your computer or other storage device.

Caption A property setting that displays a name for a field in a table, query, form, or report different from the one listed as the field name.

Common field A field included in two or more tables that stores the same data.

Currency data type An Access data type that describes monetary values and numeric data that can be used in mathematical calculations involving values with one to four decimal places.

Custom web app A database that you can publish and share with others over the Internet.

Data Facts about people, events, things, or ideas.

Data source The table or tables from which a query, form, or report gathers its data.

Data type Classification identifying the kind of data that can be stored in a field, such as numbers, text, or dates.

Database An organized collection of facts about people, events, things, or ideas related to a specific topic or purpose.

Database management system (DBMS) Database software that controls how related collections of data are stored, organized, retrieved, and secured; also known as a DBMS.

Database template A preformatted database that contains prebuilt tables, queries, forms, and reports that perform a specific task, such as tracking events.

Datasheet view The Access view that displays data organized in columns and rows similar to an Excel worksheet.

DBMS An acronym for database management system.

Design view An Access view that displays the detailed structure of a table, query, form, or report. For forms and reports, may be the view in which some tasks must be performed, and only the controls, and not the data, display in this view.

Destination table The table to which you import or append data.

Export The process of copying data from one file into another file, such as an Access table into an Excel spreadsheet.

Field A single piece of information that is stored in every record; represented by a column in a database table.

Field properties Characteristics of a field that control how the field displays and how data can be entered in the field; vary for different data types.

First principle of good database design A principle of good database design stating that data is organized in tables so that there is no redundant data.

Flat database A simple database file that is not related or linked to any other collection of data.

Form An Access object you can use to enter new records into a table, edit or delete existing records in a table, or display existing records.

Form view The Access view in which you can view records, but you cannot change the layout or design of the form.

Import The process of copying data from another file, such as a Word table or an Excel workbook, into a separate file, such as an Access database.

Information Data that is accurate, timely, and organized in a useful manner.

Layout view The Access view in which you can make changes to a form or report while the data from the underlying data source displays.

Link A connection to data in another file.

Multiple-items form A form that enables you to display or enter multiple records in a table.

Navigation area An area at the bottom of the Access window that indicates the number of records in the table and contains controls in the form of arrows that you click to move among the records.

Navigation Pane An area of the Access window that displays and organizes the names of the objects in a database; from here, you open objects for use.

Normalization The process of applying design rules and principles to ensure that your database performs as expected.

Number data type An Access data type that represents a quantity, how much or how many, and may be used in calculations.

Object tab In the object window, a tab that identifies the object and which enables you to make an open object active.

Object window An area of the Access window that displays open objects, such as tables, queries, forms, or reports; by default, each object displays on its own tab.

Objects The basic parts of a database that you create to store your data and to work with your data; for example, tables, queries, forms, and reports.

Populate The action of filling a database table with records.

Primary key A required field that uniquely identifies a record in a table; for example, a Student ID number at a college.

Property Sheet A list of characteristics—properties—for fields or controls on a form or report in which you can make precise changes to each property associated with the field or control.

Query A database object that retrieves specific data from one or more database objects—either tables or other queries—and then, in a single datasheet, displays only the data you specify.

Record All of the categories of data pertaining to one person, place, event, thing, or idea; represented by a row in a database table.

Record selector bar The bar at the left edge of a record when it is displayed in a form, and which is used to select an entire record.

Record selector box The small box at the left of a record in Datasheet view that, when clicked, selects the entire record.

Redundant In a database, information that is duplicated in a manner that indicates poor database design.

Relational database A sophisticated type of database that has multiple collections of data within the file that are related to one another.

Report A database object that summarizes the fields and records from a table or query in an easy-to-read format suitable for printing.

Run The process in which Access searches the records in the table(s) included in the query design, finds the records that match the specified criteria, and then displays the records in a datasheet; only the fields that have been included in the query design display.

Second principle of good database design A principle stating that appropriate database techniques are used to ensure the accuracy and consistency of data as it is entered into the table.

Select query A type of Access query that retrieves (selects) data from one or more tables or queries, displaying the selected data in a datasheet; also known as a simple select query.

SharePoint A Microsoft application used for setting up websites to share and manage documents.

Short Text data type An Access data type that describes text, a combination of text and numbers, or numbers that are not used in calculations, such as the Postal Code.

Simple select query Another name for a select query.

Single-record form A form that enables you to display or enter one record at a time from a table.

Source file When importing a file, refers to the file being imported.

Structure In Access, the underlying design of a table, including field names, data types, descriptions, and field properties.

Table A format for information that organizes and presents text and data in columns and rows; the foundation of a database.

Tables and Related Views An arrangement in the Navigation Pane that groups objects by the table to which they are related.

Truncated Data that is cut off or shortened because the field or column is not wide enough to display all of the data or the field size is too small to contain all of the data.

Wizard A feature in Microsoft Office that walks you step by step through a process.

Skills Review Project 1C College Administrators

1 Identify Good Database Design

2 Create a Table and Define Fields in a Blank Desktop Database

3 Change the Structure of Tables and Add a Second Table

4 Create a Query, Form, and Report

5 Close a Database and Close Access

In the following Skills Review, you will create a database to store information about the administrators of Texas Lakes Community College and their departments. Your completed database objects will look similar to Figure 1.51.

PROJECT FILES

For Project 1C, you will need the following files:

Blank desktop database

a01C_Administrators (Excel workbook)

a01C_Departments (Excel workbook)

You will save your database as:

Lastname_Firstname_1C_College_Administrators

PROJECT RESULTS

Build From Scratch

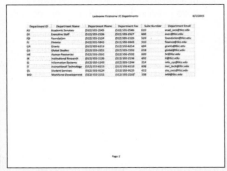

FIGURE 1.51

Access 2016, Windows 10, Microsoft Corporation

(Project 1C College Administrators continues on the next page)

1 Start Access. In the Access opening screen, click **Blank desktop database**. In the **Blank desktop database** dialog box, to the right of the **File Name** box, click **Browse**. In the **File New Database** dialog box, navigate to your **Access Chapter 1** folder. In the **File New Database** dialog box, click in the **File name** box, type **Lastname_Firstname_1C_College_Administrators** and then press Enter. In the **Blank desktop database** dialog box, click **Create**.

a. **Close** the **Navigation Pane**. In the field names row, click in the text *Click to Add*, and then click **Short Text**. Type **Title** and then press Enter.

b. In the third field name box, click **Short Text**, type **Last Name** and then press Enter. In the fourth field name box, click **Short Text**, type **First Name** and then press Enter. Create the remaining fields shown in **Table 1**, pressing Enter after the last field name. All of the data is typed on one line.

c. If necessary, scroll to bring the first column into view, and then click the **ID** field name. On the **Fields**

tab, in the **Properties group**, click **Name & Caption**. In the **Name** box, change *ID* to **Employee ID** and then click **OK**. On the ribbon, in the **Formatting group**, click the **Data Type arrow**, and then click **Short Text**.

d. In the new record row, click in the **Employee ID** field, type **ADM-9200** and press Enter. In the **Title** field, type **Vice President** and press Enter. Continue entering data in the fields shown in **Table 2**, pressing Enter or Tab to move to the next field and to the next row.

e. On the Quick Access Toolbar, click **Save**. In the **Save As** dialog box, in the **Table Name** box, using your own name, replace the selected text by typing **Lastname Firstname 1C Administrators** and then click **OK**.

f. In the new record row, enter the data for two college administrators shown in Table 3, pressing Enter or Tab to move from field to field and to the next row.

TABLE 1

Data Type		Short Text	Short Text	Short Text	**Short Text**	**Short Text**	**Short Text**	**Short Text**	**Short Text**	**Short Text**	**Short Text**	**Currency**
Field Name	ID	Title	Last Name	First Name	**Middle Initial**	**Address**	**City**	**State**	**Postal Code**	**Phone Number**	**Department ID**	**Salary**

(Return to Step 1c)

TABLE 2

Last Name	First Name	Middle Initial	Address	City	State	Postal Code	Phone Number	Department ID	Salary
Shaffer	**Lonnie**	**J**	**489 Ben Ave**	**Austin**	**TX**	**78734**	**(512) 555-6185**	**AS**	**123500**

(Return to Step 1e)

TABLE 3

Employee ID	Title	Last Name	First Name	Middle Initial	Address	City	State	Postal Code	Phone Number	Department ID	Salary
ADM-9201	Associate Vice President	Holtz	Diann	S	8416 Spencer Ln	Georgetown	TX	78627	(512) 555-1069	AS	101524
ADM-9202	Director, Enrollment Services	Fitchette	Sean	H	3245 Deer Trl	Spicewood	TX	78669	(512) 555-9012	SS	45070

(Return to Step 1g)

(Project 1C College Administrators continues on the next page)

g. **Close** your **1C Administrators** table. On the **External Data tab**, in the **Import & Link group**, click **Excel**. In the **Get External Data – Excel Spreadsheet** dialog box, click **Browse**. In the **File Open** dialog box, navigate to your student data files, and then double-click the **a01C_Administrators** Excel file.

h. Click the **Append a copy of the records to the table** option button, and then click **OK**. In the **Import Spreadsheet Wizard**, click **Next**, and then click **Finish**. In the **Get External Data – Excel Spreadsheet** dialog box, click **Close**.

i. **Open** the **Navigation Pane**. Resize the Navigation Pane so that the entire table name displays. In the **Navigation Pane**, double-click your **1C Administrators** table to open it, and then **Close** the **Navigation Pane**—there are 30 records in this table.

2 Click the **Home tab**, and then in the **Views group**, click the top of the **View** button to switch to **Design** view. In the **Field Name** column, to the left of **Middle Initial**, click the row selector box to select the entire row. On the **Design tab**, in the **Tools group**, click **Delete Rows**. In the message box, click **Yes**.

a. Click in the **Employee ID** field name box. Under **Field Properties**, click **Field Size** to select the existing text. Type **8** and then in the **Employee ID** field row, click in the **Description** box. Type **Eight-character Employee ID** and then press Enter.

b. Click in the **State** field name box. In the **Field Properties** area, click **Field Size**, and then type **2** In the **State Description** box, type **Two-character state abbreviation** and then press Enter.

c. **Save** the design changes to your table, and in the message box, click **Yes**. On the **Design tab**, in the **Views group**, click the top of the **View** button to switch to **Datasheet** view.

d. On the ribbon, click the **External Data tab**, and then in the **Import & Link group**, click **Excel**. In the **Get External Data – Excel Spreadsheet** dialog box, to the right of the **File name** box, click **Browse**. In the **File Open** dialog box, navigate to your student data files, and then double-click **a01C_Departments**. Be sure that the **Import the source data into a new table in the current database** option button is selected, and then click **OK**.

e. In the upper left corner of the wizard, select the **First Row Contains Column Headings** check box, and then click **Next**. Click **Next** again. Click the **Choose my own primary key** option button, be sure that **Department ID** displays, and then click **Next**. In the **Import to Table** box, type **Lastname Firstname 1C Departments** and then click **Finish**. In the **Get External Data – Excel Spreadsheet** dialog box, click **Close**.

f. **Open** the **Navigation Pane**, double-click your **1C Departments** table, and then **Close** the **Navigation Pane**. There are 12 records in your **1C Departments** table.

g. To the left of the **Department** field name, click **Select All**. On the ribbon, click the **Home tab**, and in the **Records group**, click **More**, and then click **Field Width**. In the **Column Width** dialog box, click **Best Fit**. Click in any field to cancel the selection, and then **Save** your table. In the object window, click the **object tab** for your **1C Administrators** table. Using the techniques you just practiced, apply **Best Fit** to the columns, cancel the selection, and then **Save** the table.

h. With your **1C Administrators** table displayed, on the ribbon, click the **File tab**, click **Print**, and then click **Print Preview**. On the **Print Preview tab**, in the **Page Layout group**, click **Landscape**. Create a paper printout or PDF electronic image as directed by your instructor—two pages result. On the ribbon, click **Close Print Preview**, and then **Close** your **1C Administrators** table.

i. With your **1C Departments** table displayed, view the table in **Print Preview**. Change the orientation to **Landscape**, and then create a paper printout or PDF electronic image as directed by your instructor—one page results. Click **Close Print Preview**, and then **Close** your **1C Departments** table.

3 On the ribbon, click the **Create tab**, and then in the **Queries group**, click **Query Wizard**. In the **New Query** dialog box, be sure **Simple Query Wizard** is selected, and then click **OK**. In the wizard, click the **Tables/Queries arrow**, and then click your **Table: 1C Administrators**.

a. Under **Available Fields**, click **Last Name**, and then click **Add Field** to move the field to the **Selected Fields** list on the right. Double-click the **First Name** field to move it to the **Selected Fields** list. By using **Add Field** or by double-clicking the field name, add

(Project 1C College Administrators continues on the next page)

the following fields to the **Selected Fields** list in the order specified: **Title**, **Department ID**, and **Phone Number**. This query will answer the question, *What is the last name, first name, title, Department ID, and phone number of every administrator?*

b. In the wizard, click **Next**. Click in the **What title do you want for your query?** box. Using your own name, edit as necessary so that the query name is **Lastname Firstname 1C All Administrators Query** and then click **Finish**. If necessary, apply Best Fit to the columns, and then Save the query. Display the query in **Print Preview**, and then create a paper printout or PDF electronic image as directed—one page results. Click **Close Print Preview**, and then **Close** the query.

c. **Open** the **Navigation Pane**, right-click your **1C Administrators** table, and then click **Open** to display the table in the object window. **Close** the **Navigation Pane**. Notice that the table has 11 fields. On the ribbon, click the **Create tab**, and in the **Forms group**, click **Form**. On the Quick Access Toolbar, click **Save**. In the **Save As** dialog box, click in the **Form Name** box, edit to name the form **Lastname Firstname 1C Administrator Form** and then click **OK**.

d. In the navigation area, click **Last Record**, and then click **Previous Record** two times to display the record for *Diann Holtz*. By using the instructions in Activity 1.15, print or create a PDF electronic image of only this record on one page. **Close** the form object, saving it if prompted. Your **1C Administrators** table object remains open.

e. **Open** the **Navigation Pane**, open your **1C Departments** table by double-clicking the table name or by right-clicking the table name and clicking Open. **Close** the **Navigation Pane**. On the **Create tab**, in the **Reports group**, click **Report**.

f. Click the **Department ID** field name, and then on the ribbon, under **Report Layout Tools**, click the **Arrange tab**. In the **Rows & Columns group**, click **Select Column**, and then press [Del]. Using the same technique, delete the **Department Email** field.

g. Click the **Department Phone** field name. Hold down [Shift], and then click the **Suite Number** field name to select the last three field names. In the **Rows & Columns group**, click **Select Column**. On the ribbon, click the **Design tab**, and then in the **Tools group**, click **Property Sheet**. In the **Property Sheet**, on the **Format tab**, click **Width**, type **1.5** and then press [Enter]. **Close** the **Property Sheet**.

h. Click the **Department Name** field name. On the ribbon, click the **Home tab.** In the **Sort & Filter group**, click **Ascending** to sort the report in alphabetic order by *Department Name*. At the bottom of the report, on the right side, click **Page 1 of 1**, and then press [Del].

i. **Save** the report as **Lastname Firstname 1C Departments Report** and then click **OK**. Display the report in **Print Preview**, and then create a paper printout or PDF electronic image of the report as directed. Click **Close Print Preview**. In the object window, right-click any **object tab**, and then click **Close All** to close all open objects, leaving the object window empty.

4 **Open** the **Navigation Pane**. If necessary, increase the width of the Navigation Pane so that all object names display fully. On the right side of the title bar, click **Close** to close the database and to close Access. As directed by your instructor, submit your database and the paper printouts or PDF electronic images of the five objects— two tables, one query, one form, and one report—that are the results of this project. Specifically, in this project, using your own name, you created the following database and printouts or PDF electronic images:

1. Lastname_Firstname_1C_College_Administrators	Database file
2. Lastname Firstname 1C Administrators	Table
3. Lastname Firstname 1C Departments	Table
4. Lastname Firstname 1C All Administrators Query	Query
5. Lastname Firstname 1C Administrator Form	Form
6. Lastname Firstname 1C Departments Report	Report

END | You have completed Project 1C

Skills Review   Project 1D Certification Events

Apply 1B skills from these Objectives:

6 Use a Template to Create a Database

7 Organize Objects in the Navigation Pane

8 Create a New Table in a Database Created with a Template

9 Print a Report and a Table

In the following Skills Review, you will create a database to store information about certification test preparation events at Texas Lakes Community College. Your completed report and table will look similar to Figure 1.52.

PROJECT FILES

For Project 1D, you will need the following files:

Desktop event management template
a01D_Certification_Events (Excel workbook)

You will save your database as:

Lastname_Firstname_1D_Certification_Events

PROJECT RESULTS

Build From Scratch

Lastname Firstname 1D All Events

Tuesday, July 28, 2015   11:49:58 AM

Title	Start Time	End Time	Location
Word 2016	7/9/2021 10:00:00 AM	7/9/2021 4:00:00 PM	Southwest Campus
Office 2016			
Excel 2016	7/16/2021 10:00:00 AM	7/16/2021 4:00:00 PM	Northeast Campus
Office 2016			
Access 2016	7/23/2021 12:00:00 PM	7/23/2021 6:00:00 PM	Southeast Campus
Office 2016			
PowerPoint 2016	7/30/2021 9:00:00 AM	7/30/2016 3:00:00 PM	Northwest Campus
Office 2016			
Word 2016	8/5/2021 10:00:00 AM	8/5/2021 4:00:00 PM	Southeast Campus
Office 2016			
Windows Server	8/6/2021 8:00:00 AM	8/6/2021 2:00:00 PM	Northeast Campus
Networking			
Excel 2016	8/12/2021 3:00:00 PM	8/12/2021 9:00:00 PM	Southeast Campus
Office 2016			
Windows 10	8/13/2021 10:00:00 AM	8/13/2021 4:00:00 PM	Southwest Campus
Networking			
Access 2016	8/19/2021 9:00:00 AM	8/19/2021 3:00:00 PM	Northeast Campus
Office 2016			
A+	8/19/2021 12:00:00 PM	8/19/2021 6:00:00 PM	Southwest Campus
Networking			
PowerPoint 2016	8/26/2021 1:00:00 PM	8/26/2021 7:00:00 PM	Northwest Campus
Office 2016			
Network+	8/26/2021 9:00:00 AM	8/26/2021 3:00:00 PM	Northwest Campus
Networking			

Page 1 of 1

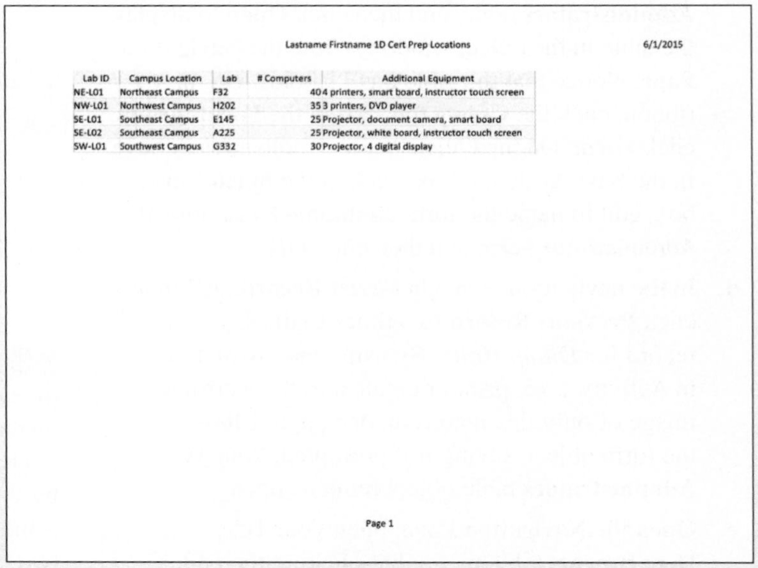

Lastname Firstname 1D Cert Prep Locations

6/1/2015

Lab ID	Campus Location	Lab	# Computers	Additional Equipment
NE-L01	Northeast Campus	F32	40	4 printers, smart board, instructor touch screen
NW-L01	Northwest Campus	H202	35	3 printers, DVD player
SE-L01	Southeast Campus	E145	25	Projector, document camera, smart board
SE-L02	Southeast Campus	A225	25	Projector, white board, instructor touch screen
SW-L01	Southwest Campus	G332	30	Projector, 4 digital display

Page 1

FIGURE 1.52

Access 2016, Windows 10, Microsoft Corporation

(Project 1D Certification Events continues on the next page)

Skills Review | Project 1D Certification Events (continued)

1 Start Access. In the Access opening screen, click in the **Search** box, type **event** and then press Enter to search for a template to manage events. Click the **Desktop event management** template. In the **Desktop event management** dialog box, to the right of the **File Name** box, click **Browse**, and then navigate to your **Access Chapter 1** folder. In the **File New Database** dialog box, click in the **File name** box to select the existing text. Using your own name, type **Lastname_Firstname_1D_ Certification_Events** and then press Enter. In the **Desktop event management** dialog box, click **Create** to download the template and to save the database. Under the ribbon, on the **Message Bar**, click **Enable Content**.

a. In the first row, click in the **Title** field, type **Word 2016** and then press Tab. In the **Start Time** field, type **7/9/21 10a** and then press Tab. In the **End Time** field, type **7/9/21 4p** and then press Tab. In the **Description** field, type **Office 2016** and then press Tab. In the **Location** field, type **Southwest Campus** and then press Tab three times to move to the **Title** field in the new record row.

b. In the form, directly above the field names row, click **New Event** to open the **Event Details** single-record form. Using Tab to move from field to field, enter the record shown in Table 1. Press Tab three times to move from the **End Time** field to the **Description** field.

c. In the **Events Detail** form, click **Close**. Using either the **Event List** multiple-items form or the **Event Details** single-record form, enter the records shown in Table 2. If you use the Events Detail form, be sure to Close it after entering records to display the records in the Event List form.

d. **Close** the **Event List** form. On the ribbon, click the **External Data tab**, and in the **Import & Link group**, click **Excel**. In the **Get External Data – Excel Spreadsheet** dialog box, click **Browse**. Navigate to your student data files, and then double-click **a01D_Certification_Events**. Click the second option button—**Append a copy of the records to the table**—and then click **OK**.

e. In the **Import Spreadsheet Wizard**, click **Next**, and then click **Finish**. In the **Get External Data – Excel Spreadsheet** dialog box, click **Close**. **Open** the **Navigation Pane**, and then double-click **Event List** to open the form that displays data stored in the Events table—12 total records display. **Close** the **Navigation Pane**.

f. To the left of the **ID** field name, click **Select All**. In the field names row, point to the right edge of any of the selected columns to display the ⊞ pointer, and then double-click to apply Best Fit to all of the columns. Click in any field to cancel the selection, and then **Save** the form.

2 **Open** the **Navigation Pane**. At the top of the Navigation Pane, click **More**. On the list, under **Navigate To Category**, click **Tables and Related Views**.

a. In the **Navigation Pane**, point to **Events: Table**, right-click, and then click **Open** to display the records in the underlying table. In the **Navigation Pane**, double-click the **Current Events** *report* (green icon) to view this predesigned report. From the **Navigation Pane**, open the **Events by Week** report to view this predesigned report.

TABLE 1

Title	Location	Start Time	End Time	Description	
Excel 2016	**Northeast Campus**	**7/16/21 10a**	**7/16/21 4p**	**Office 2016**	- ➤ (Return to Step 1c)

TABLE 2

ID	Title	Start Time	End Time	Description	Location	
3	**Access 2016**	**7/23/21 12p**	**7/23/21 6p**	**Office 2016**	**Southeast Campus**	
4	**PowerPoint 2016**	**7/30/21 9a**	**7/30/21 3p**	**Office 2016**	**Northwest Campus**	- ➤ (Return to Step 1d)

(Project 1D Certification Events continues on the next page)

b. In the object window, right-click any of the **object tabs**, and then click **Close All**. **Close** the **Navigation Pane**.

3 On the ribbon, click the **Create tab**, and in the **Tables group**, click **Table**.

a. In the field names row, click **Click to Add**, click **Short Text**, type **Campus Location** and then press Enter. In the third column, click **Short Text**, type **Lab** and then press Enter. In the fourth column, click **Number**, type **# Computers** and then press Enter. In the fifth column, click **Short Text**, type **Additional Equipment** and then press ↓.

b. Right-click the **ID** field name, and then click **Rename Field**. Type **Lab ID** and then press Enter. On the **Fields tab**, in the **Formatting group**, click the **Data Type arrow**, and then click **Short Text**.

c. In the new record row, click in the **Lab ID** field, and then enter the records shown in Table 3, pressing Enter or Tab to move from one field to the next.

d. In the **Views group**, click the upper portion of the **View** button to switch to **Design** view. In the **Save As** dialog box, in the **Table Name** box, using your own name, type **Lastname Firstname 1D Cert Prep Locations** and then click **OK**. Notice that the **Lab ID** field is the **Primary Key**. On the **Design tab**, in the **Views group**, click the upper portion of the **View** button to switch to **Datasheet** view.

e. To the left of the **Lab ID** field name, click **Select All** to select all of the columns and rows in the table. On the **Home tab**, in the **Records group**, click **More**, and then click **Field Width**. In the **Column Width** dialog box, click **Best Fit**. Click

in any field to cancel the selection, and then **Save** the changes to the table. **Close** the table, and then **Open** the **Navigation Pane**. Increase the width of the **Navigation Pane** so that your entire table name displays.

4 In the **Navigation Pane**, double-click the **All Events** report to open it in the object window. **Close** the **Navigation Pane**. On the **Home tab**, in the **Views group**, click the top of the **View** button to switch to **Layout** view. At the top of the report, click the title—*All Events*—to display a colored border around the title. Click to the left of the letter *A* to place the insertion point there. Using your own name, type **Lastname Firstname 1D** and then press Spacebar. Press Enter, and then **Save** the report.

a. On the right side of the status bar, click **Print Preview**, and notice that the report will print on one page. Create a paper printout or PDF electronic image as instructed. Click **Close Print Preview**, and then **Close** the report.

b. **Open** the **Navigation Pane**, double-click your **1D Cert Prep Locations** table, and then **Close** the **Navigation Pane**. On the ribbon, click the **File tab**, click **Print**, and then click **Print Preview**. On the **Print Preview tab**, in the **Page Layout group**, click **Landscape**. Create a paper printout or PDF electronic image as directed, and then click **Close Print Preview**. Close your **1D Cert Prep Locations** table.

c. **Open** the **Navigation Pane**. On the right side of the title bar, click **Close** to close the database and to close Access. As directed by your instructor,

TABLE 3

Lab ID	Campus Location	Lab	# Computers	Additional Equipment
NW-L01	Northwest Campus	H202	35	3 printers, DVD player
SE-L01	Southeast Campus	E145	25	Projector, document camera, smart board
NE-L01	Northeast Campus	F32	40	4 printers, smart board, instructor touch screen
SW-L01	Southwest Campus	G332	30	Projector, 4 digital display
SE-L02	Southeast Campus	A225	25	Projector, white board, instructor touch screen

(Return to Step 3d)

(Project 1D Certification Events continues on the next page)

Skills Review **Project 1D Certification Events** (continued)

submit your database and the paper printouts or PDF electronic images of the two objects—one report and one table—that are the results of this project.

Specifically, in this project, using your own name, you created the following database and printouts or PDF electronic images:

1. Lastname_Firstname_1D_Certification_Events	Database file
2. Lastname Firstname 1D Cert Prep Locations	Table
3. Lastname Firstname 1D All Events	Report

END | You have completed Project 1D

Mastering Access   Project 1E Kiosk Inventory

In the following Mastering Access project, you will create a database to track information about the inventory of items for sale in the kiosk located in the Snack Bar at the Southeast Campus of Texas Lakes Community College. Your completed database objects will look similar to Figure 1.53.

PROJECT FILES

For Project 1E, you will need the following files:

Blank desktop database
a01E_Inventory (Excel workbook)
a01E_Inventory_Storage (Excel workbook)

You will save your database as:

Lastname_Firstname_1E_Kiosk_Inventory

PROJECT RESULTS

Build From Scratch

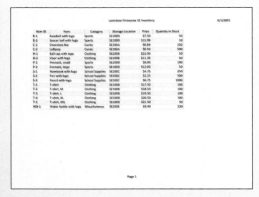

Access 2016, Windows 10, Microsoft Corporation

FIGURE 1.53

(Project 1E Kiosk Inventory continues on the next page)

Mastering Access Project 1E Kiosk Inventory (continued)

1 Start Access. Create a **Blank desktop database** in your **Access Chapter 1** folder. Name the database **Lastname_Firstname_1E_Kiosk_Inventory** and then **Close** the **Navigation Pane**. Create the fields shown in **Table 1**.

2 For the **ID** field, change the **Data Type** to **Short Text**, rename the field to **Item ID** and then enter the records shown in **Table 2**.

3 **Save** the table as **Lastname Firstname 1E Inventory** and then **Close** the table. From your student data files, import and then **Append** the data in the Excel file **a01E_Inventory** to your **1E Inventory** table. After importing, open your **1E Inventory** table—17 records display.

4 In **Design** view, delete the **Campus** field, which is redundant data. For the **Category** field, change the **Field Size** to **25** and enter a **Description** of **Enter the category of the item** For the **Item ID** field, change the **Field Size** to **10** and then **Save** the changes to your table. Switch to **Datasheet** view, apply **Best Fit** to all of the fields in the table, and then **Save** your changes. Display the table in **Print Preview**, change the orientation to **Landscape**, and then create a paper printout or PDF electronic image as directed by your instructor. **Close Print Preview**, and then **Close** the table.

5 From your student data files, import the **Excel** file **a01E_Inventory_Storage** into the database as a new table; designate the first row as column headings and the **Category** field as the primary key. In the wizard, name the table **Lastname Firstname 1E Inventory Storage** and then open your **1E Inventory Storage** table—five records display. In **Design** view, for the **Location Detail** field,

change the **Field Size** to **35** and enter a **Description** of **Room and bin number or alternate location of inventory item Save** the design changes, switch to **Datasheet** view, apply **Best Fit** to all of the fields, and then **Save** your changes. Display the table in **Print Preview**, create a paper printout or PDF electronic image as directed, **Close Print Preview**, and then **Close** the table.

6 Create a **Simple Query**, by using the **Query Wizard**, based on your **1E Inventory** table. Include only the three fields that will answer the question, *For all items, what is the storage location and quantity in stock?* In the wizard, accept the default name for the query. Display the query in **Print Preview**, create a paper printout or PDF electronic image as directed, **Close Print Preview**, and then **Close** the query.

7 Open your **1E Inventory** table, and then **Create** a **Form** for this table. **Save** the form as **Lastname Firstname 1E Inventory Form** and then display and select the fifth record. By using the instructions in Activity 1.15, create a paper printout or PDF electronic image of only this record on one page as directed by your instructor. **Close** the form object, saving changes if prompted.

8 With your **1E Inventory** table open, **Create** a **Report**. Delete the **Category** and **Price** fields, and then sort the **Item ID** field in **Ascending** order. Using the **Property Sheet**, for the **Item ID** field, change the **Width** to **0.75** and then for the **Storage Location** field, change the **Width** to **1.5** Scroll to display the bottom of the report, if necessary, and then delete the page number— **Page 1 of 1**. **Save** the report as **Lastname Firstname 1E**

TABLE 1

Data Type		Short Text	Short Text	Short Text	Short Text	Currency	Number
Field Name	ID	**Item**	**Category**	**Campus**	**Storage Location**	**Price**	**Quantity in Stock**

(Return to Step 2)

TABLE 2

Item ID	Item	Category	Campus	Storage Location	Price	Quantity in Stock
C-1	**Chocolate Bar**	**Candy**	**Southeast**	**SE100A**	**.89**	**250**
C-2	**Lollipop**	**Candy**	**Southeast**	**SE100A**	**.5**	**500**
T-1	**T-shirt**	**Clothing**	**Southeast**	**SE100B**	**17.5**	**100**

(Return to Step 3)

(Project 1E Kiosk Inventory continues on the next page)

Mastering Access Project 1E Kiosk Inventory (continued)

Inventory Report and then display the report in **Print Preview**. Create a paper printout or PDF electronic image as directed. Click **Close Print Preview**.

9 **Close All** open objects. **Open** the **Navigation Pane** and be sure that all object names display fully. **Close** the database, and then **Close** Access. As directed by your instructor, submit your database and the paper printouts or PDF electronic images of the five objects—two tables, one query, one form, and one report—that are the results of this project. Specifically, in this project, using your own name, you created the following database and printouts or PDF electronic images:

1. Lastname_Firstname_1E_Kiosk_Inventory	Database file
2. Lastname Firstname 1E Inventory	Table
3. Lastname Firstname 1E Inventory Storage	Table
4. Lastname Firstname 1E Inventory Query	Query
5. Lastname Firstname 1E Inventory Form	Form
6. Lastname Firstname 1E Inventory Report	Report

END | You have completed Project 1E

Project 1F Recruiting Events

In the following Mastering Access project, you will create a database to store information about the recruiting events that are scheduled to attract new students to Texas Lakes Community College. Your completed report and tables will look similar to Figure 1.54.

Apply **1B** skills from these Objectives:

6 Use a Template to Create a Database

7 Organize Objects in the Navigation Pane

8 Create a New Table in a Database Created with a Template

9 Print a Report and a Table

PROJECT FILES

For Project 1F, you will need the following files:

Desktop event management template
a01F_Recruiting_Events (Excel workbook)

You will save your database as:

Lastname_Firstname_1F_Recruiting_Events

PROJECT RESULTS

Build From
Scratch

Access 2016, Windows 10, Microsoft Corporation

FIGURE 1.54

(Project 1F Recruiting Events continues on the next page)

Mastering Access Project 1F Recruiting Events (continued)

1 Start Access. In the Access opening screen, search for **event** and then click the **Desktop event management** template. Save the database in your **Access Chapter 1** folder as **Lastname_Firstname_1F_Recruiting_Events** and on the **Message Bar**, click **Enable Content**.

2 In the **Event List** multiple-items form or the **Event Details** single-record form—open by clicking New Event on the Event List form—enter the records shown in Table 1.

3 Close the **Event List** form. From your student data files, import and **Append** the data from the **Excel** file **a01F_Recruiting_Events** to the **Events** table. **Open** the **Navigation Pane**, organize the objects by **Tables and Related Views**, and then open the **Events** table to display 13 records. **Close** the table, and then **Close** the **Navigation Pane**.

4 **Create** a new **Table** defining the new fields shown in Table 2.

5 For the **ID** field, change the **Data Type** to **Short Text**, rename the field to **Recruiter ID** and then enter the records shown in Table 3.

6 Apply **Best Fit** to all of the columns. **Save** the table as **Lastname Firstname 1F Recruiters** and then **Close** the table.

7 From the **Navigation Pane**, open the **Event Details** *report* (green icon). Switch to **Layout** view. In the report, click in the title—*Event Details*—and then click to position the insertion point to the left of the word *Event*. Using your own type, type **Lastname Firstname 1F** and then press Spacebar and Enter. If necessary, decrease the font size of the title so that the title does not overlap the date on the right side or does not extend to two lines.

TABLE 1

ID	Title	Start Time	End Time	Description	Location
1	**Health Professions**	**6/1/21 8a**	**6/1/21 12p**	**Science Students**	**Hill Country High School**
2	**New Students**	**6/1/21 10a**	**6/1/21 3p**	**College Fair**	**Brazos Convention Center**
3	**Information Technology**	**6/2/21 9a**	**6/2/21 12p**	**Technical Students**	**Round Rock Technical Center**
4	**International Students**	**6/2/21 2p**	**6/2/21 5p**	**Open House**	**Southeast Campus**

(Return to Step 3)

TABLE 2

Data Type		Short Text	Short Text	Short Text	Short Text	Short Text
Field Name	ID	**Location**	**Last Name**	**First Name**	**Email Address**	**Business Phone**

(Return to Step 5)

TABLE 3

Recruiter ID	Location	Last Name	First Name	Email Address	Business Phone
R-01	**Hill Country High School**	**Rostamo**	**Robyn**	**rrostamo@hillcohs.sch**	**(512) 555-3410**
R-02	**Brazos Convention Center**	**Hart**	**Roberto**	**rlhart@brazosconv.ctr**	**(512) 555-1938**
R-03	**Round Rock Technical Center**	**Sedlacek**	**Belinda**	**bsedlacek@rrocktech.sch**	**(512) 555-0471**
R-04	**Southeast Campus**	**Nguyen**	**Thao**	**tnguyen@tlcc.edu**	**(512) 555-2387**

(Return to Step 6)

(Project 1F Recruiting Events continues on the next page)

Mastering Access Project 1F Recruiting Events (continued)

Save the report, and then display it in **Print Preview**. If directed to create a paper printout, in the **Print group**, click **Print**. In the **Print** dialog box, under **Print Range**, to the right of **Pages**, click in the **From** box, type **1** and then click in the **To** box and type **1** and then click **OK** to print only the first page. If directed to create a PDF electronic image, in the **Publish as PDF or XPS** dialog box, click **Options**, and then under **Range**, click the **Page(s)** option button, and then click **OK**. **Close Print Preview**, and then **Close** the report.

8 From the **Navigation Pane**, open the **Events** table, select all of the columns, and then apply **Best Fit** to all of the columns by double-clicking the right edge of any of the selected columns. Cancel the selection, and then **Save** the table. Display the table in **Print Preview**, change the orientation to **Landscape**, change the **Margins** to **Normal**,

and then create a paper printout or PDF electronic image as directed. **Close Print Preview**, and then **Close** the table.

9 From the **Navigation Pane**, open your **1F Recruiters** table. Display the table in **Print Preview**, change the orientation to **Landscape**, and then create a paper printout or PDF electronic image as directed. **Close Print Preview**, and then **Close** the table.

10 Open the **Navigation Pane**, and be sure that all object names display fully. **Close** Access. As directed by your instructor, submit your database and the paper printouts or PDF electronic images of the three objects—one report and two tables—that are the results of this project. Specifically, in this project, using your own name, you created the following database and printouts or PDF electronic images:

1. Lastname_Firstname_1F_Recruiting_Events	Database file
2. Lastname Firstname 1F Event Details	Report
3. Lastname Firstname 1F Events	Table
4. Lastname Firstname 1F Recruiters	Table

END | You have completed Project 1F

Mastering Access Project 1G College Construction

In the following Mastering Access project, you will create one database to store information about construction projects for Texas Lakes Community College and a second database to store information about the public events related to the construction projects. Your completed database objects will look similar to Figure 1.55.

Apply 1A and 1B skills from these Objectives:

1 Identify Good Database Design
2 Create a Table and Define Fields in a Blank Desktop Database
3 Change the Structure of Tables and Add a Second Table
4 Create a Query, Form, and Report
5 Close a Database and Close Access
6 Use a Template to Create a Database
7 Organize Objects in the Navigation Pane
8 Create a New Table in a Database Created with a Template
9 Print a Report and a Table

> **NOTE** Project 1G Differs from the MyITLab Project
>
> If you are completing this project in the MYITLab Grader system, your results will differ from the following project. In Grader, the steps are all completed in one database instead of two in the project below.

PROJECT FILES

For Project 1G, you will need the following files:

Blank desktop database
a01G_Projects (Excel workbook)
a01G_Contractors (Excel workbook)
Desktop event management template

You will save your databases as:

Lastname_Firstname_1G_College_Construction
Lastname_Firstname_1G_Public_Events

PROJECT RESULTS

Build From Scratch

FIGURE 1.55

(Project 1G College Construction continues on the next page)

Access 2016, Windows 10, Microsoft Corporation

1 Start Access. Create a **Blank desktop database** in your **Access Chapter 1** folder. Name the database **Lastname_Firstname_1G_College_Construction** and then **Close** the **Navigation Pane**. Create the fields shown in **Table 1**.

2 For the **ID** field, change the **Data Type** to **Short Text**, rename the field to **Project ID** and then enter the three records shown in **Table 2**.

3 Save the table as **Lastname Firstname 1G Projects** and then **Close** the table. From your student data files, import and then **Append** the data in the **Excel** file **a01G_Projects** to your **1G Projects** table. After importing, open your **1G Projects** table—eight records display.

4 In **Design** view, for the **Project ID** field, change the **Field Size** to **5** and then enter a **Description** of **Enter the Project ID using the format P-###** Save the changes to your table. Switch to **Datasheet** view, apply **Best Fit** to all of the fields in the table, and then **Save** your changes. Display the table in **Print Preview**, change the orientation to **Landscape**, and then create a paper printout or PDF electronic image as directed by your instructor. **Close Print Preview**, and then **Close** the table.

5 From your student data files, import the **Excel** file **a01G_Contractors** into the database as a new table; designate the first row as column headings and the **ID** field as the primary key. In the wizard, name the table **Lastname Firstname 1G Contractors** and then open

your **1G Contractors** table—four records display. Apply **Best Fit** to all of the fields, and then **Save** your changes. Display the table in **Print Preview**, change the orientation to **Landscape**, and then create a paper printout or PDF electronic image as directed. **Close Print Preview**, and then **Close** the table.

6 Create, by using the **Query Wizard**, a **Simple Query** based on your **1G Projects** table. Include only the three fields that will answer the question, *For every site, what is the building project and the budget amount?* In the wizard, accept the default name for the query. Display the query in **Print Preview**, create a paper printout or PDF electronic image as directed, **Close Print Preview**, and then **Close** the query.

7 Open your **1G Projects** table, and then **Create** a **Form** for this table. **Save** the form as **Lastname Firstname 1G Project Form** and then display and select the seventh record. By using the instructions in Activity 1.15, create a paper printout or PDF electronic image of only this record on one page as directed by your instructor. **Close** the form object, saving changes if prompted.

8 With your **1G Projects** table open, **Create** a **Report**. Delete the **Budget Amount** field, and then sort the **Building Project** field in **Ascending** order. For the **Building Project**, **Site**, and **Contractor** fields, using the **Property Sheet**, change the **Width** of all three fields to **2** At the bottom of the report, delete the page

TABLE 1

Data Type		Short Text	Short Text	Short Text	Currency
Field Name	ID	**Building Project**	**Site**	**Contractor**	**Budget Amount**

(Return to Step 2)

TABLE 2

Project ID	Building Project	Site	Contractor	Budget Amount
P-356	**Student Center, 3-story**	**Northeast Campus**	**RR Construction**	**61450000**
P-823	**Student Center, 2-story**	**Southeast Campus**	**RR Construction**	**41960000**
P-157	**Health Professions Center**	**Northwest Campus**	**Marshall Ellis Construction**	**42630000**

(Return to Step 3)

(Project 1G College Construction continues on the next page)

number—**Page 1 of 1**. **Save** the report as **Lastname Firstname 1G Projects Report** and then display the report in **Print Preview**. Create a printout or PDF electronic image as directed. **Close Print Preview.**

9 **Close All** open objects. **Open** the **Navigation Pane**, arrange the objects by **Tables and Related Views**, and be sure that all object names display fully. **Close** the database, but do *not* close Access.

10 In the Access opening screen, search for **event** and then click the **Desktop Event management** template. Save the database in your **Access Chapter 1** folder as **Lastname_Firstname_1G_Public_Events** and on the **Message Bar**, click **Enable Content**.

11 In the **Event List** multiple-items form or the **Event Details** single-record form—open by clicking New Event on the Event List form—enter the three records shown in **Table 3**.

12 **Close** the **Event List** form. **Open** the **Navigation Pane**, organize the objects by **Tables and Related Views**,

and then open the **Current Events** *report* (green icon). Switch to **Layout** view. In the report, click in the title—*Current Events*—and then click to position the insertion point to the left of the letter *C*. Using your own name, type **Lastname Firstname 1G** and then press Spacebar and Enter. If necessary, decrease the font size of the title so that the title does not overlap the date on the right side or does not extend to two lines. **Save** the report, display it in **Print Preview**, and then create a paper printout or PDF electronic image as directed. **Close Print Preview**, and then **Close** the report.

13 Open the **Navigation Pane**, and be sure that all object names display fully. **Close** Access. As directed by your instructor, submit your database and the paper printouts or PDF electronic images of the six objects— two tables, one query, one form and two reports—that are the results of this project. Specifically, in this project, using your own name, you created the following database and printouts or PDF electronic images:

1. Lastname_Firstname_1G_College_Construction	Database file
2. Lastname_Firstname_1G_Public_Events	Database file
3. Lastname Firstname 1G Projects	Table
4. Lastname Firstname 1G Contractors	Table
5. Lastname Firstname 1G Projects Query	Query
6. Lastname Firstname 1G Project Form	Form
7. Lastname Firstname 1G Projects Report	Report
8. Lastname Firstname 1G Current Events	Report

TABLE 3

ID	Title	Start Time	End Time	Description	Location
1	Groundbreaking	6/13/21 10a	6/13/21 11a	Student Center groundbreaking	Northeast Campus
2	Dedication	8/26/21 12:30 p	8/26/21 2p	Gymnasium building dedication	Southwest Campus
3	Community Arts Expo	10/5/21 6p	10/5/21 9p	Book and Art Expo at Library	Southeast Campus

(Return to Step 12)

END | You have completed Project 1G

GO! Fix It	**Project 1H Scholarships**	**MyITLab**
GO! Make It	**Project 1I Theater Events**	**MyITLab**
GO! Solve It	**Project 1J Athletic Scholarships**	**MyITLab**
GO! Solve It	**Project 1K Student Activities**	

Apply a combination of the 1A and 1B skills.

 PROJECT FILES

Build From Scratch

For Project 1K, you will need the following files:

Desktop event management template
a01K_Student_Activities (Word document)

You will save your database as:

Lastname_Firstname_1K_Student_Activities

Use the Desktop event management template to create a database, and save it in your Access Chapter 1 folder as **Lastname_Firstname_1K_Student_Activities** From your student data files, use the information in the Word document a01K_Student_Activities to enter data into the Event List multiple-items form. Each event begins at 7 p.m. and ends at 10 p.m.

After entering the records, close the form, and arrange the Navigation Pane by Tables and Related Views. Open the Event Details *report*, and then add **Lastname Firstname 1K** to the beginning of the report title. If necessary, decrease the font size of the title so that it does not overlap the date and displays on one line. Create a paper printout or PDF electronic image as directed. As directed, submit your database and the paper printout or PDF electronic image that results.

Performance Level

		Exemplary: You consistently applied the relevant skills	Proficient: You sometimes, but not always, applied the relevant skills	Developing: You rarely or never applied the relevant skills
Performance Criteria	**Create database using Desktop event management template and enter data**	Database created using the correct template, named correctly, and all data entered correctly.	Database created using the correct template, named correctly, but not all data entered correctly.	Database created using the correct template, but numerous errors in database name and data.
	Modify report	Event Details report title includes name and project on one line.	Event Details report title includes name and project, but not on one line.	Event Details report title does not include name and project and does not display on one line.
	Create report printout	Event Details report printout is correct.	Event Details printout is incorrect.	Event Details report printout not created.

END | You have completed Project 1K

OUTCOMES-BASED ASSESSMENTS (CRITICAL THINKING)

RUBRIC

The following outcomes-based assessments are open-ended assessments. That is, there is no specific correct result; your result will depend on your approach to the information provided. Make Professional Quality your goal. Use the following scoring rubric to guide you in how to approach the problem and then to evaluate how well your approach solves the problem.

The *criteria*—Software Mastery, Content, Format & Layout, and Process—represent the knowledge and skills you have gained that you can apply to solving the problem. The *levels of performance*—Professional Quality, Approaching Professional Quality, or Needs Quality Improvements—help you and your instructor evaluate your result.

	Your completed project is of Professional Quality if you:	Your completed project is Approaching Professional Quality if you:	Your completed project Needs Quality Improvements if you:
1-Software Mastery	Choose and apply the most appropriate skills, tools, and features and identify efficient methods to solve the problem.	Choose and apply some appropriate skills, tools, and features, but not in the most efficient manner.	Choose inappropriate skills, tools, or features, or are inefficient in solving the problem.
2-Content	Construct a solution that is clear and well organized, contains content that is accurate, appropriate to the audience and purpose, and is complete. Provide a solution that contains no errors of spelling, grammar, or style.	Construct a solution in which some components are unclear, poorly organized, inconsistent, or incomplete. Misjudge the needs of the audience. Have some errors in spelling, grammar, or style, but the errors do not detract from comprehension.	Construct a solution that is unclear, incomplete, or poorly organized, contains some inaccurate or inappropriate content, and contains many errors of spelling, grammar, or style. Do not solve the problem.
3-Format and Layout	Format and arrange all elements to communicate information and ideas, clarify function, illustrate relationships, and indicate relative importance.	Apply appropriate format and layout features to some elements, but not others. Overuse features, causing minor distraction.	Apply format and layout that does not communicate information or ideas clearly. Do not use format and layout features to clarify function, illustrate relationships, or indicate relative importance. Use available features excessively, causing distraction.
4-Process	Use an organized approach that integrates planning, development, self-assessment, revision, and reflection.	Demonstrate an organized approach in some areas, but not others; or, use an insufficient process of organization throughout.	Do not use an organized approach to solve the problem.

Apply a combination of the 1A and 1B skills.

OUTCOMES-BASED ASSESSMENTS (CRITICAL THINKING)

GO! Think Project 1L Student Clubs

Build From Scratch

PROJECT FILES

For Project 1L, you will need the following files:

Blank desktop database
a01L_Clubs (Word document)
a01L_Student_Clubs (Excel workbook)
a01L_Club_Presidents (Excel workbook)

You will save your database as

Lastname_Firstname_1L_Student_Clubs

Dr. Daniel Martinez, Vice President of Student Services, needs a database that tracks information about student clubs. The database should contain two tables—one for club information and one for contact information for the club presidents.

Create a desktop database, and save the database in your Access Chapter 1 folder as **Lastname_Firstname_1L_Student_Clubs** From your student data files, use the information in the Word document a01L_Clubs to create the first table and to enter two records. Name the table appropriately to include your name and 1L, and then append the 23 records from the Excel workbook a01L_Student_Clubs to your table. For the Club ID and President ID fields, add a description and change the field size.

Create a second table in the database by importing 25 records from the Excel workbook a01L_Club_Presidents, and name the table appropriately to include your name and 1L. For the State and Postal Code fields, add a description and change the field size. Be sure that the field data types are correct—recall that numbers that are not used in calculations should have a data type of Short Text. Be sure all of the data and field names display in each table.

Create a simple query based on the Clubs table that answers the question, *What is the club name, meeting day, meeting time, campus, and Room ID for all of the clubs?* Create a form based on the Clubs table, saving it with an appropriate name that includes your name and 1L. Create a report based on the Presidents table, saving it with an appropriate name that includes your name and 1L, that displays the president's last name (in ascending order), the president's first name, and the phone number of every president. Change the width of the three fields so that there is less space between them, but being sure that each record prints on a single line.

Create paper printout or PDF electronic images of the two tables, the query, only Record 21 of the form, and the report as directed being sure that each object prints on one page. Organize the objects on the Navigation Pane by Tables and Related Views, and be sure that all object names display fully. As directed, submit your database and the paper printouts or PDF electronic images of the five objects—two tables, one query, one form, and one report—that are the results of this project.

END | You have completed Project 1L

Build From Scratch

GO! Think Project 1M Faculty Training   **MyItLab**

Build From Scratch

You and GO! Project 1N Personal Contacts   **MyItLab**

GO! Collaborative Team Project   Project 1O Bell Orchid Hotels   **MyItLab**

Sort and Query a Database

PROJECT
2A

OUTCOMES
Sort and query a database

OUTCOMES
Create complex queries

PROJECT
2A

PROJECT
2B

OBJECTIVES

1. Open and Save an Existing Database
2. Create Table Relationships
3. Sort Records in a Table
4. Create a Query in Design View
5. Create a New Query from an Existing Query
6. Sort Query Results
7. Specify Criteria in a Query

OBJECTIVES

8. Specify Numeric Criteria in a Query
9. Use Compound Criteria in a Query
10. Create a Query Based on More Than One Table
11. Use Wildcards in a Query
12. Create Calculated Fields in a Query
13. Calculate Statistics and Group Data in a Query
14. Create a Crosstab Query
15. Create a Parameter Query

Berni/Fotolia

In This Chapter GO! to Work with Access

In this chapter, you will sort Access database tables and create and modify queries. To convert data into meaningful information, you must manipulate your data in a way that you can answer questions. One question might be: *Which students have a grade point average of 3.0 or higher?* With this information, you could send information about scholarships or internships to students who meet the grade point average criteria.

The projects in this chapter relate to **Texas Lakes Community College**, which is located in the Austin, Texas, area. Its four campuses serve over 30,000 students and offer more than 140 certificate programs and degrees. The college has a highly acclaimed Distance Education program and an extensive Workforce Development program. The college makes positive contributions to the community through cultural and athletic programs and has maintained partnerships with businesses and nonprofit organizations.

Instructors and Courses Database

PROJECT 2A

MyITLab
Project 2A Training
Project 2A Grader

PROJECT ACTIVITIES

In Activities 2.01 through 2.17, you will assist Dr. Carolyn Judkins, Dean of the Business Division at the Northeast Campus of Texas Lakes Community College, in locating information about instructors and courses in the Division. Your completed database objects will look similar to Figure 2.1.

Please always review the downloaded Grader instructions before beginning.

PROJECT FILES

If your instructor wants you to submit Project 2A in the MyITLab Grader system, log in to MyITLab, locate Grader Project 2A, and then download the files for this project.

For Project 2A, you will need the following file:
a02A_Instructors_Courses

You will save your database as:
Lastname_Firstname_2A_Instructors_Courses

PROJECT RESULTS

GO!
Walk Thru
Project 2A

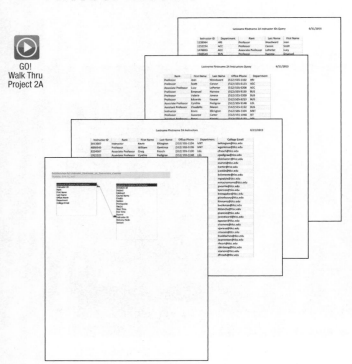

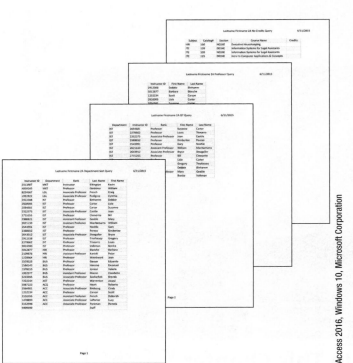

Access 2016, Windows 10, Microsoft Corporation

FIGURE 2.1 Project 2A Instructors and Courses

PROJECT RESULTS

In this project, using your own name, you will create the following database and objects. Your instructor may ask you to submit printouts or PDF electronic images:

Lastname_Firstname_2A_Instructors_Courses	Database file
Relationships for Lastname_Firstname_2A_Instructors_Courses	Relationships Report
Lastname Firstname 2A Instructors table sorted (not saved)	Table sorted (Page 1)
Lastname Firstname 2A Instructors Query	Query
Lastname Firstname 2A Instructor IDs Query	Query
Lastname Firstname 2A Department Sort Query	Query
Lastname Firstname 2A IST Query	Query
Lastname Firstname 2A Professor Query	Query
Lastname Firstname 2A No Credits Query	Query

Objective 1 | Open and Save an Existing Database

GO! Learn How
Video A2-1

There will be instances where you need to work with a database and still keep the original, unaltered version of the database. Like the other Microsoft Office 2016 applications, you can open a database file and save it with another name.

Activity 2.01 | Opening and Saving an Existing Database

ALERT!

To submit as an autograded project, log into MyITLab and download the files for this project, and begin with those files instead of the 02A_Instructors_ Courses file from your student data files. For Project 2A using Grader, read Activity 2.01 carefully. Begin working with the database in Activity 2.02. For Grader to award points accurately, when saving an object, do not include your Lastname Firstname at the beginning of the object name.

1 Start Access. In the Access opening screen, click **Open Other Files**. Under **Open**, click **Browse**. In the **Open** dialog box, navigate to the location where your student data files for this chapter are stored, and then double-click **a02A_Instructors_Courses** to open the database.

2 On the ribbon, click the **File tab**, and then click **Save As**. Under **File Types**, be sure **Save Database As** is selected. On the right, under **Database File Types**, be sure **Access Database** is selected, and then at the bottom of the screen, click **Save As**.

The Access Database file type saves your database in a format that enables the database to be opened with Access 2007, Access 2010, Access 2013, or Access 2016. If you are sharing your database with individuals who have an earlier version of Access, you can save the database in a version that will be compatible with that application, although some functionality might be lost since earlier versions of Access do not have the same features as later versions of Access. None of the features added to Access since that earlier version will be available in a database saved with backward compatibility.

3 In the **Save As** dialog box, navigate to the location where you are saving your databases. Create a **New folder** named **Access Chapter 2**, and then **Open** the folder. Click in the **File name** box to select the existing text, and using your own name, type **Lastname_Firstname_2A_Instructors_Courses** and then click **Save** or press Enter.

Use this technique when you need to keep a copy of the original database file.

4 On the **Message Bar**, notice the **SECURITY WARNING**. In the **Navigation Pane**, notice that this database contains two table objects. Compare your screen with Figure 2.2.

FIGURE 2.2

Activity 2.02 | Resolving Security Alerts and Renaming Tables

The ***Message Bar*** is the area directly below the ribbon that displays information such as security alerts when there is potentially unsafe, active content in an Office document that you open. Settings that determine the alerts that display on your Message Bar are set in the Access ***Trust Center***, an area in Access where you can view the security and privacy settings for your Access installation.

You may not be able to change the settings in the Trust Center, depending upon decisions made by your organization. To display the Trust Center, click the File tab, click Options, and then click Trust Center.

1 On the **Message Bar**, click **Enable Content**.

When working with the student data files that accompany this chapter repeat this action each time you see the security warning. Databases for this textbook are safe to use on your computer.

2 In the **Navigation Pane**, right-click the **2A Instructors** table, and then click **Rename**. With the table name selected and using your own name, type **Lastname Firstname 2A Instructors** and then press Enter to rename the table. Use the same technique to **Rename** the **2A Schedule** table to **Lastname Firstname 2A Schedule**

Including your name in the table enables you and your instructor to easily identify your work, because Access includes the table name in the header of your paper or PDF electronic image.

3 Point to the right edge of the **Navigation Pane** to display the pointer. Drag to the right to increase the width of the pane until both table names display fully.

Objective 2 Create Table Relationships

GO! Learn How
Video A2-2

Access databases are relational databases because the tables in the database can relate—actually connect—to other tables through common fields. Recall that common fields are fields in one or more tables that store the same data; for example, a Student ID number may be stored in two tables in the same database.

After you have a table for each subject in your database, you must provide a way to connect the data in the tables when you need to obtain meaningful information from the stored data. To do this, create common fields in the related tables, and then define table ***relationships***. A relationship is an association that you establish between two tables based on common fields. After the relationship is established, you can create a query, form, or report that displays information from more than one related table.

Activity 2.03 | **Selecting the Tables and Common Field to Establish the Table Relationship**

1.2.1, 1.2.4

In this Activity you will select the two tables in the database that will be used to establish the table relationship and identify the common field that is used to connect the tables.

1 In the **Navigation Pane**, double-click your **2A Instructors** table to open it in the object window. Examine the fields in the table. Double-click your **2A Schedule** table to open it, and examine the fields in the table.

In the 2A Instructors table, *Instructor ID* is the primary key field, which ensures that each instructor has only one record in the table. No two instructors have the same Instructor ID, and the table is sorted by Instructor ID.

In the 2A Schedule table, *Schedule ID* is the primary key field. Every scheduled course section during an academic term has a unique Schedule ID. The courses are sorted by Schedule ID.

2 In the **2A Schedule** table, scroll to display the **Instructor ID** field, and then compare your screen with Figure 2.3.

Both the 2A Instructors table and the 2A Schedule table include the *Instructor ID* field, which is the common field of the two tables. Because *one* instructor can teach *many* different courses, *one* Instructor ID can be present *many* times in the 2A Schedule table. When the relationship is established, it will be a **one-to-many relationship**, which is the most common type of relationship in Access.

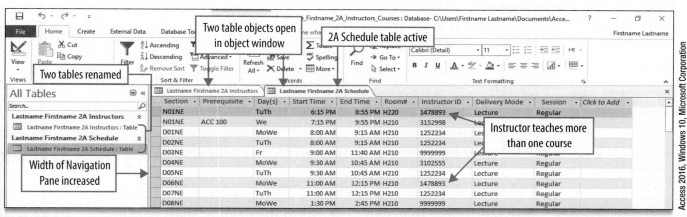

FIGURE 2.3

3 In the object window, right-click either **object tab**, and then click **Close All** to close both tables. Click the **Database Tools tab**, and then in the **Relationships group**, click **Relationships**. Compare your screen with Figure 2.4.

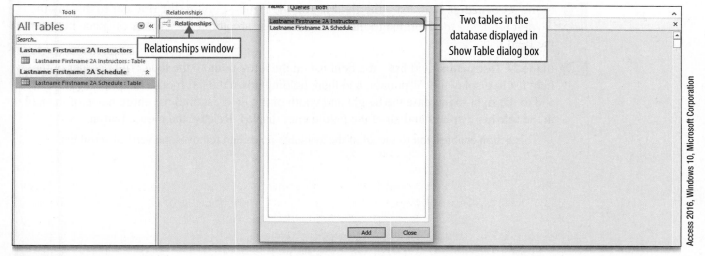

FIGURE 2.4

The Show Table dialog box displays in the Relationships window. In the Show Table dialog box, the Tables tab displays the two tables that are in this database.

4 ▸ Point to the title bar of the **Show Table** dialog box, and then, holding down the left mouse button, drag downward and slightly to the right to move the dialog box away from the top of the **Relationships** window. Release the mouse button.

Moving the Show Table dialog box enables you to see the tables as they are added to the Relationships window.

5 ▸ In the **Show Table** dialog box, if necessary, click your **2A Instructors** table, and then click **Add**. In the **Show Table** dialog box, double-click your **2A Schedule** table to add it to the **Relationships** window. In the **Show Table** dialog box, click **Close**, and then compare your screen with Figure 2.5.

You can use either technique to add a table to the Relationships window; tables are displayed in the order in which they are added. A *field list*—a list of the field names in a table—for each of the two table objects displays, and each table's primary key is identified by a key icon. Although this database has only two tables, it is not uncommon for larger databases to have many tables. Scroll bars in a field list indicate that there are fields in the table that are not currently in view.

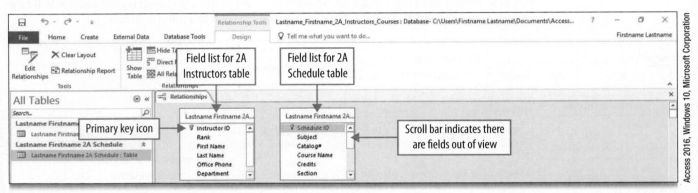

FIGURE 2.5

ALERT!   **Are there more than two field lists in the Relationships window?**

In the Show Table dialog box, if you double-click a table name more than one time, a duplicate field list displays in the Relationships window. To remove a field list from the Relationships window, right-click the title bar of the field list, and then click Hide table. Alternatively, click anywhere in the field list, and then on the Design tab, in the Relationships group, click Hide Table.

---

6 ▸ In the **2A Schedule** field list—the field list on the right—point to the title bar to display the ▧ pointer. Drag the field list to the right until there are about two inches of space between the field lists.

7 ▸ In the **2A Instructors** field list—the field list on the left—point to the lower right corner of the field list to display the ▧ pointer, and then, holding down the left mouse button, drag downward and to the right to increase the height and width of the field list until the entire name of the table in the title bar displays and all of the field names display. Release the mouse button.

This action enables you to see all of the available fields and removes the vertical scroll bar.

8 Use the same technique to resize the **2A Schedule** field list so that the table name and all of the field names display as shown in Figure 2.6.

Recall that *one* instructor can teach *many* scheduled courses. The arrangement of field lists in the Relationships window displays the *one table* on the left side and the *many table* on the right side. Recall also that the primary key in each table is the required field that contains the data that uniquely identifies each record in the table. In the 2A Instructors table, each instructor is uniquely identified by the Instructor ID. In the 2A Schedule table, each scheduled course section is uniquely identified by the Schedule ID.

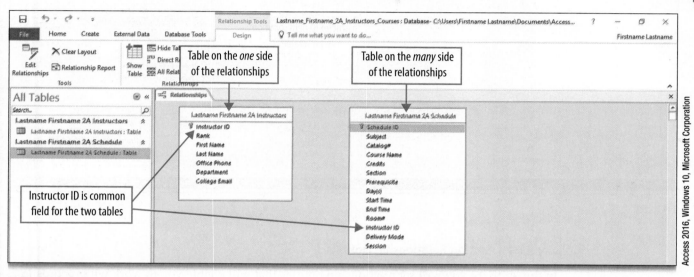

FIGURE 2.6

NOTE | **The Field That Is Highlighted Does Not Matter**

After you rearrange the field lists in the Relationships window, the highlighted field name indicates the active field list, which is the list that you moved last. This is of no consequence for this activity.

---

9 In the **2A Instructors** field list, point to **Instructor ID**, and then, holding down the left mouse button, drag the field name downward and to the right into the **2A Schedule** field list until the 🖫 pointer's arrow is on top of **Instructor ID**. Release the mouse button to display the **Edit Relationships** dialog box.

As you drag, a small graphic displays to indicate that you are dragging a field name from one field list to another. A table relationship works by matching data in two fields—the common field. In these two tables, the common field has the same name—*Instructor ID*. Common fields are not required to have the same name; however, they must have the same data type and field size.

🔄 **ANOTHER WAY** | On the Design tab, in the Tools group, click Edit Relationships. In the Edit Relationships dialog box, click Create New. In the Create New dialog box, designate the tables and fields that will create the relationship.

---

10 Point to the title bar of the **Edit Relationships** dialog box, and then, holding down the left mouse button, drag the dialog box downward and to the right below the two field lists as shown in Figure 2.7. Release the mouse button.

By dragging the common field, you create the *one-to-many* relationship. In the 2A Instructors table, Instructor ID is the primary key. In the 2A Schedule table, Instructor ID is the *foreign key* field. The foreign key is the field in the related table used to connect to the primary key in another table. The field on the *one* side of the relationship is typically the primary key.

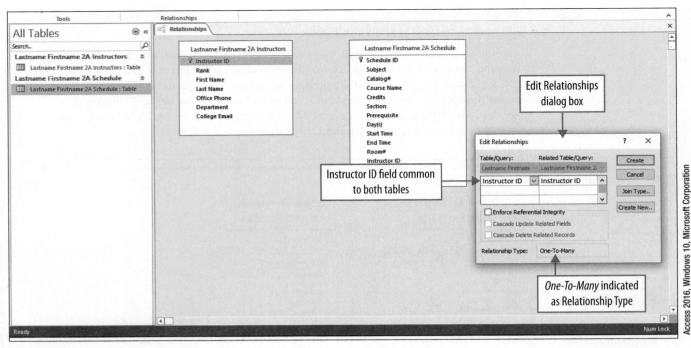

FIGURE 2.7

Activity 2.04 | Setting Relationship Options

In this Activity you will set relationship options that will enable you to work with records in the related tables.

MOS
1.2.3

1 In the **Edit Relationships** dialog box, click to select the **Enforce Referential Integrity** check box. Notice that the two options under **Enforce Referential Integrity** are now available.

Referential integrity is a set of rules that Access uses to ensure that the data between related tables is valid. Enforcing referential integrity ensures that an Instructor ID cannot be added to a course in the 2A Schedule table if the Instructor ID is *not* included in the 2A Instructors table first. Similarly, enforcing referential integrity ensures that you cannot delete an instructor from the 2A Instructors table if there is a course that has been assigned to that instructor in the 2A Schedule table.

After selecting Enforce Referential Integrity, *cascade options*—relationship options that enable you to update records in related tables when referential integrity is enforced—become available for use.

2 In the **Edit Relationships** dialog box, click to select the **Cascade Update Related Fields** check box.

The *Cascade Update Related Fields* option enables you to change the data in the primary key field for the table on the *one* side of the relationship, and updates automatically change any fields in the related table that store the same data. For example, in the 2A Instructors table, if you change the data in the Instructor ID field for one instructor, Access automatically finds every scheduled course assigned to that instructor in the 2A Schedule table and changes the data in the common field, in this case, the Instructor ID field. Without this option, if you try to change the ID number for an instructor, an error message displays if there is a related record in the related table on the *many* side of the relationship.

3 In the **Edit Relationships** dialog box, click to select the **Cascade Delete Related Records** check box, and then compare your screen with Figure 2.8

The *Cascade Delete Related Records* option enables you to delete a record in the table on the *one* side of the relationship and also delete all of the related records in related tables. For example, if an instructor retires or leaves the college and the courses that the instructor teaches must be canceled because no other instructor can be found, you can delete the instructor's record from the 2A Instructors table, and then all of the courses that are assigned to that instructor in the 2A Schedule table are also deleted. Without this option, an error message displays if you try to delete the instructor's record from the 2A Instructors table. Use caution when applying this option; in many instances, another instructor would be found so you would not want the course to be deleted. In this instance, you would need to change the Instructor ID in the related records before deleting the original instructor from the 2A Instructors table.

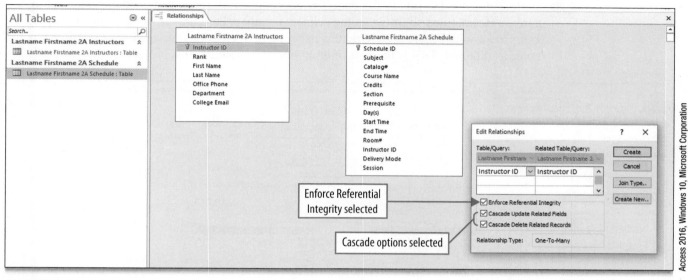

FIGURE 2.8

4 In the **Edit Relationships** dialog box, click **Create**, and then compare your screen with Figure 2.9

A *join line*—the line connecting or joining the two tables—displays between the two tables. The join line connects the primary key field—Instructor ID—in the 2A Instructors field list to the common field—Instructor ID—in the 2A Schedule field list. On the join line, *1* indicates the *one* side of the relationship, and the infinity symbol (∞) indicates the *many* side of the relationship. These symbols display when referential integrity is enforced.

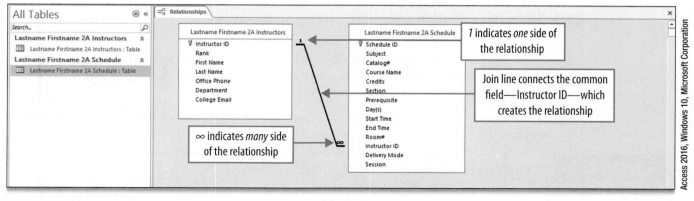

FIGURE 2.9

Activity 2.05 | Printing and Saving a Relationship Report

The Relationships window provides a map of how your database tables are related, and you can print and save this information as a report.

1▸ On the **Design tab**, in the **Tools group**, click **Relationship Report**.

The report is created and displays in the object window in Print Preview.

2▸ On the **Print Preview tab**, in the **Page Size group**, click **Margins**, and then click **Normal** to increase the margins slightly—some printers cannot print with narrow margins. Compare your screen with Figure 2.10. Create a paper or PDF electronic image of the relationship report as directed. This is the first of eight objects printed in this project.

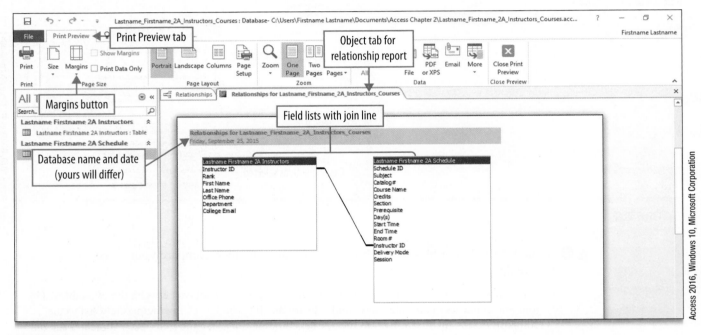

FIGURE 2.10

3▸ On the **Quick Access Toolbar**, click **Save** 🖫. In the **Save As** dialog box, click **OK** to accept the default report name.

The report name displays in the Navigation Pane under *Unrelated Objects*. Because the report is just a map of the relationship between the tables, and not a report containing records from a table, it is not associated or related with any tables.

4▸ In the object window, click **Close** ☒ to close the report, and then **Close** ☒ the **Relationships** window.

NOTE   Close Print Preview and the Relationship Report

If you click Close Print Preview when the report is displayed in Print Preview, the Relationship report will display in Design view in the object window. If this happens, you can Close the object while it is displayed in this view.

Activity 2.06 | Displaying Subdatasheet Records

When you open the table on the *one* side of the relationship, the related records from the table on the *many* side are available for you to view and to modify.

1 In the **Navigation Pane**, double-click your **2A Instructors** table to open it in the object window, and then **Close** ⟪ the **Navigation Pane**.

2 On the left side of the first record—*Instructor ID* of *1224567*—click **+**, and then compare your screen with Figure 2.11.

> A plus sign (**+**) to the left of a record in a table indicates that *related* records may exist in another table. Click the plus sign to display the related records in a ***subdatasheet***. In the first record for *Craig Fresch*, you can see that related records exist in the 2A Schedule table—he is scheduled to teach five LGL (Legal) courses. The plus signs display because you created a relationship between the two tables using the Instructor ID field—the common field.
>
> When you click **+** to display the subdatasheet, the symbol changes to a minus sign (**–**), an indication that the subdatasheet is expanded. Click **-** to collapse the subdatasheet.

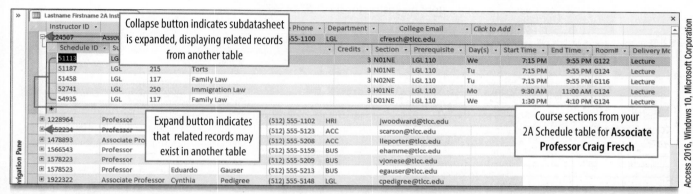

FIGURE 2.11

Activity 2.07 | Testing Cascade Options

Recall that cascade options enable you to make changes to records on the *one* side table of the relationship and update or delete records in the table on the *many* side of the relationship. In this Activity you will change the data in the Instructor ID field—the primary key field—for one instructor, and then delete all of the records associated with another instructor from both tables.

1 In the subdatasheet for the first record—*Instructor ID* of *1224567*—notice that the first course that the instructor is scheduled to teach has a *Schedule ID* of *51113—LGL 216*. In the **2A Instructors** table, to the left of the first record, click **–** (minus sign) to collapse the subdatasheet.

2 If necessary, in the first record, in the **Instructor ID** field, select the data—**1224567**. Type **8224567** and then press ⬇ to save the record.

If you had not enabled Cascade Update Related Fields in the Edit Relationships dialog box, an error message would have displayed.

3 **Open** » the **Navigation Pane**. In the **Navigation Pane**, double-click your **2A Schedule** table to open it, and then **Close** « the **Navigation Pane**.

🔄 **ANOTHER WAY**   Press F11 to open or close the Navigation Pane.

4 Scroll to locate the record with a **Schedule ID** of **51113**—*LGL 216*. If necessary, scroll to the right to display the **Instructor ID** field, and notice that for this record, the **Instructor ID** is **8224567**. Compare your screen with Figure 2.12.

The Cascade Update Related Fields option enables you to change the data in the primary key field in your 2A Instructors table, and the five related records for *Craig Fresch* in the 2A Schedule table were updated to store his Instructor ID of *8224567*.

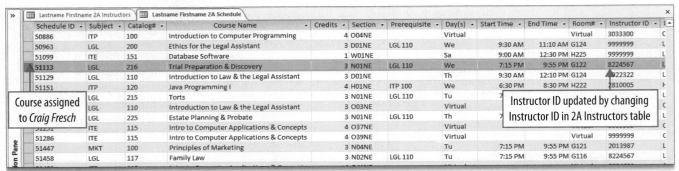

FIGURE 2.12

Access 2016, Windows 10, Microsoft Corporation

5 **Close** ✕ your **2A Schedule** table. In your **2A Instructors** table, scroll to display the last few records. On the left side of the record for **Instructor ID** of **6145288**—Professor Ivey Clarke—click + to display the subdatasheet. Notice that this instructor is scheduled to teach two courses—*Schedule ID* of *42837* and *42930*.

6 Click – to collapse the subdatasheet. For the same record—*Instructor ID* of *6145288*—point to the record selector box to display the ➡ pointer, and then click to select the record. On the **Home tab**, in the **Records group**, click **Delete**.

A message displays warning you that this record and related records in related tables will be deleted. The record you selected does not display in the table, and the next record is selected. If you had not enabled Cascade Delete Related Records, an error message would have displayed, and you would not be able to delete the record for Professor Ivey Clarke without assigning her courses to another instructor first.

🔄 **ANOTHER WAY**   With the record selected, press Del ; or with the record selected, right-click, and then click Delete Record.

7 In the message box, click **Yes**.

The record for *Instructor ID* of *6145288* is deleted. On the Quick Access Toolbar, the Undo button is unavailable—if you mistakenly delete the wrong record and the related records, you must enter them again in both tables. Access cannot use Undo to undo a Delete.

8 ▶ **Open** ⟩⟩ the **Navigation Pane**, open your **2A Schedule** table, and then **Close** ⟨⟨ the **Navigation Pane**. Scroll through the records and notice that the records for a **Schedule ID** of **42837** and **42930** have been deleted from the table.

The Cascade Delete Related Records option in the Edit Relationships dialog box enables you to delete a record in the table on the *one* side of the relationship—2A Instructors—and simultaneously delete the records in the table on the *many* side of the relationship—2A Schedule—that are related to the deleted record.

9 ▶ In the object window, right-click either **object tab**, and then click **Close All** to close both tables.

NOTE   Cascade Options—Record Must Be Edited or Deleted in Correct Table

Changes in the data in the common field must be made in the primary key field in the table on the *one* side of the relationship—you cannot change the data in the common field in the table on the *many* side of the relationship. To delete a record and all of its associated records in another table, you must delete the record in the table on the *one* side of the relationship. You can, however, delete a related record from the table on the *many* side of the relationship—the related record in the table on the *one* side of the relationship is not deleted.

Objective 3   Sort Records in a Table

GO! Learn How
Video A2-3

Sorting is the process of arranging data in a specific order based on the value in a field. For example, you can sort the names in your contact list alphabetically by each person's last name, or you can sort your music collection by the artist. As records are entered into an Access table, they display in the order in which they are added to the table. After you close the table and reopen it, the records display in order by the primary key field.

Activity 2.08 | Sorting Records in a Table in Ascending or Descending Order

MOS
2.3.6

In this Activity you will determine the departments of the faculty in the Business Division by sorting the data. Data can be sorted in either *ascending order* or *descending order*. Ascending order sorts text alphabetically (A to Z) and sorts numbers from the lowest number to the highest number. Descending order sorts text in reverse alphabetical order (Z to A) and sorts numbers from the highest number to the lowest number.

1 ▶ **Open** ⟩⟩ the **Navigation Pane**, open your **2A Instructors** table, and then **Close** ⟨⟨ the **Navigation Pane**. Notice that the records in the table are sorted in ascending order by the **Instructor ID** field, which is the primary key field.

2 ▶ In the field names row, click the **Department arrow**, click **Sort A to Z**, and then compare your screen with Figure 2.13.

To sort records in a table, click the arrow to the right of the field name in the column on which you want to sort, and then click the sort order. After a field is sorted, a small arrow in the field name box indicates the sort order. For the Department field, the small arrow points up, indicating an ascending sort, and on the ribbon, Ascending is selected.

The records display in alphabetical order by the Department field. Because the department names are now grouped together, you can quickly scroll through the table to see the instructors for each department. The first record in the table has no data in the Department field because the *Instructor ID* of *9999999* is reserved for *Staff*, a designation that is used until a scheduled course has been assigned to a specific instructor.

ANOTHER WAY   Click in the field in any record, and then on the Home tab, in the Sort & Filter group, click Ascending; or right-click in the field in any record, and then click Sort A to Z.

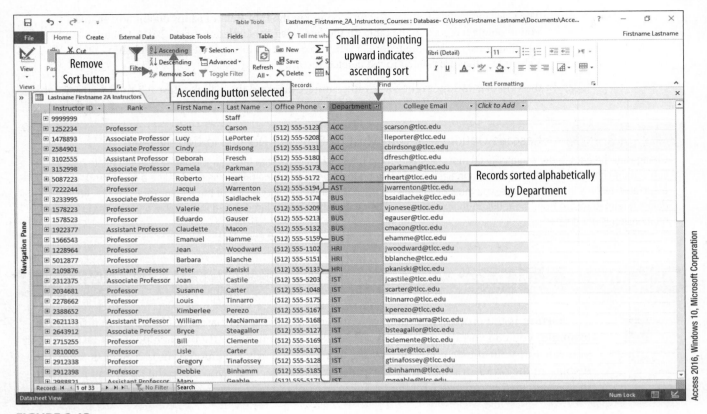

FIGURE 2.13

3 On the **Home tab**, in the **Sort & Filter group**, click **Remove Sort** to clear the sort and return the records to the default sort order, which is by the primary key field—*Instructor ID*.

4 Click the **Last Name arrow**, and then click **Sort Z to A**.

The records in the table are sorted by the Last Name field in reverse alphabetical order. The small arrow in the field name box points down, indicating a descending sort. On the ribbon, Descending is selected.

5 In the **Sort & Filter group**, click **Remove Sort** to clear the sort.

Activity 2.09 | Sorting Records in a Table on Multiple Fields

To sort a table on two or more fields, first identify the fields that will act as the ***outermost sort field*** and the ***innermost sort field***. The outermost sort field is the first level of sorting, and the innermost sort field is the second or final level of sorting. To alphabetize a table by Last Name and then First Name (also called First Name within Last Name), the Last Name field is identified as the outermost sort field. If there are duplicate last names, the records should be further sorted by the First Name field—the innermost sort field. For tables, you sort the innermost field first and then sort the outermost field.

In this Activity you will sort the records by Last Name (innermost sort field) within the Department (outermost sort field).

1 In the **Last Name** field, click in any record. On the **Home tab**, in the **Sort & Filter group**, click **Ascending**.

The records are sorted in ascending order by Last Name—the innermost sort field.

2 Point anywhere in the **Department** field, right-click, and then click **Sort Z to A**. Compare your screen with Figure 2.14.

> The records are sorted in descending order first by Department—the outermost sort field. Within each Department grouping, the records are sorted in ascending order by Last Name—the innermost sort field. Records can be sorted on multiple fields using both ascending and descending order.

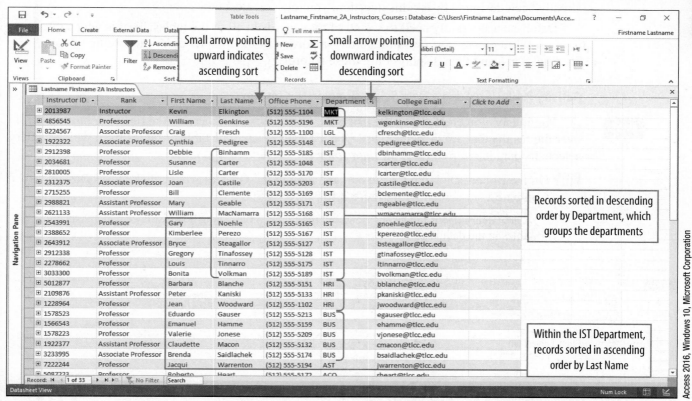

FIGURE 2.14

3 On the ribbon, click the **File tab**, click **Print**, and then click **Print Preview**. In the **Page Layout** group, click **Landscape**. In the **Zoom group**, click **Two Pages**, and notice that the table will print on two pages.

4 In the **Print group**, click **Print**. In the **Print** dialog box, under **Print Range**, click in the **From** box, type **1** and then click in the **To** box and type **1** to print only the first page. This is the second of eight objects printed in this project. If directed to submit a paper printout, click **OK**. If directed to create a PDF electronic image, in the **Publish as PDF or XPS** dialog box, click **Options**, and then under **Range**, click the **Page(s)** option button, and then click **OK**.

5 In the **Close Preview group**, click **Close Print Preview**. In the object window, **Close** ☒ the table. In the message box, click **Yes** to save the changes to the sort order.

6 **Open** ⟫ the **Navigation Pane**, double-click your **2A Instructors** table to open it, and then **Close** ⟪ the **Navigation Pane**. Notice that the table displays the sort order you specified.

7 On the **Home tab**, in the **Sort & Filter group**, click **Remove Sort**. **Close** ☒ the table, and in the message box, click **Yes** to save the table with the sort removed.

> Generally, tables are not stored with the data sorted. Instead queries are created that sort the data, and then reports are created to display the sorted data.

Objective 4 | Create a Query in Design View

GO! Learn How
Video A2-4

Recall that a select query is a database object that retrieves (selects) specific data from one or more tables and then displays the specified data in a table in Datasheet view. A query answers a question such as *Which instructors teach courses in the IST department?* Unless a query has already been designed to ask this question, you must create a new query.

Database users rarely need to see all of the records in all of the tables. That is why a query is so useful; it creates a *subset* of records—a portion of the total records—according to your specifications, and then displays only those records.

Activity 2.10 | Creating a New Select Query in Design View

3.2.2

Previously, you created a query using the Query Wizard. To create queries with more control over the results that are displayed, use Query Design view. The table or tables from which a query selects its data is referred to as the *data source*.

1 On the ribbon, click the **Create tab**, and then in the **Queries group**, click **Query Design**. Compare your screen with Figure 2.15.

> A new query opens in Design view, and the Show Table dialog box displays, which lists both tables in the database.

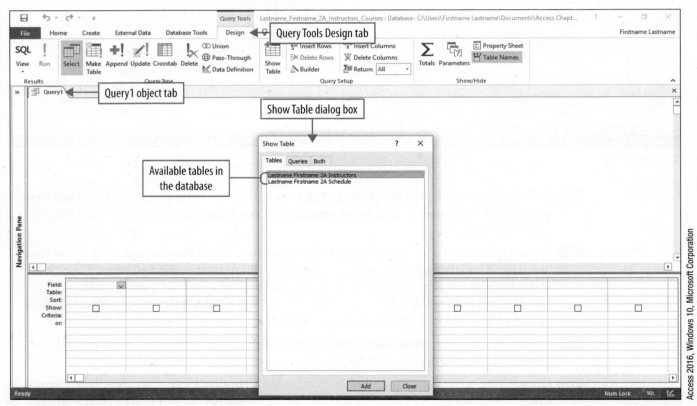

FIGURE 2.15

2 In the **Show Table** dialog box, double-click your **2A Instructors** table, and then, in the dialog box, click **Close**.

> A field list for your 2A Instructors table displays in the upper area of the Query window. Instructor ID is the primary key field in this table. The Query window has two parts: the *table area* (upper area), which displays the field lists for tables that are used in the query, and the *query design grid* (lower area), which displays the design of the query.

Is there more than one field list in the table area?

If you double-click a table more than one time, a duplicate field list displays in the table area of the Query window. To remove a field list from the Query window, right-click the title bar of the field list, and then click Remove Table.

3 Point to the lower right corner of the field list to display the ⬚ pointer, and then, holding down the left mouse button, drag downward and to the right to resize the field list, displaying all of the field names and the entire table name. Release the mouse button. In the **2A Instructors** field list, double-click **Rank**, and then look at the design grid.

The Rank field name displays in the design grid in the Field row. You limit the fields that display in the query results by placing only the desired field names in the design grid.

4 In the **2A Instructors** field list, point to **First Name**, holding down the left mouse button, drag the field name down into the design grid until the ⬚ pointer displays in the **Field** row in the second column, and then release the mouse button. Compare your screen with Figure 2.16.

This is a second way to add field names to the design grid. When you release the mouse button, the field name displays in the Field row.

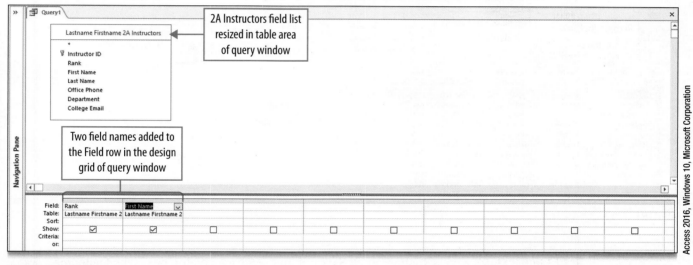

FIGURE 2.16

Access 2016, Windows 10, Microsoft Corporation

5 In the design grid, in the **Field** row, click in the third column, and then click the **arrow** that displays. From the list, click **Last Name** to add the field to the design grid.

This is a third way to add field names to the design grid.

6 Using one of the three techniques you just practiced, add the **Office Phone** field to the fourth column and the **Department** field to the fifth column in the design grid.

Is there a duplicate field name or an incorrect field name in the design grid?

If you double-click a field name more than one time, a duplicate field name displays in the design grid. To remove a duplicate field name, in the design grid, in the Field row, right-click the duplicate field name, and then click Cut. Use this same method to delete a field name that you placed in the design grid by mistake. As you progress in your study of query design, you will learn alternate ways to delete field names from the design grid.

Activity 2.11 | Running, Saving, Printing, and Closing a Query

Once a query is designed, you *run* it to display the results. When you run a query, Access looks at the records in the table (or tables) you have included in the query, finds the records that match the specified conditions (if any), and displays only those records in a datasheet. Only the fields that you have added to the design grid display in the query results. The query always runs using the current table or tables, presenting the most up-to-date information.

> **1** On the **Design tab**, in the **Results group**, click **Run**, and then compare your screen with Figure 2.17.

This query answers the question, *What is the rank, first name, last name, office phone number, and department of all of the instructors in the 2A Instructors table?* A query is a subgroup of the records in the table, arranged in Datasheet view, using the fields and conditions that you specify in the design grid. The five fields you specified in the design grid display in columns, and the records from the 2A Instructors table display in rows.

ANOTHER WAY On the Design tab, in the Results group, click the upper portion of the View button, which runs the query by switching to Datasheet view.

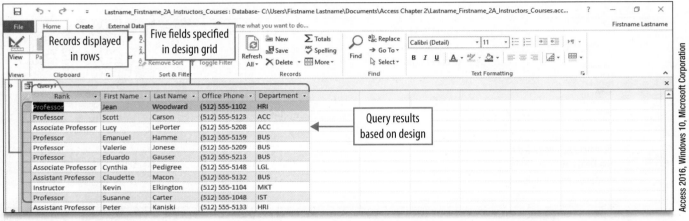

FIGURE 2.17

> **2** On the **Quick Access Toolbar**, click **Save** 🖫. In the **Save As** dialog box, type **Lastname Firstname 2A Instructors Query** and then click **OK**.

The query name displays on the object tab in the object window. Save your queries if you are likely to ask the same question again; doing so will save you the effort of creating the query again to answer the same question—just run the query again.

ALERT! **Does a message display after entering a query name?**

Query names are limited to 64 characters. For all projects, if you have a long last name or first name that results in your query name exceeding the 64-character limit, ask your instructor how you should abbreviate your name.

> **3** Click the **File tab**, click **Print**, and then click **Print Preview**. Create a paper or PDF electronic image as directed, and then click **Close Print Preview**. This is the third of eight objects printed in this project.

Queries answer questions and gather information from the data in tables. Typically, queries are created as a basis for a report, but query results can be printed like any table of data.

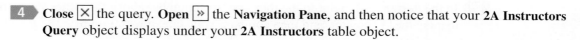

4 ▶ **Close** ⊠ the query. **Open** ⧉ the **Navigation Pane**, and then notice that your **2A Instructors Query** object displays under your **2A Instructors** table object.

> The new query name displays in the Navigation Pane under the table with which it is related—the 2A Instructors table, which is the data source. Only the design of the query is saved; the records reside in the table object. Each time you open a query, Access runs it and displays the results based on the data stored in the data source. Thus, the results of the query always reflect the most up-to-date information.

Objective 5 Create a New Query from an Existing Query

GO! Learn How
Video A2-5

You can create a new query from scratch or you can open an existing query, save it with a new name, and modify the design to answer another question. Using an existing query saves you time if your new query uses all or some of the same fields and conditions in an existing query.

Activity 2.12 │ Copying an Existing Query

MOS

3.1.6, 3.2.1

1 ▶ In the **Navigation Pane**, right-click your **2A Instructors Query**, and then click **Copy**.

2 ▶ In the **Navigation Pane**, point to a blank area, right-click, and then click Paste.

> The Paste As dialog box displays, which enables you to name the copied query.

⟳ ANOTHER WAY　　To create a copy of the query, in the Navigation Pane, click the query name to select it. On the Home tab, in the Clipboard group, click Copy. On the Home tab, in the Clipboard group, click the upper portion of the Paste button.

3 ▶ In the **Paste As** dialog box, type **Lastname Firstname 2A Instructor IDs Query** and then click **OK**.

> A new query, based on a copy of your 2A Instructors Query, is created and displays in the object window and in the Navigation Pane under its data source—your 2A Instructors table.

⟳ ANOTHER WAY　　To create a copy of an open query using a new name, click the File tab, and then click Save As. Under Save As, double-click Save Object As. In the Save As dialog box, click in the Name box and type the name of the new query.

4 ▶ In the **Navigation Pane**, double-click your **2A Instructor IDs Query** to run the query and display the query results in **Datasheet** view. **Close** ⧉ the **Navigation Pane**.

More Knowledge　　**Rename a Query**

If the query name is not correct, you can rename it as long as the query is closed. In the Navigation Pane, right-click the query name, and then click Rename. Edit the current name or type a new name, and then press Enter to accept the change.

Activity 2.13 │ Modifying the Design of a Query

MOS

3.2.2, 1.3.5,
3.2.3, 3.1.1,
3.1.6

1 ▶ On the **Home tab**, in the **Views group**, click **View** to switch to **Design** view.

⟳ ANOTHER WAY　　On the Home tab, in the Views group, click the View arrow, and then click Design View; or on the right side of the status bar, click the Design View button.

> **2** In the design grid, point to the thin gray selection bar above the **Office Phone** field name to display the ⬇ pointer, and then compare your screen with Figure 2.18.

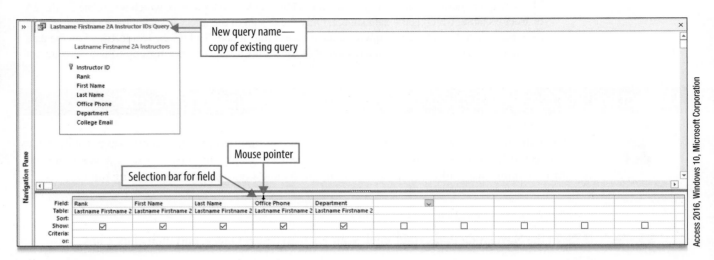

Access 2016, Windows 10, Microsoft Corporation

FIGURE 2.18

> **3** With the ⬇ pointer displayed in the selection bar above the **Office Phone** field name, click to select the column, and then press Del.

This action deletes the field from the query design only—it has no effect on the field in the data source—2A Instructors table. The Department field moves to the left. Similarly, by using the selection bar, you can drag to select multiple fields and delete them at one time.

> **ANOTHER WAY**   In the design grid, click in the field name. On the Design tab, in the Query Setup group, click Delete Columns; or right-click the field name, and then click Cut; or click in the field name, and on the Home tab, in the Records group, click Delete.

> **4** Point to the selection bar above the **First Name** column, and then click to select the column. In the selected column, point to the selection bar to display the 🔓 pointer, and then drag to the right until a dark vertical line displays on the right side of the **Last Name** column. Release the mouse button to position the **First Name** field in the third column.

To rearrange fields in a query, first select the field to move, and then drag it to a new position in the design grid.

> **5** Using the technique you just practiced, move the **Department** field to the left of the **Rank** field.

> **6** From the field list, drag the **Instructor ID** field down to the first column in the design grid until the 🔳 pointer displays, and then release the mouse button. Compare your screen with Figure 2.19.

The Instructor ID field displays in the first column, and the remaining four fields move to the right. Use this method to insert a field to the left of a field already displayed in the design grid.

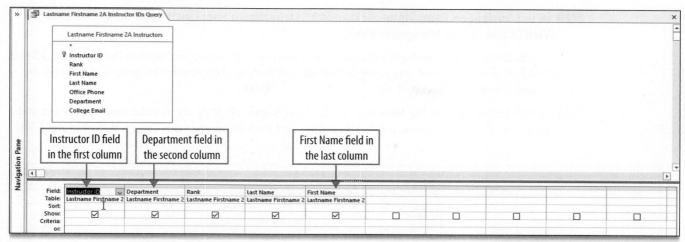

FIGURE 2.19

7 On the **Design tab**, in the **Results group**, click **Run**.

This query answers the question, *What is the instructor ID, department, rank, last name, and first name of every instructor in the 2A Instructors table?* The results of the query are a subgroup of the records stored in the 2A Instructors table. The records are sorted by the table's primary key field—Instructor ID.

8 On the **File tab**, click **Print**, and then click **Print Preview**. Create a paper or PDF electronic image as directed, and then click **Close Print Preview**. This is the fourth of eight objects printed in this project.

9 **Close** ⊠ the query. In the message box, click **Yes** to save the changes to the query design—deleting a field, moving two fields, and adding a field. **Open** ⟩⟩ the **Navigation Pane**.

The query is saved and closed, and the query name displays in the Navigation Pane under the related table. Recall that only the *design* of the query is saved; the records reside in the related table or tables.

Objective 6   Sort Query Results

GO! Learn How
Video A2-6

You can sort the results of a query in ascending or descending order in either Datasheet view or Design view. Use Design view if your query results should always display in a specified sort order, or if you intend to use the sorted results in a report.

Activity 2.14 | Sorting Query Results

MOS
3.2.5, 3.1.6

In this Activity you will save an existing query with a new name, and then sort the query results by using the Sort row in Design view.

1 In the **Navigation Pane**, right-click your **2A Instructor IDs Query**, and then click **Copy**. In the **Navigation Pane**, point to a blank area, right-click, and then click **Paste**.

2 In the **Paste As** dialog box, type **Lastname Firstname 2A Department Sort Query** and then click **OK**. Increase the width of the **Navigation Pane** so that the names of all of the objects display fully.

A new query is created based on a copy of your 2A Instructor IDs Query; that is, the new query includes the same fields in the same order as the query on which it is based. The query does not need to be open to save it with another name; you can select the object name in the Navigation Pane.

3 In the **Navigation Pane**, right-click your **2A Department Sort Query**, and then click **Design View**. **Close** ⟨«⟩ the **Navigation Pane**.

> Use this technique to display the query in Design view if you are redesigning the query. Recall that if you double-click a query name in the Navigation Pane, Access runs the query and displays the query results in Datasheet view.

4 In the design grid, in the **Sort** row, under **Last Name**, click to display the insertion point and an arrow. Click the **arrow**, click **Ascending**, and then compare your screen with Figure 2.20.

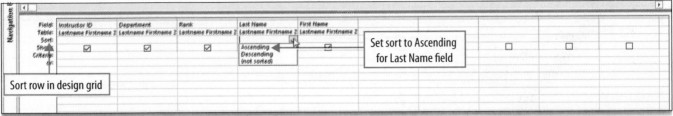

FIGURE 2.20

5 On the **Design tab**, in the **Results group**, click **Run**.

> In the query results, the records are sorted in ascending order by the Last Name field, and two instructors have the same last name of *Carter—Susanne* and *Lisle*.

6 On the **Home tab**, in the **Views group**, click the upper portion of the **View** button to switch to **Design** view.

7 In the design grid, click in the **Sort** row under **First Name**, click the **arrow**, and then click **Ascending**. **Run** the query.

> In the query results, the records are sorted first by the Last Name field. If two instructors have the same last name, then those records are sorted by the First Name field. The two instructors with the same last name of *Carter* are sorted by their first names, and the two records with the same last name of *Fresch* are sorted by their first names.

8 Switch to **Design** view. In the design grid, click in the **Sort** row under **Department**, click the **arrow**, and then click **Descending**. **Run** the query, and then compare your screen with Figure 2.21.

> In Design view, fields with a Sort setting are sorted from left to right. That is, the sorted field on the left becomes the outermost sort field, and the sorted field on the right becomes the innermost sort field. Thus, the records in this query are sorted first in descending order by the Department field—the leftmost sort field. Then, within each department, the records are sorted in ascending order by the Last Name field. And, finally, within each duplicate last name, the records are sorted in ascending order by the First Name field.

> If you run a query and the sorted results are not what you intended, be sure the fields are displayed from left to right according to the groupings that you desire.

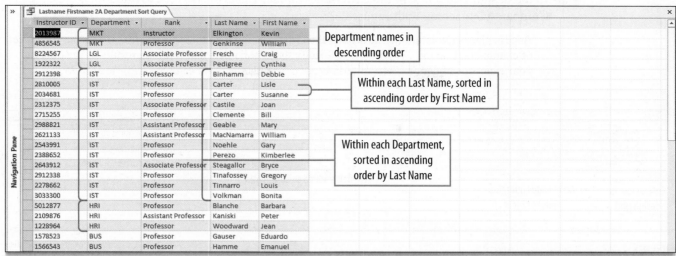

Department names in descending order

Within each Last Name, sorted in ascending order by First Name

Within each Department, sorted in ascending order by Last Name

FIGURE 2.21

Access 2016, Windows 10, Microsoft Corporation

9 Display the query results in **Print Preview**. Create a paper or PDF electronic image as directed, and then click **Close Print Preview**. This is the fifth of eight objects printed in this project. **Close** ☒ the query. In the message box, click **Yes** to save the changes to the query design.

More Knowledge | **Sorting in Design View or Datasheet View**

If you add a sort order to the *design* of a query, it remains as a permanent part of the query design. If you use the sort buttons in Datasheet view, the sort order will override the sort order of the query design and can be saved as part of the query. A sort order designated in Datasheet view does not display in the Sort row of the query design grid. As with sorting tables, in Datasheet view, a small arrow displays to the right of the field name to indicate the sort order of the field.

Objective 7 | Specify Criteria in a Query

GO! Learn How
Video A2-7

Queries locate information in a table based on ***criteria*** that you specify as part of the query design. Criteria are conditions that identify the specific records for which you are looking. Criteria enable you to ask a more specific question; therefore, you will get a more specific result. For example, to find out how many instructors are in the IST department, limit the results to display only that specific department by entering criteria in the design grid.

Activity 2.15 | Specifying Text Criteria in a Query

MOS
3.1.1, 3.2.2,
3.3.2, 3.1.6

In this Activity you will assist Dean Judkins by creating a query to answer the question, *Which instructors are in the IST Department?*.

1 On the ribbon, click the **Create tab**, and then in the **Queries group**, click **Query Design**.

2 In the **Show Table** dialog box, double-click your **2A Instructors** table to add it to the table area, and then **Close** the **Show Table** dialog box.

3 By dragging the lower right corner, resize the field list to display all of the field names and the table name. Add the following fields to the design grid in the order given: **Department**, **Instructor ID**, **Rank**, **First Name**, and **Last Name**.

4 In the design grid, click in the **Criteria** row under **Department**, type **IST** and then press Enter. Compare your screen with Figure 2.22.

> Access places quotation marks around the criteria to indicate that this is a ***text string***—a sequence of characters. Use the Criteria row to specify the criteria that will limit the results of the query to your exact specifications. The criteria is not case sensitive; you can type *ist* instead of *IST*.

FIGURE 2.22

Access 2016, Windows 10, Microsoft Corporation

NOTE	Pressing Enter After Adding Criteria

After adding criteria, when you press Enter or click in another column or row in the query design grid, you can see how Access alters the criteria so it can interpret what you have typed. Sometimes there is no change, such as when you add criteria to a field that stores a numeric or currency value. Other times, Access capitalizes a letter or adds quotation marks or other symbols to clarify the criteria. Whether or not you press Enter after adding criteria has no effect on the query results; it is used here to help you see how the program behaves.

5 **Run** the query, and then compare your screen with Figure 2.23.

> Thirteen records display. There are 13 instructors in the IST Department; or, more specifically, there are 13 records that have *IST* in the Department field.

Department	Instructor ID	Rank	First Name	Last Name
IST	2034681	Professor	Susanne	Carter
IST	2278662	Professor	Louis	Tinnarro
IST	2312375	Associate Professor	Joan	Castile
IST	2388652	Professor	Kimberlee	Perezo
IST	2543991	Professor	Gary	Noehle
IST	2621133	Assistant Professor	William	MacNamarra
IST	2643912	Associate Professor	Bryce	Steagallor
IST	2715255	Professor	Bill	Clemente
IST	2810005	Professor	Lisle	Carter
IST	2912338	Professor	Gregory	Tinafossey
IST	2912398	Professor	Debbie	Binhamm
IST	2988821	Assistant Professor	Mary	Geable
IST	3033300	Professor	Bonita	Volkman

Thirteen records match criteria—*IST* in the Department field

Access 2016, Windows 10, Microsoft Corporation

FIGURE 2.23

ALERT!	Do your query results differ?

If you mistype the criteria, or enter it under the wrong field, or make some other error, the query results will display no records. This indicates that there are no records in the table that match the criteria as you entered it. If this occurs, return to Design view and examine the query design. Verify that the criteria is entered in the Criteria row, under the correct field, and without typing errors. Then, run the query again.

6 **Save** 🖫 the query as **Lastname Firstname 2A IST Query** and then display the query results in **Print Preview**. Create a paper or PDF electronic image as directed, and then click **Close Print Preview**. This is the sixth of eight objects printed in this project.

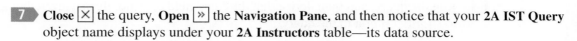
7 ⮞ **Close** ⊠ the query, **Open** ⟫ the **Navigation Pane**, and then notice that your **2A IST Query** object name displays under your **2A Instructors** table—its data source.

> Recall that in the Navigation Pane, queries display an icon of two overlapping datasheets.

Activity 2.16 | Specifying Criteria and Hiding the Field in the Query Results

3.1.1, 3.2.2,
3.3.2, 3.2.5,
3.2.4, 3.1.6

So far, all of the fields that you included in the query design have also been included in the query results. There are times when you need to use the field in the query design, but you do not need to display that field in the results—usually, when the data in the field is the same for all of the records. In this Activity you will create a query to answer the question, *Which instructors have a rank of Professor?*

1 ⮞ **Close** ⟪ the **Navigation Pane**. On the **Create tab**, in the **Queries group**, click **Query Design**.

2 ⮞ In the **Show Table** dialog box, double-click your **2A Instructors** table to add it to the table area, and then **Close** the **Show Table** dialog box.

3 ⮞ Resize the field list, and then add the following fields to the design grid in the order given: **Instructor ID**, **First Name**, **Last Name**, and **Rank**.

4 ⮞ Click in the **Sort** row under **Last Name**, click the **arrow**, and then click **Ascending**.

5 ⮞ Click in the **Criteria** row under **Rank**, type **professor** and then press Enter. Compare your screen with Figure 2.24.

> Recall that criteria is not case sensitive. As you start typing *professor*, a list of functions displays, from which you can select if a function is included in your criteria. After pressing Enter, the insertion point moves to the next criteria box, and quotation marks are added around the text string that you entered.

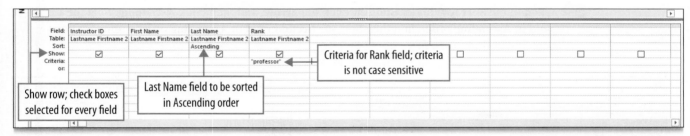

FIGURE 2.24

Access 2016, Windows 10, Microsoft Corporation

6 ⮞ In the design grid, in the **Show** row, notice that a check box is selected for every field. **Run** the query.

> Eighteen records meet the criteria—*professor* in the *Rank* field. In the Rank column, every record displays *Professor*, and the records are sorted in ascending order by the Last Name field.

7 ⮞ Switch to **Design** view. In the design grid, in the **Show** row under **Rank**, click to clear the check box.

> Because it is repetitive and not particularly useful to display *Professor* for every record in the query results, clear the Show check box so that the field is hidden or does not display. You should, however, always run the query first before clearing the Show check box to be sure that the correct records display.

8 **Run** the query, and then notice that the *Rank* field does not display even though it was used to specify criteria in the query.

> The same 18 records display, but the *Rank* field is hidden from the query results. Although the Rank field is included in the query design so that you could specify the criteria of *professor*, it is not necessary to display the field in the results. When appropriate, clear the Show check box to avoid cluttering the query results with data that is not useful.

9 **Save** 🖫 the query as **Lastname Firstname 2A Professor Query** and then display the query results in **Print Preview**. Create a paper or PDF electronic image as directed, and then click **Close Print Preview**. This is the seventh of eight objects printed in this project. **Close** ✕ the query.

Activity 2.17 │ Using *Is Null* Criteria to Find Empty Fields

MOS
3.1.1, 3.2.2,
3.3.2, 3.2.5,
3.1.6

Sometimes you must locate records where data is missing. You can locate such records by using *Is Null* as the criteria in a field. *Is Null* is used to find empty fields. Additionally, you can display only the records where data has been entered in the field by using the criteria of *Is Not Null*, which excludes record3s where the specified field is empty. In this Activity you will design a query to answer the question, *Which scheduled courses have no credits listed?*

1 On the **Create tab**, in the **Queries group**, click **Query Design**. In the **Show Table** dialog box, double-click your **2A Schedule** table to add it to the table area, and then **Close** the **Show Table** dialog box.

2 Resize the field list, and then add the following fields to the design grid in the order given: **Subject**, **Catalog#**, **Section**, **Course Name**, and **Credits**.

3 Click in the **Criteria** row under **Credits**, type **is null** and then press Enter.

> Access capitalizes *is null*. The criteria *Is Null* examines the Credits field and locates records that do *not* have any data entered in the field.

4 Click in the **Sort** row under **Subject**, click the **arrow**, and then click **Ascending**. **Sort** the **Catalog#** field in **Ascending** order, and then **Sort** the **Section** field in **Ascending** order. Compare your screen with Figure 2.25.

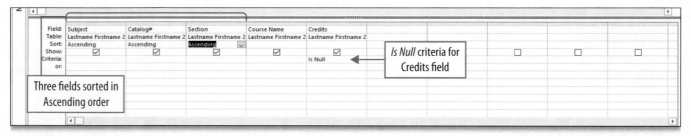

FIGURE 2.25

5 **Run** the query, and then compare your screen with Figure 2.26.

> Four scheduled courses do not have credits listed—the Credits field is empty. The records are sorted in ascending order first by the Subject field, then by the Catalog# field, and then by the Section field. Using the information displayed in the query results, a course scheduler can more easily locate the records in the table and enter the credits for these courses.

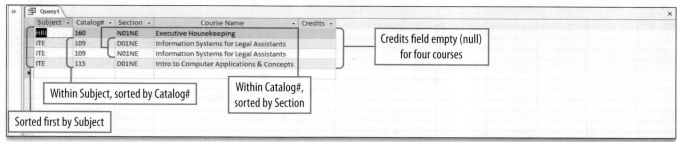

Within Subject, sorted by Catalog#

Within Catalog#, sorted by Section

Sorted first by Subject

Credits field empty (null) for four courses

Access 2016, Windows 10, Microsoft Corporation

FIGURE 2.26

6 ► **Save** 🖫 the query as **Lastname Firstname 2A No Credits Query**, and then display the query results in **Print Preview**. Create a paper or PDF electronic image as instructed, and then click **Close Print Preview**. This is the eighth of eight objects printed in this project.

7 ► **Close** ☒ the query. **Open** ⏵⏵ the **Navigation Pane**, and then notice that your **2A No Credits Query** object displays under your **2A Schedule** table object, its data source.

8 ► On the right side of the title bar, click **Close** ☒ to close the database and **Close** Access. As directed by your instructor, submit your database and the paper or PDF electronic images of the eight objects—relationship report, sorted table, and six queries—that are the results of this project.

END | You have completed Project 2A

GO! With Google

Access web apps are designed to work with Microsoft's SharePoint, a service for setting up websites to share and manage documents. Your college may not have SharePoint installed, so you will use other tools to share objects from your database so that you can work collaboratively with others. Recall that Google Drive is Google's free, web-based word processor, spreadsheet, slide show, form, and data storage and sharing service. For Access, you can export a database object to an Excel worksheet, a PDF file, or a text file, and then save the file to Google Drive.

> **ALERT!** **Working with Web-Based Applications and Services**
>
> Computer programs and services on the web receive continuous updates and improvements, so the steps to complete this web-based activity may differ from the ones shown. You can often look at the screens and the information presented to determine how to complete the activity.
>
> If you do not already have a Google account, you will need to create one before doing this activity. Go to http://google.com and in the upper right corner, click Sign In. On the Sign In screen, click Create Account. On the Create your Google Account page, complete the form, read and agree to the Terms of Service and Privacy Policy, and then click Next step. On the Welcome screen, click Get Started.

Activity | Exporting a Relationship Report to a PDF File, Saving the PDF file to Google Drive, and Sharing the File

In this Activity you will export your Relationships Report object to a PDF file, upload your PDF file to Google Drive, and then share the file.

1 Start Access, navigate to your **Access Chapter 2** folder, and then open your **2A_Instructors_Courses** database file. On the **Message Bar**, click **Enable Content**. In the **Navigation Pane**, click your **Relationships for 2A Instructors Courses** object to select it.

2 On the ribbon, click the **External Data tab**, and then in the **Export group**, click **PDF or XPS**. In the **Publish as PDF or XPS** dialog box, navigate to your **Access Chapter 2** folder. In the **File Save** dialog box, click in the **File name** box, and then using your own name, type **Lastname_Firstname_AC_2A_Web** and be sure that the **Open file after publishing** check box is selected and the **Minimum size (publishing online)** option button is selected. Click **Publish**. If necessary, choose the application with which you want to display the file.

The PDF file is created and opens in Microsoft Edge, Adobe Reader, or Adobe Acrobat, depending on the software that is installed on your computer.

3 If necessary, close the view of the PDF file. In the **Export – PDF** dialog box, click **Close**, and then **Close** ☒ Access.

4 From the desktop, open your browser, navigate to **http://google.com**, and then sign in to your Google account. Click the **Google Apps** menu ⊞, and then click **Drive** ☁. Open your **GO! Web Projects** folder—or click New to create and then open this folder if necessary.

5 On the left, click **NEW**, click **File upload**. In the **Open** dialog box, navigate to your **Access Chapter 2** folder, and then double-click your **Lastname_Firstname_AC_2A_Web** file to upload it to Google Drive. When the title bar of the message box indicates *Uploads completed*, **Close** the message box. A second message box may display temporarily.

6 In the file list, click your **Lastname_Firstname_AC_2A_Web** PDF file one time to select it.

7 At the top of the window, click **Share** 👤.

8 In the **Share with others** dialog box, with your insertion point blinking in the **Enter names or email addresses** box, type the email address that you use at your college. Click **Can edit**, and click **Can comment**. Click in the **Add a note** box, and then type **This relationship report identifies tables that can be used together to create other objects in the database.** Compare your screen with Figure A.

If you upload a table that you exported as an Excel spreadsheet or Word document and to which you want to enable others to add records, be sure that you change the Sharing permission to *Can edit*.

(GO! With Google continues on the next page)

GO! With Google

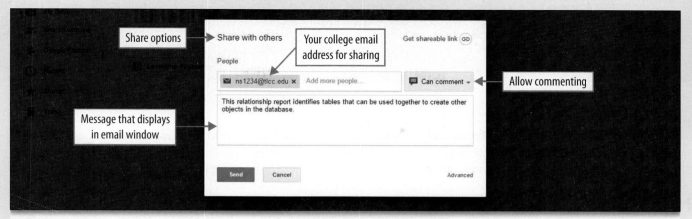

Share options → Share with others — Your college email address for sharing — Get shareable link

People

Message that displays in email window → ns1234@tlcc.edu ✕ Add more people... — Can comment ▾ ← Allow commenting

This relationship report identifies tables that can be used together to create other objects in the database.

Send   Cancel   Advanced

FIGURE A

9 In the **Share with others** dialog box, click **Send**.

If your college is not using Google accounts, you may have to confirm sending the message with a link.

10 At the top of the window, click **Share** 👤. In the **Share with others** dialog box, notice that the file has been shared with your college email account. Start the **Snipping Tool**. In the **Snipping Tool** dialog box, click the **New arrow**, and then click **Full-screen Snip**.

11 On the **Snipping Tool** toolbar, click **Save Snip** 💾. In the **Save As** dialog box, navigate to your **Access Chapter 2** folder. Click in the **File name** box, type **Lastname_Firstname_AC_2A_Web_Snip** and then be sure

that the **Save as type** box displays **JPEG file**, and then click **Save**. **Close** ✕ the **Snipping Tool** window.

12 In the **Share with Others** dialog box, click **Done** in Google Drive, click your Google Drive name, and then click **Sign out**. **Close** your browser window.

13 If directed to submit a paper printout of your PDF and snip file, follow the directions given in the Note below. As directed by your instructor, submit your file and your snip file that are the results of this project. Your instructor may also request that you submit a copy of the email that was sent to you notifying you of the shared file.

> **NOTE** Printing your PDF and Snip .JPG File
>
> Using File Explorer, navigate to your Access Chapter 2 folder. Locate and double-click your a2A_Google file. On the toolbar, click the Print file button. Then Close your default PDF reader. In your Access Chapter 2 folder, locate and double-click your AC_2A_Web_Snip file. If this is the first time you have tried to open a .jpg file, you will be asked to identify a program. If you are not sure which program to use, select Paint or Windows Photo Viewer. From the ribbon, menu bar, or toolbar, click the Print command, and then Close the program window.

Athletic Scholarships Database

PROJECT ACTIVITIES

In Activities 2.18 through 2.33, you will assist Roberto Garza, Athletic Director for Texas Lakes Community College, in creating queries to locate information about athletic scholarships that have been awarded to students. Your completed database objects will look similar to Figure 2.27.

Please always review the downloaded Grader instructions before beginning.

PROJECT FILES

MyITLab
grader

If your instructor wants you to submit Project 2B in the MyITLab Grader system, log in to MyITLab, locate Grader Project 2B, and then download the files for this project.

For Project 2B, you will need the following files:

a02B_Athletes_Scholarships
a02B_Athletes (Excel workbook)

You will save your document as:

Lastname_Firstname_2B_Athletes_Scholarships

PROJECT RESULTS

GO!
Walk Thru
Project 2B

Access 2016, Windows 10, Microsoft Corporation

FIGURE 2.27 Project 2B Athletic Scholarships

PROJECT RESULTS

In this project, using your own name, you will create the following database and objects. Your instructor may ask you to submit printouts or PDF electronic images:

Lastname_Firstname_2B_Athletes_Scholarships	Database file
Lastname Firstname 2B Relationships	Relationships Report
Lastname Firstname 2B $300 or More Query	Query
Lastname Firstname 2B Awards May-June Query	Query
Lastname Firstname 2B Football AND Over $500	Query
Lastname Firstname 2B Volleyball OR Golf AND Over $200 Query	Query
Lastname Firstname 2B Tennis OR Swimming Query	Query
Lastname Firstname 2B Wildcard Query	Query
Lastname Firstname 2B Alumni Donations Query	Query
Lastname Firstname 2B Total by Sport Query	Query
Lastname Firstname 2B Sport and Team Crosstab Query	Query
Lastname Firstname 2B City Parameter Query	Query (Round Rock)

Objective 8 Specify Numeric Criteria in a Query

GO! Learn How
Video A2-8

Criteria can be set for fields containing numeric data. When you design your table, set the appropriate data type for fields that will contain numbers, currency, or dates so that mathematical calculations can be performed.

2.2.4, 1.1.3, 1.2.2,
2.4.5, 1.3.5

Activity 2.18 | Opening, Renaming, and Saving an Existing Database and Importing a Spreadsheet as a New Table

ALERT!

To submit as an autograded project, log into MyITLab and download the files for this project, and begin with those files instead of the a02B_Athletes_Scholarships file from your student data files. For Project 2B using Grader, begin working with the database in Step 3. For Grader to award points accurately, when saving an object, do not include your Lastname Firstname at the beginning of the object name.

In this Activity you will open, rename, and save an existing database, and then import an Excel spreadsheet as a new table in the database.

1 Start Access. In the Access opening screen, click **Open Other Files**. Under **Open**, click **Browse** and then navigate to the location where your student data files are stored. Double-click **a02B_Athletes_Scholarships** to open the database.

2 On the **File tab**, click **Save As**. Under **File Types**, be sure **Save Database As** is selected, and on the right, under **Database File Types**, be sure **Access Database** is selected, and then click **Save As**. In the **Save As** dialog box, navigate to your **Access Chapter 2** folder, click in the **File name** box, type **Lastname_Firstname_2B_Athletes_Scholarships** and then press Enter.

3 On the **Message Bar**, click **Enable Content**. In the **Navigation Pane**, right-click **2B Scholarships Awarded**, and then click **Rename**. Type **Lastname Firstname 2B Scholarships Awarded** and then press Enter. Double-click the table name to open it in **Datasheet** view. **Close** « the **Navigation Pane**, and then examine the data in the table. Compare your screen with Figure 2.28.

In this table, Mr. Garza tracks the names and amounts of scholarships awarded to student athletes. Students are identified only by their Student ID numbers, and the primary key is the Scholarship ID field.

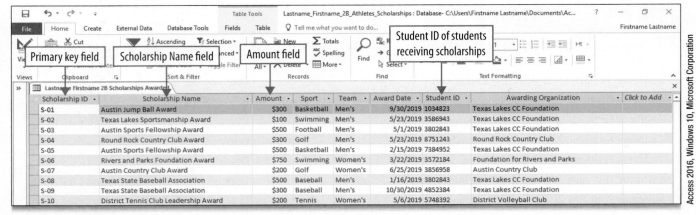

FIGURE 2.28

4 ▶ **Close** ☒ the table. On the ribbon, click the **External Data tab**, and then in the **Import & Link group**, click **Excel**. In the **Get External Data – Excel Spreadsheet** dialog box, to the right of the **File name** box, click **Browse**.

5 ▶ In the **File Open** dialog box, navigate to your student data files, and then double-click **a02B_Athletes**. Be sure that the **Import the source data into a new table in the current database** option button is selected, and then click **OK**.

> The Import Spreadsheet Wizard opens and displays the spreadsheet data.

6 ▶ In the upper left area of the wizard, select the **First Row Contains Column Headings** check box. In the wizard, click **Next**, and then click **Next** again.

7 ▶ In the wizard, click the **Choose my own primary key** option button, and then be sure that **Student ID** displays in the box.

> In the new table, Student ID will be designated as the primary key. No two students have the same Student ID.

8 ▶ Click **Next**. With the text selected in the **Import to Table** box, type **Lastname Firstname 2B Athletes** and then click **Finish**. In the **Get External Data – Excel Spreadsheet** dialog box, click **Close**.

9 ▶ **Open** ⏵⏵ the **Navigation Pane**, and increase the width of the pane so that the two table names display fully. In the **Navigation Pane**, right-click your **2B Athletes** table, and then click **Design View**. **Close** ⏴⏴ the **Navigation Pane**.

10 ▶ To the right of **Student ID**, click in the **Data Type** box, click the **arrow**, and then click **Short Text**. For the **Postal Code** field, change the **Data Type** to **Short Text**, and in the **Field Properties** area, click **Field Size**, type **5** and then press Enter. In the **Field Name** column, click **State**, set the **Field Size** to **2** and then press Enter. Compare your screen with Figure 2.29.

> Recall that numeric data that does not represent a quantity and is not used in a calculation, such as the Student ID and Postal Code, should be assigned a data type of Short Text.

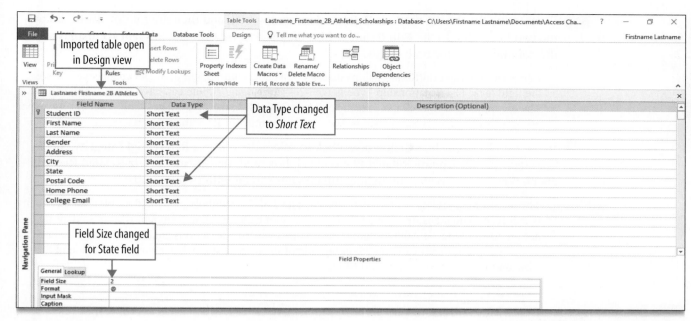

FIGURE 2.29

11 On the **Design tab**, in the **Views group**, click the top half of the **View button** to switch to **Datasheet** view. In the message box, click **Yes** to save the table. In the second message box, click **Yes**—no data will be lost. Take a moment to examine the data in the imported table.

12 In the datasheet, to the left of the **Student ID** field name, click the **Select All** button. On the **Home tab**, in the **Records group**, click **More**, and then click **Field Width**. In the **Column Width** dialog box, click **Best Fit**. Click in any record to cancel the selection, **Save** the table, and then **Close** the table.

1.2.1, 1.2.3, 1.2.4

Activity 2.19 | Creating a One-to-Many Table Relationship

In this Activity you will create a one-to-many relationship between your 2B Athletes table and your 2B Scholarships Awarded table by using the common field—*Student ID*.

1 Click the **Database Tools tab**, and then in the **Relationships group**, click **Relationships**.

2 In the **Show Table** dialog box, double-click your **2B Athletes** table, and then double-click your **2B Scholarships Awarded** table to add both tables to the **Relationships** window. **Close** the **Show Table** dialog box.

3 Point to the title bar of the field list on the right, and drag the field list to the right until there are approximately three inches of space between the field lists. By dragging the lower right corner of the field list, resize each field list to display all of the field names and the entire table name.

Repositioning and resizing the field lists are not required, but doing so makes it easier for you to view the field names and the join line when creating relationships.

4 In the **2B Athletes** field list, point to **Student ID**, and then, holding down the left mouse button, drag the field name into the **2B Scholarships Awarded** field list on top of **Student ID**. Release the mouse button to display the **Edit Relationships** dialog box.

5 Point to the title bar of the **Edit Relationships** dialog box, and then drag it downward below the two field lists. In the **Edit Relationships** dialog box, be sure that **Student ID** displays as the common field for both tables.

Repositioning the Edit Relationships dialog box is not required, but doing so enables you to see the field lists. The Relationship Type is *One-To-Many*—*one* athlete can have *many* scholarships. The common field in both tables is the *Student ID* field. In the 2B Athletes table, Student ID is the primary key. In the 2B Scholarships Awarded table, Student ID is the foreign key.

6 In the **Edit Relationships** dialog box, click to select the **Enforce Referential Integrity** check box, the **Cascade Update Related Fields** check box, and the **Cascade Delete Related Records** check box. Click **Create**, and then compare your screen with Figure 2.30.

The one-to-many relationship is established. The *1* and ∞ symbols indicate that referential integrity is enforced, which ensures that a scholarship cannot be awarded to a student whose Student ID is not included in the 2B Athletes table. Recall that the Cascade options enable you to update and delete records automatically on the *many* side of the relationship when changes are made in the table on the *one* side of the relationship.

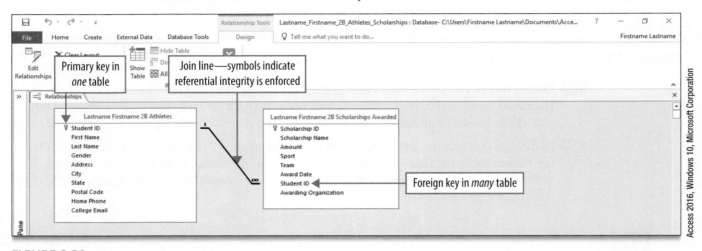

FIGURE 2.30

7 On the **Design tab**, in the **Tools group**, click **Relationship Report**. On the **Print Preview tab**, in the **Page Size group**, click **Margins**, and then click **Normal**. Save 🖫 the report as **Lastname Firstname 2B Relationships** and then create a paper or PDF electronic image as directed. This is the first of eleven objects printed in this project.

8 In the object window, right-click either **object tab**, and then click **Close All** to close the Relationships Report and the Relationships window.

9 Open ⟩⟩ the **Navigation Pane**, double-click your **2B Athletes** table to open it, and then Close ⟨⟨ the **Navigation Pane**. On the left side of the first record, click **+** (plus sign) to display the subdatasheet for the record.

In the first record, for *Joel Barthmaier*, one related record exists in the 2B Scholarships Awarded table. Joel has been awarded the *Austin Jump Ball Award* in the amount of *$300*. The subdatasheet displays because you created a relationship between the two tables using Student ID as the common field.

10 Close ☒ the **2B Athletes** table.

When you close the table, the subdatasheet will collapse—you do not need to click – (minus sign) before closing a table.

Activity 2.20 | Specifying Numeric Criteria in a Query

In this Activity you will create a query to answer the question, *Which scholarships are in the amount of $300, and for which sports?*

1 Click the **Create tab**. In the **Queries group**, click **Query Design**.

2 In the **Show Table** dialog box, double-click your **2B Scholarships Awarded** table to add it to the table area, and then **Close** the **Show Table** dialog box. Resize the field list to display all of the fields and the entire table name.

3 Add the following fields to the design grid in the order given: **Scholarship Name**, **Sport**, and **Amount**.

4 Click in the **Sort** row under **Sport**, click the **arrow**, and then click **Ascending**.

5 Click in the **Criteria** row under **Amount**, type **300** and then press Enter. Compare your screen with Figure 2.31.

> When you enter currency values as criteria, do not type the dollar sign. Include a decimal point only if you are looking for a specific amount that includes cents; for example, 300.49. Access does not insert quotation marks around the criteria because the data type of the field is Currency, which is a numeric format.

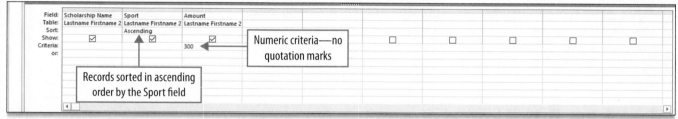

FIGURE 2.31

Access 2016, Windows 10, Microsoft Corporation

6 On the **Design tab**, in the **Results group**, click **Run** to display the query results.

> Five scholarships in the exact amount of $300 were awarded to student athletes. In the navigation area, *1 of 5* displays—1 represents the first record that is selected, and 5 represents the total number of records that meet the criteria.

7 On the **Home tab**, in the **Views group**, click **View** to switch to **Design** view.

Activity 2.21 | Using Comparison Operators in Criteria

3.3.4, 1.3.5,
3.1.6

Comparison operators are symbols that are used to evaluate data in the field to determine if it is the same (=), greater than (>), less than (<), or in between a range of values as specified by the criteria. If no comparison operator is specified, equal (=) is assumed. For example, in the previous Activity you created a query to display only those records where the *Amount* is *300*. The comparison operator of = was assumed, and the query results displayed only those records that had values in the Amount field equal to 300.

1 In the design grid, in the **Criteria** row under **Amount**, select the existing criteria—*300*—and then type **>300** and press Enter. **Run** the query.

> Fourteen records display, and each has a value *greater than* $300 in the Amount field; there are no records for which the Amount is *equal to* $300.

2 Switch to **Design** view. In the **Criteria** row under **Amount**, select the existing criteria—*>300*. Type **<300** and then press Enter. **Run** the query.

> Eleven records display, and each has a value *less than* $300 in the Amount field; there are no records for which the Amount is *equal to* $300.

3 Switch to **Design** view. In the **Criteria** row under **Amount**, select the existing criteria—*<300*. Type **>=300** and then press Enter. **Run** the query, and then compare your screen with Figure 2.32.

> Nineteen records display, including the records for scholarships in the exact amount of $300. The records include scholarships *greater than* or *equal to* $300. In this manner, comparison operators can be combined. This query answers the question, *Which scholarships have been awarded in the amount of $300 or more, and for which sports, arranged alphabetically by sport?*

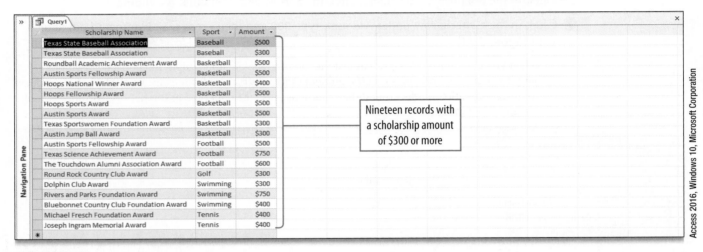

FIGURE 2.32

4 Save the query as **Lastname Firstname 2B $300 or More Query** and then display the query results in **Print Preview**. Create a paper or PDF electronic image as directed, and then click **Close Print Preview**. This is the second of eleven objects printed in this project.

5 Close ⊠ the query. **Open** ⟩⟩ the **Navigation Pane**, and notice that this new query displays under *2B Scholarships Awarded*, its data source.

Activity 2.22 | Using the Between … And Comparison Operator

3.2.2, 3.3.4,
1.3.5, 3.1.6

The ***Between … And operator*** is a comparison operator that looks for values within a range. It is useful when you need to locate records that are within a range of dates; for example, scholarships awarded between May 1 and June 30.

In this Activity you will create a new query from an existing query, and then add criteria to look for values within a range of dates. The query will answer the question, *Which scholarships were awarded between May 1 and June 30?*

1 In the **Navigation Pane**, click your **2B $300 or More Query** object to select it. On the **Home tab**, in the **Clipboard** group, click **Copy**. In the **Navigation Pane**, point to a blank area, right-click, and then click **Paste**.

2 In the **Paste As** dialog box, type **Lastname Firstname 2B Awards May-June Query** and then click **OK**.

> A new query, based on a copy of your 2B $300 or More Query, is created and displays in the Navigation Pane under its data source—your 2B Scholarships Awarded table.

3 In the **Navigation Pane**, right-click your **2B Awards May-June Query**, click **Design View**, and then **Close** ⟨«⟩ the **Navigation Pane**.

4 In the **2B Scholarships Awarded** field list, double-click **Award Date** to add it to the fourth column in the design grid.

5 In the **Criteria** row under **Amount**, select the existing criteria—>=*300*—and then press ⟨Del⟩ so that the query is not restricted by a monetary value.

6 Click in the **Criteria** row under **Award Date**, type **between 5/1/19 and 6/30/19** and then press ⟨Enter⟩.

7 In the selection bar of the design grid, point to the right edge of the **Award Date** column to display the ⟨+⟩ pointer, and then double-click to apply Best Fit to this column. Compare your screen with Figure 2.33.

> The width of the Award Date column is increased to fit the longest entry in the column, which enables you to see all of the criteria. Access places pound signs (#) around the dates and capitalizes *between* and *and*. This criteria instructs Access to look for values in the Award Date field that begin with 5/1/19 and end with 6/30/19. Both the beginning and ending dates will be included in the query results.

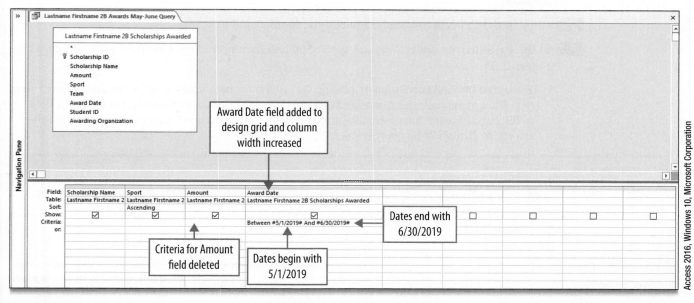

Access 2016, Windows 10, Microsoft Corporation

FIGURE 2.33

8 **Run** the query, and notice that eight scholarships were awarded between 5/1/2019 and 6/30/2019.

9 Display the query results in **Print Preview**, create a paper or PDF electronic image as directed, and then click **Close Print Preview**. This is the third of eleven objects printed in this project. **Close** ⟨✕⟩ the query, and in the message box, click **Yes** to save the changes to the query design.

GO! Learn How
Video A2-9

You can specify more than one condition—criteria—in a query; this is called *compound criteria*. Compound criteria use AND and OR *logical operators*. Logical operators enable you to enter multiple criteria for the same field or for different fields.

Activity 2.23 | Using AND Criteria in a Query

MOS
3.1.1, 3.2.2,
3.3.4, 3.3.5,
1.3.5, 3.1.6

The *AND condition* is an example of a compound criteria used to display records that match all parts of the specified criteria. In this Activity you will help Mr. Garza answer the question, *Which scholarships over $500 were awarded for football?*

1 Click the **Create tab**, and in the **Queries group**, click **Query Design**. In the **Show Table** dialog box, double-click your **2B Scholarships Awarded** table to add it to the table area, and then **Close** the **Show Table** dialog box. Resize the field list to display all of the fields and the table name.

2 Add the following fields to the design grid in the order given: **Scholarship Name**, **Sport**, and **Amount**.

3 Click in the **Criteria** row under **Sport**, type **football** and then press Enter.

4 In the **Criteria** row under **Amount**, type **>500** and then press Enter. Compare your screen with Figure 2.34.

> You create the AND condition by placing the criteria for both fields on the same line in the Criteria row. The criteria indicates that records should be located that contain *Football* in the Sport field AND a value greater than *500* in the Amount field. Both conditions must exist or be true for the records to display in the query results.

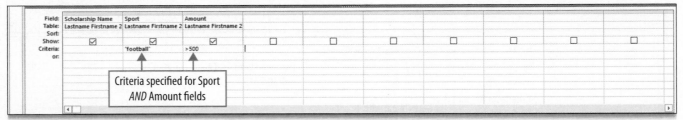

FIGURE 2.34

Access 2016, Windows 10, Microsoft Corporation

5 **Run** the query, and notice that two records display that match both conditions—*Football* in the Sport field AND a value greater than *$500* in the Amount field.

6 **Save** 🖫 the query as **Lastname Firstname 2B Football AND Over $500 Query** and then **Close** ✕ the query.

7 **Open** ⟫ the **Navigation Pane**, and then click to select your **2B Football AND Over $500 Query** object. Click the **File tab**, click **Print**, and then click **Print Preview**.

> You can view an object in Print Preview or print any selected object in the Navigation Pane—the object does not need to be open in the object window to print it.

8 Create a paper or PDF electronic image as directed, and then click **Close Print Preview**. This is the fourth of eleven objects printed in this project. **Close** ⟪ the **Navigation Pane**.

Activity 2.24 | Using OR Criteria in a Query

The **OR condition** is an example of a compound criteria used to display records that meet one or more parts of the specified criteria. The OR condition can specify criteria in a single field or in different fields. In this Activity you will help Mr. Garza answer the question, *Which scholarships over $200 were awarded for volleyball or golf, and what is the award date of each?*

1 On the **Create tab**, in the **Queries group**, click **Query Design**.

2 In the **Show Table** dialog box, double-click your **2B Scholarships Awarded** table to add it to the table area, and then **Close** the **Show Table** dialog box. Resize the field list, and then add the following fields to the design grid in the order given: **Scholarship Name**, **Sport**, **Amount**, and **Award Date**.

3 In the design grid, click in the **Criteria** row under **Sport**, type **volleyball** and then press ⬇.

The insertion point is blinking in the *or* row under Sport.

4 In the **or** row under **Sport**, type **golf** and then press Enter. **Run** the query.

Six records were located in the 2B Scholarships Awarded table that have either *volleyball* OR *golf* stored in the Sport field. This is an example of using the OR condition to locate records that meet one or more parts of the specified criteria in a single field—*Sport*.

5 Switch to **Design** view. In the **or** row under **Sport**, select *"golf"* and then press Del. In the **Criteria** row under **Sport**, select and delete *"volleyball"*. Type **volleyball or golf** and then press Enter.

6 In the **Criteria** row under **Amount**, type **>200** and then press Enter. Compare your screen with Figure 2.35.

This is an alternative way to enter the OR condition in the Sport field and is a good method to use when you add an AND condition to the criteria. Access will locate records where the Sport field contains *volleyball* OR *golf* AND where the Amount field contains a value greater than *200*.

If you enter *volleyball* in the Criteria row, and *golf* in the or row for the Sport field, then you must enter *>200* in both the Criteria row and the or row for the Amount field so that the correct records are located when the query is run.

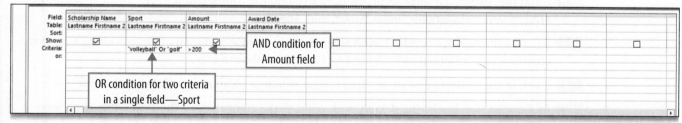

FIGURE 2.35

7 **Run** the query.

Two records were located in the 2B Scholarships Awarded table that have either *Volleyball* OR *Golf* stored in the Sport field AND a value greater than $200 in the Amount field. This is an example of using the OR condition in combination with an AND condition.

8 **Save** 🖫 the query as **Lastname Firstname 2B Volleyball OR Golf AND Over $200 Query** and then display the query results in **Print Preview**. Create a paper or PDF electronic image as directed, click **Close Print Preview**, and then **Close** ✕ the query. This is the fifth of eleven objects printed in this project.

Objective 10 | Create a Query Based on More Than One Table

GO! Learn How
Video A2-10

In a relational database, you can retrieve information from more than one table. Recall that a table in a relational database contains all of the records about a single topic. Tables are joined to one another by relating the primary key in one table to the foreign key in another table. This common field is used to create the relationship and is used to find records from multiple tables when the query is created and run.

For example, the Athletes table stores all of the data about the student athletes—name, address, and so on. The Scholarships Awarded table stores data about the scholarship name, the amount, and so on. When an athlete receives a scholarship, only the Student ID of the athlete is used to identify the athlete in the Scholarships Awarded table. It is not necessary to include any other data about the athlete in the Scholarships Awarded table; doing so would result in redundant data.

Activity 2.25 | Creating a Query Based on More Than One Table

3.1.1, 3.2.2,
3.1.5, 3.2.5,
3.3.5, 3.1.6

In this Activity you will create a query that selects records from two tables. This is possible because you created a relationship between the two tables in the database. The query will answer the questions, *What is the name, email address, and phone number of athletes who have received a scholarship for tennis or swimming, and what is the name and amount of the scholarship?*

1 On the **Create tab**, in the **Queries group**, click **Query Design**. In the **Show Table** dialog box, double-click your **2B Athletes** table, and then double-click your **2B Scholarships Awarded** table to add both tables to the table area. In the **Show Table** dialog box, click **Close**. Drag the **2B Scholarships Awarded** field list to the right so that there are approximately three inches of space between the two field lists, and then resize each field list to display all of the field names and the entire table name.

The join line displays because you created a one-to-many relationship between the two tables using the common field of Student ID; *one* athlete can have *many* scholarships.

2 From the **2B Athletes** field list, add the following fields to the design grid in the order given: **First Name**, **Last Name**, **College Email**, and **Home Phone**.

3 From the **2B Scholarships Awarded** field list, add the following fields to the design grid in the order given: **Scholarship Name**, **Sport**, and **Amount**.

4 Click in the **Sort** row under **Last Name**, click the **arrow**, and then click **Ascending** to sort the records in alphabetical order by the last names of the athletes.

5 Click in the **Criteria** row under **Sport**, type **tennis or swimming** and then press Enter.

6 In the selection bar of the design grid, point to the right edge of the **Home Phone** column to display the ⊞ pointer, and then double-click to increase the width of the column and to display the entire table name on the **Table** row. Using the same technique, increase the width of the **Scholarship Name** column. If necessary, scroll to the right to display both of these columns in the design grid, and then compare your screen with Figure 2.36.

When locating data from multiple tables, the information in the Table row is helpful, especially when different tables include the same field name, such as Address. Although the field name is the same, the data may be different—for example, an athlete's address or a coach's address from two different related tables.

FIGURE 2.36

7 ▸ **Run** the query, and then compare your screen with Figure 2.37.

Eight records display for athletes who received either a Swimming *or* Tennis scholarship, and the records are sorted in ascending order by the Last Name field. Because the common field of Student ID is included in both tables, Access can locate the specified fields in both tables by using one query. Two students—*Carla Reid* and *Florence Zimmerman*—received two scholarships, one for swimming and one for tennis. Recall that *one* student athlete can receive *many* scholarships.

FIGURE 2.37

8 ▸ **Save** 🖫 the query as **Lastname Firstname 2B Tennis OR Swimming Query** and then display the query results in **Print Preview**. Change the orientation to **Landscape**, and the **Margins** to **Normal**. Create a paper or PDF electronic image as directed, and then click **Close Print Preview**. This is the sixth of eleven objects printed in this project.

9 ▸ **Close** ✕ the query, **Open** » the **Navigation Pane**, increase the width of the **Navigation Pane** to display all object names fully, and then compare your screen with Figure 2.38.

Your *2B Tennis OR Swimming Query* object name displays under both tables from which it selected records.

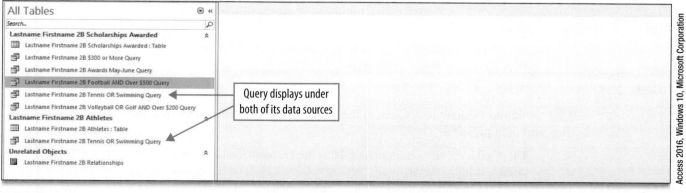

FIGURE 2.38

10 ▸ **Close** « the **Navigation Pane**.

A *wildcard character* is used to represent one or more unknown characters in a string. When you are unsure of the specific character or set of characters to include in the criteria for a query, use a wildcard character in place of the character.

Activity 2.26 | Using a Wildcard in a Query

Use the asterisk (*) wildcard character to represent one or more unknown characters. For example, entering Fo* as the criteria in a last name field will result in displaying records containing last names of Foster, Forrester, Fossil, or any other last name that begins with *Fo*. In this Activity you will use the asterisk (*) wildcard character in criteria to answer the question, *Which athletes received scholarships from local Rotary Clubs, country clubs, or foundations?*

1 On the **Create tab**, in the **Queries group**, click **Query Design**. In the **Show Table** dialog box, double-click your **2B Athletes** table, and then double-click your **2B Scholarships Awarded** table to add both tables to the table area. In the **Show Table** dialog box, click **Close**. Drag the **2B Scholarships Awarded** field list to the right so that there are approximately three inches of space between the two field lists, and then resize each field list to display all of the field names and the entire table name.

2 From the **2B Athletes** field list, add the following fields to the design grid in the order given: **First Name** and **Last Name**. From the **2B Scholarships Awarded** field list, add the **Awarding Organization** field to the design grid.

3 Click in the **Sort** row under **Last Name**, click the **arrow**, and then click **Ascending** to sort the records in alphabetical order by the last names of the athletes.

4 Click in the **Criteria** row under **Awarding Organization**, type **rotary*** and then press Enter.

The * wildcard character is a placeholder used to match one or more unknown characters. After pressing Enter, Access adds *Like* to the beginning of the criteria.

5 **Run** the query, and then compare your screen with Figure 2.39.

Three athletes received scholarships from a Rotary Club from different cities. The results are sorted alphabetically by the Last Name field.

FIGURE 2.39

6 Switch to **Design** view. Click in the **or** row under **Awarding Organization**, type ***country club** and then press Enter.

The * wildcard character can be used at the beginning, middle, or end of the criteria. The position of the * determines the location of the unknown characters. By entering **country club*, you will locate records where the Awarding Organization name ends in *Country Club*.

7 **Run** the query.

Six records display for students receiving scholarships; three from organizations with a name that begins with *Rotary*, and three from organizations with a name that ends with *Country Club*.

8 Switch to **Design** view. In the design grid under **Awarding Organization** and under **Like "*country club"**, type ***foundation*** and then press [Enter]. Compare your screen with Figure 2.40.

> This query will also display records where the Awarding Organization has *Foundation* anywhere in the organization name—at the beginning, middle, or end. Three *OR* criteria have been entered for the Awarding Organization field. When run, this query will locate records where the Awarding Organization has a name that begins with *Rotary*, OR ends with *Country Club*, OR that has *Foundation* anywhere in its name.

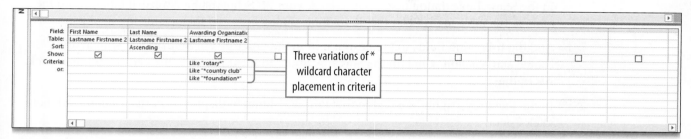

FIGURE 2.40

Access 2016, Windows 10, Microsoft Corporation

9 **Run** the query.

> Twenty-eight scholarships were awarded from organizations where the name of the organization begins with Rotary, ends with Country Club, or has Foundation anywhere in its name. The records are sorted alphabetically by the Last Name field.

10 **Save** 🖫 the query as **Lastname Firstname 2B Wildcard Query** and then display the query results in **Print Preview**. Create a paper or PDF electronic image as directed, and then click **Close Print Preview**. This is the seventh of eleven objects printed in this project.

11 **Close** ✕ the query, and then **Open** » the **Navigation Pane**. Notice that your **2B Wildcard Query** displays under both tables because the query selected data from both tables—the data sources.

More Knowledge — Using the ? Wildcard Character to Search for a Single Unknown Character

The question mark (?) wildcard character is used to search for a single unknown character. For each question mark included in the criteria, any character can be located. For example, entering *b?d* as the criteria will result in the display of words such as *bed*, *bid*, or *bud*, or any three-character word that begins with *b* and ends with *d*. Entering *b??d* as the criteria will results in the display of words such as *bard*, *bend*, or *bind*, or any four-character word that begins with *b* and ends with *d*.

Objective 12 Create Calculated Fields in a Query

GO! Learn How
Video A2-12

Queries can create calculated values that are stored in a ***calculated field***. A calculated field stores the value of a mathematical operation. For example, you can multiply the value stored in a field named Total Hours Worked by the value stored in a field named Hourly Pay to display the Gross Pay value for each work study student.

There are two steps to create a calculated field in a query. First, name the field that will store the results of the calculation. Second, enter the ***expression***—the formula—that will perform the calculation. When entering the information for the calculated field in the query, the new field name must be followed by a colon (:), and each field name from the table used in the expression must be enclosed within its own pair of brackets.

For each scholarship received by student athletes, the Texas Lakes Community College Alumni Association will donate an amount equal to 50 percent of each scholarship. In this Activity you will create a calculated field to determine the amount that the alumni association will donate for each scholarship. The query will answer the question, *How much money will the alumni association donate for each student athlete who is awarded a scholarship?*

1 Close « the **Navigation Pane**. On the **Create tab**, in the **Queries group**, click **Query Design**. In the **Show Table** dialog box, double-click your **2B Scholarships Awarded** table to add the table to the table area, **Close** the **Show Table** dialog box, and then resize the field list.

2 Add the following fields to the design grid in the order given: **Student ID**, **Scholarship Name**, and **Amount**. Click in the **Sort** row under **Student ID**, click the **arrow**, and then click **Ascending**.

3 In the **Field** row, right-click in the first empty column to display a shortcut menu, and then click **Zoom**.

> Although the calculation can be typed directly in the empty Field box, the Zoom dialog box gives you more working space and enables you to see the entire calculation as you enter it.

4 In the **Zoom** dialog box, type **Alumni Donation:[Amount]*0.5** and then compare your screen with Figure 2.41.

> The first element, *Alumni Donation*, is the new field name that will identify the result of the calculation when the query is run; the field is not added back to the table. The new field name is followed by a colon (:), which separates the new field name from the expression. *Amount* is enclosed in brackets because it is an existing field name in your 2B Scholarships Awarded table; it contains the numeric data on which the calculation is performed. Following the right square bracket is the asterisk (*), the mathematical operator for multiplication. Finally, the percentage expressed as a decimal—*0.5*—displays.

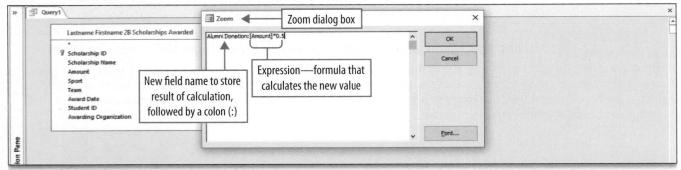

FIGURE 2.41

Access 2016, Windows 10, Microsoft Corporation

5 In the **Zoom** dialog box, click **OK**, **Run** the query, and then compare your screen with Figure 2.42.

> The query results display three fields from your 2B Scholarships Awarded table and a fourth field—*Alumni Donation*—that displays a calculated value. Each calculated value equals the value in the Amount field multiplied by 0.5 or 50%.

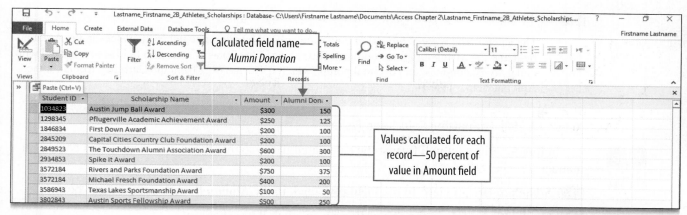

FIGURE 2.42

ALERT! **Do your query results differ from Figure 2.42?**

If your new field name does not display or if the results of the calculation do not display as shown in Figure 2.42, switch to Design view and carefully examine the expression you entered. Spelling or syntax errors prevent calculated fields from working properly.

---

6 Notice the formatting of the values in the **Alumni Donation** field—there are no dollar signs to match the formatting in the **Amount** field; you will adjust the formatting of this field later.

When using a number, such as 0.5, in an expression, the values that display in the calculated field may not be formatted the same as the existing field that was part of the calculation.

Activity 2.28 | Creating a Second Calculated Field in a Query

3.1.1, 3.3.1, 1.3.5

In this Activity you will create a calculated field to determine the total value of each scholarship after the alumni association donates an additional 50% based on the amount awarded by various organizations. The query will answer the question, *What is the total value of each scholarship after the alumni association donates an additional 50%?*

1 Switch to **Design** view. In the **Field** row, right-click in the first empty column to display a shortcut menu, and then click **Zoom**.

2 In the **Zoom** dialog box, type **Total Scholarship:[Amount]+[Alumni Donation]** and then compare your screen with Figure 2.43.

Each existing field name—*Amount* and *Alumni Donation*—must be enclosed in separate pairs of brackets.

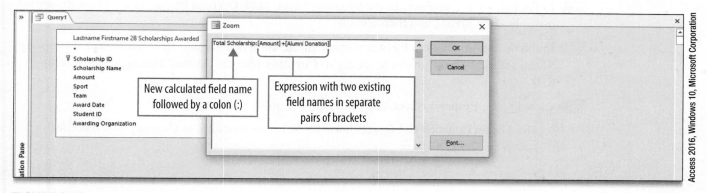

FIGURE 2.43

3 In the **Zoom** dialog box, click **OK**, and then **Run** the query.

> The value in the *Total Scholarship* field is calculated by adding together the values in the Amount field and the Matching Donation field. The values in the Total Scholarship field are formatted with dollar signs, commas, and decimal points, which is carried over from the Currency format in the Amount field.

Activity 2.29 | Formatting Calculated Fields

1.3.5, 3.2.6,
3.1.1, 3.1.6

In this Activity you will format the calculated fields so that the values display in a consistent manner.

1 Switch to **Design** view. In the **Field** row, click in the **Alumni Donation** field name box.

2 On the **Design tab**, in the **Show/Hide group**, click **Property Sheet**.

> The Property Sheet displays on the right side of your screen. Recall that a Property Sheet enables you to make precise changes to the properties—characteristics—of selected items, in this case, a field.

↻ **ANOTHER WAY**   In the design grid, on the Field row, right-click in the Alumni Donation field name box, and then click Properties.

---

3 In the **Property Sheet**, with the **General tab** active, click **Format**. In the property setting box, click the **arrow**, and then compare your screen with Figure 2.44.

> A list of available formats for the Alumni Donation field displays.

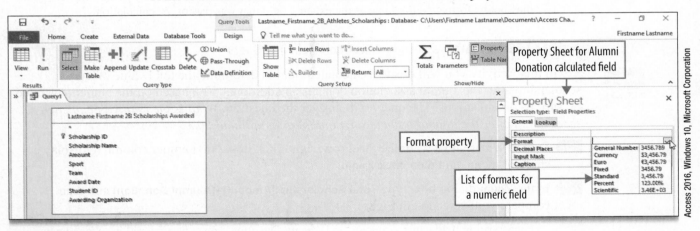

FIGURE 2.44

4 In the list, click **Currency**. In the **Property Sheet**, click **Decimal Places**. In the property setting box, click the **arrow**, and then click **0**.

5 In the design grid, in the **Field** row, click in the **Total Scholarship** field name. In the **Property Sheet**, set the **Format** property setting to **Currency** and the **Decimal Places** property setting to **0**.

6 Close ⊠ the **Property Sheet**, and then **Run** the query.

> The Alumni Donation and Total Scholarship fields are formatted as Currency with 0 decimal places.

7 To the left of the **Student ID** field name, click the **Select All** ▢ button. On the **Home tab**, in the **Records group**, click **More**, and then click **Field Width**. In the **Column Width** dialog box, click **Best Fit**. Click in any field, and then **Save** 🖫 the query as **Lastname Firstname 2B Alumni Donations Query**

> The field widths are adjusted to display fully the calculated field names.

8 Display the query results in **Print Preview**. Change the **Margins** to **Normal**. Create a paper or PDF electronic image as directed, and then click **Close Print Preview**. This is the eighth of eleven objects printed in this project. **Close** ☒ the query.

Objective 13 Calculate Statistics and Group Data in a Query

GO! Learn How
Video A2-13

Queries can be used to perform statistical calculations known as *aggregate functions* on a group of records. For example, you can find the total or average amount for a group of records, or you can find the lowest or highest number in a group of records.

Activity 2.30 | Using the Min, Max, Avg, and Sum Functions in a Query

MOS
3.1.1, 3.2.2,
3.3.3, 1.3.5

In this Activity you will use aggregate functions to find the lowest and highest scholarships amounts and the average and total scholarship amounts. The last query in this Activity will answer the question, *What is the total dollar amount of all scholarships awarded?*

1 On the **Create tab**, in the **Queries group**, click **Query Design**. In the **Show Table** dialog box, double-click your **2B Scholarships Awarded** table to add the table to the table area, **Close** the **Show Table** dialog box, and then resize the field list.

2 Add the **Amount** field to the design grid.

> Include only the field to summarize in the design grid, so that the aggregate function is applied only to that field.

3 On the **Design tab**, in the **Show/Hide group**, click **Totals** to add a **Total** row as the third row in the design grid. Notice that in the design grid, on the **Total** row under **Amount**, *Group By* displays.

> Use the Total row to select an aggregate function for the selected field.

4 In the **Total** row under **Amount**, click in the box that displays *Group By*, and then click the **arrow** to display a list of aggregate functions. Compare your screen with Figure 2.45, and then take a moment to review the available aggregate functions and the purpose of each function as shown in Figure 2.46.

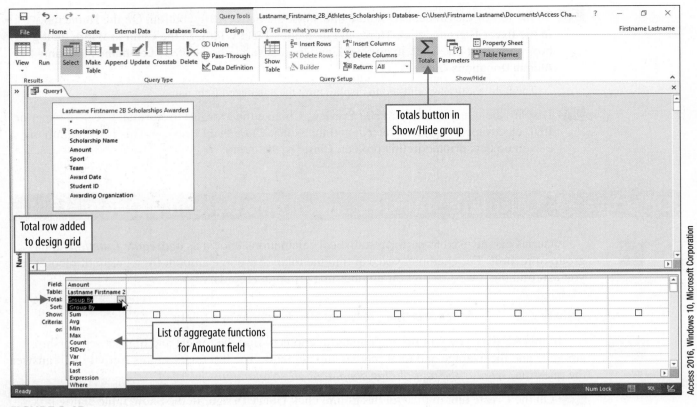

FIGURE 2.45

AGGREGATE FUNCTIONS	
FUNCTION NAME	**PURPOSE**
Group By	Combines data based on matching data in the selected field
Sum	Totals the values in a field
Avg	Averages the values in a field
Min	Locates the smallest value in a field
Max	Locates the largest value in a field
Count	Displays the number of records based on a field
StDev	Calculates the standard deviation for the values in a field
Var	Calculates the variance for the values in a field
First	Displays the first value in a field for the first record
Last	Displays the last value in a field for the last record
Expression	Creates a calculated field that includes an aggregate function
Where	Limits the records to those that match a condition specified in the Criteria row of a field

FIGURE 2.46

> **5** In the list of functions, click **Min**, and then **Run** the query. Point to the right edge of the first column to display the ⊞ mouse pointer, and then double-click to apply **Best Fit** to the field.
>
> Access locates the minimum (smallest) value—*$100*—in the Amount field for all of the records in the 2B Scholarships Awarded table. The field name *MinOfAmount* is automatically created. This query answers the question, *What is the minimum (smallest) scholarship amount awarded to athletes?*

6 Switch to **Design** view. In the **Total** row under **Amount**, click the **arrow**, and then click **Max**. **Run** the query.

> The maximum (largest) value for a scholarship award amount is *$750.00*.

7 Switch to **Design** view. In the **Total** row, select the **Avg** function, and then **Run** the query.

> The average scholarship award amount is *$358.33*.

8 Switch to **Design** view. In the **Total** row, select the **Sum** function, and then **Run** the query.

> The values in the Amount field for all records are summed and display a result of *$10,750.00*. The field name *SumOfAmount* is automatically created. The query answers the question, *What is the total dollar amount of all scholarships awarded?*

Activity 2.31 | Grouping Records in a Query

1.3.5, 3.3.3, 3.1.6, 3.2.6

You can use aggregate functions and group the records by the data in a field. For example, to group (summarize) the amount of scholarships awarded to each student, you include the Student ID field in addition to the Amount field. Using the Sum aggregate function, the records will be grouped by the Student ID so you can see the total amount of scholarships awarded to each student. Similarly, you can group the records by the Sport field so you can see the total amount of scholarships awarded for each sport.

1 Switch to **Design** view. From the field list, drag the **Student ID** field to the first column of the design grid—the **Amount** field moves to the second column. In the **Total** row under **Student ID**, notice that *Group By* displays.

> This query will group—combine—the records by Student ID and will calculate a total amount for each student.

2 **Run** the query, and then compare your screen with Figure 2.47.

> The query calculates the total amount of all scholarships for each student.

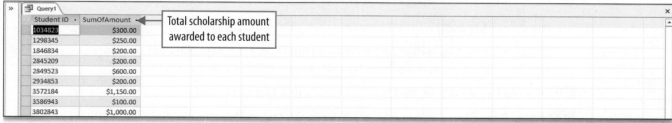

FIGURE 2.47

3 Switch to **Design** view. In the design grid, above **Student ID**, point to the selection bar to display the ⬇ pointer. Click to select the column, and then press Del to remove the **Student ID** field from the design grid.

4 From the field list, drag the **Sport** field to the first column in the design grid—the **Amount** field moves to the second column. Click in the **Sort** row under **Amount**, click the **arrow**, and then click **Descending**.

5 On the **Design tab**, in the **Show/Hide group**, click **Property Sheet**. In the **Property Sheet**, set the **Format** property to **Currency**, and then set the **Decimal Places** property to **0**. **Close** ☒ the **Property Sheet**.

> **6** **Run** the query, and then compare your screen with Figure 2.48.

Access groups—summarizes—the records by each sport and displays the groupings in descending order by the total amount of scholarships awarded for each sport. Basketball scholarships were awarded the largest total amount—*$3,500*—and Volleyball scholarships were awarded the smallest total amount—*$650*.

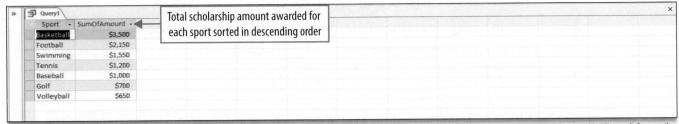

Sport	SumOfAmount
Basketball	$3,500
Football	$2,150
Swimming	$1,550
Tennis	$1,200
Baseball	$1,000
Golf	$700
Volleyball	$650

Total scholarship amount awarded for each sport sorted in descending order

Access 2016, Windows 10, Microsoft Corporation

FIGURE 2.48

> **7** **Save** 🖫 the query as **Lastname Firstname 2B Total by Sport Query** and then display the query results in **Print Preview**. Create a paper or PDF electronic image as directed, click **Close Print Preview**, and then **Close** ☒ the query. This is the ninth of eleven objects printed in this project.

Objective 14 | Create a Crosstab Query

GO! Learn How
Video A2-14

A ***crosstab query*** uses an aggregate function for data that can be grouped by two types of information, and displays the data in a compact, spreadsheet-like format with column headings and row headings. A crosstab query always has at least one row heading, one column heading, and one summary field. Use a crosstab query to summarize a large amount of data in a compact space that is easy to read.

Activity 2.32 | Creating a Crosstab Query Using the Query Wizard

MOS
3.1.2, 3.2.6

In this Activity you will create a crosstab query that displays the total amount of scholarships awarded for each sport and for each type of team—men's or women's.

> **1** On the **Create tab**, in the **Queries group**, click **Query Wizard**.

> **2** In the **New Query** dialog box, click **Crosstab Query Wizard**, and then click **OK**.

> **3** In the **Crosstab Query Wizard**, click your **Table: 2B Scholarships Awarded**, and then click **Next**.

> **4** In the wizard under **Available Fields**, double-click **Sport** to group the scholarship amounts by the sports—the sports will display as row headings. Click **Next**, and then compare your screen with Figure 2.49.

The sport names will be grouped and displayed as row headings, and you are prompted to select column headings.

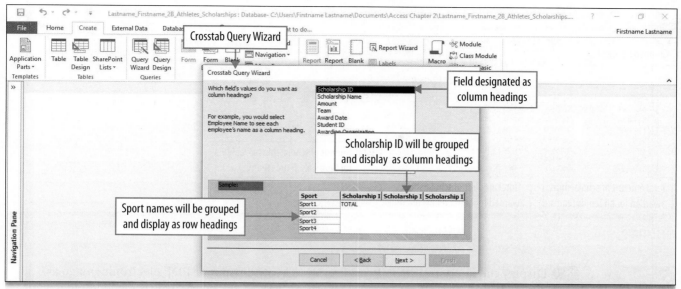

FIGURE 2.49

5 In the wizard, in the field list, click **Team** to select the column headings. Click **Next**, and then compare your screen with Figure 2.50.

The Team types—*Men's* and *Women's*—will display as column headings, and you are prompted to select a field to summarize.

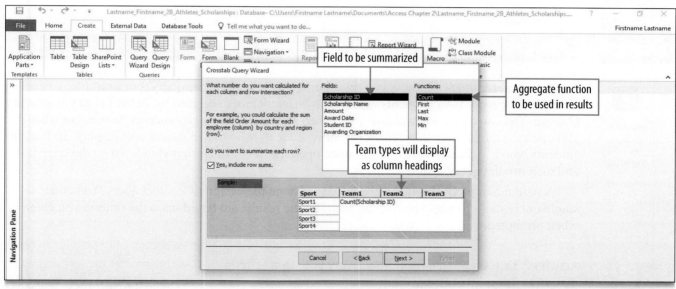

FIGURE 2.50

6 In the wizard under **Fields**, click **Amount**. Under **Functions**, click **Sum**.

The crosstab query will calculate the total scholarship amount for each sport and for each type of team.

7 Click **Next**. In the **What do you want to name your query?** box, select the existing text, type **Lastname Firstname 2B Sport and Team Crosstab Query** and then click **Finish**. Apply **Best Fit** to the datasheet, click in any field to cancel the selection, **Save** 🖫 the query, and then compare your screen with Figure 2.51.

The field widths are adjusted to display fully the calculated field names.

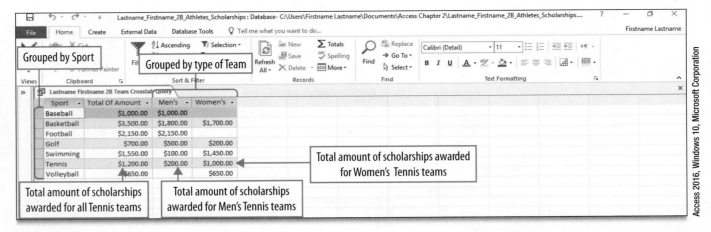

FIGURE 2.51

> **8** Display the query results in **Print Preview**. Create a paper or PDF electronic image as directed, click **Close Print Preview**, and then **Close** ☒ the query. This is the tenth of eleven objects printed in this project.

More **Knowledge**	**Creating a Crosstab Query Using Data from Two Related Tables**

To create a crosstab query using fields from more than one table, you must first create a select query with the fields from both tables, and then use the query as the data source for the crosstab query.

Objective 15 Create a Parameter Query

GO! Learn How
Video A2-15

A ***parameter query*** prompts you for criteria before running the query. For example, you need to display the records for students who live in different cities serviced by Texas Lakes Community College. You can create a select query and enter the criteria for a city such as Austin, but when you open the query, only the records for those students who live in Austin will display. To find the students who live in Round Rock, you must open the query in Design view, change the criteria, and then run the query again.

A parameter query eliminates the need to change the design of a select query. You create a single query that prompts you to enter the city; the results are based upon the criteria you enter when prompted.

Activity 2.33 | Creating a Parameter Query with One Criteria

3.1.1, 3.2.2,
3.1.3, 3.2.5,
3.1.6

In this Activity you will create a parameter query that displays student athletes from a specific city in the areas serviced by Texas Lakes Community College.

> **1** On the **Create tab**, in the **Queries group**, click **Query Design**.

> **2** In the **Show Table** dialog box, double-click your **2B Athletes** table to add it to the table area, **Close** the **Show Table** dialog box, and then resize the field list.

> **3** Add the following fields to the design grid in the order given: **First Name**, **Last Name** **Address**, **City**, **State**, and **Postal Code**.

> **4** In the **Sort** row under **Last Name**, click the **arrow**, and then click **Ascending**.

5 In the **Criteria** row under **City**, type **[Enter a City]** and then press Enter. Compare your screen with Figure 2.52.

The bracketed text indicates a *parameter*—a value that can be changed—rather than specific criteria.

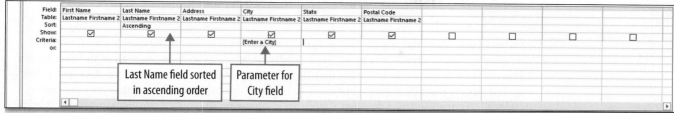

FIGURE 2.52

6 **Run** the query. In the **Enter Parameter Value** dialog box, type **austin** and then compare your screen with Figure 2.53.

The Enter Parameter Value dialog box prompts you to *Enter a City*, which is the text enclosed in brackets that you entered in the criteria row under City. The city you enter will be set as the criteria for the query. Because you are prompted for the criteria, you can reuse this query without having to edit the criteria row in Design view. The value you enter is not case sensitive—you can enter *austin*, *Austin*, or *AUSTIN*.

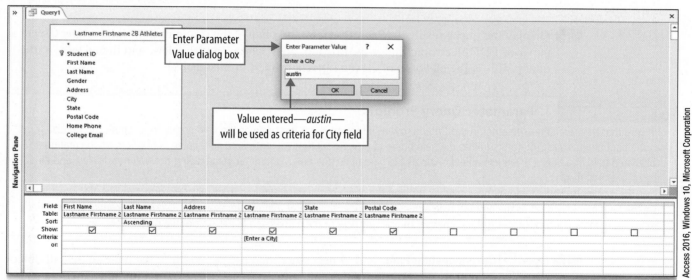

FIGURE 2.53

ALERT! **Did the Enter Parameter Value dialog box not display?**

If the Enter Parameter Value dialog box does not display, you may have typed the parameter incorrectly in the design grid. Common errors include using parentheses or curly braces instead of brackets around the parameter text, which Access interprets as specific criteria, resulting in no records matching the criteria. If you typed curly braces instead of brackets, the query will not run. To correct, display the query in Design view and change the parameter entered in the Criteria row.

---

7 In the **Enter Parameter Value** dialog box, click **OK**.

Twenty-three students live in the city of Austin, and the records are sorted in alphabetical order by the Last Name field.

8 Save 🖫 the query as **Lastname Firstname 2B City Parameter Query**, and then **Close** ☒ the query.

9 Open ⏩ the **Navigation Pane**. In the **Navigation Pane**, under your **2B Athletes** table, double-click your **2B City Parameter Query**. In the **Enter Parameter Value** dialog box, type **round rock** and then click **OK**. **Close** ⏪ the **Navigation Pane**. Compare your screen with Figure 2.54.

Nine students live in the city of Round Rock. Every time you open a parameter query, you are prompted to enter criteria. You may have to apply Best Fit to the columns if all of the data in the fields does not display and you wish to print the query results—the length of the data in the fields changes as new records display depending upon the criteria entered. Recall that only the query design is saved; each time you open a query, it is run using the most up-to-date information in the data source.

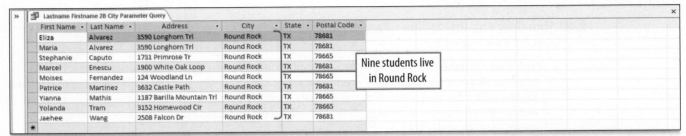

FIGURE 2.54

10 Display the query results in **Print Preview**, and change the orientation to **Landscape**. Create a paper or PDF electronic image as directed, click **Close Print Preview**, and then **Close** ☒ the query. This is the eleventh of eleven objects printed in this project.

More Knowledge   **Parameter Query Prompts**

Be sure that the parameter you enter in the Criteria row as a prompt is not the same as the field name. For example, do not use *[City]* as the parameter. Access interprets this as the field name of *City*. Recall that you entered a field name in brackets when creating a calculated field in a query. If you use a field name as the parameter, the Enter Parameter Value dialog box will not display, and all of the records will display.

The parameter should inform the individual running the query of the data required to display the correct results. If you want to use the field name by itself as the prompt, type a question mark at the end of the text; for example, *[City?]*. You cannot use a period, exclamation mark (!), curly braces ({ }), another set of brackets ([ ]), or the ampersand (&) as part of the parameter.

---

11 Open ⏩ the **Navigation Pane**, and, if necessary increase the width of the pane so that all object names display fully. On the right side of the title bar, click **Close** ☒ to close the database and **Close** Access. As directed by your instructor, submit your database and the paper or PDF electronic images of the 11 objects—relationship report and 10 queries—that are the results of this project.

> **END | You have completed Project 2B**

GO! With Google

Objective | Export an Access Query to an Excel Spreadsheet, Save It in Google Drive, and Create a Chart

Access web apps are designed to work with Microsoft's SharePoint, a service for setting up websites to share and manage documents. Your college may not have SharePoint installed, so you will use other tools to share objects from your database so that you can work collaboratively with others. Recall that Google Drive is Google's free, web-based word processor, spreadsheet, slide show, form, and data storage and sharing service. For Access, you can export a database object to an Excel worksheet, a PDF file, or a text file, and then save the file to Google Drive.

ALERT! **Working with Web-Based Applications and Services**

Computer programs and services on the web receive continuous updates and improvements, so the steps to complete this web-based activity may differ from the ones shown. You can often look at the screens and the information presented to determine how to complete the activity.

If you do not already have a Google account, you will need to create one before doing this activity. Go to http://google.com and in the upper right corner, click Sign In. On the Sign In screen, click Create Account. On the Create your Google Account page, complete the form, read and agree to the Terms of Service and Privacy Policy, and then click Next step. On the Welcome screen, click Get Started.

Activity | Exporting an Access Query to an Excel Spreadsheet, Saving the Spreadsheet to Google Drive, Editing a Record in Google Drive, and Saving to Your Computer

In this Activity you will export your 2B Sport and Team Crosstab Query table to an Excel spreadsheet, upload the Excel file to your Google Drive as a Google Sheet, edit a record in Google Drive, and then download a copy of the edited spreadsheet to your computer.

1 Start Access, navigate to your **Access Chapter 2** folder, and then open your **2B_Athletes_Scholarships** database file. If necessary, on the Message Bar, click **Enable Content**. In the **Navigation Pane**, click your **2B Sport and Team Crosstab** Query one time to select it—do not open it.

2 Click the **External Data tab**, and then in the **Export group**, click **Excel**. In the **Export – Excel Spreadsheet** dialog box, click **Browse**, and then navigate to your **Access Chapter 2** folder. In the **File Save** dialog box, click in the **File name** box, type **Lastname_Firstname_AC_2B_Web** and then click **Save**.

3 In the **Export – Excel Spreadsheet** dialog box, under **Specify export options**, select the first two check boxes—**Export data with formatting and layout** and **Open the destination file after the export operation is complete**—and then click **OK**. Take a moment to examine the data in the file, and then **Close** Excel. In the **Export – Excel Spreadsheet** dialog box, click **Close**, and then **Close Access**.

4 From the desktop, open your browser, navigate to **http://google.com**, and then sign in to your Google account. Click the **Google Apps** menu ▦, and then click **Drive** ▲. Open your **GO! Web Projects**

folder—or click New to create and then open this folder if necessary.

5 In the upper right corner, click **Settings** ⚙▾, and then on the menu click **Settings**. In the **Settings** dialog box, next to *Convert uploads*, be sure that **Convert uploaded files to Google Docs editor format** is selected. In the upper right, click **Done**.

If this setting is not selected, your document will upload as a PDF file and cannot be edited without further action.

6 On the left, click **NEW**, and then click **File upload**. In the **Open** dialog box, navigate to your **Access Chapter 2** folder, and then double-click your **Lastname_Firstname_AC_2B_Web** Excel file to upload it to Google Drive. In the lower right corner, when the title bar of the message box indicates *Uploads completed*, **Close** ✕ the message box. A second message box may display temporarily.

7 In the file list, double-click your **Lastname_Firstname_AC_2B_Web** file to open it in Google Sheets. Compare your screen with Figure A.

The worksheet displays column letters, row numbers, and data.

(GO! With Google continues on the next page)

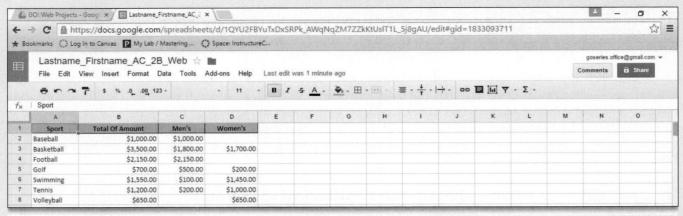

FIGURE A

8 Select the range **A1:B8**. On the menu bar, click **Insert**, and then click **Chart**. At the bottom of the **Chart Editor** dialog box, click **Insert** to insert the column chart in the spreadsheet.

The chart is placed in the spreadsheet, covering some of the data.

9 Click the **Chart title**, type **Lastname Firstname Total Scholarships by Sport** Above the title, click the **font size arrow**, click **12**, and then press Enter to apply the title. On the right side of the chart, point to the legend, right-click, and click **Clear legend**.

10 Click to select the chart, if necessary. Point to the top of the chart window until the 🖐 pointer displays. Hold down the left mouse button, and then drag the chart below the data in the spreadsheet.

11 On the menu, click **File**, point to **Download as**, and then click **Microsoft Excel (.xlsx)**. Use your browser commands to save the file in your **Access Chapter 2** folder as **Lastname_Firstname_AC_2B_Web_Download**

> **NOTE** Saving The Downloaded File to the Access Chapter 2 Folder
>
> Depending on the browser you are using, you may need to open the file in Excel and then save the AC_2B_Web_Download worksheet to your Access Chapter 2 folder.

12 In Google Drive, in the upper right corner, click your name, and then click Sign out. Close your browser window.

13 Start Excel. In the Excel opening screen, in the lower left corner, click **Open Other Workbooks**. Navigate to your **Lastname_Firstname_AC_2B_Web_Download** file and then open the file.

14 If directed to submit a paper printout of your AC_2B_Web_Download file, follow the directions given in the Note below. As directed by your instructor, submit your Excel file created in this project. Your instructor may also request that you submit a copy of the email that was sent to you notifying you of the shared file.

> **NOTE** Printing or Creating a PDF Electronic Image of an Excel Spreadsheet
>
> To print on paper, click Print. To create a PDF electronic image of your printout, on the left side of your screen, click Export. Under Export, be sure Create PDF/XPS Document is selected, and then click Create PDF/XPS. Navigate to your Access Chapter 2 folder, and then click Publish to save the file with the default name and an extension of pdf.

GO! To Work

MICROSOFT OFFICE SPECIALIST (MOS) SKILLS IN THIS CHAPTER

PROJECT 2A		PROJECT 2B	
1.2.1	Create and modify relationships	**1.2.1**	Create and modify relationships
1.2.3	Enforce referential integrity	**1.2.2**	Set the primary key
1.2.4	Set foreign keys	**1.2.3**	Enforce referential integrity
1.3.5	Change views of objects	**1.2.4**	Set foreign keys
1.5.1	Print reports	**1.3.5**	Change views of object
1.5.2	Print records	**2.2.4**	Rename tables
2.2.4	Rename tables	**3.1.1**	Run a query
2.3.3	Delete records	**3.1.2**	Create a crosstab query
2.3.6	Sort records	**3.1.3**	Create a parameter query
3.1.1	Run a query	**3.1.5**	Create a multi-table query
3.1.6	Save a query	**3.1.6**	Save a query
3.2.1	Rename a query	**3.2.2**	Add fields
3.2.2	Add fields	**3.2.5**	Sort data within queries
3.2.3	Remove fields	**3.2.6**	Format fields within queries
3.2.4	Hide fields	**3.3.1**	Add calculated fields
3.2.5	Sort data within queries	**3.3.2**	Set filtering criteria
3.3.2	Set filtering criteria	**3.3.3**	Group and summarize data
		3.3.4	Group data by using comparison operators
		3.3.5	Group data by using arithmetic and logical operators

BUILD YOUR E-PORTFOLIO

An E-Portfolio is a collection of evidence, stored electronically, that showcases what you have accomplished while completing your education. Collecting and then sharing your work products with potential employees reflects your academic and career goals. Your completed documents from the following projects are good examples to show what you have learned: 2G, 2K, and 2L.

GO! FOR JOB SUCCESS

Video: Making Ethical Choices

Your instructor may assign this video to your class, and then ask you to think about, or discuss with your classmates, these questions:

FotolEdhar / Fotolia

Which behaviors in this video do you think were unethical?

Is it unethical to "borrow" things from your employer? Why? What would you do if you saw this behavior going on?

What do you think an employer could do to prevent unethical behavior?

END OF CHAPTER

SUMMARY

Table relationships are created by joining the common fields in tables providing a means for you to modify data simultaneously and use data from multiple tables to create queries, forms, and reports.

Queries are created to answer questions and to extract information from your database tables; saving a query with your database saves you time when you need to answer the question many times.

Queries range from simple queries where you ask a single question to complex queries where you use compound criteria, wildcard characters, logical operators, and create calculated fields.

A crosstab query displays information grouped by two fields, an easy way to display complex data, and a parameter query prompts you to enter the criteria each time you open or run the query.

GO! LEARN IT ONLINE

Review the concepts and key terms in this chapter by completing these online challenges, which you can find at **MyITLab**.

Matching and Multiple Choice: Answer matching and multiple-choice questions to test what you learned in this chapter.

Lessons on the GO!: Learn how to use all the new apps and features as they are introduced by Microsoft.

MOS Prep Quiz: Answer questions to review the MOS skills that you have practiced in this chapter.

GO! COLLABORATIVE TEAM PROJECT (available in **MyITLab** and Instructor Resource Center)

If your instructor assigns the project to your class, you can expect to work with one or more of your classmates—either in class or by using Internet tools—to create work products similar to those you created in this chapter. A team is a group of workers who work together to solve a problem, make a decision, or create a work product. Collaboration is when you work together with others as a team in an intellectual endeavor to complete a shared task or achieve a shared goal.

Your instructor will assign Projects from this list to ensure your learning and assess your knowledge.

REVIEW AND ASSESSMENT GUIDE FOR ACCESS CHAPTER 2

Project	Apply Skills from These Chapter Objectives	Project Type	Project Location
2A **MyITLab**	Objectives 1–7 from Project 2A	**2A Instructional Project (Grader Project)** Guided instruction to learn the skills in Project 2A.	MyITLab and in text
2B **MyITLab**	Objectives 8–15 from Project 2B	**2A Instructional Project (Grader Project)** Guided instruction to learn the skills in Project 2B.	MyITLab and in text
2C	Objectives 1–7 from Project 2A	**2C Chapter Review (Scorecard Grading)** A guided review of the skills from Project 2A.	In text
2D	Objectives 8–15 from Project 2B	**2D Chapter Review (Scorecard Grading)** A guided review of the skills from Project 2B.	In text
2E **MyITLab**	Objectives 1–7 from Project 2A	**2E Mastery (Grader Project)** **Mastery and Transfer of Learning** A demonstration of your mastery of the skills in Project 2A with extensive decision making.	MyITLab and in text
2F **MyITLab**	Objectives 8–15 from Project 2B	**2F Mastery (Grader Project)** **Mastery and Transfer of Learning** A demonstration of your mastery of the skills in Project 2B with extensive decision making.	MyITLab and in text
2G **MyITLab**	Combination of Objectives from Projects 2A and 2B	**2G Mastery (Grader Project)** **Mastery and Transfer of Learning** A demonstration of your mastery of the skills in Projects 2A and 2B with extensive decision making.	MyITLab and in text
2H	Combination of Objectives from Projects 2A and 2B	**2H GO! Fix It (Scorecard Grading)** **Critical Thinking** A demonstration of your mastery of the skills in Projects 2A and 2B Resource by creating a correct result from a document that contains errors Center (IRC) you must find.	Instructor Resource Center (IRC) and MyITLab
2I	Combination of Objectives from Projects 2A and 2B	**2I GO! Make It (Scorecard Grading)** **Critical Thinking** A demonstration of your mastery of the skills in Projects 2A and 2B by creating a result from a supplied picture.	IRC and MyITLab
2J	Combination of Objectives from Projects 2A and 2B	**2J GO! Solve It (Rubric Grading)** **Critical Thinking** A demonstration of your mastery of the skills in Projects 2A and 2B, your decision-making skills, and your critical-thinking skills. A task-specific rubric helps you self-assess your result.	IRC and MyITLab
I2K	Combination of Objectives from Projects 2A and 2B	**2K GO! Solve It (Rubric Grading)** **Critical Thinking** A demonstration of your mastery of the skills in Projects 2A and 2B, your decision-making skills, and your critical-thinking skills. A task-specific rubric helps you self-assess your result.	In text
2L	Combination of Objectives from Projects 2A and 2B	**2L GO! Think (Rubric Grading)** **Critical Thinking** A demonstration of your understanding of the chapter concepts applied in a manner that you would outside of college. An analytic rubric helps you and your instructor grade the quality of your work by comparing it to the work an expert in the discipline would create.	In text
2M	Combination of Objectives from Projects 2A and 2B	**2M GO! Think (Rubric Grading)** **Critical Thinking** A demonstration of your understanding of the chapter concepts applied in a manner that you would outside of college. An analytic rubric helps you and your instructor grade the quality of your work by comparing it to the work an expert in the discipline would create.	IRC and MyITLab
2N	Combination of Objectives from Projects 2A and 2B	**2N You and GO! (Rubric Grading)** **Critical Thinking** A demonstration of your understanding of the chapter concepts applied in a manner that you would in a personal situation. An analytic rubric helps you and your instructor grade the quality of your work.	IRC and MyITLab
2O	Combination of Objectives from Projects 2A and 2B	**2O Collaborative Team Project for ACCESS Chapter 2** **Critical Thinking** A demonstration of your understanding of concepts and your ability to work collaboratively in a group role-playing assessment, requiring both collaboration and self-management.	IRC and MyITLab

GLOSSARY

GLOSSARY OF CHAPTER KEY TERMS

Aggregate functions Calculations such as Min, Max, Avg, and Sum that are performed on a group of records.

AND condition A compound criteria used to display records that match all parts of the specified criteria.

Ascending order A sorting order that arranges text alphabetically (A to Z) and numbers from the lowest number to the highest number.

Between … And operator A comparison operator that looks for values within a range.

Calculated field A field that stores the value of a mathematical operation.

Cascade Delete Related Records A cascade option that enables you to delete a record in a table and also delete all of the related records in related tables.

Cascade options Relationship options that enable you to update records in related tables when referential integrity is enforced.

Cascade Update Related Fields A cascade option that enables you to change the data in the primary key field in the table on the *one* side of the relationship and update that change to any fields storing that same data in related tables.

Comparison operators Symbols that are used to evaluate data in the field to determine if it is the same (=), greater than (>), less than (<), or in between a range of values as specified by the criteria.

Compound criteria Multiple conditions in a query or filter.

Criteria Conditions in a query that identify the specific records you are looking for.

Crosstab query A query that uses an aggregate function for data that can be grouped by two types of information and displays the data in a compact, spreadsheet-like format with column headings and row headings.

Data source The table or tables from which a form, query, or report retrieves its data.

Descending order A sorting order that arranges text in reverse alphabetical order (Z to A) and numbers from the highest number to the lowest number.

Expression A formula that will perform the calculation.

Field list A list of field names in a table.

Foreign key The field that is included in the related table so the field can be joined with the primary key in another table for the purpose of creating a relationship.

Innermost sort field When sorting on multiple fields in Datasheet view, the field that will be used for the second level of sorting.

Is Not Null A criteria that searches for fields that are not empty.

Is Null A criteria that searches for fields that are empty.

Join line In the Relationships window, the line joining two tables that visually indicates the common fields and the type of relationship.

Logical operators Operators that combine criteria using AND and OR. With two criteria, AND requires that both conditions be met and OR requires that either condition be met for the record to display in the query results.

Message Bar The area directly below the ribbon that displays information such as security alerts when there is potentially unsafe, active content in an Office document that you open.

One-to-many relationship A relationship between two tables where one record in the first table corresponds to many records in the second table—the most common type of relationship in Access.

OR condition A compound criteria used to display records that match at least one of the specified criteria.

Outermost sort field When sorting on multiple fields in Datasheet view, the field that will be used for the first level of sorting.

Parameter A value that can be changed.

Parameter query A query that prompts you for criteria before running the query.

Query design grid The lower area of the query window that displays the design of the query.

Referential integrity A set of rules that Access uses to ensure that the data between related tables is valid.

Relationship An association that you establish between two tables based on common fields.

Run The process in which Access looks at the records in the table(s) included in the query design, finds the records that match the specified criteria, and then displays the records in a datasheet; only the fields included in the query design display.

Sorting The process of arranging data in a specific order based on the value in a field.

Subdatasheet A format for displaying related records when you click the plus sign (+) next to a record in a table on the *one* side of the relationship.

Subset A portion of the total records available.

Table area The upper area of the query window that displays field lists for the tables that are used in a query.

Text string A sequence of characters.

Trust Center An area of Access where you can view the security and privacy settings for your Access installation.

Wildcard character In a query, a character that represents one or more unknown characters in criteria; an asterisk (*) represents one or more unknown characters, and a question mark (?) represents a single unknown character.

Apply 2A skills from these Objectives:

1 Open and Save an Existing Database
2 Create Table Relationships
3 Sort Records in a Table
4 Create a Query in Design View
5 Create a New Query from an Existing Query
6 Sort Query Results
7 Specify Criteria in a Query

Skills Review   Project 2C Freshman Orientation

In the following Skills Review, you will assist Dr. Wendy Bowie, the Director of Counseling at the Southwest Campus, in using her database to answer several questions about the freshman orientation sessions that will be held prior to class registration. Your completed database objects will look similar to Figure 2.55.

PROJECT FILES

For Project 2C, you will need the following file:

a02C_Freshman_Orientation

You will save your database as:

Lastname_Firstname_2C_Freshman_Orientation

PROJECT RESULTS

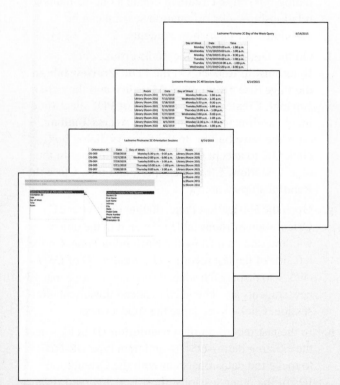
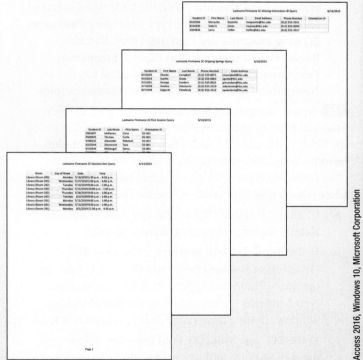

FIGURE 2.55

(Project 2C Freshman Orientation continues on the next page)

1 ▶ **Start** Access. In the Access opening screen, click **Open Other Files**. Under **Open**, click Browse and then navigate to the location where your student data files are stored. Double-click **a02C_Freshman_Orientation** to open the database.

a. Click the **File tab**, and then click **Save As**. Under **File Types**, be sure **Save Database As** is selected. On the right, under **Database File Types**, be sure **Access Database** is selected, and then click **Save As**.

b. In the **Save As** dialog box, navigate to your **Access Chapter 2** folder. Click in the **File name** box, type **Lastname_Firstname_2C_Freshman_Orientation** and then press Enter. On the **Message Bar**, click **Enable Content**.

c. In the **Navigation Pane**, right-click **2C New Students**, and then click **Rename**. With the table name selected and using your own name, type **Lastname Firstname 2C New Students** and then press Enter. **Rename** the 2C Orientation Sessions table to **Lastname Firstname 2C Orientation Sessions** and resize the **Navigation Pane** to display both tables names fully.

2 ▶ In the **Navigation Pane**, double-click your **2C New Students** table to open it in the object window, and examine the fields in the table. Double-click your **2C Orientation Sessions** table, and examine the fields in the table. In the object window, right-click either **object tab**, and then click **Close All** to close both tables. **Close** the **Navigation Pane**.

a. Click the **Database Tools tab**, and then in the **Relationships group**, click **Relationships**.

b. In the **Show Table** dialog box, click your **2C Orientation Sessions** table, and then click **Add**. In the **Show Table** dialog box, double-click your **2C New Students** table to add it to the **Relationships** window. In the **Show Table** dialog box, click **Close**.

c. In the **2C New Students** field list—the field list on the right—point to the title bar, and holding down the left mouse button, drag the field list to the right until there are approximately four inches of space between the field lists. In the **2C New Students** field list, point to the lower right corner of the field list to display the 🔲 pointer, and then drag downward and to the right to resize the field list and display all of the field names and the entire table name. Use the same technique to resize the **2C Orientation Sessions** field list—the field list on the left—so that the table name displays fully.

d. In the **2C Orientation Sessions** field list, point to **Orientation ID**, and, holding down the left mouse button, drag the field name downward and to the right into the **2C New Students** field list until the 🔲 pointer's arrow is on top of **Orientation ID**. Release the mouse button to display the **Edit Relationships** dialog box. Drag the **Edit Relationships** dialog box downward and to the right below the two field lists.

e. In the **Edit Relationships** dialog box, click to select the **Enforce Referential Integrity** check box, the **Cascade Update Related Fields** check box, and the **Cascade Delete Related Records** check box. In the **Edit Relationships** dialog box, click **Create** to create a one-to-many relationship—*one* orientation session can be scheduled for *many* new students.

f. On the **Design tab**, in the **Tools group**, click **Relationship Report**. On the **Print Preview tab**, in the **Page Size group**, click **Margins**, and then click **Normal**. Create a paper printout or PDF electronic image as directed. On the **Quick Access Toolbar**, click the **Save** button. In the **Save As** dialog box, click **OK** to accept the default report name. In the object window, **Close** the report, and then **Close** the **Relationships** window.

g. **Open** the **Navigation Pane**, double-click your **2C Orientation Sessions** table to open it in the object window, and then **Close** the **Navigation Pane**. On the left side of the last record—*Orientation ID* of *OS-1*—click **+** to display the subdatasheet, and notice that 13 new students are scheduled to attend this orientation session. Click **-** to collapse the subdatasheet.

h. In the last record, in the **Orientation ID** field, select the existing data—*OS-1*—and then type **OS-001** to make the data consistent with the Orientation IDs of the other sessions; the 13 related records are updated with the new Orientation ID because you selected Cascade Update Related Fields in the Edit Relationships dialog box.

i. Display the subdatasheet for the record with an **Orientation ID** of **OS-010**, and notice that one student—*Student ID* of *8273485*—is scheduled for this orientation session. Collapse the subdatasheet. To the left of the record, point to the record selector box to display the ➡ pointer, and then click to

(Project 2C Freshman Orientation continues on the next page)

select the record. On the **Hometab**, in the **Records group**, click **Delete**. In the message box, click **Yes** to delete this record and the related student record in the **2C New Students** table.

3 In the **Date** field, click in any record. On the **Hometab**, in the **Sort & Filter group**, click **Ascending** to sort the records by the date. In the field names row, click the **Room arrow**, and then click **Sort Z to A** to sort the rooms from Room 203 to Room 201. The records are sorted first by the Room and then by the Date. On the **File tab**, click **Print**, and then click **Print Preview**. Create a paper or PDF electronic image as directed, and then click **Close Print Preview**. On the **Home tab**, in the **Sort & Filter group**, click **Remove Sort**. **Close** the table, and in the message box, click **No**; you do not need to save any design changes to the table.

4 Click the **Create tab**, and then in the **Queries group**, click **Query Design**. In the **Show Table** dialog box, double-click your **2C Orientation Sessions** table, and then **Close** the **Show Table** dialog box. Resize the field list, displaying all of the field names and the entire table name.

a. In the field list, double-click **Date** to add the field to the first column in the design grid. In the design grid, in the **Field** row, click in the second column, click the **arrow**, and then click **Day of Week** to add the field to the design grid. In the field list, point to **Room**, drag the field name down into the design grid until the pointer displays in the **Field** row in the first column, and then release the mouse button. Using one of the three techniques you just practiced, add the **Time** field to the fourth column

b. On the **Design tab**, in the **Results group**, click **Run**. This query answers the question, *What is the room, date, day of week, and time for all of the orientation sessions in the 2C Orientation Sessions table?*

c. On the **Quick Access Toolbar**, click **Save**. In the **Save As** dialog box, type **Lastname Firstname 2C All Sessions Query** and then click **OK**. On the **File tab**, click **Print**, and then click **Print Preview**. Create a paper printout or PDF electronic image as directed, and then click **Close Print Preview**. **Close** the query.

5 **Open** the **Navigation Pane**. Right-click the **2C All Sessions Query** and click **Copy**. Right-click in a blank area of the **Navigation Pane**, and click **Paste**. In the **Paste As** dialog box, type **Lastname Firstname 2C Day of the Week Query** and then click **OK** to create a new query based on an existing query. **Close** the **Navigation Pane**.

a. In the **Navigation Pane**, right-click the **2C Day of the Week Query** and click **Design View**. In the design grid, point to the thin gray selection bar above the **Room** field name to display the ↓ pointer, click to select the column, and then press Delete.

b. Point to the selection bar above the **Day of Week** field name to display the ⬚ pointer, and then drag to the left until a dark vertical line displays on the left side of the **Date** column. Release the mouse button to position the **Day of Week** field in the first column.

c. **Run** the query. The query results display three fields. This query answers the question, *What is the day of week, date, and time for every orientation session in the 2C Orientation Sessions table?*

d. On the **File tab**, click **Print**, and then click **Print Preview**. Create a paper or PDF electronic image as directed, and then click **Close Print Preview**. **Close** the query, and in the message box, click **Yes** to save the changes to the design—you deleted one field and moved another field. **Open** the **Navigation Pane**.

6 Right-click the **2C Day of the Week Query** and click **Copy**. Right-click in a blank area of the **Navigation Pane**, and click **Paste**. In the **Paste As** dialog box, type **Lastname Firstname 2C Sessions Sort Query** and then click **OK** to create a new query based on an existing query. Increase the width of the **Navigation Pane** so that the names of all of the objects display fully.

a. In the **Navigation Pane**, right-click your **2C Sessions Sort Query**, click **Design View**, and then **Close** the **Navigation Pane**. In the field list, drag the **Room** field to the left of the **Day of Week** field to position it in the first column. In the design grid, in the **Sort** row under **Room**, click the **arrow**, and then click **Descending**. In the **Sort** row under **Date**, click the **arrow**, and then click **Ascending**.

b. **Run** the query. This query answers the question, *For every session, within each room (with the Room field sorted in descending order), what is the day of week, date (with the Date field sorted in ascending order), and time?*

c. Display the query results in **Print Preview**, create a paper printout or PDF electronic image as directed, and then click **Close Print Preview**. **Close** the query, and in the message box, click **Yes** to save the changes to the query design.

(Project 2C Freshman Orientation continues on the next page)

7 ▶ Click the **Create tab**, and then in the **Queries group**, click **Query Design**. In the **Show Table** dialog box, double-click your **2C New Students** table to add it to the table area, and then **Close** the **Show Table** dialog box. Resize the field list to display all of the field names and the table name. Add the following fields to the design grid in the order given: **Student ID**, **Last Name**, **First Name**, and **Orientation ID**.

a. In the design grid, click in the **Criteria** row under **Orientation ID**, type **OS-001**—the first character is the letters *O* and *S* followed by a hyphen, two zeros, and the number *1*—and then press Enter.

b. **Run** the query to display 13 records that meet the specified criteria—records that have *OS-001* in the *Orientation ID* field. **Save** the query as **Lastname Firstname 2C First Session Query** and then display the query results in **Print Preview**. Create a paper printout or PDF electronic image as directed, click **Close Print Preview**, and then **Close** the query.

c. On the **Create tab**, in the **Queries group**, click **Query Design**. In the **Show Table** dialog box, double-click your **2C New Students** table to add it to the table area, and then **Close** the **Show Table** dialog box. Resize the field list, and then add the following fields to the design grid in the order given: **Student ID**, **First Name**, **Last Name**, **Phone Number**, **Email Address**, and **City**. Click in the **Criteria** row under **City**, type **dripping springs** and then press Enter.

d. **Run** the query to display the five new students who live in *Dripping Springs*. Switch to **Design** view. In the design grid, in the **Show** row under **City**, click to clear the check box. Recall that if all of the results use the same criteria, such as *dripping springs*, it is not necessary to display that field in the query

results. **Run** the query again. **Save** the query as **Lastname Firstname 2C Dripping Springs Query** and then display the query results in **Print Preview**. Create a paper printout or PDF electronic image as directed, click **Close Print Preview**, and then **Close** the query.

e. On the **Create tab**, in the **Queries group**, click **Query Design**. In the **Show Table** dialog box, double-click your **2C New Students** table to add it to the table area, and then **Close** the **Show Table** dialog box. Resize the field list, and then add the following fields to the design grid in the order given: **Student ID**, **First Name**, **Last Name**, **Email Address**, **Phone Number**, and **Orientation ID**. Click in the **Sort** row under **Last Name**, click the **arrow**, and then click **Ascending**. Click in the **Criteria** row under **Orientation ID**, type **is null** and then press Enter.

f. **Run** the query to display the three new students who have not signed up for an orientation session. **Save** the query as **Lastname Firstname 2C Missing Orientation ID Query** and then display the query results in **Print Preview**. On the **Print Preview** tab, in the **Page Size group**, click **Margins**, and then click **Normal**. Create a paper printout or PDF electronic image as directed, click **Close Print Preview**, and then **Close** the query.

g. **Open** the **Navigation Pane**. If necessary, increase the width of the pane so that all object names display fully. On the right side of the title bar, click **Close** to close the database and to Close Access. As directed by your instructor, submit your database and the paper printout or PDF electronic images of the eight objects—relationship report, sorted table, and six queries—that are the results of this project.

1. Lastname_Firstname_2C_Freshman_Orientation	Database file
2. Relationships for Lastname_Firstname_2C_Freshman_Orientation Relationships	Report
3. Lastname Firstname 2C Orientation Sessions table sorted (not saved)	Table sorted
4. Lastname Firstname 2C All Sessions Query	Query
5. Lastname Firstname 2C Day of the Week Query	Query
6. Lastname Firstname 2C Sessions Sort Query	Query
7. Lastname Firstname 2C First Session Query	Query
8. Lastname Firstname 2C Dripping Springs Query	Query
9. Lastname Firstname 2C Missing Orientation ID Query	Query

End | You have completed Project 2C

Apply **2B** skills from these Objectives:

- **8** Specify Numeric Criteria in a Query
- **9** Use Compound Criteria in a Query
- **10** Create a Query Based on More Than One Table
- **11** Use Wildcards in a Query
- **12** Create Calculated Fields in a Query
- **13** Calculate Statistics and Group Data in a Query
- **14** Create a Crosstab Query
- **15** Create a Parameter Query

Skills Review Project 2D Club Fundraisers

In the following Skills Review, you will assist Dr. Michael Bransford, the Student Activities Director for Texas Lakes Community College, in answering his questions about fundraisers, clubs, donations, dates of fundraiser events, and fundraiser locations. Your completed database objects will look similar to Figure 2.56.

PROJECT FILES

For Project 2D, you will need the following files:

a02D_Clubs_Fundraisers
a02D_Clubs (Excel workbook)

You will save your database as:

Lastname_Firstname_2D_Clubs_Fundraisers

PROJECT RESULTS

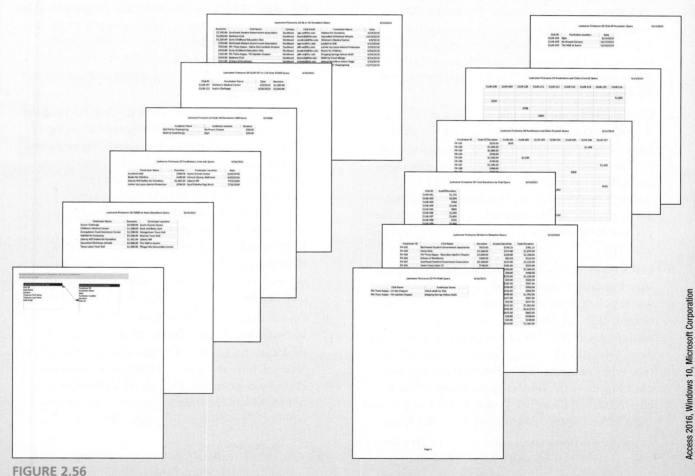

FIGURE 2.56

(Project 2D Club Fundraisers continues on the next page)

Skills Review **Project 2D Club Fundraisers** (continued)

1 **Start** Access. In the Access opening screen, click **Open Other Files**. Under **Open**, click **Browse** and then navigate to the location where your student data files are stored. Double-click **a02D_Clubs_Fundraisers** to open the database.

a. Click the **File tab**, and then click **Save As**. Under **File Types**, be sure **Save Database As** is selected. On the right, under **Database File Types**, be sure **Access Database** is selected, and then at the bottom of the screen, click **Save As**. In the **Save As** dialog box, navigate to your **Access Chapter 2** folder. Click in the **File name** box, type **Lastname_Firstname_2D_Clubs_Fundraisers** and then press Enter. On the **Message Bar**, click **Enable Content**.

b. In the **Navigation Pane**, right-click **2D Fundraisers**, click **Rename**, type **Lastname Firstname 2D Fundraisers** and then press Enter. Increase the width of the **Navigation Pane** to display the entire table name. Double-click the table name to open it, examine the fields in the table, and then **Close** the table.

c. Click the **External Data tab**, and then in the **Import & Link group**, click **Excel**. In the **Get External Data – Excel Spreadsheet** dialog box, to the right of the **File name** box, click **Browse**. In the **File Open** dialog box, navigate to your student data files, and then double-click **a02D_Clubs**. Be sure that the **Import the source data into a new table in the current database** option button is selected, and then click **OK**.

d. In the upper left area of the wizard, select the **First Row Contains Column Headings** check box. In the wizard, click **Next**, and then click **Next** again. In the wizard, click the **Choose my own primary key** option button, be sure that **Club ID** displays, and then click **Next**. With the text selected in the **Import to Table** box, type **Lastname Firstname 2DClubs** and then click **Finish**. In the **Import Spreadsheet Wizard**, click **Next**, and then click **Finish**. In the **Get External Data – Excel Spreadsheet** dialog box, click **Close**.

e. In the **Navigation Pane**, right-click your **2D Clubs** table, and then click **Design View**. **Close** the **Navigation Pane**. In the **Field Name** column, click **Club ID**. In the **Field Properties** area, click **Field Size**, type **8** and then press Enter. On the **Design**

tab, in the **Views group**, click **View** to switch to **Datasheet** view. In the message box, click **Yes** to save the design changes. In the second message box, click **Yes**—no data will be lost. Examine the fields and data in the table. To the left of the **Club ID** field name, click the **Select All** button. On the **Home tab**, in the **Records group**, click **More**, and then click **Field Width**. In the **Column Width** dialog box, click **Best Fit**. Click in any record to cancel the selection, **Save** the table, and then **Close** the table.

f. Click the **Database Tools tab**, and then in the **Relationships group**, click **Relationships**. In the **Show Table** dialog box, double-click your **2D Clubs** table, and then double-click your **2D Fundraisers** table to add both tables to the **Relationships** window. **Close** the **Show Table** dialog box. Point to the title bar of the field list on the right, and drag the field list to the right until there are approximately three inches of space between the field lists. By dragging the lower right corner of the field list, resize each field list to display all of the field names and the entire table name.

g. In the **2D Clubs** field list, point to **Club ID**, drag the field name into the **2D Fundraisers** table on top of **Club ID**, and then release the mouse button. Point to the title bar of the **Edit Relationships** dialog box, and then drag it downward below the two field lists. In the **Edit Relationships** dialog box, select the **Enforce Referential Integrity** check box, the **Cascade Update Related Fields** check box, the **Cascade Delete Related Records** check box, and then click **Create**. A *one-to-many* relationship is established; *one* student club can raise money for *many* fundraising events.

h. On the **Design tab**, in the **Tools group**, click **Relationship Report**. On the **Print Preview tab**, in the **Page Size group**, click **Margins**, and then click **Normal**. **Save** the report as **Lastname Firstname 2D Relationships** and then create a paper printout or PDF electronic image as directed. In the object window, right-click either **object tab**, and then click **Close All**.

2 Click the **Create tab**. In the **Queries group**, click **Query Design**. In the **Show Table** dialog box, double-click your **2D Fundraisers** table to add it to the table area, and then **Close** the **Show Table** dialog box. Resize

(Project 2D Club Fundraisers continues on the next page)

the field list. Add the following fields to the design grid in the order given: **Fundraiser Name**, **Donation**, and **Fundraiser Location**.

a. Click in the **Sort** row under **Fundraiser Name**, click the **arrow**, and then click **Ascending**. Click in the **Criteria** row under **Donations**, type **>=1000** and then press [Enter]. **Run** the query, and notice that seven records match the criteria. This query answers the question, W*here was each fundraiser held (in alphabetical order by the Fundraiser Name field) for fundraisers with donations greater than or equal to $1,000?*

b. **Save** the query as **Lastname Firstname 2D $1000 or More Donations Query** and then display the query results in **Print Preview**. Create a paper printout or PDF electronic image as directed, and then click **Close Print Preview**. **Close** the query.

c. In the **Navigation Pane**, right-click your **2D $1000 or More Donations Query**, and click **Copy**. In a blank area in the Navigation Pane, right-click and click **Paste**. In the **Paste As** dialog box, type **Lastname Firstname 2D Fundraisers June-July Query** and then click **OK**. In the **Navigation Pane**, right-click your **2D Fundraisers June-July Query** query, and then click **Design View**.

d. In the **2D Fundraisers** field list, double-click **Date** to add it to the fourth column in the design grid. Click in the **Sort** row under **Fundraiser Name**, click the **arrow**, and then click (**not sorted**). Click in the **Sort** row under **Date**, click the **arrow**, and then click **Ascending**.

e. In the **Criteria** row under **Donation**, select the existing criteria, *>=1000,* and then press [Del] so that the query results are not restricted by a monetary value. Click in the **Criteria** row under **Date**, type **between 6/1/19 and 7/31/19** and then press [Enter]. **Run** the query, and notice that four records match the criteria. This query answers the question, *What is the fundraiser name, donation, fundraiser location, and date (in chronological order) for events held between June 1, 2019 and July 31, 2019?*

f. Display the query results in **Print Preview**, create a paper printout or PDF electronic image as directed, and then click **Close Print Preview**. **Close** the query, and in the message box, click **Yes** to save the changes to the query design.

3 Click the **Create tab**, and in the **Queries group**, click **Query Design**. In the **Show Table** dialog box, double-click your **2D Fundraisers** table to add it to the table area, and then **Close** the **Show Table** dialog box. Resize the field list. Add the following fields to the design grid in the order given: **Fundraiser Name**, **Fundraiser Location**, **Donation**, and **Club ID**.

a. Click in the **Sort** row under **Fundraiser Name**, click the **arrow**, and then click **Ascending**. Click in the **Criteria** row under **Club ID**, type **club-109** and then press [Enter]. Click in the **Criteria** row under **Donation**, type **<=1000** and then press [Enter]. **Run** the query, and notice that two records match the criteria. Switch back to **Design** view, and in the **Show** row under **Club ID**, clear the check box. **Run** the query again. This query answers the question, *Which fundraiser events with their locations listed had donations of $1,000 or less raised by CLUB-109?*

b. **Save** the query as **Lastname Firstname 2D CLUB-109 Donations <=1000 Query** and then display the query results in **Print Preview**. Create a paper printout or PDF electronic image as directed, click **Close Print Preview**, and then **Close** the query.

c. On the **Create tab**, in the **Queries group**, click **Query Design**. In the **Show Table** dialog box, double-click your **2D Fundraisers** table to add it to the table area, and then **Close** the **Show Table** dialog box. Resize the field list. Add the following fields to the design grid in the order given: **Club ID**, **Fundraiser Name**, **Date**, and **Donation**.

d. Click in the **Sort** row under **Date**, click the **arrow**, and then click **Ascending**. Click in the **Criteria** row under **Club ID**, type **club-107 or club-115** and then press [Enter]. Click in the **Criteria** row under **Donation**, type **>1000** and then press [Enter]. **Run** the query, and notice that two records match the criteria. This query answers the question, *Which fundraiser events received donations over $1,000 from either CLUB-107 or CLUB-115, and on what dates (in chronological order) were the fundraiser events held?*

e. **Save** the query as **Lastname Firstname 2D CLUB 107 or 115 Over $1000 Query** and then display the query results in **Print Preview**. Create a paper printout or PDF electronic image as directed, click **Close Print Preview**, and then **Close** the query.

(Project 2D Club Fundraisers continues on the next page)

4 On the **Create tab**, in the **Queries group**, click **Query Design**. In the **Show Table** dialog box, double-click your **2D Clubs** table, and then double-click your **2D Fundraisers** table to add both tables to the table area. **Close** the **Show Table** dialog box. Drag the field list on the right side to the right until there are approximately two inches of space between the field lists, and then resize each field list.

a. From the **2D Clubs** field list, add the following fields to the design grid in the order given: **Club Name**, **Campus**, and **Club Email**. From the **2D Fundraisers** field list, add the following fields to the design grid in the order given: **Fundraiser Name**, **Date**, and **Donation**. In the design grid, drag the **Donation** field to position it as the first column.

b. Click in the **Sort** row under **Donation**, click the **arrow**, and then click **Descending**. Click in the **Criteria** row under **Campus**, type **southeast** and then press Enter. Click in the **or** row under **Campus**, type **northeast** and then press Enter. **Run** the query, and notice that 10 records match the criteria. This query answers the question, *For the Southeast and Northeast campuses, what is the donation (in descending order), club name, campus name, club email address, fundraiser name, and date of all fundraising events?*

c. **Save** the query as **Lastname Firstname 2D SE or NE Donations Query** and then display the query results in **Print Preview**. In the **Page Layout group**, click **Landscape**. In the **Page Size group**, click **Margins**, and then click **Normal**. Create a paper printout or PDF electronic image as directed, click **Close Print Preview**, and then **Close** the query.

5 On the **Create tab**, in the **Queries group**, click **Query Design**. In the **Show Table** dialog box, double-click your **2D Clubs** table, and then double-click your **2D Fundraisers** table to add both tables to the table area. **Close** the **Show Table** dialog box. Drag the field list on the right side to the right until there are approximately two inches of space between the field lists, and then resize each field list. From the **2D Clubs** field list, add the **Club Name** field to the design grid. From the **2D Fundraisers** field list, add the **Fundraiser Name** field to the design grid.

a. Click in the **Sort** row under **Club Name**, click the **arrow**, and then click **Ascending**. Click in the

Criteria row under **Club Name**, type **phi*** and then press Enter. In the **Criteria** row under **Fundraiser Name**, type ***walk*** and then press Enter. **Run** the query, and notice that two records match the criteria—Club Name begins with *Phi* and Fundraiser Name has *Walk* anywhere in its name. This query answers the question, *Which clubs (in alphabetical order) that have names starting with Phi have raised money for fundraisers that involve walking?*

b. **Save** the query as **Lastname Firstname 2D Phi Walk Query** and then display the query results in **Print Preview**. Create a paper printout or PDF electronic image as directed, click **Close Print Preview**, and then **Close** the query.

6 On the **Create tab**, in the **Queries group**, click **Query Design**. In the **Show Table** dialog box, double-click your **2D Clubs** table, and then double-click your **2D Fundraisers** table to add both tables to the table area. **Close** the **Show Table** dialog box. Drag the field list on the right side to the right until there are approximately two inches of space between the field lists, and then resize each field list. From the field lists, add the following fields to the design grid in the order given: **Fundraiser ID**, **Club Name**, and **Donation**.

a. Click in the **Sort** row under **Fundraiser ID**, click the **arrow**, and then click **Ascending**. Alumni will donate an additional 25 percent based on the value in the Donation field. In the **Field** row, right-click in the fourth column, and then click **Zoom**. In the **Zoom** dialog box, type **Alumni Donation:[Donation]*0.25** and then click **OK**. **Run** the query to be sure the new field—*Alumni Donation*—displays. In the first record, the *Alumni Donation* displays as *156.25*.

b. Switch to **Design** view. In the **Field** row, right-click in the first empty column, and then click **Zoom**. In the **Zoom** dialog box, type **Total Donation:[Donation]+[Alumni Donation]** and then click **OK**. **Run** the query to be sure that the new field—*Total Donation*—displays. In the first record, the *Total Donation* displays as *$781.25*.

c. Switch to **Design** view. In the **Field** row, click in the **Alumni Donation** field name box. On the **Design tab**, in the **Show/Hide group**, click **Property Sheet**. In the **Property Sheet**, click **Format**. In the property setting box, click the **arrow**, and then

(Project 2D Club Fundraisers continues on the next page)

click **Currency**. **Close** the **Property Sheet**, and then **Run** the query. This query answers the question, *In ascending order by Fundraiser ID, what is the club name, donation, alumni donation, and total donation for each fundraising event if the alumni donate an additional 25 percent based on the value in the Donation field?*

d. To the left of the **Fundraiser ID** field name, click the **Select All** button. On the **Home tab**, in the **Records group**, click **More**, and then click **Field Width**. In the **Column Width** dialog box, click **Best Fit**. Click in any field to cancel the selection, **Save** the query as **Lastname Firstname 2D Alumni Donation Query** and then display the query results in **Print Preview**. In the **Page Layout group**, click **Landscape**. Create a paper printout or PDF electronic image as directed, click **Close Print Preview**, and then **Close** the query.

7 On the **Create tab**, in the **Queries group**, click **Query Design**. In the **Show Table** dialog box, double-click your **2D Fundraisers** table to add the table to the table area. **Close** the **Show Table** dialog box. Resize the field list, and then add the **Donation** field to the design grid.

a. On the **Design tab**, in the **Show/Hide group**, click **Totals** to add a **Total** row as the third row in the design grid. In the **Total** row under **Donation**, click in the box that displays *Group By*, click the **arrow**, and then click **Sum**. In the **Show/Hide group**, click **Property Sheet**. In the **Property Sheet**, set **Decimal Places** to **0**, and then **Close** the **Property Sheet**. **Run** the query. Apply Best Fit to the field. The sum of the Donations field is *$20,259.*

b. Switch to **Design** view. From the field list, drag the **Club ID** field to the first column in the design grid—the **Donation** field moves to the second column. **Run** the query. This query answers the question, *For each club ID, what are the total donations?*

c. **Save** the query as **Lastname Firstname 2D Total Donations by Club Query** and then display the query results in **Print Preview**. Create a paper printout or PDF electronic image as directed, click **Close Print Preview**, and then **Close** the query.

8 On the **Create tab**, in the **Queries group**, click **Query Wizard**. In the **New Query** dialog box, click

Crosstab Query Wizard, and then click **OK**. In the **Crosstab Query Wizard**, click your **Table: 2D Fundraisers**, and then click **Next**. In the wizard under **Available Fields**, double-click **Fundraiser ID** to group the records by this field and display the Fundraiser IDs as row headings. Click **Next**.

a. In the wizard, in the field list, click **Club ID** to select the column headings, and then click **Next**. Under **Fields**, click **Donation**. Under **Functions**, click **Sum**, and then click **Next**. In the **What do you want to name your query?** box, select the existing text, type **Lastname Firstname 2D Fundraisers and Clubs Crosstab Query** and then click **Finish**.

b. Click the **Home** tab, and then switch to **Design** view. In the design grid, click in the **Donation** column. On the **Design tab**, in the **Show/Hide group**, click **Property Sheet**. In the **Property Sheet**, set **Decimal Places** to **0**, and then **Close** the **Property Sheet**. **Run** the query. Select all of the columns, apply **Best Fit**, and then **Save** the query. This query answers the question, *Grouped by Fundraiser ID and Club ID, what are the total donations?*

c. Display the query results in **Print Preview**. In the **Page Layout group**, click **Landscape**. Create a paper printout or PDF electronic image as directed—two pages result. Click **Close Print Preview**, and then **Close** the query.

9 On the **Create tab**, in the **Queries group**, click **Query Design**. In the **Show Table** dialog box, double-click your **2D Fundraisers** table to add the table to the table area. **Close** the **Show Table** dialog box, and then resize the field list. Add the following fields to the design grid in the order given: **Club ID**, **Fundraiser Location**, and **Date**.

a. In the **Sort** row under **Date**, click the **arrow**, and then click **Ascending**. In the **Criteria** row under **Club ID**, right-click, and then click **Zoom**. In the **Zoom** dialog box, type **[Enter a Club ID in the format club-###]** and then click **OK**. **Save** the query as **Lastname Firstname 2D Club ID Parameter Query**

b. **Run** the query. In the **Enter Parameter Value** dialog box, type **club-109** and then click **OK**. Three records

(Project 2D Club Fundraisers continues on the next page)

Skills Review   Project 2D Club Fundraisers (continued)

match the criteria. Display the query results in **Print Preview**. Create a paper printout or PDF electronic image as directed, click **Close Print Preview**, and then **Close** the query.

c. **Open** the **Navigation Pane**, and increase the width of the pane so that all object names display fully.

On the right side of the title bar, click **Close** to close the database and **Close** Access. As directed by your instructor, submit your database and the paper printout or PDF electronic images of the 11 objects—relationship report and 10 queries, that are the results of this project.

1. Lastname_Firstname_2D_Clubs_Fundraisers	Database file
2. Lastname Firstname 2D Relationships Relationships	Report
3. Lastname Firstname 2D $1000 or More Donation Query	Query
4. Lastname Firstname 2D Fundraisers June-July Query	Query
5. Lastname Firstname 2D CLUB-109<=1000 Query	Query
6. Lastname Firstname 2D CLUB 107 OR 115 Over $1000 Query	Query
7. Lastname Firstname 2D SE OR NE Donations Query	Query
8. Lastname Firstname 2D Phi Walk Query	Query
9. Lastname Firstname 2D Alumni Donation Query	Query
10. Lastname Firstname 2D Total Donations by Club Query	Query
11. Lastname Firstname 2D Fundraisers and Clubs Crosstab Query	Query (2 pages)
12. Lastname Firstname 2D Club ID Parameter Query	Query (CLUB 109)

END | You have completed Project 2D

Mastering Access Project 2E Biology Supplies

In the following Mastering Access project, you will assist Greg Franklin, Chair of the Biology Department at the Southwest Campus, in using his database to answer questions about biology laboratory supplies. Your completed database objects will look similar to Figure 2.57.

PROJECT FILES

For Project 2E, you will need the following file:

a02E_Biology_Supplies

You will save your database as:

Lastname_Firstname_2E_Biology_Supplies

PROJECT RESULTS

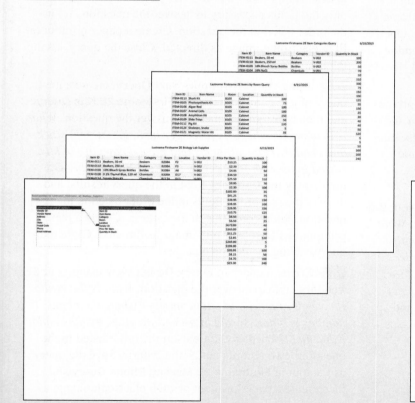

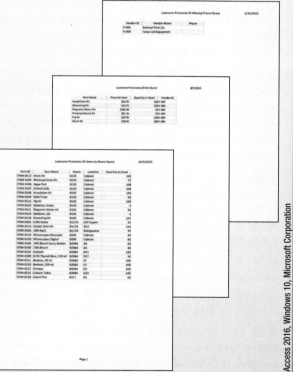

Access 2016, Windows 10, Microsoft Corporation

FIGURE 2.57

(Project 2E Biology Supplies continues on the next page)

Mastering Access Project 2E Biology Supplies (continued)

1 Start Access. From your student data files, open **a02E_Biology_Supplies**. Save the database in your **Access Chapter 2** folder as **Lastname_Firstname_2E_Biology_Supplies** and then enable the content. In the **Navigation Pane**, **Rename** each table by adding **Lastname Firstname** to the beginning of the table name. Increase the width of the **Navigation Pane** so that all object names display fully.

2 Open both tables to examine the fields and data, and then **Close** both tables. Create a *one-to-many* relationship between your **2E Vendors** table and your **2E Biology Lab Supplies** table using the common field **Vendor ID**. **Enforce Referential Integrity**, and enable both cascade options. *One* vendor can supply *many* supplies. Create a **Relationship Report** with **Normal Margins**, saving it with the default name. Create a paper or PDF electronic image as directed, and then **Close All** open objects. Open your **2E Vendors** table. In the last record, in the **Vendor ID** field, select **V-100**, type **V-001** and then press ⬇ to save the record. **Close** the table.

3 Open your **2E Biology Lab Supplies** table. Sort the records first in **Descending** order by **Price Per Item** and then in **Ascending** order by **Category**. Using **Landscape** orientation, create a paper printout or PDF electronic image as directed. **Close** the table, and do *not* save changes to the table.

4 Create a query in **Query Design** view using your **2E Biology Lab Supplies** table to answer the question, *What is the item ID, item name, room, location, and quantity in stock for all of the items, sorted in ascending order by the Room field and the Location field?* Display the fields in the order listed in the question. **Save** the query as **Lastname Firstname 2E Items by Room Query** and then create a paper printout or PDF electronic image as directed. **Close** the query.

5 In the **Navigation Pane**, use your **2E Items by Room Query** to create a new query object named **Lastname Firstname 2E Item Categories Query** and then redesign the query to answer the question, *What is the*

item ID, item name, category, vendor ID, and quantity in stock for all items, sorted in ascending order by the Category field and the Vendor ID field? Display only the fields necessary to answer the question and in the order listed in the question. Create a paper printout or PDF electronic image as directed. **Close** the query, saving the design changes.

6 In the **Navigation Pane**, use your **2E Items by Room Query** to create a new query object named **Lastname Firstname 2E Supplies Sort Query** and then open the new query in **Design** view. Redesign the query to answer the question, *What is the item name, category, price per item, and quantity in stock for all supplies, sorted in ascending order by the Category field and then in descending order by the Price Per Item field?* Display only the fields necessary to answer the question and in the order listed in the question. Create a paper printout or PDF electronic image as directed. **Close** the query, saving the design changes.

7 Using your **2E Supplies Sort Query**, create a new query object named **Lastname Firstname 2E Kits Query** and then redesign the query to answer the question, *What is item name, category, price per item, quantity in stock, and vendor ID for all items that have a category of kits, sorted in ascending order by the Item Name field?* Do not display the **Category** field in the query results, and display the rest of the fields in the order listed in the question. Six records match the criteria. Create a paper printout or PDF electronic image as directed. **Close** the query, saving the design changes.

8 Create a query in **Query Design** view using your **2E Vendors** table to answer the question, *What is the vendor ID, vendor name, and phone number where the phone number is blank, sorted in ascending order by the Vendor Name field?* Display the fields in the order listed in the question. Two records match the criteria. **Save** the query as **Lastname Firstname 2E Missing Phone Query** and then create a paper printout or PDF electronic image as directed. **Close** the query.

(Project 2E Biology Supplies continues on the next page)

Mastering Access   Project 2E Biology Supplies (continued)

9 ▶ Be sure all objects are closed. **Open** the **Navigation Pane**, be sure that all object names display fully, and then **Close Access**. As directed by your instructor, submit your database and the paper printout or PDF electronic images of the seven objects—relationship report, sorted table, and five queries—that are the results of this project.

1. Lastname_Firstname_2E_Biology_Supplies	Database file
2. Relationships for Lastname_Firstname_2E_Biology_Supplies Relationships	Report
3. Lastname Firstname 2E Biology Lab Supplies table sorted (not saved)	Table sorted
4. Lastname Firstname 2E Items by Room Query	Query
5. Lastname Firstname 2E Item Categories Query	Query
6. Lastname Firstname 2E Supplies Sort Query	Query
7. Lastname Firstname 2E Kits Query	Query
8. Lastname Firstname 2E Missing Phone Query	Query

END | You have completed Project 2E

Mastering Access Project 2F Student Publications

Apply **2B** skills from
these Objectives:

8 Specify Numeric Criteria
in a Query

9 Use Compound Criteria
in a Query

10 Create a Query Based
on More Than One Table

11 Use Wildcards in a Query

12 Create Calculated Fields
in a Query

13 Calculate Statistics and
Group Data in a Query

14 Create a Crosstab Query

15 Create a Parameter Query

In the following Mastering Access project, you will assist Siabhon Reiss, the English Writing Lab Coordinator, in using her database to answer questions about student publications. Your completed database objects will look similar to Figure 2.58.

PROJECT FILES

For Project 2F, you will need the following files:

a02F_Student_Publications
a02F_Student_Papers (Excel workbook)

You will save your database as:

Lastname_Firstname_2F_Student_Publications

PROJECT RESULTS

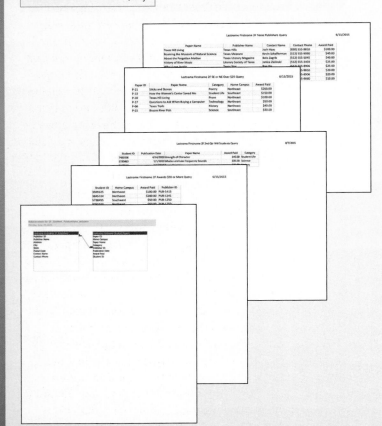

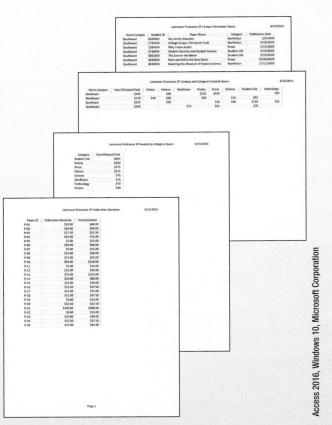

FIGURE 2.58

(Project 2F Student Publications continues on the next page)

1 **Start** Access. From your student data files, open **a02F_Student_Publications**. Save the database in your **Access Chapter 2** folder as **Lastname_Firstname_2F_Student_Publications** and then enable the content. In the **Navigation Pane**, **Rename** the table by adding **Lastname Firstname** to the beginning of the table name. From your student data files, import **a02F_Student_Papers** as a new table in the database. Designate the first row of the spreadsheet as column headings, and designate **Paper ID** as the primary key. Name the new table **Lastname Firstname 2F Student Papers** and then increase the width of the **Navigation Pane** so that all object names display fully.

Open your **2F Student Papers** table in **Design** view. For the **Student ID** field, change the **Data Type** to **Short Text**. Switch to **Datasheet** view, apply **Best Fit** to all of the columns, and then **Save** the table. Examine the fields and data in this table. Open your **2F Publishers** table, examine the fields and data, and then **Close All** open objects.

Create a *one-to-many* relationship between your **2F Publishers** table and your **2F Student Papers** table using the common field **Publisher ID**. **Enforce Referential Integrity**, and enable both cascade options. *One* publisher can publish *many* student papers. Create a **Relationship Report** with **Normal Margins**, saving it as **Lastname Firstname 2F Relationships** and then create a paper printout or PDF electronic image as directed. **Close All** open objects.

2 **Create** a query in **Query Design** view using your **2F Student Papers** table to answer the question, *What is the student ID, home campus, award paid, and publisher ID for awards greater than or equal to $50, sorted in ascending order by the Student ID field?* Display the fields in the order listed in the question. Five records match the criteria. **Save** the query as **Lastname Firstname 2F Awards $50 or More Query** and then create a paper printout or PDF electronic image as directed.

3 Using your **2F Awards $50 or More Query**, create a new query object named **Lastname Firstname 2F 2nd Qtr NW Students Query** and then redesign the query to answer the questions, *Which students (Student ID) from the Northwest campus had papers published between 4/1/19 and 6/30/19, and what was the paper name, the award paid, and the category, sorted in ascending order by the Publication Date field?* Do not restrict the results by **Award Paid**. Do not display the **Home Campus** field in the query results,

and display the rest of the fields in the order listed in the question. Three records match the criteria. Using **Landscape** orientation, create a paper printout or PDF electronic image as directed. **Close** the query, saving the design changes.

4 **Create** a query in **Query Design** view using your **2F Student Papers** table to answer the question, *Which paper IDs, paper names, and category for students from the Southeast and Northeast campuses were published that had an award paid greater than $25, sorted in descending order by the Award Paid field?* Display the fields in the order listed in the question. Six records match the criteria. **Save** the query as **Lastname Firstname 2F SE or NE Over $25 Query** and then using **Normal Margins**, create a paper printout or PDF electronic image as directed. **Close** the query.

5 **Create** a query in **Query Design** view using both tables to answer the questions, *Which paper names were published with a publisher name that has Texas as part of its name, what is the contact name and contact phone number, and what was the award paid, sorted in descending order by the Award Paid field?* (Hint: Use a wildcard character in the criteria row.) Display the fields in the order listed in the question. Eight records match the criteria. **Save** the query as **Lastname Firstname 2F Texas Publishers Query** and then using **Landscape** orientation, create a paper printout or PDF electronic image as directed. **Close** the query.

6 The college's Federation of English Faculty will donate money to the English Writing Lab based on 50 percent of the awards paid to the students. **Create** a query in **Query Design** view using your **2F Student Papers** table to answer the question, *In ascending order by the Paper ID field, what will be the total of each donation to the Writing Lab if the Federation donates an additional 50 percent of each award paid to students?* (Hint: First calculate the amount of the donation, naming the new field **Federation Donation**, and then run the query to be sure the correct results display. Then calculate the total donation, naming the new field **Total Donation**.) Change the property settings of the **Federation Donation** field to display with a **Format** of **Currency** and with **Decimal Places** set to **2**. For the **Publisher ID** of **P-20**, the *Federation Donation* is *$22.50*, and the *Total Donation* is *$67.50*. Apply **Best Fit** to all of the columns, **Save** the query as **Lastname Firstname 2F Federation Donation Query** and then create a paper printout or PDF electronic image as directed. **Close** the query.

(Project 2F Student Publications continues on the next page)

7 **Create** a query in **Query Design** view using your **2F Student Papers** table and the **Sum** aggregate function to answer the question, *What are the total awards paid for each category, sorted in descending order by the Award Paid field?* Display the fields in the order listed in the question. Change the property settings of the **Award Paid** field to display with a **Format** of **Currency** and with **Decimal Places** set to **0**. For the **Category** of **Student Life**, total awards paid are *$265*. Apply **Best Fit** to the **SumOfAward Paid** column. **Save** the query as **Lastname Firstname 2F Awards by Category Query** and then create a paper printout or PDF electronic image as directed. **Close** the query.

8 By using the **Query Wizard**, create a crosstab query based on your **2F Student Papers** table. Select **Home Campus** as the row headings and **Category** as the column headings. **Sum** the **Award Paid** field. Name the query **Lastname Firstname 2F Campus and Category Crosstab Query** In **Design** view, change the property settings of the last two fields to display with a **Format** of **Currency** and with **Decimal Places** set to **0**. This query answers the question, *What are the total awards paid for student publications by each home campus and by each*

category? Apply **Best Fit** to all of the columns, and then **Save** the query. Using **Landscape** orientation and **Normal Margins**, create a paper printout or PDF electronic image as directed. **Close** the query.

9 **Create** a query in **Query Design** view using your **2F Student Papers** table that prompts you to enter the **Home Campus**, and then answers the question, *What is the home campus, student ID, paper name, category, and publication date for student publications, sorted in ascending order by the Publication Date field?* Display the fields in the order listed in the question. **Run** the query, entering **southwest** when prompted for criteria. Seven records match the criteria. **Save** the query as **Lastname Firstname 2F Campus Parameter Query** and then using **Normal Margins**, create a paper printout or PDF electronic image as directed. **Close** the query.

10 Open the **Navigation Pane**, and be sure that all object names display fully. **Close Access**. As directed by your instructor, submit your database and the paper printout or PDF electronic images of the nine objects—relationship report and eight queries—that are the results of this project.

1. Lastname_Firstname_2F_Student_Publications	Database file
2. Lastname Firstname 2F Relationships Relationships	Report
3. Lastname Firstname 2F Awards $50 or More Query	Query
4. Lastname Firstname 2F 2nd Qtr NW Students Query	Query
5. Lastname Firstname 2F SE OR NE Over $25 Query	Query
6. Lastname Firstname 2F Texas Publishers Query	Query
7. Lastname Firstname 2F Federation Donation Query	Query
8. Lastname Firstname 2F Awards by Category Query	Query
9. Lastname Firstname 2F Campus and Category Crosstab Query	Query
10. Lastname Firstname 2F Campus Parameter Query	Query

END | You have completed Project 2F

Mastering Access Project 2G Student Scholarships

In the following Mastering Access project, you will assist Kim Ngo, Director of Academic Scholarships, in using her database to answer questions about scholarships awarded to students. Your completed database objects will look similar to Figure 2.59.

Apply 2A and 2B skills from these Objectives:

1 Open and Save an Existing Database
2 Create Table Relationships
3 Sort Records in a Table
4 Create a Query in Design View
5 Create a New Query from an Existing Query
6 Sort Query Results
7 Specify Criteria in a Query
8 Specify Numeric Criteria in a Query
9 Use Compound Criteria in a Query
10 Create a Query Based on More Than One Table
11 Use Wildcards in a Query
12 Create Calculated Fields in a Query
13 Calculate Statistics and Group Data in a Query
14 Create a Crosstab Query
15 Create a Parameter Query

PROJECT FILES

For Project 2G, you will need the following file:

a02G_Student_Scholarships

You will save your database as:

Lastname_Firstname_2G_Student_Scholarships

PROJECT RESULTS

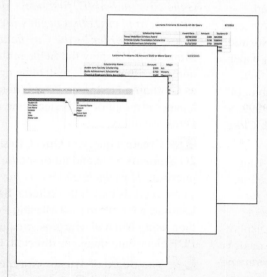

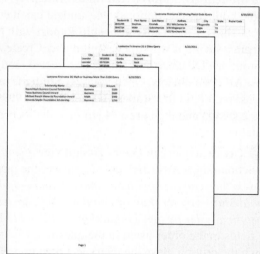

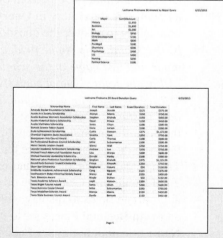

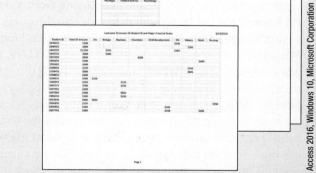

FIGURE 2.59

(Project 2G Student Scholarships continues on the next page)

Mastering Access   Project 2G Student Scholarships (continued)

1 **Start** Access. From your student data files, open **a02G_Student_Scholarships**. Save the database in your **Access Chapter 2** folder as **Lastname_Firstname_2G_Student_Scholarships** and then enable the content. In the **Navigation Pane**, **Rename** each table by adding **Lastname Firstname** to the beginning of the table name. Increase the width of the **Navigation Pane** so that all object names display fully.

2 Open both tables to examine the fields and data, and then **Close** both tables. Create a *one-to-many* relationship between your **2G Students** table and your **2G Scholarships Awarded** table using the common field **Student ID**. **Enforce Referential Integrity**, and enable both cascade options. *One* student can have *many* scholarships. Create a **Relationship Report** with **Normal Margins**, saving it with the default name. Create a paper printout or PDF electronic image as directed, and then **Close All** open objects. Open your **2G Students** table. In the last record, in the **Student ID** field, select **9999999**, type **2839403** and then press ↓ to save the record. **Close** the table.

3 **Create** a query in **Query Design** view using your **2G Scholarships Awarded** table to answer the question, *What is the scholarship name, amount, and major for scholarships greater than or equal to $500, sorted in ascending order by the Scholarship Name field?* Display the fields in the order listed in the question. Eight records match the criteria. **Save** the query as **Lastname Firstname 2G Amount $500 or More Query** and then create a paper printout or PDF electronic image as directed. Click **Close Print Preview**, and leave the query open.

4 Use your **2G Amount $500 or More Query** to create a new query object named **Lastname Firstname 2G Awards 4th Qtr Query** and then redesign the query to answer the question, *Which scholarships (Scholarship Name) were awarded between 10/1/19 and 12/31/19, for what amount, and for which student (Student ID), sorted in ascending order by the Award Date field?* Display only the fields necessary to answer the question and in the order listed in the question. Do not restrict the results by amount, and sort only by the field designated in the question. Five records match the criteria. Create a paper printout or PDF electronic image as directed. **Close** the query, saving the design changes.

5 **Create** a query in **Query Design** view using your **2G Scholarships Awarded** table to answer the question,

Which scholarships (Scholarship Name) were awarded for either Math or Business majors for amounts of more than $200, sorted in descending order by the Amount field? Display the fields in the order listed in the question. Four records match the criteria. (Hint: If six records display, switch to Design view and combine the majors on one criteria line using OR.) **Save** the query as **Lastname Firstname 2G Math or Business More Than $200 Query** and then create a paper printout or PDF electronic image as directed. **Close** the query.

6 **Create** a query in **Query Design** view using your **2G Students** table to answer the question, *What is the city, student ID, first name, and last name of students from cities that begin with the letter L, sorted in ascending order by the City field and by the Last Name field?* Display the fields in the order listed in the question. Five records match the criteria. **Save** the query as **Lastname Firstname 2G L Cities Query** and then create a paper printout or PDF electronic image as directed. **Close** the query.

7 **Create** a query in **Query Design** view using your **2G Students** table and all of the fields to answer the question, *For which students is the Postal Code missing?* Three records match the criteria. **Save** the query as **Lastname Firstname 2G Missing Postal Code Query** and then using **Normal Margins**, create a paper printout or PDF electronic image as directed. **Close** the query.

8 The Board of Trustees for the college will donate an amount equal to 50 percent of each scholarship amount. **Create** a query in **Query Design** view using both tables to answer the question, *In ascending order by the Scholarship Name field, and including the first name and last name of the scholarship recipient, what will be the total value of each scholarship if the Board of Trustees donates an additional 50 percent of each award paid to students?* (Hint: First calculate the amount of the donation, naming the new field **Board Donation**, and then run the query to be sure the correct results display. Then calculate the total donation, naming the new field **Total Donation**.) Change the property settings of the appropriate fields to display with a **Format** of **Currency** and with **Decimal Places** set to **0**. For the **Scholarship Name** of **Amanda Snyder Foundation Scholarship**, the *Board Donation* is *$125*, and the *Total Donation* is *$375*. Apply **Best Fit** to all of the columns, **Save** the query as **Lastname Firstname 2G Board Donation Query** and then

(Project 2G Student Scholarships continues on the next page)

using **Landscape** orientation, create a paper printout or PDF electronic image as directed. **Close** the query.

9 **Create** a query in **Query Design** view using your **2G Scholarships Awarded** table and the **Sum** aggregate function to answer the question, *For each major, what is the total scholarship amount, sorted in descending order by the Amount field?* Display the fields in the order listed in the question. Change the property settings of the **Amount** field to display with a **Format** of **Currency** and with **Decimal Places** set to **0**. For the **Major** of **History**, the total scholarship amount is *$1,850.* Apply **Best Fit** to all of the columns. **Save** the query as **Lastname Firstname 2G Amount by Major Query** and then create a paper printout or PDF electronic image as directed. **Close** the query.

10 By using the **Query Wizard**, create a crosstab query based on your **2G Scholarships Awarded** table. Select **Student ID** as the row headings and **Major** as the column headings. **Sum** the **Amount** field. Name the query **Lastname Firstname 2G Student ID and Major Crosstab Query** In **Design** view, change the property settings of the last two fields to display with a **Format** of **Currency** and with **Decimal Places** set to **0**. This query answers the question, *What are the total scholarship amounts paid*

by each student ID and by each major? Apply **Best Fit** to all of the columns, and then **Save** the query. Using **Landscape** orientation, create a paper printout or PDF electronic image as directed—two pages result. **Close** the query.

11 **Create** a query in **Query Design** view using your **2G Scholarships Awarded** table that prompts you to enter the **Major** of the student, and then answers the question, *What is the scholarship name and amount for a major, sorted in ascending order by the Scholarship Name field?* Display the fields in the order listed in the question. **Run** the query, entering **history** when prompted for criteria. Four records match the criteria. Hide the **Major** field from the results, and then **Run** the query again, entering **history** when prompted for criteria. **Save** the query as **Lastname Firstname 2G Major Parameter Query** and then create a paper printout or PDF electronic image as directed. **Close** the query.

12 Open the **Navigation Pane**, and be sure that all object names display fully. **Close Access**. As directed by your instructor, submit your database and the paper printout or PDF electronic images of the ten objects—relationship report and nine queries, one of which prints on two pages—that are the results of this project.

1. Lastname_Firstname_2G_Student_Scholarships	Database file
2. Relationships for Lastname_Firstname_2G_Student_Scholarships Relationships	Report
3. Lastname Firstname 2G Amount $500 or More Query	Query
4. Lastname Firstname 2G Awards 4th Qtr Query	Query
5. Lastname Firstname 2G Math OR Business Over $200 Query	Query
6. Lastname Firstname 2G L Cities Query	Query
7. Lastname Firstname 2G Missing Postal Code Query	Query
8. Lastname Firstname 2G Board Donation Query	Query
9. Lastname Firstname 2G Amount by Major Query	Query
10. Lastname Firstname 2G Student ID and Major Crosstab Query	Query (2 pages)
11. Lastname Firstname 2G Major Parameter Query (using History)	Query

END | You have completed Project 2G

Apply a combination of the 2A and 2B skills.	GO! Fix It	Project 2H Social Sciences	MyITLab
	GO! Make It	Project 2I Faculty Awards	MyITLab
	GO! Solve It	Project 2J Student Refunds	MyITLab
	GO! Solve It	Project 2K Leave	

PROJECT FILES

For Project 2K, you will need the following file:

a02K_Leave

You will save your database as:

Lastname_Firstname_2K_Leave

Start Access, navigate to your student data files, open a02K_Leave, and then save the database in your Access Chapter 2 folder as **Lastname_Firstname_2K_Leave** Add **Lastname Firstname** to the beginning of both table names, create a one-to-many relationship with cascade options between the two tables—*one* employee can receive *many* leave transactions—and then create a relationship report saving it as **Lastname Firstname 2K Relationships**

Create and save four queries to answer the following questions; be sure that all data displays fully:

- What is the last name and first name of employees who have used personal leave, sorted in ascending order by the Last Name and First Name fields? Do not display the Leave field in the query results.
- What is the last name, first name, and email address of employees who have no phone number listed, sorted in ascending order by the Last Name and First Name fields?
- Grouped by the Leave Classification field, what is the total of each type of leave used? (Hint: Use the aggregate function Count.)
- What is the total number of leave transactions grouped in rows by the Employee# field and grouped in columns by the Leave Classification field?

As directed, create paper or PDF electronic images of the relationship report and the four queries. Be sure that each object prints on one page, and that the object names display fully in the Navigation Pane. As directed, submit your database and the paper printouts or PDF electronic images of the five objects that are the results of this project.

(Project 2K Leave continues on the next page)

GO! Solve It **Project 2K Leave** (continued)

Performance Criteria

	Performance Level		
	Exemplary: You consistently applied the relevant skills	**Proficient: You sometimes, but not always, applied the relevant skills**	**Developing: You rarely or never applied the relevant skills**
Create relationship and relationship report	Relationship and relationship report created correctly.	Relationship and relationship report created with one error.	Relationship and relationship report created with two or more errors, or missing entirely.
Create 2K Personal Leave query	Query created with correct name, fields, sorting, and criteria.	Query created with one element incorrect.	Query created with two or more elements incorrect, or missing entirely.
Create 2K Missing Phone query	Query created with correct name, fields, sorting, and criteria.	Query created with one element incorrect.	Query created with two or more elements incorrect, or missing entirely.
Create 2K Type of Leave query	Query created with correct name, fields, and aggregate function.	Query created with one element incorrect.	Query created with two or more elements incorrect, or missing entirely.
Create 2K Crosstab query	Query created with correct name, row headings, column headings, and aggregate function.	Query created with one element incorrect.	Query created with two or more two elements incorrect, or missing entirely.

END | You have completed Project 2K

RUBRIC

The following outcomes-based assessments are open-ended assessments. That is, there is no specific correct result; your result will depend on your approach to the information provided. Make Professional Quality your goal. Use the following scoring rubric to guide you in how to approach the problem and then to evaluate how well your approach solves the problem.

The *criteria*—Software Mastery, Content, Format and Layout, and Process— represent the knowledge and skills you have gained that you can apply to solving the problem. The *levels of performance*—Professional Quality, Approaching Professional Quality, or Needs Quality Improvements—help you and your instructor evaluate your result.

	Your completed project is of Professional Quality if you:	Your completed project is Approaching Professional Quality if you:	Your completed project Needs Quality Improvements if you:
1-Software Mastery	Choose and apply the most appropriate skills, tools, and features and identify efficient methods to solve the problem.	Choose and apply some appropriate skills, tools, and features, but not in the most efficient manner.	Choose inappropriate skills, tools, or features, or are inefficient in solving the problem.
2-Content	Construct a solution that is clear and well organized, contains content that is accurate, appropriate to the audience and purpose, and is complete. Provide a solution that contains no errors of spelling, grammar, or style.	Construct a solution in which some components are unclear, poorly organized, inconsistent, or incomplete. Misjudge the needs of the audience. Have some errors in spelling, grammar, or style, but the errors do not detract from comprehension.	Construct a solution that is unclear, incomplete, or poorly organized, contains some inaccurate or inappropriate content, and contains many errors of spelling, grammar, or style. Do not solve the problem.
3-Format and Layout	Format and arrange all elements to communicate information and ideas, clarify function, illustrate relationships, and indicate relative importance.	Apply appropriate format and layout features to some elements, but not others. Overuse features, causing minor distraction.	Apply format and layout that does not communicate information or ideas clearly. Do not use format and layout features to clarify function, illustrate relationships, or indicate relative importance. Use available features excessively, causing distraction.
4-Process	Use an organized approach that integrates planning, development, self-assessment, revision, and reflection.	Demonstrate an organized approach in some areas, but not others; or, use an insufficient process of organization throughout.	Do not use an organized approach to solve the problem.

Apply a combination of the **2A** and **2B** skills.	GO! Think Project 2L Coaches

PROJECT FILES

For Project 2L, you will need the following file:

a02L_Coaches

You will save your database as

Lastname_Firstname_2L_Coaches

Start Access, navigate to your student data files, open a02L_Coaches, and then save the database in your Access Chapter 2 folder as **Lastname_Firstname_2L_Coaches** Add **Lastname Firstname** to the beginning of both table names, create a one-to-many relationship with cascade options between the two tables—*one* coach can participate in *many* activities—and then create a relationship report saving it as **Lastname Firstname 2L Relationships**

Create queries to assist Randy Garza, the Athletic Director, answer the following questions about the coaches at Texas Lakes Community College:

- What is the last name and first name of every coach involved in *Dive* activities, sorted in ascending order by the Last Name field? Do not display the activity name.
- What is the last name and first name of every coach involved in basketball or football activities, sorted in ascending first by the Activity Name field and then by the Last Name field?
- Grouped by division, what is the total number of activity names, sorted in descending order by the total number? (Hint: Use the Count aggregate function.)
- What is the skill specialty, first name, last name, and phone number for coaches in a specified position that is entered when prompted for the Position, sorted in ascending order first by the Skill Specialty field and then by the Last Name field? (When prompted, enter the position of *director* for your paper or PDF electronic image.)

As directed, create paper or PDF electronic images of the relationship report and the four queries. Be sure that each object prints on one page, and that the object names display fully in the Navigation Pane. As directed, submit your database and the paper printout or PDF electronic images of the five objects that are the results of this project.

> End | You have completed Project 2L

GO! Think	Project 2M Club Donations	MyITLab

Build From Scratch

You and GO!	Project 2N Personal Inventory	MyITLab

GO! Collaborative Team Project	Project 2O Bell Orchid Hotels	MyITLab

Forms, Filters, and Reports

PROJECT 3A

OUTCOMES
Create forms to enter and delete records and to display data in a database.

OBJECTIVES
1. Create and Use a Form to Add and Delete Records
2. Filter Records
3. Create a Form by Using the Form Wizard
4. Modify a Form in Layout View and in Design View

PROJECT 3B

OUTCOMES
Create reports to display database information.

OBJECTIVES
5. Create a Report by Using the Report Tool and Modify the Report in Layout View
6. Create a Report by Using the Report Wizard
7. Modify the Design of a Report
8. Keep Grouped Data Together in a Printed Report

EM Karuna/Shutterstock

In This Chapter GO! to Work with Access

In this chapter, you will create forms to enter and delete data and to view data in database tables. Forms can display one record at a time with fields placed in the same order to match a paper source document. Records in a form or table can be filtered to display a subset of the records based on matching specific values. You will modify forms by adding fields, changing field widths, and adding labels to the forms. You will create professional-looking reports that summarize the data from a query or table. You will modify the reports by changing the fields in the report, by changing the layout of the report, by grouping data, and by making sure that groupings of data stay together on the printed page.

The projects in this chapter relate to **Texas Lakes Community College**, which is located in the Austin, Texas, area. Its four campuses serve over 30,000 students and offer more than 140 certificate programs and degrees. The college has a highly acclaimed Distance Education program and an extensive Workforce Development program. The college makes positive contributions to the community through cultural and athletic programs, and has significant partnerships with businesses and nonprofit organizations. Popular fields of study include nursing and health care, solar technology, computer technology, and graphic design.

Students and Majors Database

PROJECT 3A

PROJECT ACTIVITIES

In Activities 3.01 through 3.15, you will assist Sean Fitchette, Director of Enrollment Services at Texas Lakes Community College, in using his Access database to track new students and their major fields of study. Your completed forms will look similar to Figure 3.1.

Please always review the downloaded Grader instructions before beginning.

 PROJECT FILES If your instructor wants you to submit Project 3A in the MyITLab Grader system, log in to MyITLab, locate Grader Project 3A, and then download the files for this project.

For Project 3A, you will need the following file:
a03A_Students_Majors

You will save your database as:
Lastname_Firstname_3A_Students_Majors

PROJECT RESULTS

GO!
Walk Thru
Project 3A

Lastname Firstname 3A Majors

Major ID	339.555.22
Major Name	Network Security

Lastname Firstname 3A New Students

Student ID	9712345
First Name	Firstname
Last Name	Lastname
Address	5820 Sweet Basil Ct
City	Austin
State	TX
Postal Code	78726
Home Phone	(512) 555-5712
College Email	flastname@tlcc.edu
Major ID	339

Lastname Firstname 3A Student Major Change Form

Student ID	9712345
Last Name	Lastname
First Name	Firstname
Major ID	339

Texas Lakes Community College

Access 2016, Windows 10, Microsoft Corporation

FIGURE 3.1 Project 3A Students and Majors

In this project, using your own name, you will create the following database and objects. Your instructor may ask you to submit printouts or PDF electronic images:

Lastname_Firstname_3A_Students_Majors   Database file
Lastname Firstname 3A New Student Form   Form (Record 102)
Lastname Firstname 3A Major Form   Form (Record 33)
Lastname Firstname 3A Student Major Change Form   Form (Record 102)

Objective 1   Create and Use a Form to Add and Delete Records

GO! Learn How
Video A3-1

A *form* is a database object that you can use to display existing records in a table, or to edit, delete, or enter new records into a table. A form is useful to control access to the data. For example, you can design a form for college registration assistants so that they can see and enter the courses scheduled and fees paid by an individual student. However, they cannot see or enter grades for a student.

Some forms display only one record at a time; other forms display multiple records at the same time. A form that displays only one record at a time is useful not only to the individual who performs the *data entry*—entering the actual records—but also to anyone who has the job of viewing information in a database. For example, when you request a transcript from your college, someone displays your record on the screen. For the individual viewing your transcript, it is much easier to look at one record at a time, using a form, than to look at all of the student transcripts in the database.

1.2.5, 2.2.4

Activity 3.01 | Opening and Saving an Existing Database, Renaming Tables, and Viewing a Table Relationship

To submit this as an autograded project, log on to MyITLab and download the files for this project, and begin with those files instead of a03A_Students_Majors. For Project 3A using Grader, begin working with the database in Step 4. For Grader to award points accurately, when saving an object, do not include your Lastname Firstname at the beginning of the object name.

1 ▶ Start Access. In the Access opening screen, click **Open Other Files**. Under **Open**, click **Browse**. In the **Open** dialog box, navigate to the location where your student data files for this chapter are stored, and then double-click **a03A_Students_Majors** to open the database.

2 ▶ Display **Backstage** view, and then click **Save As**. Under **File Types**, be sure **Save Database As** is selected. On the right, under **Database File Types**, be sure **Access Database** is selected, and then at the bottom of the screen, click **Save As**.

3 ▶ In the **Save As** dialog box, navigate to the location where you are saving your databases. Create a **New folder** named **Access Chapter 3**, and then **Open** the folder. In the **File name** box and using your own name, replace the existing text with **Lastname_Firstname_3A_Students_Majors** and then click **Save** or press Enter.

4 On the **Message Bar**, click **Enable Content**. In the **Navigation Pane**, right-click the **3A Majors** table, and then click **Rename**. With the table name selected and using your own name, type **Lastname Firstname 3A Majors** and then press Enter to rename the table. Use the same technique to **Rename** the **3A New Students** table to **Lastname Firstname 3A New Students**

5 Point to the right edge of the **Navigation Pane** to display the ⟷ pointer. Drag to the right to increase the width of the pane until both table names display fully.

6 On the ribbon, click the **Database Tools tab**. In the **Relationships group**, click **Relationships**. Under Relationship Tools, on the **Design tab**, in the **Relationships group**, click **All Relationships**. If necessary, resize and move the field lists so that the entire table name and fields display for each field list.

> Because you renamed the tables, the field lists do not automatically display in the Relationships window.

7 In the **Relationships** window, click the **join line** between the two field lists. In the **Tools group**, click **Edit Relationships**. Point to the title bar of the **Edit Relationships** dialog box, and drag the dialog box to the right of the two field lists. Compare your screen with Figure 3.2.

> *One* major is associated with *many* students. A one-to-many relationship is established between your 3A Majors table and your 3A New Students table using the Major ID field as the common field. Recall that Cascade Update Related Fields enables you to change the primary key in the 3A Majors table, and then the data in the foreign key field in the 3A New Students field is automatically updated. Recall that Cascade Delete Related Records enables you to delete a record in the 3A Majors table, and then all related records in the 3A New Students table are automatically deleted.

🔄 **ANOTHER WAY**   In the Relationships window, double-click the join line to display the Edit Relationships dialog box.

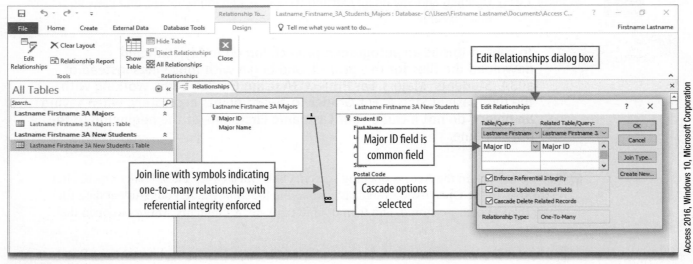

FIGURE 3.2

ALERT!	**Is your edit relationships dialog box empty?**

The Edit Relationships dialog box does not display any information if you do not first click the join line. If this happens, close the Edit Relationships dialog box, and then be sure that you click the join line—when selected, the join line is darker.

8 ▶ **Close** ☒ the **Edit Relationships** dialog box, and then **Close** ☒ the **Relationships** window. In the message box, click **Yes** to save changes to the layout of the relationships.

Activity 3.02 | Creating a Form and Viewing Records

MOS
4.1.1, 4.1.3

There are several ways to create a form in Access, but the fastest and easiest way is to use the ***Form tool***. With a single mouse click, all fields from the data source are placed on the form. You can modify the form in Layout view or in Design view, or you can switch to Form view and use the new form immediately.

The Form tool uses all of the field names and all of the records from an existing table or query. Records that you create or edit using a form are automatically updated in the underlying table or tables. In this Activity, you will create a form and then view records from the underlying table—the data source.

1 ▶ In the **Navigation Pane**, double-click your **3A New Students** table to open it. Scroll as needed to view all 10 fields—*Student ID*, *First Name*, *Last Name*, *Address*, *City*, *State*, *Postal Code*, *Home Phone*, *College Email*, and *Major ID*. **Close** ☒ the table.

2 ▶ In the **Navigation Pane**, be sure your **3A New Students** table is selected. On the ribbon, click the **Create tab**, and then in the **Forms group**, click **Form**. **Close** ≪ the **Navigation Pane**, and then compare your screen with Figure 3.3.

The form is created based on the currently selected object—your 3A New Students table—and displays in ***Layout view***. In Layout view, you can modify the form with the data displayed in the fields. For example, you can adjust the size of the text boxes to fit the data.

The form is created in a simple top-to-bottom layout, with all 10 fields from your 3A New Students table lined up in a single column. The data for the first record in the data source displays.

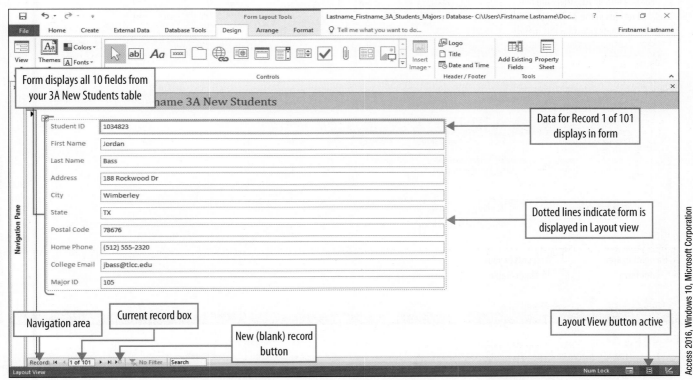

FIGURE 3.3

> **3** In the navigation area, click **Next record** ▶ four times to display the fifth record—*Student ID 1298345*. In the navigation area, select the text in the Current record box, type **62** and then press Enter to display the record for *Student ID 5720358*. In the navigation area, click **Last record** ▶| to display the record for *Student ID 9583924*, and then click **First record** |◀ to display the record for *Student ID 1034823*.

> Use the navigation buttons to scroll among the records or the Current record box to display any single record.

> **4** Save 🖫 the form as **Lastname Firstname 3A New Student Form** and then **Close** ☒ the form object.

> **5** Open ≫ the **Navigation Pane**. Notice that your new form displays under the table with which it is related—your **3A New Students** table.

Activity 3.03 | Creating a Second Form

[MOS]
4.1.1, 4.1.3

In this Activity, you will use the Form tool to create a form for your 3A Majors table.

> **1** In the **Navigation Pane**, click your **3A Majors** table to select it. On the ribbon, click the **Create tab**, and then in the **Forms group**, click **Form**. **Close** ≪ the **Navigation Pane**, and then compare your screen with Figure 3.4.

> Because a one-to-many relationship is established, the form displays related records in the 3A New Students table for each record in the 3A Majors table. Five new students have selected a major of *Diagnostic Medical Sonography—Major ID 105*.

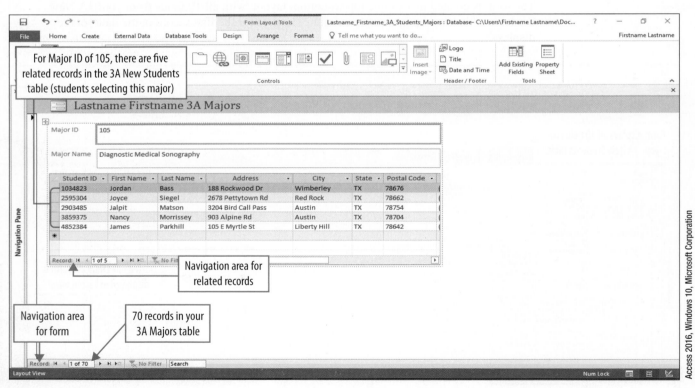

FIGURE 3.4

2 **Close** ☒ your **3A Majors** form. In the message box, click **Yes**. In the **Save As** dialog box, in the **Form Name** box, type **Lastname Firstname 3A Major Form** and then click **OK**.

> Recall that if you do not save an object, you are prompted to do so when you close the object.

3 **Open** ⫸ the **Navigation Pane**. Notice that your new form displays under the table with which it is related—your **3A Majors** table.

Activity 3.04 | Adding Records to a Table by Using a Form

By using a single-record form to add, modify, and delete records, you can reduce the number of data entry errors, because the individual performing the data entry is looking at only one record at a time. Recall that your database is useful only if the information is accurate—just like your contact list is useful only if it contains accurate phone numbers and email addresses.

Forms are based on—also referred to as *bound* to—the table where the records are stored. When a record is entered in a form, the new record is added to the underlying table. The reverse is also true—when a record is added to the table, the new record can be viewed in the related form.

In this Activity, you will add a new record to both tables by using the forms that you just created.

1 In the **Navigation Pane**, double-click your **3A New Student Form** object to open it, and then **Close** ⫷ the **Navigation Pane**. In the navigation area, click **New (blank) record** ▶⊞ to display a new blank form.

> When you open a form, the first record in the underlying table displays in *Form view*, which is used to view, add, modify, and delete records stored in the table.

2 In the **Student ID** field, type **9712345** and then press `Tab`.

> Use the `Tab` key to move from field to field in a form. *Tab order* is the order in which the insertion point moves from one field to the next when you press the `Tab` key. As you start typing, the pencil icon displays in the *record selector bar* at the left—the bar used to select an entire record. The pencil icon displays when a record is being created or edited.

⟳ ANOTHER WAY   Press the `Enter` key, provided there are no special links on the form, such as a link to create a new form or a link to print the form.

---

3 Using your own first name and last name and using the first initial of your first name and your last name for the *College Email* field, continue entering the data shown in the following table, and then compare your screen with Figure 3.5.

Student ID	First Name	Last Name	Address	City	State	Postal Code	Home Phone	College Email	Major ID
9712345	First Name	Last Name	5820 Sweet Basil Ct	Austin	TX	78726	(512) 555-5712	flastname@ tlcc.edu	339

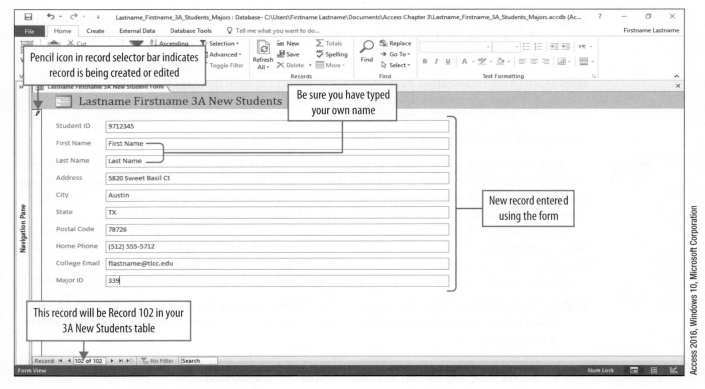

FIGURE 3.5

4 ▸ With the insertion point positioned in the last field, press Enter to save the record and display a new blank record. **Close** ✕ your **3A New Student Form** object.

5 ▸ **Open** ⟫ the **Navigation Pane**, and then double-click your **3A New Students** table to open it. In the navigation area, click **Last record** ▸I to verify that the record you entered in the form is stored in the underlying table. **Close** ✕ your **3A New Students** table.

6 ▸ In the **Navigation Pane**, double-click your **3A Major Form** object to open it. At the bottom of the screen, in the navigation area for the form—*not* the navigation area for the subdatasheet—click **New (blank) record** ▸✱. In the blank form, enter the data shown in the following table:

Major ID	Major Name
339.555.22	**Network Security**

7 ▸ **Close** ✕ your **3A Major Form** object. In the **Navigation Pane**, double-click your **3A Majors** table, and then scroll to verify that the record for *Major ID 339.555.22 Network Security* displays in the table—records are sorted by the *Major ID* field. **Close** ✕ the table.

Activity 3.05 | Deleting Records from a Table by Using a Form

2.3.3, 2.3.5

You can delete records from a database table by using a form. In this Activity, you will delete the record for *Major ID 800.03* because the program has been discontinued.

1 ▸ In the **Navigation Pane**, double-click your **3A Major Form** object to open it, and then **Close** ⟪ the **Navigation Pane**. On the **Home tab**, in the **Find group**, click **Find** to open the **Find and Replace** dialog box.

🔁 **ANOTHER WAY** Press Ctrl + F to open the Find and Replace dialog box.

2 In the **Look In** box, notice that *Current field* displays. In the **Find What** box, type **800.03** and then click **Find Next**. Compare your screen with Figure 3.6, and verify that the record for *Major ID 800.03* displays.

Because the insertion point was positioned in the *Major ID* field before opening the dialog box, Access will search for data in this field—the *Current field*.

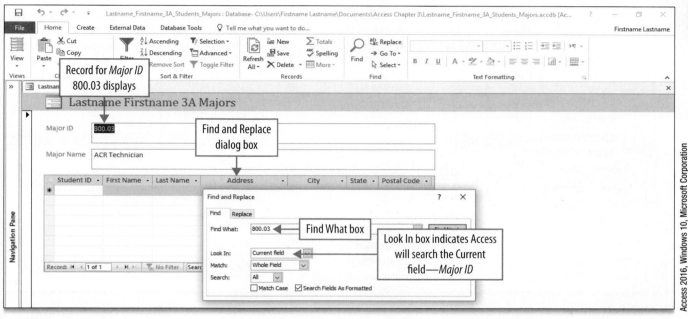

FIGURE 3.6

3 Close ⊠ the **Find and Replace** dialog box. On the **Home tab**, in the **Records group**, click the **Delete arrow**, and then click **Delete Record**.

The record is removed from the screen, and a message displays alerting you that you are about to delete *1 record(s)*. Once you click *Yes*, you cannot click Undo to reverse this action. If you delete a record by mistake, you must re-create the record by reentering the data. Because no students are associated with this major and the program is being discontinued, you can delete it from the table.

4 In the message box, click **Yes** to delete the record. In the navigation area for the form, notice that the total number of records in the table is *70*. Close ⊠ your **3A Major Form** object.

5 Open ⊠ the **Navigation Pane**, and then double-click your **3A Majors** table to open it. Examine the table to verify that the *Major ID 800.03* record has been deleted from the table, and then **Close** ⊠ the table.

Adding and deleting records in a form updates the records stored in the underlying table.

Activity 3.06 | Printing a Form

When a form is displayed, clicking Print causes *all* of the records to print in the form layout. In this Activity, you will print only *one* record.

1 In the **Navigation Pane**, double-click your **3A New Student Form** object to open it, and then **Close** ⊠ the **Navigation Pane**. Press Ctrl + F to open the **Find and Replace** dialog box. In the **Find What** box, type **9712345** and then click **Find Next** to display the record with your name. **Close** ⊠ the **Find and Replace** dialog box.

2 On the **File tab**, click **Print**, and then on the right, click **Print**. In the **Print** dialog box, under **Print Range**, click the **Selected Record(s)** option button. In the lower left corner of the dialog box, click **Setup**.

3 In the **Page Setup** dialog box, click the **Columns tab**. Under **Column Size**, double-click in the **Width** box to select the existing value, type **7.5** and then compare your screen with Figure 3.7.

Change the width of the column in this manner so that the form prints on one page. Forms are not typically printed, so the width of the column in a form might be greater than the width of the paper on which you are printing. The maximum column width that you can enter is dependent upon the printer that is installed on your system. This setting is saved when you save or close the form.

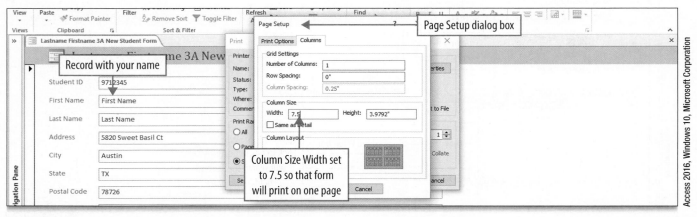

FIGURE 3.7

4 In the **Page Setup** dialog box, click **OK**. To create a paper printout, in the **Print** dialog box click **OK**. To create a PDF electronic image of this single form, click **Cancel** and then follow the instructions in the Note below.

> **NOTE**   Printing a Single Form as a PDF Electronic Image
>
> To create a PDF electronic image of a single form as a PDF electronic image, change the column width to 7.5 as described in Step 3 above, and then in the Print dialog box, click Cancel. On the left side of the form, click the Record Selector bar so that it is black—selected. Click the External Data tab. In the Export group, click PDF or XPS.
>
> In the Publish as PDF or XPS dialog box, navigate to your chapter folder. In the File name box, the file has the same name as the form. Be sure that the Open file after publishing check box is selected, and that the Minimum size (publishing online) option button is selected. In the Publish as PDF or XPS dialog box, click Options. In the Options dialog box, under Range, click the Selected records option button, click OK, and then click Publish. Close the Windows Edge Reader, Adobe Reader or Adobe Acrobat window, and then submit the file as directed by your instructor.

---

5 **Close** ☒ your **3A New Student Form** object, **Open** ⇒ the **Navigation Pane**, and then double-click your **3A Major Form** object to open it. **Close** ⇐ the **Navigation Pane**.

6 Use the techniques you just practiced to **Find** the record for the **Major ID** of **339.555.22**, and then create a paper printout or PDF electronic image as directed by your instructor of that record only on one page. After printing, **Close** ☒ your **3A Major Form** object.

If there are no related records in the subdatasheet, the empty subdatasheet does not display in the printed form.

GO! Learn How
Video A3-2

Filtering records in a form displays only a portion of the total records—a *subset*—based on matching specific values. Filters are commonly used to provide a quick answer to a question, and the result is not generally saved for future use. For example, by filtering records in a form, you can quickly display a subset of records for students majoring in Information Systems Technology, which is identified by the Major ID of 339.

A form provides an interface for the database. For example, because of security reasons, the registration assistants at your college may not have access to the entire student database. Rather, by using a form, they can access and edit only some information—the information necessary for them to do their jobs. Filtering records within a form provides individuals who do not have access to the entire database a way to ask questions of the database without constructing a query. You can save the filter with the form if you are going to use the filter frequently.

Activity 3.07 | Filtering Data by Selection of One Field

2.3.7

In this Activity, you will assist a counselor at the college who wants to see records for students majoring in Information Systems Technology. In a form, you can use the *Filter By Selection* command to display only the records that contain the value in the selected field and to hide the records that do *not* contain the value in the selected field.

1 **Open** ⟩⟩ the **Navigation Pane**, double-click your **3A New Student Form** object to open it in **Form** view, and then **Close** ⟨⟨ the **Navigation Pane**.

2 In the first record, click the **Major ID** field name—or you can click in the field box. Press Ctrl + F to display the **Find and Replace** dialog box. In the **Find What** box, type **339** If necessary, in the Match box, click the arrow, and then click Whole Field. Click **Find Next**, and then compare your screen with Figure 3.8.

This action finds and displays a record with a *Major ID* of *339*—the major of *Information Systems Technology*. You will use this action to filter the records using the value of *339*.

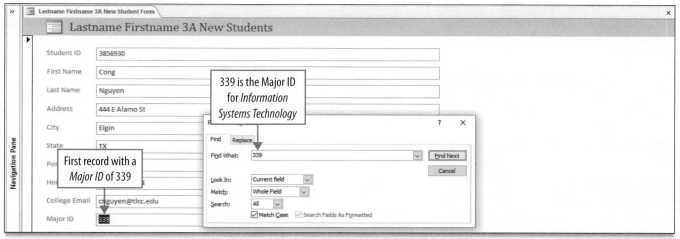

FIGURE 3.8

3 Close ☒ the **Find and Replace** dialog box. On the **Home tab**, in the **Sort & Filter group**, click **Selection**, and then click **Equals "339"**. Compare your screen with Figure 3.9.

> Seven records match the contents of the selected Major ID field—*339*—the Major ID for the Information Systems Technology major. In the navigation area, *Filtered* with a funnel icon displays next to the number of records. *Filtered* also displays on the right side of the status bar to indicate that a filter is applied. On the Home tab, in the Sort & Filter group, Toggle Filter is active.

ANOTHER WAY   With the data selected in the field, right-click the selection, and then click Equals "339".

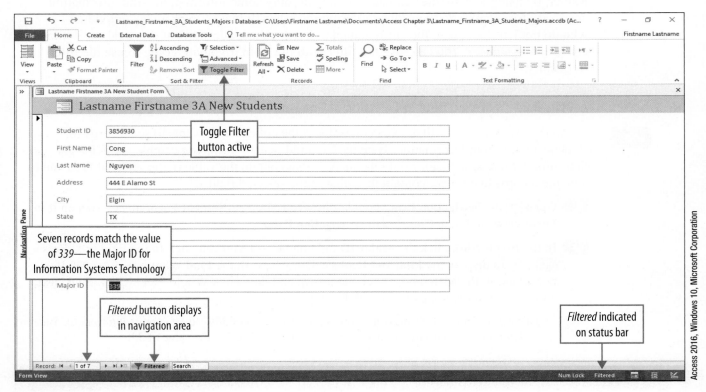

FIGURE 3.9

4 On the **Home tab**, in the **Sort & Filter group**, click **Toggle Filter** to remove the filter and display all 102 records. Notice *Unfiltered* in the navigation area, which indicates a filter is created but is not active.

ANOTHER WAY   Click Filtered in the navigation area to remove the filter.

NOTE   The Toggle Filter Button

On the Home tab, in the Sort & Filter group, the Toggle Filter button is used to apply or remove a filter. If no filter is created, the button is not available. After a filter is created, the button becomes available. Because it is a toggle button used to apply or remove a filter, the ScreenTip that displays for this button alternates between Apply Filter—when a filter is created but is not currently applied—and Remove Filter—when a filter is applied.

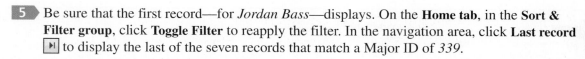

5 Be sure that the first record—for *Jordan Bass*—displays. On the **Home tab**, in the **Sort & Filter group**, click **Toggle Filter** to reapply the filter. In the navigation area, click **Last record** ⏭ to display the last of the seven records that match a Major ID of *339*.

> The record for *Student ID 9712345* displays—the record with your name. Use Toggle Filter to apply or remove filters as needed.

6 In the navigation area, click **Filtered** to remove the filter and display all of the records.

> In the navigation area, *Filtered* changes to *Unfiltered*.

7 In the first record for *Jordan Bass*, in the **Last Name** field, select the first letter—**B**—in *Bass*. In the **Sort & Filter group**, click **Selection**, and then click **Begins with "B"**.

> A new filter is applied that displays eight records in which the *Last Name* begins with the letter *B*.

↻ ANOTHER WAY   With the letter *B* selected, right-click the selection, and then click Begins with "B".

---

8 Use either **Toggle Filter** in the **Sort & Filter group** or **Filtered** in the navigation area to remove the filter and display all of the records.

9 In the **Sort & Filter group**, click **Advanced**, and then click **Clear All Filters**. Notice, that in the navigation area, *Unfiltered* changed to *No Filter*.

> The filter is removed from the form and must be re-created to apply it. If you toggle the filter off and save the form, the filter is saved with the form even though the filter is not currently applied.

Activity 3.08 │ Using Filter By Form

Use the *Filter By Form* command to filter the records based on one or more fields, or based on more than one value in the same field. The Filter By Form command offers greater flexibility than the Filter By Selection command and can be used to answer a question that requires matching multiple values. In this Activity, you will filter records to help Mr. Fitchette determine how many students live in Dripping Springs or Austin.

1 On the **Home tab**, in the **Sort & Filter group**, click **Advanced**, and then click **Filter By Form**. Compare your screen with Figure 3.10.

> The Filter by Form window displays all of the field names, but without any data. In the empty text box for each field, you can type a value or select a value from a list. The *Look for* and *Or* tabs display at the bottom.

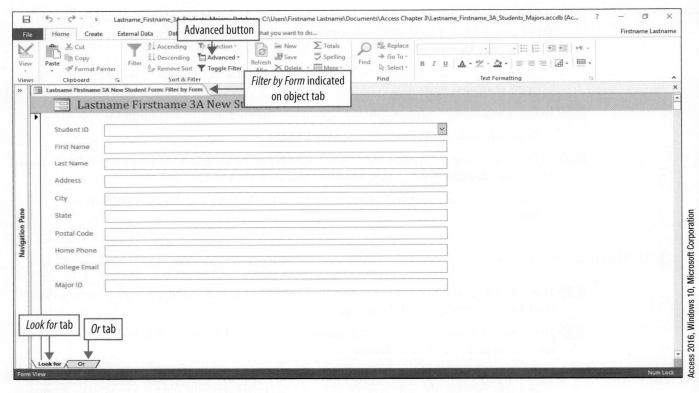

FIGURE 3.10

2 In the form, click the **City** field name to position the insertion point in the **City** field box. At the right edge of the **City** field box, click the **arrow**, and then click **Dripping Springs**. In the **Sort & Filter group**, click **Toggle Filter**.

As displayed in the navigation area, four student records have *Dripping Springs* stored in the City field.

3 In the **Sort & Filter group**, click **Advanced**, and then click **Filter By Form**. In the lower left corner of the form, click the **Or tab**. Click the **City** field box **arrow**, and then click **Austin**. In the **Sort & Filter group**, click **Toggle Filter**, and then compare your screen with Figure 3.11.

As displayed in the navigation area, 28 student records have either *Dripping Springs* OR *Austin* stored in the City field. You have created an ***OR condition***; that is, records display where, in this instance, either of two values—Dripping Springs *or* Austin—is present in the selected field.

ANOTHER WAY   Click in the field box, and type the criteria separated by the word *or*. For example, in the City field box, type *Dripping Springs or Austin*.

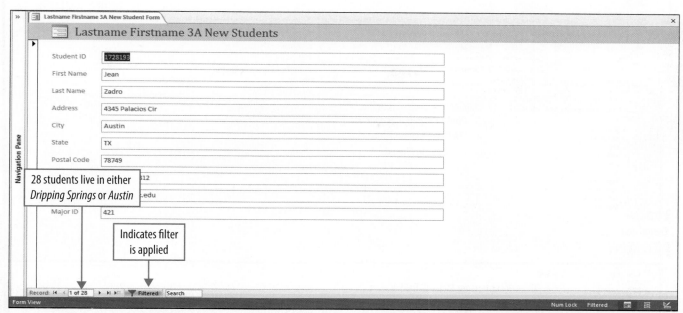

Lastname Firstname 3A New Student Form

Lastname Firstname 3A New Students

Student ID	1728193
First Name	Jean
Last Name	Zadro
Address	4345 Palacios Cir
City	Austin
State	TX
Postal Code	78749

28 students live in either *Dripping Springs* **or** *Austin*

412

.edu

Major ID	421

Indicates filter is applied

Record: I◄ ◄ 1 of 28 ► ►I ►✱ ▼ Filtered   Search

Form View

Num Lock   Filtered

Access 2016, Windows 10, Microsoft Corporation

FIGURE 3.11

---

4 In the **Sort & Filter group**, click **Advanced**, and then click **Clear All Filters** to display all 102 records.

Activity 3.09 | Using Advanced Filter/Sort

MOS
2.3.7

In this Activity, you will use the Advanced Filter/Sort command to filter records to locate students who live in Austin with a Major ID of *339*—Information Systems Technology.

1 In the **Sort & Filter group**, click **Advanced**, and then click **Advanced Filter/Sort**.

The Advanced Filter design grid displays, which is similar to the query design grid, although not all rows display in the bottom half of the window. A field list for the underlying table of the form displays.

2 In the table area, resize the field list so that the entire table name and all of the field names display.

3 In the **3A New Students** field list, double-click **City**, and then double-click **Major ID** to add both fields to the design grid. In the **Criteria** row, under **City**, type **Austin** and then press Enter. In the **Criteria** row, under **Major ID**, type **339** and then press Enter. Compare your screen with Figure 3.12.

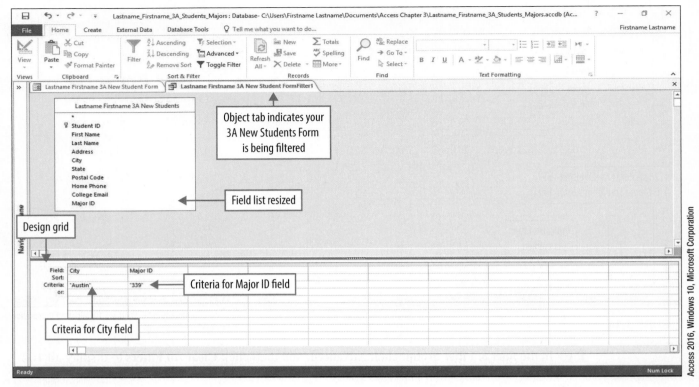

FIGURE 3.12

4 In the **Sort & Filter group**, click **Toggle Filter** to display the filtered records.

> Three records match the criteria. You have created an *AND condition*; that is, only records where both values—Austin *and* 339—are present in the selected fields display. There are three students who live in Austin who have declared a major of Information Systems Technology.

5 In the **Sort & Filter group**, click **Toggle Filter** to remove the filter and to display all of the records.

> In the navigation area, *Unfiltered* displays, which indicates that a filter has been created for this form. Unless you click Clear All Filters, the filter is saved with the form when the form is closed. When you reopen the form, you can click Toggle or Unfiltered to reapply the filter.

6 **Close** ☒ your **3A New Student Form** object, and notice that the Advanced Filter grid also closes.

More **Knowledge** | **Using the Filter Button**

You can filter a table in a manner similar to the way you filter records in a form. With a table open in Datasheet view, click in the field you wish to use for the filter. On the Home tab, in the Sort & Filter group, click Filter to display a shortcut menu. Select the (Select All) check box to clear the option, and then select the data by which you want to filter your records by clicking the check boxes preceding the data. To remove the filter, redisplay the menu, and then select the (Select All) check box.

Objective 3 | Create a Form by Using the Form Wizard

GO! Learn How
Video A3-3

The *Form Wizard* walks you step by step through the creation of a form and gives you more flexibility in the design, layout, and number of fields in a form than the Form tool. Design a form for the individuals who use the form—either for entering new records or viewing records. For example, when your college counselor displays student information, it may be easier for the counselor to view the information if the fields are arranged in a layout that more closely matches a paper form.

4.1.1, 4.1.3

In this Activity, you will create a form to match the layout of a paper form that a student at Texas Lakes Community College completes when that student changes his or her major. This will make it easier for the individual who changes the data in the database.

1 On the ribbon, click the **Create tab**, and then in the **Forms group**, click **Form Wizard**.

The Form Wizard walks you step by step through the process of creating a form by asking questions. In the first wizard screen, you select the fields to include on the form. The fields can come from more than one table or query.

2 In the **Tables/Queries** box, click the **arrow** to display a list of available tables and queries from which you can create the form.

There are two tables in the database from which you can create a new form. The selected table is the one that you last worked with.

3 Click **Table: Lastname Firstname 3A New Students**, and then compare your screen with Figure 3.13.

In the Available Fields list, the field names from your 3A New Students table display.

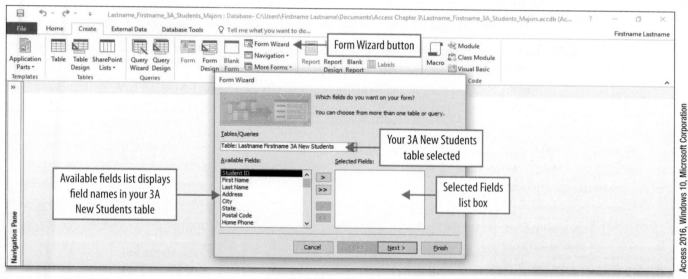

FIGURE 3.13

4 In the **Available Fields** list, double-click the following field names in the order given to move them to the **Selected Fields** list: **First Name**, **Last Name**, and **Major ID**. Compare your screen with Figure 3.14.

Three field names from your 3A New Students table display in the Selected Fields list.

ANOTHER WAY Click the field name, and then click Add Field [>] to move a field from the Available Fields list to the Selected Fields list.

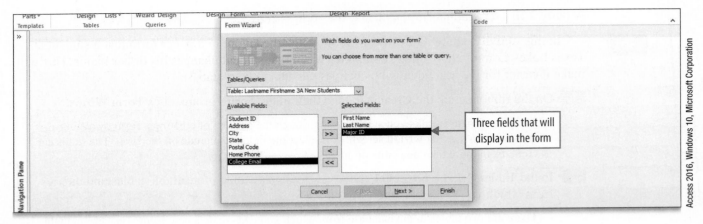

FIGURE 3.14

5 ⯈ Click **Next**. In the wizard, verify that **Columnar** is selected as the layout, and then click **Next**. In the **What title do you want for your form?** box, select the existing text, type **Lastname Firstname 3A Student Major Change Form** and then click **Finish** to close the wizard and create the form.

> The three fields and the data from the first record in your 3A New Students table display in Form view.

6 ⯈ **Open** ⯈ the **Navigation Pane**. If necessary, increase the width of the Navigation Pane so that all object names display fully. Compare your screen with Figure 3.15.

> In the Navigation Pane, the form displays under its data source—your 3A New Students table.

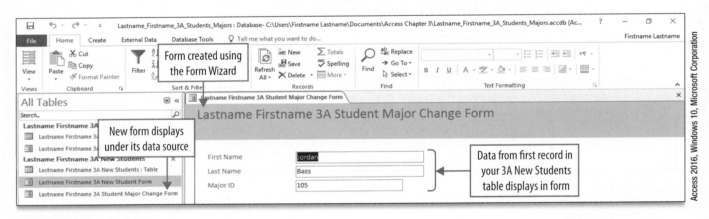

FIGURE 3.15

Objective 4 Modify a Form in Layout View and in Design View

GO! Learn How
Video A3-4

After you create a form, you can make changes to it. For example, you can group the fields, resize the fields, add more fields to the form, and change the style of the form. Layout view enables you to see the data in the form as you modify the form. Most changes to a form can be made in Layout view.

Activity 3.11 | Grouping Controls in Layout View

MOS
4.2.5

In this Activity, you will group **controls** in the form so that you can work with them as one unit. Controls are objects on a form that display data or text, perform actions, and let you view and work with information.

1 Close |«| the **Navigation Pane**, and be sure that your **3A Student Major Change Form** object displays in the object window. On the **Home tab**, in the **Views group**, click the top portion of the **View** button to switch to **Layout** view. If the Field List pane displays on the right side of your screen, click Close |X| to close the pane. Compare your screen with Figure 3.16.

The field names and data for the first record in your 3A New Students record display in controls. The data for the first record displays in *text box controls*. The most commonly used control is the text box control, which typically displays data from a field in the underlying table. A text box control is a *bound control*—its data comes from a field in a table or query.

The field names—*First Name*, *Last Name*, and *Major ID*—display in *label controls*. A label control displays to the left of a text box control and contains descriptive information that displays on the form, usually the field name. A control that does not have a data source is an *unbound control*. Another example of an unbound control is a label control that displays the title of a form.

↻ **ANOTHER WAY**   On the right side of the status bar, click Layout View 🗒 to switch from Form view to Layout view.

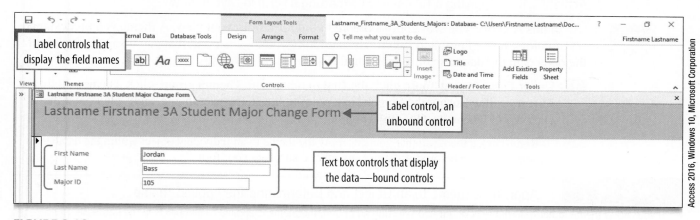

FIGURE 3.16

2 Click the **First Name label control**. Hold down Shift, and then click the **Last Name label control**, the **Major ID label control**, and the three **text box controls** to select all of the label and text box controls on the form.

3 With all six controls selected—surrounded by a colored border—on the ribbon, under **Form Layout Tools**, click the **Arrange tab**. In the **Table group**, click **Stacked**. Click the **First Name label control** to cancel the selection of all of the controls and to surround the **First Name label control** with a dotted border. Compare your screen with Figure 3.17.

This action groups the controls together in the *Stacked layout* format—a layout similar to a paper form, with labels to the left of each field. Because the controls are grouped, you can move and edit the controls more easily as you redesign your form.

A dotted line forms a border around the controls, which indicates that the controls are grouped together. Above and to the left of the first label control that displays *First Name*, the *layout selector* 🔲 displays. The layout selector is used to select and move or format the entire group of controls.

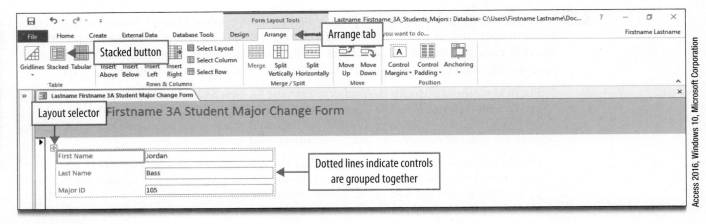

FIGURE 3.17

Activity 3.12 | Applying a Theme and Formatting a Form in Layout View

4.2.6, 4.3.4

In this Activity, you will apply a *theme* to the form in Layout view. A theme is a predesigned set of colors, fonts, lines, and fill effects that look good together and that can be applied to all of the objects in the database or to individual objects in the database.

1 Under **Form Layout Tools**, click the **Design tab**. In the **Themes group**, click **Themes**. In the **Themes** gallery, using the ScreenTips, point to the **Retrospect** theme, right-click, and then click **Apply Theme to This Object Only**.

> Right-click a theme so that you can apply the theme to an individual object within the database. Apply a theme before formatting any other controls in your form.

> **NOTE** Applying a Theme to an Object and Determining the Applied Theme
>
> If you click a theme rather than right-clicking it and selecting an option, the theme is applied to all objects in the database. You cannot click Undo to cancel the application of the theme to all objects. To determine the applied theme, in the Themes group, point to Themes. The ScreenTip displays the name of the current theme.

2 Click anywhere in the title of the form—*Lastname Firstname 3A Student Major Change Form*—to select the title. Under **Form Layout Tools**, click the **Format tab**. In the **Font group**, click the **Font Size arrow** 11 ▾ , and then click **14**. In the **Font group**, click **Bold** B . Click the **Font Color arrow** A ▾ , and then under **Theme Colors**, in the fourth column, click the last color—**Olive Green, Text 2, Darker 50%**.

Activity 3.13 | Adding, Resizing, and Moving Controls in Layout View

4.2.1, 4.2.2,
4.2.3, 4.2.5,
4.2.6

In Layout view, you can change the form's *control layout*—the grouped arrangement of controls.

1 Be sure that your **3A Student Major Change Form** object displays in **Layout** view. On the **Design tab**, and in the **Tools group**, click **Add Existing Fields**. Compare your screen with Figure 3.18.

> The Field List pane displays, which lists the fields in the underlying table—your 3A New Students table.

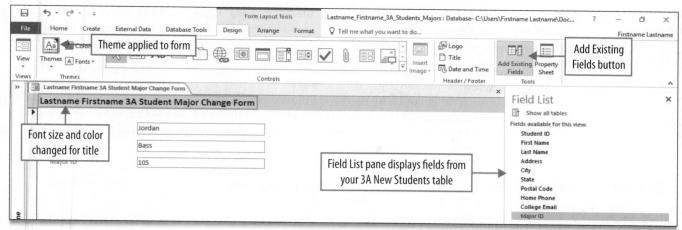

FIGURE 3.18

2 In the **Field List** pane, click **Student ID**, and then drag the field name to the left until the pointer displays above the **First Name label control** and a colored line displays above the control. Release the mouse button, and then compare your screen with Figure 3.19. If you are not satisfied with the result, click Undo, and begin again.

This action adds the Student ID label control and text box control to the form above the First Name controls.

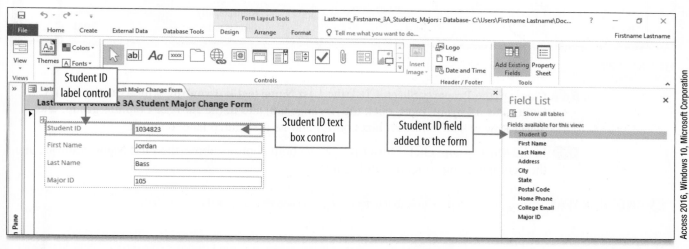

FIGURE 3.19

3 Close ☒ the **Field List** pane. Click the **Student ID text box control**, which displays *1034823*, to surround it with a border and to remove the border from the label control.

4 On the **Design tab**, in the **Tools group**, click **Property Sheet**.

The Property Sheet for the Student ID text box control displays. Recall that each control has an associated Property Sheet where precise changes to the properties—characteristics—of selected controls can be made. At the top of the Property Sheet, to the right of *Selection type: Text Box* displays because you selected the Student ID text box control.

5 In the **Property Sheet**, if necessary, click the **Format tab**. Click **Width** to select the property setting, type **1.5** and then press `Enter` to decrease the width of the text box controls. Compare your screen with Figure 3.20.

> All four text box controls are resized simultaneously. Because the controls are grouped together in a stacked layout, you can adjust the width of all of the text box controls at one time without having to select all of the controls. By decreasing the width of the text box controls, you have more space in which to rearrange the form controls. Because you can see the data in Layout view, you can determine visually that the space you have allotted is adequate to display all of the data in every field for every record.

ANOTHER WAY   With the text box control selected, point to the right edge of the text box control until the ⟺ pointer displays, and then drag left to the desired location.

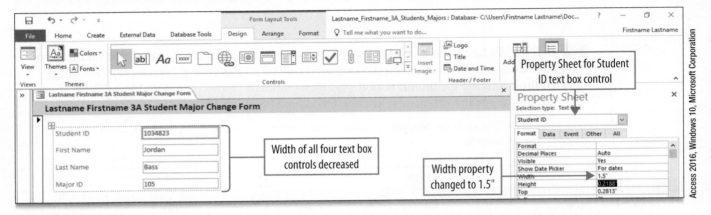

FIGURE 3.20

6 **Close** ⊠ the **Property Sheet**. Click the **Last Name text box control**, which displays *Bass*. Under **Form Layout Tools**, click the **Arrange tab**, and in the **Rows & Columns group**, click **Select Row** to select the text box control and its associated label control.

7 In the **Move group**, click **Move Up** to move both controls above the **First Name** controls, and then compare your screen with Figure 3.21.

ANOTHER WAY   Drag the selected controls to the desired location and then release the mouse button.

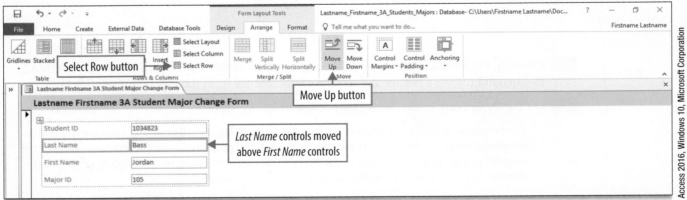

FIGURE 3.21

Did the last name label control not move with the last name text box control?

Be sure to select both the text box control and the label control before moving the controls; otherwise, only one of the controls will move. If this happens, click Undo, select both controls, and try again. Controls are stacked from top to bottom, not right to left.

---

8 **Save** 🖫 the changes you have made to the design of your form.

Activity 3.14 | Formatting Controls in Layout View

In this Activity, you will format and change the property settings for multiple controls.

1 With the form displayed in **Layout** view, click the **Student ID text box control**, which displays *1034823*. On the **Arrange tab**, in the **Rows & Columns group**, click **Select Column** to select all four text box controls.

🔄 **ANOTHER WAY**   Click the first text box control, hold down Shift, and then click the last text box control to select all four text box controls.

2 With all four text box controls selected, on the **Format tab**, in the **Font group**, click the **Background Color arrow** 🎨▾. Under **Theme Colors**, in the last column, click the second color—**Green, Accent 6, Lighter 80%**.

All of the text box controls display a background color of light green. This formatting is not applied to the label controls on the left.

3 Click the **Student ID label control**. On the ribbon, click the **Arrange tab**, and then in the **Rows & Columns group**, click **Select Column**. On the **Format tab**, click the **Font Color arrow** 🅰▾—*not* the Background Color arrow. Under **Theme Colors**, in the fourth column, click the first color—**Olive Green, Text 2**. Click **Bold** 🅱. Click in a blank area of the form to cancel the selection, and then compare your screen with Figure 3.22.

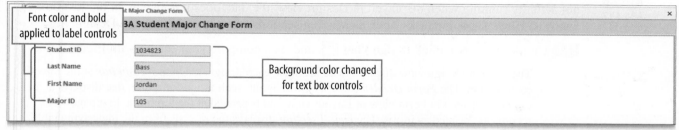

FIGURE 3.22

4 Click any **label control** to display the **layout selector** ⊞, and then click the **layout selector** ⊞ to select all of the grouped controls.

Recall that the layout selector, which displays to the left and above the Student ID label control, enables you to select and move the entire group of controls in Layout view.

🔄 **ANOTHER WAY**   Click any control, and then on the Arrange tab, in the Rows & Columns group, click Select Layout.

5 On the **Format tab**, in the **Font group**, click the **Font Size arrow** 11 ▾, and then click **12** to change the font size of all of the text in all of the controls.

6 With all of the controls still selected, click the **Design tab**. In the **Tools group**, click **Property Sheet**, and then compare your screen with Figure 3.23.

> The Property Sheet for the selected controls displays. At the top of the Property Sheet, to the right of *Selection type: Multiple selection* displays because you have more than one control selected.

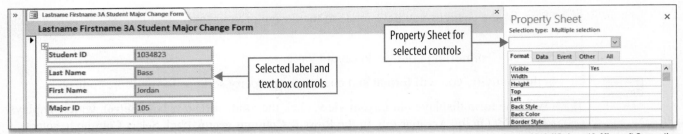

FIGURE 3.23

7 In the **Property Sheet**, click **Height**, type **0.25** and then press Enter to change the height of each selected control.

8 Click the **Student ID label control** to cancel the selection of all of the controls and to select only this label control. In the **Property Sheet**, click **Width**, type **1.25** and then press Enter.

> The width of every label control changed to 1.25 inches. Recall that because the label controls are arranged in a stacked layout, you can change the width of all controls by selecting only one control. This is one of the few properties that can be changed without first selecting the column.

9 **Close** ☒ the **Property Sheet**, and then **Save** 🖫 the design changes to your form.

Activity 3.15 | Modifying a Form in Design View

Design view presents a detailed view of the structure of your form. Because the form is not actually running when displayed in Design view, the data does not display in the text box controls. However, some tasks, such as resizing sections, must be completed in Design view.

1 On the status bar, click **Design View** 🗾, and then compare your screen with Figure 3.24.

> The form in Design view displays three sections, each designated by a *section bar* at the top of each section. The *Form Header* contains information, such as the form title, that displays at the top of the screen in Form view or Layout view and is printed at the top of the first page when records are printed as forms. The *Detail section* displays the records from the underlying table, and the *Form Footer* displays at the bottom of the screen in Form view or Layout view and is printed after the last detail section on the last page of a printout.

🔄 **ANOTHER WAY**   On the Home tab, in the Views group, click the View arrow, and then click Design view; or right-click the object tab, and then click Design View.

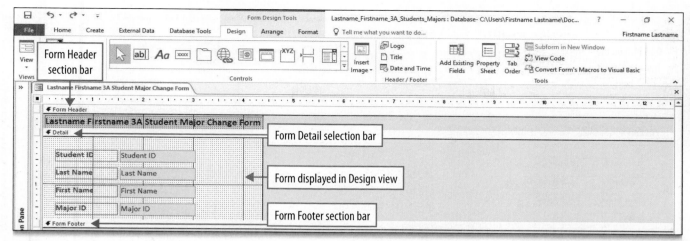

FIGURE 3.24

> **2** At the bottom of the form, click the **Form Footer section bar** to select it. On the ribbon, click the **Design tab**, and in the **Tools group**, click **Property Sheet**. In the **Property Sheet**, on the **Format tab**, click **Height**, type **0.5** and then press Enter. Compare your screen with Figure 3.25.
>
> In addition to properties for controls, you can make precise changes to sections of the form. Because you selected the Form Footer section bar, the Property Sheet displays a *Selection type* of *Section*, and the section is identified as *Form Footer*.

ANOTHER WAY At the bottom of the form, point to the lower edge of the Form Footer section bar to display the ⊞ pointer, and then drag downward approximately 0.5 inch to increase the height of the section.

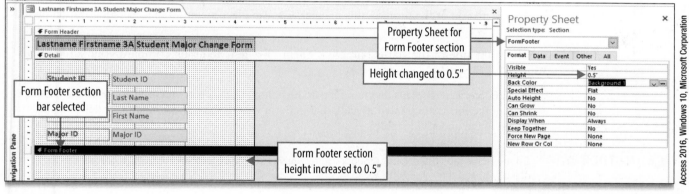

FIGURE 3.25

> **3** On the **Design tab**, in the **Controls group**, click **Label** Aa. Move the ⁺A pointer into the **Form Footer** section and then position the plus sign of the ⁺A pointer at approximately **0.25 inch on the horizontal ruler** and even with the lower edge of the **Form Footer section bar**—the position does not need to be precise. Compare your screen with Figure 3.26.

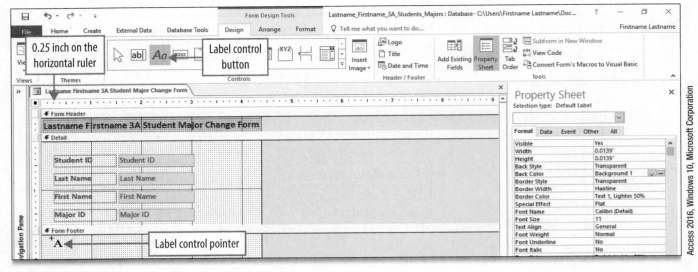

FIGURE 3.26

4 Click one time. Type **Texas Lakes Community College** and then press Enter. With the **label control** selected, click the **Format tab**. In the **Font group**, click **Bold** B. Click the **Font Color arrow**, and then under **Theme Colors**, in the fourth column, click the first color—**Olive Green, Text 2**.

5 With the **label control** still selected, in the **Property Sheet**, click **Top**, type **0.1** and then press Enter. In the **Property Sheet**, in the **Left** property setting, type **0.6** and then press Enter. **Close** X the **Property Sheet**, and then **Save** 🖫 the design changes to your form.

The top edge of the label control in the Form Footer section displays 0.1 inch from the lower edge of the Form Footer section bar. The left edge of the label control aligns at 0.6 inch from the left margin of the form. In this manner, you can place a control in a specific location on the form.

6 On the right side of the status bar, click **Form View** 📧, and then compare your screen with Figure 3.27.

Form Footer text displays on the screen at the bottom of the form and prints only on the last page if all of the forms are printed. Recall, that in Form view, you can add, modify, or delete records stored in the underlying table.

ANOTHER WAY On the Home tab, in the Views group, click the View arrow, and then click Form View; or right-click the object tab, and then click Form View.

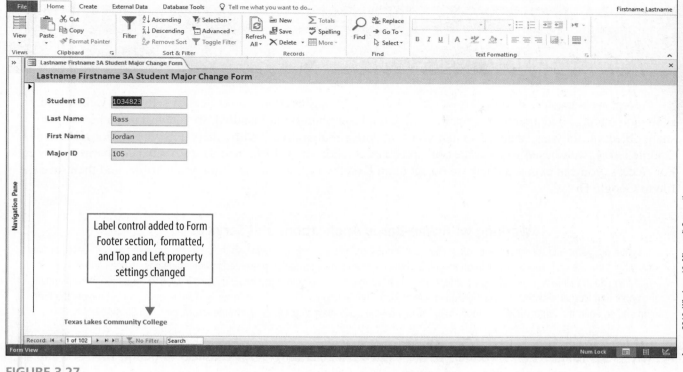

FIGURE 3.27

7 In the navigation area, click **Last record** ▶| to display the record containing your name.

8 On the **File tab**, click **Print**, and then on the right, click **Print**. In the **Print** dialog box, under **Print Range**, click the **Selected Records(s)** option button. Create a paper printout or electronic printout as directed by your instructor. To create a PDF electronic image, follow the directions given in the Note in Activity 3.06.

Because you decreased the width of the text box controls, you do *not* have to adjust the column size width in the Page Setup dialog box as you did with the form you created by using the Form tool.

9 **Close** ☒ all open objects, and then **Open** ≫ the **Navigation Pane**. On the right side of the title bar, click **Close** ☒ to close the database and to close Access. As directed by your instructor, submit your database and the paper printouts or PDF electronic images of the three forms that are the results of this project.

> **END | You have completed Project 3A**

GO! With Google

Objective	Export an Access Form to an Excel Spreadsheet, Save to Google Drive as a Google Sheet, Edit a Record, and Save to Your Computer

Access web apps are designed to work with Microsoft's SharePoint, a service for setting up websites to share and manage documents. Your college may not have SharePoint installed, so you will use other tools to share objects from your database so that you can work collaboratively with others. Recall that Google Drive is Google's free, web-based word processor, spreadsheet, slide show, form, and data storage and sharing service. For Access, you can export a database object to an Excel worksheet, a PDF file, or a text file, and then save the file to Google Drive.

ALERT! **Working with Web-Based Applications and Services**

Computer programs and services on the web receive continuous updates and improvements, so the steps to complete this web-based activity may differ from the ones shown. You can often look at the screens and the information presented to determine how to complete the activity.

If you do not already have a Google account, you will need to create one before you begin this activity. Go to http://google.com and in the upper right corner, click Sign In. On the Sign In screen, click Create account. On the Create your Google Account page, complete the form, read and agree to the Terms of Service and Privacy Policy, and then click Next step. On the Welcome screen, click Get Started.

Activity | Exporting an Access Form to an Excel Spreadsheet, Saving the Spreadsheet to Google Drive, Editing a Record in Google Sheets, and Saving to Your Computer

In this Activity, you will export your 3A Student Major Change Form object to an Excel spreadsheet, upload your Excel file to Google Drive, edit a record in Google Sheets, and then download a copy of the edited spreadsheet to your computer.

1 Start Access, on the left click **Open Other Files**, navigate to your **Access Chapter 3** folder, and then **Open** your **Lastname_Firstname_3A_Students_Majors** database file. If necessary, on the Message Bar, click Enable Content. In the **Navigation Pane**, click your **3A Student Major Change Form** object to select it.

2 On the **External Data tab**, in the **Export group**, click **Excel**. In the **Export – Excel Spreadsheet** dialog box, click **Browse**, and then navigate to your **Access Chapter 3** folder. In the **File Save** dialog box, click in the **File name** box, type **Lastname_Firstname_AC_3A_Web** and then click **Save**.

3 In the **Export – Excel Spreadsheet** dialog box, under **Specify export options**, select the second check box—**Open the destination file after the export operation is complete**—and then click **OK**.

The records from the underlying table of the form display in Excel. When you export a form to Excel, the formatting and layout are automatically saved. For example, notice the olive green background color of the cells, which was the color that was applied to the text box controls in the form.

4 In the **Microsoft Excel** window, in the column headings row, to the left of column A, click **Select All**. On the **Home tab**, in the **Cells group**, click **Format**, and then click **AutoFit Column Width**. Click in cell **A1** to cancel the selection, and then compare your screen with Figure A.

5 **Save** the spreadsheet, and then **Close** Excel. In the **Export – Excel Spreadsheet** dialog box, click **Close**, and then **Close** Access.

6 From the desktop, open your browser, navigate to **http://google.com**, and then sign in to your Google account. Click the **Google Apps menu** [⚏], and then click **Drive** [☁]. Open your **GO! Web Projects** folder—or click New to create and then open this folder if necessary.

7 In the upper right corner, click **Settings** [⚙▾], and then on the menu click **Settings**. In the **Settings** dialog box, next to **Convert uploads**, be sure that **Convert uploaded files to Google Docs editor format** is selected. In the upper right, click **Done**.

If this setting is not selected, your document will upload as a PDF file and cannot be edited without further action.

(GO! With Google continues on the next page)

GO! With Google

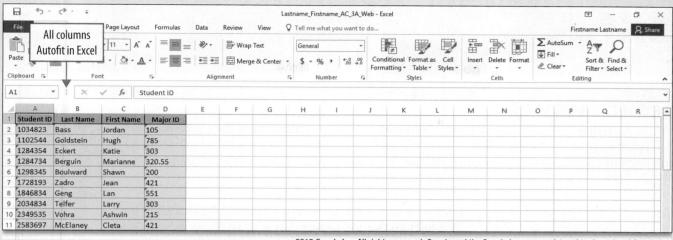

FIGURE A

8 On the left, click **NEW**, and then click **File upload**. In the **Open** dialog box, navigate to your **Access Chapter 3** folder, and then double-click your **Lastname_Firstname_AC_3A_Web** file to upload it to Google Drive. When the title bar of the message box indicates *Uploads completed*, **Close** the message box. A second box may display temporarily.

9 In your **GO! Web Projects** folder, double-click your **Lastname_Firstname_AC_3A_Web** file to open it in Google Sheets.

10 In the second record (row 3), click in the **Last Name** field, using your own last name, type **Lastname** and then press Enter. In the **First Name** field, using your

own first name, type **Firstname** and then press Enter to save the record. Compare your screen with Figure B.

11 On the menu bar, click **File**, point to **Download as**, and then click **Microsoft Excel (.xlsx)**. As necessary, open the downloaded file in Excel, enable editing, and then **Save** the file in your **Access Chapter 3** folder as **Lastname_Firstname_AC_3A_Web_Download**

12 **Close** Excel. In Google Drive, in the upper right corner, click your user name, and then click **Sign out**. **Close** your browser window.

13 As directed by your instructor, submit your two workbooks.

NOTE   Printing or Creating a PDF Electronic Image of an Excel Spreadsheet

To print on paper, click Print. To create a PDF electronic image of your printout, on the left side of your screen, click Export. Under Export, be sure Create PDF/XPS Document is selected, and then click Create PDF/XPS. Navigate to your Access Chapter 3 folder, and then click Publish to save the file with the default name and an extension of PDF.

FIGURE B

PROJECT 3B   Job Openings Database

MyITLab
Project 3B Training
Project 3B Grader

PROJECT ACTIVITIES

In Activities 3.16 through 3.24, you will assist Jack Woods, director of the Career Center for Texas Lakes Community College, in using his Access database to track the employees and job openings advertised for the annual job fair. Your completed reports will look similar to Figure 3.28.

Please always review the downloaded Grader instructions before beginning.

PROJECT FILES

MyITLab grader   If your instructor wants you to submit Project 3B in the MyITLab Grader system, log in to MyITLab, locate Grader Project 3B, and then download the files for this project.

For Project 3B, you will need the following file:
a03B_Job_Openings

You will save your database as:
Lastname_Firstname_3B_Job_Openings

PROJECT RESULTS

GO!
Walk Thru
Project 3B

Access 2016, Windows 10, Microsoft Corporation

FIGURE 3.28 Project 3B Job Openings

Objective 5 | Create a Report by Using the Report Tool and Modify the Report in Layout View

GO! Learn How
Video A3-5

A **report** is a database object that summarizes the fields and records from a query or from a table in an easy-to-read format suitable for printing. A report consists of information extracted from queries or tables and report design controls, such as labels, headings, and graphics. The queries or tables that provide the underlying data for a report are referred to as the report's **record source**.

Activity 3.16 | Opening and Saving an Existing Database, Renaming Objects, and Viewing a Table Relationship

> **ALERT!**
>
> **To submit this as an autograded project, log on to MyITLab and download the files for this project, and begin with those files instead of a03B_Job_Openings. For Project 3B using Grader, begin working with the database in Step 3. For Grader to award points accurately, when saving an object, do not include your Lastname Firstname at the beginning of the object name.**

MOS
1.2.5, 2.2.4

1 Start Access. In the Access opening screen, click **Open Other Files**. Under **Open**, click **Browse**, and then navigate to the location where your student data files are stored. Double-click **a03B_Job_Openings** to open the database.

2 On the **File tab**, click **Save As**. Under **File Types**, be sure **Save Database As** is selected. On the right, under **Database File Types**, be sure **Access Database** is selected, and then click **Save As**. In the **Save As** dialog box, navigate to your **Access Chapter 3** folder. In the **File name** box, replace the existing text with **Lastname_Firstname_3B_Job_Openings** and then press Enter.

3 On the **Message Bar**, click **Enable Content**. In the **Navigation Pane**, right-click the **3B Employers** table, and then click **Rename**. With the table name selected and using your own name, type **Lastname Firstname 3B Employers** and then press Enter to rename the table. Use the same technique to **Rename** the **3B Job Openings** table to **Lastname Firstname 3B Job Openings** and then **Rename** the first **3B Salary $40,000 or More Query** object to **Lastname Firstname 3B Salary $40,000 or More Query**

> Recall that a query that selects data from more than one table displays under both table names in the Navigation Pane. When you rename one of the query objects, the name of the second occurrence automatically changes.

4 Point to the right edge of the **Navigation Pane** to display the ⟷ pointer. Drag to the right to increase the width of the pane until all object names display fully.

5 On the **Database Tools tab**, in the **Relationships group**, click **Relationships**. Under **Relationship Tools**, on the **Design tab**, in the **Relationships group**, click **All Relationships**. Resize and move the field lists so that the entire table name and fields display for each field list.

> Because you renamed the tables, the field lists do not automatically display in the Relationships window.

6 In the **Relationships** window, click the **join line** between the two field lists. In the **Tools group**, click **Edit Relationships**. Point to the title bar of the **Edit Relationships** dialog box, and then drag the dialog box downward below the **3B Job Openings** field list. Compare your screen with Figure 3.29.

> *One* employer is associated with *many* job openings. Thus, a one-to-many relationship is established between the 3B Employers table and the 3B Job Openings table by using Employer ID as the common field. Referential integrity is enforced, and cascade options are selected.

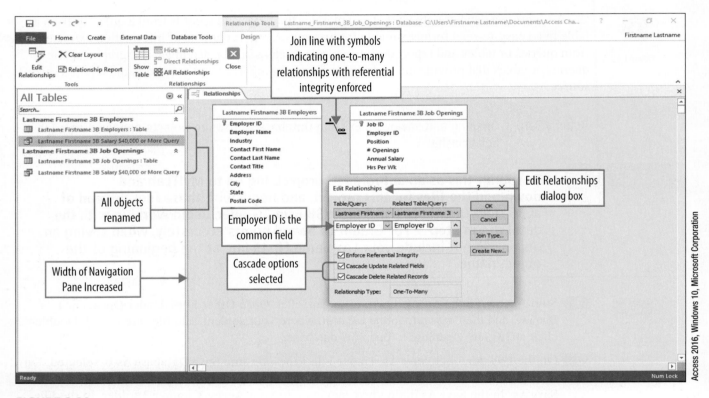

FIGURE 3.29

7 Close ☒ the **Edit Relationships** dialog box, and then Close ☒ the **Relationships** window. In the message box, click **Yes** to save changes to the layout of the relationships.

8 In the **Navigation Pane**, double-click each table, and then examine the fields and data in each table. Double-click the query object to run the query and examine the query results, apply **Best Fit** to the query results, and then **Save** the query. Switch to **Design** view to examine the design grid.

> Because you renamed the tables that are the underlying source of data for the query, you have to reapply Best Fit to the query results. The query answers the question, *What is the Job ID, position, employer name, number of job openings, and annual salary for job openings that have an annual salary of $40,000 or more, in ascending order by the Employer Name field within the Position field?*

9 In the object window, right-click any **object tab**, and then click **Close All**.

Activity 3.17 | Creating a Report by Using the Report Tool and Applying a Theme to the Report

MOS
5.1.1, 5.3.8

The **Report tool** is the fastest way to create a report, because it displays all of the fields and records from the record source that you select. You can use the Report tool to look at the underlying data quickly in an easy-to-read format, after which you can save the report and modify it in Layout view or in Design view.

In this Activity, you will use the Report tool to create a report from a query that lists all of the job openings with an annual salary of at least $40,000 and apply a theme to the report.

1 In the **Navigation Pane**, if necessary, click to select your **3B Salary $40,000 or More Query** object. On the **Create tab**, in the **Reports group**, click **Report**. **Close** ⟪ the **Navigation Pane**, and then compare your screen with Figure 3.30.

The report is created using the query as the record source and displays in Layout view. The report includes all of the fields and all of the records from the query and the title of the query. In Layout view, the broken lines indicate the page margins in the report.

FIGURE 3.30

Access 2016, Windows 10, Microsoft Corporation

2 Under **Report Layout Tools**, on the **Design tab**, in the **Themes group**, click **Themes**. In the **Themes** gallery, use the ScreenTips to locate the **Integral** theme, right-click the **Integral** theme, and then click **Apply Theme to This Object Only**.

Recall that right-clicking a theme enables you to apply a predefined format to the active object only, which is a quick way to apply a professional look to a report. Apply a theme before formatting any other controls on the report.

Activity 3.18 | Modifying a Report in Layout View

MOS
5.2.1, 5.2.4,
5.3.2, 5.3.4

After you create a report, you can make changes to it. For example, you can add or delete fields, resize the fields, and change the style of the report. Layout view enables you to see the data in the report as you modify the report. Most changes to a report can be made in Layout view.

1 Click the **Job ID** field name. On the **Report Layout Tools**, click the **Arrange tab**, in the **Rows & Columns group**, click **Select Column** to select the field name and all of the data for each record in the field. Press ⟮Del⟯ to remove the field from the report.

The Job ID field is deleted, and the remaining fields move to the left. No fields extend beyond the right margin of the report.

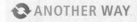 **ANOTHER WAY**   With the column selected, on the Home tab, in the Records group, click Delete; or right-click the selected column, and then click Delete or Delete Column.

2 In the **Employer Name** field, click in the **text box control** that displays *Monroe Heating & Air Conditioning* to select all of the text box controls in this field.

3 ▶ On the **Report Layout Tools**, click the **Design tab**, in the **Tools group**, click **Property Sheet**. In the **Property Sheet**, on the **Format tab**, click **Width**, type **2.5** and then press Enter. Compare your screen with Figure 3.31.

Recall that you can use the Property Sheet to make precise changes to control properties.

⟳ **ANOTHER WAY**   Point to the right edge of the text box control to display the ⟺ pointer. Drag to the right slightly until the data in the text box control displays on correctly.

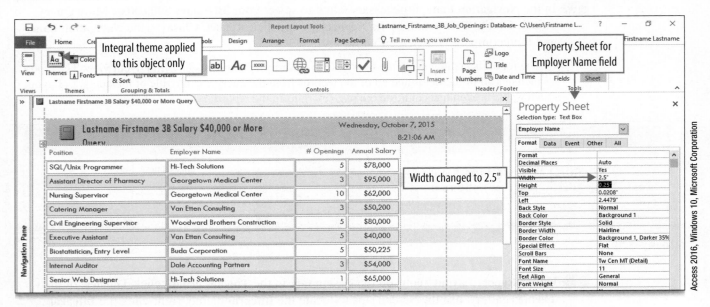

FIGURE 3.31

4 ▶ **Close** ☒ the **Property Sheet**. Click the **Position** field name, and then on the **Home tab**, in the **Sort & Filter group**, click **Ascending** to sort the records in ascending order by the Position field.

⟳ **ANOTHER WAY**   Right-click the selected field name and then click Sort A to Z.

5 ▶ Scroll to the bottom of the report, and then click the **calculated control** that displays *$2,157,625*, which is shortened at the bottom cutting off part of the data. Press Del to remove this control.

In a report created by using the Report tool, a ***calculated control*** is automatically created to sum any field that is formatted as currency. A calculated control contains an expression, often a formula or a function. Here, the total is not a useful number and thus can be deleted.

6 ▶ Scroll to the bottom of the report again, and then under the last column, click the horizontal line that is the border between the last record and the calculated control that you deleted. Press Del to remove this line, and then scroll to the bottom of the report to verify that the line has been deleted.

7 ▶ Scroll to the top of the report, and then click the **# Openings** field name. On the **Design tab**, in the **Grouping & Totals group**, click **Totals**, and then click **Sum**.

8 ▶ Scroll to the bottom of the report, and then click the **calculated control** that displays *100*. On the **Design tab**, in the **Tools group**, click **Property Sheet**. In the **Property Sheet**, on the **Format tab**, click **Height**, type **0.25** and then press Enter. Compare your screen with Figure 3.32.

The total number of job openings for positions with a salary of $40,000 or more is 100.

ANOTHER WAY Point to the lower edge of the text box control to display the ⬍ pointer, and then double-click to resize the control, or drag downward to increase the height of the control.

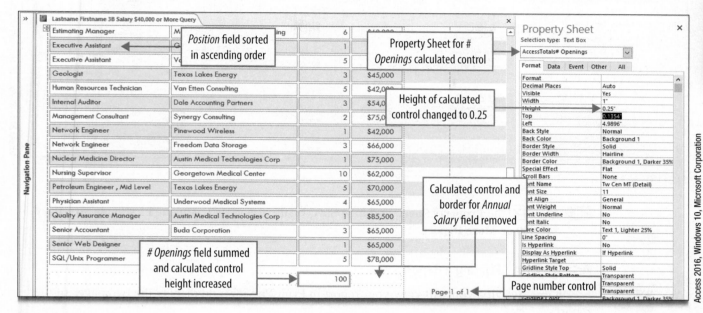

FIGURE 3.32

9 At the bottom of the report to the right of the calculated control, notice that the control that displays the page number does not fit entirely within the margins of the report. Click the **control** that displays *Page 1 of 1*. In the **Property Sheet**, click **Left**, type **2.5** and then press Enter.

The control moves within the margins of the report with the left edge of the control 2.5 inches in from the left margin of the report. When you click different controls in a report or form, the Property Sheet changes to match the selected control. Before printing, always scroll through the report to be sure that all of the controls display on one page and not outside of the margins.

ANOTHER WAY Click the control, point to the selected control to display the ⊹ pointer, and then drag the control to the left within the margins of the report.

10 Scroll to the top of the report, and then click the **label control** that displays the title of the report—*Lastname Firstname 3B Salary $40,000 or More Query*. On the **Report Layout Tools**, click the **Format tab**. In the **Font group**, click the **Font Size arrow** ⌞11 ▾⌟, and then click **14**.

11 With the **label control** for the title still selected, double-click **Query** to select the word, type **Report** and then press Enter to change the name of the report to *Lastname Firstname 3B Salary $40,000 or More Report*.

12 Click the **Position** field name. In the **Property Sheet**, click **Left**, type **0.5** and then press Enter to move this field 0.5 inch in from the left margin of the report. Compare your screen with Figure 3.33.

The other fields adjust by moving to the right. The fields are centered approximately within the margins of the report.

ANOTHER WAY Click the layout selector ⊞ to select all of the controls, and then drag it slightly downward and to the right until the columns are visually centered between the margins of the report. If your columns rearrange, click Undo and begin again.

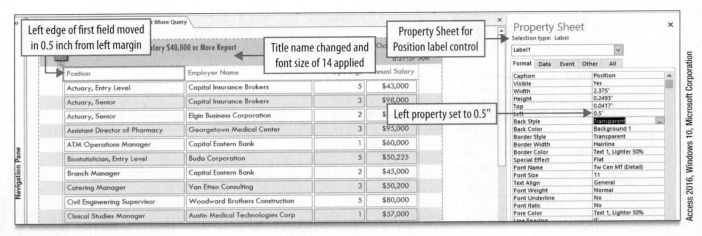

FIGURE 3.33

13 ▸ **Close** ☒ the **Property Sheet**, and then **Save** ⊟ the report as **Lastname Firstname 3B Salary $40,000 or More Report**.

Activity 3.19 | Printing a Report

MOS
1.5.1

In this Activity, you will view your report in Print Preview and display the two pages of the report.

1 ▸ On the right side of the status bar, click **Print Preview** ▤.

⟳ **ANOTHER WAY**   On the Design tab or the Home tab, in the Views group, click the View arrow, and then click Print Preview; or, in the object window, right-click the object tab, and then click Print Preview.

2 ▸ On the **Print Preview tab**, in the **Zoom group**, click **Two Pages** to view the two pages of your report. Notice that the page number displays at the bottom of each page.

3 ▸ Create a paper printout or PDF electronic image as directed—two pages result, and then click **Close Print Preview**. **Close** ☒ the report, and then **Open** ⟫ the **Navigation Pane**.

The report displays under both tables from which the query was created. The report object name displays with a small green notebook icon.

4 ▸ **Close** ⟪ the **Navigation Pane**.

Objective 6   Create a Report by Using the Report Wizard

Use the ***Report Wizard*** when you need more flexibility in the design of your report. You can group and sort data by using the wizard and use fields from more than one table or query if you have created the relationships between tables. The Report Wizard is similar to the Form Wizard; the wizard walks you step by step through the process of creating the report by asking you questions and then designs the report based on your answers.

GO! Learn How
Video A3-6

Activity 3.20 | Creating a Report by Using the Report Wizard

MOS
5.1.3, 5.2.1,
5.3.1

In this activity, you will prepare a report for Mr. Woods that displays the employers, grouped by industry, and the total fees paid by employers for renting a booth at the Job Fair.

1 On the **Create tab**, in the **Reports group**, click **Report Wizard**.

In the first wizard screen, you select the fields to include on the report. The fields can come from more than one table or query.

2 In the **Tables/Queries** box, click the **arrow**, and then click **Table: Lastname Firstname 3B Employers**. In the **Available Fields** list, double-click the following field names in the order given to move them to the **Selected Fields** list: **Industry**, **Employer Name**, and **Fee Paid** (scroll as necessary to locate the *Fee Paid* field). Compare your screen with Figure 3.34.

Three field names from your 3B Employers table display in the Selected Fields list.

ANOTHER WAY   Click the field name, and then click One Field [**>**] to move a field from the Available Fields list to the Selected Fields list.

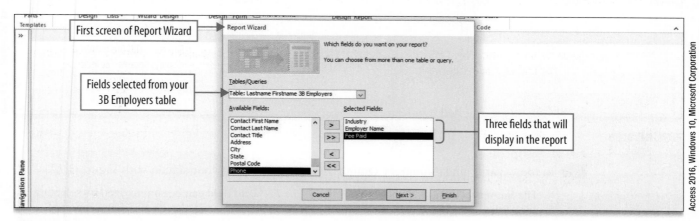

FIGURE 3.34

3 Click **Next**. In the wizard, notice that you can add grouping levels and that a preview of the grouping level displays on the right.

Grouping data helps to organize and summarize the data in your report.

4 On the left, double-click **Industry**, and then compare your screen with Figure 3.35.

The preview displays how the data will be grouped in the report. Grouping data in a report places all of the records that have the same data in a field together as a group—in this instance, the records will be grouped by *Industry*. Within each Industry name, the Employer Name and Fee Paid will display.

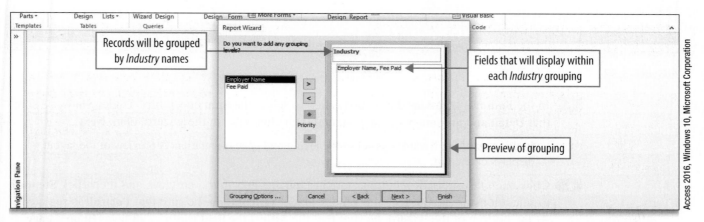

FIGURE 3.35

5 Click **Next**. Click the **1** box **arrow**, click **Employer Name**, and then compare your screen with Figure 3.36.

In this step of the wizard, you indicate how you want to sort the records and summarize the information. You can sort up to four fields. The Summary Options button displays because the data is grouped, and at least one of the fields—*Fee Paid*—contains numerical or currency data. Within each Industry grouping, the records will be sorted alphabetically by the Employer Name. Sorting records in a report presents a more organized view of the records.

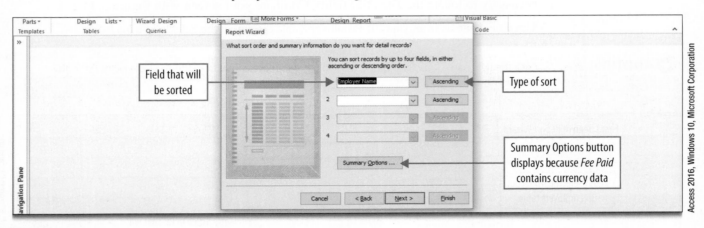

FIGURE 3.36

6 In the wizard, click **Summary Options**, and then compare your screen with Figure 3.37.

The Summary Options dialog box displays. The *Fee Paid* field can be summarized by selecting one of the four check boxes for Sum, Avg, Min, or Max. You can also display only summary information or display both the details—each record—and the summary information. The default setting is to display *Detail and Summary*.

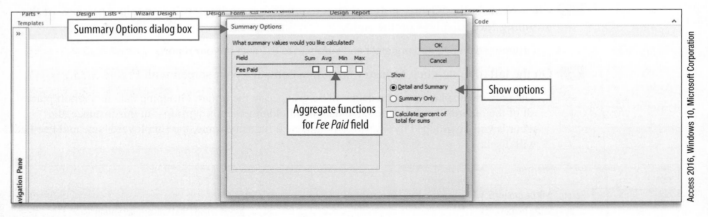

FIGURE 3.37

7 In the **Summary Options** dialog box, click to select the **Sum** check box. Under **Show**, be sure that **Detail and Summary** is selected, and then click **OK**. In the wizard, click **Next**.

In this step of the wizard, you select the layout and page orientation. A preview of the layout displays on the left.

8 Click each **Layout** option button, noticing the changes in the preview, and then click **Stepped** to select it as the layout for your report. Under **Orientation**, be sure that **Portrait** is selected. At the bottom of the wizard, be sure that the **Adjust the field width so all fields fit on a page** check box is selected, and then click **Next**.

9 In the **What title do you want for your report?** box, select the existing text, type **Lastname Firstname 3B Booth Fees by Industry Report** and then click **Finish**. Compare your screen with Figure 3.38.

The report is saved and displays in Print Preview using the specifications you defined in the Report Wizard. The records are grouped by Industry. Within each Industry, the records display in ascending order by the Employer Name. Within each Industry grouping, the Fee paid is summed or totaled—the word *Sum* displays at the end of each grouping.

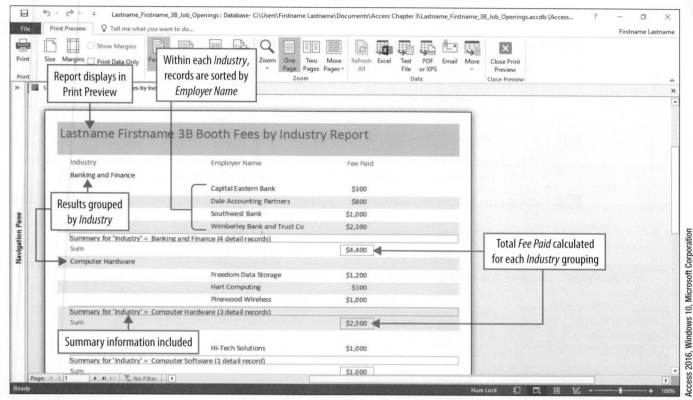

FIGURE 3.38

10 In the object window, right-click the **object tab** for the report, and then click **Layout View**.

 ANOTHER WAY On the status bar, click Layout View ▤ ; or click Close Print Preview, and then on the Home tab or the Design tab, click the View arrow, and then click Layout View.

Objective 7 Modify the Design of a Report

GO! Learn How
Video A3-7

You can modify the design of a report that is created using the Report Wizard by using the same techniques and tools that you use to modify a report created with the Report tool. Recall that most report modifications can be made in Layout view.

Activity 3.21 │ Formatting and Deleting Controls in Layout View

MOS
5.2.1, 5.2.4,
5.3.4, 5.3.8

In this Activity, you will apply a theme to the report, format the title of the report, and delete the summary information controls.

1 Be sure that your **3B Booth Fees by Industry Report** object is displayed in **Layout** view. Under **Report Layout Tools**, on the **Design tab**, in the **Themes group**, click **Themes**. In the

Themes gallery, use the ScreenTips to locate the **Ion Boardroom** theme, right-click the **Ion Boardroom** theme, and then click **Apply Theme to This Object Only**.

Recall that you should apply a theme before applying any other formatting changes. Also, recall that if you click a theme—instead of right-clicking—the theme is applied to all of the objects in the database.

2 At the top of the report, click the title—*Lastname Firstname 3B Booth Fees by Industry*—to display a border around the label control. On the **Report Layout Tools**, click the **Format tab**. In the **Font group**, click the **Font Size arrow** `11 ▾`, and then click **14**. In the **Font group**, click **Bold** `B`.

By changing the font size, the report name is no longer truncated and includes the word *Report*.

3 Within each *Industry* grouping, notice the **Summary for 'Industry'** information.

Because you selected Summary Options, a summary line is included at the end of each grouping that details what is being summarized—in this case, summed—and the number of records that are included in the summary total. Now that Mr. Woods has viewed the report, he has decided that this information is not necessary and can be removed.

4 Click any one of the controls that begins with **Summary for 'Industry'**.

The control that you clicked is surrounded by a border, and all of the other summary information controls are surrounded by paler borders to indicate that all controls are selected.

5 Press `Del` to remove the controls from the report, and then compare your screen with Figure 3.39.

🔄 **ANOTHER WAY**   Right-click any of the selected controls, and then click Delete to remove the controls from the report.

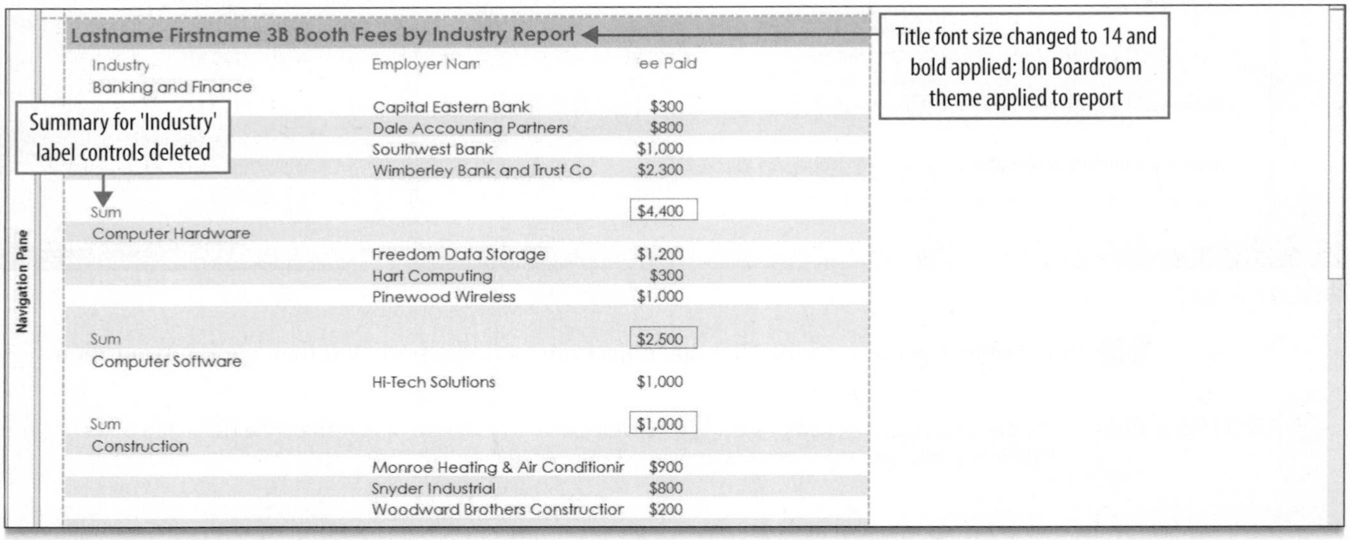

Lastname Firstname 3B Booth Fees by Industry Report ◄			Title font size changed to 14 and bold applied; Ion Boardroom theme applied to report
Industry	Employer Nam	ee Paid	
Banking and Finance			
Summary for 'Industry' label controls deleted	Capital Eastern Bank	$300	
	Dale Accounting Partners	$800	
	Southwest Bank	$1,000	
	Wimberley Bank and Trust Co	$2,300	
Sum		$4,400	
Computer Hardware			
	Freedom Data Storage	$1,200	
	Hart Computing	$300	
	Pinewood Wireless	$1,000	
Sum		$2,500	
Computer Software			
	Hi-Tech Solutions	$1,000	
Sum		$1,000	
Construction			
	Monroe Heating & Air Conditionir	$900	
	Snyder Industrial	$800	
	Woodward Brothers Constructior	$200	

Access 2016, Windows 10, Microsoft Corporation

FIGURE 3.39

6 **Save** 💾 the changes you have made to the design of the report.

Activity 3.22 | Modifying Controls in Layout View

5.2.4, 5.3.4

In this Activity, you will modify the text in controls, move controls, resize controls, and add a control to the report in Layout view.

1 On the left side of the report, click a **Sum label control**, which selects all of the related controls. Double-click the control to select the text—*Sum*. Type **Total Booth Fees by Industry** and then press `Enter`. Compare your screen with Figure 3.40.

This text states more clearly what is being summed.

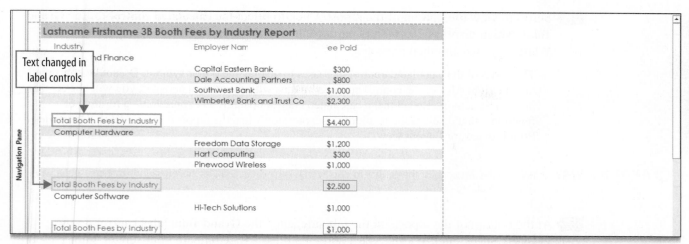

FIGURE 3.40

2 At the top of the report, click the **Industry label control** to select it. Hold down Shift, click the **Employer Name label control**, and then click the **Fee Paid label control** to select all three field names. On the **Format tab**, in the **Font group**, click **Bold** B.

Applying bold also increases the size of the controls so that the text is no longer truncated.

3 At the top of the report, under the **Fee Paid label control**, click the **text box control** that displays *$300* to select the text box controls for all of the records for this field. On the **Design tab**, in the **Tools group**, click **Property Sheet**. In the **Property Sheet**, on the **Format tab**, click **Left**, type **7** and then press Enter. Compare your screen with Figure 3.41.

All of the Fee Paid text box controls move to the right—7" in from the left margin. Do not be concerned that the summary total and the field name are not aligned with the data; you will correct this in the next activity. The field is moved to the right so that you can increase the width of the Employer Name text box controls so that all of the data for every record displays.

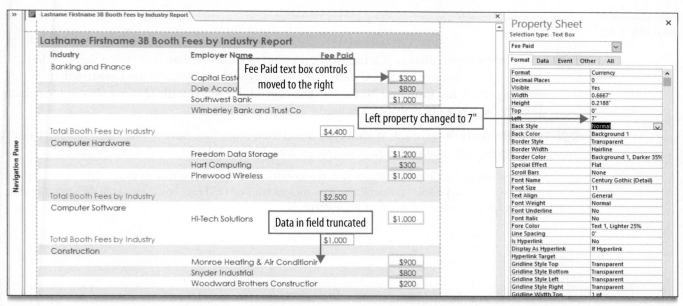

FIGURE 3.41

4 Scroll to view the bottom of the report. Click to select the **calculated control** for the **Grand Total**, which displays *20,400* and part of the dollar symbol. In the **Property Sheet**, click **Width**, type **0.8** and then press Enter.

> The width of the calculated control increases to display the dollar symbol. Do not be concerned that the right edge of the control no longer aligns with the control above it; you will correct this in the next activity. Recall that a calculated control contains an expression—a formula or function—that displays the result of the expression when the report is displayed in Report view, Print Preview, or Layout view.

ANOTHER WAY   Point to the left edge of the control to display the ⟷ pointer. Drag to the left slightly to increase the width of the calculated control.

5 At the bottom of the report, on the left side, click the **Grand Total label control**. In the **Property Sheet**, click **Width**, type **1** and then press Enter. Compare your screen with Figure 3.42.

> The width of the label control is increased so that all of the text displays.

ANOTHER WAY   Point to the right edge of the control to display the ⟷ pointer, and then double-click to resize the control.

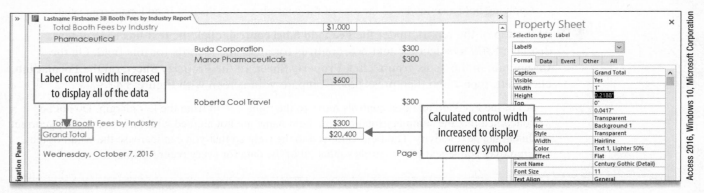

FIGURE 3.42

6 Scroll to the top to display the Industry grouping of **Construction**, and notice that the first and third records have truncated data in the **Employer Name** field. In the **Construction** grouping, click the **Employer Name text box control** that starts with *Monroe Heating* to select all of the text box controls for this field.

7 In the **Property Sheet**, click **Width**, type **3** and then press Enter. **Save** 🖫 the design changes to your report, and then compare your screen with Figure 3.43.

> The width of the Employer Name text box controls is increased so that all of the data in this field for every record displays. Recall that you moved the Fee Paid text box controls to the right to make room for the increased width of these controls.

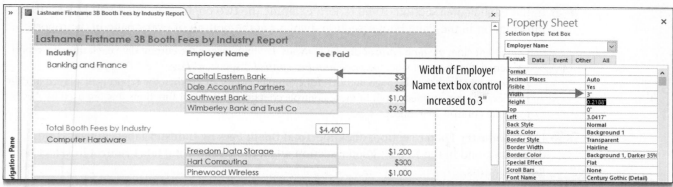

FIGURE 3.43

Activity 3.23 | Aligning Controls in Design View

MOS
5.2.4, 5.3.6

Design view gives you a more detailed view of the structure of your report. You can see the header and footer sections for the report, for the page, and for groups. In Design view, your report is not running, so you cannot see the data from the table in the controls. In the same manner as forms, you can add labels to the Page Footer section or increase the height of sections. Some tasks, such as aligning controls, must be completed in Design view.

1 Close ☒ the **Property Sheet**. On the status bar, click **Design View** 🗹, and then compare your screen with Figure 3.44.

> Design view for a report is similar to Design view for a form. You can modify the layout of the report in this view, and use the dotted grid pattern to align controls. This report has several sections. The **Report Header** displays information at the top of the *first page* of a report. The **Page Header** displays information at the top of *every page* of a report. The **Group Header** displays the name of data in the field by which the records are grouped; in this case, the *Industry* name. The *Detail* section displays the data for each record. The **Group Footer** displays the summary information for each grouping; in this case, the Industry name. The **Page Footer** displays information at the bottom of *every page* of the report. The **Report Footer** displays information at the bottom of the *last page* of the report.
>
> If you do not group data in a report, the Group Header section and Group Footer section will not display. If you do not summarize the data, the Group Footer section will not display.

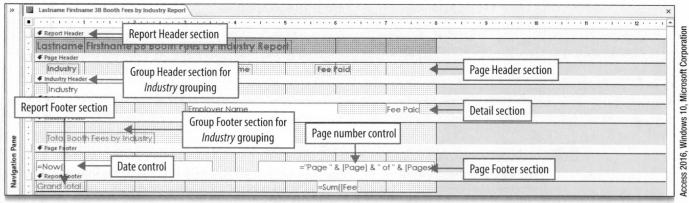

FIGURE 3.44

2 In the **Page Footer** section of the report, examine the two controls in this section. Recall that information in the Page Footer section displays at the bottom of every page in the report.

On the left side, the ***date control*** displays *=Now( )*, which inserts the current date each time the report is opened. On the right side, the ***page number control*** displays *="Page " & [Page] & " of " & [Pages]*, which inserts the page number, for example, *Page 1 of 2*, when the report is displayed in Print Preview or when printed. Both of these controls contain examples of functions that are used by Access to create controls in a report.

3 In the **Industry Footer** section, click the **Total Booth Fees by Industry label control**. Hold down Shift, and in the **Report Footer** section, click the **Grand Total label control** to select both label controls.

4 Under **Report Design Tools**, click the **Arrange tab**. In the **Sizing & Ordering group**, click **Align**, and then click **Left**.

The left edge of the *Grand Total label control* is aligned with the left edge of the *Total Booth Fees by Industry label control*. When using the Align Left command, the left edges of the selected controls are aligned with the control that is the farthest to the left in the report.

5 In the **Page Header** section, click the **Fee Paid label control**. Hold down Shift while you click the following: in the **Detail** section, click the **Fee Paid text box control**; in the **Industry Footer** section, click the **calculated control** that begins with *=Sum*; and in the **Report Footer** section, click the **calculated control** that begins with *=Sum*.

Four controls are selected.

6 On the **Arrange tab**, in the **Sizing & Ordering group**, click **Align**, and then click **Right**. **Save** 🖫 the design changes to your report, and then compare your screen with Figure 3.45.

The right edges of the four selected controls are aligned with the right edge of the *Fee Paid text box control*. When using the Align Right command, the right edges of the selected controls are aligned with the control that is the farthest to the right in the report.

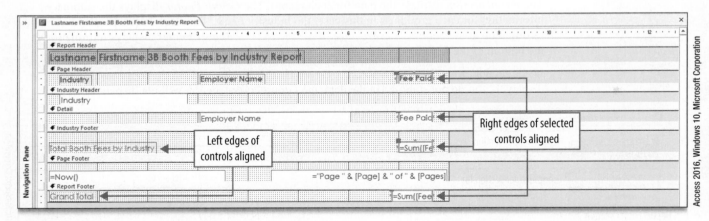

FIGURE 3.45

7 On the status bar, click **Layout View** 🖩 to display the underlying data in the controls. Scroll to view the bottom of the report. On the left side, notice that the **Total Booth Fees by Industry label control** and the **Grand Total label control** are left aligned. Also, notice the right alignment of the controls in the **Fee Paid** column.

Before you print a report, examine the report in Print Preview to be sure that all of the labels and data display fully and to be sure that all of the data is properly grouped. Sometimes a page break occurs in the middle of a group of data, leaving the labels on one page and the data or summary information on another page.

Activity 3.24 | Keeping Grouped Data Together in a Printed Report

1.5.1, 5.3.4

In this Activity, you will preview the document and then will keep the data in each group together so a grouping is not split between two pages of the report. This is possible if the data in a grouping does not exceed the length of a page.

1 On the status bar, click **Print Preview** [icon]. On the **Print Preview tab**, in the **Zoom group**, click **Two Pages**, and then compare your screen with Figure 3.46.

The report will print on two pages. For the Industry grouping of *Hotel and Food Service*, one record and the summary data display at the top of Page 2 and are separated from the rest of the grouping that displays at the bottom of page 1. Your display may differ depending upon your printer configuration.

In Print Preview, the One Page or Two Pages Zoom view causes the records to be compressed slightly and might display with the bottoms of records truncated. The records, however, will print correctly.

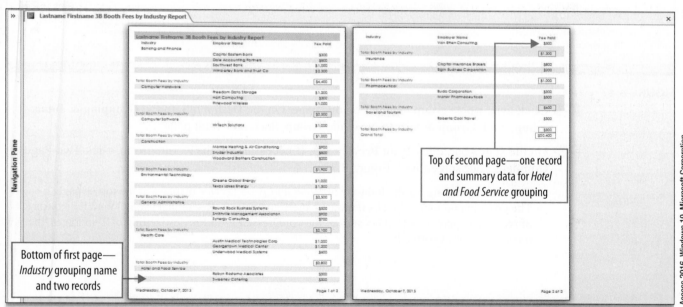

Top of second page—one record and summary data for *Hotel and Food Service* grouping

Bottom of first page—*Industry* grouping name and two records

Access 2016, Windows 10, Microsoft Corporation

FIGURE 3.46

2 Click **Close Print Preview** to return to **Layout** view. On the **Design tab**, in the **Grouping & Totals group**, click **Group & Sort**.

At the bottom of the screen, the *Group, Sort, and Total pane* displays. This pane is used to control how information is grouped, sorted, or totaled. Layout view is the preferred view in which to accomplish these tasks because you can see how the changes affect the display of the data in the report.

3 In the **Group, Sort, and Total** pane, on the **Group on Industry** bar, click **More**. To the right of **do not keep group together on one page**, click the **arrow**, and then compare your screen with Figure 3.47.

The *keep whole group together on one page* command keeps each industry group together, from the name in the Group Header section through the summary information in the Group Footer section. The default setting is *do not keep group together on one page*. Next to *Group on Industry*, *with A on top* indicates that the industry names are sorted in ascending order.

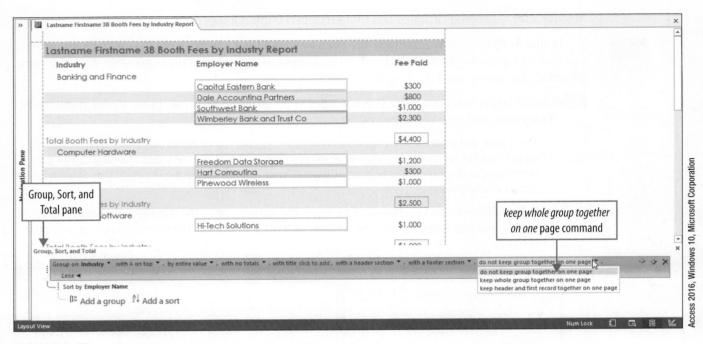

FIGURE 3.47

4 Click **keep whole group together on one page**. On the **Design tab**, in the **Grouping & Totals group**, click **Group & Sort** to close the **Group, Sort, and Total** pane.

5 On the status bar, click **Print Preview** 🔍. If necessary, in the Zoom group, click Two Pages. Compare your screen with Figure 3.48.

The entire grouping for the Industry of *Hotel and Food Service* displays at the top of page 2. The grouping no longer breaks between page 1 and page 2. Recall that even though the bottoms of records display truncated because of the compressed Print Preview setting of Two Pages, the records will print correctly.

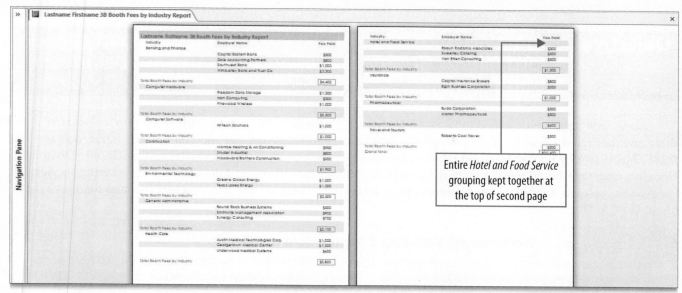

FIGURE 3.48

Access 2016, Windows 10, Microsoft Corporation

6 ▸ **Save** 🖫 the design changes to your report, and then create a paper printout or electronic printout of the report as directed—two pages result.

7 ▸ **Close** ☒ the report, and then **Open** ⟫ the **Navigation Pane**. If necessary, increase the width of the Navigation Pane so that all object names display fully.

8 ▸ On the right side of the title bar, click **Close** ☒ to close the database and to close Access. As directed by your instructor, submit your database and the paper printouts or PDF electronic images of the two reports—each report is two pages—that are the results of this project.

> **END | You have completed Project 3B**

GO! With Google

Objective Export an Access Report to a Word File, Upload the Word File to Google Drive, and Edit the Report in Google Docs

Access web apps are designed to work with Microsoft's SharePoint, a service for setting up websites to share and manage documents. Your college may not have SharePoint installed, so you will use other tools to share objects from your database so that you can work collaboratively with others. Recall that Google Drive is Google's free, web-based word processor, spreadsheet, slide show, form, and data storage and sharing service. For Access, you can export a database object to an Excel worksheet, a PDF file, or a text file, and then save the file to Google Drive.

> **ALERT!** **Working with Web-Based Applications and Services**
>
> Computer programs and services on the web receive continuous updates and improvements, so the steps to complete this web-based activity may differ from the ones shown. You can often look at the screens and the information presented to determine how to complete the activity.
>
> If you do not already have a Google account, you will need to create one before you begin this activity. Go to http://google.com and in the upper right corner, click Sign In. On the Sign In screen, click Create account. On the Create your Google Account page, complete the form, read and agree to the Terms of Service and Privacy Policy, and then click Next step. On the Welcome screen, click Get Started.

Activity | Exporting an Access Report to a Word File, Uploading the Word File to OneDrive, and Editing the Report in Google Docs

In this Activity, you will export your 3B Salary $40,000 or More Report object to a Word file, upload your Word file to OneDrive, and then edit the report in Google Docs.

1 Start Access, on the left click **Open Other Databases**, navigate to your **Access Chapter 3** folder, and then open your **Lastname_Firstname_3B_Job_Openings** database file. If necessary, on the Message Bar, click Enable Content. In the **Navigation Pane**, click one time to select the report **Lastname Firstname 3B Salary $40,000 or More Report** object to select it.

2 On the **External Data tab**, in the **Export group**, click **More**, and then click **Word**.

The report will be exported as a *Rich Text Format (RTF)*—a standard file format that contains text and some formatting such as underline, bold, italic, font sizes, and colors. RTF documents can be opened in many word processing programs and text editors.

3 In the **Export – RTF File** dialog box, click **Browse**, and then navigate to your **Access Chapter 3** folder. In the **File Save** dialog box, click in the **File name** box to select the existing text. Type **Lastname_Firstname_AC_3B_Web** and then click **Save**. In the **Export – RTF File** dialog box, select the **Open the destination file after the export operation is complete** check box, and then click **OK**.

4 In Word, click the **File tab**, click **Save As**, and then click **Browse**. In the **Save As** dialog box, navigate to your **Access Chapter 3** folder. In the **File name** box,

type **Lastname_Firstname_AC_3B_Web_Word** and then in the **Save as** type box, click the arrow and select **Word Document**. In the **Save As** dialog box, click **Save**. In the message box, click **OK**, and then compare your screen with Figure A.

The file is saved as a Word document in the .docx format to preserve the formatting of the document originally created in Access.

5 Close Word. In the **Export – RTF File** dialog box, click **Close**, and then **Close** Access.

6 From the desktop, open your browser, navigate to **http://google.com**, and then sign in to your Google account. Click the **Google Apps** menu [⊞], and then click **Drive** [☁]. Open your **GO! Web Projects** folder—or click New to create and then open this folder if necessary.

7 In the upper right, click **Settings** [⚙▾], and then on the menu click **Settings**. In the **Settings** dialog box, next to *Convert uploads*, be sure that **Convert uploaded files to Google Docs editor format** is selected. In the upper right, click **Done**.

If this setting is not selected, your document will upload as a PDF file and cannot be edited without further action.

(GO! With Google continues on the next page)

GO! With Google

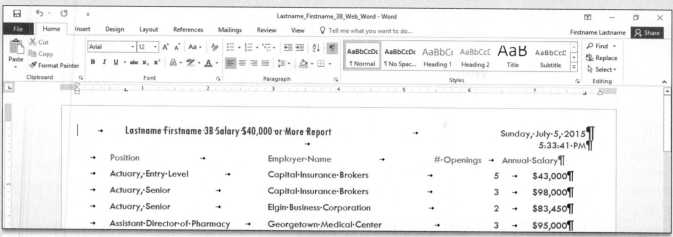

FIGURE A

8 On the left, click **NEW**, and then click **File upload**. In the **Open** dialog box, navigate to your **Access Chapter 3** folder, and then double-click your **Lastname_Firstname_AC_3B_Web_Word** file to upload it to Google Drive. In the lower right corner, when the title bar of the message box indicates *Uploads completed*, **Close** ✕ the message box. A second message box may display temporarily.

9 In the file list, double-click your **AC_3B_Web_Word** file to open it in Google Docs.

10 Drag across the four column headings—**Position**, **Employer Name**, **# Openings**, and **Annual Salary**—to select them, and then on the toolbar, click **Bold** **B** and **Underline** **U**. Compare your screen with Figure B.

11 Start the **Snipping Tool**. In the Snipping Tool dialog box, click the **New arrow**, and then click **Full-screen Snip**.

12 On the Snipping Tool toolbar, click **Save Snip** 🖫. In the **Save As** dialog box, navigate to your **Access Chapter 3** folder. Click in the **File name** box, type **Lastname_Firstname_AC_3B_Web_Snip** and then be sure that the **Save as type** box displays **JPEG file**. Click **Save**. **Close** ✕ the Snipping Tool window.

13 In **Google Drive**, at the upper right, click your user name, and then click **Sign out**. **Close** your browser window.

14 Submit your file as directed by your instructor.

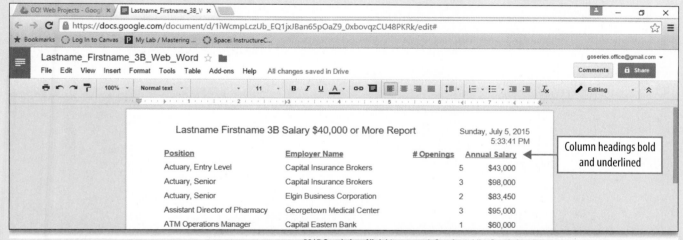

FIGURE B

GO! To Work

MICROSOFT OFFICE SPECIALIST (MOS) SKILLS IN THIS CHAPTER

3A MOS SKILLS		3B MOS SKILLS	
1.2.5	View relationships	**1.2.5**	View relationships
1.5.2	Print records	**1.5.1**	Print reports
2.2.4	Rename tables	**2.2.4**	Rename tables
2.3.2	Add records	**5.1.1**	Create a report based on the query or table
2.3.3	Delete records	**5.1.3**	Create a report by using a wizard
2.3.5	Find and replace data	**5.2.1**	Group and sort fields
2.3.7	Filter records	**5.2.4**	Add and modify labels
4.1.1	Create a form	**5.3.1**	Format reports into multiple columns
4.1.3	Save a form	**5.3.2**	Add calculated fields
4.2.1	Move form controls	**5.3.4**	Format report elements
4.2.2	Add form controls	**5.3.6**	Insert header and footer information
4.2.3	Modify data sources	**5.3.8**	Apply a theme
4.2.5	Set form control properties		
4.2.6	Manage labels		
4.3.2	Configure print settings		
4.3.4	Apply a theme		
4.3.7	Insert headers and footers		

BUILD YOUR E-PORTFOLIO

An E-Portfolio is a collection of evidence, stored electronically, that showcases what you have accomplished while completing your education. Collecting and then sharing your work products with potential employers reflects your academic and career goals. Your completed documents from the following projects are good examples to show what you have learned: 3G, 3K, and 3L.

GO! FOR JOB SUCCESS

Video: Performance Evaluations

Your instructor may assign this video to your class, and then ask you to think about, or discuss with your classmates, these questions:

FotolEdhar / Fotolia

What kind of message is Sara sending by forgetting to do the self-assessment review she was assigned for her evaluation? Why is it important to do a self-assessment for a review?

How should Sara react to her supervisor's criticisms in her review?

How important is it to follow a company's dress code policy? Do you think Sara's response to not following the dress code is appropriate? Why or why not?

END OF CHAPTER

SUMMARY

A form is a database object that you can use to enter new records into a table, or to edit, delete, or display existing records in a table and can be used to control access to the data in a database.

Filter records in a form to display only a subset of the total records based on matching specific values to provide a quick answer to a question. Filters are generally not saved with a form.

A report is a database object that summarizes the fields and records from a query or from a table, in an easy-to-read format suitable for printing. You can group records and summarize the data in a report.

Most changes to forms and reports can be done in Layout view where the underlying data displays in the controls; however, some modifications, such as aligning controls, must be done in Design view.

GO! LEARN IT ONLINE

Review the concepts and key terms in this chapter by completing these online challenges, which you can find at **MyITLab**.

Matching and Multiple Choice: Answer matching and multiple-choice questions to test what you learned in this chapter.

Lessons on the GO!: Learn how to use all the new apps and features as they are introduced by Microsoft.

MOS Prep Quiz: Answer questions to review the MOS skills that you have practiced in this chapter.

GO! COLLABORATIVE TEAM PROJECT (Available in **MyITLab** and Instructor Resource Center)

If your instructor assigns this project to your class, you can expect to work with one or more of your classmates—either in person or by using Internet tools—to create work products similar to those that you created in this chapter. A team is a group of workers who work together to solve a problem, make a decision, or create a work product. Collaboration is when you work together with others as a team in an intellectual endeavor to complete a shared task or achieve a shared goal.

PROJECT GUIDE FOR ACCESS CHAPTER 3

Your instructor will assign Projects from this list to ensure your learning and assess your knowledge.

	Review and Assessment Guide for Access Chapter 3		
Project	**Apply Skills from These Chapter Objectives**	**Project Type**	**Project Location**
3A **MyITLab**	Objectives 1–4 from Project 3A	**3A Instructional Project (Grader Project)** Guided instruction to learn the skills in Project 3A.	In MyITLab and in text
3B **MyITLab**	Objectives 5–8 from Project 3B	**3B Instructional Project (Grader Project)** Guided instruction to learn the skills in Project 3B.	In MyITLab and in text
3C	Objectives 1–4 from Project 3A	**3C Chapter Review (Scorecard Grading)** A guided review of the skills from Project 3A.	In text
3D	Objectives 5–8 from Project 3B	**3D Chapter Review (Scorecard Grading** A guided review of the skills from Project 3B.	In text
3E **MyITLab**	Objectives 1–4 from Project 3A	**3E Mastery (Grader Project)** **Mastery and Transfer of Learning** A demonstration of your mastery of the skills in Project 3A with extensive decision-making.	In MyITLab and in text
3F **MyITLab**	Objectives 5–8 from Project 3B	**3F Mastery (Grader Project)** **Mastery and Transfer of Learning** A demonstration of your mastery of the skills in Project 3B with extensive decision making.	In MyITLab and in text
3G **MyITLab**	Combination of Objectives from Projects 3A and 3B	**3G Mastery (Grader Project)** **Mastery and Transfer of Learning** A demonstration of your mastery of the skills in Projects 3A and 3B with extensive decision making.	In MyITLab and in text
3H	Combination of Objectives from Projects 3A and 3B	**3H GO! Fix It (Scorecard Grading)** **Critical Thinking** A demonstration of your mastery of the skills in Projects 3A and 3B by creating a correct result from a document that contains errors you must find.	Instructor Resource Center (IRC) and MyITLab
3I	Combination of Objectives from Projects 3A and 3B	**3I GO! Make It (Scorecard Grading)** **Critical Thinking** A demonstration of your mastery of the skills in Projects 3A and 3B by creating a result from a supplied picture.	IRC and MyITLab
3J	Combination of Objectives from Projects 3A and 3B	**3J GO! Solve It (Rubric Grading)** **Critical Thinking** A demonstration of your mastery of the skills in Projects 3A and 3B, your decision-making skills, and your critical thinking skills. A task-specific rubric helps you self-assess your result.	IRC and MyITLab
3K	Combination of Objectives from Projects 3A and 3B	**3K GO! Solve It (Rubric Grading)** **Critical Thinking** A demonstration of your mastery of the skills in Projects 3A and 3B, your decision-making skills, and your critical thinking skills. A task-specific rubric helps you self-assess your result.	In text
3L	Combination of Objectives from Projects 3A and 3B	**3L GO! Think (Rubric Grading)** **Critical Thinking** A demonstration of your understanding of the chapter concepts applied in a manner that you would outside of college. An analytic rubric helps you and your instructor grade the quality of your work by comparing it to the work an expert in the discipline would create.	In text
3M	Combination of Objectives from Projects 3A and 3B	**3M GO! Think (Rubric Grading)** **Critical Thinking** A demonstration of your understanding of the chapter concepts applied in a manner that you would outside of college. An analytic rubric helps you and your instructor grade the quality of your work by comparing it to the work an expert in the discipline would create.	IRC and MyITLab
3N	Combination of Objectives from Projects 3A and 3B	**3N You and GO! (Rubric Grading)** **Critical Thinking** A demonstration of your understanding of the chapter concepts applied in a manner that you would in a personal situation. An analytic rubric helps you and your instructor grade the quality of your work.	IRC and MyITLab
3O	Combination of Objectives from Projects 3A and 3B	**3O Collaborative Team Project for ACCESS Chapter 3** **Critical Thinking** A demonstration of your understanding of concepts and your ability to work collaboratively in a group role-playing assessment, requiring both collaboration and self-management.	IRC and MyITLab
Capstone Project for Access Chapters 1–3	Combination of Objectives from Projects 1A, 1B, 2A, 2B, 3A, and 3B	A demonstration of your mastery of the skills in Chapters 1–3 with extensive decision making. **(Grader Project)**	IRC and MyITLab

GLOSSARY

GLOSSARY OF CHAPTER KEY TERMS

AND condition A condition in which records display only when all of the specified values are present in the selected fields.

Bound A term used to describe objects and controls that are based on data that is stored in tables.

Bound control A control that retrieves its data from an underlying table or query; a text box control is an example of a bound control.

Calculated control A control that contains an expression, often a formula or function, that most often summarizes a field that contains numerical data.

Control An object on a form or report that displays data or text, performs actions, and lets you view and work with information.

Control layout The grouped arrangement of controls on a form or report; for example, the Stacked layout.

Data entry The action of entering the data into a record in a database table or form.

Date control A control on a form or report that inserts the current date each time the form or report is opened.

Design view The Access view that displays the detailed structure of a query, form, or report; for forms and reports, may be the view in which some tasks must be performed, and displays only the controls, not the data.

Detail section The section of a form or report that displays the records from the underlying table or query.

Filter by Form An Access command that filters the records in a form based on one or more fields, or based on more than one value in the field.

Filter by Selection An Access command that displays only the records that contain the value in the selected field and hides the records that do not contain the value.

Filtering The process of displaying only a portion of the total records (a subset) based on matching specific values to provide a quick answer to a question.

Form A database object that you can use to enter new records into a table, or to edit, delete, and display existing records in a table.

Form Footer Information displayed at the bottom of the screen in Form view or Layout view that is printed after the last detail section on the last page of a printout.

Form Header Information such as a form's title that displays at the top of the screen in Form view or Layout view and is printed at the top of the first page when records are printed as forms.

Form tool An Access tool that creates a form with a single mouse click, which includes all of the fields from the underlying data source (table or query).

Form view The Access view in which you can view, modify, delete, or add records in a table but you cannot change the layout or design of the form.

Form Wizard An Access tool that walks you step by step through the creation of a form and that gives you more flexibility in the design, layout, and number of fields in a form.

Group Footer Information printed at the end of each group of records to display summary information for the group.

Group Header Information printed at the beginning of each new group of records; for example, the group name.

Group, Sort, and Total pane A pane that displays at the bottom of the window in Design view in which you can control how information is sorted and grouped in a report; provides the most flexibility for adding or modifying groups, sort orders, or totals options on a report.

Label control A control on a form or report that contains descriptive information, usually a field name or title.

Layout selector A small symbol that displays in the upper left corner of a selected control layout in a form or report that is displayed in Layout view or Design view and is used to move or format an entire group of controls.

Layout view The Access view in which you can make changes to a form or report while the data from the underlying data source displays.

OR condition A condition in which records display that match at least one of the specified values.

Page Footer Information printed at the bottom of every page in a report and most often includes the page number.

Page Header Information printed at the top of every page in a report.

Page number control A control on a form or report that inserts the page number when displayed in Print Preview or when printed.

Record selector bar The vertical bar at the left edge of a record used to select an entire record in Form view.

Record source The tables or queries that provide the underlying data for a form or report.

Report A database object that summarizes the fields and records from a query or table in an easy-to-read format suitable for printing.

Report Footer Information printed at the bottom of the last page of a report.

Report Header Information printed on the first page of a report that is used for logos, titles, and dates.

Report tool An Access tool that creates a report with one mouse click and displays all of the fields and records from the record source that you select.

Report Wizard An Access tool that walks you step by step through the creation of a report and that gives you more flexibility in the design, layout, and number of fields in a report.

Rich Text Format (RTF) A standard file format that contains some formatting such as underline, bold, font sizes, and colors. RTF documents can be opened in many applications.

Section bar In Design view, a gray bar in a form or report that identifies and separates one section from another; used to select the section and to change the size of the section.

Stacked layout A control layout format that is similar to a paper form, with label controls placed to the left of each text box control; the controls are grouped together for easy editing.

Subset A portion of the total records available.

Tab order The order in which the insertion point moves from one field to another in a form when you press the Tab key.

Text box control A bound control on a form or report that displays the data from the underlying table or query.

Theme A predesigned set of colors, fonts, lines, and fill effects that look good together and that can be applied to all of the objects in the database or to individual objects in the database.

Unbound control A control that does not have a source of data, such as the title in a form or report.

Apply 3A skills from these Objectives:

1 Create and Use a Form to Add and Delete Records

2 Filter Records

3 Create a Form by Using the Form Wizard

4 Modify a Form in Layout View and in Design View

Skills Review Project 3C Student Internships

In the following Skills Review, you will assist Erinique Jerlin, the Dean of Business at the Northwest Campus, in using her database to track business students and their internship placements for the current semester. Your completed forms will look similar to Figure 3.49.

PROJECT FILES

For Project 3C, you will need the following file:

a03C_Student_Internships

You will save your database as:

Lastname_Firstname_3C_Student_Internships

PROJECT RESULTS

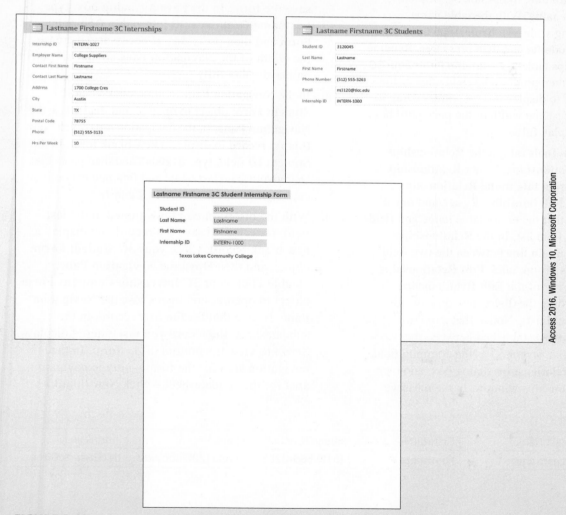

Access 2016, Windows 10, Microsoft Corporation

FIGURE 3.49

(Project 3C Student Internships continues on the next page)

1 Start Access. In the Access opening screen, click **Open Other Files**. Under **Open**, click **Browse** and then navigate to the location where your student data files are stored. Double-click **a03C_Student_Internships** to open the database.

a. On the **File tab**, click **Save As**. Under **File Types**, be sure **Save Database As** is selected. On the right, under **Database File Types**, be sure **Access Database** is selected, and then click **Save As**.

b. In the **Save As** dialog box, navigate to your **Access Chapter 3** folder. In the **File name** box, replace the existing text with **Lastname_Firstname_3C_Student_Internships** and then press Enter. On the **Message Bar**, click **Enable Content**.

c. In the **Navigation Pane**, right-click **3C Students**, and then click **Rename**. With the table name selected and using your own name, type **Lastname Firstname 3C Students** and then press Enter. **Rename** the **3C Internships** table to **Lastname Firstname 3C Internships** and then point to the right edge of the **Navigation Pane** to display the ↔ pointer. Drag to the right to increase the width of the pane until both tables names display fully.

d. On the **Database Tools tab**, in the **Relationships group**, click **Relationships**. Under **Relationship Tools**, on the **Design tab**, in the **Relationships group**, click **All Relationships**. Resize and move the field lists so that the entire table name and fields display for each field list. In the **Relationships** window, click the **join line** between the two field lists. In the **Tools group**, click **Edit Relationships**. Point to the title bar of the **Edit Relationships** dialog box, and drag the dialog box downward below the two field lists. Notice that a *one-to-many* relationship is established between the two tables by using *Internship ID* as the common field. **Close** the **Edit Relationships** dialog box, and then **Close** the **Relationships** window. In the message

box, click **Yes** to save changes to the layout of the relationships.

e. In the **Navigation Pane**, click your **3C Students** table to select it. On the **Create tab**, and then in the **Forms group**, click **Form**. **Save** the form as **Lastname Firstname 3C Student Form** and then **Close** the form object.

f. In the **Navigation Pane**, click your **3C Internships** table to select it. On the **Create tab**, and then in the **Forms group**, click **Form**. Notice that for the first record—*Internship ID INTERN-1000* for *Lakes Realty Inc*—there are two student records in the subdatasheet—two students have been assigned internships for this employer. **Close** the form, and in the message box, click **Yes** to save the form. In the **Save As** dialog box, type **Lastname Firstname 3C Internship Company Form** and then press Enter. If necessary, increase the width of the Navigation Pane so that all object names display fully.

g. In the **Navigation Pane**, double-click your **3C Student Form** object to open it, and then **Close** the **Navigation Pane**. In the navigation area, click **New (blank) record** to display a new blank form. In the **Student ID** field, type **3120045** and then press Enter. Using your own last name and first name, continue entering the data as shown in Table 1.

h. With the insertion point positioned in the last field, press Enter to save the record and display a new blank record. **Close** your **3C Student Form** object, and then **Open** the **Navigation Pane**. Double-click your **3C Internship Company Form** object to open it, and then **Close** the **Navigation Pane**. Notice that for the first record, in the subdatasheet, the record you just entered displays. Scroll to view the bottom of the form. In the navigation area for the form—*not* the navigation area for the subdatasheet—click **New (blank)**

TABLE 1

Student ID	Last Name	First Name	Phone Number	Email	Internship ID
3120045	**Lastname**	**Firstname**	**(512) 555-3263**	**ns3120@tlcc.edu**	**INTERN-1000**

(Project 3C Student Internships continues on the next page)

record. In the blank form, using your own first name and last name, enter the data as shown in Table 2.

i. In the navigation area for the form, click **First record**. Click in the **Employer Name** field, and then on the **Home tab**, in the **Find group**, click **Find**. In the **Find and Replace** dialog box, in the **Find What** box, type **Jones Consulting** and then click **Find Next**. **Close** the **Find and Replace** dialog box. On the **Home tab**, in the **Records group**, click the **Delete arrow**, and then click **Delete Record**. In the message box, click **Yes** to delete the record. In the navigation area for the form, notice that the total number of records is *27*.

j. Use the technique you just practiced to **Find** the form for the **Internship ID** of **INTERN-1027**, and then **Close** the **Find and Replace** dialog box. On the **File tab**, click **Print**, and then on the right, click **Print**. In the **Print** dialog box, under **Print Range**, click the **Selected Record(s)** option button. In the lower left corner of the dialog box, click **Setup**. In the **Page Setup** dialog box, click the **Columns tab**. Under **Column Size**, double-click in the **Width** box to select the existing value, type **7.5** and then click **OK**. If directed to print the form, in the **Print** dialog box, click **OK**. If directed to submit a PDF electronic image of the form, click **Cancel**, and then follow the directions given in the Note in Activity 3.06.

k. **Close** your **3C Internship Company Form** object, and then **Open** the **Navigation Pane**. In the **Navigation Pane**, double-click your **3C Student Form** object to open it, and then **Close** the **Navigation Pane**. Use the **Find** command to display the record where the **Last Name** field contains your last name, and then create a paper printout or electronic printout of only that record, being sure to change the **Column Size Width** to **7.5**

2 With your **3C Student Form** object displayed in **Form** view, in the navigation area, click **First record**, and then click the **Internship ID** field name to select the text in the field box. Press Ctrl + F to display the **Find and Replace** dialog box. In the **Find What** box, type **INTERN-1009** and then click **Find Next** to find and display the record for *Michael Fresch*. **Close** the **Find and Replace** dialog box. On the **Home tab**, in the **Sort & Filter group**, click **Selection**, and then click **Equals "INTERN-1009"**. In the navigation area, notice that two students are assigned internships with the company identified as INTERN-1009.

a. In the **Sort & Filter group**, click **Toggle Filter** to remove the filter and display all 52 records. **Close** the form. If prompted, click **Yes** to save the form.

b. **Open** the **Navigation Pane**, double-click your **3C Internship Company Form** object to open it, and then **Close** the **Navigation Pane**. On the **Home tab**, in the **Sort & Filter group**, click **Advanced**, and then click **Filter By Form**. In the form, click the **City** field name to position the insertion point in the **City** field box, click the **arrow**, and then click **Georgetown**. In the **Sort & Filter group**, click **Toggle Filter** to display the filtered records. In the navigation area for the form, notice that three internships are located in the *City* of *Georgetown*.

c. In the **Sort & Filter group**, click **Advanced**, and then click **Filter By Form**. In the lower left corner of the form, click the **Or tab**. Click the **City** field box **arrow**, and then click **Elgin**. In the **Sort & Filter group**, click **Toggle Filter**. In the navigation area for the form, notice that five internships are located in either *Georgetown* or *Elgin*. In the **Sort & Filter group**, click **Advanced**, and then click **Clear All Filters** to display all 27 records.

d. In the **Sort & Filter group**, click **Advanced**, and then click **Advanced Filter/Sort**. Resize the field

TABLE 2

Internship ID	Employer Name	Contact First Name	Contact Last Name	Address	City	State	Postal Code	Phone	Hrs Per Week
INTERN-1027	**College Suppliers**	**Firstname**	**Lastname**	**1700 College Cres**	**Austin**	**TX**	**78755**	**(512) 555-3133**	**10**

(Project 3C Student Internships continues on the next page)

list. In the **3C Internships** field list, double-click **City**, and then double-click **Hrs Per Week** to add both fields to the design grid. Click in the **Criteria** row under **City**, type **Austin** and then press Enter. In the **Criteria** row under **Hrs Per Week**, type **>10** and then press Enter. In the **Sort & Filter group**, click **Toggle Filter** to display the filtered records, and notice that that there are five internships in the *City of Austin* offering *more than 10* hours per week of work. In the **Sort & Filter group**, click **Toggle Filter** to remove the filter and display all 27 records. **Save** and then **Close** your **3C Internship Company Form** object, which also closes the Advanced Filter grid.

3 On the **Create tab**, and in the **Forms group**, click **Form Wizard**. In the **Tables/Queries** box, click the **arrow**, and then click **Table: Lastname Firstname 3C Students**. In the **Available Fields** list, double-click the following field names in the order given to move them to the **Selected Fields** list: **First Name**, **Last Name**, and **Internship ID**. Click **Next**. In the wizard, be sure **Columnar** is selected as the layout, and then click **Next**. In the **What title do you want for your form?** box, select the existing text, type **Lastname Firstname 3C Student Internship Form** and then click **Finish** to close the wizard and create the form.

4 On the **Home tab**, in the **Views group**, click the top portion of the **View** button to switch to **Layout** view. If the **Field List** pane displays on the right side of your screen, close the pane. Click the **First Name label control**. Hold down Shift, and then click the **Last Name label control**, the **Internship ID label control**, and the three **text box controls** to select all of the controls. On the **Form Layout Tools**, click the **Arrange tab**. In the **Table group**, click **Stacked** to group all of the controls. Click the **First Name label control** to cancel the selection of all of the controls.

a. On the **Form Layout Tools**, click the **Design tab**. In the **Themes group** click **Themes**. In the **Themes** gallery, using the ScreenTips, point to the **Wisp** theme, right-click, and then click **Apply Theme to This Object Only**. Click anywhere in the title—*Lastname Firstname 3C Student Internship Form*—to select the title. On the **Form Layout Tools**, click the **Format tab**, and In the **Font group**, click the **Font Size arrow**, and then click **14**. In the **Font group**, click **Bold**. Click the **Font Color arrow**, and

then under **Theme Colors**, in the sixth column, click the last color—**Orange, Accent 2, Darker 50%**.

b. On the **Design tab**, in the **Tools group**, click **Add Existing Fields**. In the **Field List** pane, click **Student ID**, and then drag the field name to the left until the ⬚ pointer displays above the **First Name label control** and a colored line displays above the control. Release the mouse button to add the *Student ID* controls to the form, and then **Close** the **Field List** pane.

c. Click the **First Name text box control**, which displays *Jordan*, to select it. On the **Design tab**, in the **Tools group**, click **Property Sheet**. In the **Property Sheet**, on the **Format tab**, click **Width**, type **1.75** and then press Enter to decrease the width of the text box controls. **Close** the **Property Sheet**. Be sure that the **First Name text box control** is still selected. On the **Arrange tab**, in the **Rows & Columns group**, click **Select Row**. In the **Move group**, click **Move Down** to move both controls below the **Last Name** controls. **Save** the changes you have made to the design of your form.

d. Click the **Student ID text box control**, which displays *1010101*. On the **Arrange tab**, in the **Rows & Columns group**, click **Select Column** to select all four text box controls. On the **Format tab**, in the **Font group**, click the **Background Color arrow**. Under **Theme Colors**, in the fourth column, click the second color—**Brown, Text 2, Lighter 80%**.

e. Click the **Student ID label control**, and then click the **Arrange tab**. In the **Rows & Columns group**, click **Select Column** to select all four label controls. Click the **Format tab**, and then click the **Font Color arrow**—*not* the **Background Color arrow**. Under **Theme Colors**, in the fourth column, click the first color—**Brown, Text 2**. In the **Font group**, click **Bold**.

f. Click the **layout selector** ⊞ to select all of the controls. In the **Font group**, click the **Font Size arrow**, and then click **12**. With all of the controls still selected, on the ribbon, click the **Design tab**, and in the **Tools group**, click **Property Sheet**. In the **Property Sheet**, on the **Format tab**, click **Height**, type **0.25** and then press Enter to change the height of each selected control.

(Project 3C Student Internships continues on the next page)

g.   Click the **Student ID label control** to select only that control. In the **Property Sheet**, click **Width**, type **1.75** and then press Enter to change the width of all of the label controls. **Save** the design changes to your form.

h.   On the status bar, click **Design View**. At the bottom of the form, click the **Form Footer section bar** to select it. In the **Property Sheet**, click **Height**, type **0.5** and then press Enter to increase the height of the **Form Footer** section.

i.   Under **Form Layout Tools**, click the **Design tab**. In the **Controls group**, click **Label**. Move the pointer into the **Form Footer** section and then position the plus sign of the pointer at approximately **0.25 inch on the horizontal ruler** and even with the lower edge of the **Form Footer section bar**—the placement does not need to be precise. Click one time, type **Texas Lakes Community College** and then press Enter.

j.   With the **label control** selected, click the **Format tab**. In the **Font group**, click **Bold**. Click the **Font Color arrow**, and then under **Theme Colors**, in the fourth column, click the first color—**Brown, Text 2**. If necessary, double-click the right edge of the label control to resize the control so that all of the data displays.

k.   With the **label control** still selected, in the **Property Sheet**, click **Top**, type **0.1** and then press Enter. In the **Property Sheet**, in the **Left** property setting box, type **0.9** and then press Enter. **Close** the **Property Sheet**, and then **Save** the design changes to your form.

l.   On the right side of the status bar, click **Form View**. In the navigation area, click **Last record** to display the record containing your name. On the **File tab**, click **Print**. In the **Print** dialog box, under **Print Range**, click the **Selected Records(s)** option button. Because you changed the field widths, you do not need to change the Column Size Width in the **Print** dialog box. Create a paper printout or PDF electronic image as directed by your instructor. To create a PDF electronic image, follow the directions given in the Note in Activity 3.06.

m.   **Close** all open objects, and then **Open** the **Navigation Pane**. If necessary, increase the width of the pane so that all object names display fully. On the right side of the title bar, click **Close** to close the database and to close Access. As directed by your instructor, submit your database and the paper printouts or PDF electronic images of the three forms that are the results of this project. Specifically, in this project, using your own name, you created the following database and printouts or PDF electronic images:

1. Lastname_Firstname_3C_Student_ Internships	Database file
2. Lastname Firstname 3C Student Form	Form (Record 52)
3. Lastname Firstname 3C Internship Company Form	Form (Record 27)
4. Lastname Firstname 3C Student Internship Form	Form (Record 52)

END | You have completed Project 3C

Skills Review Project 3D Student Parking

In the following Skills Review, you will assist Carlos Medina, the Chief of Security, in using his Access database to track the details about students who have paid for parking in designated lots at the Southeast Campus of Texas Lakes Community College. Your completed reports will look similar to Figure 3.50.

PROJECT FILES

For Project 3D, you will need the following file:

a03D_Student_Parking

You will save your database as:

Lastname_Firstname_3D_Student_Parking

PROJECT RESULTS

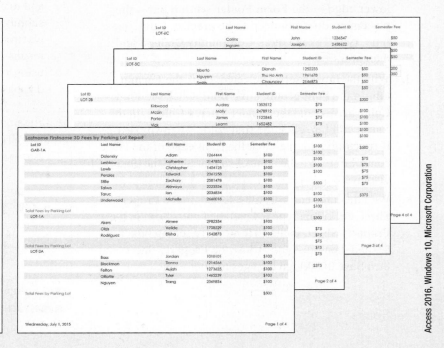

FIGURE 3.50

Access 2016, Windows 10, Microsoft Corporation

(Project 3D Student Parking continues on the next page)

1 Start Access. In the Access opening screen, click **Open Other Files**. Under **Open**, click **Browse** and then navigate to the location where your student data files are stored. Double-click **a03D_Student_Parking** to open the database.

a. On the **File tab**, click **Save As**. Under **File Types**, be sure **Save Database As** is selected. On the right, under **Database File Types**, be sure **Access Database** is selected, and then at the bottom of the screen, click **Save As**. In the **Save As** dialog box, navigate to your **Access Chapter 3** folder. In the **File name** box, replace the existing text with **Lastname_Firstname_3D_Student_Parking** and then press Enter. On the **Message Bar**, click **Enable Content**.

b. In the **Navigation Pane**, right-click the **3D Parking Lots** table, and then click **Rename**. Using your own name, type **Lastname Firstname 3D Parking Lots** and then press Enter. Use this same technique to add your last name and first name to the beginning of the names of the two queries and the **3D Students** table. Increase the width of the **Navigation Pane** so that all object names display fully.

c. On the **Database Tools tab**, in the **Relationships group**, click **Relationships**. On the **Design tab**, in the **Relationships group**, click **All Relationships**. Resize and move the field lists so that the entire table name and fields display for each field list. In the **Relationships** window, click the **join line** between the two field lists. In the **Tools group**, click **Edit Relationships**. Point to the title bar of the **Edit Relationships** dialog box, and drag the dialog box downward below the two field lists. Notice that a *one-to-many* relationship is established between the two tables by using *Lot ID* as the common field. **Close** the **Edit Relationships** dialog box, and then **Close** the **Relationships** window. In the message box, click **Yes** to save changes to the layout of the relationships.

d. In the **Navigation Pane**, double-click each table to open them, and then examine the fields and data in each table. In the **Navigation Pane**, double-click your **3D Building G Student Parking Query** object to run the query and view the results. Apply **Best Fit** to the query results, and then **Save** the query. Switch to **Design** view to examine the design grid. This query answers the question, *What is the*

lot ID, lot location, student ID, student last name, student first name, license plate, state, and semester fee for students who have paid for parking in front of Building G, in ascending order by the Last Name field? In the **Navigation Pane**, double-click your **3D Student Parking by Lots Query** object, apply **Best Fit** to the query results, **Save** the query, and then switch to **Design** view to examine the design grid. This query answers the question, *What is the lot ID, student ID, student last name, student first name, license plate, state, and semester fee for all students?* In the object window, right-click any **object tab**, and then click **Close All**.

e. In the **Navigation Pane**, click to select your **3D Building G Student Parking Query** object. On the **Create tab**, in the **Reports group**, click **Report**. **Close** the **Navigation Pane**. Under **Report Layout Tools**, on the **Design tab**, in the **Themes group**, click **Themes**. In the **Themes** gallery, use the ScreenTips to locate the **Retrospect** theme, right-click the **Retrospect** theme, and then click **Apply Theme to This Object Only**.

f. Click the **Lot Location** field name. On the **Report Layout Tools**, click the **Arrange tab**. In the **Rows & Columns group**, click **Select Column** to select the field name and all of the data for each record in the field. Press Del to remove the field from the report.

g. Click the **Last Name** field name, hold down Shift, and then click the **First Name** field name. On the **Design tab**, in the **Tools group**, click **Property Sheet**. In the **Property Sheet**, on the **Format tab**, click **Width**, type **1.25** and then press Enter to decrease the width of the two fields. **Close** the **Property Sheet**.

h. Click the **Last Name** field name to cancel the selection of both fields and to select only this field. On the **Home tab**, in the **Sort & Filter group**, click **Ascending** to sort the records in ascending order by the Last Name field.

i. If necessary, scroll to the bottom of the report, and notice that the *Semester Fee* column is automatically totaled. At the top of the report, click the **Student ID** field name. On the **Design tab**, in the **Grouping & Totals group**, click **Totals**, and then click **Count Records**. If necessary, scroll to the bottom of the report, and notice that *14* students have paid for parking in front of Building G.

(Project 3D Student Parking continues on the next page)

j. At the bottom of the report, under **Student ID**, click the **calculated control** that displays *14*. Hold down Ctrl, and then under **Semester Fee**, click the **calculated control** that displays *$1,075*—the two calculated controls are selected. On the **Design tab**, in the **Tools group**, click **Property Sheet**. In the **Property Sheet**, click **Height**, type **0.25** and then press Enter to increase the height of both controls. At the bottom of the report, to the right of the **calculated control** that displays *$1,075*, click the **control** that displays *Page 1 of 1*. In the **Property Sheet**, click **Left**, type **2.5** and then press Enter to move the page number within the margins of the report.

k. At the top of the report, click the **label control** that displays the title of the report—*Lastname Firstname 3D Building G Student Parking Query*. On the **Report Layout Tools**, click the **Format tab**. In the **Font group**, click the **Font Size arrow**, and then click **14**. With the **label control** still selected, double-click **Query** to select the word, type **Report** and then press Enter to change the title of the report to *Lastname Firstname 3D Building G Student Parking Report*.

l. Click the **Lot ID** field name. In the **Property Sheet**, click **Left**, type **0.25** and then press Enter to move all of the fields slightly to the right from the left margin. **Close** the **Property Sheet**, and then **Save** the report as **Lastname Firstname 3D Building G Student Parking Report**.

m. On the right side of the status bar, click **Print Preview**. On the **Print Preview tab**, in the **Zoom group**, click **Two Pages**, and notice that the report will print on one page. Create a paper printout or PDF electronic image as directed, click **Close Print Preview**, and then **Close** the report.

2 On the **Create tab**, in the **Reports group**, click **Report Wizard**. In the **Tables/Queries** box, click the **arrow**, and then click **Query: Lastname Firstname 3D Student Parking by Lots Query**. In the **Available Fields** list, double-click the following field names in the order given to move them to the **Selected Fields** list: **Lot ID**, **Last Name**, **First Name**, **Student ID**, and **Semester Fee**.

a. Click **Next**. In the **How do you want to view your data?** box, click **by Lastname Firstname 3D**

Students, and then click **Next**. In the list on the left, double-click **Lot ID** to group the records by this field, and then click **Next**. Click the **1** box **arrow**, and then click **Last Name** to sort the records by the student's last name within each Lot ID.

b. In the wizard, click **Summary Options**. In the **Summary Options** dialog box, to the right of **Semester Fee**, click to select the **Sum** check box. Under **Show**, be sure that **Detail and Summary** is selected, and then click **OK**. In the wizard, click **Next**.

c. In the wizard, under **Layout**, be sure that **Stepped** is selected. Under **Orientation**, click **Landscape**. At the bottom of the wizard, be sure that the **Adjust the field width so all fields fit on a page** check box is selected, and then click **Next**. In the **What title do you want for your report?** box, select the existing text, type **Lastname Firstname 3D Fees by Parking Lot Report** and then click **Finish**. In the object window, right-click the **object tab** for the report, and then click **Layout View**.

3 Under **Report Layout Tools**, on the **Design tab**, in the **Themes group**, click **Themes**. In the **Themes** gallery, use the ScreenTips to locate the **Ion Boardroom** theme, right-click the **Ion Boardroom** theme, and then click **Apply Theme to This Object Only**. In the report, click the title—*Lastname Firstname 3D Fees by Parking Lot Report*—to display a border around the label control. On the **Report Layout Tools**, click the **Format tab**. In the **Font group**, click the **Font Size arrow**, and then click **14**. In the **Font group**, click **Bold**. In the body of the report, click any one of the controls that begins with **Summary for 'Lot ID'**, and then press Del. **Save** the design changes to your report.

a. On the left side of the report, click a **Sum label control**, which will select all of the related controls. Double-click the control to select the text—*Sum*. Type **Total Fees by Parking Lot** and then press Enter.

b. At the top of the report, click the **Lot ID label control** to select it. Hold down Shift, and then click each one of the four other label controls that display the field names to select all five label controls. On the **Format tab**, in the **Font group**, click **Bold**.

c. In the report, under **Last Name**, click the **text box control** that displays *Dolensky*. Hold down Shift, and

(Project 3D Student Parking continues on the next page)

then under **First Name**, click the **text box control** that displays *Adam*. On the **Design tab**, in the **Tools group**, click **Property Sheet**. In the **Property Sheet**, click **Width**, type **1.5** and then press Enter.

d. In the report, click the **Student ID label control**. In the **Property Sheet**, click **Left**, type **7.25** and then press Enter. Do not be concerned that the data in the field is not aligned with the field name; you will adjust this later in this project. Scroll to the bottom of the report, and then click the **Grand Total label control**. In the **Property Sheet**, click **Width**, type **1** and then press Enter. **Close** the **Property Sheet**, and then **Save** the design changes to your report.

e. On the status bar, click **Design View**. In the **Lot ID Footer** section, click the **Total Fees by Parking Lot label control**. Hold down Shift, and in the **Report Footer** section, click the **Grand Total label control** to select both controls. Under **Report Design Tools**, click the **Arrange tab**. In the **Sizing & Ordering group**, click **Align**, and then click **Left**.

f. In the report, in the **Page Header** section, click the **Student ID label control**. Hold down Shift, and in the **Detail** section, click the **Student ID text box control**. On the **Arrange tab**, in the **Sizing & Ordering group**, click **Align**, and then click **Left**. On the status bar, click **Layout View** and notice the left alignment of the two sets of controls.

4 On the status bar, click **Print Preview**. On the **Print Preview tab**, in the **Zoom group**, click **More Pages**, and then click **Four Pages** to view how your report is currently laid out. In the **Zoom group**, click the **Zoom arrow**, and then click **50%**. Notice at the bottom of Page 1 and the top of Page 2, that the grouping for **LOT-2B** breaks across these two pages. Notice at the bottom of Page 2 and the top of Page 3, that the grouping for **LOT-6A** breaks across these two pages. Your pages may display differently depending upon the printer that is installed on your system.

a. Click **Close Print Preview** to return to **Layout** view. On the **Design tab**, in the **Grouping & Totals group**, click **Group & Sort**. In the **Group, Sort, and Total** pane, on the **Group on Lot ID** bar, click **More**. Click the **do not keep group together on one page arrow**, and then click **keep whole group together on one page**. On the **Design tab**, in the **Grouping & Totals group**, click **Group & Sort** to close the **Group, Sort, and Total** pane. **Save** the design changes to your report.

b. On the status bar, click **Print Preview**. Notice that the entire grouping for **LOT-2B** displays at the top of Page 2. Keeping this group together forced the groupings for **LOT-5C** and **LOT-6A** to move to the top of Page 3—your groupings may display differently depending upon the printer that is installed on your system. Create a paper printout or PDF electronic image as directed—multiple pages result.

c. **Close** the report, and then **Open** the **Navigation Pane**. If necessary, increase the width of the pane so that all object names display fully. On the right side of the title bar, click **Close** to close the database and to close Access. As directed by your instructor, submit your database and the paper printouts or PDF electronic images of the two reports—one report is four pages—that are the results of this project. Specifically, in this project, using your own name, you created the following database and printouts or PDF electronic images:

1. Lastname_Firstname_3D_Student_Parking	Database file
2. Lastname Firstname 3D Building G Student Parking Report	Report
3. Lastname Firstname 3D Fees by Parking Lot Report	Report

END | You have completed Project 3D

Mastering Access   Project 3E Textbook Publishers

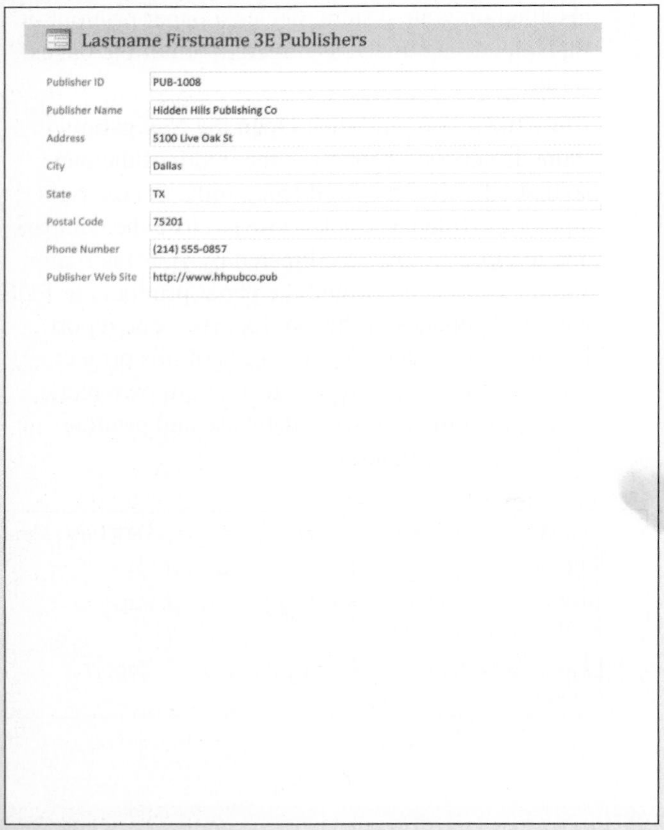

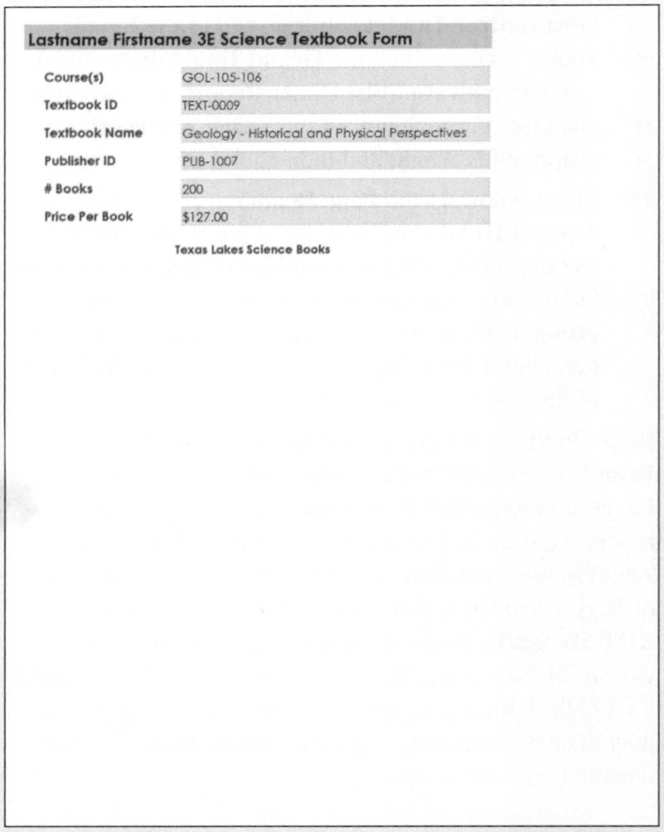

Access 2016, Windows 10, Microsoft Corporation

Apply 3A skills from these Objectives:

1 Create and Use a Form to Add and Delete Records

2 Filter Records

3 Create a Form by Using the Form Wizard

4 Modify a Form in Layout View and in Design View

In the following Mastering Access project, you will assist Donna Rider, Manager of the bookstore, in using her database to track textbooks and publishers for courses being offered by the Science Department at the Northeast Campus of Texas Lakes Community College. Your completed forms will look similar to Figure 3.51.

PROJECT FILES

For Project 3E, you will need the following file:

a03E_Textbook_Publishers

You will save your database as:

Lastname_Firstname_3E_Textbook_Publishers

PROJECT RESULTS

Lastname Firstname 3E Publishers	
Publisher ID	PUB-1008
Publisher Name	Hidden Hills Publishing Co
Address	5100 Live Oak St
City	Dallas
State	TX
Postal Code	75201
Phone Number	(214) 555-0857
Publisher Web Site	http://www.hhpubco.pub

Lastname Firstname 3E Science Textbook Form	
Course(s)	GOL-105-106
Textbook ID	TEXT-0009
Textbook Name	Geology - Historical and Physical Perspectives
Publisher ID	PUB-1007
# Books	200
Price Per Book	$127.00

Texas Lakes Science Books

FIGURE 3.51

(Project 3E Textbook Publishers continues on the next page)

Mastering Access Project 3E Textbook Publishers (continued)

1 Start Access. From your student data files, open **a03E_Textbook_Publishers**. Save the database in your **Access Chapter 3** folder as **Lastname_Firstname_3E_Textbook_Publishers** and then enable the content. In the **Navigation Pane**, **Rename** each table by adding **Lastname Firstname** to the beginning of the table name. Increase the width of the **Navigation Pane** so that all object names display fully. View the relationship between the *3E Publishers* table and the *3E Science Textbooks* table; *one* publisher can provide *many* textbooks for the science courses. Save the changes to the layout of the relationships.

2 Based on your **3E Publishers** table, use the **Form** tool to create a form. **Save** the form as **Lastname Firstname 3E Publisher Form** and then switch to **Form** view. Using the form, add a new record to the underlying table as shown in Table 1.

3 Display the first record, and click in the **Publisher ID** field. **Find** the record for the **Publisher ID** of **PUB-1006**, and then **Delete** the record. Display the record you entered for **PUB-1008**, and then, as directed, create a paper or PDF electronic image of only that record, changing the **Column Size Width** in the **Print** dialog box to **7.5**. **Save** the design changes to your form.

4 Use the **Filter By Form** tool in your **3E Publisher Form** object to create a filter that displays records with a **State** of **CA** or **TX**. After verifying that three records match this criteria, click **Toggle Filter** to display all seven records. **Save** your form, and then **Close** your form.

5 Use the **Form Wizard** to create a form based on your **3E Science Textbooks** table that includes the following fields in the order given: **Course(s)**, **Textbook Name**, **Publisher ID**, **Price Per Book**, and **# Books**. Apply a **Columnar** layout, and name the form **Lastname Firstname 3E Science Textbook Form**.

6 In **Layout** view, apply the **Stacked** layout to all of the controls, and then apply the **Ion Boardroom** theme to this form only. For the title of the form, change the **Font Size** to **16**, apply **Bold**, and then change the **Font Color** to **Dark Purple, Text 2**—under **Theme Colors**, in the fourth column, the first color. **Save** the design changes to the form.

7 From the **Field List** pane, add the **Textbook ID** field to the form directly above the **Textbook Name** field. Move the **# Books** controls directly above the **Price Per Book** controls. **Close** the **Field List** pane. Display Record 9—this record's textbook name is the longest entry of all records. Click the **Textbook Name text box control**, set the **Width** property to **4"** and then **Save** the design changes to your form.

8 Select all six **text box controls**, and change the **Background Color** to **Orange, Accent 4, Lighter 80%**—under **Theme Colors**, in the eighth column, the second color. Select all six **label controls**, and change the **Font Color** to **Orange, Accent 4, Darker 50%**—under **Theme Colors**, in the eighth column, the last color. With the **label controls** still selected, set the **Width** property to **1.75** and then select all of the **label controls** and all of the **text box controls**. Change the **Font Size** to **12**, set the **Height** property to **0.25** and then **Save** the design changes to your form.

9 In **Design** view, set the **Form Footer** section **Height** property to **0.5**. Add a **Label control** to the **Form Footer** section that displays **Texas Lakes Science Books.** For this **label control**, change the **Font Color** to **Orange, Accent 4, Darker 50%**—under **Theme Colors**, in the eighth column, the last color—and then apply **Bold**. For this **label control**, set the **Width** property to **2.25**, set the **Top** property to **0.1** and then set the **Left** property to **1.95**.

10 **Close** the **Property Sheet**, **Save** your form, and then switch to **Form** view. **Find** the record for the **Textbook ID** of **TEXT-0009**, and then, as directed, create a paper printout or PDF electronic image of only this record. Because you changed the field widths, you do not need to change the Column Size Width in the **Print** dialog box.

TABLE 1

Publisher ID	Publisher Name	Address	City	State	Postal Code	Phone Number	Publisher Web Site
PUB-1008	**Hidden Hills Publishing Co**	**5100 Live Oak St**	**Dallas**	**TX**	**75201**	**(214) 555-0857**	**http://www .hhpubco.pub**

(Project 3E Textbook Publishers continues on the next page)

Mastering Access | **Project 3E Textbook Publishers** (continued)

11 **Close** all open objects, and then **Open** the **Navigation Pane**. If necessary, increase the width of the pane so that all object names display fully. **Close** Access. As directed by your instructor, submit your database and the paper printouts or PDF electronic images of the two forms that are the results of this project. Specifically, in this project, using your own name, you created the following database and printouts or PDF electronic images:

1. Lastname_Firstname_3E_Textbook_Publishers	Database file
2. Lastname Firstname 3E Publisher Form	Form (Record 7)
3. Lastname Firstname 3E Science Textbook Form	Form (Record 9)

END | You have completed Project 3E

3 ACCESS

Apply 3B skills from these Objectives:

5 Create a Report by Using the Report Tool and Modify the Report in Layout View

6 Create a Report by Using the Report Wizard

7 Modify the Design of a Report

8 Keep Grouped Data Together in a Printed Report

In the following Mastering Access project, you will assist Tom Catogrides, the Registrar, in using his database to track degrees and grade point averages for honor students in the health professions program in preparation for graduation. Your completed database objects will look similar to Figure 3.52.

PROJECT FILES

For Project 3F, you will need the following file:

a03F_Degrees_Students

You will save your database as:

Lastname_Firstname_3F_Degrees_Students

PROJECT RESULTS

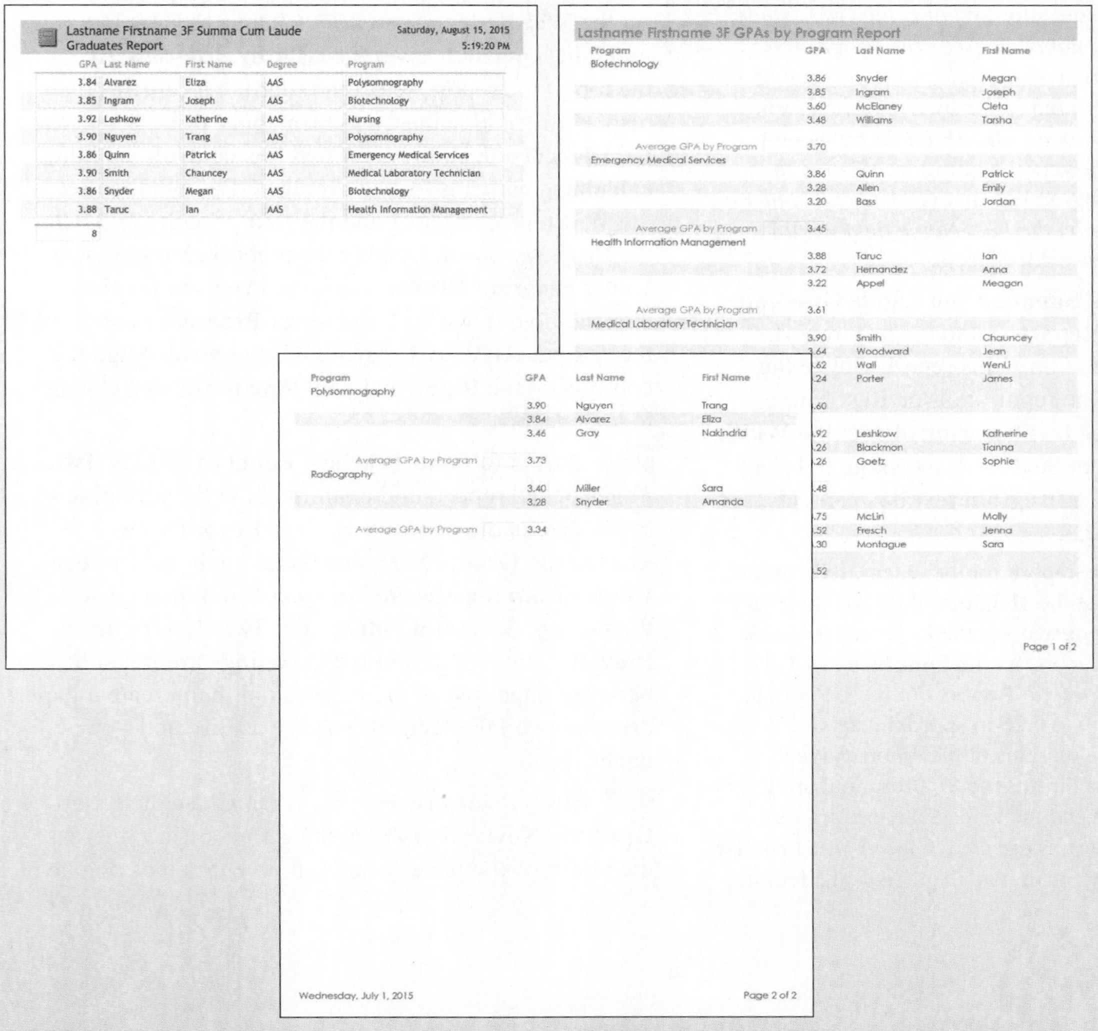

Lastname Firstname 3F Summa Cum Laude Graduates Report   Saturday, August 15, 2015   5:19:20 PM

GPA	Last Name	First Name	Degree	Program
3.84	Alvarez	Eliza	AAS	Polysomnography
3.85	Ingram	Joseph	AAS	Biotechnology
3.92	Leshkow	Katherine	AAS	Nursing
3.90	Nguyen	Trang	AAS	Polysomnography
3.86	Quinn	Patrick	AAS	Emergency Medical Services
3.90	Smith	Chauncey	AAS	Medical Laboratory Technician
3.86	Snyder	Megan	AAS	Biotechnology
3.88	Taruc	Ian	AAS	Health Information Management

8

Lastname Firstname 3F GPAs by Program Report

Program	GPA	Last Name	First Name
Biotechnology			
	3.86	Snyder	Megan
	3.85	Ingram	Joseph
	3.60	McElaney	Cleta
	3.48	Williams	Tarsha
Average GPA by Program	3.70		
Emergency Medical Services			
	3.86	Quinn	Patrick
	3.28	Allen	Emily
	3.20	Bass	Jordan
Average GPA by Program	3.45		
Health Information Management			
	3.88	Taruc	Ian
	3.72	Hernandez	Anna
	3.22	Appel	Meagan
Average GPA by Program	3.61		
Medical Laboratory Technician			
	3.90	Smith	Chauncey
	3.64	Woodward	Jean
	3.62	Wall	WenLi
	3.24	Porter	James
	3.60		
	3.92	Leshkow	Katherine
	3.26	Blackmon	Tianna
	3.26	Goetz	Sophie
	3.48		
	3.75	McLin	Molly
	3.52	Fresch	Jenna
	3.30	Montague	Sara
	3.52		

Page 1 of 2

Program	GPA	Last Name	First Name
Polysomnography			
	3.90	Nguyen	Trang
	3.84	Alvarez	Eliza
	3.46	Gray	Nakindria
Average GPA by Program	3.73		
Radiography			
	3.40	Miller	Sara
	3.28	Snyder	Amanda
Average GPA by Program	3.34		

Wednesday, July 1, 2015   Page 2 of 2

Access 2016, Windows 10, Microsoft Corporation

FIGURE 3.52

(Project 3F Degrees and Students continues on the next page)

Mastering Access Project 3F Degrees and Students (continued)

1 Start Access. From your student data files, open **a03F_Degrees_Students**. **Save** the database in your **Access Chapter 3** folder as **Lastname_Firstname_3F_Degrees_Students** and then enable the content. In the **Navigation Pane**, **Rename** the two tables and two queries by adding **Lastname Firstname** to the beginning of each object name, and then increase the width of the **Navigation Pane** so that all object names display fully. View the relationship that is established between the *3F Degrees* tables and the *3F Students* table—*one* type of degree can be awarded to *many* students. Save the changes to the layout of the relationships. **Run** each query to display the query results, apply **Best Fit**, and then **Save** each query.

Open each query in **Design** view to examine the design grid. The *3F Summa Cum Laude Graduates Query* answers the question, *What is the GPA, student ID, last name, first name, degree, and program for students graduating with a grade point average of 3.8 or higher, in descending order by GPA and ascending order by Last Name?* The *3F GPAs by Degree Program Query* answers the question, *What is the program, last name, first name, and GPA for all students, in ascending order by the Last Name field within the Program field?* **Close All** objects.

2 Based on your **3F Summa Cum Laude Graduates Query** object, use the **Report** tool to create a report. Apply the **Facet** theme to only this report. Delete the **Student ID** field from the report. For the **Last Name**, **First Name**, and **Degree text box controls**, set the **Width** property to **1.25** and then **Sort** the **Last Name** field in **Ascending** order. For the **Program text box controls**, set the **Width** property to **2.5**.

At the bottom of the report, for the **calculated control**, which displays *8*, set the **Height** to **0.25** and then for the **page number control**, set the **Left** property to **5**. For the title of the report, set the **Font Size** to **14** and change the word *Query* to **Report** For the **GPA** field, set the **Left** property to **0.25** to approximately center the fields within the margins of the report. **Save** the report as **Lastname Firstname 3F Summa Cum Laude Graduates Report** and then create a paper printout or PDF electronic image as directed. **Close Print Preview**, **Close** the **Property Sheet**, and then **Close** the report.

3 Use the **Report Wizard** to create a report based on your **3F GPAs by Degree Program Query** object that includes the following fields in the order given: **Program**, **GPA**, **Last Name**, and **First Name**. View your data by **3F Degrees** and do not add any other grouping to the report. Sort first in **Descending** order by **GPA**, and second in **Ascending** order by **Last Name**. Summarize the report by averaging the **GPA** field for each degree. Be sure the layout is **Stepped** and the orientation is **Portrait**. For the report title, type **Lastname Firstname 3F GPAs by Program Report** and then switch to **Layout** view.

4 Apply the **Wisp** theme to only this report. For the report title, change the **Font Size** to **16**, and then apply **Bold**. Delete the controls that begin with **Summary for 'Program'**. Under **Program**, for the **text box controls**, set the **Width** property to **2.75**. Change the text in the **Avg label control** to **Average GPA by Program**. At the top of the report, select the four **label controls** that display the field names, and then apply **Bold**. Select the **GPA label control**, the **GPA text box controls**, and the **calculated controls** for the average GPA, and then set the **Width** property to **1** and the **Left** property to **3**. **Close** the **Property Sheet**. Display the report in **Design** view. Under **Program Header**, click the **Program text box control**, hold down Shift, and under **Program Footer**, click the **Average GPA by Program label control**. **Align** the controls on the **Right**, and then **Save** the design changes to your report.

5 Switch to **Print Preview**, **Zoom** to display **Two Pages** of the report, and examine how the groupings break across the pages. Switch to **Layout** view, display the **Group, Sort, and Total** pane, select **keep whole group together on one page**, and then close the **Group, Sort, and Total** pane. Switch to **Print Preview**, and notice that the groupings are not split between pages. **Save** the report, and then create a paper printout or PDF electronic image as directed—two pages result.

6 **Close Print Preview**, and then **Close** the report. **Open** the **Navigation Pane**, and, if necessary, increase the width of the pane so that all object names display

(Project 3F Degrees and Students continues on the next page)

Mastering Access | Project 3F Degrees and Students (continued)

fully. On the right side of the title bar, click **Close** to close the database and to close Access. As directed by your instructor, submit your database and the paper printouts or PDF electronic images of the two reports—one report is two pages—that are the results of this project. Specifically, in this project, using your own name, you created the following database and printouts or PDF electronic images:

1. Lastname_Firstname_3F_Degrees_ Students	Database file
2. Lastname Firstname 3F Summa Cum Laude Graduates Report	Report
3. Lastname Firstname 3F GPAs by Program Report	Report

END | You have completed Project 3F

Mastering Access Project 3G Career Books

In the following Mastering Access project, you will assist Rebecca Hennelly, Head Librarian at the Southwest Campus of Texas Lakes Community College, in using her database to track publishers and book titles that assist students in finding employment. Your completed forms and report will look similar to Figure 3.53.

Apply 3A and 3B skills from these Objectives:

1 Create and Use a Form to Add and Delete Records

2 Filter Records

3 Create a Form by Using the Form Wizard

4 Modify a Form in Layout View and in Design View

5 Create a Report by Using the Report Tool and Modify the Report in Layout View

6 Create a Report by Using the Report Wizard

7 Modify the Design of a Report

8 Keep Grouped Data Together in a Printed Report

PROJECT FILES

For Project 3G, you will need the following file:

a03G_Career_Books

You will save your database as:

Lastname_Firstname_3G_Career_Books

PROJECT RESULTS

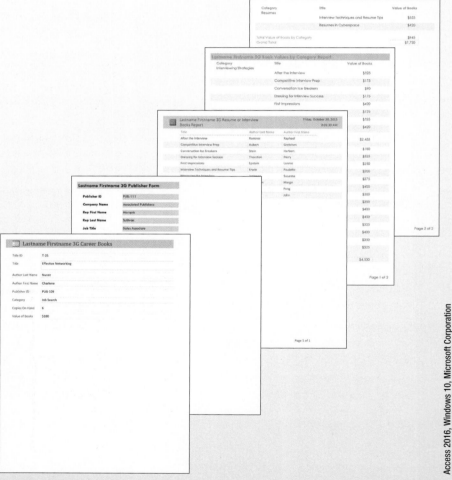

FIGURE 3.53

Access 2016, Windows 10, Microsoft Corporation

(Project 3G Career Books continues on the next page)

1 Start Access. From your student data files, open **a03G_Career_Books**. Save the database in your **Access Chapter 3** folder as **Lastname_Firstname_3G_Career_Books** and then enable the content. In the **Navigation Pane**, **Rename** the two tables and one query by adding **Lastname Firstname** to the beginning of each object name. Increase the width of the **Navigation Pane** so that all object names display fully. View the relationship that is established between the *3G Publishers* table and the *3G Career Books* table—*one* publisher can publish *many* career books. Save the changes to the layout of the relationships.

Open the **3G Resume or Interview Books Query**, apply **Best Fit**, and then **Save** the query. Switch the query to **Design** view, examine the design of the query, and then **Close** the query object.

2 Based on your **3G Career Books** table, use the **Form** tool to create a form. **Save** the form as **Lastname Firstname 3G Career Book Form** and then switch to **Form** view. Using the form, add a new record to the underlying table as shown in **Table 1**.

3 Display the first record, and click in the **Title ID** field. **Find** the record for the **Title ID** of **T-19**, and then **Delete** the record. Display the record you entered for **T-25**, and then, as directed, create a paper printout or electronic printout of only that record, changing the **Column Size Width** in the **Print** dialog box to **7.5**. **Save** the design changes to your form.

4 Use the **Filter By Form** tool in your **3G Career Book Form** object to create a filter that displays records with a **Category** of **Interviewing Strategies** or **Resumes**. After verifying that 10 records match this criteria, click **Toggle Filter** to display all 24 records. **Save** the form, and then **Close** the form.

5 Use the **Form Wizard** to create a form based on your **3G Publishers** table that includes the following fields in the order given: **Company Name, Rep Last**

Name, Rep First Name, Job Title, and **Phone Number**. Apply a **Columnar** layout, and name the form **Lastname Firstname 3G Publisher Form**.

6 In **Layout** view, apply the **Stacked** layout to all of the controls, and then apply the **Integral** theme to this form only. For the title of the form, change the **Font Size** to **16**, apply **Bold**, and then change the **Font Color** to **Dark Teal, Text 2, Darker 50%**—under **Theme Colors**, in the fourth column, the last color. **Save** the design changes to the form.

7 From the **Field List** pane, add the **Publisher ID** field to the form directly above the **Company Name** field. **Close** the **Field List** pane. Move the **Rep First Name** controls directly above the **Rep Last Name** controls. Click the **Job Title text box control**, set the **Width** property to **2.5** and then **Save** the design changes to your form.

8 Select all six **text box controls**, and change the **Background Color** to **Turquoise, Accent 1, Lighter 80%**—under **Theme Colors**, in the fifth column, the second color. Select all six **label controls**, and change the **Font Color** to **Dark Teal, Text 2, Darker 50%**—under **Theme Colors**, in the fourth column, the last color. Apply **Bold** to the **label controls**. With the **label controls** still selected, set the **Width** property to **1.75** and then select all of the **label controls** and all of the **text box controls**. Change the **Font Size** to **12**, set the **Height** property to **0.25** and then **Save** the design changes to your form.

9 In **Design** view, set the **Form Footer** section **Height** property to **0.5**. Add a **Label** control to the **Form Footer** section that displays **Texas Lakes Southwest Campus**. For this **label control**, change the **Font Color** to **Dark Teal, Text 2, Darker 50%**—under **Theme Colors**, in the fourth column, the last color —and then apply **Bold**. For this **label control**, set the **Width** property to **2.2**, set the **Top** property to **0.1** and then set the **Left** property to **1.25**. **Close** the **Property Sheet**, **Save** your form, and then

TABLE 1

Title ID	Title	Author Last Name	Author First Name	Publisher ID	Category	Copies On Hand	Value of Books
T-25	Effective Networking	Nunez	Charlene	PUB-109	Job Search	6	180

(Project 3G Career Books continues on the next page)

switch to **Form** view. Using the form, add a new record to the underlying table as shown in **Table 2**.

10 ▶ Display the record that you just created, and then, as directed, create a paper printout or PDF electronic image of only this record. Because you changed the field widths, you do not need to change the Column Size Width in the **Print** dialog box. **Close** the form.

11 ▶ Based on your **3G Resume or Interview Books Query** object, use the **Report** tool to create a report. Apply the **Retrospect** theme to only this report. Delete the following fields from the report: **Publisher ID**, **Category**, and **Company Name**. For the **Title text box controls**, set the **Width** property to **3** and then **Sort** the **Title** field in **Ascending** order. For the **Author Last Name text box controls** and the **Author First Name text box controls**, set the **Width** property to **1.5**.

12 ▶ Click the **Title** field name, and then add a calculated control that counts the number of records. At the bottom of the report, for the **calculated control**, which displays *10*, set the **Height** to **0.25** and then for the **page number control**, set the **Left** property to **5**. For the title of the report, set the **Font Size** to **14** and change the word *Query* to **Report**. Click the **Title** field name, and then set the **Left** property to **0.75** to move all of the controls to the right. **Save** the report as **Lastname Firstname 3G Resume or Interview Books Report** and then create a paper printout or PDF electronic image as directed. **Close Print Preview**, **Close** the **Property Sheet**, and then **Close** the report.

13 ▶ Use the **Report Wizard** to create a report based on your **3G Career Books** table that includes the following fields in the order given: **Category, Title**, and **Value of Books**. Group your data by **Category**, sort in **Ascending** order by **Title**, and then summarize the report by summing the **Value of Books** field. Be sure the layout is **Stepped** and the orientation is **Portrait**. For the report title, type **Lastname Firstname 3G**

Book Values by Category Report and then switch to **Layout** view.

14 ▶ Apply the **Ion Boardroom** theme to only this report. For the report title, change the **Font Size** to **14**, and then apply **Bold**. Delete the controls that begin with **Summary for 'Category'**. Select the **Category**, **Title**, and **Value of Books label controls**, and then apply **Bold**. Under **Title**, for the **text box controls**, set the **Width** property to **3.5**. For the **Value of Books label control**, set the **Left** property to **6** and then **Save** the design changes to your report.

15 ▶ At the bottom of the report in the last column, select the following three controls: **text box control** that displays *$420*, **calculated control** that displays *$945*, and the **calculated control** that displays *7,730 (Grand Total control, may be too small to view number)*. Set the **Width** property to **1.25** and the **Left** property to **6**. For the **Grand Total label control**, set the **Width** property to **1** and then change the text in the **Sum label control** to **Total Value of Books by Category**. Click any **Title text box control**, set the **Height** property to **0.35** and then **Save** your report.

16 ▶ **Close** the **Property Sheet**, and then display your report in **Design** view. Under **Category Footer**, click the **label control** that displays *Total Value of Books by Category*, hold down [Shift], and then under **Report Footer**, click the **Grand Total label control**. **Align** the controls on the **Left**, and then **Save** the design changes to your report.

17 ▶ Switch to **Print Preview**, **Zoom** to display **Two Pages** of the report, and examine how the groupings break across the pages. Switch to **Layout** view, display the **Group, Sort, and Total** pane, select **keep whole group together on one page**, and then close the **Group, Sort, and Total** pane. Switch to **Print Preview**, and notice that the groupings are no longer split between pages. **Save** the report, and then create a paper printout or PDF electronic image as directed—two pages result.

TABLE 2

Publisher ID	Company Name	Rep First Name	Rep Last Name	Job Title	Phone Number
PUB-111	**Associated Publishers**	**Marquis**	**Sullivan**	**Sales Associate**	**(512) 555-7373**

(Project 3G Career Books continues on the next page)

Mastering Access **Project 3G Career Books** (continued)

18 **Close Print Preview**, and then **Close** the report. **Open** the **Navigation Pane**, and, if necessary, increase the width of the pane so that all object names display fully. On the right side of the title bar, click **Close** to close the database and to close Access. As directed by your instructor, submit your database and the paper printout or PDF electronic images of the two forms and two reports—one report is two pages—that are the results of this project. Specifically, in this project, using your own name, you created the following database and printouts or PDF electronic images:

1. Lastname_Firstname_3G_Career_Books	Database file
2. Lastname Firstname 3G Career Book Form	Form (Record 24)
3. Lastname Firstname 3G Publisher Form	Form (Record 12)
4. Lastname Firstname 3G Resume or Interview Books Report	Report
5. Lastname Firstname 3G Book Values by Category Report	Report

END | You have completed Project 3G

CONTENT-BASED ASSESSMENTS (CRITICAL THINKING)

GO! Fix It	Project 3H Resume Workshops	MyITLab
GO! Make It	Project 3I Study Abroad	MyITLab
GO! Solve It	Project 3J Job Offers	MyITLab
GO! Solve It	Project 3K Financial Aid	

PROJECT FILES

For Project 3K, you will need the following file:

a03K_Financial_Aid

You will save your database as:

Lastname_Firstname_3K_Financial_Aid

Start Access, navigate to your student data files, open **a03K_Financial_Aid**, and then save the database in your **Access Chapter 3** folder as **Lastname_Firstname_3K_Financial_Aid**. Using your own name, add **Lastname Firstname** to the beginning of all objects. Sivia Long, the Financial Aid Director, would like you to create an form and a report, using the following guidelines:

- In the form, move the Last Name field above the First Name field. Enter a new record using your own information with a Student ID of **9091246** and Financial Aid ID of **FA-07** and a Home Phone of **(512) 555-9876** and a College Email of **ns246@tlcc.edu** Create a filter to display the only those students whose last name begin with the letter *S*. Add a footer that displays **Texas Lakes Community College Financial Aid**. Save the form as **Lastname Firstname 3K FA Student Update Form** and then create a paper printout or PDF electronic image of your record only.

- The report will use the query and list the Award Name, Student ID, and Award Amount, viewed by students, grouped by the Award Name field, and sorted in ascending order by the Student ID field. Include a total for the Award Amount field, save the report as **Lastname Firstname 3K FA Amount by Award Report** and be sure the groupings do not break across pages. Create a paper printout or PDF electronic image as directed—multiple pages result.

Open the Navigation Pane, be sure that all object names display fully, and then close Access. As directed, submit your database and the paper printout or PDF electronic images of the form and report that are the results of this project.

Performance Level

Performance Criteria	Exemplary: You consistently applied the relevant skills	Proficient: You sometimes, but not always, applied the relevant skills	Developing: You rarely or never applied the relevant skills
Create 3K FA Student Update Form	Form created with correct fields, new record, footer, and filter in an attractive format.	Form created with no more than two missing elements.	Form created with more than two missing elements.
Create 3K FA Amount by Award Report	Report created with correct fields, grouped, sorted, and summarized correctly, with groupings kept together in an attractive format.	Report created with no more than two missing elements.	Report created with more than two missing elements.

END | You have completed Project 3K

RUBRIC

The following outcomes-based assessments are *open-ended assessments*. That is, there is no specific correct result; your result will depend on your approach to the information provided. Make *Professional Quality* your goal. Use the following scoring rubric to guide you in *how* to approach the problem and then to evaluate *how well* your approach solves the problem.

The *criteria*—Software Mastery, Content, Format & Layout, and Process—represent the knowledge and skills you have gained that you can apply to solving the problem. The *levels of performance*—Professional Quality, Approaching Professional Quality, or Needs Quality Improvements—help you and your instructor evaluate your result.

	Your completed project is of Professional Quality if you:	Your completed project is Approaching Professional Quality if you:	Your completed project Needs Quality Improvements if you:
1-Software Mastery	Choose and apply the most appropriate skills, tools, and features and identify efficient methods to solve the problem.	Choose and apply some appropriate skills, tools, and features, but not in the most efficient manner.	Choose inappropriate skills, tools, or features, or are inefficient in solving the problem.
2-Content	Construct a solution that is clear and well organized, contains content that is accurate, appropriate to the audience and purpose, and is complete. Provide a solution that contains no errors in spelling, grammar, or style.	Construct a solution in which some components are unclear, poorly organized, inconsistent, or incomplete. Misjudge the needs of the audience. Have some errors in spelling, grammar, or style, but the errors do not detract from comprehension.	Construct a solution that is unclear, incomplete, or poorly organized; contains some inaccurate or inappropriate content; and contains many errors in spelling, grammar, or style. Do not solve the problem.
3-Format & Layout	Format and arrange all elements to communicate information and ideas, clarify function, illustrate relationships, and indicate relative importance.	Apply appropriate format and layout features to some elements, but not others. Overuse features, causing minor distraction.	Apply format and layout that does not communicate information or ideas clearly. Do not use format and layout features to clarify function, illustrate relationships, or indicate relative importance. Use available features excessively, causing distraction.
4-Process	Use an organized approach that integrates planning, development, self-assessment, revision, and reflection.	Demonstrate an organized approach in some areas, but not others; or, use an insufficient process of organization throughout.	Do not use an organized approach to solve the problem.

OUTCOMES-BASED ASSESSMENTS (CRITICAL THINKING)

GO! Think | Project 3L Food Services

PROJECT FILES

For Project 3L, you will need the following file:

a03L_Food_Services

You will save your database as:

Lastname_Firstname_3L_Food_Services

Start Access, navigate to your student data files, open **a03L_Food_Services**, save the database in your **Access Chapter 3** folder as **Lastname_Firstname_3L_Food_Services** and then enable the content. Using your own name, add **Lastname Firstname** to the beginning of both table names. Luciano Gonzalez, the Hospitality Director, would like you to create an attractive form and a report to assist him with the staff scheduling of food services for a two-day student orientation workshop using the following guidelines:

- The form will be used to update records in the 3L Staff table. Be sure that the Last Name field displays above the First Name field. After the form is created, enter a new record using your own last name and first name with a Staff ID of **STAFF-1119** and a Phone Number of **(512) 555-0845** and a Title of **Server**. Create a filter that when toggled on displays the records for staff with a Title of *Server*. Add a footer to the form that displays **Texas Lakes Community College Hospitality Services**. Save the form as **Lastname Firstname 3L Staff Update Form** and then create a paper printout or PDF electronic image of your record only.

- The report will be used by Mr. Gonzalez to call staff members when the schedule changes, so it should be grouped by title. Add a report footer that displays **Texas Lakes Community College Hospitality Services** and then save the report as **Lastname Firstname 3L Staff Phone List**. Create a paper printout or PDF electronic image as directed.

Open the Navigation Pane, be sure that all object names display fully, and then close Access. As directed, submit your database and the paper or electronic printout of the form and report that are the results of this project. Specifically, in this project, using your own name, you created the following database and printouts or PDF electronic images.

END | You have completed Project 3L

GO! Think | Project 3M Donor Gifts | MyITLab

Build From Scratch

You and GO! | Project 3N Personal Inventory | MyITLab

GO! Collaborative Team Project | Project 3O Bell Orchid Hotels | MyITLab

Introducing Microsoft PowerPoint 2016

P
PowerPoint 2016

Surpasspro/Fotolia

PowerPoint 2016: Introduction

Communication skills are critical to your success in a business career, and when it comes to communicating *your* ideas, presentation is everything! Whether you are planning to deliver your presentation in person or online—to a large audience or to a small group—Microsoft PowerPoint 2016 is a versatile business tool that will help you create presentations that make a lasting impression. Additionally, collaborating with others to develop a presentation is easy because you can share the slides you create by using your free Microsoft OneDrive cloud storage.

Microsoft PowerPoint 2016 includes a variety of themes that you can apply to a new presentation. Each theme includes several theme variants that coordinate colors, fonts, and effects. The benefit of this approach is that the variations evoke different moods and responses, yet the basic design remains the same. As a result, you can use a similar design within your company to brand your presentations, while still changing the colors to make the presentation appropriate to the audience and topic. You do not have to determine which colors work well together in the theme you choose, because professional designers have already done that for you. So you can concentrate on how best to communicate your message. Focus on creating dynamic, interesting presentations that keep your audience engaged!

Getting Started with Microsoft PowerPoint

PROJECT 1A

OUTCOMES
Create a company overview presentation.

PROJECT 1B

OUTCOMES
Create a new product announcement presentation.

OBJECTIVES

1. Create a New Presentation
2. Edit a Presentation in Normal View
3. Add Pictures to a Presentation
4. Print and View a Presentation

OBJECTIVES

5. Edit an Existing Presentation
6. Format a Presentation
7. Use Slide Sorter View
8. Apply Slide Transitions

Jeff McGraw/Fotolia

In This Chapter

GO! to Work with PowerPoint

In this chapter, you will study presentation skills, which are among the most important skills you will learn. Good presentation skills enhance your communications—written, electronic, and interpersonal. In this technology-enhanced world, communicating ideas clearly and concisely is a critical personal skill. Microsoft PowerPoint 2016 is presentation software with which you create electronic slide presentations. Use PowerPoint to present information to your audience effectively. You can start with a new, blank presentation and add content, pictures, and themes, or you can collaborate with colleagues by inserting slides that have been saved in other presentations.

The projects in this chapter relate to **Kodiak West Travel**, which is a travel agency with offices in Juneau, Anchorage, and Victoria. Kodiak West Travel works closely with local vendors to provide clients with specialized adventure travel itineraries. The company was established in 2001 in Juneau and built a loyal client base that led to the expansion into Anchorage and Victoria. As a full-service travel agency, Kodiak West Travel agents strive to provide their clients with travel opportunities that exceed their expectations. The company works with all major airlines, cruise lines, hotel chains, and vehicle rental companies as well as with small, specialized, boutique hotels.

PROJECT Company Overview

PROJECT ACTIVITIES

In Activities 1.01 through 1.16, you will create the first five slides of a new presentation that Kodiak West Travel tour manager Ken Dakano is developing to introduce the tour services that the company offers. Your completed presentation will look similar to Figure 1.1.

Please always review the downloaded Grader instructions before beginning.

PROJECT FILES

MyITLab grader

If your instructor wants you to submit Project 1A in the MyITLab Grader system, log in to MyITLab, locate Grader Project 1A, and then download the files for this project.

For Project 1A, you will need the following files:

New blank PowerPoint presentation
p01A_Glacier
p01A_Bay

You will save your presentation as:

Lastname_Firstname_1A_KWT_Overview

PROJECT RESULTS

Build From Scratch

GO!
Walk Thru
Project 1A

PowerPoint 2016, Windows 10, Microsoft Corporation

FIGURE 1.1 Project 1A KWT Overview

NOTE	If You Are Using a Touchscreen
	Tap an item to click it.
	Press and hold for a few seconds to right-click; release when the information or command displays.
	Touch the screen with two or more fingers and then pinch together to zoom out or stretch your fingers apart to zoom in.
	Slide your finger on the screen to scroll—slide left to scroll right and slide right to scroll left.
	Slide to rearrange—similar to dragging with a mouse.
	Swipe to select—slide an item a short distance with a quick movement—to select an item and bring up commands, if any.

Objective 1 Create a New Presentation

GO! Learn How
Video P1-1

Microsoft PowerPoint 2016 is software you can use to present information to your audience effectively. You can edit and format a blank presentation by adding text, a presentation theme, and pictures. When you start PowerPoint, presentations you have recently opened, if any, display on the left. On the right you can select either a blank presentation or a *theme*—a set of unified design elements that provides a look for your presentation by applying colors, fonts, and effects. A presentation consists of one or more slides. Similar to a page in a document—a presentation *slide* can contain text, pictures, tables, charts, and other multimedia or graphic objects.

Activity 1.01 | Identifying Parts of the PowerPoint Window

ALERT!	To submit as an autograded project, log into MyITLab, download the files for this project, and begin with those files instead of a new blank presentation.

1.1.1

In this Activity, you will start PowerPoint and identify the parts of the PowerPoint window.

1 Start PowerPoint. On the right, click **Facet** to view a preview of the Facet theme and the color variations associated with this theme. Below the theme preview, click either the left- or right-pointing **More Images** ◀ and ▶ arrows to view how various types of slides in this theme display. To the right of the preview, click each of the color variations. After you have viewed each color, click the original green color.

2 On either the left or right side of the preview window, notice the arrow, and then compare your screen with Figure 1.2.

You can use the arrows to the left and right of the preview window to scroll through the available themes.

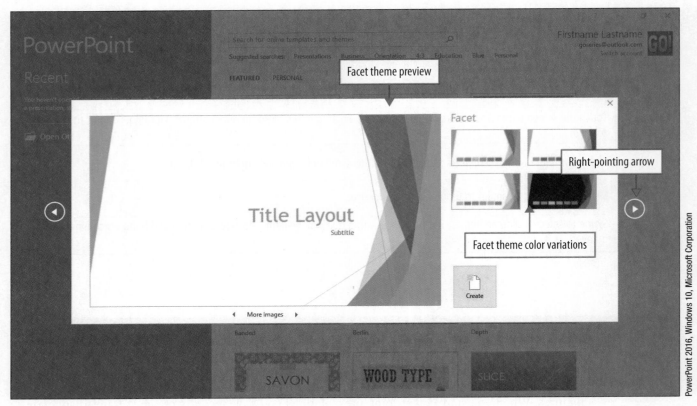

FIGURE 1.2

3 Click the right- or left-pointing arrow several times to view other available themes, and then return to the **Facet** theme. In the lower right area of the preview window, click **Create** to begin a new presentation using the **Facet** theme.

4 Compare your screen with Figure 1.3, and then take a moment to study the parts of the PowerPoint window described in the table in Figure 1.4.

The presentation displays in *Normal view*, which is the primary editing view in PowerPoint where you write and design your presentations. On the left, a pane displays miniature images—*thumbnails*—of the slides in your presentation. On the right, the *Slide pane* displays a larger image of the active slide.

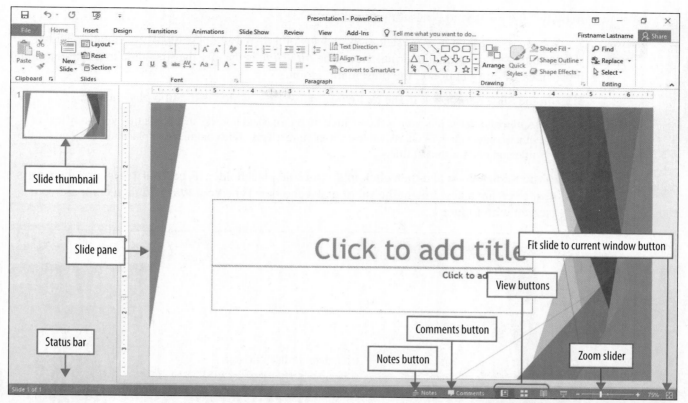

FIGURE 1.3

PowerPoint 2016, Windows 10, Microsoft Corporation

MICROSOFT POWERPOINT SCREEN ELEMENTS	
SCREEN ELEMENT	**DESCRIPTION**
Slide pane	Displays a large image of the active slide.
Slide thumbnails	Miniature images of each slide in the presentation. Clicking a slide thumbnail displays the slide in the Slide pane.
Status bar	Displays, in a horizontal bar at the bottom of the presentation window, the current slide number, number of slides in a presentation, Notes button, Comments button, View buttons, Zoom slider, and Fit slide to current window button; you can customize this area to include additional information.
Notes button	When clicked, displays an area below the Slide pane in which presentation notes can be typed.
Comments button	When clicked, displays a Comments pane to the right of the Slide pane, in which reviewers can type comments.
View buttons	Controls the look of the presentation window with a set of commands.
Zoom slider	Zooms the slide displayed in the Slide pane, in and out.
Fit slide to current window button	Fits the active slide to the maximum view in the Slide pane.

FIGURE 1.4

Activity 1.02 | Entering Presentation Text

2.1.1

When you create a new presentation, PowerPoint displays a new blank presentation with a single slide—a title slide in Normal view. The ***title slide*** is usually the first slide in a presentation; it provides an introduction to the presentation topic.

> **1** In the **Slide pane**, click in the text *Click to add title*, which is the title placeholder.
>
> A ***placeholder*** is a box on a slide with dotted or dashed borders that holds title and body text or other content such as charts, tables, and pictures. This slide contains two placeholders, one for the title and one for the subtitle.

> **2** Type **Kodiak West** and then click in the subtitle placeholder. Type **Your Travel** and then press
> Enter to create a new line in the subtitle placeholder. Type **Your Way** and then compare your screen with Figure 1.5.

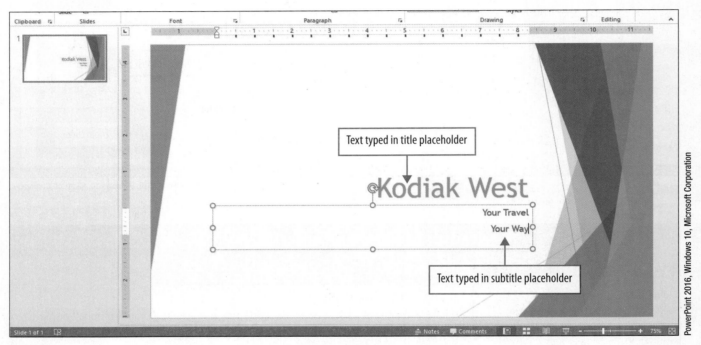

PowerPoint 2016, Windows 10, Microsoft Corporation

FIGURE 1.5

> **3** On the **Quick Access Toolbar**, click **Save** 🖫. Under **Save As**, click **Browse**. Navigate to the location where you are saving your files for this chapter, and then create and open a new folder named **PowerPoint Chapter 1** In the **File name** box, using your own name, replace the existing text with **Lastname_Firstname_1A_KWT_Overview** and then click **Save**.

Activity 1.03 | Applying a Presentation Theme

A theme is a set of unified design elements that provides a look for your presentation by applying colors, fonts, and effects. After you create a presentation, you can change the look of your presentation by applying a different theme. Kodiak West Travel wants a theme that evokes a feeling of nature.

> **1** On the ribbon, click the **Design tab**. In the **Themes group**, click **More** ⧩ to display the **Themes** gallery. Compare your screen with Figure 1.6.
>
> The themes displayed on your system may differ from Figure 1.6.

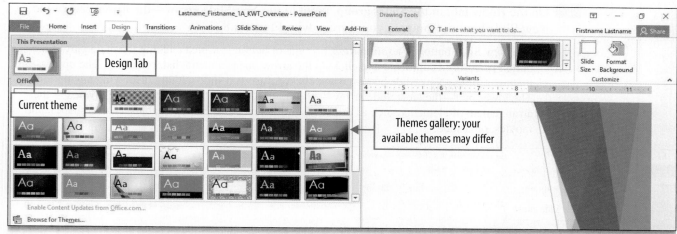

FIGURE 1.6

2 Under **Office**, point to several of the themes and notice that a ScreenTip displays the name of each theme, and the Live Preview feature displays how each theme would look if applied to your presentation.

The first theme that displays is the Office Theme.

3 Use the ScreenTips to locate the **Organic** theme shown in Figure 1.7.

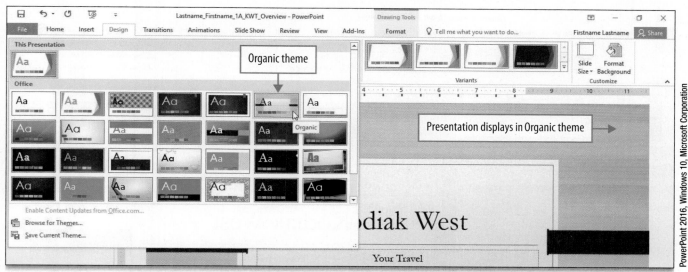

FIGURE 1.7

4 Click **Organic** to change the presentation theme and then **Save** 🖫 your presentation.

Objective 2 Edit a Presentation in Normal View

GO! Learn How
Video P1-2

Editing is the process of modifying a presentation by adding and deleting slides or by changing the contents of individual slides.

Activity 1.04 │ Inserting a New Slide

1.2.1

Your presentation consists of a single slide. You can insert additional slides in any order. If you have more than one slide, to insert a new slide in a presentation, display the slide that will come before the slide that you want to insert.

1 On the **Home tab**, in the **Slides group**, point to the **New Slide arrow**—the lower part of the New Slide button. Compare your screen with Figure 1.8.

The New Slide button is a ***split button***—a type of button in which clicking the main part of the button performs a command and clicking the arrow opens a menu, list, or gallery. The upper, main part of the New Slide button, when clicked, inserts a slide without displaying any options. The lower part—the New Slide arrow—when clicked, displays a gallery of slide ***layouts***— the arrangement of elements, such as title and subtitle text, lists, pictures, tables, charts, shapes, and movies, on a slide.

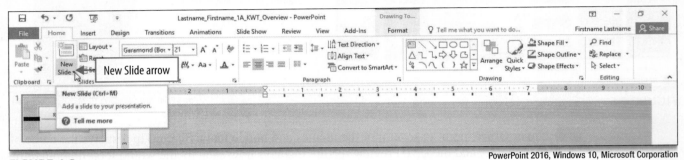

FIGURE 1.8

2 In the **Slides group**, click the lower portion of the **New Slide** button—the **New Slide arrow**—to display the gallery, and then compare your screen with Figure 1.9.

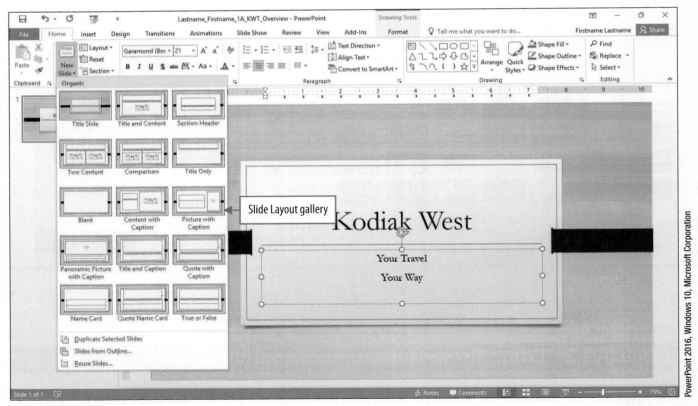

FIGURE 1.9

3 In the gallery, click the **Panoramic Picture with Caption** layout to insert a new slide. Notice that the new blank slide displays in the **Slide pane**, and a slide thumbnail displays at the left. Compare your screen with Figure 1.10.

🔄 **BY TOUCH**   In the gallery, tap the desired layout to insert a new slide.

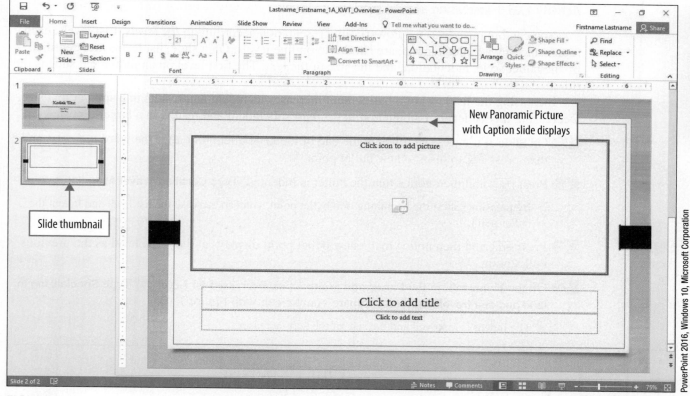

FIGURE 1.10

4 ▶ On the new slide, below the picture placeholder, click the text *Click to add title*, and then type **Your Dreams**

5 ▶ Below the title placeholder, click in the text placeholder. Type **Whether you want to trek on a glacier or spend your time in quiet solitude, Kodiak West Travel can make your dream a reality.** Compare your screen with Figure 1.11.

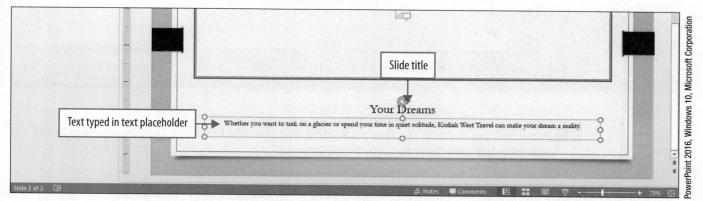

FIGURE 1.11

6 ▶ On the **Home tab**, in the **Slides group**, click the **New Slide arrow** to display the gallery, and then click **Title and Content**. In the title placeholder, type **Our Expertise** and then below the title placeholder, click in the content placeholder. Type **Over 20 years of experience in the travel industry**

7 ▶ **Save** 🖫 your presentation.

Activity 1.05 | Increasing and Decreasing List Levels

You can organize text in a PowerPoint presentation according to *list levels*. List levels, each represented by a bullet symbol, are similar to outline levels. On a slide, list levels are identified by the bullet style, indentation, and the size of the text. The first level on an individual slide is the title.

Increasing the list level of a bullet point increases its indent and results in a smaller text size. Decreasing the list level of a bullet point decreases its indent and results in a larger text size.

1 ▶ On **Slide 3**, if necessary, click at the end of the last bullet point after the word *industry*, and then press Enter to insert a new bullet point.

2 ▶ Press Tab, and then notice that the bullet is indented. Type **Certified Travel Associates**

By pressing Tab at the beginning of a bullet point, you can increase the list level and indent the bullet point.

3 ▶ Press Enter, and then notice that a new bullet point displays at the same level as the previous bullet point.

4 ▶ On the **Home tab**, in the **Paragraph group**, click **Decrease List Level** . Type **Specializing in land and sea travel** and then compare your screen with Figure 1.12.

The indent is removed and the size of the text increases.

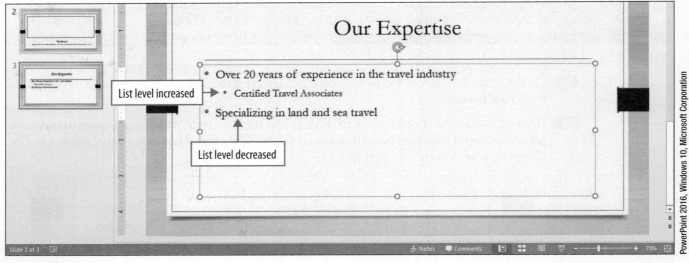

FIGURE 1.12

5 ▶ Press Enter, and then on the **Home tab**, click **Increase List Level** . Type **Pacific Northwest including U.S. and Canada**

You can use the Increase List Level button to indent the bullet point.

6 ▶ Compare your screen with Figure 1.13, and then **Save** your presentation.

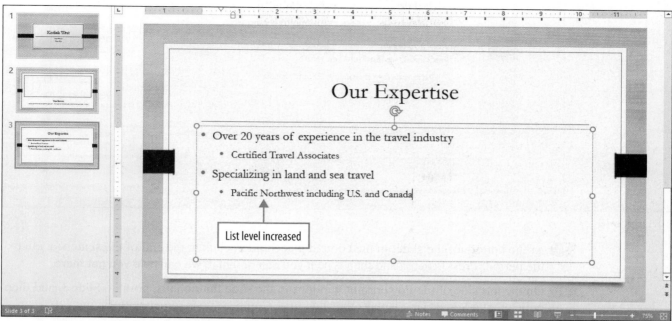

FIGURE 1.13

Activity 1.06 | Adding Speaker Notes to a Presentation

The **Notes pane** is an area of the Normal view window that displays below the Slide pane with space to type notes regarding the active slide. You can refer to these notes while making a presentation, reminding you of the important points that you want to discuss.

1 With **Slide 3** displayed, in the **Status bar**, click **Notes** 🔺, and then notice that below the Slide pane, the Notes pane displays. Click in the **Notes pane**, and then type **Kodiak West Travel has locations in Juneau, Anchorage, and Victoria.**

2 Compare your screen with Figure 1.14, and then **Save** 🖫 your presentation.

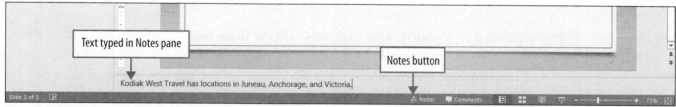

FIGURE 1.14

Activity 1.07 | Displaying and Editing Slides in the Slide Pane

1 At the left side of the PowerPoint window, look at the slide thumbnails, and then notice that the presentation contains three slides. At the right side of the PowerPoint window, in the vertical scroll bar, point to the scroll box, and then hold down the left mouse button to display a ScreenTip indicating the slide number and title.

2 Drag the scroll box up until the ScreenTip displays *Slide: 2 of 3 Your Dreams*. Compare your screen with Figure 1.15, and then release the mouse button to display **Slide 2**.

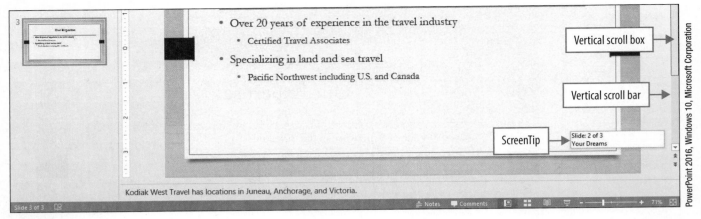

FIGURE 1.15

3 At the bottom of the slide, in the content placeholder, click at the end of the sentence, after the period. Press [Spacebar], and then type **If you can dream it, we can help you get there.**

4 On the left side of the PowerPoint window, in the slide thumbnails, point to **Slide 3**, and then notice that a ScreenTip displays the slide title. Compare your screen with Figure 1.16.

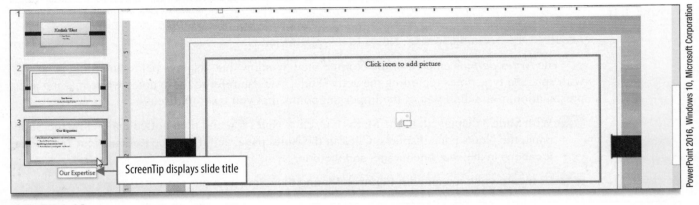

FIGURE 1.16

5 Click **Slide 3** to display it in the Slide pane. On the **Home tab**, in the **Slides group**, click the **New Slide arrow** to display the **Slide Layout** gallery, and then click **Section Header**.

A *section header* is a type of slide layout that changes the look and flow of a presentation by providing text placeholders that do not contain bullet points.

6 Click in the title placeholder, and then type **About Our Company**

7 Click in the content placeholder below the title, and then type **Kodiak West Travel was established in May of 2001 by Ken Dakona and Mariam Dorner, two Alaska residents whose sense of adventure and commitment to ecotourism is an inherent aspect of their travel itineraries.** Compare your screen with Figure 1.17.

The placeholder text is resized to fit within the placeholder. The AutoFit Options button displays.

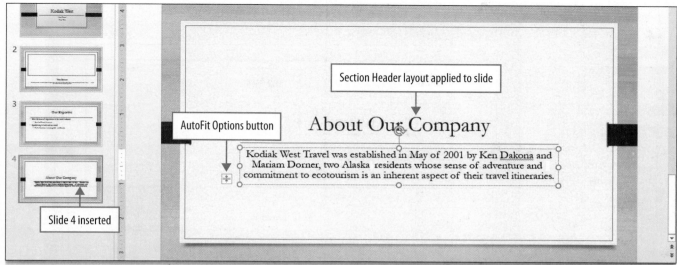

FIGURE 1.17

PowerPoint 2016, Windows 10, Microsoft Corporation

8 Click **AutoFit Options** ⊞, review the AutoFit options, and then click outside the menu to close it.

> The *AutoFit Text to Placeholder* option keeps the text contained within the placeholder by reducing the size of the text. The *Stop Fitting Text to This Placeholder* option turns off the AutoFit option so that the text can flow beyond the placeholder border; the text size remains unchanged. You can also choose to split the text between two slides, continue on a new slide, or divide the text into two columns.

9 In the slide thumbnails, click **Slide 1** to display it in the **Slide pane**, and then in the slide title, click at the end of the word *West*. Press ⟨Spacebar⟩, and then type **Travel**

> Clicking a slide thumbnail is the most common method used to display a slide in the Slide pane.

10 **Save** ⊟ your presentation.

Objective 3 Add Pictures to a Presentation

GO! Learn How
Video P1-3

Photographic images add impact to a presentation and help the audience visualize your message.

Activity 1.08 │ Inserting a Picture from a File

Many slide layouts in PowerPoint accommodate digital picture files so that you can easily add pictures you have stored. The agency has a collection of photographs to be inserted in the presentation that highlight the beauty of the region.

1 Display **Slide 2**, and then compare your screen with Figure 1.18.

> In the center of the picture placeholder, the *Pictures* button displays.

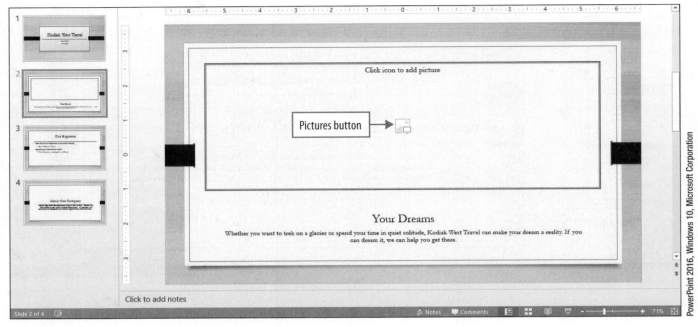

FIGURE 1.18

> **2** In the picture placeholder, click **Pictures** 🖼 to open the **Insert Picture** dialog box. Navigate to the location where your student data files are stored, click **p01A_Glacier**, and then click **Insert** to insert the picture in the placeholder. Compare your screen with Figure 1.19.
>
> > Small circles—*sizing handles*—surround the inserted picture and indicate that the picture is selected and can be modified or formatted. The *rotation handle*—a circular arrow above the picture—provides a way to rotate a selected image. The Picture Tools are added to the ribbon, providing picture formatting commands.

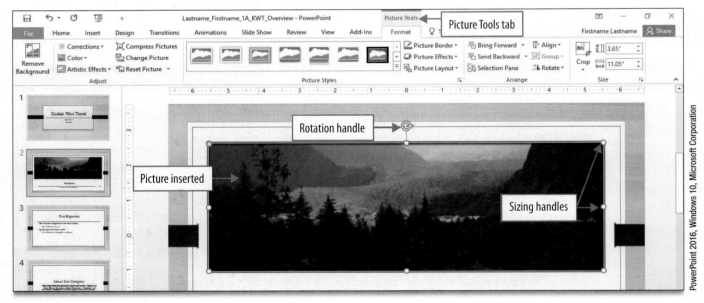

FIGURE 1.19

> **3** Display **Slide 3**. On the **Home tab**, in the **Slides group**, click the **New Slide arrow**, and then click **Title and Content**. In the title placeholder, type **Your Vacation**
>
> **4** In the content placeholder, click **Pictures** 🖼. Navigate to your student data files, and then click **p01A_Bay**. Click **Insert**, and then compare your screen with Figure 1.20. **Save** 💾 the presentation.

FIGURE 1.20

Activity 1.09 | Applying a Style to a Picture

2.3.3

When you select a picture, the Picture Tools display, adding the Format tab to the ribbon. The Format tab provides numerous styles that you can apply to your pictures. A *style* is a collection of formatting options that you can apply to a picture, text, or an object.

1 With **Slide 4** displayed, if necessary, click the picture to select it. On the ribbon, notice that the *Picture Tools* are active and the *Format* tab displays.

2 On the **Format tab**, in the **Picture Styles group**, click **More** ⮟ to display the **Picture Styles** gallery, and then compare your screen with Figure 1.21.

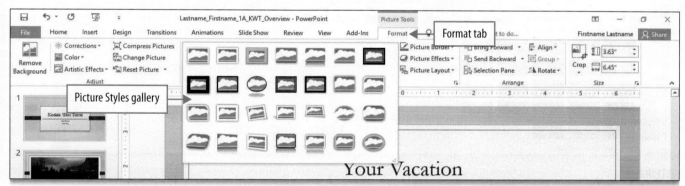

FIGURE 1.21

3 In the gallery, point to several of the picture styles to display the ScreenTips and to view the effect on your picture. In the second row, click the second style—**Simple Frame, Black**. Click in a blank area of the slide, compare your screen with Figure 1.22, and then **Save** 🔲 the presentation.

FIGURE 1.22

Activity 1.10 | Applying and Removing Picture Artistic Effects

MOS
2.3.3

Artistic effects are formats applied to images that make pictures resemble sketches or paintings.

1 On **Slide 4**, click the picture to select it. On the **Format tab**, in the **Adjust group**, click **Artistic Effects** to display the **Artistic Effects** gallery. Compare your screen with Figure 1.23.

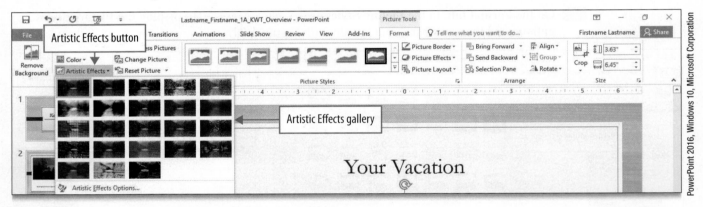

FIGURE 1.23

2 In the gallery, point to several of the artistic effects to display the ScreenTips and to have Live Preview display the effect on your picture. Then, in the second row, click the **Glow Diffused** effect.

3 With the picture still selected, on the **Format tab**, in the **Adjust group**, click **Artistic Effects** again to display the gallery. In the first row, click the first effect—**None**—to remove the effect from the picture and restore the previous formatting.

4 **Save** 🔲 the presentation.

GO! Learn How
Video P1-4

There are several print options in PowerPoint. For example, you can print full page images of your slides, presentation handouts to provide your audience with copies of your slides, or Notes pages displaying speaker notes below an image of the slide.

Activity 1.11 | Viewing a Slide Show

When you view a presentation as an electronic slide show, the entire slide fills the computer screen, and an audience can view your presentation if your computer is connected to a projection system.

1 On the ribbon, click the **Slide Show tab**. In the **Start Slide Show group**, click **From Beginning**. Compare your slide with Figure 1.24.

The first slide fills the screen, displaying the presentation as the audience would see it if your computer was connected to a projection system.

ANOTHER WAY Press F5 to start the slide show from the beginning. Or, display the first slide you want to show and click the Slide Show button on the lower right side of the status bar.

PowerPoint 2016, Windows 10, Microsoft Corporation

FIGURE 1.24

2 Click the left mouse button or press Spacebar to advance to the second slide.

3 Continue to click or press Spacebar until the last slide displays, and then click or press Spacebar one more time to display a *black slide*—a slide that displays after the last slide in a presentation indicating that the presentation is over.

> **4** With the black slide displayed, click the left mouse button to exit the slide show and return to the presentation.

↻ ANOTHER WAY   Press ⌈Esc⌋ to exit the slide show.

Activity 1.12 | Using Presenter View

Presenter View shows the full-screen slide show on one monitor or projection screen for the audience to see, while enabling the presenter to view a preview of the next slide, notes, and a timer on another monitor.

> **1** On the **Slide Show tab**, in the **Monitors** group, if necessary, select the **Use Presenter View** check box. Hold down ⌈Alt⌋ and press ⌈F5⌋. Take a moment to study the parts of the PowerPoint Presenter View window described in the table in Figure 1.25.

If you do not have two monitors, you can practice using Presenter View by pressing ⌈Alt⌋ + ⌈F5⌋. You will only see the presenter's view—not the audience view—in this mode.

MICROSOFT POWERPOINT PRESENTER VIEW ELEMENTS	
SCREEN ELEMENT	**DESCRIPTION**
`0:00:00 ‖ ↺`	**Timer:** running time, pause timer, and reset timer options
✏	**Pen and laser pointer tools:** point to or annotate slides during a presentation
▦	**See all slides:** display all slides on the screen to easily navigate between them
🔍	**Zoom into the slide:** focus on a part of a slide while presenting
▧	**Black or unblack slide show:** hide or unhide the presentation
⊙	**More slide show options:** including hide presenter view, help, pause, and end show
◀ and ▶	**Navigation buttons:** move back and forth through the presentation
SHOW TASKBAR DISPLAY SETTINGS ▼ END SLIDE SHOW	**Presenter View ribbon:** control slide presentation display options
A˄ or A˅	**Notes pane text size adjustment:** make notes text larger or smaller

FIGURE 1.25

PowerPoint 2016, Windows 10, Microsoft Corporation

> **2** Below the current slide, click the **Advance to the next slide arrow** ⊙ to display **Slide 2**.

↻ BY TOUCH   Advance to the next slide by swiping the current slide to the left.

> **3** In the upper right corner of the **Presenter View** window, point to the next slide—*Our Expertise*—and then click. Notice that the notes that you typed on **Slide 3** display. Compare your screen with Figure 1.26.

Clicking the image of the next slide advances the presentation.

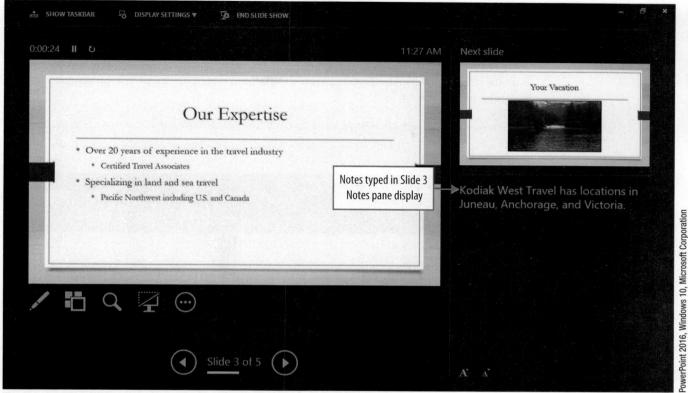

FIGURE 1.26

4 Below the notes, click **Make the text larger** ▲ to increase the font size of the notes in Presenter view to make the notes easier to read.

5 Below the current slide, click the second button—**See all slides** ▦. Compare your screen with Figure 1.27.

> A thumbnail view of all of the slides in your presentation displays. Here you can quickly move to another slide, if, for example, you want to review a concept or answer a question related to a slide other than the current slide.

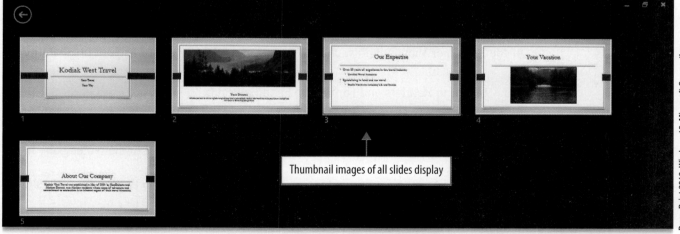

FIGURE 1.27

> **6** ▸ Click **Slide 4** to make Slide 4 the current slide in Presenter View. Below the current slide, click the third button—**Zoom into the slide** 🔍. Move the 🔍 pointer to the middle of the picture on the current slide, and then click to zoom in on the picture. Notice that the ✋ pointer displays. Compare your slide with Figure 1.28.
>
> With the ✋ pointer displayed, you can move the zoomed image to draw close-up attention to a particular part of your slide.

🔄 **BY TOUCH**   Touch the current slide with two fingers and then pinch together to zoom out or stretch your fingers apart to zoom in.

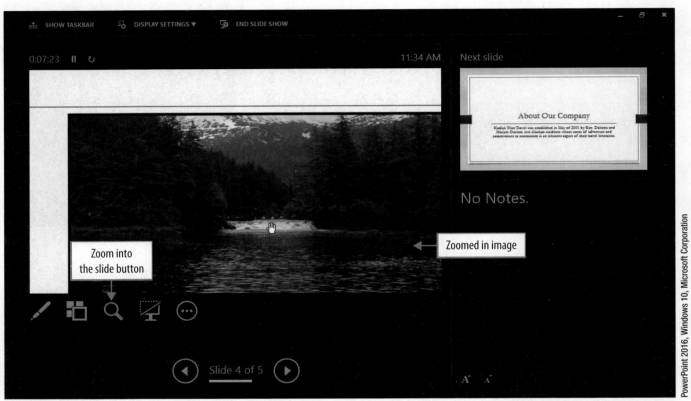

FIGURE 1.28

> **7** ▸ Below the current slide, click the **Advance to the next slide arrow** 🔘 to display **Slide 5.** At the top of the Presenter View window, click **END SLIDE SHOW** to return to your presentation.

Activity 1.13 │ Inserting Headers and Footers on Slide Handouts

1.2.7

A *header* is text that prints at the top of each sheet of *slide handouts* or *notes pages*. Slide handouts are printed images of slides on a sheet of paper. Notes pages are printouts that contain the slide image on the top half of the page and notes that you have created in the Notes pane in the lower half of the page.

In addition to headers, you can insert *footers*—text that displays at the bottom of every slide or that prints at the bottom of a sheet of slide handouts or notes pages.

> **1** ▸ Click the **Insert tab**, and then in the **Text group**, click **Header & Footer** to display the **Header and Footer** dialog box.

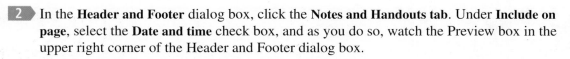

2 In the **Header and Footer** dialog box, click the **Notes and Handouts tab**. Under **Include on page**, select the **Date and time** check box, and as you do so, watch the Preview box in the upper right corner of the Header and Footer dialog box.

The two narrow rectangular boxes at the top of the Preview box are placeholders for the header text and date. When you select the Date and time check box, the placeholder in the upper right corner is outlined, indicating the location in which the date will display.

3 Be sure that the **Update automatically** option button is selected so that the current date prints on the notes and handouts each time the presentation is printed. If it is not selected, click the Update automatically option button.

4 Verify that the **Page number** check box is selected and select it if it is not. If necessary, clear the Header check box to omit this element. Notice that in the **Preview** box, the corresponding placeholder is not selected.

5 Select the **Footer** check box, and then click in the **Footer** box. Using your own name, type **Lastname_Firstname_1A_KWT_Overview** so that the file name displays as a footer, and then compare your dialog box with Figure 1.29.

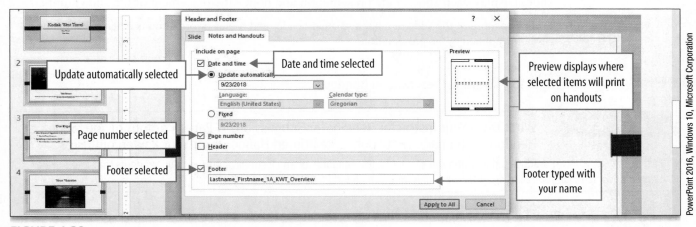

FIGURE 1.29

6 In the lower right corner of the dialog box, click **Apply to All**. Save 🖫 your presentation.

Activity 1.14 │ Inserting Slide Numbers on Slides

MOS

1.2.7

In this Activity, you will insert the slide numbers on the presentation slides.

1 Display **Slide 1**. On the **Insert tab**, in the **Text group**, click **Header & Footer** to display the **Header and Footer** dialog box.

2 In the **Header and Footer** dialog box, if necessary, click the Slide tab. Under **Include on slide**, select the **Slide number** check box, and then select the **Don't show on title slide** check box. Verify that all other check boxes are cleared, and then compare your screen with Figure 1.30.

Selecting the *Don't show on title slide* check box omits the slide number from the first slide in a presentation.

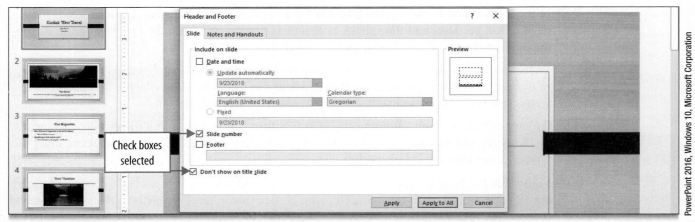

PowerPoint 2016, Windows 10, Microsoft Corporation

FIGURE 1.30

> **3** ▸ Click **Apply to All**, and then notice that on the first slide, the slide number does not display.

> **4** ▸ Display **Slide 2**, and then notice that the slide number displays in the lower right area of the slide. Display each slide in the presentation and notice the placement of the slide number.
>
> The position of the slide number and other header and footer information is determined by the theme applied to the presentation.

Activity 1.15 | Printing Presentation Handouts

NOTE	What Does Your Instructor Require for Submission? A Paper Printout of Your Slide Handouts, an Image That Looks Like Printed Handouts, or Your PowerPoint File?

In this Activity, you can produce a paper printout of your Slides Handouts or an electronic image of your handouts that looks like a printed document. Or, your instructor may want only your completed PowerPoint file.

1.6.3, 1.5.3, 1.6.4

Use Backstage view to preview the arrangement of slides and to print your presentation.

> **1** ▸ Display **Slide 1**. Click the **File tab** to display **Backstage** view, and then click **Print**.
>
> The Print tab in Backstage view displays the tools you need to select your settings and also to view a preview of your presentation. On the right, Print Preview displays your presentation exactly as it will print. If your system is not connected to a color printer, your slide may display in black and white.

> **2** ▸ Under **Settings**, click **Full Page Slides**, and then compare your screen with Figure 1.31.
>
> The gallery displays either the default print setting—Full Page Slides—or the most recently selected print setting. This button might indicate the presentation Notes Pages, Outline, or one of several arrangements of slide handouts—depending on the most recently used setting.

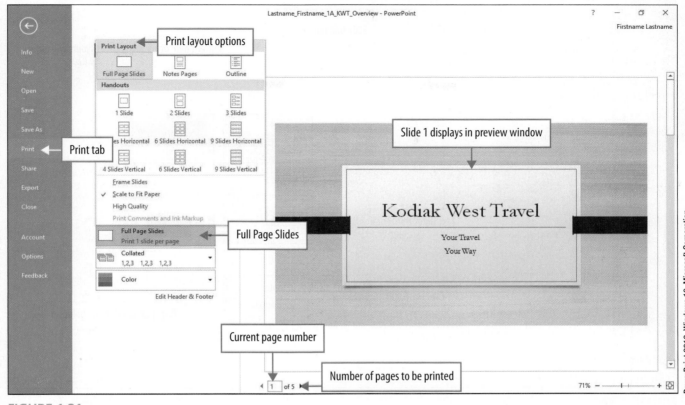

FIGURE 1.31

3 ▶ In the gallery, under **Handouts**, click **6 Slides Horizontal**. Notice that the **Print Preview** on the right displays the slide handout, and that the current date, file name, and page number display in the header and footer. Compare your screen with Figure 1.32.

In the Settings group, the Portrait Orientation option displays; here you can change the print orientation from Portrait to Landscape. The Portrait Orientation option does not display when Full Page Slides is chosen.

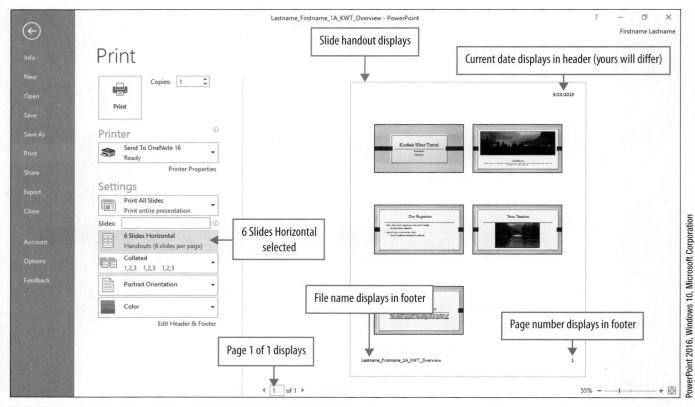

FIGURE 1.32

4 To create an electronic image of your handouts that looks like printed handouts, skip this step and continue to Step 5. To print your handout document on paper using the default printer on your system, in the upper left portion of the screen, click **Print**.

> The handout will print on your default printer—on a black and white printer, the colors will print in shades of gray. To save the cost of color ink, you can print in grayscale by clicking the Color button. Backstage view closes and your file redisplays in the PowerPoint window.

5 To create an electronic image of your document that looks like a printed document, on the left click **Export**. On the right, click the **Create PDF/XPS** button to display the **Publish as PDF or XPS** dialog box.

6 In the **Publish as PDF or XPS** dialog box, click **Options**. Under **Publish what**, click the **Slides arrow**, and then click **Handouts**. Be sure **Slides per page** is set to **6**, and **Order** is set to **Horizontal**. Click **OK**.

ANOTHER WAY Under Printer, click the printer arrow, click Print as a PDF, and then click Print to print your presentation to a PDF file. Microsoft Print to PDF is an automatically installed printer option in Windows 10, which enables you to create an image that looks like a printed document.

7 Navigate to your **PowerPoint Chapter 1** folder, and then click **Publish**. If your Adobe Acrobat or Reader program displays your PDF, close the PDF file. If your PDF displays in Microsoft Edge (on a Windows 10 computer), in the upper right corner click Close ⊠. Notice that your presentation redisplays in PowerPoint.

Activity 1.16 | **Printing Speaker Notes**

1.6.2

1 On the **File tab**, click **Print**. Under **Settings**, click **6 Slides Horizontal**, and then under **Print Layout**, click **Notes Pages** to view the presentation notes for **Slide 1**; recall that you created notes for **Slide 3**.

> Indicated below the Notes page are the current slide number and the number of pages that will print when Notes Pages is selected. You can use the Next Page and Previous Page arrows to display each Notes page in the presentation.

2 At the bottom of the **Print Preview**, click **Next Page** ▶ two times so that **Page 3** displays. Notice that the notes that you typed for Slide 3 display below the image of the slide. Compare your screen with Figure 1.33.

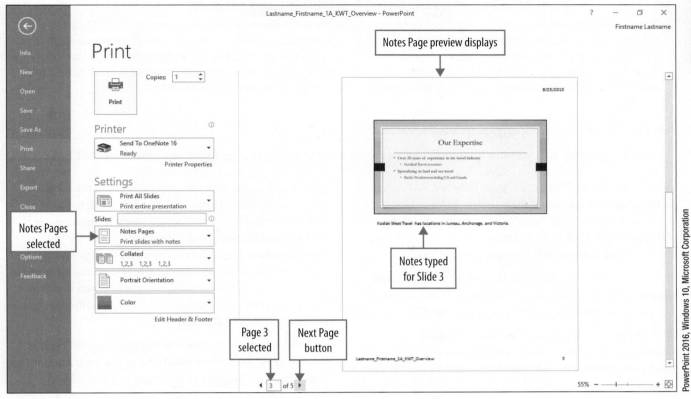

FIGURE 1.33

3 Under **Settings**, click in the **Slides box**. Type **3** and then click **Notes Pages**. In the lower section, click **Frame Slides**. Under **Printer**, click the printer arrow, click **Print as a PDF**, and then click **Print** to print your presentation to a PDF file.

> Microsoft Print to PDF is an automatically installed printer option in Windows 10, which enables you to create an image that looks like a printed document.

ALERT! **No Print as a PDF Printer Option Available**

If you are using Windows 7 or 8, select the Microsoft XPS Document Writer printer instead to print your presentation to the XPS format, a Microsoft file format that also creates an image of your document and that opens in the XPS viewer.

---

4 Navigate to the location where you store your files for this chapter, name the file **Lastname_ Firstname_1A_KWT_Overview_Notes**, and then click **Save**.

5 Redisplay **Backstage** view. On the right, at the bottom of the **Properties** list, click **Show All Properties**. On the list of **Properties**, click to the right of **Tags**, and then type **company overview**

6 Click to the right of **Subject**, and then type your course name and section number. Under **Related People**, be sure that your name displays as the author, and edit if necessary.

7 Click **Save**. On the right end of the title bar, click **Close** ✕ to close the presentation and close PowerPoint.

END | You have completed Project 1A

GO! With Google

Objective | Create a Company Overview Presentation in Google Slides

> **ALERT!** **Working with Web-Based Applications and Services**
>
> Computer programs and services on the web receive continuous updates and improvements, so the steps to complete this web-based activity may differ from the ones shown. You can often look at the screens and the information presented to determine how to complete the activity.
>
> If you do not already have a Google account, you will need to create one before you begin this activity. Go to http://google.com and in the upper right corner, click Sign In. On the Sign In screen, click Create Account. On the Create your Google Account page, complete the form, read and agree to the Terms of Service and Privacy Policy, and then click Next step. On the Welcome screen, click Get Started.

Activity | Creating a Company Overview Presentation in Google Slides

In this Activity, you will use Google Slides to create a presentation similar to the one you created in Project 1A.

1 From the desktop, open your browser, navigate to **http://google.com**, and then sign in to your Google account. Click **Google Apps** ⊞, and then click **Drive** ☁. Open your **GO! Web Projects** folder—or click New to create and then open this folder if necessary.

2 In the left pane, click **NEW**, and then click **Google Slides**. In the **Themes** pane, click **Tropic**. If this theme is not available, select another theme. **Close** the **Themes** pane.

3 At the top of the window, click **Untitled presentation** and then, using your own name, type **Lastname_Firstname_1A_Web** as the file name and then press Enter.

4 In the title placeholder, type **Kodiak West Travel** and then in the subtitle placeholder type **Your Travel - Your Way**

5 On the **toolbar**, click the **New slide arrow** ➕, and then click **Caption**.

6 On the **toolbar**, click **Image** 🖼. In the **Insert image** dialog box, click **Choose an image to upload**. Navigate to your student data files, and then click **p01_1A_Web_ Glacier**. Click **Open**.

7 Type **Your Dreams** in the text placeholder.

8 On the **toolbar**, click the **New slide arrow** ➕, and then click **Title and body**. Type **Our Expertise** in the title placeholder.

9 Click in the content placeholder. On the toolbar, if necessary, click **More** More▾, click **Bulleted list** ☰. In the placeholder, type **Over 20 years of experience in the travel industry** and then press Enter. Press Tab. Type **Certified Travel Associates** and then press Enter. On toolbar, if necessary, click More, and then click **Decrease indent** ☰. Type **Specializing in land and sea travel** and then press Enter. Press Tab and then type **Pacific Northwest including U.S. and Canada**

10 Below the slide, click in the Notes pane. Type **Kodiak West Travel has locations in Juneau, Anchorage, and Victoria.** Compare your screen to Figure A.

11 In the upper right, click the **Present arrow**, click **Present from beginning**. Click the left mouse button to progress through the presentation. When the last slide displays, press Esc or click **Exit**.

12 Your presentation will be saved automatically. If you are instructed to submit your file, click the File menu, point to Download as, and then click Microsoft PowerPoint, PDF Document, or another format as directed by your instructor. The file will download to your default download folder as determined by your browser settings. Sign out of your Google account and close your browser.

(GO! With Google continues on the next page)

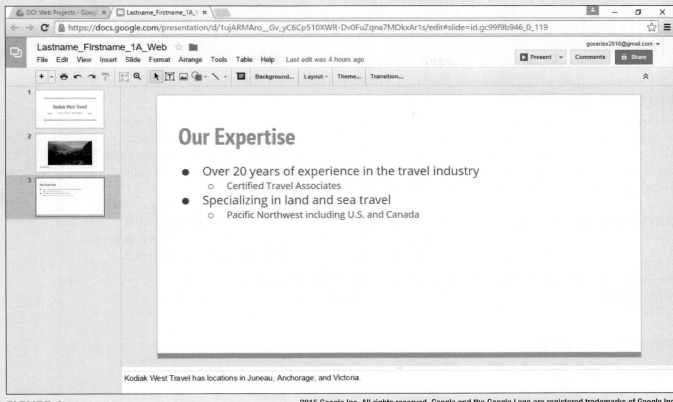

FIGURE A

Itinerary Presentation

PROJECT ACTIVITIES

In Activities 1.17 through 1.33, you will combine two presentations that the marketing team at Kodiak West Travel developed describing itinerary ideas when visiting Seattle before or after a cruise. You will insert slides from one presentation into another, and then you will rearrange and delete slides. You will also apply font formatting and slide transitions to the presentation. Your completed presentation will look similar to Figure 1.34.

Please always review the downloaded Grader instructions before beginning.

 ## PROJECT FILES

 If your instructor wants you to submit Project 1B in the MyITLab Grader system, log in to MyITLab, locate Grader Project 1B, and then download the files for this project.

For Project 1B, you will need the following files:

p01B_Seattle
p01B_Slides

You will save your presentation as:

Lastname_Firstname_1B_Seattle

 ## PROJECT RESULTS

GO!
Walk Thru
Project 1B

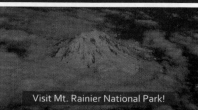

PowerPoint 2016, Windows 10, Microsoft Corporation

FIGURE 1.34 Project 1B Seattle

GO! Learn How
Video P1-5

MOS
1.5.1

Recall that editing refers to the process of adding, deleting, and modifying presentation content. You can edit presentation content in either the Slide pane or in the presentation outline.

Activity 1.17 | Changing Slide Size

ALERT! **To submit as an autograded project, log into MyITLab, download the files for this project, and begin with these files instead of the student data files.**

Presentations created with one of the new themes in PowerPoint 2016 default to a widescreen format using a 16:9 *aspect ratio*—the ratio of the width of a display to the height of the display. This slide size is similar to most television and computer monitor screens. PowerPoint 2010 and earlier versions of PowerPoint used a squarer format with a 4:3 aspect ratio. The widescreen format utilizes screen space more effectively.

1 Start PowerPoint. On the left, under the list of recent presentations, click **Open Other Presentations**. Under **Open**, click **Browse**. In the **Open** dialog box, navigate to your student data files, and then click **p01B_Seattle**. Click **Open**. On the **File tab**, click **Save As**, navigate to your **PowerPoint Chapter 1** folder, and then using your own name, save the file as **Lastname_Firstname_1B_Seattle**

2 Notice that **Slide 1** displays in a square format.

3 On the **Design tab**, in the **Customize group**, click **Slide Size**, and then click **Widescreen (16:9)**. Compare your screen with Figure 1.35, and notice that the slide fills the slide pane. **Save** 🖫 the presentation.

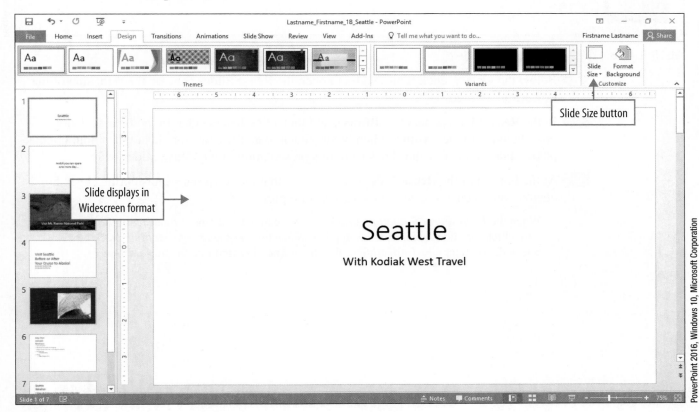

FIGURE 1.35

Activity 1.18 | Inserting Slides from an Existing Presentation

5.1.1

Presentation content is commonly shared among group members in an organization. Rather than re-creating slides, you can insert slides from an existing presentation into the current presentation. In this Activity, you will insert slides from an existing presentation into your 1B_Seattle presentation.

1 With **Slide 1** displayed, on the **Home tab**, in the **Slides group**, click the **New Slide arrow** to display the **Slide Layout** gallery and additional commands for inserting slides. Compare your screen with Figure 1.36.

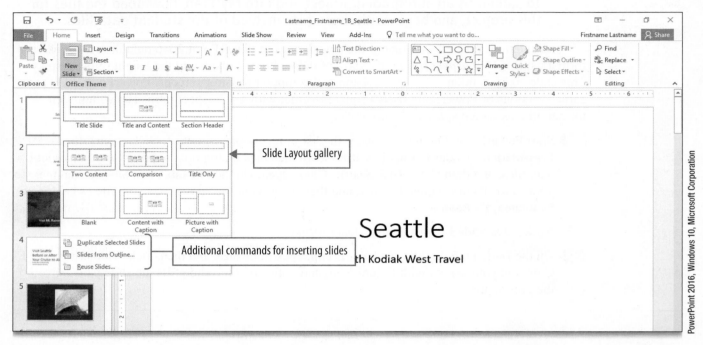

FIGURE 1.36

2 Below the gallery, click **Reuse Slides** to open the Reuse Slides pane on the right side of the PowerPoint window.

3 In the **Reuse Slides** pane, click **Browse**, and then click **Browse File**. In the **Browse** dialog box, navigate to the location where your student data files are stored, and then double-click **p01B_Slides** to display the slides from this presentation in the Reuse Slides pane.

4 At the bottom of the **Reuse Slides** pane, be sure that the **Keep source formatting** check box is *cleared*, and then compare your screen with Figure 1.37.

When the *Keep source formatting* check box is cleared, the theme formatting of the presentation into which the slides are inserted is applied. When the *Keep source formatting* check box is selected, you retain the formatting of the slides when inserted into the presentation.

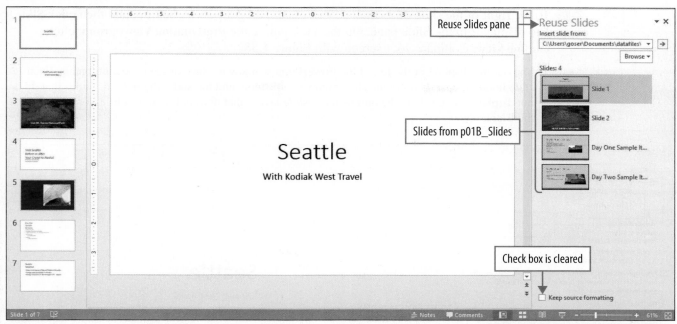

FIGURE 1.37

PowerPoint 2016, Windows 10, Microsoft Corporation

5 ▶ In the **Reuse Slides** pane, point to each slide to view a ScreenTip displaying the file name and the slide title.

6 ▶ In the **Reuse Slides** pane, click the first slide to insert the slide after **Slide 1** in your Seattle presentation. Notice that the inserted slide adopts the color of your Seattle presentation theme.

NOTE Inserting Slides

You can insert slides into your presentation in any order; remember to display the slide that will come before the slide that you want to insert.

---

7 ▶ In your **1B_Seattle** presentation, in the slide thumbnails, click **Slide 7** to display it in the **Slide pane**.

8 ▶ In the **Reuse Slides** pane, click the fourth slide to insert it after **Slide 7**.

Your presentation contains nine slides. When a presentation contains a large number of slides, a scroll box displays to the right of the slide thumbnails so that you can scroll and then select the thumbnails.

9 ▶ **Close** ✕ the **Reuse Slides** pane, and then **Save** 🖫 the presentation.

More **Knowledge** **Inserting All Slides**

You can insert all of the slides from an existing presentation into the current presentation at one time. In the Reuse Slides pane, right-click one of the slides that you want to insert, and then click Insert All Slides.

Activity 1.19 | Displaying and Editing the Presentation Outline

Outline View displays the presentation outline to the left of the Slide pane. You can use the outline to edit the presentation text. Changes that you make in the outline are immediately displayed in the Slide pane.

1 To the right of the slide thumbnails, if necessary, drag the scroll box up, and then click **Slide 1** to display it in the Slide pane. On the **View tab**, in the **Presentation Views group**, click **Outline View**. Compare your screen with Figure 1.38.

The outline displays at the left of the PowerPoint window in place of the slide thumbnails. Each slide in the outline displays the slide number, slide icon, and the slide title in bold. Slides that do not display a slide title in the outline use a slide layout that does not include a title, for example, the Blank layout.

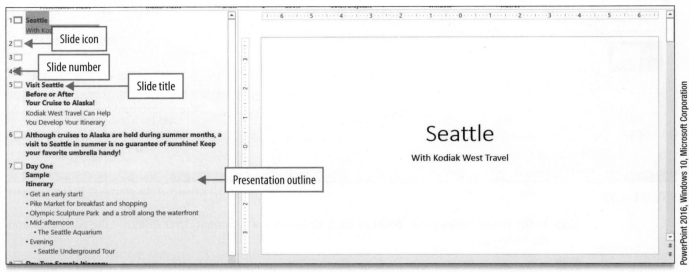

FIGURE 1.38

2 In the **Outline**, in **Slide 7**, drag to select the text of the second and third bullet points—*Pike Market for breakfast and shopping*, and *Olympic Sculpture Park and a stroll along the waterfront*. Compare your screen with Figure 1.39.

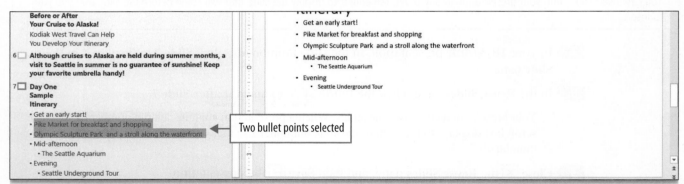

FIGURE 1.39   PowerPoint 2016, Windows 10, Microsoft Corporation

3 On the **Home tab**, in the **Paragraph group**, click **Increase List Level** 📑 one time to increase the list level of the selected bullet points.

When you type in the outline or change the list level, the changes also display in the Slide pane.

4 In the **Outline**, in **Slide 7**, click at the end of the last bullet point after the word *Tour*. Press Enter to create a new bullet point at the same list level as the previous bullet point. Type **Pike Place Market for dinner** and then compare your screen with Figure 1.40.

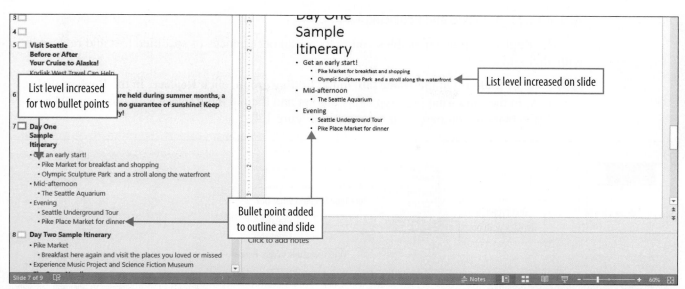

FIGURE 1.40

5 ▶ In the **Status bar**, click **Normal** 🖼 to close Outline View and redisplay the slide thumbnails. **Save** 🖫 the presentation.

> You can type text in the Slide pane or in the Outline. Displaying the Outline enables you to view the entire flow of the presentation text.

MOS
1.2.4

Activity 1.20 | Deleting and Moving a Slide

1 ▶ To the right of the slide thumbnails, locate the vertical scroll bar and scroll box. If necessary, drag the scroll box down so that **Slide 9** displays in the slide thumbnails. Click **Slide 9** to display it in the Slide pane. Press [Delete] to delete the slide from the presentation.

> Your presentation contains eight slides.

2 ▶ If necessary, scroll the slide thumbnails so that **Slide 4** displays. Point to **Slide 4**, hold down the left mouse button, and then drag down to position the **Slide 4** thumbnail below the **Slide 8** thumbnail. Release the mouse button, and then compare your screen with Figure 1.41. **Save** 🖫 the presentation.

> You can easily rearrange your slides by dragging a slide thumbnail to a new location in the presentation.

🔄 **BY TOUCH**   Use your finger to drag the slide you want to move to a new location in the presentation.

FIGURE 1.41

Activity 1.21 | Finding and Replacing Text

The Replace command enables you to locate all occurrences of specified text and replace it with alternative text.

1 Display **Slide 1**. On the **Home tab**, in the **Editing group**, click **Replace**. In the **Replace** dialog box, in the **Find what** box, type **Pike Market** and then in the **Replace with** box, type **Pike Place Market** Compare your screen with Figure 1.42.

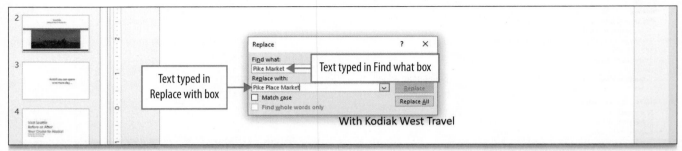

PowerPoint 2016, Windows 10, Microsoft Corporation

FIGURE 1.42

2 In the **Replace** dialog box, click **Replace All** to display a message box indicating that two replacements were made.

3 In the message box, click **OK**. **Close** the **Replace** dialog box, and then click **Save** 🖫.

Objective 6 | Format a Presentation

GO! Learn How
Video P1-6

Formatting refers to changing the appearance of the text, layout, and design of a slide.

Activity 1.22 | Applying a Theme Variant

Recall that a theme is a set of unified design elements that provides a look for your presentation by applying colors, fonts, and effects. Each PowerPoint theme includes several *variants*—variations on the theme style and color. The themes and variants that are available on your system may vary.

1 On the **Design tab**, in the **Variants group**, notice that four variants of the current theme display and the second variant is applied.

2 Point to each of the variants to view the change to **Slide 1**.

If you do not see the same variants, refer to the figures for this activity.

3 With **Slide 1** displayed, in the **Variants group**, point to the **third variant**, and then right-click. Compare your screen with Figure 1.43.

The shortcut menu displays options for applying the variant.

PowerPoint 2016, Windows 10, Microsoft Corporation

FIGURE 1.43

4 Click **Apply to Selected Slides** to apply the variant to **Slide 1** only.

5 In the **Variants group**, right-click the **second variant**. On the shortcut menu, click **Apply to All Slides** so that the original variant color is applied to all of the slides in the presentation. Compare your screen with Figure 1.44. **Save** 🔲 your presentation.

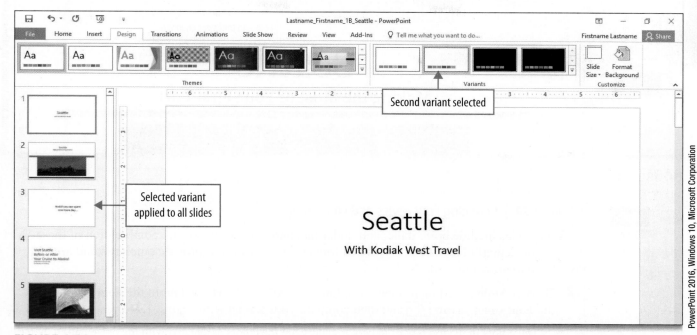

FIGURE 1.44

🔄 **ANOTHER WAY**   Click Undo to remove the variant you applied in step 4.

MOS
2.1.2

Activity 1.23 | Changing Fonts and Font Sizes

A font is a set of characters with the same design and shape, and fonts are measured in points. Font styles include bold, italic, and underline, and you can apply any combination of these styles to presentation text. Font styles and font color are useful to provide emphasis and are a visual cue to draw the reader's eye to important text.

1 Display **Slide 2**. Select all of the text in the title placeholder, point to the mini toolbar, and then click the **Font arrow** to display the available fonts. Scroll the font list, and then click **Georgia**.

2 Select the first line of the title—*Seattle*. On the mini toolbar, click the **Font Size arrow** and then click **80**.

3 Select the second line of the title—*Making the Most of Your First Port*. On the **Home tab**, in the **Font group**, click the **Font Size arrow**, and then click **36**. Click in a blank area of the slide to cancel your selection, and then compare your screen with Figure 1.45. **Save** 🔲 your presentation.

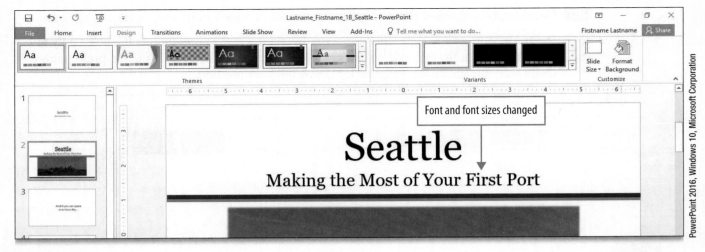

FIGURE 1.45

 Activity 1.24 | Changing Font Styles and Font Colors

2.1.2

Font styles include bold, italic, and underline, and you can apply any combination of these styles to presentation text. Font styles and font color are useful to provide emphasis and are a visual cue to draw the reader's eye to important text.

1 Display **Slide 3**, and then select both lines of text. On the **Home tab**, in the **Font group**, click the **Font Color arrow** [A ▾] and then compare your screen with Figure 1.46.

The colors in the top row of the color gallery are the colors associated with the presentation theme. The colors in the rows below the first row are light and dark variations of the theme colors.

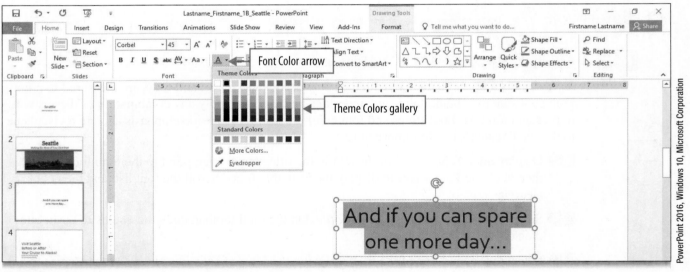

FIGURE 1.46

2 Point to several of the colors and notice that a ScreenTip displays the color name and Live Preview displays the selected text in the color to which you are pointing.

3 In the fifth column of colors, click the last color—**Dark Green, Accent 1, Darker 50%**—to change the font color. Notice that on the **Home tab**, the lower part of the **Font Color** button displays the most recently applied font color— *Dark Green, Accent 1, Darker 50%*.

> When you click the Font Color button instead of the Font Color button arrow, the color displayed in the lower part of the Font Color button is applied to selected text without displaying the color gallery.

4 With the two lines of text still selected, right-click within the selected text to redisplay the mini toolbar, and then from the mini toolbar, apply **Bold** and **Italic**.

5 Display **Slide 4**, and then select the title—*Visit Seattle Before or After Your Cruise to Alaska!* On the mini toolbar, click **Font Color** 🅰 ⋅ to apply the font color **Dark Green, Accent 1, Darker 50%** to the selection. Select the subtitle—*Kodiak West Travel Can Help You Develop Your Itinerary*—and then change the **Font Color** to **Dark Green, Accent 1, Darker 50%**. Click anywhere on the slide to cancel the selection, and then compare your screen with Figure 1.47. **Save** 🖫 your presentation.

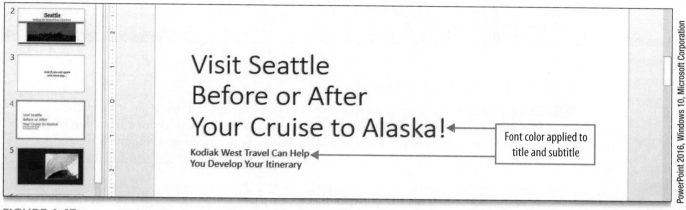

PowerPoint 2016, Windows 10, Microsoft Corporation

FIGURE 1.47

Activity 1.25 | Aligning Text

In PowerPoint, *text alignment* refers to the horizontal placement of text within a placeholder. You can align text left, centered, right, or justified.

1 Display **Slide 5**, and then, click anywhere in the paragraph. On the **Home tab**, in the **Paragraph group**, click **Center** ☰ to center the text within the placeholder.

2 Display **Slide 4**, and then click anywhere in the slide title. Press Ctrl + E to use the keyboard shortcut to center the text.

3 On **Slide 4**, using one of the methods that you practiced, **Center** the subtitle. Click in a blank area of the slide. Compare your screen with Figure 1.48 and then **Save** 🖫 the presentation.

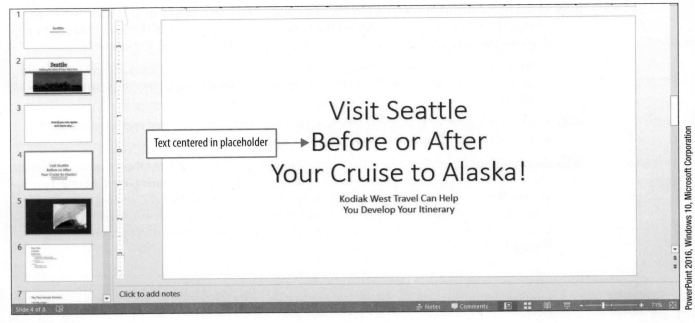

FIGURE 1.48

Activity 1.26 | Changing Line Spacing

1 Display **Slide 5**, and then click anywhere in the paragraph. On the **Home tab**, in the **Paragraph group**, click **Line Spacing**. In the list, click **2.0** to change from single spacing to double spacing between lines of text. Compare your screen with Figure 1.49.

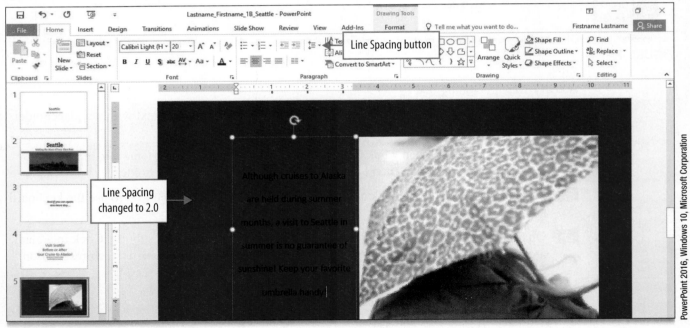

FIGURE 1.49

2 **Save** your presentation.

Activity 1.27 | Changing the Slide Layout

1.2.5

The slide layout defines the placement of the content placeholders on a slide. PowerPoint includes predefined layouts that you can apply to your slide for the purpose of arranging slide elements. For example, a Title Slide contains two placeholder elements—the title and the subtitle. When you design your slides, consider the content that you want to include, and then choose a layout with the elements that will display the message you want to convey in the best way.

1 Display **Slide 1**. On the **Home tab**, in the **Slides group**, click **Layout** to display the **Slide Layout** gallery. Notice that *Title Slide* is selected, indicating the layout of the current slide.

2 Click **Section Header** to change the slide layout. Compare your screen with Figure 1.50, and then **Save** 🖫 your presentation.

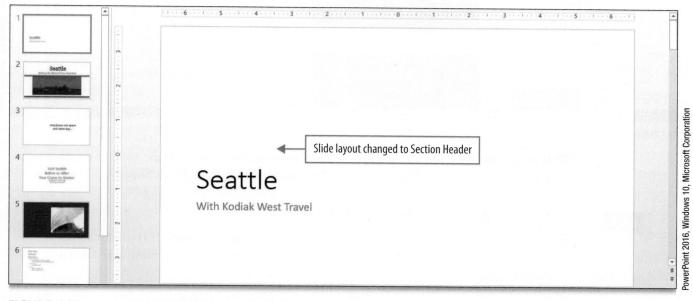

> Slide layout changed to Section Header

FIGURE 1.50

PowerPoint 2016, Windows 10, Microsoft Corporation

Objective 7 Use Slide Sorter View

GO! Learn How
Video P1-7

Slide Sorter view displays thumbnails of all of the slides in a presentation. Use Slide Sorter view to rearrange and delete slides and to apply formatting to multiple slides.

1.2.4, 1.5.2

Activity 1.28 | Deleting Slides in Slide Sorter View

1 In the lower right corner of the PowerPoint window, click **Slide Sorter** ⊞ to display all of the slide thumbnails. Compare your screen with Figure 1.51.

Your slides may display larger or smaller than those shown in Figure 1.51.

🔄 **ANOTHER WAY**   On the View tab, in the Presentation Views group, click Slide Sorter.

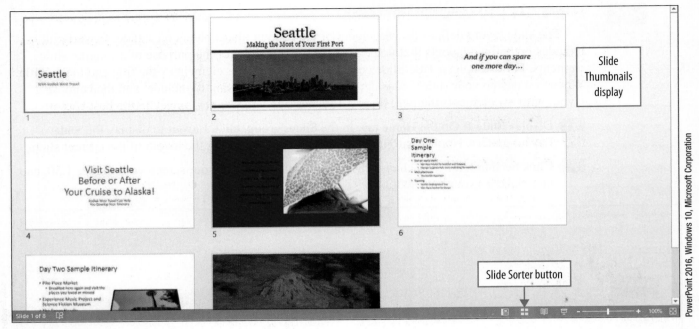

FIGURE 1.51

PowerPoint 2016, Windows 10, Microsoft Corporation

2 If necessary, click **Slide 1**, and notice that a thick outline surrounds the slide, indicating that it is selected. On your keyboard, press Delete to delete the slide. Click **Save** 🖫.

MOS
1.4.2

Activity 1.29 | Moving a Single Slide in Slide Sorter View

1 With the presentation displayed in Slide Sorter view, point to **Slide 2**. Hold down the left mouse button, and then drag to position the slide to the right of **Slide 6**, as shown in Figure 1.52.

FIGURE 1.52

PowerPoint 2016, Windows 10, Microsoft Corporation

2 Release the mouse button to move the slide to the **Slide 6** position in the presentation. **Save** 🖫 your presentation.

Activity 1.30 | Selecting Contiguous and Noncontiguous Slides and Moving Multiple Slides

Contiguous slides are slides that are adjacent to each other in a presentation. *Noncontiguous slides* are slides that are not adjacent to each other in a presentation.

1 Click **Slide 2**, hold down Ctrl, click **Slide 4**, release Ctrl. Notice that both slides are selected.

The noncontiguous slides—Slides 2 and 4—are outlined, indicating that both are selected. By holding down Ctrl, you can select noncontiguous slides.

2 Click **Slide 3**, so that only Slide 3 is selected. Hold down Shift, click **Slide 5**, and then release Shift. Compare your screen with Figure 1.53.

The contiguous slides—Slides 3, 4, and 5—are outlined, indicating that all three slides are selected. By holding down Shift, you can create a group of contiguous selected slides.

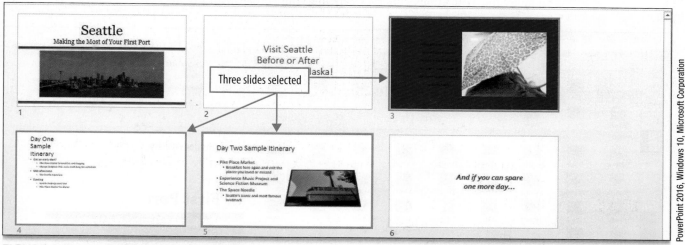

FIGURE 1.53

3 With **Slides 3, 4,** and **5** selected, hold down Ctrl, and then click **Slide 3**. Notice that only **Slides 4** and **5** are selected.

With a group of selected slides, you can press Ctrl and then click a selected slide to *deselect* it.

4 Point to either of the selected slides, hold down the left mouse button, and then drag to position the two slides to the right of **Slide 2**. Compare your screen with Figure 1.54.

The selected slides are dragged as a group, and the number 2 in the upper left area of the selected slides indicates the number of slides that you are moving.

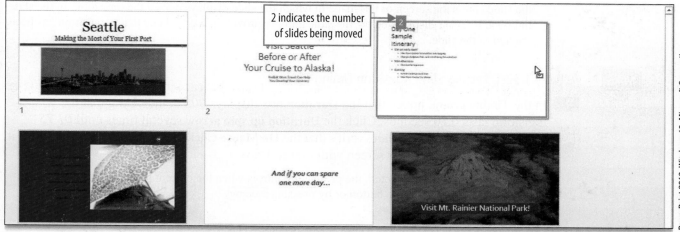

FIGURE 1.54

5 In the status bar, click **Normal** 📧 to return to Normal view. **Save** 🖫 your presentation.

Objective 8 | Apply Slide Transitions

GO! Learn How
Video P1-8

Slide transitions are the motion effects that occur in Slide Show view when you move from one slide to the next during a presentation. You can choose from a variety of transitions, and you can control the speed and method with which the slides advance.

Activity 1.31 | Applying Slide Transitions to a Presentation

4.1.1

1 Display **Slide 1**. On the **Transitions tab**, in the **Transition to This Slide group**, click **More** ⏷ to display the **Transitions** gallery. Compare your screen with Figure 1.55.

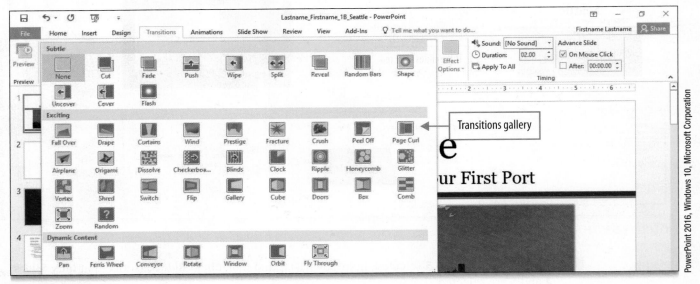

FIGURE 1.55

2 Under **Subtle**, click **Fade** to apply and view the transition. In the **Transition to This Slide group**, click **Effect Options** to display the way the slide enters the screen. Click **Smoothly**. In the **Timing group**, click **Apply To All** to apply the *Fade*, *Smoothly* transition to all of the slides in the presentation. **Save** 🖫 your presentation.

The Effect Options vary depending on the selected transition and include the direction from which the slide enters the screen or the shape in which the slide displays during the transition. In the slide thumbnails, a star displays below the slide number providing a visual cue that a transition has been applied to the slide.

Activity 1.32 | Setting Slide Transition Timing Options

4.1.2

1 In the **Timing group**, notice that the **Duration** box displays *00.70*, indicating that the transition lasts 0.70 seconds. Click the **Duration up spin arrow** several times until *01.75* displays. Under **Advance Slide**, verify that the **On Mouse Click** check box is selected; select it if necessary. Compare your screen with Figure 1.56.

With On Mouse Click selected, the presenter controls when the current slide advances to the next slide by clicking the mouse button or by pressing Spacebar.

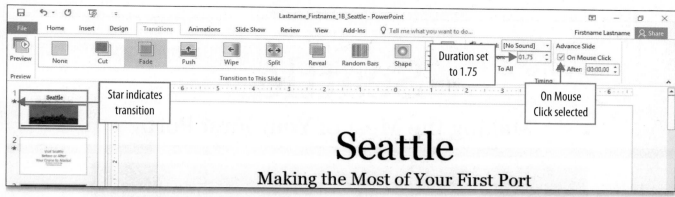

FIGURE 1.56

PowerPoint 2016, Windows 10, Microsoft Corporation

Callouts in figure: "Duration set to 1.75", "Star indicates transition", "On Mouse Click selected"

2 In the **Timing group**, click **Apply To All** so that the Duration of *1.75* seconds transition is applied to all of the slides in the presentation.

3 Click the **Slide Show tab**. In the **Start Slide Show group**, click **From Beginning**, and then view your presentation, clicking the mouse button to advance through the slides. When the black slide displays, click the mouse button one more time to display the presentation in Normal view. **Save** 🖫 your presentation.

More Knowledge | **Applying Multiple Slide Transitions**

You can apply more than one type of transition in your presentation by displaying the slides one at a time, and then clicking the transition that you want to apply instead of clicking Apply To All.

MOS
1.5.2

Activity 1.33 | **Displaying a Presentation in Reading View**

Organizations frequently conduct online meetings when participants are unable to meet in one location. The ***Reading view*** in PowerPoint displays a presentation in a manner similar to a slide show but the taskbar, title bar, and status bar remain available in the presentation window. Thus, a presenter can easily facilitate an online conference by switching to another window without closing the slide show.

1 In the lower right corner of the PowerPoint window, click **Reading View** 🔲. Compare your screen with Figure 1.57.

In Reading view, the status bar contains the Next and Previous buttons, which are used to navigate in the presentation, and the Menu button, which is used to print, copy, and edit slides.

♻ ANOTHER WAY   On the View tab, in the Presentation Views group, click Reading View.

FIGURE 1.57

2 Press Spacebar to display **Slide 2**. Click the left mouse button to display **Slide 3**. In the status bar, click **Previous** ◀ to display **Slide 2**.

3 In the status bar, click **Menu** 🔳 to display the Reading view menu, and then click **End Show** to return to Normal view.

🔄 **ANOTHER WAY**   Press Esc to exit Reading view and return to Normal view.

4 On the **Insert tab**, in the **Text group**, click **Header & Footer**, and then click the **Notes and Handouts tab**. Under **Include on page**, select the **Date and time** check box, and if necessary, select Update automatically. If necessary, select the **Page number** check box and clear the **Header** check box. Select the **Footer** check box, in the **Footer** box, using your own name, type **Lastname_Firstname_1B_Seattle** and then click **Apply to All**.

5 Display **Backstage** view, and then on the right, at the bottom of the **Properties** list, click **Show All Properties**. On the list of properties, click to the right of **Tags**, and then type **Seattle** To the right of **Subject**, type your course name and section number. Under **Related People**, be sure that your name displays as the author; edit if necessary.

6 On the left, scroll up as necessary, and then click **Save**. As directed by your instructor, create and submit a paper printout or an electronic image of your presentation that looks like a printed document; or, submit your completed PowerPoint file.

7 **Close** ✕ PowerPoint.

◀ **END | You have completed Project 1B**

GO! With Google

Objective Create an Itinerary Presentation in Google Slides

ALERT! **Working with Web-Based Applications and Services**

Computer programs and services on the web receive continuous updates and improvements, so the steps to complete this web-based activity may differ from the ones shown. You can often look at the screens and the information presented to determine how to complete the activity. If you do not already have a Google account, you will need to create one before you begin this activity.

Activity | Creating an Itinerary Presentation in Google Slides

In this Activity, you will use Google Slides to create a presentation similar to the one you created in Project 1B.

1 From the desktop, open your browser, navigate to **http://google.com**, and then sign in to your Google account. Click **Google Apps** ⊞ and then click **Drive**. ☁ Open your **GO! Web Projects** folder—or create and then open this folder if necessary.

2 In the left pane, click **NEW**, and then click **File upload** 🔒. Navigate to your student data files, click **p01_1B_Web**, and then click **Open**.

3 Wait a moment for the upload to complete, point to the uploaded file **p01_1B_Web.pptx**, and then right-click. On the shortcut menu, click **Rename**. Delete the existing text, and then using your own last name and first name, type **Lastname_Firstname_ 1B_Web** Click **OK** to rename the file.

4 Right-click the file that you just renamed, point to **Open with**, and then click **Google Slides**.

5 On **Slide 1**, in the Title placeholder, drag to select the two lines of text. On the **toolbar**, click the **Font arrow** ▾ and then click **Georgia**.

6 Select the text *Making the Most of Your First Port*. On the **toolbar**, click the **Font Size arrow**, and then click **24**.

7 Click **Slide 2**. Click the **Edit menu**, and then click **Delete** to remove the slide from the presentation.

8 With **Slide 2**—*Seattle Weather*—displayed, press Delete to remove the slide from your presentation. Notice that the presentation contains 7 slides.

9 Display **Slide 3**, and then click in the paragraph on the left side of the slide. Drag to select the text, and then on the **toolbar**, click the **Text color arrow** 🅰. Under **Theme**, click the second color—**Theme Color white**. With the paragraph still selected, on the toolbar, click **Bold** **B** and **Italic** *I*. Click the **Align** button ☰ ▾ and click **Center** ☰. Click anywhere in a blank area of the slide to cancel the selection and view your changes.

10 In the slide thumbnails, point to **Slide 4**, hold down the left mouse button, and then drag up slightly. Notice that a black bar displays above **Slide 4**. Continue to drag up until the black bar displays above **Slide 3**. Release the mouse button to move the slide.

11 Using the technique that you just practiced, move **Slide 5** to position it above **Slide 4**.

12 Display **Slide 6**. Select all three lines of text. Click the **Align** button ☰ ▾, and then click **Center** ☰. Click anywhere on the slide to cancel the selection. Click **Slide 1** and compare your screen with Figure A.

(GO! With Google continues on the next page)

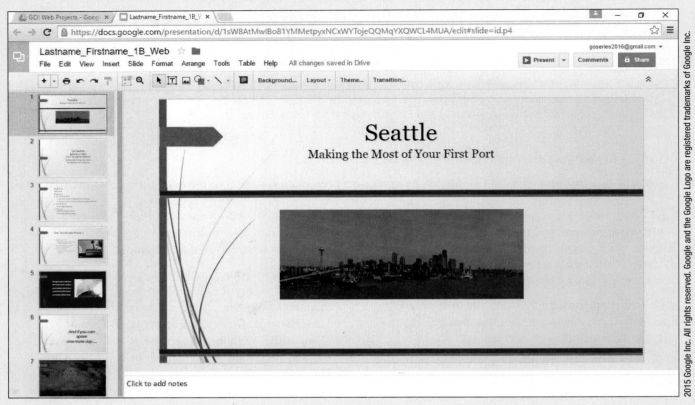

FIGURE A

13 At the right end of the toolbar, click **Transition** to open the **Animations** pane. On the right, in the Animations pane, click the **No transition button**, click **Slide from right**, and then click **Apply to all slides**.

14 To the right of the **menu bar**, click the **Present button arrow**, and then click **Present from beginning**. If necessary, click Allow. Click the left mouse button to progress through the presentation. When the last slide displays, press Esc or in the lower left corner, click **Exit**.

15 Your presentation will be saved automatically. Download as Microsoft PowerPoint, PDF Document, or another format and submit as directed by your instructor. Sign out of your Google account and close your browser.

GO! To Work

MICROSOFT OFFICE SPECIALIST (MOS) SKILLS IN THIS CHAPTER

PROJECT 1A	PROJECT 1B
1.1.1 Create a new presentation	**1.2.4** Delete slides
1.2.1 Insert specific slide layouts	**1.2.5** Apply a different slide layout
1.2.7 Insert slide headers, footers, and page numbers	**1.4.2** Modify slide order
1.5.3 Set file properties	**1.5.1** Change slide size
1.6.2 Print notes pages	**1.5.2** Change views of a presentation
1.6.3 Print handouts	**2.1.2** Apply formatting and styles to text
1.6.4 Print in color, grayscale, or black and white	**4.1.1** Insert slide transitions
1.7.4 Present a slide show by using Presenter View	**4.1.2** Set transition effect options
2.1.1 Insert text on a slide	**5.1.1** Insert slides from another presentation
2.3.3 Apply styles and effects	

BUILD YOUR E-PORTFOLIO

An E-Portfolio is a collection of evidence, stored electronically, that showcases what you have accomplished while completing your education. Collecting and then sharing your work products with potential employers reflects your academic and career goals. Your completed documents from the following projects are good examples to show what you have learned: 1G, 1K, and 1L.

GO! FOR JOB SUCCESS

Video: Managing Priorities and Workspace

Your instructor may assign this video to your class, and then ask you to think about, or discuss with your classmates, these questions:

FotolEdhar / Fotolia

What kind of scheduling tool do you use? Is it on your computer, your cell phone, or other electronic device, or do you write in a notebook or physical calendar? Which kind of scheduling tool will be most effective for you and why?

Name one lifestyle change that you can make today that will help you create more time for your work projects.

What is the one touch rule and how do you think it will help you be more efficient?

END OF CHAPTER

SUMMARY

In this chapter, you started a new presentation in PowerPoint. You inserted slides with various layouts and you entered, edited, and formatted text. You also inserted text from another PowerPoint file.

Use a presentation theme to establish a unified presentation design. You can change the color of the presentation theme by applying one of the predefined variants that are supplied with each theme.

Presentations are often organized in a manner similar to outlines. List levels represent outline levels and are identified by the bullet style, indentation, and text size.

Slide layout defines the placement of content placeholders on a slide. Each presentation theme includes predefined layouts that you can apply to slides for the purpose of arranging slide elements.

GO! LEARN IT ONLINE

Review the concepts, key terms, and MOS skills in this chapter by completing these online challenges, which you can find at **MyITLab**.

Matching and Multiple Choice: Answer matching and multiple choice questions to test what you learned in this chapter.

Lessons on the GO!: Learn how to use all the new apps and features as they are introduced by Microsoft.

MOS Prep Quiz: Answer questions to review the MOS skills that you practiced in this chapter.

GO! COLLABORATIVE TEAM PROJECT (Available in **MyITLab** and Instructor Resource Center)

If your instructor assigns this project to your class, you can expect to work with one or more of your classmates—either in person or by using Internet tools—to create work products similar to those that you created in this chapter. A team is a group of workers who work together to solve a problem, make a decision, or create a work product. Collaboration is when you work together with others as a team in an intellectual endeavor to complete a shared task or achieve a shared goal.

PROJECT GUIDE FOR POWERPOINT CHAPTER 1

Your instructor will assign Projects from this list to ensure your learning and assess your knowledge.

	Project Guide for Powerpoint Chapter 1		
Project	**Apply Skills from These Chapter Objectives**	**Project Type**	**Project Location**
1A **MyITLab**	Objectives 1–4 from Project 1A	**1A Instructional Project (Grader Project)** Guided instruction to learn the skills in Project 1A.	In MyITLab and in text
1B **MyITLab**	Objectives 5–8 from Project 1B	**1B Instructional Project (Grader Project)** Guided instruction to learn the skills in Project 1B.	In MyITLab and in text
1C	Objectives 1–4 from Project 1A	**1C Skills Review (Scorecard Grading)** A guided review of the skills from Project 1A.	In text
1D	Objectives 5–8 from Project 1B	**1D Skills Review (Scorecard Grading)** A guided review of the skills from Project 1B.	In text
1E **MyITLab**	Objectives 1–4 from Project 1A	**1E Mastery (Grader Project)** **Mastery and Transfer of Learning** A demonstration of your mastery of the skills in Project 1A with extensive decision making.	In MyITLab and in text
1F **MyITLab**	Objectives 5–8 from Project 1B	**1F Mastery (Grader Project)** **Mastery and Transfer of Learning** A demonstration of your mastery of the skills in Project 1B with extensive decision making.	In MyITLab and in text
1G **MyITLab**	Objectives 1–8 from Projects 1A and 1B	**1G Mastery (Grader Project)** **Mastery and Transfer of Learning** A demonstration of your mastery of the skills in Projects 1A and 1B with extensive decision making.	In MyITLab and in text
1H	Combination of Objectives from Projects 1A and 1B	**1H GO! Fix It (Scorecard Grading)** **Critical Thinking** A demonstration of your mastery of the skills in Projects 1A and 1B by creating a correct result from a document that contains errors you must find.	Instructor Resource Center (IRC) and MyITLab
1I	Combination of Objectives from Projects 1A and 1B	**1I GO! Make It (Scorecard Grading)** **Critical Thinking** A demonstration of your mastery of the skills in Projects 1A and 1B by creating a result from a supplied picture.	IRC and MyITLab
1J	Combination of Objectives from Projects 1A and 1B	**1J GO! Solve It (Rubric Grading)** **Critical Thinking** A demonstration of your mastery of the skills in Projects 1A and 1B, your decision-making skills, and your critical thinking skills. A task-specific rubric helps you self-assess your result.	IRC and MyITLab
1K	Combination of Objectives from Projects 1A and 1B	**1K GO! Solve It (Rubric Grading)** **Critical Thinking** A demonstration of your mastery of the skills in Projects 1A and 1B, your decision-making skills, and your critical thinking skills. A task-specific rubric helps you self-assess your result.	In text
1L	Combination of Objectives from Projects 1A and 1B	**1L GO! Think (Rubric Grading)** **Critical Thinking** A demonstration of your understanding of the chapter concepts applied in a manner that you would outside of college. An analytic rubric helps you and your instructor grade the quality of your work by comparing it to the work an expert in the discipline would create.	In text
1M	Combination of Objectives from Projects 1A and 1B	**1M GO! Think (Rubric Grading)** **Critical Thinking** A demonstration of your understanding of the chapter concepts applied in a manner that you would outside of college. An analytic rubric helps you and your instructor grade the quality of your work by comparing it to the work an expert in the discipline would create.	IRC and MyITLab
1N	Combination of Objectives from Projects 1A and 1B	**1N You and GO! (Rubric Grading)** **Critical Thinking** A demonstration of your understanding of the chapter concepts applied in a manner that you would in a personal situation. An analytic rubric helps you and your instructor grade the quality of your work.	IRC and MyITLab
1O	Combination of Objectives from Projects 1A and 1B	**1O Collaborative Team Project for PowerPoint Chapter 1** **Critical Thinking** A demonstration of your understanding of concepts and your ability to work collaboratively in a group role-playing assessment, requiring both collaboration and self-management.	IRC and MyITLab

GLOSSARY

GLOSSARY OF CHAPTER KEY TERMS

Artistic effects Formats applied to images that make pictures resemble sketches or paintings.

Aspect ratio The ratio of the width of a display to the height of the display.

Black slide A slide that displays after the last slide in a presentation, indicating that the presentation is over.

Contiguous slides Slides that are adjacent to each other in a presentation.

Editing The process of modifying a presentation by adding and deleting slides or by changing the contents of individual slides.

Footer Text that displays at the bottom of every slide or that prints at the bottom of a sheet of slide handouts or notes pages.

Formatting The process of changing the appearance of the text, layout, and design of a slide.

Header Text that prints at the top of each sheet of slide handouts or notes pages.

Layout The arrangement of elements, such as title and subtitle text, lists, pictures, tables, charts, shapes, and movies, on a slide.

List level An outline level in a presentation represented by a bullet symbol and identified in a slide by the indentation and the size of the text.

Noncontiguous slides Slides that are not adjacent to each other in a presentation.

Normal view The primary editing view in PowerPoint where you write and design your presentations.

Notes page A printout that contains the slide image on the top half of the page and notes that you have created on the Notes pane in the lower half of the page.

Notes pane An area of the Normal view window that displays below the Slide pane with space to type notes regarding the active slide.

Outline view A PowerPoint view that displays the presentation outline to the left of the Slide pane.

Placeholder A box on a slide with dotted or dashed borders that holds title and body text or other content such as charts, tables, and pictures.

Presenter view A view that shows the full-screen slide show on one monitor or projection screen while enabling the presenter to view a preview of the next slide, notes, and a timer on another monitor.

Reading view A view in PowerPoint that displays a presentation in a manner similar to a slide show but in which the taskbar, title bar, and status bar remain available in the presentation window.

Rotation handle A circular arrow that provides a way to rotate a selected image.

Section header A type of slide layout that changes the look and flow of a presentation by providing text placeholders that do not contain bullet points.

Sizing handles Small circles surrounding a picture that indicate that the picture is selected.

Slide A presentation page that can contain text, pictures, tables, charts,

and other multimedia or graphic objects.

Slide handout Printed images of slides on a sheet of paper.

Slide pane A PowerPoint screen element that displays a large image of the active slide.

Slide Sorter view A presentation view that displays thumbnails of all of the slides in a presentation.

Slide transitions Motion effects that occur in Slide Show view when you move from one slide to the next during a presentation.

Split button A type of button in which clicking the main part of the button performs a command and clicking the arrow opens a menu, list, or gallery.

Style A collection of formatting options that you can apply to a picture, text, or an object.

Text alignment The horizontal placement of text within a placeholder.

Theme A set of unified design elements that provides a look for your presentation by applying colors, fonts, and effects.

Thumbnails Miniature images of presentation slides.

Title slide A slide layout—most commonly the first slide in a presentation—that provides an introduction to the presentation topic.

Variant A variation on the presentation theme style and color.

Apply 1A skills from these Objectives:

1 Create a New Presentation
2 Edit a Presentation in Normal View
3 Add Pictures to a Presentation
4 Print and View a Presentation

Skills Review Project 1C Glaciers

In the following Skills Review, you will create a new presentation by inserting content and pictures, adding notes and footers, and applying a presentation theme. Your completed presentation will look similar to Figure 1.58.

PROJECT FILES

For Project 1C, you will need the following files:

New blank PowerPoint presentation
p01C_Glacier_Bay
p01C_Ice

Build From Scratch **p01C_Ship**

You will save your presentation as:

Lastname_Firstname_1C_Glaciers

PROJECT RESULTS

FIGURE 1.58

PowerPoint 2016, Windows 10, Microsoft Corporation

(Project 1C Glaciers continues on the next page)

1 Start PowerPoint. On the right, click **Ion**, and then click **Create**. In the **Slide pane**, click in the text *Click to add title*. Type **Glacier Bay** and then click in the subtitle placeholder. Type **Part One in a Series of Alaskan Passage Adventures**

a. On the **Quick Access Toolbar**, click **Save**. Under **Save As**, click **Browse**. Navigate to your **PowerPoint Chapter 1** folder. In the **File name** box, using your own name, replace the existing text with **Lastname_Firstname_1C_Glaciers** and then click **Save**.

b. On the **Home tab**, in the **Slides group**, click the **New Slide arrow**, and then in the gallery, click **Two Content**. Click the text *Click to add title*, and then type **About the Park**

2 On the left side of the slide, click in the content placeholder. Type **Located in the Southeast Alaskan Wilderness** and then press [Enter]. Press [Tab]. Type **3.3 million acres** and then press [Enter]. Type **A national park and preserve** and then press [Enter].

a. On the **Home tab**, in the **Paragraph group**, click **Decrease List Level**. Type **Visitor season** and then press [Enter]. On the **Home tab**, in the **Paragraph group**, click **Increase List Level**. Type **May to September**

b. On the **Home tab**, in the **Slides group**, click the **New Slide arrow**, and then in the gallery, click **Panoramic Picture with Caption**. In the lower portion of the slide, click the text **Click to add title**, and then type **Prepare to be Amazed!**

c. Click in the text placeholder. Type **Before you reach Glacier Bay, walk around your cruise ship to find the best viewing locations. Make sure your camera battery is charged!**

d. On the **Home tab**, in the **Slides group**, click the **New Slide arrow**, and then in the gallery, click **Content with Caption**. In the title placeholder, type **Learn More!**

e. Click in the text placeholder, and then type **A national park ranger will board your ship during your visit to Glacier Bay. Check your ship's itinerary for presentation information and locations.**

3 With **Slide 4** displayed, in the **Status bar**, click **Notes**. Click in the **Notes pane**, and then type **Your cruise ship will spend between 6 and 8 hours in Glacier Bay.**

a. On the left side of the PowerPoint window, in the slide thumbnails, click **Slide 1**. Click in the subtitle placeholder after the *n* in *ALASKAN*. Press [Spacebar], and then type **Inside**

b. In the slide thumbnails, click **Slide 2**, and then click at the end of the last bullet point after the word *September*. Press [Enter], and then type **Be prepared for rain**

4 With **Slide 2** displayed, in the placeholder on the right side of the slide, click **Pictures**. Navigate to your student data files, and then click **p01C_Glacier_Bay**. Click **Insert**.

a. With the picture selected, on the **Format tab**, in the **Picture Styles group**, click **More** [▾] to display the **Picture Styles** gallery. In the second row, click the third style—**Beveled Oval, Black**.

b. Display **Slide 3**. In the Picture placeholder, click **Pictures**. Navigate to your student data files, and then click **p01C_Ice**. Click **Insert**.

c. Display **Slide 4**. In the content placeholder on the right side of the slide, click **Pictures**. Navigate to your student data files, and then insert **p01C_Ship**. On the **Format tab**, in the **Picture Styles group**, click **More** [▾] to display the **Picture Styles** gallery. In the third row, click the sixth style—**Soft Edge Oval**.

d. With the picture still selected, on the **Format tab**, in the **Adjust group**, click **Artistic Effects** to display the gallery. In the fourth row, click the third effect—**Crisscross Etching**.

5 On the **Slide Show tab**, in the **Start Slide Show group**, click **From Beginning**.

a. Click the left mouse button or press [Spacebar] to advance to the second slide. Continue to click or press [Spacebar] until the last slide displays, and then click or press [Spacebar] one more time to display a black slide.

b. With the black slide displayed, click the left mouse button or press [Spacebar] to exit the slide show and return to the presentation.

6 Click the **Insert tab**, and then in the **Text group**, click **Header & Footer** to display the **Header and Footer** dialog box.

a. In the **Header and Footer** dialog box, click the **Notes and Handouts tab**. Under **Include on page**, select the **Date and time** check box. If necessary,

(Project 1C Glaciers continues on the next page)

click the Update automatically option button so that the current date prints on the notes and handouts.

b. Select the **Page number** check box. If necessary, clear the Header check box to omit this element. Select the **Footer** check box. In the **Footer** box, type **Lastname_Firstname_1C_Glaciers** and then click **Apply to All**.

c. In the upper left corner of your screen, click the **File** tab to display **Backstage** view. On the right, at the bottom of the **Properties list**, click **Show All Properties**.

d. On the list of Properties, click to the right of **Tags** to display an empty box, and then type **Glacier Bay** Click to the right of **Subject** to display an empty box, and then type your course name and section number. Under **Related People**, be sure that your name displays as the author; edit if necessary.

e. **Save** your presentation. As directed by your instructor, create and submit a paper printout or an electronic image of your presentation that looks like a printed document; or, submit your completed PowerPoint file. **Close** PowerPoint.

END | You have completed Project 1C

Skills Review | Project 1D Photography

In the following Skills Review, you will edit an existing presentation by inserting slides from another presentation, applying font and slide formatting, and applying slide transitions. Your completed presentation will look similar to Figure 1.59.

PROJECT FILES

For Project 1D, you will need the following files:

p01D_Photography
p01D_Photography_Slides

You will save your presentation as:

Lastname_Firstname_1D_Photography

PROJECT RESULTS

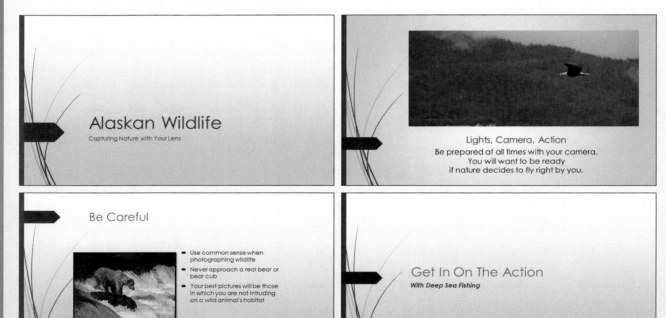

FIGURE 1.59

(Project 1D Photography continues on the next page)

1 Start PowerPoint. On the left, under the list of recent presentations, click **Open Other Presentations**. Under **Open**, click **Browse**. Navigate to your student data files, and then click **p01D_Photography**. Click **Open**. On the **File tab**, click **Save As**, navigate to your **PowerPoint Chapter 1** folder, and then using your own name, save the file as **Lastname_Firstname_1D_Photography**

a. On the **Design tab**, in the **Customize group**, click **Slide Size**, and then click **Widescreen (16:9)**.

b. With **Slide 1** displayed, on the **Home tab**, in the **Slides group**, click the **New Slide arrow**, and then click **Reuse Slides**. In the **Reuse Slides** pane, click **Browse**, and then click **Browse File**. In the **Browse** dialog box, navigate to your student data files, and then double-click **p01D_Photography_Slides** to display the slides from this presentation in the **Reuse Slides** pane.

c. At the bottom of the **Reuse Slides** pane, be sure that the **Keep source formatting** check box is *cleared*. In the **Reuse Slides** pane, click the first slide to insert the slide after Slide 1.

d. At the left of your screen, in the slide thumbnails, click **Slide 6** to display it in the **Slide pane**. In the **Reuse Slides** pane, click the second slide to insert it after **Slide 6**. **Close** the **Reuse Slides** pane.

2 Display **Slide 1**. On the **View tab**, in the **Presentation Views group**, click **Outline View**.

a. In the **Outline**, in **Slide 7**, drag to select the second and third bullet points—beginning with *Never approach* and ending with *animal's home*.

b. On the **Home tab**, in the **Paragraph group**, click **Decrease List Level** one time.

c. In the **Outline**, in the same slide, click at the end of the first bullet point after the word *sense*. Press Spacebar, and then type **when photographing wildlife**

d. In the **Status bar**, click **Normal** to display the slide thumbnails.

3 Display **Slide 8**, and then press Delete to delete the slide from the presentation.

a. Display **Slide 1**. On the **Home tab**, in the **Editing group**, click **Replace**. In the **Replace** dialog box, in the **Find what** box, type **home** and then in the **Replace with** box, type **habitat**

b. In the **Replace** dialog box, click **Replace All** to display a message box indicating that one

replacement was made. In the message box, click **OK**. **Close** the **Replace** dialog box.

c. On the **Design tab**, in the **Variants group**, right-click the third variant. On the shortcut menu, click **Apply to All Slides** so that the variant color is applied to all of the slides in the presentation.

4 Display **Slide 5**. Select all of the text in the placeholder. On the **Home tab**, in the **Font group**, click the **Font arrow**, scroll the font list, and then click **Arial Black**. Click the **Font Size arrow**, and then click **32**. In the **Paragraph group**, click **Line Spacing**, and then click **1.5**.

a. Display **Slide 2**. On the **Home tab**, in the **Slides group**, click **Layout** to display the **Slide Layout** gallery. Click **Title Slide** to change the slide layout.

b. On **Slide 2**, select the title—*Alaskan Wildlife*. On the **Home tab**, in the **Font group**, click the **Font Color arrow**. In the fourth column, click the first color— **Dark Teal, Text 2**.

c. Display **Slide 3**, and then select the title—*Lights, Camera, Action*. On the mini toolbar, click **Font Color** to apply the font color **Dark Teal, Text 2**.

d. Display **Slide 4**, and then, click anywhere in the text. On the **Home tab**, in the **Paragraph group**, click **Center** to center the text within the placeholder.

e. Display **Slide 6**, and then select the subtitle. From the mini toolbar, apply **Bold** and **Italic**.

f. In the slide thumbnails, point to **Slide 7**, hold down the left mouse button, and then drag up to position the slide between **Slides 3** and **4**.

5 In the lower right corner of the PowerPoint window, click **Slide Sorter** to display all of the slide thumbnails. Click **Slide 1**, so that it is selected. On your keyboard, press Delete to delete the slide.

a. Click **Slide 4**, and then hold down Ctrl and click **Slide 5**. With both slides selected, point to either of the selected slides, hold down the left mouse button, and then drag to position the two slides to the right of **Slide 6**. Release the mouse button to move the two slides. In the status bar, click **Normal** to return to Normal view.

b. Display **Slide 1**. On the **Transitions tab**, in the **Transition to This Slide group**, click **More** ⨆ to display the **Transitions** gallery.

(Project 1D Photography continues on the next page)

c. Under **Exciting**, click **Gallery** to apply and view the transition. In the **Transition to This Slide group**, click **Effect Options**, and then click **From Left**. In the **Timing group**, click **Apply To All** to apply the *Gallery, From Left* transition to all of the slides in the presentation.

d. In the **Timing group**, click the **Duration up spin arrow** so that *01.75* displays. Under **Advance Slide**, verify that the **On Mouse Click** check box is selected; select it if necessary. In the **Timing group**, click **Apply To All**.

e. Click the **Slide Show tab**. In the **Start Slide Show group**, click **From Beginning**, and then view your presentation, clicking the mouse button to advance through the slides. When the black slide displays, click the mouse button one more time to display the presentation in Normal view.

6 On the **Insert tab**, in the **Text group**, click **Header & Footer** to display the **Header and Footer** dialog box.

a. In the **Header and Footer** dialog box, click the **Notes and Handouts tab**. Under **Include on page**, select the **Date and time** check box. If necessary, click the Update automatically option button so that the current date prints on the notes and handouts.

b. Select the **Page number** check box. If necessary, clear the Header check box to omit this element. Select the **Footer** check box. In the **Footer** box, type **Lastname_Firstname_1D_Photography** and then click **Apply to All**.

c. In the upper left corner of your screen, click the **File** tab to display **Backstage** view. On the right, at the bottom of the **Properties list**, click **Show All Properties**.

d. On the list of Properties, click to the right of **Tags**, and then type **photography** Click to the right of **Subject**, and then type your course name and section number. Under **Related People**, be sure that your name displays as the author. If necessary, right-click the author name, click Edit Property, type your name, and click OK.

e. **Save** your presentation. As directed by your instructor, create and submit a paper printout or an electronic image of your presentation that looks like a printed document; or, submit your completed PowerPoint file. **Close** the presentation.

END | You have completed Project 1D

Apply 1A skills from these Objectives:

1 Create a New Presentation
2 Edit a Presentation in Normal View
3 Add Pictures to a Presentation
4 Print and View a Presentation

   In the following Mastering PowerPoint project, you will create a new presentation that Kodiak West Travel will use in their promotional materials to describe activities in the city of Juneau. Your completed presentation will look similar to Figure 1.60.

PROJECT FILES

For Project 1E, you will need the following files:

New blank PowerPoint presentation
p01E_Aerial_View
p01E_Whale
p01E_Falls

Build From Scratch

You will save your presentation as:

Lastname_Firstname_1E_Juneau

PROJECT RESULTS

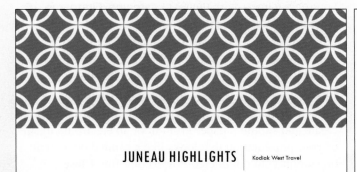

FIGURE 1.60

(Project 1E Juneau continues on the next page)

Mastering PowerPoint   Project 1E Juneau (continued)

1 Start PowerPoint and create a presentation using the **Integral** theme. Use the default color variant.

2 As the title of this presentation type **Juneau Highlights** and as the subtitle type **Kodiak West Travel** Save the presentation in your **PowerPoint Chapter 1** folder as **Lastname_Firstname_1E_Juneau**

3 Insert a **New Slide** using the **Content with Caption** layout. In the title placeholder, type **The View from Above**

4 In the content placeholder on the right side of the slide, from your student data files, insert the picture **p01E_Aerial_View**. Format the picture with the **Beveled Matte, White** picture style.

5 In the text placeholder on the left, type **View a glacial ice field from above by plane or helicopter. If you are more adventurous, try glacier trekking in Juneau where you can land on a glacier and climb an ice wall.**

6 Insert a **New Slide** using the **Two Content** layout. In the title placeholder, type **On Land and Sea**

7 In the content placeholder on the left, type the following text, increasing and decreasing the list level as shown below. In this presentation theme, the first level bullet points do not include a bullet symbol.

> **On the water**
> > **Whale watching**
> > **Kayaking**
> **Mount Roberts tramway**
> > **Spectacular views of Juneau**
> > **Recreational hiking trails**

8 In the content placeholder on the right, from your student data files, insert the picture **p01E_Whale**. Apply the **Rotated, White** picture style.

9 Insert a new slide with the **Picture with Caption** layout. In the title placeholder, type **Mendenhall Glacier** and then in the picture placeholder, from your student data files, insert the picture **p01E_Falls**.

10 In the text placeholder, type **Walk to Mendenhall Glacier from the Visitor Center to get a close-up view of Nugget Falls.**

11 In the **Notes pane**, type **Mendenhall Glacier is the most famous glacier in Juneau and in some years is visited by over 400,000 people.**

12 Insert a **Header & Footer** on the **Notes and Handouts**. Include the **Date and time** updated automatically, the **Page number**, and a **Footer**—using your own name—with the text **Lastname_Firstname_1E_Juneau** and apply to all the slides.

13 Display the **Document Properties**. As the **Tags** type **Juneau** As the **Subject** type your course and section number. Be sure your name is indicated as the Author.

14 **Save** your presentation, and then view the slide show from the beginning. As directed by your instructor, create and submit a paper printout or an electronic image of your presentation that looks like a printed document; or, submit your completed PowerPoint file. **Close** PowerPoint.

> **END | You have completed Project 1E**

Mastering PowerPoint Project 1F Refuge

In the following Mastering PowerPoint project, you will edit a presentation regarding a wildlife refuge where Kodiak West Travel conducts tours. Your completed presentation will look similar to Figure 1.61.

PROJECT FILES

For Project 1F, you will need the following files:

p01F_Refuge
p01F_Excursions

You will save your presentation as:

Lastname_Firstname_1F_Refuge

PROJECT RESULTS

FIGURE 1.61

PowerPoint 2016, Windows 10, Microsoft Corporation

(Project 1F Refuge continues on the next page)

Mastering PowerPoint   Project 1F Refuge (continued)

1 Start PowerPoint, and then from your student data files, open the file **p01F_Refuge**. In your **PowerPoint Chapter 1** folder, **Save** the file as **Lastname_Firstname_1F_Refuge**

2 Change the **Slide Size** to **Widescreen (16:9)**.

3 Display the presentation **Outline**. In the **Outline**, on **Slide 2**, increase the list level of the third and the fifth bullet points. Click at the end of the last bullet point after the word *roads*, and then type **or facilities**

4 Return the presentation to **Normal view**, and then display **Slide 4**. Display the **Reuse Slides** pane. Browse to open from your student data files, **p01F_Excursions**. Make sure the **Keep source formatting** check box is *cleared*. With **Slide 4** in your presentation displayed, insert the last two slides from the **Reuse Slides** pane.

5 Display **Slide 1**, and then change the layout to **Title Slide**.

6 Select the subtitle—*Experience Alaska with Kodiak West Travel*. Change the **Font** to **Arial**, and the **Font Size** to **28**. Change the **Font Color** to **Black, Text 1**. **Center** the title and the subtitle.

7 Display **Slide 5**, and then select the paragraph in the content placeholder. Apply **Bold** and **Italic**, and then change the **Font Size** to **16**.

8 **Center** the paragraph text, and then change the **Line Spacing** to **1.5**. **Center** the slide title.

9 In **Slide Sorter** view, delete **Slide 3**. Move **Slide 5** to position it after **Slide 2**.

10 Move **Slide 4** to the end of the presentation.

11 In **Normal** view, display **Slide 1**. Apply the **Split** transition and change the **Effect Options** to **Horizontal Out**. Change the **Duration** to **1.75** and apply the transition to all of the slides in the presentation. View the slide show from the beginning.

12 **Insert** a **Header & Footer** on the **Notes and Handouts**. Include the **Date and time** updated automatically, the **Page number**, and a **Footer** with the text **Lastname_Firstname_1F_Refuge**

13 Display the **Document Properties**. As the **Tags** type **refuge, tours** As the **Subject** type your course and section number. Be sure your name is indicated as the Author.

14 **Save** your presentation, create and submit a paper printout or an electronic image of your presentation that looks like a printed document; or, submit your completed PowerPoint file as directed by your instructor. **Close** PowerPoint.

END | You have completed Project 1F

Mastering PowerPoint   Project 1G Northern Lights

In the following Mastering PowerPoint project, you will edit an existing presentation that describes the Northern Lights and ideal viewing areas. Your completed presentation will look similar to Figure 1.62.

Apply 1A and 1B skills from these Objectives:

1 Create a New Presentation
2 Edit a Presentation in Normal View
3 Add Pictures to a Presentation
4 Print and View a Presentation
5 Edit an Existing Presentation
6 Format a Presentation
7 Use Slide Sorter View
8 Apply Slide Transitions

PROJECT FILES

For Project 1G, you will need the following files:

p01G_Northern_Lights
p01G_Lights
p01G_Slides

You will save your presentation as:

Lastname_Firstname_1G_Northern_Lights

PROJECT RESULTS

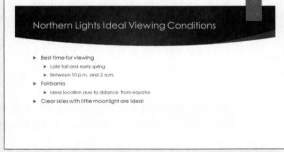
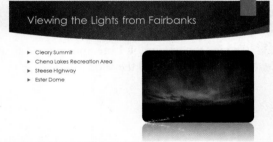

PowerPoint 2016, Windows 10, Microsoft Corporation

FIGURE 1.62

(Project 1G Northern Lights continues on the next page)

Mastering PowerPoint   Project 1G Northern Lights (continued)

1 Start PowerPoint, and then from your student data files, open the file **p01G_Northern_Lights**. In your **PowerPoint Chapter 1** folder, **Save** the file as **Lastname_Firstname_1G_Northern_Lights**

2 Replace all occurrences of the text **North** with **Northern** and then change the layout of **Slide 1** to **Title Slide**.

3 Apply the **Ion Boardroom** theme, with the default purple variant option.

4 Change the **Slide Size** to **Widescreen (16:9)**.

5 Display **Slide 2**, open the **Reuse Slides** pane, and then from your student data files browse for and open the presentation **p01G_Slides**. If necessary, clear the Keep source formatting check box, and then insert the last two slides from the **p01G_Slides** file.

6 Display **Slide 2**. In either the slide pane or in the slide outline, click at the end of the first bullet point after the word *time*. Add the words **for viewing** and then in the same slide, increase the list level of the second and third bullet points.

7 With **Slide 2** still displayed, select the title and change the **Font Size** to **32**. In the **Notes pane**, type the following notes: **The lights reach their peak in September and March.**

8 Display **Slide 3**. Select the paragraph of text, and then change the **Font Color** to **Purple, Accent 6, Lighter 60%**—in the last column, the third color. Change the **Font Size** to **16**, and then apply **Bold**.

9 Change the paragraph **Line Spacing** to **1.5**, and then **Center** the paragraph and the slide title.

10 With **Slide 3** still displayed, format the picture with the **Soft Edge Rectangle** picture style and the **Marker** artistic effect.

11 Display **Slide 4**. In the content placeholder on the right, from your student data files, insert the picture **p01G_Lights**. Change the **Height** to 3.0. Modify the **Picture Effect** by applying a **10 Point Soft Edges** effect.

12 Move **Slide 3** between **Slides 1** and **2**.

13 Display **Slide 4**. Insert a **New Slide** with the **Section Header** layout. In the title placeholder type **Visit Fairbanks and View the Northern Lights!** In the text placeholder type **With Kodiak West Travel**

14 Apply the **Uncover** transition and change the **Effect Options** to **From Top**. Change the **Timing** by increasing the **Duration** to **01.25**. Apply the transition effect to all of the slides. View the slide show from the beginning.

15 **Insert** a **Header & Footer** on the **Notes and Handouts**. Include the **Date and time** updated automatically, the **Page number**, and a **Footer**, using your own name, with the text **Lastname_Firstname_1G_Northern_Lights**

16 Display the **Document Properties**. As the **Tags** type **northern lights, Fairbanks** As the **Subject** type your course and section number. Be sure your name is indicated as the Author.

17 **Save** your presentation, create and submit a paper printout or an electronic image of your presentation that looks like a printed document; or, submit your completed PowerPoint file as directed by your instructor. **Close** PowerPoint.

END | You have completed Project 1G

Apply a combination of the 1A and 1B skills.

Build From Scratch

GO! Fix It	Project 1H Rain Forest	MyITLab
GO! Make It	Project 1I Eagles	MyITLab
GO! Solve It	Project 1J Packrafting	MyITLab
GO! Solve It	Project 1K Packing	

PROJECT FILES

For Project 1K, you will need the following file:

p01K_Packing

You will save your presentation as:

Lastname_Firstname_1K_Packing

Open the file p01K_Packing and save it as **Lastname_Firstname_1K_Packing** Complete the presentation by applying a theme and changing the variant. Format the presentation by applying appropriate font formatting and by changing text alignment and line spacing. Change the layout of the last slide to an appropriate layout. On Slide 2, insert a picture that you have taken yourself, or use one of the pictures in your student data files that you inserted in other projects. Apply a style to the picture. Apply slide transitions to all of the slides in the presentation, and then insert a header and footer that includes the date and time updated automatically, the file name in the footer, and the page number. Add your name, your course name and section number, and the tags **packing, weather** to the properties. Save and print or submit as directed by your instructor.

Performance Level

Performance Criteria		Exemplary: You consistently applied the relevant skills	Proficient: You sometimes, but not always, applied the relevant skills	Developing: You rarely or never applied the relevant skills
	Apply a theme and a variant	An appropriate theme and variant were applied to the presentation.	A theme was applied but the variant was not changed.	Neither a theme nor the variant theme were applied.
	Apply font and slide formatting	Font and slide formatting is attractive and appropriate.	Adequately formatted but difficult to read or unattractive.	Inadequate or no formatting.
	Use appropriate pictures and apply styles attractively	An appropriate picture was inserted and a style is applied attractively.	A picture was inserted but a style was not applied.	Picture was not inserted.
	Apply appropriate slide layout to Slide 4	An appropriate layout was applied to the last slide.	The slide layout was changed but is not appropriate for the type of slide.	The slide layout was not changed.

END | You have completed Project 1K

RUBRIC

The following outcomes-based assessments are open-ended assessments. That is, there is no specific correct result; your result will depend on your approach to the information provided. Make Professional Quality your goal. Use the following scoring rubric to guide you in how to approach the problem and then to evaluate how well your approach solves the problem.

The *criteria*—Software Mastery, Content, Format and Layout, and Process—represent the knowledge and skills you have gained that you can apply to solving the problem. The *levels of performance*—Professional Quality, Approaching Professional Quality, or Needs Quality Improvements—help you and your instructor evaluate your result.

	Your completed project is of Professional Quality if you:	Your completed project is Approaching Professional Quality if you:	Your completed project Needs Quality Improvements if you:
1-Software Mastery	Choose and apply the most appropriate skills, tools, and features and identify efficient methods to solve the problem.	Choose and apply some appropriate skills, tools, and features, but not in the most efficient manner.	Choose inappropriate skills, tools, or features, or are inefficient in solving the problem.
2-Content	Construct a solution that is clear and well organized, contains content that is accurate, appropriate to the audience and purpose, and is complete. Provide a solution that contains no errors in spelling, grammar, or style.	Construct a solution in which some components are unclear, poorly organized, inconsistent, or incomplete. Misjudge the needs of the audience. Have some errors in spelling, grammar, or style, but the errors do not detract from comprehension.	Construct a solution that is unclear, incomplete, or poorly organized; contains some inaccurate or inappropriate content; and contains many errors in spelling, grammar, or style. Do not solve the problem.
3-Format & Layout	Format and arrange all elements to communicate information and ideas, clarify function, illustrate relationships, and indicate relative importance.	Apply appropriate format and layout features to some elements, but not others. Overuse features, causing minor distraction.	Apply format and layout that does not communicate information or ideas clearly. Do not use format and layout features to clarify function, illustrate relationships, or indicate relative importance. Use available features excessively, causing distraction.
4-Process	Use an organized approach that integrates planning, development, self-assessment, revision, and reflection.	Demonstrate an organized approach in some areas, but not others; or, use an insufficient process of organization throughout.	Do not use an organized approach to solve the problem.

Apply a combination of the 1A and 1B skills.

Build From Scratch

GO! Think Project 1L Bears

PROJECT FILES

For Project 1L, you will need the following files:

New blank PowerPoint presentation
p01L_Bear

You will save your presentation as:

Lastname_Firstname_1L_Bears

Cindy Barrow, Tour Operations Manager for Kodiak West Travel, is developing a presentation describing brown bear viewing travel experiences that the company is developing. In the presentation, Cindy will be describing the brown bear habitat and viewing opportunities.

Kodiak bears are the largest known size of brown bears on record; they can weigh as much as 2,000 pounds and can get as large as polar bears. Kodiak bears are active during the day and are generally solitary creatures. The Kodiak Bear Travel Experience is a small, personalized travel adventure available to only eight participants at a time. It is an opportunity to peer into the life of these majestic mammals.

The adventure takes place on Kodiak Island near a lake with a high concentration of salmon, making it the perfect natural feeding ground for the Kodiak bears. Travelers can view the bears from boats, kayaks, and recently constructed viewing platforms, and guides are available.

This is a true wildlife experience as the area is home to deer, fox, and river otter. Accommodations are available at the Kodiak West Breakfast Inn from mid-June to the end of August. Peak season is early August and reservations can be made up to one year in advance. The cost is $1,800 per person for one week, and includes all meals, use of watercraft, and guided tours.

Using the preceding information, create a presentation that Cindy can show at a travel fair. The presentation should include four to six slides describing the travel experience. Apply an appropriate theme and use slide layouts that will effectively present the content. Insert at least one picture and apply appropriate picture formatting. You may use your own image file, search for one online, or from your student data files, use the file p01L_Bear. Apply font formatting and slide transitions, and modify text alignment and line spacing as necessary.

Save the file as **Lastname_Firstname_1L_Bears** and then, on the Notes and Handouts, insert a header and footer that include the date and time updated automatically, the file name in the footer, and the page number. Add your name, your course name and section number, and the tags **bears, tours** to the properties. Save and print or submit as directed by your instructor.

END | You have completed Project 1L

Build From Scratch

GO! Think Project 1M Sitka MyITLab

Build From Scratch

You and GO! Project 1N Travel MyITLab

GO! Collaborative Team Project Project 1O Bell Orchid Hotels MyITLab

Formatting PowerPoint Presentations

OUTCOMES
Format a presentation to add visual interest and clarity

OUTCOMES
Enhance a presentation with WordArt and SmartArt

OBJECTIVES
1. Format Numbered and Bulleted Lists
2. Insert Online Pictures
3. Insert Text Boxes and Shapes
4. Format Objects

OBJECTIVES
5. Remove Picture Backgrounds and Insert WordArt
6. Create and Format a SmartArt Graphic

Moccabunny/Fotolia

In This Chapter GO! to Work with PowerPoint

A well-designed PowerPoint presentation helps the audience understand complex information while keeping them focused on your message. Color is an important element that enhances your slides and draws the audience's interest by creating focus. When designing the background and element colors for your presentation, be sure that the colors you use provide contrast so that the text is visible on the background. Use elements such as images, shapes, and other graphics to enhance your presentation and illustrate your message.

The projects in this chapter relate to **Sensation Park Entertainment Group**, an entertainment company that operates 15 regional theme parks across the United States, Mexico, and Canada. Park types include traditional theme parks, water parks, and animal parks. This year the company will launch three of its new "Sensation Parks" where attractions combine fun and the discovery of math and science information, and where teens and adults enjoy the free Friday night concerts. The company focuses on safe and imaginative attractions that appeal to guests with a variety of entertainment interests, including adventure, science, and the arts.

Employee Training Presentation

PROJECT ACTIVITIES

In Activities 2.01 through 2.21, you will format a presentation for Marc Johnson, Director of Operations for Sensation Park Entertainment Group, which describes important safety guidelines for employees. Your completed presentation will look similar to Figure 2.1.

PROJECT FILES

 If your instructor wants you to submit Project 2A in the MyITLab Grader system, log in to MyITLab, locate Grader Project 2A, and then download the files for this project.

For Project 2A, you will need the following file:
p02A_Safety

You will save your presentation as:
Lastname_Firstname_2A_Safety

Please always review the downloaded Grader instructions before beginning.

PROJECT RESULTS

GO!
Walk Thru
Project 2A

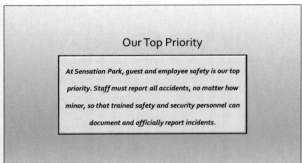

PowerPoint 2016, Windows 10, Microsoft Corporation

FIGURE 2.1 Project 2A Safety

2
POWERPOINT

GO! Learn How
Video P2-1

The font, color, and style of a numbered or bulleted list are determined by the presentation theme; however, you can format these elements by changing the bulleted and numbered list styles and colors. A *bulleted list*, sometimes called an unordered list, is a list of items preceded by small dots or other shapes, which do not indicate order or rank. In a *numbered list*, or ordered list, items are preceded by numbers, which indicate sequence or rank of the items.

Activity 2.01 | Selecting Placeholder Text

A placeholder is a box on a slide with dotted or dashed borders that holds title and body text or other content such as charts, tables, and pictures. You can format placeholder contents by selecting text or by selecting the entire placeholder.

1 Start PowerPoint. From the student data files for this chapter, locate and open **p02A_Safety**. Display the **Save As** dialog box, create a **New Folder** with the name **PowerPoint Chapter 2** and then using your own name, save the file in the folder you created as **Lastname_ Firstname_2A_Safety**

2 Display **Slide 2**, and then click anywhere in the content placeholder with the single bullet point.

3 Point to the dashed border surrounding the placeholder to display the [pointer icon] pointer, and then click one time to display the border as a solid line. Compare your screen with Figure 2.2.

When a placeholder's border displays as a solid line, all of the text in the placeholder is selected, and any formatting changes that you make will be applied to *all* of the text in the placeholder.

FIGURE 2.2

PowerPoint 2016, Windows 10, Microsoft Corporation

4 With the border of the placeholder displaying as a solid line, change the **Font Size** `60 ▾` to **24**. Notice that the font size of *all* of the placeholder text increases.

5 **Save** 🖫 your presentation.

Activity 2.02 | **Changing a Bulleted List to a Numbered List**

2.1.5

You can easily change a bulleted list to a numbered list. In this safety presentation, the list of steps to follow should be a numbered list.

1 Display **Slide 3**, and then click anywhere in the bulleted list. Point to the placeholder dashed border to display the ⬚ pointer, and then click one time to display the border as a solid line indicating that all of the text is selected.

2 On the **Home tab**, in the **Paragraph group**, click **Numbering** 📑 ▾ and then compare your slide with Figure 2.3. **Save** 🖫 your presentation.

All of the bullet symbols are converted to numbers. The color of the numbers is determined by the presentation theme.

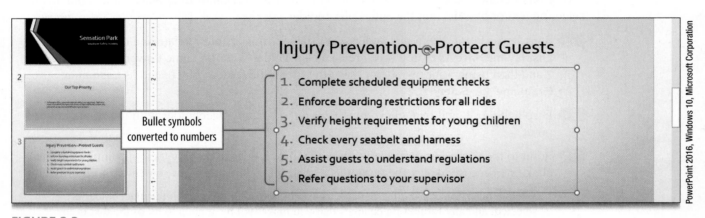

FIGURE 2.3

ALERT! **Did You Display the Numbering Gallery?**

If you clicked the Numbering arrow instead of the Numbering button, the Numbering gallery displays. Click the Numbering arrow again to close the gallery, and then click the Numbering button to convert the bullets to numbers.

Activity 2.03 | **Changing the Shape and Color of a Bulleted List Symbol**

2.1.5

The presentation theme includes default styles for the bullet points in content placeholders. You can customize a bullet by changing its style, color, and size.

1 Display **Slide 4**, and then select the three second-level bullet points—*Ride entrances*, *Visitor center*, and *Rest areas*.

2 On the **Home tab**, in the **Paragraph group**, click the **Bullets button arrow** ⬚ ▾ to display the **Bullets** gallery, and then compare your screen with Figure 2.4.

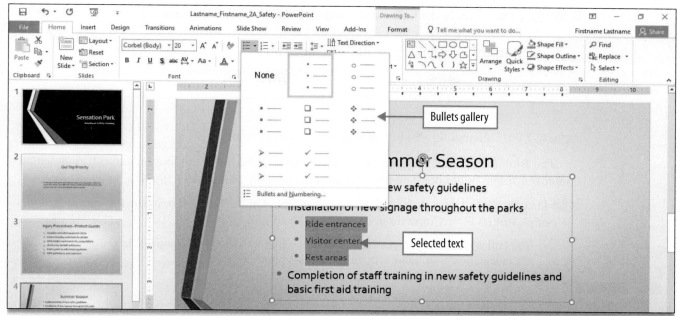

FIGURE 2.4

PowerPoint 2016, Windows 10, Microsoft Corporation

3. Below the **Bullets** gallery, click **Bullets and Numbering**. In the **Bullets and Numbering** dialog box, point to each bullet style to display its ScreenTip. Then, in the second row, click **Star Bullets**. If the Star Bullets are not available, in the second row of bullets, click the second bullet style, and then click the Reset button.

4. Below the gallery, in the **Size** box, select the existing number, type **100** and then click **Color** 🅰. Under **Theme Colors**, in the eighth column, click the last color—**Red, Accent 4, Darker 50%**, and then compare your dialog box with Figure 2.5.

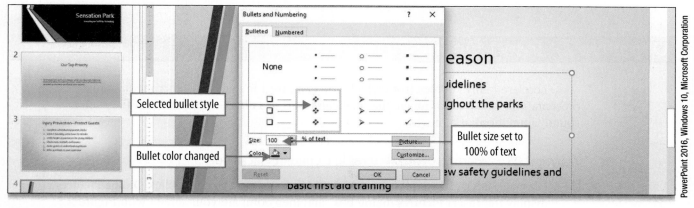

FIGURE 2.5

PowerPoint 2016, Windows 10, Microsoft Corporation

5 Click **OK** to apply the bullet style, and then **Save** 🔲 your presentation.

Activity 2.04 | Removing a Bullet Symbol from a Bullet Point

The Bullets button is a toggle, enabling you to turn the bullet symbol on and off. A slide that contains a single bullet point can be formatted as a single paragraph *without* a bullet symbol.

1 Display **Slide 2**, and then click in the paragraph. On the **Home tab**, in the **Paragraph group**, click **Bullets** 🔳. Compare your screen with Figure 2.6.

> The bullet symbol no longer displays, and the Bullets button is no longer selected. Additionally, the indentation associated with the list level is removed.

FIGURE 2.6

2 Click the dashed border to display the solid border and to select all of the text in the paragraph, and then apply **Bold** 🅱 and **Italic** 𝐼. **Center** ≡ the paragraph. On the **Home tab**, in the **Paragraph group**, click **Line Spacing** 🔳, and then click **2.0**. **Save** 🔲 your presentation.

Objective 2 | Insert Online Pictures

GO! Learn How
Video P2-2

There are many sources from which you can insert images and other media into a presentation. One type of image that you can insert is a *clip*—a single media file such as art, sound, animation, or a movie.

2.3.1

Activity 2.05 | Inserting Online Pictures in a Content Placeholder

1 Display **Slide 5**. In the placeholder on the right side of the slide, click **Online Pictures** 🔳 to display the **Insert Pictures** dialog box, and then compare your screen with Figure 2.7.

PowerPoint 2016, Windows 10, Microsoft Corporation

FIGURE 2.7

2 ▶ With the insertion point in the **Bing Image Search** box, type **pouring water** and then press Enter to search for images that contain the keywords *pouring water*. Point to any of the results, and notice that keywords display. Select a vertical image of water being poured, similar to Figure 2.8.

> You can use various keywords to find images that are appropriate for your documents. The results shown indicate the images are licensed under Creative Commons, which, according to **www.creativecommons.org** is "a nonprofit organization that enables the sharing and use of creativity and knowledge through free legal tools."

> Creative Commons helps people share and use their photographs, but does not allow companies to sell them. For your college assignments, you can use these images so long as you are not profiting by selling the images.

> To find out more about Creative Commons, go to **https://creativecommons.org/about** and watch their video.

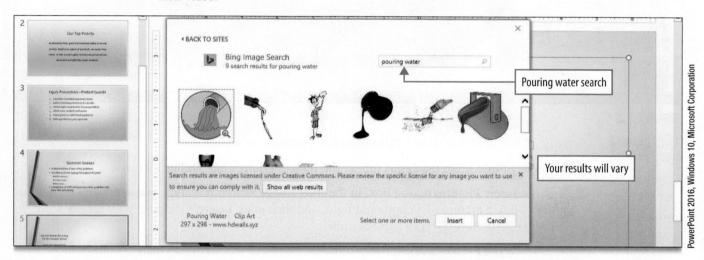

PowerPoint 2016, Windows 10, Microsoft Corporation

FIGURE 2.8

3 With the water picture selected, click **Insert**. Compare your screen with Figure 2.9, and then **Save** 🔲 your presentation.

> On the ribbon, the Picture Tools display, and the pouring water image is surrounded by sizing handles, indicating that it is selected.

◐ BY TOUCH   Tap the picture that you want to insert, and then tap Insert.

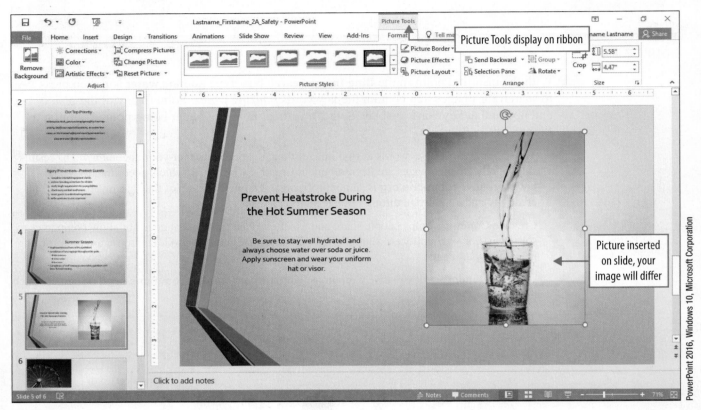

FIGURE 2.9

2.3.1

Activity 2.06 | **Inserting Online Pictures in Any Location on a Slide**

1 Display **Slide 1**. On the **Insert tab**, in the **Images group**, click **Online Pictures**.

2 In the **Insert Pictures** dialog box, in the **Bing Image Search** box, type **red lights** and then press Enter. Click a picture of a single red light, and then click **Insert**. Compare your screen with Figure 2.10. **Save** 🔲 your presentation.

> When you use the Online Pictures button on the ribbon instead of the Online Pictures button in a content placeholder, PowerPoint inserts the image in the center of the slide.

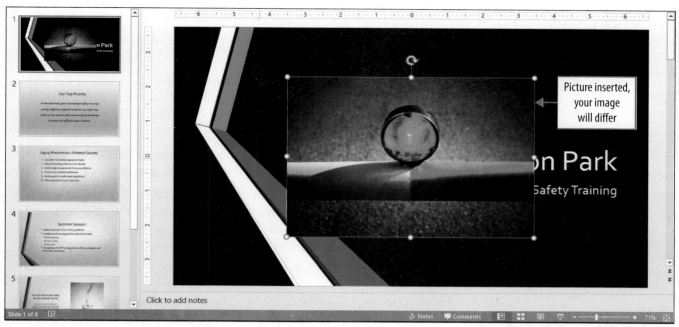

FIGURE 2.10

MOS
2.3.2

Activity 2.07 | Sizing a Picture

A selected image displays sizing handles that you can drag to resize the image. You can also resize an image using the Shape Height and Shape Width boxes on the Format tab.

1 If necessary, select the picture of the red light. On the **Picture Tools Format tab**, in the **Size group**, click in the **Shape Height** box 🔲, and then replace the selected number with **3.5**

2 Press Enter to resize the image. Notice that the picture is resized proportionately, and the **Width** box of this image displays *5.26*—or another measurement; your width will vary depending upon the image you select. Compare your screen with Figure 2.11 and then **Save** 🔲 your presentation.

When a picture is resized in this manner, the width adjusts in proportion to the picture height.

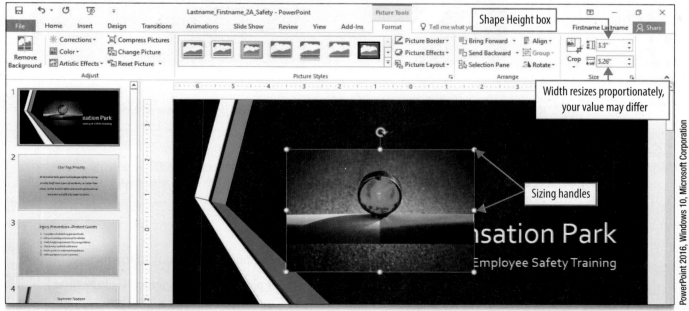

FIGURE 2.11

🔁 **BY TOUCH** Drag the corner sizing handle with your finger or mouse to resize the picture proportionately.

Activity 2.08 | **Using Smart Guides and the Ruler to Position a Picture**

2.4.4

Smart guides are dashed lines that display on your slide when you are moving an object to assist you with alignment.

1 On **Slide 1**, on the **View tab**, in the **Show group**, verify that the **Ruler** check box is selected and if necessary, select the check box. On the horizontal and vertical rulers, notice that *0* displays in the center. Point to the picture, and then drag up so that the top edge of the picture aligns with the top edge of the slide.

Horizontally, the PowerPoint ruler indicates measurements from the center of the slide *out* to the left and to the right. Vertically, the PowerPoint ruler indicates measurements from the center up and down.

2 Point to the picture to display the 🔲 pointer. Hold down Shift, and then slowly drag the picture to the right and notice that dashed red Smart Guides periodically display along the edges of the picture. When the dashed red Smart Guide displays on the right edge of the picture at approximately **6 inches to the right of zero on the horizontal ruler**, compare your screen with Figure 2.12.

Smart Guides display when you move an object and it is aligned with another object on the slide. Here, the Smart Guide displays because the right edge of the picture is aligned with the right edge of the title placeholder. Pressing Shift while dragging an object constrains object movement in a straight line either vertically or horizontally. Here, pressing Shift maintains the vertical placement of the picture at the top edge of the slide.

FIGURE 2.12

3 Release the mouse button and Shift key, and then **Save** 🔲 the presentation.

More Knowledge **Moving an Object by Using the Arrow Keys**

You can use the directional arrow keys on your keyboard to move a picture, shape, or other object in small increments. Select the object so that its outside border displays as a solid line. Then, on your keyboard, press the directional arrow keys to move the selected object in small, precise increments.

 Activity 2.09 | **Cropping a Picture**

2.4.2

When you *crop* a picture you remove unwanted or unnecessary areas of the picture.

1 Display **Slide 6**, and then select the Ferris wheel picture. On the **Picture Tools Format tab**, in the **Size group**, click the upper portion of the **Crop** button to display the crop handles on the edges of the picture. Compare your screen with Figure 2.13.

Use the *crop handles* like sizing handles to remove unwanted areas of the picture.

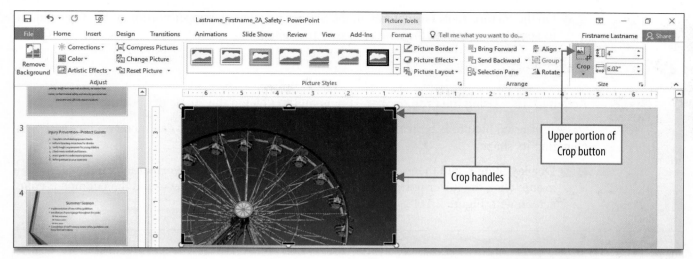

FIGURE 2.13

2 ▶ Point to the center right crop handle to display the crop pointer ⊢. Compare your screen with Figure 2.14.

The *crop pointer* is the mouse pointer that displays when cropping areas of a picture.

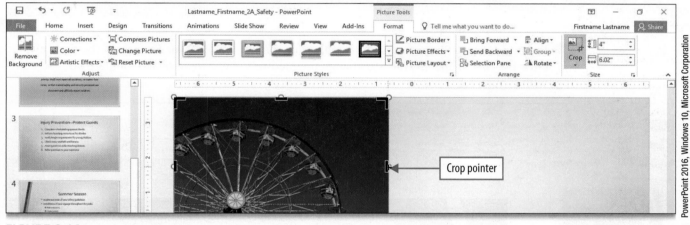

Crop pointer

FIGURE 2.14

3 ▶ With the crop pointer displayed, hold down the left mouse button and drag to the left to approximately **1.5 inches to the left of zero on the horizontal ruler**, and then release the mouse button. Compare your screen with Figure 2.15.

The portion of the picture to be removed by the crop displays in gray.

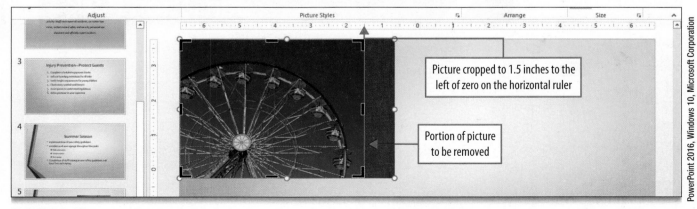

Picture cropped to 1.5 inches to the left of zero on the horizontal ruler

Portion of picture to be removed

FIGURE 2.15

> **4** On the **Picture Tools Format tab**, in the **Size group**, click the upper portion of the **Crop** button to apply the crop, and then **Save** 🖫 your presentation.

🔄 **ANOTHER WAY**   Press Enter or click outside the picture to apply the crop.

MOS
2.3.2

Activity 2.10 | Using the Crop to Shape Command to Change the Shape of a Picture

An inserted picture is typically rectangular in shape; however, you can modify a picture by changing its shape.

> **1** Display **Slide 1**, and then select the picture. On the **Picture Tools Format tab**, in the **Size group**, click the lower portion of the Crop button—the **Crop arrow**—and then compare your screen with Figure 2.16.

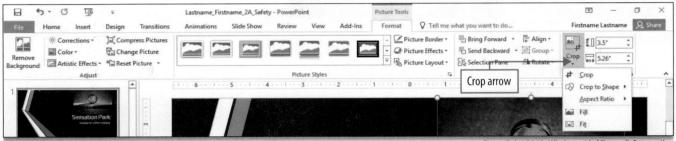

FIGURE 2.16

PowerPoint 2016, Windows 10, Microsoft Corporation

> **2** Point to **Crop to Shape** to display a gallery of shapes. Under **Basic Shapes**, in the first row, click the first shape—**Oval**—to change the picture's shape to an oval. Compare your screen with Figure 2.17.

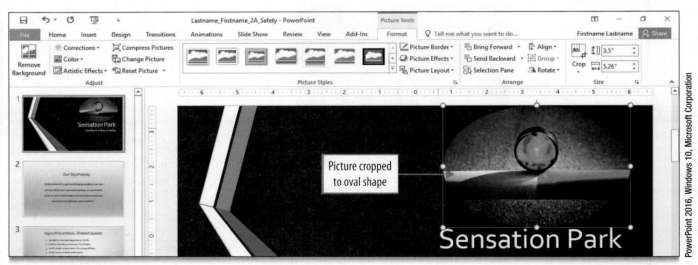

FIGURE 2.17

PowerPoint 2016, Windows 10, Microsoft Corporation

> **3** **Save** 🖫 your presentation.

GO! Learn How
Video P2-3

You can use objects, including text boxes and shapes, to draw attention to important information or to serve as containers for slide text. Many shapes, including lines, arrows, ovals, and rectangles, are available to insert and position anywhere on your slides.

2.2.2

Activity 2.11 │ Inserting a Text Box

A *text box* is an object with which you can position text anywhere on a slide.

1 Display **Slide 3** and verify that the rulers display. On the **Insert tab**, in the **Text group**, click **Text Box**.

2 Move the ⬇ pointer to several different places on the slide, and as you do so, in the horizontal and vertical rulers, notice that *ruler guides*—dotted red vertical and horizontal lines that display in the rulers indicating the pointer's position—move also.

Use the ruler guides to help you position objects on a slide.

3 Position the pointer so that the ruler guides are positioned on the **left half of the horizontal ruler at 4.5 inches** and on the **lower half of the vertical ruler at 2 inches**, and then compare your screen with Figure 2.18.

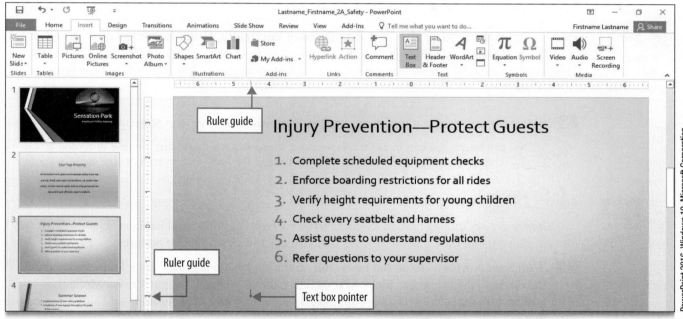

FIGURE 2.18

4 Click one time to create a narrow rectangular text box surrounded by sizing handles. With the insertion point blinking inside the text box, type **If Safety is Questionable** Notice that as you type, the width of the text box expands to accommodate the text. Compare your screen with Figure 2.19.

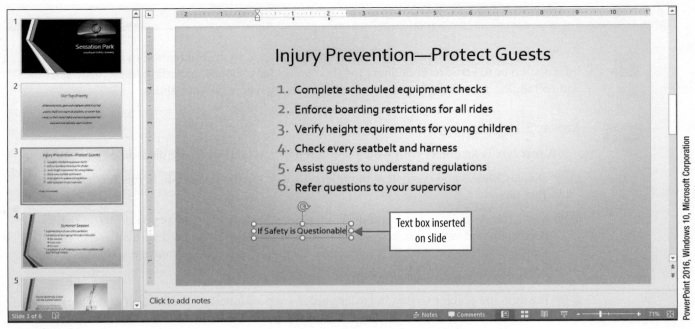

FIGURE 2.19

PowerPoint 2016, Windows 10, Microsoft Corporation

ALERT!   **Does the Text in the Text Box Display Vertically, One Character at a Time?**

If you move the pointer when you click to create the text box, PowerPoint sets the width of the text box and does not widen to accommodate the text. If this happens, your text may display vertically instead of horizontally or it may display on two lines. Click Undo, and then repeat the steps again, being sure that you do not move the mouse when you click to insert the text box.

5 Select the text that you typed, change the **Font Size** to **24** and then **Save** 🖫 your presentation.

You can format the text in a text box by using the same techniques that you use to format text in any other placeholder. For example, you can change the font, font style, font size, and font color.

Activity 2.12 │ Inserting and Sizing a Shape

Shapes are slide objects such as lines, arrows, boxes, callouts, and banners. You can size and move a shape using the same techniques that you use to size and move pictures.

1 With **Slide 3** displayed, on the **Insert tab**, in the **Illustrations group**, click **Shapes** to display the **Shapes** gallery. Under **Block Arrows**, click the first shape—**Right Arrow**. Move the pointer into the slide until the ⊞ pointer—called the *crosshair pointer*—displays, indicating that you can draw a shape.

2 Move the ⊞ pointer to position the ruler guides at approximately **0 on the horizontal ruler** and on the **lower half of the vertical ruler at 2 inches**. Compare your screen with Figure 2.20.

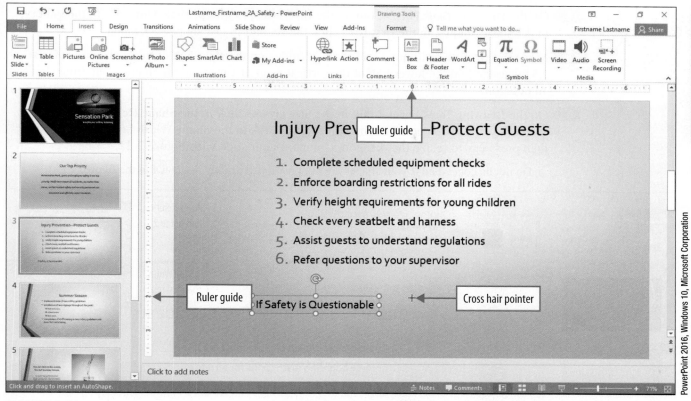

FIGURE 2.20

3 Click to insert the arrow. On the **Drawing Tools Format tab**, in the **Size group**, click in the **Shape Height** box [⊥] to select the number. Type **0.5** and then press Enter. Click in the **Shape Width** box [↔]. Type **2** and then press Enter to resize the arrow. Compare your screen with Figure 2.21.

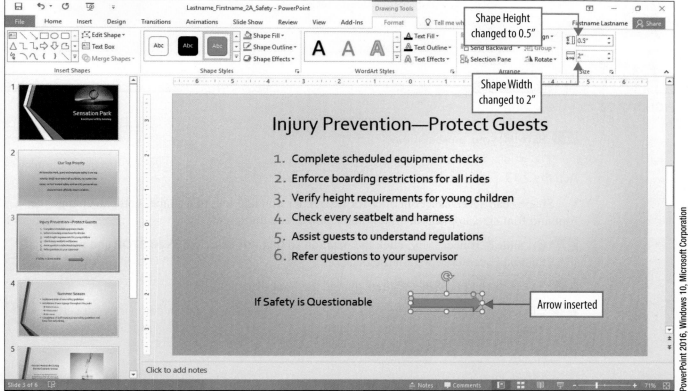

FIGURE 2.21

4 On the **Drawing Tools Format tab**, in the **Insert Shapes group**, click **More**. In the gallery, under **Basic Shapes**, in the first row, click the second to last shape—**Octagon**.

5 Move the ⊞ pointer to position the ruler guides on the **right half of the horizontal ruler at 3.5 inches** and on the **lower half of the vertical ruler at 1 inch**, and then click one time to insert an octagon.

6 On the **Drawing Tools Format tab**, in the **Size group**, click in the **Shape Height** box to select the number. Type **2** and then press Enter. Click in the **Shape Width** box. Type **2** and then press Enter to resize the octagon. Compare your slide with Figure 2.22.

Do not be concerned if your shapes are not positioned exactly as shown in the figure.

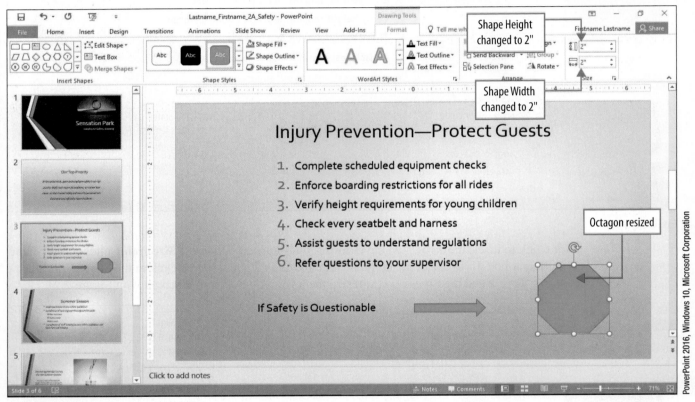

FIGURE 2.22

7 **Save** your presentation.

Activity 2.13 | Adding Text to Shapes

Shapes can serve as a container for text. After you add text to a shape, you can change the font and font size, apply font styles, and change text alignment.

1 On **Slide 3**, if necessary, click the octagon so that it is selected. Type **STOP** and notice that the text is centered within the octagon.

2 Select the text **STOP**, and then change the **Font Size** to **32**.

3 Click in a blank area of the slide to cancel the selection, and then compare your screen with Figure 2.23. **Save** your presentation.

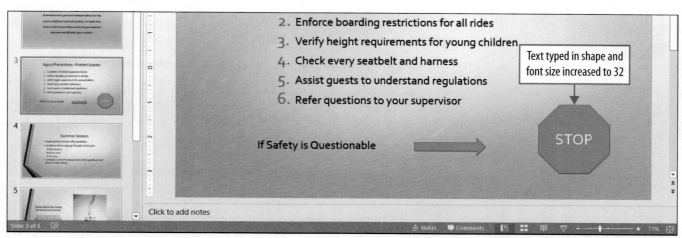

FIGURE 2.23

PowerPoint 2016, Windows 10, Microsoft Corporation

Objective 4 | Format Objects

GO! Learn How
Video P2-4

2.2.4, 2.2.5

Apply styles and effects to pictures, shapes, and text boxes to complement slide backgrounds and colors.

Activity 2.14 | Applying Shape Fills and Outlines

A distinctive way to format a shape is by changing the *fill color*—the inside color of text or of an object—and the outside line color. Use the Shape Styles gallery to apply predefined combinations of these fill and line colors and also to apply other effects.

1 Display **Slide 2**, and then click anywhere in the paragraph of text to select the content placeholder.

2 On the **Drawing Tools Format tab**, in the **Shape Styles group**, click the **Shape Fill arrow**. Point to several of the theme colors and watch as Live Preview changes the inside color of the text box. In the fifth column, click the second color—**Blue, Accent 1, Lighter 80%**.

3 In the **Shape Styles group**, click the **Shape Outline arrow**. Point to **Weight**, click **3 pt**, and notice that a thick outline surrounds the text placeholder. Click in a blank area of the slide so that nothing is selected, and then compare your slide with Figure 2.24. **Save** your presentation.

You can use combinations of shape fill, outline colors, and weights to format an object.

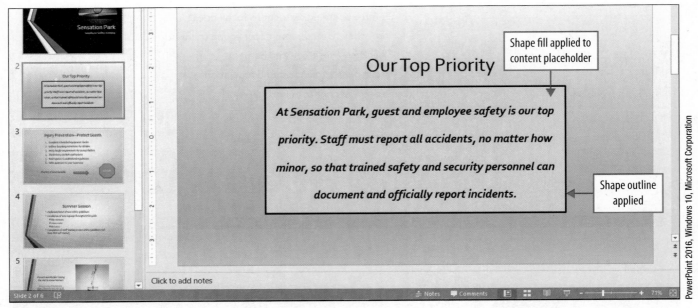

FIGURE 2.24

Activity 2.15 | Using the Eyedropper to Change Color

The **eyedropper** is a tool that captures the exact color from an object on your screen and then applies it to any shape, picture, or text. You can use the eyedropper to give your presentation a cohesive look by matching a font color, fill color, border color, or other slide element to any color on any slide.

1 Display **Slide 6**, and then select the title text—**At Sensation Park**.

2 On the **Home tab**, in the **Font group**, click the **Font Color arrow**. Below the gallery, click **Eyedropper**, and then move the 🖊 pointer into the upper right corner of the Ferris wheel picture. Compare your screen with Figure 2.25.

A small square displays next to the pointer indicating the exact color to which you are pointing. When you hover over a color, its **RGB** color coordinates display in a ScreenTip, replacing the block of color. RGB is a color model in which the colors red, green, and blue are added together to form another color.

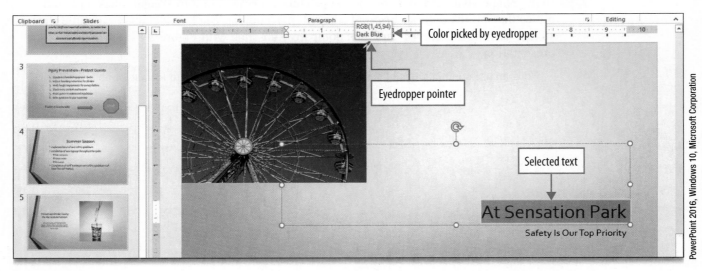

FIGURE 2.25

3 With the pointer in the upper right corner of the picture, click one time. Notice that the color is applied to the selected text. Click a blank area of the slide to deselect the text and compare your screen with Figure 2.26.

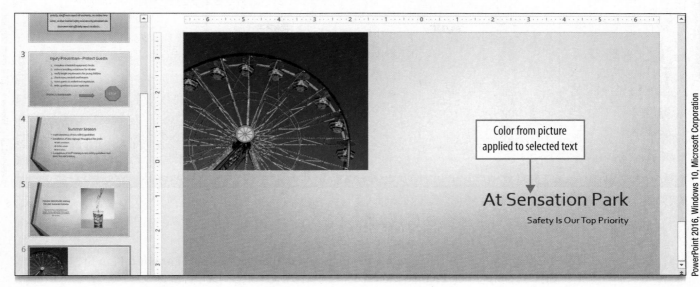

Color from picture applied to selected text

At Sensation Park

Safety Is Our Top Priority

FIGURE 2.26

4 Display **Slide 5**, and then select the title. On the mini toolbar, click the **Font Color arrow**. Under **Recent Colors**, notice that the color you selected with the eyedropper displays. Point to the color to display the ScreenTip—*Dark Blue*. Click **Dark Blue** to apply the color to the selection.

> After a color has been selected with the eyedropper, it remains available in the presentation each time the color gallery is displayed. When you use the eyedropper in this manner, you can consistently apply the same color throughout your presentation.

5 **Save** 🖫 your presentation.

MOS
2.2.5

Activity 2.16 | **Applying Shape Styles**

1 Display **Slide 3**, and then select the **arrow shape**. On the **Drawing Tools Format tab**, in the **Shape Styles group**, click **More** ⊽ to display the **Shape Styles** gallery. Under **Theme Styles**, in the last row, click the second style—**Intense Effect - Blue, Accent 1**.

2 Click anywhere in the text *If Safety is Questionable* to select the text box. On the **Drawing Tools Format tab**, in the **Shape Styles group**, click **More** ⊽.

3 Under **Theme Styles**, in the last row, click the fifth style—**Intense Effect - Red, Accent 4**.

4 Select the **octagon shape**, and then apply the same style you applied to the text box—**Intense Effect - Red, Accent 4**.

5 **Save** 🖫 your presentation and then compare your screen with Figure 2.27.

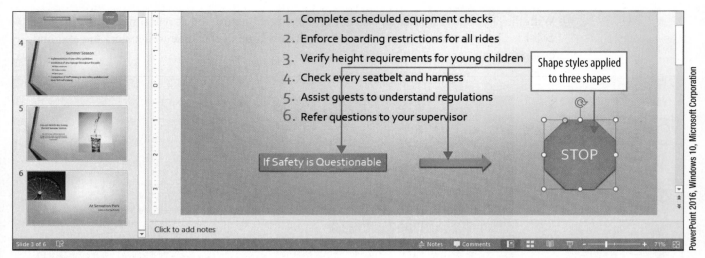

1. Complete scheduled equipment checks
2. Enforce boarding restrictions for all rides
3. Verify height requirements for young children
4. Check every seatbelt and harness
5. Assist guests to understand regulations
6. Refer questions to your supervisor

Shape styles applied to three shapes

If Safety is Questionable

STOP

Click to add notes

Slide 3 of 6

Notes   Comments   71%

PowerPoint 2016, Windows 10, Microsoft Corporation

FIGURE 2.27

2.3.3

Activity 2.17 │ Applying Shape and Picture Effects

1 Display **Slide 1**, and then select the picture. On the **Picture Tools Format tab**, in the **Picture Styles group**, click **Picture Effects**.

A list of effects that you can apply to pictures displays. These effects can also be applied to shapes and text boxes.

2 Point to **Soft Edges**, and then in the **Soft Edges** gallery, point to each style to view its effect on the picture. Click the last **Soft Edges** effect—**50 Point**, and then compare your screen with Figure 2.28.

The soft edges effect softens and blurs the outer edge of the picture so that it blends into the slide background.

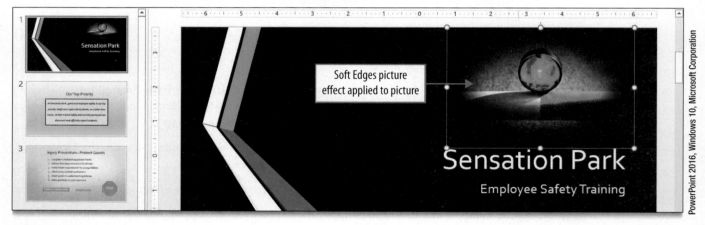

Soft Edges picture effect applied to picture

Sensation Park

Employee Safety Training

PowerPoint 2016, Windows 10, Microsoft Corporation

FIGURE 2.28

3 Display **Slide 2**, and then select the light blue content placeholder. On the **Drawing Tools Format tab**, in the **Shape Styles group**, click **Shape Effects**. Point to **Bevel** to display the **Bevel** gallery. Point to each bevel to view its ScreenTip and to use Live Preview to examine the effect of each bevel on the content placeholder. Then, in the last row, click the last bevel—**Round Convex**.

4 Click in a blank area of the slide and then compare your screen with Figure 2.29.

FIGURE 2.29

5 Display **Slide 5**, and then select the picture. On the **Picture Tools Format tab**, in the **Picture Styles group**, click **Picture Effects**, and then point to **Glow**.

6 Point to several of the effects to view the effect on the picture, and then under **Glow Variations**, in the second row, click the first glow effect—**Blue, 8 pt glow, Accent color 1**.

The glow effect applies a colored, softly blurred outline to the selected object.

7 **Save** 🖫 your presentation.

Activity 2.18 | Duplicating Objects

1 Display **Slide 6**, and then select the picture.

2 Press and hold down Ctrl, and then press D one time. Release Ctrl.

Ctrl + D is the keyboard shortcut to duplicate an object. A duplicate of the picture overlaps the original picture and the duplicated image is selected.

3 **Save** 🖫 your presentation, click a blank area of the slide, and then compare your screen with Figure 2.30.

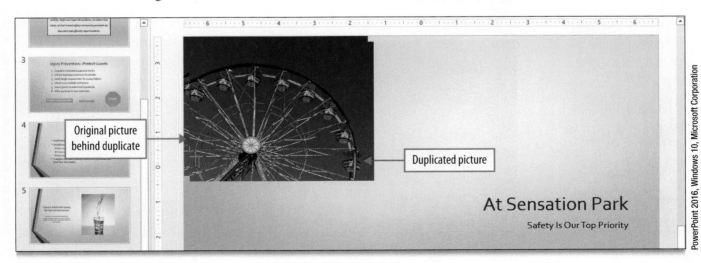

FIGURE 2.30

Activity 2.19 | Aligning and Distributing Objects Relative to the Slide

You can select multiple slide objects, and then use ribbon commands to align and distribute the objects precisely.

> **1** With **Slide 6** displayed, click the image in the upper left corner of the slide to select it. Hold down Shift and then click the second image so that both images are selected. Release the Shift key, and then compare your screen with Figure 2.31.

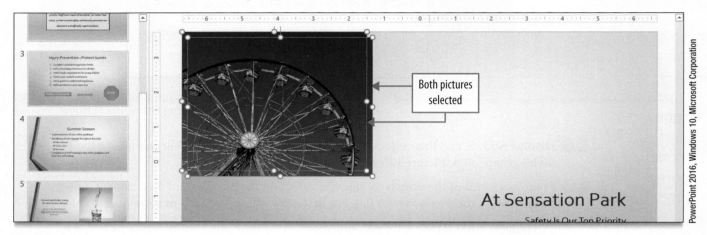

FIGURE 2.31

 Position the pointer in the gray area of the Slide pane just outside the upper left corner of the slide to display the ⬚ pointer. Drag down and to the right to draw a transparent, gray, selection rectangle that encloses both pictures.

> **2** On the **Picture Tools Format tab**, in the **Arrange group**, click **Align** ⬚. At the bottom of the menu, click **Align to Slide** to activate this setting. On the **Picture Tools Format tab**, in the **Arrange group**, click **Align** ⬚ again, click **Align Left**, and then compare your screen with Figure 2.32.

The Align to Slide setting tells PowerPoint to align each selected object with the slide, rather than with each other. In combination with the Align Left option, this aligns the left edge of each picture with the left edge of the slide.

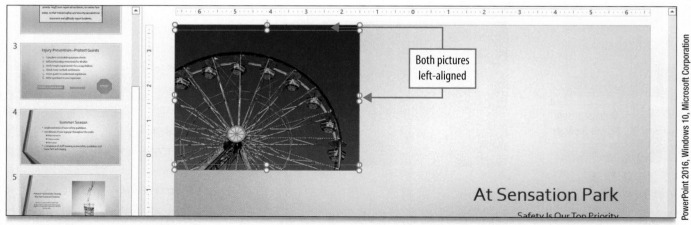

FIGURE 2.32

> **3** With both pictures still selected, on the **Picture Tools Format tab**, in the **Arrange group**, click **Align** ⬚ again, and then click **Distribute Vertically**.

The pictures are distributed evenly down the left edge of the slide between the top and bottom edges of the slide.

4 With both pictures selected, on the **Picture Tools Format tab**, in the **Picture Styles group**, click **Picture Effects**. Point to **Soft Edges**, and then click **50 Point** to apply the picture effect to both images. Click in a blank area of the slide and compare your screen with Figure 2.33.

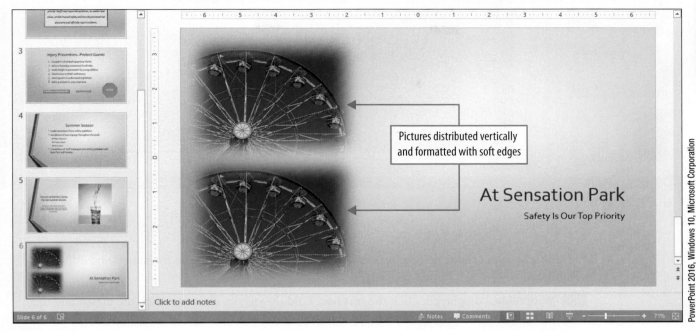

FIGURE 2.33

5 **Save** 🖫 the presentation.

2.4.2

Activity 2.20 | Aligning and Distributing Objects Relative to Each Other

1 Display **Slide 3**, hold down Shift, and then at the bottom of the slide, click the **text box**, the **arrow**, and the **octagon** to select all three objects. Release Shift.

🔄 **BY TOUCH**   Tap the text box, hold down Shift, and then tap the arrow and the octagon.

2 With the three objects selected, on the **Drawing Tools Format tab**, in the **Arrange group**, click **Align** 🖫. Click **Align Selected Objects**.

The *Align Selected Objects* option will cause the objects that you select to align relative to each other, rather than relative to the edges of the slide.

3 On the **Drawing Tools Format tab**, in the **Arrange group**, click **Align** 🖫, and then click **Align Middle**. Click **Align** again, and then click **Distribute Horizontally**.

The midpoint of each object aligns and the three objects are distributed evenly between the left edge of the leftmost object—the text box—and the right edge of the rightmost object—the octagon.

4 Click anywhere on the slide so that none of the objects are selected. Compare your screen with Figure 2.34, and then **Save** 🖫 the presentation.

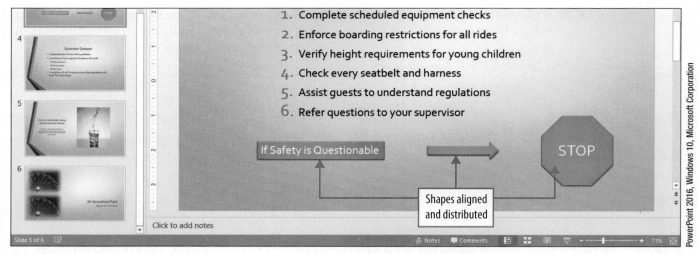

FIGURE 2.34

MOS
2.4.3

Activity 2.21 │ Grouping Objects

You can select multiple objects and group them so that they can be formatted and edited as one object.

1 With **Slide 3** displayed, click the **text box**, hold down Shift, and then click the **arrow** and the **octagon** so that all three objects are selected.

Sizing handles surround each individual object.

2 On the **Drawing Tools Format tab**, in the **Arrange group**, click **Group,** 🔲 and then click **Group**. Compare your screen with Figure 2.35.

The sizing handles surround all three shapes as one, indicating that the three shapes are grouped into one object. The individual objects are not selected. The grouped object can be formatted, aligned, and moved as one object.

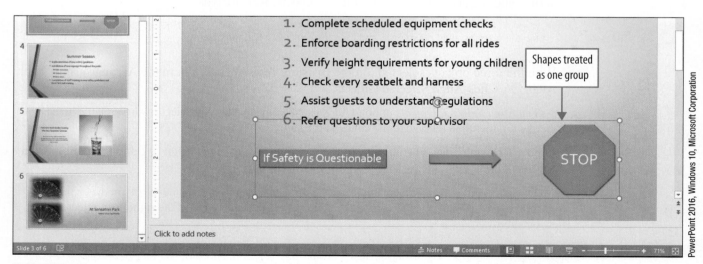

FIGURE 2.35

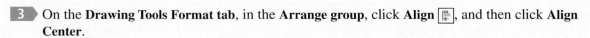

3 On the **Drawing Tools Format tab**, in the **Arrange group**, click **Align** [icon], and then click **Align Center**.

The group is centered horizontally on the slide.

4 On the **Slide Show tab**, in the **Start Slide Show group**, click **From Beginning**, and then view the slide show. When the black slide displays, press [Esc].

5 On the **Insert tab**, in the **Text group**, click **Header & Footer** to display the **Header and Footer** dialog box. Click the **Notes and Handouts tab**. Under **Include on page**, select the **Date and time** check box, and then select **Update automatically**. If necessary, clear the Header check box. Select the **Page number** and **Footer** check boxes. In the **Footer** box, using your own name, type **Lastname_Firstname_2A_Safety** and then click **Apply to All**.

6 Display the document properties. As the **Tags** type **safety presentation** and as the **Subject**, type your course and section number. Be sure your name displays as author, and then **Save** your file. As directed by your instructor, create and submit a paper printout or an electronic image of your presentation that looks like a printed document—either as the Notes and Handouts or as the presentation slides—or, submit your completed PowerPoint file.

7 **Close** PowerPoint.

> **END | You have completed Project 2A**

GO! With Google

ALERT!   Working with Web-Based Applications and Services

Computer programs and services on the web receive continuous updates and improvements, so the steps to complete this web-based activity may differ from the ones shown. You can often look at the screens and the information presented to determine how to complete the activity.

If you do not already have a Google account, you will need to create one before beginning this activity. Go to http://google.com and in the upper right corner, click Sign In. On the Sign In screen, click Create Account. On the Create your Google Account page, complete the form, read and agree to the Terms of Service and Privacy Policy, and then click Next step. On the Welcome screen, click Get Started.

Activity | Creating an Informational Presentation in Google Slides

In this Activity, you will use Google Slides to create a presentation similar to the one you created in Project 2A.

1 From the desktop, open your browser, navigate to **http://google.com**, and then sign in to your Google account. Click **Google Apps** ⊞, and then click **Drive** ☁. Open your **GO! Web Projects** folder—or if necessary, click New to create and then open this folder.

2 In the left pane, click **NEW**, click **File upload** ⬆, and then in the **Open** dialog box, navigate to your student data files. Select **p02_2A_Web**. Click **Open**. When the upload is complete and the file name displays in the file list, right-click **p02_2A_Web**, and then click **Rename**. In the Rename dialog box, select and delete the text. Using your own name, as the file name type **Lastname_Firstname_2A_Web** and then press Enter. Right-click your file, click **Open with**, and then click **Google Slides**.

3 Display **Slide 5**. On the **toolbar**, click **Image** ⬜. In the **Insert image** dialog box, click **Search**. In the **Search** box, type **pouring water** and then press Enter. Select a picture similar to the one that you inserted in Project 2A, and then in the lower left, click **Select**. Drag the image to the right and use the sizing handles to position and resize the image so that there is an even amount of space above, below, and to the right of the image.

4 Display **Slide 2**, and then click anywhere in the paragraph. At the right end of the toolbar, if necessary, click **More** ⏷, and then click **Bulleted list** ☰ to remove the bullet symbol from the paragraph. Click **More** ⏷ to close the menu.

5 Click **Align** ☰, click **Center**, and then select the entire paragraph. Change the **Font size** to **24** and apply **Bold**.

ALERT!   No Align Menu

If the Align icon is not visible on the toolbar, click More to display it.

6 With **Slide 2** displayed and the paragraph selected, on the **toolbar**, click **Fill color** 🎨, and then in the eighth column, select the fifth color—**light blue 1**.

7 Click **Line color** ✏, and then, in the eighth column, select the second color—**blue**. Click **Line weight** ☰, and then click **4px**. Click a blank area of the slide to deselect the text box, and then compare your screen with Figure A.

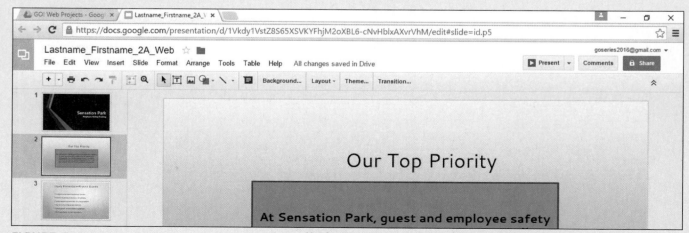

FIGURE A

(GO! With Google continues on the next page)

GO! With Google

8 Display **Slide 3**, and then click in the bulleted list. Click **More** 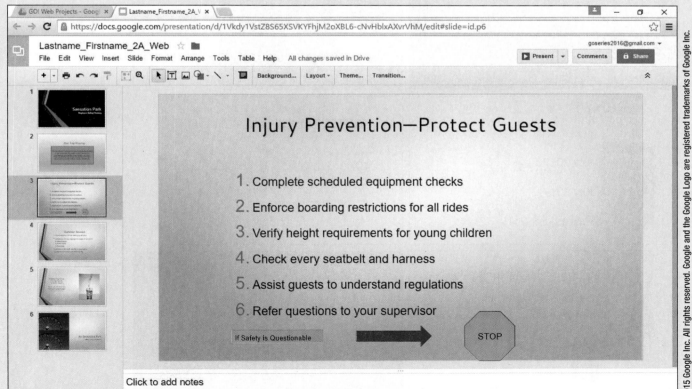, and then click **Numbered list** to apply numbers to all of the bullet points. It is not necessary to select the text; bullets and numbering are applied to all of the bullet points in a content placeholder. Click **More** to close the menu.

9 With **Slide 3** displayed, on the **toolbar**, click **Text box** to insert a text box in your slide. Click below the content placeholder and drag to create the textbox near the bottom of the slide—the exact size and placement need not be precise.

10 With the insertion point blinking in the text box, type **If Safety is Questionable** and then on the **toolbar**, click **Fill color**. In the first column, click the fourth color—**light red berry 2**. If necessary, drag the sizing handles of the textbox to shorten the text box to fit the text. Click outside the text box to deselect it.

11 On the **toolbar**, click **Shape**, point to **Arrows**, and then click **Right Arrow**. Position the mouse pointer to the right of the text box and click to insert an arrow in the middle of your slide. Drag the arrow so that it is aligned horizontally with the text box—a red guide will display to assist you—and its left edge aligns with the *y* in *your*, and then on the **toolbar**, click **Fill color**. In the eight column, click the second color—**blue**.

12 On the **toolbar**, click **Shape**, point to **Shapes**, and then click **Octagon**. Position the mouse pointer to the right of the arrow, and then click to insert an octagon on your slide. Drag the octagon so that its center sizing handle aligns with the arrow point and its left edge aligns with the *s* in *regulations*, and then on the **toolbar**, click **Fill color**. In the first column, click the fourth color—**light red berry 2**.

13 Click in the octagon. Type **STOP**, select the text, change the **Font size** to 18, **Align Center**, and then click in a blank area of the slide. Compare your screen with Figure B and make adjustments to the position of the shapes as necessary.

14 Your presentation will be saved automatically. If you are instructed to submit your file, click the File menu, point to Download, and then click PDF or PowerPoint as directed by your instructor. The file will download to your default download folder as determined by your browser settings. Sign out of your Google account.

FIGURE B

PROJECT ACTIVITIES

In Activities 2.22 through 2.34, you will format slides in a presentation for the Sensation Park Entertainment Group Marketing Director that informs employees about upcoming events at the company's amusement parks. You will enhance the presentation using SmartArt and WordArt graphics. Your completed presentation will look similar to Figure 2.36.

PROJECT FILES

MyITLab
grader

If your instructor wants you to submit Project 2B in the MyITLab Grader system, log in to MyITLab, locate Grader Project 2B, and then download the files for this project.

For Project 2B, you will need the following files:

p02B_Canada_Contact
p02B_Celebrations
p02B_Mexico_Contact
p02B_US_Contact

You will save your presentation as:

Lastname_Firstname_2B_Celebrations

Please always review the downloaded Grader instructions before beginning.

PROJECT RESULTS

GO!
Walk Thru
Project 2B

PowerPoint 2016, Windows 10, Microsoft Corporation

FIGURE 2.36 Project 2B Celebrations

Objective 5 | Remove Picture Backgrounds and Insert WordArt

GO! Learn How
Video P2-5

To avoid the boxy look that results when you insert an image into a presentation, use the **Background Removal** command, which removes unwanted portions of a picture so that the picture does not appear as a self-contained rectangle. This enables you to flow a picture into the content of the presentation.

WordArt is a gallery of text styles with which you can create decorative effects, such as shadowed or mirrored text. You can choose from the gallery of WordArt styles to insert a new WordArt object or you can customize existing text by applying WordArt formatting.

Activity 2.22 | Removing the Background from a Picture and Applying Soft Edge Options

ALERT! **To submit as an autograded project, log into MyITLab, download the files for this project, and begin with those files instead of the student data files.**

1 ▶ Start PowerPoint. From your student data files, open **p02B_Celebrations**. In your **PowerPoint Chapter 2** folder, **Save** the file as **Lastname_Firstname_2B_Celebrations**

2 ▶ Display **Slide 6**. Click the fireworks picture to select it, and then on the **Picture Tools Format tab**, in the **Adjust group**, click **Remove Background**. Compare your screen with Figure 2.37.

PowerPoint determines what portion of the picture is the foreground—the portion to keep—and which portion is the background—the portion to remove. The background is overlaid in magenta, leaving the remaining portion of the picture as it will look when the background removal is complete. A rectangular selection area displays that can be moved and sized to select additional areas of the picture. The Background Removal options display in the Refine group on the ribbon.

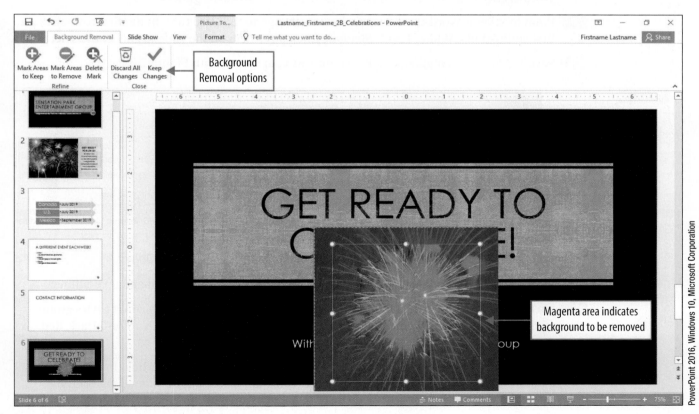

FIGURE 2.37

3 On the **Background Removal tab**, in the **Close group**, click **Keep Changes** to remove the background.

4 With the picture selected, on the **Picture Tools Format tab**, in the **Picture Styles group**, click **Picture Effects**, point to **Soft Edges**, and then click **50 Point**. **Save** 🖫 your presentation, and then compare your slide with Figure 2.38.

Background removed and soft edge picture style applied

PowerPoint 2016, Windows 10, Microsoft Corporation

FIGURE 2.38

2.1.3

Activity 2.23 | Applying WordArt Styles to Existing Text

1 On **Slide 6**, click anywhere in the word *Get* to activate the title placeholder, and then select the title—*Get Ready to Celebrate!* Click the **Drawing Tools Format tab**, and then in the **WordArt Styles group**, click **More** 🔻 to display the WordArt gallery.

2 Point to several WordArt styles to view the change to the slide title. In the first row, click the first style—**Fill – White, Text 1, Shadow**. Click anywhere on the slide to cancel the selection.

3 **Save** 🖫 your presentation, and then compare your screen with Figure 2.39.

WordArt style applied to title

PowerPoint 2016, Windows 10, Microsoft Corporation

FIGURE 2.39

Activity 2.24 | Changing the Text Fill and Text Outline Colors of a WordArt Object

You can modify a WordArt object by changing the colors of the text fill and text outline.

1 On **Slide 6**, select the title. On the **Drawing Tools Format tab**, in the **WordArt Styles group**, click **Text Fill**. Under **Theme Colors**, in the sixth column, click the fifth color—**Dark Red, Accent 2, Darker 25%**.

2 With the text still selected, in the **WordArt Styles group**, click **Text Outline**. In the second column, click the first color—**White, Text 1**. Click anywhere on the slide to cancel the selection.

3 **Save** 🖫 your presentation, and then compare your screen with Figure 2.40.

FIGURE 2.40

Activity 2.25 | Inserting and Aligning a WordArt Object

In addition to formatting existing text using WordArt, you can insert a new WordArt object anywhere on a slide.

1 Display **Slide 3**. On the **Insert tab**, in the **Text group**, click **WordArt**. In the gallery, in the second row, click the third WordArt style—**Gradient Fill – Brown, Accent 4, Outline – Accent 4**.

> In the center of your slide, a WordArt placeholder displays *Your text here*. Text that you type will replace this text, and the placeholder will expand to accommodate the text. The WordArt is surrounded by sizing handles that you can use to adjust its size.

2 Type **Schedule of Events** to replace the WordArt placeholder text. Compare your screen with Figure 2.41.

WordArt inserted

FIGURE 2.41

3 With the WordArt selected, on the **Drawing Tools Format tab**, in the **Arrange group**, click **Align**, and then click **Align Top** to move the WordArt to the top of the slide.

4 Click in a blank area of the slide, and then compare your screen with Figure 2.42.

FIGURE 2.42

5 > **Save** your presentation.

Activity 2.26 | Adding Text Effects to a WordArt

Text effects are formats applied to text that include shadows, reflections, glows, bevels, and 3-D rotations.

1 > With **Slide 3** displayed, select the **WordArt** text. Change the **Font** to **Arial** and the **Font Size** to **66**.

2 > On the **Drawing Tools Format tab**, in the **WordArt Styles group**, click **Text Effects**. Point to **Shadow**, and then compare your screen with Figure 2.43.

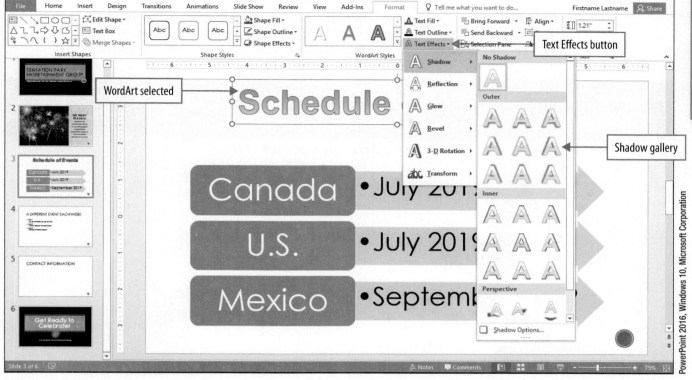

FIGURE 2.43

3 Under **Outer**, click the last style—**Offset Diagonal Top Left**. Click in a blank area of the slide, and then compare your screen with Figure 2.44.

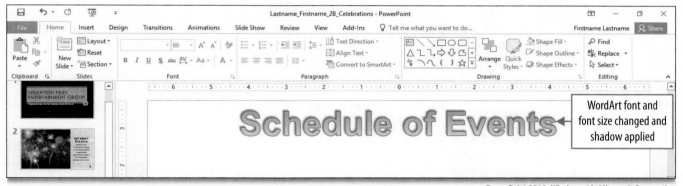

FIGURE 2.44

4 **Save** 🖫 your presentation.

Objective 6 | Create and Format a SmartArt Graphic

GO! Learn How
Video P2-6

A **SmartArt graphic** is a visual representation of information that you create by choosing from among various layouts to communicate your message or ideas effectively. SmartArt graphics can illustrate processes, hierarchies, cycles, lists, and relationships. You can include text and pictures in a SmartArt graphic, and you can apply colors, effects, and styles that coordinate with the presentation theme.

3.3.2

Activity 2.27 | Creating a SmartArt Graphic from Bulleted Points

You can convert an existing bulleted list into a SmartArt graphic. When you create a SmartArt graphic, consider the message that you are trying to convey, and then choose an appropriate layout. The table in Figure 2.45 describes types of SmartArt layouts and suggested purposes.

MICROSOFT POWERPOINT SMARTART GRAPHIC TYPES		
GRAPHIC TYPE	**EXAMPLE LAYOUT**	**PURPOSE OF GRAPHIC**
List	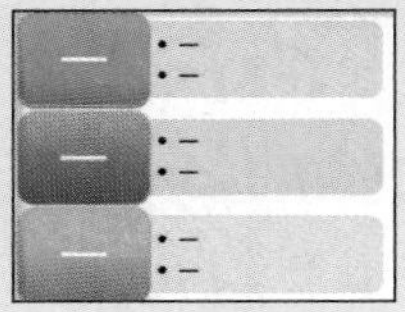	Shows nonsequential information
Process	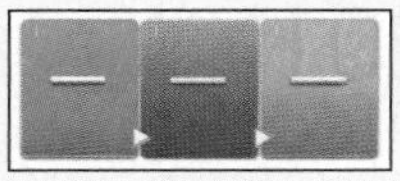	Shows steps in a process or timeline
Cycle	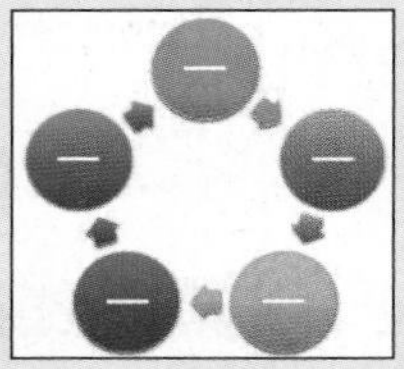	Shows a continual process
Hierarchy	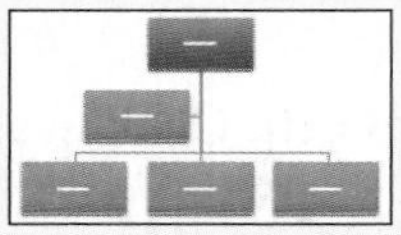	Shows a decision tree or displays an organization chart
Relationship		Illustrates connections
Matrix	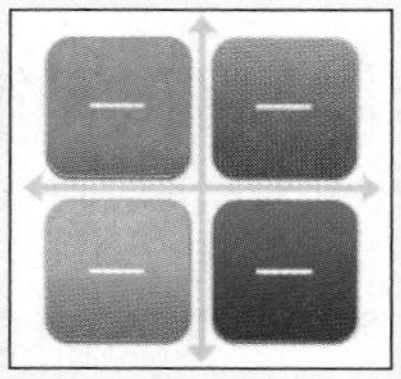	Shows how parts relate to a whole
Pyramid	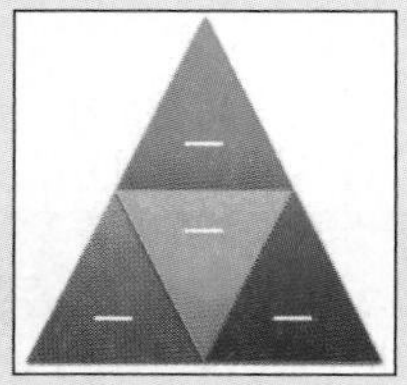	Shows proportional relationships with the largest component on the top or bottom
Picture	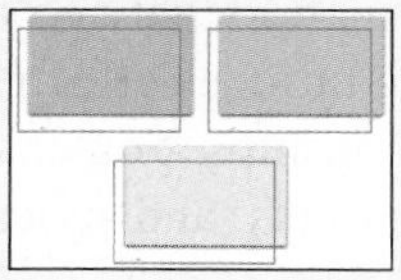	Includes pictures in the layout to communicate messages and ideas
Office.com		Additional layouts available from **Office.com**

FIGURE 2.45

PowerPoint 2016, Windows 10, Microsoft Corporation

1 Display **Slide 4**, and then click anywhere in the bulleted list placeholder. On the **Home tab**, in the **Paragraph group**, click **Convert to SmartArt**. Below the gallery, click **More SmartArt Graphics**.

Three sections comprise the Choose a SmartArt Graphic dialog box. The left section lists the SmartArt graphic types. The center section displays the SmartArt layouts according to type. The third section displays the selected SmartArt graphic, its name, and a description of its purpose.

ANOTHER WAY Right-click on a bulleted list to display the shortcut menu, point to Convert to SmartArt, and then click More SmartArt Graphics.

2 On the left side of the **Choose a SmartArt Graphic** dialog box, click **List**. Use the ScreenTips to locate and then click **Vertical Box List**. Compare your screen with Figure 2.46.

ALERT! **Vertical Box List Layout Missing**

If the Vertical Box List option is not available, choose another vertical list style.

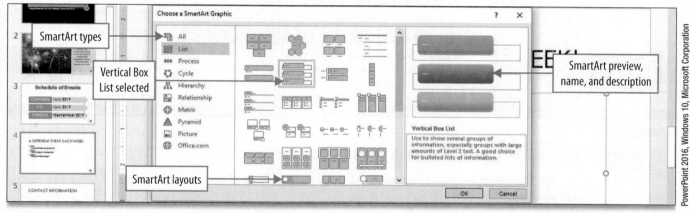

FIGURE 2.46

3 In the **Choose a SmartArt Graphic** dialog box, click **OK**. If necessary, close the Text pane on the left. **Save** 🖫 your presentation, and then compare your screen with Figure 2.47.

It is not necessary to select all of the text in the list. By clicking in the list, PowerPoint converts all of the bullet points to the selected SmartArt graphic. On the ribbon, the SmartArt contextual tools display two tabs—Design and Format. The border surrounding the SmartArt graphic indicates that it is selected and displays the area that the object will cover on the slide.

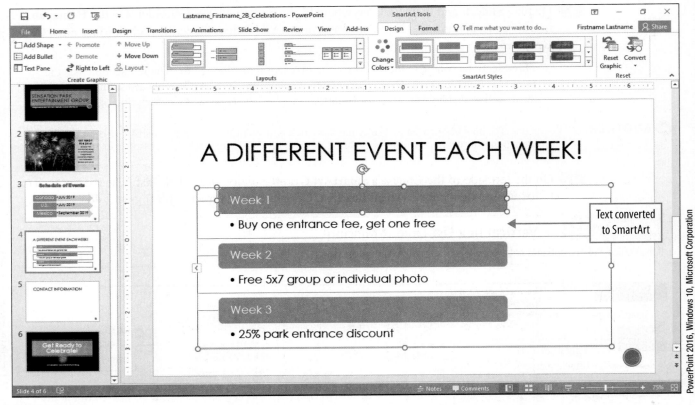

FIGURE 2.47

MOS
3.3.3

Activity 2.28 | Adding Shapes in a SmartArt Graphic

If a SmartArt graphic does not have enough shapes to illustrate a concept or display the relationships, you can add more shapes.

1 Click in the shape that contains the text *Week 3*. On the **SmartArt Tools Design tab**, in the **Create Graphic group**, click the **Add Shape arrow**, and then click **Add Shape After** to insert a shape at the same level. Type **Week 4**

The text in each of the SmartArt shapes resizes to accommodate the added shape.

ANOTHER WAY   Right-click the shape, point to Add Shape, and then click Add Shape After.

2 On the **SmartArt Tools Design tab**, in the **Create Graphic group**, click **Add Bullet** to add a bullet below the *Week 4* shape.

3 Type **25% discount on food and beverages** Click a blank area of the slide and compare your slide with Figure 2.48.

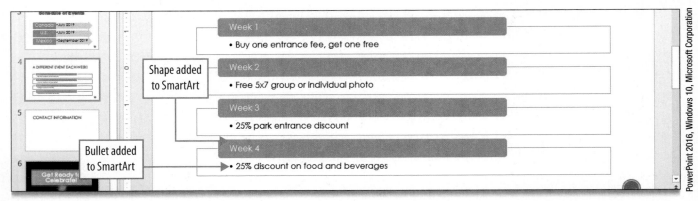

FIGURE 2.48

4 **Save** 🖫 your presentation.

MOS 3.3.1 **Activity 2.29 | Inserting a SmartArt Graphic Using a Content Layout**

1 Display **Slide 5**. In the center of the content placeholder, click **Insert a SmartArt Graphic** 🖼 to open the **Choose a SmartArt Graphic** dialog box.

2 On the left, click **Picture**, and then scroll as necessary and use the ScreenTips to locate, and then click **Picture Strips**. Compare your screen with Figure 2.49.

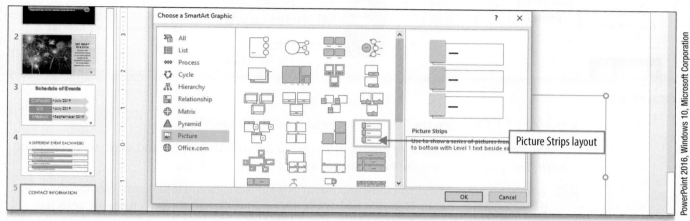

FIGURE 2.49

3 Click **OK** to insert the SmartArt graphic.

You can type text directly into the shapes or you can type text in the Text Pane, which may display to the left of your SmartArt graphic. You can toggle the Text Pane display by clicking the Text Pane tab—the small left arrow on the left side of the SmartArt graphic border—or by clicking the Text Pane button on the SmartArt Tools Design tab, in the Create Graphic group.

Activity 2.30 | Inserting Pictures and Text in a SmartArt Graphic

1 In the SmartArt graphic, in the upper left text rectangle shape, type **Sophia Ackerman** and then press Enter. Type **United States** and then click in the text rectangle on the right. Type **Joseph Mercado** and then press Enter. Type **Mexico** and then click in the lower text rectangle. Type **Michael Lewis** and then press Enter. Type **Canada**

2 In the top left picture placeholder, click **Insert Picture** 🖾. In the **Insert Pictures** dialog box, to the right of **From a file**, click **Browse**. Navigate to your student data files, click **p02B_US_Contact**, and then click **Insert** to insert the picture.

3 Using the technique you just practiced, in the right picture placeholder, insert **p02B_Mexico_Contact**. In the lower picture placeholder, insert **p02B_Canada_Contact**.

4 **Save** 🖫 your presentation, and then compare your screen with Figure 2.50.

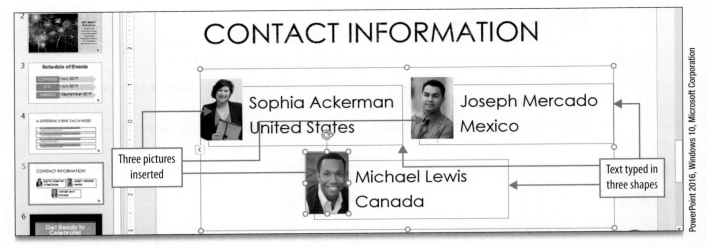

FIGURE 2.50

Activity 2.31 | Changing the Size and Shape of SmartArt Elements

You can select individual or groups of shapes in a SmartArt graphic and make them larger or smaller, and you can change selected shapes to another type of shape.

1 With **Slide 5** displayed, click the picture of *Sophia Ackerman*. Hold down Shift, and then click the pictures of *Joseph Mercado* and *Michael Lewis* so that all three pictures are selected. Release Shift.

2 On the **SmartArt Tools Format tab**, in the **Shapes group**, click **Larger** two times to increase the size of the three pictures.

3 With the three pictures selected, on the **SmartArt Tools Format tab**, in the **Shapes group**, click **Change Shape**. Under **Rectangles**, click the second shape—**Rounded Rectangle**.

4 Click in an empty area of the slide to cancel the selection, and then compare your screen with Figure 2.51.

FIGURE 2.51

5 **Save** 🖫 your presentation.

Activity 2.32 | Changing the SmartArt Layout

1 Display **Slide 3**, and then click anywhere in the SmartArt graphic. On the **SmartArt Tools Design tab**, in the **Layouts group**, click **More** ⊡, and then click **More Layouts**. In the **Choose a SmartArt Graphic** dialog box, click **List**. Scroll up or down as necessary to locate and then click **Tab List**. Compare your screen with Figure 2.52.

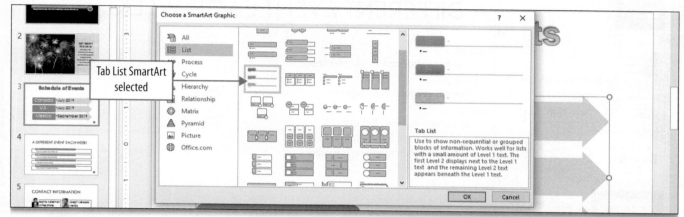

FIGURE 2.52

2 Click **OK**, and then **Save** ⊟ the presentation.

Activity 2.33 | Changing the Color and Style of a SmartArt Graphic

MOS
3.3.5

SmartArt Styles are combinations of formatting effects that you can apply to SmartArt graphics.

1 With **Slide 3** displayed, if necessary, select the SmartArt. On the **SmartArt Tools Design tab**, in the **SmartArt Styles group**, click **Change Colors**. In the color gallery, under **Colorful**, click the second style—**Colorful Range - Accent Colors 2 to 3**—to change the colors.

2 On the **SmartArt Tools Design tab**, in the **SmartArt Styles group**, click **More** ⊡ to display the **SmartArt Styles gallery**. Under **3-D**, click the third style, **Cartoon**. Compare your slide with Figure 2.53.

FIGURE 2.53

3 Save ⊟ your presentation.

Activity 2.34 | Converting a SmartArt to Text

1 Display **Slide 4**, and then click anywhere in the SmartArt graphic. On the **SmartArt Tools Design tab**, in the **Reset group**, click **Convert**, and then click **Convert to Text** to convert the SmartArt graphic back to a bulleted list. Compare your screen with Figure 2.54.

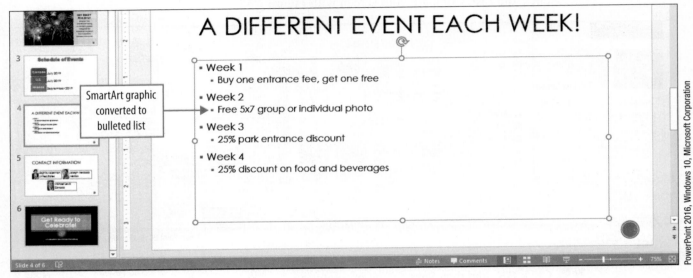

FIGURE 2.54

2 Insert a **Header & Footer** on the **Notes and Handouts**. Include the **Date and time updated automatically**, the **Page number**, and a **Footer**—using your own name—with the text **Lastname_Firstname_2B_Celebrations**

3 Display the document properties. As the **Tags** type **independence day, celebrations** and as the **Subject** type your course and section number. Be sure your name displays as the author, and then **Save** your file.

4 View the slide show from the beginning, and then make any necessary adjustments. **Save** your presentation. As directed by your instructor, create and submit a paper printout or an electronic image of your presentation that looks like a printed document—either as the Notes and Handouts or as the presentation slides—or, submit your completed PowerPoint file.

5 **Close** PowerPoint.

More Knowledge	**Move Text within SmartArt Shapes and Reverse Order**

You can change the position of text within SmartArt using commands on the Home tab in the Paragraph group. The options include Align Text—Top, Middle, Bottom; Text Direction—Horizontal, Rotate all text 90°, Rotate all text 270°, Stacked; Align—Left, Right, Center, Justify; and Line Spacing—1.0, 1.5, 2.0, 2.5, 3.0. You can reverse the order of the SmartArt graphic using commands on the Design tab, in the Create Graphic group. The options include Promote, Demote, Right to Left, Left to Right, Move Up, and Move Down.

END | You have completed Project 2B

GO! With Google

ALERT! **Working with Web-Based Applications and Services**

Computer programs and services on the web receive continuous updates and improvements, so the steps to complete this web-based activity may differ from the ones shown. You can often look at the screens and the information presented to determine how to complete the activity.

If you do not already have a Google account, you will need to create one before beginning this activity. Go to http://google.com and in the upper right corner, click Sign In. On the Sign In screen, click Create Account. On the Create your Google Account page, complete the form, read and agree to the Terms of Service and Privacy Policy, and then click Next step. On the Welcome screen, click Get Started.

Activity | Creating an Advertisement Presentation in Google Slides

In this Activity, you will use Google Slides to format a presentation similar to the one you created in Project 2B.

1 From the desktop, open your browser, navigate to **http://google.com**, and then sign in to your Google account. Click **Google Apps** ⊞, and then click **Drive** ☁. Open your **GO! Web Projects** folder—or create and then open this folder if necessary.

2 On the left, click **NEW**, and then click **File upload**. Navigate to your student data files, click **p02_2B_Web**, and then click **Open**. When the upload is complete and the file name displays in the file list, right-click **p02_2B_Web**, and then click **Rename**. In the **Rename** dialog box, select and delete the existing text. Using your own name, as the file name, type **Lastname_Firstname_2B_Web** and then press Enter. Right-click the file that you just renamed, click **Open with**, and then click **Google Slides**.

3 Display **Slide 5**. Click the picture to select it, and then on the **toolbar**, click the **Mask image arrow** ▾, point to **Callouts**, and then click **32-Point Star**.

4 With the picture selected, on the **toolbar**, click **Image options**, and then drag the **Transparency** slider to **20%**. **Close** the Image Options pane.

5 Display **Slide 3**. On the **Insert** menu, click **Word art**. In the center of the slide, with the insertion point blinking in the placeholder, type **Schedule of Events** and press Enter. The Word art is surrounded by sizing handles with which you can adjust its size.

6 With the **Word art** selected, on the **toolbar**, click **Fill color** ▾, and then in the first column, click the eighth color—**dark red berry 3**. On the **toolbar**, click **Line color**, and then in the first column, click the third color—**light red berry 3**.

7 Drag the **Word art** upward until there is an even amount of white space above and below it. On the menu bar, click **Arrange**, point to **Center on page**, and then click **Horizontally**.

8 With **Slide 3** displayed, select the **Word art**. On the **toolbar**, change the **Font** to **Georgia**. Compare your screen to Figure A.

9 Your presentation will be saved automatically. Download as a PDF or PowerPoint file and submit as instructed by your instructor. Sign out of your Google account.

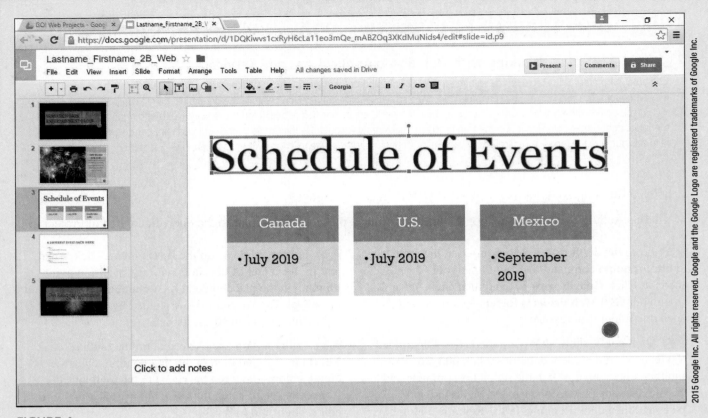

FIGURE A

GO! To Work

MICROSOFT OFFICE SPECIALIST (MOS) SKILLS IN THIS CHAPTER

PROJECT 2A

2.1.5 Create bulleted and numbered lists
2.2.1 Insert or replace shapes
2.2.2 Insert text boxes
2.2.3 Resize shapes and text boxes
2.2.4 Format shapes and text boxes
2.2.5 Apply styles to shapes and text boxes
2.3.2 Resize and crop images
2.3.3 Apply styles and effects
2.4.2 Align objects
2.4.3 Group objects
2.4.4 Display alignment guides

PROJECT 2B

2.1.3 Apply WordArt styles to text
3.3.1 Create SmartArt graphics
3.3.2 Convert lists to SmartArt graphics
3.3.3 Add shapes to SmartArt graphics
3.3.4 Reorder shapes in SmartArt graphics
3.3.5 Change the color of SmartArt graphics

BUILD YOUR E-PORTFOLIO

An E-Portfolio is a collection of evidence, stored electronically, that showcases what you have accomplished while completing your education. Collecting and then sharing your work products with potential employers reflects your academic and career goals. Your completed documents from the following projects are good examples to show what you have learned: 2G, 2K, and 2L.

GO! FOR JOB SUCCESS

Video: Business Lunch Interpersonal Communications

Your instructor may assign this video to your class, and then ask you to think about, or discuss with your classmates, these questions:

FotolEdhar / Fotolia

In what specific ways did Sara and Jordan demonstrate improper interpersonal communication during their lunch with Karen?

As a manager, did Chris follow the rules of interpersonal communication with his client? Explain your answer.

In what ways did Sara, Jordan, and Theo demonstrate proper or improper nonverbal communication skills?

END OF CHAPTER

SUMMARY

Use numbered and bulleted lists in a presentation to focus attention on specific items. The theme that you select includes default styles for bullets, but you can change the shape and color of the symbols.

Use pictures to illustrate an idea. The Online Pictures feature enables you to search the web for images that emphasize important points. Using good keywords is critical to a successful search to find a great picture!

Objects are easily modified in PowerPoint. Removing the picture background and cropping eliminate unnecessary picture parts. Smart guides and alignment options are used to position pictures and shapes.

Use SmartArt graphics to present information to illustrate processes, hierarchies, cycles, lists, and relationships. SmartArt graphics may include text and pictures, and can be formatted with styles and color combinations for maximum impact.

GO! LEARN IT ONLINE

Review the concepts, key terms, and MOS skills in this chapter by completing these online challenges, which you can find at **MyITLab**.

Matching and Multiple Choice: Answer matching and multiple choice questions to test what you learned in this chapter.

Lessons on the GO!: Learn how to use all the new apps and features as they are introduced by Microsoft.

MOS Prep Quiz: Answer questions to review the MOS skills that you practiced in this chapter.

GO! COLLABORATIVE TEAM PROJECT (Available in **MyITLab** and Instructor Resource Center)

If your instructor assigns this project to your class, you can expect to work with one or more of your classmates—either in person or by using Internet tools—to create work products similar to those that you created in this chapter. A team is a group of workers who work together to solve a problem, make a decision, or create a work product. Collaboration is when you work together with others as a team in an intellectual endeavor to complete a shared task or achieve a shared goal.

PROJECT GUIDE FOR POWERPOINT CHAPTER 2

Your instructor will assign Projects from this list to ensure your learning and assess your knowledge.

		PROJECT GUIDE FOR POWERPOINT CHAPTER 2	
PROJECT	**APPLY SKILLS FROM THESE CHAPTER OBJECTIVES**	**PROJECT TYPE**	**PROJECT LOCATION**
2A	Objectives 1–4 from Project 2A	**2A Instructional Project (Grader Project)** Guided instruction to learn the skills in Project 2A.	In MyITLab and in text
2B	Objectives 5–6 from Project 2B	**2B Instructional Project (Grader Project)** Guided instruction to learn the skills in Project 2B.	In MyITLab and in text
2C	Objectives 1–4 from Project 2A	**2C Skills Review (Scorecard Grading)** A guided review of the skills from Project 2A.	In text
2D	Objectives 5–6 from Project 2B	**2D Skills Review (Scorecard Grading)** A guided review of the skills from Project 2B.	In text
2E **MyITLab**	Objectives 1–4 from Project 2A	**2E Mastery (Grader Project) Mastery and Transfer of Learning** A demonstration of your mastery of the skills in Project 2A with extensive decision making.	In MyITLab and in text
2F **MyITLab**	Objectives 5–6 from Project 2B	**2F Mastery (Grader Project) Mastery and Transfer of Learning** A demonstration of your mastery of the skills in Project 2B with extensive decision making.	In MyITLab and in text
2G **MyITLab**	Objectives 1–6 from Projects 2A and 2B	**2G Mastery (Grader Project) Mastery and Transfer of Learning** A demonstration of your mastery of the skills in Projects 2A and 2B with extensive decision making.	In MyITLab and in text
2H	Combination of Objectives from Projects 2A and 2B	**2H GO! Fix It (Scorecard Grading) Critical Thinking** A demonstration of your mastery of the skills in Projects 2A and 2B by creating a correct result from a document that contains errors you must find.	Instructor Resource Center (IRC) and MyITLab
2I	Combination of Objectives from Projects 2A and 2B	**2I GO! Make It (Scorecard Grading) Critical Thinking** A demonstration of your mastery of the skills in Projects 2A and 2B by creating a result from a supplied picture.	IRC and MyITLab
2J	Combination of Objectives from Projects 2A and 2B	**2J GO! Solve It (Rubric Grading) Critical Thinking** A demonstration of your mastery of the skills in Projects 2A and 2B, your decision-making skills, and your critical-thinking skills. A task-specific rubric helps you self-assess your result.	IRC and MyITLab
2K	Combination of Objectives from Projects 2A and 2B	**2K GO! Solve It (Rubric Grading) Critical Thinking** A demonstration of your mastery of the skills in Projects 2A and 2B, your decision-making skills, and your critical-thinking skills. A task-specific rubric helps you self-assess your result.	In text
2L	Combination of Objectives from Projects 2A and 2B	**2L GO! Think (Rubric Grading) Critical Thinking** A demonstration of your understanding of the chapter concepts applied in a manner that you would outside of college. An analytic rubric helps you and your instructor grade the quality of your work by comparing it to the work an expert in the discipline would create.	In text
2M	Combination of Objectives from Projects 2A and 2B	**2M GO! Think (Rubric Grading) Critical Thinking** A demonstration of your understanding of the chapter concepts applied in a manner that you would outside of college. An analytic rubric helps you and your instructor grade the quality of your work by comparing it to the work an expert in the discipline would create.	IRC and MyITLab
2N	Combination of Objectives from Projects 2A and 2B	**2N You and GO! (Rubric Grading) Critical Thinking** A demonstration of your understanding of the chapter concepts applied in a manner that you would in a personal situation. An analytic rubric helps you and your instructor grade the quality of your work.	IRC and MyITLab
2O	Combination of Objectives from Projects 2A and 2B	**2O Collaborative Team Project for PowerPoint Chapter 2 Critical Thinking** A demonstration of your understanding of concepts and your ability to work collaboratively in a group role-playing assessment, requiring both collaboration and self-management.	IRC and MyITLab

GLOSSARY

GLOSSARY OF CHAPTER KEY TERMS

Background Removal A feature that removes unwanted portions of a picture so that the picture does not appear as a self-contained rectangle.

Bulleted list A list of items preceded by small dots or other shapes, which do not indicate order or rank. Sometimes called an unordered list.

Clip A single media file such as art, sound, animation, or a movie.

Crop A command that removes unwanted or unnecessary areas of a picture.

Crop handles Handles used to remove unwanted areas of a picture.

Crop pointer The pointer used to crop areas of a picture.

Crosshair pointer The pointer used to draw a shape.

Eyedropper A tool that captures the exact color from an object on your screen and then applies it to any shape, picture, or text.

Fill color The inside color of text or of an object.

Numbered list A list of items preceded by numbers, which indicate sequence or rank of the items. Sometimes called an ordered list.

RGB A color model in which the colors red, green, and blue are added together to form another color.

Ruler guides Dotted red vertical and horizontal lines that display in the rulers, indicating the pointer's position.

Shape A slide object such as a line, arrow, box, callout, or banner.

Smart guides Dashed lines that display on your slide when you are moving an object to assist you with alignment.

SmartArt graphic A visual representation of information that you create by choosing from among various layouts to communicate your message or ideas effectively.

SmartArt Styles Combinations of formatting effects that you can apply to SmartArt graphics.

Text box An object with which you can position text anywhere on a slide.

Text effects Formats applied to text that include shadows, reflections, glows, bevels, and 3-D rotations.

WordArt A gallery of text styles with which you can create decorative effects, such as shadowed or mirrored text.

Apply 2A skills from these Objectives:

1 Format Numbered and Bulleted Lists
2 Insert Online Pictures
3 Insert Text Boxes and Shapes
4 Format Objects

Skills Review Project 2C Concerts

In the following Skills Review, you will format a presentation that describes annual Concert in the Park events at several Sensation Park Entertainment Group amusement parks. Your completed presentation will look similar to Figure 2.55.

PROJECT FILES **MyITLab** grader

For Project 2C, you will need the following file:

p02C_Concerts

You will save your presentation as:

Lastname_Firstname_2C_Concerts

PROJECT RESULTS

Sensation Park Entertainment Group

Concerts in the Park

Your picture may differ

Every Friday in June and July

Your Paid Admission is Your Entrance Fee

Your picture may differ

▶ Located in the main plaza at each park
▶ Grandstand seating will be available
  ❑ Seating is limited
  ❑ Reserved seating is available
▶ Concerts begin at 7:30 pm

Join Us as We Rock the Night!

A Different Band Each Week!

1. Classic Rock
2. Top Forty
3. Country Hits
4. Fifties and Sixties
5. Jazz

Concerts begin June 21!

Your picture may differ

FIGURE 2.55

(Project 2C Concerts continues on the next page)

1 Start PowerPoint. From your student data files, locate and open **p02C_Concerts**. On the **File tab**, click **Save As**, navigate to your **PowerPoint Chapter 2** folder, and then using your own name, save the file as **Lastname_Firstname_2C_Concerts**

a. If necessary, display the rulers. With **Slide 1** displayed, on the **Insert tab**, in the **Illustrations group**, click **Shapes**, and then under **Basic Shapes**, in the second row, click the fifth shape—**Frame**.

b. Move the pointer to align the ruler guides with the **left half of the horizontal ruler at 3 inches** and with the **upper half of the vertical ruler at 2.5 inches**, and then click to insert the Frame.

c. On the **Format tab**, in the **Size group**, click in the **Shape Height** box to select the number, and then type **1.7** Click in the **Shape Width** box. Replace the selected number with **5.5** and then press Enter to resize the shape.

d. With the frame selected, type **Sensation Park Entertainment Group** and then change the **Font Size** to **28**. Change the **Font Color** to **Gray-25%, Background 2**—under Theme Colors, in the third column, the first color. On the **Format tab** in the **Shape Styles group**, click **Shape Fill**, and then under **Theme Colors**, in the third column, click the first color—**Gray-25%, Background 2**.

2 On the **Insert tab**, in the **Images group**, click **Online Pictures**. In the **Bing Image Search** box, type **sheet music** and then press Enter.

a. Click a horizontal picture of lines of music on a music sheet of your choosing, and then click **Insert**.

b. On the **Format tab**, in the **Size group**, click in the **Shape Height** box. Replace the selected number with **2.5** and then press Enter to resize the image.

c. Drag the picture down and to the right until intersecting red dashed Smart Guides display, indicating that the picture is center aligned with the title and its top edge aligns with the bottom edge of the title placeholder.

d. With the picture selected, on the **Format tab**, in the **Size group**, click the **Crop arrow**, and then point to **Crop to Shape**. Under **Basic Shapes**, click the first shape—**Oval**. In the **Picture Styles group**, click **Picture Effects**, point to **Soft Edges**, and then click **25 Point**.

e. With the picture selected, hold down Shift, and then click the **frame shape** and the **title placeholder** so that all three objects are selected. On the **Format tab**, in the **Arrange group**, click **Align**, and then click **Align to Slide**. Click **Align** again, and then click **Align Center**. **Save** the presentation.

3 Display **Slide 2**. On the right side of the slide, in the content placeholder, click **Online Pictures**. In the **Bing Image Search** box, type **drum kit** and then press Enter. Insert a horizontal picture of a colored drum set on a white background. Do not choose a black and white image. With the picture selected, on the **Format tab**, in the **Size group**, click the **Crop arrow**, and then point to **Crop to Shape**. Under **Basic Shapes**, click the first shape—**Oval**. In the **Picture Styles group**, click **Picture Effects**, point to **Soft Edges**, and then click **50 Point**.

a. Click in the placeholder containing the text *Every Friday in June and July*. On the **Home tab**, in the **Paragraph group**, click **Bullets** to remove the bullet symbol from the title.

b. Select the text *Every Friday in June and July*. On the **Home tab**, in the **Font group**, click the **Font Color button arrow**. Below the gallery, click **Eyedropper**, and then move the eyedropper pointer so that it is pointing to any bright colored area of the drum on the right side of the picture. Click one time to apply the color to the selected text. Apply **Bold** and **Italic** and change the **Font Size** to **32**.

4 Display **Slide 3**, and then select the third and fourth bullet points—*Seating is limited* and *Reserved seating is available*.

a. On the **Home tab**, in the **Paragraph group**, click the **Bullets button arrow**, and then click **Bullets and Numbering**. In the second row, click the first style—**Hollow Square Bullets**. Replace the number in the **Size** box with **90** and then click the **Color arrow**. Under **Recent Colors**, apply the color chosen using the eyedropper on Slide 2. Click **OK**.

b. Display **Slide 4**, and then click the bulleted list placeholder. Click the dashed border so that it displays as a solid line, and then on the **Home tab**, in the **Paragraph group**, click **Numbering** to change the bullet symbols to numbers.

(Project 2C Concerts continues on the next page)

c. On the left side of the slide, select the title text, and then on the mini toolbar, click the **Font Color button arrow**. Under **Recent Colors**, apply the color chosen using the eyedropper on Slide 2.

5 Display **Slide 5**. On the **Insert tab**, in the **Images group**, click **Online Pictures**. In the **Bing Image Search** box, type **electric guitar** and then press Enter. Insert a vertical picture of a guitar of your choosing.

a. Change the picture **Height** to **5.25** and then drag the picture so that its upper left corner aligns with the upper left corner of the purple area on the slide. On the **Format tab**, in the **Picture Styles group**, click **Picture Effects**, and then point to **Soft Edges**. Click **2.5 Point**.

b. Press Ctrl + D and then drag the duplicated picture to the right about 1 inch. Press Ctrl + D to insert a third picture.

c. Point to the third guitar picture that you inserted and then drag to the right so that its upper right corner aligns with the upper right corner of the purple area on the slide.

d. Hold down Shift and then click the first two guitar pictures so that all three pictures are selected. On the **Format tab**, in the **Arrange group**, click **Align**, and then click **Align to Slide**. Click **Align** again, and then click **Align Middle**.

e. With the three pictures selected, click **Align**, and then click **Align Selected Objects**. Click **Align** again, and then click **Distribute Horizontally**.

6 With **Slide 5** displayed, on the **Insert tab**, in the **Text group**, click **Text Box**. Move the pointer to align the ruler guides with the **left half of the horizontal ruler at 2 inches** and with the **lower half of the vertical ruler at 2.5 inches**, and then click to insert the text box.

a. Type **Concerts Begin June 21!** Select the text and then change the **Font Size** to **32**. On the **Format tab**, in the **Arrange group**, click **Align**, and then click **Align Center**.

b. Insert a **Header & Footer**, on the **Notes and Handouts tab**. Include the **Date and time updated automatically**, the **Page number,** and a **Footer** with the text **Lastname_Firstname_2C_Concerts**

c. Display the document properties. As the **Tags,** type **concerts** and as the **Subject,** type your course and section number. Be sure your name displays as author, and then **Save** your file.

d. View the slide show from the beginning. As directed by your instructor, create and submit a paper printout or an electronic image of your presentation that looks like a printed document; or, submit your completed PowerPoint file. **Close** PowerPoint.

END | You have completed Project 2C

Apply 2B skills from these Objectives:

5 Remove Picture Backgrounds and Insert WordArt

6 Create and Format a SmartArt Graphic

Skills Review | Project 2D Corporate Events

In the following Skills Review, you will format a presentation by inserting and formatting WordArt and SmartArt graphics. Your completed presentation will look similar to Figure 2.56.

PROJECT FILES

For Project 2D, you will need the following file:

p02D_Corporate_Events

You will save your presentation as:

Lastname_Firstname_2D_Corporate_Events

PROJECT RESULTS

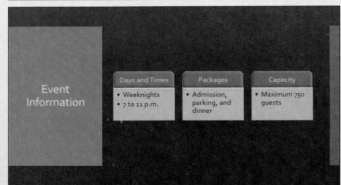

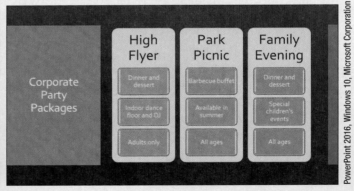

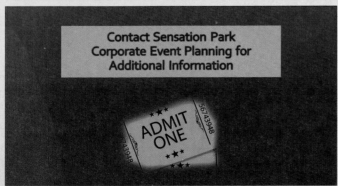

PowerPoint 2016, Windows 10, Microsoft Corporation

FIGURE 2.56

(Project 2D Corporate Events continues on the next page)

Skills Review | Project 2D Corporate Events (continued)

1 Start PowerPoint. From your student data files, locate and open **p02D_Corporate_Events**. **Save** the presentation in your **PowerPoint Chapter 2** folder as **Lastname_Firstname_2D_Corporate_Events**

a. With **Slide 1** displayed, select the text *Corporate Event Planning*. On the **Format tab**, in the **WordArt Styles group**, click **More**. In the third row, click the last style—**Fill – Brown, Background 2, Inner Shadow**. Click outside the placeholder.

b. On the **Insert tab**, in the **Text group**, click **WordArt**. In the **WordArt gallery**, in the first row, click the fourth style—**Fill – White, Outline – Accent 1, Shadow**. With the text *Your text here* selected, type **Sensation Park**

c. With the WordArt selected, hold down Shift, and then click the subtitle. On the **Format tab**, in the **Arrange group**, click **Align**, and then click **Align Selected Objects**. Click **Align** again, and then click **Align Left**.

2 Display **Slide 3**. In the center of the content placeholder, click **Insert a SmartArt Graphic** to open the **Choose a SmartArt Graphic** dialog box. On the left, click **List**, and then scroll as necessary and locate and click **Horizontal Bullet List**. Click **OK**.

a. In the SmartArt graphic, in the first gold rectangle, click **Text**. Type **Days and Times** and then click in the rectangle below the text you typed. Type **Weeknights** and then click in the second bullet point. Type **7 to 11 p.m.**

b. In the second gold rectangle, type **Packages** and then click in the rectangle below the text you typed. Type **Admission, parking, and dinner** and then delete the second text bullet point in the rectangle.

c. In the third gold rectangle, type **Capacity** and then click in the rectangle below the text you typed. Type **Maximum 750 guests** and then delete the second text bullet point in the rectangle.

d. On the **SmartArt Tools Design tab**, in the **SmartArt Styles group**, click **Change Colors**, and then under **Colorful**, click the last style **Colorful Range - Accent Colors 5 to 6**. In the **SmartArt Styles group**, click **More**, and then under **3-D**, in the first row, click the fourth style—**Powder**.

e. Click in the **Days and Times** rectangle, hold down Shift, and then click the **Packages** and **Capacity** rectangles. On the **SmartArt Tools Format tab**,

in the **Shapes group**, click **Change Shape**. Under **Rectangles**, click the fourth shape—**Snip Same Side Corner Rectangle**.

3 Display **Slide 4**, and then click anywhere in the bulleted list. On the **Home tab**, in the **Paragraph group**, click **Convert to SmartArt**. At the bottom of the gallery, click **More SmartArt Graphics**. On the left side of the **Choose a SmartArt Graphic** dialog box, click **List**. Locate and click **Grouped List**, and then click **OK** to convert the list to a SmartArt graphic.

a. Under **Family Evening**, click in the **Dinner and dessert** shape, and then on the **SmartArt Tools Design tab**, in the **Create Graphic group**, click **Add Shape**. In the inserted shape, type **Special children's events**

b. With the *Special children's events* shape selected, add another shape, and then type **All ages**

c. On the **SmartArt Tools Design tab**, in the **SmartArt Styles group**, click **Change Colors**. In the **Color** gallery, under **Colorful**, click the last style—**Colorful Range - Accent Colors 5 to 6**.

d. On the **Design tab**, in the **SmartArt Styles group**, click **More** to display the **SmartArt Styles gallery**. Under **3-D**, in the first row, click the third style—**Cartoon**.

4 Display **Slide 5**. Select the picture of the admission tickets, and then on the **Format tab**, in the **Adjust group**, click **Remove Background**. In the **Close group**, click **Keep Changes**.

a. With the picture selected, on the **Format tab**, in the **Picture Styles group**, click **Picture Effects**. Point to **Soft Edges**, and then click **25 Point**.

b. Insert a **Header & Footer** on the **Notes and Handouts**. Include the **Date and time updated automatically**, a **Page number**, and a **Footer** with the text **Lastname_Firstname_2D_Corporate_Events**

c. Display the document properties. As the **Tags** type **corporate events** and as the **Subject** type your course and section number. Be sure your name displays as author, and then **Save** your file.

d. View the slide show from the beginning. As directed by your instructor, create and submit a paper printout or an electronic image of your presentation that looks like a printed document; or, submit your completed PowerPoint file. **Close** PowerPoint.

END | You have completed Project 2D

Mastering PowerPoint Project 2E Coasters

In the following Mastering PowerPoint project, you will format a presentation describing new roller coasters being constructed at several Sensation Park Entertainment Group amusement parks. Your completed presentation will look similar to Figure 2.57.

PROJECT FILES

For Project 2E, you will need the following file:

p02E_Coasters

You will save your presentation as:

Lastname_Firstname_2E_Coasters

PROJECT RESULTS

FIGURE 2.57

(Project 2E Coasters continues on the next page)

Mastering PowerPoint | **Project 2E Coasters** (continued)

1 Start PowerPoint. From your student data files, locate and open **p02E_Coasters**. In your **PowerPoint Chapter 2** folder, **Save** the file as **Lastname_Firstname_2E_Coasters**

2 On **Slide 2**, remove the bullet symbol from the paragraph, and then **Center** the paragraph.

3 With the content placeholder selected, display the **Shape Styles** gallery, and then apply the **Subtle Effect – Blue-Gray, Accent 5** style. Apply the **Round Convex** beveled shape effect to the placeholder.

4 On **Slide 3**, apply **Numbering** to the first-level bullet points—*Intensity, Hang Time,* and *Last Chance*. Change all of the second-level bullets to **Star Bullets**, and then change the bullet color to **Aqua, Accent 1, Lighter 40%**—in the fifth column, the fourth color.

5 On **Slide 3**, select the title. Using the **Eyedropper**, select the light yellow color of the stripe on the roller coaster car at the right side of the picture and change the font color of the title. On **Slides 1** and **2**, apply the same light yellow color to the slide title on each slide.

6 Display **Slide 3**, and then apply an **Aqua, 5 pt glow, Accent color 2** picture effect to the picture.

7 Display **Slide 4**. Insert an **Online Picture** by searching for **roller coaster** and then insert a picture of people riding a roller coaster. **Crop** the picture by dragging the crop handles so that it's roughly square in shape.

8 Align the upper left corner of the picture with the top left corner of the slide, and then change the **Height** to **4.5** Modify the **Picture Effect** by applying a **50 Point Soft Edges** effect.

9 Duplicate the picture, and then use the **Align to Slide** option to align the pictures with the left edge of the slide and to distribute the pictures vertically.

10 Insert a **Text Box** aligned with the **horizontal ruler at 0 inches** and with the **lower half of the vertical ruler at 2.5 inches**. In the text box, type **Starting Summer 2019!** Change the **Font Size** to **28**. Change the **Shape Fill** to the last color in the last column—**Blue, Accent 6, Darker 50%**.

11 Select the title and the text box, and then, using the **Align Selected Objects** option, apply **Align Right** alignment. View the slide show from the beginning.

12 **Insert** a **Header & Footer** on the **Notes and Handouts**. Include the **Date and time updated automatically**, the **Page number**, and a **Footer** with the text **Lastname_Firstname_2E_Coasters**

13 Display the document properties. As the **Tags** type **coasters** and as the **Subject** type your course and section #. Be sure your name displays as author, and then **Save** your file.

14 As directed by your instructor, create and submit a paper printout or an electronic image of your presentation that looks like a printed document; or, submit your completed PowerPoint file. **Close** PowerPoint.

END | You have completed Project 2E

Mastering PowerPoint Project 2F Attractions

Apply 2B skills from these Objectives:

5 Remove Picture Backgrounds and Insert WordArt

6 Create and Format a SmartArt Graphic

In the following Mastering PowerPoint project, you will format a presentation describing new attractions at several of the Sensation Park Entertainment Group amusement parks. Your completed presentation will look similar to Figure 2.58.

PROJECT FILES

For Project 2F, you will need the following file:

p02F_Attractions

You will save your presentation as:

Lastname_Firstname_2F_Attractions

PROJECT RESULTS

FIGURE 2.58

(Project 2F Attractions continues on the next page)

Mastering PowerPoint | Project 2F Attractions (continued)

1 Start PowerPoint. From your student data files, open **p02F_Attractions**, and then **Save** the file in your **PowerPoint Chapter 2** folder as **Lastname_Firstname_2F_Attractions**

2 On **Slide 1**, select the title and display the **WordArt** gallery. In the third row, apply the first WordArt style—**Fill – Black, Text 1, Outline – Background 1, Hard Shadow – Background 1**. Change the **Text Outline** by applying, in the fourth column, the fourth color—**Dark Green, Text 2, Lighter 40%**.

3 On **Slide 2**, in the content placeholder, insert a **List** type **SmartArt** graphic—**Vertical Bracket List**. In the upper left Text placeholder, type **Location** and then in the bullet point to the right of *Location*, type **Brookside** In the lower text placeholder, type **Availability** and then in the rectangle to the right of *Availability*, type **June 2019**

4 Click the *Availability* placeholder, and then add a shape after the placeholder. In the new placeholder, type **Specifications** and then add a bullet. Type **Course located around park perimeter**

5 Change the SmartArt color to **Colorful Range - Accent Colors 4 to 5**, and then apply the **3-D Cartoon** style.

6 Select the three left bracket shapes, and then change the shapes to the **Right Arrow** shape. On the **Format tab**, in the **Shapes group**, click the **Smaller** button two times to decrease the size of the arrows.

7 On **Slide 3**, convert the bulleted list to a **SmartArt** graphic by applying the **Vertical Box List** graphic.

8 Change the SmartArt color to **Colorful Range - Accent Colors 4 to 5**, and then apply the **Polished 3-D** SmartArt style.

9 On **Slide 5**, insert a **WordArt**—in the first row, the last style—**Fill – Dark Teal, Accent 4, Soft Bevel**. Replace the WordArt text with **To Accept the Challenge?** Change the **Font Size** to **48**.

10 Hold down Shift and then drag the WordArt down so that its top edge is positioned on the **lower half of the vertical ruler at 1**.

11 Apply the **Peel Off** transition to all the slides, and then view the slide show from the beginning.

12 Insert a **Header & Footer** on the **Notes and Handouts**. Include the **Date and time updated automatically**, the **Page number**, and a **Footer** with the text **Lastname_Firstname_2F_Attractions**

13 Display the document properties. As the **Tags** type **zip line, rock wall** and as the **Subject,** type your course and section #. Be sure your name displays as author, and then **Save** your file.

14 As directed by your instructor, create and submit a paper printout or an electronic image of your presentation that looks like a printed document; or, submit your completed PowerPoint file. **Close** PowerPoint.

END | You have completed Project 2F

Mastering PowerPoint | Project 2G Orientation

Apply 2A and 2B skills from these Objectives:

1 Format Numbered and Bulleted Lists
2 Insert Online Pictures
3 Insert Text Boxes and Shapes
4 Format Objects
5 Remove Picture Backgrounds and Insert WordArt
6 Create and Format a SmartArt Graphic

In the following Mastering PowerPoint project, you will edit an existing presentation that is shown to Sensation Park Entertainment Group employees on their first day of a three-day orientation. Your completed presentation will look similar to Figure 2.59.

PROJECT FILES

For Project 2G, you will need the following files:

p02G_Orientation

You will save your presentation as:

Lastname_Firstname_2G_Orientation

PROJECT RESULTS

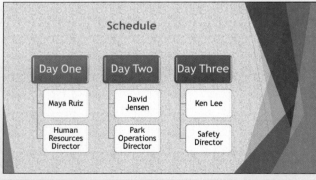

FIGURE 2.59

PowerPoint 2016, Windows 10, Microsoft Corporation

(Project 2G Orientation continues on the next page)

Mastering PowerPoint | Project 2G Orientation (continued)

1 Start PowerPoint, and then from your student data files, open the file **p02G_Orientation**. In your **PowerPoint Chapter 2** folder, **Save** the file as **Lastname_Firstname_2G_Orientation**

2 On **Slide 1**, format the subtitle—*New Employee Orientation*—as **WordArt** using the second style in the first row—**Fill - Orange, Accent 1, Shadow**. Change the **Text Fill** to **Dark Red, Accent 2, Darker 50%**.

3 Select the picture and then **Crop** the image from the left side so that the center left crop handle aligns with the **left half of the horizontal ruler at 5 inches**.

4 Change the picture **Height** to **3.5** and then apply an **Orange, 8 pt glow, Accent color 1** picture effect to the image. Use the **Align Selected Objects** command to apply **Align Middle** to the title and the picture.

5 On **Slide 2**, remove the bullet symbol from the paragraph, and then change the **Shape Fill** to **Tan, Background 2, Darker 50%**, and the **Shape Outline** to **Black, Text 1**.

6 On **Slide 3**, convert the bulleted list to the **Hierarchy** type **SmartArt** graphic—**Hierarchy List**. Change the color to **Colorful Range - Accent Colors 3 to 4**, and then apply the **3-D Inset** style.

7 On **Slide 4**, change the two bulleted lists to **Numbering**.

8 On **Slide 5**, change the bullet symbols to **Filled Square Bullets**, change the **Color** to **Tan, Background 2, Darker 50%**, and then change the **Size** to **100**

9 On **Slide 5**, in the placeholder on the right, insert an **Online Picture** by searching for **fire alarm** and then insert a picture of a **fire alarm** with a background.

10 If the option is available, remove the background from the picture, and then apply the **Brown, 18 pt glow, Accent color 3** picture effect.

11 On **Slide 5**, insert a **Text Box** below the content placeholder on the left side of the slide. In the text box, type **All employees will be tested on park safety procedures!** Using the **Align to Slide** option **Align Center** the text box and apply **Align Bottom**.

12 On **Slide 6**, from the **Shapes** gallery, under **Basic Shapes**, insert a **Diamond** of any size anywhere on the slide. Resize the diamond so that its **Shape Height** is **6** and its **Shape Width** is **8**

13 Using the **Align to Slide** option, apply the **Align Center** and **Align Middle** alignment commands to the diamond shape. Apply the **Moderate Effect - Brown, Accent 3** shape style.

14 In the diamond, type **Sensation Park Entertainment Group Welcomes You!** Change the **Font Size** to **28**, and then apply the **Round Convex Bevel** effect to the diamond shape.

15 Insert a **Header & Footer** on the **Notes and Handouts**. Include the **Date and time updated automatically**, the **Page number**, and a **Footer** with the text **Lastname_Firstname_2G_Orientation**

16 Display the document properties. As the **Tags** type **orientation** and as the **Subject** type your course and section number. Be sure your name displays as author, and then **Save** your file.

17 As directed by your instructor, create and submit a paper printout or an electronic image of your presentation that looks like a printed document; or, submit your completed PowerPoint file. **Close** PowerPoint.

END | You have completed Project 2G

Apply a combination of the 2A and 2B skills.

Build
From
Scratch

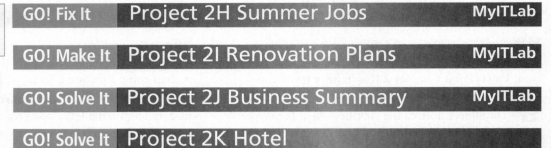

GO! Fix It	Project 2H Summer Jobs	MyITLab
GO! Make It	Project 2I Renovation Plans	MyITLab
GO! Solve It	Project 2J Business Summary	MyITLab
GO! Solve It	Project 2K Hotel	

PROJECT FILES

For Project 2K, you will need the following file:

p02K_Hotel

You will save your presentation as:

Lastname_Firstname_2K_Hotel

Open the file **p02K_Hotel** and save it in your **PowerPoint Chapter 2** folder as **Lastname_Firstname_2K_Hotel** Complete the presentation by inserting an online picture on the first slide and applying picture effects. On Slide 2, format the bullet point as a single paragraph, change the line spacing to 2.0, apply a shape style, and then on Slide 3, convert the bulleted list to a SmartArt graphic. Change the SmartArt color and apply a style. On Slide 4, insert and position a WordArt with the text **Save the Date!** On the Notes and Handouts, insert a header and footer that includes the date and time updated automatically, the file name in the footer, and the page number. Add your name, your course name and section number, and the tags **hotel, accommodations** to the properties. Save your presentation. As directed by your instructor, create and submit a paper printout or an electronic image of your presentation that looks like a printed document; or, submit your completed PowerPoint file.

(Project 2K Hotel continues on the next page)

GO! Solve It | **Project 2K Hotel** (continued)

Performance Level

Performance Criteria		Exemplary: You consistently applied the relevant skills	Proficient: You sometimes, but not always, applied the relevant skills	Developing: You rarely or never applied the relevant skills
	Insert and format an appropriate online picture	An appropriate online picture was inserted and formatted in the presentation.	An online picture was inserted but was not appropriate for the presentation or was not formatted.	An online picture was not inserted.
	Insert and format appropriate SmartArt graphic	Appropriate SmartArt graphic was inserted and formatted in the presentation.	SmartArt graphic was inserted but was not appropriate for the presentation or was not formatted.	SmartArt graphic was not inserted
	Insert and format appropriate WordArt	Appropriate WordArt was inserted and formatted in the presentation.	WordArt was inserted but was not appropriate for the presentation or was not formatted.	WordArt was not inserted.
	Remove bullet point and apply appropriate shape style	Bullet point was removed and an appropriate shape style was applied.	Either the bullet point was not removed or the shape style was not applied.	Bullet point was not removed and a shape style was not applied.

END | You have completed Project 2K

RUBRIC

The following outcomes-based assessments are *open-ended assessments*. That is, there is no specific correct result; your result will depend on your approach to the information provided. Make *Professional Quality* your goal. Use the following scoring rubric to guide you in *how* to approach the problem and then to evaluate *how well* your approach solves the problem.

The *criteria*—Software Mastery, Content, Format and Layout, and Process—represent the knowledge and skills you have gained that you can apply to solving the problem. The *levels of performance*—Professional Quality, Approaching Professional Quality, or Needs Quality Improvements—help you and your instructor evaluate your result.

	Your completed project is of Professional Quality if you:	Your completed project is Approaching Professional Quality if you:	Your completed project Needs Quality Improvements if you:
1-Software Mastery	Choose and apply the most appropriate skills, tools, and features and identify efficient methods to solve the problem.	Choose and apply some appropriate skills, tools, and features, but not in the most efficient manner.	Choose inappropriate skills, tools, or features, or are inefficient in solving the problem.
2-Content	Construct a solution that is clear and well organized, contains content that is accurate, appropriate to the audience and purpose, and is complete. Provide a solution that contains no errors in spelling, grammar, or style.	Construct a solution in which some components are unclear, poorly organized, inconsistent, or incomplete. Misjudge the needs of the audience. Have some errors in spelling, grammar, or style, but the errors do not detract from comprehension.	Construct a solution that is unclear, incomplete, or poorly organized; contains some inaccurate or inappropriate content; and contains many errors in spelling, grammar, or style. Do not solve the problem.
3-Format & Layout	Format and arrange all elements to communicate information and ideas, clarify function, illustrate relationships, and indicate relative importance.	Apply appropriate format and layout features to some elements, but not others. Overuse features, causing minor distraction.	Apply format and layout that does not communicate information or ideas clearly. Do not use format and layout features to clarify function, illustrate relationships, or indicate relative importance. Use available features excessively, causing distraction.
4-Process	Use an organized approach that integrates planning, development, self-assessment, revision, and reflection.	Demonstrate an organized approach in some areas, but not others; or, use an insufficient process of organization throughout.	Do not use an organized approach to solve the problem.

Apply a combination of the 2A and 2B skills.

GO! Think | Project 2L Interactive Ride

PROJECT FILES

For Project 2L, you will need the following file:

New blank PowerPoint presentation

You will save your presentation as:

Lastname_Firstname_2L_Interactive_Ride

As part of its mission to combine fun with the discovery of math and science, Sensation Park Entertainment Group is opening a new, interactive roller coaster at its South Lake Tahoe location. Sensation Park's newest coaster is designed for maximum thrill and minimum risk. In a special interactive exhibit located next to the coaster, riders can learn about the physics behind this powerful coaster and even try their hand at building a coaster.

Guests will begin by selecting the height of the first hill, which determines the coaster's maximum potential energy to complete its journey. Next they will plan the exit path, and build additional hills, loops, and corkscrews. When completed, riders can submit their coaster for a safety inspection to find out whether the ride passes or fails.

Whether the ride passes or fails, riders can take a virtual tour of the ride they created to see the maximum speed achieved, the amount of negative G-forces applied, the length of the track, and the overall thrill factor. They can also see how their coaster compares with other Sensation Park coasters, and they can email the coaster simulation to their friends.

Using the preceding information, create a presentation that the Marketing Director, Annette Chosek, will present at a travel fair describing the new attraction. The presentation should include four to six slides with at least one SmartArt graphic and one online picture. Apply an appropriate theme and use slide layouts that will effectively present the content, and use text boxes, shapes, and WordArt if appropriate. Apply font formatting and slide transitions, and modify text alignment and line spacing as necessary. Save the file as **Lastname_Firstname_2L_Interactive_Ride** and then insert a header and footer that includes the date and time updated automatically, the file name in the footer, and the page number. Add your name, your course name and section number, and the tags **roller coaster, new rides** to the Properties area. As directed by your instructor, create and submit a paper printout or an electronic image of your presentation that looks like a printed document; or, submit your completed PowerPoint file.

END | You have completed Project 2L

GO! Think | Project 2M Research | MyITLab

You and GO! | Project 2N Theme Park | MyITLab

GO! Collaborative Team Project | Project 2O Bell Orchid Hotels | MyITLab

Enhancing a Presentation with Animation, Video, Tables, and Charts

PROJECT **3A**

OUTCOMES
Customize a presentation with animation and video

PROJECT **3B**

OUTCOMES
Create a presentation that includes data in tables and charts

OBJECTIVES

1. Customize Slide Backgrounds and Themes
2. Animate a Slide Show
3. Insert a Video

OBJECTIVES

4. Create and Modify Tables
5. Create and Modify Charts

Fotolia

In This Chapter GO! to Work with PowerPoint

In this chapter, you will learn how to customize a presentation by modifying the theme, formatting the slide background, and applying animation to slide elements. Additionally, you will learn how to enhance your presentations by inserting tables and charts that help your audience understand numeric data and trends just as pictures and diagrams help illustrate a concept. The data that you present should determine whether a table or a chart would most appropriately display your information. Styles applied to your tables and charts unify these slide elements by complementing your presentation theme.

The projects in this chapter relate to the city of **Pacifica Bay**, a coastal city south of San Francisco. The city's access to major transportation provides both residents and businesses an opportunity to compete in the global marketplace. The city's mission is to create a more beautiful and more economically viable community for its residents. Each year the city welcomes a large number of tourists who enjoy exploring the rocky coastline and seeing the famous landmarks in San Francisco. The city encourages best environmental practices and partners with cities in other countries to promote sound government at the local level.

Informational Presentation

PROJECT ACTIVITIES

In Activities 3.01 through 3.17, you will edit and format a presentation that Carol Lehman, Director of Pacifica Bay Parks and Recreation, has created to inform residents about the benefits of using the city's parks and trails. Your completed presentation will look similar to Figure 3.1.

PROJECT FILES

MyITLab
grader

If your instructor wants you to submit Project 3A in the MyITLab grader system, log in to MyITLab, locate Grader Project 3A, and then download the files for this project.

For Project 3A, you will need the following files:

p03A_Hills
p03A_Trails
p03A_Video

You will save your presentation as:

Lastname_Firstname_3A_Trails

Please always review the downloaded Grader instructions before beginning.

PROJECT RESULTS

GO!
Walk Thru
Project 3A

Improve your physical fitness by exploring Pacifica Bay's many paths, trails, and parks.

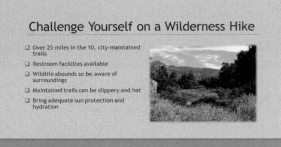

PowerPoint 2016, Windows 10, Microsoft Corporation

FIGURE 3.1 Project 3A Trails

GO! Learn How
Video P3-1

You have practiced customizing presentations by applying themes with unified design elements, backgrounds, and colors that provide a consistent look in your presentation. Additional ways to customize a slide include changing theme fonts and colors, applying a background style, modifying the background color, or inserting a picture on the slide background.

Activity 3.01 | Changing Theme Colors

ALERT!   **To submit as an autograded project, log into MyITLab, download the files for this project, and begin with those files instead of the student data files.**

The presentation theme is a coordinated, predefined set of colors, fonts, lines, and fill effects. In this Activity, you will open a presentation in which the Retrospect theme is applied, and then you will change the **theme colors**—a set of coordinating colors that are applied to the backgrounds, objects, and text in a presentation.

1 From the student data files for this chapter, locate and open **p03A_Trails**. Display the **Save As** dialog box, create a **New Folder** with the name **PowerPoint Chapter 3** and then using your own name, **Save** the file in the folder you created as **Lastname_Firstname_3A_Trails**

2 Click the **Design tab**, and then in the **Variants group**, click **More**. Point to **Colors** to display the sets of theme colors. Point to several sets and notice the color changes on **Slide 1**.

3 Click **Green** to change the presentation colors, and then compare your screen with Figure 3.2. **Save** your presentation.

Changing the colors does not change the overall design of the presentation. In this presentation, the *Retrospect* presentation theme is still applied to the presentation. By modifying the theme colors, you retain the design of the *Retrospect* theme but apply colors that coordinate with the pictures in the presentation, and that are available as text, accent, and background colors.

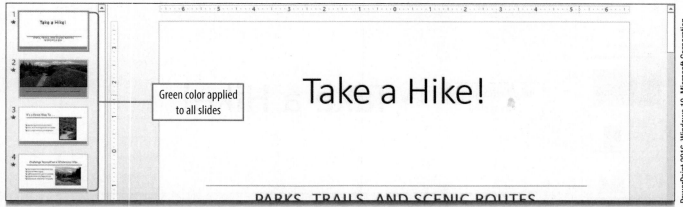

FIGURE 3.2

In addition to theme colors, every presentation theme includes *theme fonts* that determine the font to apply to two types of slide text—headings and body. The ***Headings font*** is applied to slide titles and the ***Body font*** is applied to all other text. When you apply a new theme font to the presentation, the text on every slide is updated with the new heading and body fonts.

1 With **Slide 1** displayed, click anywhere in the title placeholder. On the **Home tab**, in the **Font group**, click the **Font arrow**. Notice that at the top of the **Font** list, under **Theme Fonts**, Calibri Light (Headings) and Calibri (Body) display. Compare your screen with Figure 3.3.

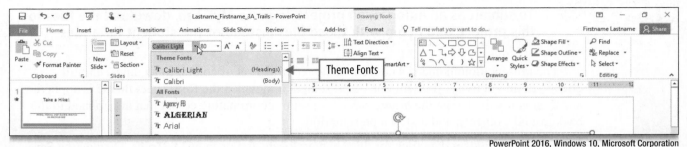

PowerPoint 2016, Windows 10, Microsoft Corporation

FIGURE 3.3

2 Click anywhere on the slide to close the Font list. On the **Design tab**, in the **Variants group**, click **More**. Point to **Fonts**.

This list displays the name of each theme and the pair of fonts in the theme. The first and larger font in each pair is the Headings font and the second and smaller font in each pair is the Body font.

3 Point to several of the themes and watch as Live Preview changes the title and subtitle text. Scroll to the bottom of the **Fonts** list, and then click **TrebuchetMS**. **Save** your presentation and then compare your screen with Figure 3.4.

TrebuchetMS theme fonts applied

Take a Hike!

PARKS, TRAILS, AND SCENIC ROUTES IN PACIFICA BAY

PowerPoint 2016, Windows 10, Microsoft Corporation

FIGURE 3.4

MOS
1.2.6

1 ▶ With **Slide 1** displayed, on the **Design tab**, in the **Variants group**, click **More** ⬛. Point to **Background Styles**, and then compare your screen with Figure 3.5.

A **background style** is a predefined slide background fill variation that combines theme colors in different intensities or patterns.

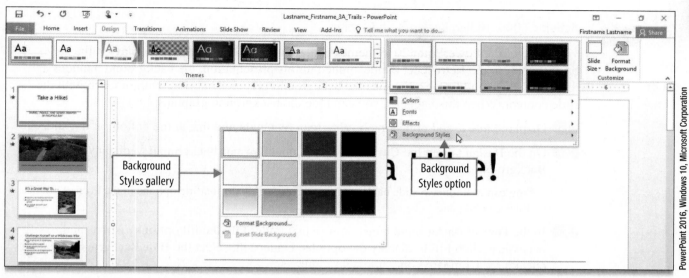

FIGURE 3.5

2 ▶ Point to each of the background styles to view the style on **Slide 1**. Then, in the first row, click **Style 2**. Compare your screen with Figure 3.6.

The background style is applied to all the slides in the presentation.

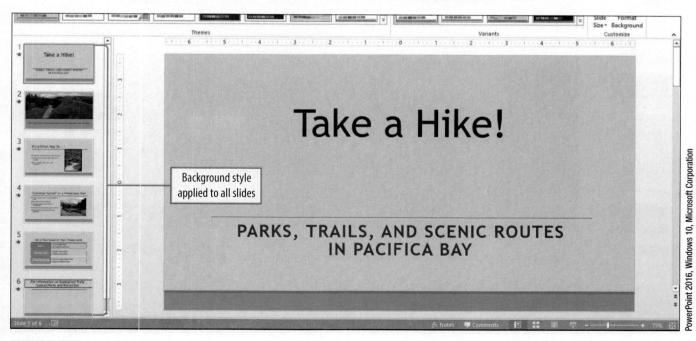

FIGURE 3.6

3 Display **Slide 5**. On the **Design tab**, in the **Variants group**, click **More** ⊡. Point to **Background Styles**, and then in the third row, *right-click* the third style—**Style 11**—to display the shortcut menu. On the shortcut menu, click **Apply to Selected Slides** to apply the style to Slide 5.

You can select individual slides to which you apply a background style.

4 **Save** 🖫 your presentation.

Activity 3.04 | **Hiding Background Graphics**

Many of the PowerPoint 2016 themes contain graphic elements that display on the slide background. In the Retrospect theme applied to this presentation, the background includes a rectangle shape and line. Sometimes the background graphics interfere with or clash with the slide content. When this happens, you can hide the background graphics.

1 Display **Slide 2**, and notice the bright green rectangle and line at the bottom of the slide.

2 On the **Design tab**, in the **Customize group**, click **Format Background** to display the Format Background pane.

You can customize a slide background by changing the formatting options in the Format Background pane.

3 In the **Format Background** pane, be sure that under **Fill**, the fill options display, and if necessary, click Fill to display the options. Under **Fill**, select the **Hide Background Graphics** check box. Compare your slide with Figure 3.7.

The background objects—the rectangle and line below the picture—no longer display.

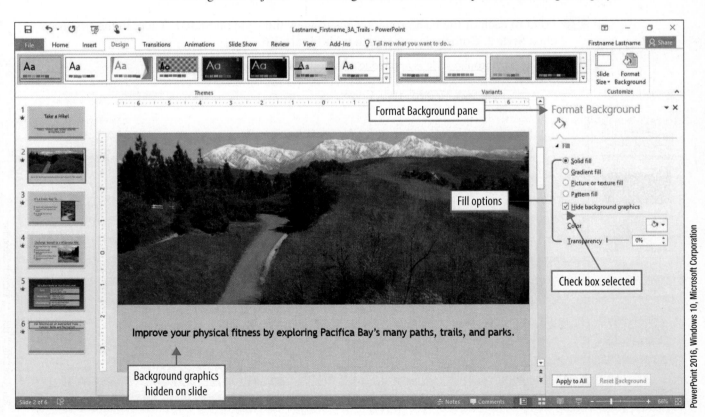

FIGURE 3.7

> 4 ▶ Leave the **Format Background** pane open for the next Activity. **Save** 🔲 your presentation.

More Knowledge | **Hiding Background Objects from All Slides in a Presentation**

To hide the background objects from all of the slides in a presentation, in the Format Background pane, select the Hide background graphics check box, and then at the bottom of the Format Background pane, click Apply to All.

MOS
1.2.6

Activity 3.05 | Applying a Background Fill Color to a Slide

In addition to applying predefined background styles, you can apply a fill color to one or all of the slides in your presentation.

> 1 ▶ Display **Slide 1**.

> 2 ▶ In the **Format Background** pane, under **Fill**, verify that **Solid fill** is selected, and select it if it is not. To the right of **Color**, click **Fill Color** 🎨. Under **Theme Colors**, in the third column, click the second color—**Tan, Background 2, Darker 10%**. Compare your screen with Figure 3.8.

The solid fill color is applied to the slide background.

FIGURE 3.8

> 3 ▶ Leave the **Format Background** pane open for the next Activity. **Save** 🔲 your presentation.

More Knowledge | **Applying a Fill Color to All the Slides in a Presentation**

To apply a fill color to all of the slides in a presentation, in the Format Background pane, select the fill color that you want to apply, and then at the bottom of the Format Background pane, click Apply to All.

MOS
1.2.6

Activity 3.06 | Applying a Background Texture

> 1 ▶ Display **Slide 2**, and then in the slide thumbnails, hold down Shift and click **Slide 4** to select **Slides 2**, **3**, and **4**.

Recall that you can select contiguous slides in this manner.

> 2 ▶ In the **Format Background** pane, under **Fill**, click **Picture or texture fill**.

A background picture that is part of the Retrospect theme may display on the slide background of the three selected slides.

3 Under **Insert picture from**, to the right of **Texture**, click **Texture** 🖼. In the **Texture gallery**, in the third row, point to the fourth texture—**Recycled paper**. Compare your screen with Figure 3.9.

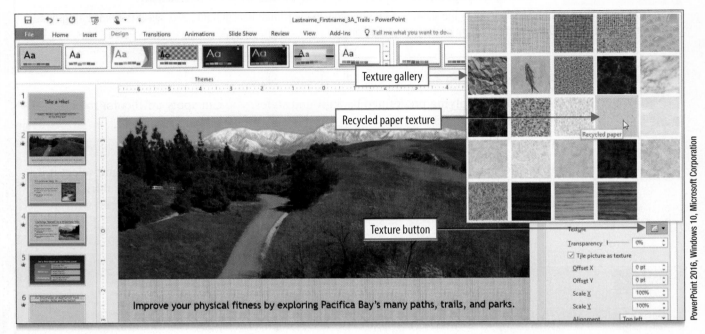

FIGURE 3.9

4 Click **Recycled paper** to apply the textured background to the three selected slides.

5 Leave the **Format Background** pane open for the next Activity, and then **Save** 🖫 your presentation.

MOS
1.2.6

Activity 3.07 | **Applying a Picture to the Slide Background and Adjusting Transparency**

You can insert a picture on a slide background so that the image fills the entire slide.

1 Display **Slide 6**. In the **Format Background** pane, select the **Hide background graphics** check box.

2 Under **Fill**, click **Picture or texture fill**. Under **Insert picture from**, click **File**. Navigate to your student data files, click **p03A_Hills**, and then click **Insert**. Compare your slide with Figure 3.10 and notice that the picture displays as the background of Slide 6.

When a picture is applied to a slide background using the Format Background option, the picture is not treated as an object. The picture fills the entire background and you cannot move it or size it.

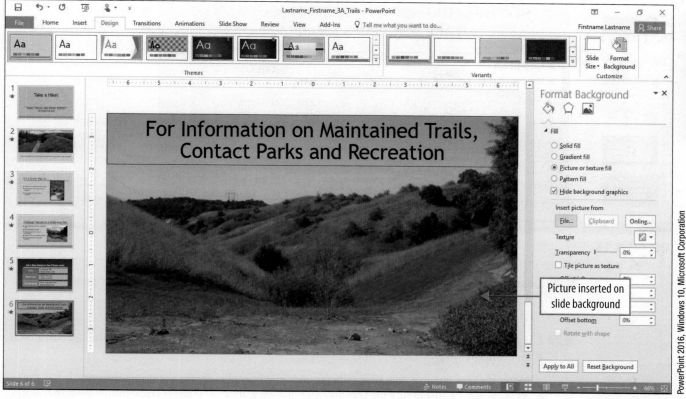

FIGURE 3.10

3 In the **Format Background** pane, to the right of **Transparency**, notice that *0%* displays, indicating that the picture is inserted in full color. Click in the **Transparency box**, and then replace the number with **50**

The transparency setting lightens the picture on the slide background. You can use the transparency option when there are other objects on the slide that do not display well against the slide background.

ANOTHER WAY Drag the Transparency slider to the left or right to adjust the transparency of the figure.

4 Replace the number in the **Transparency box** with **10**

The 10% transparency setting provides good contrast for the title while still displaying the picture in a vibrant color.

5 Click in the title placeholder. On the **Format tab**, in the **Shape Styles group**, click **More**. In the fourth row, click the second style—**Subtle Effect – Green, Accent 1**. Click anywhere on the slide outside of the title placeholder. Compare your screen with Figure 3.11.

Adequate contrast between the slide background and slide text is important as it improves slide readability. Use combinations of transparency and text placeholder styles and fills to improve contrast.

FIGURE 3.11

> **6** Leave the **Format Background** pane open for the next Activity. **Save** 🔲 your presentation.

Activity 3.08 | Resetting a Slide Background

> **1** Display **Slide 5**. At the bottom of the **Format Background** pane, click **Reset Background**, and then compare your slide with Figure 3.12.

> After making changes to a slide background, you may decide that the original formatting is the best choice for displaying the text and graphics on a slide. The Reset Background feature restores the theme and color theme formatting to a slide.

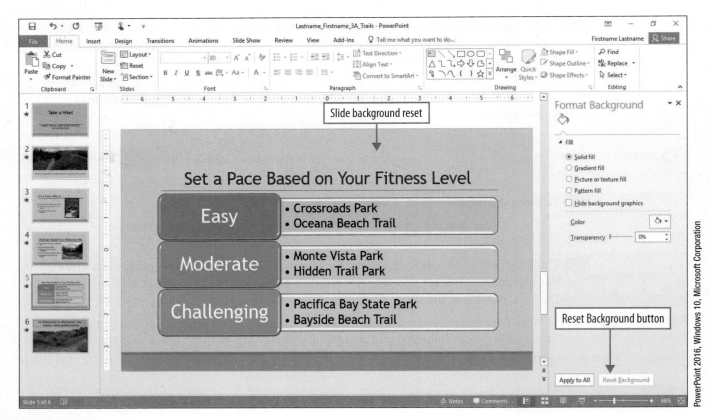

FIGURE 3.12

> **2** **Close** ✕ the **Format Background** pane, and then **Save** 🔲 your presentation.

GO! Learn How
Video P3-2

Animation is a visual or sound effect added to an object or text on a slide. Use animation to focus the audience's attention, providing the speaker with an opportunity to emphasize important points using the slide element as an effective visual aid.

4.2.1, 4.2.2,
4.2.3, 4.2.4

Activity 3.09 | Applying Animation Entrance Effects and Effect Options

Entrance effects are animations that bring a slide element onto the screen. Use the animation Effect Options command to modify an entrance effect.

> 1 ▸ Display **Slide 3**, and then click anywhere in the bulleted list placeholder. On the **Animations tab**, in the **Animation group**, click **More** ⊟, and then compare your screen with Figure 3.13.

> An entrance effect is animation that brings an object or text onto the screen. An *emphasis effect* is animation that emphasizes an object or text that is already displayed. An *exit effect* is animation that moves an object or text off the screen.

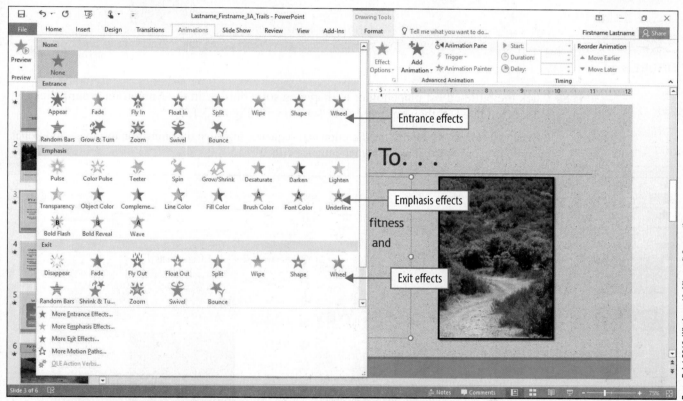

FIGURE 3.13

> 2 ▸ Under **Entrance**, click **Fly In**, and then notice the animation applied to the list. Compare your screen with Figure 3.14.

> The numbers *1, 2,* and *3* display to the left of the bulleted list placeholder, indicating the order in which the bullet points will be animated during the slide show.

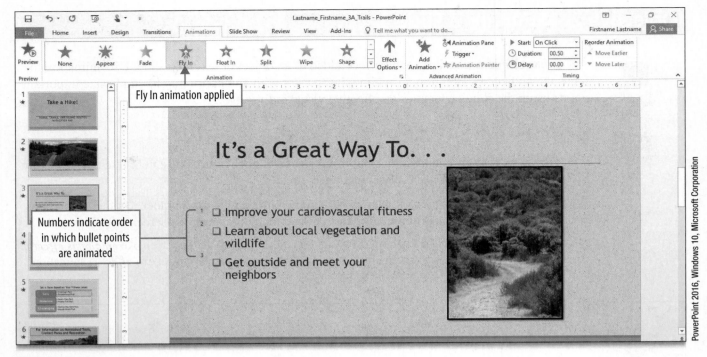

FIGURE 3.14

3 Click the bulleted list placeholder to display a solid border. In the **Animation group**, click **Effect Options**, and then compare your screen with Figure 3.15.

The Effect Options control the direction and sequence in which the animation displays. Additional options may be available with other entrance effects.

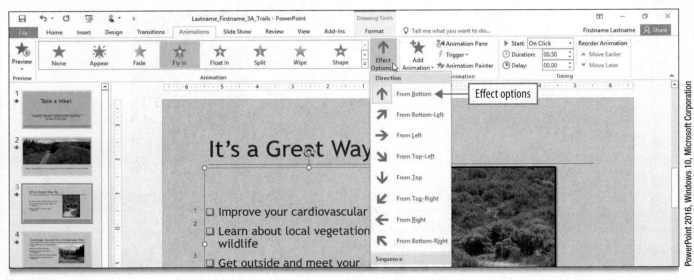

FIGURE 3.15

4 Click **From Top** and notice the bullets enter from the top of the slide.

5 Select the picture. In the **Animation group**, click **More** ▾, and then below the gallery, click **More Entrance Effects**. In the lower left corner of the **Change Entrance Effect** dialog box, verify that the **Preview Effect** check box is selected. Compare your screen with Figure 3.16.

The Change Entrance Effect dialog box displays additional entrance effects grouped in four categories: Basic, Subtle, Moderate, and Exciting.

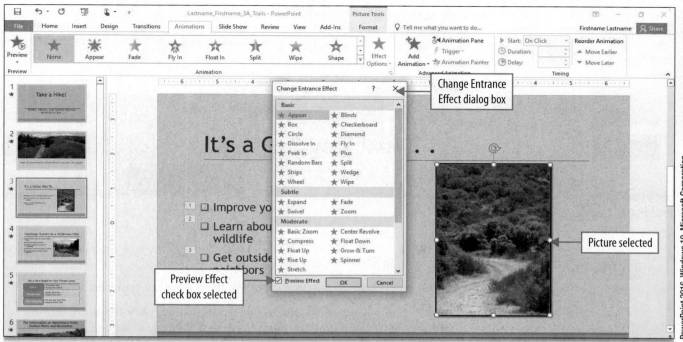

FIGURE 3.16

6 Under **Subtle**, click **Fade**, and then watch as Live Preview displays the picture with the selected entrance effect. Click **OK**.

> The number *4* displays next to the picture, indicating that it is fourth in the slide animation sequence.

7 Select the title placeholder. On the **Animations tab**, in the **Animation group**, click **More** ⊟, and then under **Entrance**, click **Fade** to apply the animation to the title.

> The number *5* displays next to the title, indicating that it is fifth in the slide animation sequence.

8 **Save** 🖫 the presentation.

MOS
4.3.3

Activity 3.10 │ **Reordering Animation**

1 With **Slide 3** displayed, on the **Animations tab**, in the **Preview group**, click **Preview**.

> The list displays first, followed by the picture, and then the title. The order in which animation is applied is the order in which objects display during the slide show.

2 Select the title placeholder. On the **Animations tab**, in the **Timing group**, under **Reorder Animation**, click **Move Earlier** two times, and then compare your screen with Figure 3.17.

> To the left of the title placeholder, the number *1* displays. You can use the Reorder Animation buttons to change the order in which text and objects are animated during the slide show.

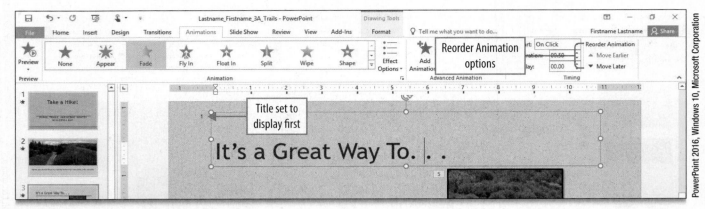

FIGURE 3.17

PowerPoint 2016, Windows 10, Microsoft Corporation

Activity 3.11 | Setting Animation Start Options

4.3.2

Timing options control when animated items display in the animation sequence.

1 With the title selected, on the **Animations tab**, in the **Timing group**, click the **Start arrow** to display three options—*On Click*, *With Previous*, and *After Previous*. Compare your screen with Figure 3.18.

The *On Click* option begins the animation sequence for the selected slide element when the mouse button is clicked or the Spacebar is pressed. The *With Previous* option begins the animation sequence at the same time as the previous animation or slide transition. The *After Previous* option begins the animation sequence for the selected slide element immediately after the completion of the previous animation or slide transition.

FIGURE 3.18

PowerPoint 2016, Windows 10, Microsoft Corporation

2 Click **After Previous**, and then notice that next to the title, the number *1* is changed to *0*, indicating that the animation will begin immediately after the slide transition; the presenter does not need to click the mouse button or press Spacebar to display the title.

3 Select the picture, and then in the **Timing group**, click the **Start arrow**. Click **With Previous** and notice that the number is changed to *3*, indicating that the animation will begin at the same time as the last bullet in the bulleted list.

4 On the **Animations tab**, in the **Preview group**, click **Preview** and notice that the title displays first, and that the picture displays at the same time as the last bullet in the bulleted list.

5 Display **Slide 1**, and then click in the title placeholder. On the **Animations tab**, in the **Animation group**, click the **Entrance** effect **Fly In**, and then click **Effect Options**. Click **From Top**. In the **Timing group**, click the **Start arrow**, and then click **After Previous**.

The number *0* displays to the left of the title indicating that the animation will begin immediately after the slide transition.

6 **Save** 💾 your presentation.

Activity 3.12 | **Setting Animation Duration and Delay Timing Options**

> **1** On **Slide 1**, if necessary, select the title. In the **Timing group**, click the **Duration up arrow** so that *00.75* displays in the **Duration** box. Compare your screen with Figure 3.19.

Duration controls the speed of the animation. You can set the duration of an animation by typing a value in the Duration box, or you can use the spin box arrows to increase and decrease the duration in 0.25-second increments. When you decrease the duration, the animation speed increases. When you increase the duration, the animation is slowed.

FIGURE 3.19

PowerPoint 2016, Windows 10, Microsoft Corporation

> **2** Select the subtitle, and then in the **Animation group**, apply the **Fade** entrance effect. In the **Timing group**, click the **Start arrow**, and then click **After Previous**. In the **Timing group**, select the value in the **Delay** box, type **00.50** and then press Enter. Compare your screen with Figure 3.20.

You can use Delay to begin a selected animation after a specified amount of time has elapsed. Here, the animation is delayed by one-half of a second after the completion of the previous animation—the title animation. You can type a value in the Delay or Duration boxes, or you can use the up and down arrows to change the timing.

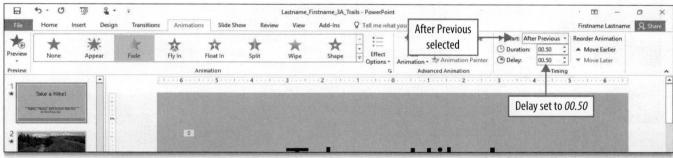

FIGURE 3.20

PowerPoint 2016, Windows 10, Microsoft Corporation

> **3** View the slide show from the beginning and notice the animation on Slides 1 and 3. When the black slide displays, press Esc to return to Normal view, and then **Save** 🖫 your presentation.

Activity 3.13 | **Using Animation Painter and Removing Animation**

Animation Painter is a feature that copies animation settings from one object to another.

> **1** Display **Slide 3**, and then click anywhere in the bulleted list. On the **Animations tab**, in the **Advanced Animation group**, click **Animation Painter**. Display **Slide 4**, and then point anywhere in the bulleted list placeholder to display the Animation Painter pointer 📎. Compare your screen with Figure 3.21.

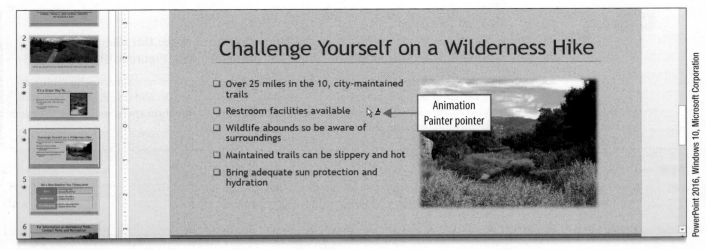

FIGURE 3.21

2 Click the bulleted list to copy the animation settings from the list on **Slide 3** to the list on **Slide 4**.

3 Display **Slide 3**, and then select the picture. Using the technique that you just practiced, use **Animation Painter** to copy the animation from the picture on **Slide 3** to the picture on **Slide 4**. With **Slide 4** displayed, compare your screen with Figure 3.22.

The numbers displayed to the left of the bulleted list and the picture indicate that animation is applied to the objects.

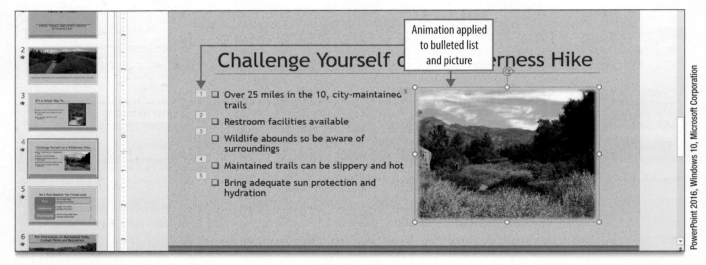

FIGURE 3.22

4 Display **Slide 3**, and then click in the title placeholder. On the **Animations tab**, in the **Animation group**, click **More**. At the top of the gallery, click **None** to remove the animation from the title placeholder. Compare your screen with Figure 3.23, and then **Save** your presentation.

FIGURE 3.23

Objective 3 | Insert a Video

GO! Learn How
Video P3-3

You can insert, size, and move videos in a PowerPoint presentation, and you can format videos by applying styles and effects. Video editing features in PowerPoint 2016 enable you to trim parts of a video and to compress the video to make the presentation easier to share.

MOS

3.4.1

Activity 3.14 | Inserting a Video and Using Media Controls

1 Display **Slide 1**. On the **Insert tab**, in the **Media group**, click **Video**, and then click **Video on My PC**. In the **Insert Video** dialog box, navigate to your student data files, and then click **p03A_Video**. Click **Insert**, and then compare your screen with Figure 3.24.

The video displays in the center of the slide, and media controls display in the control panel below the video.

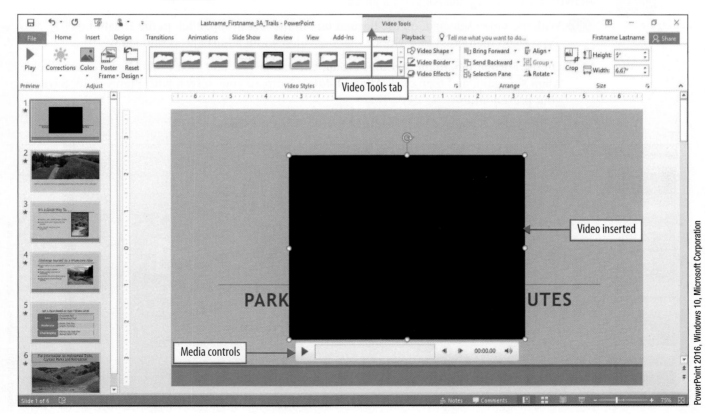

FIGURE 3.24

2 Below the video, in the media controls, click **Play/Pause** ▶ to view the video and notice that as the video plays, the media controls display the time that has elapsed since the start of the video.

3 View the slide show from the beginning. On **Slide 1**, after the subtitle displays, point to the video to display the 👆 pointer, and then compare your screen with Figure 3.25.

When you point to the video during the slide show, the media controls display.

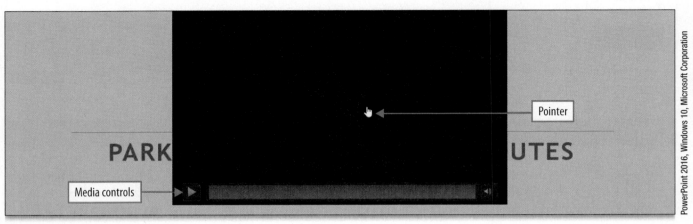

FIGURE 3.25

4 With the 👆 pointer displayed, click the mouse button to view the video. Move the pointer away from the video and notice that the media controls no longer display. When the video is finished, press Esc to exit the slide show.

5 **Save** 🖫 your presentation.

3.4.3

Activity 3.15 | **Sizing and Aligning a Video**

1 With the video selected, on the **Format tab**, in the **Size group**, click in the **Height** box ↕. Type **2** and then press Enter. Notice that the video width adjusts proportionately.

2 On the **Format tab**, in the **Arrange group**, click **Align** 🖼, and then click **Align Center**. Click **Align** 🖼 again, and then click **Align Middle**. Compare your screen with Figure 3.26. **Save** 🖫 your presentation.

The video is centered horizontally and vertically on the slide.

FIGURE 3.26

Activity 3.16 | Changing the Style and Shape of a Video

You can apply styles and effects to a video and change the video shape and border. You can also recolor a video so that it coordinates with the presentation theme.

1 With **Slide 1** displayed, if necessary, select the video. On the **Format tab**, in the **Video Styles group**, click **More** ⊡ to display the **Video Styles** gallery.

2 Using the ScreenTips to view the style name, under **Subtle**, in the second row, click the last style—**Drop Shadow Rectangle**. Compare your screen with Figure 3.27.

PowerPoint 2016, Windows 10, Microsoft Corporation

FIGURE 3.27

3 In the **Video Styles group**, click **Video Shape**, and then under **Rectangles**, click the second shape—**Rounded Rectangle**. Compare your screen with Figure 3.28.

You can format a video with any combination of styles, shapes, and effects.

PowerPoint 2016, Windows 10, Microsoft Corporation

FIGURE 3.28

3.4.2, 3.4.4, 3.4.5, 5.2.4

Activity 3.17 | Trimming and Compressing a Video and Setting Playback Options

You can *trim*—delete parts of a video to make it shorter—and you can compress a video file to reduce the file size of your PowerPoint presentation.

1 If necessary, select the video. On the **Playback tab**, in the **Editing group**, click **Trim Video**, and then compare your screen with Figure 3.29.

At the top of the displayed Trim Video dialog box, the file name and the video duration display. Below the video, a timeline displays with start and end markers indicating the video start and end time. Start Time and End Time boxes display the current start and end of the video. The Previous Frame and Next Frame buttons move the video forward and backward one frame at a time.

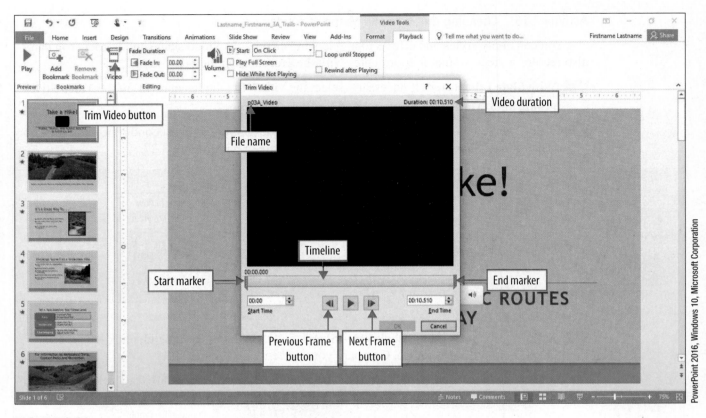

FIGURE 3.29

2 In the **End Time** box, replace the number with **00:09.425** and then compare your screen with Figure 3.30.

The blue section of the timeline indicates the portion of the video that will play during the slide show. The gray section indicates the portion of the video that is trimmed. The image in the Trim Video dialog box displays the last frame in the video based on the trim setting.

FIGURE 3.30

ANOTHER WAY   Drag the red ending marking until its ScreenTip displays the ending time that you want.

3 Click **OK** to apply the trim settings.

4 Click **File**, and then click **Compress Media**. Read the description of each video quality option, and then click **Low Quality**. Compare your screen with Figure 3.31.

> The Compress Media dialog box displays the slide number on which the selected video is inserted, the video file name, the original size of the video file, and when compression is complete, the amount that the file size was reduced.

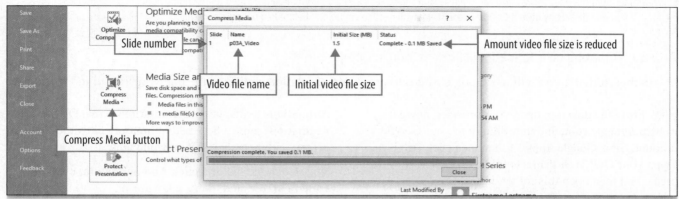

FIGURE 3.31

5 In the **Compress Media** dialog box, click **Close**, and then on the left, click **Save**.

6 If necessary, select the video. On the **Playback tab**, in the **Video Options group**, click the **Start arrow**, and then click **Automatically** so that during the slide show, the video will begin automatically. Compare your screen with Figure 3.32.

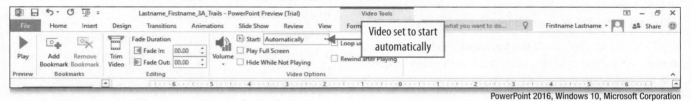

FIGURE 3.32

7 Click the **Slide Show tab**, in the **Start Slide Show group**, click **From Beginning**, and then view the slide show. Notice that on Slide 1, the video begins playing immediately after the subtitle displays. After you view the video, click the mouse button to advance to the next slide and then continue to view the presentation. Press Esc when the black slide displays.

8 Insert a **Header & Footer** on the **Notes and Handouts**. Include the **Date and time** updated automatically, the **Page Number**, and a **Footer**. In the **Footer** box, type **Lastname_Firstname_3A_Trails** and then click **Apply to All**.

9 Display the document properties. As the **Tags**, type **walking trails** and as the **Subject**, type your course and section number. Be sure your name displays as author, and then **Save** your file.

10 As directed by your instructor, create and submit a paper printout or an electronic image of your presentation that looks like a printed document—either as the Notes and Handouts or as the presentation slides—or, submit your completed PowerPoint file.

11 **Close** PowerPoint.

END | You have completed Project 3A

GO! With Google

ALERT! **Working with Web-Based Applications and Services**

Computer programs and services on the web receive continuous updates and improvements, so the steps to complete this web-based activity may differ from the ones shown. You can often look at the screens and the information presented to determine how to complete the activity. If you do not already have a Google account, you will need to create one before beginning this activity.

Activity | Creating an Informational Presentation in Google Slides

In this Activity, you will use Google Slides to create a presentation similar to the one you created in Project 3A.

1 From the desktop, open your browser, navigate to **http://google.com,** and then sign in to your Google account. Click **Google Apps** ⊞ , and then click **Drive** ☁ . Open your **GO! Web Projects** folder—or click New to create and then open this folder, if necessary.

2 In the left pane, click **NEW**, click **File upload** 🔼 , and then in the **Open** dialog box, navigate to your student data files. Select **p03_3A_Web**. Click **Open**. When the upload is complete, if necessary, close the Uploads completed message box. Right-click **p03_3A_Web**, and then click **Rename**. Using your own name, as the file name, type **Lastname_Firstname_3A_Web** and then press Enter. Right-click your file, point to **Open with**, and then click **Google Slides**.

3 On the toolbar, click **Background**, click the **Color arrow**, in the fifth column, click the fourth color—**light green 2**. Click **Done** to apply the light green background to Slide 1.

4 On **Slide 1**, in the title placeholder, select the title text—*Take a Hike!* Click the **Font arrow** ▾ , and then click **Cambria**.

5 Display **Slide 2**, and then at the bottom of the slide, click in the text placeholder. On the toolbar, click **Fill color** 🖌 ▾ , and then in the fifth column, click the fourth color—**light green 2**. Select the text, and then change the **Font Size** to **36**.

6 With the placeholder selected, point to the center-left sizing handle, and then drag as far to the left as possible without exceeding the left edge of the slide. Repeat this process on the right side of the slide, and then click outside of the placeholder.

7 Display **Slide 3**, and then click anywhere in the bulleted list. On the menu bar click **View**, and then click

Animations to display the **Animations pane**. On the **Animations pane**, click **Add animation**, click the **Fade in arrow**, and then click **Fly in from right**.

8 Click the picture, click **Add animation**, click the **Fade in arrow**, and then click **Appear**.

9 Click anywhere in the title text, click **Add animation**, click the **Fade in arrow**, and then click **Fly in from top**. Notice the animation sequencing in the Animations pane, which indicates that the title animation *Fly in from top* will display last. At the bottom of the **Animations pane**, click the **Play** button, and then point to the slide and click the slide two times to preview the animations in sequence.

10 With **Slide 3** displayed, click the title to select it, in the **Animations pane**, click the title animation *Fly in from top* and drag it to the top of the list so that it will appear first. At the bottom of the **Animations pane**, click the **Play** button, and then point to the slide and click the slide two times to preview the animations in sequence.

11 Display **Slide 4**, and then click the title. On the **Animations pane**, click **Add animation**, click the **Fade in arrow**, and then click **Fly in from top**.

12 Click the bulleted list. On the **Animations pane**, click **Add animation**, click the **Fade in arrow**, and then click **Fly in from right**.

13 Click the picture, click **Add animation**, click the **Fade in arrow**, and then click **Appear**.

14 Display **Slide 6**, and then click in the title. On the **Animations pane**, click **Add animation**, click the **Fade in arrow**, and then click **Fly in from top**.

(GO! With Google continues on the next page)

15 ▶ On the **Animations pane**, if necessary, click ▶ to expand **Slide: No transition**. Click the **No transition arrow**, click **Slide from left**, and then click **Apply to all slides**. **Close** ✕ the **Animations pane**.

16 ▶ Display **Slide 1**. In the upper right, click the **Present arrow**, and then click **Present from beginning**. If necessary, click **Allow**. Click the left mouse button to progress through the presentation. When the last slide displays, press [Esc] or click **Exit**.

17 ▶ Your presentation will be saved automatically. If you are instructed to submit your file, click the File menu, point to Download as, and then click PDF Document or Microsoft PowerPoint as directed by your instructor. The file will download to your default download folder as determined by your browser settings. Sign out of your Google account and close your browser.

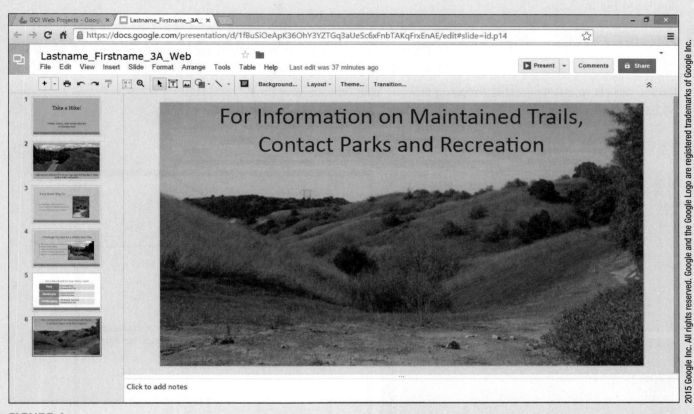

FIGURE A

Summary and Analysis Presentation

PROJECT ACTIVITIES

In Activities 3.18 through 3.29, you will add a table and two charts to a presentation that Mindy Walker, Director of Parks and Recreation, is creating to inform the City Council about enrollment trends in Pacifica Bay recreation programs. Your completed presentation will look similar to Figure 3.33.

Please always review the downloaded Grader instructions before beginning.

PROJECT FILES

MyITLab grader

If your instructor wants you to submit Project 3B in the MyITLab grader system, log in to MyITLab, locate Grader Project 3B, and then download the files for this project.

For Project 3B, you will need the following file:
p03B_Enrollment

You will save your presentation as:
Lastname_Firstname_3B_Enrollment

PROJECT RESULTS

GO!
Walk Thru
Project 3B

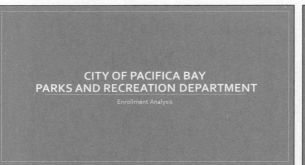

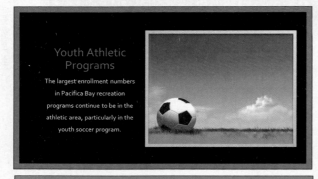

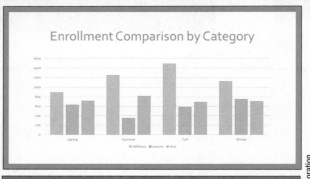

FIGURE 3.33 Project 3B Enrollment

PowerPoint 2016, Windows 10, Microsoft Corporation

GO! Learn How
Video P3-4

A *table* is a format for information that organizes and presents text and data in columns and rows. The intersection of a column and row is referred to as a *cell* and is the location in which you type text in a table.

Activity 3.18 | Creating a Table

MOS
3.1.1

There are several ways to insert a table in a PowerPoint slide. For example, you can insert a slide with a Content Layout and then click the Insert Table button. Or, click the Insert tab and then click Table.

1 ▶ Start PowerPoint. From your student data files, open **p03B_Enrollment**, and then **Save** the presentation in your **PowerPoint Chapter 3** folder as **Lastname_Firstname_3B_Enrollment**

2 ▶ Display **Slide 2**. In the content placeholder, click **Insert Table** ▦ to display the **Insert Table** dialog box. In the **Number of columns** box, type **3** and then press Tab. In the **Number of rows** box, if necessary, type **2** and then compare your screen with Figure 3.34.

Enter the number of columns and rows that you want the table to contain.

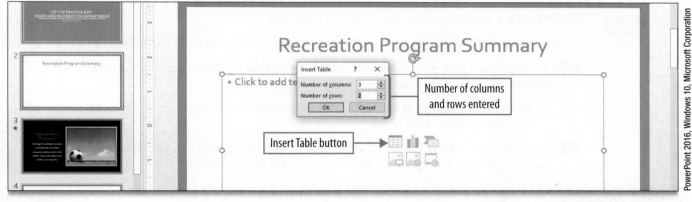

FIGURE 3.34

3 ▶ Click **OK** to create a table with three columns and two rows. Notice that the insertion point is blinking in the upper left cell of the table.

The table extends from the left side of the content placeholder to the right side, and the three columns are equal in width. By default, a style is applied to the table.

4 ▶ With the insertion point positioned in the first cell of the table, type **Athletics** and then press Tab.

Pressing Tab moves the insertion point to the next cell in the same row.

A L E R T ! **Did You Press Enter Instead of Tab?**

In a table, pressing Enter creates another line in the same cell. If you press Enter by mistake, you can remove the extra line by pressing Backspace.

5 With the insertion point positioned in the second cell of the first row, type **Leisure** and then press Tab. Type **Arts** and then press Tab to move the insertion point to the first cell in the second row. Compare your table with Figure 3.35.

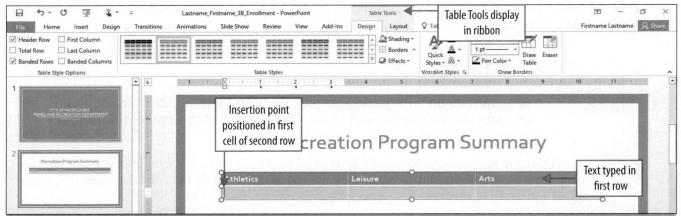

FIGURE 3.35

6 With the insertion point positioned in the first cell of the second row, type **Team sports** and then press Tab. Type **Personal development classes** and then press Tab. Type **Music and dance classes**

7 Save 🖫 your presentation.

Activity 3.19 | Inserting Rows and Columns in a Table

3.1.2

You can modify the layout of a table by inserting or deleting rows and columns.

1 With the insertion point positioned in the last cell of the table, press Tab and notice that a new blank row is inserted.

> When the insertion point is positioned in the last cell of a table, pressing Tab inserts a new blank row at the bottom of the table.

2 In the first cell of the third row, type **Youth** and then press Tab. Type **Older adults** and then press Tab. Type **Young adults** and then compare your table with Figure 3.36.

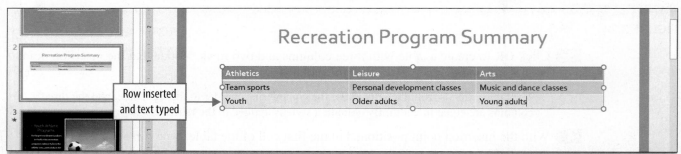

FIGURE 3.36

ALERT!   **Did You Add an Extra Row to the Table?**

When the insertion point is positioned in the last cell of the table, pressing Tab inserts a new blank row. If you inadvertently inserted a blank row in the table, on the Quick Access Toolbar, click Undo.

---

3 Click in any cell in the first column, and then click the **Layout tab**. In the **Rows & Columns group**, click **Insert Left**.

A new first column is inserted and the width of the columns is adjusted so that all four columns are the same width.

4 In the *second* row, click in the first cell, and then type **Largest Enrollments**

5 In the third row, click in the first cell, type **Primary Market** and then compare your table with Figure 3.37.

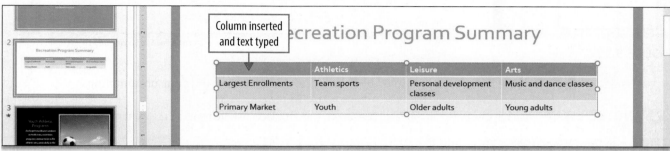

FIGURE 3.37

6 With the insertion point positioned in the third row, on the **Layout tab**, in the **Rows & Columns group**, click **Insert Above** to insert a new third row. In the first cell, type **Average Enrollment** and then press Tab. Type the remaining three entries, pressing Tab to move from cell to cell: **85% of capacity** and **62% of capacity** and **78% of capacity**

7 Save 🖫 your presentation.

More Knowledge	**Deleting Rows and Columns**

To delete a row or column from a table, click in the row or column that you want to delete. Click the Layout tab, and then in the Rows & Columns group, click Delete. In the displayed list, click Delete Columns or Delete Rows.

Activity 3.20 | Sizing a Table

A selected table is surrounded by sizing handles and can be resized in the same manner in which a shape or picture is resized.

1 Point to the bottom center sizing handle to display the 🔄 pointer. Compare your screen with Figure 3.38.

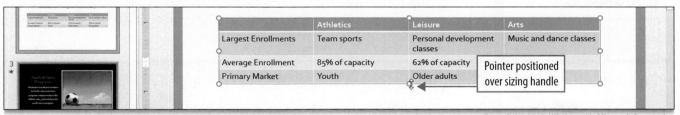

FIGURE 3.38

2 Drag down until the ruler guide is positioned on the **lower half of the vertical ruler at 2 inches**. Compare your screen with Figure 3.39.

A dim border and the red dotted ruler guides display, indicating the size of the table.

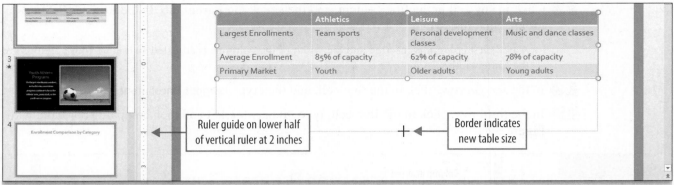

FIGURE 3.39

PowerPoint 2016, Windows 10, Microsoft Corporation

3 ▶ Release the mouse button to size the table, and then **Save** 🔲 your presentation.

ANOTHER WAY On the Layout tab, in the Table Size group, type an exact measurement in the Height or Width boxes.

Activity 3.21 | Distributing Rows and Aligning Table Text

1 ▶ Click in the first cell of the table. On the **Layout tab**, in the **Cell Size group**, click **Distribute Rows**. Compare your table with Figure 3.40.

The Distribute Rows command adjusts the height of the rows in the table so that they are equal.

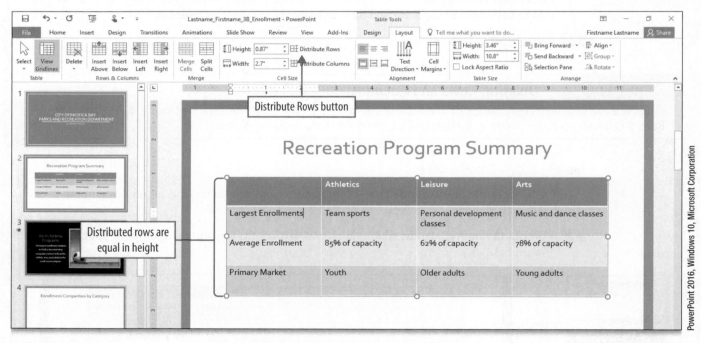

PowerPoint 2016, Windows 10, Microsoft Corporation

FIGURE 3.40

2 ▶ On the **Layout tab**, in the **Table group**, click **Select**, and then click **Select Table**. In the **Alignment group**, click **Center** 🔲, and then click **Center Vertically** 🔲.

All of the table text is centered horizontally and vertically within the cells.

3 ▶ **Save** 🔲 your presentation.

More Knowledge   **Distributing Columns**

To distribute columns, click anywhere in the table, and then on the Layout tab, in the Cell Size group, click Distribute Columns.

Activity 3.22 | Applying and Modifying a Table Style

You can modify the design of a table by applying a *table style*. A table style formats the entire table so that it is consistent with the presentation theme. There are color categories within the table styles—Best Match for Document, Light, Medium, and Dark.

1 ▶ Click in any cell in the table. On the **Table Tools Design tab**, in the **Table Styles group**, click **More** ⬚. In the **Table Styles** gallery, point to several of the styles to view the Live Preview of the style.

2 ▶ Under **Light**, in the third row, click the fourth style—**Light Style 3 – Accent 3**—to apply the style to the table.

3 ▶ On the **Table Tools Design tab**, in the **Table Style Options group**, clear the **Banded Rows** check box, and then select the **Banded Columns** check box. Compare your screen with Figure 3.41. **Save** 🖫 the presentation.

The check boxes in the Table Style Options group control where Table Style formatting is applied.

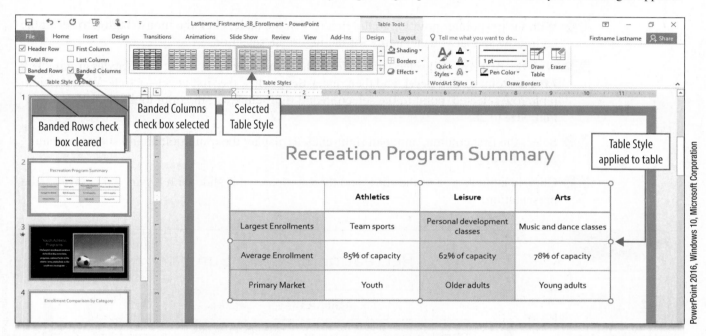

FIGURE 3.41

Activity 3.23 | Applying Table Effects and Font Formatting

1 ▶ Move the pointer outside of the table so that it is positioned to the left of the first row in the table to display the ➡ pointer, as shown in Figure 3.42.

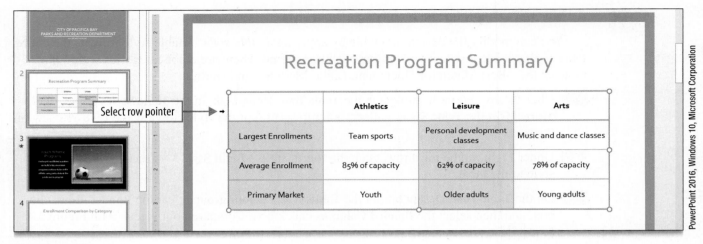

FIGURE 3.42

> **2** With the ➡ pointer pointing to the first row in the table, click the mouse button to select the entire row so that you can apply formatting to the selection.

> **3** With the first row still selected, on the **Table Tools Design tab**, in the **Table Styles group**, click **Effects**. Point to **Cell Bevel**, and then under **Bevel**, click the first bevel—**Circle**. With the first table row selected, point to the selection and right-click. On the mini toolbar, change the **Font Size** to **28**.

> **4** Select the first column, and then right-click to display the mini toolbar and shortcut menu. Apply **Bold**.

> **5** Click in a blank area of the slide, and then compare your slide with Figure 3.43. **Save** 🖫 the presentation.

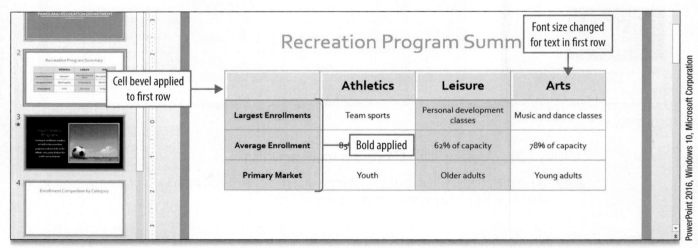

FIGURE 3.43

Objective 5 | Create and Modify Charts

GO! Learn How
Video P3-5

A ***chart*** is a graphic representation of numeric data. Commonly used chart types include bar and column charts, pie charts, and line charts. A chart that you create in PowerPoint is stored in an Excel worksheet that is incorporated into the PowerPoint file.

Activity 3.24 | Inserting a Column Chart

A ***column chart*** is useful for illustrating comparisons among related numbers. In this Activity, you will create a column chart that compares enrollment in each category of recreation activities by season.

1 Display **Slide 4**. In the content placeholder, click **Insert Chart** 📊 to display the **Insert Chart** dialog box. Compare your screen with Figure 3.44.

Along the left side of the dialog box, the types of charts that you can insert in your presentation display. Along the top of the dialog box, subtypes of the selected chart type display. By default, Column is selected and a Clustered Column chart displays in the preview area on the right side of the dialog box.

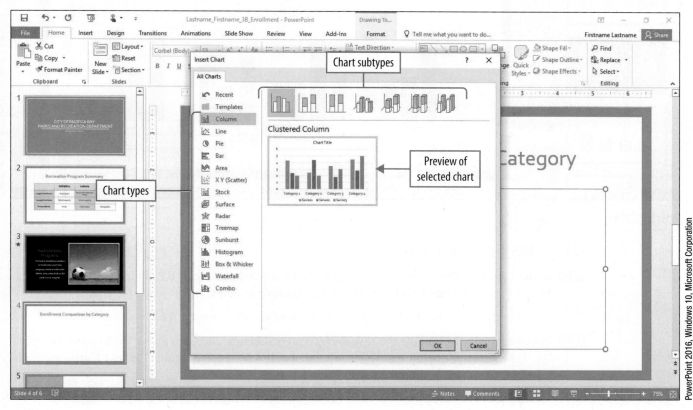

FIGURE 3.44

2 Along the top of the dialog box, point to each column chart to view the ScreenTip. Then, with the **Clustered Column** chart selected, click **OK**. Compare your screen with Figure 3.45.

The PowerPoint window displays a column chart in the content placeholder. A *Chart in Microsoft PowerPoint* worksheet window displays with cells, columns, and rows. A cell is identified by the intersecting column letter and row number, forming the ***cell reference***.

The worksheet contains sample data from which the chart on the PowerPoint slide is generated. The column headings—*Series 1*, *Series 2*, and *Series 3*—display in the chart ***legend*** and the row headings—*Category 1*, *Category 2*, *Category 3*, and *Category 4*—display as ***category labels***. The legend identifies the patterns or colors that are assigned to the data series in the chart. The category labels display along the bottom of the chart to identify the categories of data.

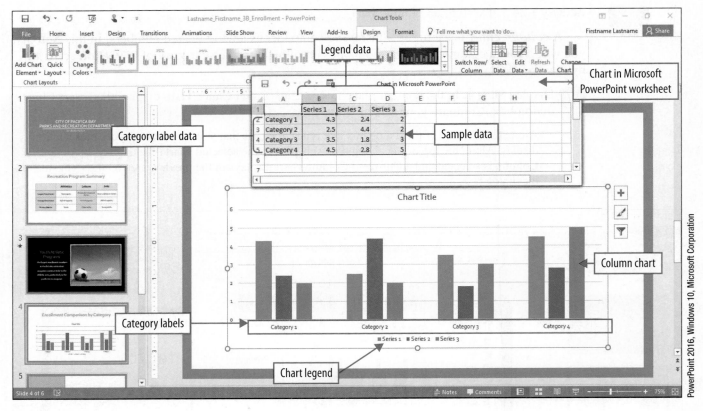

FIGURE 3.45

Activity 3.25 | Entering Chart Data

1 In the *Chart in Microsoft PowerPoint* worksheet window, in cell **B1**, which contains the text *Series 1*, type **Athletics** and then press Tab to move to cell **C1**.

> Below the chart, the chart legend is updated to reflect the change in the Excel worksheet.

2 In cell **C1**, which contains the text *Series 2*, type **Leisure** and then press Tab to move to cell **D1**. Type **Arts** and then press Tab. Notice that cell **A2**, which contains the text *Category 1*, is selected. Compare your screen with Figure 3.46.

> The outlined cells define the area in which you are entering data. When you press Tab in the rightmost cell, the first cell in the next row becomes active.

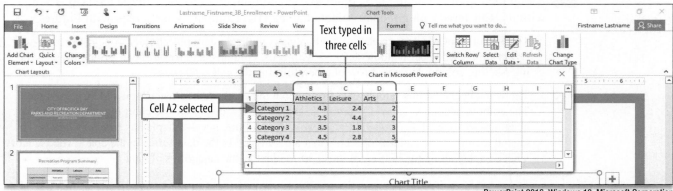

FIGURE 3.46

3 Beginning in cell **A2**, type the following data (starting with *Spring*), pressing [Tab] to move from cell to cell. Notice that as you enter the data, the chart columns resize to display the entered amounts.

	ATHLETICS	LEISURE	ARTS
Spring	895	630	720
Summer	1250	350	820
Fall	1490	585	690
Winter	1130	750	

4 In cell D5, which contains the value 5, type **710** and then press [Enter].

Pressing [Enter] in the last cell of the outlined area maintains the existing data range.

ALERT! **Did You Press [Tab] After the Last Entry?**

If you pressed [Tab] after entering the data in cell D5, you expanded the chart range. In the Excel window, click Undo.

5 Compare your worksheet and your chart with Figure 3.47. Correct any typing errors by clicking in the cell that you want to change, and then retype the data.

Each of the 12 cells containing the numeric data that you entered is a ***data point***—a value that originates in a worksheet cell. Each data point is represented in the chart by a ***data marker***—a column, bar, area, dot, pie slice, or other symbol in a chart that represents a single data point. Related data points form a ***data series***; for example, there is a data series for *Athletics*, *Leisure*, and *Arts*. Each data series has a unique color or pattern represented in the chart legend. A placeholder for the chart title displays above the chart.

To the right of the chart, three buttons display. The ***Chart Elements button*** ⊞ enables you to add, remove, or change chart elements such as the title, legend, gridlines, and data labels. The ***Chart Styles button*** 🖋 enables you to set a style and color scheme for your chart. The ***Chart Filters button*** 🔽 enables you to change which data displays in the chart.

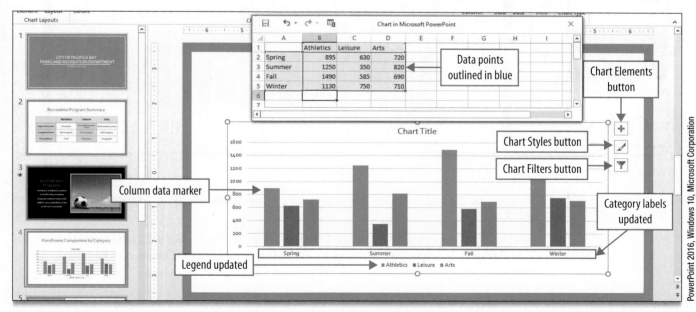

FIGURE 3.47

6 In the upper right corner of the *Chart in Microsoft PowerPoint* worksheet window, click **Close** ☒. **Save** 🖫 the presentation.

When you save the presentation, the worksheet data is saved with it.

More Knowledge — **Editing the Chart Data After Closing the Worksheet**

You can redisplay the worksheet and make changes to the data after you have closed it. To do so, click the chart to select it, and then on the Chart Tools Design tab in the Data group, click Edit Data.

3.2.4, 3.2.5

Activity 3.26 | Applying a Chart Style and Modifying Chart Elements

A *chart style* is a set of predefined formats applied to a chart, including colors, backgrounds, and effects. *Chart elements* are the various components of a chart, including the chart title, axis titles, data series, legend, chart area, and plot area.

1 Click the outer edge of the chart, if necessary, to select it. On the **Chart Tools Design tab**, in the **Chart Styles group**, click **More** ⊡ to display the **Chart Styles** gallery.

2 In the **Chart Styles** gallery, point to each style to Live Preview the style. Notice that as you point to a chart style, a ScreenTip indicates the chart style number. Click **Style 5**. Compare your screen with Figure 3.48.

This style includes lightly shaded column data markers. Horizontal gridlines display behind the columns.

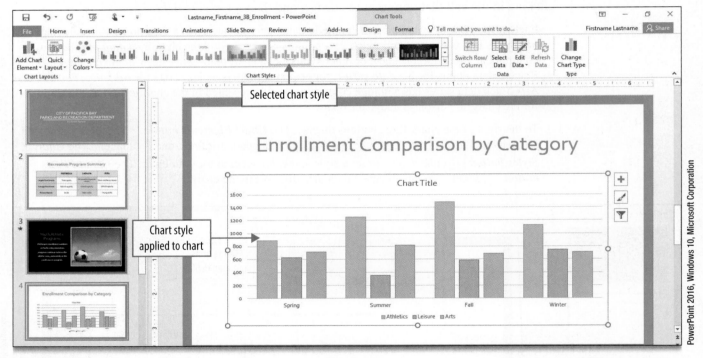

FIGURE 3.48

3 To the right of the chart, click **Chart Elements** ⊞, and then compare your screen with Figure 3.49.

A list of chart elements displays to the left of the chart. You can select the chart elements that you wish to display in your chart. In this slide, the slide title describes the chart so a chart title is not necessary.

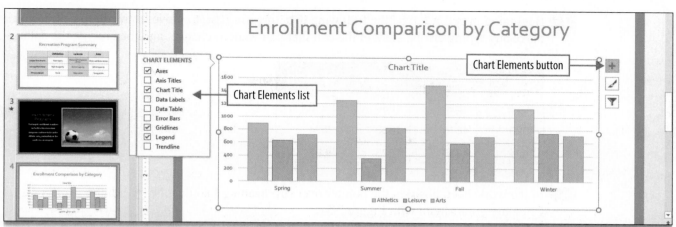

FIGURE 3.49

4 Under **Chart Elements**, click **Chart Title** to clear the check box and remove the chart title placeholder from the chart. Click **Chart Elements** ⊞ to close the Chart Elements list.

5 Click in a blank area of the slide, and then compare your screen with Figure 3.50. **Save** 🖫 your presentation.

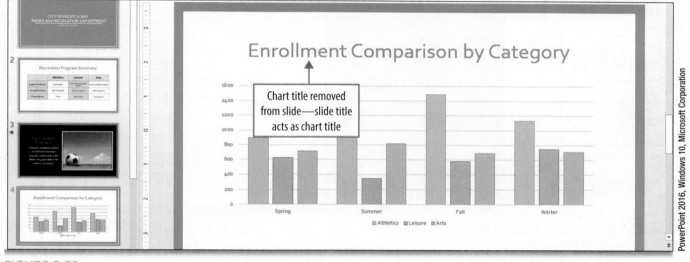

FIGURE 3.50

Activity 3.27 | Creating a Line Chart and Deleting Chart Data

To analyze and compare annual data over a three-year period, the presentation requires an additional chart. Recall that there are a number of different types of charts that you can insert in a PowerPoint presentation. In this Activity, you will create a *line chart*, which is commonly used to illustrate trends over time.

1 Display **Slide 5**. In the content placeholder, click **Insert Chart** 📊. On the left side of the **Insert Chart** dialog box, click **Line**, and then on the right, click the fourth chart—**Line with Markers**. Click **OK**.

2 In the worksheet, in cell **B1**, which contains the text *Series 1*, type **Youth** and then press ⎇Tab. In cell **C1**, type **Adult** and then press ⎇Tab. In cell **D1**, type **Senior** and then press ⎇Tab.

3 Beginning in cell **A2**, type the following data, pressing `Tab` to move from cell to cell. If you make any typing errors, click in the cell that you want to change, and then retype the data.

	YOUTH	ADULT	SENIOR
2019	3822	1588	2240
2020	4675	1833	2534
2021	4535	1925	2897

4 In the worksheet, position the pointer over **row heading 5** so that the ➡ pointer displays. Compare your screen with Figure 3.51.

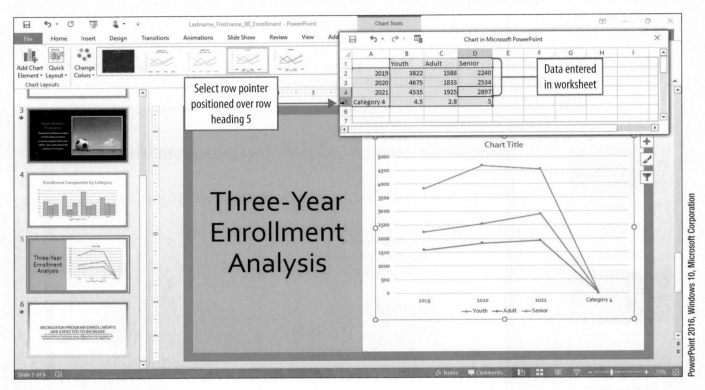

FIGURE 3.51

5 With the ➡ pointer displayed, *right-click* to select the row and display the shortcut menu. On the shortcut menu, click **Delete** to delete the extra row from the worksheet, and then compare your screen with Figure 3.52.

The data in the worksheet contains four columns and four rows, and the outline area defining the chart data range is resized. You must delete columns and rows from the sample worksheet data that you do not want to include in the chart. You can add additional rows and columns by typing column and row headings and then entering additional data. When data is typed in cells adjacent to the chart range, the range is resized to include the new data.

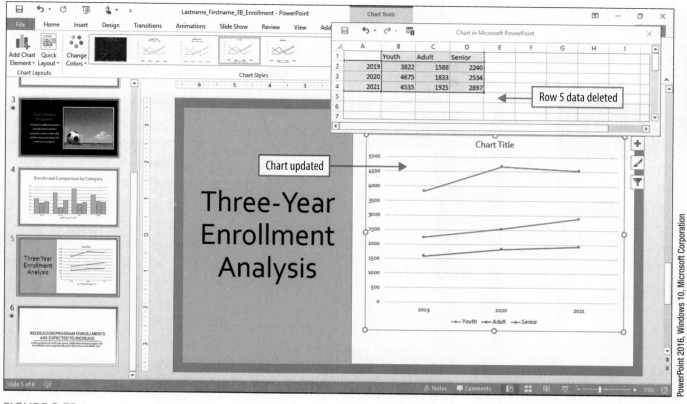

FIGURE 3.52

PowerPoint 2016, Windows 10, Microsoft Corporation

Activity 3.28 | **Formatting a Line Chart**

3.2.5

1 **Close** ☒ the worksheet window. To the right of the chart, click **Chart Styles** 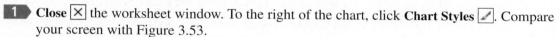. Compare your screen with Figure 3.53.

> The Chart Style gallery displays on the left side of the chart and the Style tab is active. The chart styles display in a vertical gallery.

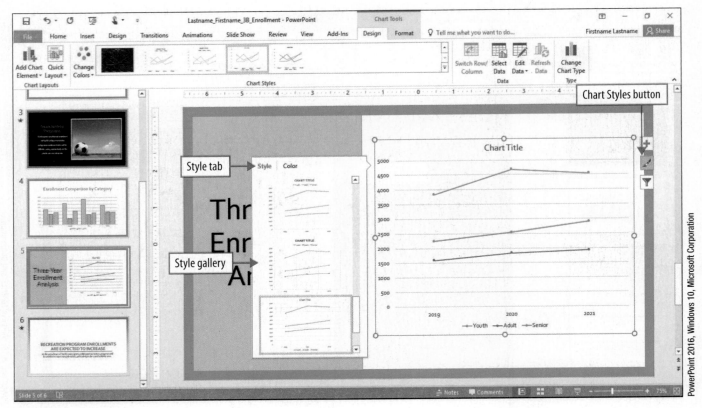

FIGURE 3.53

2 In the **Chart Style** gallery, be sure that **Style** is selected. Scroll the list, and point to various styles to view the ScreenTips and the effect of the style on the chart. Click **Style 6** and then click anywhere outside of the chart to close the Chart Style gallery.

> The styles that display when you click the Chart Styles button are the same as those that display in the Chart Styles gallery on the ribbon. Apply chart styles using the technique that you prefer.

3 In the chart, click the text **Chart Title**, and then type **By Age Category**

4 Click in a blank area of the slide, and then compare your screen with Figure 3.54. **Save** 🖫 your presentation.

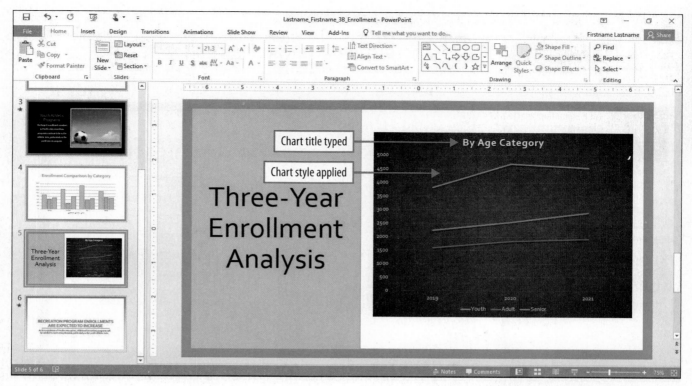

FIGURE 3.54

PowerPoint 2016, Windows 10, Microsoft Corporation

Activity 3.29 | Animating a Chart

4.2.1

1 Display **Slide 4**, and then click the column chart to select it. On the **Animations tab**, in the **Animation group**, click **More** ⏷, and then under **Entrance**, click **Fade**.

2 In the **Animation group**, click **Effect Options**, and then under **Sequence**, click **By Series**. In the **Preview group**, click **Preview** to preview the By Series effect. On **Slide 4**, notice the chart animation sequence. Compare your screen with Figure 3.55.

> The By Series option displays the chart one data series at a time, and the numbers 1, 2, 3, and 4 to the left of the chart indicate the four parts of the chart animation sequence. The chart animation sequence includes the background, followed by the Athletics data series for each season, and then the Leisure series, and then the Arts series.

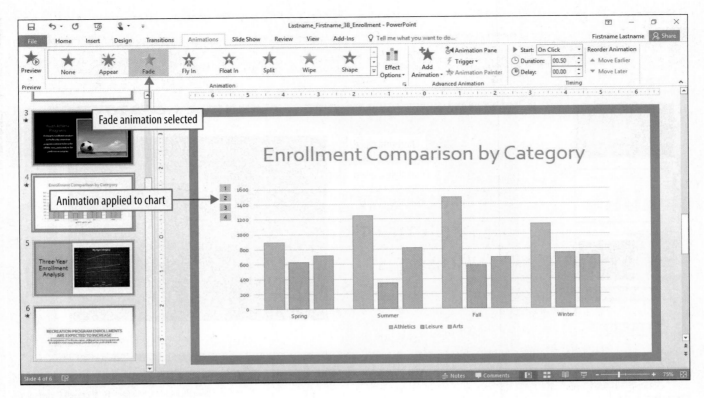

FIGURE 3.55

3 In the **Animation group**, click **Effect Options**, and then under **Sequence**, click **As One Object**. View the slide show from the beginning. On **Slide 4**, notice the chart animation sequence returns to a *1*.

4 Insert a **Header & Footer** on the **Notes and Handouts**. Include the **Date and time** updated automatically, the **Page Number**, and a **Footer**. In the Footer box, type **Lastname_Firstname_3B_Enrollment** and then click **Apply to All**.

5 Display the document properties. As the **Tags**, type **recreation enrollment** and as the **Subject**, type your course and section number. Be sure your name displays as author, and then **Save** your file.

6 As directed by your instructor, create and submit a paper printout or an electronic image of your presentation that looks like a printed document—either as the Notes and Handouts or as the presentation slides—or, submit your completed PowerPoint file.

7 **Close** PowerPoint.

END | You have completed Project 3B

GO! With Google

Objective | Create a Summary and Analysis Presentation in Google Slides

ALERT! **Working with Web-Based Applications and Services**

Computer programs and services on the web receive continuous updates and improvements, so the steps to complete this web-based activity may differ from the ones shown. You can often look at the screens and the information presented to determine how to complete the activity. If you do not already have a Google account, you will need to create one before beginning this activity.

Activity | Creating a Summary and Analysis Presentation in Google Slides

In this Activity, you will use Google Slides to create a presentation similar to the one you created in Project 3B.

1 From the desktop, open your browser, navigate to **http://google.com**, and then sign in to your Google account. Click **Google Apps** , and then click **Drive** . Open your **GO! Web Projects** folder—or click New to create and then open this folder if necessary.

2 In the left pane, click **NEW**, click **File upload** , and then in the **Open** dialog box, navigate to your student data files. Select **p03_3B_Web**. Click **Open**. When the upload is complete, if necessary, close the Uploads complete message box. Right-click **p03_3B_Web**, and then click **Rename**. Using your own name, as the file name type **Lastname_Firstname_3B_Web** and then press Enter. Right-click your file, point to **Open with**, and then click **Google Slides**.

3 Display **Slide 3**. In the text placeholder on the left side of the slide, type **The largest enrollment numbers in Pacifica Bay recreation programs continue to be in the athletic area, particularly in the youth soccer program.** Click outside of the placeholder to deselect the text placeholder.

4 Click the image placeholder on the right. On the toolbar, click **Replace image**. In the **Replace image** dialog box, click **Choose an image to upload**. Navigate to your student data files, and then click **p03B_Web_Picture**. Click **Open**. Click in a blank area of the slide.

5 Display **Slide 4**, and then click in the title placeholder. On the menu bar, click **View**, and then

click **Animations**. On the **Animations pane**, click **Add animation**, click the **Fade in arrow**, and then click **Fly in from top**.

6 Display **Slide 5**, and then click in the title placeholder. Type **Three-Year Enrollment Analysis** and then click outside of the placeholder to deselect it.

7 On **Slide 5**, click the chart to select it. On the **Animations pane**, click **Add animation.** If necessary, click the Fade in arrow to apply the Fade in animation to the chart.

8 Display **Slide 6**. In the title placeholder, type **Recreation Program Enrollments are Expected to Increase** and then click outside of the placeholder. **Close** ☒ the **Animations** pane.

9 Display **Slide 1**. In the upper right, click the **Present arrow**, and then click **Present from beginning**. If necessary, click **Allow**. Click the left mouse button to progress through the presentation. When the last slide displays, press Esc or click **Exit**.

10 Your presentation will be saved automatically. If you are instructed to submit your file, click the File menu, point to Download as, and then click PDF Document or Microsoft PowerPoint as directed by your instructor. The file will download to your default download folder as determined by your browser settings. Sign out of your Google account.

(GO! With Google continues on the next page)

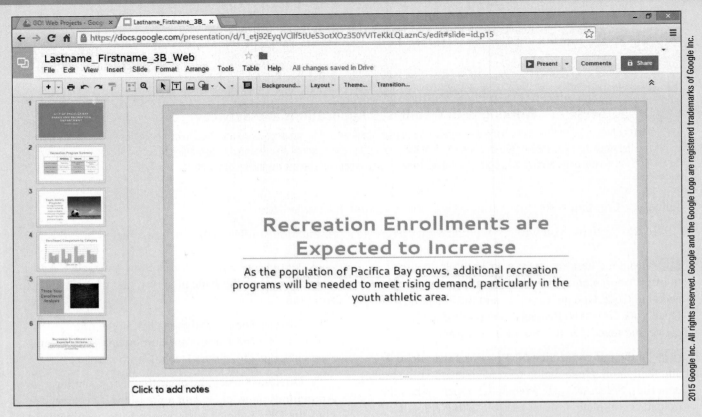

FIGURE A

GO! To Work

MICROSOFT OFFICE SPECIALIST (MOS) SKILLS IN THIS CHAPTER

PROJECT 3A		PROJECT 3B	
1.2.6	Modify individual slide backgrounds	3.1.1	Create a table
3.4.1	Insert audio and video clips	3.1.2	Insert and delete table rows and columns
3.4.2	Configure media playback options	3.1.3	Apply table styles
3.4.3	Adjust media window size	3.2.1	Create a chart
3.4.4	Set the video start and stop time	3.2.4	Add a legend to a chart
3.4.5	Set media timing options	3.2.5	Change the chart style of a chart
4.2.1	Apply animations to objects	4.2.1	Apply animations to objects
4.2.2	Apply animations to text		
4.2.3	Set animation effect options		
4.2.4	Set animation paths		
4.3.1	Set transition effect duration		
4.3.2	Configure transition start and finish options		
4.3.3	Reorder animations on a slide		
5.2.4	Preserve presentation content		

BUILD YOUR E-PORTFOLIO

An E-Portfolio is a collection of evidence, stored electronically, that showcases what you have accomplished while completing your education. Collecting and then sharing your work products with potential employers reflects your academic and career goals. Your completed documents from the following projects are good examples to show what you have learned: 3G, 3K, and 3L.

GO! FOR JOB SUCCESS
Video: Making Ethical Choices

Your instructor may assign this video to your class, and then ask you to think about, or discuss with your classmates, these questions:

Which behaviors in this video do you think were unethical?

Is it unethical to "borrow" things from your employer? Why? What would you do if you saw this behavior going on?

What do you think an employer could do to prevent unethical behavior?

FotolEdhar / Fotolia

END OF CHAPTER

SUMMARY

There are many ways to modify a presentation theme and customize a presentation. You can apply background styles, insert pictures and textures on slide backgrounds, and change theme fonts and colors.

One way to enhance a presentation and engage an audience is by inserting interesting and informative video. Styles, shapes, and effects can be applied to videos. A video can be trimmed and compressed to make the file size smaller.

Use animation to focus audience attention on a particular slide element in order to draw attention to important points. Apply animation to slide elements in the order in which you want them to display.

Use tables to present information in an organized and attractive manner. Use charts to visually represent data. Apply styles to charts and tables to give your presentations a consistent and informative look.

GO! LEARN IT ONLINE

Review the concepts, key terms, and MOS skills in this chapter by completing these online challenges, which you can find at **MyITLab**.

Matching and Multiple Choice: Answer matching and multiple-choice questions to test what you learned in this chapter.

Lessons on the GO!: Learn how to use all the new apps and features as they are introduced by Microsoft.

MOS Prep Quiz: Answer questions to review the MOS skills that you practiced in this chapter.

GO! COLLABORATIVE TEAM PROJECT (Available in **MyITLab** and Instructor Resource Center)

If your instructor assigns this project to your class, you can expect to work with one or more of your classmates—either in person or by using Internet tools—to create work products similar to those that you created in this chapter. A team is a group of workers who work together to solve a problem, make a decision, or create a work product. Collaboration is when you work together with others as a team in an intellectual endeavor to complete a shared task or achieve a shared goal.

Your instructor will assign Projects from this list to ensure your learning and assess your knowledge.

		PROJECT GUIDE FOR POWERPOINT CHAPTER 3	
Project	**Apply Skills from These Chapter Objectives**	**Project Type**	**Project Location**
3A **MyITLab**	Objectives 1–3 from Project 3A	**3A Instructional Project (Grader Project)** Guided instruction to learn the skills in Project 3A.	In MyITLab and in text
3B **MyITLab**	Objectives 4–5 from Project 3B	**3B Instructional Project (Grader Project)** Guided instruction to learn the skills in Project 3B.	In MyITLab and in text
3C	Objectives 1–3 from Project 3A	**3C Skills Review (Scorecard Grading)** A guided review of the skills from Project 3A.	In text
3D	Objectives 4–5 from Project 3B	**3D Skills Review (Scorecard Grading)** A guided review of the skills from Project 3B.	In text
3E **MyITLab**	Objectives 1–3 from Project 3A	**3E Mastery (Grader Project) Mastery and Transfer of Learning** A demonstration of your mastery of the skills in Project 3A with extensive decision making.	In MyITLab and in text
3F **MyITLab**	Objectives 4–5 from Project 3B	**3F Mastery (Grader Project) Mastery and Transfer of Learning** A demonstration of your mastery of the skills in Project 3B with extensive decision making.	In MyITLab and in text
3G **MyITLab**	Objectives 1–5 from Projects 3A and 3B	**3G Mastery (Grader Project) Mastery and Transfer of Learning** A demonstration of your mastery of the skills in Projects 3A and 3B with extensive decision making.	In MyITLab and in text
3H	Combination of Objectives from Projects 3A and 3B	**3H GO! Fix It (Scorecard Grading) Critical Thinking** A demonstration of your mastery of the skills in Projects 3A and 3B by creating a correct result from a document that contains errors you must find.	Instructor Resource Center (IRC) and MyITLab
3I	Combination of Objectives from Projects 3A and 3B	**3I GO! Make It (Scorecard Grading) Critical Thinking** A demonstration of your mastery of the skills in Projects 3A and 3B by creating a result from a supplied picture.	IRC and MyITLab
3J	Combination of Objectives from Projects 3A and 3B	**3J GO! Solve It (Rubric Grading) Critical Thinking** A demonstration of your mastery of the skills in Projects 3A and 3B, your decision-making skills, and your critical thinking skills. A task-specific rubric helps you self-assess your result.	IRC and MyITLab
3K	Combination of Objectives from Projects 3A and 3B	**3K GO! Solve It (Rubric Grading) Critical Thinking** A demonstration of your mastery of the skills in Projects 3A and 3B, your decision-making skills, and your critical thinking skills. A task-specific rubric helps you self-assess your result.	In text
3L	Combination of Objectives from Projects 3A and 3B	**3L GO! Think (Rubric Grading) Critical Thinking** A demonstration of your understanding of the chapter concepts applied in a manner that you would outside of college. An analytic rubric helps you and your instructor grade the quality of your work by comparing it to the work an expert in the discipline would create.	In text
3M	Combination of Objectives from Projects 3A and 3B	**3M GO! Think (Rubric Grading) Critical Thinking** A demonstration of your understanding of the chapter concepts applied in a manner that you would outside of college. An analytic rubric helps you and your instructor grade the quality of your work by comparing it to the work an expert in the discipline would create.	IRC and MyITLab
3N	Combination of Objectives from Projects 3A and 3B	**3N You and GO! (Rubric Grading) Critical Thinking** A demonstration of your understanding of the chapter concepts applied in a manner that you would in a personal situation. An analytic rubric helps you and your instructor grade the quality of your work.	IRC and MyITLab
3O	Combination of Objectives from Projects 3A and 3B	**3O Collaborative Team Project for PowerPoint Chapter 3 Critical Thinking** A demonstration of your understanding of concepts and your ability to work collaboratively in a group role-playing assessment, requiring both collaboration and self-management.	IRC and MyITLab
Capstone Project for PowerPoint Chapters 1–3	Combination of Objectives from Chapters 1–3	A demonstration of your mastery of the skills in Chapters 1–3 with extensive decision making. **(Grader Project)**	IRC and MyITLab

GLOSSARY

GLOSSARY OF CHAPTER KEY TERMS

After Previous An animation option that begins the animation sequence for the selected slide element immediately after the completion of the previous animation or slide transition.

Animation A visual or sound effect added to an object or text on a slide.

Animation Painter A feature that copies animation settings from one object to another.

Background style A predefined slide background fill variation that combines theme colors in different intensities or patterns.

Body font A font that is applied to all slide text except slide titles.

Category labels Text that displays along the bottom of a chart to identify the categories of data.

Cell The intersection of a column and row in a table.

Cell reference The intersecting column letter and row number that identify a cell.

Chart A graphic representation of numeric data.

Chart elements The various components of a chart, including the chart title, axis titles, data series, legend, chart area, and plot area.

Chart Elements button A button that displays options for adding, removing, or changing chart elements.

Chart Filters button A button that displays options for changing the data displayed in a chart.

Chart style A set of predefined formats applied to a chart, including colors, backgrounds, and effects.

Chart Styles button A button that displays options for setting the style and color scheme for a chart.

Column chart A type of chart used for illustrating comparisons among related numbers.

Data marker A column, bar, area, dot, pie slice, or other symbol in a chart that represents a single data point.

Data point A chart value that originates in a worksheet cell.

Data series A group of related data points.

Emphasis effect Animation that emphasizes an object or text that is already displayed.

Entrance effect Animation that brings a slide element onto the screen.

Exit effect Animation that moves an object or text off the screen.

Headings font A font that is applied to all slide title text.

Legend A chart element that identifies the patterns or colors that are assigned to the data series in the chart.

Line chart A type of chart commonly used to illustrate trends over time.

On Click An animation option that begins the animation sequence for the selected slide element when the mouse button is clicked or the Spacebar is pressed.

Table A format for information that organizes and presents text and data in columns and rows.

Table style A format applied to a table that is consistent with the presentation theme.

Theme colors A set of coordinating colors that are applied to the backgrounds, objects, and text in a presentation.

Theme fonts The fonts that apply to two types of slide text—headings and body.

Timing options Animation options that control when animated items display in the animation sequence.

Trim A command that deletes parts of a video to make it shorter.

With Previous An animation option that begins the animation sequence at the same time as the previous animation or slide transition.

Apply 3A skills from these Objectives:

1 Customize Slide Backgrounds and Themes
2 Animate a Slide Show
3 Insert a Video

Skills Review | **Project 3C Park**

In the following Skills Review, you will format a presentation by applying slide background styles, colors, pictures, and animation. Your completed presentation will look similar to Figure 3.56.

PROJECT FILES

For Project 3C, you will need the following files:

p03C_Park
p03C_Park_Scenery
p03C_Park_Video

You will save your presentation as:

Lastname_Firstname_3C_Park

PROJECT RESULTS

FIGURE 3.56

(Project 3C Park continues on the next page)

1 Start PowerPoint, from your student data files, open **p03C_Park**, and then **Save** the presentation in your **PowerPoint Chapter 3** folder as **Lastname_Firstname_3C_Park**

a. On the **Design tab**, in the **Variants group**, click **More**, point to **Colors**, and then click **Orange Red** to change the theme colors.

b. On the **Design tab**, in the **Variants group**, click **More**, point to **Fonts**, and then click **Candara** to change the theme fonts.

c. On the **Design tab**, in the **Customize group**, click **Format Background**. In the **Format Background** pane, under **Fill**, click **Picture or texture fill**. Under **Insert picture from**, to the right of **Texture**, click **Texture**, and then in the third row, click the fourth texture—**Recycled Paper**.

d. **Close** the **Format Background** pane.

2 Display **Slide 2**. Hold down Ctrl and click **Slide 4** so that both **Slides 2** and **4** are selected. On the **Design tab**, in the **Variants group**, click **More**, and then point to **Background Styles**. In the second row, *right-click* the third style—**Style 7**, and then on the shortcut menu, click **Apply to Selected Slides**.

a. Display **Slide 3**. On the **Design tab**, in the **Customize group**, click **Format Background**. Select the **Hide Background Graphics** check box.

b. In the **Format Background** pane, under **Fill**, click **Picture or texture fill**. Under **Insert picture from**, click **File**, and then navigate to your student data files. Click **p03C_Park_Scenery**, and then click **Insert**.

c. In the **Transparency** box, type **10%**

3 Display **Slide 5**. If necessary, display the **Format Background** pane.

a. In the **Format Background** pane, under **Fill**, verify that **Solid Fill** is selected.

b. To the right of **Color**, click **Fill Color**. In the third column, click the first color—**Tan, Background 2**.

c. **Close** the **Format Background** pane.

4 With **Slide 5** displayed, on the **Insert tab**, in the **Media group**, click **Video**, and then click **Video on My PC**. Navigate to your student data files, and then click **p03C_Park_Video**. Click **Insert** to insert the video.

a. With the video selected, on the **Format tab**, in the **Size group**, replace the value in the **Height** box with **2.5** and then press Enter.

b. On the **Format tab**, in the **Arrange group**, click **Align**, and then click **Align Center**. Click **Align** again, and then click **Align Bottom** so that the video is centered and aligned with the lower edge of the slide.

c. With the video selected, on the **Format tab**, in the **Video Styles** group, click **More**, and then under **Subtle**, click the third style—**Soft Edge Rectangle**.

d. In the **Video Styles group**, click **Video Shape**, and then under **Rectangles**, click the second shape—**Rounded Rectangle**.

e. With the video selected, on the **Playback tab**, in the **Video Options group**, click the **Start arrow**, and then click **Automatically**.

f. On the **Playback tab**, in the **Editing group**, click **Trim Video**. Select the number in the **End Time** box, and then type **00:14** and notice that the video ends with a picture of the park. Click **OK** to apply the trim settings.

5 Display **Slide 2**, and then select the text in the bulleted list placeholder. On the **Home tab**, in the **Font group**, click **Font Color**, and then in the second column, click the first color—**White, Text 1** so that the text displays with more contrast against the slide background.

a. With the bulleted list selected, on the **Animations tab**, in the **Animation group**, click **More**, and then under **Entrance**, click **Split**.

b. In the **Animation group**, click **Effect Options**, and then click **Vertical Out**.

c. In the **Timing group**, click the **Start arrow**, and then click **After Previous** so that the list displays after the slide transition.

d. In the **Timing group**, click the **Duration up arrow** two times so that *01.00* displays in the **Duration** box. Click the **Delay up arrow** one time so that *00.25* displays in the **Delay** box.

(Project 3C Park continues on the next page)

6 Display **Slide 3**, and then click in the title placeholder. On the **Animations tab**, in the **Animation group**, click **More**, and then under **Entrance**, click **Wipe**. In the **Timing group**, click the **Start arrow**, and then click **After Previous** so that the title displays immediately after the slide transition.

a. With the title selected, in the **Advanced Animation group**, click **Animation Painter**. Click **Slide 1**, and then click the subtitle—*Remodel Update*—to apply the animation effect to the subtitle.

b. On **Slide 1**, select the title. On the **Animations tab**, in the **Animation group**, click **More**, and then click **None** to remove the animation from the title.

c. Insert a **Header & Footer** for the **Notes and Handouts**. Include the **Date and time updated automatically**, the **Page number**, and a **Footer** with the file name **Lastname_Firstname_3C_Park**

d. On the **Slide Show tab**, in the **Start Slide Show group**, click **From Beginning**, and then view your

presentation, clicking the mouse button to advance through the slides. When the video on Slide 5 finishes, press [Esc] to return to the presentation.

7 Click the **File tab**, and then click **Compress Media**. Click **Low Quality** to make the presentation size smaller and easier to submit. When the compression is complete, in the **Compress Media** dialog box, click **Close**.

a. Display the document properties. As the **Tags,** type **park remodel** and as the **Subject,** type your course and section number. Be sure your name displays as author, and then **Save** your file.

b. As directed by your instructor, create and submit a paper printout or an electronic image of your presentation that looks like a printed document— either as the Notes and Handouts or as the presentation slides—or, submit your completed PowerPoint file. **Close** PowerPoint.

END | You have completed Project 3C

Apply 3B skills from
these Objectives:

4 Create and Modify
Tables

5 Create and Modify
Charts

Skills Review | Project 3D Budget

In the following Skills Review, you will format a presentation by inserting and formatting a table, a column chart, and a line chart. Your completed presentation will look similar to Figure 3.57.

PROJECT FILES

For Project 3D, you will need the following file:

p03D_Budget

You will save your presentation as:

Lastname_Firstname_3D_Budget

PROJECT RESULTS

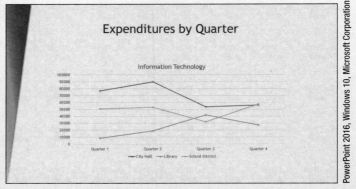

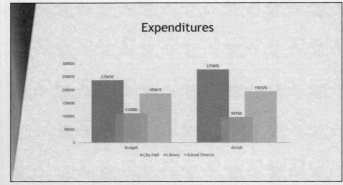

FIGURE 3.57

(Project 3D Budget continues on the next page)

1 Start PowerPoint, from your student data files, open **p03D_Budget**, and then **Save** the presentation in your **PowerPoint Chapter 3** folder as **Lastname_Firstname_3D_Budget**

a. Display **Slide 2**. In the content placeholder, click **Insert Table** to display the **Insert Table** dialog box. In the **Number of columns box**, type **3** and then press Tab. In the **Number of rows** box, if necessary, type **2** and then click **OK** to create the table.

b. In the first row of the table, click in the second cell. Type **City Hall** and then press Tab. Type **School District** and then press Tab to move the insertion point to the first cell in the second row.

c. With the insertion point positioned in the first cell of the second row, type **Network Upgrade** and then press Tab. Type **75% complete** and then press Tab. Type **50% complete** and then press Tab to insert a new blank row. In the first cell of the third row, type **Software Training** and then press Tab. Type **50% complete** and then press Tab. Type **20% complete**

d. With the insertion point positioned in the last column, on the **Layout tab**, in the **Rows & Columns group**, click **Insert Left** to insert a new column. Click in the top cell of the inserted column, and then type **Library** In the second and third rows of the inserted column, type **85% complete** and **65% complete**

e. With the insertion point positioned in the third row, on the **Layout tab**, in the **Rows & Columns group**, click **Insert Above**. Click in the first cell of the row you inserted, type **Software Testing** and then press Tab. Type the remaining three entries in the row as follows: **Complete** and **Complete** and **40% complete**

2 At the center of the lower border surrounding the table, point to the sizing handle, and make the table larger by dragging down until the lower edge of the table aligns **on the lower half of the vertical ruler at 2 inches**.

a. Click in the first cell of the table. On the **Layout tab**, in the **Cell Size group**, click **Distribute Rows**.

b. On the **Layout tab**, in the **Table group**, click **Select**, and then click **Select Table**. In the **Alignment group**, click **Center**, and then click **Center Vertically**.

c. Click in any cell in the table. On the **Table Tools Design tab**, in the **Table Styles group**, click **More**.

Under **Medium**, in the third row, click the second style—**Medium Style 3 – Accent 1**—to apply the style to the table.

d. Move the pointer outside of the table so that is positioned to the left of the first row in the table to display the ➡ pointer, and then click one time to select the entire row. On the **Design tab**, in the **Table Styles group**, click **Effects**. Point to **Cell Bevel**, and then under **Bevel**, click the first bevel—**Circle**. Change the **Font Size** of the text in the first row to **24**.

3 Display **Slide 3**. In the content placeholder, click **Insert Chart** to display the **Insert Chart** dialog box. With the **Clustered Column** chart selected, click **OK**.

a. In the worksheet window, click in cell **B1**, which contains the text *Series 1*. Type **City Hall** and then press Tab to move to cell **C1**.

b. In cell **C1**, which contains the text *Series 2*, type **Library** and then press Tab to move to cell **D1**, which contains the text *Series 3*. Type **School District** and then press Tab.

c. Beginning in cell **A2**, type the following data, pressing Tab to move from cell to cell.

	City Hall	Library	School District
Budget	235650	110500	185635
Actual	275895	95760	192570

d. In the worksheet window, position the pointer over **row heading 4** so that the ➡ pointer displays. Then, drag down to select both **rows 4** and **5**. *Right-click* in one of the selected rows to display the shortcut menu. On the shortcut menu, click **Delete**. **Close** the worksheet window.

e. With the chart selected, on the **Chart Tools Design tab**, in the **Chart Styles group**, click **More**. In the **Chart Styles** gallery, in the second row, click **Style 13** to apply the style to the chart.

f. To the right of the chart, click **Chart Elements**, and then *clear* the **Chart Title** box to remove it from the chart. Select the **Data Labels** box to add the data labels to the chart.

(Project 3D Budget continues on the next page)

g. With the chart selected, click the **Animations tab**, and then in the **Animation group**, click **More**. Under **Entrance**, click **Split**. In the **Animation group**, click **Effect Options**, and then under **Sequence**, click **By Series**.

4 Display **Slide 4**. In the content placeholder, click **Insert Chart**. On the left side of the displayed **Insert Chart** dialog box, click **Line**, and then under **Line**, click the fourth chart—**Line with Markers**. Click **OK**.

a. In the worksheet, click in cell **B1**, which contains the text *Series 1*. Type **City Hall** and then press [Tab]. Type **Library** and then press [Tab]. Type **School District** and then press [Tab].

b. Beginning in cell **A2**, type the following data, pressing [Tab] to move from cell to cell. After you finish entering the data, close the worksheet window.

	City Hall	Library	School District
Quarter 1	76575	8265	50665
Quarter 2	89670	18675	52830
Quarter 3	53620	41730	31560
Quarter 4	56030	27090	57515

c. Click in the **Chart Title**, and then type **Information Technology**

d. Insert a **Header & Footer** for the **Notes and Handouts**. Include the **Date and time updated automatically**, the **Page number**, and a **Footer** with the file name **Lastname_Firstname_3D_Budget**

e. Display the document properties. As the **Tags,** type **technology budget** and as the **Subject,** type your course and section number. Be sure your name displays as author, and then **Save** your file.

f. As directed by your instructor, create and submit a paper printout or an electronic image of your presentation that looks like a printed document—either as the Notes and Handouts or as the presentation slides—or, submit your completed PowerPoint file. **Close** PowerPoint.

End | You have completed Project 3D

In the following Mastering PowerPoint project, you will format a presentation created by the Pacifica Bay Public Relations department that describes the City of Pacifica Bay Botanical Gardens. Your completed presentation will look similar to Figure 3.58.

Apply 3A skills from these Objectives:

1 Customize Slide Backgrounds and Themes
2 Animate a Slide Show
3 Insert a Video

PROJECT FILES

For Project 3E, you will need the following files:

p03E_Garden
p03E_Flower
p03E_Video

You will save your presentation as:

Lastname_Firstname_3E_Garden

PROJECT RESULTS

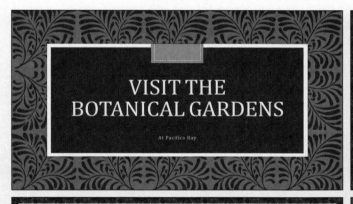

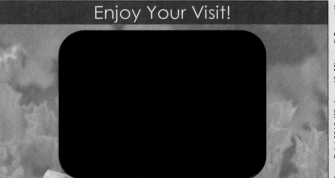

FIGURE 3.58

(Project 3E Gardens continues on the next page)

1 Start PowerPoint. From the student data files that accompany this textbook, locate and open **p03E_ Garden**. Save the presentation in your **PowerPoint Chapter 3** folder as **Lastname_Firstname_3E_Garden**

2 Change the **Colors** for the presentation to **Violet**, and the **Fonts** to **Cambria**.

3 On **Slide 1**, format the background by changing the **Fill Color** to **Gray – 25%, Text 2, Darker 90%**—in the fourth column, the last color.

4 Select **Slides 2** and **3**, and then format the background of the two selected slides with the **Green marble Texture**.

5 On **Slide 2**, select the paragraph on the right side of the slide, and then apply the **Split** entrance effect. Change the **Effect Options** to **Horizontal Out**. Change the **Start** setting to **After Previous**, and then change the **Duration** to **01.00**.

6 Use the **Animation Painter** to apply the same animation from the paragraph on **Slide 2** to the bulleted list on **Slide 3**. Then, on Slide 3, remove the animation from the title.

7 On **Slide 4,** hide the background graphics, and then format the background with a picture from your student data files—**p03E_Flower**. Change the **Transparency** to **50%**

8 Format the title placeholder with a **Shape Fill** color—in the fifth column, the last color—**Lavender, Accent 1, Darker 50%**.

9 From your student data files, insert the video **p03E_Video**. Change the **Video Height** to **6.25**

10 Using the **Align to Slide** option, apply the **Align Center** and **Align Bottom** options.

11 Format the video by applying, from the **Video Styles** gallery, an **Intense** style—**Bevel Rectangle**.

12 Change the video **Start** setting to **Automatically**, and then trim the video to **00:14** Compress the video using the **Low Quality** setting.

13 **Insert** a **Header & Footer** on the **Notes and Handouts**. Include the **Date and time updated automatically**, the **Page number**, and a **Footer** with the text **Lastname_Firstname_3E_Garden**

14 Display the document properties. As the **Tags,** type **botanical gardens** and as the **Subject,** type your course and section number. Be sure your name displays in the **Author box**, and then **Save** your file.

15 View the slide show from the beginning, and then as directed by your instructor, create and submit a paper printout or an electronic image of your presentation that looks like a printed document—either as the Notes and Handouts or as the presentation slides—or, submit your completed PowerPoint file. **Close** PowerPoint.

END | You have completed Project 3E

(Project 3E Gardens continues on the next page)

Mastering PowerPoint | Project 3F Report

In the following Mastering PowerPoint project, you will format several of the slides in a presentation that the City Manager is developing for an upcoming City Council meeting. Your completed presentation will look similar to Figure 3.59.

Apply 3B skills from these Objectives:

4 Create and Modify Tables

5 Create and Modify Charts

PROJECT FILES

For Project 3F, you will need the following file:

p03F_Report

You will save your presentation as:

Lastname_Firstname_3F_Report

PROJECT RESULTS

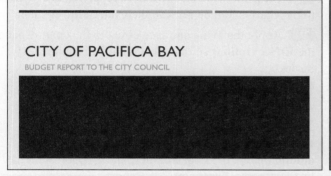

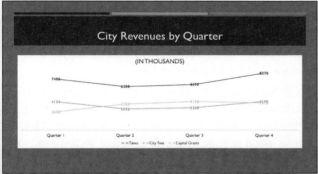

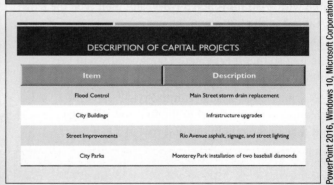

FIGURE 3.59

(Project 3F Report continues on the next page)

PowerPoint 2016, Windows 10, Microsoft Corporation

Mastering PowerPoint Project 3F Report (continued)

1 Start PowerPoint. From your student data files, open **p03F_Report**, and then **Save** the presentation in your **PowerPoint Chapter 3** folder as **Lastname_Firstname_3F_Report**

2 On **Slide 3**, in the content placeholder, insert a **Line with Markers** chart. In the worksheet, in cell B1, type **Taxes** and then enter the following data:

	Taxes	City Fees	Capital Grants
Quarter 1	7480	4154	2650
Quarter 2	6380	3092	3785
Quarter 3	6695	3260	4150
Quarter 4	8370	4190	3970

3 **Close** the worksheet window. Apply **Chart Style 7**, and then apply the **Wipe** entrance effect to the chart.

4 Including the parentheses, change the **Chart Title** to **(IN THOUSANDS)**

5 On **Slide 4**, in the content placeholder, insert a **Table** with **2 columns** and **5 rows**, and then type the text in **Table 1** at the bottom of the page.

6 Change the height of the table to **4.36"**. Align the table text so that it is centered horizontally and vertically within the cells.

7 Apply table style **Medium Style 3 - Accent 2**, and then apply a **Circle Bevel** to the first row. Change the **Font Size** of the text in the first row to **24**.

Item	Description
Flood Control	Main Street storm drain replacement
City Buildings	Infrastructure upgrades
Street Improvements	Rio Avenue asphalt, signage, and street lighting
City Parks	Monterey Park installation of two baseball diamonds

TABLE 1

8 On **Slide 5**, in the content placeholder, insert a **Clustered Column** chart. In the worksheet, in cell **B1**, type **2017** and then enter the following data:

	2017	2018	2019
Land	71534	72823	83653
Structures	95746	95920	97812
Equipment	35042	33465	39767
Infrastructure	111586	121860	125873

9 **Close** the worksheet window. Apply **Chart Style 4** to the chart, and then remove the **Chart Title** element.

10 Apply the **Wipe** entrance effect to the chart. Change the **Effect Options** so that the animation is applied **By Series**.

11 Change the chart animation **Timing** so that the animation starts **After Previous**.

12 **Insert** a **Header & Footer** on the **Notes and Handouts**. Include the **Date and time updated automatically**, the **Page number**, and a **Footer** with the text **Lastname_Firstname_3F_Report**

13 Display the document properties. As the **Tags**, type **city council report** and as the **Subject**, type your course and section number. Be sure your name displays as author, and then **Save** your file.

14 View the slide show from the beginning, and then as directed by your instructor, create and submit a paper printout or an electronic image of your presentation that looks like a printed document—either as the Notes and Handouts or as the presentation slides—or, submit your completed PowerPoint file. **Close** PowerPoint.

END | You have completed Project 3F

Mastering PowerPoint | **Project 3G Travel**

In the following Mastering PowerPoint project, you will format a presentation that the Pacifica Bay Travel and Tourism Director will show at a conference for California Travel Agents. Your completed presentation will look similar to Figure 3.60.

Apply 3A and 3B skills from these Objectives:

1 Customize Slide Backgrounds and Themes
2 Animate a Slide Show
3 Insert a Video
4 Create and Modify Tables
5 Create and Modify Charts

PROJECT FILES

For Project 3G, you will need the following files:

p03G_Travel
p03G_Video
p03G_Background

You will save your presentation as:

Lastname_Firstname_3G_Travel

PROJECT RESULTS

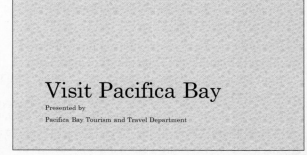

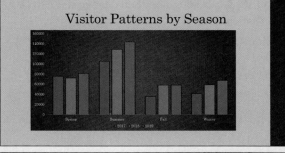

FIGURE 3.60

(Project 3G Travel continues on the next page)

Mastering PowerPoint Project 3G Travel (continued)

1 Start PowerPoint. From the student data files that accompany this textbook, locate and open **p03G_ Travel**. Save the presentation in your **PowerPoint Chapter 3** folder as **Lastname_Firstname_3G_Travel**

2 Change the **Colors** for the presentation to **Blue Warm**.

3 On **Slide 1**, format the background with the **Water droplets Texture**, and then change the **Transparency** to **50%**.

4 Select **Slides 2 through 4**, and then apply a **Solid fill** to the background of the selected slides—in the second to last column, the third color—**Teal, Accent 5, Lighter 60%**.

5 On **Slide 2**, hide the background graphics.

6 Insert a **Table** with **3 columns** and **4 rows**. Apply table style **Medium Style 3 - Accent 3**, and then type the information in **Table 1**, shown at the bottom of this page, into the inserted table.

7 Resize the table so that its lower edge extends to **3 inches on the lower half of the vertical ruler (height 4.72")**, and then distribute the table rows. Align the table text so that it is centered horizontally and vertically within the cells.

8 Change the **Font Size** of the first row of the table text to **24**. Apply a **Circle** style **Cell Bevel** to the first row.

9 On **Slide 3**, animate the picture using the **Wipe** entrance effect starting **After Previous**. Change the **Duration** to **01:00**. Apply the **Split** entrance effect to the bulleted list placeholder, and then change the **Effect Options** to **Vertical Out**.

10 On **Slide 4**, insert a **Clustered Column** chart. In the worksheet, in cell **B1** type **2017** and then enter the following data:

	2017	2018	2019
Spring	75600	72300	81460
Summer	105300	128730	143600
Fall	35900	58300	58320
Winter	41600	58430	67300

11 **Close** the worksheet window, apply **Chart Style 8** to the chart, and then remove the **Chart Title** element. Apply the **Wipe** entrance effect to the chart and change the **Effect Options** to **By Series**.

12 On **Slide 5**, apply the **Style 1** background style to this slide only. From your student data files, insert the video **p03G_Video**.

13 Change the **Video Height** to **6** and use the **Align Center** and **Align Top** options to position the video. Apply the **Soft Edge Rectangle** video style.

14 On the **Playback tab**, change the **Video Options** to **Start** the video **Automatically**. **Trim** the video so that the **End Time** is **00:09** and then compress the media in **Low Quality**.

15 On **Slide 6**, hide the background graphics, and then format the slide background by inserting a picture from your student data files—**p03G_Background**. Set the **Transparency** to **0%**.

16 Insert a **Header & Footer** on the **Notes and Handouts**. Include the **Date and time updated automatically**, the **Page number**, and a **Footer** with the text **Lastname_Firstname_3G_Travel**

17 Display the document properties. As the **Tags,** type **travel, tourism** and as the **Subject,** type your course and section number. Be sure your name displays as author, and then **Save** your file.

18 View the slide show from the beginning, and then as directed by your instructor, create and submit a paper printout or an electronic image of your presentation that looks like a printed document—either as the Notes and Handouts or as the presentation slides—or, submit your completed PowerPoint file. **Close** PowerPoint.

Trip Type	Day One	Day Two
Adventure Seeker	Kayak and Snorkel	Nature Preserve Hike
Family Friendly	Pacifica Bay Zoo	Beach Day and Horseback Riding
Arts & Culture	Pacifica Bay Art Museum	Artisan Walk

TABLE 1

End | You have completed Project 3G

Apply a combination of the 3A and 3B skills.

CONTENT-BASED ASSESSMENTS (CRITICAL THINKING)

GO! Fix It Project 3H Housing Developments **MyITLab**

Build
From
Scratch

GO! Make It Project 3I Water Usage **MyITLab**

GO! Solve It Project 3J Aquatic Center **MyITLab**

GO! Solve It Project 3K Power

PROJECT FILES

For Project 3K, you will need the following files:

p03K_Power
p03K_Tower

You will save your presentation as:

Lastname_Firstname_3K_Power

Open the file p03K_Power and save it as **Lastname_Firstname_3K_Power** Complete the presentation by applying a theme and then formatting the slide background for the title slide with the picture found in your student data files—p03K_Tower. Adjust the size, position, fill color, and font color on the title slide as necessary so that the title text displays attractively against the background picture. Format the background of at least one other slide using a background style, solid fill color, or texture. On Slide 3, insert a table with the following information:

Power Sources	Percent Used by City
Natural gas	32%
Hydroelectric	17%
Renewables	18%
Coal	23%
Nuclear	10%

On Slide 4, insert and format an appropriate chart to demonstrate the revenue collected from residential power sales over the past three years. Revenue in 2014 was 35.5 million dollars, in 2015 revenue was 42.6 million dollars, and in 2016 revenue was 48.2 million dollars. Apply appropriate animation and slide transitions to the slides. Insert a header and footer that includes the date and time updated automatically, the file name in the footer, and the page number. Add your name, your course name and section number, and the keywords **power sources, revenue** to the Properties area. Save and then as directed by your instructor, create and submit a paper printout or an electronic image of your presentation that looks like a printed document—either as the Notes and Handouts or as the presentation slides—or, submit your completed PowerPoint file. **Close** PowerPoint.

(Project 3K Power continues on the next page)

GO! Solve It | **Project 3K Power** (continued)

Performance Level

Performance Elements	Exemplary: You consistently applied the relevant skills	Proficient: You sometimes, but not always, applied the relevant skills	Developing: You rarely or never applied the relevant skills
Format two slide backgrounds with pictures and styles	Two slide backgrounds were formatted attractively and text displayed with good contrast against backgrounds.	Slide backgrounds were formatted but text did not display well against the chosen background, or only one slide background was formatted.	Slide backgrounds were not formatted with pictures or styles.
Insert and format appropriate table and chart	Appropriate table and chart were inserted and formatted and the entered data was accurate.	A table and a chart were inserted but were not appropriate for the presentation or either a table or a chart was omitted.	Table and chart were not inserted.
Apply appropriate animation	Appropriate animation was applied to the presentation.	Animation was applied but was not appropriate for the presentation.	Animation was not applied.

END | You have completed Project 3K

RUBRIC

The following outcomes-based assessments are open-ended assessments. That is, there is no specific correct result; your result will depend on your approach to the information provided. Make Professional Quality your goal. Use the following scoring rubric to guide you in how to approach the problem and then to evaluate how well your approach solves the problem.

The *criteria*—Software Mastery, Content, Format and Layout, and Process—represent the knowledge and skills you have gained that you can apply to solving the problem. The *levels of performance*—Professional Quality, Approaching Professional Quality, or Needs Quality Improvements—help you and your instructor evaluate your result.

	Your completed project is of Professional Quality if you:	Your completed project is Approaching Professional Quality if you:	Your completed project Needs Quality Improvements if you:
1-Software Mastery	Choose and apply the most appropriate skills, tools, and features and identify efficient methods to solve the problem.	Choose and apply some appropriate skills, tools, and features, but not in the most efficient manner.	Choose inappropriate skills, tools, or features, or are inefficient in solving the problem.
2-Content	Construct a solution that is clear and well organized, contains content that is accurate, appropriate to the audience and purpose, and is complete. Provide a solution that contains no errors in spelling, grammar, or style.	Construct a solution in which some components are unclear, poorly organized, inconsistent, or incomplete. Misjudge the needs of the audience. Have some errors in spelling, grammar, or style, but the errors do not detract from comprehension.	Construct a solution that is unclear, incomplete, or poorly organized; contains some inaccurate or inappropriate content; and contains many errors in spelling, grammar, or style. Do not solve the problem.
3-Format & Layout	Format and arrange all elements to communicate information and ideas, clarify function, illustrate relationships, and indicate relative importance.	Apply appropriate format and layout features to some elements, but not others. Overuse features, causing minor distraction.	Apply format and layout that does not communicate information or ideas clearly. Do not use format and layout features to clarify function, illustrate relationships, or indicate relative importance. Use available features excessively, causing distraction.
4-Process	Use an organized approach that integrates planning, development, self-assessment, revision, and reflection.	Demonstrate an organized approach in some areas, but not others; or, use an insufficient process of organization throughout.	Do not use an organized approach to solve the problem.

OUTCOMES-BASED ASSESSMENTS (CRITICAL THINKING)

GO! Think | Project 3L Animal Sanctuary

Build From Scratch

PROJECT FILES

For Project 3L, you will need the following file:

New blank PowerPoint presentation

You will save your presentation as:

Lastname_Firstname_3L_Animal_Sanctuary

The Pacifica Bay Animal Sanctuary, a nonprofit organization, provides shelter and care for animals in need, including dogs, cats, hamsters, and guinea pigs. The sanctuary, which celebrates its tenth anniversary in July, has cared for more than 12,000 animals since it opened and is a state-of-the-art facility. Funding for the sanctuary comes in the form of business sponsorships, individual donations, and pet adoption fees. The following table indicates revenue generated by the sanctuary during the past three years.

	Fees	Donations	Sponsorships
2014	125,085	215,380	175,684
2015	110,680	256,785	156,842
2016	132,455	314,682	212,648

In addition to shelter services, the sanctuary offers community service and training programs, veterinarian services, and vaccine clinics. Examples of these services include Canine Obedience classes, microchipping ($25 fee), and the Healthy Pet Hotline (free). Canine Obedience classes are for puppies and adult dogs to improve obedience, socialization, and behavior. Classes last two, three, or four months and cost $150 to $250.

Using the preceding information, create the first five slides of a presentation that the director of the Pacifica Bay Animal Sanctuary will show at an upcoming pet fair. Apply an appropriate theme and use slide layouts that will effectively present the content. Include a line chart with the revenue data, a table with the community service programs information, and at least one slide formatted with a dog or cat on the slide background. Apply styles to the table and chart, and apply animation and slide transitions to the slides. Use the techniques that you practiced in this chapter so that your presentation is professional and attractive. Save the file as **Lastname_Firstname_3L_Animal_Sanctuary** and then insert a header and footer that includes the date and time updated automatically, the file name in the footer, and the page number. Add your name, your course name and section number, and the keywords **animals, pets** to the properties. As directed by your instructor, create and submit a paper printout or an electronic image of your presentation that looks like a printed document—either as the Notes and Handouts or as the presentation slides—or, submit your completed PowerPoint file. **Close** PowerPoint.

END | You have completed Project 3L

Build from Scratch

GO! Think	Project 3M Water Sources	**MyITLab**

Build from Scratch

You and GO!	Project 3N Recreation Programs	**MyITLab**

GO! Collaborative Team Project	Project 3O Bell Orchid Hotels	**MyITLab**

3
POWERPOINT

Integrating Word, Excel, Access, and PowerPoint

PROJECT 1A

OUTCOMES
Create an Excel workbook that includes data exported from Access and data copied from Word and PowerPoint.

OBJECTIVES

1. Export Access Data to Excel
2. Create an Excel Worksheet from a Word Table
3. Copy and Paste an Excel Chart into Other Programs
4. Copy and Paste an Object from PowerPoint into Excel

PROJECT 1B

OUTCOMES
Link Excel data to a Word document and complete a mail merge in Word using Access data.

OBJECTIVES

5. Link Excel Data to a Word Document
6. Modify Linked Data and Update Links
7. Create a Table in Word from Access Data
8. Use Access Data to Complete a Mail Merge in Word

EpicStockMedia/Fotolia

In This Chapter

All applications in a software suite, for example, Microsoft Office, are designed to work well with one another. You can input data or create objects, such as a chart or table, in one application and then export the data to another application without retyping the data or re-creating the object. It is important to identify the appropriate software within the suite to produce solutions that best utilize the functions of the various applications. In this chapter, you will copy and paste data and objects between applications. You will link, modify, and update data and use mail merge to create individualized documents.

The projects in this chapter relate to **Ultimate Action Sports Gear**, one of the country's leading retailers of sports equipment and outdoor recreational merchandise. The company has a growing online business in addition to large retail stores in Colorado, New Mexico, Oregon, and Washington. Major merchandise categories include fishing, camping, golf, rock climbing, winter sports, action sports, aquatic sports, team sports, racquet sports, fitness and athletic apparel, and footwear. Inventory is constantly updated to provide customers with the newest products in the action sports industry.

PROJECT

1A State Sales

PROJECT ACTIVITIES

In Activities 1.01 through 1.12, you will export Access data into an Excel workbook, and then you will copy and paste Word data into the Excel workbook. In Excel, you will create a chart based on the data, and then copy the chart into a PowerPoint presentation. Your completed documents will look similar to Figure 1.1.

PROJECT FILES

For Project 1A, you will need the following files:

New blank Excel workbook
i01A_Store_Locations
i01A_State_Sales
i01A_Sales_Presentation

You will save your files as:

Lastname_Firstname_1A_Sales_Chart
Lastname_Firstname_1A_Store_Locations
Lastname_Firstname_1A_State_Sales
Lastname_Firstname_1A_Sales_Presentation

PROJECT RESULTS

Build From
Scratch

GO!
Walk Thru
Project 1A

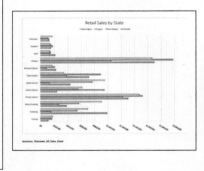

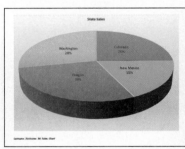

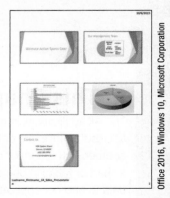

FIGURE 1.1 Project 1A State Sales

NOTE	If You Are Using a Touchscreen
👆	Tap an item to click it.
👆	Press and hold for a few seconds to right-click; release when the information or commands display.
🤏	Touch the screen with two or more fingers and then pinch together to zoom out or stretch your fingers apart to zoom in.
👉	Slide your finger on the screen to scroll—slide left to scroll right and slide right to scroll left.
👆	Slide to rearrange—similar to dragging with a mouse.
👆	Swipe to select—slide an item a short distance with a quick movement—to select an item and bring up commands, if any.

Objective 1 Export Access Data to Excel

Access includes a tool to export data from an Access database into an Excel workbook. When you export Access data, you create a copy of the data in Excel.

Activity 1.01 | Exporting Access Data to Excel

In the following Activity, you will export Access data into an Excel workbook.

1 Start Access. On the left of the opening screen, click **Open Other Files**, and then click **Browse**. In the **Open** dialog box, navigate to the Student Data Files that accompany this chapter, and then open the Access database **i01A_Store_Locations**. Click the **File tab**, and then click **Save As**. On the **Save As** screen, with **Save Database As** selected, on the right, click **Save As**.

2 In the **Save As** dialog box, navigate to the location where you are saving your files. Click **New folder**, type **Integrated Projects** and then press Enter. In the **File name** box, type **Lastname_Firstname_1A_Store_Locations** and then press Enter. On the **Message Bar** that displays a Security Warning, click **Enable Content**.

3 In the **Navigation Pane**, double-click the **Managers** table. At the bottom of the table, select **Firstname**, and then type your own first name. Press Tab to select **Lastname**, type your own last name, and then press Enter.

4 In the **Navigation Pane**, double-click the query **Store Locations by Manager**, and then be sure that your name displays. Compare your screen with Figure 1.2.

FIGURE 1.2

5 On the **External Data tab**, in the **Export group**, click **Excel**. In the **Export - Excel Spreadsheet** dialog box, click **Browse**. Navigate to your **Integrated Projects** folder, using your own name, type the file name **Lastname_Firstname_1A_Sales_Chart** and then click **Save**.

6 In the **Export - Excel Spreadsheet** dialog box, be sure that the **File format** is **Excel Workbook (*.xlsx)**. Select the **Export data with formatting and layout** check box, and then compare your screen with Figure 1.3.

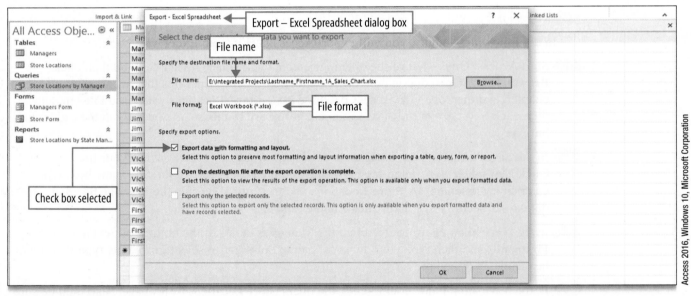

FIGURE 1.3

7 In the **Export – Excel Spreadsheet** dialog box, click **OK**. In the dialog box, be sure that the **Save export steps** check box is *not* selected, and then click **Close**.

8 Close ⊠ Access.

9 Start Excel. Near the bottom left of the screen, click **Open Other Workbooks**, and then click **Browse**. In the **Open** dialog box, navigate to your **Integrated Projects** folder, and then open the Excel workbook **Lastname_Firstname_1A_Sales_Chart**.

   The sheet tab at the bottom of the worksheet indicates that the worksheet name is changed to the exported Access query name—*Store Locations by Manager*.

Activity 1.02 | Creating and Sorting an Excel Table

To easily manage and analyze a group of related data, you can convert a range of cells to an Excel table. An Excel table typically contains data in a series of rows and columns; the Excel table can be managed independently from the data in other rows and columns in the worksheet. In the following activity, you will change a range of data into an Excel table, and then sort the data.

1 Click cell **A1**. On the **Insert tab**, in the **Tables group**, click **Table**. In the **Create Table** dialog box, under **Where is the data for your table?**, be sure that the range is **=$A$1:$E$21** and that the **My table has headers** check box is selected. Compare your screen with Figure 1.4.

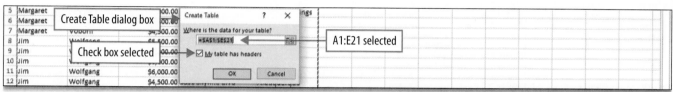

FIGURE 1.4

Excel 2016, Windows 10, Microsoft Corporation

2 In the **Create Table** dialog box, click **OK**.

3 Click cell **E1**, click **Filter** ▼, and then click **Sort A to Z** to sort the entire table alphabetically by City name. Compare your screen with Figure 1.5.

After a column is sorted in ascending or descending order, a small arrow displays on the Filter button to indicate the sort order.

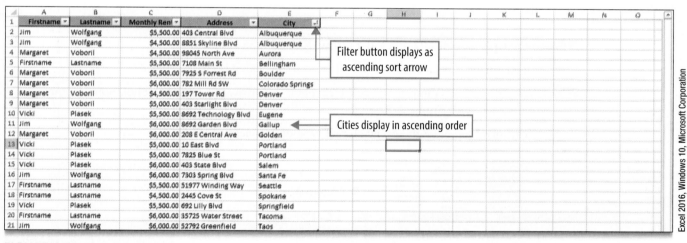

FIGURE 1.5

Excel 2016, Windows 10, Microsoft Corporation

4 Save 🖫 your Excel workbook.

Activity 1.03 | Inserting a Total Row in an Excel Table

To quickly total the data in the columns of an Excel table, display a total row at the end of the table, and then use the functions that are provided for each cell in the total row.

1 If necessary, click cell **E1**, and then on the **Design tab**, in the **Table Style Options group**, select the **Total Row** check box. Click cell **E22**, and then compare your screen with Figure 1.6.

Cell E22 displays the number 20. Because the values in Column E are not numbers, instead of totaling, Excel counts the number of cells containing text in column E. The header row is not included in the Total Row calculations.

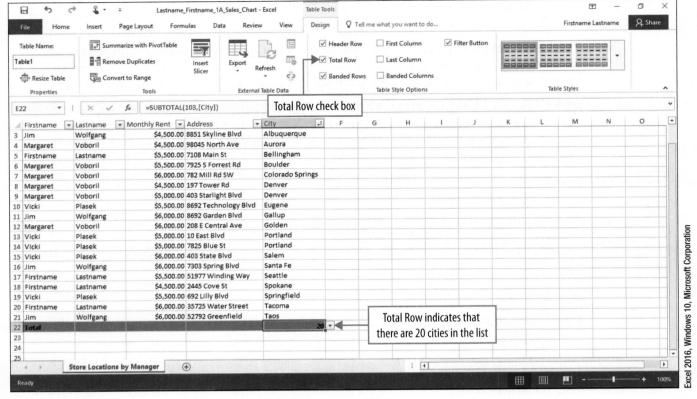

FIGURE 1.6

> **2** To the right of cell **E22**, click the arrow ▼, and then click **None**.
>
> Because the cells in column E contain text, a calculation is not required.
>
> **3** Click cell **C22**. To the right of cell **C22**, click the arrow ▼, and then click **Sum**. Compare your screen with Figure 1.7.
>
> The total Monthly Rent revenue for all locations displays in cell C22.

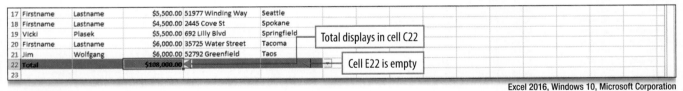

FIGURE 1.7

> **4** **Save** 🖫 your Excel workbook.

Objective 2 Create an Excel Worksheet from a Word Table

You can use data stored in one file in a different file so that you do not have to reenter the data.

Activity 1.04 | Formatting a Word Table

> **1** With your Excel workbook still open, start Word. On the left, click **Open Other Documents**, navigate to the student data files, and then open the document **i01A_State_Sales**. Click the

File tab, click **Save As**, navigate to your **Integrated Projects** folder, and then using your own name, **Save** the document as **Lastname_Firstname_1A_State_Sales**

2 ▶ With the Word document displayed, on the **Insert tab**, in the **Header & Footer group**, click **Footer**. At the bottom of the **Footer** gallery, click **Edit Footer**. On the ribbon, under **Header & Footer Tools**, on the **Design tab**, in the **Insert group**, click **Document Info**, and then click **File Name**. In the **Close group**, click **Close Header and Footer**. Display the ruler and formatting marks, if necessary.

3 ▶ Scroll down to view the table. Click anywhere in the first cell in the table, and then compare your screen with Figure 1.8.

When the entire table or a table element is selected, the Table Tools tabs—Design and Layout—display.

FIGURE 1.8

Word 2016, Windows 10, Microsoft Corporation

4 ▶ On the ribbon, under **Table Tools**, on the **Design tab**, in the **Table Styles group**, click **More** . In the **Table Styles** gallery, scroll down, and then under **List Tables**, in the third row, click the last style—**List Table 3 - Accent 6**.

5 ▶ On the **Table Tools Layout tab**, in the **Cell Size group**, click **AutoFit**, and then click **AutoFit Contents**. In the **Table group**, click **Properties**. In the **Table Properties** dialog box, under **Alignment**, click **Center**. Compare your screen with Figure 1.9.

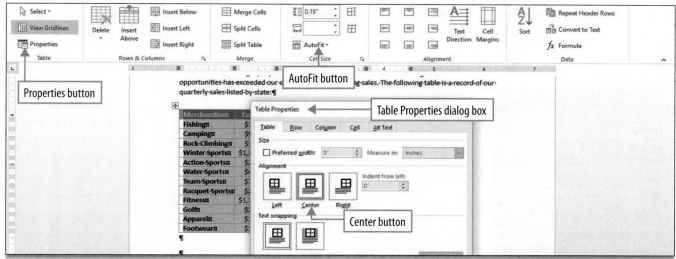

FIGURE 1.9

Word 2016, Windows 10, Microsoft Corporation

6 ▶ In the **Table Properties** dialog box, click **OK** to center the table horizontally on the page.

7 ▶ **Save** 🖫 your Word document.

After entering data in a Word document, you might decide that you can manipulate the data better in another program, such as Excel. Instead of starting over and retyping the data, you can copy the data from the Word document, and then paste the data into an Excel workbook.

NOTE   Working with Multiple Open Windows

In this chapter, you will work with a number of different files and will have a number of different windows open. When you have completed the work in one file, save the file, and then minimize the window. When you need to use the file again, click the appropriate program icon on the taskbar to maximize that window.

---

1 Be sure that Word is the active window. On the **Table Tools Layout tab**, in the **Table group**, click **Select**, and then click **Select Table**. On the **Home tab** in the **Clipboard group**, click **Copy** 📋.

The entire table is selected and copied.

2 On the taskbar, click the **Excel** icon 📊 to make the Excel window active.

3 At the bottom of the worksheet, click **New sheet** ⊕ to insert a new blank worksheet. Right-click the **Sheet1** worksheet tab, and then click **Rename**. Type **Sales** and then press Enter. Compare your screen with Figure 1.10.

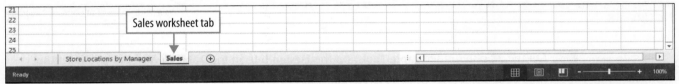

FIGURE 1.10

Excel 2016, Windows 10, Microsoft Corporation

4 On the **Page Layout tab**, in the **Themes group**, click **Themes**, and then under **Office**, click **Office**.

5 Click cell **A4** to make it the active cell. On the **Home tab**, in the **Clipboard group**, click the upper portion of the **Paste** button. Compare your screen with Figure 1.11.

The Word data is pasted into the Excel worksheet, starting in cell A4—the active cell.

The pound sign (#) will display if a column is not wide enough to display an entire number.

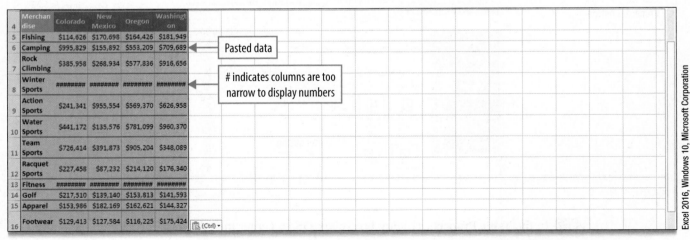

FIGURE 1.11

Excel 2016, Windows 10, Microsoft Corporation

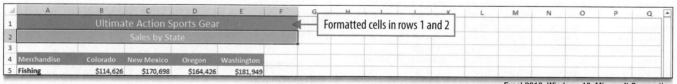

6 ▶ Click cell **A4**. On the **Home tab**, in the **Cells group**, click **Format**, and then click **Column Width**. In the **Column Width** dialog box, type **16** and then click **OK**.

7 ▶ Select the range **B4:E4**. In the **Cells group**, click **Format**, and then click **Column Width**. In the **Column Width** dialog box, type **12** and then click **OK**.

By widening the columns, all data displays in the worksheet.

8 ▶ Select the range **A4:A16**. In the **Cells group**, click **Format**, and then click **Row Height**. In the **Row Height** dialog box, type **17** and then click **OK**. Click in an empty cell, and then compare your screen with Figure 1.12.

	A	B	C	D	E	F	G	H	I	J	K	L	M	N	O	P	Q
3																	
4	Merchandise	Colorado	New Mexico	Oregon	Washington												
5	Fishing	$114,626	$170,698	$164,426	$181,949		Column widths adjusted										
6	Camping	$995,829	$155,892	$553,209	$709,689												
7	Rock Climbing	$385,958	$268,934	$577,836	$916,656												
8	Winter Sports	$1,311,794	$1,235,790	$1,529,598	$1,482,004												
9	Action Sports	$241,341	$955,554	$569,370	$626,958		Row heights adjusted										
10	Water Sports	$441,172	$135,576	$781,099	$960,370												
11	Team Sports	$726,414	$391,873	$905,204	$348,089												
12	Racquet Sports	$227,458	$87,232	$214,120	$176,340												
13	Fitness	$1,705,677	$1,057,227	$1,991,815	$1,675,831												
14	Golf	$217,510	$139,140	$153,813	$141,593												
15	Apparel	$153,986	$182,169	$162,621	$144,327												
16	Footwear	$129,413	$127,584	$116,225	$175,424												
17																	

FIGURE 1.12

Excel 2016, Windows 10, Microsoft Corporation

9 ▶ In cell **A1**, type **Ultimate Action Sports Gear** and then press Enter. In cell **A2**, type **Sales by State** and then press Enter. Select the range **A1:F1**, and then on the **Home tab**, in the **Alignment group**, click **Merge & Center**. In the **Styles group**, click **Cell Styles**, and then click **Accent 6**. In the **Font group**, click the **Font Size button arrow** `11 ▾`, and then click **16**.

10 ▶ Select the range **A2:F2**. Click **Merge & Center**, apply the cell style **60% - Accent 6**, and then change the **Font Size** to **14**. Compare your screen with Figure 1.13.

	A	B	C	D	E	F	G	H	I	J	K	L	M	N	O	P	Q
1			Ultimate Action Sports Gear					Formatted cells in rows 1 and 2									
2			Sales by State														
3																	
4	Merchandise	Colorado	New Mexico	Oregon	Washington												
5	Fishing	$114,626	$170,698	$164,426	$181,949												

FIGURE 1.13

Excel 2016, Windows 10, Microsoft Corporation

11 ▶ **Save** 🖫 your Excel workbook.

Activity 1.06 | **Using the SUM Function and Fill Handle in Excel**

In the following Activity, you will use the SUM function to add numbers.

1 ▶ Click cell **F4**, type **Total Sales** and then press Enter.

2 ▶ Be sure that **F5** is the active cell. On the **Home tab**, in the **Editing group**, click **AutoSum**, and then on the **Formula Bar**, click **Enter** ✓ to confirm the entry and keep cell **F5** as the active cell. Using the technique you previously practiced, change the width of column **F** to **13**

ALERT! **The Formula Bar May Not Display**

If the Formula Bar does not display, on the View tab, in the Show group, select the Formula Bar check box.

3 In cell **F5**, point to the fill handle until the ⊞ pointer displays, hold down the left mouse button, and then drag down to cell **F16**. Release the mouse button. In the **Font group**, click **Increase Font Size** A˙ one time, and then compare your screen with Figure 1.14.

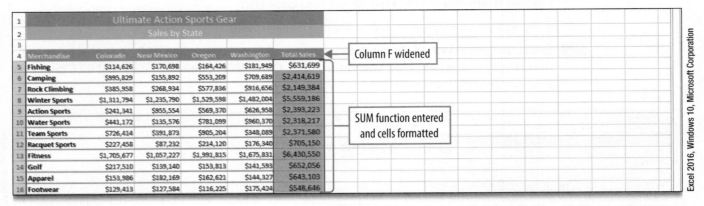

FIGURE 1.14

4 Click cell **A17**, type **Total** and then press Tab.

5 With cell **B17** selected, in the **Editing group**, click **AutoSum**, and then on the **Formula Bar**, click **Enter** ✓. Using the technique you just practiced, use the fill handle to copy the formula to cells **C17:F17**.

6 Select the range **A5:E16**. In the **Font group**, click the **Border button arrow** ⊞ ▾, and then click **No Border**. Select the range **B17:F17**. In the **Styles group**, click **Cell Styles**, and then under **Titles and Headings**, click **Total**. In the **Font group**, click **Increase Font Size** A˙ one time. Click in an empty cell, and then compare your screen with Figure 1.15.

Merchandise	Colorado	New Mexico	Oregon	Washington	Total Sales	
Fishing	$114,626	$170,698	$164,426	$181,949	$631,699	
Camping	$995,829	$155,892	$553,209	$709,689	$2,414,619	
Rock Climbing	$385,958	$268,934	$577,836	$916,656	$2,149,384	← No border applied
Winter Sports	$1,311,794	$1,235,790	$1,529,598	$1,482,004	$5,559,186	
Action Sports	$241,341	$955,554	$569,370	$626,958	$2,393,223	
Water Sports	$441,172	$135,576	$781,099	$960,370	$2,318,217	
Team Sports	$726,414	$391,873	$905,204	$348,089	$2,371,580	
Racquet Sports	$227,458	$87,232	$214,120	$176,340	$705,150	
Fitness	$1,705,677	$1,057,227	$1,991,815	$1,675,831	$6,430,550	SUM function entered
Golf	$217,510	$139,140	$153,813	$141,593	$652,056	and cells formatted
Apparel	$153,986	$182,169	$162,621	$144,327	$643,103	
Footwear	$129,413	$127,584	$116,225	$175,424	$548,646	
Total	$6,651,178	$4,907,669	$7,719,336	$7,539,230	$26,817,413	

Excel 2016, Windows 10, Microsoft Corporation

FIGURE 1.15

7 Save 🖫 your Excel workbook.

Objective 3 │ Copy and Paste an Excel Chart into Other Programs

A chart displays numerical data in a visual format. You can copy an Excel chart, and then paste it in files created with other applications.

Activity 1.07 │ Creating and Formatting a Bar Chart in Excel

In the following Activity, you will create and format a bar chart showing a comparison of merchandise sales by state.

1 Select the range **A4:E16**. On the **Insert tab**, in the **Charts group**, click the **Insert Column or Bar Chart arrow** , and then under **3-D Bar**, click the first chart—**3-D Clustered Bar**. On the **Design tab**, in the **Location group**, click **Move Chart**. In the **Move Chart** dialog box, click the **New sheet** option button, type **Merchandise Chart** and then click **OK**. Compare your screen with Figure 1.16.

A 3-D bar chart is created and moved to a new chart sheet named Merchandise Chart.

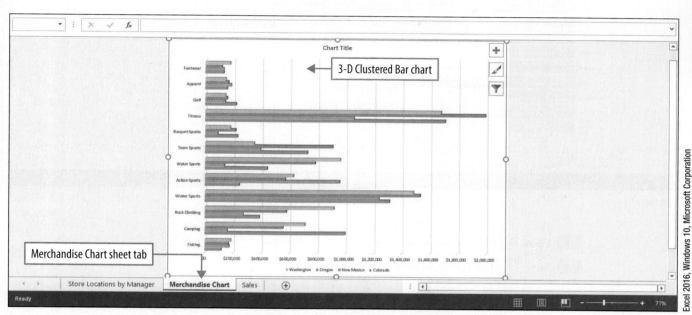

FIGURE 1.16

2 In the chart, select the text *Chart Title*, and then type **Retail Sales by State** Click in a blank area of the chart to deselect the chart title.

3 To the right of the chart, click **Chart Styles** . In the Style gallery, scroll down, and then click **Style 10**.

4 To the right of the chart, click **Chart Elements** . Under **Chart Elements**, point to **Legend**, click the **Legend arrow**, and then click **Top**.

5 Under **Chart Elements**, point to **Axes**, click the **Axes arrow**, and then click **More Options**. In the **Format Axis** pane, under **Axis Options**, click **Size & Properties** . Under **Alignment**, in the **Custom angle** box, type **30** and then press Enter. Compare your screen with Figure 1.17.

The numbers on the horizontal axis display at an angle of 30 degrees.

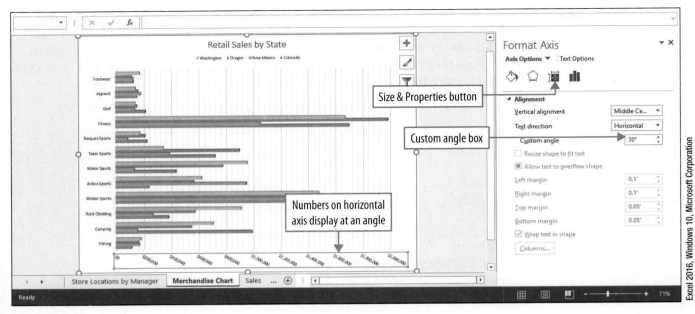

FIGURE 1.17

6 ▸ **Close** ⊠ the **Format Axis** pane.

7 ▸ **Save** 🖫 your Excel workbook.

Activity 1.08 | Creating and Formatting a Pie Chart in Excel

In the following Activity, you will create a pie chart to show each state's percentage of total sales.

1 ▸ Click the **Sales** worksheet tab. Select the range **B4:E4**, press and hold Ctrl, and then select the range **B17:E17**.

> The range B4:E4 and the range B17:E17 are selected. Recall that holding down Ctrl enables you to select nonadjacent cells.

2 ▸ On the **Insert tab**, in the **Charts group**, click the **Insert Pie or Doughnut Chart arrow** 🥧▾, and then under **3-D Pie**, click **3-D Pie**. On the ribbon, under **Chart Tools**, on the **Design tab**, in the **Location group**, click **Move Chart**. In the **Move Chart** dialog box, click the **New sheet** option button, type **State Sales Chart** and then click **OK**.

3 ▸ To the right of the chart, click **Chart Styles** 🖌. In the **Style** gallery, scroll down, and then click **Style 5**. Press Esc to close the gallery. Compare your screen with Figure 1.18.

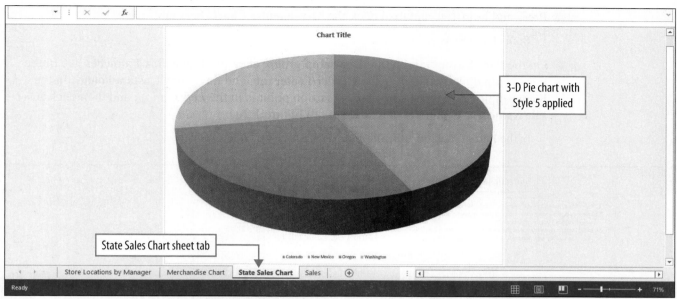

FIGURE 1.18

4 In the chart, select the text **Chart Title**, type **State Sales** and then click in a blank area of the chart.

5 Click **Chart Elements** ➕, and then under **Chart Elements**, click **Legend** to remove the legend from the chart.

6 Under **CHART ELEMENTS**, select the **Data Labels** check box. Point to **Data Labels**, click the **Data Labels arrow**, and then click **More Options**. In the **Format Data Labels** pane, if necessary, expand the Label Option. Under **Label Contains** click the **Category Name** check box, deselect the **Value** check box, and then click the **Percentage** check box. Under **Label Position**, click the **Center** option button. With the data labels selected, on the **Home tab**, change the **Font Size** 11 ▾ to **16**. Click in a blank area just inside chart to deselect the data labels.

The Format Chart Area displays on the right.

7 In the **Format Chart Area** pane, under **Chart Options**, click **Fill & Line** 🎨. Click **Fill**, and then click the **Gradient fill** option button. Click the **Preset gradients arrow**, and then in the first row, click the third gradient—**Light Gradient – Accent 3**. **Close** ✕ the **Format Chart Area** pane, and then compare your screen with Figure 1.19.

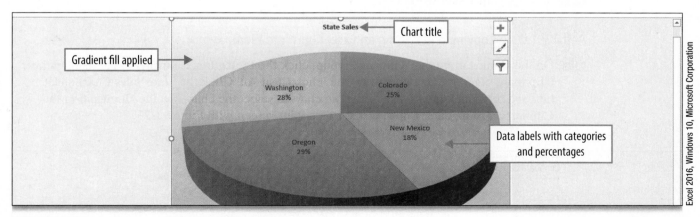

FIGURE 1.19

8 ▶ Press and hold ⌈Ctrl⌉, and then click the **Merchandise Chart** sheet tab.

Both chart sheets are selected.

9 ▶ On the **Page Layout tab**, in the **Page Setup** group, click the **Dialog Box Launcher** ⌐. In the **Page Setup** dialog box, click the **Header/Footer tab**, and then click **Custom Footer**. In the **Footer** dialog box, be sure that the insertion point is in the *Left section*, and then click **Insert File Name** ⌐. Compare your screen with Figure 1.20.

In the Left section box, the file name is inserted—*&[File]* displays.

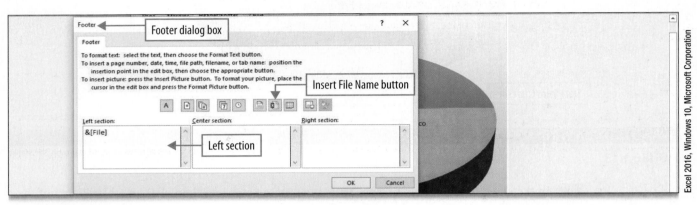

FIGURE 1.20

10 ▶ In the **Footer** dialog box, click **OK**, and then in the **Page Setup** dialog box, click **OK**.

The file name is inserted in the footer of both chart sheets.

11 ▶ Click the **Sales** worksheet tab to make it the active worksheet and to deselect the chart sheets. Press and hold ⌈Ctrl⌉, and then click the **Store Locations by Manager** worksheet tab.

12 ▶ On the **Page Layout tab**, in the **Page Setup** group, click the **Dialog Box Launcher** ⌐. In the **Page Setup** dialog box, click the **Header/Footer tab**, and then click **Custom Footer**. In the **Footer** dialog box, with the insertion point in the *Left section*, click **Insert File Name** ⌐. Click **OK** two times to close the dialog boxes.

You must insert footers in worksheets separately from inserting them in chart sheets. In this instance, the file name is inserted in the footer of both worksheets.

13 ▶ Press ⌈Ctrl⌉ + ⌈Home⌉ to display the top of the worksheet. Right-click the **Sales** sheet tab, and then click **Ungroup Sheets**.

14 ▶ **Save** ⌐ your Excel workbook.

Activity 1.09 │ Copying and Pasting an Excel Chart into Word

1 ▶ On the **Home tab**, in the **Clipboard group**, click the **Dialog Box Launcher** ⌐ to display the Clipboard pane. In the **Clipboard** pane, click **Clear All**. Click the **State Sales Chart** sheet tab, and then click the border of the pie chart to select the chart. On the **Home tab** in the **Clipboard group**, click **Copy** ⌐. Compare your screen with Figure 1.21.

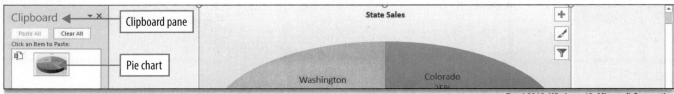

Excel 2016, Windows 10, Microsoft Corporation

FIGURE 1.21

2 Click the **Merchandise Chart** sheet tab, and then click the border of the bar chart to select the chart. In the **Clipboard group**, click **Copy** 🖻.

3 At the bottom of the screen, on the taskbar, click the **Word** icon 🔳. Press Ctrl + End to move the insertion point to the end of the document.

4 Press Ctrl + Enter.

A new blank Page 2 is inserted.

5 With the insertion point at the top of **Page 2**, type **In the chart below, our state sales managers can view their sales results.** Press Enter.

6 On the **Home tab**, in the **Clipboard group**, click the **Dialog Box Launcher** 🔲 to display the Clipboard pane, as shown in Figure 1.22.

FIGURE 1.22

Word 2016, Windows 10, Microsoft Corporation

7 In the **Clipboard** pane, click the **bar chart**.

The bar chart is pasted into the Word document.

8 **Close** ✕ the **Clipboard** pane, and then press Ctrl + Home.

9 Click the **File tab**, and then in the lower right portion of the screen, at the bottom of the **Properties** list, click **Show All Properties**. In the **Tags** box, type **memo, state sales chart** and in the **Subject** box, type your course name and section number. Be sure your name displays as the author; edit if necessary.

10 On the left, click **Save**, and then **Close** ✕ Word.

Activity 1.10 │ Pasting an Excel Chart in PowerPoint

1 With your Excel workbook still open, start PowerPoint. On PowerPoint's opening screen, on the left, click **Open Other Presentations**, click **Browse**, navigate to the student data files, and then open the presentation **i01A_Sales_Presentation**. Click the **File tab**, on the left, click **Save As**, and then click **Browse** to display the **Save As** dialog box. Navigate to your **Integrated Projects** folder, and then using your own name, **Save** the presentation as **Lastname_Firstname_1A_Sales_Presentation**

2 On the **Insert tab**, in the **Text group**, click **Header & Footer**. In the **Header and Footer** dialog box, click the **Notes and Handouts** tab. Select the **Footer** check box, click in the **Footer** box, using your own name, type **Lastname_Firstname_1A_Sales_Presentation** and then compare your screen with Figure 1.23.

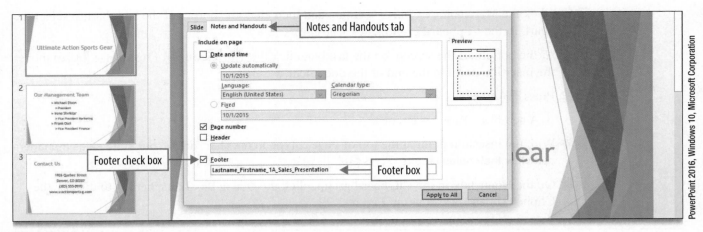

FIGURE 1.23

3 ▶ Click **Apply to All**.

4 ▶ Display **Slide 2**. On the **Home tab**, in the **Slides group**, click the **New Slide button arrow**, and then from the **Slides** gallery, click **Blank**. On the **Design tab**, in the **Customize group**, click **Format Background**. In the **Format Background** pane, under **Fill**, select the **Hide background graphics** check box. Compare your screen with Figure 1.24.

A new blank Slide 3 is inserted into the presentation, and the background graphics do not display.

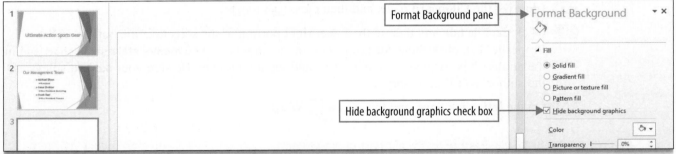

FIGURE 1.24

5 ▶ **Close** ☒ the **Format Background** pane. On the **Home tab**, in the **Clipboard group**, click the **Dialog Box Launcher** ⌐. In the **Clipboard** pane, click the bar chart.

The bar chart is pasted into Slide 3 of the presentation.

6 ▶ On the **Home tab**, in the **Slides group**, click the **New Slide button arrow**, and then from the **Slides** gallery, click **Blank**. Using the technique you practiced, select the **Hide background graphics** check box. In the **Clipboard** pane, click the pie chart. Compare your screen with Figure 1.25.

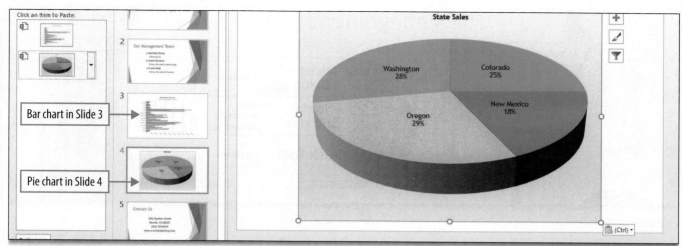

FIGURE 1.25

7 ▶ **Close** ☒ the **Clipboard** pane, and then **Save** 🖫 the presentation.

Objective 4 Copy and Paste an Object from PowerPoint into Excel

In PowerPoint, bullet points can be converted into a SmartArt graphic to illustrate your message visually. After you create a SmartArt graphic in PowerPoint, you can copy the graphic and paste it into a file created with another program. This can save you time because there is no need to re-create the graphic.

Activity 1.11 | Inserting a SmartArt Graphic

1 ▶ Click **Slide 2** to make it the active slide. Click in the placeholder containing the names of the managers. On the **Home tab**, in the **Paragraph group**, click **Convert to SmartArt**. In the **SmartArt** gallery, in the first row, click the fourth layout—**Target List**. If the Text Pane displays to the left of the SmartArt placeholder, click Close ☒.

2 ▶ On the ribbon, under **SmartArt Tools**, on the **Design tab**, in the **SmartArt Styles group**, click **More** ⊽. In the **SmartArt Styles** gallery, under **3-D**, in the first row, click the third style— **Cartoon**.

3 ▶ With the **SmartArt** graphic selected, on the **Animations tab**, in the **Animation group**, click **More** ⊽. In the **Animation** gallery, under **Entrance**, click **Wheel**. Click in a blank area of the slide to deselect the SmartArt graphic, and then compare your screen with Figure 1.26.

The number 1 displays to the left of the SmartArt graphic, which indicates that an animation effect is applied to the object.

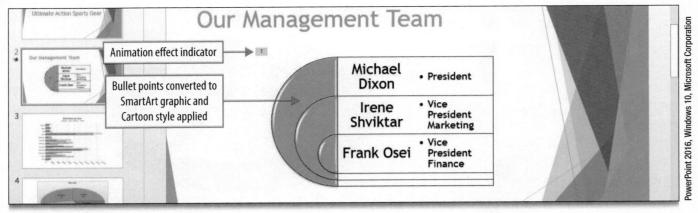

FIGURE 1.26

4 ▸ On the **Slide Show tab**, in the **Start Slide Show group**, click **From Beginning** to view the presentation. Press Enter to view the second slide.

5 ▸ Continue to press Enter to view the remaining slides, and then press Enter to return to **Normal** view.

6 ▸ **Save** 🖫 the presentation.

Activity 1.12 | Copying and Pasting a SmartArt Graphic

After you create an object in one file, you can copy the object and paste it in a file created with a different program. In this Activity, you will copy the SmartArt graphic in the PowerPoint presentation, and then paste it in an Excel workbook.

1 ▸ Click the border of the SmartArt graphic.

> By clicking the border of an object, you select the entire object, not just a part of the object.

2 ▸ On the **Home tab**, in the **Clipboard group**, click **Copy** 📋.

3 ▸ On the taskbar, click the **Excel** icon 🗙.

4 ▸ In **Excel**, click the **Sales** worksheet tab, and then click cell **A20**. On the **Home tab**, in the **Clipboard group**, click the upper portion of the **Paste** button.

> The SmartArt graphic is pasted into the Sales worksheet. The top left corner of the graphic is in cell A20.

5 ▸ Scroll down to view the entire graphic. On the ribbon, under **SmartArt Tools**, on the **Format tab**, click **Size**, if necessary. Click in the **Height** box, and then type **3.5** Click in the **Width** box, type **5.5** and then press Enter.

6 ▸ Right-click the border of the SmartArt graphic, and then above the shortcut menu, click **Color**. In the **Color** gallery, under **Colorful**, click the fourth color—**Colorful Range – Accent Colors 4 to 5**. Compare your screen with Figure 1.27.

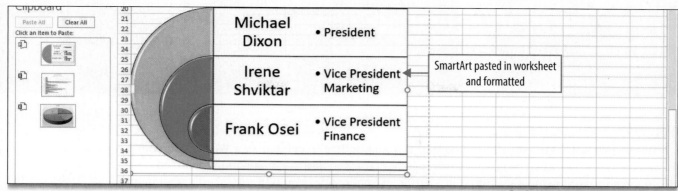

FIGURE 1.27

Excel 2016, Windows 10, Microsoft Corporation

7 In the **Clipboard** pane, click **Clear All**, and then **Close** ☒ the **Clipboard** pane.

8 Click the **File tab**, and then at the right, at the bottom of the **Properties** list, click **Show All Properties**. In the **Tags** box, type **charts, SmartArt** In the **Subject** box, type your course name and section number. Be sure your name displays as the author; edit if necessary.

9 On the left, click **Save**, and then **Close** ☒ Excel.

10 If necessary, in PowerPoint, **Close** ☒ the **Clipboard** pane.

11 Click the **File tab**, and then at the right, at the bottom of the **Properties** list, click **Show All Properties**. In the **Tags** box, type **company info, charts, SmartArt** In the **Subject** box, type your course name and section number. Be sure your name displays as the author; edit if necessary.

12 On the left, click **Save**, and then **Close** ☒ PowerPoint.

13 Submit your printed or electronic files as directed by your instructor.

> **END | You have completed Project 1A**

Taos Welcome

PROJECT ACTIVITIES

In Activities 1.13 through 1.19, you will link and update Excel data in a Word document. Because Microsoft Office programs work together, you can quickly create individualized documents in Word using data stored in a different application. You will use Word's mail merge feature and data stored in an Access database to create individualized memos. Your completed files will look similar to Figure 1.28.

PROJECT FILES

For Project 1B, you will need the following files:

i01B_Welcome_Memo
i01B_Taos_Inventory
i01B_All_Associates

You will save your files as:

Lastname_Firstname_1B_Welcome_Memo
Lastname_Firstname_1B_Taos_Memo
Lastname_Firstname_1B_Taos_Inventory
Lastname_Firstname_1B_All_Associates
Lastname_Firstname_1B_Store_Location

PROJECT RESULTS

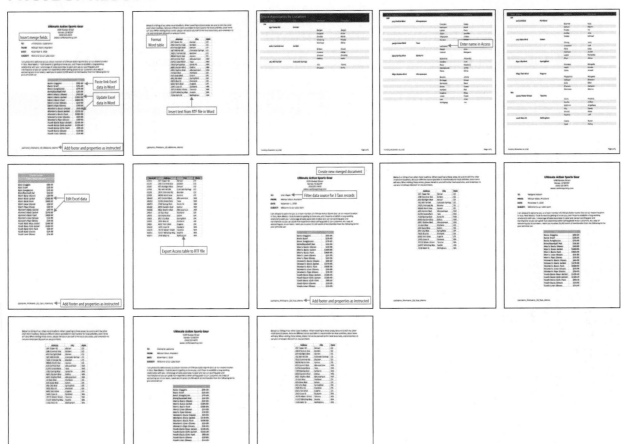

FIGURE 1.28 Project 1B Taos Welcome

Objective 5 | Link Excel Data to a Word Document

Use the linking tools in Office to connect the data in an Excel worksheet to a Word document. When you link an Excel workbook to a Word document, changes you make to data in the Excel workbook will be updated in the linked Word document. Information about the link is saved with the Word document. By default, when you open the Word document, Word checks all linked files and prompts you to apply any changes.

Activity 1.13 | Using Paste Special to Link Files

In this Activity, you will insert Excel data into a Word document. By selecting options in the Paste Special dialog box, you can link your Word document to the data in the Excel workbook.

1 Start Word. Navigate to the student data files and then open the document **i01B_Welcome_Memo**. Display the **Save As** dialog box, and then **Save** the document in your **Integrated Projects** folder as **Lastname_Firstname_1B_Welcome_Memo** If necessary, display the ruler and formatting marks.

2 Start Excel. Navigate to the student data files, and then open the Excel workbook **i01B_Taos_Inventory**. Display the **Save As** dialog box, and then **Save** the workbook in your **Integrated Projects** folder as **Lastname_Firstname_1B_Taos_Inventory**

3 On the **Page Layout tab**, in the **Page Setup group**, click the **Dialog Box Launcher** . In the **Page Setup** dialog box, click the **Header/Footer tab**, and then click **Custom Footer**. In the **Footer** dialog box, with the insertion point in the **Left section**, click **Insert File Name** —*&[File]* displays. Click **OK** two times to close the dialog boxes.

4 Press Ctrl + Home to display the top of the worksheet, and then **Save** the Excel workbook.

5 Select the range **A3:B22**. On the **Home tab** in the **Clipboard group**, click **Copy**. Compare your screen with Figure 1.29.

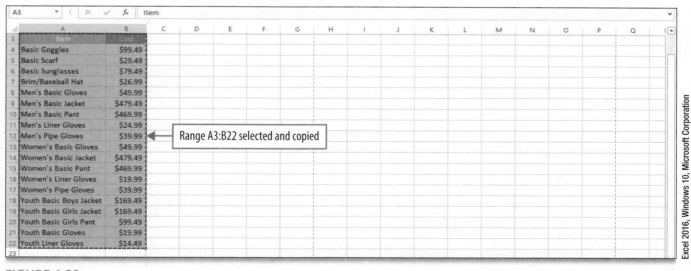

FIGURE 1.29

6 On the taskbar, click the **Word** icon . In the Word document, below the paragraph that begins *I am pleased to welcome you*, click in the blank paragraph.

7 On the **Home tab**, in the **Clipboard group**, click the **Paste button arrow**, and then click **Paste Special**. In the **Paste Special** dialog box, click the **Paste link** option button, and then under **As**, click **Microsoft Excel Worksheet Object**. Compare your screen to Figure 1.30.

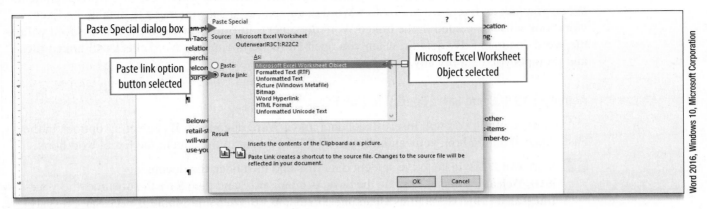

 label callouts: Paste Special dialog box; Paste link option button selected; Microsoft Excel Worksheet Object selected

Word 2016, Windows 10, Microsoft Corporation

FIGURE 1.30

8 In the **Paste Special** dialog box, click **OK**.

The linked data from Excel is pasted into the Word document.

9 Click the edge of the inserted table to select the object (sizing handles display), and then on the **Home tab**, in the **Paragraph group**, click **Center**.

10 **Save** your Word document.

11 Click the **File tab**, and then click **Close** to close the document but leave Word open.

> **NOTE** | Updating Links
>
> From this point forward, when you reopen a Word document that has a link to an external file, a Security Notice will automatically display. The notice will inform you that the file contains links and you have the option of updating the links or not updating them. If you trust the source of the file, you can update links. If you do not know where a file originated, you should cancel the update and investigate where the file came from before continuing.

12 In Word, click the **File tab**, click **Open**, click **Browse**, navigate to your **Integrated Projects** folder, and then open the file **Lastname_Firstname_1B_Welcome_Memo**. A message box displays, as shown in Figure 1.31.

The message box informs you that the Word document is linked to another file, and it asks whether you want to update the data in the document.

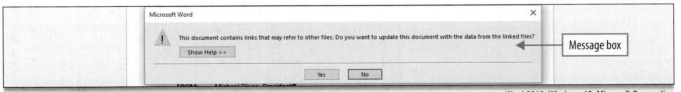

Message box

Word 2016, Windows 10, Microsoft Corporation

FIGURE 1.31

13 In the message box, click **Yes**.

The linked information is updated.

It is common to make changes to your data in saved files. You can modify the data in the source file and all linked data to that source file is updated to reflect the changes.

Activity 1.14 | Updating the Linked Data

In the following Activity, you will edit data in the linked Excel workbook, and then verify that the updated data displays in the Word document.

1 Double-click the pasted data in the Word document to display the source file—the linked Excel workbook.

Excel becomes the active window.

2 If necessary, maximize the Excel worksheet, and then press [Esc] to cancel the moving border. Click cell **B9**, type **389.99** and then press [Enter]. Click cell **B14**, type **379.99** and then press [Enter]. Compare your screen with Figure 1.32.

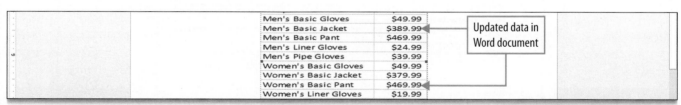

7	Brim/Baseball Hat	$26.99	
8	Men's Basic Gloves	$49.99	
9	Men's Basic Jacket	$389.99	◄— Edited data in worksheet
10	Men's Basic Pant	$469.99	
11	Men's Liner Gloves	$24.99	
12	Men's Pipe Gloves	$39.99	
13	Women's Basic Gloves	$49.99	
14	Women's Basic Jacket	$379.99	◄—
15	Women's Basic Pant	$469.99	

FIGURE 1.32

Excel 2016, Windows 10, Microsoft Corporation

3 **Save** 🖫 the Excel workbook.

4 On the taskbar, click the **Word** icon 📰. Compare your screen to Figure 1.33.

The changes made in the Excel workbook are reflected in the linked Word document.

ALERT! **What If the Data Is Not Updated?**

If you do not see the new numbers in the Word document, click one time in the data to select it, and then press [F9] to update the Excel data.

Men's Basic Gloves	$49.99
Men's Basic Jacket	$389.99	◄— Updated data in Word document
Men's Basic Pant	$469.99
Men's Liner Gloves	$24.99
Men's Pipe Gloves	$39.99
Women's Basic Gloves	$49.99
Women's Basic Jacket	$379.99
Women's Basic Pant	$469.99	◄—
Women's Liner Gloves	$19.99

FIGURE 1.33

Word 2016, Windows 10, Microsoft Corporation

5 **Save** 🖫 the Word document.

6 On the taskbar, click the **Excel** icon 📊 to display the workbook.

7 Click the **File tab**, and then at the right, at the bottom of the **Properties** list, click **Show All Properties**. In the **Tags** box, type **edited data, linked** In the **Subject** box, type your course name and section number. Under Related People, if your name does not display, right-click the author name, click Edit Property, type your name, and then click OK.

8 On the left, click **Save**, and then **Close** ☒ Excel.

Objective 7 Create a Table in Word from Access Data

You can export data from an Access file to another file—for example, an Excel worksheet, a Word document, or another database. Exporting is similar to copying and pasting. In Access, you can export large amounts of data by selecting the name of the object that contains the data you want to export. Exporting data eliminates the need to retype information; and, as a result, the possibility of data entry errors is reduced.

Activity 1.15 | Exporting an Access Table to an RTF File

1 Start Access. Navigate to the student data files and then open the Access database **i01B_All_Associates**. Click the **File tab**, click **Save As**, and then with **Save Database** selected, click **Save As**.

2 In the **Save As** dialog box, navigate to your **Integrated Projects** folder, and then **Save** the database as **Lastname_Firstname_1B_All_Associates** On the **Message Bar** that displays a Security Warning, click **Enable Content**.

3 In the **Navigation Pane**, click the **Store Location** table one time to select it. On the **External Data tab**, in the **Export group**, click **More**, and then click **Word**.

The Export - RTF File dialog box displays.

4 In the **Export – RTF File** dialog box, click **Browse**, and then navigate to your **Integrated Projects** folder. In the **File name** box, type **Lastname_Firstname_1B_Store_Location** and then click **Save**. Compare your screen with Figure 1.34.

The Access table is saved as a rich text format file. Rich text format is a universal file format, using the .rtf file extension, which can be read by many word processing programs.

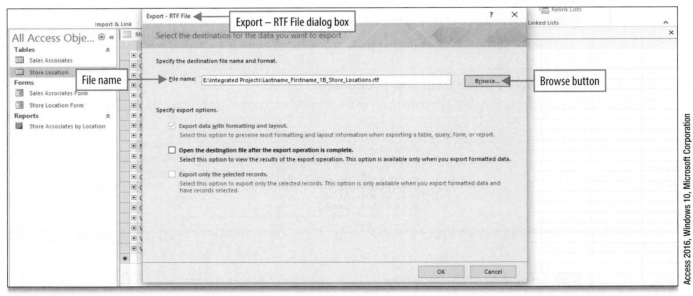

FIGURE 1.34

5 In the **Export – RTF File** dialog box, click **OK**. In the dialog box asking if you want to save these export steps, be sure the **Save export steps** check box is not selected. Click **Close**.

Activity 1.16 | Inserting Access Data into a Word Document

1 On the taskbar, click the **Word** icon. Press Ctrl + End to move to the end of the document.

2 On the **Insert tab**, in the **Text group**, click the **Object button arrow**, and then click **Text from File**. In the **Insert File** dialog box, navigate to your **Integrated Projects** folder, click the file name **Lastname_Firstname_1B_Store_Location**, and then click **Insert**. Compare your screen with Figure 1.35.

Store ID¤	Address¤	City¤	State¤	¤
CO19¤	197·Tower·Rd¤	Denver¤	CO¤	¤
CO20¤	208·E·Central·Ave¤	Golden¤	CO¤	¤
CO40¤	403·Starlight·Blvd¤	Denver¤	CO¤	¤
CO78¤	782·Mill·Rd·SW¤	Colorado·Springs¤	CO¤	¤
CO79¤	7925·S·Forrest·Rd¤	Boulder¤	CO¤	¤
CO98¤	98045·North·Ave¤	Aurora¤	CO¤	¤
NM40¤	403·Central·Blvd¤	Albuquerque¤	NM¤	¤
NM52¤	52792·Greenfield¤	Taos¤	NM¤	¤
NM73¤	7303·Spring·Blvd¤	Santa·Fe¤	NM¤	¤
NM86¤	8692·Garden·Blvd¤	Gallup¤	NM¤	¤
NM88¤	8851·Skyline·Blvd¤	Albuquerque¤	NM¤	¤
OR10¤	10·East·Blvd¤	Portland¤	OR¤	¤
OR40¤	403·State·Blvd¤	Salem¤	OR¤	¤
OR69¤	692·Lilly·Blvd¤	Springfield¤	OR¤	¤
OR78¤	7825·Blue·St¤	Portland¤	OR¤	¤
OR86¤	8692·Tech·Blvd¤	Eugene¤	OR¤	¤
WA24¤	2445·Cove·St¤	Spokane¤	WA¤	¤
WA35¤	35725·Water·Street¤	Tacoma¤	WA¤	¤
WA51¤	51977·Winding·Way¤	Seattle¤	WA¤	¤
WA71¤	7108·Main·St¤	Bellingham¤	WA¤	¤

Table inserted in Word document

FIGURE 1.35

Word 2016, Windows 10, Microsoft Corporation

3 In the inserted table, click in the first cell, **Store ID**, to make the cell the active cell. On the ribbon, under **Table Tools**, on the **Design tab**, in the **Table Styles group**, click **More** ⮟ . In the **Table Styles** gallery, scroll down, and then under **List Tables**, in the third row, click the third style—click **List Table 3 - Accent 2**.

4 Click in the cell **Store ID**, and then on the **Table Tools Layout tab**, in the **Rows & Columns group**, click **Delete**. On the displayed list, click **Delete Columns** to delete the Store ID column.

5 On the **Table Tools Layout tab**, in the **Cell Size group**, click **AutoFit**, and then click **AutoFit Contents**.

The columns are automatically resized to fit the contents of the cells.

6 In the **Table group**, click **Properties**, and then on the **Table tab**, under **Alignment**, click **Center**. Click **OK**, and then compare your screen with Figure 1.36.

The table is centered horizontally on the page.

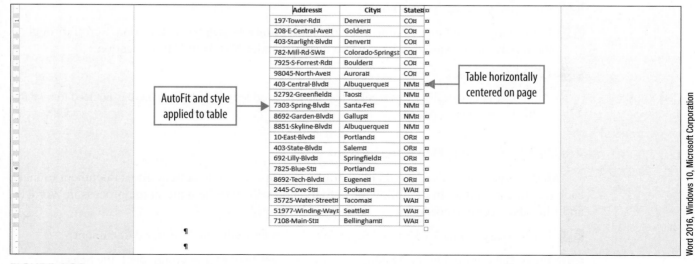

Address¤	City¤	State¤	¤
197·Tower·Rd¤	Denver¤	CO¤	¤
208·E·Central·Ave¤	Golden¤	CO¤	¤
403·Starlight·Blvd¤	Denver¤	CO¤	¤
782·Mill·Rd·SW¤	Colorado·Springs¤	CO¤	¤
7925·S·Forrest·Rd¤	Boulder¤	CO¤	¤
98045·North·Ave¤	Aurora¤	CO¤	¤
403·Central·Blvd¤	Albuquerque¤	NM¤	¤
52792·Greenfield¤	Taos¤	NM¤	¤
7303·Spring·Blvd¤	Santa·Fe¤	NM¤	¤
8692·Garden·Blvd¤	Gallup¤	NM¤	¤
8851·Skyline·Blvd¤	Albuquerque¤	NM¤	¤
10·East·Blvd¤	Portland¤	OR¤	¤
403·State·Blvd¤	Salem¤	OR¤	¤
692·Lilly·Blvd¤	Springfield¤	OR¤	¤
7825·Blue·St¤	Portland¤	OR¤	¤
8692·Tech·Blvd¤	Eugene¤	OR¤	¤
2445·Cove·St¤	Spokane¤	WA¤	¤
35725·Water·Street¤	Tacoma¤	WA¤	¤
51977·Winding·Way¤	Seattle¤	WA¤	¤
7108·Main·St¤	Bellingham¤	WA¤	¤

AutoFit and style applied to table

Table horizontally centered on page

Word 2016, Windows 10, Microsoft Corporation

FIGURE 1.36

7 **Save** 🖫 the Word document.

If you already have information in an existing data source—for example, an Access database—you do not need to enter the data again during the mail merge process. You can filter data to quickly find a portion of the total records available. Filtered data displays only the records that meet the conditions you specify and hides the records that do not meet the conditions.

Activity 1.17 | Adding Records to an Access Table

One of the most powerful features of Access is the ability to add, edit, or delete existing records without changing the structure of the existing objects—tables, queries, forms, and reports—in the database. In the following activity, you will use a form to add a record to a database.

1 On the taskbar, click the **Access** icon 📘. In the **Navigation Pane**, double-click the **Sales Associates Form**.

2 In the navigation area at the bottom of the form, click the **New (blank) record** button ▶. In the **ID** field, type **10-60531** and then press Tab. Type your own first name, press Tab, type your own last name, and then press Tab. Type **Sales Associate** press Tab, type **NM52** and then compare your screen with Figure 1.37.

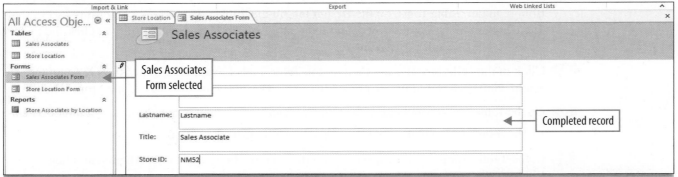

Access 2016, Windows 10, Microsoft Corporation

FIGURE 1.37

3 Press Tab to accept your record.

4 In the **Navigation Pane**, double-click the report **Store Associates by Location**. Scroll through the report and be sure that your name displays under **NM** for the **Taos** location.

5 **Close** ☒ Access.

> Access automatically saves records that have been added to a database; there is no need to save the file before closing Access.

Activity 1.18 | Starting Mail Merge in Word

Mail Merge can be used to add placeholders for inserting a data field into a document to make each document unique. In the following activity, you will start the mail merge process in Word and filter the Access records.

1 If necessary, on the taskbar, click the Word icon 📄 to display the Word document.

2 Press Ctrl + Home. On the **Mailings tab**, in the **Start Mail Merge group**, click the **Select Recipients** button, and then click **Use an Existing List**.

3 In the **Select Data Source** dialog box, navigate to your **Integrated Projects** folder, select the **Lastname_Firstname_1B_All_Associates** database, and then click **Open** to display the **Select Table** dialog box. Compare your screen with Figure 1.38.

> The Access database contains more than one table. You need to select which table will be used for the mail merge.

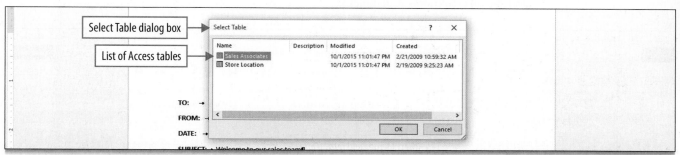

FIGURE 1.38

4 In the **Select Table** dialog box, be sure that **Sales Associates** is selected, and then click **OK**.

5 In the **Start Mail Merge group**, click **Edit Recipient List**.

> You can add or edit fields in the Mail Merge Recipients dialog box.

6 In the **Mail Merge Recipients** dialog box, under **Refine recipient list**, click **Filter**.

7 In the **Filter and Sort** dialog box, with the **Filter Records tab** selected, click the **Field arrow**, and then click **Store ID**. Under **Comparison**, be sure that **Equal to** is selected. In the **Compare to** box, type **NM52** and then compare your screen with Figure 1.39.

> You can filter on any of the fields.

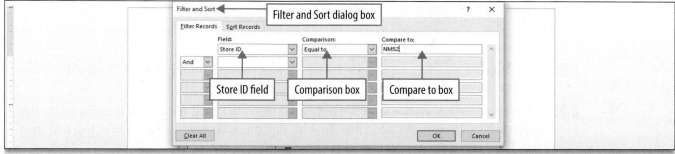

FIGURE 1.39

8 At the bottom of the **Filter and Sort** dialog box, click **OK**.

> The three Taos records—including your record—display.

9 In the **Mail Merge Recipients** dialog box, click **OK**.

Activity 1.19 | Inserting Merge Fields

You can add merge fields as placeholders in the Word document for the information that will be inserted from the Access database. In the mail merge process, you combine a data source and a main document to create a new Word document—for example, a document that contains individualized memos, letter, or mailing labels.

1 Near the top of the document, in the heading *TO*, click to position the insertion point to the left of the paragraph mark.

> **2** On the **Mailings tab**, in the **Write & Insert Fields group**, click the **Insert Merge Field button arrow**, and then click **Firstname**. Compare your screen with Figure 1.40.

The Firstname field is inserted in the memo.

A merge field is surrounded by double angle brackets (« »). These formatting marks help distinguish the merge fields in the main document and do not display in the final document—after the merge process is completed.

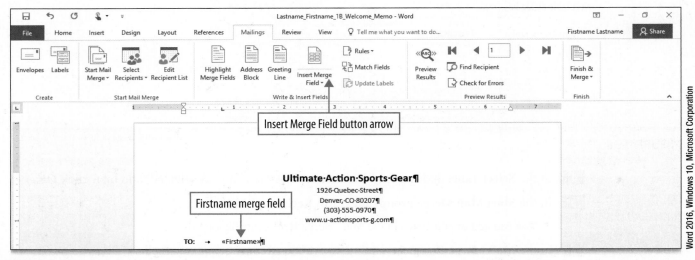

Insert Merge Field button arrow

Firstname merge field

FIGURE 1.40

> **3** Press Spacebar. Click the **Insert Merge Field button arrow**, and then click **Lastname**.

This is the location in the memo where the sales associate names will be inserted.

> **4** In the **Preview Results group**, click **Preview Results**. In the **Preview Results group**, click **Next Record** ▶ two times to preview the three memos.

The memo—the main document—displays with changes based on each record in the filtered data source—in this case, the sales associate's name.

> **5** In the **Preview Results** group, click **Preview Results** to turn off the feature. Notice the merge fields display in the document.

> **6** In the **Finish group**, click **Finish & Merge**, and then click **Edit Individual Documents**. In the **Merge to New Document** dialog box, be sure that the **All** option button is selected, and then click **OK**. Compare your screen with Figure 1.41.

A new Word document—Letter1—displays. The six-page document contains three individualized memos and is no longer connected to the Access database. The associate's first name and last name in the first record display on Page 1.

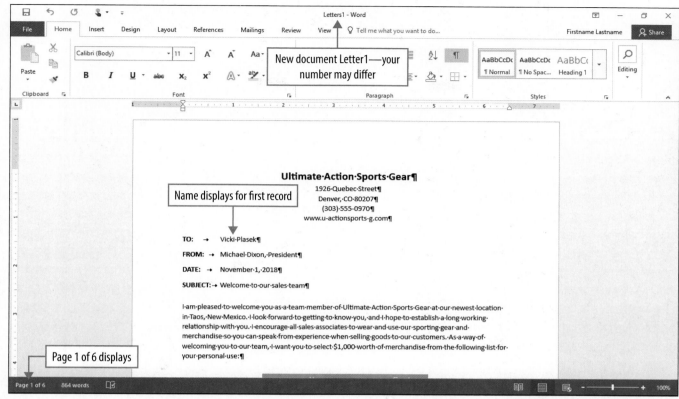

FIGURE 1.41

7 Display the **Save As** dialog box, and then save the new merged document in your **Integrated Projects** folder with the file name **Lastname_Firstname_1B_Taos_Memo**

8 Right-click in the footer area, and then click **Edit Footer**. On the ribbon, under **Header & Footer Tools**, on the **Design tab**, in the **Insert group**, click **Document Info**, and then click **File Name**. In the **Close group**, click **Close Header and Footer**.

9 Click the **File tab**, and then at the right, at the bottom of the **Properties** list, click **Show All Properties**. In the **Tags** box, type **linked table, merged** In the **Subject** box, type your course name and section number. Be sure your name displays as the author; edit if necessary.

10 On the left, click **Save**. With the Word document redisplayed, click the **File tab**, and then on the left, click **Close** ☒ to close the file and display your Welcome Memo document.

11 In **Lastname_Firstname_1B_Welcome_Memo**, right-click in the footer area, and then click **Edit Footer**. On the ribbon, under **Header & Footer Tools**, on the **Design tab**, in the **Insert group**, click **Document Info**, and then click **File Name**. In the **Close group**, click **Close Header and Footer**.

12 Click the **File tab**, and then at the right, at the bottom of the **Properties** list, click **Show All Properties**. In the **Tags** box, type **linked table, merge fields** In the **Subject** box, type your course name and section number. Be sure your name displays as the author; edit if necessary.

13 On the left, click **Save**, and then **Close** ☒ Word.

14 Submit your printed or electronic files as directed by your instructor.

> **END | You have completed Project 1B**

Appendix

MICROSOFT OFFICE SPECIALIST WORD 2016			
Obj Number	**Objective text**	**GO! Activity**	**Page Number**
1.0 Create and Manage Documents			
1.1	**Create a document**		
1.1.1	create a blank document	OF 1.01, 1.01	98, 153
1.1.2	create a blank document using a template	2.13	236
1.1.3	open a PDF in Word for editing	3.14	292
1.1.4	insert text from a file or external source	1.02, 2.03	154, 219
1.2	**Navigate through a document**		
1.2.1	search for text	2.17	242
1.2.2	insert hyperlinks	3.23	307
1.2.3	create bookmarks	OF 1.20	137
1.2.4	move to a specific location or object in a document	3.11	288
1.3	**Format a Document**		
1.3.1	modify page setup	1.17	174
1.3.2	apply document themes	Online Supplemental	Online Supplemental
1.3.3	apply document style sets	2.12	235
1.3.4	insert headers and footers	OF 1.07, 1.15	111, 168
1.3.5	insert page numbers	3.02	276
1.3.6	format page background elements	OF 1.04	103
1.4	**Customize Options and Views for Documents**		
1.4.1	change document views	3.13	290
1.4.2	customize views by using zoom settings	OF 1.14, 3.20	126, 305
1.4.3	customize the Quick Access toolbar	OF 1.11	120
1.4.4	split the window	Online Supplemental	Online Supplemental
1.4.5	add document properties	1.16, 3.12	169, 289
1.4.6	show or hide formatting symbols	1.01	153
1.5	**Print and Save Documents**		
1.5.1	modify print settings	Online Supplemental	Online Supplemental
1.5.2	save documents in alternative file formats	3.14	292
1.5.3	print all or part of a document	1.16	169
1.5.4	inspect a document for hidden properties or personal information	OF 1.19	137
1.5.5	inspect a document for accessibility issues	OF 1.19	137
1.5.6	inspect a document for compatibility issues	OF 1.19	137

2.0 Format Text, Paragraphs, and Sections

2.1	**Insert Text and Paragraphs**			
2.1.1	find and replace text		2.17	242
2.1.2	cut, copy and paste text		OF 1.17	131
2.1.3	replace text by using AutoCorrect		2.15	239
2.1.4	insert special characters		3.25	309
2.2	**Format Text and Paragraphs**			
2.2.1	apply font formatting		OF 1.15, 3.24	127, 308
2.2.2	apply formatting by using Format Painter		OF 1.16	129
2.2.3	set line and paragraph spacing and indentation		1.19, 1.20, 1.21, 3.02	176, 178, 179, 276
2.2.4	clear formatting		Online Supplemental	Online Supplemental
2.2.5	apply a text highlight color to text selections		Online Supplemental	Online Supplemental
2.2.6	apply built-in styles to text		OF 1.05	105
2.2.7	change text to WordArt		OF 1.18	135
2.3	**Order and Group Text and Paragraphs**			
2.3.1	format text in multiple columns		3.15	296
2.3.2	insert page, section, or column breaks		3.17	299
2.3.3	change page setup options for a section		Online Supplemental	Online Supplemental

3.0 Create Tables and Lists

3.1	**Create a Table**			
3.1.1	convert text to tables		Online Supplemental	Online Supplemental
3.1.2	convert tables to text		Online Supplemental	Online Supplemental
3.1.3	create a table by specifying rows and columns		2.01	217
3.1.4	apply table styles		2.19	245
3.2	**Modify a Table**			
3.2.1	sort table data		Online Supplemental	Online Supplemental
3.2.2	configure cell margins and spacing		Online Supplemental	Online Supplemental
3.2.3	merge and split cells		2.07	224
3.2.4	resize tables, rows, and columns		2.05	222
3.2.5	split tables		Online Supplemental	Online Supplemental
3.2.6	configure a repeating row header		Online Supplemental	Online Supplemental
3.3	**Create and Modify a List**			
3.3.1	create a numbered or bulleted list		2.04	221
3.3.2	change bullet characters or number formats for a list level		1.24	184
3.3.3	define a custom bullet character or number format		Online Supplemental	Online Supplemental

3.3.4	increase or decrease list levels	Online Supplemental	Online Supplemental
3.3.5	restart or continue list numbering	Online Supplemental	Online Supplemental
3.3.6	set starting number value	Online Supplemental	Online Supplemental
4.0 Create and Manage References			
4.1	**Create and Manage Reference Markers**		
4.1.1	insert footnotes and endnotes	3.03	278
4.1.2	modify footnote and endnote properties	3.04	279
4.1.3	create bibliography citation sources	3.09	286
4.1.4	modify bibliography citation sources	3.06	283
4.1.5	insert citations for bibliographies	3.05	282
4.1.6	insert figure and table captions	Online Supplemental	Online Supplemental
4.1.7	modify caption properties	Online Supplemental	Online Supplemental
4.2	**Create and Manage Simple References**		
4.2.1	insert a standard table of contents	Online Supplemental	Online Supplemental
4.2.2	update a table of contents	Online Supplemental	Online Supplemental
4.2.3	insert a cover page	Online Supplemental	Online Supplemental
5.0 Insert and Format Graphic Elements			
5.1	**Insert Graphic Elements**		
5.1.1	insert shapes	1.11	164
5.1.2	insert pictures	1.04	156
5.1.3	insert a screen shot or screen clipping	3.23	307
5.1.4	insert text boxes	1.13	166
5.2	**Format Graphic Elements**		
5.2.1	apply artistic effects	1.09	162
5.2.2	apply picture effects	1.08	161
5.2.3	remove picture backgrounds	3.20	305
5.2.4	format objects	1.12, 1.14, 3.19	165, 167, 302
5.2.5	apply a picture style	OF 1.12	121
5.2.6	wrap text around objects	1.05, 3.18	157, 300
5.2.7	position objects	1.07, 1.11, 3.18	160, 164, 300
5.2.8	add alternative text to objects for accessibility	OF 1.18	135
5.3	**Insert and Format SmartArt Graphics**		
5.3.1	create a SmartArt graphic	1.27	189
5.3.2	format a SmartArt graphic	1.28	190
5.3.3	modify SmartArt graphic content	Online Supplemental	Online Supplemental

Appendix

MICROSOFT OFFICE SPECIALIST EXCEL 2016			
Obj Number	**Objective text**	**GO! Activity**	**Page Number**
1.0 Create and Manage Worksheets and Workbooks			
1.1	**Create Worksheets and Workbooks**		
1.1.1	create a workbook	1.01	351
1.1.2	import data from a delimited text file	Online Supplemental	Online Supplemental
1.1.3	add a worksheet to an existing workbook	2.30	452
1.1.4	copy and move a worksheet	2.34	455
1.2	**Navigate in Worksheets and Workbooks**		
1.2.1	search for data within a workbook	2.11	428
1.2.2	navigate to a named cell, range, or workbook element	Online Supplemental	Online Supplemental
1.2.3	insert and remove hyperlinks	Online Supplemental	Online Supplemental
1.3	**Format Worksheets and Workbooks**		
1.3.1	change worksheet tab color	2.21	441
1.3.2	rename a worksheet	2.21	441
1.3.3	change worksheet order	2.34	455
1.3.4	modify page setup	1.14, 1.17	372, 375
1.3.5	insert and delete columns or rows	1.25, 3.17	389, 506
1.3.6	change workbook themes	1.10	365
1.3.7	adjust row height and column width	1.26	390
1.3.8	insert headers and footers	1.14	372
1.4	**Customize Options and Views for Worksheets and Workbooks**		
1.4.1	hide or unhide worksheets	Online Supplemental	Online Supplemental
1.4.2	hide or unhide columns and rows	Online Supplemental	Online Supplemental
1.4.3	customize the Quick Access toolbar	OF 1.11	120
1.4.4	change workbook views	Online Supplemental	Online Supplemental
1.4.5	change window views	2.13, 2.19	430, 435
1.4.6	modify document properties	1.15	373
1.4.7	change magnification by using zoom tools	2.18	435
1.4.8	display formulas	1.17	375
1.5	**Configure Worksheets and Workbooks for Distribution**		
1.5.1	set a print area	1.16	374
1.5.2	save workbooks in alternative file formats	Online Supplemental	Online Supplemental
1.5.3	print all or part of a workbook	1.15, 2.35	373, 457
1.5.4	set print scaling	1.17, 2.20	375, 436

1.5.5	display repeating row and column titles on multipage worksheets	2.20	436
1.5.6	inspect a workbook for hidden properties or personal information	Online Supplemental	Online Supplemental
1.5.7	inspect a workbook for accessibility issues	Online Supplemental	Online Supplemental
1.5.8	inspect a workbook for compatibility issues	Online Supplemental	Online Supplemental

2.0 Manage Data Cells and Ranges

2.1	**Insert Data in Cells and Ranges**		
2.1.1	replace data	2.11	428
2.1.2	cut, copy, or paste data	2.24	446
2.1.3	paste data by using special paste options	2.24, 3.16	446, 503
2.1.4	fill cells by using Auto Fill	1.03	355
2.1.5	insert and delete cells	Online Supplemental	Online Supplemental
2.2	**Format Cells and Ranges**		
2.2.1	merge cells	1.08	363
2.2.2	modify cell alignment and indentation	Online Supplemental	Online Supplemental
2.2.3	format cells by using Format Painter	3.14	501
2.2.4	wrap text within cells	1.26	390
2.2.5	apply number formats	1.09, 1.24	364, 388
2.2.6	apply cell formats	1.26	390
2.2.7	apply cell styles	1.08	363
2.3	**Summarize and Organize Data**		
2.3.1	insert sparklines	1.13, 2.33	371, 454
2.3.2	outline data	Online Supplemental	Online Supplemental
2.3.3	insert subtotals	Online Supplemental	Online Supplemental
2.3.4	apply conditional formatting	2.10	427

3.0 Create Tables

3.1	**Create and Manage Tables**		
3.1.1	create an Excel table from a cell range	2.14	431
3.1.2	convert a table to a cell range	Online Supplemental	Online Supplemental
3.1.3	add or remove table rows and columns	Online Supplemental	Online Supplemental
3.2	**Manage Table Styles and Options**		
3.2.1	apply styles to tables	2.14	431
3.2.2	configure table style options	Online Supplemental	Online Supplemental
3.2.3	insert total rows	2.16	433
3.3	**Filter and Sort a Table**		
3.3.1	filter records	2.16	433
3.3.2	sort data by multiple columns	2.15	432

Appendix

MICROSOFT OFFICE SPECIALIST ACCESS 2016			
Obj Number	**Objective text**	**GO! Activity**	**Page Number**
1.0 Create and Manage a Database			
1.1	**Create and Modify Databases**		
1.1.1	create a blank desktop database	1.02	543
1.1.2	create a database from a template	1.18	579
1.1.3	create a database by using import objects or data from other sources	2.18	649
1.1.4	delete database objects	GO! Access Comprehensive 10.04	Access Comprehensive
1.2	**Manage Relationships and Keys**		
1.2.1	create and modify relationships	2.03, 2.19	623, 651
1.2.2	set the primary key	2.18	649
1.2.3	enforce referential integrity	2.04, 2.19	626, 651
1.2.4	set foreign keys	2.03, 2.19	623, 651
1.2.5	view relationships	3.01, 3.16	705, 733
1.3	**Navigate through a Database**		
1.3.1	navigate specific records	GO! Access Comprehensive 4.07, 4.08	Access Comprehensive
1.3.2	create and modify a navigation form	GO! Access Comprehensive 10.01	Access Comprehensive
1.3.3	set a form as the startup option	GO! Access Comprehensive 10.07	Access Comprehensive
1.3.4	display objects in the Navigation Pane	1.21	585
1.3.5	change views of objects	1.08, 2.13, 2.18, 2.21, 2.22, 2.23, 2.24, 2.28, 2.29, 2.30, 2.31	554, 637, 649, 653, 654, 656, 657, 663, 664, 665, 667
1.4	**Protect and Maintain Databases**		
1.4.1	compact a database	GO! Access Comprehensive 10.07	Access Comprehensive
1.4.2	repair a database	GO! Access Comprehensive 10.07	Access Comprehensive
1.4.3	back up a database	GO! Access Comprehensive 4.01	Access Comprehensive
1.4.4	split a database	GO! Access Comprehensive 10.09	Access Comprehensive
1.4.5	encrypt a database with a password	GO! Access Comprehensive 10.10	Access Comprehensive
1.4.6	recover data from backup	GO! Access Comprehensive 4.01, 9.07	Access Comprehensive
1.5	**Print and Export Data**		
1.5.1	print reports	1.16, 1.24, 2.05, 3.19, 3.24	572, 589, 628, 738, 747
1.5.2	print records	1.13, 1.25, 2.09, 3.06	562, 589, 632, 711

1.5.3	save a databases as a template	GO! Access Comprehensive 10.08	Access Comprehensive	
1.5.4	export objects to alternative formats	GO! Access Comprehensive 9.09, 9.10, 9.11, 9.12, 9.14, 9.15	Access Comprehensive	

2.0 Build Tables

2.1	**Create Tables**		
2.1.1	create a table	1.03, 1.22	545, 586
2.1.2	import data into tables	1.11	558
2.1.3	create linked tables from external sources	GO! Access Comprehensive 9.08	Access Comprehensive
2.1.4	import tables from other databases	GO! Access Comprehensive 9.07	Access Comprehensive
2.1.5	create a table from a template with application parts	1.22	586
2.2	**Manage Tables**		
2.2.1	hide fields in tables	GO! Access Comprehensive 4.09	Access Comprehensive
2.2.2	add total rows	GO! Access Comprehensive 5.03	Access Comprehensive
2.2.3	add table descriptions	1.09	556
2.2.4	rename tables	1.05, 2.02, 2.18, 3.01, 3.16	549, 622, 649, 705, 733
2.3	**Manage Records in Tables**		
2.3.1	update records	1.19	581
2.3.2	add records	1.05, 1.06, 1.23, 3.04	549, 550, 587, 709
2.3.3	delete records	2.07, 3.05	629, 710
2.3.4	append records from external data	1.07, 1.20	551, 584
2.3.5	find and replace data	3.05	710
2.3.6	sort records	2.08, 2.09	631, 632
2.3.7	filter records	3.07, 3.08, 3.09	713, 715, 717
2.4	**Create and Modify Fields**		
2.4.1	add fields to tables	1.03	545
2.4.2	add validation rules to fields	GO! Access Comprehensive 4.22	Access Comprehensive
2.4.3	change field captions	1.04	548
2.4.4	change field sizes	1.09	556
2.4.5	change field data types	2.18	649
2.4.6	configure fields to auto-increment	1.04	548
2.4.7	set default values	GO! Access Comprehensive 4.20	Access Comprehensive
2.4.8	using input masks	GO! Access Comprehensive 4.17, 4.18	Access Comprehensive
2.4.9	delete fields	1.08	554

3.0 Create Queries

3.1	**Create a Query**		
3.1.1	run a query	1.14, 2.11, 2.13, 2.15, 2.16, 2.17, 2.20, 2.23, 2.24, 2.25, 2.26, 2.27, 2.28, 2.29, 2.30, 2.33	567, 636, 637, 641, 643, 644, 653, 656, 657, 658, 660, 662, 663, 664, 665, 670
3.1.2	create a crosstab query	2.32	668
3.1.3	create a parameter query	2.33	670
3.1.4	create an action query	GO! Access Comprehensive 5.12, 5.13, 5.14, 5.15, 5.16	Access Comprehensive
3.1.5	create a multi-table query	2.25	658
3.1.6	save a query	2.11, 2.12, 2.13, 2.14, 2.15, 2.16, 2.17, 2.21, 2.22, 2.23, 2.24, 2.25, 2.26, 2.29, 2.33	636, 637, 637, 639, 641, 643, 644, 653, 654, 656, 657, 658, 660, 664, 670
3.2	**Modify a Query**		
3.2.1	rename a query	2.12	637
3.2.2	add fields	2.10, 2.13, 2.15, 2.16, 2.17, 2.20, 2.22, 2.23, 2.24, 2.26, 2.27, 2.30, 2.31, 2.33	634, 637, 641, 643, 644, 653, 654, 656, 657, 660, 662, 665, 667, 670
3.2.3	remove fields	2.13	637
3.2.4	hide fields	2.16, 2.20	643, 653
3.2.5	sort data within queries	2.14, 2.16, 2.17, 2.25, 2.27	639, 643, 644, 658, 662
3.2.6	format fields within queries	2.29, 2.31, 2.32	664, 667, 668
3.3	**Create Calculated Fields and Grouping within Queries**		
3.3.1	add calculated fields	2.27, 2.28	662, 663
3.3.2	set filtering criteria	2.15, 2.16, 2.17, 2.20, 2.22, 2.23, 2.24	641, 643, 644, 653, 654, 656, 657
3.3.3	group and summarize data	2.30, 2.31	665, 667
3.3.4	group data by using comparison operators	2.21, 2.22, 2.23, 2.24,	653, 654, 656, 657
3.3.5	group data by using arithmetic and logical operators	2.23, 2.24, 2.25. 2.26	656, 657, 658, 660

4.0 Create Forms

4.1	**Create a Form**		
4.1.1	create a form	1.15, 3.02, 3.03, 3.10	569, 707, 708, 719
4.1.2	create a form from a template with application parts	GO! Access Comprehensive 7.05	Access Comprehensive
4.1.3	save a form	1.15, 3.02, 3.03, 3.10	569, 707, 708, 719
4.2	**Configure Form Controls**		
4.2.1	move form controls	3.13	722
4.2.2	add form controls	GO! Access Comprehensive 3.13, 3.15, 6.01, 6.04, 7.02, 7.05, 7.08	Access Comprehensive
4.2.3	modify data sources	GO! Access Comprehensive 3.13, 6.01, 7.08	Access Comprehensive

4.2.4	remove form controls	GO! Access Comprehensive 7.02, 7.06	Access Comprehensive
4.2.5	set form control properties	3.11, 3.13, 3.14, 3.15	720, 722, 725, 726
4.2.6	manage labels	3.12, 3.13, 3.14, 3.15	722, 722, 725, 726
4.2.7	add sub-forms	GO! Access Comprehensive 7.04, 7.05, 7.07	Access Comprehensive
4.3	**Format a Form**		
4.3.1	modify tab order	GO! Access Comprehensive 6.10	Access Comprehensive
4.3.2	configure print settings	GO! Access Comprehensive 3.06, 6.10, 7.02, 7.03	Access Comprehensive
4.3.3	sort records by form field	GO! Access Comprehensive 6.10, 7.04	Access Comprehensive
4.3.4	apply a theme	3.12	722
4.3.5	control form positioning	GO! Access Comprehensive 6.10, 7.04	Access Comprehensive
4.3.6	insert backgrounds	GO! Access Comprehensive 6.05, 6.06	Access Comprehensive
4.3.7	insert headers and footers	3.15	726
4.3.8	insert images	GO! Access Comprehensive 6.02, 6.04, 6.06, 7.02. 7.06	Access Comprehensive

5.0 Create Reports

5.1	**Create a Report**		
5.1.1	create a report based on the query or table	1.16, 3.17	572, 735
5.1.2	create a report in Design view	GO! Access Comprehensive 6.13	Access Comprehensive
5.1.3	create a report by using a wizard	3.20	738
5.2	**Configure Report Controls**		
5.2.1	group and sort fields	3.18, 3.20, 3.21	735, 738, 741
5.2.2	modify data sources	GO! Access Comprehensive 6.13, 7.09, 7.11	Access Comprehensive
5.2.3	add report controls	GO! Access Comprehensive 6.13, 6.15, 6.16, 6.18, 7.09, 7.10	Access Comprehensive
5.2.4	add and modify labels	3.18, 3.21, 3.23	735, 741, 745
5.3	**Format a Report**		
5.3.1	format a report into multiple columns	3.20	738
5.3.2	add calculated fields	3.18	735
5.3.3	control report positioning	GO! Access Comprehensive 6.17, 7.12, 7.13	Access Comprehensive
5.3.4	format report elements	3.18, 3.21, 3.22, 3.24	735, 741, 742, 747
5.3.5	change report orientation	GO! Access Comprehensive 6.11	Access Comprehensive
5.3.6	insert header and footer information	3.23	745
5.3.7	insert images	GO! Access Comprehensive 6.14, 6.16, 9.05	Access Comprehensive
5.3.8	apply a theme	3.17, 3.21	735, 741

Appendix

MICROSOFT OFFICE SPECIALIST POWERPOINT 2016			
Obj Number	**Objective text**	**GO! Activity VOL 1**	**Page Number**
1.0 Create and Manage Presentations			
1.1	**Create a Presentation**		
1.1.1	create a new presentation	1.01	783
1.1.2	create a presentation based on a template	GO! PowerPoint Comprehensive 4.10	PowerPoint Comprehensive
1.1.3	import Word document outlines	GO! PowerPoint Comprehensive 8.10	PowerPoint Comprehensive
1.2	**Insert and Format Slides**		
1.2.1	insert specific slide layouts	1.04	787
1.2.2	duplicate existing slides	GO! PowerPoint Comprehensive 6.12	PowerPoint Comprehensive
1.2.3	hide and unhide slides	GO! PowerPoint Comprehensive 6.12	PowerPoint Comprehensive
1.2.4	delete slides	1.20, 1.28	813, 819
1.2.5	apply a different slide layout	1.27	819
1.2.6	modify individual slide backgrounds	3.03, 3.04, 3.05, 3.06, 3.07	913, 914, 915, 915, 916
1.2.7	insert slide headers, footers, and page numbers	1.13, 1.14	800, 801
1.3	**Modify Slides, Handouts, and Notes**		
1.3.1	change the slide master theme or background	GO! PowerPoint Comprehensive 4.01, 4.02, 4.04	PowerPoint Comprehensive
1.3.2	modify slide master content	GO! PowerPoint Comprehensive 4.03, 4.11	PowerPoint Comprehensive
1.3.3	create a slide layout	GO! PowerPoint Comprehensive 4.05	PowerPoint Comprehensive
1.3.4	modify a slide layout	GO! PowerPoint Comprehensive 4.06	PowerPoint Comprehensive
1.3.5	modify the handout master	GO! PowerPoint Comprehensive 4.07	PowerPoint Comprehensive
1.3.6	modify the notes master	GO! PowerPoint Comprehensive 4.08	PowerPoint Comprehensive
1.4	**Order and Group Slides**		
1.4.1	create sections	GO! PowerPoint Comprehensive 7.10	PowerPoint Comprehensive
1.4.2	modify slide order	1.29	820
1.4.3	rename sections	GO! PowerPoint Comprehensive 7.10	PowerPoint Comprehensive
1.5	**Change Presentation Options and Views**		
1.5.1	change slide size	1.17	809
1.5.2	change views of a presentation	1.28, 1.33	819, 823

1.5.3	set file properties	1.15	802
1.6	**Configure a Presentation for Print**		
1.6.1	print all or part of a presentation	GO! PowerPoint Comprehensive 6.16	PowerPoint Comprehensive
1.6.2	print notes pages	1.16	804
1.6.3	print handouts	1.15	802
1.6.4	print in color, grayscale, or black and white	1.15	802
1.7	**Configure and Present a Slide Show**		
1.7.1	create custom slide shows	GO! PowerPoint Comprehensive 6.10, 6.11	PowerPoint Comprehensive
1.7.2	configure slide show options	GO! PowerPoint Comprehensive 6.15	PowerPoint Comprehensive
1.7.3	rehearse slide show timing	GO! PowerPoint Comprehensive 6.15	PowerPoint Comprehensive
1.7.4	present a slide show by using Presenter View	1.12	798
2.0 Insert and Format Text, Shapes, and Images			
2.1	**Insert and Format Text**		
2.1.1	insert text on a slide	1.02	786
2.1.2	apply formatting and styles to text	1.23, 1.24	815, 816
2.1.3	apply WordArt styles to text	2.23	876
2.1.4	format text in multiple columns	GO! PowerPoint Comprehensive 8.04	PowerPoint Comprehensive
2.1.5	create bulleted and numbered lists	2.02, 2.03	850, 850
2.1.6	insert hyperlinks	GO! PowerPoint Comprehensive 6.06, 6.07, 6.08	PowerPoint Comprehensive
2.2	**Insert and Format Shapes and Text Boxes**		
2.2.1	insert or replace shapes	2.12	860
2.2.2	insert text boxes	2.11	859
2.2.3	resize shapes and text boxes	2.12	860
2.2.4	format shapes and text boxes	2.14	863
2.2.5	apply styles to shapes and text boxes	2.14, 2.16	863, 865
2.3	**Insert and Format Images**		
2.3.1	insert images	2.05, 2.06	852, 854
2.3.2	resize and crop images	2.07, 2.09, 2.10	855, 856, 858
2.3.3	apply styles and effects	1.09, 1.10, 2.17	795, 796, 866
2.4	**Order and Group Objects**		
2.4.1	order objects	GO! PowerPoint Comprehensive 5.01	PowerPoint Comprehensive
2.4.2	align objects	2.19, 2.20	868, 869
2.4.3	group objects	2.21	870
2.4.4	display alignment tools	2.08	856

3.0 Insert Tables, Charts, SmartArt, and Media

3.1	**Insert and Format Tables**		
3.1.1	create a table	3.18	933
3.1.2	insert and delete table rows and columns	3.19	934
3.1.3	apply table styles	3.22	937
3.1.4	import a table	GO! PowerPoint Comprehensive 7.02, 7.03	PowerPoint Comprehensive
3.2	**Insert and Format Charts**		
3.2.1	create a chart	3.24	939
3.2.2	import a chart	GO! PowerPoint Comprehensive 7.11, 7.12	PowerPoint Comprehensive
3.2.3	change the Chart Type	GO! PowerPoint Comprehensive 7.14	PowerPoint Comprehensive
3.2.4	add a legend to a chart	3.26	942
3.2.5	change the chart style of a chart	3.26, 3.28	942, 945
3.3	**Insert and Format SmartArt graphics**		
3.3.1	create SmartArt graphics	2.29	883
3.3.2	convert lists to SmartArt graphics	2.27	880
3.3.3	add shapes to SmartArt graphics	2.28	882
3.3.4	reorder shapes in SmartArt graphics	2.34	886
3.3.5	change the color of SmartArt graphics	2.33	885
3.4	**Insert and Manage Media**		
3.4.1	insert audio and video clips	3.14	925
3.4.2	configure media playback options	3.17	927
3.4.3	adjust media window size	3.15	926
3.4.4	set the video start and stop time	3.17	927
3.4.5	set media timing options	3.17	927

4.0 Apply Transitions and Animations

4.1	**Apply Slide Transitions**		
4.1.1	insert slide transitions	1.31	822
4.1.2	set transition effect options	1.32	822
4.2	**Animate Slide Content**		
4.2.1	apply animations to objects	3.09, 3.29	919, 947
4.2.2	apply animations to text	3.09	919
4.2.3	set animation effect options	3.09	919
4.2.4	set animation paths	3.09	919
4.3	**Set Timing for Transitions and Animations**		
4.3.1	set transition effect duration	3.12	923
4.3.2	configure transition start and finish options	3.11	922
4.3.3	reorder animations on a slide	3.10	921

5.0 Manage Multiple Presentations			
5.1	**Merge Content from Multiple Presentations**		
5.1.1	insert slides from another presentation	1.18	810
5.1.2	compare two presentations	GO! PowerPoint Comprehensive 4.16	PowerPoint Comprehensive
5.1.3	insert comments	GO! PowerPoint Comprehensive 4.12	PowerPoint Comprehensive
5.1.4	review comments	GO! PowerPoint Comprehensive 4.13, 4.14	PowerPoint Comprehensive
5.2	**Finalize Presentations**		
5.2.1	protect a presentation	GO! PowerPoint Comprehensive 4.20, 4.21	PowerPoint Comprehensive
5.2.2	inspect a presentation	GO! PowerPoint Comprehensive 4.17, 4.18, 4.19	PowerPoint Comprehensive
5.2.3	proof a presentation	GO! PowerPoint Comprehensive 8.03	PowerPoint Comprehensive
5.2.4	preserve presentation content	3.17	921
5.2.5	export presentations to other formats	GO! PowerPoint Comprehensive 8.05, 8.06, 8.07, 8.08, 8.09	PowerPoint Comprehensive

Glossary

3-D The shortened term for *three-dimensional*, which refers to an image that appears to have all three spatial dimensions—length, width, and depth.

Absolute cell reference A cell reference that refers to cells by their fixed position in a worksheet; an absolute cell reference remains the same when the formula is copied.

Accounting Number Format The Excel number format that applies a thousand comma separator where appropriate, inserts a fixed U.S. dollar sign aligned at the left edge of the cell, applies two decimal places, and leaves a small amount of space at the right edge of the cell to accommodate a parenthesis for negative numbers.

Action Center A vertical panel that displays on the right side of your screen when you click the icon in the notifications area of the taskbar; the upper portion displays notifications you have elected to receive such as mail and social network updates and the lower portion displays buttons for frequently used system commands.

Active cell The cell, surrounded by a border, ready to receive data or be affected by the next Excel command.

Address bar (File Explorer) The area at the top of a File Explorer window that displays your current location in the folder structure as a series of links separated by arrows.

Administrator account A user account that lets you make changes that will affect other users of the computer; the most powerful of the three types of accounts, because it permits the most control over the computer.

After Previous An animation option that begins the animation sequence for the selected slide element immediately after the completion of the previous animation or slide transition.

Aggregate functions Calculations such as Min, Max, Avg, and Sum that are performed on a group of records.

Alignment The placement of text or objects relative to the left and right margins.

Alignment guides A green vertical or horizontal line that displays when you are moving or sizing an object to assist you with object placement.

All apps A command that displays all the apps installed on your computer in alphabetical order on the Start menu.

Alt text Another name for alternative text.

Alternative text Text added to a picture or object that helps people using a screen reader understand what the object is.

American Psychological Association (APA) One of two commonly used style guides for formatting research papers.

AND condition A compound criteria used to display records that match all parts of the specified criteria.

Animation A visual or sound effect added to an object or text on a slide.

Animation Painter A feature that copies animation settings from one object to another.

App The shortened version of the term *application*, and which typically refers to a smaller application designed for a single purpose, is self-contained, and that run on smartphones and other mobile devices.

App bar A term used to describe a horizontal or vertical array of command icons in a Windows app.

Append To add on to the end of an object; for example, to add records to the end of an existing table.

Application A set of instructions that a computer uses to accomplish a task; also called a program.

Application developer An individual who writes computer applications.

Apps for Office A collection of downloadable apps that enable you to create and view information within Office programs and that combine cloud services and web technologies within the user interface of Office.

Arguments The values that an Excel function uses to perform calculations or operations.

Arithmetic operators The symbols +, −, *, /, %, and ^ used to denote addition, subtraction (or negation), multiplication, division, percentage, and exponentiation in an Excel formula.

Artistic effects Formats applied to images that make pictures resemble sketches or paintings.

Ascending order A sorting order that arranges text alphabetically (A to Z) and numbers from the lowest number to the highest number.

Aspect ratio The ratio of the width of a display to the height of the display.

Auto Fill An Excel feature that generates and extends values into adjacent cells based on the values of selected cells.

AutoCalculate A feature that displays three calculations in the status bar by default—Average, Count, and Sum—when you select a range of numerical data.

AutoComplete A feature that speeds your typing and lessens the likelihood of errors; if the first few characters you type in a cell match an existing entry in the column, Excel fills in the remaining characters for you.

AutoCorrect A feature that corrects common typing and spelling errors as you type, for example, changing *teh* to *the*.

AutoFit An Excel feature that adjusts the width of a column to fit the cell content of the widest cell in the column.

AutoNumber data type A data type that describes a unique sequential or random number assigned by Access as each record is entered and that is useful for data that has no distinct field that can be considered unique.

AutoSum A button that provides quick access to the SUM function.

AVERAGE function An Excel function that adds a group of values, and then divides the result by the number of values in the group.

Axis A line that serves as a frame of reference for measurement and that borders the chart plot area.

Background Removal A feature that removes unwanted portions of a picture so that the picture does not appear as a self-contained rectangle.

Background style A predefined slide background fill variation that combines theme colors in different intensities or patterns.

Backstage tabs The area along the left side of Backstage view with tabs to display screens with related groups of commands.

Backstage view A centralized space for file management tasks; for example, opening, saving, printing, publishing, or sharing a file. A navigation pane displays along the left side with tabs that group file-related tasks together.

Badge An icon that displays on the Lock screen for lock screen apps that you have selected.

Base The starting point when you divide the amount of increase by it to calculate the rate of increase.

Best Fit An Access command that adjusts the width of a column to accommodate the column's longest entry.

Between ... And operator A comparison operator that looks for values within a range.

Bevel A shape effect that uses shading and shadows to make the edges of a shape appear to be curved or angled.

Bibliography A list of cited works in a report or research paper; also referred to as Works Cited, Sources, or References, depending upon the report style.

Bing Microsoft's search engine, which powers Cortana.

Black slide A slide that displays after the last slide in a presentation, indicating that the presentation is over.

Blank desktop database A database that has no data and has no database tools—you must create the data and tools as you need them; the database is stored on your computer or other storage device.

Body The text of a letter.

Body font A font that is applied to all slide text except slide titles.

Bookmark A command that identifies a word, section, or place in a document so that you can find it quickly without scrolling.

Booting the computer The process of turning on a computer when the computer has been completely shut down and during which the BIOS program will run.

Bound A term used to describe objects and controls that are based on data that is stored in tables.

Bound control A control that retrieves its data from an underlying table or query; a text box control is an example of a bound control.

Brightness The relative lightness of a picture.

Bulleted list A list of items with each item introduced by a symbol such as a small circle or check mark, and which is useful when the items in the list can be displayed in any order.

Bullets Text symbols such as small circles or check marks that precede each item in a bulleted list.

Calculated control A control that contains an expression, often a formula or function, that most often summarizes a field that contains numerical data.

Calculated field A field that stores the value of a mathematical operation.

Caption A property setting that displays a name for a field in a table, query, form, or report different from the one listed as the field name.

Cascade Delete Related Records A cascade option that enables you to delete a record in a table and also delete all of the related records in related tables.

Cascade options Relationship options that enable you to update records in related tables when referential integrity is enforced.

Cascade Update Related Fields A cascade option that enables you to change the data in the primary key field in the table on the *one* side of the relationship and update that change to any fields storing that same data in related tables.

Category axis The area along the bottom of a chart that identifies the categories of data; also referred to as the x-axis.

Category labels The labels that display along the bottom of a chart to identify the categories of data; Excel uses the row titles as the category names.

Cell (Word) The box at the intersection of a row and column in a Word table.

Cell (Excel) The intersection of a column and a row.

Cell address Another name for a cell reference.

Cell content Anything typed into a cell.

Cell reference The identification of a specific cell by its intersecting column letter and row number.

Cell style A defined set of formatting characteristics, such as font, font size, font color, cell borders, and cell shading.

Center alignment The alignment of text or objects that is centered horizontally between the left and right margin.

Chart The graphic representation of data in a worksheet; data presented as a chart is usually easier to understand than a table of numbers.

Chart area The entire chart and all of its elements.

Chart elements The various components of a chart, including the chart title, axis titles, data series, legend, chart area, and plot area.

Chart Elements button A button that enables you to add, remove, or change chart elements such as the title, legend, gridlines, and data labels.

Chart Filters button A button that displays options for changing the data displayed in a chart.

Chart layout The combination of chart elements that can be displayed in a chart such as a title, legend, labels for the columns, and the table of charted cells.

Chart sheet A workbook sheet that contains only a chart.

Chart style A set of predefined formats applied to a chart, including colors, backgrounds, and effects.

Chart Styles button A button that displays options for setting the style and color scheme for a chart.

Chart Styles gallery A group of predesigned chart styles that you can apply to an Excel chart.

Chart types Various chart formats used in a way that is meaningful to the reader; common examples are column charts, pie charts, and line charts.

Check Accessibility A command that checks the document for content that people with disabilities might find difficult to read.

Check Compatibility A command that searches your document for features that may not be supported by older versions of Office.

Citation A note inserted into the text of a research paper that refers the reader to a source in the bibliography.

Click The action of pressing the left mouse button.

Clip A single media file such as art, sound, animation, or a movie.

Clipboard A temporary storage area for information that you have copied or moved from one place and plan to use somewhere else.

Cloud computing Applications and services that are accessed over the Internet, rather than accessing applications that are installed on your local computer.

Cloud storage Storage space on an Internet site that may also display as a drive on your computer.

Collaborate To work with others as a team in an intellectual endeavor to complete a shared task or to achieve a shared goal.

Column A vertical group of cells in a worksheet.

Column break indicator A dotted line containing the words *Column Break* that displays at the bottom of the column.

Column chart A chart in which the data is arranged in columns and that is useful for showing data changes over a period of time or for illustrating comparisons among items.

Column heading The letter that displays at the top of a vertical group of cells in a worksheet; beginning with the first letter of the alphabet, a unique letter, or combination of letters identifies each column.

Comma Style The Excel number format that inserts thousand comma separators where appropriate and applies two decimal places; Comma Style also leaves space at the right to accommodate a parenthesis when negative numbers are present.

Commands Instructions to a computer program that cause an action to be carried out.

Common field A field included in two or more tables that stores the same data.

Comparison operators Symbols that are used to evaluate data in the field to determine whether it is the same (=), greater than (>), less than (<), or in between a range of values as specified by the criteria.

Complimentary closing A parting farewell in a business letter.

Compound criteria Multiple conditions in a query or filter.

Compressed file A file that has been reduced in size and that takes up less storage space and can be transferred to other computers faster than uncompressed files.

Compressed Folder Tools File Explorer tools, available on the ribbon, to assist you in extracting compressed files.

Conditional format A format that changes the appearance of a cell—for example, by adding cell shading or font color—based on a condition; if the condition is true, the cell is formatted based on that condition, and if the condition is false, the cell is *not* formatted.

Constant value Numbers, text, dates, or times of day that you type into a cell.

Content app An app for Office that integrates web-based features as content within the body of a document.

Context menus Menus that display commands and options relevant to the selected text or object; also called *shortcut menus*.

Context sensitive commands A command associated with the currently selected or active object; often activated by right-clicking a screen item.

Contextual tabs Tabs that are added to the ribbon automatically when a specific object, such as a picture, is selected, and that contain commands relevant to the selected object.

Contiguous slides Slides that are adjacent to each other in a presentation.

Contrast The difference between the darkest and lightest area of a picture.

Control An object on a form or report that displays data or text, performs actions, and lets you view and work with information.

Control layout The grouped arrangement of controls on a form or report; for example, the Stacked layout.

Control Panel An area of Windows 10 where you can manipulate some of the Windows 10 basic system settings—a carryover from previous versions of Windows.

Copy A command that duplicates a selection and places it on the Clipboard.

Cortana Microsoft's intelligent personal assistant that is part of the Windows 10 operating system.

COUNT function A statistical function that counts the number of cells in a range that contains numbers.

COUNTIF function A statistical function that counts the number of cells within a range that meet the given condition and that has two arguments—the range of cells to check and the criteria.

Cover letter A document that you send with your resume to provide additional information about your skills and experience.

Creative Commons A nonprofit organization that enables sharing and use of images and knowledge through free legal tools.

Criteria (Access) Conditions in a query that identify the specific records you are looking for.

Criteria (Excel) Conditions that you specify in a logical function.

Crop A command that removes unwanted or unnecessary areas of a picture.

Crop handles Handles used to define unwanted areas of a picture.

Crop pointer The pointer used to crop areas of a picture.

Crosshair pointer The pointer used to draw a shape.

Crosstab query A query that uses an aggregate function for data that can be grouped by two types of information and displays the data in a compact, spreadsheet-like format with column headings and row headings.

Currency data type An Access data type that describes monetary values and numeric data that can be used in mathematical calculations involving values with one to four decimal places.

Custom web app A database that you can publish and share with others over the Internet.

Cut A command that removes a selection and places it on the Clipboard.

Dashboard A descriptive term for the Windows 10 Start menu because it provides a one-screen view of links to information and programs that matter most to the signed-in user.

Data (Access) Facts about people, events, things, or ideas.

Data (Excel) Text or numbers in a cell.

Data (Windows) All the files—documents, spreadsheets, pictures, songs, and so on—that you create and store during the day-to-day use of your computer.

Data bar A cell format consisting of a shaded bar that provides a visual cue to the reader about the value of a cell relative to other cells; the length of the bar represents the value in the cell—a longer bar represents a higher value and a shorter bar represents a lower value.

Data entry The action of entering the data into a record in a database table or form.

Data management The process of managing your files and folders in an organized manner so that you can find information when you need it.

Data marker A column, bar, area, dot, pie slice, or other symbol in a chart that represents a single data point; related data points form a data series.

Data point A value that originates in a worksheet cell and that is represented in a chart by a data marker.

Data series Related data points represented by data markers; each data series has a unique color or pattern represented in the chart legend.

Data source The table or tables from which a form, query, or report retrieves its data.

Data Source (Word) A document that contains a list of variable information, such as names and addresses, that is merged with a main document to create customized form letters or labels.

Data type Classification identifying the kind of data that can be stored in a field, such as numbers, text, or dates.

Database An organized collection of facts about people, events, things, or ideas related to a specific topic or purpose.

Database management system (DBMS) Database software that controls how related collections of data are stored, organized, retrieved, and secured; also known as a DBMS.

Database template A preformatted database that contains prebuilt tables, queries, forms, and reports that perform a specific task, such as tracking events.

Datasheet view The Access view that displays data organized in columns and rows similar to an Excel worksheet.

Date & Time A command with which you can automatically insert the current date and time into a document in a variety of formats.

Date control A control on a form or report that inserts the current date each time the form or report is opened.

Dateline The first line in a business letter that contains the current date and which is positioned just below the letterhead if a letterhead is used.

DBMS An acronym for database management system.

Default The term that refers to the current selection or setting that is automatically used by a computer program unless you specify otherwise.

Descending order A sorting order that arranges text in reverse alphabetical order (Z to A) and numbers from the highest number to the lowest number.

Deselect The action of canceling the selection of an object or block of text by clicking outside of the selection.

Design view An Access view that displays the detailed structure of a table, query, form, or report. For forms and reports, it may be the view in which some tasks must be performed, and only the controls, and not the data, display in this view.

Desktop The main Windows 10 screen that serves as a starting point and surface for your work, like the top of an actual desk.

Desktop app A computer program that is installed on the hard drive of a personal computer and that requires a computer operating system like Microsoft Windows or Apple OSX to run.

Desktop background Displays the colors and graphics of your desktop; you can change the desktop background to look the way you want.

Desktop shortcuts Desktop icons that link to any item accessible on your computer or on a network, such as a program, file, folder, disk drive, printer, or another computer.

Destination table The table to which you import or append data.

Detail section The section of a form or report that displays the records from the underlying table or query.

Detail sheet The worksheets that contain the details of the information summarized on a summary sheet.

Details pane Displays the most common properties associated with the selected file.

Details view A view in File Explorer that displays a list of files or folders and their most common properties.

Dialog box A small window that displays options for completing a task.

Dialog Box Launcher A small icon that displays to the right of some group names on the ribbon and that opens a related dialog box or pane providing additional options and commands related to that group.

Displayed value The data that displays in a cell.

Document properties Details about a file that describe or identify it, including the title, author name, subject, and keywords that identify the document's topic or contents; also known as *metadata*.

Dot leader A series of dots preceding a tab that guides the eye across the line.

Double-click The action of pressing the left mouse button twice in rapid succession while holding the mouse still.

Download The action of transferring or copying a file from another location—such as a cloud storage location or from an Internet site—to your computer.

Downloads folder A folder that holds items that you have downloaded from the Internet.

Drag The action of moving something from one location on the screen to another while holding down the left mouse button; the action of dragging includes releasing the mouse button at the desired time or location.

Drag and drop The action of moving a selection by dragging it to a new location.

Drawing objects Graphic objects, such as shapes, diagrams, lines, or circles.

Drive An area of storage that is formatted with a file system compatible with your operating system and is identified by a drive letter.

Edit The process of making changes to text or graphics in an Office file.

Editing The process of modifying a presentation by adding and deleting slides or by changing the contents of individual slides.

Ellipsis A set of three dots indicating incompleteness; an ellipsis following a command name indicates that a dialog box will display if you click the command.

Em dash A punctuation symbol used to indicate an explanation or emphasis.

Embed code A code that creates a link to a video, picture, or other type of rich media content.

Emphasis effect Animation that emphasizes an object or text that is already displayed.

Enclosures Additional documents included with a business letter.

Endnote In a research paper, a note placed at the end of a document or chapter.

Enhanced ScreenTip A ScreenTip that displays more descriptive text than a normal ScreenTip.

Enterprise fund A municipal government fund that reports income and expenditures related to municipal services for which a fee is charged in exchange for goods or services.

Entrance effect Animation that brings a slide element onto the screen.

Excel pointer An Excel window element with which you can display the location of the pointer.

Excel table A series of rows and columns that contains related data that is managed independently from the data in other rows and columns in the worksheet.

Exit effect Animation that moves an object or text off the screen.

Expand Formula Bar button An Excel window element with which you can increase the height of the Formula Bar to display lengthy cell content.

Expand horizontal scroll bar button An Excel window element with which you can increase the width of the horizontal scroll bar.

Explode The action of pulling out one or more pie slices from a pie chart for emphasis.

Export The process of copying data from one file into another file, such as an Access table into an Excel spreadsheet.

Expression A formula that will perform the calculation.

Extract The action of decompressing—pulling out—files from a compressed form.

Eyedropper A tool that captures the exact color from an object on your screen and then applies it to any shape, picture, or text.

Field (Access) A single piece of information that is stored in every record; represented by a column in a database table.

Field (Word) In a mail merge, the column headings in the data source.

Field list A list of field names in a table.

Field properties Characteristics of a field that control how the field displays and how data can be entered in the field; vary for different data types.

File A collection of information that is stored on a computer under a single name, for example, a text document, a picture, or a program.

File Explorer window A window that displays the contents of the current location and contains helpful parts so that you can navigate within the file organizing structure of Windows.

File History A backup and recovery tool that automatically backs up your files to a separate location.

File list Displays the contents of the current folder or location; if you type text into the Search box, only the folders and files that match your search will display here—including files in subfolders.

File name extension A set of characters at the end of a file name that helps Windows 10 understand what kind of information is in a file and what program should open it.

File properties Information about a file such as its author, the date the file was last changed, and any descriptive tags.

Fill The inside color of an object.

Fill color The inside color of text or of an object.

Fill handle The small square in the lower right corner of a selected cell.

Filter The process of displaying only a portion of the data based on matching a specific value to show only the data that meets the criteria that you specify.

Filter by Form An Access command that filters the records in a form based on one or more fields, or based on more than one value in the field.

Filter by Selection An Access command that displays only the records that contain the value in the selected field and hides the records that do not contain the value.

Filtered list A display of files that is limited based on specified criteria.

Filtering The process of displaying only a portion of the total records (a subset) based on matching specific values to provide a quick answer to a question.

Find and Replace A command that searches the cells in a worksheet—or in a selected range—for matches and then replaces each match with a replacement value of your choice.

First principle of good database design A principle of good database design stating that data is organized in tables so that there is no redundant data.

Flash Fill Recognizes a pattern in your data, and then automatically fills in values when you enter examples of the output that you want. Use it to split data from two or more cells or to combine data from two cells.

Flat database A simple database file that is not related or linked to any other collection of data.

Flip A command that creates a reverse image of a picture or object.

Floating object A graphic that can be moved independently of the surrounding text characters.

Folder A container in which you store files.

Folder structure The hierarchy of folders in Windows 10.

Font styles Formatting emphasis such as bold, italic, and underline.

Font A set of characters with the same design and shape.

Footer Text that displays at the bottom of every slide or that prints at the bottom of a sheet of slide handouts or notes pages.

Footnote In a research paper, a note placed at the bottom of the page.

Foreign key The field that is included in the related table so the field can be joined with the primary key in another table for the purpose of creating a relationship.

Form An Access object you can use to enter new records into a table, edit or delete existing records in a table, or display existing records.

Form Footer Information displayed at the bottom of the screen in Form view or Layout view that is printed after the last detail section on the last page of a printout.

Form Header Information such as a form's title that displays at the top of the screen in Form view or Layout view and is printed at the top of the first page when records are printed as forms.

Form tool An Access tool that creates a form with a single mouse click, which includes all of the fields from the underlying data source (table or query).

Form view The Access view in which you can view, modify, delete, or add records in a table but you cannot change the layout or design of the form.

Form Wizard An Access tool that walks you step by step through the creation of a form and that gives you more flexibility in the design, layout, and number of fields in a form.

Format Changing the appearance of cells and worksheet elements to make a worksheet attractive and easy to read.

Formatting The process of establishing the overall appearance of text, graphics, and pages in an Office file—for example, in a Word document.

Formatting marks Characters that display on the screen, but do not print, indicating where the Enter key, the Spacebar, and the Tab key were pressed; also called *nonprinting characters*.

Formula An equation that performs mathematical calculations on values in a worksheet.

Formula AutoComplete An Excel feature that, after typing an = (equal sign) and the beginning letter or letters of a function name, displays a list of function names that match the typed letter(s).

Formula Bar An element in the Excel window that displays the value or formula contained in the active cell; here, you can also enter or edit values or formulas.

Free-form snip When using Snipping Tool, the type of snip that lets you draw an irregular line, such as a circle, around an area of the screen.

Freeze Panes A command that enables you to select one or more rows or columns and freeze (lock) them into place; the locked rows and columns become separate panes.

Full-screen snip When using Snipping Tool, the type of snip that captures the entire screen.

Function A predefined formula—a formula that Excel has already built for you—that performs calculations by using specific values in a particular order or structure.

Fund A sum of money set aside for a specific purpose.

Gallery An Office feature that displays a list of potential results instead of just the command name.

General format The default format that Excel applies to numbers; this format has no specific characteristics—whatever you type in the cell will display, with the exception that trailing zeros to the right of a decimal point will not display.

General fund The term used to describe money set aside for the normal operating activities of a government entity such as a city.

Get Started A feature in Windows 10 to learn about all the things that Windows 10 can do for you.

Goal Seek A what-if analysis tool that finds the input needed in one cell to arrive at the desired result in another cell.

Google Drive Google's cloud storage.

Gradient fill A fill effect in which one color fades into another.

Graphical user interface The system by which you interact with your computer and which uses graphics such as an image of a file folder or wastebasket that you click to activate the item represented.

Graphics Pictures, charts, or drawing objects.

Group Footer Information printed at the end of each group of records to display summary information for the group.

Group Header Information printed at the beginning of each new group of records; for example, the group name.

Group, Sort, and Total pane A pane that displays at the bottom of the window in Design view in which you can control how information is sorted and grouped in a report; provides the most flexibility for adding or modifying groups, sort orders, or totals options on a report.

Groups On the Office ribbon, the sets of related commands that you might need for a specific type of task.

GUI The acronym for a graphical user interface, pronounced *GOO-ee*.

Hamburger Another name for the hamburger menu.

Hamburger menu An icon made up of three lines that evoke a hamburger on a bun.

Hanging indent An indent style in which the first line of a paragraph extends to the left of the remaining lines and that is commonly used for bibliographic entries.

Hard disk drive The primary storage device located inside your computer and where most of your files and programs are typically stored; usually labeled as drive C.

Header (PowerPoint) Text that prints at the top of each sheet of slide handouts or notes pages.

Header (Word) A reserved area for text or graphics that displays at the top of each page in a document.

Headings font A font that is applied to all slide title text.

Hierarchy An arrangement where items are ranked and where each level is lower in rank than the item above it.

HoloLens A see-through holographic computer developed by Microsoft.

Hub A feature in Microsoft Edge where you can save favorite websites and create reading lists.

iCloud Apple's cloud storage that is integrated into its Mac and iOS operating systems.

Icons Small images that represent commands, files, or other windows.

IF function A function that uses a logical test to check whether a condition is met, and then returns one value if true, and another value if false.

Import The process of copying data from another file, such as a Word table or an Excel workbook, into a separate file, such as an Access database.

Info tab The tab in Backstage view that displays information about the current file.

Information Data that is accurate, timely, and organized in a useful manner.

Inline object An object or graphic inserted in a document that acts like a character in a sentence.

Innermost sort field When sorting on multiple fields in Datasheet view, the field that will be used for the second level of sorting.

Insertion point A blinking vertical line that indicates where text or graphics will be inserted.

Inside address The name and address of the person receiving the letter and positioned below the date line.

Inspect Document A command that searches your document for hidden data or personal information that you might not want to share publicly.

Interactive media Computer interaction that responds to your actions; for example, by presenting text, graphics, animation, video, audio, or games. Also referred to as rich media.

Internet of Things A growing network of physical objects that will have sensors connected to the Internet.

IoT The common acronym for the Internet of Things.

Is Not Null A criteria that searches for fields that are not empty.

Is Null A criteria that searches for fields that are empty.

Join line In the Relationships window, the line joining two tables that visually indicates the common fields and the type of relationship.

JPEG An acronym for Joint Photographic Experts Group, and which is a common file type used by digital cameras and computers to store digital pictures; JPEG is popular because it can store a high-quality picture in a relatively small file.

Jump list A list that displays when you right-click a button on the taskbar, and which displays locations (in the upper portion) and tasks (in the lower portion) from a program's taskbar button.

Justified alignment An arrangement of text in which the text aligns evenly on both the left and right margins.

Keyboard shortcut A combination of two or more keyboard keys, used to perform a task that would otherwise require a mouse.

KeyTip The letter that displays on a command in the ribbon and that indicates the key you can press to activate the command when keyboard control of the Ribbon is activated.

Keywords Custom file properties in the form of words that you associate with a document to give an indication of the document's content; used to help find and organize files. Also called *tags*.

Label Another name for a text value, and which usually provides information about number values.

Label control A control on a form or report that contains descriptive information, usually a field name or title.

Landscape orientation A page orientation in which the paper is wider than it is tall.

Layout The arrangement of elements, such as title and subtitle text, lists, pictures, tables, charts, shapes, and movies, on a slide.

Layout Options A button that displays when an object is selected and that has commands to choose how the object interacts with surrounding text.

Layout selector A small symbol that displays in the upper left corner of a selected control layout in a form or report that is displayed in Layout view or Design view and is used to move or format an entire group of controls.

Layout view The Access view in which you can make changes to a form or report while the data from the underlying data source displays.

Leader character Characters that form a solid, dotted, or dashed line that fills the space preceding a tab stop.

Left alignment The cell format in which characters align at the left edge of the cell; this is the default for text entries and is an example of formatting information stored in a cell.

Legend A chart element that identifies the patterns or colors that are assigned to the categories in the chart.

Lettered column headings The area along the top edge of a worksheet that identifies each column with a unique letter or combination of letters.

Letterhead The personal or company information that displays at the top of a letter.

Line break indicator A nonprinting character in the shape of a bent arrow that indicates a manual line break.

Line chart A chart type that displays trends over time; time displays along the bottom axis and the data point values are connected with a line.

Line spacing The distance between lines of text in a paragraph.

Link A connection to data in another file.

List level An outline level in a presentation represented by a bullet symbol and identified in a slide by the indentation and the size of the text.

Live Layout A feature that reflows text as you move or size an object so that you can view the placement of surrounding text.

Live Preview A technology that shows the result of applying an editing or formatting change as you point to possible results—*before* you actually apply it.

Live tiles Tiles on the Windows 10 Start menu that are constantly updated with fresh information relevant to the signed-in user; for example, the number of new email messages, new sports scores of interest, or new updates to social networks such as Facebook or Twitter.

Location Any disk drive, folder, or other place in which you can store files and folders.

Lock screen The first screen that displays after turning on a Windows 10 device and that displays the time, day, and date, and one or more icons representing the status of the device's Internet connection, battery status on a tablet or laptop, and any lock screen apps that are installed such as email notifications.

Lock screen apps Apps that display on a Windows 10 lock screen and that show quick status and notifications, even if the screen is locked.

Logical functions A group of functions that test for specific conditions and that typically use conditional tests to determine whether specified conditions are true or false.

Logical operators Operators that combine criteria using AND and OR. With two criteria, AND requires that both conditions be met and OR requires that either condition be met for the record to display in the query results.

Logical test Any value or expression that can be evaluated as being true or false.

Mail app An app for Office that displays next to an Outlook item.

Mail merge A feature that joins a main document and a data source to create customized letters or labels.

Main document In a mail merge, the document that contains the text or formatting that remains constant.

Major unit The value in a chart's value axis that determines the spacing between tick marks and between the gridlines in the plot area.

Manual column break An artificial end to a column to balance columns or to provide space for the insertion of other objects.

Manual line break A break that moves text to the right of the insertion point to a new line while keeping the text in the same paragraph.

Manual page break The action of forcing a page to end and placing subsequent text at the top of the next page.

Margins The space between the text and the top, bottom, left, and right edges of the paper.

MAX function An Excel function that determines the largest value in a selected range of values.

Maximize The command to display a window in full-screen view.

MEDIAN function An Excel function that finds the middle value that has as many values above it in the group as are below it; it differs from AVERAGE in that the result is not affected as much by a single value that is greatly different from the others.

Menu A list of commands within a category.

Menu bar A group of menus.

Menu icon Another name for the hamburger menu.

Merge & Center A command that joins selected cells in an Excel worksheet into one larger cell and centers the contents in the merged cell.

Message Bar The area directly below the ribbon that displays information such as security alerts when there is potentially unsafe, active content in an Office document that you open.

Metadata Details about a file that describe or identify it, including the title, author name, subject, and keywords that identify the document's topic or contents; also known as *document properties*.

Microsoft account A single login account for Microsoft systems and services.

Microsoft Edge The web browser program included with Windows 10.

MIN function An Excel function that determines the smallest value in a selected range of values.

Mini toolbar A small toolbar containing frequently used formatting commands that displays as a result of selecting text or objects.

Mobile device platform The hardware and software environment for smaller-screen devices such as tablets and smartphones.

Modern Language Association (MLA) One of two commonly used style guides for formatting research papers.

Mouse pointer Any symbol that displays on your screen in response to moving your mouse.

MRU Acronym for *most recently used*, which refers to the state of some commands that retain the characteristic most recently applied; for example, the Font Color button retains the most recently used color until a new color is chosen.

Multiple-items form A form that enables you to display or enter multiple records in a table.

Name Box An element of the Excel window that displays the name of the selected cell, table, chart, or object.

Nameplate The banner on the front page of a newsletter that identifies the publication.

Navigate (Excel) The process of moving within a worksheet or workbook.

Navigate (Windows) Explore within the file organizing structure of Windows 10.

Navigation area An area at the bottom of the Access window that indicates the number of records in the table and contains controls in the form of arrows that you click to move among the records.

Navigation Pane (Access) An area of the Access window that displays and organizes the names of the objects in a database; from here, you open objects for use.

Navigation Pane (Windows) The area on the left side of a folder window in File Explorer that displays the Quick Access area and an expandable list of drives and folders.

Network and Sharing Center A Windows 10 feature in the Control Panel where you can view your basic network information.

Newsletter A periodical that communicates news and information to a specific group.

No Paragraph Space Style The built-in paragraph style—available from the Paragraph Spacing command—that inserts *no* extra space before or after a paragraph and uses line spacing of 1.

Noncontiguous slides Slides that are not adjacent to each other in a presentation.

Nonprinting characters Characters that display on the screen, but do not print, indicating where the Enter key, the Spacebar, and the Tab key were pressed; also called *formatting marks*.

Normal template The template that serves as a basis for all Word documents.

Normal view (Excel) A screen view that maximizes the number of cells visible on your screen and keeps the column letters and row numbers close to the columns and rows.

Normal view (PowerPoint) The primary editing view in PowerPoint where you write and design your presentations.

Normalization The process of applying design rules and principles to ensure that your database performs as expected.

Note In a research paper, information that expands on the topic, but that does not fit well in the document text.

Notepad A basic text-editing program included with Windows 10 that you can use to create simple documents.

Notes page A printout that contains the slide image on the top half of the page and notes that you have created on the Notes pane in the lower half of the page.

Notes pane An area of the Normal view window that displays below the Slide pane with space to type notes regarding the active slide.

NOW function An Excel function that retrieves the date and time from your computer's calendar and clock and inserts the information into the selected cell.

Number data type An Access data type that represents a quantity, how much or how many, and may be used in calculations.

Number format A specific way in which Excel displays numbers in a cell.

Number values Constant values consisting of only numbers.

Numbered list A list of items preceded by numbers, which indicate sequence or rank of the items. Sometimes called an *ordered list*.

Numbered row headings The area along the left edge of a worksheet that identifies each row with a unique number.

Object A text box, picture, table, or shape that you can select and then move and resize.

Object anchor The symbol that indicates to which paragraph an object is attached.

Object tab In the object window, a tab that identifies the object and which enables you to make an open object active.

Object window An area of the Access window that displays open objects, such as tables, queries, forms, or reports; by default, each object displays on its own tab.

Objects The basic parts of a database that you create to store your data and to work with your data; for example, tables, queries, forms, and reports.

Office 365 A version of Microsoft Office to which you subscribe for an annual fee.

Office Presentation Service A Word feature to present your Word document to others who can watch in a web browser.

Office Store A public marketplace that Microsoft hosts and regulates on Office.com.

On Click An animation option that begins the animation sequence for the selected slide element when the mouse button is clicked or the is pressed.

One-click Row/Column Insertion A Word table feature with which you can insert a new row or column by pointing to the desired location and then clicking.

OneDrive A free file storage and file-sharing service provided by Microsoft when you sign up for a free Microsoft account.

One-to-many relationship A relationship between two tables where one record in the first table corresponds to many records in the second table—the most common type of relationship in Access.

Open dialog box A dialog box from which you can navigate to, and then open on your screen, an existing file that was created in that same program.

Operating system A specific type of computer program that manages the other programs on a computer—including computer devices such as desktop computers, laptop computers, smartphones, tablet computers, and game consoles.

Operators The symbols with which you can specify the type of calculation you want to perform in an Excel formula.

Option button In a dialog box, a round button that enables you to make one choice among two or more options.

Options dialog box A dialog box within each Office application where you can select program settings and other options and preferences.

OR condition A compound criteria used to display records that match at least one of the specified criteria.

Order of operations The mathematical rules for performing multiple calculations within a formula.

Outermost sort field When sorting on multiple fields in Datasheet view, the field that will be used for the first level of sorting.

Outline view A PowerPoint view that displays the presentation outline to the left of the Slide pane.

Page break indicator A dotted line with the text *Page Break* that indicates where a manual page break was inserted.

Page Footer Information printed at the bottom of every page in a report and most often includes the page number.

Page Header Information printed at the top of every page in a report.

Page number control A control on a form or report that inserts the page number when displayed in Print Preview or when printed.

Page Width A view that zooms the document so that the width of the page matches the width of the window. Find this command on the View tab, in the Zoom group.

Pane A portion of a worksheet window bounded by and separated from other portions by vertical and horizontal bars.

Paragraph symbol The symbol ¶ that represents the end of a paragraph.

Parameter A value that can be changed.

Parameter query A query that prompts you for criteria before running the query.

Parent folder In the file organizing structure of File Explorer, the location where the folder you are viewing is saved—one level up in the hierarchy.

Parenthetical references References that include the last name of the author or authors, and the page number in the referenced source.

Paste The action of placing cell contents that have been copied or moved to the Clipboard into another location.

Paste area The target destination for data that has been cut or copied using the Office Clipboard.

Paste Options gallery A gallery of buttons that provides a Live Preview of all the Paste options available in the current context.

Path A sequence of folders (directories) that leads to a specific file or folder.

PC Reset A backup and recovery tool that returns your PC to the condition it was in the day you purchased it.

PDF The acronym for *Portable Document Format*, which is a file format that creates an image that preserves the look of your file, but that cannot be easily changed; a popular format for sending documents electronically, because the document will display on most computers.

PDF Reflow The ability to import PDF files into Word so that you can transform a PDF back into a fully editable Word document.

Pen A pen-shaped stylus that you tap on a computer screen.

Percent for new value = base percent + percent of increase The formula for calculating a percentage by which a value increases by adding the base percentage—usually 100%—to the percent increase.

Percentage rate of increase The percent by which one number increases over another number.

Personal folder A folder created for each user account on a Windows 10 computer, labeled with the account holder's name, and that contains the subfolders *Documents, Pictures, Music.*

Picture effects Effects that enhance a picture, such as a shadow, glow, reflection, or 3-D rotation.

Picture element A point of light measured in dots per square inch on a screen; 64 pixels equals 8.43 characters, which is the average number of characters that will fit in a cell in an Excel worksheet using the default font.

Picture styles Frames, shapes, shadows, borders, and other special effects that can be added to an image to create an overall visual style for the image.

Pie chart A chart that shows the relationship of each part to a whole.

PIN Acronym for personal identification number; in Windows 10 Settings, you can create a PIN to use in place of a password.

.png An image file format, commonly pronounced *PING*, that stands for Portable Network Graphic; this is an image file type that can be transferred over the Internet.

Pixel The abbreviated name for a picture element.

Placeholder text Nonprinting text that holds a place in a document where you can type.

Placeholder A box on a slide with dotted or dashed borders that holds title and body text or other content such as charts, tables, and pictures.

Platform An underlying computer system on which application programs can run.

Plot area The area bounded by the axes of a chart, including all the data series.

Point and click method The technique of constructing a formula by pointing to and then clicking cells; this method is convenient when the referenced cells are not adjacent to one another.

Point to The action of moving the mouse pointer over a specific area.

Pointer Any symbol that displays on your screen in response to moving your mouse and with which you can select objects and commands.

Pointing device A mouse, touchpad, or other device that controls the pointer position on the screen.

Points A measurement of the size of a font; there are 72 points in an inch.

Populate The action of filling a database table with records.

Portable Document Format A file format that creates an image that preserves the look of your file, but that cannot be easily changed; a popular format for sending documents electronically, because the document will display on most computers; also called a *PDF*.

Portrait orientation A page orientation in which the paper is taller than it is wide.

Presenter view A view that shows the full-screen slide show on one monitor or projection screen while enabling the presenter to view a preview of the next slide, notes, and a timer on another monitor.

Primary key A required field that uniquely identifies a record in a table; for example, a Student ID number at a college.

Print Preview A view of a document as it will appear when you print it.

Print Titles An Excel command that enables you to specify rows and columns to repeat on each printed page.

Program A set of instructions that a computer uses to accomplish a task; also called an application.

Progress bar In a dialog box or taskbar button, a bar that indicates visually the progress of a task such as a download or file transfer.

Property Sheet A list of characteristics—properties—for fields or controls on a form or report in which you can make precise changes to each property associated with the field or control.

Protected View A security feature in Office 2016 that protects your computer from malicious files by opening them in a restricted environment until you enable them; you might encounter this feature if you open a file from an e-mail or download files from the Internet.

pt The abbreviation for *point*; for example, when referring to a font size.

Query A database object that retrieves specific data from one or more database objects—either tables or other queries—and then, in a single datasheet, displays only the data you specify.

Query design grid The lower area of the query window that displays the design of the query.

Quick access The navigation pane area in File Explorer where you can pin folders you use frequently and that also adds folders you are accessing frequently.

Quick Access Toolbar (Windows File Explorer) The small row of buttons in the upper left corner of a File Explorer window from which you can perform frequently used commands.

Quick Access Toolbar In an Office program window, the small row of buttons in the upper left corner of the screen from which you can perform frequently used commands.

Quick Analysis Tool A tool that displays in the lower right corner of a selected range, with which you can analyze your data by using Excel tools such as charts, color-coding, and formulas.

Range Two or more selected cells on a worksheet that are adjacent or nonadjacent; because the range is treated as a single unit, you can make the same changes or combination of changes to more than one cell at a time.

Range finder An Excel feature that outlines cells in color to indicate which cells are used in a formula; useful for verifying which cells are referenced in a formula.

Rate = amount of increase/base The mathematical formula to calculate a rate of increase.

Read Mode A view in Word that optimizes the Word screen for the times when you are reading Word documents on the screen and not creating or editing them.

Reading view A view in PowerPoint that displays a presentation in a manner similar to a slide show but in which the taskbar, title bar, and status bar remain available in the presentation window.

Read-only A property assigned to a file that prevents the file from being modified or deleted; it indicates that you cannot save any changes to the displayed document unless you first save it with a new name.

Recently added On the Start menu, a section that displays apps that you have recently downloaded and installed.

Recolor A feature that enables you to change all colors in the picture to shades of a single color.

Recommended Charts An Excel feature that displays a customized set of charts that, according to Excel's calculations, will best fit your data based on the range of data that you select.

Record All of the categories of data pertaining to one person, place, event, thing, or idea; represented by a row in a database table.

Record selector bar The bar at the left edge of a record when it is displayed in a form, and which is used to select an entire record.

Record source The tables or queries that provide the underlying data for a form or report.

Rectangular snip When using Snipping Tool, the type of snip that lets you draw a precise box by dragging the mouse pointer around an area of the screen to form a rectangle.

Recycle Bin A folder that stores anything that you delete from your computer, and from which anything stored there can be retrieved until the contents are permanently deleted by activating the Empty Recycle Bin command.

Redundant In a database, information that is duplicated in a manner that indicates poor database design.

Referential integrity A set of rules that Access uses to ensure that the data between related tables is valid.

Relational database A sophisticated type of database that has multiple collections of data within the file that are related to one another.

Relationship An association that you establish between two tables based on common fields.

Relative cell reference In a formula, the address of a cell based on the relative positions of the cell that contains the formula and the cell referred to in the formula.

Relative cell reference In a formula, the address of a cell based on the relative positions of the cell that contains the formula and the cell referred to in the formula.

Removable storage device A portable device on which you can store files, such as a USB flash drive, a flash memory card, or an external hard drive, commonly used to transfer information from one computer to another.

Report A database object that summarizes the fields and records from a query or table in an easy-to-read format suitable for printing.

Report Footer Information printed at the bottom of the last page of a report.

Report Header Information printed on the first page of a report that is used for logos, titles, and dates.

Report tool An Access tool that creates a report with one mouse click and displays all of the fields and records from the record source that you select.

Report Wizard An Access tool that walks you step by step through the creation of a report and that gives you more flexibility in the design, layout, and number of fields in a report.

Resources A term used to refer collectively to the parts of your computer such as the central processing unit (CPU), memory, and any attached devices such as a printer.

Restore Down A command to restore a window to its previous size before it was maximized.

RGB A color model in which the colors red, green, and blue are added together to form another color.

Ribbon The area at the top of a folder window in File Explorer that groups common tasks such as copying and moving, creating new folders, emailing and zipping items, and changing views on related tabs.

Rich media Computer interaction that responds to your actions; for example, by presenting text, graphics, animation, video, audio, or games. Also referred to as interactive media.

Rich Text Format (RTF) A standard file format that contains some formatting such as underline, bold, font sizes, and colors. RTF documents can be opened in many applications.

Right alignment An arrangement of text in which the text aligns at the right margin, leaving the left margin uneven.

Right-click The action of clicking the right mouse button one time.

Rotation handle A symbol with which you can rotate a graphic to any angle; displays above the top center sizing handle.

Rounding A procedure in which you determine which digit at the right of the number will be the last digit displayed and then increase it by one if the next digit to its right is 5, 6, 7, 8, or 9.

Row A horizontal group of cells in a worksheet.

Row heading The numbers along the left side of an Excel worksheet that designate the row numbers.

Ruler guides Dotted red vertical and horizontal lines that display in the rulers, indicating the pointer's position.

Run The process in which Access looks at the records in the table(s) included in the query design, finds the records that match the specified criteria, and then displays the records in a datasheet; only the fields included in the query design display.

Salutation The greeting line of a business letter.

Sans serif font A font design with no lines or extensions on the ends of characters.

Scale A command that resizes a picture to a percentage of its size.

Scale to Fit Excel commands that enable you to stretch or shrink the width, height, or both, of printed output to fit a maximum number of pages.

Scaling The process of shrinking the width and/or height of printed output to fit a maximum number of pages.

Screen reader Software that enables visually impaired users to read text on a computer screen to understand the content of pictures.

Screenshot An image of an active window on your computer that you can paste into a document.

ScreenTip Useful information that displays in a small box on the screen when you perform various mouse actions, such as pointing to screen elements or dragging.

Scroll arrow An arrow at the top, bottom, left, or right, of a scroll bar that when clicked, moves the window in small increments.

Scroll bar A bar that displays on the bottom or right side of a window when the contents of a window are not completely visible; used to move the window up, down, left, or right to bring the contents into view.

Scroll box The box in a vertical or horizontal scroll bar that you drag to reposition the document on the screen.

Second principle of good database design A principle stating that appropriate database techniques are used to ensure the accuracy and consistency of data as it is entered into the table.

Section A portion of a document that can be formatted differently from the rest of the document.

Section bar In Design view, a gray bar in a form or report that identifies and separates one section from another; used to select the section and to change the size of the section.

Section break A double dotted line that indicates the end of one section and the beginning of another section.

Section header A type of slide layout that changes the look and flow of a presentation by providing text placeholders that do not contain bullet points.

Select To specify, by highlighting, a block of data or text on the screen with the intent of performing some action on the selection.

Select All box A box in the upper left corner of the worksheet grid that, when clicked, selects all the cells in a worksheet.

Select query A type of Access query that retrieves (selects) data from one or more tables or queries, displaying the selected data in a datasheet; also known as a simple select query.

Selecting Highlighting, by dragging with your mouse, areas of text or data or graphics, so that the selection can be edited, formatted, copied, or moved.

Series A group of things that come one after another in succession; for example, January, February, March, and so on.

Serif font A font design that includes small line extensions on the ends of the letters to guide the eye in reading from left to right.

Shapes Lines, arrows, stars, banners, ovals, rectangles, and other basic shapes with which you can illustrate an idea, a process, or a workflow.

Share button Opens the Share pane from which you can save your file to the cloud—your OneDrive—and then share it with others so you can collaborate.

SharePoint Collaboration software with which people in an organization can set up team sites to share information, manage documents, and publish reports for others to see.

Sheet tab scrolling buttons Buttons to the left of the sheet tabs used to display Excel sheet tabs that are not in view; used when there are more sheet tabs than will display in the space provided.

Sheet tabs The labels along the lower border of the workbook window that identify each worksheet.

Short Text data type An Access data type that describes text, a combination of text and numbers, or numbers that are not used in calculations, such as the Postal Code.

Shortcut menu A menu that displays commands and options relevant to the selected text or object; also called a *context menu*.

Show Formulas A command that displays the formula in each cell instead of the resulting value.

Shut down Turning off your computer in a manner that closes all open programs and files, closes your network connections, stops the hard disk, and discontinues the use of electrical power.

Simple select query Another name for a select query.

Single spacing The common name for line spacing in which there is *no* extra space before or after a paragraph and uses line spacing of 1.

Single-record form A form that enables you to display or enter one record at a time from a table.

Sizing handles Small circles surrounding a picture that indicate that the picture is selected.

Skype A Microsoft product with which you can make voice calls, make video calls, transfer files, or send messages—including instant messages and text messages—over the Internet.

Sleep Turning off your computer in a manner that automatically saves your work, stops the fan, and uses a small amount of electrical power to maintain your work in memory.

Slide A presentation page that can contain text, pictures, tables, charts, and other multimedia or graphic objects.

Slide handout Printed images of slides on a sheet of paper.

Slide pane A PowerPoint screen element that displays a large image of the active slide.

Slide Sorter view A presentation view that displays thumbnails of all of the slides in a presentation.

Slide transitions Motion effects that occur in Slide Show view when you move from one slide to the next during a presentation.

Small caps A font effect that changes lowercase letters to uppercase letters, but with the height of lowercase letters.

Smart guides Dashed lines that display on your slide when you are moving an object to assist you with alignment.

SmartArt A designer-quality visual representation of your information that you can create by choosing from among many different layouts to effectively communicate your message or ideas.

SmartArt graphic A visual representation of information that you create by choosing from among various layouts to communicate your message or ideas effectively.

SmartArt Styles Combinations of formatting effects that you can apply to SmartArt graphics.

Snap Assist The ability to drag windows to the edges or corners of your screen, and then having Task View display thumbnails of other open windows so that you can select what other windows you want to snap into place.

Snip The image captured using Snipping Tool.

Snipping Tool A program included with Windows 10 with which you can capture an image of all or part of a computer screen, and then annotate, save, copy, or share the image via email.

Sort The process of arranging data in a specific order based on the value in each field.

Sorting The process of arranging data in a specific order based on the value in a field.

Source file When importing a file, refers to the file being imported.

Sparkline A tiny chart in the background of a cell that gives a visual trend summary alongside your data; makes a pattern more obvious.

Spin box A small box with an upward- and downward-pointing arrow that lets you move rapidly through a set of values by clicking.

Split Splits the window into multiple resizable panes that contain views of your worksheet. This is useful to view multiple distant parts of your worksheet at one time.

Split button A button that has two parts—a button and an arrow; clicking the main part of the button performs a command and clicking the arrow opens a menu with choices.

Spreadsheet Another name for a worksheet.

Stacked layout A control layout format that is similar to a paper form, with label controls placed to the left of each text box control; the controls are grouped together for easy editing.

Start menu The menu that displays when you click the Start button, which consists of a list of installed programs on the left and a customizable group of app tiles on the right.

Statistical functions Excel functions, including the AVERAGE, MEDIAN, MIN, and MAX functions, which are useful to analyze a group of measurements.

Status bar The area along the lower edge of the Excel window that displays, on the left side, the current cell mode, page number, and worksheet information; on the right side, when numerical data is selected, common calculations such as Sum and Average display.

Structure In Access, the underlying design of a table, including field names, data types, descriptions, and field properties.

Style A group of formatting commands, such as font, font size, font color, paragraph alignment, and line spacing that can be applied to a paragraph with one command.

Style guide A manual that contains standards for the design and writing of documents.

Style set A collection of character and paragraph formatting that is stored and named.

Subdatasheet A format for displaying related records when you click the plus sign (+) next to a record in a table on the *one* side of the relationship.

Subfolder A folder within another folder.

Subject line The optional line following the inside address in a business letter that states the purpose of the letter.

Subset A portion of the total records available.

SUM function A predefined formula that adds all the numbers in a selected range of cells.

Summary sheet A worksheet where totals from other worksheets are displayed and summarized.

Suppress A Word feature that hides header and footer information, including the page number, on the first page of a document.

Switch Row/Column A charting command to swap the data over the axis—data being charted on the vertical axis will move to the horizontal axis and vice versa.

Synchronization The process of updating computer files that are in two or more locations according to specific rules—also called *syncing*.

Syncing The process of updating computer files that are in two or more locations according to specific rules—also called *synchronization*.

Synonyms Words with the same or similar meaning.

System image backup A backup and recovery tool that creates a full system image backup from which you can restore your entire PC.

System tray Another name for the notification area on the taskbar.

Tab order The order in which the insertion point moves from one field to another in a form when you press the Tab key.

Tab stop A specific location on a line of text, marked on the Word ruler, to which you can move the insertion point by pressing the Tab key, and which is used to align and indent text.

Table An arrangement of information organized into rows and columns.

Table (Access) A format for information that organizes and presents text and data in columns and rows; the foundation of a database.

Table area The upper area of the query window that displays field lists for the tables that are used in a query.

Table style A format applied to a table that is consistent with the presentation theme.

Tables and Related Views An arrangement in the Navigation Pane that groups objects by the table to which they are related.

Tabs (ribbon) On the Office ribbon, the name of each task-oriented activity area.

Tags Custom file properties in the form of words that you associate with a document to give an indication of the document's content; used to help find and organize files. Also called *keywords*.

Task pane app An app for Office that works side-by-side with an Office document by displaying a separate pane on the right side of the window.

Taskbar The area of the desktop that contains program buttons, and buttons for all open programs; by default, it is located at the bottom of the desktop, but you can move it.

Tell Me A search feature for Microsoft Office commands that you activate by typing what you are looking for in the Tell Me box.

Tell me more A prompt within a ScreenTip that opens the Office online Help system with explanations about how to perform the command referenced in the ScreenTip.

Template An existing document that you use as a starting point for a new document; it opens a copy of itself, unnamed, and then you use the structure—and possibly some content, such as headings—as the starting point for new a document.

Text alignment The horizontal placement of text within a placeholder.

Text box A movable resizable container for text or graphics.

Text box control A bound control on a form or report that displays the data from the underlying table or query.

Text effects Decorative formats, such as shadowed or mirrored text, text glow, 3-D effects, and colors that make text stand out.

Text string A sequence of characters.

Text values Constant values consisting of only text, and which usually provide information about number values; also referred to as labels.

Text wrapping The manner in which text displays around an object.

Theme A predesigned set of colors, fonts, lines, and fill effects that look good together and that can be applied to all of the objects in the database or to individual objects in the database.

Theme colors A set of coordinating colors that are applied to the backgrounds, objects, and text in a presentation.

Theme fonts The fonts that apply to two types of slide text—headings and body.

Thesaurus A research tool that provides a list of synonyms.

This PC An area on the navigation pane that provides navigation to your internal storage and attached storage devices including optical media such as a DVD drive.

Thumbnail A reduced image of a graphic.

Thumbnails (PowerPoint) Miniature images of presentation slides.

Tiles Square and rectangular boxes on the Windows 10 Start menu from which you can access apps, websites, programs, and tools for using the computer by simply clicking or tapping them.

Timing options Animation options that control when animated items display in the animation sequence.

Title bar The bar at the top edge of the program window that indicates the name of the current file and the program name.

Title slide A slide layout—most commonly the first slide in a presentation—that provides an introduction to the presentation topic.

Toggle button A button that can be turned on by clicking it once, and then turned off by clicking it again.

Toolbar In a folder window, a row of buttons with which you can perform common tasks, such as changing the view of your files and folders or burning files to a CD.

Trim A command that deletes parts of a video to make it shorter.

Triple-click The action of clicking the left mouse button three times in rapid succession.

Truncated Data that is cut off or shortened because the field or column is not wide enough to display all of the data or the field size is too small to contain all of the data.

Trust Center An area of Access where you can view the security and privacy settings for your Access installation.

Trusted Documents A security feature in Office that remembers which files you have already enabled; you might encounter this feature if you open a file from an e-mail or download files from the Internet.

.txt file A simple file consisting of lines of text with no formatting that almost any computer can open and display.

Unbound control A control that does not have a source of data, such as the title in a form or report.

Underlying formula The formula entered in a cell and visible only on the Formula Bar.

Underlying value The data that displays in the Formula Bar.

Universal apps Windows apps that use a common code base to deliver the app to any Windows device.

Unzip Extracting files.

User account A collection of information that tells Windows 10 what files and folders the account holder can access, what changes the account holder can make to the computer system, and what the account holder's personal preferences are.

Value Another name for a constant value.

Value after increase = base x percent for new value The formula for calculating the value after an increase by multiplying the original value—the base—by the percent for new value (see the *Percent for new value* formula).

Value axis A numerical scale on the left side of a chart that shows the range of numbers for the data points; also referred to as the Y-axis.

Variant A variation on the presentation theme style and color.

Virtual desktop An additional desktop display to organize and quickly access groups of windows.

Volatile A term used to describe an Excel function that is subject to change each time the workbook is reopened; for example, the NOW function updates itself to the current date and time each time the workbook is opened.

Wallpaper Another term for the desktop background.

Watermark A text or graphic element that displays behind document text.

Web browser Software with which you display webpages and navigate the Internet.

What-if analysis The process of changing the values in cells to see how those changes affect the outcome of formulas in a worksheet.

Wildcard character In a query, a character that represents one or more unknown characters in criteria; an asterisk (*) represents one or more unknown characters, and a question mark (?) represents a single unknown character.

Window snip When using Snipping Tool, the type of snip that captures the entire displayed window.

Windows 10 An operating system developed by Microsoft Corporation designed to work with mobile computing devices of all types and also with traditional PCs.

Windows apps An app that runs on all Windows device families—including PCs, Windows phones, Windows tablets, and the Xbox gaming system.

Windows Defender Protection built into Windows 10 that helps prevent viruses, spyware, and malicious or unwanted software from being installed on your PC without your knowledge.

Windows Firewall Protection built into Windows 10 that can prevent hackers or malicious software from gaining access to your computer through a network or the Internet.

Windows Journal A desktop app that comes with Windows 10 with which you can type or handwrite—on a touchscreen—notes and then store them or email them.

Windows Store The program where you can find and download Windows apps.

With Previous An animation option that begins the animation sequence at the same time as the previous animation or slide transition.

Wizard A feature in Microsoft Office that walks you step by step through a process.

WordArt An Office feature in Word, Excel, and PowerPoint that enables you to change normal text into decorative stylized text.

Wordwrap The feature that moves text from the right edge of a paragraph to the beginning of the next line as necessary to fit within the margins.

Work access A Windows 10 feature with which you can connect to your work or school system based on established policies.

Workbook An Excel file that contains one or more worksheets.

Works Cited In the MLA style, a list of cited works placed at the end of a research paper or report.

Worksheet The primary document that you use in Excel to work with and store data, and which is formatted as a pattern of uniformly spaced horizontal and vertical lines.

Worksheet grid area A part of the Excel window that displays the columns and rows that intersect to form the worksheet's cells.

Writer's identification The name and title of the author of a letter, placed near the bottom of the letter under the complimentary closing—also referred to as the *writer's signature block*.

Writer's signature block The name and title of the author of a letter, placed near the bottom of the letter, under the complimentary closing—also referred to as the *writer's identification*.

X-axis Another name for the horizontal (category) axis.

XML Paper Specification A Microsoft file format that creates an image of your document and that opens in the XPS viewer.

XPS The acronym for XML Paper Specification—a Microsoft file format that creates an image of your document and that opens in the XPS viewer.

Y-axis Another name for the vertical (value) axis.

Zip Compressing files.

Zoom The action of increasing or decreasing the size of the viewing area on the screen.

Index

V

value after increase = base × percent for new value, 502
value axis, 368, 508
values
  calculating, 501–503
  definition, 354
  editing in worksheets, 388
  pie charts, 483–484
variants
  definition, 814
  themes (presentations), 814–815
video
  changing the style and shape of, 927
  sizing and aligning, 926
  trimming and compressing, 927–929
viewing
  records, 707–708
  table relationships, 705–707, 733–734
views, Details, 67
virtual desktop, 33
volatile, 430

W

wallpaper, 12
watermarks, 289
web browsers, 39
Websites
  adding citations, 284–285
  downloading files from, 48–49
what-if analysis
  definition, 494
  Goal Seek, 494–496
  worksheets for, 499–503
    format painter, 501
    using parentheses for percentage rate of increase, 499–501
    value calculation, 501–503
what-if questions, 503–506
Whatsapp, 3
wildcards
  definition, 660
  query, 660–661
  question mark (?), 661
windows
  Access database elements, 549
  object, 550
Windows 10
  colors' variation, 5
  creating PIN, 13–14
  described, 2
  desktop, 12–13
  environment, 2–14

  features, 28–42
  File Explorer, 14–25
  functionality, 5
  functions of, 26–28
  lock screen, 8–9
    apps, 8
  managing, 45–46
  personalization, 13
  screen organization, 5
  signing out of, 43–44
  sign-in screen, 8–11
  Start menu, 10, 11
  touchscreen commands, 9
  user accounts, 5–6
    Microsoft account, 6–7
Windows apps, 3–4
  definition, 97
  using, 28–32
Windows Defender, 46
Windows Firewall, 46
Windows Journal, 57
window snip, 22
Windows Store, 13
Windows Store app, 11
With Previous option, 922
wizard, definition, 556
WordArt
  definition, 875
  adding text effects to, 878–879
WordArt objects
  aligning, 877–878
  changing the text fill and text outline colors of, 876–877
  inserting, 877–878
WordArt styles, 486
  applying to existing text, 876
Word documents
  adding document properties, 111–112
  checking spelling, 102–103
  entering and editing text in, 100–102
  inserting document info, 111–112
  inserting headers & footers, 111–112
  show/hide in, 100
  Undo, 105–106
wordwrap, 153
Work access, 8
workbooks
  adding document properties, 373–374
  chart sheets, 495–496
  copying/pasting tables (Word) in, 980–981
  creating, 351–353
  definition, 351
  editing, 493–494

  importing data to Access databases, 555–558, 562–565, 649–651
  navigating, 351–353, 441–442
  printing, 373–374
  renaming, 441–442
  saving, 351–353
  tab color of, 441–442
  themes, 365
Works Cited, 281, 286
worksheets
  centering, 372–373
  copying, 442
  data entry
    AutoComplete, 354–355
    AutoFill, 355–356
    column size, 357–358
    keyboard shortcuts, 355–356
    Name Box, 354–355
    numbers, 358–359
    text, 354–355
    text alignment, 357–358
  definition, 351
  editing values, 388
  formatting, 389–392, 455–457
    grouped, 451
  grouping, 447–448
  inserting, 452
  modifying, 435
  page orientation, 375–377
  printing, 374–375, 455–457
  shrinking, 435
  spell check in, 380–382
  splitting into panes, 435–436
  ungrouping, 452
  for what-if analysis, 499–503
writer's identification, 239
writer's signature block, 239

X

x-axis, 368, 508
XML Paper Specification (XPS), 113
XPS. *See* **XML Paper Specification (XPS)**

Y

y-axis, 368, 508

Z

zip, 48
zoom
  definition, 113
  Page Width, 127
Zoom dialog box, 435